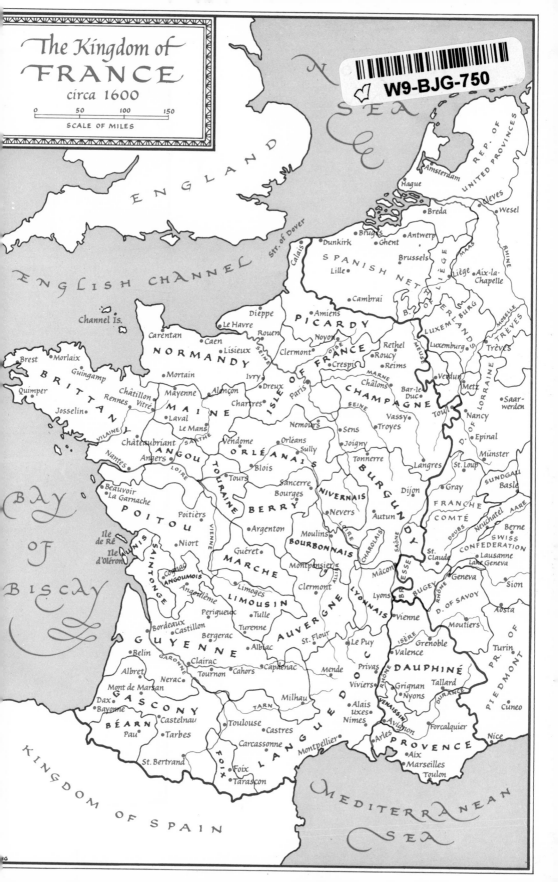

The Kingdom of FRANCE
circa 1600

SCALE OF MILES
0   50   100   150

N
SEA

REP. OF UNITED PROVINCES

Amsterdam
Hague
Cleves
Wesel
Breda

ENGLAND

SPANISH NETHERLANDS

Bruges
Dunkirk
Ghent
Antwerp
Brussels
Lille
B. OF LIÈGE
Liège
Aix-la-Chapelle

Calais
Cambrai

LUXEMBURG
Luxemburg
Trèves

ENGLISH CHANNEL
STR. OF DOVER

Channel Is.

Dieppe
Le Havre
Rouen
PICARDY
Amiens
Noyon
Clermont
Crespi
Rethel
Roucy
Reims
Verdun
Metz
Saar-werden

Carentan
Caen
Lisieux
NORMANDY
Mortain
Ivry
Dreux
ISLE OF FRANCE
Paris
Châlons
Bar-le-Duc
Toul
Nancy

Brest
Morlaix
Guingamp
Quimper

BRITTANY
Rennes
Châtillon
Vitré
Josselin

Mayenne
Alençon
Chartres
MAINE
Laval
Le Mans
SARTHE

CHAMPAGNE
SEINE
Vassy
Troyes
Sens
Joigny
Tonnerre
Langres
St. Loup
Münster
Epinal

MARNE

Nemours
Orléans
Sully

BURGUNDY
Dijon
Autun
Gray
SUNDGAU
Basle

Nantes
VILAINE
Châteaubriant
Angers
ANGOU
LOIRE
Vendôme
Blois
ORLÉANAIS
Tours
TOURAINE

Sancerre
Bourges
NIVERNAIS
Nevers

FRANCHE COMTÉ
DOUBS
Neuchatel
AARE
Berne
SWISS CONFEDERATION
Lausanne
Lake Geneva

BAY
OF
BISCAY

Beauvoir
La Garnache
POITOU
Poitiers
Niort
Ile de Ré
Ile d'Oléron
AUNIS
SAINTONGE

Argenton
BERRY
VIENNE
Guéret
MARCHE
Moulins
BOURBONNAIS
Montpensier
ALLIER

St. Claude
Mâcon
CHAROLAIS
SAÔNE
BRESSE
Geneva
Sion

Cognac
ANGOUMOIS
Angoulême
LIMOUSIN
Limoges
Clermont

Lyons
LYONNAIS
Vienne
BUGEY
RHÔNE
D. OF SAVOY
Moutiers
Aosta

Périgueux
Tulle
Turenne
AUVERGNE
St. Flour
ISÈRE

Bordeaux
Castillon
Bergerac
GUYENNE
Albiac
Le Puy
Grenoble
Valence
DAUPHINÉ
PR. OF PIEDMONT
Turin
Cuneo

Belin
Clairac
GARONNE
Tournon
Cahors
Capdenac
Mende
Privas
Viviers
Grignan
Nyons
Tallard
Forcalquier
Nice

Albret
Nerac
Mont de Marsan
Dax
Bayonne
GASCONY

Milhau
TARN
Alais
uxes
Nîmes
VENAISSIN
Avignon
Arles
PROVENCE
Aix
Marseilles
Toulon

BÉARN
Pau
Castelnau
Tarbes
Toulouse
Castres
Carcassonne
LANGUEDOC
Montpellier

St. Bertrand
FOIX
Foix
Tarascon

KINGDOM OF SPAIN

MEDITERRANEAN SEA

BY WILL DURANT

The Story of Philosophy
Transition
The Pleasure of Philosophy
Adventures in Genius

BY WILL AND ARIEL DURANT

THE STORY OF CIVILIZATION

1. *Our Oriental Heritage*
2. *The Life of Greece*
3. *Caesar and Christ*
4. *The Age of Faith*
5. *The Renaissance*
6. *The Reformation*
7. *The Age of Reason Begins*
8. *The Age of Louis XIV*
9. *The Age of Voltaire*
10. *Rousseau and Revolution*
11. *The Age of Napoleon*

The Lessons of History
Interpretation of Life
A Dual Autobiography

THE AGE OF LOUIS XIV

A History of European Civilization in the Period
of Pascal, Molière, Cromwell, Milton,
Peter the Great, Newton, and Spinoza: 1648–1715

by

Will and Ariel Durant

SIMON AND SCHUSTER

NEW YORK

ISBN 0-671-01215-0
LIBRARY OF CONGRESS CATALOG CARD NUMBER 35-10016
MANUFACTURED IN THE UNITED STATES OF AMERICA

TO OUR BELOVED
GRANDDAUGHTER
MONICA

Dear Reader:

THIS volume is Part VIII in a history whose beginning has been forgotten, and whose end we shall never reach. The subject is civilization, which we define as social order promoting cultural creation; therefore it includes government, economy (agriculture, industry, commerce, finance), morality, manners, religion, art, literature, music, science, and philosophy. The aim is integral history—to cover all phases of a people's activity in one perspective and one unified narrative; that aim has been very imperfectly achieved. The scene is Europe. The time is from the Treaty of Westphalia (1648) to the death of Louis XIV, whose reign (1643–1715) dominated and named the age.

The pervading theme is the Great Debate between faith and reason. Faith was on the throne in this period, but reason was finding new voices in Hobbes, Locke, Newton, Bayle, Fontenelle, and Spinoza; this "Classical Age was throughout what it called itself at its close, the Age of Reason."* Almost a third of the book is devoted to the "Intellectual Adventure" out of superstition, obscurantism, and intolerance to scholarship, science, philosophy. An attempt is made to report the discussion fairly, despite the authors' evident prejudice; hence the extended and sympathetic treatment of such able defenders of the faith as Pascal, Bossuet, Fénelon, Berkeley, Malebranche, and Leibniz. Our children will live a new chapter in this conflict of ideals, where every victory must be repeatedly rewon.

We hope to present Part IX, *The Age of Voltaire*, in 1965, and Part X, *Rousseau and Revolution*, in 1968. Some difficulties have arisen, partly from the wealth of material offered by the eighteenth century, all demanding study and space. Meanwhile we shall rely on the Great Powers not to destroy our subject before it destroys us.

May, 1963   WILL AND ARIEL DURANT

ACKNOWLEDGMENTS

One of the associated publishers with whom we began this "word business" in 1926 has passed away; we shall never forget his bright spirit. The other is still our friend, always enthusiastic, generous, and forgiving, a publisher who remains a poet.

---

* Albert Guérard, *The Life and Death of an Ideal*, p. 18.

We trust that it will not be interpreted as "a lively sense of future favors" if we take this—which could be our last—chance to express our gratitude to the many critics who have won us an audience for these volumes. Without their help we should have been voices moaning in the wilderness.

We owe a substantial debt to our daughter Ethel for her devoted transformation of our not quite legible second draft into an almost perfect typescript, with wise emendations. And to our sisters and brother—Sarah, Flora, Mary, and Harry Kaufman—for their patient classification of some forty thousand notes under some twelve thousand headings. To Mrs. Anne Roberts of the Los Angeles Public Library, and Miss Dagny Williams of the Hollywood Regional Library, for their precious aid in securing rare books from all over America; these volumes could never have been written without our magnificent, open-handed libraries. And to Mrs. Vera Schneider, of the editorial staff of Simon and Schuster, for such scholarly editing of this and the preceding volume as probably few manuscripts have ever received.

1. Dates of birth or death have usually been omitted from the narrative, where they tend to be forgotten or lost; they will be found always available in the Index.

2. The value of coins in any age is subject to so many influences and variations that no reliable system can be set up for equating them with current currencies. The livre in this period sank in value to the level of a franc. Voltaire reported* a silk weaver of Lyon in 1768 supporting a wife and eight children on 45 sous daily, or (since he received nothing on Sundays or holidays) 639 livres per year. A similar family would need at least $50 per week, or $2,600 per year, in the United States of 1962; this would equate a livre with $4.07. In the London of 1779 a worker with wife and children required about 19 shillings per week for rent, food, and common necessaries;† this would make a shilling equal to $2.50. From such comparisons we derive the following hazardous and loose equivalents:

crown, $12.50	guilder, $10.50	pound, $50.00
ducat, $12.50	gulden, $10.50	reale, $.50
écu, $8.00	livre, $2.50	ruble, $10.00
florin, $12.50	louis d'or, $50.00	scudo, $1.16
franc, $2.50	mark, $30.00	shilling, $2.50
guinea, $52.50	penny, $.21	sou, $.15
		thaler, $8.00

3. The location of works of art, when not indicated in the text, will usually be found in the Notes. In allocating such works the name of the city will imply its leading gallery, as follows:

Amsterdam—Rijksmuseum
Berlin—Staatsmuseum
Bologna—Accademia di Belle Arti
Brussels—Museum
Budapest—Museum of Fine Arts
Cassel—Museum
Chantilly—Musée Condé
Chatsworth—Duke of Devonshire Collection
Chicago—Art Institute
Cincinnati—Art Institute
Cleveland—Museum of Art

Detroit—Institute of Art
Dresden—Gemälde-Galerie
Dulwich—College Gallery
Edinburgh—National Gallery
Ferrara—Galleria Estense
Frankfurt—Städelsches Kunstinstitut
Geneva—Musée d'Art et d'Histoire
Haarlem—Frans Hals Museum
The Hague—Mauritshuis
Kansas City—Nelson Gallery
Leningrad—Hermitage
Lisbon—National Museum

---

* Article "Feasts" in the *Philosophical Dictionary*.
† Dorothy George, *London in the XVIIIth Century* (London, 1925), p. 166.

London—National Gallery
Madrid—Prado
Milan—Brera
Minneapolis—Institute of Arts
Munich—Haus der Kunst
Naples—Museo Nazionale
New York—Metropolitan Museum of Art
Nuremberg—Germanisches National-museum
Philadelphia—Johnson Collection
Rouen—Musée Municipale

St. Louis—Art Museum
San Diego—Fine Arts Gallery
San Francisco—De Young Museum
San Marino, Calif.—Henry E. Huntington Art Gallery
Sarasota, Fla.—Ringling Museum of Art
Seville—Art Museum
Stockholm—National Museum
Vienna—Kunsthistorisches Museum
Washington—National Gallery

4. Reduced type has occasionally been used to indicate passages of only remote or special interest, or exceptionally dull.

Table of Contents

BOOK II: ENGLAND: 1649–1714

Chapter VII. Cromwell: 1649–60 183

Chapter VIII. Milton: 1608–74 207

Chapter IX. The Restoration: 1660–85 244

Chapter X. The Glorious Revolution: 1685–1714 288

Chapter XI. From Dryden to Swift: 1660–1714 312

List of Illustrations

THE page number in the captions refers to a discussion in the text of the subject or the artist, and sometimes both.

The authors wish to express their gratitude to the following organizations for certain illustrative materials used in this book:

Bettmann Archive, New York; French Cultural Services, New York; French Embassy Press Information Division, New York; Italian State Tourist Office, New York; Netherlands Information Service, New York; New York Public Library; Photographie Giraudon, Paris; Royal Academy of Arts, London.

BOOK I

THE FRENCH ZENITH

1643–1715

CHAPTER I

The Sun Rises

1643–84

I. MAZARIN AND THE FRONDE: 1643–61

WHY is it that from 1643 France exercised an almost hypnotic dominance over Western Europe, in politics till 1763, in language, literature, and art till 1815? Not since Augustus had any monarchy been so
adorned with great writers, painters, sculptors, and architects, or so widely
admired and imitated in manners, fashions, ideas, and arts, as the government of Louis XIV from 1643 to 1715. Foreigners came to Paris as to a
finishing school for all graces of body and mind. Thousands of Italians,
Germans, even Englishmen, preferred Paris to their native lands.

One reason for French domination was manpower. France had a population of 20,000,000 in 1660, while Spain and England had 5,000,000 each,
Italy 6,000,000, the Dutch Republic 2,000,000. The Holy Roman Empire,
which included Germany, Austria, Bohemia, and Hungary, had some 21,-
000,000; but it was an empire only in name, recently impoverished by the
Thirty Years' War, and divided into over four hundred jealously "sovereign" states, nearly all small and weak, each with its own ruler, army,
currency, and laws, and none with more than 2,000,000 inhabitants. France,
after 1660, was a geographically compact nation, united under one strong
central government; so Richelieu's painful midwifery had helped the birth
of *le grand siècle.*

In the long duel between the Hapsburgs and the French kings the Bourbons won where the Valois had lost. Decade after decade some portion of
the Empire fell to France, and Hapsburg Spain surrendered her pride and
leadership at Rocroi (1643) and the Peace of the Pyrenees (1659). Thereafter the French state was the strongest in Christendom, confident in its
natural resources, the skills and loyalty of its people, the strategy of its
generals, the destiny of its King. It was of some moment, too, that this
youth was to reign for almost three quarters of a century, adding unity of
government and policy to unity of race and soil. Now for fifty years France
would support and import geniuses in science and letters, build colossal
palaces, equip immense armies, frighten and inspire half the world. It was
to be a picture of almost unprecedented glory, painted in all the forms and
colors of art, and in the blood of men.

3

When Louis XIV, aged five, came to the throne (1643), France was not yet unified, and another cardinal had to complete the work of Richelieu. In Italy Jules Mazarin had been Guilio Mazarini, born in the Abruzzi of poor Sicilian parentage, educated by the Jesuits in Rome, serving the popes as a diplomatic agent, and suddenly catching the eye of Europe by negotiating, at a critical moment, an end to the Mantuan War (1630). Sent as papal nuncio to Paris, he tied his fortunes to the commanding genius of Richelieu, who rewarded his fidelity with a cardinal's hat. When Richelieu heard the summons of death, he "assured the King that he knew of no one more capable than Mazarin of filling his place."[1] Louis XIII took the advice.

On the death of this obedient sovereign (1643), Mazarin remained in the background while the Queen Mother, Anne of Austria, took the regency for her son, and Louis de Condé and Gaston d'Orléans, princes of the blood, maneuvered to be the power behind the throne. They never forgave her for passing them by and calling the handsome Italian, now forty-one, to be her chief minister. On the day after his appointment Paris hailed the news of the epochal victory at Rocroi; Mazarin's rule began auspiciously, and was buttressed by many successes in diplomacy and war. His choice of policies, generals, and negotiators proved his intelligence. It was under his guidance that the Peace of Westphalia (1648) confirmed to France the supremacy that her arms had won.

Not dowered with Richelieu's unity and strength of will, Mazarin had to rely on patience, craft, and charm. He had the disadvantage of foreign birth. He assured France that though his tongue was Italian his heart was French, but he was never quite believed; his head was Italian, and his heart was his own. We do not know how much of it he gave to the Queen; he served her and his ambition zealously, and won her affection, perhaps her love. He knew that his safety and hers lay in continuing Richelieu's policy of building up the power of the monarchy against the feudal lords. To feather his nest in the event of a fall, he accumulated wealth with all the greed of poverty remembered or feared; and France, which was beginning to admire measure, condemned him as a parvenu. It resented his Italian accent, his costly relatives, especially his nieces, whose beauty demanded a lavish equipage. Cardinal de Retz, himself no Grandison of virtue, scorned him as "a sordid soul . . . a complete trickster . . . a villainous heart";[2] but de Retz; defeated by Mazarin, was in no condition to be just. If the wily minister gathered riches without dignity, he spent them with taste, filling his rooms with books and art that he later bequeathed to France. He had a gay and courtly way that pleased the ladies and baffled the men. The judicious Mme. de Motteville described him as "full of gentleness, and far removed from the severity of" Richelieu.[3] He readily pardoned opposition, and readily forgot benefits. All agreed that he labored tirelessly in the government of France, but even his industry could offend, for sometimes he left titled visitors waiting fretfully in his anterooms. He thought everybody corruptible, and was insensitive to integrity. His personal morals were proper enough if we set aside the gossip that he made a mistress of his Queen. Many persons at the court were shocked by his skeptical wit about religion,[4] for such irreverence was not yet fashionable; they attributed his religious toleration to lack of religious belief.[5] One of his first acts was to confirm the Edict of Nantes. He allowed the Huguenots to hold their synods in peace; and during his ministry no Frenchman suffered religious persecution by the central government.

It is astonishing how long he held his power despite his unpopularity. The peasants hated him because they were bitterly burdened by the taxes with which he waged war. The merchants hated him because his imposts injured commerce. The nobles hated him because he did not agree with them about the virtues of feudalism. The *parlements* hated him because he set himself and the King above the law. The Queen heightened his unpopularity by forbidding criticism of his rule. She supported him because she found herself challenged by two groups that saw in the infancy of the King and the supposed weakness of the woman an opening to power: the nobles who hoped to restore their former feudal privileges at the expense of the monarchy, and the *parlements* that aspired to make the government an oligarchy of lawyers. Against these two forces—the old aristocracy of the sword (*noblesse d'épée*) and the younger aristocracy of magistrates (*noblesse de robe*)—Anne sought a shield in the subtle, flexible pertinacity of Mazarin. His enemies made two violent attempts to unseat him and govern her; and these constitute the Fronde.

The Parlement of Paris launched the first Fronde (1648–49), seeking to duplicate in France the movement that in England had just raised Parliament above the king as the source and judge of law. The Paris Parlement was, below the king, the supreme court of France; and by tradition no law or tax received public acceptance until these magistrates (nearly all lawyers) had registered the law or the tax. Richelieu had reduced or ignored these powers; now the Parlement was resolved to assert them. It felt that the time had come to make the French monarchy constitutional, subject to the national will as expressed by some representative assembly. The twelve *parlements* of France, however, were not legislative chambers chosen by the nation, like the Parliament of England; they were judiciary and administrative bodies whose members inherited their seats or magistracies from their fathers, or were appointed by the king. The success of the first Fronde would have made the French government an aristocracy of lawyers. The States-General, composed of delegates from the three *états* (states or classes)—nobles, clergy, and the remainder of the people—

could have been developed into a representative assembly checking the monarchy; but the States-General could be summoned only by the king; no king had summoned it since 1614, none would summon it till 1789; hence the Revolution.

The Parlement of Paris became indirectly and momentarily representative when its members dared to speak for the nation. So Omer Talon, early in 1648, denounced the taxes that under Richelieu and Mazarin had impoverished the people:

> For ten years France has been reduced to ruin. The peasantry must sleep upon straw, for their effects have been sold to pay taxes. To enable certain people to live in luxury in Paris, countless innocent persons must survive on the meanest bread . . . owning nothing but their souls—and that merely because nobody has devised a means to put them up for sale.[6]

On July 12 the Parlement, meeting in the Palais de Justice with other courts of Paris, addressed to the King and his mother several demands that must have seemed to them revolutionary. All personal taxes were to be reduced by one quarter; no new taxes were to be levied without the freely voted consent of the Parlement; the royal commissioners (intendants), who had been ruling the provinces over the heads of local governors and magistrates, were to be dismissed; and no person was to be kept in prison beyond twenty-four hours without being brought before the proper judges. If these demands had been met they would have made the French government a constitutional monarchy, and would have put France abreast of England in political development.

The Queen Mother had stronger roots in the past than vision of the future. She had never experienced any other form of government than absolute monarchy; such a surrender of royal power as was now proposed must, she felt, irreparably crack the established mold of rule, undermine its psychological support in tradition and custom, and bring it down, sooner or later, into the chaos of the sovereign crowd. And what a disgrace it would be to transmit to her son anything less than the power that his father (or Richelieu) had enjoyed! This would be a dereliction of duty, and condemn her at the bar of history. Mazarin agreed with her, seeing his own evaporation in these insolent demands from the pedants of the law. On August 26 he ordered the arrest of Pierre Broussel and other leaders of Parlement. But the aged Broussel had become popular with his motto, *Pas d'impostes*—"No taxes." A mob gathered before the Palais-Royal and clamored for his release. The slings or catapults that many in the crowd carried earned them the name *frondeurs*, throwers, and gave a name to the revolt. Jean François Paul de Gondi—later de Retz—coadjutor and prospective successor to the Archbishop of Paris, advised the Queen to release Broussel. When she refused he retired in anger and helped to rouse the people against the government. Meanwhile he pulled wires in an effort to obtain a cardinal's hat, and attended to three mistresses.

On August 27 the members of Parlement, 160 in number, made their way to the royal palace through crowds and barricades. They were spurred on by cries of *"Vive le roi! À mort Mazarin!"* The cautious minister thought it time for discretion rather than valor; he advised the Queen to order Broussel's release. She consented; then, furious at this concession to the crowd, she withdrew with the boy King to the suburb Rueil. Mazarin provisionally granted the demands of the Parlement, but dallied in their enforcement. The barricades remained in the streets; when the Queen ventured to return to Paris the crowd shouted its scorn at her, and she heard its jokes about her relations with Mazarin. On January 6, 1649, she again fled from the city, this time with the royal family and the court to St.-Germain, where silk slept on straw and the Queen pawned her jewels to buy food. The young King never forgave that crowd, never loved his capital.

On January 8 the Parlement, in full rebellion, issued a decree outlawing Mazarin, and urging all good Frenchmen to hunt him down as a criminal. Another decree ordered the seizure of all royal funds, and their use in the common defense. Many nobles saw in the revolt a chance to win the Parlement to the restoration of feudal privileges; perhaps also they feared that the uprising would get out of hand without pedigreed leadership. Great lords like the Ducs de Longueville, de Beaufort, and de Bouillon, even the Prince de Conti of royal Bourbon blood, joined the rebellion, and brought to it soldiers, funds, and romance. The Duchesse de Bouillon and the Duchesse de Longueville—beautiful despite smallpox—came with their children to live in the Hôtel de Ville as voluntary hostages guaranteeing the fidelity of their husbands to the Parlement and the people. While Paris became an armed camp, titled ladies danced in the City Hall, and the Duchesse de Longueville carried on a liaison with the Prince de Marsillac, who was not yet the Duc de La Rochefoucauld, and not yet cynical. On January 28 the Duchesse raised the morale of the revolt by giving birth to Marsillac's son.[7] Many Frondeurs bound themselves as chivalric servitors to highborn ladies, who bought their blood with a condescending smile.

The situation was saved for the Queen by a feud between the Prince de Conti and his older brother Louis II de Bourbon, Prince de Condé—the "Great Condé" who had led French arms to victory at Rocroi and Lens. Turning up his powerful nose at the insurgence of lawyers and populace, he offered his services to Queen and King. Gladly she commissioned him to lead an army against rebellious Paris—against his brother, against his sister the Duchesse de Longueville—and take the royal family back in safety to the Palais-Royal. Condé gathered troops, laid siege to Paris, captured the fortified outpost of Charenton. The rebel nobles appealed for aid to Spain and the Empire. It was a mistake; the sentiment of patriotism was stronger in Parlement and people than the feeling of class. Most members of Parlement refused to annul the work and victories of Richelieu by restoring the Hapsburg ascendancy over France; and they began to see that they themselves were being used as pawns in an attempt to restore a feudalism that would again divide France into regions individually independent and collectively impotent. In a revulsion of humility they sent a deputation to the approaching Queen; they offered their submission, and protested that they had always loved her. She granted a general amnesty to all who would lay down their arms. Parlement dismissed its troops, and informed the people that obedience to the King was the order of the day. The barricades were removed; Anne, Louis, and Mazarin returned to the royal seat (August 28, 1649); the court reassembled, and the rebel nobles joined it as if nothing but a trifling unpleasantness had occurred. All was forgiven, nothing was forgotten. The first Fronde was ended.

There was a second. Condé felt that his services entitled him to subordinate Mazarin. They quarreled; Condé flirted with the discontented nobles; Mazarin, in his boldest moment, had Condé, Conti, and Longueville imprisoned at Vincennes (January 18, 1650). Mme. de Longueville rushed up to Normandy, raised rebellion there, passed on to the Spanish Netherlands, and charmed Turenne into treason; the great general agreed to lead a Spanish army against Mazarin. "All parties," said Voltaire, "came into collision with each other, made treaties, and betrayed each other in turn. . . . There was not a man who did not frequently change sides."[8] "We were ready to cut one another's throats ten times every morning," recalled de Retz;[9] he himself was nearly killed by La Rochefoucauld. Everybody, however, professed loyalty to the King, who must have wondered what kind of monarchy this was that had fallen into pieces in his hands.

A royal force maneuvered Bordeaux into surrender; and Mazarin, playing Mars, led an army toward Flanders and defeated the invincible Turenne. Meanwhile de Retz, eager to replace the Queen's minister and lover, persuaded the Parlement to renew its demand for the exile of Mazarin. Losing his nerve, the Cardinal ordered the release of the imprisoned princes (February 13, 1651), and then, fearing for his life, he fled to Brühl, near Cologne. Condé, hot for revenge against minister and Queen, brought his brother Conti, his sister Longueville, and the Ducs de Nemours and de La Rochefoucauld into a new alliance. In September they declared war, captured Bordeaux, and made it again a citadel of revolt. Condé signed an alliance with Spain, negotiated with Cromwell, and promised to establish a republic in France.

On September 8 Louis XIV, aged thirteen, announced that he was ending the regency of his mother, and was taking the government into his own hands. To appease the Parlement he confirmed Mazarin's banishment; but in November, gaining courage, he recalled the minister, who came back to France at the head of an army. Gaston d'Orléans now played neutral, but Turenne came over to the royal cause. In March, 1652, Louis sent Molé, keeper of the seals, to demand the allegiance of the city of Orléans. Its magistrates dispatched a message to Gaston that unless he or his daughter came to inspire the citizens to resist, they would deliver the city to the King.

At this point one of the most famous of France's many famous women rode upon the scene, like another Joan rescuing Orléans. Anne Marie Louise d'Orléans had become a rebel in her childhood, when Richelieu exiled her father. Gaston, as brother of Louis XIII, was officially "Monsieur"; his wife, Marie de Bourbon, Duchesse de Montpensier, was the current "Madame"; their daughter was thereby "Mademoiselle"; and because she was strong and tall, she came to be called La Grande Mademoiselle de Montpensier. As the Montpensier fortune was immense, she grew up with the double pride of money and ancestry. "I am of a birth," she said, "that does nothing that is not great and noble."[10] She aspired to marry Louis XIV, though he was her cousin; when she received no encouragement she nursed revolt. Hearing the appeal of her city, and seeing her father loath to commit himself, she won his consent to go in his place. She had long resented the limitations put upon her sex by custom; especially she recognized no reason why women should not be warriors. Now she arrayed herself in armor and helmet, gathered about her some highborn Amazons and a small force of soldiery, and led them gaily to Orléans. The magistrates refused to admit her, fearing the wrath of the King. She ordered some of her men to break a hole in the walls; through this she and two countesses entered, while the guardians napped or winked. Once within, her flaming oratory captured the citizens; Molé was sent away without his prize, and Orléans vowed fidelity to its new Maid.

The second Fronde reached its climax at the gates of Paris. Condé marched up from the south, defeated a royal army, and came within an ace of capturing King, Queen, and Cardinal, which would have been checkmate indeed. As his army neared Paris the populace, again Frondeurs, carried a shrine of the city's patron St. Geneviève through the streets in processional prayer for the victory of Condé and the overthrow of Mazarin. La Grande Mademoiselle, hurrying up from Orléans to the Luxembourg Palace, where her father was still playing with pros and cons, begged him to support Condé; he refused. Turenne and the King's army now approached, and met Condé's forces outside the walls, near the Porte St.-Antoine (now the Place de la Bastille). Turenne was winning when Mademoiselle rushed into the Bastille and prodded its governor to turn its cannon upon the royal troops. Then, in the name of her absent father, she commanded the people within the walls to open the gates just long enough to let Condé's army in and shut out the King's (July 2, 1652). Mademoiselle was the heroine of the day.

Condé was master of Paris, but level heads were turning against him. He could not pay his troops; they began to desert, and the populace ran riot. On July 4 a mob attacked the City Hall, demanding that all supporters of Mazarin be given up to them; to indicate their temper they set fire to the building, and killed thirty citizens. Economic operations were disrupted; the food supply fell into chaos; every second family in Paris feared starvation. The propertied classes began to wonder whether royal autocracy, or even government by Mazarin, was not better than mob rule. Mazarin helped by going into voluntary exile, leaving the Frondeurs without a unifying cause. De Retz, having obtained his coveted red hat, thought it time to consolidate his gains, and now used his influence to encourage loyalty to the King.

On October 21 the royal family re-entered Paris peacefully. The sight of the young monarch, fourteen, handsome, and brave, charmed the Parisians; the streets resounded with "*Vive le roi!*" Almost overnight public agitation subsided, and order was restored, not by force but by the aura of royalty, the prestige of legitimacy, the half-unconscious belief of the people in the divine right of kings. By February 6, 1653, Louis felt strong enough to recall Mazarin again, and to re-establish him in all his former powers. The second Fronde was over.

Condé fled to Bordeaux, Parlement submitted gravely, the rebel nobles retired to their châteaux. Mme. de Longueville, no longer lovely, sought solace among the nuns of Port-Royal. La Grande Mademoiselle was banished to one of her estates, where she ate her heart out recalling the remark ascribed to Mazarin, that her cannonade from the Bastille had killed her husband—i.e., ended her chance of marrying the King. At the age of forty she fell in love with Antoine de Caumont, Comte de Lauzun, who was much younger and shorter; the King refused permission for the marriage; when they proposed to marry nevertheless, Louis imprisoned him for ten years (1670–80). Mademoiselle remained bravely loyal to him through all that time; when he was released she married him, and she lived in turmoil with him till her death (1693). De Retz was arrested, escaped, was pardoned, served the King as a diplomat in Rome, retired to a corner in Lorraine, and composed his memoirs, remarkable for their objective analysis of character, including his own:

I did not act the devotee, because I could not be sure how long I should be able to play the counterfeit. . . . Finding I could not live without some amorous intrigue, I managed an amour with Mme. de Pommereux, a young coquette, who had so many sparks, not only in her house but at her devotions, that the apparent business of others was a cover for mine. . . . I came to a resolve to go on in my sins . . . but I was fully determined to discharge all the duties of my [religious] profession faithfully, and exert my utmost to save other souls, though I took no care of my own.[11]

As for Mazarin, he had landed safely on his feet, and was again master of the realm, under a King still willing to learn. To the scandal of France, the minister arranged a treaty with Protestant England and regicide Cromwell (1657), who sent six thousand troops to help fight Condé and the Spanish; together the French and the English won the "Battle of the Dunes" (June 13, 1658). Ten days later the Spanish surrendered Dunkirk; Louis entered it in state, and then, pursuant to the treaty, gave it to England. Exhausted in money and men, Spain signed with France the Peace of the Pyrenees (November 7, 1659), ending twenty-three years of one war and establishing the basis of another. Spain ceded Roussillon, Artois, Gravelines, and Thionville to France, and abandoned all claim to Alsace. Philip IV gave his daughter María Teresa in marriage to Louis XIV, on terms that later involved all Western Europe in the War of the Spanish Succession: he promised to send her a dowry of 500,000 crowns within eighteen months, but exacted from her and Louis a renunciation of her rights to succeed to the Spanish throne. The Spanish King made the pardon of Condé a condition of the Peace. Louis did not merely forgive the impetuous Prince, he restored him to all his titles and estates, and welcomed him to his court.

The Peace of the Pyrenees marked the fulfillment of Richelieu's program—the reduction of the Hapsburg power, and the replacement of Spain by France as the dominant nation in Europe. Mazarin was given the credit for carrying this policy through triumphantly; though few men liked him, they recognized him as one of the ablest ministers in French history. But France, which so soon forgave Condé's treason, never forgave Mazarin's greed. Amid the destitution of the people he amassed a fortune reckoned by Voltaire at 200,000,000 francs.[12] He deflected military appropriations into his personal coffers, sold crown offices for his own benefit, lent money to the King at a high rate of interest, and gave one of his nieces a necklace which is still among the most costly pieces of jewelry in the world.[13]

Dying, he advised Louis to be his own chief minister, and never to leave major matters of policy to any of his aides.[14] After his death (March 9, 1661), the hiding place of his hoard was revealed to the King by Colbert.

Louis confiscated it to the general satisfaction, and became the richest monarch of his time. The wits of Paris acclaimed as a public benefactor Mazarin's physician Guénot: "Make way for his honor! It is the good doctor who killed the Cardinal."[15]

II. THE KING

The most famous of French kings was only one-quarter French. He was half Spanish by his mother, Anne of Austria; he was one-quarter Italian by his grandmother Marie de Médicis. He took readily to Italian art and love, afterward to Spanish piety and pride; in his later years he resembled his maternal grandfather, Philip III of Spain, far more than his paternal grandfather, Henry IV of France.

At birth (September 5, 1638) he was called Dieudonné, God-given; perhaps the French could not believe that Louis XIII had really achieved parentage without divine assistance. The estrangement between father and mother, the father's early death, and the prolonged disorders of the Fronde hurt the boy's development. Amid the struggles of Anne and Mazarin to maintain themselves in power Louis was often neglected; at times, in those unroyal days, he knew poverty in shabby dress and stinted food. No one seemed to bother about his education; and when tutors took him in hand their most earnest endeavor was to convince him that all France was his patrimony, which he would rule by divine right, with no responsibility except to God. His mother found time to train him in Catholic doctrine and devotion, which would return to him in force when passion was spent and glory had worn thin. Saint-Simon assures us that Louis "was scarcely taught to read or write, and remained so ignorant that the most familiar historical and other facts were utterly unknown to him"[16]—but this is probably one of the Duke's furious exaggerations. Certainly Louis showed little taste for books, though his patronage of authors, and his friendship with Molière, Boileau, and Racine suggest a sincere appreciation of literature. Later he regretted that he had come so tardily to the study of history. "The knowledge of the great events produced in the world through many centuries, and digested by solid and active minds," he wrote, "will serve to fortify the reason in all important deliberations."[17] His mother labored to form in him not merely good manners but a sense of honor and chivalry, and much of this remained in him, sullied with a reckless will to power. He was a serious and submissive youth, apparently too good for government, but Mazarin declared that Louis "has in him the stuff to make four kings and an honorable man."[18]

On September 7, 1651, John Evelyn, from the Paris apartment of

Thomas Hobbes, watched the procession that escorted the boy monarch, now thirteen, to the ceremony that was to mark the end of his minority. "A young Apollo," the Englishman described him. "He went almost the whole way with his hat in hand, saluting the ladies and acclamators who filled the windows with their beauty, and the air with *Vive le Roi!*"[19] Louis might then have taken over full authority from Mazarin, but he respected his minister's suave resourcefulness, and allowed him to hold the reins for nine years more. Nevertheless, when the Cardinal died he confessed, "I do not know what I should have done if he had lived much longer."[20] After Mazarin's death the heads of the departments came to Louis and asked to whom henceforth they should address themselves for instructions. He answered, with decisive simplicity, "To me."[21] From that day (March 9, 1661) till September 1, 1715, he governed France. The people wept with joy that now, for the first time in half a century, they had a functioning king.

They gloried in his good looks. Seeing him in 1660, Jean de La Fontaine, a man not easily deceived, exclaimed: "Do you think that the world has many kings of figure so beautiful, of appearance so fine? I do not think so, and when I see him I imagine I see Grandeur herself in person."[22] He was only five feet five inches tall, but authority made him seem taller. Well built, robust, a good horseman and good dancer, a skillful jouster and fascinating raconteur, he had just the combination to turn a woman's head and unlock her heart. Saint-Simon, who disliked him, wrote: "Had he been just a private individual, he would have created the same havoc with his love affairs."[23] And this Duke (who could never forgive Louis for not letting dukes rule), acknowledged the royal courtesy that now became a school to the court, through the court to France, and through France to Europe:

> Never did man give with better grace than Louis XIV, or augment so much in this way the value of his benefits. . . . Never did disobliging words escape him; and if he had to blame, to reprimand, or to correct, which was rare, it was nearly always with goodness, never, except on one occasion . . . , with anger or severity. Never was a man so naturally polite. . . . Towards women his politeness was without parallel. Never did he pass the humblest petticoat without raising his hat, even to chambermaids whom he knew to be such. . . . If he accosted ladies he did not cover himself until he had quitted them.[24]

His mind was not as good as his manners. He almost matched Napoleon in his penetrating judgment of men, but he fell far short of Caesar's philosophical intellect, or Augustus' humane and farseeing statesmanship. "He had nothing more than good sense," said Sainte-Beuve, "but he had a

great deal of it,"[25] and perhaps that is better than intellect. Hear again
Saint-Simon: "He was by disposition prudent, moderate, discreet, the
master of his movements and his tongue."[26] "He had a soul greater than
his mind," said Montesquieu,[27] and a power of attention and will that in his
heyday made up for the limitation of his ideas. We know his defects
chiefly from the second period (1683–1715) of his reign, when bigotry
had narrowed him, and success and flattery had spoiled him. Then we shall
find him as vain as an actor and as proud as a monument—though some of
this pride may have been put on by the artists who portrayed him, and
some may have been due to his conception of his office. If he "acted the
part" of *Le Grand Monarque*, he may have thought this necessary to the
technique of rule and the support of order; there had to be a center of
authority, and this authority had to be propped up with pomp and
ceremony. "It seems to me," he told his son, "that we should be at once
humble for ourselves and proud for the place we hold."[28] But he rarely
achieved humility—perhaps once, when he took no offense at Boileau's
correcting him on a point of literary taste. In his memoirs he contemplated
his own virtues with great equanimity. The chief of these, he judged, was
his love of glory; he "preferred to all things," he said, "and to life itself, a
lofty reputation."[29] This love of glory became his nemesis because of its
excess. "The ardor that we feel for *la gloire*," he wrote, "is not one of
those feeble passions that cool with possession. Her favors, which can
never be obtained except with effort, never cause disgust, and he who can
refrain from longing for fresh ones is unworthy of all those he has received."[30]

Until his love of glory ruined his character and his country, he had his
share of estimable qualities. His court was impressed by his justice, lenience,
generosity, and self-control. "In this respect," said Mme. de Motteville, who
saw him almost daily in this period, "all preceding reigns . . . must yield
precedence to the happy beginning of this one."[31] Those near him noted
the fidelity with which, despite a multitude of affairs, he visited his
mother's apartments several times each day; later they saw his tenderness
for his children, his solicitude for their health and rearing—no matter who
their mother had been. He had more sympathy for individuals than for
nations; he could make war upon the inoffensive Dutch, and order the
devastation of the Palatinate, but he grieved at the death of the Dutch
Admiral de Ruyter, who had inflicted defeats upon the French navy; and
his pity for the dethroned queen and son of James II cost him the worst
of his wars.

He seems seriously to have believed that he was ordained by God to
govern France, and with absolute power. He could of course quote
Scripture to his purpose, and Bossuet was happy to show him that both

the Old and the New Testament upheld the divine right of kings. The memoirs* which he prepared for the guidance of his son informed him that "God appoints kings the sole guardians of the public weal," and that they "are God's vicars here below." For the proper exercise of their divine functions they need unlimited authority; hence they should have "full and free liberty to dispose of all property, whether in the hands of the clergy or the laity."[32] He did not say, "*L'état, c'est moi,*" but he believed it in all simplicity. The people do not appear to have resented these assumptions, which Henry IV had made popular in reaction against social chaos; they even looked up to this royal youth with religious devotion, and took a collective pride in his magnificence and power; the only alternative they knew was feudal fragmentation and arrogance. After the tyranny of Richelieu, the disorder of the Fronde, and the peculations of Mazarin, the middle and lower classes welcomed the centralized power and leadership of a "legitimate" ruler who seemed to promise order, security, and peace.

He gave expression to his absolutism when, in 1665, the Parlement of Paris wished to discuss some of his decrees. He drove from Vincennes in hunting dress, entered the hall in top boots, whip in hand, and said, "The misfortunes that your assemblies have brought about are well known. I order you to break up this assembly which has met to discuss my decrees. Monsieur le Premier Président, I forbid you to allow these meetings, and any single one of you to demand them."[33] The function of the Parlement as a superior court was taken over by a royal Conseil Privé always subject to the King.

The place of the nobles in the government was radically changed. They furnished the dress and glamour of the court and the army, but they seldom held administrative posts. The leading nobles were invited to leave their estates through most of the year and live at the court—most of them in their Paris *hôtels*, or mansions, the greater of them in the royal palaces as royal guests; hence the acres of apartments at Versailles. If they refused the invitation they could expect no favors from the King. The nobles were exempt from taxation, but they were required, in time of crisis, to rush back to their rural châteaux, organize and equip their retainers, and lead them to join the army. The tedium of court life made them relish war. They were expensive idlers, but their bravery in battle became a compulsion of their caste. Custom and etiquette forbade them to engage

---

* The *Notes pour servir aux Mémoires,* begun in 1661, were continued at intervals till 1679, when he added *Réflexions sur le métier de roi—Thoughts on the Business of Being a King.* Despite their theory of absolutism they contain much good sense, and make the treatises of philosophers on this subject seem jejune. They were apparently dictated to secretaries, who tidied them up into literary form. They are as well worth reading as anything in the literature of the age.

in commerce or finance—though they took tolls on trade passing through their lands, and borrowed freely from the bankers. Their estates were worked by sharecroppers (*métayers*), who paid them a part of the produce and rendered them various feudal services and dues. The seigneur was expected to maintain local order, justice, and charity; in some localities he did this reasonably well, and was respected by the peasants; in others he gave a poor return for his privileges, and his long absences at court undermined the humanizing intimacy of master and man. Louis forbade the private wars of feudal factions, and put an end, for a time, to dueling, which had revived during the Fronde—and had become doubly serious, since seconds as well as principals fought and killed, and cheated Mars of prey. Gramont reckoned nine hundred deaths from dueling in nine years (1643–52).[34] Perhaps one cause of the frequent wars was the desire to provide an outlet, at the expense of foreigners, for domestic pugnacity and pride.

For the actual operation of the government Louis preferred those leaders of the middle class who had proved their ability by their rise, and could be depended upon to support the absolutism of the King.[35] Administration was directed chiefly by three councils, each meeting under the King's presidency, and serving to prepare the information and recommendations upon which he based his decisions. A Conseil d'État of four or five men met thrice weekly to deal with major questions of action or policy; a Conseil des Dépêches managed provincial affairs; and a Conseil des Finances attended to taxation, revenue, and expenditure. Additional councils dealt with war, commerce, religion. Local government was taken out of the hands of irresponsible nobles and entrusted to royal intendants, and municipal elections were manipulated to produce mayors satisfactory to the King. Today we should consider so centralized a government to be oppressive; it was, but probably less so than the preceding rule by municipal oligarchies or feudal lords. When a royal commission entered the Auvergne district (1665) to inquire into local abuses of seignorial power, the people welcomed this grand inquest (*les grands jours d'Auvergne*) as their liberation from tyranny; they were delighted to see a *grand seigneur* beheaded for murdering a peasant, and lesser nobles punished for malfeasance or cruelty.[36] By such procedures monarchical replaced feudal law.

The laws were revised into as much order and logic as comported with aristocracy, and the Code Louis so formed (1667–73) governed France till the Code Napoléon (1804–10). The new code was superior to anything of the kind since Justinian, and it "powerfully contributed to advance French . . . civilization."[37] A system of police was established to check the crime and filth of Paris. Marc René, Marquis de Voyer d'Argenson, serving through twenty-one years as lieutenant general of police left a noble record for just and energetic administration of a difficult post. Under his surveillance the streets of Paris were paved, were moderately cleaned, were lighted by five thousand lamps, and were made passably safe for the citizens; in such matters Paris was now far ahead of any other city in Europe. But the code legalized much barbarism and tyranny. A net of informers was spread through France, spying on words as well as actions. Arbitrary arrests could be made by *lettres de cachet*—secret orders of the king or his ministers. Prisoners could be kept for years without trial, and without being told the cause of their arrest. The code forbade accusations of witchcraft, and it ended capital punishment for blasphemy, but it retained the use of torture to elicit confessions. A great variety of offenses could be punished by condemnation to the war galleys —large, low ships rowed by convicts chained to the benches. Six men were allotted to each fifteen-foot oar, and were forced to hold a pace set by an overseer's whistle. Their bodies were naked except for a loincloth; their hair, beards, and eyebrows were shaved. Their sentences were long, and could be arbitrarily extended for inadequate submission; sometimes they were kept to their slavery for years after their sentences had expired. They knew relief only when, in port, still coupled in chains, they could sell trifles or beg for charity.

Louis himself was placed above the law, free to decree any punishment for anything. In 1674 he decreed that all prostitutes found with soldiers within five miles of Versailles should have their noses and ears cut off.[38] He was often humane, but often severe. "A measure of severity," he told his son, "was the greatest kindness I could do to my people; the opposite policy would have brought in an endless series of evils. For as soon as a king weakens in that which he has commanded, authority perishes, and with it the public peace. . . . Everything falls upon the lowest ranks, oppressed by thousands of petty tyrants, instead of by a legitimate king."[39]

He labored conscientiously at what he called *le métier de roi*. He required frequent and detailed reports from his ministers, and was the best-informed man in the kingdom. He did not resent ministerial advice contrary to his own views, and sometimes yielded to his councilors. He maintained the most friendly relations with his aides, provided that they remembered who was king. "Continue to write to me whatever comes into your mind," he told Vauban, "and do not be discouraged though I do not always do what you suggest."[40] He kept an eye on everything—the army, the navy, the courts, his household, the finances, the Church, the drama, literature, the arts; and though, in this first half of his reign, he was supported by devoted ministers of high ability, the major policies and decisions, and the union of all phases of the complex government into a consistent whole, were his. He was every hour a king.

It was hard work. He was waited on at every step, but paid for it by being watched in every move. His getting out of bed and getting into it (when unaccompanied) were public functions. After his *lever*, or official rising, he heard Mass, breakfasted, went to the council chamber, emerged toward one o'clock, ate a big meal, usually at a single small table, but surrounded by courtiers and servitors. Then, usually, a walk in the garden, or a hunt, attended by the favorites of the day. Returning, he spent three or four hours in council. From seven till ten in the evening he joined the court in its amusements—music, cards, billiards, flirtation, dancing, receptions, balls. At several stages in this daily routine "anyone spoke to him who wished,"[41] though few took the liberty. "I gave my subjects, without distinction, the freedom to address me at all hours, in person or by petition."[42] About 10 P.M. the King supped in state with his children and grandchildren, and, sometimes, the Queen.

France was edified to note how punctually, seven or eight hours six days a week, the King attended to the tasks of government. "It is unbelievable," wrote the Dutch ambassador, "with what promptness, clarity, judgment, and intelligence this young prince treats and expedites business, which he accompanies with a great agreeableness to those with whom he deals, and with a great patience in listening to that which one has to say to him: which wins all hearts."[43] He continued his devotion to administration through fifty-four years, even when ill in bed.[44] He came to councils and conferences carefully prepared. He "never decided on the spur of the moment, and never without consultation."[45] He chose his aides with remarkable acumen; he inherited some of them, like Colbert, from Mazarin, but he had the good sense to keep them, usually till their death. He gave them every courtesy and reasonable trust, but he kept an eye on them. "After choosing my ministers I made it a point to enter their offices when they least expected it . . . In this way I learned thousands of things useful in determining my course."[46]

Despite or because of the concentration of authority and direction, despite or because all threads of rule were drawn into one hand, France, in those days of her ascendant sun, was better governed than ever before.

III. NICOLAS FOUQUET: 1615–80

The first task was to reorganize finance, which under Mazarin had fallen through a sieve of embezzlements. Nicolas Fouquet, as *surintendant des finances* since 1653, had managed taxation and expenditure with sticky fingers and lordly hand. He had reduced the hindrances to internal trade, and had stimulated the growth of French commerce overseas; and he had dutifully shared the spoils of his office with the "farmers" of the taxes and with Mazarin. The "farmers-general" were capitalists who advanced large sums to the state, and were in return, and for a fixed sum, empowered to collect taxes. This they did with such efficient rapacity that they were the most hated persons in the kingdom; twenty-four such men were executed during the French Revolution. In collusion with these *fermiers-généraux* Fouquet amassed the greatest private fortune of his time.

In 1657 he engaged the architect Louis Le Vau, the painter Charles Le Brun, and the landscape artist André Le Nôtre to design, build, and decorate the immense and magnificent Château Vaux-le-Vicomte, to lay out the gardens and adorn them with statuary. The project employed eighteen thousand men at one time,[47] cost eighteen million livres,[48] and covered the area of three villages. There Fouquet collected paintings, sculpture, objects of art, and a library of 27,000 volumes, impartially including Bibles, Talmuds, and Korans. To these elegant rooms (we are told) "women of the highest nobility went secretly to keep him company at an extravagant price."[49] With similar taste but at less cost he brought poets like Corneille, Molière, and La Fontaine to grace his salon.

Louis envied this splendor, and suspected its source. He asked Colbert to examine the Surintendant's methods and accounts; Colbert reported that they were incredibly corrupt. On August 17, 1661, Fouquet invited the young King to a fete at Vaux. The six thousand guests were served on six thousand plates of silver or gold; Molière presented, in the gardens, his comedy *Les Fâcheux*. That evening cost Fouquet 120,000 livres, and his liberty. Louis felt that this man was "stealing beyond his station." He did not like the motto *Quo non ascendam?*—"To what may I not ascend?" —accompanied by the figure of a squirrel climbing a tree; and he thought that one of Le Brun's paintings contained a portrait of Mlle. de La Vallière, already a royal mistress. He would have arrested Fouquet on the spot, but his mother convinced him that it would spoil an enchanting evening.

The King bided his time until the evidence of the minister's peculations was overwhelming. On September 5 he ordered the chief of his musketeers to arrest him. (This *mousquetaire* was Charles de Baatz, Sieur d'Artagnan, hero of Dumas *père*.) The trial, dragging on for three years, became the *cause* most *célèbre* in the history of the reign. Mme. de Sévigné, La Fontaine, and other friends worked and prayed for Fouquet's acquittal, but the papers found in his château convicted him. The court condemned him to banishment and the confiscation of his property; the King changed this to life imprisonment. For sixteen years the once joyous minister languished in the fortress of Pignerol (Pinerolo) in Piedmont, consoled by the faithful comradeship of his wife. It was a harsh sentence, but it checked

political corruption, and served notice that the appropriation of public
funds for private pleasure was a prerogative of the king.

IV. COLBERT REBUILDS FRANCE

"To keep an eye on Fouquet," Louis wrote, "I associated with him
Colbert as . . . intendant, a man in whom I had all possible confidence, for
I knew his intelligence, application, and honesty."[50] Fouquet's friends
thought that Colbert had pursued him vindictively; some envy may have
been involved, but in all the France of that age no man rivaled Colbert in
tireless devotion to the public good. Mazarin, dying, is reported to have
said to the King, "Sire, I owe everything to you; but I pay my debt . . .
by giving you Colbert."[51]

Jean Baptiste Colbert was the son of a clothier in Reims, and the nephew
of a rich merchant. Bourgeois in blood and economist by contagion, he
was trained to hate confusion and incompetence, and was fitted by nature
and time to transform the economy of France from peasant changelessness
and feudal fragmentation into a nationally unified system of agriculture,
industry, commerce, and finance, marching with a centralized monarchy,
and providing it with the material basis of grandeur and power.

Entering the war office as a minor secretary at the age of twenty (1639),
Colbert toiled his way into notice, was taken into the service of Mazarin,
and became the successful manager of the Cardinal's fortune. When
Fouquet fell, Colbert was given the critical task of reorganizing the nation's
finances. In 1664 he was made also superintendent of buildings, royal manufactures, commerce, and fine arts; in 1665 he was named controller general
of finances; in 1669, secretary of the navy, and secretary of state for the
King's household. No other man under Louis XIV rose so rapidly, worked
so hard, or accomplished so much. He sullied his rise with nepotism, dower-
ing countless Colberts with place and pay, and remunerated himself almost
in proportion to his worth. He was subject to vanity, insisting on his
alleged descent from Scottish kings. Sometimes, in his hurry to get things
done, he rode roughly over existing laws, and circumvented opposition
with superior bribery. As his power grew he became imperious, and
angered the nobility by stepping on toes that bled blue blood. In remolding
the French economy he used the same dictatorial methods that Richelieu
had used in remolding the French state. He was no better than a cardinal.

He began by looking into the ways of the financiers who collected
taxes, supplied the army with weapons, clothing, and food, and advanced
loans to feudal lords or the national treasury. Some of these bankers were

as rich as kings; Samuel Bernard had 33,000,000 livres.[52] Many of them infuriated the aristocracy by marrying into it, by buying or earning titles, and by living in luxury unattainable by mere pedigree. They charged up to eighteen per cent for their loans, according to the uncertainty of repayment. At Colbert's request the King set up a Chamber of Justice to inquire into all financial malfeasance since 1635 "by any person of any quality or condition whatsoever."[53] All fiscal agents, tax collectors and rentiers were summoned to open their records and explain the legitimacy of their gains. Everyone had to show clean hands or suffer confiscation and other penalties. The Chamber spread its agents through France, and encouraged informers. Several men of wealth were imprisoned, some were sent to the galleys, some were hanged. The upper classes were shocked by this "Colbert Terror"; the lower classes applauded. In Burgundy the money men organized a revolt against the minister, but the populace rose in arms against them, and the government was hard put to save them from the public wrath. Some 150,000,000 francs were restored to the treasury, and fear, for a generation, tempered the corruptions of finance.[54]

Colbert marched through the fisc with an economizing scythe. He dismissed half the officials in the department of finance. Probably at his suggestion Louis abolished, in the royal household, all offices that carried emoluments without duties. Twenty "secretaries to the king" were sent out to earn their bread. The number of attorneys, sergeants, ushers, and other minor functionaries at the court was drastically reduced. All fiscal agents were ordered to keep and submit accurate and intelligible accounts. Colbert converted old governmental debts into new ones at a lower rate of interest. He simplified the collection of taxes. Recognizing the difficulty of collecting arrears, he persuaded the King to cancel all taxes still due for 1647–58. He lowered the tax rate in 1661, and mourned when he had to raise it again in 1667 to finance the "War of Devolution" and the extravagance of Versailles.

His greatest failure was in retaining the old system of taxation. Perhaps a basic reconstruction would have entailed disorder endangering the flow of revenue. The state was financed chiefly by two taxes—the taille and the gabelle. In some provinces the taille (cut) was assessed on real property, in others on income. The nobles and the clergy were exempt from this tax, so that it fell entirely upon the "third estate"—which was all the rest of the population. Each district was required to collect a stated amount, and the principal citizens were held responsible for raising the allotted sum. The gabelle was a tax on salt. The government held a monopoly on its sale, and compelled all subjects to buy periodically a prescribed quantity at prices fixed by the government. To these basic taxes were added a variety of minor imposts, and the tithe of the peasant's produce to be paid to the Church.

This, however, was usually much less than a tenth,[55] and was collected with mercy.

Colbert's reforms affected agriculture least. The technique of tillage was still so primitive that it could not support twenty million people reproducing without restraint. Many couples had twenty children; the population would have doubled every twenty years except for war, famine, disease, and infant mortality.[56] Yet Colbert, instead of seeking to increase the fertility of the soil, gave tax exemptions for early marriage, and rewards for large families: a thousand livres to parents of ten children, two thousand livres to parents of twelve.[57] He protested the multiplication of convents as a threat to the manpower of France.[58] Nevertheless the French birth rate declined during the reign, as war raised taxes and deepened poverty. Even so, war did not kill enough to keep a balance between births and food, and pestilence had to co-operate with war. Two successive crop failures could bring famine, for transportation was not developed to the point of effectively supplying the deficiencies of one region with the surplus of another. There was no year without famine somewhere in France.[59] The years 1648–51, 1660–62, 1693–94, and 1709–10 were periods of starvation terror, when, in some districts, thirty per cent of the population died. In 1662 the King imported corn, sold it at a low price or gave it to the poor, and remitted three million francs of taxes due.[60]

Legislation alleviated some rural griefs. The seizure of peasants' beasts, carts, or implements for debt was forbidden, even for debts owed the Crown; stud farms were established where the peasants might have their mares serviced without charge; hunters were forbidden to traverse sown fields; and tax exemptions were offered to those who restored abandoned lands to cultivation. But these palliatives could not reach the heart of the problem—the disbalance between human and soil fertility, and the lack of mechanical invention. All the peasantries of Europe suffered likewise, and the French *paysans* were probably better off than their fellows in England or Germany.[61]

Colbert sacrificed agriculture to industry. To feed the rising population of the towns, and the expanding armies of the King, he kept the price of grain from rising commensurately with other staples. He took it as elementary that a government, to be strong, must have ample revenues and an army of sturdy soldiers well equipped; a peasantry inured to hardships would provide a tough infantry; a growing industry and commerce must supply the wealth and the tools. Therefore Colbert's persisting aim was to stimulate industry. Even trade was to be subordinate; home industries were to be protected by tariffs that would exclude dangerous competition from abroad. Continuing the economic policies of Sully and Richelieu, he brought all but the minor enterprises of France under the control of the corporative state: each industry, with its guilds, finances, masters, apprentices, and journeymen, formed a corporation regulated by the government in practices, prices, wages, and sales. He established high standards for each industry, hoping to win foreign markets by the refinement of design and finish in French products. He and Louis believed that the aristocratic taste for elegance supported and improved the luxury trades; so the goldsmiths, engravers, cabinetmakers, and tapestry weavers found employment, stimulus, and renown.

Colbert completely nationalized the Gobelin factory in Paris, and made it a model of method and arrangement. He encouraged new enterprises by tax exemptions, state loans, and lowering the interest rate to five per cent. He allowed new industries a monopoly until they were well established. Inducements were offered to foreign artisans to bring their skills into France; Venetian glassworkers were settled at St.-Gobain; ironworkers were brought in from Sweden; and a Dutch Protestant, assured freedom of worship, and capital advanced by the state, established at Abbeville the manufacture of fine cloth. By 1669 there were 44,000 looms in France; Tours alone had 20,000 weavers. France planted its own mulberry trees, and was already famous for its silks. As the armies of Louis XIV grew, textile factories multiplied to clothe them. Under these stimuli French industries rapidly expanded. Many of them produced for a national or an international market, and some reached a capitalistic stage of investment, equipment, and management. The King fell in with Colbert's industrializing mission; he visited workshops, allowed fine products to be stamped with the royal arms, raised the social status of the businessman, and ennobled great entrepreneurs.

The state encouraged or provided scientific and technical education. Workshops in the Louvre, the Tuileries, Les Gobelins, and the naval shipyards became schools for apprentices. Anticipating Diderot's *Encyclopédie*, Colbert sponsored an encyclopedia of arts and crafts, and an illustrated description of all known machinery.[62] The Academy of Sciences published treatises on machines and mechanical arts; the *Journal des savants* recorded new industrial techniques. Perrault, building the eastern front of the Louvre, marveled at a machine that raised a stone block weighing 100,000 kilos (1,100 tons).[63] Colbert, however, opposed the introduction of machinery that would throw employees out of work.[64]

Burning with a passion for order and efficiency, he nationalized, and expanded almost to suffocation, the regulation of industry by communes or guilds. Hundreds of ordinances prescribed methods of manufacture, the size, color, and quality of products, the hours and conditions of labor. Boards were established in all town halls to check defects in the output of local crafts and factories. Specimens of faulty workmanship were publicly exposed, with the name of the worker or manager attached. If the offender repeated the offense, he was censured at a meeting of the guild; if he offended a third time he was tied to a post for public exhibition and disgrace.[65] Every ablebodied male was put to work; orphans were drafted from asylums into industry; beggars were taken from the streets and placed in factories; and Colbert remarked happily to the King that now even children could earn something in the shops.

Workers were subjected to an almost military discipline. Laziness, incompetence, cursing, indecent conversation, disobedience, drunkenness, frequentation of taverns, concubinage, irreverence in church—all these were to be punished by the employer, sometimes by flogging. Working hours were long—twelve or more, with interruptions of thirty or forty minutes for meals. Wages were low, and were partly paid in goods priced by the employer. Vauban calculated the average daily wage of artisans in the large towns at twelve sous (thirty cents) a day; however, a sou could buy a pound of bread.[66] The government cut down the number of religious feast days that exempted men from work; thirty-eight such holydays remained, so that the people had ninety days of rest in the year.[67] Strikes were outlawed, meetings of workers to improve their conditions were forbidden; at Rochefort some workers were jailed for complaining that their wages were too low. The wealth of the business class grew, the revenues of the state rose; the condition of the workers was probably lower under Louis XIV than in the Middle Ages.[68] France was disciplined in industry as well as in war.

And in commerce. Colbert, like nearly all statesmen of his time, believed that the economy of a nation should produce the maximum of wealth and self-sufficiency within the nation; and that, since gold and silver were so valuable as mediums of exchange, commerce should be so regulated as to secure for the nation a "favorable balance of trade"—i.e., an excess of exports over imports, and therefore an influx of silver or gold. Only in this way could France, England, and the United Provinces, which had no gold in their soil, procure their needs, and supply their troops, in time of war. This was "mercantilism"; and though some economists ridiculed it, there was, and will be, much to be said for it in an age of frequent wars. It applied to the nation the system of protective tariffs and regulations which in the Middle Ages had been applied to the commune; the unit of protection grew when the state replaced the commune as the unit of production and government. Hence, in Colbert's theory, the wages of workers had to be low to enable their products to compete in foreign markets and thereby bring in gold; the rewards of employers had to be high to stimulate them to industrial enterprises in manufacturing goods, especially luxuries, that would be of no use in war, but could be exported at little cost for a high return; and interest rates had to be low to tempt entrepreneurs to borrow capital. The competitive nature of man, in the lawless jungle of states, geared their nationalistic economies to the chances and needs of war. Peace is war by other means.

Therefore the function of commerce, in the view of Colbert (and, indeed, of Sully, Richelieu, and Cromwell) was to export manufactured articles in exchange for precious metal or raw materials. In 1664, and again in 1667, he raised the duties on imports that threatened to outsell in France the products of domestic industries considered necessary in war; and when such imports persisted, he forbade them completely. He laid heavy export dues upon vital materials, but reduced the tax on the export of luxuries.

Meanwhile he tried to free domestic commerce from internal tolls. He found French trade clogged by provincial, municipal, and manorial barriers and tariffs. Goods moving from Paris to the Channel, or from Switzerland to Paris, paid tolls at sixteen points; from Orléans to Nantes, at twenty-eight points. These dues may have had sense when, because of difficulties of transport, and possibilities of feudal or intercommunal strife, each locality aspired to self-sufficiency, and strove to protect its own industries. Now that France was politically unified, these internal tolls were an irritating impediment to a national economy. By an edict of 1664 Colbert tried to suppress all internal tolls. The resistance was obdurate; in half of France the tolls continued, some of them till the Revolution, of which they were a minor cause. Colbert almost nullified his work for commercial expansion by issuing complex regulations that aimed to remedy abuses but hampered trade sometimes to frustration. "Liberty," he (or one of his critics) said, "is the soul of commerce. We must let men choose the most convenient ways" (*Il faut laissez faire les hommes*);[69] here was a phrase destined to make history.

He labored to open new avenues of internal transport. He began a system of royal highways, military in their primary purpose, but also a boon to commerce in general. Land travel was still arduous and slow; Mme. de Sévigné took eight days to go by coach from Paris to her estate at Vitré in Brittany. At the suggestion of Pierre Paul de Riquet, Colbert put twelve thousand men to work digging the great Languedoc Canal, 162 miles long, and rising at times to 830 feet above sea level; by 1681 the Mediterranean was connected by the Rhone, the canal, and the Garonne with the Bay of Biscay, and the commerce of France could bypass Portugal and Spain.

Colbert envied the Dutch, who had fifteen thousand of the twenty thousand commercial vessels on the seas, while France had only six hundred. He built up the French navy from its twenty ships to 270; he repaired harbors and docks; he impressed men ruthlessly into naval service; he organized or reformed trading companies for the West Indies, the East

Indies, the Levant, and the northern seas. He gave these companies protective privileges, but again the regulations that he laid upon them hindered them fatally. Nevertheless foreign commerce grew; French goods competed with Dutch or English products in the Caribbean and the Near, Middle, and Far East. Marseilles, which had declined through lack of French shipping, became the biggest port on the Mediterranean. After ten years of experience, consultation and labor, Colbert issued (1681) a maritime code for French shipping and commerce; soon other nations adopted it. He organized insurance for commercial ventures overseas. He sanctioned French participation in the slave trade, but strove to mitigate it with humane regulations.[70]

He encouraged exploration and the establishment of colonies, hoping to sell them manufactured articles for raw materials, and to use them as feeders to a merchant marine that would prove useful in war. French colonists were already spreading in Canada, West Africa, and the West Indies, and were entering Madagascar, India, and Ceylon. Courcelle and Frontenac explored the Great Lakes (1671–73). Cadillac founded a large French colony at what is now Detroit. La Salle (having been granted a monopoly in the slave trade in any regions that he should open up) discovered the Mississippi (1672), and descended it in a frail bark, reaching the Gulf of Mexico after two months of adventurous navigation. He took possession of the delta, and named it after the King. France now controlled the valleys of the St. Lawrence and the Mississippi through the heart of North America.

All in all—and we have noted as yet but a part of Colbert's activity, having said nothing of his work for science, literature, and art—this was one of the most devoted and overspreading lives in history. Not since Charlemagne had a single mind so remade in so many phases so great a state. Those regulations were a nuisance, and made Colbert unpopular, but they created the economic form of modern France; and Napoleon only continued and revised Colbert in government and code. For ten years France knew such prosperity as never before. Then the faults of the system and the King brought it down. Colbert protested against the extravagance of King and court, and the disease of war that was consuming France in his old age; yet it was his high tariffs, as well as Louis' love of power and glory, that led to some of those wars; France's commercial rivals denounced the closing of her ports to their goods. The peasants and the artisans bore the brunt of Colbert's reforms, and even the businessmen whom they enriched charged that his regulations clogged development; said one of them to the minister, "You found the carriage overturned on one side, and you have upset it on the other."[71] When, broken and defeated, he died (September 6, 1683), his body had to be buried by night lest it be insulted by the people in the streets.[72]

V. MANNERS AND MORALS

It was an age of strict manners and loose morals. Dress was the sacrament of status. In the middle classes clothing was almost puritanically simple—a black coat modestly covering shirt and trousers and legs. But in the elite it was magnificent, and more so in men than in women. Hats were large and soft, with a broad brim trimmed with gold braid, tilted up on one or three sides, and sporting a plume of feathers caught in a metal clasp. When Louis came to the throne he—and soon the court—discarded the perukes that had come into style with his bald father, for the young King's waves of chestnut hair were too splendid to be concealed; but when, after 1670, his hair began to thin, he took to wigs; and presently every head of any pretensions, in France, England, or Germany, was crowned with borrowed and powdered curls falling to the shoulders or lower, and making all men look alike except to their bedfellows. Beards were shaved, mustaches were cherished. Gloves were gauntleted and adorned, and both sexes carried muffs on cold days. The high ruff was now replaced by the silk cravat, loosely tied around the neck. The doublet was giving way to a long and ornamented vest; the thighs were graced with *culottes*—trousers ending at the knees, and buckled or ribboned there; and these garments were covered, except in front, by a swirling coat whose sleeves ended in large cuffs trimmed with lace. By law only nobles were permitted to deck their raiment with gold embroidery or precious stones, but moneyed men of any class overrode the law. Stockings were usually of silk. Male feet were shod in boots, even for a dance.

The dress of courtly women was free and flowing to accord with their morals. Their bodices were laced, but in front, as Panurge had urged in Rabelais, and swelling bosoms leaped to the roving eye. Farthingales and puffed sleeves went out with Richelieu. Robes were richly embroidered and gaily colored; entrancing high-heeled shoes covered tired feet; and hair was daintily beribboned, bejeweled, perfumed, and curled. The first fashion magazine appeared in 1672.

Manners were stately, though under the flourish of the saluting hat and trailing skirt many crudities remained. Men spat on floors, and urinated on the stairways of the Louvre.[73] Humor could be brutal or obscene. But conversation was elegant and polite, even when dealing with physiology and sex. Men were learning from women the graces of conduct and speech; they spoke clearly and correctly, avoided sententiousness and pedantry, and touched all topics, however profound, with a light gaiety of spirit and phrase. To dispute earnestly was bad form. Table manners were improving. The King ate with his fingers to the end of his life, but by that time forks were in general use. About 1660 napkins came into vogue, and guests were no longer expected to wipe their fingers on the tablecloth.

Social morality was not outstanding in this age of etiquette and protocol. Charity declined as the wealth of the upper classes grew. Morals were soundest in the lower middle class, where good behavior was made possible by security, and stimulated by the desire to rise. In all classes the ideal was *l'honnête homme*—not the honest man, but the honorable man, who added good breeding and manners to good conduct. Honesty was hardly expected. Despite Colbert's regulations and royal espionage, venality in office was widespread, and it was encouraged by the sale of governmental appointments as a source of public revenue. Crime sprouted from the greed of the rich, the need of the poor, and the passionate outbreaks of all classes. So some highborn dames enjoyed the services of Catherine Monvoisin or the Marquise de Brinvilliers, both skilled in concocting poisons of lingering subtlety; poisoning was so popular that special courts were set up to deal with it.[74] Catherine Montvoisin practiced medicine, midwifery, and witchcraft; she assisted a renegade priest in celebrating the "Black Mass," soliciting the aid of Satan; she procured abortion and sold poisons and love potions. Among her clients were Olympe Mancini, niece of Mazarin, the Comtesse de Gramont, and Mme. de Montespan, mistress of the King. In 1679 a commission investigated the activities of "La Voisin," and found evidence involving so many members high at the court that Louis ordered suppression of the record.[75] La Voisin was burned alive (1680).

Private morals included the usual aberrations. In law homosexuality was punishable with death; a nation preparing for war and paying for babies could not let the sexual instincts be diverted from reproduction; but it was difficult to pursue such deviates when the King's own brother was a noted invert, beneath contempt but above the law. Love between the sexes was accepted as a romantic relief from marriage, but not as a reason for marriage; the acquisition, protection, or transmission of property was judged more important in marriage than the attempt to fix for a lifetime the passions of a day. As most marriages in the aristocracy were arrangements of property, French society condoned concubinage; nearly every man who could afford it had a mistress; men plumed themselves on their liaisons almost as much as on their battles; a woman felt desolate if no man but her husband pursued her; and some faithless husbands winked at their wives' infidelities. "Is there in all the world," asks a character in Molière, "another town where the husbands are as patient as here?"[76] It was in this cynical atmosphere that La Rochefoucauld's maxims grew. Prostitution was despised if it had no manners, but a woman like Ninon de Lenclos, who gilded it with literature and wit, could become almost as famous as the King.

Her father was a nobleman, freethinker and duelist. Her mother was a woman of strict morals but (if we may believe her daughter) "with no sensory feelings . . . She procreated three children, scarcely noticing it."[77] Without formal education, Ninon picked up considerable knowledge; she learned to speak Italian and Spanish, perhaps as aids in international commerce; she read Montaigne, Charron, even Descartes, and followed her father into skepticism. Later her discussions of religion made Mme. de Sévigné shudder.[78] "If a man needs a religion to conduct himself properly in this world," said Ninon, "it is a sign that he has either a limited mind or a corrupt heart."[79] She might thence have concluded to the almost universal necessity of religion; instead she slipped into prostitution at the age of fifteen (1635). "Love," she said recklessly, "is a passion involving no moral obligation."[80] When Ninon allowed her promiscuity to be too prominent, Anne of Austria ordered her confinement in a convent; there, we are told, she charmed the nuns by her wit and vivacity, and enjoyed her imprisonment as a restful vacation. In 1657 she was released by order of the King.

There was so much more in her than the courtesan that she soon enlisted among her devotees many of the most distinguished men in France, including several members of the court,[81] ranging from the composer Lully to the Great Condé himself. She played the harpsichord well, and sang; Lully came to her to try out his new airs. Three generations of Sévignés were on her list—the husband, then the son, then the grandson, of the amiable letter writer.[82] Men came from foreign lands to court her. Her lovers, she said, "never quarreled over me; they had confidence in my inconsistency; each awaited his turn."[83]

In 1657 she opened a salon; she invited men of letters, music, art, politics, or war, and sometimes their wives; and she astonished Paris by showing an intelligence equal to that of any woman, and most men, of her time; behind the face of Venus they found the mind of Minerva. Says a severe judge, Saint-Simon:

> It was useful to be received by her, on account of the connections thus formed. There was never any gambling there, nor loud laughing, nor disputes, nor talk about religion or politics, but much elegant wit . . . [and] news of gallantries, yet without scandal. All was delicate, light, measured; and she herself maintained the conversation by her wit and her great knowledge.[84]

At last the King himself became curious about her; he asked Mme. de Maintenon to invite her to the palace; from behind a curtain he listened to her; charmed, he revealed and introduced himself. But by this time (1677?) she had become quasi-respectable. Her simple honesty and many kindnesses gave her a brighter renown; men left large sums with her for

safekeeping, and could always rely on regaining them at will; and Paris had
noted how, when the poet Scarron was incapacitated by paralysis, Ninon
visited him almost daily, bringing him the delicacies that he could not afford.

She outlived nearly all her friends, even the nonagenarian Saint-Évremond, whose letters from England were the consolation of her old age.
"Sometimes," she wrote to him, "I am tired of always doing the same
things, and I admire the Swiss who throw themselves into the river for that
very reason."[85] She resented wrinkles. "If God had to give a woman wrinkles,
He might at least have put them on the soles of her feet."[86] As she neared
death, in her eighty-fifth year, the Jesuits competed with the Jansenists for
the honor of converting her; she yielded to them graciously, and died in
the arms of the Church (1705).[87] In her will she left only ten écus for her
funeral, "so that it might be as simple as possible"; but "I humbly request
M. Arouet"—her attorney—"to allow me to leave his son, who is at the
Jesuits, one thousand francs for books."[88] The son bought books, read them,
and became Voltaire.

It was the crowning charm of French society that the sexual stimulus
extended to the mind, that the women were roused to add intelligence to
beauty, and that the men were tamed by the women to courteous conduct,
good taste, and polished speech; in this regard the century from 1660 to
1760 in France marks the zenith of civilization. In that society intelligent
women were numerous beyond any precedent; and if they were also attractive in face or figure, or in the solicitude of kindliness, they became a pervasive civilizing force. The salons were training men to be sensitive to
feminine refinement, and women to be responsive to masculine intellect.
In those gatherings the art of conversation was developed to an excellence
never known before or since—the art of exchanging ideas without exaggeration or animosity, but with courtesy, tolerance, clarity, vivacity, and
grace. Perhaps the art was more nearly perfect under Louis XIV than in
the days of Voltaire—not so brilliant and witty, but more substantial and
friendly. "After dinner," wrote Mme. de Sévigné to her daughter, "we
went to talk in the most agreeable woods in the world; we were there till
six o'clock, engaged in various sorts of conversation so kind, so tender, so
amiable, so obliging . . . that I am touched to the heart by it."[89] Many men
ascribed nine tenths of their education to such converse and social intercourse.[90]

In the Blue Room at the Hôtel de Rambouillet the first of the salons was
in its final glory. Condé came there, though he did not shine; Corneille
came, La Rochefoucauld, Mmes. de La Fayette and de Sévigné, the Duchesse
de Longueville, and La Grande Mademoiselle. There les femmes précieuses
laid down the laws of nice conduct and polished speech. The Fronde interrupted these gatherings; Mme. de Rambouillet moved to the country; and

though her *hôtel* later reopened its doors to the genius of France, the première of Molière's *Les Précieuses ridicules* (1659) was a mortal blow. The first famous salon ended with the death of its founder in 1665.

Other salons continued the tradition, in the homes of Mmes. de La Sablière, de Lambert, and de Scudéry—the last the most famous novelist of the reign, the first a woman who attracted men by beauty despite her love of physics, astronomy, mathematics, and philosophy. In such salons flourished the *femmes savantes* who provoked Molière's laughter in 1672. But every satire is a half-truth; in his philosophical moments Molière might have recognized the right of women to share in the intellectual life of their times. It is the women of France, even more than her writers and artists, who are the crown of her civilization, and the special glory of her history.

VI. THE COURT

The King and the court helped to civilize France. The court, in 1664, comprised some six hundred persons: the royal family, the higher nobility, the foreign envoys, and the servant staff. In the fullness of Versailles it grew to ten thousand souls,[91] but this included notables in occasional attendance, all the entertainers and servitors, and the artists and authors whom the King had singled out for reward. To be invited to the court became a passion only third to hunger and sex; even to be there for a day was a memorable ecstasy, worth half a lifetime's savings.

The splendor of the court lay partly in the luxurious furnishings of the apartments, partly in the dress of the courtiers, partly in the sumptuous entertainments, partly in the fame of the men and the beauty of the women drawn there by the magnets of money, reputation, and power. Some notable women, like Mmes. de Sévigné and de La Fayette, were seldom seen there, for they had sided with the Fronde; but enough remained to please a King extremely sensitive to feminine charms. In the portraits that have come down to us these ladies seem a bit ponderous, overflowing their corsages; but apparently the men of that time liked an adipose warmth in their amours.

The morals of the court were decorous adultery, extravagance in dress and gambling, and passionate intrigues for prestige and place, all carried on a rhythm of external refinement, elegant manners, and compulsory gaiety. The King set the fashion of costly dress, especially in ambassadorial receptions; so in receiving the envoys of Siam he wore a robe laced with gold and bordered with diamonds, the whole worth 12,500,000 livres;[92] such display was part of the psychology of government. Nobles and their ladies consumed half the income of their estates on clothing, lackeys, and equipage; the most modest had to have eleven servants and two coaches;

richer dignitaries had seventy-five attendants in their household, and forty horses in their stables.[93] When adultery was no longer prohibited it lost its charm, and gambling at cards became the chief recreation of the court. Louis again gave the lead, bidding for high stakes, urged on by his mistress Montespan, who herself lost and won four million francs in one night's play.[94] The mania spread from the court to the people. "Thousands ruin themselves in gambling," wrote La Bruyère; "a frightful game . . . in which the player contemplates the total ruin of his adversary, and is transported with the lust for gain."[95]

Competition for the royal favor, for a lucrative appointment or a place in the royal bed, led to an atmosphere of mutual suspicion, calumny, and tense rivalry. "Every time I fill a vacant post," said Louis, "I make a hundred people discontented, and one ungrateful."[96] There were quarrels for precedence at table or in attending the King; even Saint-Simon worried lest the Duc de Luxembourg should walk five steps in advance of him in a procession, and Louis had to banish three dukes from court because they refused to yield precedence to foreign princes. The King laid great stress on protocol, and frowned when, at dinner, he found an untitled lady seated above a duchess.[97] Doubtless some fixed order was necessary to keep six hundred beribboned egos from trampling upon one another's toes, and visitors praised the external harmony of the enormous entourage. From the palaces, receptions, and entertainments of the King a code of etiquette, standards of manners and taste, spread through the upper and middle classes, and became a part of the European heritage.

To keep all these lords and ladies from being bored into regicide, artists of every kind were engaged to arrange amusements—tournaments, hunts, tennis, billiards, bathing or boating parties, dinners, dances, balls, masques, ballets, operas, concerts, plays. Versailles seemed heaven on earth when the King led the court into boats on the canal, and voices and instruments made music, and torches helped the moon and the stars to illuminate the scene. And what could be more splendid or more suffocating than the formal balls, when the Galerie des Glaces reflected in its massive mirrors the grace and sparkle of men and women in stately dances under a thousand lights? To celebrate the birth of the Dauphin (1662) the King arranged a ballet in the square before the Tuileries, attended by fifteen thousand people. The Commune of 1871 destroyed the palace, but the site of that famous fete is still called the Place du Carrousel.

Louis loved dancing, praised it as "one of the most excellent and important disciplines for training the body,"[98] and established at Paris (1661) the Académie Royale de Danse. He himself took part in ballets, and the nobility followed suit. The composers at his court were kept busy preparing music for dances and ballets; there the dance suite developed which was so skillfully used by Purcell in England and the Bachs in Germany. Not since Imperial Rome had the dance reached such graceful and harmonious forms.

In 1645 Mazarin imported Italian singers to establish opera in Paris. The Cardinal's death interrupted this initiation, but when the King grew up he founded an Académie de l'Opéra (1669), and commissioned Pierre Perrin to present operas in several cities of France, beginning with Paris in 1671. When Perrin bankrupted himself through excessive outlays for scenery and machinery, Louis transferred the *privilège des académies de musique* to Jean Baptiste Lully, who soon made the whole court dance to his tunes.

He too was a gift of Italy. The Chevalier de Guise brought him, as a peasant boy of seven, from Florence to France in 1646 "as a present" to his niece, La Grande Mademoiselle, who gave him work as an assistant in her kitchen (*sousmarmiton*). He annoyed his fellow servants by practicing the violin, but Mademoiselle recognized his talent, and provided him with an instructor. Soon he was playing in the royal band of twenty-four violins. Louis took a liking to him, and gave him a small ensemble to conduct. Through this little string orchestra he learned to conduct and to compose —dance music, songs, violin solos, cantatas, church music, thirty ballet suites, twenty operas. He became friendly with Molière, collaborated with him in several ballets, and composed *divertissements* for some of Molière's plays.

His success as a courtier rivaled his triumphs as a musician. In 1672, through Mme. de Montespan's influence, he succeeded in acquiring a monopoly on opera in Paris. He found in Philippe Quinault a librettist who was also a poet. Together they produced a succession of operas that constituted a revolution in French music. Not only did these performances delight the court at Versailles, they brought the elite of Paris to the theater that had been built for Lully in the Rue St.-Honoré, and in such numbers that the street was blocked with carriages, and patrons in many cases had to get out and walk, often through mud, lest they miss Act One. Boileau frowned upon opera as an enervating effeminacy,[99] but the King granted a charter to the Académie de Musique (1672), and authorized "gentlemen and ladies to sing at the representations of the said Academy without derogation" to their rank.[100] Louis raised Lully to the nobility as a secretary to the king; other secretaries complained that this was too high a post for a musician; but Louis told Lully, "I have honored them, not you, by placing a man of genius among them."[101] Everything prospered for Lully till 1687; then, while conducting, he accidentally struck his foot with the cane that he used as a baton; the wound, maltreated by a quack, developed gangrene, and the ebullient composer died at the age of forty-eight. French opera still feels his influence.

One more name survives from the music of that lordly reign. The Couperins were another case of heredity in art, contributing composers to France for two centuries, and ruling from 1650 to 1826 the great organ in the Church of St.-Gervais. François Couperin "le Grand" held that post for forty-eight years; he was also *organiste du roi* in the King's chapel at Versailles, and was the most famous harpsichordist of the "great century." His compositions for that instrument were closely studied by Johann Sebastian Bach; and his treatise *L'Art de toucher le clavecin* (the French name for the clavichord) influenced the great German's *Das wohltemperirte Clavier*. Was music in the Couperin blood, or only in the Couperin home? Probably it is social, not biological, heredity that makes civilization.

VII. THE KING'S WOMEN

Louis was not a rake. We must always remember, in the case of kings even to our own century, that custom required them to sacrifice their personal preferences in order to contract marriages of some political utility to the state. Consequently society—and often the Church—winked an eye when a king sought the exhilaration of sex and the romance of love outside the marriage bond. If Louis had had his way he would have begun with a marriage of love. He was deeply moved by the beauty and charm of Marie Mancini, a niece of Mazarin; he begged his mother and the Cardinal to let him marry her (1658); Anne of Austria reproved him for allowing passion to interfere with politics; and Mazarin regretfully sent Marie off to marry a Colonna. Then for a year the subtle minister pulled wires to get as Louis' bride María Teresa, daughter of Philip IV. What if, by some failure of the male line in the Spanish kings, this Infanta should bring all Spain as her dowry to the King of France? So in 1660, with all the costly splendor that mesmerized the taxpayers, Louis married María, both of them twenty-two years old.

Marie Thérèse was a proud woman, pious and virtuous; her example and influence helped to improve the morals of the court, at least in her entourage. But a severe discipline had made her somber and dull, and her great appetite was amplifying her, just when the beauties of Paris were ogling her handsome mate. She gave him six children, of whom only one, the Dauphin, survived infancy.* It was her misfortune that in the very year of

---

* Mme. de Montespan, who was a bit biased, related in her memoirs how an African prince presented Marie with a Negro dwarf, and how Marie gave birth to "a fine, healthy girl, black from head to toe." The Queen ascribed the color to being frightened by the dwarf during her pregnancy. The Paris *Gazette* announced that the girl had died shortly after birth, but apparently she survived, was brought up by a colored family, and became a nun.[102]

their marriage Louis had discovered in his sister-in-law Henrietta Anne all
the charms of young womanhood.

Henrietta Anne was the daughter of England's Charles I. Her mother,
Henrietta Maria (daughter of Henry IV of France), had shared with her
husband the tragedy of the Civil War. When the Parliament army approached Charles's headquarters at Oxford, the English Queen fled to
Exeter, and there, so ill that she expected death, she gave birth (1644) to
"a lovely little princess." Pursued by Parliamentary agents, the ailing
mother fled again, and made her way clandestinely to the coast, where a
Dutch vessel, narrowly escaping English guns, took her to France. The
child, left behind with Lady Anne Dalkeith, lived through two years of
concealment in England before she too could be safely gotten across the
Channel. Soon she had to experience the vicissitudes of the Fronde; in
January, 1649, she joined her mother and Anne of Austria in the flight from
barricaded Paris to St.-Germain. In that month the news came—doubtless
kept from her for a time—that her father had been beheaded by the victorious Roundheads. After the Fronde subsided, Princess Henrietta was
brought up in comfort and piety by her mother, and both lived to see
Charles II restored to the English throne (1660). A year later, aged sixteen,
she married the brother of Louis XIV, "Monsieur" Philippe Duc d'Orléans,
and became "Madame."

Monsieur was a little round-bellied man on high-heeled shoes, who
loved feminine adornments and masculine forms; as brave as any knight
in battle, but as painted, perfumed, beribboned, and begemmed as the
vainest woman in this vainest land. It was a grief and a shame to Henrietta
that her husband preferred the company of the Chevaliers de Lorraine and
de Châtillon to her own. Almost everybody else fell in love with her, not
so much for her frail beauty—though she was considered the fairest
creature at the court[103]—as for her gentle and kindly spirit, her almost
childlike vivacity and gaiety, the fresh vernal breeze that she brought
wherever she went. Racine—one of the many authors whom she inspired
and helped—called her "the arbiter of all that is beautiful."[104]

At first Louis XIV found her too weak and slender for his vigor and
taste; but as he came to feel the *douceur et lumière*, "sweetness and light,"[105]
of her character, he found increasing pleasure in her presence, delighted to
dance with her, frolic with her, plan games with her, go walking in the
park at Fontainebleau or boating on the canal with her, until all Paris
assumed that she had become his mistress, and thought it a just revenge on
the "King of Sodom."[106] But probably Paris misjudged. Louis loved her
this side of adultery, and she, who spent her devotion in love for her
brothers Charles and James, accepted the King as another brother, and
took it as her mission to bind all three in alliance or amity.

In 1670, at Louis' request, she crossed to England to persuade Charles to join France against Holland, even to urge him to proclaim his Catholic faith. Charles so promised in the secret Treaty of Dover (June 1, 1670), and Henrietta returned to France loaded with gifts and victory. A few days after reaching her palace at St.-Cloud she fell violently ill. She thought she had been poisoned, and so all Paris believed. The King and his Queen hurried to her bedside, along with the penitent Monsieur, and Condé, Turenne, Mme. de La Fayette, and Mademoiselle de Montpensier; and Bossuet came to pray with her. At last, on June 30, her suffering ended. A post-mortem examination revealed that she had died not of poison but of peritonitis.[107] Louis gave her such a funeral as was usually reserved for crowned heads, and over her remains in St.-Denis Bossuet preached a funeral sermon that has reverberated through the centuries.

It was Henrietta who gave the King the first of his more public mistresses. Born at Tours in 1644, Louise de La Vallière received with unquestioning faith the religious education given her by her mother and her priestly uncle, the future bishop of Nantes. She had barely reached the age of First Communion when her father died. Her mother remarried; the new husband, maître d'hôtel for Gaston, Duc d'Orléans, secured a place for Louise as lady in waiting to the daughters of the Duke; and when, after Gaston's death, his nephew and successor Philippe married, he took Louise with him as a maid of honor to Henrietta (1661). In that capacity she frequently saw the King. She was dazzled by his splendor, power, and personal fascination. Like a hundred other women she fell in love with him, but hardly dreamed of speaking to him.

Her beauty was more of character than of form. She was delicate in health, limped a bit, and "had no bosom to speak of," said a critic; and she was alarmingly thin. But her frailty was itself a charm, for it engendered in her a modesty and gentleness that disarmed even women. Henrietta, to discourage the gossip that she herself was the royal mistress, had the King's attention drawn to Louise. The scheme worked too well; Louis was attracted by this timid girl of seventeen, so different from the proud and aggressive ladies who surrounded him at the court. One day, finding her alone in the gardens at Fontainebleau, he offered himself to her, with no very honorable intentions. She surprised him by confessing that she loved him, but she long resisted his importunities. She pleaded with him not to make her betray both Henrietta and the Queen. Nevertheless, by August, 1661, she was his mistress. Everything seemed good if it was the King's will.

Then the King in turn fell in love, and was never so happy as with this diffident fledgling. They picnicked like children, danced at balls, and pranced in ballets; by his side in the hunt she lost her timidity and rode so impetuously that, said the Duc d'Enghien, "not even the men can keep up with her."[108] She took no advantage of her triumph; she refused to accept gifts or to join in intrigues; she remained modest in adultery. She was ashamed of her position, and suffered when the King introduced her to the Queen. She bore him several children; two died early; a third and a fourth, legitimized by royal decree, became the Conte de Vermandois and the very beautiful Mlle. de Blois. During these maternal crises she saw prettier faces than hers drawing the eyes of the King; by 1667 he was enamored of Mme. de Montespan; and Louise began to think of expiating her sins by spending the remainder of her life in a nunnery.

Sensing this mood, Louis gave her many signs of lingering affection, and thought to keep her in his world by making her a duchess. But between Montespan and war he found less and less time for her, and at the court she cared for no one but him. In 1671 she renounced her worldly possessions, put on the simplest dress she could find, slipped out of the palace on a winter morning, and fled to the convent of Ste.-Marie-de-Chaillot. Louis sent after her, protesting his love and anguish; and she, still a maid in mind, consented to return to the court. She stayed there three years more, torn between her love for the faithless King and her longing for religious cleansing and peace; already, in secret, she practiced in the palace the austerities of conventual life. Finally she persuaded the King to release her. She joined the barefoot Carmelite nuns in the Rue d'Enfer (1674), became Sister Louise de la Miséricorde, and lived there in ascetic penitence for her remaining thirty-six years. "My soul is so content, so tranquil," she said, "that I worship the goodness of God."[109]

Her successor in the King's favor has not won such universal forgiveness. Françoise Athénaïs Rochechouart came to the court in 1661, served the Queen as a maid of honor, and married the Marquis de Montespan (1663). According to Voltaire she was one of the three most beautiful women in France, and the other two were her sisters.[110] Her pearl-studded blond curls, her languorous proud eyes, her sensuous lips and laughing mouth, her caressing hands, her skin with the color and texture of lilies—so her contemporaries breathlessly described her, and so Henri Gascard painted her in a famous portrait. She was pious, she fasted strictly on fast days, and attended church devoutly and frequently. She had a bad temper and a cutting wit, but that was at first a challenge.

Michelet quoted her as having said she had come up to Paris resolved to capture the King;[111] but Saint-Simon reports that when she saw that she was quickening the royal pulse, she begged her husband to take her back at once to Poitou.[112] He refused, confident of his hold on her, and loving the aura of the court. One night at Compiègne she went to sleep in a room usually assigned to the King. For a while he tried to sleep in an adjoining room; he found it difficult; at last he took possession of his room and her

(1667). The Marquis, hearing of it, put on widower's garb, draped his carriage in black, and adorned its corners with horns. Louis with his own hand wrote the bill of divorcement between the Marquis and the Marquise, sent him 100,000 écus, and bade him leave Paris. The court, quite shorn of morals, smiled.

For seventeen years Mme. de Montespan was mistress of the royal bed. She gave Louis what La Vallière could not give him—intelligent conversation and stimulating vivacity. She boasted that she and dullness could never be in the same place at the same time; and it was so. She bore six children to the King. He loved them, and was grateful to her; but he could not resist the opportunity to sleep, now and then, with Mme. de Soubise or the young Mlle. de Scorraille de Roussilles, whom he made the Duchesse de Fontanges. Such aberrations led Mme. de Montespan to consult sorceresses for magic potions or other means to keep the King's love; but the story that she planned to poison him or her rivals was probably a legend spread by her enemies.[113]

Her children were her undoing. She needed someone to take care of them; Mme. Scarron was recommended, and was engaged; Louis, going frequently to see his brood, observed that the governess was beautiful. Mme. Scarron, nee Françoise d' Aubigné, was the granddaughter of Théodore Agrippa d'Aubigné, Huguenot aide to Henry IV. Born in a prison at Niort in Poitou, where her father was serving one of many sentences for a variety of crimes, she was baptized a Catholic, and was brought up amid the disorder and poverty of a divided family. Some Protestants took pity on her, fed her, and made her so firm in the Reformed faith that she turned her back upon Catholic altars. When she was nine her parents took her to Martinique, where she nearly died under the harsh discipline of her mother. The father dying a year later (1645), the widow and her three children returned to France. In 1649 Françoise, aged fourteen, again a Catholic, was placed in a convent, and earned her bread with menial tasks. Probably we should never have heard of her had she not married Paul Scarron.

He was a famous writer, a brilliant wit, an almost complete cripple, hideously deformed. The son of a lawyer of note, he had expected a prosperous career, but his widowed father married again, the new wife rejected Paul, the father sent him off with a small pension, just enough to entertain Marion Delorme and other ladies of a night. He contracted syphilis, surrendered himself to a quack, and imbibed strong drugs that ruined his nervous system. At last he was so paralyzed that he could move hardly anything but his hands. He described himself:

> Reader, . . . I am going to tell you as nearly as possible what I am like. My figure was well made, though small. My malady has shortened it by a good foot. My head is rather large for my body. My face is full, while my body is that of a skeleton. My sight is fairly good, but my

eyes protrude, and one of them is lower than the other. . . . My legs and thighs formed at first an obtuse, next a right, and finally an acute, angle; my thighs and body form another; and with my head bent down on my stomach I resemble not badly the letter Z. My arms have shrunk as well as my legs, and my fingers as well as my arms. To sum up, I am a condensation of human misery.[114]

He solaced his misery by writing a picaresque *Roman comique* (1649), which had considerable success, and by staging farces hilarious in their humor and scandalous in their wit. Paris honored him for keeping his gaiety amid his pains; Mazarin and Anne of Austria gave him pensions, which he forfeited by supporting the Fronde. He earned much, spent more, and was repeatedly in debt. Propped up in a box from which his head and arms emerged, he presided with zest and erudition over one of the famous salons of Paris. As his debts multiplied, he made his guests pay for their dinner. Still they came.

Who would marry such a man? In 1652 Françoise d'Aubigné, now sixteen, was living with a miserly female relative, who so grudged her keep that she resolved to send Françoise back to a convent. A friend introduced the girl to Scarron, who received her with painful grace. He offered to pay her board and lodging in the convent, so exempting her from taking the vows; she refused. Finally he proposed marriage to her, making it clear that he could not claim a husband's rights. She accepted him, served him as nurse and secretary, and played hostess at his salon, pretending not to hear the *double-entendres* of the guests. When she joined in the conversation they were surprised by her intelligence. She gave to Scarron's gatherings a degree of respectability sufficient to attract Mlle. de Scudéry, and, now and then, Mme. de Sévigné; Ninon, Gramont, and Saint-Évremond were already habitués. There is a hint in Ninon's letters that Mme. Scarron alleviated this sexless marriage with a liaison; but Ninon also reported that she "was virtuous from weakmindedness. I wanted to cure her, but she feared God too much."[115] Her devotion to Scarron was the talk of a Paris that unconsciously hungered for instances of decency. As his paralysis increased, even his fingers stiffened immovably; he could not turn a page or hold a pen. She read to him, wrote at his dictation, and ministered to all his wants. Before his death (1660) he composed his epitaph:

Celui qui ici maintenant dort	He who lies here
Fit plus de pitié que d'envie,	Awoke more pity than envy,
Et suffrit mille fois la mort	And suffered death a thousand times
Avant que perdre la vie.	Before losing life.
Passant, ne fais ici de bruit,	Passing, make here no noise,
Garde bien que tu ne l'éveille;	Take care not to wake him;
Car voici la première nuit	For this is the first night
Que le pauvre Scarron sommeille.[116]	That poor Scarron sleeps.

He left nothing but creditors. The "Widow Scarron," still a young woman of twenty-five, was again thrown destitute upon the world. She appealed to the Queen Mother to renew the canceled pension; Anne settled upon her two thousand livres annually. Françoise took a room in a convent, lived and dressed modestly, and accepted various minor employments in good homes.[117] In 1667 Mme. de Montespan, about to give birth, sent an emissary to ask her to receive and bring up the expected child. Françoise refused, but when Louis himself seconded the request she consented, and for several years thereafter she received the royal infants as they emerged.

She learned to love these children, and they looked up to her as a mother. The King, who at first had laughed at her as a prude, came to admire her, and was moved by the grief she showed when one of the children, despite her constant care, died. "She knows how to love," he said; "it would be a pleasure to be loved by her."[118] In 1673 he legitimized the children; Mme. Scarron had no longer to practice secrecy; she was admitted to the court as a lady in waiting to Mme. de Montespan. The King gave her a present of 200,000 livres to maintain her new status. She used them to buy an estate at Maintenon, near Chartres. She never lived there, but it gave her a new name; she became the Marquise de Maintenon.

It was a dizzy rise for one so lately destitute, and perhaps it turned her head for a time. She took upon herself to advise Mme. de Montespan to end her life of sin; Montespan resented the counsel, and thought that Maintenon was scheming to replace her. And indeed, by 1675, Louis was becoming more impatient with Montespan's tantrums, and was finding pleasure in talking with the new Marquise. Perhaps with the King's connivance Bishop Bossuet warned him that the Easter Sacrament would be refused him unless he dismissed his concubine. He bade her leave the court. She did; Louis received Communion, and remained continent for a while. Mme. de Maintenon approved his course, apparently without selfish intent,[119] for soon she left with the sickly Duc de Maine (one of Montespan's children) to seek the boy's cure in the sulphur baths of Barèges in the Pyrenees. Louis went off to the wars. Returning famished, he repulsed Bossuet, and invited Montespan to reoccupy her apartment in Versailles. There he fell into her waiting arms, and she conceived again.

Maintenon, returning with the cured Duke from the Pyrenees, was welcomed by the King and his mistress, but was alarmed to see him in the full swing of several simultaneous liaisons. In 1679 he ended his adulteries with Montespan by appointing her surintendante of the Queen's household —one of the many indelicacies to which he subjected Marie Thérèse. Montespan raged and wept, but was comforted by great gifts. A year later Maintenon received a similar post—lady of the bedchamber to the

Dauphine, the wife of Louis' one surviving legitimate child. The King now frequently visited the Dauphine, to converse with Maintenon. There seems no doubt that he wished to make the Marquise his mistress, and that she refused. On the contrary, she urged him to abandon his irregularities and return penitent to the Queen.[120] He yielded to her and Bossuet, and in 1681, after twenty years of philandering, he became a model husband. The Queen, who had long since reconciled herself to his infidelities, and even to his mistresses, enjoyed the royal favor for only two years, dying in 1683.

Louis thought that Maintenon would now consent to be his mistress, but he found in her a politic restraint: it must be marriage or nothing.[121] At some date not precisely known, but probably in 1684, he married her, he forty-seven, she fifty. It was a morganatic union, whereby the mate of lower status acquired no new rank, and no hereditary rights. The King's councilors had difficulty in dissuading him from giving his wife full rights, and crowning her as queen; they pointed out how discontent the royal family and the court would be to find themselves curtsying to a governess. So the marriage was not made public, and there are some who think it never took place. Saint-Simon, always a stickler for caste, thought it "a frightful marriage";[122] but it was the King's best and happiest union, the only one whose vows he appears to have kept. It had taken him almost half a century to discover that to be loved is worth monogamy.

VIII. *LE ROI S'EN VA-T-EN GUERRE*

The successes of Richelieu and Mazarin had left France the strongest power in Europe. The Empire was weakened by the exhaustion and division of Germany, and by renewed danger from the Turks. Spain was weakened by the exhaustion of her gold and men in eighty years of futile war in the Netherlands. England, after 1660, was bound to France by secret subsidies to its King. France too had been divided and weakened, but by 1667 the wounds of the Fronde had healed, and France was one. Meanwhile first-rate men had been found to rebuild the French armies: Louvois, a genius of military organization and discipline, Vauban, a genius of fortification, trench warfare, and siege, and two superlative generals— Condé and Turenne. Now, it seemed to the young and adulated King, was the time for France to reach to her natural geographical boundaries—the Rhine, the Alps, the Pyrenees, and the sea.

First, then, to the Rhine. The Dutch controlled it; they must be subdued; and soon thereafter they must be brought back to the faith that for a thousand years had been the helpful ally of kings. Once the many mouths of the great river were under French control, all the Rhineland, and therefore half of German commerce, would be in the power of France. The Spanish Netherlands ("Belgium") were in the way; they must be conquered. Philip IV, dying in 1665, left the Spanish Netherlands to Charles II, his son by his second marriage. Louis saw a diplomatic opening. He quoted the old custom of Hainaut and Brabant, by which the children of a first marriage inherited in preference to those of a second; Louis' wife was the daughter of Philip IV's first marriage; therefore, by this *ius devolutionis* —the right or law of devolution or transmission—the Spanish Netherlands belonged to Marie Thérèse. It was true that Marie, at her marriage, had renounced her right of succession; but this renunciation had been made conditional upon the payment of her dowry—500,000 gold crowns—by Spain to France;[123] this dowry had not been paid; *ergo* . . . Spain denied the syllogism, Louis declared the "War of Devolution." Let his own memoirs reveal the motives of the royal chess player:

> The death of the King of Spain and the war of the English against the Dutch (1665) offered me at once two important occasions for making war: one against Spain for the pursuance of rights which had fallen to me; the other against England for the defense of the Dutch. I saw with pleasure the plan of these two wars as a vast field where great occasions might arise for distinguishing myself. Many brave men whom I saw devoted to my service seemed always to be begging me to offer them an opportunity for valor. . . . Moreover, since I was obliged in any case to maintain a large army, it was more expedient for me to throw it into the Low Countries than to feed it at my expense. . . . Under pretext of a war with England I would dispose of my forces and my information [espionage] service to begin more successfully my enterprise in Holland.[124]

This was the royal view of war; it might make one's country greater in extent, security, or revenue; it would open roads to renown and power; it would provide outlets for combative impulses; it would let the costly army feed on alien food; it would improve the position of the state for the next war. As for the human lives that would be lost, men must die in any case; how absurd to die of some lingering disease in bed!—how better could men die than in the anesthesia of battle, on the field of glory, and for their fatherland?

On May 24, 1667, French troops crossed into the Spanish Netherlands. There was no effectual resistance; the French had 55,000, the Spanish 8,000, men; soon the King entered Charleroi, Tournai, Courtrai, Douai, Lille, as if in a triumphal procession; and Vauban fortified the conquered towns. Louvois had supplies ready at every step, even to silver service for the officers in camp or trench. Artois, Hainaut, Walloon Flanders were annexed to France. Spain appealed to the Emperor Leopold I for help; Louis proposed to Leopold to divide the Spanish empire with him; Leopold agreed, and gave no help to Spain. The conquest of Flanders had been so easy that Louis hurried to take also Franche-Comté—the region around Besançon, between Burgundy and Switzerland. It was a dependency of Spain, and yet a thorn in the very side of France. In February, 1668, a French army, twenty thousand strong, descended upon Franche-Comté under the lead of Condé; it was everywhere victorious, for French bribes had softened local commanders. Louis himself led the siege of Dôle; it fell in four days; and in three weeks all Franche-Comté submitted. He returned to Paris in glory.

But he had overreached himself. The United Provinces persuaded Sweden and England to join them in a Triple Alliance against France (January, 1668); all three states recognized that their political or commercial freedom would wither if the power of France should extend to the Rhine. Louis saw that he had moved too precipitately toward his goal. The secret agreement with Leopold had stipulated that on the death of Charles II of Spain all the Netherlands and Franche-Comté were to go to France; it seemed only a matter of a year or so when the sickly Charles would die; perhaps it was better for France to wait and let the fruit fall peacefully into her lap. Louis offered terms to the Alliance; his trained diplomats worked on England and Sweden; at the Treaty of Aix-la-Chapelle (May 2, 1668) the War of Devolution was ended. France returned Franche-Comté to Spain, but she retained Charleroi, Douai, Tournai, Audenaarde, Lille, Armentières, and Courtrai. Louis had kept half the spoils.

In 1672 he resumed his march to the Rhine, and now his real goal appeared—not Flanders but Holland. We shall see this tragedy later from the standpoint of the Dutch; in summary, the attack reached almost to Amsterdam and The Hague before it was checked by the opening of the dykes. But again Europe rose against the new threat to the balance of power. In October, 1672, Emperor Leopold joined the United Provinces and Brandenburg in a "Great Coalition"; Spain and Lorraine entered it in 1673; Denmark, the Palatinate, and the duchy of Brunswick-Lüneburg, in 1674; and in that year the English Parliament compelled its Francophile King to make peace with the Dutch.

Louis faced bravely this nemesis of his pride. Despite Colbert's complaints that he was impoverishing France, he raised more taxes, built a navy, and expanded his armies to 180,000 men. In June, 1674, he directed one force to a second siege of Besançon; in six weeks Franche-Comté was again conquered. Meanwhile Turenne, in the most brilliant and ruthless of his campaigns, led twenty thousand soldiers to victory over seventy thousand Imperial troops; to prevent the enemy from feeding itself, he laid waste the Palatinate, Lorraine, and part of Alsace; along the Rhine the desolation of the Thirty Years' War was renewed. On July 27, 1675, Turenne was killed while reconnoitering near Sulzbach in Baden. Louis had him buried in St.-Denis with almost royal honors, knowing that that one death equaled a dozen defeats. The Great Condé, after bloody victories in the Netherlands, replaced Turenne, and drove the Imperials from Alsace; then the Prince, worn out by years of passion and war, retired to a life of philosophy and government at Chantilly. Louis now took charge of the campaign in the Netherlands; he besieged and captured Valenciennes, Cambrai, St.-Omer, Ghent, and Ypres (1677–78). France acclaimed the King as a general.

But the drain upon his people had become unbearable. Revolts broke out in Bordeaux and Brittany; in south France the peasantry neared starvation; in the Dauphiné the populace was living on bread made of acorns and roots.[125] When the Dutch offered peace, Louis signed with them (August 11, 1678) a treaty restoring to the United Provinces all the territory that France had taken from them, and lowering the tariffs that had kept Dutch products out of France. He made up for these surrenders by forcing Spain, now in disintegration, to yield to him Franche-Comté, and a dozen towns that advanced the northeastern frontier of France into the Spanish Netherlands. A treaty with the Emperor kept for France the strategic cities of Breisach and Freiburg-im-Breisgau; Alsace and Lorraine remained in French hands. These treaties of Nijmegen (1678–79) and St.-Germain-en-Laye (1679) were a triumph for the United Provinces, but not a defeat for Louis; he had prevailed over the Empire and Spain, and, here and there, he had reached the coveted Rhine.

Despite the peace he kept up his immense army, knowing that an army in being is a force in diplomacy. With that power behind him, and taking scandalous advantage of the Emperor's preoccupation with the advancing Turks, he established in Alsace, Franche-Comté, and Breisgau "Chambers of Reunion" to reclaim certain frontier districts that had formerly belonged to them; these were occupied by French troops; and the great city of Strasbourg was induced, by the lavish lubrication of its officials, to acknowledge Louis as its sovereign (1681). In the same year, by like means, the Duke of Milan was led to cede to France the town and fortress of Casale, which controlled the road between Savoy and Milan.* When Spain dallied in handing over the Netherland cities, Louis again sent his

---

* The Man in the Iron Mask was probably the Count Mattioli who sold to Spain (1679) the secret of the negotiations between Louis and the Duke of Milan. Speculation has identified him with a mysterious prisoner Marchioli, whose face was hidden behind a velvet (not iron) mask, and who died in the Bastille in 1703.[126]

armies into Flanders and Brabant, overcame resistance with indiscriminate bombardment, and absorbed the duchy of Luxembourg en route (June, 1684). In the Truce of Regensburg (August 15) these conquests were provisionally recognized by Spain and the Emperor, for the Turks were besieging Vienna. By an alliance with the Elector of Cologne Louis in effect extended French power to the Rhine. Part of the Gallic aspiration to reach natural boundaries was realized.

This was the zenith of the Roi Soleil. Not since Charlemagne had France been so extended or so powerful. Immense and costly spectacles celebrated the successes of the Sun King. The Council of Paris officially declared him Louis le Grand (1680). Le Brun painted him as a god on the vaults of Versailles; and a theologian argued that Louis' victories proved the existence of God.[127] The populace, amid its destitution, idealized its ruler, and took pride in his apparent invincibility. Even foreigners praised him, seeing some geographical logic in his campaigns; the philosopher Leibniz hailed him as "that great prince who is the acknowledged glory of our time, and for whom succeeding ages will long in vain."[128] North of the Alps and the Pyrenees, west of the Vistula, all educated Europe began to speak his language and imitate his court, his arts, and his ways. The sun was high.

CHAPTER II

The Crucible of Faith

1643–1715

I. THE KING AND THE CHURCH

THE historian, like the journalist, tends to lose the normal background of an age in the dramatic foreground of his picture, for he knows that his readers will relish the exceptional and will wish to personify processes and events. Behind the rulers, ministers, courtiers, mistresses, and warriors of France were men and women competing for bread and mates, scolding and loving their children, sinning and confessing, playing and quarreling, going wearily to work, stealthily to brothels, humbly to prayer. The quest for eternal salvation occasionally interruped the struggle for daily survival; the dream of heaven grew as the lust for life declined; the cool naves of the churches gave respite from the heat of strife. The marvelous myths were the people's poetry; the Mass was the consoling drama of their redemption; and though the priest himself might be a covetous worldling, the message he brought lifted up the hearts of the defeated poor. The Church still rivaled the state as a pillar of society and power, for it was through hope that men submitted patiently to labor, law, and war.

The higher Catholic clergy knew their importance in the miracle of order, and shared with the nobility and the King the revenues of the nation and the splendor of the court. Bishops and archbishops associated in polished intimacy with the Condés, the Montpensiers, and the Sévignés; and a thousand abbés, half-ordained, half-married, flirted with women and ideas. By and large, however, the mentality and morals of the Catholic clergy— perhaps under the stimulus of competition from Huguenot ministers—were better than for centuries before.[1]

The nunneries were not the "hotbeds of vice" imagined by the mythopoetic frenzy of religious hate. Many were retreats of sincere, some-times ascetic piety, like the Carmelite convent to which Louise de la Vallière retired. Some others served as havens for genteel young women whose parents could find no husband or dowry for them, or who had committed some offense, or had offended some potentate. In such nunneries the inmates thought it no sin to receive a visitor from the outisde world, to dance with one another, to read secular literature, or to mitigate the tedium of their lives with billiards or cards. It was by reforming such a convent that Jacqueline Arnauld made Port-Royal the most famous nunnery in the history of France.

Of the monastic orders we cannot speak so leniently; many of them had relaxed their rules, and led lives of idleness, formal prayer, and mendicant importunity. Armand Jean de Rancé reformed the Monastery of Notre-Dame de la Trappe in Normandy, and established the austere Trappist order that still silently survives. The Jesuits entered more actively into the life and history of France. At the beginning of the seventeenth century they were under a cloud as defenders of regicide; at the end they were the confessors and guides of the King. They were experts in psychology. When the nun Marguerite Marie Alacoque, inspired by a mystic vision, founded (1675) the society devoted to the public worship of the Sacred Heart of Jesus, the Jesuits encouraged the movement as an outlet and stimulus for popular piety. At the same time they made religion easier for sinners by recognizing the naturalness of sin, and developing the science of casuistry as a means of mitigating the difficulties of the Ten Commandments and the neuroses of remorse. They were soon in demand as confessors, and gained authority as "directors of conscience," especially for the women who dominated French society, and who sometimes influenced national policy.

The word "casuistry" did not have in the seventeenth century the derogatory connotation left upon it by Pascal's *Provincial Letters*. As a confessor or spiritual director, every priest was expected to know just what was to be considered a mortal sin, or a venial sin, or no sin at all; and he had to be prepared to apply his knowledge, and adjust his judgment, his counsel, and the penance, to the special circumstances of the penitent and the case (*casus*). The rabbis had developed this art of moral distinctions to great length in the legal portions of the Talmud; modern jurisprudence and psychiatry have followed suit. Long before the establishment of the Society of Jesus, Catholic theologians had drawn up voluminous treatises on casuistry to guide the priest in moral doctrine and confessional practice. In what cases might the letter of the moral law be set aside for its spirit or intent? When might one lie or steal or kill, or reasonably break a promise, or violate an oath, or even deny the faith?

Some casuists demanded strict interpretation of the moral law, and thought that in the long run severity would prove more beneficial than laxity. Other casuists—especially the Jesuits Molina, Escobar, Toledo, and Busenbaum—favored a lenient code. They urged that allowances should be made for human nature, for environmental influences, for ignorance of the law, for extreme hardship of literal compliance, for the semi-insanity of transports of passion, and for any circumstances that hindered the freedom of the will. To facilitate this complaisant morality, the Jesuits developed the doctrine of probabilism—that where any recognized authority on moral theology favored a particular view, the confessor might at his discretion judge in accordance with that view, even though the majority of experts opposed it. (The word *probabilis* at that time meant approvable, admitting of approbation.[2]) Moreover, said some Jesuit casuists, it was sometimes permissible to lie, or to withhold the truth by a "mental reservation"; so a captured Christian, forced to choose between Mohammedanism and death, might without sin pretend to accept Islam. Again, said Escobar, the moral quality of an action lies not in the deed itself, which in itself is amoral, but in the moral intention of the agent; there is no sin unless there is a conscious and voluntary departure from the moral law.

Much Jesuit casuistry was a reasonable and humane adjustment of medievally ascetic rules to a society that had discovered the legitimacy of pleasure. But in France especially, and to a lesser degree in Italy, the Jesuits developed casuistry to such lenience with human frailty that earnest men like Pascal in Paris and Sarpi in Venice, and many Catholic theologians, including several Jesuits,[3] protested against what seemed to them a surrender of Christianity to sin. The Huguenots of France, inheriting the rigorous code of Calvin, were shocked by the Jesuit compromise with the world and the flesh. A powerful movement within Catholicism itself—Jansenism—raised at the convent of Port-Royal the flag of an almost Calvinistic ethic in an anti-Jesuit war that agitated France, and French literature, for a century. That war involved Louis XIV, for his confessors were Jesuits and his practice was not puritan. In 1674 Père La Chaise—"an even-tempered man," Voltaire described him, "with whom reconciliation was always easy"[4]—took charge of the royal conscience. He occupied the post for thirty-two years, forgiving everything and loved by all. "He was so good," said Louis, "that I sometimes reproached him for it."[5] But in his quiet and patient way he had great influence over the King, and helped to steer him to monogamy at last, and obedience to the pope.

For Louis was not always a good "papist." He was pious in his official way, and rarely failed to attend daily Mass.[6] In his memoirs he told his son:

> Partly out of gratitude for all the good fortune I had received, and partly to win the affection of my people . . . , I continued the exercises of piety in which my mother had brought me up. . . . And to tell you the truth, my son, we lack not only gratitude and justice, but prudence and good sense, when we fail in veneration of Him of whom we are but the lieutenants. Our submission to Him is the rule and example of that which is due to us.[7]

This, however, did not include submission to the papacy. Louis inherited the Gallican tradition—the Pragmatic Sanction of Bourges (1438) and the

Concordat of Francis I (1516)—which had established the right of French kings to appoint the bishops and abbots of France, to determine their income, and to appoint to all benefices in a diocese between the death of its bishop and the installation of his successor. Louis held that he was the vicar or representative of God in France, that his submission to the pope (as also a divine viceroy) should be limited to matters of faith and morals, and that the French clergy should obey the king in all matters affecting the French state.

A part of the French clergy—the Ultramontanes—repudiated these claims, and upheld the absolute authority of the popes over kings, councils, and episcopal nominations; but the majority—the Gallicans—defended the full independence of the king in temporal affairs, denied the infallibility of the pope except in agreement with an ecumenical council, and saw an advantage to the French clergy in evading the dominance of Rome. The Prince de Condé declared it his opinion that if it pleased the King to go over to Protestantism, the French clergy would be the first to follow him.[8] In 1663 the Sorbonne—the faculty of theology at the University of Paris— issued Six Articles emphatically affirming the Gallican position. The French *parlements* took the same stand, and supported Louis in claiming the right to determine which papal bulls should be published and accepted in France. In 1678 Pope Innocent XI protested against Gallicanism, and excommunicated the archbishop of Toulouse for deposing an anti-Gallican bishop. The King convoked an assembly of the clergy, nearly all chosen by him. In March, 1682, it reaffirmed the Six Articles of the Sorbonne, and drew up for the assembly the famous Four Articles that almost divorced the French Church from Rome.

1. The pope has jurisdiction in spiritual concerns, and has no authority to depose princes or release their subjects from obedience.

2. Ecumenical councils are above the pope in authority.

3. The traditional liberties of the French Church are inviolable.

4. The pope is infallible only when in accord with the council of bishops.

Innocent declared the decisions of the assembly null and void, and refused canonical institution to all new bishops who approved the articles. Since Louis appointed only such candidates, some thirty-five dioceses were without canonical bishops in 1688. But by that time age and Mme. de Maintenon had mollified the King, and death had taken the resolute pope. In 1693 Louis allowed his nominees to disavow the articles; Pope Innocent XII recognized the royal right over episcopal nominations; and Louis was again *Rex Christianissimus*, the Most Christian King.

II. PORT-ROYAL: 1204–1626

The old war between Church and state was the least of the three religious dramas that inflamed this reign. Deeper by far was the conflict between the orthodox Catholicism of state and clergy and the almost Protestant Catholicism of the Jansenists and Port-Royal; and deepest and most tragical, the destruction of the Huguenots in France. But what was Port-Royal, and why so much ado about it in French history? It was a Cistercian nunnery situated some sixteen miles from Paris and six miles from Versailles, on a low and marshy site in what Mme. de Sévigné called "a dreadful valley, just the place in which to find salvation."[9] Founded about 1204, it barely survived a hundred vicissitudes in the Hundred Years' War and the Wars of Religion. Discipline and membership fell; and probably the convent would have disappeared from notice had it not fallen under the rule of Jacqueline Arnauld, and enlisted in its defense the pen of Blaise Pascal.

Antoine Arnauld I (1560–1619) made history by his eloquence and his fertility. In 1593, after Barrière's attempt to assassinate Henry IV, Arnauld addressed the Paris Parlement in an indignant demand for the expulsion of the Jesuits from France. They never forgave him, and they looked with critical and ominous eye upon the operations of his family at Port-Royal. Of his twenty or more children at least four were involved in the story of that convent. Jacqueline Arnauld was made coadjutrix to the abbess of Port-Royal at the age of seven (1598), and a year later her sister Jeanne, aged six, became abbess of St.-Cyr. These nominations were made by Henry IV, and were confirmed by papal bulls obtained through falsifying the ages of the girls.[10] Presumably the father had sought these places for his daughters as an alternative to finding husbands and dowries for them.

When Jacqueline, as Mère Angélique, became nominal abbess at Port-Royal (1602), she found only the most genial discipline among the thirteen nuns. Each had her own property, displayed her hair, used cosmetics, and dressed in the fashion of the day. They took the Sacrament infrequently, and had heard no more than seven sermons in thirty years.[11] As she grew more conscious of the life to which her parents had committed her, the young abbess became discontent, and meditated flight (1607). "I thought of leaving Port-Royal and returning to the world, without notifying my father or my mother, to escape this unbearable yoke, and to be married."[12] She fell ill, and was taken home, where she was nursed by her mother with such tender care that, on recovering, she returned to Port-Royal resolved, for love of her mother, to keep her conventual vows. However, she ordered a whalebone corset to keep her figure in fashionable bounds.[13] She remained secretly averse to the religious life until, at Easter of 1608, now in the full glow of puberty, she heard a sermon by a Capuchin monk on the sufferings of Christ. "During this sermon," she later reported, "God touched me in such a way that from that moment I found myself happier in the life of a nun . . . and I know not what I would not have done for God if He had continued the movement which His grace had given me."[14] This, in her language, was the "first work of grace."

On November 1 of that year another sermon—the "second work of grace"—filled her with shame that she and her nuns were so lax in observing their vows of poverty and seclusion. Torn between affection for the nuns and desire to enforce the Cistercian rule, she became melancholy, practiced austerities beyond her strength, and fell into a fever. She must have been lovable, for when the nuns asked the reason of her sadness, and she revealed her wish that they should return to the full rule of their order, they consented, pooled their private property, and pledged themselves to perpetual poverty.

The next step, seclusion from the world, was more painful. Mère Angélique forbade the nuns to leave the premises, or to receive visitors—even their nearest relatives—without express permission, and then only in the parlor. They complained that this would be a great hardship. To give them a fortifying example, she resolved not to see her parents on their next visit, except through a grate or lattice window in the door between the parlor and the convent rooms. When her father and mother came they were shocked to find that she would talk to them only through this *guichet*. The *journée du guichet* (September 25, 1609) became famous in the literature about Port-Royal.

The anger of the excluded family subsided, and the piety of Mère Angélique (now eighteen years old) so moved them that one Arnauld after another entered Port-Royal. In 1618 Anne Eugénie, sister of the abbess, took the vows. Soon other sisters joined them—Catherine, Marie, Madeleine. In 1629 their mother, now a widow, knelt at the feet of Mère Angélique, and begged to be admitted as a novice. In due time she took the vows, and lived humbly and happily under her daughter, whom she henceforth called Mother. When she died (1641) she thanked God that she had given six daughters to the religious life. Five of her granddaughters later entered Port-Royal. Her son Robert and three of her grandsons became "solitaries" there; her most brilliant son, Antoine Arnauld II, member of the Sorbonne, became the philosopher and theologian of Port-Royal. We marvel at such fertility, and cannot but respect such depth of devotion, loyalty, and faith.*

---

* Sainte-Beuve noted that "several of the young ladies who became the outstanding nuns of Port-Royal had had smallpox, which at an early age had disfigured their faces," and added slyly, "I do not wish to say that we give to God only that which no longer has value in the world."[15]

Step by step Mère Angélique led her flock back to the full Cistercian rule. The nuns, now thirty-six in number, observed all fasts with canonical strictness, maintained long periods of silence, rose at two o'clock in the morning to chant matins, and out of their communal property dispensed charity to the local poor. From Port-Royal the reforms spread; nuns trained there were sent to convents throughout France to spur them back to their rule. A convent at Maubuisson was especially lax: Henry IV had used it as a place of assignation with his mistress Gabrielle d'Estrées; its abbess was surrounded by her own illegitimate daughters; the nuns moved freely from their home to meet and dance with the monks of a neighboring monastery.[16] In 1618 Mère Angélique was requested by her superiors to replace the abbess at Maubuisson; she stayed there for five years; when she returned to Port-Royal thirty-two Maubuisson nuns followed her into the mother convent of the reform.

In 1626 an epidemic of ague broke out at Port-Royal. Advised that the damp climate there was dangerous, Angélique and her nuns moved to a house in Paris, where, under the influence of Jansenism, they entered upon their historic conflict with the Jesuits and the King. The deserted and dilapidated buildings at Port-Royal-des-Champs—"of the Fields"—were soon occupied by the Solitaries, men who, while not taking monastic vows, wished to lead an almost monastic life. Here came several of the Arnaulds— Antoine II, his brother Robert Arnauld d'Andilly, his nephews Antoine Lemaistre and Simon Lemaître de Séricourt, and his grandson Isaac Louis de Sacy; some ecclesiastics joined them, like Pierre Nicole and Antoine Singlin; even some nobles—the Duc de Luynes and the Baron de Pontchâteau. Together they drained swamps, dug ditches, repaired the buildings, and tended the orchards and gardens. Together or individually they practiced austerities, fasted, chanted, and prayed. They wore the dress of peasants, and during the coldest winter they allowed no heat in their rooms. They studied the Bible and the Fathers of the Church; they wrote works of devotion and scholarship; one of these, *L'Art de penser* (*The Art of Thinking*), by Nicole and the younger Arnauld, remained a popular manual of logic till the twentieth century.

In 1638 the Solitaries opened *petites écoles*, "little schools," to which they invited selected children of age nine or ten. These were taught French, Latin, Greek, and the orthodox aspects of Descartes' philosophy. They were required to shun dancing and the theater (both of which the Jesuits approved); they were to pray frequently, but not to the saints; and in the chapel where they heard Mass there were no religious images. At Port-Royal-des-Champs and at Port-Royal-de-Paris the challenge of Arnauld piety to the immorality of the court became also the challenge of the stern

Jansenist theology and ethic to the Jesuit mitigation of Christianity to the nature of man.

III. THE JANSENISTS AND THE JESUITS

Cornelis Jansen was a Dutchman, born in the province of Utrecht of Catholic parentage, but closely touched by the Augustinian theology of his Calvinist neighbors. When he entered the Catholic University of Louvain (1602) he found it in the heat of a violent controversy between the Jesuit or Scholastic party and a faction that followed the Augustinian views of Michael Baius on predestination and divine grace. Jansen inclined to the Augustinians. In the interval between his undergraduate studies and his professorial work, Jansen accepted the invitation of his fellow student Jean Duvergier de Hauranne to live with him at Bayonne. They studied St. Paul and St. Augustine, and agreed that the best way of defending Catholicism against the Dutch Calvinists and the French Huguenots was to follow the Augustinian emphasis on grace and predestination, and to establish in the Catholic clergy and laity a rigorous moral code that would shame current laxity in court and convent, and the easygoing ethic of the Jesuits.

In 1616 Jansen, as head of a hostel of Dutch students at Louvain, attacked the Jesuit theology of free will, and preached a mystical puritanism akin to the Pietism that was taking form in Holland, England, and Germany. He continued the war as professor of Scriptural exegesis at Louvain, and as bishop of Ypres. At his death (1638) he left, not quite finished, a substantial treatise, *Augustinus,* which, soon after its publication in 1640, became the doctrinal platform of Port-Royal, and the center of contention in French Catholic theology for almost a century.

Though the book ended with a curtsy of submission to the Roman Church, the Calvinists of the Netherlands acclaimed it as the very essence of Calvinism.[17] Like Augustine, Luther, and Calvin, Jansen fully accepted predestinarianism: God, even before the creation of the world, had chosen those men and women who should be saved, and had determined who should be damned; the good works of men, though precious, could never earn salvation without the aid of divine grace; and even among the good minority only a few would be saved. The Catholic Church had not explicitly repudiated the predestinarianism of St. Paul and St. Augustine, but she had let it sink into the background of her teaching as hard to reconcile with that freedom of the will which seemed logically indispensable to moral responsibility and the idea of sin. But man's will is not free, said Jansen; it lost its freedom by Adam's sin; man's nature is now corrupt beyond self-redemption; and only God's grace, earned by Christ's death, can save him. The Jesuit defense of free will seemed to Jansen to exaggerate the role of good works in earning salvation, and to render almost superfluous the redeeming death of Christ. Moreover, he urged, we must not take logic too seriously; reason is a faculty far inferior to trustful, unquestioning faith, just as ritual observances are an inferior form of religion as compared with the direct communion of the soul with God.

These ideas came to Port-Royal through Duvergier, who meanwhile had become abbot of St.-Cyran. Fired with zeal to reform theology and morals, and to replace external religion with internal devotion, M. de Saint-Cyran, as he was now called, came up to Paris, and was soon (1636) accepted as spiritual director of the nuns at Port-Royal-de-Paris and of the *solitaires* at Port-Royal-des-Champs; that double institution now became the voice and exemplar of Jansenism in France. Richelieu thought the reformer a troublesome fanatic, and jailed him in Vincennes (1638). Saint-Cyran was released in 1642, but he died a year later of an apoplectic stroke.

Even from his prison he had continued to inspire innumerable Arnaulds. Antoine II, "the Great Arnauld," published in 1643 a treatise *De la Fréquente Communion*, which carried on his father's war against the Jesuits. He did not name them, but he denounced the idea, which he felt that some confessors had tolerated, that repeated sinning could be compensated by frequent confession and Communion. The Jesuits felt that the attack was meant for them, and they mounted up the score against the Arnaulds. Anticipating trouble, Antoine left Paris for Port-Royal-in-the-Fields. In 1648 the nuns, frightened by the Fronde, also left the capital, and returned to their former home. The Solitaries vacated the rooms there, and moved to a nearby farmhouse, Les Granges.

Pope Urban VIII had already (1642) condemned the general doctrine of Jansen's *Augustinus*. In 1649 a professor in the Sorbonne asked the faculty to condemn seven propositions which, he said, were gaining too much popularity. The matter was referred to Innocent X, and the Jesuits took the opportunity to impress upon the Pope the dangers of Jansenism as essentially a Calvinist theology in Catholic guise. At last they prevailed upon him to issue the bull *Cum occasione* (May 31, 1653), which condemned as heretical five propositions allegedly taken from the *Augustinus*:

    1. There are divine precepts which good men, though willing, are absolutely unable to obey.

    2. No person can resist the influence of divine grace.

    3. In order to render human actions meritorious or otherwise, it is not requisite that they be exempt from necessity but only free from constraint.

4. The semi-Pelagian heresy consisted in allowing the human will to be endued with a power of resisting grace, or of complying with its influence.

5. Whoever says that Christ died, or shed his blood, for all mankind, is a semi-Pelagian.[18]

These propositions were not taken verbatim from the *Augustinus*: they were formulated by a Jesuit as a summary of the book's teaching. As a summary they were fair enough,[19] but the Jansenists contended that the propositions, as such, were not to be found in Jansen—though Arnauld slyly suggested that they could all be found in St. Augustine. Meanwhile nobody seems to have read the book.

Antoine Arnauld was a fighter. He acknowledged the infallibility of the pope in matters of faith and morals, but not in questions of fact; and as a matter of fact he denied that Jansen had stated the propositions condemned. In 1655 he again carried the war to the Jesuits by publishing two *Lettres à un duc et pair* (*Letters to a Duke and Peer*), attacking what he claimed to be Jesuit methods in the confessional. The Sorbonne entertained a motion to expel him. He prepared his defense, and read it to his friends at Port-Royal. It did not impress them. One of them was a new adherent named Blaise Pascal. Turning to him, Arnauld pleaded, "You, who are young, why cannot you produce something?"[20] Pascal retired to his room, and wrote the first of the *Provincial Letters*, a classic in the literature and philosophy of France. We should listen to Pascal at some length, for he was not only the greatest writer of French prose, but the most brilliant defender of religion in all the Age of Reason.

IV. PASCAL: 1623–62

1. Himself

His father, Étienne Pascal, was president of the Court of Aides at Clermont-Ferrand in south-central France. His mother died three years after his birth, leaving also an elder sister, Gilberte, and a younger sister, Jacqueline. When Blaise was eight the family moved to Paris. Étienne was a student of geometry and physics, sufficiently advanced to gain him the friendship of Gassendi, Mersenne, and Descartes. Blaise eavesdropped on some of their meetings, and became, in the first period of his life, a devotee of science. At the age of eleven he composed a short treatise on the sounds of vibrating bodies. The father thought that the boy's passion for geometry would injure his other studies, and forbade his further pursuit of mathematics for a while. But one day (story tells), Étienne found him writing on the wall, with a piece of coal, the proof that the three angles of a triangle equal two right angles;[21] thenceforth the boy was allowed to study Euclid. Before he was sixteen he composed a treatise on conic sections; most of it is lost, but one theorem was a lasting contribution to that science, and still bears his name. Descartes, shown the manuscript, refused to believe that the composition was not by the father but by the son.

In that year, 1639, his pretty sister Jacqueline, then thirteen years old, played a dramatic part in the life of the family. The father had invested in municipal bonds; Richelieu reduced the rate of interest paid on these bonds; Étienne criticized him; the Cardinal threatened to arrest him; Étienne hid in Auvergne. But the Cardinal liked plays and girls; Scudéry's *L'Amour tyrannique* was performed before him by a group of girls including Jacqueline; he was especially pleased by her acting; she took the opportunity to ask him to forgive her father; he did, and appointed him intendant at Rouen, the capital of Normandy. Thither the family moved in 1641.

It was there that Blaise, now nineteen, contrived the first of several computing machines, some of which are still preserved in the Conservatoire des Arts et Métiers at Paris. Their principle was a succession of wheels, each divided into nine digits and zero, each geared to turn one tenth of a revolution for each full revolution of the wheel at its right, and each showing its uppermost figure in a slot at the top. The machine could only add, and was not commercially practicable, but it stands near the head of a development that now astonishes the world. Pascal sent one of his computers to Christina of Sweden, with a very eloquent letter of adulation. She invited him to her court, but he felt himself too frail for that heroic climate.

The eager young scientist was intensely interested in the experiments that Torricelli had published on the weight of the atmosphere. Independently of Torricelli, but probably on a suggestion from Descartes,[22] Pascal conceived the idea that the mercury in a Torricelli tube would rise to different heights in different places according to variations in atmospheric pressure. He sent a request to his brother-in-law in Auvergne to carry a tube of mercury to a mountaintop, and observe any difference, at diverse levels, in the height of the mercury in the closed portion of a tube whose other end was open to the pressure of the atmosphere. Florin Périer did as asked: on September 19, 1648, with several friends, he ascended the Puy de Dôme, a mountain five thousand feet above the town of Clermont-Ferrand; there the mercury rose to a level of twenty-three inches in the tube, whereas at the base of the mountain it rose to twenty-six inches. The experiment was hailed throughout Europe as finally establishing the principle and value of the barometer.

Pascal's fame as a scientist brought him (1648) a stimulating appeal from a gambler to formulate the mathematics of chance. He accepted the challenge, and shared with Fermat in developing the calculus of probabilities, which now enters so profitably into insurance tables of sickness and mortality. At this stage of his growth there was no sign that he would ever transfer his devotion from science to religion, or lose his faith in reason and experiment. He continued for ten years to work at scientific problems, chiefly mathematical. As late as 1658 he offered, anonymously, a prize for the quadrature of a cycloid—the curve traced by a point on a circle rolling in a straight line on a plane. Solutions were offered by Wallis, Huygens, Wren, and others; then Pascal, under a pseudonym, published his own solution. A controversy followed in which the competitors, including Pascal, behaved less than philosophically.

Meanwhile two basic influences had come to the fore in his life: sickness and Jansenism. As early as his eighteenth year he suffered from a nervous ailment that left him hardly a day without pain. In 1647 a paralytic attack so disabled him that he could not move without crutches. His head ached, his bowels burned, his legs and feet were continually cold, and required wearisome aids to circulation of the blood; he wore stockings steeped in brandy to warm his feet. Partly to get better medical treatment he moved with Jacqueline to Paris. His health improved, but his nervous system had been permanently damaged. Henceforth he was subject to a deepening hypochondria, which affected his character and his philosophy. He became irritable, subject to fits of proud and imperious anger, and he seldom smiled.[23]

His father had always been a devout, even an austere, Catholic amid his scientific avocations, and had taught his children that religious faith was their most precious possession, something far beyond the reach or judgment of the frail reasoning powers of mankind. At Rouen, when the father was seriously injured, a Jansenist physician treated him successfully; through this contact a Jansenist tinge colored the family's faith. When Blaise and Jacqueline moved to the capital they frequently attended Mass at Port-Royal-de-Paris. Jacqueline wished to enter the convent as a nun, but her father could not bring himself to let her go out of his daily life. He died in 1651, and soon thereafter Jacqueline became a nun in Port-Royal-des-Champs. Her brother tried in vain to dissuade her.

For a time they engaged in a dispute over the division of their patrimony. When this was settled Blaise found himself both rich and free—a condition hostile to sanctity. He took a sumptuously furnished home, staffed it with many servants, and drove about Paris in a coach behind four or six horses.[24] His temporary recovery gave him a deceptive euphoria, which turned him from piety to pleasure. We must not grudge him his few years "in the world" (1648–54), when he enjoyed the company of Parisian wits and

games and belles, and for an exciting while pursued in Auvergne a lady of
beauty and learning, the "Sappho of the countryside."[25] About this time he
wrote a *Discours sur les passions de l'amour*, and apparently he contemplated
marriage—which he was later to describe as "the lowest of the conditions
of life permitted to a Christian."[26] Among his friends were some *libertins*,
who combined free morals with free thought. Perhaps through them Pascal
became interested in Montaigne, whose *Essais* now entered deeply into his
life. Their first influence probably inclined him to religious doubt.

Jacqueline, hearing of his new frivolity, reproached him, and prayed
for his reform. It was characteristic of his emotional nature that an accident
reinforced her prayers. One day, as he was driving over the Pont de Neuilly,
the four horses took fright, and plunged over the parapet into the Seine.
The carriage almost followed them; fortunately the reins broke, and the
coach hung half over the edge. Pascal and his friends emerged, but the
sensitive philosopher, terrified by the nearness of death, fainted away, and
remained unconscious for some time. On recovering he felt that he had
had a vision of God. In an ecstasy of fear, remorse, and gratitude he recorded his vision on a parchment which henceforth he carried sewn in
the lining of his coat:

> The year of grace 1654.
> Monday, Nov. 23rd, . . . from about half past six in the
>   evening to half an hour after midnight.
> The late
> God of Abraham, God of Isaac, God of Jacob,
>   not of the philosophers and the scholars.
> Certainty, certainty, feeling, joy, peace.
>   God of Jesus Christ . . .
> He is not to be found except by ways taught in the Gospel.
> Grandeur of the human soul.
> Just Father, the world has never known you, but I have
>   known you.
>   Joy, joy, joy, tears of joy . . .
> My God, will you abandon me? . . .
>   Jesus Christ
>   Jesus Christ . . .
> I was separated from Him, I fled Him, renounced Him,
>   crucified Him.
> May I never be separated from Him . . .
> Reconciliation sweet and complete.[27]

He resumed his visits to Port-Royal and Jacqueline, gladdening her
heart with his new mood of humility and penitence. He listened to the
sermons of Antoine Singlin. In December, 1654, he became a member of

the Port-Royal community.[28] In January he had a long conversation there with Sacy, who undertook to convince him of the superficiality of science and the futility of philosophy. Arnauld and Nicole discovered in the new recruit an ardor of conversion, and a skill in literary expression, that seemed a providential instrument placed in their hands to defend Port-Royal against its enemies. They begged him to devote his pen to answering the Jesuits who were trying to make Jansenism a sin. He responded with such brilliance and force that to this day the Society of Jesus feels his sting.

2. *The* Provincial Letters

On January 23 and 29, 1656, Pascal published the first and second of what he called *Lettres écrites par Louis de Montalte à un provincial de ses amis, et aux RR. PP. Jésuites, sur la morale et la politique de ces Pères*— "Letters written by Louis de Montalte" (a fictitious name) "to a provincial friend, and to the reverend Jesuit Fathers, on their ethics and politics." The framework was clever: it pretended to be the report of a Parisian to a friend in the provinces on the moral and theological issues then exciting the intellectual and religious circles in the capital. Arnauld and Nicole helped Pascal with facts and references; Pascal, combining the fervor of a convert with the wit and polish of a man of the world, provided the style that reached a new level in French prose.

The first letters sought public support for those Jansenist views on grace and salvation which Arnauld had defended; they were designed to influence the Sorbonne against the motion to expel Arnauld. In this they failed; Arnauld was solemnly degraded and expelled (January 31). The failure stimulated Pascal and Arnauld to attack the Jesuits as undermining morality by the laxity of their confessors and the loopholes of their casuistry. They explored the tomes of Escobar and other Jesuits, and denounced the doctrines of "probabilism," "direction of intention," and "mental reservation"; even the Jesuit missionaries' accommodation of Christian theology to Chinese ancestor worship was condemned[29]—though they made no explicit charge that the Jesuits justified means by ends. As the letters proceeded, and Arnauld revealed more and more of Escobar's casuistry to Pascal, the convert's passion rose. After the tenth letter he abandoned the fiction of a Parisian writing to a provincial; he spoke now in his own person, and addressed the Jesuits directly with indignant eloquence and sarcastic wit. Sometimes he gave twenty days to composing one letter, then rushed it off to the printer lest the public interest should cool. He gave a unique apology for the length of Letter XVI: "I had no time. to make it shorter."[30] In the eighteenth and final letter (March 24, 1657) he defied the Pope himself. Alexander VII had issued (October 16, 1656) another denunciation of Jansenism; Pascal reminded his readers that the papal judgment might err, as (he felt) it had done in the case of Galileo.[31] The Pope condemned the letters (September 6, 1657), but all educated France read them.

Were they fair to the Jesuits? Were the excerpts from Jesuit writers correctly quoted? "It is quite true," says a learned rationalist, "that qualifying phrases have at times been improperly omitted, a few phrases have been wrongly translated, and the condensing of long passages into short sentences has in a few instances the effect of an injustice"; but, he adds, "these cases are relatively few and unimportant";[32] and the essential accuracy of the extracts is now generally acknowledged.[33] It must be admitted, however, that Pascal took out of their context the most alarming and questionable passages of some casuists, and led a part of the public to the exaggerated view that these theological jurists were conspiring to destroy the morality of Christendom. Voltaire praised the excellence of the Letters as literature, but thought that "the whole book rested on a false basis. The author skillfully ascribed to the whole of the Society the extravagant ideas of a few Spanish and Flemish Jesuits,"[34] from whom many other Jesuits had differed. D'Alembert regretted that Pascal had not lampooned the Jansenists too, for "the shocking doctrine of Jansen and Saint-Cyran afforded at least as much room for ridicule as the pliant doctrine of Molina, Tambourin, and Vásquez."[35]

The influence of the Letters was immense. They did not immediately lessen the power of the Jesuits—certainly not with the King—but they so shamed the excesses of the casuists that Alexander VII himself, while continuing his opposition to Jansenism, condemned "laxism," and ordered a revision of casuistical texts (1665–66).[36] It was the Letters that gave the word "casuistry" its connotation of specious subtleties defending wrong actions or ideas. Meanwhile a masterpiece of style had been added to French literature. It was as if Voltaire had lived a century before Voltaire —for here were the gay wit, the cutting irony, the skeptical humor, the passionate invective of Voltaire, and, in the later letters, that warm resentment of injustice which redeemed Voltaire from being an encyclopedia of persiflage. Voltaire himself called the Letters "the best-written book that has yet appeared in France";[37] and the most penetrating and discriminating of all critics held that Pascal "invented fine prose in France."[38] Bossuet, being asked what book he would rather have written had he not written his own, answered, the Provincial Letters of Pascal.[39]

3. In Defense of Faith

Pascal returned to Paris in 1656 to superintend the publication of the *Letters*, and lived there through his six remaining years. He had not abandoned the world; in the very year of his death he shared in organizing a regular coach service in the capital—the germ of the present omnibus network. But two events occurred which renewed his piety, and led to his culminating contribution to literature and religion. On March 15, 1657, the Jesuits secured from the Queen Mother an order closing the schools of the Solitaries and forbidding the admission of new members to Port-Royal. The order was peacefully obeyed; the children, now including Racine, were sent to the houses of friends, and the teachers sadly dispersed. Nine days later (the date of the last of the *Provincial Letters*) an apparent miracle occurred in the chapel of the troubled nunnery. Pascal's ten-year-old niece, Marguerite Périer, suffered from a painful lachrymal fistula that exuded noisome pus through eyes and nose. A relative of Mère Angélique had presented to Port-Royal what he and others claimed to be a thorn from the crown that had tortured Christ. On March 24 the nuns, in solemn ceremony and singing psalms, placed the thorn on their altar. Each in turn kissed the relic, and one of them, seeing Marguerite among the worshipers, took the thorn and with it touched the girl's sore. That evening, we are told, Marguerite expressed surprise that her eye no longer pained her; her mother was astonished to find no sign of the fistula; a physician, summoned, reported that the discharge and the swelling had disappeared. He, not the nuns, spread word of what he termed a miraculous cure. Seven other physicians who had had previous knowledge of Marguerite's fistula subscribed a statement that in their judgment a miracle had taken place. The diocesan officials investigated, came to the same conclusion, and authorized a Te Deum Mass in Port-Royal. Crowds of believers came to see and kiss the thorn; all Catholic Paris acclaimed a miracle; the Queen Mother ordered all persecution of the nuns to stop; the Solitaries returned to Les Granges. (In 1728 Pope Benedict XIII referred to the case as proving that the age of miracles had not passed.) Pascal made himself an armorial emblem of an eye surrounded by a crown of thorns, with the inscription *Scio cui credidi*—"I know whom I have believed."[40]

He now set himself to write, as his last testament, an elaborate defense of religious belief. All that he found strength to do was to jot down isolated thoughts and group them into a tentative but telling order. Then (1658) his old ailments returned, and with such crippling severity that he was never able to give these notes coherent sequence or structural form. After his death his devoted friend the Duc de Roannez and the scholars of Port-Royal edited and published the material as *Pensées de M. Pascal sur la réligion, et sur quelques autres sujets* (1670). They feared that as Pascal had left these fragmentary "thoughts" they might lead to skepticism rather than to piety; they concealed the skeptical pieces, and modified some of the rest lest King or Church should take offense;[41] for at that time the persecution of Port-Royal had ceased, and the editors deprecated a renewal of controversy. Not till the nineteenth century were the *Pensées* of Pascal published in their full and authentic text.

If we may venture to impose an order upon them, we may place their starting point in the Copernican astronomy. We feel again, as we listen to Pascal, the tremendous blow that the Copernican-Galilean astronomy was dealing to the traditional form of Christianity.

> Let man contemplate Nature entire in her full and lofty majesty; let him put far from his sight the lowly objects that surround him; let him regard that blazing light, placed like an eternal lamp to illuminate the world; let the earth appear to him but a point within the vast circuit which that star describes; and let him marvel that this immense circumference is itself but a speck from the viewpoint of the stars that move in the firmament. And if our vision is stopped there, let imagination pass beyond. . . . All this visible world is but an imperceptible element in the great bosom of nature. No thought can go so far. . . . It is an infinite sphere whose center is everywhere, and whose circumference is nowhere.[42] This is the most perceivable feature of the almightiness of God, so that our imagination loses itself in this thought.

And Pascal adds, in a famous line characteristic of his philosophical sensitivity, "The eternal silence of these infinite spaces frightens me."[43]

But there is another infinity—the infinitely small, the endless theoretical divisibility of the "uncuttable" atom: no matter how tiny the minim to which we reduce anything, we cannot but believe that it too has parts smaller than itself. Our reason wavers perplexed and appalled between the infinitely vast and the infinitely minute.

> He who sees himself thus will be frightened by himself, and, perceiving himself sustained . . . between these two abysses of infinity and nothing, will tremble . . . and will be more disposed to contemplate these marvels in silence than to explore them with presumption. For in the end, what is man in nature? A nothing in respect to the infinite, everything in respect to the nothing, a halfway between nothing and all. Infinitely far from comprehending the extremes, both the end and the beginning or principle of things are invincibly hidden in an im-

penetrable secret; he is equally incapable of seeing the nothing whence he has been drawn, and the infinite in which he is engulfed.[44]*

Science, therefore, is a silly presumption. It is based on reason, which is based on the senses, which deceive us in a hundred ways. It is limited by the narrow bounds within which our senses operate, and by the corruptible brevity of the flesh. Left to itself, reason cannot understand—or offer a solid base to—morality, the family, or the state, much less perceive the real nature and order of the world, not to speak of comprehending God. There is more wisdom in custom, even in imagination and myth, than in reason, and "the wisest reason takes as her own principles those which the imagination of man has everywhere rashly introduced."[46] There are two kinds of wisdom: that of the simple and "ignorant" multitude, who live by the wisdom of tradition and imagination (ritual and myth); and that of the sage who has pierced through science and philosophy to realize his ignorance.[47] Therefore "there is nothing so conformable to reason as to disavow reason," and "to make light of philosophy is to be a true philosopher."[48]

So Pascal thought it unwise to rest religion on reason, as even some Jansenists tried to do. Reason cannot prove God, nor immortality; in either case the evidence is too contradictory. Nor can the Bible serve as the final basis of faith, for it is full of passages ambiguous or obscure, and the prophecies which piety interprets as pointing to Christ may have had quite other significance.[49] Moreover, God in the Bible speaks through figures, whose literal sense is misleading, and whose real meaning is perceived only by those blessed with divine grace. "We understand nothing of the works of God unless we take it as a principle that He wishes to blind some and to enlighten others."[50] (Here Pascal seems to take literally the story of Yahveh hardening Pharaoh's heart.)

Everywhere, if we rely on reason, we find the unintelligible. Who can understand, in man, the union and interaction of an obviously material body and an obviously immaterial mind? "There is nothing so inconceivable as that matter should be conscious of itself."[51] Philosophers who have mastered their passions—"what matter could do that?"[52] And the nature of man, so mingled of angel and brute,[53] repeats the contradiction of mind and body, and reminds us of the Chimera, which, in Greek mythology, was a she-goat with a lion's head and a serpent's tail.

What a Chimera is man! What a novelty, a monster, a chaos, a contradiction, a prodigy! Judge of all things, and imbecile norm of

---

* "The French language," said Sainte-Beuve, "has no finer pages than the simple and severe lines of this incomparable picture."[45]

the earth; depository of truth, and sewer of error and doubt; the glory and refuse of the universe. Who shall unravel this confusion?[54]

Morally man is a mystery. All kinds of wickedness appear or lie hidden in him. "Man is only a disguise, a liar, and a hypocrite, both to himself and to others."[55] "All men naturally hate one another; there could not be four friends in the world."[56] "How hollow is the heart of man, and how full of excrement!"[57] And what bottomless, insatiable vanity! "We would never travel on the sea if we had no hope of telling about it later. . . . We lose our lives with joy provided people talk about it. . . . Even philosophers wish for admirers."[58] Yet it is part of man's greatness that out of his wickedness, his hatred, and his vanity he evolved a code of law and morals to control his wickedness, and drew out of his lust an ideal of love.[59]

The misery of man is another mystery. Why should the universe have labored so long to produce a species so fragile in its happiness, so subject to pain in every nerve, to grief in every love, to death in every life? And yet "the grandeur of man is great in that he knows himself to be miserable."[60]

> Man is but a reed, the most feeble thing in nature; but he is a thinking reed.* The entire universe need not arm itself to crush him; a vapor, a drop of water, suffice to kill him. But when the universe has crushed him man will still be nobler than that which kills him, because he knows that he is dying, and of its victory the universe knows nothing.[61]

None of these mysteries finds an answer in reason. If we trust to reason alone we shall condemn ourselves to a Pyrrhonism that will doubt everything except pain and death, and philosophy could be at best a rationalization of defeat. But we cannot believe that man's fate is as reason sees it—to struggle, to suffer, and to die, having begotten others to struggle, to suffer, and to die, generation after generation, aimlessly, stupidly, in a ridiculous and superabundant insignificance. In our hearts we feel that this cannot be true, that it would be the greatest of all blasphemies to think that life and the universe have no meaning. God and the meaning of life must be felt by the heart, rather than by reason. "The heart has its reasons, which reason does not know,"[62] and we do right to listen to our hearts, to "place our faith in feeling."[63] For all belief, even in practical matters, is a form of will, a direction of attention and desire." (The "will to believe.") The mystical experience is profounder than the evidence of the senses or the arguments of reason.

What answer, then, does feeling give to the mysteries of life and thought?

---

* L'homme n'est qu'un roseau, le plus faible de la nature, mais c'est un roseau pensant.

The answer is religion. Only religion can restore meaning to life, and nobility to man; without it we flounder ever more deeply into mental frustration and mortal futility. Religion gives us a Bible; the Bible tells us of man's fall from grace; only that original sin can explain the strange union, in human nature, of hate and love, of bestial wickedness and our longing for redemption and God. If we let ourselves believe (however absurd it may seem to the philosophers) that man began with divine grace, that he forfeited this by sin, and that he can be redeemed only by divine grace through the crucified Christ, then we shall find a peace of mind never granted to philosophers. He who cannot believe is cursed, for he reveals by his unbelief that God has not chosen to give him grace.

Belief is a wise wager. Granted that faith cannot be proved, what harm will come to you if you gamble on its truth and it proves false? "You *must* wager; it is not optional . . . Let us weigh the gain and the loss in wagering that God exists . . . If you gain, you gain all; if you lose, you lose nothing. Wager, then, without hesitation, that He exists."[64] If at first you find it difficult to believe, follow the customs and rituals of the Church as if you did believe. "Bless yourself with holy water, have Masses said, and so on; by a simple and natural process this will make you believe, and will dull you" (*cela vous fera croire, et vous abêtira*)—will quiet your proudly critical intellect.[65] Go to confession and communion; you will find it a relief and a strengthening.[66]

We do injustice to this historic apologia by letting it end on so unheroic a note. We may be sure that Pascal, when he believed, did so not as a gambler but as a soul baffled and buffeted by life, humbly recognizing that his intellect, whose brilliance had astonished friends and foes, was no match for the universe, and finding in faith the only way to give meaning and pardon to his pain. "Pascal is sick," said Sainte-Beuve; "we must always remember this in reading him."[67] But Pascal would have replied: Are we not all sick? Let him who is perfectly happy reject faith. Let him reject it who is content with no more meaning in life than a helpless trajectory from a filthy birth to an agonizing death.

> Picture a number of men in chains, and all condemned to death; each day some are strangled in the sight of the rest; those who remain see their own condition in that of these their fellows, looking at one another with sorrow and without hope, each awaiting his turn. This is the picture of the condition of man.[68]

How shall we redeem this obscene slaughter called history except by believing, with or against the evidence, that God will right all wrongs in the end?

Pascal argued so earnestly because he had never really recovered from the doubts suggested to him by Montaigne, by the *libertins* of his "years in the world," and by the merciless neutrality of nature between "evil" and "good."

> This is what I see, and what troubles me. I look on all sides, and everywhere I see nothing but obscurity. Nature offers me nothing that is not a matter of doubt and disquiet. If I saw no signs of a divinity, I would fix myself in denial. If I saw everywhere the marks of a Creator, I would repose peacefully in faith. But seeing too much to deny [Him], and too little to assure me, I am in a pitiful state, and I would wish a hundred times that if a God sustains nature it would reveal Him without ambiguity.[69]

It is this profound uncertainty, the paralyzing ability to see both sides, that makes Pascal a fascination to believer and doubter alike. This man had felt the atheist's angry resentment of evil, and the believer's trust in the triumph of the good; he had passed through the intellectual gyrations of Montaigne and Charron to the happy humility of St. Francis of Assisi and St. Thomas à Kempis. It is this cry from the depths of doubt, this desperate forging of a faith against death, that make the *Pensées* the most eloquent book in French prose. Again, for the third time in the seventeenth century, philosophy became literature, not with the cool pithiness of Bacon, nor with the ingratiating intimacy of Descartes, but with the emotional power of a poet feeling philosophy, writing to his own heart in his own blood. In the apex of the classic age rose this romantic appeal, strong enough to survive Boileau and Voltaire, and to be heard across a century by Rousseau and Chateaubriand. Here, in the morning of the Age of Reason, in the very decades of Hobbes and Spinoza, reason found a challenger in a dying man.

In his final years, said his sister Mme. Périer, Pascal suffered "continual and ever-increasing maladies."[70] He came to think that "sickness is the natural state of Christians."[71] Sometimes he welcomed his pains as distracting him from temptations. "One hour's pain," he said, "is a better teacher than all the philosophers put together."[72] He renounced every pleasure, took to ascetic practices, flogged himself with a girdle studded with iron spikes.[73] He rebuked Mme. Périer for allowing her children to caress her. He opposed the marriage of her daughter, saying that "the marriage state is no better than paganism in the eyes of God."[74] He would not allow anyone, in his presence, to speak of the beauty of woman.

In 1662, as one of many charitable acts, he took a poor family into his home. When one of the children developed smallpox Pascal, instead of asking the family to leave, moved to the house of his sister. Soon afterward he took to his bed, racked with colic pains. He drew up his will, leaving nearly half his fortune to the poor. He confessed to a priest, and received viaticum. He died after a violent convulsion, August 19, 1662, in the fortieth year of his age. Upon opening his body it was found that his stomach and liver were diseased, and his intestines gangrened.[75] His brain, reported the doctors, "was of prodigious abundance, its substance solid and condensed," but only one of the cranial sutures had properly closed; hence, perhaps, his terrible headaches. On the cortex were two depressions, "as large as if made by fingers laid in wax."[76] He was buried in the church of his parish, St.-Étienne-du-Mont.

V. PORT-ROYAL; 1656–1715

The *Provincial Letters* intensified the resolution of the Jesuits and the bishops to suppress Jansenism as Protestantism in disguise. At the urging of French bishops, Pope Alexander VII issued (October 6, 1656) a bull requiring all French ecclesiastics to subscribe to the following formulary:

> I submit myself sincerely to the constitution of Pope Innocent X, dated May 31, 1653, according to its true sense, which has been determined by the constitution of our Holy Father, Pope Alexander VII, dated October 6, 1656. And I acknowledge that I am bound in conscience to obey these constitutions; and I condemn with heart and mouth the doctrine of the Five Propositions of Cornelis Jansen, contained in his book entitled *Augustinus*.

Mazarin refrained from enforcing signatures to this formulary, but on April 13, 1661, soon after Mazarin's death, Louis XIV promulgated the order. A friendly diocesan vicar prefaced the formulary with a conciliatory statement. In this form Arnauld and the Solitaries signed it, and advised the nuns of Port-Royal to do likewise. Mère Angélique, bedridden with dropsy, refused, and persisted till her death on August 6, 1661, aged seventy. Pascal and his sister Jacqueline, now subprioress, also refused. "Since the bishops have the courage only of girls," said Jacqueline, "girls must have the courage of bishops."[77] Finally all the surviving nuns signed; but Jacqueline, exhausted by her long resistance, died on October 4, aged thirty-six; and Pascal followed her within a year.

Meanwhile the King repudiated the conciliatory preamble, and insisted that the nuns should sign the formulary without any addition or change. Those few who did this were transferred to Port-Royal in Paris. The great majority of the nuns, led by Mère Agnès, announced that they could not in conscience sign a document so contrary to their beliefs. In August,

1665, the archbishop disqualified the seventy nuns and their fourteen lay sisters from receiving the sacraments, and forbade them to have any communication with the outside world. During the next three years a sympathetic priest scaled the walls of Port-Royal-des-Champs to give viaticum to dying nuns. In 1666 Sacy, Lemaître, and three other Solitaries were arrested by order of the King. Arnauld, disguised with wig and sword, was sheltered by the Duchesse de Longueville, who waited upon him in person during his concealment.[78] She and other titled ladies took up the cause of the nuns; they prevailed upon Louis to relent; and in 1668 Pope Clement IX issued a new bull, so wisely ambiguous as to allow all parties to accept it. The prisoners were released, the dispersed nuns were restored to Port-Royal-des-Champs; once again the bells tolled there, which had been silent for three years. Arnauld was received amicably by the King, and wrote a book against the Calvinists. Nicole, however, wrote another book against the Jesuits.

This "Peace of the Church" lasted eleven years. Then Mme. de Longueville died, and the peace died with her. As the King aged, and his victories turned into defeats, his religion became a mess of bigotry and fear. Was God punishing him for tolerating heresy? His dislike of Jansenism took on a personal tinge. When a M. Fontpertuis was recommended for office Louis rejected him as suspected of Jansenism, but when he was assured that the man was merely an atheist he confirmed the nomination.[79] He could never forgive the nuns for defying his order to sign the undiluted formulary. To ensure the early disappearance of this center of disaffection, he forbade it to accept new members. He appealed to Clement XI to issue an unmistakable condemnation of Jansenism; after two years of prodding, the Pope fulminated the bull *Vineam Domini* (1705). By that time only twenty-five nuns survived at Port-Royal, the youngest sixty years old. The King impatiently awaited their death.

In 1709 the Jesuit Michel Tellier, aged sixty-six, succeeded Père La Chaise as the royal confessor. He urged upon Louis, now seventy-one, that the eternal fate of his soul depended upon the immediate and outright extermination of Port-Royal. Many of the secular clergy, including Louis Antoine de Noailles, Archbishop of Paris, protested against such haste, but the King overruled them. On August 29, 1709, the abbey was surrounded by troops; the nuns were shown a *lettre de cachet* ordering their dispersal without delay; they were given fifteen minutes to gather up their belongings. Their cries and tears availed nothing. They were loaded into coaches, and were scattered among various conformist convents sixty to 150 miles away. In 1710 the buildings of the famous nunnery were razed to the ground.

Jansenism survived. Arnauld and Nicole died in Flanders exile (1694–95), but in 1687 Pasquier Quesnel, a priest of the Paris Oratory, defended the Jansenist theology in *Réflexions morales sur le Nouveau Testament*. Imprisoned (1703), he escaped to Amsterdam, where he established a Jansenist church. As his book won much support among the French secular clergy, Louis induced Clement XI to issue the bull *Unigenitus* (September 8, 1713), which condemned 104 propositions ascribed to Quesnel. Many French prelates resented the bull as a papal interference with the Gallican Church, and Jansenism merged with a revival of the Gallican movement. When Louis XIV died, there were more Jansenists in France than ever before.[80]

Today we find it hard to understand why a nation should have been divided, and a king so excited, about abstruse problems of divine grace, predestination, and free will; we forget that religion was then as important as politics seem now. Jansenism was the final effort of the Reformation in France, and the last flare of the Middle Ages. In the perspective of history it appears as a reaction rather than an advance. But in several aspects its influence was progressive. For a while it fought for a measure of religious freedom—though we shall find it in Voltaire's days more intolerant than the papacy.[81] It checked the excesses of casuistry. Its moral fervor was a wholesome counterweight to a policy of confessional lenience that may have shared in the deterioration of French morality. Its educational influence was good; the *petites écoles* were the best of their time. Its literary influence emerged not only in Pascal but moderately in Corneille, vividly in Racine, pupil and historian of Port-Royal. Its philosophical influence was indirect and unintentional: its concept of God as damning to everlasting torture the larger part of the human race—including all unbaptized children, all Mohammedans, and all Jews—may have had some part in leading the Voltaires and the Diderots into rebellion against the entire Christian theology.

VI. THE KING AND THE HUGUENOTS: 1643–1715

The King had not yet saved his soul, for there were 1,500,000 Protestants in France. Mazarin had continued and developed Richelieu's policy of protecting the religious freedom of the Huguenots so long as they remained politically obedient. Colbert recognized how valuable they were in the commerce and industry of France. In 1652 Louis confirmed the Edict of Nantes (1598) of his grandfather Henry IV; and in 1666 he expressed his appreciation of Huguenot loyalty during the Fronde. But it grieved him that the unity of France could not be religious as well as political; and about 1670 he wrote an ominous passage in his memoirs:

As to that great number of my subjects of the so-called Reformed religion, an evil . . . that I regard with sorrow . . . , it seems to me that those who wished to employ violent remedies did not know the nature of this evil, caused in part by the warmth of minds, which must be left to pass away and to die out insensibly, instead of exciting it anew by such strong contradictions. . . . I believed that the best means, in order to reduce the Huguenots of my kingdom by degrees, was, in the first place, not to constrain them at all by any new rigor, to cause that to be observed toward them that they had obtained from my predecessors, but to accord them nothing beyond this, and even to confine its execution within the narrowest limits which justice and propriety could permit.[82]

This has an air of sincere intolerance. It is the view of an absolute king who has taken from Bossuet the motto *Un roi, une loi, une foi*—"One king, one law, one faith." It is no longer the tolerance of Richelieu, who appointed to office able men of any creed; Louis goes on to say that he would appoint only good Catholics to office, and trust thereby to encourage conversions.

The Church herself had never approved the toleration guaranteed by the Edict of Nantes. An assembly of the clergy in 1655 called for a stricter interpretation of the edict; their assembly of 1660 asked the King to close all Huguenot colleges and hospitals, and to exclude Huguenots from public office; their assembly of 1670 recommended that children who had reached their seventh birthday should be deemed legally capable of abjuring the Huguenot heresy, and that those who so abjured should be removed from their parents; in 1675 their assembly demanded that mixed marriages be declared null, and that the offspring of such marriages be classed as illegitimate.[83] Pious and kindly priests like Cardinal de Bérulle contended that forcible repression by the state was the only practical way of dealing with Protestantism.[84] One prelate after another urged upon the King the argument that the stability of his government rested on social order, which rested on morality, which would collapse without the support of the state religion. Catholic laymen joined in the argument. Magistrates reported troublesome conflicts between the rival creeds in the towns—Catholic attacks upon Protestant churches, funerals, and homes, and Protestant reprisals in kind.

Louis, against his better nature, yielded bit by bit to this campaign. Perpetually in need of money for war and elegance, he found the clergy offering him substantial grants on condition of accepting their views. Other factors drove him in the same direction. He was encouraging—bribing—Charles II to turn England toward Catholicism; how could he meanwhile allow Protestantism in France? Had not the Protestants, in the Peace of

Augsburg (1555) and later, agreed to the principle *Cuius regio eius religio*—that the religion of the ruler should be made obligatory upon his subjects? Were not Protestant rulers in Germany and the United Provinces banishing families that rejected the religion of the prince?

From the beginning of his active reign Louis—or his ministers with his consent—issued a succession of decrees that moved toward full revocation of the toleration edict. In 1661 he outlawed Protestant worship in most of the province of Gex, near the Swiss border, on the ground that Gex had been added to France since the edict; however, there were seventeen thousand Protestants in that province, and only four hundred Catholics.[85] In 1664 advancement to mastership in the guilds was made especially difficult for any but Catholics.[86] In 1665 boys of fourteen and girls of twelve were authorized to accept conversion to Catholicism and to leave their parents, who were thereafter required to pay them an annuity for their support.[87] In 1666 the Huguenots were forbidden to establish new colleges, or to maintain academies for the education of the young nobility. In 1669 the emigration of Huguenots was made punishable with arrest if they were captured, and confiscation of goods;[88] and anyone who aided a Huguenot to emigrate was subject to condemnation to the galleys for life.[89] In 1677 Louis permitted the endowment of a "treasury of conversions," from which sums averaging six livres per head were given to Huguenots accepting conversion to the Catholic faith. To ensure durability of conversions Louis decreed (1679) the banishment of all relapsed converts, and the confiscation of their property.[90] A protest from the Elector of Brandenburg, complaints from Colbert that these measures were depressing trade, and the King's absorption in campaigns interrupted the stream of prohibitions. But his reconciliation with monogamous Catholicism in 1681 turned him again to the holy war against the Huguenots. Now he told an aide that he felt himself "indispensably bound to effect the conversion of all his subjects and the extirpation of heresy."[91] In 1682 he issued—and ordered all Protestant ministers to read to their congregations —an address threatening Huguenots "with evils incomparably more terrible and deadly than before."[92] Within the next three years 570 of the 815 Huguenot churches were closed; many were torn down; and when the Huguenots tried to worship on the site of their ruined temples they were punished as rebels against the state.

Meanwhile the dragonnades had begun. It was an old custom in France to lodge troops in and at the expense of communes or homes. Louvois, minister of war, proposed to the King (April 11, 1681) that converts to Catholicism be exempt for two years from such billeting of troops. It was so ordered. Louvois now directed the military administrators of the provinces of Poitou and Limousin to house their dragoons (mounted

soldiers) among Huguenots, especially among the well-to-do. In Poitou
Maréchal de Marillac let his troops understand that he would not resent
some apostolic zeal in their treatment of their heretic hosts. Soon the
soldiers were robbing, beating, raping the Huguenots. When Louis heard
of these excesses he reproved Marillac, and when they continued he dismissed him.[93] On May 19 he ordered the suspension of conversion by
billeting, and condemned the acts of violence committed in some places
against the Reformers.[94] Louvois notified provincial administrators that
they might continue the dragonnades, but warned them to keep all knowledge of this from the King. The dragonnades spread through a large part
of France, and brought in thousands of converts; some towns and provinces
—Montpellier, Nîmes, Béarn—abjured wholesale their Calvinistic faith.
The majority of the Huguenots, terrified, pretended conversion; but thousands, defying the laws, abandoned their homes and property and fled
across frontiers or overseas. Louis was told that very few Huguenots were
left in France, and that the Edict of Nantes had become meaningless. In
1684 the general assembly of the clergy petitioned the King that the edict
be completely annulled, and that "the undisturbed reign of Jesus Christ . . .
be re-established in France."[95]

On October 17, 1685, the King revoked the Edict of Nantes as now
unnecessary in a France almost entirely Catholic. All Huguenot worship
and schooling were henceforth forbidden. All Huguenot conventicles were
to be destroyed or transformed into Catholic churches. Huguenot clergymen were ordered to leave France within fourteen days, but emigration
of other Huguenots was prohibited on pain of condemnation to the galleys
for life. Half the goods of lay emigrants was pledged to informers.[96] All
children born in France were to be baptized by priests, and were to be
brought up in the Catholic faith. A final clause promised that the few
remaining Huguenots would be allowed to dwell peacefully in certain
towns. This article was carried out in Paris and its suburbs; Huguenot
tradesmen there were protected and reassured by the lieutenant of police;
there were no dragonnades in or near Paris; the dancing could go on at
Versailles, and the King could sleep with a good conscience. But in many
provinces, under Louvois' urging,[97] the dragonnades continued, and obdurate Huguenots were subjected to pillage and torture. Says the leading
French authority on the Revocation of the Edict of Nantes:

> All was permitted to the soldiers except murder. They made the
> Huguenots dance till exhausted; they tossed them up in blankets;
> they poured boiling water down their throats . . . ; they beat the
> soles of their feet; they pulled out the hair of beards . . . ; they burned
> the arms and legs of their hosts with candle flame . . . ; they forced

them to hold burning charcoal in their hands . . . They burned the
feet of many, holding them long before a great fire . . . They forced
women to stand naked in the street, to bear the mockery and outrages
of passersby. They bound a nursing mother to a bedpost, and held
away from her the infant crying for her breast; and when she opened
her mouth to plead with them they spat into her mouth.[98]

This holy terror of 1685, Michelet thought, was far worse than the
Revolutionary Terror of 1793.[99] Some 400,000 "converts" were forced to
attend Mass and receive the Eucharist; a few who spat out the consecrated
wafers when they left the church were condemned to be burned alive.[100]
Obstinate Huguenot males were imprisoned in subterranean dungeons or
unheated cells. Obdurate Huguenot women were sent to confinement in
convents, where they received unexpectedly merciful treatment from the
nuns.[101]

Two provinces resisted with special valor. Of the Vaudois in French
Dauphiné and Savoyard Piedmont we shall hear later. In the valleys of
the Cevennes range in Languedoc thousands of "converted" Huguenots
secretly retained their faith, waiting for time and chance to free them;
and their "prophets," claiming divine inspiration, assured them that the
time was near at hand. When the War of the Spanish Succession seemed
to absorb French arms, the peasants formed rebel groups of "Camisards,"
who donned white shirts to be recognized by one another at night. In
one foray they killed the Abbé du Chayla, who had persecuted them with
special ardor. A regiment of soldiery suddenly came down upon them,
massacred them indiscriminately, and destroyed their houses and crops
(1702). A remnant fought back ferociously until the conciliatory methods
of Maréchal de Villars pursuaded them to peace.

Of the 1,500,000 Huguenots who had been living in France in 1660,
some 400,000, in the decade before and after the Revocation, escaped across
guarded borders at the risk of their lives. A thousand tales of heroism
survived for a century from those desperate years. Protestant countries
welcomed the fugitives. Geneva, a city of sixteen thousand souls, found
room for four thousand Huguenots. Charles II and James II, despite their
Catholicism, offered Huguenots material aid, and eased their absorption
into English economic and political life. The Elector of Brandenburg gave
them so friendly a reception that by 1697 over a fifth of Berlin's population was French. Holland opened its doors, built a thousand homes to
house the newcomers, lent them money to set up business, and guaranteed
them all the rights of citizenship; Dutch Catholics joined Protestants and
Jews in raising funds for Huguenot relief. The grateful refugees not only
enriched industry and trade in the United Provinces, they enlisted in
Dutch and English armies fighting France. Some of them accompanied

or followed William III to England to help him against James II; the French Calvinist Marshal Schomberg, who had won victories for Louis XIV, led an English army against the French, and died in defeating them in the battle of the Boyne (1690). Everywhere in these hospitable lands the Huguenots brought their skills in crafts, commerce and finance; all Protestant Europe profited from the victory of Catholicism in France. An entire quarter of London was occupied by French silk workers. Huguenot exiles in England became interpreters of English thought to France, and prepared the conquest of the French mind by Bacon, Newton, and Locke.

A minority of French Catholics privately condemned the massacres of the Revocation, and gave secret help and refuge to many victims. But the vast majority hailed the destruction of the Huguenots as the King's culminating achievement; now at last, they said, France was Catholic and one. The greatest writers—Bossuet, Fénelon, La Fontaine, La Bruyère, even the Jansenist patriarch Arnauld—extolled the courage of the King in implementing what they conceived to be the national will. "Nothing could be finer," wrote Mme. de Sévigné; "no king has done or will do anything more memorable."[102] Louis himself was happy at having apparently completed a disagreeable but holy task. Says Saint-Simon:

> He believed himself to have renewed the days of the preaching of the Apostles . . . The bishops wrote panegyrics of him, the Jesuits made the pulpit resound with his praises . . . He heard nothing but eulogies, while the good and true Catholics and bishops groaned in spirit to see the orthodox act toward error and heretics as heretical tyrants and heathen had acted against the truth, the confessors, and the martyrs. They could not endure this immensity of perjury and sacrilege.[103]

Saint-Simon and Vauban were among the few Frenchmen who realized, at the outset, the economic loss to France through the exodus of so many industrious citizens. Caen lost its textile manufactures, Lyon and Tours lost three fourths of their silk looms. Of sixty paper mills in the province of Angoumois only sixteen remained; of 109 shops in the town of Mézières eight survived; of four hundred tanneries in Tours, fifty-four were left.[104] Ports like Marseilles declined through the loss of markets in countries that now, by the work and instructions of Huguenots, produced what formerly they had imported from France. The great reconstruction of the French economy by Colbert was partly undone; the industries that he had labored to develop in France went to nourish her competitors. As revenues from industry were sharply reduced, the government fell back into the hands of the moneylenders from whom Colbert had rescued it. The French navy lost nine thousand sailors, the army six hundred officers and twelve thousand troops; perhaps this depletion shared in the defeats that almost shattered France in the War of the Spanish Succession. And the will of Protestant Europe to unite against France had been strengthened by the ominous barbarity of the persecution, and by the pleas of the emigrés.

The Revocation may have been indirectly helpful to the arts, the manners, and the graces of life in France. The Calvinistic spirit, distrusting adornment, graven images, and levity, discouraged art, elegance, and wit; a Puritan France would have been an anomaly and a mistake. But the Revocation was a disaster for French religion. Bacon had remarked that the spectacle of the religious wars would have made Lucretius "seven times more epicure and atheist than he was";[105] what would he have said now? No stopping point was left for the Gallic mind between Catholicism and unbelief. Whereas in Switzerland, Germany, Holland, and England Protestantism had served to express rebellion against the Church, no such vehicle of resentment remained in France; the reaction against Romanism found it safer to be thoroughly skeptical than openly Protestant. The French Renaissance, unimpeded by Protestantism, passed directly into the Enlightenment after the death of the King.

VII. BOSSUET: 1627–88

For the present, however, the French Church was triumphant, and stood at the summit of splendor and authority. Intolerant in its corporate spirit, and cruel in its power, it had nonetheless the best-educated body of men in Europe, and its tyrants were rivaled by its saints. Several of its bishops were humanitarians sincerely devoted to the public good as they saw it; and two of them entered almost as brilliantly as Pascal, and in their time more prominently, into the literature of France. Rarely had French ecclesiastics rivaled the prestige of Bossuet, or the popularity of Fénelon.

Jacques Bénigne Bossuet (whose middle name better fitted Fénelon) was born prosperous to a prominent lawyer and member of the Parlement of Dijon (1627). His parents dedicated him to the priesthood, had him tonsured at eight, and made him at thirteen a canon in the cathedral of Metz. At fifteen he was sent to the Collège de Navarre in Paris. At sixteen he was already so eloquent that the bluestockings at the Hôtel de Rambouillet persuaded him, shyly proud, to preach a sermon to them in mid-salon. Graduating with honors, he returned to Metz, was ordained, and soon advanced to a doctorate in theology. He was scandalized to find that ten thousand of Metz's thirty thousand souls were God-damned Protestants. He entered into a polite controversy with Paul Ferry, a Huguenot leader; he admitted some evils in Catholic practice, but argued that schism was a greater evil still. He remained on friendly terms with Ferry for twelve years, just as, later, he was to labor amicably with Leibniz for a reunion of Christendom. Anne of Austria, hearing him preach at Metz, thought him too good for so unseemly an environment, and persuaded the King to invite him to Paris. Thither he moved in 1659.

At first he preached to simple audiences in the Monastery of St.-Lazare, under the auspices of Vincent de Paul. In 1660 he addressed the fashionable congregation at the Church of Les Minimes near the Place Royale. The King heard him, and recognized in the young orator a judicious union of eloquence, orthodoxy, and strong character. He invited him to preach the Lenten sermons of 1662 in the Louvre; he attended these discourses with conspicuous piety, except on the Sunday when he galloped off to recapture Louise de La Vallière from a convent. The presence of the King stimulated Bossuet to clear his style of provincial crudities, scholastic scaffolding, and dialectical argument; the refinement of the court passed to the upper clergy, and generated an age of pulpit eloquence rivaling the forensic oratory of Demosthenes and Cicero. During the next eight years Bossuet made himself the favorite preacher in the chapels of the court. He became director of conscience to highborn ladies like Henrietta "Madame" d'Orléans, Mme. de Longueville, and Mlle. de Montpensier.[106] Sometimes in his sermons he addressed the King directly, usually with excessive flattery, once with an earnest call to abandon his adulteries and return to his wife. For a while he forfeited the royal smile, but he regained it by converting Turenne. In 1667 Louis chose him to deliver the funeral oration at the burial of Anne of Austria. Two years later he preached over the remains of Henrietta Maria, dowager Queen of England, and in 1670 he had the melancholy task of delivering the burial sermon for the younger Henrietta, his beloved penitent, who had died in his arms in the precarious charm of her youth.

Those sermons over the mother and the sister of England's Charles II are the most renowned in the literature of France—for the still more famous address of Pope Urban II, calling Europe to the First Crusade (1095), was spoken in Latin, though on French soil. The earlier of these oraisons funèbres began with Bossuet's brave and favorite theme: that kings should learn from the lessons of history, and that a divine nemesis of revenge will punish them if they do not use their power for the public good. But instead of seeing in Charles I of England an example of such retribution, he found no fault in him except too great clemency, and none at all in his devoted wife. He apostrophized the dead Queen as a saint who had labored to make her husband and England Catholic. He digressed at length on another topic dear to him: the endless variations of Protestantism, and the disorder of morals that results from the disturbance of faith; the Great Rebellion had been God's punishment for England's apostasy from Rome. But how exemplary had been the behavior of the Queen after the horrible and criminal execution of her husband! She had accepted her sorrows as an atonement and a blessing, had thanked God for them, and had lived for eleven years in humble and patient prayer. At last she had been rewarded; her son was restored to his throne, and the Queen Mother might again have dwelt in palaces. She had preferred to live in a convent in France, making no use of her new fortune except to multiply her charities.

More moving, and closer to history and French memories, was the sermon that Bossuet delivered ten months later over Henrietta Anne. He had recently been made bishop of Condom in southwest France; for this oration he came to the abbey church of St.-Denis in full episcopal state, preceded by heralds and crowned with the miter; and on his finger shone the great emerald given him by the dead princess. Usually, in these sermons, the emotion of the speaker had been checked by his thinking of death in general terms; now it was the death of one who only yesterday had been the joy of the King and the radiance of the court; and the stately prelate broke into tears as he recalled the bitter suddenness of the blow that had set all France mourning and marveling at the ways of God. He described Henrietta with no cold objectivity, but with the prejudice of love—"always sweet and peaceful, generous and benevolent"[107]—and he merely hinted, with discreet brevity, that her happiness had not been proportioned to her deserts. For a moment even the careful bishop, pillar and guardian of orthodoxy, dared to ask God why so much evil and injustice flourish on the earth.[108] He consoled himself and his auditors with the remembrance of Henrietta's dying piety, of the sacraments that had cleansed her of all worldly attachments; surely so tender and purified a spirit merited salvation, and would grace Paradise itself!

It was through a rare mistake in judging character that Louis, moved by such eloquence, appointed Bossuet (1670) preceptor to the Dauphin, and trusted him to train the stolid, backward lad in the knowledge and character required to rule France. Bossuet gave himself faithfully to this task; he resigned his bishopric to be near his ward and the court, and he wrote for the young Louis such earnest manuals of world history, logic, the Christian faith, government, and the duties of a king, as should have made the boy a monster of perfection and power.

In one of these treatises, *Politique tirée des propres paroles de l'Écriture sainte* (1679, 1709)—*Politics as Drawn from the Very Words of Holy Scripture*—Bossuet defended absolute monarchy and the divine right of kings with more than the ardor of Cardinal Bellarmine upholding the supremacy of the popes. Was it not said in the Old Testament that "God has given to every people its ruler"?[109] And in the New Testament, with all the authority of St. Paul, that "the powers that be are ordained of God"?[110] Yes, and the Apostle had added: "Whosoever, therefore, resisteth the power, resisteth the ordinance of God; and they that resist shall receive to themselves eternal damnation." Obviously, anyone who accepts the Bible as the word of God must honor the king as God's vice-regent, or, as Isaiah called Cyrus, "the anointed of the Lord."[111] Consequently the royal person is sacred, the royal power is divine and absolute, the king is responsible only to God. But that responsibility lays upon him severe obligations: he must in every word and deed obey the laws of God. Fortunately for Louis, the God of the Bible had been well disposed toward polygamy.

For the Dauphin, too, Bossuet wrote (1679) his famous *Discours sur l'histoire universelle*. Scandalized by Descartes' suggestion that—given one initial push by God—all events in the objective world could be explained mechanically as following from the laws and constitution of nature, Bossuet retorted that on the contrary every major event in history was part of a divine plan, was an act of Providence leading up to the sacrifice of Christ and the development of Christianity into an expanding City of God. Again taking the Bible as divinely inspired, he centered all history on the career of the Old Testament Jews and the nations enlightened by Christianity. "God used the Assyrians and the Babylonians to chastise His chosen people, the Persians to restore them, Alexander to protect them, Antiochus to test them, the Romans to preserve Jewish liberty against Syrian kings." If this seems foolish, we must remember that it was also the view of the authors of the Bible, whom Bossuet confidently identified with God. So he began with a summary of Old Testament history, and he performed that task with his usual flair for order, compactness, and vigorous eloquence. The chronology was taken from Archbishop Ussher's scheme, dating the creation at 4004 B.C. Bossuet took only passing notice of the nations that lay outside the Biblical reference, but of these he gave synoptical accounts of remarkable insight and power, and showed a sympathetic understanding of pagan virtues and accomplishments. Through all the kaleidoscope of rising and falling empires he saw some advance; in him, as in Charles Perrault and other contemporary defenders of the moderns versus the ancients, the idea of progress took form and flesh, and prepared, from afar off, for Turgot and Condorcet. With all its faults, the book created the modern philosophy of history, which is achievement enough for one man.

Bossuet's royal pupil did not appreciate the honor of having great books written for his instruction. And Bossuet's spirit was too serious and severe

Fig. 1—Girardon: *Louis XIV.* Louvre, Paris

Fig. 4—Pierre Mignard: *Cardinal Mazarin*. Musée de Condé, Chantilly (Photo Giraudon)

FIG. 5—UNKNOWN ARTIST: *Ninon de Lenclos.*
Château de Versailles   PAGE 28

FIG. 6—PIERRE MIGNARD: *Madame de Montespan.*
From Pierre Pradel, *L'Art au siècle de Louis XIV*
(Paris: Éditions de Clairefontaine, 1949; Photo by
J. E. Bulloz)   PAGE 37

LOUIS DE BOURB
D. LE GRAND, PRINCE
DE CONDÉ

Fɪɢ. 7—Jᴏᴏsᴛ ᴠᴀɴ Eɢᴍᴏɴᴛ: *The Great Condé*. Château de Versailles

Fig. 8—N. DE L'ARMESSIN: *Louise de La Vallière* (Bettmann Archive) PAGE 36

Fig. 9 — HYACINTHE RIGAUD: *Henrietta Anne, Duchess of Orléans*. Private Collection, Paris (Bettmann Archive)
PAGE 35

FIG. 10—*Death Mask of Blaise Pascal.* From Ernst Benkard, *Undying Faces* (London: Hogarth Press, 1929)   PAGE 55

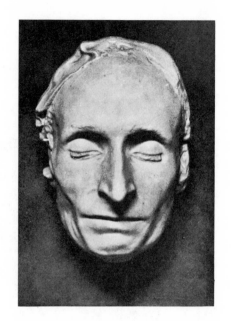

FIG. 11—JOSEPH VIVIEN: *Fénelon.* Alte Pinakothek, Munich (Bettmann Archive)   PAGE 81

Fig. 12—Hyacinthe Rigaud: *Jacques Bossuet*. Louvre, Paris (Bettmann Archive) PAGE 75

Fig. 13—*Church of Val-de-Grâce* (1645), Paris. Courtesy of the French Cultural Services, New York (Photo by Molinard, Couleurs du Monde) PAGE 90

Fig. 14—GIRARDON: *Bathing Nymphs*. Château de Versailles PAGE 99

FIG. 15—ANDRÉ CHARLES BOULLE: *Ebony cabinet*. The Wallace Collection, London

FIG. 16—*The Louvre Colonnade* (Photo Giraudon) PAGE 94

FIG. 17—*Church of St.-Louis-des-Invalides* (1670), Paris. Courtesy of the French Embassy Press and Information Division, New York PAGE 90

Fig. 18—Charles Le Brun: *Gobelin Tapestry: The Family of Darius at the Feet of Alexander*. Louvre, Paris (Bettmann Archive)

PAGE 96

Fig. 19—*Chapel at Versailles* (1699). Château de Versailles

PAGE 92

FIG. 20—ANTOINE COYSEVOX: *Duchess of Burgundy*. Château de Versailles
PAGE 100

FIG. 21—DESJARDINS: *Pierre Mignard*. Louvre, Paris   PAGE 98

FIG. 22—PIERRE MIGNARD: *Duchess of Maine as a Child*. Château de Versailles　　PAGE 98

FIG. 23—*La Rochefoucauld.* From *Memoirs of Madame de Motteville*, Vol. II (Boston: Hardy, Pratt & Co., 1901)

PAGE 155

FIG. 24—HOUDON: *Molière.* Joseph Duveen Collection (Bettmann Archive)

PAGE 105

to be an ingratiating teacher. He was more in his element when he gently guided Louise de La Vallière out of adultery into a nunnery. He preached the sermon when she took the vows; and in that year 1675 he spoke up again in reproof of the philandering King. Louis heard him impatiently, but restored him to the episcopate as bishop of Meaux (1681), near enough to Versailles to let Bossuet savor the pomp and splendor of the court. Through that proud generation he was the authoritative exponent and leader of the French clergy. For them he drew up the Four Articles that reaffirmed the "Gallican liberties" of the French Church as against papal domination. Bossuet forfeited thereby a cardinal's hat, but he became the pope of France.

He was not a bad pope. Though he insisted on the dignity and ceremony of the episcopal state, he remained humane and kind, and spread his mantle over many varieties of Catholic belief. Without condoning the passion and scorn that sharpened the *Provincial Letters*, he agreed in condemning the excesses of casuistry; in 1700 he persuaded the assembly of the clergy to repudiate 127 propositions taken from Jesuit casuists; and he remained on friendly terms with Arnauld and other Jansenists. He was reputed to be lenient in the confessional, and deprecated austerities in laymen, but he warmly approved the asceticism of Rancé, went into frequent retreat at La Trappe, and wished at times that he might win the peace of a monastic cell. The glamour of the court, however, overcame his aspirations to sanctity, and tarnished his theology with ambitions to rise in the hierarchies of Church and state. "Pray for me," he asked the abbess at Meaux, "that I may not love the world."[112] In his later years he became more severe. We must excuse him for denouncing the theater and Molière in his *Maximes sur la comédie* (1694), for Molière had shown religion only in its puritanical and hypocritical forms, hardly doing justice to men like Vincent de Paul.

Bossuet was more intolerant in theory than in practice. He thought it absurd that any individual mind, however brilliant, should think to acquire in one lifetime the knowledge and wisdom fitting him to sit in judgment upon the traditions and beliefs of the family, the community, the state, and the Church. The *sens commun* was more trustworthy than individual reasoning; not "common sense" as the thought of common persons, but as the collective intelligence of generations taught by centuries of experience, and taking form in the customs and creeds of mankind. What man could pretend to know better than so many men the needs of the human soul, and the answers to questions unanswerable by knowledge alone? Consequently the human mind needs an authority to give it peace, and free thought can only destroy that peace; human society needs an authority to give it morals, and free thought, by questioning the divine origin of the moral code, brings the whole moral order into ruin. Hence heresy is treason to society and the state as well as to the Church, and "those who believe that a prince should not use force in religious matters . . . are guilty of an impious error."[113] The bishop favored persuasion rather than force in the conversion of heretics, but he defended force as a last resort, and hailed the Revocation as "the pious edict that will give the deathblow to heresy." In his own district he enforced the decree with such lenience that the intendant reported, "Nothing can be done in the diocese of Meaux; the weakness of the Bishop is a hindrance to conversion."[114] Most of the Huguenots in that area persisted in their faith.

He hoped to the last that argument could win even Holland, Germany, and England to the old faith, and we shall see him negotiate for years with Leibniz over the philosopher's plan for reuniting the severed segments of Christianity. In 1688 he wrote his masterpiece, *Histoire des variations des églises protestantes*, which Buckle rated as "probably the most formidable work ever directed against Protestantism."[115] The four volumes were distinguished by painstaking scholarship; every page was propped up with references—a type of conscience that was just beginning to take form. The bishop made an attempt at fairness. He acknowledged the ecclesiastical abuses against which Luther had rebelled; he saw much to admire in Luther's character; but he could not stomach the jolly coarseness that mingled, in Luther, with patriotic courage and masculine piety. He drew almost a loving picture of Melanchthon. Nevertheless he hoped, by showing the personal weaknesses and theological disputes of the Reformers, to loosen the attachment of their followers. He ridiculed the idea that every man should be free to interpret the Bible for himself and found a new religion on a new reading; anyone acquainted with human nature could have foreseen that this, if unopposed, would result in the fragmentation of Christianity into a wilderness of sects, and of morals into an individualism in which the instincts of the jungle could be checked only by the endless multiplication of police. From Luther to Calvin to Socinus—from the rejection of the papacy to the rejection of the Eucharist to the rejection of Christ—and then from Unitarianism to atheism: these were easily descending steps in the dissolution of belief. From religious to social revolt, from Luther's theses to the Peasants' War, from Calvin to Cromwell to the Levellers to regicide: these were slippery steps in the disintegration of social order and peace. Only a religion of authority could give sanction to morals, stability to the state, and strength to the human spirit in the face of bewilderment, bereavement, and death.

It was a powerful argument, impressive with learning and eloquence, containing pages unsurpassed in the French prose of that age except by the polemics and *Pensées* of Pascal. It might have had more success if its

appeal to reason had not been stultified by the appeal to force in the barbarities of the Revocation. A hundred refutations appeared in Protestant
lands excoriating the pretense to reason in a man who approved spoliation,
banishment, confiscation, and galley slavery as arguments for Catholic
Christianity. And—asked the rejoinders—were there not variations in
Catholicism too? What century had passed without divisions in the Church
—Roman Catholics, Greek Catholics, Armenian Catholics, Uniates? Were
not the Jansenists of Port-Royal at that moment warring with their fellow
Catholics of the Society of Jesus? Was not the Gallican clergy, led by
Bossuet himself, in bitter dispute with the Ultramontanes, almost to the
point of schism with Rome? Was not Bossuet fighting Fénelon?

VIII. FÉNELON: 1651–1715

Nobly born and trebly named, François de Salignac de La Mothe-Fénelon
was also orthodox and ambitious, a bishop and courtier, a royal tutor and
master of prose, but elsewise all the world away from Bossuet. Saint-Simon
was impressed:

> A very tall, thin man, well-built, pale, with a large nose, and eyes
> that flashed with fire and intelligence. His physiognomy seemed
> composed of contradictions, yet, somehow, these contradictions were
> not disagreeable. It was grave yet gallant, serious yet gay; it expressed
> equally the doctor, the bishop, and the aristocrat; and, perceptible
> above everything else, in his face as in himself, were delicacy, modesty,
> and, supremely, nobility of mind. It required an effort to take one's
> eyes from his face.[116]

Michelet thought him *un peu vieux dès sa naissance*[117]—"a bit old from
his birth"—as the fruit of the final flowering of an aging seigneur in Périgord, who, over the groans of his grown sons, had married a poor but noble
demoiselle. The new son was put out of the money by being dedicated to
the Church. Brought up by his mother, he developed an almost feminine
grace of speech and delicacy of feeling. Well educated in classical lore by
a tutor and the Jesuits of Paris, he became a scholar as well as a priest. He
could bandy pagan quotations with any heretic, and wrote a French style
nervous, delicate, and refined, at the other end of the scale from the masculine and rotund oratory of Bossuet.

Ordained at twenty-four (1675), he was soon made superior of the
Convent of New Catholics, where he had the difficult task of reconciling
to the Roman faith young women recently separated from Protestantism.
They listened to him at first unwillingly, then resignedly, then affection-

ately, for it was easy to fall in love with Fénelon, and he was the only man available. In 1686 he was sent to the region of La Rochelle to aid in the conversion of Huguenots. He approved the Revocation, but deprecated the violence, and warned the King's ministers that forced conversions would be superficial and transient. Returning to the convent in Paris, he published (1687) a *Traité de l'éducation des filles,* almost Rousseauian in its advocacy of gentle methods. When the Duc de Beauvilliers was appointed by the King as governor of his eight-year-old grandson Louis, Duke of Burgundy, he called upon Fénelon to tutor the boy (1689).

The young Duke was proud, headstrong, passionate, sometimes ferocious and cruel, but possessed of a brilliant mind and a vivacious wit. Fénelon felt that only religion could tame him; he instilled in him both the fear and the love of God; at the same time he won the respect of his pupil by a discipline tempered with sympathetic understanding of adolescence. He dreamed of reforming France by forming its prospective king. He taught the lad the absurdity of war, and the necessity of promoting agriculture instead of discouraging the peasantry with taxes to build luxurious cities and finance aggressive wars. In the *Dialogues of the Dead* that he wrote for his pupil he stigmatized as "barbarous that government where there are no laws but the will of one man. . . . He who rules should be pre-eminently obedient to the law; detached from the law, his person is nothing." All wars are civil wars, since all men are brothers; "each one owes infinitely more to the human race—which is the great country—than to the particular country in which he was born."[118] The King, not privy to this esoteric instruction, and seeing a wondrous improvement in his grandson's character, rewarded Fénelon with the archbishopric of Cambrai (1695). Fénelon put many prelates to shame by living nine months of each year at his see. The rest he spent at the court, anxious to influence policy, and occasionally continuing his instruction of the Duke.

Meanwhile he had met the woman who was to be, in a real sense, his *femme fatale.* Mme. Jeanne Marie de La Motte-Guyon, married at sixteen, widowed and pretty and wealthy at twenty-eight, had the world of suitors at her feet. But she had received an intensive religious training as a necessary protection against ambitious males; she had found no adequate outlet for her piety in the external observance of Catholic worship; and she listened responsively to the mystics of her time, who offered peace of soul not so much through confession, Communion, and the Mass as through absorption in the contemplation of an omnipresent deity, a complete and loving surrender of the self to God. In such a divine love affair no worldly matters counted; in that exaltation of the spirit one might neglect all religious ritual and yet attain to heaven not only after death but in life as well. The Spanish priest Miguel de Molinos had been condemned by the Inquisition (1687) for preaching such "quietism" in Italy; but the movement was spreading throughout Europe—in the "Pietism" of Germany and the Netherlands, among the Quakers and the Cambridge Platonists in England, among the *dévots* in France.

Mme. Guyon, in several books, expounded her views with moving eloquence. Souls, she taught, are torrents that have issued from God, and that find no quiet until they lose themselves in Him like rivers swallowed by the sea. Then individuality fades away; there is no further consciousness of self or the world, no consciousness at all, only identity with God. In such a state the soul is infallible, beyond good and evil, virtue and sin; whatever it does is right, and no force can injure it. She could not ask forgiveness for her sins, Mme. Guyon told Bossuet, because in her world of ecstasy there was no sin.[119] Some ladies of the aristocracy saw in this mysticism a noble form of piety; Mme. Guyon numbered among her disciples the Mmes. de Beauvilliers, de Chevreuse, de Mortemart, even, in a degree, Mme. de Maintenon. Fénelon himself was attracted by this fascinating union of piety, wealth, and loveliness; his own character was a complex of mysticism, ambition, and sentiment. He persuaded Mme. de Maintenon to let Mme. Guyon teach in the school that the secret wife of the King had founded at St.-Cyr. Maintenon asked her confessor to advise her about Mme. Guyon; he consulted Bossuet, who invited the mystic to expound her doctrines to him. She did. The cautious bishop saw in them a threat to the theology and practices of the Church, for they seemed to dispense not only with the sacraments and the priest, but with the Gospels and Christ. He reproved her, gave her the Eucharist, and asked her to leave Paris and cease teaching. At first she consented, then she refused. Bossuet had her confined in a convent for eight years (1695–1703), after which she was released on condition that she live quietly on her son's estate near Blois. There she died in 1717.

To define the limits of permissible mysticism Bossuet composed an *Instruction on the States of Prayer* (1696). He showed Fénelon a copy of the manuscript, and asked his approval. Fénelon demurred, and wrote an opposed work, *Explanation of the Maxims of the Saints on the Internal Life* (1697). The two books, published almost simultaneously, became a matter of widespread discussion as lively as in the furor over Port-Royal. The King, trusting Bossuet, removed Fénelon from his position as instructor to the Duke of Burgundy, and bade him stay in his diocese at Cambrai Urged on by Bossuet, Louis demanded a papal condemnation of Fénelon's book. Innocent XII, remembering Bossuet's Gallicanism and Fénelon's Ultramontane defense of the papacy, hesitated; pressure was brought upon him; he yielded, but condemned the *Maxims* as mildly as he could (March, 1699). Fénelon submitted quietly.

At Cambrai he performed his duties with a devotion and conscience that won him the respect of France. Bossuet and the King might have been appeased had not a printer published (April, 1699), with the consent of the author, a romance that Fénelon had written for his royal pupil under the apparently harmless title of *Suite de l'Odicée d'Homère* (*Continuation of Homer's Odyssey*), known to us as *Les Aventures de Télémaque, fils d'Ulysse*. Here, in a style of smooth grace and almost feminine tenderness, the ingratiating teacher had expounded again his idealistic political philosophy. Mentor, his mouthpiece, having persuaded the kings to peace, warns them:

> Henceforth, under divers names and chiefs, you will be all one people . . . All the human race is one family . . . All peoples are brothers . . . Unhappy the impious men who seek a cruel glory in the blood of their brothers. . . . War is sometimes necessary, but it is the shame of the human race. . . . Do not tell me, O kings, that one should desire war to acquire glory. . . . Whoever prefers his own glory to sentiments of humanity is a monster of pride and not a man; he will gain only false glory, for true glory is found only in moderation and goodness. . . . Men should not think well of him, since he has thought so little of them, and has shed their blood prodigally for a brutal vanity.[120]

Fénelon admitted the divine right of kings, but only as a power given them by Providence to make men happy, and as a right limited by laws:

> Absolute power degrades every subject to the condition of a slave. The tyrant is flattered, even to the point of adoration, and everyone trembles at the glance of his eye; but at the least breath of revolt this monstrous power perishes by its own excess. It drew no strength from the love of the people.[121]

In these bold lines Louis XIV saw himself described and his wars condemned. The friends of Fénelon hastily vanished from the court. The printer of *Télémaque* was arrested, and the police were told to confiscate all copies. But the book was reprinted in Holland, and soon it was being read throughout the French-reading world; for a century and a half it was the most widely read, and best loved, of all French books.[122] Fénelon protested that he had not had Louis in mind in these critical passages; no one believed him. Two years passed before the Duke of Burgundy dared to write to his former teacher; then the King relented, and allowed him to visit Fénelon at Cambrai. The Archbishop lived in hopes that his pupil would soon inherit the throne, and might then call upon him to be his

Richelieu. But the grandson died three years before the King; and Fénelon himself (January 7, 1715) preceded Louis by nine months to the grave.

Bossuet had gone long before them. He was unhappy in his later years; he had triumphed against Fénelon, the Ultramontanes, and the mystics, and he had seen the Church triumphant against the Huguenots; but all these victories could not enable him to pass the stones from his bladder. Pain so racked him that he could hardly bear to take the place he so loved to hold in the ceremonies of the court; and heartless cynics asked why he could not go and die privately at Meaux. He saw about him the rise of skepticism, of Biblical criticism, of Protestant polemics impiously aimed at his own head; here, for example, was Jurieu, the banished Huguenot, telling the world that he, Bossuet, the bishop of bishops and the very image of virtue and probity, was a ranting liar living with concubines.[123] He began some new books to rout these scurrilous foes, but life ran out on him as he wrote; and on April 12, 1704, his pains ceased.

At first sight Bossuet seems to mark the zenith of Catholicism in modern France. The old faith appeared to have recovered all the ground that had been lost to Luther and Calvin. The clergy were reforming their morals, Racine was devoting his final dramas to religion, Pascal had turned skepticism upon the skeptics, the state had made itself an obedient agent of the Church, the King had become almost a Jesuit.

And yet the situation was not perfect. The Jesuits were still under the cloud raised by the *Lettres à un provincial*; Jansenism was not destroyed; the Huguenot fugitives were stirring up half of Europe against the pious King; Montaigne was read more widely than Pascal; and Hobbes, Spinoza, and Bayle were striking terrible blows at the edifice of faith. According to St. Vincent de Paul (1648), "several pastors complain that they have fewer communicants than before; St.-Sulpice three thousand less; the pastor of St.-Nicolas-du-Chardonnet found that 1,500 of his parishioners had omitted Easter communion."[124] Said Bayle in 1686: "The age we live in is full of freethinkers and deists; people are amazed at their number";[125] "a prodigious indifference to religion reigns everywhere";[126] and he attributed this to the wars and controversies of Christendom. "You must know," said Nicole, "that the great heresy in the world is not Calvinism or Lutheranism, but atheism."[127] Said the Princess Palatine in 1699: "One now rarely finds a young man who does not wish to be an atheist."[128] In the Paris of 1703, Leibniz reported, the "so-called *esprits forts* are in the fashion, and piety is there turned to ridicule. . . . Under a King devout, severe, and absolute, the disorder of religion has gone beyond anything ever seen in the Christian world."[129] Among these *esprits forts*—"minds strong" enough to doubt almost everything—were Saint-Évremond, Ninon de Lenclos, Gassendi's epitomizer Bernier, the Ducs de Nevers and de Bouillon. The Temple, once the headquarters of the Knights Templar in Paris, became the center of a little group of freethinkers—Chaulieu, Sirvien, La Fare, etc.—who passed down their irreverence to the Regency. And Fontenelle, the indestructible near-centenarian destined to bandy quips with the Encyclopedists, was already in 1687 publishing his *Histoire des oracles,* slyly undermining the miraculous basis of Christianity. In the ecstasy of his piety Louis XIV had cleared the road for Voltaire.

CHAPTER III

The King and the Arts

1643–1715

I. THE ORGANIZATION OF THE ARTS

NEVER before or after, excepting perhaps under Pericles, has a government so stimulated, nourished, or dominated art as under Louis XIV. *Artes virumque cano.*

Richelieu's fine taste and judicious purchases had helped the recovery of French art from the Religious Wars. During the regency of Anne of Austria private collectors—nobles and financiers—had begun to vie with one another in gathering works of art. Pierre Crozat, a banker, had a hundred paintings by Titian, a hundred by Veronese, two hundred by Rubens, over a hundred by Vandyck. Fouquet, as we have seen, amassed paintings, statues, and lesser objects of art at Vaux, with more discrimination than discretion. Louis, destroying him, inherited his acquisitions; and in time several other private collections were gathered into the Louvre or Versailles. Mazarin had put part of his hoard into art more likely than money to escape depreciation. His fine Italian taste shared in forming the classical bias of the King, and it was probably he who taught Louis XIV that it redounded to the glory of a ruler to accumulate, display, and foster art. These collections provided the stimulating exemplars and stabilizing norms for art education and development in France.

The next step was to organize the artists. Here too Mazarin led the way. In 1648 he founded the Académie de Peinture et de Sculpture; in 1655 this received a charter from the King, and became the first in a series of academies designed to train artists and direct them into the service and adornment of the state. Colbert took up where Mazarin left off, and brought to a head this centralization of French art. Though himself laying no claim to artistic judgment, he aspired "to make the arts flourish better in France than anywhere else."[1] He began by buying for the King the tapestry works of the Gobelins (1662). In 1664 he acquired the post of superintendent of buildings, which gave him control of architecture and its ancillary arts. In that year he reorganized the Academy of Painting and Sculpture as the Académie Royale des Beaux-Arts. Henry IV had housed in the Louvre a guild of artisans to adorn the royal palaces; Colbert made these men the nucleus of the Manufacture Royale des Meubles de la Couronne—the Royal

Manufactory of Furniture for the Crown (1667). In 1671 he established the Académie Royale de l'Architecture, where artists were induced to build and decorate in *le bon goût* approved by the King. In all these societies the artisans were brought under the direction of artists, and these under the guidance of one policy and style.

To reinforce the classical bent that French art had received under Francis I, and cleanse it from Flemish influences, Colbert and Charles Le Brun set up in Rome the Académie Royale de France (1666). Students who had won the Prix de Rome in the Paris academies were sent to Italy, and were maintained there for five years at the expense of the French government. They were required to rise at five o'clock in the morning and to retire at ten o'clock at night; they were trained in copying and imitating classical and Renaissance models; they were expected to produce a "masterpiece" (in the guild sense) every three months; and when they returned to France the state had first option on their services.

The result of this fostering and nationalization of art was an impressive, overwhelming production of palaces, churches, statues, pictures, tapestries, pottery, medallions, engravings, and coins, all stamped with the pride and taste—often with the features—of Le Roi Soleil. It was not a subjection of French art to Rome, as some complained; it was a subjection of Roman art to Louis XIV. The style aimed to be classical, for that style agreed with the majesty of states and kings. Colbert poured French money into Italy to buy classical or Renaissance art. Everything was done to transport the glory of the Roman emperors to the King and capital of France. The result amazed the world.

Louis XIV became the greatest patron of art that history has known. He "gave greater encouragement to the arts" (in the judgment of Voltaire) "than all his fellow kings together."[2] He was, of course, the most openhanded collector. He enlarged the number of paintings in his galleries from two hundred to twenty-five hundred; and many of these pictures were the product of royal commissions to French artists. He bought so many pieces of classical or Renaissance sculpture that Italy feared artistic denudation, and the Pope forbade the further export of art. Louis engaged men of talent like Girardon or Coysevox to make copies of statues that he could not buy; and seldom have copies so rivaled their originals. The palaces, gardens, and parks of Paris, Versailles, and Marly were peopled with statuary. The surest way to the King's favor was to present him with a work of unquestioned beauty or established repute; so the city of Arles gave him its famous *Venus* in 1683. Louis was not stingy; each year, in Voltaire's estimate, he bought French art products to the value of 800,000 livres, and made gifts of them to cities, institutions, and friends,[3] aiming at once to support the artists and to disseminate a sense of beauty and a feeling for art. The taste of the King was good, and immensely benefited French art, but it was narrowly class-ical. When he was shown some paintings by the younger Teniers he com-manded, "*Enlevez-moi ces grotesques!* Take away these crudities!"[4] Under his favor artists rose considerably in earnings and social status. He gave the cue by personally honoring them; and when someone complained of the patents of nobility that he conferred on the painter Le Brun and the archi-tect Jules Hardouin-Mansard, he replied, with some warmth, "I can make twenty dukes or peers in a quarter of an hour, but it takes centuries to make a Mansard."[5] Mansard was paid eighty thousand livres per year; Le Brun reveled in the opulence of his mansions at Paris, Versailles, and Montmor-ency; Largillière and Rigaud received six hundred livres per portrait. "No artist of worth was left in poverty."[6]

In honoring and rewarding art the provinces emulated the capital, and nobles followed the lead of the King. The cities developed art schools of their own—at Rouen, Beauvais, Blois, Orléans, Tours, Lyons, Aix-en-Provence, Toulouse, Bordeaux. The role of the nobles as patrons diminished as the state absorbed the available talent, but it continued; and the trained taste of the most developed aristocracy in Europe contributed to establish the exquisite style of art productions under Louis XIV. Men and women born to privilege and wealth, and reared in good manners amid handsome surroundings and objects of beauty, acquired standards and tastes from their elders and their environment; and the artists had to meet those stand-ards and satisfy those tastes. As moderation, self-restraint, elegant expression, graceful movement, and polished form were ideals of the French aristoc-racy in this age, it demanded these qualities in art; the social structure favored the classic style. Art profited from these influences and controls, but it paid a price. It lost touch with the people, it could not express them as Dutch and Flemish art expressed the Netherlands; it became the voice not of the nation but of a class, the state, and the King. We shall not find in the art of this period much warmth or depth of feeling, not the rich tints and abundant flesh of Rubens, nor the profound shadows enveloping Rembrandt's rabbis, saints, and financiers; we shall see no peasants, no workers, no beggars, but only the pretty happiness of the top of the world.

To the joy of Colbert and his master, they found in Charles Le Brun a man who could be at once a zealous servant of the government and a dominating magistrate of this classic style. In 1666, on Colbert's recom-mendation, Le Brun was made chief painter to the King, and director of the Académie des Beaux-Arts; a year later he was put in charge of the Gobelin factory. He was commissioned to superintend the education and operation of artists, with a view to developing in their products a harmony of style distinctive and representative of the reign. With the help of like-minded subordinates Le Brun established in the Academy (1667) the *con-*

férences, or lectures, by which the principles of the classic style were inculcated with precepts, examples, and authority. Raphael among the Italians, Poussin among the French, were the favored models; every painting was judged by the canons derived from their art. Le Brun and Sébastien Bourdon formulated these rules; they exalted line above color, discipline above originality, order above freedom; the task of the artist was not to copy Nature but to make her beautiful, not to mirror her disorder, imperfections, and monstrosities as well as her incidental loveliness, but to select those features of her that would enable the soul of man to express its deepest feelings and highest ideals. The architects, the painters, the sculptors, the potters, the woodworkers, the metalworkers, the glassworkers, the engravers were to utter with one harmonious voice the aspirations of France and the grandeur of the King.

II. ARCHITECTURE

However, these French artists Italianate had returned from Rome unconsciously coated with baroque. That now pervasive style has been previously described; it may be summarized as replacing the calm simplicity of classic forms with an exuberance of feeling and ornament. While the classic—more specifically the Hellenistic—ideal was approximated in the sculpture, painting, and literature of this *grand siècle*, the architecture and decoration borrowed from the elegant and ornate styles that had triumphed in Italy after the death of Michelangelo (1564). The King's builders aimed at the classical and achieved the baroque—at Versailles the full baroque, in the façades of the Louvre a successful synthesis of baroque and classical.

The first architectural *chef-d'oeuvre* of the reign was the Church of Val-de-Grâce in Paris. Anne of Austria had registered a vow to build a handsome shrine if God and Louis XIII would give her a son. When her regency provided her with funds, she engaged François Mansart to draw up plans. The first stone was laid by Louis XIV, then seven years old, in 1645. Mansart's design was carried out by Lemercier in Italian classic style, with a dome that is still the admiration of architects. Libéral Bruant built the Church of St.-Louis-des-Invalides (1670) for the veterans housed in the Hôtel des Invalides; and in 1676 Louvois commissioned Jules Hardouin-Mansard (grandnephew of François Mansart) to finish the church with a choir and a dome. In elegant beauty that dome is the architectural masterpiece of the reign. Hardouin-Mansard triumphed again in designing the chapel at Versailles (1699). Here and at the Invalides his work was completed with luxurious ornament by his brother-in-law Robert de Cotte who raised also the Hôtel de Ville at Lyons, the Abbey of St.-Denis, and the façade of St.-Roche.

Royal replaced ecclesiastical architecture as the state surpassed the Church in wealth and prestige. The problem now was to express not devotion but power. In meeting this requirement the Louvre had the advantage of tradition; many generations had seen it grow, and many kings had marked its history. Lemercier, working for Mazarin, raised the western front of the main wing, and began the north wing along the present Rue de Rivoli. Le Vau, who succeeded him, finished that wing, reconstructed the façade of the south wing (facing the Seine), and laid the foundations of the east wing. At this juncture Colbert became superintendent of buildings. Rejecting Le Vau's plans for the east wing, he conceived the project of continuing the Louvre westward until it should join the Tuileries in a single palace. He announced to the architects of France and Italy a competition to design a new façade. To make sure to get the best, he persuaded the King to send a special invitation to Giovanni Lorenzo Bernini (1665), then the acknowledged prince of European artists, to come to Paris at the royal expense and submit a design. Bernini came with great pomp, angered the French artists with his scorn of their work, and drew up a massive, costly plan that required the demolition of nearly all the existing Louvre. Colbert found the plan deficient in plumbing and other facilities for living; Bernini fumed that "M. Colbert treats me like a little boy, with all his idle talk about privies and underground conduits."[7] A compromise was reached: the King laid the foundation stone of Bernini's design; then the artist, after six months in Paris, was sent back to Italy with honors and livres, which he tried to repay with the bust of Louis XIV now at Versailles, and the equestrian statue of Louis in the Galleria Borghese in Rome. His design for the Louvre was abandoned; the existing structure was retained, and Charles Perrault was awarded the commission to build the eastern front. Now rose the famous Colonnade du Louvre, whose palpable defects let loose a flood of criticism,[8] but which is now accepted as one of the most magnificent façades on earth.

Colbert had hoped that the King would move from the cramped quarters at St.-Germain into the renovated Louvre. But Louis still remembered that he and his mother had had to flee from the Paris populace during the Fronde; he thought that the voice of the people was the voice of violence; and he did not care to subject himself to such checks on his absolute rule. To the dismay of Colbert he decided to build Versailles.

Louis XIII had erected there a modest hunting lodge in 1624. André Le Nôtre saw in the gently rising slope of the site, and its rich forestation, a tempting chance for garden artistry. In 1662 he presented to Louis XIV a general plan for the grounds; and if today the buildings are inferior to the lawns and the lake, the flowers and shrubs and varied trees, that may be as Le Nôtre conceived it. It was to be not so much a masterpiece of architecture as an invitation to live outdoors, amid a nature tamed and improved by art: to breathe the fragrance of flowers and trees, to feast the eyes and fancied touch on classically sculptured forms, to hunt prey and women in the woods, to dance and picnic on the grass, to boat on the canal and the lake, to hear Lully and Molière under the open sky. Here was a garden of the gods, built with the pennies of twenty million Frenchmen who would rarely see it, but who gloried in the glory of their King. It is pleasant to learn that except on royal occasions the park at Versailles was open to the public.

The art of landscape gardening, like so much else, had come from Italy, bringing a hundred devices and surprises; bowers, trellises, grottoes, caves, grotesques, colored stones, bird houses, statues, vases, brooks, fountains, waterspouts, even organs played by running water. Le Nôtre had already designed the gardens at Vaux for Fouquet; soon he would design the Jardins des Tuileries for the Queen, and the gardens at St.-Cloud for Madame Henrietta, and the gardens at Chantilly for Le Grand Condé. At Versailles, from 1662 onward, Louis gave him carte blanche, and Colbert was appalled at the expense incurred in transforming a disheveled wilderness into acres of paradise. The King fell in love with Le Nôtre, who cared not for money but only for beauty, and in whom there was no guile.[9] He was the Boileau of gardens, resolved to turn the "disorder" of nature into order, harmony, and reasonable, intelligible form. Perhaps he was too insistently classical, but his creation remains, after three hundred years, one of the meccas of mankind.

Still envious of Fouquet, Louis brought Vaux's architect, Le Vau, to enlarge the hunting lodge into a royal palace. Jules Hardouin-Mansard took over the direction in 1670, and began the vast apartments, galleries, reception rooms, dance halls, guardrooms, and administrative offices that are now Versailles. By 1685 there were thirty-six thousand men and six thousand horses laboring on the enterprise, sometimes working in night and day shifts. Colbert long ago had warned the King that such architecture, added to war after war, would bankrupt the treasury; but in 1679 Louis built another palace at Marly as an escape from the crowds at Versailles, and in 1687 he added the Grand Trianon as a retreat for Mme. de Maintenon. He ordered an army of men, including many of his regular troops, to divert the River Eure and carry its waters through ninety miles of the "Aqueduc of Maintenon" to supply the lakes, streams, fountains, and baths of Versailles; in 1688, after huge expenditures, this enterprise was abandoned at the call of war. All in all, Versailles—buildings, furniture, decoration, gardens, and aqueducts—had by 1690 cost France 200,000,000 francs ($500,000,000?).[10]

Architecturally, Versailles is too complex and haphazard to approach perfection. The chapel is brilliant, but such flaunting of decoration hardly accords with the humility of prayer. Parts of the palace are beautiful, and the stairways to the gardens are majestic; but the compulsion laid upon the designers to leave the hunting lodge intact, merely adding wings and ornament, injured the appearance of the whole. Sometimes the proliferating pile leaves an impression of cold monotony and labyrinthine repetition— one room after another to a spread of 1,320 frontal feet. The internal arrangements seem to have ignored physiological convenience, and to have presumed upon remarkable retentive power in noble vesicles. Half a dozen rooms had to be traversed to reach the goal of desire; no wonder we hear of stairways and hallways serving in such emergencies. The rooms themselves appear too small for comfort. Only the Grande Galerie is spacious, extending 320 feet along the garden front. There the decorators deployed all their skills—hanging Gobelin and Beauvais tapestries, scattering sculpture along the walls, making every piece of furniture lovingly perfect, and reflecting all the splendor in those great mirrors that gave the room its second name, Galerie des Glaces. On the ceiling Le Brun, rising to the height of his art, painted through five years (1679–84) and mythological symbols the triumphs of the long reign, and unwittingly its tragedy; for these pictured victories over Spain, Holland, and Germany were to arouse the Furies against the war-fond King.

Louis lived there, on and off, from 1671, spending part of his time at Marly, St.-Germain, and Fontainebleau; after 1682 it was his permanent home. But we do him injustice when we think of Versailles as his residence and playground; he himself occupied a moderate fraction of the structure; the rest housed his wife, children, and grandchildren, his mistresses, the foreign legations, the chief administrators, the court, and all the servantry required by royalty. Doubtless some part of the magnificence had a political purpose—to awe the ambassadors, who were expected to judge from this luxury the resources and power of the state. They and other visitors were duly impressed, and they spread through Europe such reports of Versailles' splendor that it became the envy and model of a dozen courts and palaces throughout the Continent. In the aftermath of the reign the great mass seemed to people an insolent symbol of despotism, a reckless challenge of human pride to unchanging human fate.

III. DECORATION

The arts of decoration had never known, even under the Renaissance popes, such encouragement and display. Thickly carpeted floors, ornamental columns, massive tables and chimneypieces, porcelain vases, silver candelabra, crystal chandeliers, marble clocks inlaid with gems, walls paneled or frescoed or hung with pictures or tapestries, cornices elegantly molded, ceilings coffered or painted—these and a dozen other forms of art, in Versailles, Fontainebleau, Marly, the Louvre, even in private palaces, made almost every room a museum of objects charming eye and soul with the mystery of perfection. From Raphael and his aides—Giulio Romano, Perino del Vaga, Giovanni da Udine—and the Loggie of the Vatican, Le Brun and his aides took their palette of gods, goddesses, Cupids, trophies, emblems, arabesques, garlands of flowers and leaves, cornucopias of the fruits of the earth, to decorate the record of the royal triumphs over women and states.

In the style of Louis XIV furniture was lavish and gorgeous; here classic simplicity yielded to baroque ornament. Chairs were often so carved, upholstered, and petitpointed as to frighten away all but the most exquisite bottoms; on the other hand, tables could be heavy and solid to the point of apparent immobility. Writing tables and "secretaries" were of an elegance inviting the pen to compose with the pithy precision of La Rochefoucauld or the bubbling vivacity of Mme. de Sévigné. Chests and cabinets were in many cases laboriously carved, and/or inlaid with designs in metal or jewelry. André Charles Boulle, who was settled in the Louvre (1672) as the favorite cabinetmaker of Louis XIV, gave his name ("buhlwork") to his special art of inlaying furniture—preferably ebony—with engraved metal, tortoise shell, mother-of-pearl, etc., and adding floral or animal scrolls of the most graceful design. One of his inlaid cabinets brought £3,000 in 1882, probably equal to $50,000 in 1960;[11] Boulle, however, died in extreme poverty in his ninetieth year (1732). More to our taste are the carved stalls that were set up in this period in Notre-Dame-de-Paris.

Tapestry was now specifically a royal art. Not content with bringing the Gobelin and Aubusson factories under the King's control, Colbert persuaded him also to take over the *tapissiers* of Beauvais. Tapestries were still the favored decoration for the walls and screens of palaces and châteaux, for pageants, tournaments, state ceremonies, and religious festivals. At Beauvais the Flemish painter Adam van der Meulen designed an outstanding series, *The Conquests of Louis the Great*, for which the artist prepared himself by following the King to the wars, and drawing or painting on the spot the sites, forts, and villages involved in the campaigns. The Gobelin factory employed eight hundred artisans, who made not only tapestry but fine textiles, woodwork, silverwork, metalwork, and marble marquetry. There, under Le Brun's direction, were woven the great tapestries from the cartoons of Raphael's massive frescoes in the Stanze of the Vatican. Hardly less renowned were the several series designed by Le Brun himself: *The Elements, The Seasons, The History of Alexander, The Royal Residences,* and *The History of the King.* The last group ran to seventeen pieces and took ten years of labor. A superb specimen still hangs in the Gobelin exhibition rooms—the figures astonishingly individualized, the details fully visualized, even to the landscape picture on the wall; all in colored threads patiently woven by subtle hands under tired eyes. Rarely has so much human industry been devoted to the adulation of one man. Louis excused himself by explaining to Colbert that these apotheoses gave employment and income to dyers and weavers, and served as impressive gifts in the lubrication of diplomacy.

Under the lavish royal hand all the minor arts rejoiced. Splendid carpets were made at La Savonnerie near Paris. Fine faïence was produced at Rouen and Moustiers, good majolica at Nevers, soft-paste porcelain at Rouen and St.-Cloud. Toward the end of the seventeenth century French craftsmen, prodded by Colbert, learned the Venetian secrets of casting, rolling, and polishing plate glass; so were made the vast and brilliant mirrors of the Galerie des Glaces.[12] Goldsmiths like Julien Defontaine and Vincent Petit were organized by Colbert and Le Brun, were given lodgings in the Louvre, and made for the King and the rich a thousand articles in silver or gold—until Louis and the grandees melted down these ornaments to finance war. Jewels, medals, coins were cut and engraved in designs that set the pace for all Europe but Italy. Not since the Renaissance had the art of the medallion reached such excellence as came now with Antoine Benoist and Jean Mauger. Leaving no stone uncarved, Colbert founded in 1662 the Academy of Medals and Inscriptions, "in order to render the acts of the King immortal by . . . medals struck in his honor"[13]—which was the great minister's way of enlisting moneyed vanity behind expensive art. In 1667 the École de Gravures was established in the Louvre; and the burins of Robert Nanteuil, Sébastien Le Clerc, Robert Bonnart, and Jean Lepautre illustrated with meticulous refinement the personalities and events of the reign. Even miniature painting survived, though fallen from its medieval estate, in the *Livre d'heures* presented to the King by his pensioners in the Invalides. It is the minor arts, above all the rest, that display the taste and craftsmanship of the great century.

IV. PAINTING

Two pictorial stars of the second magnitude fall into the outer orbit of this age: Philippe de Champaigne and Eustache Le Sueur. Philippe came from Brussels at the age of nineteen (1621), shared in decorating the Palais du Luxembourg, and made not only the full-length *Richelieu* in the Louvre, but the bust and profiles of the Cardinal in the London National Gallery. His sympathetic flair as a portrait painter brought him as sitters half the leaders of France in the generation that succeeded Richelieu: Mazarin, Turenne, Colbert, Lemercier . . . He had already, before coming to France, portrayed Jansen and accepted Jansenism; he loved Port-Royal, and made portraits of Mère Angélique, Robert Arnauld, and Saint-Cyran. For Port-Royal he painted his greatest picture, *Les Religieuses* (Louvre)—Mère Agnès, somber yet sweet, with the artist's nun daughter Suzanne. Champaigne's range was limited, but his art comes warmly to us with its feeling and sincerity.

A kindred but more orthodox piety made Eustache Le Sueur uncomfortable in an age whose painting was dominated by his rival Le Brun and by a pagan mythology dedicated to the deification of a not-yet-pious King. The two artists studied together under Vouet, worked together in the same cellar, used the same model, and were alike praised by Poussin on his visit to Paris. Le Brun followed Poussin to Rome and imbibed the classical spirit; Le Sueur tied himself to Paris with a fertile wife, and seldom escaped from poverty. About 1644 he painted five pictures, describing events in the life of Eros, for the ceiling of the Cabinet de l'Amour in the palace of his patron Lambert de Thorigny; and in another room of this Hôtel Lambert he executed a major fresco, *Phaeton Asks to Guide the Chariot of the Sun.* In 1645 Le Sueur stumbled into a duel, killed his man, hid himself in a Carthusian monastery, and there painted twenty-two pictures from the life of St. Bruno, founder of the Carthusian order; in these the artist reached his apogee. In 1776 the series was bought from the Carthusian monks for 132,000 livres; today they occupy a special room in the Louvre. When Le Brun returned from Italy (1647) he carried everything before him, and Le Sueur fell back into poverty. He died in 1655, only thirty-eight years old.

Charles Le Brun ruled the arts in Paris and Versailles, because he had the ability to co-ordinate and direct as well as to conceive and execute. Son of a sculptor who had painter friends, he grew up in an environment where he learned to draw as other children learn to write. At fifteen, with a never sleeping eye to the main chance, he painted an allegory of Richelieu's life and success; the minister leaped to the bait, and commissioned him to paint some mythological subjects for the Palais-Cardinal. Taken to Rome by Poussin, he steeped himself in the mythologies and decorations of Raphael, Giulio Romano, and Pietro da Cortona. When he reappeared in Paris his style of luscious ornamentation was fully developed. Here again Fouquet gave Louis a lead by engaging Le Brun for the palace at Vaux. The brilliance of the resulting frescoes, the voluptuous grace of the female figures, the rich detail in cornices and moldings appealed to Mazarin, Colbert, and the King. By 1660 Le Brun was painting frescoes from the career of Alexander for the royal palace at Fontainebleau. Louis, pleased to recognize his own features under Alexander's helmet, came daily to watch the artist at work on *The Battle of Arbela* and *The Family of Darius at the Feet of Alexander*—both now in the Louvre. The King rewarded him with a royal portrait inset with diamonds, made him his *premier peintre*, and gave him a pension of twelve thousand livres a year.

Le Brun did not slacken his industry. In 1661 fire ruined the central gallery of the Louvre. Le Brun designed the restoration, and painted the ceiling and cornices with scenes from the legends of Apollo; hence the name Galerie d'Apollon. Meanwhile the ambitious artist studied architecture, sculpture, metalwork, woodwork, tapestry design, and the diverse arts that were now conscripted to adorn the palaces of the great. All these arts were fused in his varied skills, so that he seemed made by fortune to bring the artists of France into unified action to produce *le style Louis Quatorze*.

Even before appointing him director of the Académie des Beaux-Arts, Louis gave him a free hand and purse to decorate Versailles. There he labored for seventeen years (1664–81), co-ordinating the art work, designing the Ambassador's Staircase, and himself painting, in the Halls of War and Peace, and in the Grand Gallery, twenty-seven frescoes describing the glories of the King from the Peace of the Pyrenees (1659) to the Treaty of Nijmegen (1679). Amid a profusion of gods and goddesses, clouds and rivers, horses and chariots, he showed Louis in war and peace: hurling thunderbolts, crossing the Rhine, besieging Ghent, but also administering justice and finance, feeding the poor in famine, establishing hospitals, nourishing art. Individually these pictures are not masterpieces; the classical basis is overgrown with baroque profusion of ornament; but taken together they constitute the most brilliant work done by French painters in this age. The exaltation of the King offends us as revealing in him a *hybris* of pride, but such adulation of princes was in the manner of the time. No wonder Louis, seeing some paintings by Le Brun near others by Veronese and Poussin, said to his painter, "Your works sustain themselves well among those of the great masters; they require only the death of their author to make them more valued. But we hope they will not soon have that advantage."[14] Through all the jealousies with which Le Brun was soon surrounded, the King supported him, as he was supporting the harassed Molière. It was characteristic of Louis that when he was in administrative conference and word was brought to him that Le Brun had come to show him his latest work, *The Elevation of the Cross*,[15] he excused himself from the conference to go and examine the painting and express his pleasure; then he invited all the conferees to come and join him in viewing the picture.[16] So, in this reign, government and art went hand in hand, and artists shared rewards and plaudits with generals.

Le Brun's artistry, though it stemmed from Italian decoration, was something new; it was a decorative composition in which a dozen arts were brought together to make one aesthetic whole. When he tried his hand at individual canvases he slipped into mediocrity. As the King's victories turned into defeats, and his mistresses gave way to priests, the mood of the reign changed, and the gay ornaments of Le Brun fell out of place. When Louvois succeeded Colbert as superintendent of buildings, Le Brun lost his role as master of the arts, though he remained president of the Academy. He died in 1690, a symbol of glory finished and gone.

Many artists rejoiced to be freed from his authority. Pierre Mignard in particular had resented that domination. Nine years older than Le Brun, he had preceded him as a pilgrim coming with palette to Rome; like Poussin, he so loved the Eternal City that he decided to live there the rest of his life, and he did remain there for twenty-two years (1635–57). His portraits so pleased their sitters that at last Pope Innocent X, who may have resented the face that Velázquez had given him, sat for Mignard, who interpreted him more amiably. In 1646, aged thirty-four, Mignard married an Italian beauty; but he had barely settled down to legitimate parentage when he received a summons from France to come and serve his King. He went reluctantly. In Paris he rebelled against accepting directions from Le Brun, refused to join the Academy, and fretted to see the younger man reaping ribbons and gold. Molière recommended him to Colbert, but the minister was probably right in preferring Le Brun; Mignard would not rise to the grandiose scale that the *grand siècle* required. However, Louis, then twenty, wanted a fetching portrait of himself with which to lure a bride from Spain. Mignard obliged, Louis and María Teresa were charmed, and Mignard became the most successful portrait painter of the age. One after another he pictured his contemporaries: Mazarin, Colbert, de Retz, Descartes, La Fontaine, Molière, Racine, Bossuet, Turenne, Ninon de Lenclos, Louise de La Vallière, Mmes. de Montespan, de Maintenon, de La Fayette, de Sévigné; and he did justice to Anne of Austria's hands, which were considered the most beautiful in the world. She rewarded him with a commission to decorate the vault of the dome in the Church of Val-de-Grâce; this fresco was his masterpiece, which Molière celebrated in a poem. He painted the King many times, most famously in the equestrian portrait at Versailles, but we find him there at his best in the lovely portrait of the *Duchess of Maine as a Child*. After Colbert's death Mignard at last triumphed over Le Brun; he succeeded his rival as court painter in 1690, and was made a member of the Academy by royal decree. Five years later, still painting and fighting, he died, aged eighty-five.

A dozen other painters labored for the all-absorbing King. Charles Dufresnoy, Sébastien Bourdon, Noël Coypel and his son Antoine, Jean François de Troy, Jean Jouvenet, Jean Baptiste Santerre, Alexandre François Desportes—they beg to be listed as also present at the feast. Two others stand out commandingly at the end of the reign. Nicolas de Largillière followed Mignard as the favorite painter of the aristocracy, not only in France but for a time (1674–78) in England. He won Le Brun's heart with the splendid portrait of him that now hangs in the Louvre. His rosy colors and light touch illustrate the transition from the somber decline of Louis XIV to the gay Regency and Watteau.

Hyacinthe Rigaud was of tougher fiber; he too buttered his bread with portraits (see his fine *Bossuet* in the Louvre), but not with flattery. Though his dominating figure of Louis XIV, rising at the end of the Grande Galerie of the Louvre, appears at a distance to be a compliment, we note, at closer range, the hard and swollen features of the King, standing at the top of power and on the edge of fate (1701). It was the best-paid, as it is the best-displayed, picture of the time. Louis gave Rigaud forty thousand francs for it ($100,000?)—perhaps as much as he had paid for the awesome robes that here adorned his decay.

V. SCULPTURE

The sculptors were less favored and rewarded in this age than the painters. Yet it was the antique marbles on whose lines Le Brun wished all arts to be formed, and great sums and talents were spent in buying or copying such statuary as had survived the collapse of the classic world. Louis, of course, was not content with copies. Mindful of the Roman gardens of Sallust and Hadrian, he engaged a band of able sculptors to set the park at Versailles alive with statuary. Massive vases, like Coysevox' *Vase de la Guerre*, were raised in the basin of Neptune, and on the terrace; the brothers Gaspard and Balthasar de Marsy carved the great *Basin of Bacchus;* Jean Baptiste Tuby projected from the lake the magnificent *Chariot of Apollo*, with the Sun God symbolizing the King; and François Girardon cut in stone such *Bathing Nymphs* as Praxiteles himself might not have scorned to sign.

Girardon looked back across a century to see how Primaticcio and Goujon had idealized the female form. The fluid grace of Hellenic art returned to him, perhaps in excess; not all our searching has yet found such perfect females as in his *Rape of Proserpine*.[17] But he was capable of stronger moods. For the Place Vendôme he executed the figure of Louis XIV, now in the Louvre; and for the church of the Sorbonne he carved a stately tomb of Richelieu. Le Brun warmed to him for falling in so amiably with the taste and purposes of the Academy. He succeeded Le Brun as chief sculptor to the King, and presided over the Academy after the passing of Mignard. Born ten years before Louis, he outlived him by some months, dying in 1715 at the age of eighty-seven.

Antoine Coysevox was smoother than his name, and as lovable as his *Duchesse de Bourgogne*. Born in Lyons, he was carving a place for himself there as a sculptor when Le Brun called him to help decorate Versailles. He began by making excellent copies or adaptations of classical statuary. From an antique marble in the Villa Borghese he cut the *Nymph of the Shell*; from a statue in the Medici Palace at Florence he made a *Crouching Venus*—both now in that Fortunatus' purse of art called the Louvre. Still in place at Versailles is his *Castor and Pollux*, from a group in the Ludovisi Gardens at Rome. Soon he was producing original works of considerable power. For the park at Versailles he carved large figures representing the rivers Garonne and Dordogne, and for the grounds at Marly two similar symbols of the Seine and the Marne. Four marbles that he made for Marly—*Flora*, *Fame*, *Hamadryad*, and *Mercury Mounted on Pegasus*—are now in the Jardins des Tuileries. From his chisel came much of the sculptural decoration in the major rooms at Versailles.

He labored eight years there, and fifty-five in the service of the King. He made twelve statues of him; the best known is the bust in Versailles. He became in sculpture what Mignard was in painting—the most popular portraitist in France. Instead of quarreling with his rivals he carved them in marble or cast them in bronze, usually sparing both their vanity and their purse. When he was sent fifteen hundred livres for his bust of Colbert he judged himself overpaid, and returned seven hundred.[18] He left firm likenesses of Le Brun, Le Nôtre, Arnauld, Vauban, Mazarin, and Bossuet; of himself a simple rendering of an honest, rugged, troubled face;[19] of the Great Condé two busts, one in the Louvre, the other at Chantilly, of uncompromising veracity and masculine force. In quite another style is the graceful *Duchess of Burgundy as Diana*,[20] and the lovely bust of the same princess in Versailles. He designed imposing tombs for Mazarin,[21] Colbert, Vauban, and Le Brun. His works feel the baroque spirit in their dramatic emotionalism and occasional exaggeration; but at their best they well express the classical ideal of the King and the court. They are Racine in marble and bronze.

Around him and Girardon were gathered a sculptural Pléiade: François Anguier and his brother Michel, Philippe Coffier and his son François, Martin Desjardins, Pierre Legros, and Guillaume Coustou, whose *Horses of Marly* still leap into the air at the Place de la Concorde.

Aside and afar from all these, and defying the soft idealism of the official sculpture, Pierre Puget made his chisel voice the anger and misery of France. Born at Marseilles (1622), he began his art career as a wood carver; but he longed to be, like his idol Michelangelo, at once painter, sculptor, and architect; the supreme artist, he felt, should have all these arts at his command. Dreaming of the Italian masters, he walked from

Marseilles to Genoa to Florence to Rome. He worked eagerly under Pietro da Cortona in decorating the Palazzo Barberini; he absorbed every echo and vestige of Buonarroti, and envied Bernini's varied fame. Returning to Genoa, he executed a *St. Sebastian* that brought him his first renown. Fouquet, again the forerunner of Louis XIV in art, commissioned Puget to carve a *Hercules*[22] for the Château of Vaux. But Fouquet fell, and Pierre hurried south to brood in poverty at Toulon. Engaged to cut *Atlantes* (each a marble Atlas) to support the balcony of the Hôtel de Ville, he modeled the figures on the toiling porters of the docks, and gave almost a revolutionary cry to their straining muscles and pain-distorted faces—the oppressed proletariat upholding the world. This would hardly do at Versailles.

Nevertheless Colbert, his arms open to every talent, asked him for statuary, preferably in a harmless mythological vein. Puget sent him three pieces now in the Louvre: a pleasant bas-relief of *Alexander and Diogenes,* a laborious overdone *Perseus and Andromeda,* and a violent *Milo of Crotona*—the mighty vegetarian struggling to free himself from the jaws and claws of an unconverted lion. In 1688 Puget visited Paris, but, finding his proud temper and angry chisel out of tune with the wit and art of the court, he moved back to Marseilles. There he designed the Hospice de la Charité and the Halle au Poisson—in France even a fish market can be a work of art. His greatest sculpture was probably intended as a commentary on the martial exploits of the King: an equestrian statue of Alexander, handsome and debonair, dagger in hand, carelessly trampling under his horse's feet the victims of war.[23] Puget escaped the formalism, but also the discipline, of Le Brun and Versailles; his ambition to rival Bernini, even Michelangelo, led him to exaggerations of musculature and expression; see the horrible *Head of Medusa* in the Louvre. But all in all he was the most powerful sculptor of his land and time.

As the great reign neared its end, and defeats brought France to desperation, the royal pride turned toward piety, and art passed from the lordliness of Versailles to the humility of Coysevox' *Louis XIV Kneeling in Notre Dame*—the King, now seventy-seven, still flaunting regal robes, yet laying his crown humbly at the Virgin's feet. In those final years the outlay for Versailles and Marly was restrained, but the choir of Notre Dame was restored and beautified. The idolatry of ancient art was cooled by its own excess; the natural began to encroach upon the classical; the pagan *élan* of art was finished by the Revocation of the Edict of Nantes and the ascendancy of Mme. de Maintenon and Le Tellier over the King. The new decorative themes stressed religion, not glory; Louis recognized God.

The history of art under Le Grand Monarque teases us with difficult questions. Was the nationalization of the arts an injury or a boon? Did the influence of Colbert, Le Brun, and the King divert the development of France from its native and natural bent into an enfeebling imitation of an enfeebled Hellenistic "antiquity," confused by a baroque elaboration of ornament? Did these forty years of *le style Louis Quatorze* prove that art flourishes better under a monarchy patronizing it with concentrated wealth, and directing talents into a harmonious unity?—or under an aristocracy preserving, transmitting, and cautiously modifying standards of excellence and taste, and precepts of order and discipline?—or under a democracy opening a career to every talent, freeing ability from the bondage of tradition, and compelling it to submit and adjust its products to the judgment of the people? Would Italy and France be the favored homes of art and beauty today if they had not been embellished by the means and tastes of the Church, the nobles, and the kings? Would great art have been possible without the concentration of wealth?

An ecumenical wisdom would be needed to answer these queries modestly and fruitfully, and every such answer would have to be hedged and obscured with distinctions and doubts. Presumably art lost something in naturalness, initiative, and energy through being protected, directed, and controlled by a central power. The art of Louis XIV was a disciplined and academic art, majestic in its orderly splendor and unsurpassed in its artistic finish; but it was crippled in inventiveness by authority, and fell short of that alliance with the people which gave warmth and depth to Gothic art. The harmony of the arts under Louis was impressive, but it sounded too often the same chord, so that at last it became the expression not of an age and a nation, but only of an ego and a court. Wealth is necessary to great art, but wealth is disgraceful and art is unpleasant when they flourish at the expense of widespread poverty and debasing superstition; for the beautiful cannot long be divorced from the good. An aristocracy could be a beneficent repository and vehicle of manners, standards, and tastes if means could be found to keep it open to fresh talent, and to prevent it from being an agent of class privilege and vain luxury. Democracies too can accumulate wealth and dignify it with the nourishment of knowledge, letters, charity, and art; their problems lie in the hostility of immature freedom to order and discipline, the tardy development of taste in young societies, and the tendency of unmoored ability to waste itself in bizarre experiments that mistake originality for genius and novelty for beauty.

In any case the judgment of Europe's aristocracies was decidedly in favor of French art. The palace architecture, the classic sculpture and literary style, the baroque decoration of furniture and dress, spread from France to almost every ruling class in Western Europe, even into Italy and Spain. The courts of London, Brussels, Cologne, Mainz, Dresden,

Berlin, Cassel, Heidelberg, Turin, and Madrid looked to Versailles as their model of manners and art. French architects were engaged to design palaces as far east as Moravia; Le Nôtre laid out gardens at Windsor and Cassel; Wren and other foreign architects came to Paris for ideas. French sculptors spread out over Europe, until nearly every prince had an equestrian statue like the French King's. The mythological allegories of Le Brun appeared in Sweden, Denmark, Spain, and Hampton Court. Foreign sovereigns begged to sit for Rigaud, or, that failing, for one of his pupils. A Swedish ruler ordered Beauvais tapestries to commemorate his victories. Not since the extension of ancient Latin culture through Western Europe had history seen a cultural conquest so rapid and complete.

CHAPTER IV

Molière

1622–73

I. THE FRENCH THEATER

IT REMAINED for French drama and poetry to bring Europe under their sway.

The humor of history arranged that French literature in this age should take to the stage; that the drama, so long outlawed by the Church, should be encouraged by Cardinal Richelieu; that Italian comedy should be imported into France by Cardinal Mazarin; and that Louis XIV should inherit a taste for the theater from these two ecclesiastics who had prepared or preserved his power.

The modern drama had reached literary form in Italy under the highly cultured popes of the Renaissance, and Leo X had attended plays without demanding that they be fit for virgins. But the Reformation, and the consequent Council of Trent, had put an end to this ecclesiastical lenience. The drama continued to be tolerated in Italy, said Benedict XIV, to avoid greater evils, and in Spain because it served the Church. In France, however, the clergy, shocked by the sexual freedom of the comic stage, condemned the theater as an enemy to public morals. A long succession of bishops and theologians ruled that actors were excommunicated *ipso facto*, by their very profession; the Paris clergy, through the authoritative voice of Bossuet, refused them the sacraments or burial in consecrated ground unless they repented and renounced their calling. Unable to secure priestly administration of sacramental matrimony, actors had to content themselves with common-law marriages of hectic impermanence. French law too pronounced actors infamous, and excluded them from every honorable employment. Magistrates were forbidden to attend theatrical representations.

It is one of the outstanding features of modern history that the theater overcame this resistance. The popular demand for make-believe to alleviate and avenge reality generated a long supply of farces and comedies; and the pains of monogamy provided an especially paying audience for dramas of licit or illicit love. Richelieu apparently agreed with Leo X that the easiest way to keep the theater within bounds was to patronize the best rather than condemn all; thereby he might give a lead to public taste, and bread to decent companies. Note Voltaire's report: "Since Cardinal Richelieu introduced regular performances of plays at court, which have now made Paris the rival of Athens, not only was there a special bench for the Academy, which included several ecclesiastics among its members, but also one for the bishops."[1] In 1641, presumably at the Cardinal's request, Louis XIII took under his protection a group of actors thereafter known as the Troupe Royale or the Comédiens Royaux, gave them a pension of twelve hundred livres per year, issued an edict acknowledging the theater to be a legitimate form of entertainment, and expressed the royal wish that the calling of an actor should no longer be held prejudicial to his social standing.[2] This troupe established its theater at the Hôtel de Bourgogne, received the official patronage of Louis XIV, and continued throughout his reign to excel in the production of tragedies.

To raise the standards of French comedy, Mazarin invited Italian players to Paris. One of these was Tiberio Fiorelli, whose performance of the boasting buffoon Scaramuccia made him a favorite with Paris and the court. He and his fellows probably shared in giving the theatrical fever to Jean Coquelin IV, and in teaching him the arts of the comic theater.[3] When "Scaramouche" returned to Italy (1659) Jean Coquelin, known to the stage and the world as Molière, became the chief comedian to the King, and soon, in the fond judgment of Boileau, the greatest writer of the reign.

II. APPRENTICESHIP

A building at 96 Rue St.-Honoré in Paris bears an inscription in letters of gold:

> *Cette maison a été construite sur l'emplacement*
> *de celle où est né*
> MOLIÈRE
> *le 15 janvier 1622*

——"This house was built on the site of that where Molière was born January 15, 1622." It was the home of Jean Baptiste Coquelin III, upholsterer and decorator. His wife Marie Cressé had brought him a dowry of 2,200 livres. She gave him six children, and then died, after ten years of marriage. Jean Baptiste Coquelin IV, her first child, remembered her only vaguely, and never mentioned her in his plays. The father married again (1633), but, as this stepmother died in 1637, it was the father who bore the brunt of his son's genius, directed his education, and thought to mold his career. In 1631 Jean Coquelin III became *valet tapissier de chambre du roi* —superintendent of the royal upholstery, with the privilege of making the

royal bed and of living in the King's household, at an annual salary of
three hundred livres; a modest sum, but only three months of attendance
were required in any year. The father had bought the office from his
brother, and planned to transmit it to his son. In 1637 Louis XIII recognized
Jean Coquelin IV as rightful heir to the position; and if the father's aspirations had been realized Molière might have been known to history—if at
all—as the man who made the King's bed. However, a grandfather had a
liking for the theater, and took the boy with him now and then to the
performances.

To fit him for making the King's bed, Jean IV was sent to the Jesuit
Collège de Clermont, the alma mater of heretics. He learned considerable
Latin, read Terence profitably, and doubtless took interest, perhaps part,
in the dramas staged by the Jesuits as a device for educating their students
in Latin, literature, and speech. According to Voltaire, Jean also received
instruction from the philosopher Gassendi, who had been engaged as tutor
for a rich classmate; in any case Jean learned much about Epicurus, and
translated a considerable portion of Lucretius' Epicurean epic, *De rerum
natura*. (Some lines in *Le Misanthrope*[4] are almost a translation of a
passage in Lucretius.[5]) It is probable that Jean, before ending his youth,
had lost his faith.[6]

After five years at college Jean studied law; he appears to have practiced
briefly in the courts. For some months he followed his father's profession
(1642). In that year he met Madeleine Béjart, then a gay lady of twenty-
four. Five years earlier she had been the mistress of the Comte de Modène;
he graciously acknowledged the child she bore him, and let his son act as
godfather at the christening. Jean, now twenty, was attracted by her
beauty, her cheerful and kindly disposition. In all probability she accepted
him as a lover. Her passion for the theater joined with other factors in
deciding him to turn his back upon upholstery, to sign away, for 630
livres, his right to succeed his father as a *valet tapissier* to the King, and
to plunge into the profession of an actor (1643). He left his father, and
went to live in the home of Madeleine Béjart.[7] With her, her two brothers,
and some others, he entered into a formal contract establishing the Illustre
Théâtre (June 30, 1643). The Comédie-Française regards that contract
as the beginning of its long and distinguished career. As was the custom
with actors, Jean now took a stage name, and became Molière.

The new company hired a tennis court for its theater, presented a variety
of plays, and went bankrupt; in the year 1645 Molière was thrice arrested
for debt. His father, hoping that the youth had been cured of stage fever,
paid his debts and secured his release. But Molière reorganized the Illustre
Théâtre, and went off on a tour of the provinces. The Duc d'Épernon,
governor of Guienne, gave the company his support. In a wearing series

of successes and failures, the troupe passed from Narbonne to Toulouse, Albi, Carcassonne, Nantes, Agen, Grenoble, Lyons, Montpellier, Bordeaux, Béziers, Dijon, Avignon, Rouen. Molière rose to be manager (1650), and by a hundred expedients kept the company solvent and fed. In 1653 the Prince de Conti, his old schoolfellow, lent his name and support to the players, probably because his secretary admired the actress Mlle. du Parc. But in 1655 the Prince had a religious stroke, and informed the company that his conscience forbade his connection with the theater. Later he publicly denounced the stage, and Molière in particular, as a corrupter of youth, an enemy to morality and Christianity.

Gradually, amid these vicissitudes, the troupe improved its competence, income, and repertoire. Molière learned the art and tricks of the theater. By 1655 he was writing as well as acting plays. By 1658 he felt strong enough to challenge the pre-emption of the Paris stage by the King's players at the Hôtel de Bourgogne, and a private troupe that was operating the Théâtre du Marais. From Rouen he and Madeleine Béjart came to Paris to prepare the ground. He visited his father, and won forgiveness for his sins and his career. He persuaded Philippe I Duc d'Orléans, to take the company under his protection, and to secure for it a hearing at the court.

On October 24, 1658, this "Troupe de Monsieur" presented before the King, in the guardroom of the Louvre, Corneille's tragedy *Nicomède*. Molière played the main part, not very successfully, for he suffered, Voltaire tells us, "from a kind of hiccup which was quite unsuited to serious roles," but which "served only to make his acting in comedy the more enjoyable."[8] He saved the day by following the tragedy with a comedy now lost; he acted it with a verve and gaiety, a rising eyebrow and babbling mouth, that made the audience wonder why he had ever played tragedy at all. The King was young enough to enjoy the fun, and man enough to appreciate Molière's courage. He issued instructions that the Troupe de Monsieur should share the Salle du Petit Bourbon with the Italian company of Scaramouche. There too the newcomers failed when they attempted tragedies, in which they fell short of the royal players at the Hôtel de Bourgogne, and they succeeded in comedies, above all in those that Molière composed. They continued nevertheless to produce tragedies. The leading ladies felt that they shone better in serious drama, and Molière himself was never content to be a comedian. The struggles and absurdities of life had developed in him a vein of melancholy, and he found it tragical to be always comical. Moreover, he had tired of the comedies of amorous intrigue, of the old stock characters and whipping boys, mostly echoes of Italy. Looking about him in Paris, he saw things that seemed to him quite as laughable as Polichinelle and Scaramouche.

"No longer need I take Plautus and Terence for my masters, or despoil Menander," he was quoted as saying; "I have only to study the world."[9]

III. MOLIÈRE AND THE LADIES

There was, for example, the Hôtel de Rambouillet, where men and women were making a fetish of delicate manners and perfumed speech. Molière wrote *Les Précieuses ridicules;* its production (November 18, 1659) began the French comedy of manners and Molière's fortune and fame. *The Laughable Exquisites* was brief enough to be absorbed in an hour, and sharp enough to leave a lasting sting. Two cousins, Magdalon and Cathos, enveloped in seven veils of refinement, protest against their matter-of-fact short-of-francs elders' anxiety to have them marry.

> GORGIBUS. What see you in them to find fault with?
> MAGDALON. Fine gallantry of theirs, indeed! What, to begin immediately with matrimony! . . . Were the whole world like you, romance would be ended at once. . . . Matrimony should never be brought about till after other adventures. A lover, to be agreeable, must understand how to utter fine sentiments, to sigh forth the soft, the tender, the passionate, and his address must be according to the rules. In the first place he should behold, either at church or in the park, or at some public ceremony, the person of whom he becomes enamored, or else he should be fatally introduced to her by a relation or friend, and go from her melancholy and pensive. He conceals his passion for some time from the beloved object, but pays her several visits, at which some discourse about gallantry never fails to be brought upon the carpet to exercise the wits of all the company. . . . The day comes for him to declare himself, which usually should be done in the walk of some garden, while the company is at a distance. This declaration is met by immediate resentment, which appears by our coloring, and which, for a while, banishes the lover from our presence. He finds afterwards the way to pacify us, to accustom us insensibly to hear his passion, and to draw from us that confession which causes so much trouble. Then follow the adventures: the rivals that thwart an established inclination, the persecutions of fathers, the jealousies arising from false appearances, the complainings, the despair, the running off with, and its consequences. Thus are things carried on in a handsome manner, and these are the rules that cannot be dispensed with in a genteel piece of gallantry. But to come point blank to the conjugal union!—to make no love but by the marriage contract, and to take a romance by the tail—

> once more, dear father, nothing can be more mechanic than such a proceeding, and I'm sick at heart with merely the idea that it gives me. . . .
>
> CATHOS. For myself, uncle, all I can say is that I think matrimony a mighty shocking thing. How can one endure the thought of lying by a man that's really naked?[10]

Two valets borrow their masters' raiment, disguise themselves as a marquis and a general, and court the two ladies with all the paraphernalia of gallantry and persiflage. Their masters break in upon them, tear off their plumage, and leave the young women faced with the almost naked truth. As in most of Molière's comedies of sex, there are some rough passages, and some horseplay, but so keen a satire of social follies that the effect became an event in the history of manners. An uncertain tradition credits a woman in the audience with rising amid the audience and crying out, "Courage! Courage! Molière, this is good comedy."[11] One habitué of Mme. de Rambouillet's salon, emerging from the performance, was reported to have said, "Yesterday we admired all the absurdities which have been so delicately and sensibly criticized; but, in the words of St. Remy to Clovis, we must now burn what we have adored, and adore what we have burned."[12] The Marquise de Rambouillet met the attack with genius by arranging with Molière to give a special performance of the play for the benefit of her salon; he repaid her courtesy with a preface in which he claimed to have satirized not her circle but its imitators. In any case the reign of the *précieuses* ended. Boileau, in his tenth satire, referred to "those *beaux esprits*, yesterday so renowned, whom Molière has deflated with one blow of his art."

The play succeeded so well that the price of admission was doubled after the première. In its first year it was performed forty-four times. The King commanded three performances for the court, attended all three, and gave the company three thousand livres. By February of 1660 the grateful company had paid the author 999 livres in royalties. But he had made a mistake by inserting into the play a satirical reference to

> the actors of the Théâtre Royal [Troupe Royale]: none but they are capable of gaining things a reputation; the rest are ignorant creatures who speak their parts just as one talks; these don't understand how to make the verses roar, or to pause at a beautiful passage. How can it be known where the fine lines are if the actor does not stop at them, and apprize you thereby to applaud?[13]

The troupe at the Hôtel de Bourgogne expressed open contempt of Molière as unable to produce tragedy, and as capable only of coarse comedy. Molière strengthened their case by writing and presenting a middling farce, *Le Cocu imaginaire*—*The Imaginary Cuckold*—though the King was pleased to see this nine times.

Meanwhile the old Louvre was undergoing alterations; the Salle du Petit Bourbon was incontinently demolished, and for a time it seemed that Molière's Troupe de Monsieur would be stageless. The King, always friendly, came to his rescue by assigning to him, in the Palais-Royal, the *salle* in which Richelieu had had plays performed. There, as an almost physical part of the court, Molière's company remained till his death. His first production in this new home was his last attempt at tragedy, *Don Garcie*. He thought, with some reason, that the pompous rhetorical style of tragedy as developed by Corneille and played at the Hôtel de Bourgogne was unnatural; he aspired to a simpler and more natural style. Had the classical dominance (and his hiccup) allowed him he might have produced successful combinations of tragedy with comedy, as in Shakespeare; and, indeed, his greatest comedies have a touch of tragedy. But *Don Garcie* failed, despite the efforts of the King to buttress it by attending three performances. Molière was designed to suffer tragedy, not to play it.

So he returned to comedy. *L'École des maris*—*The School for Husbands*—had a solacing success, playing daily from June 24 to September 11, 1661. It foreshadowed the marriage of Molière, then thirty-nine, with Armande Béjart, then eighteen; its problem was, How should a young woman be trained to be a good and faithful wife? The brothers Ariste and Sganarelle are fortunate in being the guardians of the girls they plan to marry. Ariste, who is sixty, treats his eighteen-year-old ward, Léonor, quite leniently:

> I've not made crimes of little liberties. I've continually complied with her youthful desires; and, thank Heaven, I don't repent it. I've given her leave to see good company, diversions, plays, and balls; these are things which, for my part, I always judge very proper to form the minds of young people; and the world is a school which, in my opinion, teaches the way of living better than any book. She likes to spend money on clothes, linen, and new fashions. . . . I try to gratify her wishes; these are pleasures we should allow young women when our circumstances can afford it.[14]

Sganarelle, the younger brother, derides Ariste as a fool seduced by the latest fancies. He laments the passing of the old morality, the looseness of the new, the insolence of liberated youth. He proposes a stern discipline to train his ward Isabelle to be an obedient wife:

> She shall be dressed in becoming clothes . . . Staying at home like a discreet person, she shall apply herself entirely to affairs of house-

wifery, darning linen in her leisure hours, or knitting stockings for her diversion. She . . . shall not stir abroad without someone to watch her. . . . I will not wear horns if I can help it.

After an incredible intrigue (imitated from a Spanish comedy) Isabelle runs away with an ingenious lover, while Léonor marries Ariste and remains faithful to him to the end of the play.

Molière was evidently debating with himself. On February 20, 1662, now forty, he married a woman less than half his age. Moreover, Armande Béjart was the daughter of Madeleine Béjart, with whom Molière had cohabited twenty years before. His enemies accused him of marrying his own illegitimate daughter. Montfleury, leader of the rival troupe at the Hôtel de Bourgogne, wrote to Louis XIV to this effect in 1663; Louis replied by standing godfather to Molière's first child by Armande. Madeleine, when Molière met her, had been too lavish of her person to give us any certainty of Armande's parentage. Molière apparently did not think himself her father; and we may allow that he was slightly better informed on the point than we can be.

Armande had grown up as the spoiled pet of the troupe; Molière had seen her almost every day; he had loved her as a child long before he had known her as a woman. She was by this time an accomplished actress. With such a background she was not made for monogamy, least of all with a man who had outworn the spirit of youth. She loved the pleasures of life, and indulged in flirtations that were widely interpreted as infidelities. Molière suffered, his friends and foes gossiped. Ten months after his marriage he tried to salve his wounds by criticizing male jealousy and defending female emancipation. He tried to be Ariste, but Armande could not be Léonor. Perhaps he failed to be Ariste, for he was as impatient as any theatrical producer. In the *Impromptu of Versailles* (October, 1663) he described himself as saying to his wife, "Hold your peace, wife; you are an ass"; whereto she replies, "Thank you, good husband. See how it is: matrimony alters people strangely; you would not have said this a year and a half ago."[15]

He continued his meditations on jealousy and liberty in *L'École des femmes*, which had its première on December 26, 1662. Almost the opening lines struck the theme of cuckoldry. Arnolphe, played by Molière, is again the old-fashioned tyrant who believes that a woman loosed is a loose woman, and that the only means of guaranteeing a wife's fidelity is to train her to modest servitude, keep her under strict watch, and skimp her education. Agnès, his ward and prospective bride, grows up in such delectable innocence that she asks Arnolphe, in a line that echoed through France, *"si les enfants . . . se faisoient par l'oreille"*—if children are begotten through the ear.[16] As Arnolphe has told her nothing about love, she accepts with guileless pleasure the attentions of Horace, who finds his way to her during her guardian's brief absence. When Arnolphe returns she gives him an objective account of Horace's procedure:

ARNOLPHE. Well, but what did he do when he was alone with you?

AGNÈS. He said he loved me with an unequalled passion, and told me, in the finest language in the world, things that nothing ever can come up to; the agreeableness whereof delighted me every time I heard him speak, and raised within me a certain, I know not what, emotion which entirely charmed me.

ARNOLPHE (aside). O tormenting inquiry into a fatal secret, where the inquirer only suffers all the pain! (Aloud.) Besides all this talk, all these pretty ways, didn't he bestow some kisses on you, too?

AGNÈS. Oh, to that degree! He took my hands and arms, and was never weary of kissing 'em.

ARNOLPHE. Did he take nothing else from you, Agnès? (Seeing her at a loss.) Hah?

AGNÈS. Why, he did—

ARNOLPHE. What?

AGNÈS. Take—

ARNOLPHE. How?

AGNÈS. The—

ARNOLPHE. What d'ye mean?

AGNÈS. I durst not tell you; for, maybe, you'll be angry wi' me.

ARNOLPHE. No.

AGNÈS. Yes, but you will.

ARNOLPHE. Lack-a-day, I won't.

AGNÈS. Swear faith, then.

ARNOLPHE. Well, faith.

AGNÈS. He took—You'll be in a passion.

ARNOLPHE. No.

AGNÈS. Yes.

ARNOLPHE. No, no, no, no. What the deuce is this mystery? What did he take from you.

AGNÈS. He—

ARNOLPHE (aside). I suffer damnation.

AGNÈS. He took away the ribbon you gave me; to tell you the truth, I could not help it.

ARNOLPHE (recovering himself). No matter for the ribbon. But I want to know whether he did nothing but kiss your hands.

AGNÈS. Why! do people do other things?

ARNOLPHE. No, no. . . . But in short I must tell you, that to accept caskets and hearken to the idle stories of these powdered fops, to permit 'em, in a languishing way, to kiss your hands and charm your heart in this manner, is a mortal sin, the greatest that can be committed.

AGNÈS. A sin, d'ye say! The reason, pray?

ARNOLPHE. The reason? Why, the reason is, because it's declared that Heaven is offended at such doings.

AGNÈS. Offended! But wherefore should it be offended? Lack-a-day! 'tis so sweet, so pleasant! I admire at the delight one finds in't, and didn't know these things before.

ARNOLPHE. Ay, there's a great deal of pleasure in all these tendernesses, these complaisant discourses, these fond embraces; but they should be tasted in an honest manner, and the sin should be taken away by marrying.

AGNÈS. Is it no more a sin when a body's married?

ARNOLPHE. No.

AGNÈS. Then marry me out of hand, I pray.[17]

Of course Agnès soon runs off to Horace. Arnolphe recaptures her, and is about to beat her when her sweet voice and form unnerve him; and perhaps when Molière wrote Arnolphe's lines he was thinking of Armande:

That speech and that look disarm my fury, and produce a return of tenderness which effaces all her guilt. How strange it is to be in love! and that men should be subject to such weakness for these traitresses! Everybody knows their imperfection; they're nothing but extravagance and indiscretion; their mind is wicked and their understanding weak; nothing is more frail, nothing more unsteady, nothing more false, and yet, for all that, one does everything in the world for the sake of these animals.[18]

In the end she eludes him and marries Horace; and Arnolphe's friend Chrysalde consoles him with the thought that abstention from marriage is the only sure way of avoiding the growth of horns.

The play delighted the audience; it was performed thirty-one times in its first ten weeks, and the King was young enough to enjoy its laxity. But the more conservative elements at the court condemned the comedy as immoral; procreation through the ear proved unpopular with the ladies; the Prince de Conti denounced, as the most scandalous thing ever staged, the second-act scene between Arnolphe and Agnès quoted above; Bossuet anathematized the entire play; some magistrates called for its suppression as a threat to morality and religion. The rival troupe laughed at the vulgarities of the dialogue, the contradictions in characterization, and the hasty incredibilities of the plot. For a time the play "made the conversation of every house in Paris."[19]

Molière was too much of a fighter to let these criticisms go unnoticed.

In a one-act piece presented at the Palais-Royal June 1, 1663, *La Critique de l'École des femmes*, he pictured a gathering of his critics, allowed them to voice their objections forcefully, and made hardly any answer except to let the critique weaken itself through exaggeration, and be voiced by ridiculous characters. The Hôtel de Bourgogne kept up this *guerre comique* by producing a skit called *The Countercritic;* and Molière satirized the royal troupe in *L'Impromptu de Versailles* (October 18, 1663). The King stood loyally by Molière, invited him to dinner,[20] and now gave him an annual pension of a thousand livres, not as *comédien*, but as *excellent poète*.[21] Time also gave the victory to Molière, and today, *L'École des femmes* is rated as the first great comedy of the French theater.

IV. *L'AFFAIRE TARTUFFE*

Molière paid a price for the King's favor. Louis so liked his wit and courage that he made him a leading organizer of the entertainments at Versailles and St.-Germain. One such fete, *Les Plaisirs de l'île enchantée*, filled a week (May 7–13, 1664) with jousts, feasting, music, ballet, dancing, and drama, all presented in the park and palace of Versailles under illumination by torches and chandeliers holding four thousand candles. Molière received six thousand livres for his labors on this festival. Some scholars have mourned that the King used so much of Molière's genius to provide lighthearted entertainment at the court, and they have imagined the masterpieces that might have matured if the poet in the comedian had had more time to think and write. But he was under pressure from his company too, and in any case his cares and responsibilities as manager and actor would have kept him from any ivory tower. Many an author writes better under pressure than at leisure; leisure relaxes the mind, urgency stimulates it. Molière's greatest play was first produced on May 12, 1664, during the height, and as part, of the *Plaisirs de l'île enchantée*.

Tartuffe, in this première, hardly fitted the festival, for it was a merciless exposure of hypocrisy taking a pious and moralistic dress. A religious fraternity of laymen, the Compagnie du Saint Sacrement, later known as the Cabale des Dévots, had already pledged its members to work for the suppression of the play. The King, whose liaison with La Vallière had aroused much criticism from the devout, was in a mood to agree with Molière; but, having seen the comedy in its private performance at Versailles, he withheld permission to present it to the public of Paris in the Palais-Royal. He solaced Molière by inviting him to read *Tartuffe* at Fontainebleau to a select group including a papal legate, who raised no objection known to history (July 21, 1664). In that month the drama was performed in the home of the Duke and Duchess (Henrietta Anne) of Orléans, in the presence of the Queen, the Queen Mother, and the King. The way was being prepared for a public presentation when, in August, Pierre Roullé, vicar of St.-Barthélemy, published a tribute to the King for prohibiting the play, and took occasion to denounce Molière as "a man, or rather a demon in flesh and habited as a man, the most notably impious creature and libertine who ever lived." For writing *Tartuffe*, "to the derision of the whole Church," said Père Roullé, Molière "should be burned at the stake as a foretaste of the fires of hell."[22] The King rebuked Roullé, but continued to withhold permission for a public performance of *Tartuffe*. To show where he stood the King raised Molière's annual pension to six thousand livres, and took over from "Monsieur" the protection of Molière's company; henceforth it was the Troupe du Roi.

The controversy simmered for two years. Then Molière read to Louis a revised version of the play, with some added lines pointing out that the satire was not of honest faith but only of hypocrisy. Madame Henrietta supported the author's plea for permission to produce. Louis gave a verbal consent; and while he went off to war in Flanders the first public presentation of *Tartuffe* was staged at the Palais-Royal on August 5, 1667, three years after its court première. The next morning the president of the Parlement of Paris, who belonged to the Company of the Blessed Sacrament, ordered the theater closed, and all its posters torn down. On August 11 the Archbishop of Paris forbade, on pain of excommunication, the reading, hearing, or performance of the comedy, in public or in private. Molière announced that if this triumph of "*les Tartuffes*" continued he would retire from the stage. The King, returning to Paris, bade the angry dramatist be patient. Molière managed it, and was rewarded at last by the removal of the royal prohibition. On February 5, 1669, the play began a successful run of twenty-eight consecutive performances. At the public première the crowd seeking admission was so large and eager that many persons came near to suffocation. It was the *drame célèbre* of Molière's career. Of all French classic dramas it has received the greatest number of performances —2,657 (to 1960) at the Comédie-Française alone.

How far do the contents of the play explain its long postponement, and its continuing popularity? They explain the first by their frontal attack upon hypocritical piety; they explain the second by the power and brilliance of their satire. Everything in that satire is, of course, exaggerated: hypocrisy is rarely so reckless and complete as in Tartuffe, stupidity is seldom so extravagant as in Orgon, and no maid is so successfully insolent as Dorine. The denouement is incredible, as almost always in Molière; this did not trouble him; after he had presented his picture and indictment of hypocrisy, any *deus* or *rex ex machina* would do to untangle the plot into triumphant virtue and punished vice. Quite likely the satire was aimed at the Compagnie du Saint Sacrement, whose members, even if laymen, undertook to direct consciences, to report private sins to public authorities, and to interfere in families to promote religious loyalty and devotion. The play twice referred to a *cabale* (lines 397 and 1705), evidently alluding to the Cabale des Dévots. Soon after the play's public première the Company of the Blessed Sacrament was dissolved.

Orgon, the rich bourgeois, first sees Tartuffe in church, and is impressed.

> Ah, had you but seen him . . . you would have loved him as well as I do. He came every day to church, with a composed mien, and knelt just near me. He attracted the eyes of the whole congregation by the fervency with which he sent up his prayers to Heaven. He sighed and groaned very heavily, and at every moment he humbly kissed the earth. And when I was going out he would advance before me to offer me holy water at the door. Understanding . . . his lowly condition, . . . I made him presents, but he always modestly would offer to return me part. . . . At length Heaven moved me to take him home, since which everything seems to prosper. I see he reproves without distinction, and that even with regard to my wife he is extremely cautious of my honor. He acquaints me who ogles her.[23]

But Tartuffe does not similarly impress Orgon's wife and children. His hearty appetite, his love for tidbits, his round paunch and rubicund face, dull for them the point of his homilies. Orgon's brother-in-law, Cléante, begs him to see the difference between hypocrisy and religion:

> As I see no character in life greater or more valuable than to be truly devout, nor anything nobler or fairer than the fervor of a sincere piety, so I think nothing more abominable than the outside daubing of a pretended zeal, than those mountebanks, those devotees in show . . . who make a trade of godliness, and who would purchase honors and reputation with a hypocritical turning up of the eyes and affected transports.

Orgon, however, continues to take Tartuffe at phrase value, submits to his guidance, invokes God's aid upon him when he belches, and proposes to give him in marriage his daughter Mariane, who violently prefers Valère. The real heroine of the piece is Mariane's maid Dorine, who, as in classic comedy, seems to prove that Providence has distributed genius in inverse ratio to money. Delightful is her reception of Tartuffe's first entry upon the stage:

> TARTUFFE [seeing Dorine, speaks aloud to his servants]. Laurence, lock up my hair-cloth and scourge, and beg of Heaven ever to en-

lighten you with grace. If anybody comes to see me, I am gone to the prisons to distribute my alms.

DORINE (aside). What affectation and roguery!

TARTUFFE. What do you want?

DORINE. To tell you—

TARTUFFE (drawing a handkerchief out of his pocket). Oh! lack-a-day! pray take me this handkerchief before you speak.

DORINE. What for?

TARTUFFE. Cover that bosom, which I can't bear to see. Such objects hurt the soul, and usher in sinful thoughts.

DORINE. You mightily melt, then, at a temptation, and the flesh makes a great impression upon your senses? Truly, I can't tell what heat may inflame you; but, for my part, I am not so apt to hanker. Now, I could see you stark naked from head to foot, and that whole hide of yours not tempt me at all.[24]

The next scene is the core of the comedy. Tartuffe tries to make love to Orgon's wife, Elmire, and uses pious language in his plea. His treachery is reported to Orgon, who refuses to believe it; and to show his trust in Tartuffe he gives over to him all his property. Tartuffe resigns himself to accept it, saying, "Heaven's will be done in all things."[25] The situation is dissolved by Elmire, who, having hidden her husband under a table, sends for Tartuffe, gives him a little encouragement, and soon lures him into attempts at amorous exploration. She pretends compliance, but professes scruples of conscience, which Tartuffe handles with expert casuistry; evidently Molière had read and relished Pascal's *Provincial Letters*.

> TARTUFFE. If nothing but Heaven obstructs my wishes, 'tis a trifle with me to remove such an obstacle. Heaven, 'tis true, forbids certain gratifications. But there are ways of compounding those matters. It is a science to stretch the strings of conscience according to the different exigencies of the case, and to rectify the immorality of the action by the purity of our intention.[26]

Orgon comes out from his hiding, and angrily bids Tartuffe leave the house, but Tartuffe explains to him that the house, by Orgon's recently signed deed, belongs to Tartuffe. Molière, not very ingeniously, cuts this knot by having the King's agents opportunely discover that Tartuffe is a long-sought-for criminal. Orgon recovers his property, Valère gets Mariane, and the play concludes with a melodious paean to the justice and benevolence of the King.

V. THE AMOROUS ATHEIST

The royal benevolence must have been strained by the next audacity of Molière. At the height of the war over *Tartuffe,* and while the Dévots were still in triumph over the suppressing of the play, he staged at the Palais-Royal (February 15, 1665) *Le Festin de pierre—The Feast of the Stone Statue*—telling in rollicking prose the already oft-told tale of Don Juan, and turning that reckless Casanova into an arrogant atheist. Taking the shell of the story from Tirso de Molina and others, Molière filled it with a remarkable study of a man who enjoys wickedness for its own sake and as a challenge to God. The play is an astonishing echo of the great debate that was embroiling religion with philosophy.

Don Juan Tenorio is a marquis, and acknowledges obligations to his caste; otherwise he proposes to enjoy any pleasure he has an itch for. His valet, Sganarelle, calculates at 1,003 the number of women whom his master has seduced and deserted. "Constancy," says Juan, "is only fit for fools. . . . I can't refuse my heart to any lovely creature I see."[27] Such an ethic craves a corresponding theology, so Juan, for his own comfort, is an atheist. His servant tries to reason with him:

SGANARELLE. Is it possible that you don't believe in Heaven?
JUAN. Forget it.
SGAN. That is, you don't. And Hell?
JUAN. Eh!
SGAN. Likewise. And the Devil, if you please?
JUAN. Yes, yes.
SGAN. Again very little. Don't you believe at all in another life?
JUAN. Ha, ha, ha.
SGAN. Here's a man I'll be hard put to convert. But tell me, surely you
        believe in *le moine bourru?* *
JUAN. Plague on the fool.
SGAN. Now, that I can't suffer; for there's nothing better established
        than this *moine bourru,* and I'll be hanged if he isn't real. But a
        man must believe something. What *do* you believe? . . .
JUAN. I believe that two and two are four, and that four and four are
        eight.
SGAN. A lovely creed, and beautiful articles of faith! Your religion,
        then, so far as I can see, is arithmetic? As for me, sir, . . . I under-
        stand full well that this world is not a mushroom that grew in a
        single night. I would like to ask you who made these trees, these

---

* Literally, "the surly monk"—a pretended ghost used by nurses and mothers to frighten children.

rocks, this earth, and that sky up there; was all this built by itself? Look at yourself, for example; here you are; did you make yourself, or wasn't it necessary that your father should enlarge your mother to make you? Can you behold all the inventions of which the human machine is composed, without admiring how one part sets another working? ... Whatever you may say, there is something marvelous in man, which all the pundits will never explain. Isn't it wonderful to see me here, and that I have in my head something that thinks a hundred different things in a moment, and makes my body do what I wish? I want to clap my hands, raise my arm, lift my eyes to the sky, lower my head, move my feet, go to the right, to the left, forward, to the rear, turn. (He falls while turning.)

JUAN. Good! Your argument has a broken nose.[28]

In the next scene the tilt between Juan and religion takes another form. He meets a beggar, who tells him that he prays every day for those who give him alms. "Surely," says Juan, "a man who prays every day must be very well off." On the contrary, answers the beggar, "most often I have not even a piece of bread." Juan offers him a louis d'or if he will swear an oath; the beggar refuses—"I'd rather die of hunger." Juan is a bit startled by this fortitude. He hands over the coin, as he says, "for love of humanity."[29] All the opera-going world knows the denouement. Juan comes upon a statue of the Commander, whose daughter he had seduced, and whose life he had taken. The statue invites Juan to dinner; Juan comes, gives him his hand, and is led into hell. The infernal apparatus of the medieval stage appears; "thunder and lightning fall with great noise upon Don Juan; the earth opens and swallows him; a vast fire rises from the spot where he has fallen."

The first night's audience was shocked by Molière's exposition of Juan's unbelief. It may have allowed that he had exposed Juan's worthless character as well as his lack of theology, that the Don had been revealed as a brute without conscience or tenderness, spreading deception and grief wherever he went; and it may have observed that the villain's victims were presented with all the author's sympathy. But it noted that the answer to atheism had been put into the mouth of a fool who believed in bogeys more firmly than in God, and it was not mollified by Juan's final damnation, for it saw him descending into hell without a word of repentance or fear. After the première Molière toned down the most offensive passages, but public opinion was not appeased. On April 18, 1665, the Sieur de Rochemont, *avocat en Parlement*, published *Observations sur une comédie de Molière*, in which he described *Le Festin de pierre* as "truly devilish . . . Nothing more impious has ever appeared, even in pagan times"; and the King was exhorted to suppress the play:

> While this noble prince devotes all his care to maintaining religion, Molière is working to destroy it. . . . There is no man so little enlightened in the doctrine of the faith who, having seen this play . . . , can affirm that Molière, so long as he persists in presenting it, is worthy to participate in the sacraments, or to be received into penitence without a public reparation.[30]

Louis continued his favor to Molière. *Le Festin de pierre* ran three days a week from February 15 to Palm Sunday, when it was withdrawn. It did not return to the boards till four years after the dramatist's death, and then only in a verse adaptation by Thomas Corneille, who omitted the scandalous scene quoted above. The original version disappeared; it was rediscovered in 1813 in a pirated edition that had been published in Amsterdam in 1683. Till 1841 the Corneille version alone held the stage; and in some editions of Molière's works[31] it still replaces the original.

VI. MERIDIAN

Not content with the enemies that he had made, Molière proceeded to attack the medical profession. He had pictured Don Juan as being "impious in medicine" and rating medicine "one of the greatest errors of mankind."[32] He had discovered in person the deficiencies and pretenses of seventeenth-century physicians. He thought that doctors had killed his son by prescribing antimony, and he saw that they were helpless against his own advancing tuberculosis.[33] The King too was rebelling against weekly purges and bleedings; according to Molière it was Louis who prompted him to put the doctors on the grill. So, borrowing from old comedies on this ancient theme, he wrote in five days *L'Amour médecin*. It was produced at Versailles on September 15, 1665, before the King, who "was heartily amused"; and it met with an hilarious reception when it was staged a week later at the Palais-Royal. A woman is ill; four doctors are called in; they enter into private consultation, but discuss only their own affairs. When the father insists upon a decision and a remedy, one prescribes an enema, another swears that an enema will kill the patient. She gets better without medicine, which infuriates the doctors. "It is better to die according to the rules," cries Dr. Bahys, "than to recover contrary to them."[34]

On August 6, 1666, Molière presented another short piece, *Le Médecin malgré lui*, as a merry prelude to *Le Misanthrope*, designed to offset the gloom of that paean to pessimism. It does not repay reading today. Molière hardly intended these satires on medicine to be taken seriously. We note that he kept on excellent terms with his own physician, M. de Mauvilain, and that he interceded with the King to get a sinecure for the doctor's son (1669). He once explained how it was that he and Mauvilain got along so well: "We reason with one another; he prescribes remedies; I omit to take them, and I recover."[35]

Still amid the battle over *Tartuffe*, Molière presented, on June 4, 1666, another satire hardly calculated to please either the public or the court. If action is the soul of drama, *Le Misanthrope* is rather a philosophical dialogue than a play. One sentence can tell the story: Alceste, who demands a strict morality and complete honesty from himself and all, loves Célimène, who favors him but relishes a multiplicity of suitors and compliments. To Molière this is but a scaffolding for a study of morality. Should we always speak the truth, or should we substitute courtesy for truth in order to get along in the world? Alceste resents the compromises that society makes with the truth; he condemns the hypocrisy of the court, where everyone pretends to the loftiest sentiments and the "warmest regards," while at heart each one is scheming for himself, is critical of all the rest, and uses flattery as a lever to position or power. Alceste scorns all this, and proposes to be honest even to the point of suicide. Orontes, a scribbling courtier, insists on reading his verses to Alceste and asks for sincere criticism; he gets it, and vows revenge. Célimène flirts; Alceste reproves her; she calls him a prig; we almost hear Molière rebuking his gay wife, and indeed it was he who played Alceste, and she Célimène.

ALCESTE. Madame, will you have me be plain with you? I am very much dissatisfied with your ways of behavior. . . . I don't quarrel with you, but your disposition, madame, opens to the first comer too ready an access to your heart. You have too many lovers whom we see besieging you; and my soul cannot reconcile itself to this.
CÉLIMÈNE. Do you blame me for attracting lovers? Can I help it if people find me lovable? And when they make delectable efforts to see me should I take a stick and drive them out?
ALCESTE. No, it is not a stick that you must use, but a spirit less yielding and melting before their vows. I know that your beauty follows you everywhere, but your welcome holds further those whom your eyes attract; and your sweetness to all who surrender to you completes in their hearts the work of your charms.[36]

The philosophical foil to Alceste is his friend Philinte, who advises him to adjust himself amiably to the natural defects of mankind, and to recognize politeness as the lubrication of life. The zest of the play lies in Molière's division of his sentiments between Alceste and Philinte. Alceste is Molière the husband who fears that he is a cuckold, and the *valet tapissier du roi* who, to make the King's bed, has to run the gantlet of a hundred nobles as proud of their pedigree as he of his genius. Philinte is Molière the philosopher, bidding himself be reasonable and lenient in judging humanity. Says Philinte-Molière to Molière-Alceste, in a passage which we may take as a sample of Molière the poet:

> *Mon Dieu, des moeurs du temps mettons-nous moins en peine,*
> *Et faisons un peu grâce à la nature humaine;*
> *Ne l'examinons point dans la grande rigueur,*
> *Et voyons ses défauts avec quelque douceur.*
> *Il faut, parmi le monde, une vertu traitable;*
> *A force de sagesse on peut être blâmable;*
> *La parfaite raison fuit toute extrémité*
> *Et veut que l'on soit sage avec sobriété.*
> *Cette grande raideur des vertus des vieux âges*
> *Heurte trop notre siècle et les communs usages;*
> *Elle veut aux mortels trop de perfection:*
> *Il faut fléchir au temps sans obstination,*
> *Et c'est une folie à nulle autre seconde*
> *De vouloir se mêler de corriger le monde.*
> *J'observe, comme vous, cent choses tous les jours,*
> *Qui pourraient mieux aller, prenant un autre cours;*
> *Mais quoi qu'à chaque pas je puisse voir paraître,*
> *En courroux, comme vous, on ne me voit point être;*
> *Je prends tout doucement les hommes comme ils sont,*
> *J'accoutume mon âme à souffrir ce qu'ils font,*
> *Et je crois qu'à la cour, de même qu'à la ville,*
> *Mon flegme est philosophe autant que votre bile.*[*][37]

Napoleon thought that Philinte had the better of the argument; Jean Jacques Rousseau thought Philinte a liar, and approved Alceste's rigorous morality.[38] In the end Alceste, like Jean Jacques, renounces the world and retires to a sterilized solitude.

---

* "My God! Let us give ourselves less trouble about the manners of the age, and make some small allowances to human nature; let us not examine it with so great rigor, but look upon its defects with some indulgence. This world requires a tractable virtue; one may be blameworthy by stress of wisdom; right reason avoids every extremity, and would have us be wise with sobriety. That great stiffness in the virtues of ancient times too much shocks our age and common usage; it would have mortals too perfect; we must yield to the times without obstinacy, and 'tis an extremity of folly to busy ourselves in correcting the world. I observe, as you do, a thousand things every day, which might go better taking another course; but whatever I may discover in every transaction, people don't see me in a rage, like you. I take men with great calmness, just as they are; I accustom myself to bear with what they do; and I think that at court, as well as in the city, my phlegm is as much a philosopher as your bile."

The play had only a moderate success. The courtiers did not relish the satire of their fine manners, and the pit could hardly enthuse over an Alceste who frankly despised everybody but himself. The critics, however, being neither of the pit nor of the court, applauded the play as a brave attempt to write a drama of ideas; and later pundits judge it the most perfect of Molière's works. In the course of time, when its pilloried generation was dead, it won public acceptance; between 1680 and 1954 it had 1,571 performances at the Comédie-Française—only less than *Tartuffe* and *L'Avare*.

Unable to live in peace with a young wife to whom monogamy and beauty seemed a contradiction in terms, Molière left her (August, 1667), and went to live with his friend Chapelain at Auteuil, in the western end of Paris. Chapelain gently derided him for taking love so seriously; but Molière was more poet than philosopher, and (if we may believe one poet reporting another) confessed:

"I have determined to live with her as if she were not my wife; but if you knew what I suffer you would pity me. My passion has reached such a point that it even enters with compassion into all her interests. When I consider how impossible it is for me to conquer what I feel for her, I tell myself that she may have the same difficulty in conquering her inclination to be coquettish, and I find myself more disposed to pity her than to blame her. You will tell me, no doubt, that a man must be a poet to feel this; but for my part I feel that there is but one kind of love, and that those who have not felt these delicacies of sentiment have never truly loved. All things in the world are connected with her in my heart . . . When I see her, an emotion, transports that may be felt but not described, take from me all power of reflection; I have no longer any eyes for her defects; I can see only all that she has that is lovable. Is not that the last degree of madness?"[39]

He tried to forget her by losing himself in his work. In 1667 he busied himself arranging entertainment for the King at St.-Germain. His comedy *Amphitryon* (January 13, 1668) celebrated again the amours of Jupiter, who seduces Amphitryon's wife Alcmène. When Jupiter explains to her that

> *Un partage avec Jupiter*
> *N'a rien du tout qui déshonore*

—i.e., for a lady to share her bed with Jove is not at all dishonorable—the lines were interpreted by many auditors as condoning the royal liaison with Mme. de Montespan; if so, it was a very generous sycophancy, for

Molière was in no mood to sympathize with seducers. Like everybody else he buttered the King with flattery, as at the end of *Tartuffe*. In another comedy, produced before the court on July 15, *George Dandin, ou le Mari confondu*, we have again the story of the husband confounded, suspecting his wife of adultery, unable to prove it, and eating his heart out with suspicion and jealousy; Molière was pouring salt into his wounds.

It was a busy year, for only a few months later (September 9) he produced one of his most famous plays. *L'Avare* (*The Miser*) took its theme, and part of its plot, from Plautus' *Aulularia*; but Plautus had taken that from the New Comedy of the Greeks; the miser, and satire of him, are probably as old as money. No one has ever handled the subject with more vivacity and power than Molière. Harpagon so loves his hoard that he lets his horses starve and go without hoofs; he has such an aversion to giving that he does not "give you good day," but *prête le bonjour*—"lends you good day." Seeing two candles lit for dinner, he blows one out. He refuses a dowry to his daughter, and trusts that his children will predecease him.[40] The satire, as usual in Molière, verges on caricature. The audience found the picture distasteful, and after eight performances the play was withdrawn. But Boileau's praise helped to revive it; it was shown forty-seven times in its first four years, and is second only to *Tartuffe* in frequency of presentation.

Le Bourgeois Gentilhomme had less merit and more success. In December, 1669, a Turkish ambassador came to France. The court put on all its splendor to impress him; he responded with haughty stolidity; after his departure Louis invited Molière and Lully to compose a comedy-ballet in which the ambassador would be parodied in a *turquerie*. Molière enlarged the scheme into a satire on the increasing number of middle-class Frenchmen who were struggling to dress and speak like born aristocrats. The comedy had its première before King and court at Chambord, October 14, 1670. When presented at the Palais-Royal in November it atoned financially for the losses of *L'Avare*. Molière played M. Jourdain; Lully played the Mufti. To invest himself with nobility, M. Jourdain hires a music master, a dancing master, a fencing master, a philosophy master. They come to blows over the relative importance of their arts—whether it is more vital to achieve harmony, to be in step, to be able to kill neatly, or to speak elegant French. In the claims of the music master we suspect a sly dig at pompous, climbing Lully. Half the world knows the scene in which M. Jourdain learns that all language is either prose or verse.

M. JOURDAIN. What? When I say, "Nicole, bring me my slippers, and give me my night bonnet"—this is prose?
PHILOSOPHY MASTER. Yes, Monsieur.

M. JOURDAIN. By my faith! for over forty years I've been speaking
prose without knowing anything about it. I am for all the world
most obliged to you for informing me of this.[41]

Some courtiers, who had not long since graduated from commerce into
lace, felt that the satire was aimed at them, and they pooh-poohed the play
as nonsense; but the King assured Molière, "You have never written anything yet which has amused me so much." Hearing this, says Guizot, "the
court was at once seized with a fit of admiration."[42]

Molière and Lully collaborated again to produce before the court (January, 1671), a tragedy-ballet, *Psyché*, to which Pierre Corneille and Quinault contributed most of the verse. Lully was winning the battle against
Molière: comedy was giving way to opera, dialogue to machinery; gods
and goddesses had to be lowered from heaven or hoisted from hell. The
stage at the Palais-Royal had to be rebuilt for *Psyché*, at a cost of 1,98'
livres. But the production was a financial success.

Romance, however, was not Molière's forte; he was more at home when
roasting the absurdities of the age on the point of his wit. It seemed to him
that a learned woman was an uncomfortable anomaly and an impediment
to marriage. He had heard such women pruning vocabularies, debating
niceties of grammar, quoting the classics, and talking philosophy; this,
to Molière's ears, sounded like a sexual perversion. Moreover two men, the
Abbé Cotin and the poet Ménage, had been inveighing against Molière's
plays; here was a chance to prick them. So, on March 11, 1672, he offered
Les Femmes savantes. Philaminte discharges a maid for using a word condemned by the Academy; her daughter Armande rejects matrimony as a
disgusting contact of bodies rather than a fusion of minds; Trissotin reads
his awful poetry to these admiring prudes; Vadius riddles the poetry and
presents more of his own and the same. Against all these Molière defends
Henriette, who abominates alexandrines and wants a husband who can give
her children instead of epigrams. Had Armande Béjart become a *précieuse*?
Or was Molière showing his age?

VII. CURTAIN

He was only fifty, but his hectic life, his tuberculosis, his marriage, and
his bereavements had drained his vitality. The portrait by Mignard caught
him at his prime: large nose, sensual lips, and comically elevatable eyebrows, but already a wrinkled forehead and wistful eyes. Moving in the
vortex of the theater from town to town and from day to day, dealing with
high-strung prima donnas, a lively wife, and a sensitive King, seeing two of

his three children die—this was no primrose path to optimism, but an open road to bad digestion and early death. Understandably he became "a self-devouring volcano,"[48] melancholy, sharp-tempered, frankly critical but sympathetically generous. His troupe understood him and was devoted to him, knowing that he used himself up to give it sustenance and success. His friends were always ready to do battle for him—above all, Boileau and La Fontaine, who, sometimes with Racine, made with Molière *les Quatre Amis*, the famous "Four Friends." They found him well educated and informed, witty but seldom merry, a Grimaldi on the stage, but in private sadder than Shakespeare's Jaques.

After four and a half years of separation he returned to his wife (1671). The child that resulted from this reconciliation died after a month of life. At Auteuil he had lived on a milk diet prescribed by his doctor; now he resumed his usual consumption of wine, and attended late suppers to please Armande. Despite his increasing cough he decided to play the leading role, Argan, in his final play, *Le Malade imaginaire* (February 10, 1673).

Argan imagines himself afflicted with a dozen diseases, and spends half his fortune on doctors and drugs. His brother Béralde derides him:

> ARGAN. What must we do, then, when we are sick?
> BÉRALDE. Nothing, brother. . . . We must only keep ourselves quiet. Nature herself, when we let her alone, will gently deliver herself from the disorder she's fallen into. 'Tis our ingratitude, 'tis our impatience, that spoils all; and almost all men die of their medicines, not of their diseases.[44]

To further ridicule the profession, Argan is told that he himself can become a doctor in short order, and can easily pass the examination for a medical license. There follows the famous mock examination:

> FIRST DOCTOR. *Demandabo causam* and *rationem quare opium facit dormire.* . . .
> ARGAN.   *Quia est in eo*
>   *Virtus dormitiva.*
>   *Cujus est natura*
>   *Sensus stupifire.* . . .
> SECOND DOCTOR. *Quae sunt remedia*
>   *Quae in maladia*
>   Called *hydropsia*
>   *Convenit facere?*
> ARGAN.   *Clisterium donare,*
>   *Postea bleedare,*
>   Afterwards *purgare.*

CHORUS. *Bene, bene, bene respondere,*
Dignus, dignus est intrare
In nostro docto corpore.

Molière's death was almost a part of this play. On February 17, 1673, Armande and others, perceiving his fatigue, begged him to close the theater for a few days while he regained strength. But "How can I do that?" he asked. "There are fifty poor workmen here who are paid by the day; what will they do if we don't play? I should reproach myself for having neglected to give them their bread for a single day so long as I was able to act."[45] In the final act, as Molière, in the part of Argan (who had twice pretended death), uttered the word *Juro*, "I swear," in taking the oath as a physician, he was seized with a convulsive cough. He covered it with a false laugh, and finished the play. He was hurried to his home by his wife and the young actor Michel Baron. He asked for a priest, but none came. His cough became more violent; he burst a blood vessel, choked with the blood in his throat, and died.

Harlay de Champvallon, Archbishop of Paris, ruled that since Molière had not made his final penitence and received absolution, he could not be buried in Christian ground. Armande, who had always loved him even while deceiving him, went to Versailles, threw herself at the feet of the King, and said, not wisely but boldly and truly, "If my husband was a criminal, his crimes were sanctioned by your Majesty in person."[46] Louis sent some secret word to the Archbishop. Harlay compromised: the body must not be taken into a church for Christian rites, but it was allowed a quiet burial, after sunset, in a remote corner of the Cemetery of St.-Joseph in the Rue Montmartre.

Molière remains by common consent one of the greatest figures in the literature of France. Not by perfection of dramatic technique, nor by any splendor of poetry. Almost all his plots are borrowed, almost all their denouements are artificial and absurd; almost all his characters are personified qualities, several, like Harpagon, are exaggerated to the point of caricature; and too often his comedies fall into farce. We are told that the court, as well as the general public, liked him best when he was most farcical, and did not relish his mordant satires on failings widely shared. Probably he would have omitted the farce if he had not felt compelled to keep his company solvent.

Like Shakespeare mourning that he must make himself a motley to the view, he wrote: "I think it a very grievous punishment, in the liberal arts, to display oneself to fools, and to expose our compositions to the barbarous judgment of the stupid."[47] It irked him to be always required to make people laugh; this, he has one of his characters say, "is a queer enterprise."[48]

He aspired to write tragedies, and, though he fell short of his aim, he managed to give to his greatest comedies a tragic significance and depth.

So it is the philosophy in his plays, as well as their humor and pungent satire, that makes almost every literate Frenchman read Molière.[49] It was essentially a rationalistic philosophy, which gladdened the hearts of the eighteenth-century *philosophes*. "There is in Molière not a trace of supernatural Christianity," and "the religion expounded by his mouthpiece Cléante" in *Tartuffe* "might be endorsed by Voltaire."[50] He never attacked the Christian creed, he acknowledged the beneficence of religion in innumerable lives, he respected sincere devotion; but he scorned the surface piety that put a weekly face on daily selfishness.

His moral philosophy was pagan in the sense that it legitimized pleasure, and had no sense of sin. It savored of Epicurus and Seneca rather than of St. Paul or Augustine; harmonized better with the laxity of the King than with the austerities of Port-Royal. He deprecated excess even in virtue. He admired *l'honnête homme*, the sensible man of the world who threaded his way with sane moderation among competing absurdities, and adjusted himself without fuss to the shortcomings of mankind.

Molière himself did not reach that plane of moderation. His profession as a comic dramatist compelled him to satire, and often to hyperbole; he was too hard on learned women, too indiscriminate in attacking physicians; and he might have shown more respect for enemas. But overemphasis is in the blood of satire, and dramas seldom make their point without it. Molière would have been greater if he could have found a way to satirize the fundamental evil of the reign—the military greed and ruinous despotism of Louis XIV; but it was this gracious autocrat who protected him against his enemies and made possible his war against bigotry. How lucky he was to die before his master had become the most destructive bigot of them all!

France loves Molière, and still plays him, as England loves and plays Shakespeare. We cannot, as some fervent Gauls would do, equate him with England's bard; he was only a part of Shakespeare, whose other parts were Racine and Montaigne. Nor can we, as many do, place him at the head of French literature. We are not even sure that Boileau was right when he told Louis XIV that Molière was the greatest poet of the reign; when Boileau said this, Racine had not yet written *Phèdre* or *Athalie*. But in Molière it is not only the writer who belongs to the history of France, it is the man: the harassed and faithful manager, the deceived and forgiving husband, the dramatist covering his griefs with laughter, the ailing actor carrying on to the hour of death his war against pedantry, bigotry, superstition, and sham.

CHAPTER V

The Classic Zenith in French Literature

1643–1715

I. MILIEU

THE zenith in French classical literature was not coterminous with the age of Louis XIV; it came, rather, under the ministry of Mazarin and in the halcyon youth of the reign (1661–67), before Mars had sent the Muses to the rear. The initial stimulus to the literary outburst was given by Richelieu's encouragement of drama and poetry; the second spur came from the martial triumphs at Rocroi (1643) and Lens (1648); the third flowed from the diplomatic victories of France in the treaties of Westphalia (1648) and the Pyrenees (1659); the fourth, from the association of men of letters with men of breeding and women of culture in the salons; only the final impulse was the patronage of literature by the King and the court. Many of the literary masterpieces of the reign—Pascal's *Letters* (1656) and *Thoughts*, Molière's *Tartuffe* (1664), *Le Festin de pierre* (1665), and *Le Misanthrope* (1666), La Rochefoucauld's *Maxims* (1665), Boileau's *Satires* (1667), Racine's *Andromaque* (1667)—were written before 1667 by men who had grown up under Richelieu and Mazarin.

It remains nevertheless that Louis was the most lavish patron of literature in all history. Hardly two years after taking over the government (1662–63)—consequently before all but two of the works just mentioned—he asked Colbert and others to have competent persons draw up a list of authors, scholars, and scientists, of whatever land, who merited aid. From these lists forty-five Frenchmen and fifteen foreigners received royal pensions.[1] The Dutch scholars Heinsius and Vossius, the Dutch physicist Christian Huygens, the Florentine mathematician Viviani, and many other foreigners were surprised to receive letters from Colbert apprising them that they had been voted pensions by the French King, subject to approval by their own governments. Some of these pensions ran as high as three thousand livres per year. Boileau, the unofficial president of poetry, lived on his pensions like a *grand seigneur*, and left 286,000 francs in cash; Racine received 145,000 francs over a period of ten years as royal historian.[2] Probably the international pensions were motived in part by the wish to have a favorable press abroad; and the domestic gifts aimed to bring thought, like industry and art, under governmental co-ordination and control. This aim was achieved: all publication was subjected to state censorship, and the French mind submitted, with only sporadic and negligible resistance, to royal supervision of its printed expression. Moreover, the King was persuaded that these pensioned pens would sing his praises in prose and verse and send a rosy picture of him down to history. They did their best.

Louis not only pensioned men of letters, he protected and respected them, raised their social status, and welcomed them at court. "Remember," he said to Boileau, "that I shall always have a half hour to give you."[3] His literary taste may have leaned too far toward classical order, dignity, and good form; but these virtues seemed to him not only to stabilize government but to ennoble France. In some ways he was ahead of the people and the court in his literary judgments. We have seen him protecting Molière against noble and ecclesiastical sniping; we shall see him encouraging the highest flights of Racine.

Again at the suggestion of Colbert, and again following in the steps of Richelieu, Louis declared himself the personal protector of the French Academy, raised it to the rank of a major state institution, provided it with ample funds, and gave it lodgings in the Louvre. Colbert himself became a member. When an Academician who was also a *grand seigneur* had an easy chair installed in the Academy for his own comfort, Colbert sent for thirty-nine more such seats to maintain an equality of dignity above distinctions of class; so *"les quarante fauteuils"* became a synonym for the Académie Française. In 1663 a subsidiary Academy of Inscriptions and Belles-Lettres was organized to record the events of the reign.

Colbert saw to it that the forty Immortals earned their keep by dutiful attendance, and by work on the Dictionary. This undertaking, begun in 1638, was progressing so slowly that Boisrobert could express alphabetically his longing for longevity:

> Six months they've been engaged on *F*;
> Oh, that my fate would guarantee
> That I should keep alive till *G*.[4]

The plan of the Dictionary was elaborate: it proposed to trace each *permissible* word through the history of its uses and spellings, with abundant illustrative quotations; so fifty-six years elapsed between its inception and its first publication (1694). It screened too strictly the language of the people, the professions, and the arts; it pruned Rabelais, Amyot, and Montaigne; it outlawed a thousand expressions that favored vivid speech.

The same logic, precision, and clarity that made geometry the ideal of seventeenth-century science and philosophy, the same authority and discipline by which Colbert ruled the economy and Le Brun the arts, the same dignity and refinement that governed the court of the King, the same classic cleaving to rules that molded the style of Bossuet, Fénelon, La Rochefoucauld, Racine, and Boileau—these dictated the Dictionary of the Academy. Periodically it has been revised and reissued, struggling to maintain order in a living growth, its classical citadel repeatedly assaulted, and often conquered, by the errors of the people, the terminology of the sciences, the jargon of the trades, the argot of the streets; a dictionary, like history and government, is a composition of forces between the weight of the many and the power of the few. Something was lost to the language in vitality, much was gained in purity, precision, elegance, and prestige. It produced no turbulent and wanton Shakespeare, but it became the most respected language in Europe, the medium of diplomacy, the speech of aristocracies. For a century and more, Europe aspired to be French.

II. CORNEILLE POSTSCRIPT: 1643–84

The language reached its zenith in the flexible facility of Molière's dialogue, in the sonorous rhetoric of Corneille, and in the melodious refinement of Racine.

Corneille was apparently in his prime—aged thirty-seven—when Louis became King. He began the reign with *Le Menteur*, which raised the tone of French comedy as *Le Cid* had raised that of tragedy. Thereafter he staged tragedies almost annually: *Rodogune* (1644), *Théodore* (1645), *Heraclius* (1646), *Don Sancho d'Aragon* (1649), *Andromède* (1650), *Nicomède* (1651), *Pertharite* (1652). A few were well received, but, as each trod on its predecessor's heels, it became evident that Corneille was working too hastily, and that the sap of his genius was running thin. His flair for portraying nobility was lost in a river of argument; his eloquence defeated itself by continuance. "My friend Corneille," said Molière, "has a familiar who inspires him with the finest verses in the world. But sometimes the familiar leaves him to shift for himself, and then he fares very badly."[5] *Pertharite* was so unfavorably received that Corneille for six years retired from the theater (1653–59). He dealt with his critics in a series of *Examens*, and in three *Discours* on dramatic poetry; these showed his critical faculty rising as his poetic talent fell; they became a fountainhead of modern literary criticism, and served as models when Dryden defended his middling poetry in excellent prose.

In 1659 a thoughtful gift from Fouquet called Corneille back to the boards. *Oedipe* won some acclaim in the wake of the young King's praise; but the works that followed—*Sertorius* (1662), *Sophonisbe* (1663), *Othon* (1664), *Agésilas* (1666), *Attila* (1667)— were so mediocre that Fontenelle could hardly believe that they were by Corneille; and Boileau emitted a cruel epigram: "*Après l'*Agésilas, *hélas! Mais après l'*Attila, *holà!*—After *Agésilas*, alas! But after *Attila*, stop!" Madame Henrietta, usually the soul of kindness, made matters worse by inviting both Corneille and Racine, each with the knowledge of the other, to write a play on the same theme— Berenice, the Jewish princess with whom the future Emperor Titus fell in love. Racine's *Bérénice* was played at the Hôtel de Bourgogne on November 21, 1670, almost five months after Henrietta's death, and met with full success; Corneille's *Tite et Bérénice* was performed a week later by Molière's company, and was coldly received. The failure broke Corneille's spirit. He tried again with *Pulchérie* (1672) and *Suréna* (1674); they too failed; and Corneille spent the remaining decade of his life in quiet and somber piety.

He was so careless of money that, despite a pension of two thousand livres and other gifts from Louis XIV, he ended his life in poverty. Through some oversight the pension was interrupted for four years; then Corneille appealed to Colbert, who had it restored; but after the death of Colbert it lapsed again. Boileau, hearing of it, informed Louis XIV, and offered to give up his own pension in favor of Corneille. The King immediately sent two hundred livres to the old poet, who soon thereafter died (1684), aged seventy-eight. A eulogy memorable for generosity and eloquence was pronounced upon him in the French Academy by the rival who had succeeded him, and who had already raised French drama and poetry to the peak of their history.

III. RACINE: 1639–99

Like Molière, he was of middle-class origin. His father was controller of the state's salt monopoly at La Ferté-Milon, some fifty miles northeast of Paris; his mother was the daughter of an attorney at Villers-Cotterêts. She died in 1641, when Jean was not yet two; his father died a year later; and the boy was brought up by his paternal grandparents. There was a strong Jansenist bent in the family; a grandmother and an aunt joined the Port-Royal sisterhood, and Jean himself, at the age of sixteen, was sent to the *petite école* kept there by the Solitaries. He received from them an intensive training in religion and Greek—two influences that were to take turns in dominating his life. He was fascinated by the plays of Sophocles and Euripides, and translated some of them himself. At the Collège d'Harcourt in Paris he learned some philosophy and more classical lore, and discovered the mysterious charms of young womanhood, new and used. For two years he lived on the Quai des Grands-Augustins with his cousin Nicolas Vitart, who fluctuated between Port-Royal and the theater. Racine heard several plays, wrote one, and presented it to Molière. It was not good enough for production, but Molière gave him a hundred louis nevertheless, and encouraged him to try again. Racine decided upon a literary career.

Alarmed by this madness, and by reports of his amours, his relatives sent him to Uzès in south France (1659) as understudy to an uncle who, as canon of the cathedral, promised him an ecclesiastical benefice if he would study theology and be ordained. For a year the young poet, still simmering with Paris, covered his fire with a black robe, and read St. Thomas Aquinas —with a little Ariosto and Euripides on the side. Now he wrote to La Fontaine:

> All the women are brilliant . . . *corpus solidum et succi plenum* [flesh firm and succulent]; but as the first thing that was said to me was to be on my guard, I do not wish to say more about them. Besides, it would be profaning the house of a beneficed priest, in which I live, to make a long discourse on the matter; *domus mea domus orationis* [my house is the house of prayer]. . . . I was told, "Be blind." If I can't be that entirely, I can at least be mute; for . . . one must be a monk with monks, just as I was a wolf with you and the other wolves of your pack.[6]

The canon fell into difficulties, the promised benefice became uncertain, Racine discovered that he had no vocation to the priesthood. He changed his garb, closed the *Summa*, and returned to Paris (1663).

Arrived, he published an ode that drew a hundred louis from the royal purse. Molière suggested to him a theme which Racine turned into his second play, *La Thébaïde*. Molière produced it on June 20, 1664, but had to withdraw it after four performances. However, it made enough noise to be heard at Port-Royal-des-Champs. His nun aunt sent him thence a letter that deserves to be quoted as part of a drama as eloquent and touching as anything in Racine:

> Having learned that you are planning to come here, I have asked of our Mother permission to see you. . . . But I have heard news, these last days, that has moved me deeply. I write to you in the bitterness of my heart, shedding tears that I should wish to lay in abundance before God to obtain from him your salvation, which is what I long for with more ardor than anything else in the world. I have learned

with sorrow that you frequent, more than ever, people whose name
is an abomination to all who have any measure of piety, and with
reason, since they are forbidden entry to the church, or access to the
Sacrament. . . . Judge, then, my dear nephew, in what state I must
be, for you must know the tenderness I have always had for you, and
that I have asked for nothing except that you should belong to God
in some honorable employment. I beg you, then, my dear nephew,
to have pity on your soul, to look into your heart and consider
seriously into what an abyss you have cast yourself. I hope that
what has been told me is not true; but if you are so unfortunate as
to be continuing a commerce which dishonors you before God and
men, you must not think of coming to see us, for you well understand
that I could not speak with you, knowing you to be in a state so
deplorable and so contrary to Christianity. Meanwhile I shall not
cease to pray God to have mercy upon you and thereby upon me,
since your salvation is so dear to me.[7]

Here is quite another world than that which our pages usually record—a
world of profound belief in the Christian creed, and of loving devotion to
its moral code. We cannot but sympathize with a woman who could write
with such sincerity of feeling, and not without excuse in her view of the
French drama as it had been in her youth. Not quite so tender was a
public statement by Nicole, who had taught Racine at Port-Royal:

Everyone knows that this gentlemen has written . . . stage plays. . . .
In the eyes of right-minded people such an occupation is in itself
not a very honorable one; but, viewed in the light of the Christian
religion and the Gospel teaching, it becomes really a dreadful one.
Novelists and dramatists are poison-mongers who destroy not men's
bodies but their souls.[8]

Corneille, Molière, and Racine separately answered this indictment, Racine
with an angry vigor that he keenly repented in later years.

His break with Port-Royal was soon followed by a break with Molière.
On December 4, 1665, Molière's company presented Racine's third play,
Alexandre. Molière was characteristically generous; he knew that Racine
did not admire him as a tragic actor, and that the young author was in love
with the most beautiful but not the most capable of his actresses; he kept
himself and the Béjarts out of the cast, gave the leading female role to
Thérèse du Parc, and spared no expense on the production. It met with a
good reception, but Racine was dissatisfied with the acting. He arranged a
private performance of his play by the Troupe Royale; he was so pleased
that he withdrew it from Molière and gave it to this rival company. He
persuaded Mlle. du Parc, who had become his mistress, to leave Molière's

company and join the older one. In its new home at the Hôtel de Bourgogne the play ran through thirty performances in little more than two months. It was not one of Racine's masterpieces, but it established him as the successor of Corneille, and won him the guiding friendship of the critic Boileau. When Racine boasted, "I have a surprising facility in writing my verses," Boileau replied, "I want to teach you to write them with difficulty."[9] Henceforth the great critic taught the poet the rules of classic art.

We do not know with what difficulty Racine wrote *Andromaque;* in any case he reached in it the full perfection of his dramatic power and poetic style. Its dedication to Madame Henrietta recalls that he read the play to her, and that she wept. Yet it is a drama of terror rather than of sentiment, with all the inevitable catastrophe that we expect in Aeschylus or Sophocles. The plot is a tangle of loves. Orestes loves Hermione, who loves Pyrrhus, who loves Andromache, who loves Hector, who is dead. Pyrrhus, son of Achilles, has been awarded three prizes for his share in the Greek victory over Troy: Epirus as his kingdom, Andromache (Hector's widow) as his captive, and Hermione (daughter of Menelaus and Helen) as his wife. Andromache is still young and beautiful, though always in tears; she lives only to remember her noble husband, and to fear for their child Astyanax, whom Racine, by dramatic license, rescues from the death allotted him in Euripides to use him here as a hinge of fate. Orestes, son and slayer of Clytemnestra, comes to Epirus as envoy of the Greeks to demand of Pyrrhus the surrender and death of Astyanax as a possible future avenger of Troy. Pyrrhus rejects the proposal in a passage of untranslatable music:

> On craint qu'avec Hector Troie un jour ne renaisse,
> Son fils peut me ravir le jour que je lui laisse.
> Seigneur, tant de prudence entraîne trop de soin:
> Je ne sais point prévoir les malheurs de si loin.
> Je songe quelle était autrefois cette ville,
> Si superbe en ramparts, en héros si fertile,
> Maîtresse de l'Asie; et je regarde enfin
> Quel fut le sort de Troie et quel est son destin.
> Je ne vois que des tours que la cendre a couvertes,
> Un fleuve teint de sang, des campagnes désertes,
> Un enfant dans les fers; et je ne puis songer
> Que Troie en cet état aspire à se venger.
> Ah! si du fils d'Hector la perte était jurée,
> Pourquoi d'un an entier l'avons-nous différée?
> Dans le sein de Priam n'a-t-on pu l'immoler?
> Sous tant de morts, sous Troie il fallait l'accabler.
> Tout était juste alors: la vieillesse et l'enfance
> En vain sur leur faiblesse appuyaient leur defense;

La victoire et la nuit, plus cruelles que nous,
Nous excitaient au meurtre, et confondaient nos coups.
Mon courroux aux vaincus ne fut que trop sévère.
Mais que ma cruauté survive à ma colère?
Que malgré la pitié dont je me sens sáisir,
Dans le sang d'un enfant je me baigne à loisir?
Non, Seigneur. Que les Grecs cherchent quelque autre proie;
Qu'ils poursuivent ailleurs ce qui reste de Troie:
De mes inimitiés le cours est achevé;
L'Épire sauvera ce que Troie a sauvé.*10

There is one defect here: Pyrrhus, and perhaps Racine, do not recognize how much the conqueror's pity owes to the fact that he has fallen in love with the child's mother—even to offering to marry her (whom he might have made his slave), and to adopt Astyanax as his son and heir. She refuses him; she cannot forget Hector, whom Pyrrhus' father killed. He threatens to abandon the child to the Greeks, and, terrified, she consents to marriage. But Hermione—as powerful a conception as Lady Macbeth—burns with anger at being cast aside; while still loving Pyrrhus, she resolves to kill him; she accepts Orestes' proffered devotion, on condition that he shall slay Pyrrhus. Reluctantly he agrees. At every step and in every character of this drama there is a conflict of motives mounting to a psychological complex as subtle as any in literature. Greek soldiers, violating sanctuary, kill Pyrrhus at the altar where he is exchanging marriage vows with Andromache. Hermione scorns Orestes, runs to the altar, plunges a knife into the dead Pyrrhus, stabs herself, and dies. This is Racine's greatest play, worthy to stand comparison with Shakespeare or Euripides: a plot well constructed, characters revealed in depth, feelings studied in their full complexity and intensity,† and poetry of such splendor and harmony as France had not heard since Ronsard.

Andromaque was at once recognized as a masterpiece, establishing

---

* "They fear that Hector and Troy may one day be reborn; that his son may take from me the life that in him I have spared. Sir, so much foresight is too cautious; I cannot see evils at so great a distance. I think what Troy used to be—so proud within its ramparts, so fertile in heroes, mistress of Hither Asia; and then I behold its fate and destiny. I see nothing but towers covered with sand, a river colored with blood, fields deserted, a child in chains; and I cannot imagine that Troy in this condition aspires to revenge. Ah, if the death of Hector's son had been promised, why have deferred it an entire year? Could we not have immolated him on the breast of Priam? He might have been crushed under Troy amid a thousand deaths. All might have been allowable then; old age and infancy would in vain have sought in their weakness their defense; victory and might, more cruel than ourselves, would have excited us to murder in the confusion of our blows. My fury against the vanquished was only too severe. But should my cruelty survive my wrath? Should I leisurely bathe in the blood of a child despite the pity that I feel rising in me? No, sir, let the Greeks seek another prey; let them pursue elsewhere the relics of Troy; the course of my enmity is run. Epirus will save that which Troy has preserved."

† Montfleury burst a blood vessel acting it, and died soon afterward.

Racine as the successor, and perhaps the superior, of Corneille. He entered now his happiest decade, passing from one triumph to another, and even challenging Molière with a comedy. *Les Plaideurs* (1668), a burlesque on greedy lawyers, false witnesses, and corrupt judges, echoed Racine's own experience of the law. He had solicited and obtained a lien on the income of a priory; his claim was disputed by a monk; a long lawsuit followed, which so disgusted Racine that he abandoned the case, and avenged himself with the play. It did not please its first audience; but when it was shown at court Louis XIV laughed so heartily at its sallies that the public changed its mind; and this mediocre comedy played its part in filling Racine's purse.

One minor note intervened. On December 11, 1668, his mistress Mlle. du Parc died in mysterious circumstances—of which more later on. After due delay he took another actress, Marie Champmeslé. She had an attentive husband but a bewitching voice; Racine eluded the one and surrendered to the other. The liaison lasted from *Bérénice* to *Phèdre*, after which, as a wit expressed it, the lady was *déracinée*—torn from the root—by the Comte de Clermont-Tonnerre.

Racine thought that *Britannicus* (1669) was his most careful work; and like *Phèdre* and *Athalie* it is often ranked above *Andromaque*. The modern reader, even if steeped in Tacitus, will likely find it distasteful: a termagant Agrippina, a whining Britannicus, a floundering Burrhus, a slimy Narcissus, a Nero all evil—no character here shows us complexity or development, none offers us that strain of nobility which should somewhere redeem any tragedy worthy of a poet's pen.

As *Britannicus* looked into Tacitus' chamber of horrors, so *Bérénice* (1670) took an emperor's love story from a compact line in Suetonius: *Berenicem statim ab urbe demisit invitus invitam*[12]—"He, unwillingly, at once sent the unwilling Berenice from the city." Titus, besieging Jerusalem (A.D. 70), had fallen in love with the Jewish princess. Though already thrice married, she follows him to Rome as his mistress; but when he inherits the throne he realizes that the Empire would not tolerate an alien queen, and he dismisses her in a royal burst of common sense. The play was warm with sentiment, and succeeded well with both the public and the King, who must have recognized with pleasure his own court and victories in Berenice's description of the young Emperor's glory:

> *De cette nuit . . . as tu vu la splendeur?*
> *Tes yeux ne sont-ils pas tout plein de sa grandeur?*
> *Ces flambeaux, ce bûcher, cette nuit enflaminée,*
> *Ces aigles, ces faisceaux, ce peuple, cette armée,*
> *Cette foule de rois, ces consuls, ce sénat,*
> *Qui tous de mon amant empruntaient leur éclat;*
> *Cette poupre, cet or, que rehaussait sa gloire,*

Et ces lauriers encore témoins de sa victoire;
Tous ces yeux qu'on voyait venir de toutes parts
Confondre sur lui seul leurs avides regards;
Ce port majestueux, cette douce présence.
Ciel! avec quel respect et quelle complaisance
Tous les coeurs en secret l' assuraient de leur foi!
Parle: peut-on le voir sans penser comme moi
Qu'en quelque obscurité que le sort l'eut fait naître,
Le monde, en le voyant, eut reconnu son maître?*13

Is it any wonder that Racine, so skillful in adulation, rose rapidly in favor with the King?

We pass respectfully by some lesser plays, all of them still holding the French stage: *Bajazet* (1672), *Mithridate* (1673), which Louis liked best of all, and *Iphigénie* (1674), which Voltaire ranked with *Athalie* as one of the finest poems ever written.[14] *Iphigénie* had its première in the Versailles gardens, by the light of crystal chandeliers hung in the orange and pomegranate trees; violins played; half the elite audience melted; Racine stepped forward to acknowledge the most cherished plaudits of his career. Produced in Paris, it ran for forty performances in three months. Meanwhile (1673) he had been elected to the French Academy. Nothing seemed lacking to his happiness.

But it is still not given to poets to be happy, unless beauty proves a joy forever, and praise encounters no discordant voice. "The applause I have met with," Racine told his son, "has often flattered me a great deal; but the smallest critical censure . . . always caused me more vexation than all the pleasure given me by praise."[15] He himself was not only thin-skinned, as he had to be, but he was short-tempered, and returned every unkind word. At the height of his success he found half of Paris carping at him, even working for his fall. Corneille had outlived himself, but his followers remembered the heroic tone and topics of his earlier tragedies, the air of nobility in his eloquence, the lofty level on which he raised the calls of honor and the state above the romances of the heart. They accused Racine of debasing the tragic drama with the half-mad passions of ignoble creatures, introducing to the stage the gallantries of courtly love, and drenching it with the tears of his heroines. They were resolved to bring him down.

---

* "Have you seen the splendor of this night? These torches, this pyre, this night with sacred flames, these eagles, these fasces, this assemblage, this army, this crowd of kings, these consuls, this senate—all taking their luster from my lover; this purple and gold made brighter by his glory, and these laurels still bearing witness to his victories; all these eyes that we see come from all parts to unite upon him alone their eager glances; this majestic bearing, this sweet presence. Heaven, with what respect and what willingness all hearts secretly assure him of their trust! Speak: can one see him without thinking, with me, that in whatever obscurity fate had given him birth, the world, beholding him, would have recognized its master?"

When it became known that he was writing *Phèdre*, a group of his enemies persuaded Nicolas Pradon to write a rival play on the same theme. Both dramas had originally the same title—*Phèdre et Hippolyte*—and stemmed from the legend that Euripides had told with classic restraint. Phedra, wife of Theseus, developed an uncontrollable passion for Hippolytus, son of Theseus by an earlier marriage; finding him frigid to women, Phedra hanged herself, leaving in revenge a note accusing Hippolytus of an attempt against her virtue; Theseus banished his innocent son, who was soon afterward killed while driving horses along Troezen's shores. Racine altered the sequence, making Phedra poison herself after hearing of Hippolytus' death. This version was produced at the Hôtel de Bourgogne on January 1, 1677; Pradon's was staged two days later at the Théâtre de Guénégaud. Both for a time had equal success; but Pradon's play is now forgotten, while Racine's is usually rated as his masterpiece; the role of Phèdre is the goal of all French actresses, as that of Hamlet lures the tragedians of the English theater.* Racine, model of the classic style, rivaled the romantics in the emotionalism of Phedra's love, and Hippolytus (quite contrary to the legend) burns for the Princess Aricia. Phedra learns of this passion, and Racine gives us in excited detail a study of a woman scorned. He redeems these romantic ecstasies with a powerful description of how the frightened horses of Hippolytus dragged him to death.

In the preface to *Phèdre* (the religious element in him now rising as the sexual subsided) Racine offered an olive branch to Port-Royal:

> I do not dare assure myself that this . . . is the best of my tragedies . . . But I am sure that I have written none in which virtue has been put in a better light. The slightest faults are here severely punished; the mere thought of crime is here regarded with as much horror as the crime itself. The weaknesses of love are here seen as real weaknesses. The passions are brought to view only to show all the disorder of which they are the cause; and vice is here painted throughout in colors that make us see and hate its deformity. This is the proper end that every man who works for the public should propose to himself. . . . It would perhaps be a means of reconciling the tragic drama with many persons famous for their piety and their teaching who have lately condemned it, but who would judge it more favorably if authors thought as much of instructing their spectators as of entertaining them, and if they followed in this the true intention of tragedy.[17]

Arnauld, famous for his piety and his teaching, welcomed this new note, and announced his approval of *Phèdre*. Perhaps in writing the preface

---

* Adam Smith thought *Phèdre* "the finest tragedy, perhaps, that is extant in any language."[16]

Racine, now thirty-eight, was looking forward to settling down from multiplicity to unity. On June 1 of this year 1677 he took a well-dowered wife. He discovered the comforts of domesticity, and found more delight in his first child than in his most successful play. The jealousies and cabals of competitors had soured his taste for the theater. He put aside the plots and notes that he had made for future dramas, and for twelve years he confined himself to writing occasional verse and prose—chiefly a filial and reverent history of Port-Royal.

A bitter contretemps disturbed his exemplary peace. In 1679 the special court investigating the charges of poisoning made against Catherine Monvoisin drew from her the accusation that Racine had poisoned his mistress Thérèse du Parc. "La Voisin" gave details, but there was no corroboration. Being confident of death, she had nothing to lose by making false accusations; and it was noted that one of her clients and friends was the Comtesse de Soissons, a member of the clique that had opposed Racine in the *affaire Phèdre*.[18] Nevertheless Louvois wrote to the commissioner Bazin de Bézons, on January 1, 1680: "The royal warrant for the arrest of the Sieur Racine will be sent to you as soon as you ask for it." But as the investigation proceeded and seemed to implicate Mme. de Montespan, the King ordered the suppression of the trial record, and no action was taken against Racine.[19]

Louis showed continued faith in the dramatist. In 1664 he assigned him a pension; in 1674 he gave him a sinecure worth 2,400 livres per year, in the department of finance; in 1677 he appointed Racine and Boileau court historiographers; in 1690 the poet became gentleman in ordinary to the King, which brought him an additional two thousand livres annually. In 1696 he was rich enough to buy the office of secretary to the King.

His active fulfillment of his duties as *historiographe royal* shared in withdrawing him from the theater. He accompanied the King on campaigns to record the events more faithfully. Otherwise he remained at home, busying himself with the development of his two sons and five daughters, but sometimes, amid their turbulence, wishing that he had become a monk. He might never have written another play had not Mme. de Maintenon appealed to him to compose a religious drama, purified of all love interest, to be played by the young women whom she had gathered into the Academy of St.-Cyr. *Andromaque* had already been played there, but the virtuous Maintenon noted that the girls enjoyed the passages of amorous passion. To bring them back to piety Racine wrote *Esther*.

He had never before taken a theme from the Bible, but he had studied that book for forty years, and knew all the complex history recorded in the Old Testament. He himself coached the young ladies in their parts, and the King contributed 100,000 francs to provide the Persian costumes required. When it was produced (January 25, 1689) Louis was among the few men in the audience. The clergy, then the court, clamored to see it; St.-Cyr gave twelve more performances. *Esther* did not reach the general public till 1721, six years after the death of the King, and then (religion having lost its royal patronage) it met with indifferent success.

On January 5, 1691, St.-Cyr produced Racine's latest play, *Athalie*. Athaliah was the wicked queen who for six years led many of the Jews into the pagan worship of Baal, until she was deposed by a priestly revolution.[20] Racine made from the story a drama whose power can be felt only by those who come to it familiar with the Bible narrative, and still warm with orthodox Jewish or Christian faith; others will find its long speeches and somber spirit discouraging. The play seemed to applaud the expulsion of the Huguenots and the triumph of the Catholic hierarchy; on the other hand it contained, in the high priest's warning to the young King Joad, a strong denunciation of absolute rule:

> Brought up far from the throne, you have not felt its poisonous charm; you do not know the drunkenness of absolute power, and the enchantment of cowardly flatterers. Soon they will tell you that the holiest laws ... should obey the king; that a king has no other restraint than his own will; that he should sacrifice everything to his supreme grandeur ... Alas! they have misled the wisest of kings.[21]

The lines won much applause during the eighteenth century, and may have moved Voltaire and others[22] to rank *Athalie* as the greatest of French dramas. Subsequent lines suggest that the highpriest was merely arguing for the subordination of kings to priests.

Louis, whose piety now exceeded Racine's, saw no harm in the play, and continued to receive Racine at court despite the poet's known sympathy with Port-Royal. But in 1698 the royal favor lapsed. At the request of Mme. de Maintenon Racine drew up a statement of the sufferings that were afflicting the people of France in the final years of the reign. The King surprised her reading this document, took it, drew from her the author's name, and flew into a rage. "Does he think, because he is a perfect master of verse, that he knows everything? And because he is a great poet does he want also to be minister?" Maintenon, all apologies to Racine, assured him that the storm would soon pass. It did; Racine returned to the court and was received graciously, though, he thought, not as warmly as before.[23]*

---

* Says Racine's son: "He returned several times to the court, and always had the honor of approaching his Majesty."[24] Saint-Simon gives a different account: Racine fell from favor by criticizing Scarron's comedies in the presence of Mme. de Maintenon and the King. "At this the poor widow blushed, not for the reputation of the cripple attacked, but at hearing his name uttered in the presence of his successor. The King was also embarrassed ... The end was that the King sent Racine away, saying that he was going to work. ... Neither the King nor Mme. de Maintenon ever spoke to Racine again, or even looked at him." This explanation of Racine's fall from grace is now generally rejected.[25]

What killed the poet was not a cold look from the King, but an abscess of the liver. He submitted to an operation, and was for a time relieved; but he was not deceived when he said, "Death has sent in its bill."[26] Boileau, himself ailing, came to stay at his friend's bedside. "I rejoice," said Racine, "to be allowed to die before you."[27] He drew up a simple will, whose central paragraph was a plea to Port-Royal:

> I desire that my body shall be taken to Port-Royal-des-Champs, and that it shall be buried in the cemetery there . . . I most humbly beg the Mother Abbess and the nuns to grant me this honor, though I know that I am unworthy of it, both by the scandals of my past life and by the little use that I have made of the excellent education that I formerly received in that house, and the great examples of piety and penitence that I saw there. . . . But the more I have offended God, the more do I need the prayers of so holy a community.[28]

He died April 21, 1699, aged fifty-nine. The King pensioned the widow and the children till the death of the last survivor.

France ranks Racine among her greatest poets, as representing, with Corneille, the highest development of the modern classic drama. Under Boileau's urging he accepted a strict interpretation of the "three unities," and achieved thereby an unrivaled concentration of feeling and power through a single action transpiring in one place and completed in one day. He avoided the intrusion of secondary plots, and all mingling of tragedy and comedy; he excluded commoners from his tragedies, and dealt usually with princes and princesses, kings and queens. His vocabulary was purged of all words that might have been out of place in the salons or the court, or might have raised an eyebrow in the French Academy. He complained that he did not dare mention, in his plays, so vulgar an operation as eating, though Homer was full of it.[29] The aim was to achieve a style that would reflect in literature the speech and manners of the French aristocracy. These restrictions limited Racine's range; each of his dramas, before *Esther*, was like its predecessors, and in each the sentiments were the same.

Despite the classical idea of intelligence overspreading life and controlling emotion and speech, Racine verged upon romanticism in the character and intensity of the feelings he expressed. Whereas in Corneille the sentiments stressed honor, patriotism, and nobility, in Racine they centered largely about love or passion; we sense in him the influence of the romances of d'Urfé, Mme. de Scudéry, and Mme. de La Fayette. He admired Sophocles most among all dramatists, but he reminds us rather of Euripides, in whom the Sophoclean restraint and dignity of expression passed now and then into an abandon of ardor and feeling; there is more restraint of speech in *Hamlet* or *Macbeth* than in *Andromaque* or *Phèdre*.

Racine frankly stated his view that "the first rule" of drama "is to please and touch the heart."[30] He did this by dealing with the heart, by taking as his main characters persons—usually women—of emotional intensity, and turning his plays into a psychology of passion.

He accepted the classic prohibition of violent action on the stage, and therefore restricted himself to expressing passion by speech. This put a heavy burden upon style; the drama became a succession of orations, and the uninterrupted march of alexandrines—twelve-syllable lines rhyming in couplets—skirts the edge of monotony; we miss in Racine and Corneille the flexibility, naturalness, and incalculable variety of Elizabethan blank verse. What a labor of genius must have been required to lift this narrow form out of a wearying sameness by the force and beauty of style! Racine and Corneille should not be read, they must be heard, preferably at night in the court of the Invalides or the Louvre.

To compare Racine with Corneille is an old pastime among the French. Mme. de Sévigné, after seeing *Bajazet*, and before *Iphigénie* or *Phèdre* had been staged, pronounced for Corneille with her usual verve. Rashly, but perhaps rightly, she predicted:

> Racine will never be able to go beyond ... *Andromaque* ... His plays are written for [Mlle.] Champmeslé ... When he grows old and ceases to be in love, then it will be seen whether I am mistaken or not. Long live, then, our friend Corneille; and let us forgive the bad lines we meet with in him for the sake of those divine passages that so often transport us ...

It is in general the opinion of everyone of good taste.[31] But Voltaire, having undertaken to edit Corneille, shocked the French Academy by noting the faults, the crudities, the rhetoric of the great dramatist. "I confess," he wrote, "that in editing Corneille I become an idolater of Racine."[32] Time has recognized those faults, and has forgiven them in one who had not Racine's advantage of coming after Corneille. To have raised the French drama from its previous level to the height of *Le Cid* and *Polyeucte* was a more difficult achievement than to reach the passionate ecstasies and melodious beauty of *Andromaque* and *Phèdre*. Corneille and Racine are the masculine and feminine themes in the poetry of the Great Century—the powerful expression of honor and love. They must be taken together to feel the scope and strength of the French classical drama, just as we must take Michelangelo and Raphael together to judge the Italian Renaissance, or Beethoven and Mozart to understand German music at the close of the eighteenth century.

David Hume, a canny Scot well versed in the language and literature of France, thought that "with regard to the stage, the French have excelled even the Greeks, who far excelled the English."[33] This is a judgment that would have surprised Racine himself, who worshiped Sophocles as perfection, though he dared to rival Euripides. And in this he succeeded, which is praise indeed. He kept the modern drama at a level that only Shakespeare and Corneille had reached, and that no one but Goethe has touched again.

IV. LA FONTAINE: 1621-95

In that age of flamboyant literary enmities it is a pleasure to hear of the famous, half-legendary friendship of Boileau, Molière, Racine, and La Fontaine—*la société des Quatre Amis*.

Jean de La Fontaine was the black sheep of the group. Like the others, he came from the middle class; the aristocracy is too interested in the art of life to spare time for the life of art. Born at Château-Thierry in Champagne, son of the local Master of the Waters and Forests, he grew up as an eager part of surrounding nature, became a lover of fields, woods, trees, streams, and all their denizens; he learned the habits, and divined with sympathy the aims, worries, and thoughts of a hundred species of animals; all he had to do, when he wrote, was to make these multipede philosophers speak, and he became another Aesop, fused by his fables into the memory of millions.

His parents thought they would make a priest of him, but he had no flair for the supernatural. He tried to practice law, but he found poetry much more intelligible. He married a rich girl (1647), gave her a son, arranged a separation from his wife (1658), went to Paris, pleased Fouquet, and received from that amiable embezzler a pension of a thousand livres, on condition of quarterly payments in verses. When Fouquet fell La Fontaine addressed to the King a courageous petition for the financier's pardon; consequently he never basked in the royal sun. Shorn of his pension, La Fontaine, who had no notion of making a living, was housed and fed by the Duchesse de Bouillon, whom we have met as a Frondeuse. While under her wing he published (1664) the first book of his *Contes*, a collection of novelettes in verse, Boccaccianly risqué, but told with such disarming simplicity that soon half of France, even blushing maidens, read them.*

---

* Take as example *Le Faiseur d'oreilles—The Maker of Ears.* Sir William goes to the city for business, leaving his wife, Alix, pregnant. Her relative André warns her that, judging from the color of her countenance, her child will be lacking an ear. He offers himself as a surgeon, and explains that a bout of love will supply the missing member. She accepts the prescription, and takes several doses, until the thought occurs to her that the child will have too many ears. When William returns he restores the moral balance by seducing André's wife.[34]

Shortly thereafter Marguerite of Lorraine, dowager Duchess of Orléans, installed him in the Luxembourg Palace as gentleman in waiting. There he wrote more *Contes*, and thence he sent to the printer the first six books of his fabulous *Fables* (1668). He pretended that they were paraphrases of Aesop or Phaedrus; some were; some were taken from the legendary Bidpai of India, some from the *fabliaux* of France; but most of them were re-created in the bubbling rivulet of La Fontaine's mind and verse. The very first one was an unwitting summary of his careless, singing life:

La cigale, ayant chanté	The grasshopper, having sung
Tout l'été, se trouve fort dépourvue	All summer, found himself quite destitute
Quant la bise fut venue;	When the frost came;
Pas un seul petit morceau	Not a single tiny piece
De mouche ou de vermisseau;	Of fly or little worm;
Elle alla crier famine	She went to plead her hunger
Chez la fourmi, sa voisine,	To the ant her neighbor,
La priant de lui prêter	Begging her to lend her
Quelque grain pour subsister	Some grain to live on
Jusqu'à la saison nouvelle;	Until the new season.
Je vous paierai, lui dit-elle,	"I will pay you," she said,
Avant l'août, foi d'animal,	"Before harvest, on the faith of
Interêt et principal.	An animal, interest and principal."
La fourmi n'est pas prêteuse;	The ant is not a lender;
C'est là son moindre défaut;	This is his least fault;
Que faisiez vous au temps chaud?	"What were you doing in summer?"
Dit-elle à cette emprunteuse.—	He asked this borrower.
Nuit et jour à tout venant	"Night and day to every comer
Je chantois, ne vous déplaisez.—	I sang; do not be displeased."
Vous chantiez! j'en suis fort aisé.	"You sang! I am happy to hear it.
Hé bien, dansez maintenant.	Well, then, dance now."

La Fontaine was wiser than Descartes, who thought all animals to be thoughtless automata; the poet loved them, sensed their reasoning, and found in them all the livable lessens of philosophy. France was charmed to receive wisdom in such digestible doses. The fabulist became the most widely read author in the land. The critics for once agreed with the people, and joined in his praise; for though simplicity was his soul, he knew the French language in its peasant color and earthy tang, and gave his verses such supple grace, delectable turns, vivid pictures in a line, that all the *bourgeois gentilshommes* in France rejoiced to find that their animals, even their insects, had been talking poetry all the time. "I use animals," La Fontaine said, "to instruct men."[35]

In 1673 Marguerite of Lorraine died, and the poet, who had been singing improvidently and had not managed well the modest fees allowed him for his books, found himself rich in debts. He had better luck than his grasshopper, for the learned and kindly Mme. de La Sablière gave him lodging, food, and motherly care in her home on the Rue St.-Honoré, and there he lived in quiet content till her death in 1693. He divided his time (he tells us) into two parts: one part for sleep, the other for doing nothing.[36] La Bruyère described him as a man who could make animals, trees, and stones speak elegantly, but was himself dull, "heavy; and stupid" in conversation;[37] however, there are contrary reports that he could be a lively *causeur* when he found congenial ears.[38] A hundred anecdotes, largely legendary, celebrated his absent-mindedness. Being late for dinner, he excused himself: "I have just come from the funeral of an ant; I followed the procession to the cemetery, and I escorted the family home."[39]

Louis XIV opposed his election to the French Academy, on the ground that the poet's life and *Contes* were hardly exemplary; finally he relented (1684), saying that La Fontaine had promised to behave. But the old poet knew no distinction between virtue and sin, only between natural and unnatural; he had learned his ethics in the woods. Like Molière, he felt no attraction toward Port-Royal, those *bons disputeurs* (he called them) whose "lessons seem to me a bit depressing."[40] For a time he joined the coterie of freethinkers at the Temple, but when a stroke nearly felled him in the street, he thought it time to make his peace with the Church; still, he wondered, "was St. Augustine as wise as Rabelais?"[41] He died in 1695, aged seventy-four. His nurse was confident of his eternal salvation, for, she said, "he was so simple that God would not have the courage to damn him."[42]

V. BOILEAU: 1636–1711

In the meetings of the Four Friends in the Rue du Vieux Colombier the conversation was usually dominated by Nicolas Boileau, who laid down the rules of literature and morals with all the authority and confidence of Dr. Johnson at the Turk's Head Tavern in Soho. Like Johnson, Boileau was more important as a voice than as an author; his best works are middling poetry, but his edicts were of more lasting effect in literature than those of Louis XIV in politics. His friendship and critical acclaim helped Molière and Racine to survive the antics of hostile cabals.

He was the fourteenth child of a clerk in the Paris Parlement. Destined for the priesthood, he studied theology at the Sorbonne. He rebelled, took up law, and was entering practice when his father died (1657), leaving him a patrimony sufficient to support him in verse. He spent ten years sharpening his pen; then, in twelve *Satires* (1666f.), he pronounced judgment upon his fellow men. He was alarmed by "this frightful crowd of famished rhymesters";[43] he attacked it as a horde of locusts; he named names, making enemies by the rhyme; and, to bring the women too down upon his head, he ridiculed the romances with which Mmes. de Scudéry and de La Fayette were using the paper and hours of France. He praised the ancients, and, among the moderns, Malherbe and Racan, Molière and Racine. "I think," he said, "that without wounding conscience or the state, we may call bad poetry bad, and have full right to be bored by a foolish book."[44] These *Satires* bore us in their turn because their aim was achieved: the poets condemned were destroyed beyond our memory or interest; moreover, the tender-minded amongst us, especially if we are authors, prefer critics who direct us to the good rather than those who belabor the bad.

Having adopted the severity of Juvenal in the *Satires*, Boileau in a series of *Epistles* (1669–95) restrained his hatchet to Horace's milder mood, and achieved a smoother style. It was these poetic letters that led Louis to invite him to the court. The King asked him which of his own verses he thought the best. Boileau, with an eye to the main chance, read nothing from his published work, but recited as "least bad" some still unprinted lines in honor of Le Grand Monarque. He was rewarded with a pension of two thousand livres,[45] and became *persona grata* at the court. "I like Boileau," said Louis, "as a necessary scourge that we can pit against the bad taste of second-rate authors."[46] And as Louis sustained Molière against the bigots, so he raised no protest when Boileau published a mock epic, *Lutrin* (1674), poking fun at sleepy and gluttonous ecclesiastics. In 1677 the satirist was made an official historiographer along with Racine; and in 1684 he was finally admitted to the Academy at the explicit behest of the King and over the protests of those whom he had flayed.

The poem that has carried him over the whirlpools of time is *L'Art poétique* (1674), which has rivaled in influence its model, Horace's *Ars poetica*. At the outset Boileau warns young bards that Parnassus is steep; let them be sure, before they set out to climb that sacred mount of the Muses, that they have something worth saying, something that will strengthen truth and *tendra au bon sens*—will make for good sense and taste. Vary your discourse, he advises them; a style too equal and uniform (like Boileau's) puts us to sleep; and "happy the poet who, with a light touch, passes from the grave to the sweet, from the pleasant to the severe."[47] Keep a sharp ear for the cadence of your words. Follow Malherbe's rules on language and style. Study not your contemporaries but the ancients: in epic poetry Homer and Virgil, in tragic drama Sophocles, in comedy Terence, in satire Horace, in eclogue Theocritus. "Make haste slowly;

without losing courage, put your work on the anvil twenty times . . . Add occasionally, omit often."[48] "Love those who criticize you, and, bowing to reason, correct yourself without complaint."[49] "Work for glory, and let not sordid gain be ever the object of your toil."[50] If you write dramas, observe the unities:

> *Qu'en un lieu, qu'en un jour, un seul fait accompli*
> *Tienne jusqu' à la fin le théâtre rempli*

—"Let one action, completed in one place and one day, keep the theater full to the end."[51] "Study the court and familiarize yourself with the city; both are rich in models; perhaps that is how Molière won the prize in his art."[52]

Boileau joined Molière in making *les précieuses* ridiculous, and he scorned the artificial love poetry that had enfeebled French verse. Against this bathos of sentiment he raised the Cartesian worship of reason and the classic inculcation of restraint. He formulated the principles of the classic style, and summarized them in two classic lines:

> *Aimez donc la raison; que toujours vos écrits*
> *Empruntent d'elle seule et leur lustre et leur prix*

—"Love reason, then; let your writings take from it both their splendor and their worth."[53] No sentimentality, no emotionalism, no bombast; no pedantry, no artificiality, no pompous obscurity. The ideal in literature, as in life, is a stoic self-control, and "nothing in excess."

Boileau loved Molière, but regretted his descents into farce. He loved Racine, but apparently did not remark his romantic exaltation of feeling, and his emotion-bursting heroines—Hermione, Berenice, Phèdre. A warrior must exaggerate his share of the truth. Boileau was too lusty a battler to understand what Pascal had said—that the heart has its reasons which the head cannot understand, and that literature without feeling may be as smooth as marble and as cold. Horace had allowed for feeling: "If you wish me to weep," to feel what you write, "you must weep first"—you must feel the matter yourself. All the literature and art of the Middle Ages remained hidden from Boileau.

The influence of his teaching was immense. Through three generations French poetry and prose tried to adhere to his classic rules. These shared in molding the style of English literature in the "Augustan Age," whose Pope frankly imitated *L'Art poétique* in his *Essay on Criticism*. Boileau's influence did harm and good. By deprecating imagination and feeling, it put a damper on poetry in France after Racine and in England after Dryden; verse at its best took on the chiseled form of sculpture, but lost the warmth and color of painting. Nevertheless it was good that the ideal of reason should enter into belles-lettres; too much nonsense had been written about love and shepherds; Europe needed Boileau's angry scorn to cleanse the literary air of absurdity, affectation, and shallow sentiment. Perhaps it was in part through Boileau that Molière rose from farce to philosophy, and Racine perfected his art.

It was just like Boileau that when, with a gift from the King (1687), he bought a house and garden in Auteuil, he said nothing in his writings of the nature that surrounded him—except that from those fields he now took the name Despréaux. There, for nearly all his remaining years, he lived in simple peace, never visiting the court, but warmly welcoming his friends. People noted that "he had many friends, though he spoke ill of everybody."[54] He was brave enough to express sympathy for Port-Royal, and to tell a Jesuit that Pascal's *Provincial Letters* were a masterpiece of French prose. He outlived all of the circle of which he had been the honored theorist: Molière was long since gone, La Fontaine went in 1695, Racine in 1699; the old and ailing satirist spoke feelingly of "the dear friends whom we have lost, and who have disappeared *velut somnium surgentis*"—like the dream of a man rising from sleep.[55] As death neared he left Auteuil, and went to die (1711) in the rooms of his confessor in the cloister of Notre Dame. There, he hoped, Satan would not dare touch him.

VI. THE ROMANTIC PROTEST

The ladies did not take as kindly to the classic canons of reason, moderation, and restraint as old Corneille and young Racine. Their world was a realm of feeling and romance, and the *mariages de convenance* that they contracted stirred rather than checked the fantasies of love. Alongside the classic drama the romantic novel grew to immense proportions, wide acclaim, and international influence. The ladies of France never had enough of such novels, and never found them too long. When Gauthier de La Calprenède stopped his *Cléopâtre* after ten volumes (1656), his fiancée refused to marry him until he had concluded it in two more.[56]

Mlle. Madeleine de Scudéry enslaved half of France with her ten-volume novels, *Artamène, ou le Grand Cyrus* (1649-53) and *Clélie* (1654-60). French society was flattered to find that in these romantic proliferations the characters, under pseudonyms, described and revealed the celebrities of the time. Soon the ladies and gentlemen of the salons called themselves by names from the romances, and learned to sigh and deny like their heroes and heroines; Mlle. de Scudéry herself became Sappho, and was so addressed in the salons to the end of her ninety-four years. She wrote to please her brother Georges, published her books under his name, and preferred his surveillance to marriage. Her reign over literate women and perfumed men continued until Molière's *Précieuses ridicules* and *Femmes savantes* changed literary fashions; then Madeleine bravely kept the last of her ninety volumes from the press. Those who suffer from leisure may still locate in the fifteen thousand pages of *Le Grand Cyrus*, or the ten thousand of *Clélie*, passages distinguished by the delicacy of their sentiment, or remarkable for their analysis of character. And La Scudéry deserves remembrance, too, for having labored to advance the education of women in France.

Marie Madeleine Pioche de la Vergne, who became by marriage the Comtesse de La Fayette, is a more attractive figure because she not only wrote a famous romance, but lived one more famous still. She received an unusually full education. After her marriage (1655) she went to live in Auvergne. Finding life dull there, she arranged an amicable separation from her husband (1659), came to Paris, and joined the circle that met at the Hôtel de Rambouillet. She became lady in waiting to Madame Henrietta, and later commemorated her in a loving memoir. She was a relative but friend of Mme. de Sévigné, who, after forty years of intimacy, wrote of her: "Never did we have the smallest cloud upon our friendship; long habit had not made her merit stale to me; the flavor of it was always fresh and new."[57] This is an exceptional compliment to both parties, for friendships are as mortal as romantic love. We shall find a rare union of love and friendship in Mme. de La Fayette's relations with La Rochefoucauld.

When she decided to cross pens with Mlle. de Scudéry she hit upon a revolutionary innovation: she wrote a romance in one volume only two hundred pages long. She adopted the principle that, other things equal, the best book is that which omits most of its original form; every sentence omitted, she said, added a louis d'or to the value of the book, and every word omitted added twenty sous. After some minor products she composed (1672) and published (1678) her *chef-d'oeuvre*, *La Princesse de Clèves*. The plot (to mix figures) was a triangle with a tangent. Mlle. de Chartres is so modestly beautiful that the Prince de Clèves becomes her slave at first sight. On her mother's advice she marries him, but with no warmer sentiment than respect. Soon thereafter the Duc de Nemours sees her and falls precipitately in love with her. She repels him virtuously, but his feverish persistence touches her; and gradually her pity turns to love. She confesses this development to her husband, and begs him to take her away from the court and temptation. He cannot believe that she is faithful, and worries himself to death, gored, so to speak, with his own imaginary horns. The Princess, in remorse over his death, repulses the Duke, and devotes the rest of her life to charity. The skeptical Bayle remarked that if so pure and faithful a woman could be found in France he would walk twelve hundred miles to see her.[58]

The book was published anonymously, but the literary world soon decided that it was one result of an already famous intimacy. Said Mlle. de Scudéry, "M. de La Rochefoucauld and Mme. de La Fayette have written a novel . . . which I am told is admirably done";[59] but she added, "They are no longer of an age to do anything else together."[60] Both the alleged authors disclaimed authorship. "The *Princesse de Clèves*," wrote La Scudéry, "is a poor orphan, disowned by father and mother." In any case there was general agreement that this was the finest novel yet written in France. Fontenelle confessed to having read it four times, and Boileau, foe of romance, judged Mme. de La Fayette "the finest spirit and best writer among the women of France." History recognizes *La Princesse de Clèves* as one of the first, and still one of the best, psychological novels. It is the only French novel of that age that can still be read without pain.

VII. MME. DE SÉVIGNÉ: 1626–96

But there are ten volumes surviving from that reign—and also by a woman—that even in the palpitation of our time can be read with a self-surrendering delight. Marie de Rabutin-Chantal lost her parents in her childhood, and inherited their substantial fortune. Some of the best minds in France collaborated in her education, and the best families in France formed her in the arts of life. At eighteen she married Henri, Marquis de Sévigné; but this philanderer loved her fortune more than herself, squandered part of it on mistresses, fought a duel over one of these, and was killed (1651). Marie tried to forget him, but she never married again, absorbed in bringing up her son and daughter. Perhaps, as her malicious cousin Bussy-Rabutin suggested, she was of "a cold disposition";[61] or perhaps she had learned that sex depletes while parentage fulfills. Her letters are alive with happiness, almost all parental.

She loved society as much as she distrusted marriage. As a young widow with 530,000 livres,[62] she had many a noble suitor—Turenne, Rohan, Bussy . . . She saw no sense in driving all but one of them away; yet no word of scandal or liaison has clouded her name. She was loved with a less doubtful sincerity by her friends, who included de Retz, La Rochefoucauld, Mme. de La Fayette, and Fouquet. The first two were barred from the court for participation in the Fronde, the last for inexplicable wealth; Mme. de Sévigné, as warmly faithful to all four, was not welcome in the sacred precincts, though we find her receiving some gracious words from the King at a performance of *Esther* at St.-Cyr. Outside the court many circles took pleasure in her company, for she had all the graces of a cultured woman, and conversed as spiritedly as she wrote. This is the reverse of a more usual compliment; we are often advised, perhaps recklessly, to write as we speak.

Over fifteen hundred of her letters survive, nearly all to her daughter; for Françoise Marguerite married (1669) the Comte de Grignan, and soon went to live with him in Provence, where he was lieutenant governor. From 1671 to 1690 the mother dispatched a letter by almost every post—sometimes twice a day—to this young wife now separated from her by the length of France. "The correspondence I have with you," she told her, "is my well-being, the sole pleasure of my life; every other consideration is but mean when put in competition with this."[63] The love that had found no man satisfying became a passion for a daughter who felt herself unworthy of it. Françoise was of a more reserved character; she did not know how to phrase her feelings warmly; she had a husband and children to care for, and sometimes she became cross or somber; yet for twenty-five years, except when ill, she wrote to her mother twice a week, rarely missing a post, so that the fond mother worried that she was taking up too much of her daughter's time.

The most touching incident in these letters is the life and conventual death of Mme. de Grignan's first child. She came to Paris to be delivered under the care of her mother. Soon she sent an apology to her husband for having borne a girl—who would have to be reared painfully, dowered expensively, and then lost; and when Françoise returned to Provence she left little Marie Blanche for a while with the fascinated grandma. Mme. de Sévigné wrote to the father: "If you want a son, take the trouble to make him."[64] She wrote to the unappreciative parents ecstatic details of the marvel they had reluctantly begotten:

> Your little girl grows lovable. . . , white as snow, and laughing incessantly . . . Her complexion, her throat, all her little body, are wonderful. She does a hundred little things—babbling, coaxing, striking, making the sign of the cross, asking pardon, making a bow, kissing her hand, shrugging her shoulders, dancing, wheedling, plucking your chin . . . I amuse myself with her for hours together."[65]

It cost Grandma many a tear to let the plump miracle go to Provence; and many more when the parents put her into a convent when she was still but five years old. The child never came back. At the age of fifteen she took the vows, and disappeared from the world.

The lieutenant governor was extravagant, and entertained beyond his station. His wife periodically informed her mother of their approaching bankruptcy; the mother scolded them lovingly, and sent them great sums.

"How, for the love of God or man, can one keep so much gold, so much silver, so many jewels, such furniture, amid the extreme misery of the poor who surround us in these times?"[66] To keep herself solvent after these deductions, Mme. de Sévigné traveled laboriously to her property at Les Rochers in Brittany to see that it was properly tended, and its rents transmitted to her with only reasonable pilferage. She found a new happiness in the fields, the woods, and the Breton peasantry, and wrote of them as vividly as of that Parisian society of which she was the semiweekly newsletter for her daughter.

Her son was a problem of another kind. She was very fond of him, for he was good-natured, and had, she tells us, a "fund of wit and humor. . . . He used to read us some chapters out of Rabelais, which were enough to make one die of laughter."[67] Charles was a model son, except that he walked in his father's steps from one port of call to another, until—but let Madame, writing to her daughter, bear responsibility for the rest; nothing could better illustrate the tone of the time:

> A word or two concerning your brother . . . Yesterday he wanted to acquaint me with a dreadful accident that had befallen him. He had met with a happy moment; but when he came to the point— It was a strange thing! The poor damsel never had been so entertained in her life. The cavalier, quite defeated, retired, thinking himself bewitched; and, what you will find better than all the rest, he could not be easy till he had acquainted me with his disaster. We laughed very heartily at him; I told him I was overjoyed to find him punished in the sinful part . . . It was a scene for Molière.[68]

He contracted syphilis; she berated him; but she nursed him lovingly.

She tried to infuse a little religion into him, but she had so little of it herself that she could not give him much. She was moved by Bourdaloue's sermons, and had some spurts of piety, but she smiled at the religious processions that so pleased the people of the tenements. She read Arnauld, Nicole, and Pascal, and sympathized with Port-Royal, but she was repelled by their concentration on avoiding damnation; she could not bring herself to believe in hell.[69] In general she shied away from serious thought; such matters were not for women, and disturbed the charm of a comfortable life. Yet her reading was of the best—Virgil, Tacitus, and St. Augustine in Latin, Montaigne in French, and she knew intimately the plays of Corneille and Racine. Her humor was heartier, more joyous, than Molière's. Hear her on a friend given to absent-minded contemplation:

> Brancas was overturned the other day into a ditch, where he found himself so much at his ease that he asked those who came to help him

out if they had any occasion for his services. His glasses were broken, and his head would have been so too, if he had not been more lucky than wise; but all this did not seem to have interrupted his meditation in the least. I wrote him word this morning . . . to let him know that he had been overturned and was very near breaking his neck, as I supposed he was the only person in Paris that had not heard of it.[70]

Altogether, these letters make one of the most revealing portraits in literature, for the Marquise chronicles her faults and virtues carelessly. A loving mother, at home in the salons of the capital and the fields of Brittany; telling her daughter of the latest gossip of the aristocracy, but also that "the nightingale, the cuckoo, and the warbler are beginning [to sing] in the spring of the woods"; rarely uttering an ill word about the hundreds of persons who flutter through her two thousand pages; always ready to help those in trouble, and gracing her speech with delicate compliments and courtesy; guilty, now and then, of unfeeling mirth (as when she joked about the hanging of some poor Breton rebels), yet sensitive to the sufferings of the poor; condoning the immorality of her times and class, but herself of conduct irreproachable; a spirit bubbling with good will and *joie de vivre*; too modest to publish a book, but writing the best French in that age of the best French ever written.

Did she think her letters might be published? Sometimes she indulged in rhetorical flights as if smelling printers' ink; yet her letters are full of business details, emotional intimacies, and compromising revelations, which she could hardly have intended for the public eye. She knew that her daughter showed her letters to friends, but such sharing was frequent in those days, when correspondence was almost the sole means of communication through distances. Her granddaughter Pauline, whom she kept from following Blanche Marie into a nunnery, inherited and preserved the letters, but they were not published till 1726, thirty years after the Marquise's death. They are now among the most treasured classics in the literature of France, a rich bouquet whose fragrance grows with the centuries.

As she neared the end of her life she thought more about religion, and confessed her fear of death and judgment. In the mists of Brittany and the rains of Paris she developed rheumatism, lost her joy in life, and discovered that she was mortal.

> I embarked upon life without my consent, and I must go out of it; this overwhelms me. And how shall I go? . . . When will it be? . . . I bury myself in these thoughts, and I find death so terrible that I hate life more because it leads me toward death than because of the thorns with which it is planted. You will say that I want to live forever. Not at all; but if my opinion had been asked, I should have preferred to die

in my nurse's arms. That would have removed me from vexations of spirit, and would have given me Heaven full surely and easily.[71]

It was not true that she hated life because it led to death; she hated death because she had enjoyed life intensely for almost seventy years. Wishing to die in the home of her beloved daughter, she crossed France through four hundred miles and pains to the Château Grignan. When death came she faced it with a courage that surprised herself, comforted with the sacraments and hoping for immortality. It has been granted her.

VIII. LA ROCHEFOUCAULD: 1613–80

What a different spirit was the most famous of modern cynics, the most merciless unmasker of our frailties, the gloomy invalid who slandered women and love, and whom three women loved to their death?

He was the sixth François de La Rochefoucauld, born of a long line of princes and counts, eldest son of the grand master of the wardrobe to Queen and Regent Marie de Médicis. Until he inherited the ducal title on his father's death (1650), he was Prince de Marsillac. He was educated in Latin, mathematics, music, dancing, fencing, heraldry, and etiquette. Aged fourteen, he was married, by his father's arrangement, to Andrée de Vivonne, only daughter and heir of the late grand falconer of France. At fifteen he was given command of a cavalry regiment; at sixteen he bought a colonelcy. He attended the salon of Mme. de Rambouillet, which polished his manners and style. With all the idealism of youth, and its preference for mature women, he fell in love with the Queen, with Mme. de Chevreuse, with Mlle. de Hautefort. When Anne of Austria plotted against Richelieu, François served her, was detected, and was for a week imprisoned in the Bastille (1636). Soon released, he was banished to the family estate at Verteuil. He reconciled himself for a time to living with his wife, played with his young sons François and Charles, and learned that the countryside has delights that only the city can understand.

In those days, among the French upper classes, a legal marriage could not be dissolved, but it could be ignored. After a decade of restless monogamy, the Prince set out for adventure in war or love. When he set his sights on Mme. de Longueville (1646) it was no longer through idealistic devotion but in the resolve to capture a renowned and well-defended citadel; it would be a distinction to seduce the wife of a duke and the sister of the Great Condé. For her part she may have accepted him for political reasons; he could be a useful ally in the aristocratic rebellion wherein she was resolved to play an active role. When she informed him that he had made her pregnant,[72] he gave all his support to the Fronde. In 1652 she molted him, and took on the Duc de Nemours; La Rochefoucauld tried to convince himself that this was what he had desired; as he put it later, "When we have loved someone to the point of weariness . . . , most welcome . . . is some act of infidelity that may justify us in disengaging our affection."[73] In that year, fighting for the Fronde in the Faubourg St.-Antoine, he was struck by a musket shot that injured both his eyes, leaving him partly blind. He retired again to Verteuil.

He was now forty years old, beginning to suffer from gout, and embittered by misfortunes mostly of his own contrivance. His idealism had died in the wake of Mme. de Longueville, and in the shifty intrigues and ignoble end of the Fronde. He amused his hours, and defended his career, in *Mémoires* (1662) that showed him a careful master of the classic style. In 1661 he was allowed to return to the court; henceforth he divided his time between his wife at Verteuil and his friends in the Paris salons.

His favorite salon was that of Mme. de Sablé. There she and her guests occasionally played a game of *Sentences*: someone would offer a comment on human nature or conduct, and the group would toss it pro and con. Mme. de Sablé was a neighbor and devoted friend of Port-Royal-de-Paris; she adopted its view of the natural wickedness of man and the emptiness of earthly life; La Rochefoucauld's pessimism, born of disillusionments in love and war, of political treachery and physical pain, of deceiving and being deceived, may have received a minor reinforcement from the Jansenism of his hostess. He found a somber pleasure in refining at leisure his own *sentences* and those of others; he allowed these apothegms to be read, sometimes amended, by Mme. de Sablé and other friends. One of these copied them; a Dutch pirate publisher printed 189 of them, anonymously, about 1663; salon circles recognized them as La Rochefoucauld's; and the author himself issued a better edition, with 317 entries, in 1665, under the title of *Sentences et maximes morales*. The little book, soon known briefly as *Maximes*, became almost at once a classic. Readers not only admired the precise, compact, and chiseled style; they enjoyed the exposure of other people's selfishness, and only rarely realized that the story was told about themselves.

La Rochefoucauld's standpoint is stated in his second maxim: "Self-love [*amour de soi*] is the love of a man's own self, and of anything else for his own sake . . . A man's whole life is but one continued exercise and strong agitation of it." Vanity (*amour-propre*) is only one of the many forms that self-love takes, but even that form enters into almost every action and thought. Our passions may sometimes sleep, but our vanity never rests. "He that refuses praise the first time that it is offered does so because he would hear it a second time."[74] The hunger for applause is the source of all conscious literature and heroism. "All men are proud alike; the only difference is that all do not take the same methods of showing it."[75] "Virtues are lost in self-interest, as rivers are in the sea."[76] "If we reflect upon our 'secret' thoughts, we shall find within our own breast the seed of all those vices which we condemn in others," and we shall be able to judge, from our private corruption, the basic depravity of mankind.[77] We are the slaves of our passions; if one passion is overcome it is not by reason but by another passion;[78] "intellect is always the dupe of feeling"; "men never desire anything very eagerly which they desire only by the dictates of reason";[79] and "the plainest man, with the help of passion, will prevail more than the most eloquent man without it."[80]

The art of life lies in concealing our self-love sufficiently to avoid antagonizing the self-love of others. We must pretend to some degree of altruism. "Hypocrisy is a sort of homage which vice pays to virtue."[81] The philosopher's supposed contempt of riches or noble birth is just his way of exalting his own wares. Friendship is "only a kind of traffic in which self-love ever proposes to be the gainer";[82] we may measure its sincerity by noting that we find something not altogether displeasing in the misfortunes of our friends.[83] We more readily forgive those who have injured us than those whom we have injured, or who have obliged—therefore obligated—us with favors.[84] Society is a war of each against all. "True love is like ghosts—something that everyone talks of but scarcely anyone has seen";[85] and "if we had never heard discourse of love, most of us would never have fallen in love."[86] Yet love, when real, is so profound an experience that women who have once known it can have little capacity for friendship, finding the latter by comparison so cold and flat.[87] Hence women hardly exist except when in love. "Some ladies may be met with who never had any intrigue at all; but it will be exceeding hard to find any who have had one and no more."[88] "The generality of honest women are like hidden treasures, which are safe only because nobody has sought them."[89]

The ailing cynic knew quite well that these epigrams were not a just description of humanity. He hedged many of them with "almost," "nearly," or the like philosophical cautions; he confessed that "it is easier to know mankind in general than any one man in particular";[90] and his preface allowed that his maxims did not apply to those "few favorites whom Heaven is pleased to preserve . . . by an especial grace."[91] He must have ranked himself among those few, for he wrote: "I am devoted to my friends so far that I would not hesitate for a moment to sacrifice my interests to theirs"[92] —though doubtless he would have explained that this would be because he found more pleasure in making such a sacrifice than in withholding it. He talked now and then of "gratitude, the virtue of wise and generous minds";[93] and of "love, pure and untainted with any other passion (if such a thing there be), which lies hidden in the bottom of our hearts."[94] And "though it may be said, with great truth . . . , that men never act without a regard for their own interest, yet it does not follow that all that they do is corrupt, and that no such thing as justice or honesty is left in the world. Men may govern themselves by noble means, and propose [to themselves] interests full of commendation and honor."[95]

Old age softened La Rochefoucauld, even while it darkened his gloom. In 1670 his wife died, after forty-three years of patient fidelity, having given him eight children, and having nursed him for the last eighteen years. In 1672 his mother died, and he confessed that her life had been a long miracle of love. In that year two of his sons were wounded in the invasion of Holland; one succumbed to his injuries. The bastard son whom Mme. de Longueville had borne, whom he had not been allowed to claim as his own, but had deeply loved, fell in the same unholy war. "I have seen La Rochefoucauld weep," reported Mme. de Sévigné, "with a tenderness that made me adore him."[96] Was his love for his mother and his sons self-love? Yes, if we may view these as part and extensions of his self. This is the reconciliation of altruism and egoism—that altruism is the expansion of the self, and of self-love, to one's family, or friends, or community. Society can be satisfied with such embracing magn-anim-ous selfishness.

One of La Rochefoucauld's most superficial remarks was that "few women's worth lasts longer than their beauty."[97] His mother and his wife were exceptions, and it was ungenerous to ignore the thousands of women who had lost their physical beauty in the service of men and other children. In 1665 a third woman offered him most of her life. Doubtless Mme. de La Fayette pleased her own heart in seeking to comfort him. He was fifty-two, gouty, and half-blind; she was thirty-three, still beautiful, but herself an invalid, suffering from tertian fever. She had been appalled by the cynicism of the *Maximes*, and perhaps some pleasant notion of reforming and comforting this unhappy man entered into her view. She invited him to her home in Paris; he came, carried in a sedan chair; she swathed and cushioned his aching foot; she brought her friends, including the effervescent Mme. de Sévigné, to help her entertain him. He came again, and even more frequently, until his visits aroused the gossip of Paris. We do not know if sexual intimacy was involved; in any case it was a minor part in what proved to be an exchange of souls. "He gave me understanding," she said, "but reformed his heart."[98] He may have helped her with *La Princess de Clèves*, though the tenderness and delicacy of that romance are all the world apart from the harshness of the *Maximes*.

After the death of Mme. de La Rochefoucauld this historic friendship became a kind of spiritual marriage, and French literature contains many a picture of the frail little woman sitting quietly beside the old philosophe immobilized with pain. "Nothing," said Mme. de Sévigné, "could be compared to the charm and confidence of their friendship."[99] Someone said that where La Rochefoucauld ends, Christianity begins;[100] it proved true in this case. Perhaps Mme. de La Fayette, sincerely pious, persuaded him that only religion could answer the problems of philosophy. When he felt himself dying he asked Bishop Bossuet to give him the last sacraments (1680). His friend survived him for thirteen ailing years.

IX. LA BRUYÈRE: 1645–96

Eight years after La Rochefoucauld's death Jean de La Bruyère confirmed his sardonic analysis of Parisian humanity. Jean was the son of a minor civil servant. He studied law, bought a minor governmental office, became tutoɪ to the grandson of the Great Condé, served the Condé family as *écuyer gentilhomme*—gentleman in waiting—and followed it to Chantilly and Versailles. He remained a bachelor to the end of his life.

Sensitive and shy, he suffered from the sharp edge of class distinctions in France, and he could not evoke the amiable pretenses that might have smoothed his way, despite his middle-class origin, among the aristocracy and at the court. He observed the royal menagerie with a hostile and penetrating eye, and took his revenge by describing it in a book into which he poured nearly all his intellectual substance. He entitled it *Les Caractères de Théophraste traduits du grec avec les caractères ou les moeurs de ce siècle* —*The Characters of Theophrastus Translated from the Greek, with the Characters or Manners of This Age*. The book became the talk of Paris, for under recognizable disguises it portrayed persons well known in the city or at the court; and each of them reveled in the exposure of the rest. "Keys" were published, purporting to identify the portraits with their originals; La Bruyère protested that the resemblances were accidental, but no one believed it, and his fame was made. Eight editions were used up before the author's death in 1696; to each he added new "characters," in which Paris saw the mirror of the time.

To us today, who have lost the key to this gallery, the material seems a bit thin, the ideas traditional and hackneyed, the spirit a bit envious, the satire too facile, as of Menalcas, the absent-minded man.[101] La Bruyère asked for no change in the religion or government of France. He thought it good that there should be poor people; otherwise it would be difficult to get servants, and there would be no one to mine or till the earth; the fear of poverty is indispensable to the production of wealth.[102] He proudly numbered Bossuet among his friends; he repeated in the final section of his book ("Of Freethinkers") the arguments that the great preacher had ex-

pressed with better judgment and in nobler prose; he echoed the proofs
that Descartes had given of God and immortality; and with some skill he
invoked against the agnostics of his time the order and majesty of the
heavens, the signs of design in living things, and the sense of self-determina-
tion in the will, and of immateriality in the mind. He struck at the arrogance
of aristocrats, the greed of financiers, and the servility of courtiers, whom
he pictured as facing Louis, rather than the altar, in the chapel at Versailles;
but he took care to hand protective bouquets to the King.[103] In at least one
passage he put caution aside, and rose bravely to describe the bestial condition to which the peasants of France had been reduced by the wars and
taxes of the reign:

> Certains animaux farouches, des mâles et des femelles, répandus par
> la campagne, noirs, livides, et tout brûlés du soleil, attachés à la terre
> qu'ils fouillent et qu'ils remuent avec une opiniâtreté invincible; ils ont
> comme une voix articulée, et quand ils se lèvent sur leurs pieds, ils
> montrent une face humaine; et en effet ils sont des hommes.*

That page has remained a *locus classicus* in France's classic age.

X. FOR GOOD MEASURE

Shall we now, exhausted, jumble together in a cowardly appendix some Immortals who are beginning to die?

There is Jean Chapelain, who helped to organize the French Academy, and
was considered in his day (1595–1674) the greatest poet in France. There is
Jean Baptiste Rousseau, who wrote forgettable poetry, but such biting epigrams
that he was banished from France (1712) for defamations of character. Almost
every noble active in politics wrote memoirs; we have seen those of de Retz and
La Rochefoucauld, and will come later to those of Saint-Simon; only next to
these are the three volumes in which Mme. de Motteville recorded, with charming modesty, her twenty-two years at the court of Anne of Austria. We note
that she agreed with La Rochefoucauld: "The hard experience I have had of
the fictitious friendship of human beings has forced me to believe that there i
nothing so rare in this world as probity, or a good heart capable of gratitude."[10]
She was such a rarity.

Roger de Rabutin, Comte de Bussy, made a *succès de scandale* with his *His
toire amoureuse des Gaules* (1665), which described the liaisons of his contem
poraries under the guise of ancient Gauls. The King, angry at a quip on

---

* "Certain wild animals, male and female, scattered over the country, dark, livid, an
all scorched by the sun, fixed to the soil which they rummage and throw up with indom
itable pertinacity. They have a kind of articulate voice, and when they rise to their fee
they show a human face. They are, in fact, men."[104]

Madame Henrietta, sent him to the Bastille. He was released after a year on condition of retiring to his estate; there, fretting to the end of his days, he composed his lively *Mémoires*. Even more untrustworthy are the *Historiettes* in which Tallemant des Réaux drew malicious vignettes of celebrities in literature or affairs. Claude Fleury, with his conscientious *Histoire ecclésiastique* (1691), and Sébastien de Tillemont, with his *Histoire des empereurs* (1690f.), and his sixteen-volume *Mémoires pour servir à l'histoire ecclésiastique des six premiers siècles* (1693), labored painstakingly, unwittingly, to clear the wilderness for Gibbon's *Decline and Fall of the Roman Empire* (1776f.).

And there is, last of all, Charles de Marquetel, Seigneur de Saint-Évremond. He was the most genial of those *esprits forts* who shocked Catholics and Huguenots, Jesuits and Jansenists alike by questioning the basic doctrines of their common faith. His adventurous military career was leading him toward a marshal's baton when he fell into disfavor as a friend of Fouquet and a critic of Mazarin. Learning that he was scheduled for arrest, he fled to Holland, and then (1662) to England. His fine manners and skeptical wit made him a favorite in the London salon of Hortense Mancini, and at the court of Charles II. Like the Maréchal d'Hocquincourt in one of his merriest dialogues,[106] he loved war best, women next, philosophy third. Having sipped all the delights in Montaigne and studied Epicurus with Gassendi, he concluded with the maligned Greek that sense pleasure is good but intellectual pleasure better, and that we need as little concern ourselves with the gods as they seem to do with us. To eat well and write well appeared to him a reasonable combination. In 1666 he visited Holland again, met Spinoza, and was deeply impressed by the Christian life of the pantheist Jew.[107] A pension from the English government, added to the salvaged remnants of his fortune, enabled him to write a long series of minor works, all in a style of airy grace that shared in forming Voltaire. His *Réflexions sur les divers génies du peuple romain* helped Montesquieu, and his correspondence with Ninon de Lenclos made part of the fragrance that permeates French letters. On reaching the age of fifty-eight, and unaware that he had thirty-two years of life still before him, he described himself as irremediably infirm. "Without M. Descartes' philosophy, which says, 'I think, therefore I am,' I should scarcely believe myself to be; that is all the benefit I have received from studying that famous man."[108] He almost rivaled Fontenelle in longevity, dying in 1703 at the age of ninety; and he achieved for a Frenchman the rare distinction of being buried in Westminster Abbey.

"Some centuries hence," wrote Frederick the Great to Voltaire, "they will translate the good authors of the time of Louis XIV as we translate those of the age of Pericles and of Augustus."[109] Long before the King was dead many Frenchmen had already compared the art and literature of the reign to that of the ancient best. In 1687 Charles Perrault (brother of the Claude Perrault who had designed the eastern façade of the Louvre) read to the French Academy a poem, *Le Siècle de Louis le Grand*, in which he ranked his own time above any period in the history of Greece or Rome.

Though Perrault included Boileau among the contemporaries whom he considered superior to their classic analogues, the old critic leaped to the defense of antiquity, and told the Academy it was a shame to listen to such nonsense. Racine tried to smother the fire by pretending that Perrault was jesting,[110] but Perrault felt that he had a remunerative point. He returned to the battle in 1688 with *Parallèles des Anciens et des Modernes*, a long but lively dialogue upholding the superiority of the moderns in architecture, painting, oratory, and poetry—except for the *Aeneid*, which he thought finer than the *Iliad*, the *Odyssey*, or any other epic. Fontenelle supported him brilliantly, but La Bruyère, La Fontaine, and Fénelon sided with Boileau.

It was a healthy quarrel; it marked the end of the Christian and medieval theory of degeneration, and of Renaissance and humanist humility before ancient poetry, philosophy, and art. It was generally agreed that science had now advanced beyond any stage reached in Greece or Rome; even Boileau admitted this; and the court of Louis XIV readily conceded that the art of life had never been so beautifully developed as at Marly and Versailles. We shall not pretend to decide the issue; let us put it aside until all phases of this age, in all Europe, have been passed in review. We need not believe that Corneille was superior to Sophocles, or Racine to Euripides, or Bossuet to Demosthenes, or Boileau to Horace; we should hardly equate the Louvre with the Parthenon, or Girardon and Coysevox with Pheidias and Praxiteles. But it is pleasant to know that these preferences are debatable, and that those ancient models are not beyond rivalry.

Voltaire called the reign of Louis XIV "the most enlightened age the world has ever seen,"[111] not anticipating that his own epoch would be named "the Enlightenment." We should have to moderate his eulogy. Officially it was an age of obscurantism and intolerance, capped by the Revocation of the humane Edict of Nantes; "enlightenment" was the possession of a small minority discountenanced by the court and sometimes disgraced by epicurean excess. Education was controlled by a clergy dedicated to the medieval creed. Freedom of the press was hardly dreamed of; freedom of speech was a clandestine audacity amid enveloping censorship. There had been more initiative and spirit, more birth of genius, under Richelieu than under the Great King. The age was unrivaled in the royal patronage and eloquent servility of literature and art. Both the art and the literature touched grandeur, as in the Louvre Colonnade and *Andromaque;* sometimes they fell into the grandiose, as in the Palace of Versailles or the rhetoric of the later Corneille. There was something artificial in the tragic drama and major arts of the period; they leaned too heavily upon Greek, Roman, or Renaissance models; they took their subjects from an alien antiquity rather than from the history, faith, and character of France; they expressed the classical education of an exclusive caste rather than the life and soul of the people. Hence, amid all that gilded galaxy, the plebeian Molière and La Fontaine are most alive today, because they forgot Greece and Rome and remembered France. The classic age cleansed the language, chiseled the literature, gave grace to speech, and taught passion to reason; but also it chilled French (and English) poetry for almost a century after the great reign.

Nevertheless it was a great reign. Never in history had a ruler been so generous to science, letters, and the arts. Louis XIV persecuted Jansenists and Huguenots, but it was under him that Pascal wrote, Bossuet preached, and Fénelon taught. He conscripted art to his purpose and glory, but with his nourishment it gave France magnificent architecture, sculpture, and painting. He protected Molière against a swarm of enemies, and supported Racine from tragedy to tragedy. Never did France write better drama, better letters, or better prose. The King's good manners, his self-control, his patience, his respect for women, helped to spread a charming courtesy through the court, into Paris and France and Europe. He misused some women, but it was under his rule that women reached a status, in literature and life, that gave France a bisexual culture lovelier than any other in the world. After making every discount, and regretting that so much beauty was tarnished with so much cruelty, we may join the French in acclaiming the age of Louis XIV as standing with Periclean Greece, Augustan Rome, Renaissance Italy, and Elizabethan-Jacobean England among the peaks in the faltering trajectory of mankind.

CHAPTER VI

Tragedy in the Netherlands

1649–1715*

THE century from 1555 to 1648 had seen the heroic defense of the Netherlands against the world-embracing empire of Spain; the period from 1648 to 1715 saw the magnificent defense of the Dutch Republic against the swelling navy of England and the unprecedented armies of France. In each case the tiny state maintained itself with a courage and success that claim a high place in history. And amid these burdens and assaults it continued its development of commerce, science, and art; its cities offered havens of refuge to harassed thought; and its republican institutions flung an inspiring challenge to encompassing and powerful monarchies.

I. THE SPANISH NETHERLANDS

The southern or Spanish Netherlands continued till 1713 under Spanish rule. Their ethnically diverse peoples were overwhelmingly Catholic, and they preferred to be subject to a distant and weakened Spain rather than to the Protestants north of them, or to a neighboring France that threatened at any moment to engulf them. The Peace of the Pyrenees (1659) gave most of Artois to France; the Peace of Aix-la-Chapelle (1668) gave her Douai and Tournai; the Peace of Nijmegen (1678) gave her Valenciennes, Maubeuge, Cambrai, St.-Omer, and Ypres. And the Dutch Republic was as merciless as the French monarchy. By the Treaty of Westphalia (1648) Spain, eager to free its armies for continued war with France, not only ceded to the United Provinces the districts that they had captured in Flanders, Limburg, and Brabant, but agreed that the River Scheldt should be closed to foreign trade. This stifling humiliation crippled Antwerp and the whole economy of the Spanish Netherlands. *La politique n'a pas d'entrailles.*

Within such hostile walls what we now call Belgium cherished its traditional culture, welcomed the Jesuits, and followed the intellectual lead of Louvain. When the French bombarded Brussels (1695) a large section of

---

* The political and military history of the Netherlands after 1688 is deferred to Chapter XXIV below.

the city was turned into debris; all the lovely architecture of the Grand'
Place was destroyed except a guild hall and the noble Hôtel de Ville. The
Maison du Roi (in which the royal address was read to the States-General)
was rebuilt in ornate Gothic (1696); this and the Hôtel de Ville are among
the most beautiful structures in Europe today. Sculptors lavished their art
in adorning the façades of churches and civic buildings, and the pulpits,
confessionals, and tombs in church interiors. Brussels continued to make
fine tapestries.[1]

Flemish painting declined sharply after Rubens and Vandyck, as if those
two lives had exhausted the pictorial genius of a century. The rise of France
in art and wealth drew many Flemish painters, like Philippe de Champaigne.
A greater man, David Teniers the Younger, stayed. Taught by his father,
he became a "master" in the Guild of St. Luke by the age of twenty-three;
and four years later (1637) he sealed his success by marrying Anne, daughter of Jan "Velvet" Brueghel and ward of Rubens himself. In 1651 the
Archduke Leopold William summoned him from Antwerp to Brussels
to be court painter and curator of the royal museum; one of Teniers' canvases shows the Archduke and himself among the pictures of this gallery.[2]
He painted with reluctant skill old themes like *The Prodigal Son*[3] and *The
Temptation of St. Anthony*,[4] but like his Dutch contemporaries he preferred to catch within small frames the life of the peasantry, not reducing
the peasantry to brutes as in Pieter Brueghel, but joining with them in their
recreations and festivals. He showed himself acquainted in detail with the
Interior of a Cabaret,[5] but he could also paint rural landscapes transfigured
by an ever-changing sky. He loved light as Rembrandt loved shade, and he
caught it on his brush with a sensitive delicacy that has not been surpassed.

II. THE DUTCH REPUBLIC

The seven Dutch provinces were now united in a proud and victorious
republic whose wealth and expansion stirred the wonder and jealousy of
its neighbors. Here was a nation anomalously without a king; each town
was almost independently governed by a council of rich burghers; each
town council sent delegates to a provincial assembly; each such assembly
sent representatives to a States-General that ruled the interrelations of the
provinces, and their foreign affairs. So far it was an ideal government for
the merchant princes whose fortunes were swelling with the growth of
Dutch trade. Against this oligarchy of businessmen stood one aristocratic
force: the descendants of that William I and Silent of Orange and Nassau
who had led the country through the darkest days of its struggle with
Spain. The States-General had rewarded him with the title of stadholder

and command of its armies; he had been able to transmit that title and command to his descendants; and the control of the military was now a power ever threatening to transform the oligarchic republic into an aristo-cratic monarchy. In July, 1650, William II of Orange, as stadholder and captain general, tried by a *coup d'état* to establish his supreme authority over all the United Provinces; several provincial leaders resisted; William and his soldiers imprisoned six of them, including Jacob de Witt, burgo-master of Dordrecht. But smallpox defeated William in victory; he died on November 6, 1650, aged twenty-four. A week later his widow, Mary Stuart (great-granddaughter of the last Queen of Scots), gave birth to William III of Orange, destined to surpass his father's dreams by becoming King of England.

Beneath these rival ruling classes the farmers and fishermen who fed the nation shared only such remnant of its prosperity as the merchants, manu-facturers, and landowners neglected to absorb. If we may believe the Dutch painters, the peasants had been depressed by war and exploitation to an almost bestial poverty, redeemed by festivals and dulled by drink. The craftsmen in their shops, and the workers in the factories of Amsterdam, Haarlem, and Leiden were better paid than their like in England,[6] but they staged a bitter strike in 1672. Huguenot immigrants from France enriched Dutch industry with their savings and their skills. By 1700 the United Prov-inces had replaced France as the leading industrial nation in the world.

The greatest fortunes were derived from overseas commerce and devel-opment. In 1652 the Dutch made their first settlement at the Cape of Good Hope, and founded Capetown. The Dutch East India Company paid divi-dends averaging eighteen per cent over a period of 198 years.[7] The natives in the Dutch colonies were sold or worked as slaves; the investors at home heard little about this, and took their dividends with Dutch placidity. Dutch foreign trade continued till 1740 to exceed that of any other nation;[8] of twenty thousands vessels carrying the maritime commerce of Europe in 1665, fifteen thousand were Dutch.[9] The merchants and financiers of Hol-land were by general agreement the ablest of the time. The Bank of Am-sterdam had evolved practically all the techniques of modern finance; its deposits were estimated at what would now be $100,000,000;[10] accounts running into millions could be settled there in an hour; and confidence in Dutch solvency and reliability was so high that the Dutch Republic could borrow money at a lower rate of interest—sometimes as low as four per cent—than any other government.[11] Amsterdam was probably the most beautiful and civilized city in Europe in this age. We have seen Descartes' eulogy of it; Spinoza spoke likewise.[12] Pepys was equally enthusiastic about The Hague—"a most neat place in all respects, the houses so neat in all places and things as possible."[13]

These thriving provinces would have been a paradise but for the nature of man. Their prosperity invited attacks by England and France; the struggle for internal control led to the tragedy of Jan de Witt; and the rivalry of religious creeds divided an otherwise amiable people into devout hostilities. The predominant Calvinists, wherever they could, prevented the public exercise of Catholic worship. In 1682 the Synod of Dort (Dordrecht), probably retaliating the Revocation of the Edict of Nantes, drew up a confession of orthodox Calvinism, required every pastor to sign it or be dismissed, appointed Pierre Jurieu, an ex-French Huguenot, to conduct a Calvinist Inquisition, subpoenaed, tried, and excommunicated heretics, and invoked the "secular arm" to imprison them.[14] Nevertheless the Arminian heresy grew; bold men dared to think that God had not predestined the majority of mankind to everlasting hell. Dissenting sects—Mennonites, Collegiants (who sheltered Spinoza), Lucianites, Pietists, even Unitarians— found it possible to live in Holland in the interstices and slumbers of the law. Socinians had sought refuge in the United Provinces from persecution in Poland, but their Unitarian worship was forbidden by a Dutch statute of 1653. Daniel Zwicker published at Amsterdam in 1658 a treatise questioning the divinity of Christ, and subordinating the Bible to "the universal reason of mankind"; yet he managed to die as peaceably as a general. In 1668, however, one Kerbagh, for expressing similar ideas, was sentenced to ten years in prison, where he died. Hadrian Beverland was jailed for suggesting that the original sin of Adam and Eve was sexual intercourse and had little to do with apples.

Toward the close of the seventeenth century religious toleration increased. Dealing with many countries of diverse cultures, opening their ports and bourse to merchants of many faiths or none, the Dutch found it profitable to practice a degree of toleration imperfect indeed, but considerably broader than elsewhere in Christendom. Though the Calvinists were politically supreme, the Catholics were so numerous that their suppression was impracticable. Moreover, as Sir William Temple noted, the social and political dominance of the business classes left the clergy with far less influence than in other states. Refugees from other lands, contributing to the economy or the culture, demanded and received a limited religious freedom. When Cromwell seized power in England, its Royalists sought safety in Holland; when Charles II was restored, English republicans took refuge in the Dutch Republic; when Louis XIV oppressed the Huguenots, they escaped in part to the United Provinces; when Locke, Collins, and Bayle feared persecution in England or France, they found a haven in Holland; when the Portuguese synagogue of Amsterdam excommunicated Spinoza he was received and aided by Dutch scholars, and pensioned by Jan de Witt. Little Holland became "the school of Europe"[15] in business and finance, in science and philosophy.

This civilization would have been depressingly materialistic had it not been for its religious liberty, its science, its literature, and its art. Huygens and other Dutch scientists will meet us later. There were Dutch poets, dramatists, and historians, but their language confined their fame. The Dutch cities were alive with books and publishers. England had only two publishing centers, London and Oxford, France had Paris and Lyons; the United Provinces had Amsterdam, Rotterdam, Leiden, Utrecht, and The Hague, printing books in Latin, Greek, German, English, French, and Hebrew as well as in Dutch; Amsterdam alone had four hundred shops printing, publishing, and selling books.[16]

The taste for art competed with the lust for money and the bargaining for eternal salvation. The Dutch burghers, who had denuded their Protestant churches of ornament, gave to their women and their homes the decoration they had taken from the Lord. They quieted their wives with velvet, silk, and gems; they spread their tables with gold and silver plate; they brightened their walls with tapestries, and their shelves or cupboards with pottery or engraved glass. At Delft, after 1650, Dutch potters, inspired by imported Chinese and Japanese wares, produced glazed earthenware, chiefly blue on white, that gave a bright loveliness to homes that had once been puritanically bare. And there was hardly a Dutch family but had at least one of those little paintings that brought the ideal of the clean and peaceful dwelling, and the refreshment of trees, flowers, and streams, within arm's reach on domestic walls.

III. THE FLOWERING OF GENRE

The heroic age of Dutch painting had passed. The new clients were more numerous but less wealthy; they asked for small pictures that would let them see their own daily life in a distilled and refined extract, reproduced with a realism that aroused the pleasure of recognition, or touched with some delicate but homely sentiment, or inviting the soul into a landscape's liberating view. The Dutch painters met this demand with a refinement of line and light and color that crowded meticulous artistry into a little space. These artists are known throughout Europe and America, for their desperate competition with one another led them to pour forth a quick profusion of small pictures at low prices, and now there is hardly a museum that does not hang them. Letting a lazy footnote attest their abundance,*

---

* Nicolaes Berchem: *The Castle in the Forest* (Dresden). Ferdinand Bol: *Jacob before Pharaoh* (Dresden). Gerard Dou: *Old Woman at a Window* (Vienna). Barent Fabritius: *Jacob and Benjamin* (Chicago). Bartholomeus van der Helst: *A Dutch Burgomaster*, (New York). Pieter de Hooch: *Interior of a Dutch House* (London). Philips de Koninck: *Landscape* (Frankfurt). Nicolaes Maes: *Old Woman Spinning* (Amsterdam). Gabriel Metsu: *The Vegetable Market* (London). Frans van Mieris I: *Self-portrait with Wife* (The

we must look more leisurely at the unfortunate but joyful Jan Steen, and the greatest of the genre painters, Jan Vermeer, and the greatest of Dutch landscape painters, Jacob van Ruisdael.

Steen was a brewer's son in Leiden, worked in The Hague, Delft, and Haarlem, and ended as a tavernkeeper in Leiden; in between he made himself the best figure painter, barring Rembrandt, in Dutch art. At twenty-three (1649) he married Margarete, daughter of the painter Jan van Goyen; her face and figure were her only dowry, but they served him as inspiring models for a time. He was so poorly paid for his pictures that in 1670 an apothecary attached all the paintings he could find in Steen's house, and auctioned them off to cover a debt of ten gulden. His early pictures record the pleasures or penalties of intoxication. An excellent example, *Dissolute Life*,[17] shows one woman drowsy, another asleep, with liquor; seizing the moment, a child steals from a cupboard; a dog eats from the table; a nun, entering, launches into a homily on the sinfulness of rum; everything here, though picturing chaos, is composed and drawn with the order and harmony of art. A lovelier theme animates the misnamed *Menagerie*:[18] a little girl feeds milk to a lamb, garden fowl prance about, a peacock dangles his tail from a blasted tree; pigeons perch aloft, a dove soars in from the street: this is an idyl that makes all the problems of philosophy seem meaningless; it is life, each part with its own sufficient reason, ignoring ultimates. When Steen bypassed the tavern he gave bright views of Dutch civilization: pleasant interiors, music lessons, concerts, festivals, happy families, and the artist himself, smoking in *The Merry Company*,[19] or playing the lute.[20] Then, discouraged by the unappreciative prices paid for his work, he returned to selling beer, drank forgetfully, and died at the age of fifty-three, leaving four hundred paintings unsold.

One glance at a single picture by Jan Vermeer, *The Head of a Girl*,[21] reveals a world and an art almost antipodal to Steen's. This pearl beyond price was auctioned away in 1882 for two and a half gulden; a good critic now ranks it as "one of the dozen finest pictures in the world."[22] The young lady obviously comes of a good home and family; her eyes are clear of fear, unclouded with even the normal wonderment of youth; she is quietly happy, and alert to the music of life; and she is given to us with a careful craftsmanship of color, line, and light that make the brush an astonishing vehicle of understanding and sympathy.

Vermeer was born at Delft in 1632, lived there, so far as we know, all his life, and ended there (1675) at the age of forty-three; he was an almost

Hague). Willem van Mieris: *The Recognition of Preciosa* (Dresden). Aert van der Neer: *Moonlight Scene* (Berlin). Gerard Terborch: *The Music Lovers* (London). Adriaen van der Velde: *The Farm* (Berlin). Willem van der Velde II: *Zuider Zee* (Berlin). Jan Weenix II: *A Hunting Scene* (London). Adriaen van der Werff: *The Expulsion of Hagar* (Dresden). Philips Wouwerman: *Halt of a Hunting Party* (Dulwich).

exact contemporary of Spinoza (1632–77). He married at twenty, and had eight children; he received good prices for his paintings, but he toiled at them with such time-consuming care, and spent so much money in buying pictures, that he died in debt; his widow had to apply for aid to the court of bankruptcy. Yet his thirty-four surviving works suggest a background of middle-class comfort. One of them[23] shows him in his studio, with fluffy cap and particolored jerkin, stockings, rumpled but of silk, his buttocks bulging with prosperity. Doubtless he lived in one of the better quarters of Delft, perhaps in the outskirts from which he could have a *View of Delft*;[24] we feel, in that famous picture, his fondness for his native town. He seems to have been more contentedly domesticated than the artists of our time. Love of the home shines out in most Dutch painting, but in Vermeer the home becomes a little temple, and the housewife is proud of her ministrations; in his *Christ with Mary and Martha*[25] the latter shares the pedestal with Mary. His women are no longer the heavy bundles of flesh sometimes seen in Dutch art; they are of some refinement and sensitivity; they may even, like the seated lady in *Mistress and Maid*,[26] be expensively robed, delicately featured, carefully coiffured, or be rich in silk and musical instruments, like the *Lady Seated at the Virginals*.[27] Vermeer makes an epic of family life, or a lyric of simple and normal domestic moments; not group scenes of confused and multiple activity, but at his best one woman alone, quietly reading a letter,[28] or intent on her sewing,[29] or adorning herself with a necklace, or asleep at her sewing,[30] or just a girl and her smile.[31] Vermeer recorded with perfect art his gratitude for a good woman and a happy home. In the eighteenth century he was almost forgotten; his little masterpieces were ascribed to de Hooch, Terborch, or Rembrandt; only in 1858 was he disinterred. Now his name stands only after those of Rembrandt and Hals in Dutch painting.

One thing is missing in these genre painters—the life of nature that surrounded the interloping towns. Italy, and Poussin in Italy, had caught some of the fresh air and open fields; England would discover them in the next century; now Dutch painters, leaving for a while their chaste or hilarious interiors, placed their easels to capture the lure of rippling streams, silent and leisurely windmills, burgeoning farms, trees shaming our hectic transiency, exotic vessels swaying in crowded ports, clouds kaleidoscoping the sky. All the world knows the *Middelharnis Road* of Meindert Hobbema —perspective vanishing into endless space; but far more beautiful is his *Water Mill with the Great Red Roof*.[32] Aelbert Cuyp found his inspiration in plump kine wading in lush marshes,[33] horses halting thirsty at an inn, sails disappearing on the sea.[34] Salomon van Ruisdael marveled at the tremor of waters reflecting and inverting boats and trees (*Canal and Ferry*[35]), and taught his nephew to surpass him.

Jacob van Ruisdael grew in Haarlem, and left us a *View of Haarlem*[36] quite as impressive as Vermeer's *Delft*, and better conveying the vast yet huddled complexity of a great city. Moving to Amsterdam, he became a member of the Mennonite Brethren, and perhaps their mysticism helped his poverty to make him feel the tragic side of the nature in which he loved to lose himself. He knew that those fields, woods, and skies that promised peace could also destroy, that nature had moods of wrath in which even the proudest, sturdiest trees could be shorn by mad winds and torn from their roots, that deadly clefts could form in the good earth, that lightning could wreak its lethal fire upon every form of life with playful indifference. No idyl is *The Waterfall on the Cliff*,[37] but the furious surge of the sea upon rocks that it has vowed to shatter and submerge or wear away; *The Storm*[38] is the sea beating in rage against its enemy the land; *The Beach*[39] is no pleasure strand but a shore disordered by a mounting surf under a lowering sky; *Winter*[40] is no skating frolic, but a poor cottage shivering under threatening clouds; and the masterly etching of *Oak Trees* despoils them of their dignity to show their branches disheveled or bare, their trunks wounded and distorted by inclement time. *The Jewish Cemetery*[41] is itself an image of death—ruined walls, a dying tree, flood waters running over tombs. Not that Ruisdael was always gloomy; in *The Wheat Field*[42] he rendered with deep feeling the quiet of a country road, the blessing of rich crops, the exhilaration of expanding space. The Dutch seem to have felt their land and clime maligned in Ruisdael's pictures; they paid for these with a pittance, and let their author die in a poorhouse. Today some would rank him only after Poussin among the landscape painters of all time.[43]

Infinite riches in a little room—Rembrandt and Hals, Vermeer and Ruisdael, Spinoza and Huygens, Tromp and de Ruyter, Jan de Witt and William III, all at the same time within close frontiers, laboring precariously behind the dunes, keeping alive the arts of peace amid the alarms of war: this is Holland in the seventeenth century. "Size is not development."

IV. JAN DE WITT: 1625–72

Their independence won, the United Provinces, after the Treaty of Westphalia, gave themselves to the pursuit of money, pleasure, and war. They were the least self-contained nation in history; the products of their soil could support only an eighth of their population; the life of the country depended upon foreign trade and colonial exploitation; and these depended upon a navy capable of protecting Dutch vessels and settlements. The Spanish mastery of the seas had ended with the defeat of the Spanish Armada. The English navy, bouncy with victory, spread its sails out over the ocean. Soon English mercantile expansion encountered Dutch ships and Dutch settlements in India, the East Indies, Africa, even in the "New Amsterdam" that was to become New York. Some Englishmen, still warm with the fire of Hawkins and Drake, felt that these ubiquitous Dutch should be replaced by ubiquitous Britons, and that this could be done with a naval victory or two. "The merchants," reported the Earl of Clarendon, "took to discourse of 'the infinite benefit that would accrue' from a barefaced war against the Dutch, how easily they might be subdued, and the trade carried on by the English."[44] Cromwell thought it a good idea.

In 1651 the English Parliament passed a Navigation Act forbidding foreign vessels to bring into England any merchandise except that produced in their own country. The Dutch had been shipping to England the products of their colonies; now this lucrative trade was stopped. They sent an embassy to London to secure some modification of the act; the English not only refused, but demanded that Dutch vessels meeting English ships in "English waters" (i.e., all the waters between England, France, and the Netherlands) should lower their flags in recognition of English dominance of those seas. The Dutch emissaries returned empty-handed to The Hague. In February, 1652, the English seized seventy Dutch merchantmen found in "English waters." On May 19 an English fleet under Robert Blake met a Dutch squadron under Maarten Tromp; Tromp refused to lower his flag; Blake attacked; Tromp withdrew. So began the "First Dutch War."

The separatism of the supposedly United Provinces now brought them close to disaster. The unified military leadership formerly provided by the princes of Orange had lapsed; the States-General became a debating society instead of a state. The English had a strong and centralized government under the resolute Cromwell; they had a better navy; they had all the advantages of geography and prevailing westerly winds. They destroyed Dutch fishing fleets, captured Dutch merchantmen, and defeated the Dutch Admiral de Ruyter off the coast of Kent. Tromp won over Blake off Dungeness (November 30, 1652), but died in battle in the following July. The result of a year's war was the overwhelming demonstration of English naval power. English blockade of the Dutch coast brought economic life almost to a standstill in the Provinces. Thousands of their population approached starvation, and threatened revolt.

It was at this unhappy juncture that Jan de Witt undertook the leadership of the country. He came of a family long prominent in Dutch commerce and politics. His father, Jacob de Witt, was six times elected burgomaster of Dordrecht. Jan himself received all available education, traveled in France with his older brother, Cornelis, met Cromwell in England, and then settled down as a lawyer in The Hague (1647). Three years later his father was among the six republican leaders imprisoned by William II of Orange, the Stadholder, who wished to establish his political, as well as his military, authority over all the seven provinces. When William II died (1650) the States-General, perhaps influenced by the apparently successful creation (1649) of a republic in England, refused to accept his posthumous son as his successor, and discontinued the stadholdership. The internal drama of the United Provinces became a struggle between the mercantile republican and pacific spirit represented by de Witt, and the martial aristocratic spirit soon to be revived in the young and ardent William III.

On December 21, 1650, Jan de Witt, still a youth of twenty-five, was elected pensionary (chief magistrate) of Dordrecht, and its representative in the States-General of the United Provinces. In February, 1653, that body named him grand pensionary of the republic, and gave him the bitter task of negotiating peace with victorious England. Cromwell was merciless. He demanded that the Dutch acknowledge English dominance, and salute the English flag, in the Channel; that they admit the right of English captains to search Dutch vessels at sea; that they pay for the privilege of fishing in English waters, and give compensation for the murder of Englishmen by the Dutch in Amboyna in 1623; and that they perpetually exclude from office or power all members of the house of Orange—which, being allied by marriage to the Stuarts, had vowed to restore that dynasty in England. De Witt removed this last clause from the treaty as presented to the States-General and ratified by it (April 22, 1654); then he induced the Estates of the one province of Holland to accept the treaty with this clause included. William III never forgave him.

De Witt consolidated his position by marrying the wealthy Wendela Bicker; through her he became related to the mercantile princes of Amsterdam; with their support he filled the most important posts in Holland with his father, his brother, his cousins, and his friends; soon he had in his hands all the reins of government in the province. Other provinces reluctantly accepted his lead, for Holland, enriched by its ports, paid fifty-seven per cent of the Union's expenses, and provided most of the Dutch fleet. He was unpopular with the masses, but his administration was enlightened and competent. He checked extravagant outlays, reduced the interest on the federal debt, overhauled the fleet, built better ships, trained new naval personnel. Reflecting the sentiments of the merchants, he strove for peace but prepared for war. In 1658, and again in 1663, he was re-elected as grand pensionary of the United Provinces. He impressed observers with his devotion to the tasks of government, the simplicity and modesty of his bearing, and the integrity of his family life. The wealth of his wife enabled him to live in a sumptuous home, where he could receive foreign emissaries in imposing surroundings; but that home was a center of Dutch culture rather than of luxurious display; poetry mingled there with politics; science and philosophy were discussed perhaps too freely for de Witt's Calvinistic constituents; and even the dreaded heretic Spinoza found a loyal friend and protector in the Grand Pensionary.

It was always his tragedy that he loved peace more than war, while the neighbors of the rich republic gathered their forces to destroy it. In 1660 Charles II was restored to the throne of England. He pointedly recommended his nephew, William III of Orange, to the good will of Jan de Witt; soon he demanded the annulment of that "Act of Seclusion" by which William was barred from office; de Witt consented; and so the Stuart King unwittingly prepared the fall of the Stuart dynasty. In October, 1664, an English expedition seized the Dutch colony of New Amsterdam, and renamed it New York in honor of the Duke of York (the future James II), then head of the English navy. The States-General of the United Provinces protested; the protest was ignored; in March, 1665, the Second Dutch War began.

The preparations that de Witt had made were now vindicated. Weakness of leadership had passed from the States-General to the careless and incompetent government of Charles II; and while the Merrie Monarch danced with his mistress, de Witt won the applause even of his enemies by the energy and devotion with which he attended to all the aspects and details of military organization. Repeatedly he sailed with the fleet, exposed himself to all the perils of battle, and inspired the crews with his courage and zeal. The Dutch navy was not yet equal to the English in vessels, men, or discipline; and in the first major encounter of the war the English navy under the Duke of York decisively defeated the Dutch (Lowestoft, June 13, 1665). The patient burghers reconstituted the fleet, and put it under the command of one of history's ablest and most daring admirals. In June, 1667, Michel Adriaanszoon de Ruyter led sixty-six ships into the Thames, captured the fort of Sheerness (some forty miles east of London), broke the barriers that had blocked entry into the Medway (which flows into the Thames at Sheerness), and captured, burned, or sank sixteen English men-of-war that lay there unprepared for so unmannerly a visitor (June 12, 1667). Charles II, having no taste for war, bade his diplomats offer the Dutch an acceptable peace. On July 21, 1667, the two powers signed the Treaty of Breda. The Dutch surrendered the apparently unimportant New York to England, and agreed to salute the English flag in English waters; England surrendered the colony of Surinam (Dutch Guiana, in South America) to the Dutch, and modified the Navigation Act in favor of Dutch trade. The treaty was a moderate victory for de Witt, and brought him to the height of his career.

But he made now a succession of fatal blunders. He further alienated the supporters of William III by putting through the provincial assembly of Holland (August 5, 1667) a "Perpetual Edict" excluding any stadholder of any province from supreme military or naval command of the Union. Thereupon the adherents of the young Prince resigned from the army, leaving it without experienced leadership. Unfortunately, this act of family rivalry occurred while France was invading the Spanish Netherlands, thereby threatening the vital interests of the United Provinces. A France controlling the southern provinces would soon reopen the Scheldt to foreign trade; Antwerp, revived, would challenge the commercial ascendancy of Amsterdam; the whole economy of the northern provinces would be imperiled. And how long would Louis XIV stop at the Dutch frontier? If he should decide to absorb the United Provinces, and take control of the mouths of the Rhine, the country would in effect cease to exist, and Dutch Protestantism would be doomed.

De Witt offered the aggressive King a series of compromises; they were refused. He arranged with England (January 23, 1668), and shortly thereafter with Sweden, a Triple Alliance for common defense against expanding France. Louis tactfully agreed to end his "War of Devolution" on condition of retaining a cordon of cities and fortresses that he had captured in Flanders and Hainaut. These terms were accepted by England and Sweden, and therefore by the United Provinces, in the Treaty of Aix-la-Chapelle (May 2, 1668). Apparently the danger had been averted by de Witt's diplomacy. In July he was elected to a fourth term of five years as grand pensionary of the republic.

But he had misread the policies of the French and English kings. Louis never forgave the Dutch for interfering with his conquest of the Spanish Netherlands. He vowed that "if Holland should trouble him as it had done the Spanish, he would send his men with shovels and pickaxes to throw it into the sea,"[45] presumably by opening the dykes. He resented the republic and coveted the Rhine; he was resolved to destroy the one and control the other. A war of tariffs heated the conflict: Colbert had laid prohibitive duties upon Dutch goods entering France, and the Dutch had retaliated in kind. A clever exception was made for munitions; Louvois, French minister of war, persuaded the Dutch manufacturers to sell him great quantities of war material;[46] meanwhile the Dutch businessmen withheld their consent to the taxes that de Witt proposed for replenishing the army and its supplies. The French diplomatic corps proved its skill, or affluence, by detaching England and Sweden from alliance with the United Provinces. By the secret Treaty of Dover (June 1, 1670) Charles II agreed to abandon the Triple Alliance and join Louis in war against the Dutch. In 1672 Sweden, needing French help against Denmark and Germany, withdrew from the same alliance. Spain, the Empire, and Brandenburg promised aid to the republic, but their available forces were too meager or distant to count much in meeting the immense levies that were now let loose upon the United Provinces by land and sea. Again de Witt offered concessions and compromises; they were rejected.

On March 23, 1672, England began the attack upon the Dutch Republic; on April 6 France declared war. Some 130,000 men marched against the little state, under Turenne, Condé, Luxembourg, Vauban, and Louis himself; "Never had there been such a magnificent army," said Voltaire.[47] By clever and unexpected strategy the main French force passed through German territory—appeasing the villages with "gifts"—to assault less strongly fortified points. On June 12, under the fire of the Dutch and the eyes of the King, the French crossed the Rhine, swimming the sixty feet of its width that were too deep for wading; this became a favorite episode in the iconography of the King. Moving north into the heart of the United Provinces, the royal armies easily captured one city after another. Utrecht surrendered without resistance; the provinces of Overijssel and Gelderland submitted; soon only Amsterdam and The Hague remained to be taken. It availed little that on June 6 de Ruyter had defeated the combined English and French fleets at Southwold Bay. De Witt asked Louis for terms; Louis demanded a large indemnity, French control of all Dutch highways and waterways, and the re-establishment of the Catholic religion throughout the republic. Rejecting these conditions as tantamount to slavery, the Dutch resorted to their last defense: they opened the dykes, letting in their ancient enemy, the sea, as a saving friend. Soon the waters were pouring over the land, and the French armies, unprepared for such an inundation, retreated helplessly.

Nevertheless the country was devastated; the troops of the bishop of Münster and the Elector of Cologne, allied with Louis, were marching unhindered through the province of Overijssel; French and English vessels, despite de Ruyter, were raiding Dutch commerce; the economic life of the beleaguered state neared collapse. De Witt, during these bitter months, had labored as hardly any man in Dutch history before him—raising funds, equipping and provisioning the fleet, standing on deck beside de Ruyter in the battle of Southwold Bay, and striving through embassy after embassy to negotiate a saving peace. In June, 1672, he sent Louis an offer to cede to him Maastricht and parts of Dutch Brabant, and to pay all the costs of the war. But this offer too was scorned; and when de Witt's countrymen heard of it they denounced him as planning a treasonable surrender.[48] The people now cast upon him all the responsibility for their misfortunes. They charged him with naïve and reckless trust in the words of Charles II and Louis XIV; they accused him of filling a dozen lucrative offices with his relatives; above all, they could not forgive him for refusing to the house of

Orange the military and political honors that through a century had kept the Dutch provinces free. They laid at his door the incompetence and cowardice of his bourgeois generals. The Calvinist clergymen denounced him as a secret freethinker, as a follower of Descartes and friend of Spinoza.[49] Even the commercial classes, which had been his main support, turned against him now as the organizer of defeat.

His brother Cornelis, who had shared with him the emoluments of office and the burdens and perils of war, received with him the hatred and insults of the populace. On June 21, 1672, an unsuccessful attempt was made to assassinate Jan; two days later a like attempt was made upon Cornelis. On July 24 the officials of The Hague arrested Cornelis on a charge of plotting against the Prince of Orange. On August 4 Jan resigned his office as grand pensionary. On August 19 Cornelis was put to the torture, and was condemned to exile. Though warned that he was risking his life, Jan made his way through a hostile city to the Gevangenpoort prison to see his brother. Soon a crowd collected outside, urged on by a sheriff, a goldsmith, and a barber. A civic guard commissioned to hold back the mob shared its hatred of the de Witts, and made no resistance when it battered down the doors of the jail and rushed in. Jan and Cornelis were seized, dragged into the square, and beaten to death, and their bodies were hung head downward on a lamppost (August 20, 1672).

The Dutch Republic died with them, and the house of Orange returned to power.

V. WILLIAM III OF ORANGE

Mary Stuart, broken in spirit by the execution of her father, Charles I (1649), the death of her young husband, William II of Orange (1650), the abolition of the stadholdership, and the exclusion of the house of Orange from office, brought up her son to a somber self-control that would silently bide its time till persistence brought victory. Physically weak, surrounded in his development by enemies set to guard him, but inheriting from William I of Orange the motto *Je maintiendrai*—"I will maintain"— he grew up as a sickly lad hiding behind an immobile face a fire of resolution and revenge. Austere, decorous, coldly courteous, he shunned amusements and frivolity, and pursued outdoor sports to overcome his repeated headaches and his liability to fainting spells. This was a frail vessel to house the spirit that would capture the throne of England and chasten the King of France.

His mother went to England in 1660 to rejoice in her brother's coronation; she died there of smallpox on Christmas Eve. In 1666 the government of Holland province declared the sixteen-year-old Prince a ward of the state; Jan de Witt replaced his beloved guardians and tutors with persons more responsive to the policy of the provincial Estates.[50] William's hatred of de Witt grew with every year. At the height of Jan's power the Prince, eluding his new guardians, rode from The Hague to Bergen-op-Zoom (1668), and took a boat to Zeeland, the province that had been most loyal to his ancestors. The people of its capital, Middelburg, greeted him with mass demonstrations of fidelity and affection. He assumed without hesitation or opposition the presidency of the Zeeland provincial assembly. Returning to The Hague, he announced that his minority was now ending on his eighteenth birthday (November 4, 1668), and that he would henceforth dispense with the guardians that the Estates of Holland had given him. The Estates refused to remove them; he dismissed them; they remained. He bided his time.

It came when the French and German armies overran the Dutch provinces, Dutch armies surrendered town after town, and The Hague itself seemed defenseless. Yielding to the demands of the military, and hoping that the restoration of the house of Orange to leadership would restore the unity and morale of the nation, the States-General appointed William captain general of the Union (February 25, 1672). On July 2 the Estates of Zeeland, flouting the "Perpetual Edict," elected William their provincial stadholder; on July 4 the Estates of Holland followed suit; on July 8 he was made supreme commander of the Union's armed forces on land and sea. He showed his spirit when the French King offered peace in return for an indemnity of sixteen million florins and the cession of large areas to France, Münster, and Cologne; a secret offer was made to recognize William as king of the remainder. The Estates of Holland asked his advice; he replied, "Rather let us be hacked to pieces than accept such conditions."[51] When the second Duke of Buckingham, coming from England to urge William to make peace, said to him, "Do you not see that your country is lost?" he replied, "My country is in great danger, but there is a sure way never to see it lost, and that is to die in the last ditch."[52] Nevertheless, with wisdom remarkable in a youth of twenty-two, he counseled patient and courteous negotiations with the English; already he may have seen in a co-operation of the English and the Dutch the only hope of checking the aggressions of France. He took measures to strengthen the ties between the United Provinces, the Empire, and Brandenburg. The outlines of the Grand Alliance were taking form in his mind.

He proceeded to the headquarters of the army, and so was absent from The Hague when the de Witts were murdered. He had apparently no share in planning that act, which perhaps no one had planned; but when he heard of it he did not hide his satisfaction; and he protected and pensioned the men who had led the mob.[53] He tried now to be a good general; he never succeeded, but the experienced soldiers who came enthusiastically to his standard reorganized the army and the navy, and victories began to outweigh defeats. De Ruyter and Cornelis Tromp (son of Maarten) outfought the English and French fleets at Schooneveldt and Kykduin (1673); the German invaders were stopped in Groningen; William captured Naarden; the provinces of Gelderland, Utrecht, and Overijssel were cleared of the enemy; nearly everywhere the French were in retreat. For the time being, at least, the United Provinces were saved, and they hailed William as their savior.

To these successes he added diplomatic victories. On February 19, 1674, he persuaded England to a separate peace by agreeing to pay a war indemnity of two million florins; on April 22 and May 11 he signed treaties with Münster and Cologne; he confirmed the alliance of the United Provinces, Spain, Brandenburg, Denmark, and the Empire against a now isolated France. As a final stroke he won the hand of Mary, eldest daughter of James, Duke of York, brother of the English King. The two leading Protestant powers were now drawn together; the net was being closed around France; and it was no minor matter that Mary stood only after her father in line of succession to the English throne. Seldom in history has so young a statesman laid such farseeing plans, and with such success.

Meanwhile, however, the French renewed their attack, took Ypres and Ghent, and advanced to the Dutch border. De Ruyter was defeated by a French fleet off the Sicilian coast (April 22, 1676), and died a week later of his wounds. Louis offered peace to the States-General on tempting terms: he would restore all Dutch territory held by the French, provided the States would agree to his retention of Franche-Comté and Lorraine. The Emperor, Brandenburg, and Denmark protested against such a peace; William supported them; the States-General, dominated by commercial interests, overruled him, deserted its allies, and signed the separate Peace of Nijmegen with France (August 10, 1678).

William viewed the peace as merely a truce, and strove through the next ten years to reconstruct the alliance. The Dutch merchants restrained his martial temper, arguing that the exhausted provinces needed a rest from turmoil, and that prosperity was returning. Two events of the year 1685 played into William's hands. Louis revoked the Edict of Nantes; persecuted Huguenots crowded into the Netherlands, and led an active propaganda for a union of Protestant powers against France. In England James II, become King, revealed his hope to make that nation Catholic; English Protestants planned to depose him, leaving William's wife, Mary, in line for the throne. William had carried on a liaison with Mary's best friend, Elizabeth Villiers,[54] but Mary forgave him, and agreed that if she became queen of

England she would obey her husband as king. In 1686 William succeeded in arranging an alliance with the Empire, Brandenburg, Spain, and Sweden for common defense. On June 30, 1688, the English Protestant leaders invited William and Mary to enter England with armed forces and help them dethrone their Catholic King. William hesitated, for Louis XIV had a vast army awaiting the royal decision to attack either the Netherlands or the Empire. Louis sent it word to advance into Germany; William's hands were free. On November 1, 1688, he sailed with fourteen thousand men to win the throne of England.

BOOK II

ENGLAND

1649–1714

CHAPTER VII

Cromwell

1649–60

I. THE SOCIALIST REVOLT

HAVING beheaded Charles I (January 30, 1649), the victorious Puritans faced the problems of constructing a new government and restoring the security of life and property in an England disordered by seven years of civil war. The Rump Parliament—the fifty-six active members that remained of the Long Parliament after "Pride's Purge" (1648)—proclaimed the supremacy and sufficiency of the Commons, abolished the House of Lords (February 6, 1649) and the monarchy, and nominated as its executive arm a Council of State composed of three generals, three peers, three judges, and thirty members of the House, all Independents—i.e., republican Puritans. On May 19 the Commons officially established the English republic: "England shall hereafter be governed as a Commonwealth, or Free State, by the supreme authority of this nation, the representatives of the people in Parliament, and by such as they shall appoint and constitute as ministers under them for the good of the people."[1] The republic was not a democracy; the Parliament claimed a democratic base, but the expulsion of Royalist members during the war, and of Presbyterians in the Purge, had "winnowed and sifted it," said Cromwell, "and brought it to a handful."[2] In its origin the Parliament had been elected by property owners only; now whole counties were without delegates in the Rump. Its power rested not on the people but on the army. Only the army could protect it from the royalist rebels in England, the Catholic rebels in Ireland, the Presbyterian rebels in Scotland, and the radical rebels in the army itself.

To meet the expenses of the government, and the arrears of pay due to the army, the Rump levied taxes as lavishly as the late King. It proposed to confiscate the property of all who had borne arms for Charles, but in most cases it compromised by taking a fine equal to a part—from one tenth to one half—of the capital value of the estate. Many young nobles, facing impoverishment in England, migrated to America and founded aristocratic families like the Washingtons, the Randolphs, the Madisons, the Lees.* Some royalist leaders were executed, some were imprisoned. Even

---

* The American Civil War renewed the English Civil War by pitting the descendants of English aristocrats in the South against the descendants of English Puritans in the North.

so, the royalist movement remained troublesome, for royalist sentiment predominated among the people. The execution of the King had turned him from a tax collector into a martyr. Ten days after that regicide a book appeared under the title of *Eikon Basilike*—i.e., a royal portrait. It had been written by John Gauden, a Presbyterian minister, but it purported to be the thoughts and feelings of Charles as set down by his own hand shortly before his death. Some of it may have been elaborated from notes left by the King.[3] In any case the picture presented by it was that of a tender-hearted ruler who had actually been defending England against the tyranny of a merciless oligarchy. Within a year the book sold thirty-six editions; it was translated into five languages, and not all the thunder of Milton's *Eikonoklastes* (1649) could cancel its effect. It shared in promoting a public reaction against the new government, and encouraged the royalist agents who in every county of England began at once to agitate for the restoration of the Stuart dynasty. The Council of State met the movement with widespread and efficient espionage, and the prompt arrest of leaders who might have organized a revolt.

At the other extreme a minority of the populace and a large part of the army demanded a more thorough, some a socialist, democracy. The sky rained radical pamphlets; Colonel John Lilburne alone produced a hundred; Milton, at this stage, was not a poet but a pamphleteer. Lilburne attacked Cromwell as a tyrant, an apostate, a hypocrite. One writer complained that "you shall scarce speak to Cromwell about any thing but he will lay his hand on his breast, elevate his eyes, and call God to record. He will weep, howl, and repent, even while he doth smite you under the fifth rib."[4] Another pamphleteer asked: "We were ruled before by King, Lords, and Commons, now by a General, Court Martial, and Commons; and we pray you, what is the difference?"[5] The new government felt compelled to censure press and pulpit sternly. In April, 1649, Lilburne and three others were arrested for issuing two pamphlets that described England as in "new chains." The army clamored for their release, and their women threatened Cromwell's life if any harm came to the prisoners. From prison Lilburne sent to his printer a defiant *Impeachment of High Treason against Cromwell and Ireton*. In October the four writers were tried in a *cause célèbre* that drew thousands of people about the court. Lilburne challenged the judges, and appealed to a jury. When all four were acquitted there went up from the crowd "such a loud and unanimous shout as is believed was never heard in Guildhall, which lasted for about half an hour without intermission, which made the judges for fear turn pale."[6] For two years Lilburne was the hero of the army. In 1652 he was banished; he returned in 1653, was again arrested, was again acquitted (August, 1653); he was kept in prison nevertheless. In 1655 he was released; in 1657 he died, aged forty-three.

Some "Levellers" went beyond Lilburne and democracy to call for a more equal distribution of goods. Why, they asked, should there be rich and poor? Why should some starve while the rich engrossed the land? In April, 1649, a "prophet" named William Everard led four men to St. George's Hill in Surrey; they took possession of some unoccupied land, dug the earth, planted seed, and invited recruits; some thirty other "Diggers," as they came to be called, joined them, and (said a report to the Council of State) "they threaten the neighbors that they will shortly make them all come up to the hills and work."[7] Haled before Sir Thomas Fairfax, captain general of the army, Everard explained that his followers proposed to respect private property, "only to meddle with what is common and untilled, and make it fruitful," but they hoped "that the time will suddenly be when all men shall willingly come in and give up their lands and estates, and submit to this Community of Goods."[8] Fairfax released the men as harmless fanatics. One of them, Gerrard Winstanley, continued the movement with a manifesto (April 26, 1649) entitled *The True Leveller's Standard Advanced*: "In the beginning the great Creator Reason made the earth a common treasury for beasts and men"; but then man, falling into blindness, became a greater slave to his own kind than the beasts of the field to him; the earth was bought and sold and hedged in by rulers, and was kept in the possession of a few. All landlords are thieves. Only when common ownership is restored will crime and hatred cease.[9] In *The Law of Freedom* (1652) Winstanley begged the Commonwealth to establish a society in which there would be no buying or selling, no lawyers, no rich or poor; all to be compelled to work till forty, then to be absolved from toil; the franchise to be open to all adult males; marriage to be a civil ceremony, and divorce to be free.[10] The Diggers abandoned their scheme, but their propaganda entered into the memory of the English poor, and perhaps crossed the Channel to France and the sea to America.

Cromwell, himself a property owner and well versed in the nature of man, put no trust in these ideals of common ownership, or even of adult suffrage. In the confusion inevitable after the violent overthrow of a government, some centralized authority was needed, and Cromwell supplied it. Many who hated him as a regicide welcomed for a time a dictatorship that seemed the sole alternative to social and political dissolution. And even the army, when it heard that counterrevolution was brewing in Ireland and Scotland, was glad that his iron hand was ready to lead it against rebels who sought not a democratic utopia, but a restored and vengeful monarchy.

II. THE IRISH REVOLT

In Ireland the reaction against the Great Rebellion united transiently the Protestants of the Pale and the Catholics in it and beyond. Even before the execution of Charles I James Butler, Earl of Ormonde, as lord lieutenant in Ireland, signed a treaty with the Confederate Catholics at Kilkenny (January 17, 1649), by which, in return for religious freedom and an independent Irish Parliament, they agreed to furnish him with fifteen thousand infantry and five hundred horse. Ormonde sent a message to the Prince of Wales, whom he immediately recognized as Charles II, inviting him to come to Ireland and lead a combined army of Protestants and Catholics. Charles chose to go to Scotland, but Cromwell decided to meet the Irish threat first.

When he landed at Dublin in August, Ormonde had already been defeated at Rathmines by troops adhering to the Commonwealth, and had retreated with his remaining 2,300 men into the fortified town of Drogheda on the Boyne. Cromwell besieged it with ten thousand soldiers, took it by storm (September 10, 1649), and ordered all the surviving garrison killed.[11] Some civilians were included in the massacre; every priest in the town was slain;[12] altogether some 2,300 died in this triumphant slaughter. Cromwell shared the credit with God: "I wish that all honest hearts may give the glory of this to God, to whom indeed the praise of this mercy belongs."[13] He hoped that "this bitterness will save much effusion of blood, through the goodness of God";[14] and we may allow his sincere belief that one such act of terror would quickly end the rebellion and save many lives on both sides.

But the war continued for three years. From Drogheda Cromwell passed to the siege of Wexford; it was soon taken; fifteen hundred of its defenders and inhabitants were slain; "God, by an unexpected providence in His righteous justice," reported Cromwell, "brought a just judgment upon them ... with their bloods to answer the cruelties which they had exercised upon the lives of divers poor Protestants."[15] The policy of massacre failed. The towns of Duncannon and Waterford defied Cromwell's siege; Kilkenny surrendered only after receiving terms that elsewhere had been refused; Clonmel was taken, but after a loss of two thousand men. Hearing that Charles II had reached Scotland, Cromwell left the further prosecution of the Irish war to his son-in-law Henry Ireton, and sailed to England (May 24, 1650).

Ireton was an able leader, but he died of plague on November 26, 1651. The policy of massacre was abandoned, pardon was offered to the rebels, and by the Articles of Kilkenny (May 12, 1652) nearly all of them surrendered on condition of being allowed to emigrate unhindered. An "Act for the Settling of Ireland" (August 12) confiscated part or all of the property of Irishmen—of whatever faith—who could not prove that they had been loyal to the Commonwealth; in this way 2,500,000 acres of Irish soil were transferred to English or Irish soldiers or civilians who had supported Cromwell in Ireland; two thirds of the soil of Ireland passed into the hands of Englishmen.[16] The counties of Kildare, Dublin, Carlow, Wicklow, and Wexford were formed into a new English Pale, and an attempt was made to exclude from them all Irish proprietors, then all Irishmen. Thousands of Irish families were dispossessed, and were given until March 1, 1655, to find other homes. Hundreds were shipped to Barbados or elsewhere on a charge of vagrancy.

Sir William Petty calculated that out of a total population of 1,466,000 in Ireland in 1641, 616,000 had perished by 1652, by war, starvation or plague. In some counties, said an English officer, "a man might travel twenty or thirty miles and not see a living creature, either man or beast or bird." "The sun," said another, "never shined upon a nation so completely miserable."[17] The Catholic religion was outlawed; all Catholic clergymen were ordered to leave Ireland within twenty days; to harbor a priest was made punishable by death; severe penalties were decreed for absence from Protestant services on Sunday; magistrates were authorized to take away the children of Catholics and send them to England for education in the Protestant faith.[18] All the inhumanity that was to be visited by Catholics upon the Protestants of France in 1680–90 was visited by Protestants upon the Catholics of Ireland in 1650–60. Catholicism became an inseparable part of Irish patriotism because the Church and the people were fused in a community of suffering. Those bitter years remained in Irish memory as an undying heritage of hate.

III. THE SCOTTISH REVOLT

The Scots, who had surrendered Charles I to the English Parliament, were shocked by his execution, suddenly remembering that his father was a Scot. They looked upon Pride's Purge of Presbyterians from the Long Parliament as a violation of the Solemn League and Covenant by which that Parliament had sworn fidelity to Scotland and the Presbyterian faith; they feared that the victorious Puritans would attempt to force their own form of Protestantism upon Scotland as well as England. On February 5, 1649, less than a week after the beheading of Charles I, the Scottish Parliament or Estates proclaimed his son Charles II, then in the Netherlands, to be the rightful King of Great Britain, France, and Ireland.

Before they would allow his entry into Scotland they required him to sign the National Covenant and the Solemn League and Covenant, and swear to maintain or establish Presbyterian Protestantism in all his dominions and in his household. Charles II, who was already a mixture of Catholicism and skepticism, had no talent for Presbyterianism, but much relish for a throne; he reluctantly signed all these demands at Breda on May 1, 1650. Montrose, noblest of the Scots in this age, led a small force from the Orkneys into Scotland, hoping to raise for Charles an army independent of the Covenanters; he was defeated, captured, and hanged (May 21, 1650). On June 23 Charles landed in Scotland, eager to head an army against the Puritan Commonwealth that had beheaded his father. Before the Scots would fight for him they induced him to issue a declaration in which he desired to be "deeply humbled before God because of his father's opposition to the Solemn League and Covenant, and because his mother had been guilty of idolatry" (Catholicism).[19] To expiate the sins of Charles I and II the Scottish clergy ordained, for the army and the people, a solemn fast, and assured the army that now—the young King having made amends to Heaven—it would be invincible.[20] On the insistence of the ministers all officers who put loyalty to the King above loyalty to the Covenant and the Kirk were purged from the army; in this way eighty of its ablest leaders were discharged.

Cromwell proposed to the English Parliament that he invade Scotland at once, without waiting for a Scottish attack. Fairfax, who had refused to take part in the trial of Charles I, now resigned his supreme command of the Commonwealth armies. Cromwell, appointed to succeed him, organized his forces with his usual decision and speed, and crossed into Scotland (July 22, 1650) at the head of sixteen thousand men. On August 3 he sent to the Commission of the General Assembly of the Scottish Kirk a letter full of intestinal fortitude: "Is it infallibly agreeable to the Word of God, all that *you* say? I beseech you, in the bowels of Christ, think it possible that you may be mistaken."[21] At Dunbar (September 3) he routed the main Scottish armies, taking ten thousand prisoners; soon he held Edinburgh and Leith. The Scottish preachers lost face and infallibility; the purged officers were hastily recalled. Charles II was formally crowned at Scone. Cromwell took sick in Edinburgh, and for some months the conflict marked time.

Then the reorganized Scottish army, with Charles at its head, marched into England, hoping that all good royalists and Presbyterians would come to the banner of legitimacy and truth. Cromwell pursued them, gathering local militia as he passed through the English towns. At Worcester (September 3, 1651) the battle was fought that preserved the Commonwealth and made Charles again an exile; by superior strategy and courage Cromwell's lesser forces defeated thirty thousand Scots. Charles was brave but he was no general. He strove to rally his disordered troops, but they seemed awed and palsied by Cromwell's reputation as a warrior who never lost a battle; many of them threw down their arms and fled. Charles begged his officers to shoot him; they refused, and a few of his most devoted followers led him to temporary safety in a royalist home. There he cut his hair close to his head, discolored his hands and face, exchanged his clothes for those of a laborer, and began a long march, on horse and foot, hunted from one hiding place to another, sleeping in attics, barns, or woods, once in a "Royal Oak" tree in Boscobel while Commonwealth soldiers searched for him below. Often recognized, never betrayed, he and his party, after forty days of flight, found at Shoreham, in Sussex, a vessel whose captain agreed, at the risk of his life, to take them to France (October 15).

Cromwell entrusted to General George Monck the further suppression of the Scottish rebels; by February, 1652, this was complete. Scotland was made subject to England, its separate Parliament was dissolved, but the country was allowed to send thirty delegates to the London Parliament. The Kirk was chastened by the prohibition of its general assemblies, and by the toleration of all peaceful Protestant sects. Economically, Scotland benefited from the new freedom of trade with England. Politically it waited and prayed for a Stuart restoration.

IV. OLIVER ABSOLUTE

Cromwell returned in modest triumph to London. Seeing the multitude that had collected to witness his arrival, he remarked that a still greater crowd would have gathered to see him hanged.[22] The Rump Parliament gave him an annual allowance of four thousand pounds, and the once royal palace at Hampton Court. It trusted that he would be content to remain its general. It proposed a new election to raise its membership to four hundred, but the present members were to retain their seats without re-election, and were to determine the conditions of the franchise and the validity of the votes. It protected itself against criticism by rigidly restricting the freedom of pulpit and press: "Nothing by pretence of pulpit liberty shall be suffered in prejudice of the peace and honour of the government."[23] The clergy of the Anglican Established Church were dispossessed of their livings. Persons who professed the Catholic faith were condemned to forfeit two thirds of their property. Rewards were offered for the apprehension of Catholic priests.[24]

Cromwell, though slow to make up his mind, was prompt to act when he had reached a decision. He suffered impatiently the long debates that in Parliament confused policy and obstructed administration; he agreed with Charles I that the executive power should be distinct and free from the legislative. He began to wonder might it not be a blessing if Cromwell were king. He hinted the idea (December, 1652) to his friend Whitelocke, who lost his friendship by objecting.[25] On the morning of April 20, 1653, hearing that the Rump was about to make itself the unelected master of the new Parliament, he gathered a handful of soldiers, stationed them at the door of the House, entered it with Major General Thomas Harrison at his side, and for a time listened in dark silence to the discussion. When the question was put to the vote he rose and spoke, at first with moderation, soon with fury. He denounced the Rump as a self-perpetuating oligarchy unfit to govern England. "Drunkards!" he cried, indicating one member. "Whoremaster!" he shouted at another. "You are no Parliament. I say you are no Parliament. I will put an end to your sittings." Turning to Harrison, he ordered, "Call them in, call them in." His soldiery marched into the chamber; Cromwell commanded them to clear the room; the members left, protesting, "This is not honest"; the empty hall was locked, and next day a notice was found tacked to the door: "This house to lett, now unfurnished."[26] Going to the room where the Council of State was in session, Cromwell, accompanied by two generals, told it, "If you are met here as private persons, you shall not be disturbed; but if as a Council of State, this is no place for you. . . . Take notice that the Parliament is dissolved."[27] So ignominiously ended the Long Parliament, which had sat at Westminster, in full or in Rump, since 1640, and had transformed the constitution and government of England. Now there was no constitution, only an army and an untitled king.

Generally the people were glad to have done with a Parliament that had shaken England to the verge of anarchy. According to Cromwell, there was "not so much as the barking of a dog, or any . . . visible repining at its dissolution."[28] Ardent Puritans accepted the expulsion as clearing the way for the Fifth Monarchy—i.e., the promised coming and rule of Christ. Royalists took heart, and whispered that Cromwell would now call back Charles II and content himself with a dukedom, or the viceroyalty of Ireland. But Oliver was not the man to sit content under another's will. He instructed his military aides to choose—chiefly from the Puritan congregations of England—140 men, including five from Scotland and six from Ireland, to meet as a "Nominated Parliament." When it assembled at Whitehall on July 4, 1653, Cromwell confessed that it had been chosen by the army, but he hailed it as beginning a veritable reign of saints under the presidency of Jesus Christ,[29] and proposed to devolve upon it the supreme authority and the task of devising a new constitution. For five months it struggled with this assignment, but it lost itself in long debates, and divided hopelessly on questions of religion and toleration. London wits called it "Barebone's Parliament," from one of its members, Praise-God Barebon, a Fifth Monarchy saint.

The army tired of these men as it had tired of those it had expelled in April. The officers, playing Antony, proposed to Cromwell that he make himself king; Caesar gently demurred, but on December 12 eighty members of the Parliament, at the pointed suggestion of the army, announced to Cromwell that the new assembly could come to no agreement, and was voting its own dissolution. An "Instrument of Government" prepared by army leaders proposed that Cromwell be "Lord Protector of the Commonwealth of England, Scotland, and Ireland"; that another Parliament be elected on a property-qualification franchise, excluding royalists and Catholics; and that the executive power be vested in a Council of eight civilians and seven army officers, chosen for life, and serving as adviser to both the Protector and the Parliament. Cromwell accepted and signed this "first and last written English constitution,"[30] and took oath as lord protector on December 16, 1653. The Commonwealth ended, the Protectorate began—two names for Oliver Cromwell.

Was he a despot? Obviously he relished power, but this is a common taste, and most natural to conscious ability. He had thought of making himself king, and of establishing a new royal line.[31] He seems to have been sincere in offering to surrender his power to the Nominated Parliament, but its incompetence convinced him that his own executive authority was the sole present alternative to chaos; if he stepped down there seemed no one who could command sufficient support to maintain order. The radicals in the army condemned the Protectorate as just another monarchy; they denounced Cromwell as "a dissembling perjured villain," and threatened him with "a worse fate than had befallen the last tyrant."[32] Some of these rebels he sent to the Tower, including the Major General Harrison who had led the soldiers in expelling the Rump. Cromwell's fear for his own safety led him more and more toward absolutism, for he knew that half the nation would have welcomed his assassination. Like other rulers, he felt the need to surround himself with awe-inspiring splendor and dignity; he moved into Whitehall Palace (1654), refurnished it sumptuously, and adopted royal state;[33] but doubtless much of this show was to impress ambassadors and awe the populace.

Privately he was a man without airs, living simply and devotedly with his mother, wife, and children. His mother loved him fearfully, trembling for his life at every musket shot; dying at ninety-three (1654), she said, "My dear son, I leave my heart with thee."[34] He himself, in his middle fifties, was aging rapidly; crisis after crisis had shaken his supposedly iron nerves; the campaigns in Ireland and Scotland had added fever to his gout; and every day was passed in trouble and anxiety. Lely painted a remarkable portrait of him in 1650. Everyone knows Cromwell's admonition to the painter: "Mr. Lely, I desire you would use all your skill to paint my picture truly like me, and not flatter me at all; but remark all these roughnesses, pimples, warts, and everything; otherwise I never will pay a farthing for it."[35] Lely took his fee in his hands and polished the Protector considerably; nevertheless he caught well the stern strong face, incarnate will—and also a nervous spirit strained to the breaking point.

Cromwell was criticized for the somber simplicity of his usual dress—a plain black coat and suit; but on official occasions he donned a coat embroidered with gold. In public he maintained an unostentatious dignity; privately he indulged in amusements and jesting, even in practical jokes and occasional buffoonery.[36] He loved music, and played the organ well.[37] His religious piety was apparently sincere,[38] but he took the name of the Lord (not in vain) so often in support for his purposes that many accused him of hypocrisy. Probably there was some hypocrisy in his public piety, little in the private piety that all who knew him attested. His letters and speeches are half sermons; and there is no question that he assumed too readily that God was his right hand. His private morals were impeccable, his public morals were no better than those of other rulers; he used deception or force when he thought them necessary to his major purposes. No one has yet reconciled Christianity with government.

He was not technically absolute. Pursuant to the Instrument of Government, a Council of State was formed and a Parliament was elected. Despite all efforts of the Protector and the army to ensure the return of complaisant delegates, the Commons that convened on September 3, 1654, contained some troublesome republicans, even some royalists. A struggle ensued as to whether the Parliament or the Protector should control the army. Parliament proposed to reduce the number and pay of the soldiers; they rebelled, and persuaded Cromwell to dismiss the Parliament (January 22, 1655). Actually the government of England had been a military dictatorship since Pride had purged the Parliament in 1648.

Cromwell was now driven to govern without pretense of any other than martial law. In the summer of 1655 he divided England into twelve military districts, and over each district he stationed a corps of soldiers headed by a major general. To support the expense of this establishment he laid a tax of ten per cent upon all Royalist estates. The people protested, criticism and rebellion spread, voices were heard calling for the restoration of Charles II. Cromwell replied with stricter censorship, wider espionage, arbitrary arrests, and star-chamber proceedings that bypassed juries and habeas corpus.[39] "Sir Harry" Vane was among the former revolutionists who found their way to jail. Revolutions eat their fathers.

Needing more money than he dared raise by further direct taxes, Cromwell summoned another Parliament. When it assembled (September 17, 1656), his Council of State posted army officers at the door of the House, and forbade entry to 103 members duly elected but suspected of republican, royalist, Presbyterian, or Catholic sympathies. The excluded members signed a remonstrance denouncing the exclusion as a flagrant violation of their constituents' expressed will, and they branded as rank hypocrisy "the practice of the tyrant to use the name of God and religion, and formal fasts and prayer, to color the blackness of the fact."[40] Of the 352 members who passed the Council's scrutiny, 175 were army men, or appointees or relatives of Cromwell. The reduced and submissive Parliament presented to the Protector (March 31, 1657) "An Humble Petition and Advice" asking him to take the title of king. Sensing opposition to this in the army, Cromwell refused, but a compromise gave him the right to name his successor as lord protector. In January, 1658, he consented to readmit the excluded members to the House; at the same time he chose nine peers and sixty-one commoners to sit as a Second House. Many army officers refused to support this move. When they entered into an agreement with the republicans in the Commons to limit the powers of the Second House, Cromwell lost his temper, invaded Westminster Palace, and dismissed the Parliament (February 4, 1658). Now in law, as well as in fact, the English republic ended, and monarchy was restored. History had given another illustration to Plato's sardonic sequence of monarchy, aristocracy, democracy, dictatorship, and monarchy.[41]

V. PURITAN HEYDAY

The Puritan victory involved a religious revolution. The Church of England had been broken up in 1643 by the abolition of the episcopacy. The Presbyterian form of Protestantism—in which the congregations were ruled by ministers governed by district synods subject to a general assembly—had been made the official religion of the state in 1646, but this Presbyterian dominance ended two years later when Pride purged the Presbyterians from Parliament. For a time it seemed that religion was to be left free of state control or subsidy. But Cromwell (who came to agree in almost everything with the King whom he had killed) believed that a state-endowed church was indispensable to education and morals. In 1654 he appointed a "Commission of Triers" to test clergymen for fitness to receive a benefice and stipend. Only Independents (Puritans), Baptists, and Presbyterians were eligible. Each parish was allowed to choose between the presbyterian form of organization and the congregational form

—in which each congregation ruled itself. The Puritans adopted the congregational form; the presbyterian system, which prevailed in Scotland, was largely confined in England to London and Lancashire. The Anglican clergy, once so powerful, were ejected from their livings, and ministered to their followers in secret places, like the Catholic priests. In 1657 John Evelyn was arrested for attending Anglican services.[42] Catholicism was still outlawed. Two priests were hanged (1650, 1654) for "seducing the people," and in 1657 the Puritan Parliament, with Cromwell's consent, passed an act by which any person over sixteen years old who did not disavow Catholicism was to suffer the forfeiture of two thirds of his property.[43] By 1650 religion had taken on a measure of social stratification: the poor favored the dissenting sects—Baptists, Quakers, Fifth Monarchy Men, etc.—or the Catholics; the middle classes were predominantly Puritans; the aristocracy and most of the gentry (untitled landowners) adhered to the disestablished Anglican Church.

Intolerance was inverted rather than lessened. Instead of Anglicans persecuting Catholics, Dissenters, and Puritans, the triumphant Puritans, who formerly had clamored for toleration, now persecuted Catholics, Dissenters, and Anglicans. They forbade the use of the Book of Common Prayer, even in the privacy of homes. The Puritan Parliaments limited toleration to those Britons who accepted the Trinity, the Reformation, the Bible as God's Word, and the rejection of bishops. Socinians or Unitarians were therefore beyond toleration. Severe penalties were decreed for any criticism of the Calvinistic creed or ritual.[44] Cromwell was more lenient than his Parliaments. He connived at some Anglican services, and permitted a small number of Jews to live in London, even to build a synagogue. Two Anabaptist preachers denounced him as the Beast of the Apocalypse, but he bore with them patiently.[45] He used his influence to check the persecution of Huguenots in France and of Waldenses in Piedmont; but when Mazarin asked in return more toleration of Catholics in England, Cromwell pleaded his inability to control the zeal of the Puritans.[46]

Perhaps only among the Jews did religion play so pervasive a role in everyday life as among the Puritans; and indeed Puritanism agreed with Judaism in almost everything except the divinity of Christ. Literacy was encouraged in order that the Bible might be read by all. The Old Testament was loved with a special devotion, because it offered the model of a society dominated by religion. The main business of life was to escape the fires of hell; the Devil was real and everywhere, and only the grace of God could enable a chosen few to inherit salvation. Biblical phrases and imagery permeated the utterances of the Puritans; thoughts and visions of God or Christ (but never of Mary) brightened and terrified their minds. Their clothing was modest, somber, and unadorned; their speech was grave and slow. They were expected to abstain from all profane amusements and sensual pleasure. The theaters, which had been closed in 1642 because of war, remained closed till 1656 because of Puritan condemnation. Horse races, cockfights, wrestling matches, bear or bull baiting, were forbidden; and to make sure that the bears in London would be baited no more the Puritan Colonel Newson killed them all.[47] All maypoles were pulled down. Beauty was suspect. Women were respected as faithful wives and good mothers; elsewise they were in bad odor with the Puritans as temptresses, and as the cause of man's expulsion from Paradise. Music was frowned upon, except in hymns. Art was destroyed in the churches, and none was produced except for some excellent portraits by Samuel Cooper and by Peter Lely—who was a Dutchman.

The Puritan attempt to legislate morality was probably the most thoroughgoing since the Mosaic Law. Civil marriage was recognized as valid and divorce was allowed, but adultery was made a capital crime; however, after two executions on this head no jury would convict. Oaths were punished on a class-graduated scale; they cost a duke twice as much as a baron, three times as much as a squire, ten times as much as a commoner; one man was fined for saying "God is my witness."[48] Wednesday was a day of obligatory fasting from meat, even if it coincided with Christmas, and soldiers were authorized to invade homes to see that the fasts were observed. No shops were to be opened on Sunday, no games or sports were then to be played, no worldly work was to be done, and no avoidable travel was permitted; "vainly and profanely walking on the day" was prohibited.[49] Despite the Restoration and its moral relapse, the English Sunday remained "blue" till our time.

Many of these legal or social taboos proved too severe for human nature. We are told that a large proportion of the population under Cromwell became hypocrites, sinning as usual, pursuing money, women, and power, but always with a long face, a nasal twang, and religious phrases dripping from the tongue. And yet a great number of Puritans seem to have lived up to their Gospel with sincerity and courage. We shall find two thousand Puritan preachers accepting poverty under the Restoration rather than abandon their principles. The Puritan regimen narrowed the mind but stengthened the will and the character. It helped to prepare Englishmen for self-rule. If the home was darkened by fear of hell and by Puritan ordinances, the family life of the common people was given an order and purity that survived the demoralization of the elite in the reign of Charles II. All in all, the Puritan regime probably effected a moral betterment which—renewed and reinforced by Methodism in the eighteenth century—may deserve much of the credit for the comparatively high morality of the British nation today.

VI. THE QUAKERS

All the virtues of the Puritans shone in their offshoot the Quakers, however obscured for a time with fantasies and bigotry. The fear of both God and Satan was so strong in them that sometimes it set their bodies trembling, and gave them a name. Said one of them, Robert Barclay, in 1679:

> The power of God will break forth into a whole meeting, and there will be such an inward travail, while each is seeking to overcome the evil in themselves, that by the strong workings of these opposite powers, like the going of two opposite tides, every individual will be strongly exercised as in a day of battle, and thereby trembling and a motion of the body will be upon most, if not upon all, which, as the Power of Truth prevails, will from pangs and groans end with a sweet sound of thanksgiving and praise. And from this the name of *Quakers*, i.e., Tremblers, was first reproachably passed upon us.[50]

The explanation of their founder, George Fox, is slightly different: "Justice Bennet of Derby was the first that called us Quakers, because we bid them tremble at the word of the Lord. This was in 1650."[51] Their own name for their sect was the Friends of Truth, and later, more modestly, the Society of Friends.

Apparently they were at first Puritans with an especially strong conviction that their hesitations between virtue and sin were the struggles, in their minds and bodies, of two spiritual forces, one good and the other evil, to possess them here and through all eternity. They accepted the basic tenets of the Puritans—the divine inspiration of the Scriptures, the fall of Adam and Eve, the natural sinfulness of man, the redeeming death of Christ the Son of God, and the possibility of the Holy Ghost or Spirit coming from heaven to enlighten and ennoble the individual soul. To perceive and feel this Inner Light, to welcome its guidance, was to the Quaker the essence of religion; if a man followed that Light he needed no preacher or priest, and no church. That Light was superior to human reason, even to the Holy Bible itself, for it was the direct voice of God to the soul.

George Fox was a man with little education, but the *Journal* that he wrote is an English classic, revealing the literary power of unliterary speech if simple, earnest, and sincere. Son of a weaver, apprenticed to a shoemaker, he left his master and his relatives "at the command of God," and began at the age of twenty-three (1647) the perambulant preaching that ended only with his death in 1691. In those early years he was beset with temptations, and went to clergymen for counsel. One prescribed medicine and bloodletting, another recommended tobacco and psalms.[52] George lost faith in ministers, but whenever he opened the Scriptures he found solace.

> Often I took my Bible, and went and sate in hollow trees and lonesome places till night came on; and frequently in the night walked mournfully about by myself, for I was a man of sorrows in the times of the first workings of the Lord in me. . . . Then the Lord led me along, and let me see His love, which was endless and eternal, surpassing all the knowledge that men have in the natural state, and can get by history or books.[53]

Soon he felt that the divine love had chosen him to preach the Inner Light to all. At a meeting of Baptists in Leicestershire "the Lord opened my mouth, and the everlasting truth was declared amongst them, and the power of the Lord was over them all."[54] A report spread that he had "a discerning spirit," whereupon many came to hear him. "The Lord's power broke forth, and I had great openings [revelations] and prophecies."[55] "As I was walking in the fields, the Lord said unto me: 'Thy name is written in the Lamb's book of life, which was before the foundation of the world' "[56] —i.e., George was now comforted with the thought that he was among that minority of men chosen by God, before the Creation, to receive His grace and eternal bliss. Now he felt equal to any man, and the pride of this divine election forbade him "to put off my hat to any, high or low; and I was required to Thee and Thou all men and women, without respect to rich or poor, great or small."[57]

Convinced that true religion was found not in churches but only in the enlightened heart, he entered a church near Nottingham, and interrupted the sermon by crying out that the test of truth was not in the Scriptures but in the Inner Light. He was arrested (1649), but the sheriff released him, and the sheriff's wife became one of his first converts. He resumed his missionary wandering, entered another church, and: "I was moved to declare the truth to the priest and the people, but the people fell upon me in great rage, struck me down . . . , and I was cruelly beaten and bruised by them with their hands, Bibles, and sticks." He was again arrested; the magistrate let him go, but the populace stoned him out of the town.[58] At Derby he preached against churches and sacraments as vain approaches to God; he was committed to a house of correction for six months (1650). He was offered release if he would join the army; he replied by preaching against war. His jailers now put him "into a lousy, stinking place, low in the ground, without any bed, among thirty felons, where I was kept almost half a year."[59] From his prison he wrote to judges and magistrates arguing against capital punishment, and his intercession may have helped to save from the gallows a young woman who had been condemned to death for stealing.

After a year of imprisonment he resumed his peripatetic gospel. At Wakefield he converted James Nayler. At Beverley he entered a church, listened till the sermon was over, and then asked the preacher was he not ashamed to "take three hundred pounds a year for preaching the Scriptures?"[60] In another town the minister invited him to preach in the church; he refused, but addressed a crowd in the churchyard.

> I declared to the people that I came not to hold up their idol temples, nor their priests, nor their tithes, nor . . . their Jewish and heathenish ceremonies and traditions (for I denied all these), and told them that that piece of ground was no more holy than any other. . . . Therefore I exhorted the people to come off from all these things, and directed them to the spirit and grace of God in themselves, and to the light of Jesus in their own hearts.[61]

At Swarthmore, in Yorkshire, he converted Margaret Fell, and then her husband, Judge Thomas Fell; their home, Swarthmore Hall, became the first substantial meeting place of the Quakers, and is to this day a shrine of pilgrimage for Friends.

We must not follow Fox's story further. His methods were crude, but he atoned for them by the patience with which he bore a long succession of arrests and buffetings. Puritans, Presbyterians, and Anglicans attacked him, for he rejected sacraments, churches, and ministers. Magistrates sent the Quakers to jail not only for disturbing public worship, and seducing soldiers with pacifism, but also for refusing to swear allegiance to the government. The Quakers protested that oaths of any kind are immoral; Yea or Nay should be enough. Cromwell sympathized with the Quakers, gave Fox a friendly interview (1654) and, parting, said, "Come again to my house; if thou and I were but an hour of a day together, we should be nearer one to the other."[62] In 1657 the Protector ordered the release of imprisoned Quakers, and sent instructions to all justices to treat these churchless preachers "as persons under a strong delusion."[63]

The worst persecution had fallen to the lot of James Nayler, who carried the doctrine of the Inner Light to the point of believing, or pretending, that he was Christ reincarnate. Fox reprimanded him, but some devoted followers worshiped him, and one woman affirmed that he had restored her to life after she had been two days dead. When Nayler rode into Bristol women threw their scarves before his horse, and chanted, "Holy, holy, holy is the Lord God of Hosts." He was arrested on a charge of blasphemy. Questioned as to the claims made by or for him, he would make no other answer but Christ's "Thou hast said it." Parliament, then predominantly

Puritan, took up his case (1656), and for eleven days debated whether he should be put to death. The motion was lost by ninety-six to eighty-two, but by a spirit of humane compromise he was sentenced to stand for two hours with his neck in a pillory, to receive 310 lashes, to have the letter *B* (for blasphemer) burned into his forehead, and to have his tongue bored through with a red-hot iron. He suffered these atrocities bravely; his followers hailed him as a martyr; they kissed and sucked his wounds. He was committed to solitary confinement, without pen, paper, fire, or light. Gradually his spirit broke; he confessed that he had been deluded. He was released in 1659, and died destitute in 1660.[64]

The Quakers distinguished themselves by what seemed to some of their contemporaries to be troublesome peculiarities. They allowed no ornaments on their clothing. They refused to take off their hats to any person, of whatever rank, even in church or palace or at court. They addressed all persons by the singular *thou* or *thee*, instead of by the originally honorific plural *you*. They rejected the pagan names of the days of the week and the months of the year, saying, for example, "the first day of the sixth month." They worshiped as readily in the open as indoors. Each worshiper was invited to tell what the Holy Ghost had inspired him to say; then all practiced a reverent silence, probably as a sedative after enthusiasm—which originally meant "feeling a god within." Women were admitted to worship and preaching on the same terms as men. Matter-of-fact Britons resented the tendency of the early Quakers to the intemperate denunciation of other sects, and to a certain pride in election and virtue. Otherwise the Friends were model Christians. They did not resist evil, they accepted with only verbal protests the vilest conditions of imprisonment, they did not strike back at those who beat them. They gave as they could to all who asked. Their married life was beyond reproach. Their rule against marrying any but another Quaker limited their growth; nevertheless by 1660 there were sixty thousand Friends in England. Their reputation for honesty, courtesy, industry, and thrift raised them from the humble ranks in which they first appeared into the middle classes that claim most of them today.

VII. DEATH AND TAXES

It was the middle classes that prospered most under Cromwell; above all, the merchants engaged in foreign trade. Parilament now included many men representing or possessing commercial interests. It was in their behalf that the Navigation Act of 1651 required all colonial imports into Britain to be carried in English ships—a measure obviously aimed at the Dutch. Cromwell at times played with the idea of an alliance with the United

Provinces for the protection and advancement of Protestantism, but the London merchants preferred profits to piety, and soon (1652) Cromwell found himself engaged in the First Dutch War. The results, as we have seen, were encouraging.

The imperialistic fever rose as the navy grew. Memories of Hawkins and Drake suggested to the merchants and to Cromwell that the Spanish hegemony in the Americas might be broken, the lucrative trade in slaves could be captured for England, and the precious metals of the New World could be directed to London; moreover, as Cromwell explained, the conquest of the West Indies would enable English preachers to convert those islands from Catholicism to Protestantism.[65] On August 5, 1654, Cromwell sent to Philip IV of Spain assurances of friendship. In October he dispatched a fleet under Blake to the Mediterranean, and in December another, under William Penn (father of the Quaker) and Robert Venables, to seize Hispaniola from Spain. The latter attempt failed, but Penn captured Jamaica for England (1655).

On November 3, 1655, Cromwell and Mazarin, both subordinating religion to politics, signed an Anglo-French alliance against Spain. The war that Spain had continued to wage with France, after the Treaty of Westphalia (1648), had kept those powers too busy to interfere with Cromwell's rise to leadership in England; now it gave his foreign policy a brilliant if passing success. Blake for a long time watched for the Spanish Silver fleet coming from America. He found it in the harbor of Santa Cruz in the Canary Islands, and totally destroyed it (April 20, 1657). English soldiers took the lead in defeating a Spanish army in the Battle of the Dunes (June 4, 1658). When the Peace of the Pyrenees ended the war (1659), France ceded Dunkirk to England, and Cromwell appeared to have retrieved the ignominy of Mary Tudor in losing Calais a century before. He had proposed to make the name of Englishman as great as ever that of Roman had been, and he came close to realizing his aim. The mastery of the seas had now fallen to England; consequently it was only a matter of time until England would dominate North America and extend her rule in Asia. All Europe looked in awe upon this Puritan who praised God but built a navy, who preached sermons but won every battle, who founded the British Empire by martial force while invoking the name of Christ. The crowned heads who had counted him an upstart now sought his alliance, making no fuss about theology.

But John Thurloe, secretary to the Council of State, warned Cromwell that it was a mistake to help France against Spain; France was rising, Spain was declining; England's policy of supporting a balance of power on the Continent, as a surety for England's freedom, required, if not help to Spain, certainly none to France. Now (1659) France was supreme on land; the road was open for her expansion into the Netherlands, Franche-Comté, and Lorraine. Many an Englishman's life would be laid down to check the aggressive ambitions of Louis XIV.

Meanwhile the merchant princes prospered from the wars. The East India Company was reorganized in 1657 as a joint-stock enterprise; it "lent" Cromwell sixty thousand pounds to avoid governmental scrutiny of its affairs;[66] It was now a powerful factor in the economy and politics of England. The cost of the wars was met by raising taxes beyond any point reached in the reigns of Charls I or II. Most of the crown lands, those of the Anglican Church, many Royalist estates, half of Ireland, were sold by the government; even so it operated at an average annual deficit of £450,000 after 1654. The simple citizen profited little. All the goals for which the Great Rebellion of 1642–49 had been fought had now been set aside. Taxation without representation or parliamentary approval, arrest without due process of law, trial without jury, were as flagrant as before; and rule by the army and naked force was made still more offensive by being coated with religious cant. "The rule of Cromwell became hated as no government has ever been hated in England before or since."[67]

England waited impatiently for its Protector's death. Plots to assassinate him multiplied. He had to be always on the watch, and now he raised his bodyguard to 160 men. A former radical, Lieutenant Colonel Sexby, engaged one Sundercombe to kill him; the plot was detected (January, 1657). Sundercombe was arrested, and died in the Tower. In May Sexby published a pamphlet under the title *Killing No Murder*, which was an outright appeal for the murder of Cromwell. Sexby was found, and he too died in the Tower. Conspiracies against the Protector took form in the army, and in royalist circles where hope for a Stuart restoration was rising feverishly. Cromwell's eldest daughter, married to the radical Major General Charles Fleetwood, adopted republican principles, and deplored her father's dictatorship.[68]

Cares, fears, and bereavements broke the iron man's spirit. Like so many others who had tasted power to the dregs, he sometimes regretted that he had ever left the quiet of his early life as a rural squire. "I can say in the presence of God . . . I would have lived under my woodside, to have kept a flock of sheep, rather than undertook such a government as this is."[69] In August, 1658, his best-loved daughter, Elizabeth, died after a long and painful illness. Shortly after her funeral Cromwell took to bed with intermittent fever. Quinine might have cured him, but his physician rejected it as a newfangled remedy introduced into Europe by idolatrous Jesuits.[70] Cromwell seemed to recover, and spoke bravely. "Do not think that I shall die," he told his wife; "I am sure of the contrary."[71] His Council asked him to name his successor; he answered, "Richard"—his eldest son. On

September 2 he suffered a relapse, and sensed his end. He prayed God to forgive his sins and protect the Puritans. The next afternoon he died. Secretary Thurloe wrote, "He is gone to heaven, embalmed with the tears of his people, and upon the wings of the prayers of the saints."[72] When news of Cromwell's death reached Amsterdam the city "was lighted up as for a great deliverance, and children ran along the canals, shouting for joy that the Devil was dead."[73]

VIII. THE ROAD BACK: 1658–60

His son did not have the devil in him, nor the steel that might have held England in the chains that force and piety had forged. Richard Cromwell shared with his sister the tenderness of mind that had made them look with secret dread upon their father's policy of blood and iron. Richard, on his knees, had begged Cromwell to spare the life of Charles I. During the Commonwealth and the Protectorate he had lived peaceably on the rural estate that his marriage had brought him. It was through no ambition of his own that on September 4, 1658, by his father's will, he became Lord Protector of England. Lucy Hutchinson described him as "gentle and virtuous, but a peasant in his nature, and became not greatness."[74]

All the divisions that Oliver had kept in check now emerged, more boldly as they saw the weakness of Richard's fiber. The army, resenting his civil background, and wishing to keep in its hands the authority that under his father had been frankly martial, petitioned him to yield all military direction to Fleetwood. He refused, but mollified his brother-in-law by making him lieutenant general. As the treasury was empty and burdened with debt, he summoned a Parliament, which met on January 27, 1659. A rumor spread that it was planning to reinstate the Stuart monarchy. The army officers, followed by bands of soldiers, came to Richard and asked him to dismiss the Parliament. He sent for his guards to protect him; they ignored his orders. Yielding to force, he signed an order dissolving the Parliament (April 22). He was now at the mercy of the army. The ardent republicans in the army, led by Major General John Lambert, invited the surviving members of the Long Parliament to reassemble, and to assume the authority which, as the Rump, they had held until Cromwell, aided by the ardent republicans in the army, dismissed them in 1653. The new Rump convened at Westminster May 7, 1659. Richard, weary of politics, sent it his resignation (May 25). He retired into private life, and in 1660 he disappeared into France, where he lived in seclusion under the pseudonym of John Clarke. He returned to England in 1680, and died there in 1712, aged eighty-six.

"Chaos," wrote a royalist on June 3, 1659, "was a perfection compared to our present order and government."[75] The contest for power between army and Parliament continued; but those parts of the army that were stationed in Scotland or Ireland favored Parliament, and in the predominantly republican Parliament there was a strong royalist faction. On October 13 Lambert stationed soldiers at the entrance to Westminster Palace, excluded the Parliament, and announced that the army would for the present take over the government. It seemed as if the whole sequence of events that had begun with Pride's Purge was to be repeated, with Lambert a new Cromwell.

Milton called Lambert's *coup d'état* "most illegal and scandalous, I fear me barbarous . . . that a paid army . . . should thus subdue the supreme power that set them up,"[76] but the poet was powerless. The only force in Britain that could oppose the military dictatorship was another army, the ten thousand soldiers that Parliament had assigned to General George Monck to maintain its authority in Scotland. We do not know whether any personal ambitions were concealed behind Monck's resolve to challenge the London army's usurpation of power. "I am engaged in conscience and honor," he declared, "to free England from that intolerable slavery of a sword government."[77] His statement roused to courage a variety of other elements opposed to martial rule. The people refused to pay taxes; the army in Ireland, the fleet in the Downs, the apprentices in the capital declared for the Parliament. The London financiers refused to the usurping leaders the loans that had been depended upon for the payment of the troops. The mercantile and manufacturing classes, which had approved the deposition of Charles I, now felt that the deepening and spreading disorder threatened the economic life of England, and began to wonder whether political or economic stability could be restored without a king whose legitimacy would comfort the people, bring in taxes, and quiet the storm. On December 5 Monck led his forces into England. The army leaders sent troops to oppose him; they refused to fight. The usurping officers admitted defeat, restored the Parliament, and submitted themselves to its mercy (December 24).

The triumphal Parliament, numbering thirty-six men, was still republican. One of its first acts required all present and future members to abjure the Stuart line. It refused admission to the Presbyterian survivors of the pre-Rump Parliament, on the ground that they favored the restoration of Charles II. The people scorned it as merely a revived Rump unrepresentative of England, and expressed its sentiments by the "Roasting of the Rump" in effigy in a multitude of bonfires—thirty-one in a single London street. Monck, whose army had reached London on February 3, 1660, notified the Parliament that unless it called for a new and wider election, and dissolved itself by May 6, he would no longer protect it. He advised the House to admit the excluded Presbyterians; it did. The enlarged Commons re-established the presbyterian organization of religion in England, issued a call for a new election, and declared itself dissolved. Now at last the Long Parliament came to its official and legal end (March 16, 1660).

On that same day a workman blotted out with paint the inscription *Exit Tyrannus, Regum Ultimus* ("Exit the Tyrant, Last of the Kings") which the Commonwealth had set up in the Exchange; then he threw up his cap and cried, "God bless King Charles the Second!"; whereupon, we are told, "the whole Exchange joined with the greatest shout."[78] The next day Monck gave a secret interview to Charles's emissary, Sir John Greenville. Soon Greenville was on his way to Brussels with Monck's message to the throneless King.

IX. THE KING RETURNS: 1660

Since his arduous escape from England in 1650, Charles had led almost a vagabond's life on the Continent. His mother, Henrietta Maria, received him in Paris; but the French had impoverished her, and for a while Charles and his entourage lived like paupers; his faithful future Chancellor, Edward Hyde, was reduced to one meal a day; and Charles himself, having no food at home, ate in taverns, mostly on the credit of his expectations. When Louis XIV returned to affluence he gave Charles a pension of six thousand francs, and Charles began to enjoy life too freely to please his mother.

In those Paris days he learned to love with his purest affection his sister, Henrietta Anne. Mother and sister exerted themselves to win him to Catholicism; Catholic emigrés from England did not let him forget how they had fought for his father. Presbyterian emissaries promised to aid his restoration if he would accept and protect their faith. He listened to both sides courteously, but expressed his determination to adhere to that Anglican Church for which his father had suffered.[79] The arguments that besieged him may have inclined him to a skepticism of all religion. But the Catholic worship, which he saw all around him in France, seems to have made a strong impression on him; it became an open secret in his little court that if his hands were free he would join the Roman Church.[80] In 1651 he wrote to Pope Innocent X, promising, if restored to the throne of England, to repeal all laws against Catholics. The Pope made no answer, but the general of the Jesuits informed Charles that the Vatican could not support an heretical prince.[81]

When Mazarin began to negotiate an alliance with Cromwell, Charles's advisers persuaded him to leave France, and the Cardinal agreed to continue his pension. He moved to Cologne, then to Brussels. There, toward March 26, 1660, Greenville brought him Monck's message: If he would promise a general amnesty, excepting not more than four persons, grant liberty of conscience, and confirm the present possessors of confiscated property, Monck would help him; meanwhile, since England was still at war with Spain, it would be advisable for Charles to leave the Spanish Netherlands. He moved to Breda in Dutch Brabant, and there (April 14) signed an agreement accepting Monck's terms in principle, but leaving precise conditions to the new Parliament.

The elections returned an overwhelmingly royalist House of Commons, and forty-two peers took their seats in the new House of Lords. On May 1 the letters that Greenville had brought from Charles were read to both houses. In this "Declaration of Breda" the young King offered amnesty to all, "excepting only such persons as shall hereafter be excepted by Parliament"; he left to Parliament the adjustment of confiscated properties; he promised that "no man shall be disquieted or called in question for differences of opinion in matters of religion which do not disturb the peace of the Kingdom"; and he added a judicious statement prepared for him by Chancellor Hyde:

> We do assure you upon our royal word that none of our predecessors have had a greater esteem of Parliament than we have . . . We do believe them to be so vital a part of the constitution of the Kingdom, and so necessary to the government of it, that we well know neither prince nor people can be in any tolerable degree happy without them . . . We shall always look upon their counsels as the best we can receive, and shall be as tender of their privileges, and as careful to preserve and protect them, as of that which is most near to ourself, and most necessary for our own preservation.

Parliament was pleased. On May 8 it proclaimed Charles II King of England, dated his title from the moment of his father's death, and derived it not from any act of Parliament but from inherent birthright. The sum of fifty thousand pounds was voted to be sent to Charles, with an invitation to come at once and take his throne.

Nearly all England rejoiced that two decades of violence had ended in the restoration of order without the shedding of one drop of blood. Bells rang throughout the land; in London men knelt in the streets and drank to the health of the King.[82] All the crowned heads of Europe acclaimed the triumph of legitimacy; even the United Provinces, firmly republican, feted Charles as he traveled from Breda to The Hague, and the States-General, which had heretofore ignored him, offered him thirty thousand pounds for his expenses, as a persuasive to future good will. An English fleet, already decked with pennants and the initials "C. R.," came to The Hague and took Carolus Rex on board (May 23).

On May 25 the fleet reached Dover. Twenty thousand people had gathered on the beach to receive the King. When his boat neared the shore they fell on their knees; and he, touching land, knelt and thanked God. "Old men who were there," wrote Voltaire, "told me that nearly everyone was in tears. Perhaps there has never been a more moving sight."[83] Along roads lined in every mile with happy crowds Charles and his escort, followed by hundreds, rode to Canterbury, to Rochester, to London. There 120,000 citizens came out to welcome him; and even the army that had fought against him joined Monck's army in the parade. The houses of Parliament awaited him in the Palace of Whitehall. "Dread Sovereign," said the Speaker of the Lords, "you are the desire of three kingdoms, the strength and stay of the tribes of the people, for the moderating of extremities, the reconciling of differences . . . and for restoring the collapsed honor of these nations."[84] Charles accepted all compliments with grace and private humor. As he retired to his rest, exhausted with triumph, he remarked to a friend, "It must surely have been my fault that I did not come before, for I have met with no one today who did not protest that he always wished for my restoration."[85]

FIG. 25—TENIERS THE YOUNGER: *Temptation of St. Anthony*. Louvre, Paris   PAGE 165

FIG. 26—JACOB VAN RUISDAEL: *The Storm*. Louvre, Paris

PAGE 171

FIG. 27—MEINDERT HOBBEMA: *Water Mill with the Great Red Roof*. The Art Institute of Chicago, Gift of Mr. and Mrs. Frank G. Logan

PAGE 170

Fig. 28—Vermeer: *Head of a Girl*. Mauritshuis, The Hague (Photo by A. Dingjan)

PAGE 169

Fig. 31—Sir Peter Lely: *Charles II of England.* By Permission of His Grace the Duke of Grafton and the Royal Academy of Arts, London   PAGE 244

FIG. 32—SIR GODFREY KNELLER: *Henry Purcell.* National Portrait Gallery, London (Bettmann Archive)   PAGE 267

FIG. 33—PETER PAUL RUBENS: *George Villiers, Duke of Buckingham.* Albertina Museum, Vienna   PAGE 270

Fig. 34—CHRISTOPHER WREN: *Sheldonian Theatre*, Oxford (*Bettmann Archive*)

PAGE 264

Architect's original model (Bettmann Archive)

Photograph of cathedral today (Bettmann Archive)

FIG. 35—CHRISTOPHER WREN: *St. Paul's Cathedral* (1675–1710), London   PAGE 264

FIG. 36—SIR GODFREY KNELLER: *Sir Christopher Wren*. National Portrait Gallery, London (Bettmann Archive)

FIG. 37—SIR PETER LELY: *Nell Gwyn*. National Portrait Gallery, London (Bettmann Archive)

PAGES 249, 266

Fig. 40—Johann Gottfried Schidow: *Frederick the Great*. Sans Souci, Potsdam (Bettmann Archive)

PAGE 412

Fig. 41—Kupetzki the Elder: *Peter the Great*. Herzog Anton Ulrich Museum, Braunschweig, Germany   PAGE 391

Fig. 42—Baldassare Longhena: *Palazzo Rezzonico*, Venice. (Building at right) Courtesy of the Italian State Tourist Office   PAGE 433

FIG. 43—SALVATOR ROSA: *Tobias and the Angel Raphael*. Louvre, Paris

Fig. 44—Andrea Pozzo: *Altar of St. Ignatius in Church of Il Gesù*, Rome (Bettmann Archive)

Milton

1608–74

I. JOHN BUNYAN: 1628–88

IN THEIR enthusiasm for religion and morality, the Puritans felt no
need of secular literature. The King James Bible was literature enough;
nearly everything else seemed trivial or sinful dross. A member of Parliament proposed in 1653 that nothing should be studied in the universities
except the Scriptures and "the work of Jakob Böhme, and such like."[1]
This seems depressing, but we should note that at the height of the Puritan
ascendancy (1653) Sir Thomas Urquhart published his spirited translation
of Rabelais,* preferring scatology to eschatology. And in the same year
Izaak Walton cast his *Compleat Angler* upon the waters. Even today, with
judicious leaps from one fish to another, that book is refreshing in its
simple, fresh-air mood; and it is a reminder that while England was passing
through a revolution as violent as 1789, men could go quietly to snare
some eager creature in rural streams. "Turn out of the way a little, good
Scholar, toward yonder high honeysuckle hedge; there we'll sit and sing
whilst this shower falls so gently upon the teeming earth."[2]

Andrew Marvell kept his head, everywise, during the shuffling of governments between his birth in 1621 and his death in 1678. He welcomed
Cromwell's return from Ireland with a vigorous and melodious ode, but
in it he dared to write with sympathy of the dying Charles I:

> He nothing common did, or mean,
> Upon that memorable scene,
> But with his keener eye
> The axe's edge did try.
> Nor called the gods with vulgar spite
> To vindicate his helpless right,
> But bowed his comely head
> Down, as upon a bed.[3]

Marvell became assistant to Milton as Latin secretary to Cromwell, was
elected to Parliament in 1659, helped to save Milton from the vengeance

---

* Books I and II, 1653; Book III, 1693. Pierre Motteux completed the translation in 1708.

of the triumphant royalists, lived through eighteen years of the Restoration, and condemned its immorality, corruption, and incompetence in satires that he carefully refrained from publishing.

John Bunyan's classics, like Milton's epics, were written after the Restoration, but both men were molded under the Puritan regime. "I was of a low and inconsiderable generation [birth]," he tells us, "my father's house being of that rank that is meanest and most despised of all families in the land."[4] The father was a tinker—a mender of pots and kettles—in the village of Elstow, near Bedford. Thomas Bunyan earned enough to send John to Bedford School, where the boy learned at least to read and write —enough to "search the Scriptures" and write the most famous of all English books. At home he served as apprentice to his father, who taught him the catechism on Sunday afternoons. From the boys of the town he learned to lie and blaspheme; in these arts, he assures us, "I had but few equals."[5] Moreover, he was guilty of dancing, playing games, and taking a glass of ale in the tavern—all condemned by the Puritans, who in his youth (1628–48) were not yet in power. "I was the very ringleader . . . in all manner of vice and ungodliness."[6] Such confessions of mighty sins were popular among the Puritans, since they made their reform all the more remarkable, and showed the power of God's saving grace. As the Puritan teaching spread around him, Bunyan's deviltry was disturbed by thoughts of death, the Last Judgment, and hell. Once he dreamed that he saw all the sky on fire, and the earth splitting beneath him. He woke in terror, and frightened the family with his cries: "O Lord, have mercy on me! . . . The Day of Judgment is come, and I am not prepared!"[7]

At sixteen he was drafted into the Parliamentary army, and he served for thirty months in the Civil War. As a soldier, "I sinned still, and grew more and more rebellious against God, and careless of my own salvation." Demobilized, he married (1648) an orphan girl whose only dowry was two religious books and her oft-repeated memories of her father's piety. Bunyan, having succeeded to his father's shop, supported her by tinkering. He prospered, went to church regularly, and abandoned one by one his youthful sins. Almost daily he read the Bible, whose simple English became his own. Elstow talked of him as a model citizen.

But (he tells us) theological doubts harassed him. He had no conviction that God's grace had been extended to him, and without that grace he would be damned. He suspected that nearly all the inhabitants of Elstow and Bedford were already lost to everlasting hell. He was troubled with the thought that his Christian beliefs were a geographical accident. "How can you tell," he asked himself, "but that the Turks had as good scripture to prove their Mahomet the Saviour, as we have to prove our Jesus is?" "Whole floods of blasphemies against God, Christ, and the Scriptures wa poured upon my spirit . . . questions in me against the very being of God and of his only beloved Son, as whether there was in truth a God or Christ? And whether the Holy Scriptures were not rather a fable and cunning story than the holy and pure Word of God?"[10] He concluded that these doubts were due to a devil that had lodged in him. "I beheld the condition of the dog and toad, and counted the estate of everything that God had made far better than this dreadful state of mine . . . , for they had no souls to perish under the everlasting weight of hell or sin, as mine was like to do."[11]

Then one day, as he was walking into the countryside, musing on the wickedness of his heart, he remembered a line of St. Paul's: "He hath made peace through the blood of His cross."[12] The thought that Christ had died for him as well as for others grew stronger in his mind, until "I was ready to swoon . . . with solid joy and peace."[13] He joined a Baptist church in Bedford (1653), was baptized, and entered upon two years of spiritual happiness and tranquillity. In 1655 he moved to Bedford and became a deacon in this church, and in 1657 he was commissioned to preach. His message was Luther's: that unless a man had firm faith that he had been redeemed from his natural sinfulness by the death of Christ the Son of God, he would—no matter what were his virtues—join the great majority of mankind in going to hell. Only Christ's divine self-sacrifice could balance the enormity of man's sins. Children, he thought, should be told this very clearly:

> My judgment is that men go the wrong way to learn their children to pray. It seems to me a better way for people to tell their children betimes what cursed creatures they are, how they are under the wrath of God by reason of original and actual sin; also to tell them the nature of God's wrath, and the duration of misery.[14]

Amid these exhortations there was, in Bunyan's sermons, much wise counsel on the rearing of children and the treatment of employees. Like other preachers he was subjected to heckling by the Quakers, who told him that not the Scriptures but the Inner Light brought understanding and salvation. In 1656 he wrote two books against the troublesome new sect; they replied by accusing him of being a Jesuit, a highwayman, an adulterer, and a witch.[15] Worse difficulties came with the Restoration. The old Elizabethan law was renewed which required all Englishmen to attend Anglican services, and only those; all non-Anglican houses of worship were closed; all non-Anglican ministers were forbidden to preach. Bunyan obeyed to the extent of closing his conventicle in Bedford, but he met his congregation in secret places, and preached to it. He was arrested; he was offered release if he would promise not to preach publicly; he refused; he was committed to Bedford jail (November, 1660). There, with some intervals of limited liberty, he remained for twelve years. At different times the offer of release was renewed, on the same conditions and eliciting the same reply: "If you let me out today I will preach tomorrow."[16]

Perhaps domestic life had become a burden. His first wife had died in 1658, leaving him four children, one blind; and his second wife was pregnant. The neighbors helped to support the family, and Bunyan contributed by making laces in prison and arranging for their sale. His wife and children were allowed to visit him daily, and he was permitted to preach to his fellow prisoners, to leave the jail as he pleased, even to travel to London.[17] But he resumed his clandestine sermons, and was put in closer confinement. In jail he read and reread the Bible, and Foxe's *Book of Martyrs;* he warmed his faith at the pyres of Protestant heroes, and reveled in visions of the Apocalypse. He must have been well supplied with pen and paper, for in the first six years of his incarceration he wrote and published eight religious tracts, and one major work, *Grace Abounding to the Chief of Sinners.* This is his spiritual autobiography, an almost frightening revelation of the Puritan mind.

In 1666, under Charles II's first Declaration of Indulgence, he was released. He preached again, and was returned to jail. In 1672 Charles's second Declaration of Indulgence allowed nonconformist ministers to preach. Bunyan was freed, and was at once elected pastor of his old church. In 1673 this declaration was withdrawn; the old prohibitions were renewed, Bunyan disobeyed them, he was again imprisoned (1675), but he was soon released.

It was in this third and final term that he wrote Part I of *The Pilgrim's Progress from This World to That Which Is to Come.* This was published in 1678; Part II followed in 1684. (In an amusing doggerel preface Bunyan claimed that he had written the book to divert himself, without thought of publication.) He presented the story disarmingly in the form of fantasy:

> As I walked through the wilderness of this world, I lighted on a certain place where was a Den, and I laid me down in that place to sleep; and as I slept I dreamed a dream.[18]

Christian, in this vision, is obsessed with the thought that he must abandon and forget everything else, and seek only Christ and Paradise. He leaves his wife and children, and begins his progress toward the "Celestial City." He is joined by Hopeful, who expresses the Puritan faith succinctly:

> One day I was very said, I think sadder than at any time in my life, and this sadness was through a fresh sight of the greatness and vileness of my sins. And as I was then looking for nothing but hell, and the everlasting damnation of my soul, suddenly, as I thought, I saw the

Lord Jesus Christ look down from heaven upon me, and saying "Believe on the Lord Jesus Christ, and thou shalt be saved."[19] But I replied, I am a great, a very great, sinner. And he answered, "My grace is sufficient for thee." . . . And now was my heart full of joy.[20]

The pilgrims, after much tribulation and disputation, reach the Celestial City, and we learn what it is they had hoped for so fervently:

And lo, as they entered, they were transfigured, and they had raiment put on that looked like gold. There were also that met them with harps and crowns, and gave them to them—the harps to praise withal, and the crowns in token of honor. . . . And behold, the City shone like the sun; the streets also were paved with gold, and in them walked many men, with crowns on their heads, palms in their hands, and golden harps to sing praises withal.[21]

Poor Ignorance, who has followed them haltingly, not having quite the true faith, comes to the gates of the Celestial City, knocks, is asked for his passport, cannot find it, and is bundled off to hell.[22]—The story is engagingly told, but sometimes we sympathize with Obstinate, who says of Christian and his fellows, "There is a company of these crazy-headed coxcombs, that, when they take a fancy by the end, are wiser in their own eyes than even men that can render a reason."[23]

The idea of the soul's pilgrimage from earthly temptations to heavenly bliss was old; so was the medieval allegorical form; presumably Bunyan had read some of these earlier works.[24] They were now forgotten in the extraordinary success of the new story. Fifty-nine editions were printed in its first century of life; it sold 100,000 copies before Bunyan's death; it has sold millions since; it has been translated into 108 languages; in Puritan America it was in almost every home. Some of its phrases—the Slough of Despond, Vanity Fair, Mr. Worldly Wiseman—entered into common speech. In the twentieth century its popularity has rapidly declined; the Puritan mood is gone; the book is now less a part of man's belief and furniture; but it is still a well of simple English fresh and clear.

Bunyan wrote some sixty books; they are not required reading today. After his final release in 1675 he became one of the most prominent preachers of his time, the recognized leader of the Baptists in England. He expressed admiration for Charles II, and bade his followers be loyal to the Stuart King as the defender of England against the pope.[25] Three years after Charles declared his deathbed acceptance of Catholicism, Bunyan finished his own career. His end was strangely like Luther's. A quarrel at Reading having alienated a father and son of whom Bunyan was very fond, he journeyed thither on horseback from Bedford. He reconciled the parties;

but on the ride back he was caught in a storm, and was wetted through before he could find shelter on the way. A fever seized him, from which he never recovered. He was buried in the cemetery of the Dissenters at Bunhill Fields, where he still lies, in stone, on his tomb.

II. THE YOUNG POET: 1608–40

Milton's grandfather was a Roman Catholic, who was fined sixty pounds in 1601 for skipping Anglican services, and who disinherited his son for abandoning the Roman Church. This disowned John Milton earned a good living as a London scrivener—a penman skilled in writing or copying manuscripts, charters, and legal documents. He loved music, composed madrigals, had many musical instruments, including an organ, in his home; and this feeling for music passed down to the poet, who would have agreed that to write well one must have music in his soul and in his mental ear. The mother, Sarah Jeffrey, daughter of a merchant tailor, gave her husband six children, of whom our John was the third. A younger brother, Christopher, became a Stuart royalist and High Church man; John became a Cromwellian Puritan republican. The home in Bread Street was a Puritan establishment, serious and devout but not puritanic; the Renaissance love of the beautiful mingled here with the Reformation passion for the good.

John senior bought realty, prospered, engaged tutors (Puritan) for John junior, and sent him, aged eleven, to St. Paul's School. There the boy learned Latin, Greek, French, Italian, and some Hebrew. He read Shakespeare, but preferred Spenser; we note in passing that he was much impressed by an English translation of Du Bartas' *La Semaine* (1578), an epic describing the creation of the world in seven days.

> My appetite for knowledge was so voracious that from twelve years of age I hardly ever left my studies, or went to bed before midnight. This primarily led to my loss of sight. My eyes [like his mother's] were naturally weak, and I was subject to frequent headaches, which, however, could not chill the ardor of my curiosity, or retard the progress of my improvement.[26]

At sixteen he passed to Christ's College, Cambridge. There his quarrel with a tutor led to fisticuffs. Samuel Johnson was "ashamed to relate what I fear is true, that Milton was one of the last students in either university that suffered the public indignity of corporal correction."[27] Milton was expelled for a term, then was allowed to return. Already he was writing good poetry. In 1629, aged twenty-one, he celebrated with a magnificent ode "the Morning of Christ's Nativity," and a year later he composed a sixteen-

line "Epitaph," which was later accepted for publication in the Second
Folio edition (1632) of Shakespeare's works:

> What needs my Shakespeare for his honoured bones
> The labour of an Age in pilèd stones,
> Or that his hallow'd Reliques should be hid
> Under a Star-ypointing Pyramid?
> Dear Sonne of Memory, great Heire of Fame,
> What need'st thou such dull witnesse of thy Name?*

Milton stayed eight years at Cambridge, taking the bachelor's degree in
1628, the master's in 1632; then he left without the usual affection for
the scene of one's college years. His father had expected him to enter the
ministry, but the proud youth refused to take the oath of loyalty to the
Anglican creed and liturgy:

> Perceiving what tyranny had invaded the Church—that he who
> would take orders must subscribe slave, and take an oath withal,
> which unless he took with a conscience that would retch, he must
> either straight perjure or split his faith—I thought it better to prefer
> a blameless silence before the sacred office of speaking, bought . . .
> with servitude and forswearing.[29]

He retired to his father's country house at Horton, near Windsor; there,
apparently, he was paternally maintained while he pursued his studies,
chiefly classical. He became familiar with even the most minor of the
Latin authors. He wrote Latin poems that won the praise of a Roman
Catholic cardinal; soon he was to make Europe resound with his Latin
defenses of Cromwell's policies. Even when he wrote English prose he
wrote Latin, bending the English to classical inversions and convolutions,
but achieving a strange and fascinating sonority.

Probably it was at Horton, amid the lush fields and greenery of an
English countryside, that he composed (1632?) the companion pieces that
celebrated in turn the careless joys and melancholy moods of his passing
youth. Almost every line of "L'Allegro" cries out to be sung. Allegro is the
"daughter fair, . . . buxom, blithe, and debonair," born of "Zephyr with
Aurora playing." Everything in the rural scene now delights the poet: the
lark startling the night, the cock strutting before his dames, the hounds
leaping at the blowing of the hunter's horn, the sun rising "in flames and
amber light," the singing milkmaid and the nibbling flocks, the dance of
youth and maiden on the grass, the evening by the hearth or at the theater.

---

* We regret to add that when Milton was assigned the task of defending the execution
of Charles I, he listed, among the blots on that monarch's memory, a fondness for Shakespeare.[28]

> If Jonson's learnèd sock be on,
> Or sweetest Shakespeare, Fancy's child,
> Warble his native wood-notes wild;

and music

> Untwisting all the chains that tie
> The hidden soul of harmony; . . .
> These delights if thou canst give,
> Mirth, with thee I mean to live.

Here was as yet no grim or joyless Puritan, but a healthy English youth in whose veins ran some ichor of the Elizabethan bards.

But there came at times another mood, when these pleasures seemed trivial to the pensive mind remembering tragedy, seeking significance, and finding in philosophy no answers, but only questions unfelt before. Then "Il Penseroso," the thoughtful one, walks unseen

> To behold the wand'ring Moon
> Riding near her highest noon,
> Like one that had been led astray
> Through the Heav'ns' wide pathless way;

or he sits solitary by the fire

> Where glowing embers through the room
> Teach light to counterfeit a gloom,
> Far from all resort of mirth,
> Save the cricket on the hearth;

or he is in "some high lonely tower," humbled by the stars, turning Plato's leaves, and wondering where heaven is—

> What worlds, or what vast regions hold
> The immortal mind that hath forsook
> Her mansion in this fleshly nook

—or recalling the griefs of lovers and the sad deaths of kings. Then better than dour philosophy are the "studious cloister's pale" of the great cathedral, its storied windows and shadowed light;

> There let the pealing organ blow
> To the full-voiced choir below,
> In service high, and anthems clear,
> As may with sweetness, through mine ear,

> Dissolve me into ecstasies,
> And bring all Heav'n before mine eyes.

These are the pleasures that come to "the pensive one," and if they seem tied to Melancholy, then with Melancholy will the poet live. In these two lovely poems Milton reveals himself at twenty-four: a youth atremble with life's beauties and unashamed of happiness, but already touched with puzzled reveries on life and death, feeling in himself the conflict of religion with philosophy.

The poet's first chance to distinguish himself came in 1634, when he was commissioned to write a pastoral masque for the ceremonies inaugurating the Earl of Bridgewater as lord president of the Council of the West. Henry Lawes composed the middling music; Milton's verses, modestly anonymous, were so praised that he was moved to acknowledge their authorship. Sir Henry Wotton commended "a certain Doric delicacy in your songs and odes, whereunto . . . I have seen yet nothing parallel in our language."[30] Originally the piece was entitled *A Masque Presented at Ludlow Castle* (in Shropshire); today we call it *Comus*. It was performed by two young nobles and their sister, a seventeen-year-old girl from the court of Queen Henrietta Maria. Though most of the little drama is in blank verse, much trammeled with mythology, it has a lyric lilt and melodious elegance better sustained than ever again in Milton's poetry. The theme was traditional: a lovely virgin, wandering recklessly in the woods, and singing

> strains that might create a soul
> Under the ribs of death,

is accosted by the sorcerer Comus, who casts upon her a charm to loose her chastity. He begs her to make play while her youth shines; she with warm eloquence defends virtue, temperance, and "divine philosophy." All the lines went well, except perhaps an ominously republican passage that may have made that lavish gathering wince:

> If every just man that now pines with want
> Had but a modest and beseeming share
> Of that which lewdly-pamper'd Luxury
> Now heaps upon some few with vast excess,
> Nature's full blessings would be well dispenc't
> In unsuperfluous even proportion,
> And she no whit encombered with her store.[31]

In 1637 the poet's mood was darkened by the drowning of his young friend and fellow poet Edward King. To a memorial volume Milton contributed an elegy, "Lycidas," conceived in artificial pastoral form, and cluttered with dead gods, but rich in lines that still ring in grateful memory:

> Alas! what boots it with incessant care
> To tend the homely slighted shepherd's trade,*
> And strictly meditate the thankless Muse?
> Were it not better done as others use,
> To sport with Amaryllis in the shade,
> Or with the tangles of Neaera's hair?
> Fame is the spur that the clear spirit doth raise
> (That last infirmity of noble mind)
> To scorn delights, and live laborious days;
> But the fair guerdon when we hope to find,
> And think to burst out into sudden blaze,
> Comes the blind Fury with th'abhorrèd shears,
> And slits the thin-spun life.

John Milton senior seems to have felt that six years of leisurely indulgence at Horton were well earned by a talent that could sing such songs. To crown his generosity, he sent his son to travel on the Continent, all expenses paid. Equipped with a manservant, Milton left England in April, 1638, spent a few days in Paris (then in the martial grip of Richelieu), and hurried on to Italy. During a stay of two months in Florence he visited the blind and half-imprisoned Galileo, met the literati, sat in with the academies, exchanged compliments in Latin verse, and wrote Italian sonnets as if he had been reared by the Arno or the Po. In Naples he was received and escorted by that same Marquis Manso who had befriended Tasso and Marini. He spent four months in Rome, met and liked some learned cardinals, but frankly confessed his Protestant faith. Then again to Florence, and through Bologna and Ferrara to Venice, through Verona to Milan, and through Geneva, Lyons, and Paris to London (August, 1639).

In later works he made two notable statements about his travels in Italy. Rebutting the insinuations of an opponent, he wrote: "I call God to witness that in all those places in which vice meets with so little discouragement, and is practiced with so little shame, I never once deviated from the paths of integrity and virtue."[32] And, recalling how the Italian critics had praised his poetry,

> I began thus far to assent both to them and divers of my friends
> here at home, and not less to an inward prompting which now grew
> daily upon me, that by labor and intent study (which I take to be my

---

* I.e., to write poetry.

portion in this life), joined with the strong propensity of nature, I might perhaps leave something so written to aftertimes, as they should not willingly let it die.[33]

Now he began to plan a great epic that would celebrate his nation or his faith, and enshrine his name in centuries. Twenty years were to pass before he could begin it, twenty-nine before he could publish it. Between the first period of his poetry (1630–40) and the second (1658–68) he played his part in the Great Rebellion, and kept his pen for war and prose.

III. THE REFORMER: 1640–42

In 1639 Milton took a bachelor's apartment in St. Bride's Churchyard, London, where he tutored his sister's sons. A year later he moved with them to Aldersgate Street. There (1643) he received additional pupils between ten and sixteen years of age, boarded and taught them, and earned a modest income to fill out the allowance from his father. In a "Letter to Mr. Hartlib" (1644) he formulated his views on education. He gave the word a mighty definition: "I call a complete and generous education that which fits a man to perform justly, skilfully, and magnanimously all the offices, both private and public, of peace and war."[34] The first task of the teacher is to form moral character in the student, "to repair the ruins of our first parents"—i.e., to overcome the natural wickedness of man ("original sin")—or (as we should now say) to readjust to the needs of civilized life the native character formed by the needs of the hunting stage. This, Milton felt, can be done best by inculcating in the growing mind a strong faith in an all-seeing God, and inuring it to self-control by a stoic discipline. He set his pupils an example of "hard study and spare diet," seldom permitting himself a day of "festivity and enjoyment."[35] Next to religion and morals should come the Greek and Latin classics, which Milton used not merely as models of literature but as vehicles of instruction in natural science, geography, history, law, morality, physiology, medicine, agriculture, architecture, oratory, poetry, philosophy, and theology. If this unique compromise between science and the humanities assumed that very little had been added to science since the fall of Rome, we should note that this was substantially true except for Galileo; even Copernicus had had his Greek forebear in Aristarchus. Moreover, Milton proposed also to acquaint his students with some modern texts in science and history, and even some living exemplars in practical arts; he hoped to bring hunters, mariners, gardeners, anatomists, apothecaries, engineers, architects to his classroom to convey the latest knowledge in their fields.[36] He allotted considerable time to music and drama, and an hour and a half every day to athletic exercises and martial games. "In vernal seasons" his pupils would "ride out in companies with prudent and staid guides to all quarters of the land, learning and observing"; they would "join the navy for a while to learn sailing and sea-fight"; and finally, after their twenty-third year, they might travel abroad. It was an arduous curriculum; we have no evidence that it was fully followed in Milton's school; but if his students caught some of his enthusiasm and industry, it might have been realized.

He dreamed at times of developing an academy that should rival those of Plato and Aristotle, but his spirit was allured by the epochal events of the age. The gathering of the Long Parliament (1640) was a turning point in his life, an almost violent veering from poetry and scholarship to politics and reform. On December 11 the "Root and Branch" party of the Puritans, to which some of his friends belonged, presented to Parliament a monster petition, signed with fifteen thousand names (probably including Milton's[37]) and asking for the elimination of bishops from the English Church. Joseph Hall, bishop of Exeter, countered the petition with *An Humble Remonstrance to the High Court of Parliament* (January, 1641), in which he defended episcopacy as derived "from the times of the blessed Apostles, without interruption . . . unto the present age."[38] Five Presbyterian divines joined their pens in *An Answer to . . . an Humble Remonstrance* (March, 1641), which they signed "Smectymnuus," a pseudonym made up of their initials.* Hall and other episcopal-ians replied; the Commons passed the proposal, the Lords rejected it; the controversy boiled in pulpit, press, and Parliament; and Milton leaped into it with a ninety-page booklet, *Of Reformation Touching Church Discipline in England* (June, 1641).

With powerful and breathless sentences running at times to half a page, he ascribed the deterioration of the Established Church to two causes: the retention of Catholic ceremonies, and the episcopal monopoly of the power to ordain. He scorned "those senseless ceremonies which we only retain as a dangerous earnest of sliding back to Rome, and serving merely as . . . an interlude [drama] to set out the pomp of prelatism."[39] The bishops have been stealthily moving back to Catholicism in their ritual—a palpable hit at Archbishop Laud, who had been offered a cardinal's hat. Milton repudiated the claim of James I and Charles I that bishops were necessary to church government and monarchical institutions. He called upon the Presbyterian Scots to continue their old war against episcopacy; and he appealed to the Trinity to serve in the good cause:

> Thou Tripersonal godhead! look upon this thy poor and almost
> spent and expiring church; leave her not thus a prey to those impor-

---

* Stephen Marshall, Edmund Calamy, Thomas Young, Matthew Newcomen, and William (*W* as double *U*) Spurstow.

tunate wolves, that wait and think long till they devour thy tender flock; these wild boars that have broke into thy vineyard, and left the print of their polluting hoofs on the souls of thy servants. O let them not bring about their damned designs, that stand now at the entrance of the bottomless pit, expecting the watchward to open and let out those dreadful locusts and scorpions, to reinvolve us in that pitchy cloud of infernal darkness, where we shall never more see the sun of thy truth again, never hope for the cheerful dawn, never more hear the bird of morning sing.[48]

He ended by consigning the High Church party to hell:

But they . . . that by the impairing and diminution of the true faith, the distresses and servitude of their country aspire to high dignity, rule, and promotion here, after a shameful end in this life (which God grant them) shall be thrown down eternally into the darkest and deepest gulf of hell, where, under the despiteful control, the trample and spurn of all the other damned, that in the anguish of their torture shall have no other ease than to exercise a raving and bestial tyranny over them as their slaves and negroes, they shall remain in that plight forever, the basest, the lowermost, the most dejected, most underfoot and downtrodden vassals of perdition.[41]

When Bishop Hall answered and abused the "Smectymnuans," Milton came to their support with a blast that must have shaken the sixty-five-year-old prelate out of his canonicals. The *Animadversions upon the Remonstrant's Defence against Smectymnuus* appeared anonymously in July, 1641. In a preface Milton apologized for his vehemence:

In the detecting and convincing [convicting] of any notorious enemy to truth and his country's peace, especially that is conceited to have a voluble and smart influence of tongue . . . , it will be nothing disagreeing from Christian meekness to handle such a one in a rougher accent, and to send home his haughtiness well besprinkled with his own holy water.[42]

The bishop and his son came back with *A Modest Confutation* (January [?], 1642), attacking the author of the *Animadversions* in the hot manner of that infuriate age.[43] Milton retorted in *An Apology against . . . a Modest Confutation* (April ?). He further excused his rough treatment of the bishop; he denounced as a "commodious lie" the charge that he, Milton, had been "vomited" from Cambridge; he assured the world that the Fellows of Christ's College had invited him to stay with them after his graduation; and he reaffirmed his impugned chastity:

Though Christianity had been but slightly taught me, yet a certain reservedness of natural disposition, and moral discipline learned out of the noblest philosophy, was enough to keep me in disdain of far less incontinences than this of the bordello. But having had the doctrine of Holy Scripture, unfolding those chaste and high mysteries . . . , that "the body is for the Lord, and the Lord for the body," thus also I argued to myself, that if unchastity in a woman, whom St. Paul terms the glory of man, be such a scandal and dishonor, then certainly in a man, who is both the image and glory of God, it must . . . be much more deflouring and dishonorable, in that he sins both against his own body, which is the perfecter sex, and his own glory, which is in the woman, and, that which is worst, against the image and glory of God, which is in himself.[44]

Therefore Milton deplored the morality of many classic poets, and preferred to them Dante and Petrarch,

who never write but honor of them to whom they devote their verse, displaying sublime and pure thoughts, without transgression. And long it was not after, when I was confirmed in this opinion, that he who would not be frustrate of his hope to write well . . . ought himself to be a true poem; that is, a composition and pattern of the best and honorablest things; not presuming to sing high praises of heroic men, or famous cities, unless he have in himself the experience and practice of all which is praiseworthy.[45]

After this exemplary passage Milton proceeded to talk of the bishop's socks and feet sending a "fouler stench to heaven"; and if such language should seem uncongenial to theology, he defended it by "the rules of the best rhetoricians," and the example of Luther; and he reminded his readers that "Christ himself, speaking of unsavory traditions, scruples not to name the dunghill and the jakes."[46]

But enough of this dreary controversy, so quotable because of the light it sheds on Milton's character and the manners of the time, and because, amid the virulent nonsense, the grammatical chaos, and the sesquipedalian sentences, there are passages of organlike prose as splendid and moving as Milton's verse. Meanwhile (March, 1642) he had published over his own name a more impersonal booklet, *The Reason of Church Government Urged against Prelaty*—"this impertinent yoke of prelaty under whose inquisitorious and tyrannous duncery no free and splendid wit [intelligence] can flourish."[47] He admitted the necessity of moral and social discipline; indeed, he saw in the rise and fall of discipline the key to the rise and fall of states:

There is not that thing in the world of more grave and urgent importance throughout the whole life of man than discipline. What need I instance? He that hath read with judgment of nations and commonwealths . . . will readily agree that the flourishing and decaying of all civil societies, all the movements and turnings of human occasions, are moved to and fro as upon the axle of Discipline. . . . Nor is there any sociable perfection in this life, civil or sacred, that can be above Discipline; but she is that which with her musical cords preserves and holds all the parts thereof together.[48]

Such discipline, however, should be derived not from an ecclesiastical hierarchy, but from the conception of every man as a potential priest.

As at all stages Milton was conscious of his own abilities, he prefaced the second part of his treatise with an autobiographical fragment mourning that the controversy had diverted him from the composition of a great work which he had long had in mind, "that what the greatest and choicest wits of Athens, Rome, or modern Italy, and those Hebrews of old, did for their country, I, in my proportion, with this over and above, of being a Christian, might do for mine."[49] He told how already he was examining subjects for such a work, but wished it to be one that would allow him "to paint out and describe . . . the whole book of sanctity and virtue," and "whatsoever in religion is holy and sublime."[50] And as if foreseeing that sixteen years would pass before the Great Rebellion would let him set his pen to this task, he excused his tardiness:

Neither do I think it shame to covenant with any knowing reader, that for some few years yet I may go on trust with him toward the payment of what I am now indebted, as being a work not to be raised from the heat of youth, or the vapours of wine, like that which flows at waste from the pen of some vulgar amourist, or the trencher fury of a rhyming parasite; nor to be obtained by the invocation of Dame Memory and her siren daughters; but by devout prayer to that eternal Spirit who can enrich with all utterance and knowledge, and sends out his Seraphim, with the hallowed fire of his altar, to touch and purify the lips of whom he pleases: to this must be added industrious and select reading, steady observation, insight into all seemly and generous arts and affairs; till which in some measures be compassed, at mine own peril and cost, I refuse not to sustain this expectation from as many as are not loth to hazard so much credulity upon the best pledges that I can give them.[51]

IV. MARRIAGE AND DIVORCE: 1643–48

In the *Modest Confutation* Bishop Hall had charged that Milton was seeking literary fame, and advertising his abilities and background, in order to win "a rich widow" or some other reward. In the *Apology* Milton ridiculed the idea; on the contrary, he had been "bred up in plenty," needed no rich widow, and held "with them who, both in prudence and elegance of spirit, would choose a virgin of mean fortunes, honestly bred, before the wealthiest widow."[52] While England drifted into Civil War (1642), Milton drifted into marriage (1643).

He did not join the Parliamentary army; and when the King's forces neared London (November 12, 1642), he wrote a sonnet advising Royalist commanders to protect the poet's house and person, as Alexander had protected Pindar, and promising to spread their fame in verse for "such gentle acts as these."[53] However, the Royalist troops were turned back, and Milton's bower was left unharmed to greet his wife.

He had met Mary Powell in Forest Hill in Oxfordshire, where her father was a justice of the peace. This Richard Powell, far back in 1627, had acknowledged his indebtedness to Milton, then at Cambridge, in the sum of £500, which was later commuted to £312, which had not yet been paid. Apparently the poet spent a month with the Powells in May–June, 1643—whether to collect a debt or a wife we know not. John may have felt that at thirty-four it was time he should marry and beget; and Mary, seventeen, apparently had the virginity that he required. He surprised his nephews by returning to London with a wife.

No one was happy long. The nephews resented Mary as an intruder. She resented Milton's books, and missed her mother, and the "great deal of company and merriment, dancing, etc.," which she had enjoyed in Forest Hill; "Oftimes," says Aubrey, "she heard his nephews beaten and cry."[54] Finding that Mary had but a few ideas, and those Royalist, Milton sank back into his books. He spoke later of a "mute and spiritless mate," and mourned that "a man shall find himself bound fast to an image of earth and phlegm, with whom he looked to be the co-partner of a sweet and gladsome society."[55] Some inquirers into the *mésalliance* believe that Mary refused him consummation.[56] After a month she asked leave to visit her parents; he consented on the understanding that she would return; she went, and did not return. He sent letters to her, which she ignored; and finding no other outlet for his feelings, he wrote, and anonymously published, *The Doctrine and Discipline of Divorce* (August, 1643). He dedicated it "To the Parliament of England, with the Assembly"—i.e.. the Westminster Assembly that was then drawing up a confession of the

Presbyterian faith. He begged the Parliament to free itself from the bondage of tradition, and to advance the Reformation by admitting other grounds than adultery for divorce. He proposed to show

> that indisposition, unfitness, or contrariety of mind, arising from a cause in nature unchangeable, hindering and ever likely to hinder the main benefits of conjugal society, which are solace and peace, is a greater reason of divorce than natural frigidity, especially if there be no children, and that there be mutual consent.[57]

He quoted the old Jewish law of Deut. xxiv, 1: "When a man hath taken a wife and married her, and it come to pass that she find no favor in his eyes, because he hath found some uncleanness in her, let him write her a bill of divorcement, and give it in her hand, and send her out of the house." Christ had apparently rejected this part of the Mosaic Law: "It hath been said, Whoever shall put away his wife, let him give her a writing of divorcement; but I say unto you, That whosoever shall put away his wife, saving for the cause of fornication, causeth her to commit adultery." (Matt. v, 31-32.) Milton argued that "Christ meant not to be taken word for word,"[58] and had repeatedly avowed that he had not come to change one iota of the Mosaic Law. He struggled to make his broad interpretation cover his individual case, even to justifying divorce for inability to join in "a fit and matchable conversation"; for "the unfitness and defectiveness of an unconjugal mind" can reduce matrimony to "a worse condition than the loneliest single life," wherein a living soul is tied to a corpse.[59]

The little book sold rapidly, for it was universally denounced. Milton published in February, 1644, a second edition, eloquently enlarged and boldly signed. He replied to his critics learnedly in *Tetrachordon*, and in a lighter vein in *Colasterion* (both issued in March 4, 1645), heaping upon them his rich vocabulary of vituperation—clod, pork, boar, snout, cock-brained solicitor, brazen ass, odious and odorous fool.[60] Milton could leap in one page from the heights of Parnassus to a Tartarus of scurrility.

Having failed to secure from Parliament a change in the law of divorce, he decided to defy the law and take another wife, preferably a Miss Davis, of whom we know nothing except that she refused him. When rumor of this courtship reached Mary Powell, she decided to recapture her husband, for better or for worse, before it should be too late. One day, when Milton was visiting a friend, she came upon him suddenly, knelt before him, and begged to be restored to his bed and board. He hesitated; his friends pleaded her cause; he consented. With her, his father, and his pupils, he now took a larger house in Barbican Street. Soon Mary's parents, impoverished by the collapse of the Royalist cause, came also to live with the poet, making such a household as must have made for madness or philosophy. Another addition arrived in 1646—Milton's first child, Anne. Richard Powell mitigated the mess by dying (July), and John Milton senior completed a long and honorable life in the following March. The poet fell heir to two or three houses in London, some money, and perhaps some realty in the countryside. In 1647 he disbanded his school, and moved with his wife, daughter, and two nephews to High Holborn Street. A second daughter, Mary, was born in 1648.

V. FREEDOM OF THE PRESS: 1643–49

On August 13, 1644, a Presbyterian clergyman, Herbert Palmer, preaching before the two houses of Parliament, proposed that Milton's treatise on divorce should be publicly burned. It was not, but Palmer's complaint may have led the Stationers' Company, composed of the English booksellers, to point out to the Commons (August 24) that books and pamphlets were violating the law requiring them to be registered and licensed by the company. This law was as old as the reign of Elizabeth, but on June 14, 1643, Parliament had reinforced it with an ordinance specifying

> that no . . . book, pamphlet, paper, nor part of any such . . . shall . . . be printed . . . or put to sale . . . unless the same be first approved and licensed under the hands of such . . . persons as both or either of the . . . Houses shall appoint for the licensing of the same, and entered into the Register Book of the Company of Stationers according to ancient custom.[61]

Any violation was to be punished by the arrest of the authors and printers concerned.

Milton had regularly neglected to register his prose publications. Though *The Doctrine and Discipline of Divorce* appeared two months after the ordinance, he ignored the requirements. Perhaps he was *persona grata* to the Parliament because he had supported it in its conflict with the King; in any case it let him alone. But that ordinance remained over his head, and over the heads of all authors in Britain. It seemed to Milton impossible that literature could prosper under such censorship. Of what use to depose a king and a censorious episcopacy if Parliament and Church were to continue inquisition over the speech of Englishmen? On November 24, 1643, he sent forth, unregistered and unlicensed, the noblest of his prose works: *Areopagitica: A Speech of Mr. John Milton for the Liberty of Unlicensed Printing, to the Parliament of England.** Here is no invective, no vitupera-

---

* *Areopagitica* meant matters pertaining to the supreme court of Athens, which was called the Areopagus from the hill where it convened. Milton took the title from a pamphlet addressed to the Areopagus by Isocrates in 355 B. C.

tion; the "speech" is kept to a high level of language and thought. Milton respectfully asks Parliament to reconsider its censorship ordinance as tending to "the discouragement of all learning . . . by hindering and cropping the discovery that might be yet further made both in religious and civil Wisdom." And he proceeds in a famous and magnificent passage:

> I deny not but that it is of greatest concernment in the Church and Commonwealth to have a vigilant eye how books demean themselves, as well as men; and thereafter to confine, imprison, and do sharpest justice on them as malefactors. For books are not absolutely dead things, but do contain a potency of life in them to be as active as that soul was whose progeny they are; nay, they do preserve as in a vial the purest efficacy and extraction of that living intellect that bred them. I know they are as lively, and as vigorously productive, as those fabulous dragon's teeth; and being sown up and down, may chance to spring up armed men. And yet, on the other hand, unless wariness be used, as good almost kill a man as kill a good book. Who kills a man kills a reasonable creature, God's image; but he who destroys a good book, kills reason itself, kills the image of God, as it were in the eye. Many a man lives a burden to the earth; but a good book is the precious life-blood of a master spirit, embalmed and treasured up on purpose to a life beyond life. 'Tis true, no age can restore a life, whereof perhaps there is no loss; and revolutions of ages do not oft recover the loss of a rejected truth, for the want of which whole nations fare the worse.
>
> We should be wary therefore what persecution we raise against the living labours of public men, how we spill that seasoned life of man preserved and stored up in books; since we see a kind of homicide may be thus committed, sometimes a martyrdom, and if it extend to the whole impression, a kind of massacre; whereof the execution ends not in the slaying of an elemental life, but strikes at that ethereal and fifth essence, the breath of reason itself, slays an immortality rather than a life.[62]

He cites the intellectual vitality of ancient Athens, where only those writings were censored which were atheistical and libelous; "thus the books of Protagoras were by the judges of the Areopagus commanded to be burnt, and himself banished the territory, for a discourse beginning with his confessing not to know 'whether there were gods, or whether not.'" Milton praises the government of ancient Rome for allowing much freedom to writers, and then sketches the growth of censorship in Imperial Rome and the Catholic Church. This licensing ordinance, he feels, smacks of "popery." "What advantage is it to be a man, over it is to be a boy at school, if we have only scaped the ferula to come under" another Imprimatur?[63] Governments and their licensers are fallible; let them not enforce their preferences upon the people; rather let the people choose and learn, even if by costly trial and error:

> I cannot praise a fugitive and cloistered virtue, unexercised and unbreathed, that never sallies out and sees her adversaries, but slinks out of the race. . . .[64] Give me the liberty to know, to utter, and to argue freely according to conscience, above all liberties.[65] . . . Though all the winds of doctrine were let loose to play upon the earth, so Truth be in the field, we do injuriously, by licensing and prohibiting, to misdoubt her strength. Let her and Falsehood grapple; who ever knew Truth put to the worse in a free and open encounter?[66]

However, Milton does not ask for complete tolerance of publications; he believes that atheism, libel, and obscenity should be outlawed, and he refuses toleration to Catholicism because it is an enemy of the state and is itself intolerant.[67] A state otherwise free in thought and speech must, other things equal, grow into greatness.

> Methinks I see in my mind a noble and puissant nation, rousing herself like a strong man after sleep, and shaking her invincible locks. Methinks I see her as an eagle mewing her mighty youth, and kindling her undazzled eyes at the full midday bloom . . .[68]

Parliament paid no attention to Milton's plea; on the contrary, it legislated with increased severity (in 1647, 1649, and 1653) against unlicensed printing. Members of the Stationers' Company protested that Milton had not registered the *Areopagitica*; the House of Lords appointed two justices to examine him; we do not know the result, but apparently he was not molested; he was a useful voice for the triumphant Puritans.

In February, 1649, only two weeks after the execution of Charles I, Milton published a pamphlet on *The Tenure of Kings and Magistrates.* It accepted the social-contract theory that the authority of a government is derived from the sovereign people, and that "it is lawful . . . for any who have the power, to call to account a tyrant or wicked king, and, after due conviction, to depose and put him to death."[69] A month later the Council of State of the revolutionary government invited Milton to become its "secretary for foreign tongues." He put his epic aside, and for eleven years gave himself to the service of the Puritan Commonwealth and Cromwell's Protectorate.

VI. THE LATIN SECRETARY: 1649–59

The new regime needed a good Latinist to compose its foreign correspondence. Milton was the obvious choice; he could write Latin, Italian, and French like an ancient Roman, a Florentine, or a Parisian; and he had proved through dangerous years his fidelity to the Parliamentary cause against the bishops and the King. It was the Council, not Cromwell, that engaged him; he had no close relations with the new ruler, but he must have seen him frequently, and must have felt in his thought and writing the nearness of that awesome personality. The Council used Milton not merely to translate its foreign correspondence into Latin, but to explain to other governments, by Latin brochures, the justice of its domestic policies, and, above all, how reasonable had been the decapitation of the King.

In April, 1649, soon after his induction into office, Milton joined with other employees of the Council in suppressing royalist and Leveller publications against the new regime.[70] Censorship was now more severe than at any time in England's history, following the general rule that censorship increases with the insecurity of the government. The man who had written the most eloquent appeal ever made for freedom of the press was now looking at censorship from the view of the ruling power. We should note, however, that in the *Areopagitica* Milton had allowed that "it is of the greatest concernment in the Church and Commonwealth to have a vigilant eye how books demean themselves, as well as men; and *thereafter* to confine, imprison, and do sharpest justice on them as malefactors."[71]

As John Lilburne was an especially troublesome Leveller, Milton was instructed by the Council to write a reply to his radical pamphlet, *New Chains Discovered*. We do not know if he carried out this assignment. But he himself tells us[72] that he was "ordered" to answer the *Eikon Basilike*. He complied by publishing (October 6, 1649) a book of 242 pages, entitled *Eikonoklastes* ("Image Breaker"). Doubting but assuming that the *Eikon Basilike* was what it purported to be, the work of Charles I, Milton took up step by step the royalist argument, and countered it with all the force he could muster. He defended the policy of Cromwell throughout, justified the execution of the King, and expressed his scorn of the "inconstant, irrational, and image-doting rabble . . . , a credulous and helpless herd, begotten to servility . . . and enchanted with . . . tyranny."[73]

Charles II, fretting on the Continent, paid Europe's greatest scholar, Claude Saumaise, to come to the defense of the dead King. "Salmasius" hurriedly composed the *Defensio Regia pro Carolo I*, which appeared at Leiden in November, 1649. He described Cromwell and his followers as "fanatical scoundrels . . . , the common enemy of the human race," and called upon all kings, for their own sake, to

> fit out an armament for the extermination of these pests . . . Surely the blood of the great King . . . calls to its revenge all monarchs and princes of the Christian world. Nor can they appease his spirit more worthily than by restoring to his full rights the legitimate heir . . . , reseating him on his paternal throne . . . and slaying, as victims at the tomb of the saintly dead, those most outrageous beasts who conspired for the murder of so great a king.[74]

Cromwell, fearing that this attack by a scholar of European fame would intensify the resentment, general on the Continent, against his government, asked Milton to answer Salmasius. The Latin secretary labored at the task for almost a year, working at it by candlelight despite his doctor's warning that he was slowly becoming blind. One eye was already useless. On December 31, 1650, appeared *Joannis Miltoni, Angli, pro Populo Anglicano Defensio contra Claudii Salmasii Defensionem Regiam*. It began by taunting Salmasius for selling his services to Charles II, and went on to show that Salmasius only four years earlier had written against episcopacy, which now he defended.

> O you venal and fee-taking agent! . . . O the sneak and turncoat! . . . You, silliest of blockheads, are worthy of the fool's staff itself for thinking to persuade kings and princes to war with such puerile arguments . . . Do you then, without wit, without genius, a mouther and a pettifogger, born only to rifle and transcribe good authors, imagine that you can produce anything of your own that will live— you, whose foolish writings, bundled up with yourself, the next age, believe me, will consign to oblivion? Unless perchance this *Defensio regia* of yours shall owe something to the Answer to it, and shall therefore, though already for some time neglected and laid to sleep, be again taken up[75]

—which is precisely what has happened. Salmasius had idealized Charles I, Milton degrades him. He suspects Charles of having abetted the Duke of Buckingham to poison his father, James I; he accuses the dead King of "all kinds of viciousness" with the said Duke; he charges Charles with kissing women at the theater, and of publicly fondling the breasts (*papillas*) of virgins and matrons.[76] Salmasius had called Milton many names; Milton retaliates by describing Salmasius as a fool, beetle, ass, liar, slanderer, apostate, idiot, ignoramus, vagabond, slave. He taunts Salmasius with being dominated by his wife, chides him for Latin errors, invites him to hang himself, and guarantees him admission to hell.[77] Thomas Hobbes, viewing the rival books from some perch of philosophy, declared himself unable to decide whose language was best, or whose arguments were worse.[78] The Council of State gave Milton a vote of thanks.

Salmasius received a copy of Milton's *Defensio* while at the court of Queen Christina in Stockholm. He promised, but delayed, to reply. Meanwhile Milton passed from foreign to domestic affairs. In 1649 he moved to a house in Charing Cross to be nearer his work. There his wife bore a son, who soon died, and, in 1652, a daughter, Deborah, whose birth cost the mother's life. In that year Milton's blindness became complete. Now he wrote one of his greatest sonnets—"When I consider how my light is spent." The Council continued him as Latin secretary, providing him with an amanuensis.

In his darkness he suffered another loss: the republic that he had so fervently hailed collapsed (1653) into a military monarchy, and Cromwell, "Protector," became in effect king. Milton resigned himself to these developments with the remark that "the ways of Providence are inscrutable."[79] He continued to admire Cromwell, and praised him as "the greatest and most glorious of our countrymen, . . . the father of your country," and assured him that "in the coalition of human society nothing is more pleasing to God, or more agreeable to reason, than that the highest mind should have the sovereign power."[80]

He was soon called upon to defend the Protector against a powerful indictment. In 1652 there had appeared a book whose very title was a battle cry: *Regii Sanguinis Clamor ad Coelum Adversus Parracidas Anglicanos—The Cry of the Royal Blood to Heaven against the English Parricides.* It began with a description of Milton as "a monster hideous, ugly, huge, bereft of sight, . . . a hangman, . . . a gallows bird." It compared the execution of Charles I with the crucifixion of Christ, and reckoned the regicide the greater crime.[81] It scorned the religious professions of the "usurpers":

> The language of their public documents is stuffed with piety; the style of Cromwell or his tribunes is to match; it would move anyone's bile and bitter laughter to mark with what impudence the secret rogues and open robbers mask their wickedness with a pretext of religion . . . Verily an egg is not liker an egg than Cromwell's like to Mahomet.[82]

And the anonymous author, like Salmasius, appealed to the Continental powers to invade England and restore the Stuart monarchy. The book closed with an address "To the Bestial Blackguard John Milton, Advocate of Parricides and Parricide," and a hope that he would soon be mercilessly flogged:

Round this perjured head
Ply well the stick; lard every inch with weals,
Till you have thonged the carcass to one jelly.
Cease you already? Lay on, till he shed
Gall from his liver through his bleeding eyes.[83]

The Council of State urged Milton to reply to this fury. He waited a while, expecting a blast from Salmasius, and hoping to impale both antagonists upon one pen. But Salmasius died (1653), leaving his rebuttal unfinished. Milton was misled into believing that the author of the *Regii Sanguinis Clamor* was Alexander Morus, a pastor and scholar at Middelburg. He asked his correspondents in the United Provinces to send him data about Morus' public and private life.[84] Adrian Ulacq, the printer of the book, wrote to Milton's friend Hartlib, assuring him that Morus was not the author,[85] but Milton refused to believe this, and Amsterdam gossip agreed with him. In April, 1654, John Drurie wrote to Milton warning him that he was mistaken in ascribing the *Clamor* to Morus; Milton ignored the warning. On May 30 he published *Joannis Miltoni pro Populo Anglicano Defensio Secunda*.

The eloquence of these 173 pages is remarkable, for they were dictated in Latin by a man completely blind. His enemies had described that blindness as a divine punishment for egregious sins; Milton replies that this cannot be, for he has led an exemplary life. He rejoices that his first *Defensio*

> so routed my opponent . . . that he yielded at once, broken alike in spirit and reputation, and in the whole three years of his subsequent life, though threatening and fuming much, gave us no further trouble, save that he called to his aid the obscure labor of some utterly despicable person, and suborned I know not what silly and extravagant adulations to repatch by their eulogies, as far as might be, the unexpected and recent ruin of his character.[86]

Turning upon his new enemy, Milton notes that *morus* in Greek meant fool; he accuses him of heresy, profligacy, and fornication, of getting Salmasius' maidservant with child and then abandoning her. Even the printer of the *Clamor* gets a lashing; everyone knows that he is a "notorious cheat and bankrupt."[87]

In better humor Milton reviews the career of Cromwell. He defends the campaigns in Ireland, the dissolutions of Parliament, the assumption of supreme power. He addresses the Protector:

> We all yield to your insuperable worth . . . Go on, therefore, in your magnanimous course, O Cromwell, . . . the liberator of your

country, the author of its freedom, . . . you who have excelled by your actions hitherto not only the exploits of kings, but even the legendary adventures of our Heroes.[88]

But after this obeisance he does not hesitate to advise the Protector on policy. Cromwell should surround himself with men like Fleetwood and Lambert (radicals); he should establish freedom of the press; he should leave religion entirely separate from the state. No tithes should be collected for the clergy; these men are already overfed; "all in general is fat about them, even their intellects not excepted."[89] Milton warns Cromwell that "if he, than whom none among us is reckoned more just, more saintly, or a better man, should afterwards invade that Liberty which he has defended . . . , the result would be disastrous and deadly, not only to himself but also to the universal interests of virtue and piety."[90] By "Liberty" Milton makes plain that he does not mean democracy. He asks the people:

> Why should anyone assert for you the right of free suffrage, or the power of electing whom you will to the Parliament? Is it that you should be able . . . to elect in the cities men of your faction, or that person in the boroughs, however worthy, who may have feasted yourselves most sumptuously, or treated the country people and boors to the greatest quantity of drink? Then we should have our members of Parliament made for us not by prudence and authority, but by faction and feeding; we should have vintners and hucksters from city taverns, and graziers and cattlemen from the country districts. Should one entrust the Commonwealth to those to whom nobody would entrust a matter of private business?[91]

No, such universal suffrage would not be freedom.

> To be free is the same thing exactly as to be pious, wise, just, temperate, self-providing, abstinent from the property of other people, and in fine, to be magnanimous and brave. To be the opposite of all this is the same as being a slave. And by the judgment of God it comes to pass that a nation that cannot rule and govern itself, but has surrendered itself in slavery to its own lusts, is surrendered also to other masters . . . and made a slave both with and against its own will.[92]

In October, 1654, Ulacq reprinted Milton's *Defensio Secunda* at The Hague, with an answer by Morus entitled *Fides publica* (*Public Testimony*). In a preface the printer asserted that Morus was not the author of the *Clamor;* that the manuscript had been given him (Ulacq) by Salmasius, who had refused to reveal the author's name. Morus solemnly denied his authorship, affirmed that Milton had been repeatedly informed of this, and charged that Milton had refused to alter the *Defensio*, since very little of it would have remained if all the abuse of Morus had been taken out. In August, 1655, Milton issued a volume of 204 pages, *Pro se Defensio* (*A Self-Defense*); he refused to believe Morus' denial; he repeated the scandal about Salmasius' maid, and added that the maid, in a fair fight, had beaten Morus, knocked him down, and almost scratched his eyes out.[93] In a sequel it appeared that a French Protestant theologian, Pierre de Moulin, had written the *Clamor*, and that Morus had edited it and written its dedication.[94] When Morus was invited (1657) to become the minister of a Reformed church near Paris, the poet sent several copies of his *Defensio Secunda* to the parish to prevent the appointment.[95] The parish consistory accepted Morus nevertheless, and he ended his troubled career (1670) as the most eloquent Protestant preacher in or about Paris.

Milton appears in a softer light in his powerful sonnet on the Piedmont massacre of 1655.* It was probably he who wrote the letters by which Cromwell appealed to the Duke of Savoy to end the persecution of the Vaudois, and to Mazarin and the rulers of Sweden, Denmark, the United Provinces, and the Swiss cantons to intercede with the Duke.

In 1656, after four years of widowhood, Milton married, sight unseen, Katharine Woodcock. She proved a blessing to him, serving as patient nurse to a blind and tempestuous husband, and mothering his three daughters; but she died in 1658 in giving birth to a short-lived child. That was a bitter year for Milton, since it took Cromwell too, and left the Latin secretary to keep his post as best he could amid the chaos of factions that reduced Richard Cromwell to a benevolent nonentity. Though Milton must have known that England was now moving toward a Stuart restoration, he issued a new edition (October, 1658) of his *Pro Populo Anglicano Defensio*, justifying the execution of Charles I in terms that almost courted martyrdom. In a characteristic preface he described this first *Defense* as "a monument . . . not easily to perish," claimed for it divine inspiration, and ranked it only next to Cromwell's deeds as having saved England's liberty.[96]

He resisted with blind bravery the movement for recalling Charles II. When Monck's army reached London, and Parliament hesitated between a republic and a monarchy, Milton published (February, 1660), as an address to Parliament, an eighteen-page pamphlet, *The Ready and Easy Way to Establish a Free Commonwealth, and the Excellence Thereof Compared with Inconveniences and Dangers of Readmitting Kingship in this Nation*, and he boldly signed it "The author, J.M." He pleaded with Parliament not to make

---

* See below, Chapter XVI, Section 1.

vain and viler than dirt the blood of so many thousand faithful and valiant Englishmen who left us this liberty, bought with our own lives . . . What will they [our neighbors] at best say of us, and of the whole English name, but scoffingly, as of that foolish builder mentioned by our Saviour, who began to build a tower, and was unable to finish it? Where is this goodly tower of a commonwealth, which the English boasted they would build to overshadow kings, and be another Rome in the West? . . . What madness is it for them who might manage nobly their own affairs themselves, sluggishly and weakly to devolve all in a single person! . . . How unmanly must it needs be, to count such a one the breath of our nostrils, to hang all our felicity on him, all our safety, our wellbeing, for which, if we were aught else but sluggards and babies, we need depend on none but God and our own counsels, our own active virtue and industry![97]

He predicted that all "the old encroachments" of monarchy on the freedom of the people will return soon after restoration. He proposed to replace Parliament with a "General Council" of ablest men, elected by the people, its members to serve till death, subject to removal only by conviction of some crime, and replenished by periodical elections. This Council, however, is to allow the greatest possible freedom of speech and worship, and of local autonomy. "I trust," Milton concluded, "I shall have spoken persuasion to abundance of sensible and ingenuous men—to some perhaps whom God may raise of these stones to become Children of Liberty, and may enable and unite in their noble resolutions to give a stay to these our ruinous proceedings, and to this general defection of the unguided and abused multitude."[98]

Parliament ignored this plea to destroy itself. Attacks on Milton appeared in print; one pamphlet recommended hanging him. The Council of State, now royalist, ordered the arrest of Milton's printer, and discharged Milton from his post as Latin secretary. Milton replied by publishing a second and enlarged edition of *The Ready and Easy Way* (April, 1660). He warned Parliament that promises now made by Charles II could easily be broken after the consolidation of the new royal power. He admitted that the majority of the people desired the restoration of Charles II, but he urged that the majority had no right to enslave a minority. "More just it is . . . if it come to force, that the less number compel a greater to return . . . their liberty than that a greater number . . . compel a less most injuriously to be their fellow slaves."[99] Attacks upon Milton multiplied; one called upon Charles II, then at Breda, to remember the insults that Milton, in *Eikonoklastes* and elsewhere, had heaped upon Charles I, and suggested that Milton should be joined with the actual regicides as meriting death.[100]

Before this pamphlet could reach Charles, he had already sailed for England. On May 7 Milton, having taken leave of his children, disappeared into hiding with a friend. He was discovered and imprisoned. For three months his fate hung in the balance of the royalist Parliament. Many members argued that he, if anyone, should be hanged. The general expectation was that he would be; but Marvell, Davenant, and others pleaded his age and blindness. Parliament contented itself with ordering that certain of his books, wherever found, should be burned. On December 15 he was released. He took a house in Holborn, moved into it with his children, and passed, after eleven turbulent years of prose, into the second and noblest period of his poetry.

VII. THE OLD POET: 1660–67

He found some solace in playing the organ and singing; he had, Aubrey tells us, "a delicate, tuneable voice."[101] In 1661 he moved again, and again in 1664, this time to his final home on Artillery Walk, where a private garden allowed him to stroll without other guides than his hands and feet. His nephews, their beatings forgotten, came often to see and aid him; friends dropped in to read to him or take his dictation. His three daughters served him impatiently but arduously. Anne, the oldest, was lame and deformed, and had a defect of speech. Deborah was his amanuensis. She and Mary were taught to read to him in Latin, Greek, Hebrew, French, Italian, and Spanish, though they could not understand what they read.[102] Indeed, none of them had ever gone to school; they had had some private tutoring, but they were poorly educated at best. Milton sold most of his library before he died, as his children cared little for books. He complained that they clandestinely sold his books, that they neglected him in his need, that they conspired with the servants to rob him in household purchases.[103] They were unhappy in that somber home, under a stern, demanding, irritable father. When daughter Mary heard that he was planning another marriage, she said "that there were no news to hear of his wedding; but if she could hear of his death, that were something."[104] In 1663 Milton, aged fifty-five, took a third wife, Elizabeth Minshull, aged twenty-four. She served him faithfully to the end of his days. After seven years with this stepmother, whom Aubrey describes as "a gentle person, a peaceful and agreeable humor,"[105] the three daughters left the paternal home and went out, at Milton's expense, to learn various trades.

The Restoration had cost him much—almost his life; but it made *Paradise Lost* possible. Without it he might have exhausted himself in embattled prose, for the fighter in him was as strong as the poet. Nevertheless amid his campaigns, he had never quit hope of writing something that England would cherish for centuries to come. In 1640 he made a list of possible subjects for an epic or a drama; the story of Adam's fall was in that list, along with the legends of King Arthur. He wavered between Latin and English as the language he would use; and even when he had decided on Paradise Lost as his theme, he thought of writing it in the form of a Greek tragedy or a medieval mystery play. At various times he composed lines or passages which were later fitted into the poem. Not till Cromwell was dead did Milton have the leisure to work upon the epic daily; and then (1658) he was altogether blind—

> On evil days though fallen, and evil tongues;
> In darkness, and with dangers compass'd round.[106]

Lines came to him as he lay helpless and sleepless in bed; bursting with them he would call for an amanuensis, saying that he "wanted to be milked."[107] A fever of composition would come upon him; he would dictate forty lines "in a breath," and then laboriously correct them as they were reread to him. Probably no poem was ever written with such toil and courage. Milton found strength in his consciousness that he was playing both Homer and Isaiah to England, for he believed that the poet is the voice of God, a prophet divinely inspired to teach mankind.

In 1665, when plague struck London, an imprisoned Quaker friend, Thomas Ellwood, arranged that Milton should be guided to Chalfont St. Giles in Buckinghamshire, and occupy Ellwood's ten-room "cottage" there. In this "Pretty Box" the poet completed Paradise Lost (June, 1665). But who would publish it? London was in turmoil in 1665-66, with fire coming on the heels of plague; and what joy remained was largely Restoration roistering, in no mood for 10,558 lines on original sin. Milton had received a thousand pounds for his Pro Populo Anglicano Defensio; now (April 27, 1667) he sold all rights to Paradise Lost to Samuel Simmons for five pounds down and an agreement for additional payments of five pounds each, contingent on sales; all in all he received eighteen pounds.[108] The poem was published in August, 1667. In its first two years thirteen hundred copies were sold; in its first eleven years, three thousand. Probably not that many readers, in any year, read it through today. We have so little leisure now that we have invented so many labor-saving devices.

The poem shares with the Aeneid the drawback that it came after "Homer"; so its battle scenes and supernatural warriors lose force by being imitations. Doubtless Homer too followed earlier models, but we have forgotten them. Johnson thought that Paradise Lost, "by the nature of its subject, has the advantage, above all others, that it is universally and perpetually interesting"; but he confessed that "none ever wished it longer than it is."[109] The subject,

> Of Man's First Disobedience, and the Fruit
> Of that Forbidden Tree, whose mortal taste
> Brought Death into the World, and all our woe,

was timely enough in Milton's youth, when the Book of Genesis was received as history, and heaven and hell, angels and devils, were in the fabric of daily thought. Today the subject is the poem's greatest handicap, a fairy tale recited to adults in twelve cantos; and a sustained effort is now required to accompany from beginning to end so long an exposition of so harsh and antiquated a theology. But never has nonsense been made more sublime. The grandeur of the scene, embracing heaven, hell, and the earth; the solemn, stately march of the blank verse, the manipulation of the complicated plot, the fresh and tender descriptions of nature, the successful effort to give reality and character to Adam and Eve, the frequent passages of majestic power—these are some of the reasons why *Paradise Lost* remains the greatest poem in the English language.

The story opens in hell, where Satan, pictured as a bird of "mighty stature" and "expanded wings," exhorts his fallen angels not to despair:

> All is not lost; the unconquerable Will,
> And study of revenge, immortal hate,
> And courage never to submit or yield:
> . . . To bow and sue for grace
> With suppliant knee, and deify his power
> . . . , that were low indeed,
> That were an ignominy and shame beneath
> This downfall; . . .
>   the mind and spirit remains
> Invincible . . .[110]

This sounds like Cromwell defying one Charles, and Milton another. Several passages describing Satan remind us of Milton:

> A mind not to be changed by place or time.
> The mind is its own place, and in itself
> Can make a Heaven of Hell, a Hell of Heaven.[111]

In the early cantos Milton's eloquence lured him into drawing an almost sympathetic picture of the Devil as the leader of a revolt against established and arbitrary power. The poet saved himself from making Satan the hero of the epic by representing him later as the Father of Lies, who "squat like a toad," or as a serpent sliding sinuously in the slime.[112] But in that same canto Satan stands forth as the defender of knowledge:

> Knowledge forbidden?
> ... Why should their Lord
> Envy them that? Can it be a sin to know,
> Can it be death? And do they [Adam and Eve] only stand
> By ignorance? Is that their happy state,
> The proof of their obedience and their faith?
> ... I will excite their minds
> With more desire to know . . .[113]

And so he argues with Eve like a rationalist attacking an obscurantist Church:

> Why, then, was this forbid? Why but to awe,
> Why but to keep you low and ignorant,
> His worshipers? He knows that in the day
> You eat thereof, your eyes, that seem so clear
> Yet are but dim, shall perfectly be then
> Open'd and clear'd, and ye shall be as gods . . .[114]

The angel Raphael, however, bids Adam check his curiosity about the universe; it is not wise for man to desire to know beyond his mortal scope;[115] faith is wiser than knowledge.

We should have expected Milton to interpret the "first sin" not as desire for knowledge but as sexual intercourse. On the contrary, he sings a quite unpuritanic paean to the legitimacy of sexual pleasure, within the bounds of marriage; and he represents Adam and Eve as indulging in such tactile values while still remaining in the "state of innocence."[116] But after the "fall"—eating the forbidden fruit of the tree of knowledge—they begin to feel shame in sexual congress.[117] Now Adam sees Eve as the source of all evil, "a rib crooked by nature," and mourns that God ever created woman:

> O why did God
> ... create at last
> This novelty on Earth, this fair defect
> Of Nature, and not fill the World at once
> With men as angels without feminine,
> Or find some other way to generate
> Mankind?[118]

Whereupon, so soon in the Biblical history of marriage, the first man makes a plea for the easier divorcing of the wife by the husband. Almost forgetting Adam, Milton here repeats in verse what he had said in prose about the proper subordination of woman to man.[119] He will return to that refrain in *Samson Agonistes;*[120] it is his favorite dream. And in his secret *De Doctrina Christiana* he pleaded for the restoration of polygamy. Had not the Old Testament sanctioned it, and had not the New Testament left that wholesome and manly law unrepealed?[121]

However interpreted, "man's first disobedience" proved too narrow a theme to fill twelve cantos. An epic required action, action, and action; but as the revolt of the angels is over when the story begins, its drama can enter the poem only through reminiscence, which is a fading echo. The battle scenes are well described, with due clash of arms and cleaving of heads and limbs, but it is hard to feel the pain or ecstasy of such imaginary blows. Like the French dramatists, Milton indulges a passion for oratory; everyone from God to Eve makes speeches, and Satan finds hellfire no impediment to rhetoric. It is disturbing to learn that even in hell we shall have to listen to lectures.

God, in this poem, is not the indescribable effulgence felt in Dante's *Paradiso;* he is a Scholastic philosopher who gives long and unconvincing reasons why he, the omnipotent, allows Satan to exist, and allows him to tempt man, all the while foreseeing that man will succumb and bring all mankind to centuries of sin and misery. He argues that without freedom to sin there is no virtue, without trial there is no wisdom; he thinks it better that man should face temptation and resist it than not be tempted at all, quite unforeseeing that the Lord's Prayer would beg God not to lead man into temptation. Who can help sympathize with Satan's revolt against such an incredible sadist?

Did Milton really believe in this predestinarian horror? Apparently, for he expounded it not only in *Paradise Lost*, but in his secret essay *De Doctrina Christiana;*[122] long before the creation of man, God had determined which souls should be saved, and which should be damned. That secret essay, however, contained some heresies; Milton never published it; it was not discovered till 1823, and did not reach print till 1825.

It is a remarkable document. It begins piously enough by assuming, without argument, that every word in the Bible was inspired by God. Milton admits that the Biblical text has suffered from "corruptions, falsifications, and mutations," but even in its present form it is the work of God. He will not allow any but a literal interpretation. If the Scriptures tell us that God rested, or feared, or repented, or was angry or grieved, these statements are to be taken at their face value, and not diluted as metaphors. Even the corporeal parts and qualities ascribed to God are to be accepted as physically true.[123] But in addition to this external revelation of himself in Scripture, God has given us an internal revelation which is the Holy Spirit speaking in our hearts; and this internal revelation, "the peculiar possession of each believer, is far superior . . . , a more certain guide than Scripture."[124] However, in his arguments, Milton quotes the Bible as the final and clinching proof.

On the basis of Scripture he rejects orthodox Trinitarianism, and prefers the Arian heresy: Christ was literally the Son of God, but he was begotten by the Father in time; therefore he was not coeval with the Father, and never equal with Him. Christ is the agent created by God as the Logos through whom all else was to be created. Milton does not admit Creation *ex nihilo*, out of nothing; the world of matter, like the world of spirit, is a timeless emanation from the divine substance. Even spirit is a fine, ethereal matter, and should not be too sharply distinguished from matter; ultimately matter and spirit, and in man body and soul, are one.[125] These views bear considerable resemblance to those of Hobbes (1588–1679) and Spinoza (1632–77), both of whom died in the same decade with Milton (1608–74). Probably Milton knew the works of Hobbes, which were making considerable noise in the court of Charles II.

Milton's personal religion remained a strange mixture of theism and materialism, of Arminian freedom of will and Calvinistic predestination. He seems in his writings to have been a profoundly religious man; yet he attended no church, even before his blindness, and practiced no religious rites in his home.[126] "In the distribution of his hours," wrote Dr. Johnson, "there was no hour of prayer, either solitary or with his household; omitting public prayers, he omitted all."[127] He scorned the clergy, and lamented Cromwell's retention of a state-paid clergy as a form of "whoredom" injurious to both Church and state.[128] In one of his last pronouncements (*Treatise of True Religion, Heresy, Schism, Toleration, and the Best Means to Prevent the Growth of Popery*, 1673) he went directly counter to Charles II's second Declaration of Indulgence (1672) by warning England not to tolerate Catholics, atheists, or any sect that did not recognize the Bible as the sole basis of its creed.

It was this man, bristling with heresy, anticlericalism, and nonconformity, who gave its noblest modern exposition to the Christian creed.

VIII. THE FINAL YEARS: 1667–74

As he passed into his seventh decade, Milton still retained, except for his blindness, the physical health and pride that had upheld him through so many conflicts of religion and politics. Aubrey describes him as "a spare man . . . of middle stature, . . . a beautiful and well-proportioned body, . . . complexion exceeding fair; . . . healthy and free from all diseases; seldom taking any physic [medicine]; only towards his latter end he was visited with the gout."[129] His hair, parted in the middle, fell to his shoulders in curls; his eyes gave no sign of their blindness; his gait was still erect and firm. When he went out he dressed fastidiously and wore a sword, for he was proud of his swordsmanship.[130] A man made grave and humorless by too much certainty, yet pleasant enough in conversation if not crossed. He was not quite a Puritan: he had the Puritan consciousness of sin, hell, election, and infallible Scripture, but he relished beauty, enjoyed music, wrote a play, and wanted many wives; some echo of the Elizabethan *élan* lingered amid his humorless solemnity. He was egotistic, or revealed his natural egotism, to an unusual extreme; he was "not ignorant of his own parts," as Anthony Wood put it;[131] and, said Johnson, "scarcely any man ever wrote so much and praised so few."[132] Probably genius needs to be self-centered, buttressed with internal pride, in order to stand steadily against the crowd. What is hardest to accept in Milton is his capacity for hatred and his intemperate abuse of those who differed from him. He thought that we should pray for our enemies, but that we should also "call down curses publicly on the enemies of God and the Church, as also on false brethren, and on such as are guilty of any grievous offenses against God, or even against ourselves."[133] The other side of this hot passion was the courage of the prophet denouncing his time. Instead of being silenced by the Restoration riot, he dared to hit at the "court amours" under Charles II, the "lust and violence" in palaces, the "bought smile of harlots," the "wanton masque or midnight ball."[134]

As if flinging a last defiance at darkened time, he published in one day (September 20, 1670) two unrelentingly Miltonic works: *Paradise Regained* and *Samson Agonistes*. In 1665 Thomas Ellwood, having read the earlier epic, challenged Milton: "Thou hast said much here of Paradise lost, but what hast thou to say of Paradise found?"[135] Milton felt the point keenly, but he wondered how he could show Paradise regained at any point in history; even the death of Christ had not cleansed man of crime and lust and war. But he thought that in the resistance of Christ to Satan's temptations he saw a promise that the God in man would someday overcome the Devil in him, and make man fit to live under the rule of Christ and justice on earth.

So in the four "books" of *Paradise Regained* Milton centered the life of Christ not on the Crucifixion but on the temptation in the wilderness. Satan offers Christ "stripling youths . . . of fairer hue than Ganymede," then "nymphs . . . and Naiades . . . and ladies of the Hesperides,"[136] then wealth—all to no avail. Satan shows him Imperial Rome under a Tiberius exhausted, childless, and unpopular; would not Christ like to lead a revolution with Satan's aid, and make himself emperor of the world? As this does not appeal to Jesus, Satan shows him the Athens of Socrates and Plato; would he not like to join them and be a philosopher? Satan and Christ then engage in a strange debate on the comparative merits of Greek versus Hebrew literature. Christ upholds the Jewish prophets and poets as far superior to the Greeks:

> Greece from us these arts derived,
> Ill imitated . . .[137]

After two "books" of argument Satan acknowledges himself defeated and takes to his wings, while a chorus of angels gathers around the triumphant Christ and sings:

> . . . now thou hast avenged
> Supplanted Adam, and by vanquishing
> Temptation, hast regained lost Paradise . . .[138]

Milton tells the story not with the sonorous sublimity of the larger epic, but with his usual facility for verse and predilection for argument, all the while unfolding his erudition in geography and history. He does not continue the story to the Crucifixion; probably he did not agree with the view that it was Christ's death that reopened the gates of Paradise. Happiness could be gained only by virtue and self-control. He could never understand why England refused to take seriously this absurd rewriting of the Gospels. He thought the later epic not inferior to the earlier except in scope.[139] "He could not bear to hear *Paradise Lost* preferred to *Paradise Regained*."[140]

The Miltonic fire flared up for the last time in *Samson Agonistes*. Having challenged Homer, Virgil, and Dante with his epic, now he challenged Aeschylus and Sophocles with a play that accepted all the restraints of Greek tragedy. The preface asks the reader to note that the drama obeys the classic unities, and that it avoids "the poet's error of intermixing comic stuff with tragic sadness and gravity, or introducing trivial and vulgar persons"; here Milton turns his back upon the Elizabethans, and cleaves to the Greeks; nor does he fall far short of his Attic exemplars. Samson, his strength shorn with his hair by Delilah, and his eyes gouged out by his Philistine captors, does not merely echo Oedipus eyeless in Colonus; he is Milton himself, living in a world hostile and unseen:

> Blind among enemies, O worse than chains,
> Dungeon, or beggary, or decrepit age!
> Light, the prime work of God, to me is extinct,
> And all her various objects of delight
> Annulled, which might in part my grief have eased . . .

> O dark, dark, dark, amid the blaze of noon,
> Irrecoverably dark, total eclipse
> Without all hope of day![141]

Indeed, the whole play may be interpreted as a remarkably consistent allegory: Milton is Samson, agonizing in adversity; the defeated Jews are the Puritans, the chosen people, broken by the Restoration; the victorious Philistines are the triumphant pagan royalists, and the collapse of their temple is almost a prophecy of the "Glorious Revolution" that unseated the "idolatrous" Stuarts in 1688. Delilah is a treacherous Mary Powell, and the chorus repeats Milton's arguments for divorce.[142] Milton almost purged himself of his furies by voicing them through Samson, who accepts his coming end:

> My race of glory run, and race of shame,
> And I shall shortly be with them that rest.[143]

In July, 1674, Milton felt himself failing. For reasons not known to us he omitted writing his will; instead, he delivered to his brother Christopher a "nuncupative"—merely oral—will, which Christopher reported as follows:

> Brother, the portion due to me from Mr. Powell, my former wife's father, I leave to the unkind children I had by her; but I have received no part of it; and my will and meaning is they shall have no other benefit of my estate than the said portion and what I have besides done for them, they having been very undutiful to me. And all the residue of my estate I leave to the disposal of Elizabeth, my loving wife.[144]

This oral will was repeated to his wife and to others at various times.

He held on to life resolutely, but day to day his gout increased in pain, crippling his hands and feet. On November 8, 1674, fever consumed him, and that night he died. He had lived sixty-five years and eleven months. He was buried in the cemetery of his parish church, St. Giles, Cripplegate, beside his father.

Oral wills were recognized in English law till 1677, but were subject to close scrutiny by the courts. The daughters contested Milton's will; the judge rejected it, gave two thirds to the wife, one third, totaling three hundred pounds, to the daughters. The "portion due" from Mr. Powell was never paid.

Though we know so much more about Milton than about Shakespeare, and so much must be recorded to picture him, we still do not know enough to judge him—if this is possible of any man. We do not know how much reason his daughters gave him for his resentment, nor how they treated that third wife who so comforted his old age; we can only regret that he failed to win their love. We do not know in full his reasons for acting as a censor of the press for Cromwell after arguing so eloquently for "unlicensed printing." We may ascribe much of his abusiveness in controversy to the manners and standards of the time. We may pardon his vanity and egotism as the crutch on which genius leans when it gets little support from the applause of the world. We need not relish him as a man to admire him as a poet, and as one of England's greatest writers of prose.

Those who resolve to read *Paradise Lost* from beginning to end are surprised to find how often it soars to high levels of imagination and utterance, so that in time we forgive the dull pages of argument, science, or geography as breathing spaces between exaltations; it would be absurd to expect those lyric flights to be continuously sustained. In the short poems they are sustained. And in Milton's prose there are passages, especially in the *Areopagitica*, that are unsurpassed for vigor or splendor, for thought and music, in all the gamut of the world's secular literature.

His contemporaries gave him only a grudging fame. During the ascendancy of his party he was a warrior writing prose, and his early lyrics were forgotten. He published his larger poems under that Restoration which scorned his tribe and reluctantly consented to let him live. When Louis XIV asked his ambassador in London to name England's best living authors, the reply was that there were none of any worth except Milton, who, unfortunately, had defended the regicides who were now being hanged, alive or dead. Even in that riotous age, however, its most famous poet, John Dryden, whom Milton had reckoned as "a good rhymester but no poet,"[145] rated *Paradise Lost* as "one of the greatest, most noble and most sublime poems which either this age or nation has produced."[146] After the overthrow of the Stuarts Milton came into his own. Addison praised him generously in *The Spectator*.[147] Thereafter the image of Milton grew in splendor and sanctity in the British mind, till Wordsworth, in 1802, could apostrophize him:

> Milton! thou shouldst be living at this hour; . . .
> Thy soul was like a Star, and dwelt apart;
> Thou hadst a voice whose sound was like the sea,
> Pure as the naked heavens, majestic, free.

His soul was like a monument, and dwelt apart even from those nearest to him; but his mind spread like the majestic heavens over all the concerns of men, and his voice still sounds like Homer's *polyphloisboio thalasses*, the "many-billowed sea."

CHAPTER IX

The Restoration

1660–85

I. THE HAPPY KING

ON May 29, 1660, exactly thirty years after his birth, Charles II entered London amid such popular rejoicing as exceeded anything in England's memory. Twenty thousand men of the city militia escorted him, flaunting their banners and brandishing their swords, through streets strewn with flowers, hung with tapestry, noisy with trumpets and bells and hailing cries, and lined with half the population of the town. "I stood in the Strand and beheld it," wrote Evelyn, "and blessed God."[1] It marked the temper of England, and the failure of Puritanism, that whereas six years of war and turmoil had been required to depose Charles I, not one drop of blood had been shed in restoring his son. All through that ecstatic summer Englishmen flocked to Whitehall to greet the King. "The eagerness of men, women, and children to see his Majesty and kiss his hands," said one witness, "was so great that he had scarce leisure to eat for some days. . . . And the King, being as willing to give them that satisfaction, would have none kept out, but gave free access to all sorts of people."[2] He said he wished to make his people as happy as himself.

If he had taken any problem very seriously in those triumphant days, the difficulties bequeathed to him would have darkened his honeymoon. The cash in the Exchequer amounted to £11, 2s. 10d. The government was in debt by two million pounds. The army and navy were several years behind in pay. England was at war with Spain. Dunkirk was precariously held at a cost of £100,000 per annum. Ten thousand Cavaliers who had fought for Charles I, and had been despoiled by Cromwell, begged for compensation. Ten thousands patriots petitioned for sinecures. Charles said Yes recklessly, and trusted Parliament to find funds.

Parliament too was happy. Its first mood was one of ecstatic submission to the restored monarchy: "We submit and oblige ourselves and our posterities to your Majesty forever."[3] The House of Commons voted "that neither themselves nor the people of England could be free from the horrid guilt of the late unnatural rebellion, or from the punishments which that guilt merited unless they formally availed themselves of his Majesty's grace and pardon"—whereupon the members went in a body and knelt before the amused monarch to receive his absolution.[4] The Commons felt added guilt for having assembled without the summons or consent of the King; it called itself humbly a "Convention" until Charles eased its conscience by declaring it a legitimate Parliament.[5] These ceremonies over, the Parliament annulled all such legislation of the Long Parliament as had not received the consent of Charles I; but it reaffirmed those concessions which that King had made to Parliament, including its own supremacy in all matters of taxation; and these concessions were confirmed by Charles II. Parliament shared with the King in a crucial victory of the civil power over the military: the arrears of pay due the army that for a decade had ruled England were paid; the forty thousand men disbanded and went home.

Charles had agreed to pardon all his enemies except those that Parliament should exclude from amnesty. Parliament spent weeks debating whom to spare and whom to kill. On July 27, 1660, the King went to the House of Lords and pleaded for an early and merciful decision:

> My Lords, if you do not join with me in extinguishing this fear, which keeps the hearts of men awake . . . , you keep me from performing my promise, which if I had not made, I am persuaded neither you nor I had been now here. I knew well there had been some men who could neither forgive themselves, or be forgiven by us; and I thank you for your justice towards those—the immediate murderers of my father; but—I will deal truly with you—I never thought of excepting any others [from the amnesty] . . . This mercy and indulgence is the best way to bring men to a true repentance . . . It will make them good subjects to me, and good friends and neighbors to you.[6]

Parliament wished for a wider vengeance, but Charles insisted that pardon should be offered to all except those who had signed the death sentence of his father.[7] Of these a third were dead, a third had fled; twenty-eight were arrested and tried; fifteen were condemned to life imprisonment, thirteen were hanged, drawn, and quartered (October 13–17, 1660). Thomas Harrison, the first to suffer, "looking as cheerful," noted eyewitness Pepys, "as any man could do in that condition," spoke bravely from the scaffold, saying that his course in voting for the death of Charles I had been dictated by God.[8] "He was presently cut down," says Pepys, "and his head and heart shown to the people, at which there were great shouts of joy."[9] On December 8 Parliament ordered that the corpses of Cromwell, Ireton, and John Bradshaw should be exhumed from Westminster Abbey and be hanged; it was so done on January 30, 1661, as a way of celebrating the anniversary of Charles I's death. The heads were exposed for a day on top of Westminster Hall (where Parliament met), and then the remains were buried in a pit under the gallows of Tyburn; all of which made John Evelyn rejoice at "the stupendous and inscrutable judgments of God."[10] Another victim, Harry Vane, once governor of Massachusetts Bay Colony, was hanged (1662) for having been instrumental in procuring the execution of Strafford. In this case the King's mercy slept; he had promised to spare popular "Sir Harry," but the prisoner's boldness at trial hardened the royal heart.

On December 29, 1660, the Convention Parliament dissolved itself to make way for elections to a more representative delegation. In the interim the government faced the only hostile demonstration that questioned its popularity in the capital. It had done nothing to silence the religious sects that still hoped for a republican regime; Presbyterian, Anabaptist, Independent, and Fifth Monarchy divines preached hotly against the monarchy, and predicted that God's vengeance would fall upon it soon in earthquakes, or sheets of blood, or swarms of toads invading the houses of royal magistrates. On Sunday, January 6, 1661, while the King was at Portsmouth seeing his beloved sister Henrietta off to France, a wine cooper, Thomas Venner, raised the cry of revolt in a congregation of Fifth Monarchy "saints." His excited hearers armed themselves, ran through the streets crying out that only Jesus should be king, and slew all who resisted them. For two days and nights the city was in terror, for the Saints scattered in all directions, killing heartily; until at last a small company of guards, which the confident government had relied upon to keep order, rounded up the raiders and led them to the gallows. Charles, returning in haste to his capital, organized new regiments to police it.

On April 23, feast of England's patron St. George, the happy King was crowned in Westminster Abbey, with all the solemn gorgeous ceremony so precious to monarchy and so dear to the people; and the restored Anglican hierarchy took care to impress upon their anointed rake his obligation to defend the faith and the Church. On May 8 the new "Cavalier Parliament" convened, so called because its majority was more royalist than the King, and lusted for revenge against the Puritans. Charles had difficulty in dissuading it from resuming the slaughter of his father's enemies. It restored, theoretically, much of the royal prerogative that had been lost by Charles I: no legislation was to be valid except with the consent of both Houses and the King; and he was to have supreme command of England's armed forces on land or sea. It re-established the House of Lords, and returned to that chamber the bishops of the Established Church; but it refused to renew the Star Chamber or the Court of High Commission, and the right of habeas corpus was retained. Cavalier properties confiscated under Cromwell were restored, with little compensation to the purchasers. The old aristocracy regained wealth and power; the dispossessed families turned against the Stuarts, and later joined with the gentry and the middle classes to form the Whigs against the Tories. Charles, in the first half of his reign, was too lackadaisical to assert any absolute authority; he allowed the Cavalier Parliament to continue for seventeen years despite his legal right to dismiss it; in practice he was a constitutional king. The essential result of the Rebellion (1642–49), the passage of supremacy from king to Parliament, and from the Lords to the Commons, survived the Restoration despite the theoretical absolutism of the Crown.

It was the good fortune of Parliament that Charles had no liking for government. He behaved as if, after fourteen years of wandering and hardship, he had now been granted by Providence the right to be happy, and had been admitted to a Mohammedan Paradise. Sometimes he labored at affairs of state; his negligence of them has been exaggerated;[11] and toward the end of his reign the nation was surprised to see him take direct charge and acquit himself with skill and resolution. But in these honeymoon years he delegated to Edward Hyde, whom he made Earl of Clarendon in 1661, the administration of the government and even the determination of policy.

The character of the King entered influentially into the manners, morals, and politics of the age. He was predominantly French in parentage and education. His mother was French; his father was the great-grandson of Mary of Guise or Lorraine; add to this a Scottish, a Danish, and an Italian grandparent, and we get a rich but perhaps unstable mixture. From his sixteenth to his thirtieth year he had lived on the Continent, where he learned French ways, and saw them at their best in his sister Henrietta Anne. His dark hair and skin remembered his Italian grandmother, Marie de Médicis; his temperament was Latin, like that of his great-grandmother Mary Queen of Scots; his sensual lips, his shining eyes, his long intrusive nose, and perhaps his taste for women, came from his Gascon grandfather, Henry of Navarre.

Sexually he was the most scandalous leader of his time, for his example set loose the looseness of his court, of London society, and of the Restoration theater. We know thirteen of his mistresses by name. When, aged eighteen, he came from Holland to England to fight for his father, he found time to beget, by the "brown, beautiful, bold" Lucy Walter, a boy who grew up as James Scott, whom he later acknowledged as his son and made Duke of Monmouth. Lucy followed Charles to the Continent and served him faithfully, apparently with some now nameless aides. Soon after occupying the royal palace he called Barbara Palmer to comfort his weariness. As Barbara Villiers she had set London agog with her beauty. At eighteen (1659) she married Roger Palmer, who became Earl of Castlemaine. At nineteen she found the King's bed, and soon won such domination over his complaisant spirit that he gave her an apartment in Whitehall, lavished great sums upon her, and allowed her to sell political appointments and to influence the fate of ministers. She bore three sons and two daughters, whom he acknowledged as his own. He had his doubts, however, for amid her royal devotions she carried on liaisons with other men.[12] Her piety grew with her promiscuity. In 1663 she announced her conversion to Catholicism. Her relatives sought the King to dissuade her, but he told them that he never meddled with the *souls* of the ladies.[13]

In 1661 Charles thought it time to marry. From many suitors he chose Catherine of Braganza, daughter of John IV of Portugal, for she was offered to him with a dowry providentially fitted to the needs of a spend-thrift ruler and a merchant state: £500,000 in cash, the port of Tangier, the isle and (then small) city of Bombay, and free trade with all Portu-guese possessions in Asia and America. In return England pledged aid to maintain the independence of Portugal. When the precious Infanta reached Portsmouth Charles was on hand to greet her; they were married (May 21, 1662) at first by Roman Catholic rites, then by Anglican. He wrote to her mother that he was "the happiest man in the world," and he bore gallantly with her train of hoopskirted ladies and solemn monks. She fell in love with him at first touch. Everything went well for some weeks; but in July Lady Castlemaine gave birth to a boy, at whose christening Charles stood godfather—another case of taking God's name in vain. Having left her husband, Barbara was now completely dependent upon the King. She begged him not to desert her; he yielded, and soon resumed relations with her, with the most scandalous fidelity. Forgetting his usual good manners, he publicly presented Barbara to his wife. Catherine bled at the nose with humiliation, swooned, and was carried from the room. Clarendon, at Charles's urging, explained to her that adultery was a royal privilege, recog-nized as such by the best families on the Continent. In time the Queen ad-justed herself to her consort's Oriental ways. Once, visiting him and seeing a tiny slipper beside his bed, she graciously withdrew lest "the pretty little fool" hiding behind the curtains should catch cold;[14] this time it was the actress Moll Davis. Meanwhile Catherine tried repeatedly to bear Charles a child; but, like Catherine of Aragon with an earlier King, she had several miscarriages. In 1670 Parliament passed a bill enlarging the grounds for divorce; some courtiers, anxious for a Protestant heir, advised Charles to divorce Catherine for sterility, but he refused. By that time he had learned to love her deeply, after his own fashion.

Pepys pictures the court as of July 27, 1667:

> Fenn tells me that the King and my Lady Castlemaine are quite broke off, and she is going away, and is with child, and swears the King shall own it . . . or she will bring it into Whitehall . . . and dash the brains of it out before the King's face. He tells me that the King

and court were never in the world so bad as they are now for gaming, whoring, and drinking, and the most abominable vices that were ever in the world; so that all must come to naught.[15]

By 1668 Charles was tiring of La Castlemaine's tantrums. On one of his last visits to her he interrupted John Churchill, the future Duke of Marlborough, who, according to Bishop Burnet, jumped from the window to avoid a scene with the King.[16] Charles made her Duchess of Cleveland, and supported her, with the public money, to the end of her career.

It is pleasant to relate that one woman apparently repulsed the royal rooster: Frances Stewart, who was credited with "the finest face that perhaps was ever seen";[17] "It was hardly possible," said Anthony Hamilton, "for a woman to have less wit or more beauty."[18] The King continued to importune her even after she had married the Duke of Richmond. Pepys describes him as rowing alone at night to Somerset House, "and there, the garden door not being open, himself clambered over the wall to make a visit to her, which is a horrid shame!"[19]

In 1668 Charles saw Nell Gwynn acting at the Drury Lane Theatre. Born and bred in the lowest poverty, entertaining tavern drinkers with her songs, selling oranges in the theater, taking minor parts, rising to leading roles in comedies, she kept through all her career a spontaneity of good spirits and good will that charmed the blasé King. She made no difficulties about becoming his mistress; she drew large sums from his ailing purse, but she spent much of these in charity. Soon she had to compete with a siren sent from France (1671) to keep Charles toeing the French and Catholic line: Louise de Kéroualle, whose aristocratic airs Nell mimicked impishly. All the world knows how, when the London populace mistook Nell for her Catholic rival and jeered her, she put her pretty head out of the coach window and cried: "Be silent, good people; I am the *Protestant* whore."[20] She continued to share Charles's favor to the end of his life, and was in his thoughts at his death. La Kéroualle, soon made Duchess of Portsmouth, angered London because she was looked upon as a very expensive French agent, draining the King of forty thousand pounds a year, amassing jewelry, and living in such luxury as turned honest John Evelyn's stomach.[21] Her reign ended in 1676, when Charles discovered Hortense Mancini, the vivacious niece of Cardinal Mazarin.

Charles had other faults. In his youthful misfortunes he had lost all faith in humanity, and judged all men and women as La Rochefoucauld described them. Hence he was scarcely capable of devotion—except to his sister—but lost himself in infatuations; and no sincere and lasting friendship cast any substantial glow upon the shallow brilliance of his life. He sold his country as readily as he bought women. He set his court the example of gambling for great sums. Despite the careless charm of his manners he showed at times a lack of delicacy that could hardly have been found in his father; so, for example, he drew Gramont's attention to the fact that his household attendants served him on bended knee.[22] He was not often drunk, but was "horribly" so a few days after the issuance of an edict against drunkenness.[23] He was usually tolerant of criticism, but when Sir John Coventry, overstepping bounds, asked in open Parliament "whether the King's pleasure lay among men or the women," Charles bade his guardsmen "leave a mark" upon him; they waylaid Sir John and slit his nose to the bone.[24]

And yet there were very few who could help liking him. Not since the youth of Henry VIII had an English king been so popular with his court. His physical vitality was ingratiating. There was no meanness in him; he was considerate, kind, and generous; even after paying his courtesans he found means for charity. He made his park a sanctuary for diverse animals, and saw that no harm came to them. His favorite spaniel slept, mated, littered and gave suck in the King's bedchamber.[25] He put on no airs, was affable and approachable, and quickly set his interlocutors at their ease. Everyone but Coventry agreed in speaking of him as "the good-natured king."[26] Gramont reckoned him "of all men one of the most mild and gentle."[27] According to Aubrey he was "the pattern of courtesy."[28] He had polished his manners in France, and, like Louis XIV, he doffed his hat to the lowliest women. He was far ahead of his nation in tolerance of diverse opinions and faiths. He drank to the health of his political opponents, and delighted in satire even when of himself. His sense of humor was the delight of the court. Pepys describes him as leading an old country dance called "Cuckolds All Awry." His merrymaking was only briefly interrupted by news of plague, fire, bankruptcy, or war.

His mind was not profound, but there was remarkably little nonsense in it. He disposed of a man who claimed to tell fortunes by taking him to the races and noting that he lost three times in succession. He had a keen interest in science, made experiments, gave a charter and gifts to the Royal Society, and attended several of its meetings. He had no particular interest in literature, but much in art, and treasured his Raphaels, Titians, and Holbeins. His conversation had much of the vivacity and variety of that of the cultured circles in France; he talked well of poetry with Dryden, of music with Purcell, of architecture with Wren, and was a discriminating patron in all these fields. There must have been a great deal to be loved in a man whose sister, on her deathbed, said of him, "I have loved him better than life itself, and now my only regret in dying is to be leaving him."[29]

II. THE RELIGIOUS CALDRON

Did he have any religion? His life suggests the same attitude that we find in many contemporary Frenchmen, who lived as atheists and died as Catholics; this seemed to get the best of both worlds, and to be a great improvement on Pascal's "wager." "His sense of religion was so small," said Burnet, "that he did not so much as affect the hypocrite, but at prayers and sacraments let everyone, by his negligent behavior, see how little he thought himself concerned in these matters."[30] "My Lord, my Lord," said a preacher to a dozing peer in the congregation, "you snore so loud you will wake the King."[31] Saint-Évremond, who knew Charles well, described him as a deist[32]—i.e., one who acknowledged a Supreme Being, more or less impersonal, and interpreted the remainder of the religious creeds as popular poetry; and the Earl of Buckingham and the Marquess of Halifax agreed with Saint-Évremond.[33] "He said once to myself," reports Burnet, "that he was no atheist, but he could not think God would make a man miserable for taking a little pleasure out of the way."[34] Charles welcomed the materialist Hobbes to his friendship, and protected him against the theologians who demanded his prosecution for heresy. Voltaire thought that the King's "extreme indifference to all [religious] disputes that commonly divide men had contributed not a little to his reigning peacefully."[35]

Probably he was a skeptic with a leaning toward Catholicism; i.e., doubting the theologies, he preferred Catholicism for its colorful ritual, its marriage with the arts, its lenience to the flesh, and its support of monarchy. He had probably forgotten that the Catholic League and some Jesuit fathers had sanctioned regicide. He remembered that English Catholics had fought for his father, that a third of the nobles who had died for Charles I were Catholics,[36] that the Irish Catholics had persisted in loyalty to the Stuarts, and that a Catholic government had supported him in his long exile. His generally sympathetic spirit inclined him to desire some mitigation of England's anti-Catholic laws, which, in Hallam's judgment, "were highly severe, in some cases sanguinary."[37] He did not share the English Protestant's memory of the Gunpowder Plot (1605), or dread of subjection to the Inquisition and to Rome. He took no offense at the open adherence of his brother—and presumptive heir—to the Catholic faith. We may judge from his deathbed conversion that he too would have professed Catholicism if that had been politically practical.

So, as an amiable politician, he accepted and supported the Anglican Church. It had been loyal to his father, who had died in its defense; it had suffered under Cromwell; it had worked for the Restoration. Charles took for granted that some religion should receive state sanction and aid as an agent of education and social order. He was constitutionally horrified by Puritanism; besides, it had had a fair chance at government, and had proved too severe and unpopular. He could not forget that the Presbyterians had imprisoned, and the Puritans had beheaded, his father, and that he himself had been forced to accept their creed, and to apologize for the sins of his parents. He signed as obviously just the act of the Convention Parliament restoring to their parishes the Anglican clergymen who had been dispossessed by the Commonwealth. Nevertheless, he had promised "liberty to tender consciences," and that no man should be "disquieted" for peaceable diversities of religious belief. In October, 1660, he proposed a comprehensive toleration of all Christian sects, even mitigating the laws against Catholics, but the Presbyterians and the Puritans, fearing this relaxation, joined with the Anglicans in rejecting the plan. To reconcile Presbyterians and Anglicans he suggested a compromise liturgy, and a limited episcopacy in which bishops would be assisted and advised by elected presbyters; Parliament vetoed the idea. The "Savoy Conference" of twelve bishops and twelve Presbyterian divines (1661) reported to the King that "they could not come to an harmony."[38]

It was a lost opportunity, for the new Parliament was overwhelmingly Anglican. It opened old wounds by re-establishing episcopacy in Scotland and Ireland; it restored ecclesiastical courts for the punishment of "blasphemy" and nonpayment of tithes to the Anglican Church; it made the Anglican Book of Common Prayer obligatory on all Englishmen; by the "Corporation Act" (November 20, 1661) it disqualified from public office all persons who had not received the sacrament according to the Anglican rite before the election; and by the "Act of Uniformity" (May 19, 1662) it required all clergymen and teachers to take an oath of nonresistance to the King, and to declare their full assent to the Book of Common Prayer. Clergymen who rejected these conditions were to vacate their livings by August 24. Some twelve hundred so refused, and were ejected. These, and the eight hundred already displaced by restored Anglicans, joined, with a great part of the congregations, the swelling body of "Sects" or "Dissenters" who finally compelled the Act of Toleration of 1689.

Charles tried to modify the Act of Uniformity by asking Parliament to let him exempt from the loss of their benefices those ministers whose only objections were to the wearing of the surplice, or the use of the cross in baptism; the Lords agreed, the Commons refused. He sought to soften the blow by delaying the execution of the act for three months; this too was frustrated. On December 26, 1662, he issued a declaration announcing his intention to exempt from the penalties of the act peaceable persons whose consciences prevented them from taking the required oath; but Parliament distrusted and rejected this appeal as implying the power of the King to "dispense" from obedience to the laws. Charles indicated his feelings by releasing imprisoned Quakers (August 22, 1662), and by confirming religious toleration in the charters that he granted to Rhode Island and Carolina, and in his instructions to the governors of Jamaica and Virginia.

Parliament felt that such toleration should have no place in England. To end Quaker "conventicles" it defined these as meetings of more than five persons additional to the members of a household; and it ruled (1662) that any person attending such an assembly should be fined five pounds or suffer three months' imprisonment for the first offense, ten pounds or six months for the second, banishment to convict plantations for the third. Offenders unable to pay the cost of their transportation to the colonies were to serve five years as indentured laborers; and transported convicts who escaped or returned to England before the expiration of their terms were to be put to death. In 1664 these measures were extended to Presbyterians and Independents. The "Five Mile Act" of 1665 forbade nonjuring ministers to reside within five miles of any corporate town, or to teach in any school, public or private. These laws came to be called the Clarendon Code because they were enforced by the King's chief minister against the express wishes of the sovereign. Charles accepted this harsh legislation because he was appealing to Parliament for funds, but he never forgave Clarendon, and lost respect for the bishops who, so soon after being restored, proved so hard in vengeance and poor in charity. Charles concluded that "Presbyterianism is no religion for a gentleman, and Anglicanism is no religion for a Christian."[39]

The Anglican Church, recognizing its dependence upon the monarchy, reasserted more positively than ever the divine right of kings, and the mortal sinfulness of resistance to an established royal government. In 1680 Sir Robert Filmer's *Patriarcha, or The Natural Power of Kings Asserted*, reached publication, twenty-seven years after his death, and became the standard defense of the doctrine. In the "Judgement and Decree" of Oxford (1683) leading divines of the Anglican Church declared it "false, seditious, and impious, even heretical and blasphemous" (and therefore a capital crime) to hold that "authority is derived from the people, that if lawful governors become tyrants, they forfeit the right of governing, that the King hath but co-ordinate right with the other two estates, the Lords and the Commons"; and it added that "passive obedience is the badge and character of the Church of England."[40] This proved to be an uncomfortable doctrine when, two years later, James II tried to make England Catholic.

The restored Anglican clergy, despite its intolerance, had many admirable qualities. It allowed a wide latitude of theological opinion within its own membership, from Laudians (later known as "High Churchmen") who approached Catholic doctrine and liturgy, to Latitudinarians (later

"Broad Churchmen") who sympathized with a liberal theology, stressed the moral rather than the doctrinal element in Christianity, discouraged persecution, and sought to reconcile Puritans, Presbyterians, and Anglicans. Charles supported these "men of latitude," and appreciated the comparative brevity of their sermons.[41] Greatest of these liberal theologians was John Tillotson, whom Charles made his chaplain, and whom William III made Archbishop of Canterbury (1691), "a man of clear head and sweet temper,"[42] who opposed "popery," atheism, and persecution with equal ardor, and dared to rest Christianity on reason. "We need not desire any better evidence that a man is in the wrong," he said, "than to hear him declare against reason, and thereby to acknowledge that reason is against him."[43] The lower Anglican clergy, the "parsons," tended now to become the spiritual servants of the local lords, even of the squires, and fell into an almost plebeian status;* but in the cities and the better benefices many Anglican clergymen distinguished themselves by an erudition and literary capacity that later produced some of the best historiography in Europe. In general a spirit of doctrinal moderation came to prevail in the Anglican Church rather than among the Dissenters, in whom persecution intensified dogmatism.

The Puritans suffered now not merely political persecution but a social contumely in which they were the butt of those whose easy morals had been inconvenienced under the Puritan regime. They bore with courage this turn of the wheel. Some migrated to America, many took the required oaths. Their finest figure in this age was Richard Baxter, a man of reasonable temper who was willing to accept any compromise that would not impair his fiery theology. Though faithful to Puritan ideology to the end, he condemned the execution of Charles I and the absolutism of Cromwell, and favored the Restoration. After 1662 he was prohibited from preaching, and was repeatedly arrested for violating the prohibition. He was one of the most enlightened of the Puritans, yet he applauded the burning of witches in Salem, Massachusetts, and thought of his God in terms that made Moloch seem amiable. Who are the saved? "They are," said Baxter, "a small part of lost mankind, whom God hath from eternity predestined to this rest."[44] He emphasized, in his sermons, the tortures of hell, whose "principal author is God Himself. . . . The torments of the damned," he wrote, "must be extreme, because they are the effect of the divine vengeance. Wrath is terrible, but revenge is implacable."[45] He forbade sexual intercourse except to have offspring with a lawful mate; and if this restriction required stoic self-control, he recommended cold baths and a vegetable diet to moderate erotic desire.[46] We almost forgive his theology when we see him, aged seventy

---

* Described and exaggerated in a famous passage of Macaulay's *History of England* (I, 253-55). Cf. Lecky, *History of England in the Eighteenth Century*, I, 75-79.

(1685), standing trial before the brutal Judge Jeffreys for having uttered a few words against Anglican pretensions; he was denied all chance to defend or explain himself, and was sentenced to pay five hundred marks or remain in jail till the full sum should be paid.[47] He was freed after eighteen months, but he never recovered his health.

The Quakers continued to suffer arrest and confiscation of property for refusing to take oaths, or avoiding Anglican services, or holding illegal assemblies. In 1662 there were over 4,200 of them in English jails. "Some of them were crowded into prisons so close that there was not room for all of them to sit down. . . . They were refused straw to lie upon; they were often denied food."[48] Their patience and persistence finally won the battle; the persecutions diminished in fact if not in law. In 1672 Charles freed twelve hundred of them;[49] and in 1682 his brother James, Duke of York, gave to the Scottish Quaker Robert Barclay, the rich Friend William Penn, and some associates a patent for the province of East Jersey in America.

Penn was the son of the Admiral William Penn who had captured Jamaica for England. When the boy was twelve he went through various stages of religious excitement, during which he was so "suddenly surprised with an inward comfort and . . . an external glory in the room, that he has many times said that from thence he had the seal of divinity and immortality," the conviction "that there was a God, and that the soul of man was capable of enjoying His divine communication."[50] At Oxford he was fined and expelled for refusing to attend Anglican services (1661). Returning to his father, he was whipped and turned out of doors for his avowed Quakerism. The relenting father sent him to France to learn *la gaieté Parisienne*; there, perhaps, Penn acquired some of his courtly ways. In 1666 he had so far reconciled himself with sin as to serve in the army in Ireland, but a year later he attended a Quaker meeting in Cork, took fire again, expelled a heckling soldier, and was arrested. From his prison he wrote to the lord president of Munster a plea for freedom of worship. Returning to England, he burned his bridges behind him, became a Quaker preacher, was again and again arrested. His trial in 1669 played a role in the history of English law. The jury acquitted him; the judge fined and imprisoned the jury for contumacy; the jurors appealed to the Court of Common Pleas, which, by unanimously declaring that they had been unlawfully arrested, vindicated the right and power of juries in England. However, Penn was jailed for refusing to remove his hat in court. He was released in time to be present at his father's death (1670), which left him a fortune of fifteen hundred pounds a year, and a claim on the Crown for sixteen thousand pounds lent by his father to Charles II. Reimprisoned for preaching, he wrote in jail his most eloquent defense of toleration, *The Great Case of Liberty of Conscience* (1671). In an interval of freedom he married a wealthy woman, and bought an interest in the western half of what is now the state of New Jersey. For this colony he wrote (1677) a constitution assuring religious toleration, jury trial, and popular government; but control passed out of his hands, and the full provisions of the constitution were not applied.

In 1677 Penn, George Fox, Robert Barclay, and George Keith crossed the Channel to preach Quakerism on the Continent. Some of Penn's converts from Kirchheim founded Germantown in Pennsylvania, and were among the first to declare it wrong for Christians to have slaves. Back in England, Penn took the lead in keeping the Quakers from joining the persecution of Catholics for the "Popish Plot"; his *Address to Protestants of All Persuasions* (1679) was a powerful appeal for complete religious toleration. In 1681 the Crown accepted his proposal to surrender his debt claim in exchange for a grant of what we now know as Pennsylvania. He suggested the name Sylvania for the vast and highly wooded tract; Charles II prefixed the name Penn in memory of the admiral. Though subject ultimately to the King, the government of the new colony was democratic, the relations with the Indians were friendly and just, and religion was left free by the predominantly Quaker settlers. For two years Penn labored there; then (1684), hearing that a new and violent persecution of his sect had begun in England, he returned to London. A year later his friend the Duke of York became James II, and Penn became a man of influence in the government. We shall meet him again.

The passive resistance of the Quakers to persecution was the strongest force making for religious toleration in this intolerant age. A Dissenter estimated that there were sixty thousand arrests for religious nonconformity between 1660 and 1688, and that five thousand of those so arrested died in jail.[51] The intolerance of Parliament was worse than the immorality of the court or the stage. "In this crucial period," said one who wrote history almost as well as he made it, "the King was almost the only modern and merciful voice . . . Throughout his reign he consistently strove for toleration."[52] When (1669) three men were sentenced under an old Elizabethan law to forfeit a large sum to the Crown for failing to attend Anglican services, Charles pardoned the fines, and declared that he would not have this statute enforced hereafter, "it being his judgment that no one ought to suffer merely for conscience' sake."[53]

More Englishmen would have agreed with him had they not suspected him of wishing to relieve the disabilities of English Catholics; and England was still so fearful of papal domination, Spanish Inquisitions, and government by priests, that Presbyterians and Puritans preferred to have their own worship outlawed rather than permit the Catholic worship in England. The English Catholics were at this time approximately five per cent of the population.[54] Politically they were impotent, but the Queen was a Catholic, and the King's brother made little attempt to conceal his conversion (1668). By that time there were 266 Jesuits in England, one of them a bastard son of Charles, and they were beginning to appear confidently in public despite the most stringent laws. Catholic schools were being set up in private homes. England worried. Annually the Protestants celebrated an antipopery parade, carrying to Smithfield, and there joyously burning, effigies of the pope and the cardinals. They had not forgotten Guy Fawkes. But the Catholics waited hopefully. At any moment now a Catholic would be king.

III. THE ENGLISH ECONOMY: 1660–1702

The population of England and Wales in 1660 has been estimated at some 5,000,000;[55] probably it grew to 5,500,000 by 1700;[56] still it was hardly a fourth the population of France or Germany, and less than that of Italy or Spain.[57] About a seventh of the inhabitants—the yeomanry—owned the lands that they tilled; tenant farmers working the lands of nobility and gentry made up another seventh. The rest were in the towns.

As population rose, the supply of wood per family fell; coal was increasingly used in homes and shops; mining and metallurgy developed; Sheffield became a center of the iron industry. A fever of production and moneymaking agitated England. Manufacturers begged Parliament to pass laws forcing idlers to work. Domestic industry, particularly textiles, used more and more child labor; Defoe rejoiced that at Colchester and Taunton "there was not a child in the town, or in the villages round it, of above five years old, but, if it was not neglected by its parents and untaught, could earn its bread"; and likewise around West Riding "hardly anything above four years old but its hands were sufficient for its support."[58]

Most industry was carried on in homes or family shops, but the factory system was expanding in textiles and iron. An English publication of 1685 told how "manufacturers at great cost build whole great houses, wherein the wool sorters, combers, spinners, weavers, pressers, and even dyers work together." We hear of one such factory with 340 employees; in 1700 Glasgow had a textile factory employing 1,400 persons.[59] Division and specialization of labor were developing. "In the making of a watch," wrote Sir William Petty in 1683, "if one man shall make the wheels, another the spring, another shall engrave the dial plate, and another shall make the cases, then the watch will be better and cheaper made than if the whole work be put upon any one man."[60]

Wages for agricultural labor were still fixed by local magistrates according to the Elizabethan Statute of Apprentices (1585), and any employer who paid, or any employee who took, more, was subject to penalty. Agricultural wages in this period ranged from five to seven shillings per week, with board.[61] Wages in industry were slightly higher, averaging a shilling per day, perhaps equal in purchasing power to $2.50 in 1960. Rents were relatively low; a house of moderate size in London cost some thirty pounds a year.[62] Beer was cheap, but sugar, salt, coal, soap, shoes, and clothing cost as much in 1685 as in 1848.[63] The price of grain rose five hundred per cent between 1500 and 1700.[64] The working classes ate bread of rye, barley, or oats; wheat bread was a luxury of the well-to-do; and the poor seldom had meat. The poverty of the masses was taken as a normal condition, though it was probably greater than in the later Middle Ages.[65] So Thorold Rogers:

> During the seventeenth century the landlords strove to get all the rent they could out of their tenants. To the utmost of their power they forced famine wages on the laborer. To the utmost of their power they used the legislature in order to secure famine prices from the consumer. . . . The historical evidence on this subject is cumulative and abundant.[66]

In 1696 Gregory King estimated that a fourth of England's population was dependent upon alms, and the money collected for poor relief equaled a quarter of the whole export trade.[67] The triumph of the rich over the poor was so complete that the wage earners and peasants were too weak to revolt; and for half a century the class war in England slept.[68]

The Anglican Church, which under Charles I had dared to say an occasional word for the poor, now concluded, from the Puritan Rebellion, that its interests would be best assured by identifying them entirely with those of the possessing classes.[69] Parliament belonged to a coalition of land-owners, manufacturers, merchants, and financiers. It listened with fellow feeling to the cry of the employing class to be liberated from the laws impeding the free play of economic forces. Before the end of the seventeenth century—long before Adam Smith—England heard the employers' cry for *laissez faire*, for economic freedom, for the escape of the businessman from legal, feudal, and guild hindrances in employment, production, and trade.[70] The guild restraints were bypassed; the institution of apprenticeship decayed; the fixing of wages by magistrates was superseded by the relative bargaining power of rich employers and hungry employees.[71] It was in this clamor of entrepreneurs to be freed from legal and moral restraints that the modern ideology of liberty began.

Commerce was now so important in the English economy, and so vital in earning the funds that Parliament voted, that it soon had its way even with a government dominated by landowners. Legislation favored English trade at the expense not only of the Dutch but of the Irish and the Scots. The importation of Irish cattle, sheep, or swine into England was totally prohibited (1660); Scottish corn was excluded, and Scottish imports were heavily taxed. The alliance with Portugal, the marriage of Charles II with Catherine of Braganza, the renewed war with the United Provinces, the resolute retention of Gibraltar, were actuated by the desire to expand English commerce and give it military protection. Partly as a result of victory over the Dutch, English commerce doubled between 1660 and 1688.[72] "The thing which is nearest to the heart of this nation," wrote Charles II to his sister, "is trade, and all that belongs to it."[73] Mercantile fortunes now rivaled noble acreage.

English enterprise extended its outposts in every direction. New colonies were developed in New York, New Jersey, Pennsylvania, Carolina, and Canada. The East India Company was given full rights over all of India that it could bring under its power; it had its own navy, army, forts, coinage, and laws; it declared war and negotiated peace. Bombay was acquired by marriage in 1661, Manhattan by conquest in 1664, and in that year the English seized Dutch possessions on the west coast of Africa. To man these colonies the custom of "crimping" grew: young Englishmen were inveigled into service in the "plantation" by getting them drunk, or knocking them unconscious, then carrying them on board a departing ship, and later explaining to them that they had signed an indenture.[74] The law forbade this, but was not enforced; the conscience of Parliament was clear. While the political effect of the revolutions of 1642–49 and 1688–89 was the conquest of the king by the Parliament, a simultaneous economic revolution brought the conquest of Parliament by commerce, industry, and finance.

London had now hundreds of goldsmiths-become-bankers, who paid six per cent to depositors and charged eight per cent on loans.[75] Charles II, always seeking ways to bypass the parliamentary power over the purse, borrowed heavily from these bankers—so much so that by January 2, 1672, he owed them £1,328,526.[76] On that date his Council, about to begin war against the United Provinces, shocked the financial community by "closing the Exchequer"—i.e., stopping for a year all interest payments on the government's debts. A panic ensued. The bankers refused to meet their obligations to their depositors, or to keep their agreements with merchants. The Council quieted the storm by solemn pledges to resume payments at the end of a year. They were resumed in 1674; the principal was refunded in new governmental obligations; so that in effect January 2, 1672, marked the beginning of England's national debt, a new device in the financing of the state.

London, home of the banking firms and the merchant princes, and focus of the wealth gathered by the price system from the producers of food and goods, was now the most populous city in Europe. The mansions of the rich businessmen rivaled the aristocracy in luxury, if not in taste. A succession of stores, with their picturesque emblems, swaying signs, and mullioned windows offered to the few the products of the world.* Only the principal thoroughfares were paved, usually with round cobblestones; and after 1684 they were dimly lit till midnight on moonless nights by lanterns set up at every tenth door. There were no sidewalks. By day the streets were noisy with traffic, with hawkers peddling their wares in baskets, pushcarts, or wheelbarrows, or criers offering various household services, such as "rats or mice to kill."[77] Beggars and thieves were everywhere, but there were also street singers ballading for pence. The business center, called "the City," was governed by a lord mayor, a board of aldermen, and a common council, elected by the householders of the wards. West of this lay the political center, Westminster—with Westminster Abbey, Westminster Palace (where Parliament met), and the royal palaces of Whitehall and St. James. Outside of these lay the slum districts, pullulating with the fertile poor. There were no pavements there, and coaches proudly splashed with rain water or mud the pedestrians hugging the walls in narrow streets. Houses there were so close together, with upper stories almost meeting, that the sun had little chance to spread its fitful light. There were no sewers as yet in London; there were outhouses and cesspools; carts carried off refuse and dumped it beyond the city limits, or clandestinely and illegally into the Thames.

Air pollution was already a problem. In 1661 John Evelyn, at the King's request, prepared and published *Fumifugium*, a plan for scattering the fumes that hung over London. Said Evelyn:

> The immoderate use of . . . coal . . . exposes London to one of the foulest inconveniences and reproaches; and that not from the culinary fires, which . . . is hardly at all discernible, but from some few particular funnels and issues [smokestacks] belonging only to brewers, dyers, lime-burners, salt, and soap-boilers, and some other private trades, one of whose spiracles [vents] alone does manifestly infest the air more than all the chimneys of London put together. . . . While these are belching [from] their sooty jaws, . . . London resembles the face rather of Mt. Etna, . . . or the suburbs of hell, than an assembly of rational creatures. . . . The weary traveller, at many miles' distance, sooner smells than sees the city to which he repairs . . . This acrimonious soot . . . [ulcerates] the lungs, which is a mischief so incurable that it carries away multitudes by languishing and deep consumptions, as the bills of mortality do weekly inform us.[78]

---

* About this time sash windows began to replace casement windows, because they admitted more light.

Evelyn prepared a bill for Parliament, which, being more approachable by rich industrialists than by unorganized majorities, did nothing about it. Thirteen years later Sir Thomas Browne raised his medical voice in warning against the

> exhalations of . . . common sewers and fetid places, and decoctions used by unwholesome and sordid manufactures. . . . Mists and fog also hinder the . . . coal smoke from descending and passing away. [So] it is conjoined with the mist and drawn in by the breath, all which may produce bad effects, inquinite [defile] the blood, and produce catarrhs and coughs.[79]

Bad air, bad sanitation, bad and inadequate food darkened every year with epidemics, and only waited some conjunction of circumstances to flare up in plague. Pepys noted in his diary, October 31, 1663: "The plague is much in Amsterdam, and we in fears of it here." Ships coming from Holland to England were quarantined. In December, 1664, one person died of the plague in London; in April, 1665, two; in May, forty-three; so it grew until the hot summer, with little rain to cleanse the streets, gave the pestilence headway, and London in terror realized that it faced something like the still remembered Black Death of 1348. Defoe, then a child of six, could recall enough of it by hearsay in 1720 to write a fictitious *Journal of the Plague Year* that may almost be taken as history.[80]

> From the first week in June the infection spread in a dreadful manner, and the bills [mortality records] rose high. . . . All that could conceal their distemper did it, to prevent their neighbors shunning . . . them, and also to prevent authority shutting up their houses. . . . In June . . . the richer sort . . . thronged out of town. . . . In Whitechapel . . . nothing was to be seen but wagons and carts, with goods, women, children, etc., . . . besides innumerable numbers of men on horseback . . . a terrible and melancholy thing to see.[81]

Portents and prophecies of doom added to the terror. Theaters, dance halls, schools, and law courts were closed. The King and the court removed in June to Oxford, "where it pleased God to preserve them" untouched, though many voices rose to blame them for having brought on this plague as a divine punishment of their immorality. The Archbishop of Canterbury stayed at his post in Lambeth, and spent several hundred pounds a week caring for the sick or dead. The city officials remained, and labored heroically. The King sent a thousand pounds, the businessmen of the City six hundred, a week. Many doctors and clergymen fled, many remained, many died of the infection. Cures of every sort were tried; and when these failed, people resorted to miraculous amulets. "This week,"

said Pepys (August 31, 1665), "died 7,496, and of them 6,102 of the plague."
Gravediggers carried away in carts those who died in the streets, and buried
them in common ditches. Altogether some seventy thousand Londoners,
a seventh of the population, died of the plague in 1665. By December the
pestilence abated. People dribbled back to work. In February, 1666, the
court returned to the capital.

The survivors had hardly time to reconcile themselves to their losses
when another disaster struck the city. It was bad enough that in June,
1666, the Dutch sailed boldly into the Thames and there destroyed
English vessels with broadsides heard in London. But at three o'clock on
the morning of Sunday, September 2, in a baker's shop in Pudding Lane, a
fire began which in three days burned down most of London north of the
river. Again circumstances conspired: a dry summer, the houses nearly
all of wood and close together; many homes left vacant by families
spending the weekend in the country; stores full of oil, pitch, hemp, flax,
wine, and other readily combustible wares; a strong wind that carried the
fire from roof to roof and from street to street; and the lack of organization
and equipment to deal with such a fire at such a time of night. Evelyn,
fortunate in Southwark, ran up to the riverbank,

> where we beheld . . . the whole city in dreadful flames near the water
> side; all the houses from the [London] Bridge, all Thames street, and
> upwards towards Cheapside . . . The conflagration was so universal,
> and the people so astonished, that from the beginning, I know not by
> what despondency or fate, they hardly stirred to quench it; so that
> there was nothing heard or seen but crying out and lamentation,
> running about like distracted creatures. . . . So it burned the churches,
> public halls, Exchange, hospitals, monuments, and ornaments, . . .
> houses, furniture, and everything. Here we saw the Thames covered
> with goods floating, all the barges and boats laden with what some had
> time and courage to save, as, on the other side, the carts, etc., carry-
> ing out to the fields, which for many miles were strewn with movables
> of all sorts, and tents erected to shelter both people and what goods
> they could get away. Oh, the miserable and calamitous spectacle! such
> as haply the world had not seen since the foundation of it. . . . All the
> sky was of a fiery aspect, like the top of a burning oven. . . . God
> grant my eyes may never behold the like, who now saw above 10,000
> homes all in one flame! The noise and cracking and thunder of the
> impetuous flames, the shrieking of women and children, the hurry of
> people, the fall of towers, houses, and churches was like a hideous
> storm; and the air all about so hot . . . that they were forced to stand
> still, and let the flames burn on, which they did for nearly two miles
> in length and one in breadth.[82]

In this crisis both the King and his unpopular brother James acquitted themselves well, laboring with their own hands among the firefighters, directing and financing relief, providing food and shelter for the homeless; and it was their insistence, against much opposition, on blowing up houses to stop the progress of the fire, that saved part of the city north of the Thames.[83] The commercial City was almost wiped out; the political city—Westminster—was saved. Altogether two thirds of London was destroyed, with 13,200 houses and eighty-nine churches, including old St. Paul's. Only six lives were lost, but 200,000 lost their homes.[84] Most of the booksellers were ruined; £150,000 worth of books were burned. The whole damage was reckoned at £10,730,000,[85] perhaps equivalent to $500,000,000 today.

After the disaster the Corporation of London organized a fire department; fireplugs were placed in the main water pipes; each guild company was to appoint some of its members to be ready to turn out at once on alarm; and all workmen were to follow them when called upon by the lord mayor or the sheriff. Slowly the city was rebuilt, not more beautifully, but more substantially; by royal order brick or stone replaced wood as the material of building; projecting upper stories disappeared; streets were made wider and straighter, they were paved with smooth freestone, and posts set aside a walk for pedestrians. Sanitation was improved; the fire had destroyed much filth, many rats, fleas, and germs; London had no further plagues. And Wren rebuilt St. Paul's.

IV. ART AND MUSIC: 1660–1702

Christopher Wren was born in religion, nurtured in science, and completed in art. His father was dean of Windsor, his uncle was bishop of Ely. He went to Westminster School and to Wadham College, Oxford. At twenty-one (1653) he was a fellow at All Souls College there; at twenty-five, professor of astronomy at Gresham College, London; at twenty-nine, Savile professor of astronomy at Oxford. He seemed absorbed in science. Mathematics, mechanics, optics, meteorology, astronomy, fascinated him. He rectified the cycloid (found the straight line equivalent to the cycloid curve). He demonstrated the laws of impact, and was credited by Newton with experiments leading to the three laws of motion.[86] He labored to improve the telescope and the grinding of lenses. He investigated the rings of Saturn. He invented a device for turning salt water into fresh water. He performed for Boyle the first injection of a fluid into the bloodstream of an animal. He proved that an animal could live comfortably after the removal of its spleen. He shared with Thomas Willis in dissecting a brain, and made the drawings for Willis' *Cerebri Anatome*. He was one of the first members of the Royal Society, and wrote the preamble to its charter. No one dreamed that he would go down in history as the greatest of English architects.

Circumstances alter careers. It was probably Wren's skill in drawing that led Charles II to appoint him (1661) assistant to Sir John Denham, surveyor general of works. Soon he found in architecture that marriage of science and art, of the true becoming beautiful, which was the heart and goal of his thought. "There are two kinds of beauty," he wrote, "natural and customary. Natural is from geometry. . . . Customary [or conventional] beauty is begotten by the use [habituation] of our senses to those objects that are usually pleasing to us. . . . But always the true test is natural or geometrical beauty."[87] The geometrically correct, he thought, would of itself please us and be beautiful (like any of the great bridges of the world). From this standpoint he preferred classic to Gothic architecture, and in his first designs he followed the lead of Inigo Jones.

In 1663, for Gilbert Sheldon, bishop of London, he designed the Sheldonian Theatre at Oxford; here at the outset he adopted classical principles, raising the circular edifice on lines laid down by Vitruvius in antiquity and by Vignola in the Renaissance. A long stay in France (1664–1666) confirmed his classical predilections, but his admiration for François Mansart's Church of Val-de-Grâce inclined him to add a degree of baroque adornment to his façades; and he remembered the dome of Val-de-Grâce when he rebuilt St. Paul's.

He returned to London in March, 1666. In April, at the request of Bishop Sheldon, he drew up a plan for repairing the tottering cathedral, then almost six hundred years old. On August 27 a Commission for the Repair of St. Paul's accepted Wren's plan. Two weeks later the church was destroyed in the historic fire of London; the melted lead of its roof ran in the streets.

That conflagration, razing two thirds of the capital, gave architecture an opportunity unprecedented since the burning of Rome. The fire was still smoldering when Wren offered to Charles II a majestic design for rebuilding the city. Charles accepted it, but could not find funds for it, and it conflicted with powerful property rights. Wren busied himself with other projects. In 1673 he prepared a classical design for a new St. Paul's. The cathedral chapter objected that the design smacked of a pagan temple, and urged Wren to adhere to the Gothic style of the old church. He reluctantly agreed to a compromise by which the interior would have Gothic arches, transept, and choir, but the façade would be a Renaissance columnar portico with a classical pediment and two baroque towers. The result is an unpleasant mixture of styles, but Wren redeemed it by crowning the transept with a dome rivaling Brunelleschi's at Florence and

Michelangelo's in Rome. St. Paul's remains the finest church ever built by Protestants.

While that project went on through thirty-five years, Wren, having succeeded Denham as surveyor general, designed fifty-three other churches, many of them famous for towers and spires that united his sense of beauty with his mathematical bent. Add the Custom House in London, the Greenwich and Chelsea hospitals, the chapels of Pembroke College at Cambridge and Trinity College at Oxford, the library of Trinity College at Cambridge, the classical east wing of Hampton Court Palace, thirty-six guildhalls, a number of private houses, and it seems that "no building of importance was erected during the last forty years of the seventeenth century of which Wren was not the architect."[88] Through the reigns of Charles II, James II, William and Mary, and Anne, he retained his place as surveyor general. He retired from practice at eighty-six, but continued for five years more to superintend the work at Westminster Abbey; and some credit him with its towers. He died in his ninety-first year, and was buried in St. Paul's.

Sculpture was still an orphan in England, but wood carving was a major art. Grinling Gibbons was a worthy collaborator with Wren, carving the choir stalls and magnificent organ case in St. Paul's, and decorations at Windsor Castle, Kensington Palace, and Hampton Court.

English painting continued to import its masters and discourage its sons. Nevertheless some have ranked John Riley as the best portrait painter of the Restoration. He knew that a mature face is an autobiography; he could read its lines, and between them, with patient insight, he revealed its secrets with unprofitable courage. He was almost ruined by Charles II's comment on Riley's portrait of him: "Is that like me? Then, odds fish, I am an ugly fellow!" Much time elapsed before the court realized that this was a spontaneous compliment to the artist's honesty. Riley transmitted with similar fidelity James II the foolish king, Edmund Waller the turncoat poet, and the Earl of Arundel the vain aristocrat. But when he painted Christopher Wren and Robert Boyle he recognized genius, and caught its marks in the face and its light in the eyes. "With a quarter of Sir Godfrey Kneller's vanity," said Horace Walpole, "Riley might have persuaded the world that he was a master."[89] He died in 1691, aged forty-five.

Lely the Dutchman and Kneller the German were the fashionable portrait painters of that second Stuart age. Lely's father was a Dutch soldier, van der Faes, whose nickname Lely (from a lily painted on his house) passed down to his son. Pieter was born in Westphalia (1618), studied painting in Haarlem, and took ship to England (1641) on hearing that Charles I had taste and pounds. He succeeded Vandyck as the most sought-for portraitist in England, and continued so under Cromwell and

Charles II. He adopted Vandyck's trick of endowing his sitters with elegance, even if only in dress. The beauties of the court besieged him; so in the National Portrait Gallery we see Nell Gwyn plump and naughty, and the Countess of Shrewsbury, notorious for her gallantries; and at Hampton Court Palace Lady Castlemaine and Louise de Kéroualle still flaunt their nipples from the walls. Lovelier is John Churchill pictured as a child, with his sister Arabella;[90] who would expect this angelic boy and angelic girl to become the invincible Duke of Marlborough and the irremovable mistress of James, Duke of York? Lely achieved knighthood and riches by such portraits. Charles II and half a dozen dukes sat for him. Pepys found him "a mighty proud man . . . and full of state,"[91] living in "pomp and victuals,"[92] and dated three weeks ahead.

In 1674, six years before Lely's death, a German arrived in London, resolved to succeed Sir Peter in portraiture, profits, and knighthood; and he accomplished his program. Gottfried von Kneller was then twenty-eight. Charles II made him court painter, and Kneller kept that post under James II and William III, who dubbed him knight. Sir Godfrey painted forty-three members of the politically powerful Kit Cat Club,[93] and ten sirens of William's court,[94] and deprived Dryden and Locke of character. As everyone itched for immortality, Kneller turned his luxurious studio into a mass-production factory with an unprecedented staff of aides, each charged with some specialty—hands, drapery, lace. Sometimes he took fourteen sitters in a day. He built a mansion in the country, and commuted between it and his town house in a coach-and-six. He kept his head on his neck through all political overturns, and died in bed and honors at seventy-seven (1723). In that year Reynolds was born, Hogarth was twenty-six, and native painting was coming into its own.

The Puritans had nearly obliterated art, but they had not silenced music. All but the lowliest homes had some musical instruments. Amid the great fire Pepys noticed virginals on almost every third boat carrying salvaged goods on the Thames.[95] "Music and women," he wrote, "I cannot but give way to, whatever my business is"; and he mentions his flageolet, lute, theorbo, and "viollin" as frequently as his amours.[96] Everybody in his *Diary* plays music and sings; he takes it for granted that his friends can join in part song;[97] he and his wife and their maids sing in harmony in his garden, and so bearably that neighbors open their windows to hear them.

In the Restoration jubilation music burst forth in all its forms. Charles brought in musicians from France, and soon let it be known that he favored tuneful, cheerful, intelligible compositions that did not take mathematics for melody. Organs were built again, and rumbled in the churches of the Establishment; those designed for St. George's Chapel at Windsor and the cathedral at Exeter were among the wonders and thunders of the age. But even in church choirs solemnity was replaced by dramatic displays of instrumental virtuosos and vocal soloists. Charles II and James II ordered music for odes and masques to celebrate royal events; churches commissioned music; theaters ventured on opera. English composers and performers began to eat again.

In 1656 Sir William Davenant persuaded the Protectorate government to let him reopen a theater on the ground that he would produce not a play but an opera. The *First Dayes Entertainment* that he staged was less an opera than a series of dialogues preceded, interrupted, and followed by music; but in that same year Davenant presented, in his own Rutland House, the first English opera, *The Siege of Rhodes*.[98] The closing of the theaters by the plague and the fire interfered with these experiments, but in 1667 the enterprising Davenant offered a musical adaptation of his alleged father's *Tempest*. Purcell's *Dido and Aeneas* marked the full arrival of opera in England.

As so often in musical history, Henry Purcell's genius was in large part a product of social heredity—i.e., adolescent environment. His father was master of the choristers at Westminster Abbey; his uncle was "composer in ordinary for the violins to his Majesty"; his brother was a composer and dramatist, his son and his grandson continued his role as organist in the Abbey. He himself was allowed only thirty-seven years of life (1658–95). As a boy he sang in the Chapel Royal till his voice broke. As a youth he composed anthems that continued to be heard in English cathedrals for a century. His twelve sonatas (1683), for two violins and organ or harpsichord, brought the sonata form from Italy to England. His songs, anthems, cantatas, and chamber music, said Burney, "so far surpassed whatever our country had produced or imported before, that all other musical compositions seem to have been instantly consigned to contempt or oblivion."[99]

Busy with his work as organist and composer, it was not till 1689 that Purcell produced *Dido and Aeneas*, for a select audience at a girls' school in London. The music, even the famous overture, seems to us now thin and feeble; we have to remember that opera was still young, and that audiences did not then have our liking for noise. The final aria—Dido's lament, "When I am laid in earth"—is one of the most moving airs in the whole history of opera.

King Arthur (1691), for which Dryden wrote the words and Purcell the music, is not quite an opera, since the music seems to have little relation to the mood or events of the play—just as the play had little connection with the Arthurian cycle as we know it in Malory and Tennyson. A year later Purcell made a further advance with incidental music for *The Fairy Queen*, an anonymous adaptation of *A Midsummer Night's Dream*. He did

not live to see it produced; the music was lost, was discovered in 1901, and
is now ranked with Purcell's best.

In 1693 he composed the most elaborate of his many odes for St. Cecilia's
Day. But the finest of these is the joyful *Te Deum and Jubilate* of 1694; this
was performed annually at the festival of the Sons of the Clergy till 1713,
when it shared the honor with Handel's *Utrecht Te Deum* in alternate
years till 1743. For Queen Mary's funeral (1695) Purcell wrote a famous
anthem, "Thou knowest, Lord, the secrets of our hearts." In his final years
he contributed incidental music to Dryden's *Indian Queen*. Apparently he
fell sick before he could complete this, for the music of the concluding
masque was provided by his brother Daniel. He died, probably of consumption, on November 21, 1695.

Despite the vitality of the Restoration, English music had not yet
recovered from the cutting of its Elizabethan traditions by the Puritan
interlude. Instead of rooting itself again in English soil, it followed the
royal lead and bowed to French styles and Italian voices. After *Dido and
Aeneas* the English operatic stage was dominated by Italian operas sung
by Italians. "English music," wrote Purcell in 1690, "is yet but in its nonage,
a forward child, which gives hope of what it may be hereafter . . . when
the masters of it shall find more encouragement."[100]

V. MORALS

Let us at once distinguish the masses from the classes. The sexual riot
of the Restoration ran through the court to the upper middle class and
the "people about town" who frequented the theatres. The morals of the
unrecorded commoners were probably better than under Elizabeth, for
economic routine kept them steady, they did not have the means to be
wicked, and they still felt the stimulus and surveillance of their Puritan
faiths. But in London, and above all at the court, the release and reaction
from Puritan restraints engendered an hilarious promiscuity. Young
aristocrats uprooted from England, and at loose ends in France, left their
morals behind them in their exile, and brought a fluid chaos with them on
their return. Avenging years of oppression and spoliation, they turned
against the dress and speech, the theology and ethics, of the Puritans all
the acid of their wit, until no man of their class dared say a word for
decency. Virtue, piety, and marital fidelity became forms of rural innocence, and the most successful adulterer (as in Wycherley's *Country
Wife*) became the hero of the hour. Religion had literally lost caste; it
belonged to tradesmen and peasants; most preachers were put down as
long-faced, long-eared, long-winded hypocrites and bores. The only

religion fit for a gentleman was a polite Anglicanism wherein the master attended Sunday services to lend support to a chaplain who kept the villagers in fear of hell, and who said grace with due brevity from the foot of the master's board. It became more fashionable to be a materialist with Hobbes than a Christian with Milton, a blind old fool who took Genesis as history. Hell, overdone for the past twenty years, had lost its terrors for the possessing classes; heaven, for them, was here and now, in a society freed from social rebellion and moral inhibitions, under a court and King that gave the example and set the pace in lechery, gambling, and merriment.

There were several good men and women at the court. Clarendon was a man of principle and conduct until his daughter allowed herself to be seduced, whereupon he lost his head and recommended that she should lose hers. The fourth Earl of Southampton and the first Duke of Ormonde were decent men. There were some sincerely religious men among the Anglican clergy, even in the hierarchy. The Queen, and Lady Fanshaw, and Miss Hamilton, and, later, Mrs. Godolphin, dared to be good. There were doubtless others, lost to history because virtue makes no news.

The higher the rank, the lower the morals. The King's brother James, Duke of York, seems to have exceeded even the royal allotment of mistresses.[101] While still in exile in Holland he had found his way to the bed of Anne Hyde, daughter of the Chancellor. When she became pregnant she begged him to marry her; he procrastinated, but finally made her secretly his legal wife seven weeks before she gave birth (October 22, 1660). On hearing of the marriage Clarendon, according to his own autobiography,[102] protested to the King that he had known nothing of this alliance; that "he had much rather his daughter should be the Duke's whore than his wife"; that if they were really married, "the King should immediately cause the woman to be . . . cast into a dungeon"; and that "an act of Parliament should be immediately passed for cutting off her head, to which he would not only give his consent, but would very willingly be the first man that should propose it." Charles shrugged the matter off as much ado about nothing. Probably the Chancellor knew that Charles would not take him at his word, and spoke with such Roman severity to offset any suspicion that he had arranged the marriage in order to make his daughter a queen. Anne, however, died of cancer in 1671, aged thirty-four.

While motherhood distracted his wife, James made a mistress of Arabella Churchill, whose brother accepted the situation philosophically as favoring his advancement in the army. To aid Arabella and Anne the Duke took some supplementary bedmates; Evelyn was especially disgusted by his "bitchering" with Lady Denham (1666).[103] James's conversion to Catholicism made no apparent change in his morals. "He was perpetually in one amour or another," wrote Burnet, "without being very nice in his choice; upon which the King once said he believed his brother had his mistresses given him by his priests for penance."[104] The liaison with Arabella continued as an organ tone during these variations; it survived the death of Anne, and James's marriage (1673) to Mary of Modena.

We should add that there were some admirable qualities in the Duke of York. As Lord High Admiral (1660–73) he toiled to overcome the disorder in the navy, due to the poor pay, victualing, and training of the seamen; and he conducted himself with courage and skill in the engagements with the Dutch. He attended ably and faithfully to the tasks of administration. He never wavered in his affectionate fidelity to his brother, and waited patiently through a quarter of a century before succeeding him on the throne. He was frank and sincere and easy of access, but too conscious of his rank and authority to be popular. He was a firm friend but an unforgiving enemy. His mind was rather laborious than keen; and he was suicidally immune to advice.

Close below him at the court was George Villiers, second Duke of Buckingham. Son of James I's assassinated favorite, he fought for Charles I in the Civil War and for Charles II at Worcester; and the restored King made him a privy councilor. Handsome and witty, genial and generous, he for a time dominated the court with his charm. He wrote a brilliant comedy, *The Rehearsal*, and dallied with alchemy and the violin. But his face and his fortune ruined him. He passed from one woman to another, indulged in disgraceful frolics, and squandered his rich estate. Desiring the Countess of Shrewsbury, he challenged her husband to a duel; she, disguised as a page, held Buckingham's horse while he fought; he killed the Count; the happy widow embraced the victor, who was still covered with her husband's blood; then they returned in triumph to the victim's home.[105] Buckingham was dismissed from office (1674), abandoned himself to degeneration, and died in poverty and disgrace (1688).

His rival in figure, wit, revelry, and decay was John Wilmot, second Earl of Rochester. John received the master's degree at Oxford at the incredible age of fourteen (1661), was admitted to the court at seventeen, and became gentleman of the bedchamber to the King. At nineteen, needing money, he made love to a rich heiress; finding her dilatory, he kidnaped her, suffered imprisonment, won the lady's sympathy, then her hand, then her fortune. Charles repeatedly banished him from the court, and repeatedly let him return, relishing his wit. Like Buckingham, Rochester was an expert mimic. He delighted to disguise himself as a porter, a beggar, a merchant, a German physician, and so successfully that he deceived his closest friends. As a physician he pretended to effect difficult cures through his knowledge of astrology; he attracted hundreds of patients and cured several; soon the ladies of the court came to him for treatment, and even those who had known him well failed to recognize him.[106] In nearly all these disguises he pursued women, quite disregarding their rank, and they pursued him. He amused himself by writing satirical obscenities, ruined his health with liquor and lechery, and boasted of having been drunk uninterruptedly through five years. He died in poverty and penitence at thirty-three.

There were so many others like him at the court that Pepys, himself no amateur in adultery, wondered "what will be the end" of "so much . . . drinking, swearing, and loose amours."[107] Or, as Pope was to phrase it in his *Essay on Criticism*, not with full justice to the King:

> When love was all an easy monarch's care,
> Seldom at council, never in a war,
> Jilts ruled the state, and statesmen farces writ;
> Nay, wits had pensions, and young lords had wit; . . .
> The modest fan was lifted up no more,
> And virgins smiled at what they blushed before.[108]

It was taken for granted that wives were as unfaithful as husbands; these demanded fidelity only from their mistresses.[109] The memoirs of Count Philibert de Gramont, written in French by his brother-in-law Anthony Hamilton, read at times like a roster of roosters, a concatenation of cuckolds as seen by the Count in his happy exile at Charles's court.

Hours were given to dancing, horse races, cockfights, billiards, cards, chess, floor games, and gay masquerades. Then, says Burnet, "both the King and Queen" and "all the court went about masked, and came into houses unknown, and danced there, with a great deal of wild frolic."[110] Play was often for high stakes. "This evening," says Evelyn, "according to custom, his Majesty opened the revels . . . by throwing the dice himself in the privy chamber . . . and lost his £100. (The year before, he won £1,500.) The ladies also played very deep."[111] The example of the court in gambling and promiscuity spread through the upper classes. Evelyn speaks of the "depraved youth of England, whose prodigious debaucheries . . . far surpass the madness of all civilized nations whatsoever."[112] Homosexuality flourished, especially in the army; Rochester wrote a play entitled *Sodomy*, which was performed before the court. A number of brothels for homosexual prostitution apparently existed in England.[113]

Love marriages were increasing in number, and we hear of some pretty instances, as of Dorothy Osborne with William Temple. This proved a happy marriage; yet Dorothy wrote: "To marry for love were no reproachful thing if we did not see that of the thousand couples that do it, hardly one can be brought for example that it may be done and not repented afterward."[114] Swift, writing to a young lady about her marriage, speaks of "the person your father and mother have chosen for your husband," and adds, "Yours was a match of prudence and common good feeling, without any hindrance of the ridiculous passion" of romantic love.[115] "My first inclination to marriage," Clarendon recalled, "had no other passion in it than an appetite to a convenient estate."[116]

Theoretically the husband had full control over his wife, including the dowry she brought him. In all classes the husband's will was law. In the lower classes he used his legal rights to beat his wife, but the law forbade him to use any stick thicker than his thumb.[117] Family discipline was strong, except in upper-class London; there Clarendon complained that parents had no manner of authority over their children, nor children any obedience or submission to their parents, but "everyone did what was good in his eyes."[118] Divorce was rare, but might be allowed by act of Parliament. Bishop Burnet, like Luther and Milton, thought that polygamy might in certain cases be permitted, and offered this plan to Charles II because of the Queen's sterility; but Charles refused to further humiliate his wife.[119]

Crime continually threatened life and property. Thieves, cutpurses, and pickpockets congregated in gangs and sallied forth at night. Dueling was forbidden by law, but it remained the privilege of a gentleman; and if the killing was done according to rule, the victor usually escaped with a brief and courteous imprisonment. The law struggled to discourage crime with what seems to us barbarous punishments; but perhaps sharp measures had to be used to penetrate dull minds. For treason the penalty was torture and death; for murder, felony, or counterfeiting the currency, hanging; the wife who killed her husband was to be burned alive. Petty larceny was punished by whipping, or the loss of an ear; striking anyone in the King's court incurred loss of the right hand; forgery, cheating, false weights or measures, invited the pillory, sometimes with both ears nailed to the board, or with perforation of the tongue with a hot iron;[120] usually the spectators enjoyed witnessing these punishments,[121] and crowded in holiday spirit to see a prisoner hanged. Under the Merrie Monarch there were ten thousand persons in jail for debt. Prisons were filthy, but wardens could be bribed to provide some comforts. Punishments were more severe than in contemporary France, but the law was more liberal; there were no *lettres de cachet* in England, and there were habeas corpus and jury trial.

Social morality shared in the general laxity. Charity was growing, but the forty-one almshouses in England may have been merely another side to the greed of the strong. Nearly everyone cheated at cards.[122] Corruption was above normal in all classes. Pepys's *Diary* smells with corruption in business, in politics, in the navy, and in Pepys. Business firms watered their stock, falsified their accounts, and charged exorbitant prices to the government.[123] Funds voted to the army or navy were diverted in part into the pockets of officials and courtiers. High officers of state, even when their salaries were ample and paid, sold titles, contracts, commissions, appointments, and pardons on such a scale that "the regular salary was the smallest part of the gains."[124] Heads of government like Clarendon, Danby, and Sunderland grew rich in a few years, and bought or built estates far beyond their salaries. Members of Parliament sold their votes to ministers, even to foreign governments;[125] on some votes two hundred members were "taken off" the opposition by ministerial lubrication.[126] In 1675 it was estimated that two thirds of the Commons were in the pay of Charles II, and the other third in the pay of Louis XIV.[127] The French King found it quite feasible to bribe members to vote against Charles whenever Charles deviated troublesomely from Bourbon policies. As for Charles, he repeatedly accepted large sums from Louis to play the French game in politics, religion, or war. It was the gayest and most rotten society in history.

VI. MANNERS

As in France, manners tried to redeem morals, and gave a ceremonious grace to ornate dress, obscene literature, and profane speech. Charles himself was a model of manners; his courtesy and charm spread through the upper classes, and left their mark on English life. Men kissed each other on meeting, and kissed a lady on being introduced to her. Ladies in London, as in Paris, received gentlemen while in bed. There was an invigorating frankness, a scorn of hypocrisy, in the literature, the theater, and the court. But the candor released a flood of coarseness on the stage and in daily speech. Profanity was unparalleled. Here Charles was among the exceptions, confining himself to "Odds fish" as his favorite oath. The surviving Puritans were clean of speech except in belaboring their opponents; and the Quakers refused to swear.

Men outdid the women in fanciful dress, from powdered wigs to silk stockings and buckled shoes. The wig or periwig was another import from France. Cavaliers and others whose hair was short, and who were loath to be mistaken for close-cropped Puritan Roundheads, covered their shortage with alien cuttings; and men whose hair was turning gray or white found the wig useful in disguising their age, for then nearly all men shaved. It offset in some measure the King's Spanish complexion and Brobdingnagian nose. Pepys made his first wig a critical affair, and mourned that his own beloved hair had to be shorn to make way for his peruke and provide hair for another head;[128] periodically he had his wig "cleansed of its nits."[129] The stiff Elizabethan-Jacobean ruff had now disappeared. Doublet and long cloak were giving way to waistcoat and surcoat; the waistcoat or vest, however, reached to the calf of the leg, and was bound to the body by a sash. Breeches stopped at the knee. Swords dangled at the side of aristocratic or moneyed legs. Velvet and lace, ribbons and frills, helped to complete the courtly man; and in winter he might keep his hands warm in a muff hung from his neck.

Fashionable women powdered and perfumed their hair, curled it into ringlets over their foreheads, and supplemented it with false locks mounted on secret wires. They feathered their hats with rare plumage. They painted black spots ("patches") upon their cheeks, foreheads, or chins as added inducements to the chase. They exposed their shoulders and generous portions of their breasts; so Louise de Kéroualle had Lely paint her with one breast naked, and Nell Gwyn went her one better. Legs were alluringly concealed. Dainty articles of toilette were in rising demand. Woman was already so intricate an artifact that a Restoration play pictured her in hyperbole:

> Her teeth were made in the Blackfriars, her eyebrows in the Strand, and her hair on Silver Street. . . . She takes herself asunder, when she goes to bed, into some twenty boxes, and about noon the next day is put together again like a great German clock.[130]

Extravagance was *de rigueur*. Life, become ceremonious again, required elaborate equipment. Servants had to be hired in gross; Evelyn's father had half a hundred; Pepys had a cook, a housemaid, a lady's maid, and a serving girl. Meals were tremendous; note Pepys's dinner on January 26, 1660, long before his salad days:

> My wife had got ready a very fine dinner—viz., a dish of marrow bones, a leg of mutton, a loin of veal, a dish of fowl, three pullets, and two dozen of larks all in a dish; a great tart, a neat's tongue, a dish of anchovies, a dish of prawns and cheese.

The main meal was taken about one o'clock. Cooking was English. Gramont, when Charles explained that the servants waited on him on bended knee as a mark of respect, said (or so he tells us): "I thank your Majesty for the explanation; I thought they were begging your pardon for serving you so bad a dinner."[131]

Drinking of alcoholic beverages was no merely social function. Water was scarcely ever drunk, even by children;[132] beer was easier to find than water fit to drink. So everybody, of any age, drank beer, and the well-to-do added whiskey or imported wine. Most people visited a tavern once a day, and all classes got drunk now and then.

Coffee had come in from Turkey about 1650; till 1700 most of it was imported from the region around Mocha in the Yemen; in the eighteenth century the Dutch transplanted it to Java, the Portuguese to Ceylon and Brazil, the English to Jamaica. The use of coffee to overcome drowsiness and stimulate the wits spread its popularity. London opened its first coffeehouse in 1652; by 1700 there were three thousand of them in the capital.[133] Every man of any account made one or another of them his regular rendezvous, where he could meet his friends and learn the latest scandal and news. Charles II tried to suppress the coffeehouses as centers of political agitation and conspiracy, but the itch to talk and drink and smell tobacco smoke frustrated him. From some coffeehouses sprang the clubs that played a role in eighteenth-century politics, and then became a refuge from monogamy. The coffeehouses, however, differed from the later clubs, not only because coffee was the favorite drink, but because conversation was encouraged. Literary lions like Dryden, Addison, and Swift had their rostrums in coffeehouses. English freedom of speech was nourished there.

Tea came to England from China about 1650, but it was so expensive that a century passed before it displaced coffee in the English ritual. Pepys thought it quite an adventure when he had his first cup of tea.[134] Meanwhile the cacao bean had been imported from Mexico and Central America; about 1658 a new drink was made by adding vanilla and sugar to cacao; the resultant chocolate became a popular drink during the Restoration, and was served in many coffeehouses.

All classes, including many women and some children, now smoked tobacco, always through long pipes. The women thought it had some antiseptic value, as in averting plague. Probably from this notion the habit arose, in this period, of taking snuff—i.e., inhaling powdered tobacco.

Now that the Puritan incubus was lifted, games and sports flourished. The poor again enjoyed puppet shows, circuses, cockfighting, bear and bull baiting, tightrope walkers, wrestlers, jugglers, pugilists, conjurers. The rich took to venery in both its senses. Charles II played tennis till he was fifty-three. Evelyn liked bowling on the green, which is still a pretty sight in England today. Cricket was beginning to be a national pastime; in 1661 we find the first mention of a ground specifically reserved for it. In that year Vauxhall Gardens were laid out on the south bank of the Thames, and soon became a fashionable resort. St. James's Park was opened to the public by Charles II. Hyde Park was now established as the place where the elite, led by the King and Queen, drove carriages on pleasant afternoons. "Society" was beginning to take the waters at Bath.

All but the poorest classes traveled in stagecoaches, which had begun a regular "penny post" service in 1657, and a scheduled passenger service in 1658. "Hackney coaches" had served intracity traffic since 1625. The

very rich traveled in a "coach-and-six"; the three teams were not for display, but to pull the coach through muddy stretches; sometimes the local
cattle had to be hitched in front of the horses to tug the coach out of hub-
deep mire. Roads were mud or dust. The roadside inns, with their lively
mixture of coachmen, travelers, actors, salesmen, thieves, and tarts, were
preparing to make their contribution to the literature of England. The
rough, lusty, lovable England that Dickens knew in his youth was taking
form.

VII. RELIGION AND POLITICS

Amid this human pullulation the struggle of the faiths continued, and
the old conflict between king and Parliament was renewed. The Merrie
Monarch was saddened to find that the House of Commons, after the
honeymoon of its proferred obedience, was jealous of his power, and
sparing of its funds. Tender in heart but tough in conscience, Charles
turned to the French King for private loans. He promised—and apparently
desired—to alleviate the disabilities of the English Catholics, to support the
policy of Louis XIV against the Netherlands, and to sell to France the
Channel port of Dunkirk, which Cromwell's soldiers had won. Dunkirk
was costly to defend; it was a thorn in the side of France; Charles let it
go (1662) for five million francs, which, along with secret Bourbon subsidies, enabled him to ignore for a while the oligarchy of land and money
that now ruled Parliament.

The oligarchs, however, thought that the funds of the government should
be used to wage another profitable war against the Dutch. The same
rivalry in commerce and fisheries that had produced the First Dutch War
in 1652 supported the Second Dutch War in 1664. Charles resisted the
martial current as long as he could, for he much preferred love. "I never
saw so great an appetite for war," he wrote to his sister, "as is in both this
town and country, especially in the Parliament men. I find myself the only
man in my kingdom who doth not desire war."[135]

Everything went badly. The English navy, ill-fed, ill-clothed, ill-
munitioned, fought bravely, but lost as often as it won; and at the height
of the war plague and fire left London desolate and England bankrupt.
Toward the end of 1666 the Dutch opened negotiations for peace; Charles,
glad to come to terms, sent commissioners to Breda. Confident that an
agreement was in sight, and seeing himself at the end of his finances, he
laid up part of the English fleet in the Medway, and allowed the sailors to
take service in merchantmen. In June, 1667, de Ruyter led a Dutch squadron into the Thames and the Medway, and destroyed most of the unmanned

ships. That very night, says Pepys, "the King did sup with my Lady Castlemaine at the Duchess of Monmouth's, and they were all mad in hunting a poor moth."[136] When the news of the attack reached London every able-bodied man was called to arms. But the Dutch too wanted peace, for the French had invaded Flanders. The Treaty of Breda (July 21, 1667) ended the Second Dutch War on terms unsatisfactory to all.

The position of the King was so weakened by the fiasco and the accumulated misfortunes of London that some Englishmen thought of deposing him. Parliament demanded parliamentary supervision of governmental expenses; Charles yielded, being penniless, and another step was taken toward parliamentary supremacy. Parliament demanded the dismissal of Clarendon for mishandling foreign affairs; Charles was not unwilling to let him go, for his Chancellor had opposed his moves toward religious toleration, and had censured his absorption in mistresses. Not satisfied with Clarendon's resignation, the Commons drew up a proposal to impeach him for subservience to France. Clarendon took the King's advice and fled to the Continent. It was a pitiful and cruel end for a long career of service. The old man glorified his exile by writing the finest historical work that English literature had yet produced. He died at Rouen in 1674, aged sixty-five.

Charles appointed five men to replace him (1667): Sir Thomas Clifford, the Earl of Arlington, the Duke of Buckingham, Lord Ashley (soon to be the first Earl of Shaftesbury), and the Earl of Lauderdale. Their initials made the word *cabal*, by which the new ministry came to be called. Clifford was an avowed Catholic, Arlington was inclined toward that faith, Buckingham was a rake, Shaftesbury was a tolerant skeptic, Lauderdale was a former Covenanter who with fire and sword forced episcopacy upon his fellow Scots. Charles listened to their conflicting counsels, but more and more followed his own.

His aims were basically two: to renew absolute monarchy, and to elevate Roman Catholicism in England. He looked with hope to being succeeded by his Catholic brother James. He corresponded with the general of the Jesuits in Rome, and gave a secret interview to a papal internuncio who came to London from Brussels.[137] In January, 1669, he told his brother, Clifford, Arlington, and Lord Arundell that he wished to reconcile himself with the Church of Rome, and bring all England back to the old faith.[138] His sister Henrietta never ceased to urge him to boldly announce his conversion.

In May, 1670, Louis XIV sent Henrietta to England, aided by subtle diplomats, to bind Charles to a French and Catholic policy. On June 1, 1670, Clifford, Arundell, and Arlington signed for England the secret Treaty of Dover. The French King agreed to pay Charles £150,000 whenever Charles should announce his conversion to Catholicism; if need should arise, Louis would furnish Charles with six thousand soldiers, to be maintained at French expense; Charles, when called upon, was to join France in war against the United Provinces; he was to receive £225,000 a year while the war continued; he was to take and keep some Dutch islands; and he was to support the claims of Louis to inherit Spain.[139] To deceive the Parliament and the people of England, Charles sent Buckingham to Paris to draw up a sham treaty, which was signed on December 21, 1670, and was published to the world; it pledged England to war against the Dutch, but made no mention of religion.

Charles took his time—fifteen years—about announcing his conversion. His brother openly proclaimed himself a Catholic in 1671; but even the pro-Catholic Earl of Arlington warned the King that a similar admission might precipitate a revolution. Charles, however, moved toward his goal by issuing (March 15, 1672) his second "Declaration of Indulgence for Tender Consciences," suspending "all manner of penal laws in matters ecclesiastical, against whatsoever sort of Nonconformists or recusants." At the same time he released from prison all persons who had been jailed for not conforming to the religious legislation of Parliament. Hundreds of Dissenters, including Bunyan and many Quakers, were freed, and their leaders sent a deputation to thank the King. Presbyterians and Puritans were shocked to find that the new freedom accorded to them was extended also to Catholics and Anabaptists, and Anglicans were horrified by "papists and swarms of sectaries" meeting openly in London. For almost a year England enjoyed or suffered religious toleration.

On March 17, 1672, England opened the Third Dutch War. In this matter King and Parliament were now agreed. The Parliament voted £1,250,000 for the war, but this sum was to be doled out to the government in installments that would obviously depend upon the King's reconciliation with Parliament and its religious legislation. The Commons declared that "penal statutes in matters ecclesiastical cannot be suspended but by Act of Parliament"; and it sent a petition to the King that his Declaration of Indulgence should be withdrawn. Louis XIV, anxious to have England give united support to the war against the Dutch, advised Charles to cancel the Declaration until the war should be successfully concluded. Charles yielded, and on March 8, 1673, the Declaration was annulled.

It is probable that by that time the Protestant leaders had got wind of the secret Treaty of Dover. To contracept any royal conversion, both houses passed, at the end of March, a "Test Act," by which all holders of civil or military office in England were required to abjure the Catholic doctrine of transubstantiation, and to take the Sacrament according to the

Anglican rite. Clifford fought the bill passionately; after its passage he resigned from the government, retired to his estate, and soon died—by suicide, Evelyn thought. Shaftesbury warmly supported the bill; he was dismissed from the ministry, and made himself the leader of the "Country Party" that opposed, to the verge of revolution, the "Court Party" favoring the King. The Cabal ended (1673); the Earl of Danby became chief minister.

James resigned his offices. The opposition to him had been in some degree mollified by the fact that though his first wife had accepted Catholicism, her children, the future Queens Mary and Anne, were being brought up as Protestants. But now his marriage (September 30, 1673) to a Catholic princess roused virulent condemnation. Mary of Modena was branded as "the Pope's eldest daughter," and it was assumed that she would bring up her children as Catholics. Bills were at once introduced into Parliament that all royal children must be reared in the Protestant faith.

The turn of events soured England's taste for the war against the United Provinces. If England should have a Catholic king he would sooner or later join France and Spain in utterly destroying the Dutch Republic— which now appeared not as a commercial rival but as the bulwark of Protestantism on the Continent. If that should fall, how would English Protestantism stand? Charles willingly commissioned Sir William Temple to conclude a separate peace with the Dutch. On February 9, 1674, the Treaty of Westminster ended the Third Dutch War.

VIII. THE "POPISH PLOT"

An almost lucid interval followed. Having received an additional 500,000 crowns from Louis, Charles prorogued his troublesome Parliament and returned to his mistresses. But politics continued. Shaftesbury and other opposition leaders established (1675) the Green Ribbon Club, and from that center the Country Party issued its propaganda to defend Parliament and Protestantism against a King plotting with Catholic France and an heir apparent wedded to a Catholic wife. By 1680 these men of the Country Party had come to be called Whigs, and the defenders of the royal power were labeled Tories.* Shaftesbury seemed to Charles "the weakest and wickedest of men,"[141] and Burnet rated his "learning superficial, . . . his vanity ridiculous, . . . his reasoning loose";[142] but John Locke, who lived with Shaftesbury for fifteen years, thought him a brave defender

---

* *Whig* was apparently a shortened form of Whiggamore, the name of a band of Scots active in 1648 against Charles I. *Tory* was an Irish word for robber, and was first applied to the Court Party by Titus Oates in 1680.[140]

of civil, religious, and philosophical liberty. Burnet called him a deist; and we might suspect as much from Shaftesbury's remark that "wise men are of but one religion." When a lady asked which one that was, he answered, "Wise men never tell."[143]

The religious tension fell slightly in 1677, when William of Orange married Protestant Mary, eldest daughter of the Duke of York; if James continued to have no male issue, Mary would be next to him in line for the throne, and England would be joined in marriage with the Protestant Dutch. But on August 28, 1678, Titus Oates came before the King, and announced that he had discovered a "Popish plot": the Pope, the King of France, the Archbishop of Armagh, and the Jesuits of England, Ireland, and Spain were planning to kill Charles, enthrone his brother, and impose Catholicism in England by the sword; three thousand cutthroats were to massacre the leading Protestants of London, and London itself, the citadel of English Protestantism, was to be burned to the ground.

Oates, then twenty-nine, was the son of an Anabaptist preacher. He had become an Anglican clergyman, but had been expelled from his bene-fice for disorderly conduct.[144] He had accepted, or pretended, conversion to Catholicism, and had studied in Jesuit colleges at Valladolid and St.-Omer, from which last he had been expelled;[145] meanwhile, he now claimed, he had learned the secret plans of the Jesuits for the conquest of England. He professed to have been present on April 24, 1678, at a Jesuit conference in London, which had discussed means of killing the King. He named five Catholic peers as in the plot: Arundell, Powis, Petre, Stafford, and Bellasis. When Oates added that Bellasis was to be commander in chief of the papist army, Charles laughed, for Bellasis was bedridden with gout; the King concluded that Oates had fabricated the story in hopes of reward, and dismissed him.

The Privy Council thought it safer to assume some truth in the charges. It summoned Oates to appear before it on September 28. Fearing that he would be imprisoned, Oates went before Sir Edmund Berry Godfrey, a justice of the peace, and left with him a sworn deposition detailing the plot. The Council, impressed by his testimony, ordered the arrest of several papists implicated by him. One of these was Edward Coleman, who had been for some years (till dismissed at the King's bidding) secretary to the Duchess of York. Before the arrest, Coleman burned some of his papers, but those that he had no time to burn showed that he had carried on with Père La Chaise, the Jesuit confessor of Louis XIV, correspondence ex-pressing on both sides the hope that England would soon be made Catholic. In these letters Coleman suggested that Louis XIV should send him money to influence members of Parliament in the Catholic interest, and added: "Success will give the greatest blow to the Protestant religion that it has received since its birth, . . . the conversion of three kingdoms, and by that, perhaps, the utter subduing of a pestilent heresy."[146] The fact that Coleman had destroyed most of his correspondence led the Council to believe that he had known of, perhaps had been an agent in, the plot described by Oates. Charles himself concluded from these letters that some real plot existed.

On October 12 Justice Godfrey disappeared. Five days later his corpse was found in a suburban field. He had evidently been murdered—by agents, and for reasons, still unknown, but the Protestants ascribed the assassination to Catholics who hoped to prevent the publication of Oates's deposition. This event seemed to confirm the charges; and in the atmosphere of distrust left by the secret Treaty of Dover, and the fear of James's accession, it was natural that most of Protestant England should now credit all the accusations made by Oates, and should fall into a frenzy in which the protection of Protestantism seemed to require the arrest, if not the execution, of any Catholic named in the conspiracy.

A reign of terror began which continued for almost four years. James fled to the Netherlands. The citizens of London armed themselves to resist an expected invasion; cannon were planted in Whitehall; guards were placed in the vaults beneath the Houses of Parliament to circumvent a second Gunpowder Plot. Parliament passed a bill excluding Catholics from the House of Lords. It hailed Oates as the savior of the nation, awarded him a life pension of twelve hundred pounds a year, and gave him an apartment in Whitehall Palace. Soon the prisons were filled with Jesuits, secular priests, and Catholic laymen implicated by Oates or by William Bedloe, who came forward claiming knowledge that would substantiate Oates's charges.

On November 24 Oates laid before the Council a new and startling accusation—that he had heard the Queen consent to the poisoning of her husband by her physician. Charles caught Oates in a demonstrable lie, lost faith in his stories, and had him arrested. The Commons ordered him freed, arrested three servants of the Queen, and voted an address demanding the Queen's removal. Charles came to the upper house, defended his wife's loyalty, and persuaded the Lords to refuse concurrence in the Commons' address. On November 27 Coleman and another Catholic layman were tried, were found guilty of treason, and were executed. On December 17 six Jesuits and three secular priests were put to death, and on February 5, 1679, three men were hanged for the murder of Godfrey. These twelve were later proved innocent.

The attack pressed closer to the King. On December 19, 1678, Parliament received from Paris communications showing that Danby had accepted large sums of money from Louis XIV. The minister refused to explain that these sums were French subsidies to the King. The Commons impeached him, and Charles, fearing that his loyal councilor would be condemned to death, dissolved the "Cavalier Parliament" (January 24, 1679), which had sat, discontinuously, for almost eighteen years—longer than the Long Parliament.

But the first "Whig" Parliament, which met on March 6, was more passionately anti-Catholic and anti-King than its predecessor. The Commons charged Danby with treason; the Lords saved him by committing him to the Tower, where he remained in comfort and anxiety during the five following turbulent years. On the advice of Sir William Temple Charles named a new Council of thirty members; to appease the opposition he included in it the two leaders of the Whig Party, Shaftesbury and George Savile, Marquis of Halifax; and on the King's recommendation Shaftesbury was chosen lord president of the Council. To further calm the storm, Charles offered to Parliament a compromise substitute for the exclusion of his brother from the throne: no Catholic should be admitted to Parliament or hold any place of trust; the king should lose the power to make ecclesiastical appointments; his nomination of judges should be subject to Parliamentary approval; and Parliament should control the army and navy.[147] But Parliament felt no confidence that James would honor such an agreement. On May 11 Shaftesbury himself introduced the first exclusion bill in unmistakable terms: "to disable the Duke of York to inherit the imperial crown of this realm." On May 26 the Parliament honored itself by extending the right of habeas corpus: the right to release on bail was assured to every arrested person except those charged with treason or felony; and in these cases the prisoner was to be tried at the next session of the court, or be discharged. France was to wait 110 years before enjoying similar safeguards against arbitrary arrests. On May 27 the King, fearing that the Exclusion Bill would be passed, prorogued the Parliament.

The right of habeas corpus did not help the papists accused by Oates, for they were tried with little delay, and, if found guilty of treason, were executed with angry haste. All through 1679 they went to the scaffold or the block. Trials were expeditious because the judges, frightened by the cries of the bloodthirsty crowds outside the court, condemned many of the defendants without dissecting the evidence or allowing cross-examination of witnesses. False witnesses, noting the rewards enjoyed by Oates, arose as if by incantation, and swore to the wildest tales: one, that an army of thirty thousand men was coming from Spain; another, that he had been promised five hundred pounds and canonization if he would kill the King; another, that he had heard a rich Catholic banker vow to do the same.[148] No counsel was allowed to the accused; he was not told till the day of trial what the accusation would be; and he was assumed to be guilty unless he could prove his innocence.[149] To make conviction easier, an old Elizabethan law was revived that made it a capital crime for a priest to be in England. The surrounding crowds hooted and pelted witnesses for the defense, and shouted with joy when verdicts of guilty were announced.[150]

All this was a heartbreaking experience for the once Merrie Monarch, who saw all his hopes shattered, his powers reduced, his wife humiliated, his brother scorned and set aside. At the height of the storm he fell so seriously ill that his death was expected at any hour. Halifax summoned James from Brussels. The Whig leaders ordered the army to prevent his return; and Shaftesbury, Monmouth, Lord Russell, and Lord Grey agreed that in case Charles should die they would lead an insurrection to prevent the accession of his brother.[151] James found entry in disguise, and made his way to the bedside of the King. Charles apparently recovered, and smiled at the fears with which even his enemies had contemplated his death. He never really recovered.

The anti-Catholic fury continued till Oates blundered in the trial of Sir George Wakeman, the Queen's physician. In testimony before the Council he had exonerated the doctor; in the trial he accused him of planning to poison the King. Chief Justice Scroggs, who had prosecuted the Catholics with vigor, pointed out the contradiction. Wakeman was acquitted, and thereafter Oates's testimony was more critically heard. The false witnesses who had corroborated him fell away from his support. The execution of Oliver Plunket, the Catholic Archbishop of Armagh, was the last act of the anti-Catholic terror (July 1, 1681).

When the fear and passion had subsided, sane men realized that Oates, partly by unsupported suspicions, partly by lies, had sent many innocent men to a premature death. They concluded that there had been no plan to kill the King, or to massacre Protestants, or to burn London. But they felt, too, that a Catholic, though not a "popish," plot had been real: that leading members of the government had planned or hoped, with the help of funds (and, if necessary, of soldiers) from France, to remove the disabilities of English Catholics, to convert the King, to enthrone his converted brother, and to use every means to re-establish Catholicism as the religion of the state, and ultimately of the people. Practically all this had been contained in the secret Treaty of Dover that had been signed in 1670. Charles had retreated from that agreement, but his desires had not changed, and he was still resolved that his Catholic brother should be king.

IX. COMOEDIA FINITA

Shaftesbury was resolved to the contrary. Coleman had confessed, at his trial, that James had known and approved of his correspondence with Père La Chaise.[152] Shaftesbury felt that the accession of James would realize the first stage of the "Popish Plot." He offered his support to Charles if the King would divorce his barren Queen and marry a Protestant by whom he might have a Protestant son. Charles refused to let Catherine of Braganza repeat the role of Catherine of Aragon. Shaftesbury then turned to the Duke of Monmouth, the King's bastard, who could not forgive his father for cheating him of the throne by failing to marry his mother. Shaftesbury spread the idea that Charles had really married Lucy Walter, and that the Duke was the legal heir to the throne. Charles countered by a declaration that he had never married anyone but Catherine of Braganza. Finding Shaftesbury irreconcilable, the King dismissed him from the Council (October 13, 1679).

In this succession of crises Charles almost changed his character. He gave up his life of pleasure and ease, sold his stables, devoted himself to administration and politics, and fought his foes with strategic retreats until they overreached themselves into failure. In his final five years he showed such resolution and ability as surprised even his friends. Recovering his confidence, he called for his fourth Parliament.

It met on October 21, 1680. In November the second exclusion bill passed the Commons and was presented to the Lords. Halifax, who had heretofore voted with the Whigs, now veered to the side of the King, and began to earn and flaunt the title of "trimmer." He detested James and distrusted Catholicism, but he agreed with Charles that the principle of hereditary monarchy should be maintained, and he feared that Shaftesbury was leading England toward another civil war.[153] In a long debate his eloquence and logic persuaded the Lords to reject the bill. The Commons retaliated by refusing funds to the King, and forbidding any merchant or financier to lend him money, and it impeached Halifax, Scroggs, and Viscount Stafford—one of the five Catholic lords imprisoned in the Tower. Stafford was condemned to death on the testimony of Oates, and was beheaded (December 7). The King dismissed the Parliament (January 18, 1681).

Rather than sacrifice his brother to his need for funds, Charles decided to finance the government by becoming again a pensioner of Louis XIV. He consented to look with equanimity upon the aggressive policies of France in return for £700,000[154]—enough to make him independent of parliamentary subsidies for three years. So sinewed, he summoned his fifth

Parliament. To deprive it of support from the mobs and militia of London, he ordered it to meet at Oxford. Both sides came in arms—Charles with numerous guards, the Whig leaders with retainers carrying swords and pistols and flying banners reading "No Popery, No Slavery." The Commons at once passed the third exclusion bill. Before the measure could reach the Lords, Charles dismissed the Parliament (March 28, 1681).

Many men now expected Shaftesbury to resort to civil war; and public opinion, remembering 1642–60, turned against him and rallied to the King. The Anglican clergy zealously defended the right of Catholic James to the throne. When Shaftesbury tried to reorganize the disbanded Commons into a revolutionary convention,[155] Charles ordered his arrest. A jury acquitted Shaftesbury (November 24); and though he was now so ill that he could barely walk, he joined with the Duke of Monmouth in open revolution.[156] The King had both of them arrested. Shaftesbury escaped from the Tower, fled to Holland, and died there (January 21, 1683), worn out, but leaving his friend Locke to carry on in philosophy the struggle that had for a time been lost in politics.

Charles pardoned Monmouth, but he could not forgive the London jury that had acquitted Shaftesbury. Becoming extreme in his turn, he resolved to destroy the autonomy of the cities, for it was in these that Whig—even revolutionary—sentiment flourished. He ordered an examination of the city charters that permitted such municipal flouting of the royal will. Legal flaws were found in them; they were declared null; and new charters were issued by which all municipally elected officials were henceforth to be subject to veto or removal by the king (1683). Freedom of speech and press were now subjected to new restraints. A persecution of Dissenters (not of Catholics) was begun, for the Dissenters were mostly Whigs; and in Scotland James personally led the oppression. The triumph of royal prerogative over parliamentary privilege seemed complete, and the achievements of the Great Rebellion were apparently to be sacrificed in a royalist reaction supported by a nation fearful of renewed civil war. Halifax reflected the feeling of the country when he abandoned Shaftesbury and turned his temperate wisdom to serve the King (1682–85) as lord privy seal.

The followers of Shaftesbury made a final attempt. In January, 1683, the Duke of Monmouth, the Earl of Essex, the Earl of Carlisle, William Lord Russell, and Algernon Sidney met at the house of John Hampden (grandson of the Civil War hero), and laid plans to circumvent James and, if necessary, assassinate Charles. Sidney hoped to proceed further and reestablish the English republic. He was the grandson of a brother of Sir Philip Sidney, the "President of Chivalry." He fought on the Parliamentary side in the Civil War, and was wounded at Marston Moor. Appointed as one of the commission to try Charles I, he refused to serve, saying that the commission had received no authority from the people to try the King. Finding himself on the Continent at the Restoration, he stayed there, engaged in studies and in plots against Charles II. During the Second Dutch War he urged the Dutch to invade England, and he offered his services to the French government to raise a rebellion in England if it would supply him with 100,000 crowns.[157] Charles allowed him to return to England (1677) to attend the death of his father. Remaining in England, he joined the Country Party. In *Discourses Concerning Government* (written in 1681 but not published till 1688), he advocated semirepublican principles, anticipated Locke by attacking Filmer's defense of divine right in kings, and asserted the right of the people to judge and depose their rulers. Apparently both he and Russell accepted money from the French government, which was interested in keeping Charles II busy with domestic troubles.[158]

The "Council of Six" decided to capture the King. It was known that in March he would attend the horse races at Newmarket; on his return to London his coach would pass by Rye House, at Hoddesdon, north of the city; a cart of hay was to block the road there; the King, and perhaps his brother, were to be taken, alive or dead. But on March 22 a fire broke out at the racecourse; the races were ended a week sooner than scheduled, and Charles passed safely to London before the conspirators could advance their preparations. On June 12 one of them, fearing exposure and hoping for pardon, betrayed the plot to the government. Carlisle, arrested, confirmed the confession, and was forgiven. Monmouth protested innocence, and though Charles knew that his son was lying, he canceled the order for his arrest. Russell was tried, convicted, and executed (July 21, 1683). Essex killed himself in jail. "He needed not to have despaired of mercy," said the King, "for I owed him a life";[159] Essex' father had died for Charles I. Several minor participants in this "Rye House Plot" were hanged. Sidney was convicted on technically inadequate evidence; he defended himself ably, and met his death like a Roman (December 7). His motto had been *Manus haec inimica tyrannis*—"This hand is the foe of tyrants"; but he had chosen a double-edged sword. On the scaffold he uttered notable words: "God has left nations unto the liberty of setting up such governments as please themselves."[160] He refused any religious attendance, saying that he was already at peace with God.

Charles had won, but he was through. He enjoyed, wearily, a new popularity. England had prospered economically under his reign, and now, longing for political quiet, it rallied to a ruler who represented national continuity and order, even if that meant for a time a Catholic king. It forgave Charles his faults as it saw him fading into premature decline. It half agreed with him that a monarchy elective and not hereditary invited periodical turmoil. It respected his loyalty to his brother, even while it mourned the result. It saw James triumphant, again lord high admiral, already pursuing his enemies vengefully. In January, 1685, James brought and won a civil suit against Titus Oates for £100,000 damages; Oates, unable to pay this great sum, was imprisoned. "When I am dead and gone," said Charles sadly, "I know not what my brother will do; I am very much afraid that when he comes to wear the crown he will be obliged to travel again. And yet I will take care to leave my kingdoms to him in peace, wishing he may keep them long so. But this hath all of my fears, little of my hopes, and less of my reason."[161] When James expostulated with him for driving about London unguarded, he bade him calm his fears: "No one will kill me to make you king."[162]

He should have excepted the doctors. On February 2, 1685, he suffered a convulsion; his face was distorted, his mouth foamed. Dr. King bled him by lancing a vein, with good effect. But attendants summoned eighteen other physicians to diagnose and prescribe. For five tortured days he submitted to their united attack. They tapped his veins, put cupping glasses to his shoulders, cut off his hair to raise blisters on his scalp, and applied to the soles of his feet plasters of pitch and pigeon dung. "To remove the humours from his brain," says a medical historian, "they blew hellebores up his nostrils and set him sneezing. To make him vomit they poured antimony and sulphate of zinc down his throat. To clear his bowels they gave him strong purgatives and a brisk succession of clysters."[163]

The dying King called for his long-suffering wife, not perceiving that she was already kneeling at the foot of the bed, rubbing his feet. On February 4 some bishops offered him the last rites of the Anglican Church, but he begged them to desist. When his brother asked him did he want a Catholic priest, he answered, "Yes, yes, with all my heart."[164] Father John Huddleston, who had saved Charles's life at the battle of Worcester, and whose life Charles had saved in the Popish Terror, was sent for; Charles made profession of the Roman Catholic faith, confessed his sins, pardoned his enemies, asked pardon of all, and received extreme unction and the last sacrament. He asked pardon especially of his wife; but also he bade his brother take care of Louise de Kéroualle and his children, and "let not poor Nelly starve."[165] He apologized to those around him for taking so unconscionable a time dying.[166]

By noon of February 6 the Duke of York was King.

CHAPTER X

The Glorious Revolution

1685–1714

I. THE CATHOLIC KING: 1685–88

WHO would have fancied, from Vandyck's beautiful blue-and-gold portrait[1] of the Duke of York at the age of two, that this innocent, sensitive, diffident child would ruin the Stuart dynasty and finally complete, in the "Glorious Revolution," that transfer of power from king to Parliament which his father had ingloriously begun? But in Riley's portrait[2] of the same soul as James II the diffidence has become bewilderment, the sensitivity has changed into obstinacy, and the innocence has passed through compliant mistresses to an inflexible theology. That character determined a tragic fate in which, as in all great tragedies, every participant fought for what seemed to him right, and can claim a portion of our sympathy.

We have already noted some of his virtues. He repeatedly exposed himself to danger of death in his naval career. Men compared him favorably with his brother in administrative industry, in modesty of expenditure, in fidelity to his word. He observed Charles's dying injunction to take care of Nell Gwyn: he paid her debts, and settled upon her an estate sufficient to maintain her in comfort. After his accession he continued for a while his relations with his latest mistress, Catherine Sedley; but on the remonstrances of Father Petre he rewarded her for her services and persuaded her to leave England; for he confessed that if he saw her again he would not be able to resist the hold she had over him.[3] Bishop Burnet, who helped to dethrone him, judged him to be "naturally candid and sincere, though sometimes eager and revengeful; a very firm friend, until his religion had corrupted his first principles and inclinations."[4] He was frugal and thrifty, kept an honest coinage, and was easy on the people in taxation.[5] Macaulay, after writing eight hundred pages about James's three-year rule, concluded that "with so many virtues he might, if he had been a Protestant, nay, if he had been a moderate Roman Catholic, have had a prosperous and glorious reign."[6]

His faults grew with his power. Proud and arrogant even before his accession, scornful of the many and accessible only to a few, he adopted to the letter his father's theory that the king should have absolute authority;

288

and he had not his brother's realistic humor to see its practical limitations. We must pay respect to his fervor for his religion, and his desire to give his fellow Catholics in England freedom of worship and equality of political opportunity. He had been devoted to his Catholic mother and sister; he had, for the past fifteen years, been surrounded by Catholics in his own house; and he thought it strange that a religion that produced so many good men and women should be so checked and hated by Englishmen. He did not share the vivid memories that English Protestants transmitted of the Gunpowder Plot, or their fear that a Catholic ruler would be inclined, and be sooner or later persuaded, to adopt only such policies as would not displease an Italian pope. Protestant England felt that its religious, intellectual, and political independence would be imperiled by a Catholic king.

James's first moves after his accession slightly relieved these fears. He made Halifax lord president of his Council, Sunderland secretary of state, and Henry Hyde (second Earl of Clarendon) lord privy seal—all Protestants. In his first speech to the Council he promised to maintain the existing institutions in Church and state; he expressed his appreciation of the support that the Church of England had given to his succession, and promised to cherish her with special care. At his coronation he took the usual oath of modern English sovereigns to preserve and protect the Established Church. For some months he enjoyed an unexpected popularity.

His first pro-Catholic measure carried no direct offense to Protestantism. He ordered the release of all persons imprisoned for refusal to take the oaths of allegiance and supremacy. Thousands of Catholics were thereby freed, but also twelve hundred Quakers and many other Dissenters. He forbade any further prosecutions in matters of religion. He liberated Danby, and the Catholic lords who had been sent to the Tower on charges by Titus Oates. In a new trial Oates was convicted of perjuries that had led to the execution of several innocent persons; the court, expressing regret that it could not condemn him to death, sentenced him to pay a fine of two thousand marks, to be tied to the back of a cart, to be twice publicly whipped—once from Aldgate to Newgate, and two days later from Newgate to Tyburn—and to stand in the pillory five times every year for the remainder of his life. He survived the ordeal, and was returned to jail (May, 1685). James, asked to remit the second whipping, refused.

The precarious truce of the faiths was broken by a double revolt. In May Archibald Campbell, ninth Earl of Argyll, landed in Scotland, and in June James, Duke of Monmouth, landed on the southwest coast of England, in a joint effort to overthrow the Catholic King. Monmouth's proclamation denounced James as a usurper, tyrant, and murderer, charged him with the burning of London, the Popish Plot, and the poisoning of

Charles, and pledged the invaders to make no peace until they had rescued the Protestant religion and the liberties of the nation and the Parliament. Argyll was overcome on June 17, and executed on June 30; the northern arm of the rebellion failed. But the people of Dorsetshire, strongly Puritan, hailed Monmouth as a savior, and so many men enlisted under his banner that he confidently and solemnly assumed the title of James II, King of England. The nobility and the moneyed classes offered him no support, and his undisciplined army was defeated by the royal forces at Sedgemoor (July 6, 1685)—the last battle fought on English soil before the Second World War. Monmouth fled, begged forgiveness of the King, was refused, and was beheaded.

The royal army, led by Colonel Percy Kirke, pursued the remainder of the rebels and hanged prisoners without trial. James appointed a commission, headed by Chief Justice Jeffreys, to go into the west country and try persons accused of joining or abetting the revolt. Jury trials were given them, but the juries were so terrorized by Jeffreys that very few of the accused found mercy in these "Bloody Assizes" (September, 1685).* Nearly four hundred were hanged, and eight hundred were condemned to forced labor in the plantations of the West Indies.[7] Elizabeth in 1569 and Cromwell in 1648 had been guilty of similar barbarities, but Jeffreys outdid them by browbeating witnesses and juries, cursing his victims, gloating over them, and giving guilt the benefit of every doubt except when a substantial bribe argued for innocence.[8] James made some modest efforts to check the brutality, but when the holocaust was over he raised Jeffreys to the peerage and made him lord chancellor (September 6, 1686).

This vengeful pursuit shared in alienating the country from the King. When he asked Parliament for repeal of the Test Act (excluding Catholics from office and Parliament), for modification of the Habeas Corpus Act, and for a standing army under royal command, it refused to comply. James prorogued it (November 20), and proceeded to appoint Catholics to office. When Halifax objected to this flouting of Parliament James dismissed him from the Council, and replaced him, as its lord president, with Sunderland, who presently announced his conversion to Catholicism (1687). When James commended Louis XIV's Revocation of the Edict of Nantes,[9] England concluded that if James had power as absolute as that of the Bourbon, he would take similar measures against English Protestants. James made no concealment of his belief that his power was already absolute, and that Louis XIV was his ideal of a king. For a time he accepted subsidies from Louis, but he refused to let him dictate the policies of the English government, and the subsidies ended.

* The assizes were the periodical sittings of the superior courts in each county.

Louis was wiser about England than about his own country; while he weakened France by his persecution of the Huguenots, he cautioned James against haste in Catholicizing England. Pope Innocent XI gave him similar counsel. When James sent word to him promising England's early submission to the Roman Church,[10] he advised the King to content himself with obtaining toleration for English Catholics; he warned these to abstain from political ambitions, and directed the general of the Jesuits to rebuke Father Petre for taking so prominent a part in the government.[11] Innocent had not abated his Catholic zeal, but he feared the encompassing strength of Louis XIV, and hoped that England could be turned from a servant of French designs to be a makeweight against them. The Pope sent a nuncio to England—the first since Mary Tudor's reign—to make clear to James that a rupture between Parliament and the King would be injurious to the interests of the Roman Church.[12]

James did not profit from this advice. He felt that, being fifty-two years old at his accession, he had not much time left to effect the religious changes that were dear to his heart. He had little hope of a son; a Protestant daughter would succeed him, and would overturn his work unless this should be solidly established before his death. Father Petre and the Queen overruled all counsels of deliberation. The King not only went in royal state to hear Mass, but he asked his councilors to attend him there. Priests in growing number moved about the court. He appointed Catholics to military posts, and persuaded the judges (who were appointed and removable by him) to confirm his right to dispense such appointees from the penalties imposed upon them by the Test Act. He built up, largely under such Catholic officers, an army of thirteen thousand men, subject only to his orders, and obviously threatening the independence of Parliament. He suspended the penalties attached by law to public attendance at Catholic worship. He issued a decree (June, 1686) forbidding clergymen to preach sermons of doctrinal controversy; and when Dr. John Sharp preached on the motives of converts, James, as legal head of the English Church, ordered Henry Compton, bishop of London, to suspend him from the Anglican ministry. Compton refused. James, overriding a law of 1673, appointed a new Ecclesiastical Commission Court, dominated by Sunderland and Jeffreys; it tried Compton for disobedience to the Crown, and removed him from office. The Anglican Church, which had preached absolute obedience, began to turn against the King.

He had hoped to win the Anglican Church to reconciliation with Rome, but his precipitate action now excluded that policy; instead, he took up the plan of uniting the Catholics and Dissenters against the Establishment. William Penn, who had found his way into the King's confidence, advised him that he could bring to his ardent support all the English Protestants but the Anglicans if he should, by a few strokes of the pen, annul all laws forbidding the public worship of the Dissenting sects. On August 4, 1687, James issued his first Declaration of Indulgence. Whatever were his motives, the document holds a place in the history of toleration. It suspended all penal laws affecting religion, abrogated all religious tests, allowed freedom of worship to all, and forbade interference with peaceable religious assemblies. It released all persons who were imprisoned for religious nonconformity. It went beyond the similar declarations of Charles II, which had kept religious tests for office, and had allowed Catholic worship only in private homes. It assured the Established Church that the King would continue to protect it in all its legal rights. It was a pity that this measure had to be an implicit declaration of war against Parliament, which had decreed all the disabilities now annulled. If Parliament were to admit the authority of the King to cancel parliamentary legislation, the Civil War would have to be fought once more.

Halifax, who was at this time the most brilliant mind in England, entered the fray with an anonymous *Letter to a Dissenter* (August, 1687)—"the most successful pamphlet of the age."[13] He urged Protestants to realize that the toleration now offered them came from a prince loyal to a Church that claimed infallibility and frankly repudiated toleration. Could there be any lasting harmony between liberty of conscience and an infallible Church? How could Dissenters trust their new friends, who till yesterday had branded them as heretics? "The other day you were sons of Belial, now you are angels of light."[14] Unfortunately, the Anglican Church had agreed with Rome about the sons of Belial, and had in the last twenty-seven years subjected Dissenters to such persecution as might well have excused them from accepting freedom even at Catholic hands. The Anglican hierarchy made haste to seek peace with the Presbyterians, Puritans, and Quakers. It begged them to reject the present indulgence, and promised them soon a toleration that would have the sanction of both the Parliament and the Established Church. Some Dissenters sent letters of gratitude to the King; the majority stood aloof; and when the day of decision came, they rejected the King.

James proceeded. The universities of England, for many years past, had required of teachers and students submission to the Anglican Church. Exceptions had been made in conferring a degree upon a Lutheran candidate, and an honorary degree upon a Mohammedan diplomat; but the Anglican clergy thought of Oxford and Cambridge as institutions whose chief function was to prepare men for the Anglican ministry, and it was resolved that no Catholic should be admitted. To breach this barrier James sent a mandatory letter to the vice-chancellor at Cambridge, directing him to exempt from the Anglican oath a Benedictine monk who sought the master's degree. The vice-chancellor refused; he was suspended by order of the Ecclesiastical Commission; the university sent a delegation, including Isaac Newton, to explain its position to the King; the monk quieted the situation by withdrawing (1687). In the same year the King recommended for the presidency of Magdalen College, Oxford, a man of indifferent learning but of Catholic leaning; the fellows refused to elect him. After a long dispute James suggested a less objectionable candidate, the Anglican Bishop Parker of Oxford. The electoral fellows rejected him; they were expelled by order of the King, and Bishop Parker was installed by force.

Resentment rose as James entrusted himself more and more to Catholic advisers. His admiration for Father Petre was so great that he importuned the Pope to make him a bishop, even a cardinal; Innocent refused. In July, 1687, James made the able but reckless Jesuit a member of the Privy Council. Many English Catholics protested that this was a foolish measure, but James was in haste to fight the issues out to a conclusion. There were now six Catholics in the Council, and the favor of the King made them predominant.[15] In 1688 four Catholic bishops were appointed to govern the Catholic Church in England; James settled upon each of them an annual pension of a thousand pounds; in effect Catholics now shared with the Anglicans the position of a state-supported church.

On April 25, 1688, James republished his year-old Declaration of Indulgence, and added to it a reaffirmation of his resolve to secure to all Englishmen "freedom of conscience forever." Henceforth promotion to and in office was to depend upon merit regardless of creed. The reduction of religious hostility, he predicted, would open new markets to English trade, and would add to the prosperity of the nation. He begged his subjects to lay aside all animosity, and elect the next Parliament without any distinctions of religious faith. To ensure the widest circulation of this enlarged Declaration his Council sent instructions to all bishops to arrange with their clergy that it should be read in every parish church in England on May 20 or 27. Such use of the clergy as a means of communicating with the people had several precedents, but none in which the message was so distasteful to the Established Church. On May 18 seven Anglican bishops presented to the King a petition explaining that they could not in conscience recommend to their clergy the reading of the Declaration, for it violated the edict of Parliament that parliamentary legislation could be suspended only by Parliament's consent. James answered that their own theologians had persistently preached the necessity of obedience to the King as the head of their Church, and that there was nothing in the Declaration offensive to any conscience. He promised to consider their petition; but if they did not hear from him on the morrow, they were to obey the order.

The next morning thousands of copies of the petition were sold in the streets of London, while it was still under royal consideration. James felt that this was contrary to all protocol. He submitted the petition to the twelve judges of the royal court; they advised him that he had acted within his legal rights. He left the petition unanswered. On May 20 the petition was read in four London churches; it was ignored in the remaining ninety-six. The King felt that his authority had been flouted. He ordered the seven bishops to appear before the Council. When they came he told them that they would have to submit to trial on the charge of having published a seditious libel; however, to spare them imprisonment in the meantime, he would accept their written promise to appear when summoned. They replied that as peers of the realm they need not give any other security than their word. The Council committed them to the Tower. As they were rowed down the Thames they were cheered by people on the banks.

On June 29 and 30 the bishops were tried before the Court of King's Bench—four judges and a jury. After two days of heated argument, in a hall surrounded by ten thousand excited Londoners, the jury returned a verdict of not guilty. All Protestant England rejoiced; "Never within man's memory," said a Catholic peer, "have there been such shouts and such tears of joy as today."[16] The streets blazed with bonfires; crowds paraded behind wax figures of the Pope, the cardinals, and the Jesuits, which were burned amid wild celebrations. To the simple people the verdict meant that Catholicism was not to be tolerated; to more complex minds it meant that the privilege of Parliament to make laws irrevocable by the king had been vindicated, and that England was in fact, even if not in theory, a constitutional, not an absolute, monarchy.

James, brooding in defeat, consoled himself with the infant to which the Queen had given birth on June 10, a month before her expected time. He would bring up this precious boy as a loyal and devoted Catholic. Day by day father and son, over every opposition and discouragement, would move a step nearer to the sacred goal—the old monarchy living in concord with the old Church, in an England pacified and reconciled, in a Europe repenting its apostasy, and united again in the one true, holy, universal faith.

II. *DEPOSUIT POTENTES DE SEDE*

Perhaps it was that premature birth that brought disaster to the precipitate King. Protestant England agreed with James that this boy might continue the effort to restore Catholicism; it feared him for the same reason that the King loved him. It denied, at first, that this was the King's son; it accused the Jesuits of having brought in some purchased infant to the Queen's bed as part of a plot to keep the King's Protestant daughter Mary from inheriting the throne. It turned more and more to Mary as the hope of English Protestantism, and reconciled itself to another revolution to make her queen.

But Mary was now the wife of William III of Orange, Stadholder of the United Provinces; what would proud William say to being merely the consort of a queen? Why not offer him co-ordinate rule with Mary? After all, he too had royal English blood; his mother had been another Mary, daughter of Charles I. In any case William had no intention of playing consort to his wife. It was probably at his suggestion[17] that Bishop Burnet, who had exiled himself to the Continent on the accession of James, persuaded Mary to pledge her full obedience to William "in all things," whatever authority might devolve upon her. "The rule and authority should be his," she agreed, "for she only desired that he would obey the command of 'Husbands, love your wives,' as she should do that of 'Wives, be obedient to your husbands in all things.' "[18] William accepted the obedience, but ignored the gentle allusion to his liaison with Mrs. Villiers, his mistress.[19] After all, Protestant rulers too should be allowed to adulterate their marriages.

William, fighting Louis XIV for the preservation of Dutch independence and Protestantism, had hoped for a time to win his father-in-law to an alliance against a French King who was destroying the balance and liberties of Europe. When this hope faded, he had negotiated with those Englishmen who led the opposition to James. He had connived at the organization, on Dutch soil, of Monmouth's expedition against the King, and had allowed it to depart unhindered from a Dutch port.[20] He had reason to fear that James planned to disqualify him as a successor to the throne; and when a son was born to the King, the rights of Mary were obviously superseded. Early in 1687 William sent Everhard van Dykvelt to England to establish friendly contacts with Protestant leaders. The envoy returned with favorable letters from the Marquis of Halifax, the Earls of Shrewsbury, Bedford, Clarendon (son of the former Chancellor), Danby, Bishop Compton, and others. The letters were too vague to constitute clear treason, but they implied warm support for William as a contender for the throne.

In June, 1687, Kaspar Fagel, Grand Pensionary, issued a letter authoritatively stating William's views on toleration: the Stadholder desired freedom of religious worship for all, but opposed the abrogation of the Test Act confirming public office to adherents of the Anglican faith.[21] This cautious pronouncement won him the support of prominent Anglicans.

When the birth of a son to James apparently ended William's chances of succeeding James, the Protestant leaders decided to invite him to come and conquer the throne. The invitation (June 30, 1688) was signed by the twelfth Earl of Shrewsbury, the first Duke of Devonshire, the Earls of Danby and Scarborough, Admiral Edward Russell (cousin of the William Russell executed in 1683), Henry Sidney (brother of Algernon), and Bishop Compton. Halifax did not sign, saying that he preferred constitutional opposition; but many others, including Sunderland and John Churchill (both then in the service of James), sent William assurance of their support.[22] The signers recognized that their invitation was treason; they deliberately took their lives in their hands, and dedicated their fortunes to the enterprise. Shrewsbury, a former Catholic converted to Protestantism, mortgaged his estates for forty thousand pounds, and crossed to Holland to help direct the invasion.[23]

William could not act at once, for he was not sure of his own people, and he feared that at any moment Louis XIV would renew his attack upon Holland. The German states also feared attack by France; nevertheless they raised no objection to William's invasion, for they knew that his ultimate aim was to check the Bourbon King. The Hapsburg governments of Austria and Spain forgot their Catholicism in their hatred of Louis XIV, and approved the deposition of a Catholic ruler friendly to France. Even the Pope gave the expedition his *nihil obstat,* so that it was by permission of Catholic powers that Protestant William undertook to depose Catholic James. Louis and James themselves precipitated the invasion. Louis proclaimed that the bonds of "friendship and alliance" existing between England and France would compel him to declare war upon any invader of England. James, fearing that this statement would further unify his Protestant subjects against him, denied the existence of such an alliance, and rejected the offer of French help. Louis let his anger get the better of his strategy. He ordered his armies to attack not Holland but Germany (September 25, 1688); and the States-General of the United Provinces, freed for a time from fear of the French, agreed to let William proceed on an expedition which might win England to alliance against France.

On October 19 the armada set forth—fifty warships, five hundred transports, five hundred cavalry, eleven thousand infantry, including many Huguenot refugees from the French dragonnades. Driven back by winds, the fleet waited for a "Protestant breeze," and sailed again on November 1. An English squadron sent to intercept it was scattered by a storm. On November 5—the national holiday commemorating the Gunpowder Plot—the invaders landed at Torbay, an inlet of the Channel on the Dorsetshire coast. No resistance was encountered, but no welcome was received; the people had not forgotten Jeffreys and Kirke. James ordered his army, under command of Lord John Churchill, to assemble at Salisbury, and he himself joined it there. He found his troops so lukewarm in their allegiance that he could not trust them to give battle; he ordered a retreat. That night (November 23) Churchill and two other high officers of the King's army deserted to William with four hundred men.[24] A few days later Prince George of Denmark, husband of James's daughter Anne, joined the spreading defection. Returning to London, the unhappy King found that Anne, with Churchill's wife, Sarah Jennings, had fled to Nottingham. The spirit of the once proud monarch broke under the discovery that both his daughters had turned against him. He commissioned Halifax to treat with William. On December 11 he himself left his capital. Halifax, back from the front, found the nation leaderless, but a group of peers made him president of a provisional government. On the thirteenth they received a message from James that he was in hostile hands at Faversham in Kent. They sent troops to rescue him, and on the sixteenth the humiliated King was back in Whitehall Palace. William, advancing toward London, sent some Dutch guardsmen with instructions to carry James to Rochester, and there let him escape. It was done; James fell into the trap laid for him, and quitted England for France (December 23). He would survive his fall by thirteen years, but he would never see England again.

William reached London on December 19. He used his victory with characteristic firmness, prudence, and moderation. He put an end to the riots in which London Protestants had been pillaging and burning the houses of Catholics. At the request of the provisional government he summoned the lords, bishops, and former members of Parliament to meet at Coventry. The "Convention" that assembled there on February 1, 1689, declared that James had abdicated the throne by his flight. It offered to crown Mary as queen and accept William as her regent; they refused. It offered to crown William as king and Mary as queen; they accepted (February 13). But the Convention accompanied this offer with a "Declaration of Right," which was re-enacted by Parliament as the "Bill of Rights" on December 16, and (though not explicitly agreed to by William) became a vital part of the statutes of the realm:

> Whereas the late King James II . . . did endeavor to subvert and extirpate the Protestant religion, and the laws and liberties of this Kingdom:
> 1. By assuming and exercising a power of dispensing with, and suspending of, laws, and the execution of laws, without consent of Parliament; . . .
> 3. By . . . erecting a . . . "Court of Commission for Ecclesiastical Causes";
> 4. By levying money for and to the use of the Crown, by pretense

of prerogative, for other time and in other manner than the same was granted by Parliament.

5. By raising and keeping a standing army . . . without consent of Parliament; . . .

7. By prosecutions in the Court of King's Bench for matters and causes cognizable only in Parliament . . .

All which are utterly and directly contrary to the known laws and statutes and freedom of this realm; . . .

Having therefore an entire confidence that . . . the Prince of Orange will . . . preserve them [the Parliament] from the violation of their rights which they have here asserted, and from all other attempts upon their religion, rights, and liberties, the . . . lords spiritual and temporal and commons, assembled at Westminster, do resolve that William and Mary, Prince and Princess of Orange, be and be declared King and Queen of England, France, and Ireland . . . and that the oaths hereafter mentioned be taken by all persons of whom the oaths of allegiance and supremacy might be required by law . . .

"I, A. B., do swear that I do from my heart abhor, detest and abjure, as impious and heretical, this damnable doctrine . . . that princes excommunicated or deprived by the pope, or any author- ity of the see of Rome, may be deposed or murdered by their subjects, or any other whatsoever. And I do declare that no foreign prince, person, prelate, state, or potentate has, or ought to have, any jurisdiction, power, superiority, . . . or authority . . . within this realm. So help me God."

. . . And whereas it hath been found by experience that it is incon- sistent with the safety and welfare of this Protestant kingdom to be governed by a popish prince, or by any king or queen marrying a papist, the said lords spiritual and temporal, and commons, do further pray that it may be enacted that all and every person and persons that is, are, or shall be reconciled to, or shall hold communion with, the see or Church of Rome, or shall profess the popish religion, or shall marry a papist, shall be excluded and be forever incapable to inherit, possess, or enjoy the crown and government of this realm . . .[25]

This historic proclamation expressed the essential results of what Protestant England called the "Glorious Revolution": the explicit assertion of the legislative supremacy of Parliament, so long contested by four Stuart kings; the protection of the citizen against arbitrary governmental power; and the exclusion of Roman Catholics from holding or sharing the throne of England. Only next to these results in importance was the consoli- dation of governmental power in the landowning aristocracy; for the revolution had been initiated by great nobles and carried through with the landowning gentry as represented in the House of Commons; in effect, the "absolute" monarchy by "divine right" had been changed into a territorial oligarchy characterized by moderation, assiduity, and skill in government, co-operating with the princes of industry, commerce, and finance, and generally careless of the artisans and peasantry. The upper middle classes benefited substantially from the revolution. The cities of England recovered their freedom to be ruled by mercantile oligarchies. The merchants of London, who had shied away from helping James, lent £200,000 to finance William between his arrival in the capital and his first reception of parliamentary funds.[26] That loan cemented an unwritten agreement: the merchants would let the landowners rule England, but the ruling aristocracy would direct foreign policy to commercial interests, and would leave merchants and manufacturers increasingly free from official regulation.

There were some inglorious elements in the Glorious Revolution.[27] It seemed regrettable that England had had to call in a Dutch army to redress English wrongs, that a daughter should help oust her father from his throne, that the commander of his army should go over to the invader, and that the national Church should join in overthrowing a King whose divine and absolute authority it had sanctified against any act of rebellion or disobedience. It was regrettable that the supremacy of Parliament had to be vindicated by opposing freedom of worship. But the evil that these men and women did was interred with their bones; the good that they accomplished lived after them and grew. Even in establishing an oligarchy they laid the foundations of a democracy that would come with the broadening of the electorate. They made the Englishman's home his castle, relatively secure against the "insolence of office" and "the oppressor's wrong." They contributed some part to that admirable reconciliation of order and liberty which is the English government today. And they did all this without shedding a drop of blood—except the repeated nosebleeds of the harassed, helpless, deserted, witless King.

III. ENGLAND UNDER WILLIAM III: 1689–1702

The new King appointed as his privy councilors Danby as lord president, Halifax as lord privy seal, the Earls of Shrewsbury and Nottingham as secretaries of state, the Earl of Portland as lord of the privy purse, and Gilbert Burnet bishop of Salisbury.

The most remarkable and influential of these men was George Savile, Marquis of Halifax. As a nephew of the Lord Strafford who had been executed by the Long Parliament, he had lost much of his property in the Great Rebellion, but he had salvaged enough to live comfortably in France during the Cromwellian regime. There he discovered Montaigne's *Essays*, and became a philosopher; if, later, he graduated from politics to statesmanship, it was because the difference between politics and statesmanship is philosophy—the ability to see the moment and the part in the light of the lasting and the whole. Halifax was never content to be entirely a man of affairs. "The government of the world," he wrote, meaning the rule of nations, "is a great thing; but it is a very coarse one, too, compared with the fineness of speculative knowledge."[28] Politics had sometimes to deal with crowds, which frightened Halifax. "There is an accumulative cruelty in a number of men, though none in particular are ill-natured . . . The angry buzz of a multitude is one of the bloodiest noises in the world."[29] He had lived through the Popish Terror, when mobs terrorized the courts. Seeing so many religions in acquisitive conflict, he shed most theology, so that, says Burnet, "he passed for a bold and determined atheist; though he often protested to me he was not one, and said he believed there was not one in the world. He confessed he could not swallow down everything that divines imposed on the world; he was a Christian in submission; he believed as much as he could."[30]

Back in England, he regained his property, and wealth so extensive that he could afford to be honest. He served Charles II until he learned of the secret Treaty of Dover. He defended the right of James to succeed to the throne, but he opposed the repeal of the Test Act. He looked forward to a Protestant rule after a brief Catholic interval, and realized his hope when he took a leading part in peacefully transferring the royal power from James II to William III. He followed his own sense of right rather than cleave to any party line. "Ignorance," he wrote in *Thoughts and Reflexions*, "maketh most men go into a party, and shame keepeth them from getting out of it."[31] When he was abused for breaking party lines he defended himself in a famous pamphlet on *The Character of a Trimmer*:

> The innocent word *Trimmer* signifieth no more than this, That if men are together in a boat, and one part of the company would weigh it down on one side, another would make it lean as much to the contrary; it happeneth there is a third opinion, of those who conceive it would do as well if the boat were even.[32]

He was occasionally unscrupulous, always eloquent, and perilously witty. When the court of William III was overrun with place hunters who claimed to have helped the revolution, he made enemies by remarking, "Rome was saved by geese, but I do not remember that these geese were made consuls."[33]*

Halifax must have smiled when the Convention, having transformed itself

---

* The cackling of the frightened sacred geese on the Capitol awakened the Roman garrison to defeat a night attack by the Celts in 390 B.C.[34]

into a Parliament, proceeded to what it deemed the first necessity of government—a new oath of allegiance and submission to William III as head not only of the state but of the Established Church. It was another of history's humors that the Anglican Church, which for a century had been persecuting Calvinists (Presbyterians, Puritans, and other Dissenters), should now accept a Dutch Calvinist as its head.

Four hundred Anglican clergymen, adhering to the doctrine of the divine right of kings, and therefore questioning William's right to rule, refused to take the new oath. These "Nonjurors" were dismissed from their benefices, and formed another sect of Dissent. Many of those clergymen who took the oath did so with "a mental reservation"[35] that would have amused the few Jesuits who remained in England. "The prevarication of too many in so sacred a matter," Burnet thought, "contributed not a little to fortify the growing atheism."[36] Anglicans of all shades were shocked when William, yielding to the overwhelming preponderance of sentiment in Scotland, abolished there the episcopacy that the Stuarts had established by force. And many Anglicans grieved when they found William inclined to religious toleration.

Brought up in predestinarian Calvinism, William could not sympathize with the Anglican view that a Presbyterian should be excluded from office or Parliament. He had already encouraged toleration in the United Provinces, and had made no religious discrimination in his friendships. Predestinarian Calvinism had become for William a trust in himself as an agent of destiny; and in this assurance he could look without bigotry upon Dissent as itself an instrument of that mysterious Power, more than personal, which he variously called Fortune, Providence, or God.[37] He saw in the religious divisions of England a force that could tear the nation apart if not moderated into amity.

It was clever of the Privy Council to have its Toleration Act proposed to Parliament by Nottingham, who was known as a zealous and loyal son of the Anglican Church; his advocacy disarmed the rigorists. So this first achievement of the new reign passed both houses with little opposition (May 24, 1689). It allowed freedom of public worship to all groups that accepted Trinitarianism and Biblical inspiration, and that explicitly repudiated transubstantiation and the religious supremacy of the pope. Baptists were permitted to defer baptism to maturity, and by the Affirmation Act of 1696 the Quakers were allowed to substitute a solemn promise for an oath. Unitarians and Catholics were excluded from toleration. An attempt was made by William and his Council, in the Comprehension Bill introduced later in 1689, to have various dissenting groups admitted to the Anglican Church, but this measure failed to pass. Dissenters were still banned from the universities, and were ineligible to Parliament or public office unless they received the Sacrament according to the Anglican rite. A renewed law against blasphemy (1697) decreed imprisonment for attacks upon any basic Christian doctrine. There was no further legal extension of religious freedom in England till 1778; nevertheless toleration was greater than in any other European country after 1685, except the United Provinces. In practice toleration slowly widened as England grew strong enough to lose its fear of invasion or internal subversion by Catholic power.

Even the Catholics enjoyed, under William, an increasing security. The King explained that he could not maintain his alliances with Catholic states if he oppressed Catholics in England.[38] For a decade Catholic priests could say Mass in private homes, and were not molested if they kept a judicious disguise in public. Toward the close of the reign (1699), when the Tories and the rigorists got the upper hand in Parliament, the laws against Catholics were sharpened. Any priests convicted of saying Mass, or of discharging any other sacerdotal function, except in the house of an ambassador, was made liable to life imprisonment; and to implement the law a reward of a hundred pounds was offered to anyone who procured a conviction. The same penalty was decreed for any Catholic who undertook the public education of the young. No parent might send a child abroad to be educated in the Catholic faith. No one might purchase or inherit land except after taking the oath of royal supremacy in religion, and against transubstantiation. All persons refusing to take such oaths forfeited their inheritance to the government.[39] William pardoned and pensioned Titus Oates (1689).

The Catholics of Ireland brought a renewed persecution by organizing a revolt that aimed to restore James II. Richard Talbot, Earl of Tyrconnel, collected 36,000 troops, and invited James to come from France to lead them. Louis XIV, who had set up the deposed King in a court of his own at St.-Germain, with an annual allowance of 600,000 francs, now equipped a fleet for him, accompanied him to Brest, and bade him a famous adieu: "The best that I can wish you is that we shall never see each other again."[40] James landed in Ireland (March 12, 1689) with twelve hundred men, was escorted to Dublin by Talbot, summoned an Irish Parliament, and proclaimed freedom of worship for all loyal subjects. The Parliament met on May 7, repealed the Act of Settlement of 1652, and ordered the return to their former Irish possessors of all lands taken from them since 1641. William sent his Huguenot general Schomberg to Ireland with ten thousand men; Louis countered by dispatching seven thousand French veterans to James's aid; William himself crossed to Ireland in June, 1690. When the opposed armies met in the battle of the Boyne (July 1), James, who had once been brave, rode off in panic on seeing that his forces were giving way. Soon he was back in St.-Germain.

William would have been glad to make peace with the Irish on the *status quo ante,* but the Protestant leaders and forces under him demanded the complete eradication of rebellious elements, and a further appropriation of Irish lands. William returned to England, leaving his army in charge of Godert de Ginkel, now Earl of Athlone; Schomberg had died in his victory at the Boyne. The King instructed Ginkel to offer a free pardon, freedom of worship, exemption from the antipapal oath of supremacy, and recovery of their estates, to all rebels who should lay down their arms.[41] Ginkel secured the surrender of Galway and Limerick on these terms. By the Treaty of Limerick (October 3, 1691) the Irish rebels accepted the pacification offered by William, and in March, 1692, a royal proclamation announced the end of the Irish war.

The Protestants of Ireland denounced the treaty as a surrender to papists, and appealed to the English Parliament. That assembly at once (October 22, 1691) passed an act debarring from the Irish Parliament any man who would not take the oath of supremacy and declare against transubstantiation. The new Irish Parliament, entirely Protestant, refused to recognize the Treaty of Limerick. While William absorbed himself in organizing Europe against Louis XIV, the Dublin Parliament laid upon Irish Catholics a new series of penal acts frankly overriding the peace that William and Mary had signed. Catholic schools and colleges were made illegal; Catholic priests were subject to deportation; no Catholic was to carry arms, or possess a horse worth more than five pounds; and any Protestant heiress who married a Catholic was to suffer the forfeiture of her estate.[42] The confiscation of Irish property went on until "there was practically no more land to confiscate."[43] It was almost impossible for an Irish Catholic to win a suit in an Irish court, and crimes against Irish Catholics were rarely punished. To complete the desolation of Ireland, its woolen industry, which had grown to the point of competing with England's, was ruined by acts of the English Parliament forbidding the exportation of wool from Ireland to any country but England, and stifling even this trade by deliberately prohibitive tariffs (1696). Poverty, beggary, famine, and desperate lawlessness covered the island outside the English Pale. In the sixty years following the Glorious Revolution half the Catholic population, which had neared a million in 1688, emigrated, taking the best blood of the people to foreign lands.

In England every economic class now prospered except the proletariat and the peasantry. Textile workers suffered from foreign competition and from invention; in 1710 the stocking knitters went on strike against the introduction of stocking looms and the use of low-paid apprentices to operate them.[44] But the national product was rising; we may judge it from the increase of the average annual revenues of the government from £500,-000 in the sixteenth century to £7,500,000 in the seventeenth;[45] the increase came partly from inflation, but chiefly from the expansion of manufacturing and foreign trade.

Even so, the revenues did not suffice, for William was raising great armies to fight Louis XIV. Taxes rose beyond precedent, but more money was needed. In January, 1693, Charles Montagu, first Earl of Halifax, as lord of the treasury, revolutionized governmental finance by persuading Parliament to float a public loan of £900,000, on which the government promised to pay seven per cent yearly. Toward the end of 1693, as expenditures were dangerously outrunning receipts, a group of bankers agreed to lend the government £1,200,000 at eight per cent, secured by an added duty on shipping. The idea of such incorporated lending had been suggested by William Paterson three years before. Montagu now gave it official support, and Parliament accepted the plan. The lenders (following Genoese, Venetian, and Dutch precedents) organized themselves as "the Governors and Company of the Bank of England," which was chartered on July 27, 1694. They borrowed money at four and a half per cent from diverse sources, lent it to the government at eight per cent, and made additional profits by undertaking all the functions of a bank. So originated, the Bank of England made further loans to the government, and in 1696 it received from Parliament a monoply of such loans. After many vicissitudes it became a leading factor in the remarkable stability of the English government from the accession of William and Mary to our own day. As early as 1694 the notes of the bank, backed by deposits and payable in gold on demand, were accepted as legal tender; this was the first genuine paper money in England.[46]*

Montagu further distinguished his tenure at the treasury by reforming the metallic currency (1696). The good coins of Charles II and James II were being hoarded, melted, or exported, while the clipped or damaged coins of Elizabeth and James I bore the brunt of use, and lost in purchasing power a considerable part of their face value. Montagu called in his friends John Locke, Isaac Newton, and John Somers to give England a more stable currency. They designed new coins with a milled edge that would defy clipping; they called in the old coins, which were redeemed at their face value; the state took the loss, and England had a sound currency that was the model and envy of Europe. In 1698 the London Stock Exchange was opened, and an era of financial speculation began which soon produced the South Sea Company (1711) and the bursting of its "bubble" (1720). In 1688 Edward Lloyd set up in a London coffeehouse the insurance firm now known with proud simplicity as Lloyd's. In 1693 Edmund Halley issued the first known tables of mortality. All these financial developments emphasized and extended the role of the moneyed interest in the affairs of England, and

---

* The earliest recorded paper money was issued in the seventh century A.D. under the T'ang Dynasty in China. Marco Polo saw such paper money in China in 1275, and tried without success to introduce the device into Italy. Sweden used paper money in 1656, Massachusetts Colony in 1690.[47]

marked the rising importance of capitalists—providers and managers of capital—in Britain.

Above the expanding economy the political battle steamed with the strife for power between the landowning Tories and the moneymaking Whigs, between the English and the Scots, with plots to assassinate William, and schemes to replace James on the throne. William was not interested in the domestic affairs of England; he had conquered it chiefly to align it with his homeland and other states against Louis XIV; as Halifax put it, he had "taken England on his way to France."[48] When the English discovered that this was his absorbing passion, he lost all popularity. He was not an amiable king. He could be coldly cruel, as in ordering the extirpation of the Mac-Donald clan of Glencoe for tendering its allegiance tardily (1692). He was "silent and surly in company," for he spoke English with difficulty. He cared little for women, and had terrible manners at table, so that the ladies of London society called him "a Low-Dutch bear."[49] He surrounded himself with Dutch guards and associates, and did not hide his opinion that the Dutch were far superior to the English in economic ability, political judgment, and moral character. He knew that many nobles were secretly negotiating with James II. He found corruption so prevalent around him that he entered into it himself, and bought M.P.s like merchandise. Everything was good that made for the checking of rampant France.

Because he left domestic affairs to his ministers, the era of powerful ministries began (1695), of "cabinets" united in responsibility and action and dominated by one man, usually the lord of the treasury. In 1697 his enemies the Tories came to power in an electoral overturn. They so limited his authority and questioned his foreign policy that he thought of resigning (1699). But when he laid his bent, asthmatic, and tubercular body down to his final rest (March 8, 1702), he could console his domestic defeats with the consciousness that he had at last brought England into resolute participation in the Grand Alliance (1701) which, after twelve years of struggle, would bring the great Bourbon to his knees, save the independence of Protestant Europe, and leave England free to spread her power over the world.

IV. ENGLAND UNDER QUEEN ANNE: 1702–14

The death of Queen Mary in 1695 had left her sister Anne heiress to the throne. Brought up in danger and turmoil, Anne had become a timid girl, pure in morals, simple in mind, strong in feeling, and seeking consolation and courage in a devoted and humble friendship with her childhood companion, the lively, laughing, skeptical, positive, confident Sarah Jennings. In 1678 Sarah, who was five years older than Anne, married John Churchill, and in 1683 Anne married Prince George of Denmark. Both marriages prospered, but they did not interfere with the close intimacy of the two women. Anne waived all formality, playfully called Sarah (now her lady of the bedchamber) "Mrs. Freeman," and insisted on being called not "Princess" but "Mrs. Morley." When the two husbands deserted James for William, Anne had to make a bitter choice between father and mate. Her love for her husband and her friend decided her to leave for Nottingham (November 26, 1688). On December 19 she and Sarah returned to London and an alien King.

She never learned to like William III. She felt insulted and injured when he gave to one of his friends the estate of her father, to which she had a partial claim. By 1691 she was longing for the return of her father to the throne. William reasonably suspected both Churchill (now Earl of Marlborough) and his wife of intrigues with the deposed ruler. Queen Mary ordered Anne to dismiss Sarah from her entourage. Anne refused. On the next morning (January, 1692) Marlborough was dismissed from his offices, and he and Sarah were banished from the court. Rather than be separated from her friend, Anne, defying King and Queen, left Whitehall Palace to live with Sarah at Sion House. On May 4 Marlborough was sent to the Tower. Sarah often visited him there, and proposed to end her association with Anne to appease the Queen. Whereupon Anne wrote to her:

> The last time he [the Bishop of Worcester] was here, I told him that you had several times desired that you might go from me. . . . I beg it again for Christ Jesus' sake that you would never name it any more to me. For be assured, if you should ever do so cruel a thing as to leave me, from that moment I shall never enjoy one quiet hour. And should you do it without asking my consent (which if I ever give you, may I never see the face of Heaven) I will shut myself up and never see the world more, but live where I may be forgot by human kind.[50]

As the evidence of Marlborough's participation in any plot to restore James proved inconclusive, William, who needed good generals, released him, and restored him to favor and authority.

When Anne, now thirty-eight, became Queen, her preference for morality, fidelity, and privacy changed the character of the English court. The roisterers found no entry there, and retired disgruntled to the coffee-houses and the stews. The moral Addison replaced the riotous Rochester, and Steele wrote *The Christian Hero*. Anne's avoidance of the theater, and the example of her life, had some influence in improving the tone of the English stage. She expressed her piety by turning over to the poorer clergy of the Established Church the royal share of ecclesiastical "first fruits" and tithes (1704); this "Queen Anne's Bounty" is still paid annually by the British government. She bore children with almost yearly regularity, but all except one died in childhood; none survived her; and her spirit was darkened by many funerals.

If she could have determined national policy she would have made peace with France, and would have acknowledged her dead father's son as what he claimed to be—James III. But the strong will of William III had committed England to the Grand Alliance; the dominant man in her counsels, whom she had raised from Earl to Duke of Marlborough soon after her accession, induced her to reign unhappily over ten years of bloody and costly war. She was still under the influence of her friend, now duchess, mistress of the robes and comptroller of the privy purse—i.e., the Queen's personal finances. Sarah received £5,100 a year, and used her almost hypnotic influence over Anne to advance the fortunes of her husband. Marlborough was appointed captain general of the land forces, and it was at his suggestion that his friend Sidney Godolphin was made secretary of the treasury; for Godolphin was anomalousy honest as well as financially competent, and could be relied upon for prompt remittances to army leaders, whose soldiers adjusted their courage to their pay. It is pleasant to record that after spending half a lifetime in charge of the treasury, Godolphin died a poor man. The hardheaded Duchess of Marlborough thought him "the best man that ever lived."[51] However, he gave his leisure to cockfighting, horse racing, and gambling, which were considered such mild vices as to verge on virtue.

Anne's freedom from intellect allowed her ministers to appropriate much of the authority and initiative that Parliament had left to the Crown; the political battles hereafter (except under George III) were to be between Parliament and ministers rather than between Parliament and sovereign. In 1704 new figures entered her ministry: Robert Harley as secretary of state, and Henry St. John as secretary for war. Both of these men touched the history of literature: Harley as employer of Defoe and Swift, and St. John—under his later title of Viscount Bolingbroke—as influencing Pope and Voltaire, and as himself the author of once famous essays, *Letters on the Study of History* and *Idea of a Patriot King*. Both these ministers were hard drinkers, but this was no distinction in the England of that day. Both entered office with the support of Marlborough, but turned against him on the charge that he was unnecessarily prolonging the War of the Spanish Succession.

St. John, born (1678) under Charles II, and dying (1751) in the first yea. of the *Encyclopédie*, personified the passage of Europe from the English Restoration to the French Enlightenment. He received too much religion in his childhood, and shed too much of it in his manhood. "I was obliged while yet a boy," he tells us, "to read over the commentaries of Dr. Manton, whose pride it was to have made 119 sermons on the 119th Psalm."[52] At Eton and Oxford he sought and won pre-eminence in brilliance of mind, careless idleness, and graceful dissipation. He boasted of holding the maximum of wine without intoxication, and of keeping the most expensive prostitute in the kingdom.[53] In a monogamous moment he married a wealthy heiress; she soon abandoned him because of his infidelity, but he continued, with some interruptions, to enjoy her estates. He found it comparatively inexpensive to get elected to Parliament in 1701. There his handsome presence, his quick intelligence, and his fluid eloquence gained him great influence in the Commons. He was only twenty-six when he entered the ministry.

The outstanding achievement of that ministry was the parliamentary union of England and Scotland. The two countries, though under the same sovereign, had had their distinct parliaments, conflicting economies, and hostile faiths; each had made war upon the other; and their jealous tariffs had impeded trade. On January 16, 1707, the Scottish Parliament accepted, and on March 6 the Queen ratified, the Articles of Union by which the two kingdoms, while retaining their independent religions, were to become the United Kingdom of Great Britain, under one British Parliament, and with complete freedom of trade. Sixteen Scottish peers were to be seated in the House of Lords, forty-five Scottish members were to be elected to the House of Commons, and the crosses of St. George and St. Andrew were combined in a new flag, the Union Jack. The Scottish masses did not welcome the merger, and for half a century the old enmities luxuriated; but by 1750 the union was recognized as beneficent. Scotland was spared many duplicative expenditures, and her intellectual energy was freed to produce, in the second half of the eighteenth century, a bright flowering of literature and philosophy.

Harley and St. John were deposed from the cabinet by a Whig victory in October, 1707, but Harley continued to influence the Queen through his cousin, Mrs. Abigail Masham. This lady had been introduced to Anne by the Duchess of Marlborough. Her calm and complaisant temper soothed the Queen, whose nerves, on edge with her new responsibilities, were rasped by Sarah's rampant voice and views. Sarah for a time welcomed her release from constant attendance at the court, but she was soon alarmed on discovering how rapidly her influence with the Queen was fading. Anne was almost by nature a Tory, a pietist, and a lover of peace; Sarah was a Whig of little faith, who laughed openly at the divine right of rulers as humbug for the masses, and insisted on the Queen's support of Marlborough's desire for a war to the finish against France. Anne developed a new firmness of mind as Sarah receded; and when Sarah raged at her insolently she dismissed her from the court (1710). The Queen declared that she felt now as if she had been freed from a long captivity.

In that year a Tory victory at the polls restored Harley and Bolingbroke to power. Harley replaced Godolphin at the treasury, Bolingbroke took the war office, and Jonathan Swift became their most effective pamphleteer. Harley was made Earl of Oxford (1711), and St. John was named Viscount Bolingbroke (1712). The courtesans of London, on hearing of Bolingbroke's elevation, rejoiced, saying, "Bolingbroke gets eight thousand guineas yearly, and all for us!"* The Tory majority put through both houses (1711) a measure requiring, for eligibility to Parliament, the possession of landed property worth a minimum of three hundred pounds a year for borough representatives, and six hundred pounds yearly for county delegates.[54] Now was the hedyday of the landed aristocracy in England.

The new ministry was resolved—Marlborough refused—to end the war by making a separate peace with France. In 1711 Harley brought before the Commons an indictment of Marlborough on charges of peculation. It was alleged that the Duke was amassing a large private fortune as captain general of the British forces, and through other offices held by him; that in addition to his annual salaries of some sixty thousand pounds he had received six thousand a year from Sir Solomon Medina, the contractor who sold him bread for the army; and that he had deducted for his own use two and a half per cent of the sums received by him from foreign governments for the pay of foreign troops under his command. No one except Sir John Vanbrugh, its architect, liked the architecture of the immense Blenheim Palace that Marlborough was building at Woodstock, near Oxford, and for which the Queen had ordered the government to pay. Begun in 1705, it was only half finished in 1711, and had already cost £134,000;[55] before its completion it would cost £300,000, of which the government paid four fifths.[56]

Marlborough replied that the two-and-a-half-per-cent deduction was by custom allowed to the commander to finance, without public record, the secret service and espionage which he had guided to good results; he produced the Queen's signed warrant authorizing him to make this deduction; all the foreign allies affirmed that they too had authorized the deduction; and the Elector of Hanover added that the money had been wisely applied, and had "contributed to the gaining of so many battles."[57] On the Medina subsidy Marlborough's defense was not so convincing. The House condemned him by a vote of 276 to 175, and the Queen dismissed him from all his offices (December 31, 1711). He departed into voluntary exile,

---

* From a letter of April 24, 1769, by the often mendacious Voltaire.

and remained in Holland or Germany till the end of the reign. The ministers appointed James Butler, second Duke of Ormonde, to command the British armies, and authorized him to make the same deductions from the bread contracts and the foreign payments as those for which Marlborough had been condemned.[58] But Marlborough's fall was accepted by the British people as a step toward peace.

The Tories and the Whigs found a new source of strife in the problem of succession to the throne. In 1701, Anne's last surviving child having died, Parliament, to forestall another Stuart restoration, had passed an Act of Settlement by which, in default of issue of William III and Princess Anne, the crown of England would pass to "Princess Sophia or the heirs of her body, being Protestants." Sophia, wife of the Elector of Hanover, was safely Protestant, and fractionally of royal British blood, as a granddaughter of James I. Anne had accepted this arrangement as guaranteeing a Protestant England; but now that her life neared its end her sympathy for her disowned brother grew warmer, and she left no doubt that if James III would consent to abandon Catholicism she would support his claim to the throne. The Whigs gave their full support to the Hanoverian succession, the Tories inclined to the Queen's view. Bolingbroke negotiated with James; the Prince refused to surrender his Catholic faith; but Bolingbroke, to whom religions were but diverse garments to dignify death, pulled every wire to have the Act of Settlement repealed, and give James the succession. He quarreled with Harley for moving too slowly in this matter; at his suggestion Anne reluctantly dismissed Harley, and for two days Bolingbroke seemed supreme.

But on July 29 the Queen, agitated and depressed by the quarrels of her ministers, fell seriously ill. The Protestants of England armed themselves to resist any attempt at a Stuart restoration. The Privy Council rejected Bolingbroke's policy, and persuaded the vacillating Queen to make the Duke of Shrewsbury lord high treasurer and head of her government. On August 1, 1714, Anne died. Sophia had died two months before, but the Act of Settlement was still in force. The Council sent word to Sophia's son, the Elector of Hanover, that he was now George I, King of England.

The reigns of William and Mary and Anne (1689–1714) were vital years in the history of England. Despite moral laxity, political corruption, and internal strife, they accomplished a dynastic revolution, they declared England irrevocably Protestant, and they definitively transferred governmental supremacy from the Crown to the Parliament. They saw the development of powerful ministers still further reducing the role of the monarch, and they witnessed in 1707 the last royal veto of parliamentary legislation. They established a wider degree of religious toleration and freedom of the press. They peacefully united England and Scotland in a stronger Britain. They turned back the attempt of the most powerful of modern kings to make France the dictator of Europe; instead, they made England mistress of the seas. They expanded, to historic effects, England's possessions in America. They saw the victories of English science and philosophy in Newton's *Principia* and Locke's *Essay concerning Human Understanding*. And the brief twelve years of the gentle Anne saw such an outburst of literature—Defoe, Addison, Steele, Swift, and the first period of Alexander Pope—as was not matched in that age anywhere in the world.

CHAPTER XI

From Dryden to Swift

1660–1714

I. A FREE PRESS

WHAT could have led a Frenchman to write that "in 1712 England surpassed France in quantity and quality of literary production," that "the center of intellectual life . . . unceasingly moved toward the north," until, about 1700, the English "held the highest creative role"?[1] An Englishman schooled in French graces could return the compliment: part of the stimulus came from French manners imported by Charles II and the returning emigrés; part of it came from Descartes and Pascal, Corneille and Racine, Molière and Boileau, Mlle. de Scudéry and Mme. de La Fayette, and from Frenchmen living in England, like Saint-Évremond and Gramont. We see the French influence in the erotic comedies and heroic tragedies of the Restoration theater, and in the passage from the exuberance of Elizabethan prose, and the convolutions of Milton's periods, to the refined and reasoned prose of Dryden writing prefaces and Pope writing poetry. For a century now (1670–1770) English literature would be prose, even when it scanned and rhymed; but it would be stately, clear, and classical prose.

The French influence, however, was only a prod; the root of the matter was in England itself, in her joyous and liberating Restoration, her colonial expansion, her commercial enrichment in ideas, her naval victories over the Dutch, her triumph (1713) over the France that had triumphed over Spain. So the course of empire northward made its way. And as Louis XIV gave pensions to authors as *douceurs* to docility, in a kindred manner the English government rewarded patriotic (or partisan) poets or *proseurs*—Dryden, Congreve, Gay, Prior, Addison, Swift—with pensions, dinners with the aristocracy, introductions to royalty, sinecures in the administration; one of them became secretary of state; Voltaire noted with envy these political plums.[2] Charles II favored science and beauty rather than letters or art; William III and Anne were indifferent to literature; but their ministers—finding authors useful in an age of newspapers, pamphlets, coffeehouses, and propaganda—subsidized the pens that could serve the Crown, the party, or the sword. Writers became minor politicians; some, like Prior, became diplomats; some, like Swift and Addison, manipulated patronage and power. In grateful appreciation of favors to come, authors dedicated their works to lords and ladies with compliments that made these superior to Apollo or Venus in body, and to Shakespeare or Sappho in mind.

Freedom helped gold to release the inky flood. Milton's *Areopagitica* had failed to end the Licensing Act through which censorship had controlled the press under Tudor and Stuart rulers, and that act continued in force under Cromwell precarious and the Stuarts restored. But as the government of James II began to frighten the nation, more and more pamphleteers defied the law and pleased the people. When William III came to the throne he and his Whig supporters owed so much to the press that they opposed the renewal of the Licensing Act; it expired in 1694, and was not renewed; freedom of the press was automatically established. The royal ministers might still arrest for extreme attacks upon the government, and the Blasphemy Act of 1697 still decreed stiff penalties for questioning the fundamentals of the Christian creed; but England henceforth enjoyed a literary liberty which, though often abused, contributed immensely to the growth of the English mind.

Periodicals multiplied. Weekly newspapers had circulated since 1622. Cromwell suppressed all but two of them; Charles II allowed three, under official supervision; one of these, the *Oxford* (then *London*) *Gazette*, became the organ of the government, and has appeared biweekly or semi-weekly ever since 1665. Soon after the decease of the Licensing Act several new weeklies ventured forth. In 1695 the Tories established the first English daily, *The Post Boy*, which lasted only four days; the Whigs at once countered it with *The Flying Post*. Finally, in 1702, *The English Courant* became the first regular daily newspaper in England—a small sheet printed on one side only, and containing news but not views. From these fitful flurries came the advertising mammoths of our day.

Defoe set a new standard with *The Review* (1704-13), a weekly offering comments as well as news, and originating the serial story. Steele followed with *The Tatler* (1709-11), and he and Addison brought the development to its historic peak in *The Spectator* (1711-12). The Tory government, alarmed by the aggregate circulation (44,000) and influence of the dailies, weeklies, and monthlies, laid upon them (1712) a stamp tax ranging from a halfpenny to a penny, which was intended to make life impossible for most of the periodicals. *The Spectator* was one of those that succumbed. "All Grub Street is ruined," Swift told his Stella.[3] Bolingbroke started the weekly *Examiner* in 1710 to defend the policies of the Tory ministry; he found in Jonathan Swift a contributor formidable in knowledge, invective, and wit; money had discovered a new instrument. Gradually the power of the periodical press overtook the influence of the pulpit in forming the public mind to private purposes, and a new secularizing force entered into history.

II. THE RESTORATION DRAMA

There was another medium that between 1660 and 1700 formed, deformed, or merely expressed, the soul of soulless London. Charles II, having relished the Parisian drama, licensed two theaters: one for the King's Company in Drury Lane, one for the Duke of York's Company in Lincoln's Inn Fields. In 1705 the Queen's Theatre opened in Haymarket, but she rarely attended. Usually, under Charles II, two theaters sufficed. The Puritans still boycotted the drama, and in any case the general public was not admitted to the theaters between 1660 and 1700.[4] The audience came mostly from the roisterers of the court, the lower fringes of the "quality," and the "men about town." "A grave lawyer," said the grave Dr. Johnson, "would have debased his dignity, and a young lawyer would have impaired his credit, by appearing in those mansions of dissolute licentiousness."[5] Women were but a small part of the audience, and those that came concealed their identity behind a mask.[6] Performances began at three in the afternoon, but as street lighting improved (c. 1690) the hour was deferred to 6 P.M. Admission to the boxes cost four shillings, to the pit two and a half, to the gallery one. Stage machinery and scenic changes were much more elaborate than in Elizabethan days, though a bedroom and its approaches might have sufficed for most of the Restoration comedies. Actresses replaced boys in playing female parts. Most of the actresses were also mistresses; so Margaret Hughes, who played Desdemona in the first known appearance of a woman on the English stage (December 8, 1660), was the mistress of Prince Rupert;[7] and it was at a performance of Dryden's *Tyrannic Love* that Charles II began to yearn for Nell Gwyn, who played Valeria.[8] The character of the audience, the reaction against Puritanism, the morals of the court, the memory and revival of Elizabethan and Jacobean plays (especially those of Ben Jonson), and the influence of the French theater and royalist emigrés, all came together to form the Restoration drama.

In the tragic drama of the Restoration the great name is Dryden. We put him aside for the moment, and open Thomas Otway's *Venice Preserved* (1682), which outlived all of Dryden's plays, and was acted as late as 1904. It is a love story grafted upon the conspiracy of Count de Osuna's friends to overthrow the Venetian Senate in 1616. Its early success was due in part to its caricature of the first Earl of Shaftesbury (Charles II's foe and Locke's friend) in the character of Antonio, who loves to be beaten by his bawd; partly to the resemblance of the conspiracy to the recent Popish

Plot; partly to the acting of Thomas Betterton and Mrs. Elizabeth Barry. But the play now stands on its own feet. The comic scenes are absurd and offensive, and the finale scatters death with operatic unanimity; but the plot is well woven, the characters are distinctively drawn, the action is intensely dramatic, and the blank verse rivals anything in Elizabethan drama barring Marlowe and Shakespeare. Otway fell in love with Mrs. Barry, who preferred to amuse the Earl of Rochester. After writing some further successes the poet produced a series of failures, drifted into poverty, and (in one account) died of starvation.[9]

It is for its comedies that the Restoration drama is remembered. Their humor and wit, their bawdy dialogue and bedroom escapades, and their value as a mirror of one class in one generation, have given them a hardy if stealthy popularity which they scarcely deserve. Their range is narrow as compared with the Elizabethan comedies, or Molière's; they describe not life, but the manners of town idlers and court profligates; they ignore the countryside except as a butt of ridicule, or as a Siberia to which husbands banish prying wives. Some English dramatists saw Molière play or played in Paris; some of them borrowed his characters or plots; but none rose to his flair for discussing basic ideas. The one basic idea in these comedies is that adultery is the main purpose and most heroic business of life. Their ideal man is described in Dryden's *Mock Astrologer* as "a gentleman, a man about town, one that wears good clothes, eats, drinks, and wenches sufficiently." A character in Farquhar's *Beaux' Stratagem* says, as one gentleman to another: "I love a fine horse, but let another keep it; and just so I love a fine woman"[10]—which means not that he will not covet his neighbor's wife, but that he proposes to enjoy her favors while letting her husband support her. In Congreve's *Way of the World* the admired Mirabell says to his *friend's* wife: "You should have just so much disgust for your husband as may be sufficient to make you relish your lover."[11] Rarely, in these plays, does love rise above its physical basis of mutual itching for mutual titillation. We hunger, as we read them, for some ray of nobility, but we are offered, as an ideal, the ethics of the stews.

William Wycherley set the tone and pace. His father was a royalist of ancient family and large estate, who, when the Puritans came to power, sent the boy to France for education, resolved that he should never be a Puritan. William never was, but he shocked his family by becoming a Catholic. Restored to England and soon to Protestantism, he studied at Oxford, left without a degree, took to writing plays. At thirty-two he struck gold with *Love in a Wood* (1671), which he dedicated to Lady Castlemaine. He was received at court by the amiable King, who did not complain when he found that Wycherley, as well as Churchill, was supplementing him in Milady's love.[12]

He fought in the Dutch War of 1672 with the bravery expected of a gentleman, returned to England whole, and scored another success with *The Country Wife* (1673). The prologue invited the audience, if it disliked the play, to enter the dressing room of the actors at the close, where

> We patiently . . . give up to you
> Our poets, virgins, nay, our mistresses too.

Mr. Pinchwife has brought his spouse to London for a week, and guards her so thoroughly that she is seduced under his nose. A Mr. Horner, returning from France and desiring unhindered access to wives, spreads the rumor that he is a eunuch. Pinchwife concludes that to such an incompetent he may safely open his home. Soon he finds his wife writing a love letter to the maimed gallant. He forces her to write another, which calls Horner the vilest names; while his back is turned she substitutes her first letter for the angry one; the husband, proud in domination, delivers the original missive to Horner. Later, suspecting that Horner is an abler man than rumor described him, he thinks to keep him occupied by agreeing to take his sister Alithea to him. The wife disguises herself as Alithea, and is delivered by her husband to her paramour. The play ends with a "Dance of the Cuckolds," Horner has the last triumphant word, and an epilogue, spoken by an actress, chides the men in the audience for insufficient virility:

> And men may still believe you vigorous,
> But then we women—there's no cozening us.[13]

Wycherley had taken much of *The Country Wife* from Molière's *École des maris* and *École des femmes*. His next comedy, *The Plain Dealer* (1674), transformed the Alceste of Molière's *Misanthrope* into Captain Manly, whose notion of plain dealing is to berate all persons and all things with billingsgate. The surprising thing is that London, and even some surburbanites, liked to have life described as a round of carnal seeking seasoned with profanity. In a bookstore at Tunbridge Wells Wycherley had the ecstasy of hearing a lady ask for his recently published *Plain Dealer*. She was the Countess of Drogheda, a rich widow. He courted her, married her, and found that she kept him under surveillance with more than Pinchwife's continuity and vision. Suddenly she died, and he thought himself now possessed of her fortune; but the legacy was so cobwebbed with lawsuits that he could not use any of it. Unable to pay the debts that he had confidently contracted, he was sent to jail, where he languished for seven years, until James II, before or after Wycherley's reconversion to Catholicism, paid his debts and pensioned him. He lived to a bad old age, pursuing women beyond his capacity, and writing verses that his young friend Pope struggled to turn into poetry. At seventy-five the old rake married a young woman. Ten days later he died (January 1, 1716).

Sir John Vanbrugh was the most amiable of these adulterographers. He was John Bull incarnate, rough, jolly, good-natured, loving the food and drink of England; yet his grandfather was Gillis van Brugg, a Fleming from Ghent, who came to Britain in the reign of James I. John was promising enough to be sent to Paris at nineteen to study art. Returning at twenty-one, he joined the army, was arrested at Calais as a British spy, served a term in the Bastille, and there wrote the first draft of *The Provoked Wife*. Released, he turned his versatile hand to playwriting. In six weeks, he tells us, he conceived, wrote, and staged *The Relapse* (1696), with its hilarious satires of the London fop as Lord Foppington, of the country squire as Sir Tunbelly Clumsey, and the ruttish Miss Hoyden. Sir Tunbelly has kept her under watch and guard since puberty, and rejoices in her innocence: "Poor girl, she'll be scared out of her wits on her wedding night, for, honestly speaking, she does not know a man from a woman but by his beard and his breeches."[14] But Miss Hoyden describes herself otherwise: "It's well I have a husband a-coming, or ecod, I'd marry the baker, I would so! Nobody can knock at the gate but presently I must be locked up; and here's the young greyhound bitch can run loose about the house all day long, she can." When Tom Fashion asks for her hand, and her father wants them to wait a week, she protests: "A week! —why, I shall be an old woman by that time!"[15]

This *Relapse* succeeded so well that Vanbrugh hurried to complete *The Provoked Wife* (1697). This was one of the greatest "hits" of the time; half a century later David Garrick was still amusing London with his riotous playing of Sir John Brute, the most memorable character in all the dramatis personae of the Restoration. Sir John is a caricature of the more porcine aspects of the English squire—drinking, boasting, blustering, bullying, cursing, and complaining that " 'tis a damned atheistical age." He opens the play with his opinion of marriage:

> What cloying meat is love, when matrimony is the sauce to it! Two years' marriage has debauched my five senses. Everything I see, everything I hear, everything I feel, everything I smell, and everything I taste, methinks, has wife in't: No boy was ever so weary of his tutor, no girl of her bib, no nun of doing penance, or old maid of being chaste, as I am of being married.

His wife, knowing his views, thinks to tame him with horns:

> LADY BRUTE. He has used me so barbarously of late that I could almost resolve to play the downright wife, and cuckold him. . . .
> BELINDA. But, you know, we must return good for evil.
> LADY BRUTE. That may be a mistake in the translation.[16]

Her neighbor Lady Fanciful, similarly inclined, discusses her qualms with her French maid, who answers in French, here translated:

LADY F. My reputation, mademoiselle, my reputation!

MADEMOISELLE. Madame, when one has once lost it, one is no longer embarrassed by it.

LADY F. Fie! mademoiselle, fie! Reputation is a jewel.

MADEMOISELLE. Which costs much, madame.

LADY F. Why, sure, you would not sacrifice your honor to your pleasure?

MADEMOISELLE. I am a philosopher. . . .

LADY F. Honor is against it [a rendezvous].

MADEMOISELLE. Pleasure is for it. . . .

LADY F. But when reason corrects nature, mademoiselle—

MADEMOISELLE. Reason is then very insolent, since nature is reason's older sister.

LADY F. Do you then prefer your nature to your reason?

MADEMOISELLE. Yes, certainly.

LADY F. Why?

MADEMOISELLE. Because my nature make me very merry, my reason make me mad.[17]

It was probably this play that angered Jeremy Collier into publishing, in the year following its production, a powerful attack upon the Restoration drama, especially upon Vanbrugh. Collier was an Anglican clergyman of some learning and dogmatic courage. Having sworn allegiance to James II in 1685, he refused to take the oath of loyalty to William and Mary in 1689. He denounced the Glorious Revolution, even to inciting revolt. He was arrested, and was with difficulty persuaded to let his friends bail him out. He gave public absolution to two men about to be hanged for conspiring against what he considered a usurping government. Denounced by his bishop and indicted by the Attorney General, he refused to appear before a court. He was outlawed, and lived under the ban till his death; but the government respected his integrity, and took no further steps against him. William III expressed warm approval of Collier's historic blast.

It was called *A Short View of the Immorality and Profaneness of the English Stage*. There was much nonsense in it, as in most books; the passionate pastor denounced in the English drama many faults that now seem to us trivial or no faults at all; he protested against any irreverent reference to reverends, and generously spread this umbrella of ineffability over pagan prophets, Catholic priests, and Dissenting divines. He condemned so many dramatists, from Aeschylus to Shakespeare to Congreve and Dryden, that all the indicted might feel acquitted by their company. He weakened his case by arguing that the public stage should not deal with crime or immorality at all. But he struck some healthy blows, for shining targets faced him everywhere. He mourned the effect, upon audiences, of the admiration which several Restoration dramatists had shown for the addicts of adultery. For a year the book was the talk of London. The playwrights offered diverse defenses. Vanbrugh turned from drama to architecture, labored for a decade over Blenheim Palace, then built Castle Howard in fine Palladian style (1714). Dryden admitted his sins and expressed repentance. Congreve denied his guilt, but reformed his art.

William Congreve brought the Restoration drama to its apex and conclusion. He was born near Leeds (1670) of a family whose antiquity remained through all his triumphs his dearest pride. His father was given command of an English garrison in Ireland, so William was educated at Kilkenny School, where he sat on the same bench as Jonathan Swift; then at Trinity College, Dublin; then at Middle Temple, London. The virus of literary ambition entered his blood from an environment in which even dukes wrote books. In his first year as a law student he wrote *Incognita* (1692), which Edmund Gosse praised for its "light raillery and humour" and as "the earliest novel [of manners?] in English,"[18] but of which Samuel Johnson said, "I would rather praise than read it."[19] Fame came to Congreve at a bound with his first comedy, *The Old Bachelor* (1693). Dryden, then the acknowledged head of English letters, vowed that he had never seen so good a first play. Not sure that a gentleman should write for the theater, Congreve excused himself as having written it "to amuse myself in a slow recovery from a fit of sickness"; whereupon Collier remarked: "What his disease was, I am not to inquire; but it must be a very ill one to be worse than the remedy."[20] Halifax agreed with Dryden; he appointed Congreve to two government posts, which brought sufficient income to enable him to remain a gentleman while being a dramatist.

His next play, *The Double Dealer* (1694), had a poor reception, but Dryden's encomium, equating Congreve with Shakespeare, held up the young author's spirit; and in 1695, aged twenty-five, he returned to the boards with *Love for Love*, whose success exceeded any in living memory. Collier denounced the play as giving aid and comfort to lechers. Congreve's reply fell so flat that for three years he kept from the theater. When he returned to it with *The Way of the World* (1700) he had profited from the castigation, and showed that wit did not depend upon inverting the Decalogue. This play, which the hyperbolic Swinburne called "the unequalled and unapproached masterpiece of English comedy,"[21] has some of the faults, but none of the vices, of the Restoration drama. When merely read it may tire us with its bantering wit, reminding us of the silly word play in Shakespeare's early efforts; acted and spoken (as by Betterton and Mrs. Bracegirdle in its première), it would probably delight us with its sparkle. (Says Witwoud, "I know a lady that loves talking so incessantly, she won't give an echo fair play."[22]) The plot is too complicated; we grudge the time required to understand the schemes and quarrels of frivolous nonentities; and the denouement is unmitigated absurdity. But there is here a refinement of language and humor, a subtlety (though never a profundity) of thought, that can please the unhurried mind; no rough burlesque as in Vanbrugh, but such polite and graceful persiflage as had trickled down from Versailles to Whitehall and the Restoration court. And there is characterization. The hero, Mirabell, is an unattractive but lifelike legacy-hunter; it is remarkable that he seeks to marry Millamant, instead of seducing her—but she had a fortune worth a dozen adulteries. She is Congreve's liveliest creation, the flirt who wants a thousand lovers and demands a lifetime of adoration for a decade of charms. She consents to marry, but on conditions:

> MILLAMANT. . . . Positively, Mirabell, I'll lie abed in a morning as long as I please. . . .
> MIRABELL. Have you any more conditions to offer? . . .
> MILLAMANT. Trifles!—As liberty to . . . come to dinner when I please, dine in my dressing-room alone when I'm out of humour, without giving a reason. To have my closet inviolate; to be sole empress of my tea-table, which you must never presume to approach without first asking leave. And lastly, wherever I am, you shall always knock at the door before you come in. These articles subscribed, if I continue to endure you a little longer, I may by degrees dwindle into a wife.
> MIRABELL. . . . Have I liberty to offer conditions . . . ?
> MILLAMANT. . . . Propose your utmost . . .
> MIRABELL. *Item*, I article that you continue to like your own face as long as I shall; and while it passes current with me, that you endeavour not to new-coin it. . . . *Item*, when you shall be breeding—
> MILLAMANT. Ah! name it not.
> MIRABELL. Which may be presumed, with a blessing on our endeavours—
> MILLAMANT. Odious endeavours!
> MIRABELL. I denounce against all straight lacing, squeezing for a shape, till you mould my boy's head like a sugar-loaf . . .[23]

and so on; it is pleasant trifling and good satire, safely skimming the surface of life.

Congreve himself sampled many surfaces, preferring texture to substance and variety to unity. He never married, but serviced a succession of actresses. We hear of no children troubling or delighting him. He was a pleasant companion in coffeehouses and clubs, and was received into the best families. He ate well, and had his feet regularly blistered and anointed for the gout. When Voltaire visited him in 1726 Congreve deprecated the Frenchman's praise of his plays, brushed them aside as forgotten trifles, and asked Voltaire to consider him merely as a gentleman. "If you had been merely a gentleman," said Voltaire (according to Voltaire), "I should not have come to see you."[24]

In 1728, on a journey to take the waters at Bath, Congreve's carriage overturned, and he sustained internal injuries from which he died (January 19, 1729). He was buried in Westminster Abbey. His will left two hundred pounds to Mrs. Bracegirdle, who was living out her old age in poverty; the bulk of the estate, some ten thousand pounds, was bequeathed to the immensely wealthy second Duchess of Marlborough, his favorite hostess. She turned the sum into a necklace of pearls. She placed permanently, in his usual place at her table, a wax and ivory replica of the poet, and had its feet regularly blistered and anointed for the gout.[25]

Long before Congreve's death the English theater had begun to cleanse itself. William III ordered the Master of the Revels to exercise with greater severity his power to license or prohibit plays, and a revulsion of public opinion supported this censorship. A law of Queen Anne forbade the wearing of masks in the theater, and women, denied this disguise, boycotted plays that were not of assured decency.[26] Swift agreed with the bishops in condemning the London stage as a blot upon the English character. Steele offered his *Conscious Lovers* (1722) as moral drama, and Addison rivaled the dignity of French tragedy in his *Cato* (1713). An earlier sign of the change was the tone of Dryden's answer to Collier. He felt that the divine had often condemned the dramatists unfairly, and had "in many places . . . interpreted my words into blasphemy and bawdry, of which they were not guilty." But he added:

> I shall say the less of Mr. Collier, because in many things he has taxed me justly, and I have pleaded guilty to all thoughts and expressions of mine which can be truly argued of obscenity, profaneness, or immorality, and retract them. If he be my enemy, let him triumph; if he be my friend, as I have given him no personal occasion to be otherwise, he will be glad of my repentance.[27]

III. JOHN DRYDEN: 1631–1700

His father was of the minor gentry, having a small estate in Northamptonshire. He was sent to Westminster School in London, where the learned Richard Busby gave him, and his fellow student John Locke, much Latin and discipline. There he earned a scholarship which enabled him to go to Trinity College, Cambridge. In the year (1654) in which he took his degree his father died, and John, as the eldest of fourteen children, inherited the estate, which brought him sixty pounds a year. He moved to London, and tried to eke this out with poetry. In 1659 he published "Heroic Stanzas" to the memory of Cromwell—verses remarkably jejune for a man of twenty-nine. Dryden matured slowly, like a man climbing laboriously over a hundred obstacles to successively higher ledges of income. A year later he welcomed the Restoration in "Astræa Redux," which compared Charles II's star to the star of Bethlehem. Hardly anyone dared to accuse Dryden of inconstancy, for nearly all the poets but Milton changed their key from Puritan to royalist with practiced modulation.

But Charles was interested in the theater rather than mere poetry; so the dramatists made money while the new poets languished. Dryden felt no flair for drama, but he longed for regular bread. He tried his hand at comedy, with a result (*The Wild Gallant*, 1663) which Pepys damned as "so poor a thing as ever I saw in my life almost."[28] On December 1, 1663, Dryden married Lady Elizabeth Howard, daughter of the Earl of Berkshire. Eyebrows had risen at a lady marrying a poet, but she was twenty-five and in danger of desiccation, and her brother Sir Robert Howard, itching with authorship, had secured Dryden's collaboration in a play, *The Indian Queen*, which they produced in 1664 with lavish scenery and great success.

This tragedy made literary history by abandoning the blank verse of the Elizabethans and using as its regular medium rhymed couplets of pentameter lines. Lord Orrery had been impressed by the melody of rhyme in French tragedy, and had introduced the style in his own plays. Dryden returned to blank verse after 1675, recognizing that rhyme tends to obstruct the flow of speech and thought. He would have been a greater poet had he had less facility in verse.

He followed up his co-operative success with an independent continuation, *The Indian Emperor* (1665), whose hero was Montezuma. He was just finding a place on the English stage when the plague closed the London theaters for a year. When the plague and the fire had passed he celebrated England's re-emergence under the triple ordeal of these and war in *Annus Mirabilis* (1666), a poem of 304 quatrains, alternating between vigorous description (stanzas 212–82) and juvenile inanity (e.g., stanza 29). When the theaters reopened in 1666 Dryden hurried back to drama, and till 1681 he produced nothing but plays. His tragedies run to bombast, but they seemed to his contemporaries superior to Shakespeare's;[29] and when he joined Davenant in remodeling *The Tempest* the result was by the common consent of the collaborators a great improvement on the original. The King's Company may have agreed with them, for it gave Dryden a commission to supply it with three plays annually in return for a share in the profits, which came to some £350 a year. Dryden's comedies, though as obscene as any, had less success than his twenty-seven tragedies, for in these he caught the public interest in the New World and its wonderful savages. So in *The Conquest of Granada* Almanzor says:

> I am as free as Nature first made man,
> Ere the base law of servitude began,
> When wild in woods the noble savage ran.

Probably it was the success of this play, and the luscious eulogies of Charles II in *Annus Mirabilis*, that in 1670 won Dryden the post of royal historiographer and poet laureate. His income now averaged a thousand pounds a year.

In the epilogue to Part II of *The Conquest of Granada* Dryden claimed superiority for the Restoration drama over the Elizabethan. His competitors, while appreciating the compliment, thought that too much of its charity began at home. The wits of the town did not share the taste of the audiences for the extravagant heroics of Dryden's tragedies. The Duke of Buckingham, with some collaborators, issued in 1671 a rollicking satire, *The Rehearsal*, which made great fun of the improbabilities, absurdities, and bombast of contemporary tragedies, especially Dryden's. The poet felt the sting, but nursed his revenge for ten years; then he pilloried Buckingham as Zimri in the strongest lines of *Absalom and Achitophel*.

Meanwhile his study of Shakespeare had improved his art. In his finest tragedy, *All for Love* (1678), he turned from Racine and rhyme to Shakespeare and blank verse, put all his skill into rivaling the Elizabethan on common ground, and told again the story of Antony and Cleopatra losing the world for a liaison. If the earlier play did not exist, Dryden's might be better praised. Now and then it rises in stark simplicity of speech to noble feeling tensely contained, as in Octavia's coming to Antony with Octavian's offer of pardon.[30] Dryden's play is more compact, aiming to observe the unities; but by narrowing the action to one crisis in one place and three days he reduced the heroic theme to an amour, and lost the large perspective that in *Antony and Cleopatra* saw this romance as part of events that shook and shaped the Mediterranean world.

Today the most interesting aspects of Dryden's dramas are the prefaces with which he introduced them in print, and the essays in which he expounded his views on dramatic art. Corneille had given him the example, but Dryden made the form a vehicle of splendid prose. As we skim through these brief treatises and lively dialogues, we perceive that the age of creation in English literature was passing into that age of criticism which would culminate in Pope. But also our respect for Dryden's mind rises as we see him probing urbanely into the technique of the drama and the art of poetry, and comparing, with considerable penetration, the French with the English stage. In these essays the picturesque rambling of Elizabethan prose, the turgid and cumulative sentences of Milton, make way for a simpler, smoother, more orderly diction freed from Latin constructions, and improved by acquaintance with French literature; never quite rivaling French elegance, but transmitting to the eighteenth century—the century of prose—models of clear and graceful speech, flowing and charming, natural and strong. Here the English essay took form, and the classic age of English literature began.

But if Dryden's essays now seem superior to the plays that gave them cause, it was in satire that he dominated and almost terrorized his time. Perhaps an accident released his sting. In 1679 John Sheffield, Earl of Mulgrave, circulated in manuscript an anonymous *Essay on Satire*, which attacked the Earl of Rochester, the Duchess of Portsmouth (Louise de Kéroualle), and in general the court of Charles II. Dryden, who now derived much of his income from the King, was mistakenly supposed to be the author. On the night of December 18, in Rose Alley, Covent Garden, he was attacked and cudgeled by a band of ruffians presumably, but not certainly, in the hire of Rochester. Dryden was a man of good nature and generosity, ready to help and praise; but his success, his egotism, and his controversial affirmations had earned him many enemies. For a time he bore their attacks without public reply; even the "Rose Alley ambuscade" brought no direct response from his pen. But in 1681 he gathered several of his foes into one caldron, and boiled them in the most lethal satire in the English language.

It was the year in which Shaftesbury tried to organize a revolution to replace Charles II with Charles's bastard son; and when Part I of *Absalom and Achitophel* appeared (November), Shaftesbury was about to be tried for treason. Dryden's satire took the side of the King, and may have been suggested by the King.[31] He ridiculed Shaftesbury as Achitophel, who persuades Absalom (the Duke of Monmouth) to revolt against his father, David (Charles). And as both David and Charles loved plurally, the poem begins with an essay on the value of polygamy:

> In pious times, ere priestcraft did begin,
> Before polygamy was made a sin,
> When man on many multiplied his kind,
> Ere one to one was cursedly confined,
> When nature prompted and no law denied
> Promiscuous use of concubine and bride,
> When Israel's monarch after Heaven's own heart
> His vigorous warmth did variously impart

> To wives and slaves, and, wide as his command,
> Scattered his Maker's image through the land . . .

David rejoices in the beauty of his Absalom; Monmouth was, till the revolt,
the apple of the Merrie Monarch's eye. And the Jews are the English,

> a headstrong, moody, murmuring race
> As ever tried th' extent and stretch of grace;
> God's pampered people, whom, debauched with ease,
> No king could govern, nor no God could please . . .[32]

Astrophel is the archangel of treason; London at once recognized
Shaftesbury:

> Of these the false Achitophel was first,
> A name to all succeeding ages curst;
> For close designs and crooked counsels fit,
> Sagacious, bold, and turbulent of wit,
> Restless, unfixed in principles and place,
> In power unpleased, impatient of disgrace;
> A fiery soul, which, working out its way,
> Fretted the pigmy body to decay,
> And o'er-informed the tenement of clay.
> A daring pilot in extremity,
> Pleased with the danger when the waves went high,
> He sought the storms; but for a calm unfit,
> Would steer too nigh the sands to boast his wit.
> Great wits are sure to madness near allied,
> And thin partitions do their bounds divide;
> Else why should he, with wealth and honors blest,
> Refuse his age the needful hours of rest? . . .
> In friendship false, implacable in hate,
> Resolved to ruin or to rule the state.[33]

And now comes the revenge against Buckingham and *The Rehearsal*:

> In the first rank of these [rebels] did Zimri stand:
> A man so various that he seemed to be
> Not one, but all mankind's epitome:
> Stiff in opinions, always in the wrong,
> Was everything by starts, and nothing long,
> But in the course of one revealing moon
> Was chymist, fiddler, statesman, and buffoon;
> Then all for women, painting, rhyming, drinking,
> Besides ten thousand freaks that died in thinking. . . .

In squandering wealth was his peculiar art;
Nothing went unrewarded but desert;
Beggared by fools, whom still he found [out] too late,
He had his jest, and they had his estate.[34]

England had never known satire as merciless as this, concentrating mayhem in a line, and leaving quartered corpses on every page. The poem sold by the hundreds outside the very court in which Shaftesbury was being tried for his life. Shaftesbury was acquitted; his Whig partisans struck a medal in his honor; and a dozen poets and pamphleteers, led by Thomas Shadwell, issued triumphant replies to the man who, they were sure, had sold his wit and caustic to the King. Dryden came back with another satire, *The Medal* (March, 1682), and Shadwell was flayed with a special flail, *MacFlecknoe* (October). Here the invective was coarser, descending at times to verbal abuse undistinguished by such cutting couplets as had spread their bane with such precision and economy in the earlier satire.

Our taste for literary slaughter of this sort has declined; after centuries of argument we suspect that there is some truth in every passion, something to be loved in every foe. But even today politics is war by other means; much more so then, when the Stuart throne swung on the hinge of revolution, and to emerge on the losing side might well mean death. In any case, Dryden had shown his mettle; he had earned the gratitude of the King and of the Duke of York; and no one now questioned his pre-eminence in the realms of rhyme. When he came to Will's Tavern a chair was reserved for him near the hearth in winter, on the balcony in summer; there Pepys saw him, and heard "very witty and pleasant discourse."[35] Sir Walter Scott, with creative imagination, pictured Dryden entering Will's: "a little fat old man, with his own gray hair, and in a full trimmed black suit that sat close as a glove," and "with the pleasantest smile I ever saw."[36] "To bow to the Laureate, and to hear his opinion of Racine's last tragedy . . . , was thought a privilege. A pinch from his snuffbox was an honor sufficient to turn the head of a young enthusiast."[37] He could be the soul of kindness to friends, but fell too readily into personal abuse about rivals and enemies;[38] and he allowed no one to exceed him in praise of his own poetry. His adulation of the King, of Lady Castlemaine, and of those who paid him for dedications surpassed the customary servility of his profession in his time.[39] Yet Congreve repaid Dryden's encouragement by describing him as "exceedingly humane and compassionate, ready to forgive injuries, and capable of a sincere reconciliation with those that had offended him."[40]

Entering now upon his physical decline, he began to think more kindly of religion than in the proud vigor of his middle years. His dramas and satires had taken incidental flings at divers creeds; now, having cast in his lot with the Tories, he turned to the Anglican Church as a pillar of England's stability, and deprecated the insolence of reason invading the sanctuaries of faith. In November, 1682, he astonished his worldly friends by issuing *Religio Laici*, a poem in defense of the Established Church. An inspired Bible, even an infallible Church to interpret and supplement it, seemed to him indispensable supports of society and sanity. He was acquainted with the contentions of the deists; his answer was that their doubts were foolishly disturbing that difficult social order which only a moral code sanctioned by religion can sustain:

> For points obscure are of small use to learn,
> But common quiet is the world's concern.

The argument could serve the Roman Church too, and Dryden followed it to its conclusion by accepting conversion to Catholicism (1686). Whether the accession of a Catholic King the year before, and anxiety for the continuance of his pensions,[41] had anything to do with the conversion we cannot say. In any case Dryden gave his full poetic art to expounding the Catholic view in *The Hind and the Panther* (1687), in which a "milk-white hind" defends the Roman faith against a panther, "fairest creature of the spotted kind," representing the Anglicans. The picture of two four-footed beasts debating the Real Presence of Christ in the Eucharist[42] lent it-self to ridicule, which was soon supplied by Matthew Prior and Lord Halifax in a parody entitled *The Hind and the Panther Transversed to the Story of the Country Mouse and the City Mouse* (1687).

In 1688 James II fled to France, and Dryden found himself living again under a Protestant King. He kept to his new faith; all his three sons had employment in Rome under the Pope, and another change of key would have been cacophonous. He bore with courage the loss of his laureateship, his pension, and his post as historiographer; history, however, sharpened his sorrow by giving these honors to the Shadwell whom Dryden had crowned as King of Nonsense and paragon of stupidity. He returned in old age to supporting himself by his pen. He wrote more plays, translated selections from Theocritus, Lucretius, Horace, Ovid, and Persius, made a loose but fluent rendering of the *Aeneid* into heroic verse, and transformed into his own meters some "fables" of Homer, Ovid, Boccaccio, and Chaucer. In 1697, aged sixty-seven, he composed a celebrated ode, "Alexander's Feast," which has been too highly praised.

He died May 1, 1700. Much confusion attended his funeral, rival factions contesting for his corpse; but finally he was laid to rest beside Chaucer in Westminster Abbey.

It is difficult to love him. To all appearances he was an opportunist trimmer, who praised Cromwell's memory under the Protectorate, praised Charles and his mistresses, praised Protestantism under a Protestant King and Catholicism under a Catholic, and courted pensions with all his melody. He made so many enemies that there must have been something unlovable in him. He rivaled all his competitors in the licentiousness of his plays and the piety of his verse. His power of satire was so great as to evoke our sympathies for his victims as for martyrs burning at the stake. But he was without question the greatest English poet of his generation. Much of his poetry was written to the occasion, and time seldom preserves what was addressed to the time. But his satires still live, for no one has equaled them in etching characters in acid scorn. He developed the heroic couplet to such compactness and flexibility that it dominated English poetry for a century. His influence was better in prose: he cleared it of cumbersome involutions and alien idioms, and disciplined it to a classic clarity and ease. His contemporaries were right: they feared rather than loved him, but they knew that by the force of his will and the labor of his art he had won the right to preside over them as the arbiter of letters and the sovereign of rhyme. He was the Jonson and Johnson of his age.

IV. A CATALOGUE

Let us gather into a lifeless catalogue some minor figures who gave life and literature to this epoch, but with whom we cannot stay long enough to see them live.

The greatest poem of the pagan Restoration was a Puritan epic, but the most famous poem was an anti-Puritan mock epic, *Hudibras* (1663–78). Samuel Butler, as a lusty youth, spent uncomfortable years in the service of Sir Samuel Luke, an ardent Presbyterian colonel in Cromwell's army, stationed at Cople Hoo, a citadel of Puritan politics and prayer. When the Restoration came Butler revenged himself by publishing a rollicking satire in which Sir Hudibras, the chivalric knight, leads his squire, Ralpho, on a crusade against sin. From the beginning you may judge the whole:

> When civil dudgeon first grew high,
> And men fell out, they knew not why;
> When hard words, jealousies, and fears
> Set folks together by the ears,
> And made them fight, like mad or drunk,
> For Dame Religion as for punk; . . .
> When Gospel-trumpeter, surrounded
> With long-eared rout, to battle sounded,
> And pulpit, drum ecclesiastic,

> Was beat with fist instead of stick:
> Then did Sir Knight abandon dwelling,
> And out he rode a-colonelling. . . .
> For 't has been held by many that
> As Montaigne, playing with his cat,
> Complains she thought him but an ass,
> Much more she would Sir Hudibras . . .
> We grant, although he had much wit,
> H'was very shy of using it,
> As being loath to wear it out,
> And therefore bore it not about
> Unless on holidays or so,
> As men their best apparel do. . . .
>
> For his religion, it was fit
> To match his learning and his wit;
> 'Twas Presbyterian true blue,
> For he was of that stubborn crew
> Of errant saints, whom all men grant
> To be the true Church Militant:
> Such as do build their faith upon
> The holy text of pike and gun,
> Decide all controversies by
> Infallible artillery,
> And prove their doctrine orthodox
> By Apostolic blows and knocks; . . .
> A sect whose chief devotion lies
> In odd perverse antipathies; . . .
> That with more care keep holiday
> The wrong than others the right way;
> Compound for sins they are inclined to
> By damning those they have no mind to.[43]

And so on, to the pain of the Puritans and the delight of the King. Charles rewarded the author with three hundred pounds. Every royalist praised it except Pepys, who could not "see where the wit lies," though "the book [is] now in the greatest fashion for drollery."[44] Butler hurried to bring out continuations (1664, 1678), but he had no further arrows in his quiver, and had run out of rhymes. The strife of Protestant and Catholic replaced that of royalist and Puritan; Butler was forgotten, and died in obscure poverty (1680). Forty years later a monument was erected to him in Westminster Abbey. "He asked for bread," said an epigram, "and he received a stone."[45]

Better than such rhyme-chasing doggerel was the stately prose of

Clarendon's *History of the Rebellion*, which appeared in 1702–4, though written in 1646–74. Men could see, in Queen Anne's reign, how careful had been the composition of those eight volumes, how splendid their style, how penetrating those sketches of character, how magnanimous had been the spirit of the old beaten Chancellor. Gilbert Burnet, likewise, had played no small part in *The History of His Own Time*, which by his order was published (1724) only after his death. His *History of the Reformation of the Church of England* (1679, 1681, 1715) was a more substantial work, a labor of long research; it came at a time when Protestant England feared a Catholic revival; both houses of Parliament thanked him for it. Enemies and editors have found a thousand errors in it; it is still warm with partisanship, and occasionally sullied with invective; but it remains the greatest book on its theme. Burnet strove to widen religious toleration, and earned the hostility of the mob.

Three other men sought to enlarge the present with the past. Thomas Fuller, passing through his loved land county by county, collected his *History of the Worthies of England* (1662), enlivening his dead heros with anecdotes, epigrams, and wit. Anthony Wood told the history of Oxford, and compiled a biographical dictionary of its graduates—careful works from which many an author has nibbled stealthily. John Aubrey gathered juicy fragments about 426 English notables, hoping to co-ordinate the material into a history, but laziness and death prevented him, and his *Minutes of Lives* saw print only in 1813;[46] his relics have cheered us on our way. Colonel John Hutchinson, a Puritan gentleman, voted for the execution of Charles I, was imprisoned by Charles II, was released, died soon afterward, and was enshrined by his widow, Lucy, in a loving and illuminating *Life of Colonel Hutchinson*; but Lucy suffered from delayed periods, her sentences sometimes running through a page. John Arbuthnot, able physician and loyal friend of Swift, Pope, Queen Anne, and many others, joined in the Tory campaign to stop the war with France, by issuing (1712) a series of pamphlets satirizing the Whigs, and describing an imaginary character, John Bull, who became thenceforth a symbol of England. John, wrote John, was

> an honest, plain-dealing fellow, choleric, bold, and of a very inconstant temper. . . . If you flattered him you might lead him like a child. John's temper depended very much upon the air; his spirits rose and fell with the weather-glass. John was quick and understood his business very well; but no man alive was more careless in looking into his accounts, or more cheated by partners, apprentices, or servants. This was occasioned by his being a boon companion, loving his bottle and his diversion; for to say truth, no man kept a better house than John, nor spent his money more generously.[47]

What would Sir William Temple say if he could find himself reduced to a paragraph in a chapter culminating in his secretary? Perhaps he would say, if his fine manners would permit, that historians neglected him because he had not kept two women dangling on the edge of matrimony till the death of one and the exhaustion of the other; that he had not sold his pen to Tory ministers out of pique at Whigs, nor dipped it in acid against mankind; but had served his country quietly in successful diplomacy, and, in an age of corruption and licentiousness, had given England an unostentatious example of decent family life. For seven years he courted Dorothy Osborne, whose lively letters to him became a part of English literature;[48] she accepted him despite the opposition of both their families; and he married her after an attack of smallpox had destroyed her beauty. He entered politics, but preferred tasks that took him far away from the fever of London; and he avoided "that laborious, that invidious, that closely watched slavery which is mocked with the name of power."[49] He was among the first to warn against the territorial ambitions of Louis XIV, and he was the chief architect of the Triple Alliance that checked the French King in 1668. In 1674 and 1677 he was offered the secretaryship of state, but he preferred his diplomatic post at The Hague. His farseeing negotiations brought about the marriage of Mary, daughter of James II, to the future William III, which made possible the "Glorious Revolution." In 1681 he retired from politics to a life of studying and writing at Moor Park, his estate in Surrey. Swift thought him cold and reserved, but Sir William's wife and sister alike worshiped him as the heart of kindness and courtesy. The most famous of his essays, *Of Ancient and Modern Learning* (1690), lauded the ancients, and belittled modern science and philosophy in the very teeth of Newton, Hobbes, Spinoza, Leibniz, and Locke. Bentley caught him in a famous error. Sir William retreated into his garden, and comforted himself with Epicurus. We shall meet him again.

V. EVELYN AND PEPYS

John Evelyn agreed with Temple that "where factions were once entered and rooted in a state, they thought it madness for good men to meddle with public affairs."[50] When Civil War loomed he judged it time to travel. He left England in July, 1641, but a stroke of conscience brought him back in October. He joined the King's army at Brentford just in time to participate in its retreat. After a month of service he retired to his paternal estate at Wotton in Surrey; and on November 11, 1643, he crossed again to the Continent. He traveled leisurely through France, Italy, Switzerland, Holland, and again in France. In Paris he married an English girl. For a time he oscillated between France and England; finally, the Civil War over, he returned to his home (February 6, 1652). He paid Cromwell's government to leave him alone. He corresponded with the exiled Charles II, and in 1659 he labored to promote the Restoration. After Charles had reached the throne Evelyn was *persona grata* at the court, though he condemned its immorality. He filled some minor governmental posts, but for the most part he preferred to plant trees and write thirty books at his country home. He wrote on everything from Lucretius to Sabbatai Zevi. His *Fumifugium* failed to clear the air of London, but his *Sylva* (1664) pleaded effectively for the reforestation of England, and he spurred the government to plant trees throughout London, whose trees are now its greatest glory and delight. His *Life of Mrs. Godolphin* is an idyl of womanly virtues amid the Restoration riot.

From 1641, when he was twenty-one, to February 3, 1706, twenty-four days before his death, he kept a diary of what he saw or heard in England or on the Continent. As a man of "quality" he could not afford to record such sins and intimate views as lure us to Pepys's longer *Diary;* but his descriptions of European cities have helped us to see the color of the time. He has some vivid pages, as on the Simplon Pass;[51] and sometimes he opens his heart in tender passages, as on the death of his five-year-old son. His diary remained unpublished till 1818.

Its references to Samuel Pepys led to the examination of the six volumes, in shorthand, that had been bequeathed by Pepys to Magdalene College, Cambridge. After three years of labor the 3,012 pages were deciphered; they were published in 1825, abbreviated and purified; now, still incomplete, they fill four thick tomes. They have made Pepys one of the most intimately and erroneously known characters in history. Intimately, because his diary was obviously intended for only posthumous publication if any, and therefore included details many of which had to be kept secret in his lifetime, and some of which are still "unprintable." Erroneously, for the diary covers less than a decade (January 1, 1660, to May 31, 1669) of Pepys's life, and gives no adequate account of his work at the Admiralty— the headquarters of the English navy—where he served in more and more important capacities from 1660 to 1689. Long after his death he was remembered and honored there as an able and industrious administrator.

His father was a London tailor, one of those younger sons of the gentry who took to trade because the oldest son alone inherited the estate. Samuel went to Cambridge on a scholarship, and took the bachelor's and master's degrees with no other discount than a public reprimand for having once been "scandalously overseene in drinking," and again for writing a romance, *Love is a Cheat,* which he afterward destroyed. At the age of twenty-two (1655) he married Elizabeth St. Michel, daughter of a Hugue-

not. In 1658 he was operated on for the stone; the affair went off successfully, and he gratefully celebrated its anniversary every recorded year
thereafter.

Sir Edward Montagu, his distant kinsman, made him his secretary (1660),
and Samuel accompanied him when Montagu commanded the fleet that
brought Charles back from exile. Before that year was out, Pepys was appointed clerk of the acts in the navy office. He studied naval affairs as
sedulously as his pursuit of women would permit, and since his superiors
were also devoted to that ancient sport, he soon came to know naval details more fully than the admirals (Montagu and the Duke of York) who
depended on his information. During the war with the Dutch (1665–67)
he managed with notable competence the victualing of the fleet, and during
the plague he kept to his post after most governmental officials had run
away. When (1668) the navy office was attacked in Parliament, Pepys
was entrusted with the defense, and his three hours' speech in the Commons won for the office an unmerited exoneration. Pepys then drew up
for the Duke of York two papers exposing the incompetence of navy personnel, and these papers played a part in the reform of the fleet. He
worked hard, usually rising at 4 A.M.,[52] but he saw to it that his salary of
£350 a year was aided by presents, commissions, and other perquisites,
some of which might now be called bribes, but which in those amiable days
were considered legitimate amplifications. His own superior, Lord Montagu, had explained to him that "it was not the salary of any place that
did make a man rich, but the opportunity of getting money while he is
in the place."[53]

All of Pepys's faults are revealed in the diary with a candor unpretentious
and relatively complete. Why he kept it so honestly is not clear. He concealed it carefully during his life, and wrote it in his own system of
shorthand, using 314 different characters, and made no arrangements for
its posthumous publication. Apparently he took pleasure in so reviewing
his daily activities, his physiological disturbances, his marital quarrels, his
flirtations and adulteries; he could, on secretly rereading the record, find
the same clandestine satisfaction that we derive from looking at ourselves
in the mirror. He tells us how he had his wife cut his hair, and "found in
my head and body about twenty lice, . . . more than I have had, I believe,
these twenty years."[54] He learned to love his wife, but only after many
quarrels, some that "vexed" him "to the guts"; often, on his own telling,
he was mean to her; on one occasion he "pulled her by the nose";[55] on
another "I did strike her over her left eye such a blow as the poor wretch
did cry out and was in great pain, but yet her spirit was such as to endeavor to bite and scratch me; but I coying with her made her leave
crying."[56] He had a poultice applied to her eye, and went out to a para-

mour. He returned home for dinner, then sallied out, found "Bagwell's wife . . . and took her away to an alehouse, and there made I much of her, and then away thence to another and endeavored to caress her, but *elle ne voulait pas*, which did vex me."

It is astonishing what energy the man had—every few months another amour; he pursued women till they repulsed him with pins.[57] He confessed the "strange slavery that I stand in to beauty."[58] In Westminster Abbey "I heard a sermon, and spent (God forgive me) most of my time in looking at Mrs. Butler."[59] He looked with especial longing, almost with *lèse majesté*, upon Lady Castlemaine; seeing her in Whitehall Palace, "I glutted myself with looking at her."[60] He had to content himself with her petticoats hanging on a line; "it did me good to look upon them";[61] and "so home to supper and to bed, fancying myself to sport with Mrs. Stewart [Lady Castlemaine] with great pleasure."[62] But his taste was not confined to court beauties. A neighbor, Mrs. Diana, passed his door; he drew her "into my house upstairs, and there did dally with her a great while."[63] He took a Mrs. Lane to Lambeth, but, "after being tired of her company," he resolved "never to do so again while I live."[64] On one occasion his wife caught him hugging a girl; she threatened to leave him; he appeased her with vows, and rushed off to his latest mistress. He seduced his wife's maid, Deborah Willet; he loved to have her comb his hair; but his wife came upon him during his explorations; he made new vows; Deborah was dismissed; Pepys visited her as part of his day's work.

His lust continued even when his eyesight failed. His habit of reading and writing by candlelight began in 1664 to impair his vision. But in the critical years that followed he worked especially hard, despite the progress of his trouble. On May 31, 1669, he made the last entry in his diary:

> And thus ends all that I doubt I shall ever be able to do with my own eyes in the keeping of my Journal. . . . Whatever comes of it, I must forbear; and therefore resolve, from this time forward, to have it kept by my people in longhand, and must therefore be contented to set down no more than is fit for them and all the world to know; or, if there be anything—which cannot be much, now my amours with Deborah are past, and my eyes hindering me in almost all other pleasures—I must endeavor to keep a margin in my book open, to add, here and there, a note in shorthand with my own hand. And so I betake myself to that course, which is almost as much as to see myself go into my grave; for which, and all the discomforts that will accompany my being blind, the good God prepare me!—S.P.

He had thirty-four years of life remaining to him. He nursed carefully what remained of his eyesight, and he never went completely blind. The

FIG. 47—FRANCESCO SOLIMENA: *Rape of Oreithyia*. Kunsthistorisches Museum, Vienna

FIG. 48—ENGRAVING AFTER A PAINTING BY WILLIAM FAITHORNE: *Robert Boyle.* (Bettmann Archive)

PAGE 511

FIG. 49—ENGRAVING AFTER A PAINTING BY CASPAR NET-SCHER: *Christian Huygens.* (Bettmann Archive)

PAGE 499

FIG. 50—UNKNOWN ARTIST: *Thomas Sydenham.* Royal College of Physicians, London (Bettmann Archive)   PAGE 527

FIG. 51—UNKNOWN ARTIST: *Isaac Newton.* National Portrait Gallery, London (Bettmann Archive)   PAGE 531

FIG. 52—LOUIS GALLOCHE: *Fontenelle*. Château de Versailles

FIG. 55—PIERRE BAYLE: Original engraving used as frontispiece to his *Historical and Critical Dictionary*, third edition (Rotterdam, 1715)

PAGE 605

FIG. 56—ADRIAEN HANNEMAN: *Jan de Witt*. Museum Boymans, Rotterdam. Courtesy of Netherlands Information Bureau, New York

PAGE 625

Fig. 57—Mezzotint based on portrait sketch by Johann Gottfried Auerbach: *Gottfried Wilhelm von Leibniz.* (Bettmann Archive)   PAGE 658

Fig. 58—Unknown Artist: *Benedictus Spinoza.* Gemeente Museum, The Hague. Courtesy of Netherlands Information Bureau, New York   PAGE 620

FIG. 59—HYACINTHE RIGAUD: *Louis XIV.* Louvre, Paris (Bettmann Archive) PAGE 717

Duke and the King gave him a long leave of absence; then he returned to work. In 1673 he was made secretary of the Admiralty. Meanwhile his wife became a Catholic. When the Popish Plot broke upon England Pepys was arrested and sent to the Tower (May 22, 1679) on suspicion of having had a hand in the murder of Godfrey. He disproved the charge and was released after nine months' imprisonment. He remained out of office till 1684; then he was again appointed secretary of the Admiralty, and continued the reform of the navy. When his master became James II Pepys was in effect head of naval administration. But when James fled to France Pepys was imprisoned again. Soon released, he lived his final fourteen years in retirement as "the Nestor of the navy." He died May 26, 1703, aged seventy, full of honors and washed of sin.

Many things in the man were likable. We have noted his love of music. He pursued science too, experimented in physics, became a member of the Royal Society, was elected its president in 1684. He was as vain as a man, he took bribes, he beat his servant till his arm hurt,[65] he was cruel to his wife, and he was an arrant rake. But what royal and ducal exemplars he had, more shameless far than he! And which of us would have a spotless fame if he left so honest a diary?

VI. DANIEL DEFOE: 1659?–1731

One of the women who escaped Pepys deserves a cautious curtsy here as the mother of the Restoration novel, and the first Englishwoman to live by her pen. Aphra Behn was remarkable in a dozen ways. Born in England, brought up in South America, she returned to England at the age of eighteen (1658), married a London merchant of Dutch descent, impressed Charles II by her shrewdness and wit, was sent on secret service to the Netherlands, accomplished her missions with skill, but was so meagerly paid that she took to writing as a means of support. She composed comedies, as obscene and successful as any. In 1678 she published *Oroonoko*, the story of a Negro "royal slave" and his beloved Imoinda. It was an original blend of realism and romance. The way was open for *Robinson Crusoe*, and for the romantic novel.

Defoe too lived by his pen, and it was one of the most versatile in history. His father was James Foe, a London butcher of strong Presbyterian doctrine. Daniel was expected to become a preacher, but he preferred marriage, business, and politics. He begot seven children, became a wholesale hosier, joined Monmouth's army in rebellion (1685), and William's army in overthrowing James II. In 1692 he went bankrupt, owing £17,000; later he paid his creditors almost in full. While making and losing money he issued pamphlets on a variety of subjects, and containing an astonishing wealth of original thought. His *Essay on Projects* (1698) offered practical suggestions, much in advance of his time, on banking, insurance, roads, lunatic asylums, military colleges, the higher education of women. He moved to Tilbury, where he became secretary, then manager, then owner, of a tile factory. Introduced to William III, he was appointed to a minor post in the government, and supported the King's war policy so vigorously that he was accused of being more Dutch than English. He defended himself in a vigorous poem, *The True-born Englishman* (1701), reminding the English that the whole nation was of mixed origin and blood. Himself a Dissenter, he issued in 1702 an anonymous tract, *The Shortest Way with the Dissenters*, in which, anticipating Swift's method of stultification by exaggeration, he ridiculed the Anglican persecution of Dissent by recommending that every Dissenter who preached should be hanged, and every Dissenter who listened should be driven from England. He was arrested (February, 1703), fined, jailed, and condemned to the pillory. He was released in November, but meanwhile his tile business had gone to ruin.

The man who secured his release was Robert Harley, secretary of state. Harley recognized Defoe's ability as a journalist; apparently he struck a bargain with him for the services of his pen, and for the remainder of Anne's reign Defoe was in the employ of the government. Soon after his release he started a triweekly four-page periodical, *The Review*, which ran till 1713 and was almost entirely written by Defoe.

In 1704–5 he rode horseback through England as an election agent for Harley; *en courant* he picked up the data for his *Tour through England and Wales*. In 1706–7 he served Harley and Godolphin as a spy in Scotland. His powerful pamphlets won him many readers, but also many enemies. He was arrested again in 1713 and in 1715; and again he earned release by promising to put his pen at the service of the government.

He was full of literary devices. In 1715 he published tracts allegedly written by a Quaker, and in the same year *The Wars of Charles XII* as reported by "a Scots Gentleman in the Swedish Service." In 1717 he issued letters supposedly by a Turk, ridiculing Christian intolerance; to a magazine well called *Mist* he contributed material signed by fictitious correspondents; rarely did he write as Defoe. To this skill in impersonation he added a wide reading in geography, especially of Africa and the Americas. He was apparently fascinated by William Dampier's *New Voyage round the World* (1697). On one of Dampier's voyages his galley, the *Cinque Ports*, put in at Juan Fernández Islands, some four hundred miles west of Chile. A Scottish sailing master, Alexander Selkirk, having quarreled with his captain, asked to be left on one of the three islands, with a few necessaries. He remained alone there for four years, when he was taken back to

England. He told his story to Richard Steele, who reported it in *The Englishman* for December 3, 1713. He told it also to Defoe, and claimed to have given Defoe a written record of his adventure in solitude.[66] Defoe transformed the account into literature, and published in 1719 the most famous of English novels.

The Life and Strange Surprizing Adventures of Robinson Crusoe caught the imagination of England, running through four editions in four months. Here was a new conception of adventure and conflict—not of man against man, nor of civilized man amid savages, but of man against nature, of man alone, frankly afraid, unaided till "Friday" came, building a life out of nature's raw materials; this was the history of civilization in one volume and one man. Many readers took it as history, for seldom in all literature had a story been told with such verisimilitude of circumstantial detail. Defoe's training in literary deception had lifted him out of journalism into art.

He lived now in moderate affluence in London, but he did not abate his unparalleled productivity. While still sending forth pamphlets, he turned out full-length books as if they were novelettes. In 1720 he published *Serious Reflections during the Life and Surprizing Adventures of Robinson Crusoe; The Life and Adventures of Mrs. Duncan Campbell* (a deaf-and-dumb conjurer); a month later *The Memoirs of a Cavalier*, so *ben trovato* that the elder Pitt took it for history; and another month later *The Life, Adventures, Piracies of the Famous Captain Singleton*, which contained astonishing anticipations of discoveries in Africa. In 1722 he issued *The Fortunes and Misfortunes of Moll Flanders*, and *A Journal of the Plague Year*, and *The History of Colonel Jacque*, and *The Religious Courtship*, and *The Impartial History of Peter Alexowitz, the Present Czar of Muscovy*—his second anticipation of Voltaire's biographies. These substantial volumes were intended as potboilers to provide food for his family; but, by the man's power of imagination and fluency of style, they became literature. In *Moll Flanders* Defoe entered into the mind and character of a prostitute, made her tell her story with apparent candor and plausibility, and dared to leave her prosperous "in good heart and health" at the age of seventy.[67] The *Journal of the Plague Year* was so minutely realistic and statistical that historians look upon it as tantamount to history.

The year 1724 was slightly less astonishing: Defoe published one of his major novels, *The Fortunate Mistress*, now known as *Roxana;* the first of two volumes reporting his *Tour through the Whole Island of Great Britain;* and a *Life of John Sheppard*, purporting to be a manuscript handed to a friend by Sheppard just before his execution. This was one of several short lives that Defoe wrote of famous criminals. One of these biographies, *The Highland Rogue* (1724), prepared for Scott's *Rob Roy;* another,

An Account of Jonathan Wild (1725), prepared for Fielding. Any popular topic drew ink from Defoe's well and pounds from his publishers: *Political History of the Devil* (1726), *The Mysteries of Magic* (1720), *Secrets of the Invisible World Discovered, or History and Reality of Apparitions* (1727–28). Add to these a poem in twelve books, *Jure Divino*, defending every man's natural rights to life, liberty, and the pursuit of happiness. Amid so many breadwinning condescensions to popular taste and fancies were honest contributions to serious thought: so in *The Complete English Tradesman* (1725–27), and *A Plan of the English Commerce* (1728), and the unfinished *Complete English Gentleman*, he offered useful information and practical advice, not always geared to Gospel morality.

We cannot recommend his literary morals, but we can admire his industry. Probably never since Rameses II's 150 children has history seen such a prodigy of progeny. The only thing incredible in Defoe is that he wrote all that he wrote. For we marvel, too, at the quality of Defoe's mind, in which imagination and memory, harnessed to hard labor, produced the most plausible unrealities in literature. We recognize the genius and courage of a man who, in such a mass and haste of work, could maintain so high a level of matter and style. In all his 210 volumes (if we may speak from hearsay) there is hardly one dull page; and where Defoe is dull he is deliberately so, to add to the verisimilitude of his tale. No one has surpassed him in direct and simple narrative, convincingly natural. Here his haste was his fortune: he had no time for ornament; his journalistic training and bent compelled him to brevity and clarity. He was by all means the greatest journalist of his time, though that included Steele and Addison and Swift; his *Review* plowed the furrow in which *The Spectator* planted choicer seed. That was distinction enough; but add to it the cosmic and living popularity of *Robinson Crusoe*, and the influence it had upon novels of adventure, even upon a story so differently motivated as *Travels . . . by Lemuel Gulliver*. Barring the author of that brilliant indictment of mankind, Defoe was the greatest genius of English letters in that abounding age.

VII. STEELE AND ADDISON

"Dick" Steele, more than anyone else, marks the literary transition from the Restoration to Queen Anne. His youth had all the qualities of a Restoration roisterer: born in Dublin, son of a notary; educated at Charterhouse School and Oxford; impressionable, excitable, generous; instead of taking his degree he joined the government army in Ireland. He drank like a sieve, fought a duel, and nearly killed his antagonist. The experience sobered him transiently; he began a campaign against dueling, and wrote an essay, *The Christian Hero* (1701), in which he argued that a man might be a gentleman while remaining a Christian. He described the corruption of the age, called his readers back to the Bible as the source of true faith and pure morality, and appealed to men to respect the charm and chastity of women.

He was now twenty-nine years old. Finding that even the middle class, to which he belonged, looked upon him as a tiresome preacher, he decided to put his message into plays. He applauded Jeremy Collier's denunciation of theatrical obscenity, and in a succession of comedies he championed virtue and punished his villains decisively. These productions were failures. They contained some lively scenes and wit, but the audiences were skeptical of his denouements, and demanded entertainment at whatever cost to the Ten Commandments; while those solid Londoners who might have seconded his sentiments were seldom seen at the theater. How to reach these people?

He decided to try a medium that would find them in the coffeehouses. On April 12, 1709, taking a leaf from Defoe's *Review*, he issued the first number of a triweekly periodical, *The Tatler*, editing it, and writing most of it, under the pseudonym of Isaac Bickerstaff. He aimed it at the coffee-houses by announcing:

> All accounts of gallantry, pleasure, and entertainment shall be under the article [be dated from] White's chocolate house; poetry, under that of Will's coffee-house; learning, under the title of Grecian; foreign and domestic news you will have from St. James's coffee-house; and what else I shall on any subject offer shall be dated from my own apartment.

It was a clever scheme: it aroused the interest of the coffeehouse frequenters, it took news and topics from the discussions there, and it allowed Steele to express his views without interruption or dispute. So, in Number 25 (June 7, 1709), he told of receiving a letter "from a young lady . . . wherein she laments the misfortune of . . . her lover, who was lately wounded in a duel"; and he went on to show the absurdity of a custom by which an injured gentleman must invite the offender to add murder to insult; for what does a challenge mean but:

> "Sir, your extraordinary behaviour last night, and the liberty you were pleased to take with me, makes me this morning give you this, to tell you, because you are an illbred puppy, I will meet you in Hyde Park, an hour hence. . . . I desire you would come with a pistol in

your hand. . . . and endeavour to shoot me through the head, to teach you more manners."

Here was the voice of the middle class laughing at the aristocracy; and it was chiefly the middle class that filled the coffeehouses.

In further essays Steele made fun of aristocratic luxury, expletives, affectations, ornaments, and dress. He begged women to dress simply, and to avoid jewelry: "The cluster of diamonds upon the breast can add no beauty to the fair chest of ivory that supports it."[68] His tenderness for women rivaled his affection for alcohol. He insisted that they had intelligence as well as texture, but he lauded most of all their modesty and purity —qualities not recognized in Restoration comedy. Of one woman he said that "to have loved her was a liberal education"—which Thackeray considered "the finest compliment to a woman that perhaps ever was offered."[69] Steele described with emotion the joys of family life, the pleasant patter of children's feet, the gratitude of a husband to his aging wife:

> She gives me every day pleasure beyond what I ever knew in the possession of her beauty when I was in the vigour of youth. Every moment of her life brings me fresh instances of her complacency to my inclinations, and her prudence in regard to my fortune. Her face is to me much more beautiful than when I first saw it; there is no decay in any feature which I cannot trace from the very instant it was occasioned by some anxious concern for my welfare and interests. . . . The love of a wife is as much above the idle passion commonly called by that name, as the loud laughter of buffoons is inferior to the elegant mirth of gentlemen.[70]

When Steele wrote this he had been twice married. His letters to his second wife are models of devotion, though they soon include excuses for not coming home to dinner. He failed to be the good bourgeois that he held up as the model of life. He drank too much, spent too much, borrowed too much. He walked in side streets to avoid the friends who had lent him money; he went in hiding to elude his creditors; finally he was jailed for debt. Readers of *The Tatler* contrasted his preaching with his practice. John Dennis issued an unfeeling satire on Steele's sentiments. Subscribers fell away, and on January 2, 1711, *The Tatler* expired. Its place in the history of English literature remains, for in its pages the new morality began to express itself, the short story took its modern form, and Addison developed—as in *The Spectator* he would perfect—the modern essay.

Addison and Steele, both born in 1672, had been friends since their days together in Charterhouse School. Joseph's father was an Anglican minister, who gave him an inoculation of piety that resisted all Restoration infections. At Oxford his proficiency in Latin won him a scholarship. At twenty-two his talents so impressed Halifax that the Earl persuaded the head of Magdalen College to divert the youth from the ministry to the service of the government. "I am called an enemy of the Church," said Halifax, "but I will never do it any other injury than keeping Mr. Addison out of it."[71] As the prodigy in Latin was destitute of French, and a knowledge of French was required of diplomats, Halifax secured for him an annual pension of three hundred pounds to finance a stay on the Continent. For two years Addison wandered leisurely through France, Italy, and Switzerland.

While he was in Geneva the accession of Anne removed his friends from office and cut off his pension. Reduced to his own slender income, he engaged himself as tutor to a young English traveler, and with him toured Switzerland, Germany, and the United Provinces. This employment ending, he returned to London (1703), and for a time lived in genteel poverty. But he was a magnet for good fortune. When Marlborough won the battle of Blenheim (August 13, 1704), Godolphin, lord treasurer, looked around for someone to celebrate the victory in verse. Halifax recommended Addison; the scholar responded with a resounding poem, *The Campaign;* it was published on the very day of Marlborough's triumphant entry into the capital, and its success helped to reconcile England to continuing the war. It was Addison's highest poetic flight, which George Washington favored above all other poems. Hear the famous lines:

> But, O my Muse! what numbers wilt thou find
> To sing the furious troops in battle join'd?
> Methinks I hear the drum's tumultuous sound
> The victor's shouts and dying groans confound;
> The dreadful burst of cannon rend the skies,
> And all the thunder of the battle rise.
> 'Twas then great Marlborough's mighty soul was proved,
> That, in the shock of charging hosts unmoved,
> Amidst confusion, horror, and despair,
> Examined all the dreadful scenes of war:
> In peaceful thought the field of death surveyed,
> To fainting squadrons sent the timely aid,
> Inspired repulsed battalions to engage,
> And taught the doubtful battle where to rage.
> So when an angel, by divine command,
> With rising tempests shakes a guilty land
> (Such as of late o'er pale Britannia passed),
> Calm and serene he drives the furious blast;
> And, pleased the Almighty's orders to perform,
> Rides in the whirlwind and directs the storm.

That last line and angelic simile wafted Addison safely back into government pay, where he remained for the next ten years. In 1705 he was appointed commissioner of appeals, replacing John Locke; in 1706 he was undersecretary of state; in 1707 he was attached to the mission of Halifax to Hanover, which prepared for the accession of that house to the throne of England; in 1708 he took his seat in Parliament, and, by virtue of his offices, held it till his death; in 1709 he became chief secretary to the Lord Lieutenant of Ireland. In 1711 he was affluent enough to buy a ten-thousand-pound estate near Rugby.

In his prosperity he did not forget Steele. He chided his sins, got him a place in the government, lent him considerable sums, and in one case sued him for repayment.[72] When the anonymous *Tatler* appeared he noticed in it a remark on Virgil which he had made to Steele; in "Isaac Bickerstaff" he recognized his high-living, impecunious friend; and soon he was contributing to the journal. In 1710 the Whigs fell, Steele lost his governmental post, and Addison lost all his offices except as commissioner of appeals. *The Tatler* celebrated the new year by expiring. Steele and Addison pooled their misfortunes and hopes, and on March 1, 1711, they sent forth the first number of the most famous periodical in English literary history.

The Spectator appeared daily except Sunday, in a folded sheet of four or six pages. Instead of dating the articles from various centers, the anonymous editor invented an imaginary club whose members would represent different sectors of the English world: Sir Roger de Coverley as the English country gentleman; Sir Andrew Freeport representing the merchant class; Captain Sentry speaking for the army; Will Honeycomb the man of fashion; a lawyer of the Inner Temple standing for the world of learning; and Mr. Spectator himself, who brings all their views together in a spirit of genial humor and witty courtesy that won him entry into the homes and hearts of England. In the first number the Spectator described himself, and set the clubs and coffeehouses guessing at his identity.

> I have passed my latter years in this city, where I am frequently seen in most public places, though there are not above half a dozen of my select friends that know me; of whom my next paper shall give a more particular account. There is no place of general resort wherein I do not often make my appearance; sometimes I am seen thrusting my head into a round of politicians at Will's, and listening with great attention to the narratives that are made in those circular audiences. Sometimes I smoke a pipe at Child's, and whilst I seem attentive to nothing but the *Postman*, overhear the conversation of every table in the room. I appear on Sunday nights at St. James's coffee-house, and sometimes join the little committee of politics in the inner-room as

one who comes there to hear and improve. My face is likewise very well known at the Grecian, the Cocoa-tree, and in the theatres both of Drury-lane and Hay-market. I have been taken for a merchant upon the Exchange for above these ten years, and sometimes pass for a Jew in the assembly of stockjobbers at Jonathan's. In short, wherever I see a cluster of people, I always mix with them, though I never open my lips but in my own club.

Thus I live in the world rather as a Spectator of mankind, than as one of the species, by which means I have made myself a speculative statesman, soldier, merchant and artisan, without ever meddling with any practical part in life. I am very well versed in the theory of a husband, or a father, and can discern the errors in the economy, business, and diversion of others, better than those who are engaged in them; as standers-by discover blots which are apt to escape those who are in the game. I never espoused any party with violence, and am resolved to observe an exact neutrality between the Whigs and Tories, unless I shall be forced to declare myself by the hostilities of either side. In short, I have acted in all the parts of my life as a looker-on, which is the character I intend to preserve in this paper.

As the enterprise proceeded, *The Spectator* mingled social gossip, and studies of manners and character, with literary criticism and theatrical reviews. Addison wrote a series of essays on Milton, in which he astonished England by ranking *Paradise Lost* above the *Iliad* and the *Aeneid*. The discussions avoided politics, as leading to enmities and vicissitudes, but they stressed—and Addison willingly joined in—Steele's plea for moral reform. Something of the Puritan spirit, chastened by adversity, returned in reaction against the Restoration reaction; but now it was no long-faced theological preoccupation with Satan and damnation, but a call to moderation and decency, cheered with optimism and coated with wit. So Number 10 began:

It is with much satisfaction that I hear this great city inquiring day by day after these my papers, and receiving my morning lectures with a becoming seriousness and attention. My publisher tells me, that there are already three thousand of them distributed every day: so that if I allow twenty readers to every paper, which I look upon as a modest computation, I may reckon about three score thousand disciples in London and Westminster, who I hope will take care to distinguish themselves from the thoughtless herd of their ignorant and unattentive brethren. Since I have raised to myself so great an audience, I shall spare no pains to make their instruction agreeable, and their diversion useful. For which reason I shall endeavour to enliven morality with wit, and to temper wit with morality, that my readers may, if possible, both ways find their account in the speculation of the day. And to the end that their virtue and discretion may not be short, transient, intermitting starts of thought, I have resolved to refresh their memories from day to day, till I have recovered them out of that desperate state of vice and folly, into which the age is fallen. The mind that lies fallow but a single day, sprouts up in follies that are only to be killed by a constant and assiduous culture. It was said of Socrates, that he brought philosophy down from heaven, to inhabit among men; and I shall be ambitious to have it said of me, that I have brought philosophy out of closets and libraries, schools and colleges, to dwell in clubs and assemblies, at tea-tables, and in coffee-houses.

I would therefore in a very particular manner recommend these my speculations to all well-regulated families, that set apart an hour in every morning for tea and bread and butter; and would earnestly advise them for their good to order this paper to be punctually served up, and to be looked upon as a part of the tea-equipage.

The Spectator addressed itself to women as well as men, proposed to deal with love and sex, and to make "falsehood in love bear a blacker aspect than . . . infidelity in friendship, or villainy in business."[73] "I shall take it for the greatest glory of my work," wrote the Spectator, "if among reasonable women this paper may furnish tea-table talk."[74] Letters were invited and printed, and Steele ran a series of lovelorn epistles, some of them his own to his ladies, some invented by the editors in quite modern style. The journal joined religion with love, and provided a genial theology for a generation beginning to wonder what the decline of religious belief in the upper classes was doing to morality. It counseled science to mind its business and let the Church alone as the wise and experienced guardian of morals; the rights of feeling and the needs of order are beyond the comprehension of individual reason, always adolescent. It is better for morals and happiness to accept the old religion humbly, attend its services, observe its holydays, and help to establish in each parish the wholesome atmosphere of a quiet and worshipful Sabbath.

I am always very well pleased with a country Sunday, and think, if keeping holy the seventh day were only a human institution, it would be the best method that could have been thought of for the polishing and civilising of mankind. It is certain the country people would soon degenerate into a kind of savages and barbarians were there not such frequent returns of a stated time in which the whole village meet together with their best faces, and in their cleanliest habits, to converse with one another upon indifferent subjects, hear their duties explained to them, and join together in adoration of the Supreme Being. Sunday clears away the rust of the whole week, not only as it refreshes in their minds the notions of religion, but as it puts both the sexes upon appearing in their most agreeable forms.[75]

Now literature, which for forty years had served licentiousness, moved to the side of morality and faith; *The Spectator* shared in the revolution of manners and style that in the reign of Anne anticipated by a century the mid-Victorian spirit, making respectability respectable, and changing the English concept of the gentleman from a titled philanderer to a well-bred citizen. The virtues of the middle class found in *The Spectator* an urbane and polished defense. Prudence and thrift were more precious to society than lace and wit; merchants were the ambassadors of civilization to backward peoples; and the profits of commerce and industry were the sinews of the state.

For a year *The Spectator* enjoyed a *succès d'estime* unparalleled in English journalism. Its circulation was small, rarely exceeding four thousand, but its influence was immense. Its bound volumes sold some nine thousand copies annually,[76] as if England already recognized it to be literature. But in time the novelty wore off; the characters of the "club" began to repeat themselves; the verve of the weary authors waned; their sermons grew tiresome; the circulation declined. The stamp tax of 1712 increased costs beyond revenues, and on December 16, 1712, *The Spectator* gave up the ghost. Steele resumed the struggle with *The Guardian*, and Addison revived *The Spectator*, in 1714. Both journals were short-lived, for by that time Addison had become a successful dramatist and had been restored to his posts and emoluments in the government.

On April 14, 1713, the Drury Lane Theatre produced Addison's *Cato*. His friend Pope wrote for it a prologue bristling with Popal epigrams and heavy with Bullish patriotism. Steele undertook to pack the house with ardent Whigs; he did not quite succeed, but the Tories joined the Whigs in applauding Cato's last stand for Roman liberty (46 B.C.); and the Tory *Examiner* rivaled Steele's *Guardian* in ecstatic praise. For an entire month the tragedy played to overflowing audiences. "Cato," said Pope, "was not so much the wonder of Rome in his days as he is of Britain in ours."[77] On the Continent *Cato* was rated the finest tragic drama in the English language. Voltaire admired its adherence to the unities, and marveled that England could tolerate Shakespeare after seeing Addison's play.[78] Critics now deride it as vapid declamation, but one reader has found his attention held to the end by a well-constructed plot, and a love story skillfully integrated into the larger war.

Addison was now so popular that "I believe," said Swift, "if he had a mind to be chosen king he would hardly be refused."[79] But Addison, always a model of moderation, contented himself with being appointed secretary to the government, presently chief secretary for Ireland, then a lord commissioner of trade. He was *persona gratissima* at the clubs, for his hard drinking kept him from being the "faultless monster whom the world ne'er" loves. To crown his glory he married (1716) a countess, and lived unhappily with the proud lady at Holland House in London. In 1717 he was again a secretary of state; but his competence was questioned, and he soon resigned, with a pension of £1,500 a year. Despite his patience and good manners he slipped into quarrels with his friends, including Steele and Pope—who satirized him as a prig wont to "damn with faint praise," and,

> Like Cato, give his little senate laws,
> And sit attentive to his own applause.[80]

Steele came to a less stately end. He was elected to Parliament in 1713, but the Tory majority expelled him on a charge of seditious language. The triumph of the Whigs a year later consoled him with several lucrative places in the administration, and for a time his income equaled his expenditures. Then his debts won the race, his creditors pursued him, and he retired to his wife's estate in Wales. There he died, September 1, 1729, ten years after his collaborator. Together, Steele with originality and verve, Addison with polished artistry, they had raised the short story and the essay to new excellence, had shared in the moral regeneration of the age, and had set the tone and forms of English literature for a century—except for the most powerful and bitter genius of the age.

VIII: JONATHAN SWIFT: 1667–1745

Swift was five years older than Steele and Addison, but he outlived the one by sixteen, the other by twenty-six years, and served as a living fire that ran from century to century, from Dryden to Pope. He could never forgive his birth in Dublin, which proved an irritating handicap in England; and it was cruel that his father, steward of the King's Inns in Dublin, died before Jonathan appeared. The child was put out to nurse; the nurse took it to England, and returned it to its mother only when it was three years old. These adventures may have begotten in the boy a sense of orphaned insecurity. This must have been deepened by his being transferred to an uncle, who soon disposed of him, aged six, to a boarding school at Kilkenny. At fifteen he was sent to Trinity College, Dublin, where he remained for seven years. He barely scraped through, being especially negligent in theology. He was often delinquent, often punished, and he was reduced to precarious poverty when the uncle who was paying his expenses suffered final reverses and mental collapse (1688). On his uncle's death (1689), and amid the uprising of Ireland for James II, Jonathan fled to England and his mother, who was living at Leicester on twenty pounds a year. Despite their long separation they got along reasonably well; he learned to love her, and visited her, now and then, till her death (1710).

Toward the end of 1689 he found employment, at twenty pounds a year and board, as secretary to Sir William Temple at Moor Park. Temple was then at the height of his career, the friend and adviser of kings; we must not berate him for failing to recognize genius in the twenty-two-year-old youth who came to him with some Latin and Greek, but also an Irish brogue, and furtive uncertainty about the relative functions of knives and forks.[81] Swift sat with the upper servants at the master's table,[82] but the master always kept his distance. Yet Temple was kind. In 1692 he sent Swift to Oxford to acquire the M.A. degree; and he recommended him to William III, without result.

Meanwhile Jonathan was writing couplets. He showed some of them to Dryden, who told him, "Cousin Swift, you will never be a poet"—a prediction whose accuracy was beyond the young man's appreciation. In 1694 Swift left Temple with a recommendation from his master; he returned to Ireland, was ordained an Anglican priest (1695), and was appointed to a small benefice at Kilroot, near Belfast. In Belfast he fell in love with Jane Waring, whom he called Varina; he proposed marriage, but she held him off until time should improve her health and his income. Unable to bear the dull isolation of a country parish, he fled from Kilroot in 1696, went back to Temple, and remained in Sir William's service till the latter's death.

During his first year at Moor Park Swift had met the Esther Johnson who was to become his "Stella." Some gossip thought her the result of Sir William's rare impulsiveness; more likely she was the daughter of a London merchant, whose widow had entered Lady Temple's service. When Swift first saw her she was a girl of eight, delightful like all girls of eight, but too young to arouse in him any amorous unrest. Now, however, she was fifteen; and Swift, turning twenty-nine, soon discovered as her tutor that she had charms to rouse a savage breast priestly but starved. Black, shining eyes, raven hair, swelling bosom, "a gracefulness somewhat more than human in every motion, word, and action" (so he later described her), and "every feature of her face in perfection"[83]—how could this Héloïse avoid awakening this Abélard?

Temple, dying (1699), left a thousand pounds to Esther, a thousand to Swift. After vain hopes of governmental employment, Swift accepted an invitation to become chaplain and secretary to the Earl of Berkeley, who had just been appointed a lord justice in Ireland. He acted as secretary on the journey to Dublin; but there he was dismissed. He asked for the deanery of Derry, which was falling vacant, but the new secretary, for a bribe of a thousand pounds, gave the place to another candidate. Swift denounced the Earl and the secretary to their faces as "a couple of scoundrels." They quieted him with the rectory of Laracor, a village some twenty miles from Dublin, with a congregation of fifteen persons. Swift had now (1700) an income of £230, which Jane Waring thought might suffice for marriage. However, she was four years older than when he had proposed to her, and meanwhile he had discovered Esther. He wrote to Jane that if she would submit to enough education to make her a suitable companion in his home, if she would promise to accept all his likes and dislikes, and soothe his ill-humor, he would take her without inquiring into her looks or her income.[84] The affair ended.

Lonely in Laracor, Swift made frequent visits to Dublin. There, in 1701, he took his degree as a doctor of divinity. Later in that year he invited Esther Johnson and her companion, Mrs. Robert Dingley, to come and live in Laracor. They came, took lodgings near him, and during his absences in England they occupied the apartment he had rented in Dublin. "Stella" expected him to marry her, but he kept her waiting for fifteen years. She accepted her situation fretfully, but the force of his character and the sharpness of his intellect held her hypnotized to the end.

The quality of his mind showed alarmingly when, in 1704, he published in one volume *The Battle of the Books* and *The Tale of a Tub*. The former is a brief and negligible contribution to the controversy as to the relative merits of ancient and modern literature; but *The Tale of a Tub* is a major exposition of Swift's religious, or irreligious, philosophy. Re-reading this work in later life, he exclaimed, "Good God! what a genius I had when I wrote that book!"[85] He loved it so much that in later editions he caressed it with fifty pages of nonsense in the form of prefaces and apologies. He prided himself on its complete originality; and though the Church had long since spoken of Christianity as the once "seamless robe of Christ" torn to pieces by the Reformation, no one—least of all the Carlyle of *Sartor Resartus*—has impugned the unprecedented force with which Swift here reduced all philosophies and religions to diverse garments used to clothe our shivering ignorance or conceal our naked desires.

> What is man himself but a micro-coat, or rather a complete set of clothes with all its trimmings? . . . Is not religion a cloak; honesty a pair of shoes worn out in the dirt; self-love a surtout; vanity a shirt; and conscience a pair of breeches which, though a cover for lewdness

as well as for nastiness, is easily slipped down for the service of both?
If certain ermines and furs be placed in a certain position, we style a
judge; and so an apt conjunction of lawn and black satin we entitle a
bishop.[86]

The garment allegory is carried out with thoroughness and finesse.
Peter (Catholicism), Martin (Lutheranism and Anglicanism) and Jack
(Calvinism) received from their dying father three new and identical coats
(Bibles), and a will directing them how to wear these, and forbidding them
ever to alter, add to, or diminish them by even a single thread. The sons
fall in love with three ladies: the Duchess d'Argent (wealth), Mme. de
Grands Titres (ambition), and the Countess d'Orgueil (pride). To please
these ladies the brothers make certain changes in their inherited coats; and
when the alterations seem to contradict their father's will, they reinterpret
it by scholarly exegesis. Peter wished to add some silver fringes (papal
luxury); it was readily shown, on the most learned authority, that the word
fringe in the will meant *broomstick;* so Peter adopted silver fringes, but
denied himself broomsticks (witchcraft?). Protestants were delighted to
find the keenest edge of satire falling upon Peter: upon his purchase of
a large continent (purgatory), which he sold in various parcels (indulgences) over and over again; upon his sovereign and usually painless
remedies (penances) for worms (gnawings of conscience)—for example,
"to eat nothing after supper for three nights . . . and by no means to break
wind at both ends together without manifest occasion";[87] upon the invention of "a whispering office" (the confessional) "for the public good
and ease of all such as are hypochondriacs or troubled with the colic";
upon "an office of insurance" (more indulgences); upon the "famous universal [Catholic] pickle" (holy water) as a preventive of decay. Enriched by these wise expedients, Peter sets himself up as the representative
of God. He claps three high-crowned hats upon his head, and holds an
angling rod in his hand; and when anyone wishes to shake his hand, he,
"like a well-educated spaniel," offers them his foot.[88] He invites his brothers
to dinner, gives them nothing but bread, assures them that it is not bread
but meat, and refutes their objections: "To convince you what a couple
of blind, positive, ignorant, willful puppies you are, I will use but this
simple argument. By G——, it is true, good, natural mutton as any in
Leadenhall Market, and G—— confound you both eternally if you offer
to believe otherwise."[89] The brothers rebel, make "true copies" of the will
(vernacular translations of the Bible), and denounce Peter as an impostor;
whereupon he "kicked them out of doors, and would never let them come
under his roof from that day to this."[90] Soon thereafter the brothers quarrel
as to how much of their inherited coats they may discard or change. Martin,

after his first anger, resolves on moderation, and recalls that Peter is his brother; Jack, however, tears his coat to shreds (Calvinist sects), and falls into fits of madness and zeal. Swift proceeds to describe the strange operations of wind (inspiration) in the "Aeolists" (Calvinist preachers); and has much fun—some quite unprintable—with their nasal speech, predestination theories, and idolatry of the Scriptural word.[91]

So far the author's own creed, Anglicanism, had come off with only minor scars. But as the tale proceeds Swift, changing coats for winds, apparently reduces not only the Dissenting theologies but all religions and philosophies to vaporous delusions:

> If we take a survey of the greatest actions that have been performed in the world . . ., which are the establishment of new empires by conquest, the advance and progress of new schemes in philosophy, and the contriving, as well as the propagating, of new religions, we shall find the authors of them all to have been persons whose natural reason had admitted great revolutions, from their diet, their education, the prevalency of some certain temper, together with the particular influence of air and climate . . . For the human understanding, seated in the brain, must be troubled and overspread by vapors ascending from the lower faculties to water the invention and render it fruitful.[92]

Swift gives, in unquotable physiological detail, what seemed to him a fine example of internal secretions generating mighty ideas, even Henry IV's "Grand Design": the French King had been inspired to war against the Hapsburgs by the thought of capturing on the way a woman (Charlotte de Montmorency) whose beauty had stirred up in him sundry juices, "which ascended to the brain."[93] It was likewise with the great philosophers, who were rightly judged by their contemporaries to be "out of their wits."

> Of this kind were Epicurus, Diogenes, Apollonius, Lucretius, Paracelsus, Descartes, and others; who, if they were now in the world, . . . would, in this understanding age, incur manifest danger of phlebotomy [medical bleeding], and whips, and chains, and dark chambers, and straw. . . . Now I would gladly be informed how it is possible to account for such imaginations . . . without reference to . . . vapors ascending from the lower faculties to overshadow the brain, and there distilling into conceptions for which the narrowness of our mother-tongue has not yet assigned any other name beside that of madness or frenzy.[94]

To similar "disturbance or transposition of the brain by force of certain vapors issuing up from the lower faculties," Swift ascribes "all those

mighty revolutions that have happened in empire, philosophy, and religion."[95] He concludes that all systems of thought are winds of words,
and that the wise man will not attempt to pierce to the inner reality of
things, but will content himself with the surface; whereupon Swift uses
one of the pleasant similes to which he had a turn: "Last week I saw a
woman flayed, and you will hardly believe how much it altered her person
for the worse."[96]

This scandalous little book, blown up to 130 pages, established Swift
at once as a master of satire—a *Rabelais perfectionné*, Voltaire was to call
him. The allegory was verbally consistent with Swift's profession of
Anglican orthodoxy, but many readers felt that the author was a skeptic,
if not an atheist. Archbishop Sharp told Queen Anne that Swift was little
better than an infidel,[97] and Anne's confidante, the Duchess of Marlborough, was of opinion that Swift

> had long ago turned all religion into a Tale of a Tub and sold it for a
> jest. But he had taken it ill that the [Whig] ministry had not promoted
> him in the Church for the great zeal he had shown for religion by his
> profane drollery; and so [he] carried his atheism and his humor into
> service of their enemies.[98]

Steele too called Swift an infidel, and Nottingham, in the House of Commons, described him as a divine "who is hardly suspected of being a
Christian."[99] Swift had read Hobbes, an experience not easily forgotten.
Hobbes had begun with fear, passed to materialism, and ended as a Tory
supporting the Established Church. It was small consolation to the men
of religion that Swift made short work of philosophy:

> The various opinions of philosophers have scattered through the
> world as many plagues of the mind as Pandora's box did those of the
> body, only with this difference, that they have not left hope at the
> bottom . . . Truth is as hidden as the source of the Nile, and can be
> found only in Utopia.[100]

Perhaps because he felt that truth was not meant for man, he resented
with special warmth those religious sects that professed to have the "true
religion," and he scorned men who, like Bunyan and some Quakers, claimed
to have seen or talked with God. He concluded, with Hobbes, that it was
social suicide to let every man make his own religion; the result would
be such a maelstrom of absurdities that society would be a madhouse. So
he opposed free thought, on the ground that "the bulk of mankind is as
well qualified for flying as thinking."[101] He repudiated toleration. To the
end of his life he supported the Test Act, which excluded from political

or military office all but adherents of the Established Church.[102] He agreed with Catholic and Lutheran rulers that a nation should have only one religion; and, having been born into an England with an Established Anglican Church, he thought that a general and unified acceptance of that Church was indispensable to the process of civilizing Englishmen. These were the *Sentiments of a Church of England Man*, this the *Argument to Prove that the Abolishing of Christianity in England May . . . Be Attended with Some Inconveniences*—tracts which he published in 1708 on his way from the Whigs to the Tories.

His first political associations after leaving Temple were with the Whigs, for these seemed to be the more progressive party, and the likelier to find a place for a man with more brains than money. In 1701 he published a Whiggish pamphlet hopefully. Halifax, Sunderland, and other Whig leaders welcomed him to the party, and promised him some preferment should they come to power. The promises were not fulfilled; perhaps these men feared Swift's temper as unmanageable, and his pen as a double-edged sword. On an extended visit from Ireland to London in 1705 Swift won the friendship of Congreve, Addison, and Steele. Addison inscribed to him a copy of *Travels in Italy* with the words: "To Jonathan Swift, the most agreeable companion, the truest friend, and the greatest genius of his age, this work is presented by his most humble servant the author";[103] but this friendship, like those of Jonathan with Steele and Pope, withered in Swift's rising fire.

On another visit to London he amused himself by destroying a pretentious astrologer. John Partridge, a cobbler, sent forth each year an almanac rich in predictions based on the progress of the stars. In 1708 Swift issued a rival almanac under the pseudonym of Isaac Bickerstaff. One of Isaac's predictions was that at 11 P.M. on March 29 Partridge would die. On March 30 "Bickerstaff" published a letter triumphantly announcing that Partridge had died within a few hours of the predicted time, and stating in convincing detail the arrangements for the funeral. Partridge assured London that he was still alive, but Isaac retorted that this assurance was a forgery. The wits of the city took up the hoax; the Stationer's Office struck Partridge's name from its rolls; and Steele, inaugurating *The Tatler* in the following year, adopted Isaac Bickerstaff as its imaginary editor.

In 1710 Swift again left Laracor, this time as an emissary of the Irish bishops to ask that "Queen Anne's Bounty" be extended to the Anglican clergy of Ireland. Godolphin and Somers, Whig members of the Queen's Council, refused to grant this unless the clergy agreed to relax the Test Act. Swift strongly objected to such relaxation. The Whigs discovered that he was a Tory in religion, and Swift practically confessed himself a Tory in politics when he wrote: "I ever abominated that scheme of politics . . . of setting up a moneyed interest in opposition to the landed."[104] He applied to the Tory leaders, Harley and Bolingbroke, received a hearty welcome, and became overnight a confirmed Tory. Made editor of the Tory *Examiner,* Swift signalized his style by describing the Whig Lord Lieutenant of Ireland, whose secretary was Swift's friend Addison:

> Thomas, Earl of Wharton, . . . by the force of a wonderful constitution, has some years passed his grand climacteric without any visible effects of old age, either in his body or his mind; and in spite of a continual prostitution to those vices which usually wear out both. . . . He goes constantly to prayers . . . and will talk bawdy and blasphemy at the chapel door. He is a Presbyterian in politics, an atheist in religion; but he chooses at present to whore with a papist.[105]

Delighted with this assassination, the Tory ministers commissioned Swift to write a tract, *The Conduct of the Allies* (November, 1711), as part of their campaign to depose Marlborough and end the War of the Spanish Succession. Swift argued that the unpopular taxes levied to finance the long conflict with Louis XIV could be reduced by confining England's share in it to the sea; and he stated with force the complaint of the landholders that the cost of the war fell too much upon the land, too little upon the merchants and manufacturers, who were doing quite well out of the war. As to Marlborough: "Whether this war was prudently begun or not, it is plain that the true spring or motive of it was the aggrandizing a particular family, and in short a war of the General and the [Whig] ministry, and not of the Prince or people."[106] He summed up Marlborough's emoluments at £540,000—"and the figure was not inaccurate."[107] A month later Marlborough was condemned. His candid Duchess, who had the only tongue in England as sharp as Swift's, viewed the matter from the Whig point of view in her memoirs:

> The Rev. Mr. Swift and Mr. Prior quickly offered themselves to sale, . . . both men of wit and parts, ready to prostitute all they had in the service of well-rewarded scandal, being both of a composition past the weakness of blushing or of stumbling at anything for the interest of their new masters.[108]

These rewarded their new servants. Matthew Prior was sent as a diplomat to France, where he acquitted himself well. Swift received no office, but was now so intimate with the Tory ministers that he was able to secure many a sinecure for his friends. He was the genius of generosity to those who did not cross him. He claimed later that he had done fifty times more for fifty people than Temple had ever done for him.[109] He persuaded Bolingbroke to help the poet Gay. He saw to it that the Tory ministry should continue the pension that Congreve had received from the Whigs. When Pope asked for subscriptions to finance him while translating Homer, Swift commanded all his friends and place-seekers to subscribe, and vowed that "the author shall not begin to print till I have a thousand guineas for him."[110] He outshone Addison at the clubs. Almost every evening now he dined with the great, and brooked no superior airs from any of them. "I am so proud," he wrote to Stella, "that I make all the lords come up to me . . . I was to have supped at Lady Ashburnham's, but the drab did not call for us in her coach as she promised, but sent for us, and so I sent my excuses."[111]

It was during these three years (1710–13) in England that he wrote the strange letters published in 1766–68 as the *Journal to Stella*. He needed someone as the confidante of his ducal dinners and political victories; besides, he loved the patient woman, now approaching thirty, but still waiting for him to make up his mind. He must have loved her, for sometimes he wrote to her twice a day, and he showed his interest in everything about her except marriage. We should never have expected, from so overbearing a man, such playful delicacies and fanciful nicknames, such jokes and puns and baby talk as Swift, not expecting their publication, poured into these letters. They are rich in caresses but poor in proposals, unless Stella could have read a promise of marriage in his letter of May 23, 1711: "I will say no more, but beg you to be easy till Fortune takes her course and to believe that M.D.'s [Stella's] felicity is the greatest goal I aim at in all my pursuits."[112] Yet even in this correspondence he calls her "brat," "fool," "quean," "jade," "slut," "agreeable bitch," and other such terms of endearment. We catch the spirit of the man when he tells Stella:

> I was this forenoon with Mr. Secretary at his office, and helped to hinder a man of his pardon, who is condemned for a rape. The Under Secretary was willing to save him, upon an old notion that a woman cannot be ravished; but I told the Secretary that he could not pardon him without a favorable report from the judge; besides, he is a fiddler, and consequently a rogue, and deserved hanging for something else; and so he shall swing. What; I must stand up for the honor of the fair sex! 'Tis true, the fellow had lain with her a hundred times before; but what care I for that? What? Must a woman be ravished because she is a whore?[113]

Swift's physical ailments may help us to understand his ill-humor. As early as 1694, aged twenty-seven, he had begun to suffer from vertigo in the labyrinth of the ear; occasionally and incalculably he experienced fits of dizziness and deafness. A famous Dr. Radcliffe recommended a conplex liquid to be held in a bag inside Swift's wig. The malady became worse with the years, and may have caused his insanity. Probably in 1717 he said to the poet Edward Young, pointing to a withering tree, "I shall be like that tree: I shall die at the top."[114] This alone was enough to make him question the value of life, and certainly to doubt the wisdom of marriage. Probably he was impotent, but of this we have no certainty. He took to much walking to fend off physical decay; once he walked from Farnham to London—thirty-eight miles.

His malaise was heightened by a painful keenness of the senses, which often goes with sharpness of mind. He was especially sensitive to odors, in city streets and in human beings; he could tell at a smell the hygiene of the men and women whom he met; and he concluded that the human race stank.[115] His conception of a lovable woman was partly that

> No noisome Whiffs or sweating Streams
> Before, behind, above, below
> Could from her taintless body flow.[116]

He describes "A Beautiful Young Nymph Going to Bed," and then the same lady on arising:

> Corinna in the morning dizen'd
> Who sees, will spew, who smells, be poison'd.

And his conception of a nice young woman is olfactory:

> Her dearest comrades never caught her
> Squat on her hams to make Maid's water;
> You'd swear that so divine a creature
> Felt no necessities of nature.
> In summer, had she walked the town,
> Her armpits would not stain her gown;
> At country dances not a nose
> Could in the dog days smell her toes.[117]

He himself was finically clean. And yet the writings of this Anglican divine are among the coarsest in English literature. His anger at life made him fling his faults into the face of his time. He made no effort to please, and every effort to dominate, for domination comforted his secret uncertainty of himself. He said that he hated (feared) all those whom he could not command;[118] this, however, was not true of his affection for Harley. He was angry in adversity, and arrogant in success. He loved power more than money; when Harley sent him fifty pounds for his articles he returned the bank note, demanded an apology, received it, and wrote to Stella, "I have taken Mr. Harley into favor again."[119] He resented formality, and despised cant. The world seemed bent on defeating him, and he frankly returned its hostility. He wrote to Pope:

> The chief end I propose to myself in all my labors is to vex the world rather than divert it; and if I could compass that design without hurting my own person or fortune, I would be the most indefatigable writer you have ever seen . . . When you think of the world, give it one lash the more at my request. I have ever hated all nations, professions, and communities, and all my love is towards individuals . . . I hate the tribe of lawyers, but I love Councillor Such-a-one and Judge Such-a-one; so with physicians (I will not speak of my own trade), soldiers, English, Scotch, French, and the rest. But principally I hate and detest that animal called man—although I heartily love John, Peter, Thomas, and so forth.[120]

He appears at this distance the least lovable of men, and yet two women loved him to their deaths. During these years in London he lived near a Mrs. Vanhomrigh, a rich widow with two sons and two daughters. When he could not secure an invitation to titled tables he dined with the "Vans." The eldest daughter, Hester, then (1711) twenty-four, fell in love with him, forty-three, and told him so. He tried to pass this off as a transient humor, and explained that he was too old for her; she replied, hopefully, that he had in his books taught her to love great men (she read Montaigne at her toilet), and why should she not love a great man when she found him in the flesh? He was half melted. He composed a poem, intended for her eyes only, *Cadenus and Vanessa*, humorous and tragical. Vanessa was his name for her; Cadenus was an anagram for *decanus*, dean.

For in April, 1713, the Queen had reluctantly appointed him dean of St. Patrick's Cathedral in Dublin. In June he went to Ireland to be installed. He saw Stella, and wrote to Vanessa that he was dying of melancholy and discontent.[121] He returned to London (October, 1713), and shared in the debacle of the Tories in 1714. Politically powerless now that the Whigs whom he had attacked were triumphant under George I, he went back to hated Ireland and his deanery. He was unpopular in Dublin, for the Whigs who now ruled it hated him for his diatribes, and the Dissenters hated him for his insistence on excluding them from office. People hissed and booed him in the streets, and pelted him with gutter filth.[122] An Anglican clergyman expressed the view of his cloth in a poem which was nailed to the cathedral door:

> Today this temple gets a Dean,
>   Of parts and fame uncommon;

Used both to pray and to profane,
　　To serve both God and Mammon . . .
The place he got by wit and rhyme,
　　And many ways most odd,
And might a bishop be in time
　　Did he believe in God.[123]

He stood his ground bravely, continued to support the Tories, and offered to share Harley's imprisonment in the Tower. He attended to his religious duties, preached regularly, administered the sacraments, lived simply, and gave a third of his income in charity. On Sundays he held open house; Stella then came to play hostess for him. Soon his unpopularity waned. In 1724 he published, under the pseudonym of M. B. Drapier, six letters denouncing the attempt of William Wood to make a large profit out of supplying Ireland with a copper currency. The Irish resented the proposal, and when "Drapier" was discovered to be Swift, the gloomy Dean became almost popular.

He might have had some moments of happiness had he been able to keep the Irish Channel between the two women who loved him. In 1714 Mrs. Vanhomrigh died, and "Vanessa" moved to Ireland to occupy a small property bequeathed to her by her father at Celbridge, eleven miles west of the capital. To be nearer the Dean, she took a lodging in Turnstile Alley, Dublin, a short distance from where Stella lived. She wrote to Swift, begging him to visit her, and warned him that if he failed to come she would die of grief. He could not resist her appeal, and now (1714–23) he went repeatedly and clandestinely to see her. When his visits became less frequent, her letters became more ardent. She had been born, she told him, with "violent passions, which terminate all in one, that inexpressible passion I have for you." It would be useless, she told him, to try to turn her love to God; for "was I an enthusiast, still you'd be the deity I should worship."[124]

Perhaps he thought to break through this imprisoning triangle by marrying; perhaps Stella, conscious of a rival, demanded it as simple justice; and the balance of the evidence is that he did marry Stella in 1716.[125] Apparently he required her to keep the marriage secret; she continued to live apart; and probably the union was never consummated. Swift resumed his visits to Vanessa; not that he was merely a philanderer or altogether a brute, but presumably because he had not the heart to leave her hopeless, or he feared her suicide. His letters assured Vanessa that he loved and valued her above all things, and would do so to the end of his life. So the affair went on till 1723; then Vanessa wrote to Stella asking her point blank what was her connection with the Dean. Stella took the letter to Swift. He rode to Vanessa's lodging, flung the letter down upon her table, terrified her with his angry looks, and, without a word, left her, never to see her again.

When Vanessa recovered from her fright she realized at last that he had been deceiving her. Hopelessness combined with a consumptive tendency to destroy what was left of her health; and within two months of that last interview she died (June 2, 1723), aged thirty-four. She took revenge in her will: she revoked an earlier testament that had made Swift her heir; she bequeathed her goods to Robert Marshall and George Berkeley, the philosopher; and she bade them publish, without comment, Swift's letters to her, and his poem *Cadenus and Vanessa*. Swift fled on an obscure "southern journey" in Ireland, and did not reappear in his cathedral until four months after Vanessa's death.

When he returned he gave his leisure to composing the most famous and savage satire ever directed against mankind. He wrote to Charles Ford that he was engaged upon a book that would "wonderfully rend the world."[126] A year later it was complete, and he took the manuscript in person to London, arranged for its anonymous publication, accepted two hundred pounds for it, and went to Pope's house in Twickenham to enjoy the expected storm. So in October, 1726, England received the *Travels into Several Remote Nations of the World by Lemuel Gulliver*. The first public reaction was one of delight with the circumstantial realism of the narrative. Many readers took it as history, though one Irish bishop (said Swift) thought it full of improbabilities. Most readers went no further than the voyages to Lilliput and Brobdingnag, which were jolly narratives usefully illustrating the relativity of judgments. The Lilliputians were only six inches tall, and gave Gulliver a swelling sense of superiority. Political parties there were distinguished from each other by wearing high heels or low heels, and the religious factions were Big-Endians or Little-Endians as they believed in breaking eggs at the big end or the small end. The Brobdingnagians were sixty feet tall, giving Gulliver a new perspective of humanity. Their king mistook him for an insect, Europe for an anthill; and from Gulliver's description of human ways he concluded that "the bulk of your natives [are] the most pernicious race of little odious vermin that nature ever suffered to crawl upon the surface of the earth."[127] For his part Gulliver (suggesting the relativity of beauty) was repelled by the "monstrous breasts" of the Brobdingnagian belles.

The story weakens in Gulliver's third voyage. He is pulled up by chain and bucket to Laputa, an island floating in the air and inhabited and governed by scientists, scholars, inventors, professors, and philosophers; here the details that elsewhere lent verisimilitude to the narrative are a bit silly, like the little bladders with which servants tap the ears and mouths of the profound thinkers to rouse them from dangerous absent-mindedness in their cogitations. The Academy of Lagado, with its fanciful inventions and decrees, is a feeble satire on Bacon's *New Atlantis* and the Royal Society of London. Swift had no faith in the reform or rule of states by scientists; he laughed at their theories, and the early mortality thereof; and he predicted the overthrow of the Newtonian cosmology: "New systems of nature were but new fashions, which would vary in every age; and even those who pretend to demonstrate them from mathematical principles [*Principia Mathematica*, 1687] would flourish but a short period of time."[128]

So Gulliver moves on to the land of Luggnaggians, who condemn their greatest criminals not to death but to immortality. When these "Struldbrugs"

> came to fourscore years, which is reckoned the extremity of living in their country, they had not only all the follies and infirmities of other old men, but many more, which arose from the dreadful prospects of never dying. They were not only opinionative, peevish, covetous, morose, vain, talkative; but incapable of friendship, and dead to all natural affection, which never descended below their grandchildren. Envy and impotent desires are their prevailing passions. . . . Whenever they see a funeral, they lament and repine that others are gone to an harbor of rest, to which they themselves never can hope to arrive. . . . They were the most mortifying sight I ever beheld, and the women more horrible than the men. . . . From what I had heard and seen, my keen appetite for perpetuity of life was much abated.[129]

In Part IV Swift discarded humor for a sardonic excoriation of humanity. The land of the Houyhnhnms is governed by clean, handsome, genial horses, who speak, reason, and have all the marks of civilization, while their menial servants, the Yahoos, are men dirty, odorous, greedy, drunken, irrational, and deformed. Among these degenerates (wrote Swift in the days of George I)

> there was a . . . ruling Yahoo [king] who was always more deformed in body, and mischievous in disposition, than any of the rest. . . . This leader had usually a favorite as like himself as he could get, whose employment was to lick his master's feet . . . and drive the female Yahoos to his kennel; for which he was now and then rewarded with a piece of ass's flesh [title of nobility?]. . . . He usually continues in office till a worse can be found.[130]

By contrast the Houyhnhnms, being reasonable, are happy and virtuous; therefore they need no physicians, lawyers, clergymen, or generals. These gentlemanly horses are shocked by Gulliver's account of Europe's wars, and still more by the disputes that generated them—as "whether flesh be bread, or bread be flesh [in the Eucharist]; whether the juice of a certain berry be blood or wine";[131] and they cut Gulliver short when he boasts how many human beings could now be blown up by the marvelous inventions which his race has invented.

When Gulliver returns to Europe he can hardly bear the smell of the streets and the people, who now all seem to be Yahoos.

> My wife and family received me with great surprise and joy, because they [had] concluded me certainly dead; but I must freely confess that the sight of them filled me only with hatred, disgust, and contempt . . . As soon as I entered the house my wife took me in her arms, and kissed me; at which, having not been used to the touch of that odious animal [man] for so many years, I fell in a swoon for almost an hour. . . . During the first year I could not endure my wife or children in my presence, the very smell of them was intolerable . . . The first money I laid out was to buy two young . . . horses, which I keep in a good stable; and next to them the groom is my greatest favorite, for I feel my spirit revived by the smell he contracts in the stable.[132]

The success of *Gulliver* exceeded the author's dreams, and might have mollified his olfactory misanthropy. Readers enjoyed the spare and limpid English, the circumstantial details, the hilarious obscenities. Arbuthnot predicted for the book "as great a run as John Bunyan"—i.e., as for *Pilgrim's Progress*. Doubtless Swift owed something to that book, more to *Robinson Crusoe*, something, perhaps, to Cyrano de Bergerac's *Histoires comiques des états et empire de la lune*. What was quite new was the awful cynicism of the later parts, and even this found admirers. Marlborough's Duchess, now in her rasping old age, forgave Swift his attacks upon her husband in consideration of his attacks upon mankind. Swift, she declared, had given "the most accurate account of kings, ministers, bishops, and courts of justice that is possible to be writ." Gay reported that she "is in raptures with the book, and can dream of nothing else."[133]

Swift's triumph was soured by the publication, in the same year as *Gulliver*, of his poem *Cadenus and Vanessa*. Hester Vanhomrigh's executors had obeyed her injunction to print it, and had not asked the author's permission. It appeared in separate editions in London, Dublin, and Edinburgh. It was a cruel blow to Stella, for she saw how many of the loving phrases once addressed to her had been repeated to Vanessa. Shortly after that revelation she took sick. Swift crossed to Ireland to comfort her; she improved, and he returned to England (1727). Soon news came to him that she was dying. He sent hurried instructions to his cathedral aides that

"Stella must not die in the Deanery."[134] He came back to Dublin, and once more she rallied; but on January 28, 1728, she died, aged forty-seven. Swift broke down, and was too ill to attend her funeral.

Thereafter he lived in Dublin (as he wrote to Bolingbroke) "like a poisoned rat in a hole."[135] He extended his charities, gave a pension to Mrs. Dingley, and helped Richard Sheridan in his youthful scrapes. Apparently a cruel man, he was touched to bitter wrath by the poverty of the Irish people, and was shocked by the number of child beggars in Dublin's streets. In 1729 he issued the most ferocious of his ironies: *A Modest Proposal for Preventing the Children of Poor People from Being a Burden to Their Parents or Country.*

> I have been assured . . . that a young healthy child well nursed, is, at a year old, a most delicious, nourishing, and wholesome food, whether stewed, roasted, baked, or boiled; and I make no doubt that it will equally serve in a fricassee or ragout. I do therefore humbly offer it to public consideration, that of the hundred and twenty thousand children already computed, twenty thousand may be reserved for breed, whereof only one fourth part to be males . . . That the remaining hundred thousand may, at a year old, be offered in sale to the persons of quality and fortune throughout the Kingdom; always advising the mother to let them suck plentifully in the last month, so as to render them plump and fat for a good table. A child will make two dishes at an entertainment for friends; and when the family dines alone, the fore or hind quarter will make a reasonable dish, and, seasoned with a little pepper or salt, will be very good . . .
>
> Those who are more thrifty . . . may flay the carcass, the skin of which, artificially dressed, will make admirable gloves for ladies, and summer boots for fine gentlemen. . . .
>
> Some persons of desponding spirit are in great concern about that vast number of poor people who are aged, diseased, or maimed; and I have been desired to employ my thoughts, what course may be taken to ease the nation of so grievous an encumbrance. But I am not in the least pain upon that matter; because it is very well known that they are every day dying and rotting, by cold and famine, and filth and vermin, as fast as can be reasonably expected. . . .
>
> I think the advantages [of] the proposal which I have made are obvious and many . . . For first, . . . it would greatly lessen the number of Papists with whom we are yearly overrun, being the principal breeders of the nation, as well as our most dangerous enemies . . . Thirdly, whereas the maintenance of an hundred thousand children, from two years old and upward, cannot be computed at less than ten shillings a piece per annum, the nation's stock will be thereby increased fifty thousand pounds per annum, besides the profit of a new

dish introduced to the tables of all gentlemen of fortune . . . who have any refinement in taste . . .

The strange and sometimes revolting productions of Swift's pen, especially after Stella's death, suggest the germs of insanity. "A person of great honor in Ireland (who was pleased to stoop so low as to look into my mind) used to tell me that my mind was like a conjured spirit, that would do mischief if I would not give it employment."[136] This unhappy misanthrope, whose visible faults left him in a glass house while he pelted humanity with vengeful satire, asked a friend, "Do not the corruptions and villainies of men eat your flesh and exhaust your spirit?"[137] His anger at the world was an extension of his anger at himself; he knew that despite his genius he was diseased in body and soul, and he could not forgive life for having denied him health, normal organs, peace of mind, and advancement proportionate to his mental power.

Life's cruelty to him took its final form in the day-by-day impairment of his sanity. After 1728 his avarice grew even amid his charities; he grudged the food he fed to his guests, and the wine he served to his friends.[138] His vertigo became worse, and he could never tell at what inauspicious moment it might send him reeling in his chancel or in the street. He had refused to wear spectacles; now his sight was so poor that he had to give up reading. Some of his friends died, some shunned his temper and gloom. "I have often thought of death," he wrote to Bolingbroke, "but now it is never out of my mind,"[139] and he began to long for it. He kept his birthday as a day of mourning. "No wise man," he wrote, "ever wished to be younger."[140] His regular farewell to his visitors, in these final years, was, "Good night; I hope I shall never see you again."[141]

Definite symptoms of madness appeared in 1738. In 1741 guardians were appointed to take care of his affairs and watch lest in his outbursts of violence he should do himself harm. In 1742 he suffered great pain from the inflammation of his left eye, which swelled to the size of an egg; five attendants had to restrain him from tearing out his eye. He went a whole year without uttering a word. His misery ended on October 19, 1745, in his seventy-eighth year. His will left his fortune, twelve thousand pounds, to build an insane asylum. He was buried in his own cathedral, under an epitaph chosen by himself:

> *Ubi saeva indignatio*
> *Cor ulterius lacerare nequit*

—"where bitter indignation can no longer tear his heart."

BOOK III

THE PERIPHERY

1648–1715

CHAPTER XII

The Struggle for the Baltic

1648–1721

I. ADVENTUROUS SWEDEN: 1648–1700

HISTORY is a fragment of biology—the human moment in the pageant of species. It is also a child of geography—the operation of land and sea and air, and of their forms and products, upon human desire and destiny. See again the confrontation of countries around the Baltic in the seventeenth century: on its north, Sweden; on its east, Esthonia, Livonia, Lithuania, and, behind them, cold and hungry Russia; on its south, East Prussia, Poland, West Prussia, Germany; and on its west, Denmark, with its strategic place on the narrow outlets of the Baltic to the North Sea and the Atlantic. This was a geographical prison, whose inmates would struggle to control those waters and straits, those coasts and ports, those avenues of commerce and escape by land or sea. Here geography created history.

Denmark played now a minor role in the Baltic drama. Its freedom-monopolizing nobles had tied the hands and feet of its kings. It had surrendered control of the Skagerrak and the Kattegat (1645); it still held Norway, but in 1660 it lost the southern provinces of Sweden. Frederick III (1648–70) felt the need of a centralized authority to meet external challenges, and with the help of the clergy and the middle classes he compelled the nobles to yield him absolute and hereditary power. His son Christian V (1670–99) found in Peder Schumacher, Count Griffenfeld, an aide who won the praise of Louis XIV as one of the ablest ministers in that heyday of diplomacy. The finances were reformed, trade and industry were advanced, the army and navy were reorganized. The Count pursued a policy of peace, but the new King longed to recover the power and provinces that Denmark had once held. In 1675 he renewed the old conflict with Sweden. He was defeated, and the sovereignty of Sweden in Scandinavia was confirmed.

Sweden in this period had a remarkable succession of strong kings; for half a century (1654–1718) they were the wonder of the world, rivaled only by Louis XIV. Had they possessed a larger background of resources they might have equaled the power of France, and the Swedish people, inspired by the achievements of two Gustavs, three Karls, and their great ministers, might have financed a cultural flowering commensurate with their victories and aspirations. But the wars that exalted their power exhausted their wealth, and Sweden emerged from this age heroic but consumed. It is astonishing that a nation so weak should have accomplished so much abroad. She had a population of 1,500,000, divided into classes that had not yet learned to live with one another in peace. The nobles dominated the king, and voted themselves crown lands on easy terms. Industry was so bound and narrowed to the needs of war that it could not feed the commerce that war had freed. Foreign possessions were a proud liability. Only the statesmanship of devoted ministers staved off the bankruptcy that seemed to be the price of glory.

Charles X Gustavus was the cousin, playmate, lover, and successor of the redoubtable Christina, who had resigned the throne to him in 1654. He met the danger of bankruptcy by compelling the nobles to disgorge some of the royal estates that they had absorbed. By this "reduction" of seignorial holdings the state regained three thousands homesteads, and solvency. To supplement the coinage of silver and gold, Charles commissioned Johann Palmstruh to establish a national bank and issue paper money (1656)—the first such currency in Europe. For a while the increased circulation stimulated the economy, but the bank issued more paper than it could redeem on demand, and the experiment was discontinued. About the same time the enterprising monarch transplanted the iron and steel industry of Riga to Sweden, and so laid the foundations of a stronger industrial basis for his martial policy.

His aim was frankly expansionist. The principalities that Gustavus Adolphus had won on the mainland were threatening revolt. The Polish government had refused to recognize Charles X as King of Sweden, but Poland was weakened by the Cossack rebellion. Russia had come to the aid of the Cossacks, and was obviously hoping to cut a way to the Baltic. Sweden had a well-trained army, which it feared to demobilize and could best support by victorious war. All the conditions, in Charles's view, favored an attack upon Poland. The peasants and the clergy objected; he won them over by calling his enterprise a holy war to protect and extend the Reformation (1655).[1]

Poland proved easy to invade, difficult to subdue. Disordered and assailed in the east, it made little resistance in the west. Charles entered Warsaw, appeased the Polish nobles by promising to preserve their traditional privileges, received the homage of the Polish Protestants, and the offer of the Lithuanians to acknowledge his sovereignty. When Frederick William, the "Great Elector" of Brandenburg, tried to profit from Poland's collapse by seizing West Prussia (then a Polish fief), Charles marched his army westward with Napoleonic celerity, besieged the Elector in his capital, and forced him to sign the Treaty of Königsberg (January, 1656). The Elector did homage to Charles for East Prussia as a Swedish fief, agreed to turn over to Sweden half of that province's customs and dues, and promised to supply fifteen hundred soldiers to the Swedish army.

The religious issue which Charles had raised defeated him. Pope Alexander VII and the Emperor Ferdinand III used all their influence to raise up an anti-Swedish coalition; even the Protestant Danes and Dutch joined in the resolve to check the young conqueror lest he should next impinge upon their territory or trade. He rushed back to Poland, defeated a new Polish force, and reoccupied Warsaw (July, 1656). But now the country, religiously aroused, took up arms against him, and Charles, triumphant but friendless, found himself hemmed in by foes. The Elector of Brandenburg deserted him and pledged aid to Poland. Knowing only how to win battles, not how to consolidate his conquests in a practicable peace, Charles swept westward against Denmark, crossed the Kattegat over thirteen miles of ice (January, 1658), defeated the Danes, and compelled Frederick III to sign the Peace of Roskilde (February 27). Denmark withdrew completely from the Swedish peninsula, and agreed to close the Sound against Sweden's enemies. When the Danes delayed to carry out these terms Charles renewed the war, and besieged Copenhagen. Now he resolved to dethrone Frederick III and reunite Denmark, Sweden, and Norway under one crown.

He was defeated by sea power. The two great naval nations of the age, England and the United Provinces, normally enemies, agreed that no country should hold the key to the Baltic by controlling the Sound between Denmark and Sweden. In October a Dutch squadron forced its way through the Sound, relieved Copenhagen, and drove the small Swedish fleet into its home ports. Charles vowed to fight to the last. But the rigors of his campaigns had told upon him. While he was addressing the Swedish Diet at Göteborg he was seized with fever. He died shortly thereafter (February 13, 1660), in the prime of his life.

As his son Charles XI (1660–97) was only five years old, a Regency of nobles took charge, and brought the war to a close with the Peace of Oliva and the Treaty of Copenhagen (May, June, 1660). The Polish monarchy surrendered its claim to the Swedish crown; Livonia was confirmed to Sweden; Brandenburg received full title to East Prussia; Sweden retained her southern counties (Skåne) and her mainland provinces (Bremen, Verden, and Pomerania), but she joined Denmark in guaranteeing the access of foreign vessels to the Baltic. A year later Sweden and Poland signed at Kardis a halfhearted peace with the Czar. For fifteen years the struggle for the Baltic proceeded by other means than war.

These treaties were a substantial victory for Sweden, but she was again verging on bankruptcy. Two members of the Regency, Gustav Bonde and Per Brahe, labored to check governmental expenditures, but Magnus de la

Gardie, the Chancellor, added new debts to old ones, allowed the nobility, his friends, and himself to profit at the expense of the treasury, and, for a subsidy, allied Sweden with France (1672) only a few days before Louis XIV pounced upon Sweden's ally, the United Provinces. Soon Sweden found herself at war with Denmark, Brandenburg, and Holland. She suffered defeat by the Great Elector at Fehrbellin (June 18, 1675), her mainland provinces were overrun by her enemies, a Danish army reconquered Skåne, and the Swedish navy met disaster off Öland (June 1, 1676).

The young Charles XI, taking control, rescued Sweden by a series of campaigns in which his personal bravery so inspired his troops that they routed the Danes at Lund and Landskrona. Through these victories, and support by Louis XIV, Sweden recovered all that she had lost. A new hero of Swedish diplomacy, Count Johan Gyllenstierna, co-operated with Count Griffenfeld to arrange at Lund (1679) not only peace but a military and commercial alliance between Sweden and Denmark. They agreed to a common coinage, and the union of all Scandinavia was close to complete when the death of Gyllenstierna at the age of forty-five (1680), interrupted this development. The two nations preserved the peace for twenty years.

Gyllenstierna had taught the young King that Sweden would be unable to maintain her status as a great power if her nobles continued to absorb crown lands, thereby depressing the monarchy to poverty and the state to impotence. In 1682 Charles XI took decisive action. Supported by the clergy, the peasants, and the burghers, he resumed with angry thoroughness the "reduction," or restoration, of alienated royal estates. He investigated and punished official corruption, and brought the revenues of the government to a point where Sweden was again able to maintain her possessions and responsibilities. Charles XI was not a very lovable king, but he was a great one. Though he made an enviable record in war, he preferred the less noisy victories of peace. He established monarchical absolutism, but that was then the alternative to a chaotic and retrogressive feudalism.

In the calm of this lucid interval science, literature, and art flourished in Sweden. Swedish architecture reached its zenith in the erection of the massive and majestic royal palace at Stockholm, designed (1693–97) by Nicodemus Tessin. Lars Johansson was both the Leopardi and the Marlowe of Sweden, singing melodious misanthropy, and stabbed to death in a tavern brawl at the age of thirty-six. Gunno Dahlstierna composed in Dante's meter an epic, *Kunga-Skald* (1697), in honor of Charles XI. The King died in that year, after saving and rebuilding a Sweden that his more famous son almost destroyed.

Charles XII was now fifteen. As the map of Europe was being remade by blood and iron, he had been trained above all for war. All his sports prepared him for martial deeds; he learned mathematics as a branch of military science; and he read enough Latin to derive from Qintus Curtius' biography of Alexander the ambition to excel in arms, if not to conquer the world. Tall, handsome, strong, with no surplus ounce of flesh to burden him, he enjoyed a soldier's life, bore its privations stoically, laughed at danger and death, and demanded the same hardihood of his troops. He cared little for women, and though often courted, he never married. He hunted bears with no other weapon than a heavy wooden fork; rode his horses at reckless speed, swam in waters that were half covered with ice, and relished sham battles in which, time and again, he and his friends were nearly killed. Along with fanatical bravery and physical stamina went certain qualities of character and intellect: a candor scorning the tricks of diplomacy; a sense of honor blemished by exceptional moments of wild cruelty; a mind clear to see the point of a matter at once, but impatient of indirect approaches in thought or strategy; a taciturn pride that never forgot his royal birth and never acknowledged defeat. At his coronation he crowned himself, Napoleonwise; he took no oath limiting his power; and when a clergyman questioned the wisdom of conferring absolute authority upon a youth of fifteen, Charles at first condemned him to death, then commuted the sentence to life imprisonment.

At his accession Sweden was a major Continental power, ruling Finland, Ingria, Esthonia, Livonia, Pomerania, and Bremen; she controlled the Baltic, and kept Russia from access to that sea. Russia, Poland, Brandenburg, and Denmark saw in the youthfulness of the Swedish King an opportunity to extend their boundaries to the advantage of their commerce and revenues. The catalytic agent in this geographical solution was a Livonian knight, Johann von Patkul. As a subject of Sweden he had entered its army and had risen to a captaincy. In 1689 and 1692 he protested so forcefully against Charles XI's "reduction" of estates in Livonia that he was charged with treason. He escaped to Poland, asked Charles XII to pardon him, was refused, and in 1698 proposed to Augustus II of Poland and Saxony a coalition of Poland, Saxony, Brandenburg, Denmark and Russia against Sweden. Augustus thought the plan timely, and took the first step by entering into alliance with Denmark's Frederick IV (September 25, 1699). Patkul proceeded to Moscow. On November 22 Peter the Great signed with the envoys of Saxony and Denmark an agreement for the dismemberment of Sweden.

II. POLAND AND SOBIESKI: 1648–99

Two events at the outset of this period deeply influenced Polish history. In 1652, for the first time, a single member of the Sejm defeated a measure by exercising the *liberum veto*, which allowed any delegate in that parliament to overrule any majority. Formerly the consent of all the provinces had been required for the passage of any measure, and sometimes a small minority had made legislation impossible; but no individual had yet asserted the right to veto a proposal acceptable to all the rest. Forty-eight of the fifty-five sessions of the Sejm after 1652 were "exploded" or terminated by the "free veto" of a single deputy. The plan supposed that no majority could justly override a minority, however small. It rose not out of popular theory but out of feudal pride; every landowner considered himself supreme on his lands. The result was a maximum of local independence and collective futility. As the kings were subject to the Sejm, and this to the *liberum veto*, a consistent national policy was usually impossible. Nine years after that first veto King John Casimir made a remarkable prediction to the Sejm:

> Would God I may prove a false prophet! But I tell you that if you do not find a remedy for the present evil [the *liberum veto*] the republic will become the prey of foreign countries. The Muscovites will attempt to detach our Russian Palatinates perhaps as far as the Vistula. The House of Prussia . . . will try to seize Great Poland. Austria will hurl herself upon Cracow. Each of these Powers will prefer to partition Poland rather than possess the whole of it with such liberties as it enjoys today.[2]

This prediction was almost literally fulfilled.

Next only to this veto in historical importance was the revolt of the Cossacks in the Ukraine (1648). The consolidation of Lithuania with Poland in the Union of Lublin (1569) had brought under chiefly Polish rule the Dnieper region of the Ukraine, largely peopled by Zaporogue Cossacks accustomed to independence and war. Polish nobles, buying land in this western Ukraine, sought to establish feudal conditions there, and Polish Catholics discouraged the exercise of that freedom which the Union of Lublin had guaranteed to the Orthodox worship. Out of a now inextricable complex of dissatisfactions a Cossack rebellion took form, led for a time by a rich hetman, Bogdan Chmielnicki, and supported by the Moslem Tatars of the Crimea. On May 26, 1648, the Cossacks and the Tatars routed the main Polish army at Korsun, and enthusiasm for the revolt spread among rich and poor alike.

Meanwhile the death of Ladislas IV on May 20 had left the throne of Poland to noble debate that lasted till November 20, when the electoral Diet chose John II Casimir. Chmielnicki, fearing that the revolt could maintain itself against renewed Polish armies only by accepting alien aid and suzerainty, cast in his lot with Orthodox Russia. He offered the Ukraine to Czar Alexis; the Russian government, quite aware that this meant war with Poland, welcomed the offer; and by the "Act of Pereyaslav", January 18, 1654, the Ukraine passed under Russian rule. The region was guaranteed local autonomy under a hetman elected by the Cossacks and ratified by the Czar.

In the ensuing war between Poland and Russia the Crimean Tatars, preferring a Polish to a Russian Ukraine, shifted their aid from the Cossacks to the Poles. On August 8, 1655, the Russians took Wilno, massacred thousands of the inhabitants, and burned the city to the ground. While the Poles defended themselves on their eastern front, Charles X led a Swedish army into western Poland and took Warsaw (September 8). Polish resistance to him collapsed. The Polish gentry, even the Polish army, paid homage and swore allegiance to the conqueror.[3] Cromwell sent him congratulations on having seized one of the pope's horns,[4] and Charles assured the Protector that soon there would not be a papist left in Poland;[5] nevertheless he promised religious toleration in Poland.

His plans were frustrated by his victorious army. Escaping control, it pillaged towns, massacred inhabitants, despoiled churches and monasteries. The famous Monastery of Jasna Gora, near Częstochowa, stoutly resisted siege; this success, regarded as a miracle, aroused the religious ardor of the populace; the Catholic priests appealed to the nation to expel the impious invaders; peasants led the way in taking up arms; the garrison that Charles had left in Warsaw fled before the advancing crowd; John Casimir was restored to his capital (June 16, 1656). The Tatars turned against Russia, and Russia, preferring Poland to Sweden as a neighbor, signed a truce with Poland (1656). The sudden death of Charles X led to the Peace of Oliva (May 3, 1660), ending the war between Poland and Sweden. In 1659 the struggle with Russia was resumed. After eight years of chaos, campaigns, and vacillations of Cossack loyalty, the Peace of Andrusovo (January 20, 1667) ceded Smolensk, Kiev, and the Ukraine east of the Dnieper to Russia. This division of the Ukraine endured till the first partition of Poland (1772).

Tired of war and the *liberum veto*, John Casimir abdicated the Polish throne (1668), retired to Nevers in France, and lived a quiet life of study and prayer until his death (1672). His successor, Michael Wiśniowiecki, fought a disastrous war with the Turks; by the Peace of Buczacz (1672) Poland acknowledged Turkish sovereignty over the western Ukraine, and pledged an annual tribute of 220,000 ducats to the sultans. In that war Poland discovered the military genius of Jan Sobieski; and when Wiśniowiecki died (1673), the Diet, after the usual costly delay, elected Poland's greatest King (1674).

Jan—now John III—was already forty-four years old. He had had a propitious origin as son of the castellan (military governor) at Cracow; his mother was the granddaughter of the Polish general Stanislas Zólkiewski who had captured Moscow in 1610; Jan had arms in his blood. Education at the University of Cracow, travels in Germany, the Netherlands, England, and France, with almost a year in Paris, made him a man of culture as well as of martial courage and skill. In 1648 his father died, shortly after being chosen to represent Poland at the Peace of Westphalia. Jan hurried home, and joined the Polish army in action against the Cossack revolt. When the Swedes invaded Poland, and John Casimir fled, Sobieski was among the many Polish officials who accepted Charles X as King of Poland, and for a year he served in the Swedish army. But when the Poles rose against the invaders Sobieski came back to his national allegiance, and fought so well for his country that in 1665 he was made commander in chief of the Polish armies. In that year he married the remarkable woman who became half of his life and molder of his career.

Maria Kazimiera, of royal French blood, was born at Nevers in 1641, and brought up in France and Poland. At Warsaw, when she was thirteen, her vivacious beauty inflamed Sobieski, then twenty-five. But the fortunes of war took him away, and when he returned he found her married to Jan Zamojski, a noble debauchee. Neglected by her husband, Maria accepted Sobieski as her *cavaliere servente*. Apparently she kept her marriage vows, but she promised to marry Sobieski as soon as she could have her union with Zamojski annulled. The husband made this unnecessary by dying; the lovers were soon wed; and their long love became a legend in Polish history. Many Polish women rivaled the French in combining classic beauty of features with an almost masculine courage and intelligence, and a penchant for making or guiding kings. From the day of their marriage Maria began to plan the elevation of Sobieski to the throne.

Her love was sometimes unscrupulous, as love can be. In 1669 Sobieski seems to have accepted French money to support a French cardinal against Wiśniowiecki. After Michael's election Jan joined other nobles in plots to depose the King as a coward unfit and unwilling to defend Poland against the Turks. He himself led his men to four victories within ten days. On November 11, 1673, the day of the King's death, Sobieski routed the Turks at Khotin in Bessarabia. The achievement made him a logical candidate for a throne that only the most resolute arms could now maintain against foes on every side. To reinforce logic he appeared at the electoral Diet at the head of six thousand troops. French money played a part in his election, but this was quite in the mores of the age.

He was a king in body and soul as well as in name. Foreigners described him as "one of the handsomest and best-built men" in Europe, "of proud and noble visage, eyes of light and fire,"[6] physically strong, venereally assiduous, mentally curious and alive. His natural acquisitiveness was spurred by the extravagance of his beloved Marysienka, but he often atoned for a parsimonious Sejm by paying his soldiers out of his own pocket, and selling his property to buy them guns.[7] He deserved all that he took, for he saved both Poland and Europe.

His foreign policy was simple in aim: to drive the Turks into Asia, or at least to repel their attacks upon the bastion of Western Christendom at

Vienna. In this effort he was harassed by the alliance of his ally France with the Sultan, and by the attempts of the Emperor to embroil him in Turkish wars; Leopold I hoped thus to leave Austria free to appropriate Danubian or Hungarian territory to which both Austria and Poland laid claim. Treading angrily through the maze, Sobieski longed for the freedom to plan policy and issue directives without being subject at every step to the Sejm and the *liberum veto*. He envied the power of Louis XIV and the Emperor to make decisions definitely and to issue orders accordingly and immediately.

Soon after his election he undertook to recover the western Ukraine from the Turks, who had now advanced as far north as Lvov. There, with only five thousand cavalry, he defeated twenty thousand Turks (August 24, 1675). By the Treaty of Zuravno (October 17, 1676) he compelled the Turks to surrender their claim to tribute, and to acknowledge Polish suzerainty in the western Ukraine. He felt that the opportunity had come to expel the Ottoman power from Europe. He appealed to Leopold to join with him in war *à l'outrance* against the Turks; but Leopold objected that he had no assurance that if he sent his armies to the east, Louis XIV would not attack him in the west. Sobieski begged France to give Austria such assurance; Louis refused.[8] Sobieski turned more and more toward alliance with Austria. When French agents tried to bribe the Sejm against him, he exposed their plot and published their secret correspondence. In the resultant reaction against France the Sejm signed (April 1, 1683) an alliance with the Empire. Poland was to raise forty thousand men, the Empire sixty thousand. If Vienna or Cracow should be besieged by the Turks, the other ally would come to the rescue with his entire force.

In July the Turks moved toward Vienna. In August Sobieski and the Polish army left Warsaw with the declared purpose "to proceed to the Holy War, and with God's help to give back the old freedom to besieged Vienna, and thereby help all wavering Christendom."[9] The finest spirit of medieval chivalry seemed restored. The Poles reached the beleaguered capital just in time; disease and hunger had already decimated its defenders. Sobieski in person led the combined armies of Poland and the Empire in one of the most crucial engagements in European history (September 12, 1683). Half of the twenty-five thousand Poles who had followed him in the crusade died in battle or on the way.

He returned to Poland in triumph and disappointment. Warsaw received him proudly as the hero of Europe, but he had been rebuffed by the Emperor in his hopes of marrying his son to the Archduchess of Austria. To secure a kingdom for his son he attempted the conquest of Moldavia; he won all the battles except against weather and accident, and came back empty-handed.

Amid the turmoil of politics, and in the intervals of war, he made his court the center of a cultural revival. He himself was a man of wide reading: he had studied Galileo and Harvey, Descartes and Gassendi, he had read Pascal, Corneille, and Molière. While supporting the Catholic Church as a matter of state policy, he extended religious freedom and protection to Protestants and Jews;[10] the Jews loved him as they had loved Caesar. He had the will, but not the power, to save from death a freethinker who had expressed some doubts as to the existence of God (1689);[11] this was the first auto-da-fé in Polish history. Poland continued to produce her own poets, but to import most of her major artists. Waclaw Potocki wrote an epic on the Polish victory at Khotin; Wespazian Kochowski composed similar epics, and a Polish psalmody in poetic prose; and Andrzej Morsztyn, after translating Tasso's *Aminta* and Corneille's *Cid*, showed in his lyrics the influence of French and Italian poetry in Poland. Sobieski encouraged the French influence, admiring everything in France except its politics. He brought French and Italian painters and sculptors to work in Warsaw. He engaged architects, chiefly Italian, to build baroque palaces at Wilanów, Zólkiew, and Jaworów. Sumptuous churches were erected during his reign: St. Peter's in Wilno, and in Warsaw the churches of the Holy Cross and the Benedictine nuns. Andreas Schlüter came from Germany to carve decoration for the palace at Wilanów and the Krasiński Palace in the capital. Amid these Western influences in art, Eastern influence predominated in dress and appearance: the long cloak and the broad and colorful waistband, and mustaches turned up like double scimitars.

The old age of the King was darkened by the rebelliousness of his son Jakób, the intransigence of his wife, and his failure to have the monarchy made hereditary in his family. The *liberum veto* stood always over his head. He could not improve the condition of the peasants, for their masters dominated the Sejm; he could not compel the rich to pay taxes, for the rich were the Sejm; he could not keep the factious nobles in order, for they refused him a standing army. He died of uremia on June 17, 1696, not, as story has it, brokenhearted, but saddened by the decline of his beloved country from the pinnacle of heroism to which he had raised it.

The Diet passed over his son and sold the crown to Frederick Augustus, Elector of Saxony, who easily transformed himself from a Protestant to a Catholic to become Augustus II of Poland. He was a character in his own right. History calls him Augustus the Strong, for he was an athlete in body and bed; legend credits him with 354 illegitimate children.[12] In January, 1699, he signed at Karlowitz a treaty by which Turkey yielded all claim to the western Ukraine. Feeling safe now in south and east, Augustus listened to Patkul, and allied Poland with Denmark and Russia for the partition of Sweden.

III. RUSSIA TURNS WEST: 1645–99

Each of the conspirators could allege some excuse and provocation. Sweden's Charles X had besieged Copenhagen and tried to conquer Denmark. He had invaded Poland and captured her capital; and Gustavus Adolphus had so strengthened Swedish power in Livonia and Ingria that he could defy Russia to launch a boat on the Baltic without Sweden's consent. The imprisoned Russian bear gnawed its claws at the sight of all exits closed in the west, all outlets to the Black Sea shut off by the Crimean Tatars and the Turks. Only eastward could Russia move—into Siberia; and that seemed the way to hardships and barbarism. The comforts and graces of life beckoned Russia to the west, and the West was resolved to keep Russia Oriental.

When Alexis Mikhailovich Romanov became czar Russia was as yet overwhelmingly medieval. She had not known Roman law, or Renaissance humanism, or Reformation religious reform. Under Alexis Russian law received a new formulation (the Ulozhenie of 1649), but this merely codified existing laws based on absolutism and orthodoxy. So it remained a criminal offense to look at the new moon, or play chess, or neglect church attendance, in Lent. These and a hundred other crimes were punished by the knout. Alexis himself, though personally amiable and generous, was fanatically pious; often he spent five hours a day in church, making on one occasion fifteen hundred obeisances.[13] He delighted in feeding the beggars who gathered around his palace, but he punished severely all political or religious dissent, taxed his people heavily, and allowed exploitation of the peasantry and corruption in the government to go to such lengths that revolts broke out in Moscow, Novgorod, and Pskov, and, above all, among the Cossacks of the Don. One of these, Stenka Razin, formed a robber band, pillaged and killed the rich and made himself master of Astrakhan and Tsaritsyn (now Stalingrad). He set up a Cossack republic along the Volga, and at one time threatened to take Moscow. He was captured and was tortured till he died (1671), but his memory was cherished by the poor as a promise of revenge against the landlords and the government.

Even in this medieval milieu some modern influences appeared. The wars with Poland involved more frequent contacts with the West. Diplomats and merchants came in rising number from what the Russians called "Europe." The River Dvina and the ports of Riga and Archangel saw increasing trade with Western states. Foreign technicians were called in to develop mines, organize industries, and manufacture armament. An entire colony of immigrants grew up, about 1650, in a quarter of Moscow; Germans and Poles brought a touch of Western literature and music to this settlement, and provided Latin tutors for rich Russian families. Alexis himself maintained a German orchestra. He allowed his minister Artamon Matveev to import Western furniture and French manners, even to the social mingling of women with men. When the Russian ambassador to the Grand Duke of Tuscany sent Alexis descriptions of Florentine dramas, operas, and ballets, Alexis allowed the building of a theater in Moscow and the presentation of plays, chiefly Biblical; one of these, *Esther*, preceded Racine's play of that name by seventeen years. Feeling that he had sinned in attending these performances, Alexis mentioned them to his confessor, who permitted him the new pleasures.[14] Matveev married a Scottish lady of the famous Hamilton family; they adopted and brought up a Russian orphan, Natalia Naruishkina; Alexis took her as his second wife.

These Westernizing ventures aroused a patriotic reaction. Some Orthodox Russians condemned the study of Latin as an evil thing that might incline youth to un-Orthodox ideas. The older generation felt that any change in customs, faith, or ritual dislodged some stone in the social structure, loosened all, and might in time bring the whole precarious edifice down in ruins. Religion in Russia relied on liturgy as well as doctrine. Though the masses had as yet a very limited capacity to understand ideas, they could be trained in religious observances whose hypnotic repetition made for social and mental stability and peace. But the repetition had to be exact to produce the hypnotic effect; a change in the accustomed sequence would break the soothing charm; hence every detail of the ceremonial, every word of the prayers, had to remain as they had been for centuries. One of the bitterest disputes and divisions in Russian history came when Nikon, Patriarch of Moscow, introduced into the liturgy some reforms based upon a study of Byzantine practices and texts. Clerics who had learned Greek pointed out to the Patriarch many errors in the texts used by the Russian Orthodox Church. Nikon ordered a revision and correction of the texts and ritual: for example, Jesus was henceforth to be Jisus, not Isus; the sign of the cross was to be made with three fingers, not two; the number of genuflections during a certain prayer were to be reduced from twelve to four; icons showing Italian influence were to be destroyed and replaced by icons adhering to Byzantine patterns. In general, Russian ritual was to be brought into closer conformity with its Byzantine origins. Some Russian churchmen who refused to accept these changes were demoted or anathematized or sent to Siberia. Nikon's dictatorial methods displeased the Czar, and in 1667 he was banished to a remote monastery. The Russian Church split into two factions; the official church, supported by Alexis, accepted the reforms; the dissenters (Raskolniki), or Old Believers (Staroviertsi), developed into a schismatic body, which the new orthodoxy persecuted with fire and sword. Their leader, Avvakum, was burned at the

stake (1681) by order of Czar Feodor. Many Old Believers killed them-
selves rather than pay taxes to a government which they identified with
Antichrist. This religious chaos was part of the inheritance of Peter the
Great.

The death of Alexis (1676) prepared a violent conflict among his children. By his first wife, Maria Miloslavski, he left an ailing son, Feodor
(born 1662), a lame, half-blind, and half-imbecile son, Ivan (born 1666),
and six daughters, of whom the ablest and most ambitious was Sophia
Alekseevna (born 1657). By his second wife, Natalia Naruishkina, Alexis
begot the famous Peter (born 1672). Feodor inherited the throne, but died
in 1682. The boyars, judging Ivan helplessly incompetent, wished to make
Peter czar, with his mother as regent. But Peter's stepsisters hated Natalia,
and feared to be neglected under her rule. Led by Sophia, they stirred up
the Streltsi—soldiers of the Moscow garrison—to invade the Kremlin and
insist upon the accession of Ivan. Matveev, Natalia's foster father, pleaded
with the soldiers to withdraw. They tore him from Peter's grasp, killed him
before the eyes of the ten-year-old boy, killed Natalia's brothers and several
of her supporters, and forced the boyars to accept Ivan as czar, with Peter
as co-czar but subordinate, and with Sophia as regent. These barbarities
may have shared in producing the convulsions that later disturbed Peter's
life; in any case they gave him unforgettable lessons in violence and brutality.

Natalia withdrew with Peter to Preobrazhensky, a suburb of Moscow.
Sophia governed well. She repudiated the isolation of the *terem,* or women's
quarters; she appeared in public unveiled, and presided without a qualm
over male assemblies where old heads shook at such insolence. She had
received more education than most of the men around her; she was inclined
to reform, and to Western ideas; and she chose as her chief minister, perhaps as her lover, a man much won to Western ways. Prince Vasili Golitsyn
wrote Latin, admired France, adorned his palace with paintings and Gobelin
tapestries, and had a large library of Latin, Polish, and German books. It
was apparently due to his example and encouragement that three thousand
stone dwellings were built in Moscow in the seven years of his regency,
whereas, before, all houses had been of wood. He seems to have planned
to free the serfs.[15] Under his rule enslavement for debt was abolished, murderers were no longer buried alive, and the death penalty for seditious utterances was abolished. His work as a reformer was ruined by his failure as a
general. He reorganized the army and twice led it against the Turks; in
both cases he mismanaged the provisioning of the troops; they returned defeated and rebellious, and their disaffection gave Peter his cue to capture
power.

IV. PETER LEARNING

He had been receiving education from his mother, his tutors, and his sallies into the streets of Moscow. He was not precocious, but he was eager, curious, intelligent, fascinated by the mechanisms brought in from the West—watches, weapons, tools, and instruments. He longed for a Russia that would rival the West in industry and war. He loved to play war games with his rough companions—raising, attacking, and defending forts. Dreaming of a Russian navy before Russia had touched an ice-free sea, he built larger and larger boats, until he had to go eighty miles from Moscow to find, at Pereslavl, a lake in which he could set his little fleet afloat.

As he grew stronger he bore with rising impatience the ascendancy of a stepsister who, with Vasili Golitsyn, had appropriated the authority of both Ivan and himself. On July 18, 1689, Peter joined Ivan in the procession that annually celebrated Moscow's liberation from the Poles. Contrary to custom, Sophia walked in the procession. Peter, now seventeen, commanded her to withdraw; she persisted; he left the city in anger, and sought allies against the Regent. He found them in the boyars, who had never reconciled themselves to being ruled by a woman, and in the Streltsi, who, having suffered some rebuffs from Sophia, were ready for stratagems and spoils. Boris Golitsyn, cousin to the minister, set the *coup d'état* in motion by sending a false message to Peter that Sophia was planning to arrest him. Peter, followed by his mother, his sister, and his recently acquired wife, fled to the Troitsko-Sergievskaya Monastery, forty-five miles from Moscow. Thence he sent orders to each colonel of the Streltsi to come to the Troitsko-Sergievskaya. Sophia forbade them to obey, but many went. Soon the leaders of the nobility came, and then Joachim, Patriarch of Moscow. Vasili Golitsyn was summoned, submitted, and was exiled to a village near Archangel. Several of Sophia's supporters were captured; some were tortured, some were put to death. Peter wrote to Ivan for permission to take over the government; Ivan's consent was given or presumed. Peter ordered Sophia to remove to a convent; she protested, rebelled, yielded. She was provided with every comfort and many servants, but was forbidden to leave the convent grounds. On October 16, 1689, Peter entered Moscow, was welcomed by Ivan, and assumed supreme power. Ivan gracefully retired from public life; and seven years later he died.

Peter, however, was not yet ready to rule. He left the government to the the illiberal and reactionary Boris Golitsyn, Joachim, and others, while he himself spent much of his time in the foreign colony. There he made new friends who strongly influenced his development. One was Patrick Gordon, a Scot soldier of fortune who was now at fifty-five an officer in the Russian army; from him Peter learned more of the art of war. Another was François Lefort, born in Geneva, now at thirty-four a Russian major general. His good looks, quick mind, and pleasant ways delighted the young czar, who dined twice or thrice a week with him, to the dismay of Muscovites, who regarded all foreigners as vicious heretics. Peter preferred the company of these aliens to that of the Russians. They seemed to be more civilized, though they drank as heavily; they far excelled the Russians in industrial, scientific, and military knowledge; and their talk and amusements were on a higher plane. Peter noted their mutual toleration in religion—Gordon a Catholic, Lefort a Protestant—and smilingly served as godfather for Catholic and Protestant children at the baptismal font. From the Germans and the Dutch he acquired enough of their languages for his purposes.

These were to make Russia strong in war, and have her rival the West in the arts of peace. He learned from the Dutch resident, Baron von Keller, how the Hollanders maintained their wealth and power by building good ships. He longed to find an outlet to the sea, and to build a salt-water fleet. He had no such outlet except at Archangel, which was icebound half the year. Nevertheless he made his way there in 1693; he bought a Dutch man-of-war lying in the harbor; when he overcame his fear of the sea and set forth on this vessel, he was drunk with delight. "You shall command her," he wrote to Lefort, "and I will serve as a common sailor."[16] He dressed himself like a Dutch sea captain, and mingled happily with Dutch sailors in the wineshops of the port. The salt air of that cold sea was a bracing breath from the West, from that region of industry, power, science, and art which called to him ever more and more temptingly.

There were two practicable ways to the West: one via the Baltic, closed by Sweden and Poland, the other via the Black Sea, closed by Tatars and Turks. The Tatars and Turks controlled at Azov the mouth of the Don; they made repeated raids into Muscovite territory, capturing Russians— sometimes twenty thousand in a year—to sell them as slaves in Constantinople. In 1695 Peter ordered his army to graduate from games to war, to march through the steppes, sail down the rivers, and attack Azov. Three generals were in divided command—Golovin, Gordon, Lefort; Peter humbly served as bombardier sergeant in the Preobrazhensky regiment. The affair was badly managed, the troops were poorly disciplined; after fourteen costly weeks the siege was abandoned, and Peter returned to Moscow swearing that he would train a better army, and try again.

At Voronezh he built a fleet of transports and men-of-war. In May, 1696, he sailed down the Don with 75,000 men, and resumed the siege of Azov. In July, chiefly by the bravery of the Don Cossacks, the city was taken. Peter at once ordered a large fleet to be built at Voronezh for service on the Black Sea. All Russia, including the great landlords, was taxed for the purpose; workers were conscripted; foreign mechanics were brought in. Fifty Russian nobles were sent at their own expense to Italy, Holland, and England, to learn the art of building ships. On March 10, 1697, Peter followed them.

Russia would have been horrified at the thought of its Czar going abroad into lands soiled with heresy. Therefore he organized an embassy of fifty-five nobles and two hundred attendants, led by Lefort, to visit "Europe" and seek allies against the Turks. Among the fifty-five emissaries was a non-commissioned officer answering only to the name Peter Mikhailov, and using as a seal the image of a shipwright and the inscription "My rank is that of a pupil, and I need masters."[17] Once outside Russia, Peter wore this incognito loosely. It was as Czar of Russia that he was entertained by Elector Frederick III of Brandenburg, by King William III in England, by Emperor Leopold I in Vienna. Even in his royal state he shocked the courts by his rough manners and speech, his uncleanliness and untidiness, and his aversion to the use of knives and forks.[18] But he made his way.

The embassy encountered difficulties, which Peter never forgot, in moving through Swedish Livonia to Riga. Thence he hurried to Königsberg, where he signed with the Elector a treaty of trade and friendship. In Brandenburg he studied artillery and fortification with a Prussian military engineer, who gave him a certificate of progress. At Koppenbrügge Sophia, the widowed Electress of Hanover, and her daughter Sophia Charlotte, Electress of Brandenburg, persuaded him and his suite to dine and dance with them. The Dowager later described him:

> The Czar is very tall, his features are fine, and his figure very noble. He has great vivacity of mind, and a ready and just repartee. . . . It could be wished that his manners were a little less rustic . . . He was very gay, very talkative, and we established a great friendship for each other. . . . He told us that he worked in building ships, showed us his hands, and made us touch the callous places that had been caused by work. . . . He is a very extraordinary man. . . . He has a very good heart, and remarkably noble sentiments. . . . He did not get drunk in our presence, but we had hardly left when the people of his suite made ample amends. . . . He is sensible to the charms of beauty, but . . . I found in him no disposition to gallantry. . . . The Muscovites, in dancing, took the whalebones of our corsets for our bones, and the Czar showed his astonishment by saying that the German ladies had devilish hard bones.[19]

From Koppenbrügge the embassy sailed down the Rhine into Holland. Leaving most of the group at Amsterdam, Peter and a few intimates went on to Zaandam, then a great shipbuilding center (August 18, 1697); even in Russia he had heard much about the skill of the shipwrights in this picturesque town. In its streets he recognized a worker whom he had known in Moscow, Gerrit Kist. Asking him to respect his incognito, Peter proposed to live in Kist's small wooden cottage. There he stayed for a week, dressing in the garb of a Dutch workingman, spending his days in watching the shipwrights at work, and finding time, at night, to make love to a servant girl at the local inn. In later years Joseph II and Napoleon visited the cottage as a shrine, Czar Alexander I decorated it with a marble slab, and a Dutch poet inscribed on the wall a famous line: *"Nichts is den grooten man te klein"* (To a great man nothing is too small).[20]

Annoyed by the crowds that followed his every step at Zaandam, Peter went back to Amsterdam and his embassy. He again insisted on being incognito, but now he called himself "Carpenter Peter of Zaandam." He persuaded the Dutch East India Company to let him join its workers in the shipyards at Oostenburg. There he labored for four months with ten of his followers, helping to build and launch a ship. He allowed no distinction to be made between himself and other workingmen, and he put his shoulder to the timber like the rest. At night he studied geometry and the theory of shipbuilding; his notebooks show how thorough these studies were. He found time to visit factories, workshops, anatomical museums, botanical gardens, theaters, and hospitals. He met the great physician and botanist Boerhaave, studied microscopy with Leeuwenhoek, and took the gentlemen of his suite into Boerhaave's anatomical theater. He took up military engineering with Baron van Coehorn, architecture with Schynvoet, mechanics with van der Heyden. He learned to pull teeth, and some of his aides suffered under his zealous dentistry. He entered the homes of the Dutch to study their family life and domestic arrangements. He shopped in the markets, mingled with the people, marveled at their various trades, learned to mend his own clothes and cobble his shoes. He drank beer and wine with the Dutch in their saloons. Probably no man in history has been more eager to absorb and savor life.

In all this activity he did not lose sight of Russia. He guided by letter the actions of its deputed government. He engaged, and sent to Russia, several naval captains, thirty-five lieutenants, seventy-two pilots, fifty physicians, four cooks, 345 sailors; he dispatched to Russia 260 cases of guns, sailcloth, compasses, whalebone, cork, anchors, and tools, even eight blocks of marble for Russian sculptors to work on.[21] His interest lagged when it came to the refinement of manners, the graces of society, or the subtleties of thought; he had no time for metaphysics, balls, or salons; in any case those intangibles could wait. For the present his task was to introduce the crafts and practical sciences of the West into Russia "so that, having mastered them thoroughly, we can, when we return, be victors over the enemies of Jesus Christ"[22]—i.e., take Constantinople and let Russia pass from its prison through the Bosporus into the world.

After four months in Holland he asked William III if he might visit England, still semi-incognito. William sent the royal yacht to fetch him. Peter arrived in London in January, 1698. Though it was winter, he frequented the docks and the naval establishments. He visited the Royal Society and the Mint, where he may have met Newton. Evelyn turned over his house and carefully groomed grounds at Deptford to Peter and his staff; later the English government allowed Sir John £350 to repair the damage done by the Russians. The Czar astonished his neighbors by going to bed early, rising at four, and walking to the shipyards with an ax over his shoulder and a pipe in his mouth. He made a mistress of a leading actress, who complained that he underpaid her. He received the degree of Doctor of Laws at Oxford, and attended Protestant services with such decorum that parsons expected him to convert Russia to the Reformation. Bishop Burnet worked upon him, found him curious but noncommittal, and concluded that the Czar seemed "designed by nature rather to be a ship-carpenter than a great prince."[23]

Having spent four months in England, Peter sailed back to Amsterdam, rejoined his embassy, and moved on with it through Leipzig and Dresden to Vienna (June 26, 1698). Through an impatient month he labored in vain to bring the Emperor into an alliance against Turkey. He was pleasant to the Jesuits, who began to dream of a Roman Catholic Russia. Then, just as he was about to leave for Venice, a message reached him that the Streltsi were in revolt, and were threatening to seize Moscow and the government. He started at once for Russia, but near Cracow he received assurance that the revolt had been put down. At Rava he tarried four days with Augustus II of Poland. He was surprised and delighted to find a king who could match him in physical strength, wild hunting, and hard drinking. They fell in love with each other, kissed, and debated whether Sweden or Turkey should be the first victim of their friendship. On September 4 Peter reached Moscow, after eighteen months of a journey that in Macaulay's judgment marked "an epoch in the history not only of his own country, but . . . of the world."[24] Russia had discovered Europe, and Europe had discovered Russia. Leibniz began to study Russian.

But Peter was still a seventeenth-century Muscovite. He had never forgiven the Streltsi their share in the murder of his uncles and Matveev, and in the usurpation of power by Sophia. His plans for a new army left no room for this troublesome Praetorian Guard. When he learned that Sophia had from her convent negotiated with them to restore her to power, that they had threatened Lefort and others of the "German colony," that they had spread rumors that he was betraying the religion of Russia in his love of the West, his fury became a convulsion of revenge. He ordered a considerable number of the Streltsi to be tortured, with a view to making them confess Sophia's share in their uprising; they bore the most terrible torments without implicating her. He had her attendants tortured with the same end and result. Sophia was forced to take the vows, and was closely confined in her convent, where she died six years later. A thousand Streltsi were put to death; Peter executed five with his own hand, and compelled his aides to do likewise; Lefort refused. By 1705 the Streltsi had disappeared from history.

Peter began at once to build a new army. The old one had been composed of Streltsi, of foreign mercenaries, and of peasant levies raised by noblemen. Peter replaced this motley with a standing army of 210,000 men by conscripting one man from every twenty peasant households. These troops were dressed in "European" uniforms, and were drilled in the tactics of the West. The term of service for all ranks was for life. In addition Peter called upon 100,000 Cossacks. Ships were hurriedly built on lakes, rivers, seas; by 1705 the Russian navy had forty-eight men-of-war, eight hundred smaller vessels, and 28,000 men.

All this was still in process, far from complete, when Patkul came to Moscow and proposed that Peter join Frederick IV of Denmark and Augustus II of Poland to drive Sweden from the mainland and wrest from her the control of the Baltic. All those ships that were abuilding longed for the sea. Preferably the warm Mediterranean—but the Turkish Empire was still discouragingly strong, Constantinople was a hard nut to crack, and Austria and France were now friends with the Turks. Russia must look to the other door, must seek some outlet in the north. It was untimely that Swedish envoys had just come to Moscow and had secured Peter's consent to renew the Treaty of Kardis pledging Russia and Sweden to peace. But geography and commerce laugh at treaties. Besides, had not the Baltic littoral between the Neva and Narva rivers—the provinces of Ingria and Karelia—formerly belonged to Russia, and been surrendered to Sweden in 1616 only because Russia, then in her Time of Troubles, was powerless to resist? Why should not force recapture what force had taken away? On November 22, 1699, Peter joined the coalition against Sweden, and prepared to cut his way through to the Baltic. On August 8, 1700, he cleared his southern front as well as a treaty could, by signing peace with Turkey. On that same day he ordered his army to march into Swedish Livonia.

V. CHARLES XII AND THE GREAT NORTHERN WAR: 1700–21

Some inkling of the coalition agreement reached Stockholm. The royal Council met to discuss measures of defense. The prevailing judgment was that negotiations should be opened with one or another of the allies with a view to a separate peace. Charles listened for a long time in silence, then rose abruptly. "Gentlemen," he said, "I have resolved never to engage in an unjust war, but . . . never to conclude a just war but by the ruin of my foes."[25] He renounced all amusements, all luxuries, all intercourse with women, all use of wine. His army and navy were in readiness. With them he left Stockholm on April 24, 1700, to begin one of the most spectacular military careers in history. He never saw his capital again.

He attacked Denmark first, for he had to protect the southern provinces of Sweden from Danish assaults while he faced Poland and Russia. With characteristic daring and speed, over the protest of his admiral, he led his ships across the eastern—supposedly unnavigable—channel of the Sound, and landed in Sjaelland, only a few miles from Copenhagen (August 4, 1700). The Danish King, Frederick IV, dreading the capture of his capital, hastily signed the Peace of Travendal (August 18), paying an indemnity of 200,000 rix-dollars, and swearing that he would never attack Sweden.

In May, 1700, Augustus II tried to take Riga. He was defeated by the seventy-five-year-old Swedish general Count Erik Dahlberg, who had gained the title "the Vauban of Sweden" by his skill in fortification. Augustus, retreating, appealed to Peter to relieve him by invading Ingria. Peter responded by ordering forty thousand men to besiege Narva. Thinking to help Dahlberg, Charles XII transported his army by sea to Pernau (Parnu), on the Gulf of Riga; but finding that warrior victorious, he turned north, and marched through swamps and dangerous passes to appear suddenly in the rear of Peter's army. The Czar was surprised into what seemed disgraceful cowardice; he left the army (in which he had been serving only as a lieutenant), and fled to Novgorod and Moscow. Probably he knew that his crude conscripts would collapse in their first test; he could not afford to be captured, for he thought himself more valuable to Russia alive than dead. The forty thousand Russians, under the incompetent command of the Magyar Prince Carl Eugene de Croy, were defeated by Charles's eight thousand Swedes in the battle of Narva (November 20, 1700), the first setback in Peter's adult career.

The Swedish generals urged Charles to march upon Moscow and finish Peter. But his army was small, winter had begun, even the young Napoleon's courage must have hesitated before the engulfing distances of Russia, and the problem of feeding his army in a hostile land. Moreover (pledges being paper), could he trust the Danish King, or the Polish, not to invade Sweden while its main army and leader were so far from home? After reorganizing the government and defense of Livonia, Charles marched south into Poland, occupied Warsaw without a struggle (1702) like his grandfather forty-seven years earlier, deposed Augustus, and made Stanislas Leszczyński King of Poland (1704). Each of the allies had now been defeated; but the Russian bear had just begun to fight.

Peter had not only recovered from his fright, he had organized and equipped another army. To provide it with artillery, he ordered the bells of the churches and monasteries to be melted down; three hundred cannon were forged, and a school was set up to train artillerymen. Soon the new levies were winning victories; Peter's own battalion of artillery led in capturing Nienskans, at the mouth of the Neva (1703); and here at once the Czar began to build "Petersburg," hardly realizing as yet that this was to be his capital, but resolved that it should be one portal to the sea. While Charles was busy in Poland, Peter came up again before Narva. Charles had left too small a garrison there; the great fortress was taken by assault (August 20, 1704); the victors avenged the former failure with a frightful massacre, which Peter finally stopped by killing twelve of the blood-maddened Russians with his own hand.

In Poland the triumph of Charles seemed complete. The deposed Augustus signed a treaty acknowledging Leszczyński as king, renouncing his alliances against Sweden, and surrendering to Charles the man who had first organized the coalition; Johann von Patkul was broken on the wheel and then beheaded (1707). Peter found himself alone against the young Swedish terror. He tried to bribe the English ministry to arrange a peace, but it refused to interfere. Peter's agent went directly to Marlborough, who agreed to intercede in return for a principality in Russia;[26] Peter offered him Kiev or Vladimir or Siberia, a guarantee of fifty thousand thalers a year, and "a rock ruby such as no European potentate possesses";[27] but these negotiations fell through. Western statesmen sympathized with Charles, despised Augustus, feared Peter; some of them argued that if Russia were allowed to expand westward, all Europe would soon tremble before a Slavic inundation.[28]

On January 1, 1708, Charles crossed the Vistula on unsafe ice at the head of 44,000 men, half of them cavalry. He reached Grodno on the twenty-sixth only two hours after Peter had abandoned it. The Czar had decided on defense by depth and devastation; he ordered his armies to retreat, to draw Charles farther and farther into the Russian mattress, and to burn all crops as they passed; he commanded the peasants to hide their corn in the earth or the snow, and scatter their cattle in forests and swamps. He entrusted to the Cossack hetman Ivan Mazeppa the defense of "Little

Russia" and the Ukraine. Mazeppa had been brought up as a page at the Polish court; a Polish nobleman whom he had cuckolded had him bound naked on a wild Ukrainian horse; the horse (as Byron was to tell) was deliberately frightened by the cuts of a whip and the firing of a pistol close to his ear; the steed rushed through thickets and woods to his native haunts; Mazeppa, though torn and bloody, survived, and rose to be leader of the Zaporogue Cossacks. He pretended loyalty to Peter, but resented the Czar's autocracy, and waited for a chance to revolt. Hearing that Peter was retreating and Charles advancing, he decided that his opportunity had come. He sent Charles an offer of co-operation.

It was probably that offer that led Charles to continue his reckless march into Russia. The "scorched-earth" policy was having its effect; the Swedes found nothing but charred wilderness in their path, and began to starve. Charles had relied upon reinforcements from Riga; these tried to reach him, but were half destroyed by the Russians on their way. Charles hoped that Mazeppa would join him with provisions and the full force of the Dnieper Cossacks; but Peter, suspecting treachery, sent an army under Aleksandr Danilovich Menshikov to arrest Mazeppa; the hetman, surprised before he could raise his horsemen, fled to Charles at Horki, bringing only thirteen hundred men. Charles marched south to capture Mazeppa's capital, Baturin, and its supplies; Menshikov reached it first, burned the city to the ground, and appointed a hetman faithful to Russia. Peter, using every weapon, discouraged the Cossacks from joining the Swedes by manifestoes describing the invaders as heretics who "deny the doctrines of the true religion and spit on the picture of the Blessed Virgin."[29] Charles's hope now was that the Tatars and Turks would come to his aid in revenge for Peter's seizure of Azov.

None came, and the winter of 1708–9 proved a terrible enemy to the Swedes. It was especially severe everywhere in Europe: the Baltic froze so deeply that heavily laden wagons crossed the Sound on the ice; in Germany the fruit trees died; in France the Rhone, in Venice the canals, were covered with ice. In the Ukraine snow blanketed the ground from October 1 to April 5; birds fell dead in their flight; saliva congealed in its passage from the mouth to the ground; wine and spirits froze into solid blocks; firewood would not burn in the open air; and the wind cut like a knife over the level plains and into the face. Charles's soldiers suffered in silent fortitude while two thousand of them died of hunger or cold. "You could see," said an eyewitness, "some without hands, some without feet, some without ears or noses, many creeping along after the manner of quadrupeds."[30] Charles bade them march on, trusting that somewhere soon they would come upon Peter's main army and win all Russia with one overwhelming victory. Wherever he made contact with the enemy, at

Holowczyn, Cerkova, and Opressa, he won through superior generalship and courage, often against forces ten times greater than his own. But when that winter ended, his army had dwindled from 44,000 to 24,000 men.

On May 11, 1709, it reached Poltava, on a tributary of the Dnieper, eighty-five miles southwest of Kharkov. Here at last Charles sighted Peter's army, eighty thousand strong. While on reconnaissance he was struck in the foot by a bullet. He made nothing of the wound, and calmly extracted the bullet with his own knife; but when he regained his camp he fainted. Unable to lead in person, he delegated the command to General Carl Rehnskjoll, and ordered him to attack on the morrow (June 26). At first the Swedes, who had never lost a battle under Charles, carried everything before them. To urge them on, Charles had himself carried to the field of battle on a litter, which was shattered under him by enemy fire. Peter, though still officially a mere lieutenant, rode to the forefront, encouraging his troops; a bullet passed through his hat, another was stopped by a golden cross on his breast. His years of preparing and training artillery now served him well; his cannon fired five times to every once of the Swedes. When Swedish ammunition ran out the Swedish infantry was massacred whole-sale by the Russian artillery. Seeing the situation hopeless, the Swedish cavalry surrendered. Charles himself mounted a horse and fled with Mazeppa and a thousand men across the Dnieper into Turkish territory. The Swedish lost, in killed and wounded, four thousand men; the Russians lost 4,635, but took 18,670 prisoners, including three generals and many officers. Peter treated the officers honorably, but employed the prisoners on fortifications and public works. Leibniz hailed his humanity and concluded, from the size of the Russian battalions, that God was on the side of the Russians.[31] Peter agreed with him. "Now by God's help," he wrote, "the foundations of Petersburg are securely laid for all time."[32]

The battle had endless and far-reaching results. Leszczyński fled to Alsace, and Augustus II remounted the Polish throne. Russia appropriated the Baltic principalities and all of the Ukraine. Denmark rejoined the alliance against Sweden, invaded Skåne, but was repulsed. Frederick William of Prussia took Stettin and Holstein, and part of Pomerania. Russian prestige and pride ran high; Louis XIV offered his alliance to Peter, who rejected it but consented to receive an envoy.

Charles did not admit that he was definitely beaten. The Turks, grateful to anyone who had made trouble for Russia, gave their royal refugee all but royal honors. At Bender (now Tighina), near the Dniester, he maintained his own court, and received from Sultan Ahmed III supplies for himself and eighteen hundred Swedes still in his service. As soon as his foot healed he resumed martial exercises, and drilled his little army. His abstinence from wine, and his regular attendance at public prayers, led to the report that he was a convert to Islam. He employed every means to persuade the Sultan or the vizier to make war against Russia; and in that hope he refused to be taken back to Sweden by French vessels offered to his use. An attempt was made to poison him, but it was detected in time. Peter demanded that Mazeppa be surrendered to him as a traitorous Russian subject; Charles would not permit it, and Mazeppa cut the knot by dying (1710).

Every victory breeds new enemies or inflames old ones. Charles was able to convince the Sultan that the rising power of Russia, now unchecked in the north, would sooner or later challenge Turkish control of the Black Sea and the Bosporus. The Sultan declared war, and sent against Russia 200,000 men under his vizier. Peter, caught by surprise, could gather only 38,000 soldiers in the south to stop this avalanche. His Bulgarian and Serbian allies failed him. When the two armies met at the River Prut (now the eastern boundary of Romania), Peter had to give battle, for the surrounding country had been ravaged, and he had provisions for only two days. Expecting defeat and death, he sent instructions to Moscow for the election of a new czar in case his fears should be realized; then he retired to his tent and forbade anyone to enter. But his second wife, Catherine, agreed with his generals that surrender was better than mass suicide. She braved Peter's wrath by taking in to him for his signature a letter asking the vizier for terms. Peter signed without hope. Catherine collected all her jewels, borrowed money from the officers, and sent Vice-Chancellor Peter Shafirov, armed with 230,000 rubles, to negotiate terms with the vizier. The vizier took the rubles and jewels, and allowed Peter to withdraw his army and equipment unhindered, on his promise to surrender Azov, to dismantle the Russian forts and ships there, to allow Charles clear passage to Sweden, and to interfere no more in Polish affairs. Peter readily made these promises (August 1, 1711), and led his troops away. Charles, coming up ready for battle, raged when he found peace. He secured the dismissal of the pacific vizier and continued his efforts for war; but Shafirov, with 84,900 ducats, persuaded the new vizier to confirm the Treaty of the Prut.

Tired of these complications, the Sultan asked Charles to leave Turkey. He refused. A Turkish force of twelve thousand men was sent to compel him; with forty men he held them off for eight hours, killing ten Turks himself; finally a dozen Janissaries overpowered him (February 1, 1713). He was transported to Dimotika, near Adrianople, but was allowed to remain there for twenty months while a new vizier meditated war with Russia. When this hope faded, Charles consented to return to Sweden. He was provided with military escort, gifts, and funds. He left Dimotika (September 20, 1714), traveled through Wallachia, Transylvania, and Austria, and at midnight, November 11, reached Pomerania and its port and fort, Stralsund, on the Baltic coast due south of Sweden. This and Wismar, to the west, were the last Swedish strongholds on the mainland.

By this time Charles's insistence upon governing Sweden from Turkey, and his refusal to make any concessions to Peter, had brought the Swedish empire to collapse. On August 1, 1714, Elector George of Hanover had become King George I of England. Resolved to use his new power to add Bremen and Verden to Hanover, he joined Britain with Denmark and Prussia in a new coalition against Sweden, and the British fleet reinforced the Danish in the Straits. Charles found himself locked up in Stralsund, at war with England, Hanover, Denmark, Saxony, Prussia, and Russia. For twelve months he stood siege there by 36,000 men, frequently leading his garrison on heroic futile sallies. After the town and its walls had been shattered by the besiegers' cannon, and surrender was inevitable, Charles leaped into a small vessel, sailed through enemy fire, and reached Karlskrona on the Swedish coast (December 12, 1715).

Stockholm awaited him as its desperate hero, but he refused to return there except as a victor. He ordered new levies of men, even of youths fifteen years old; he conscripted all articles of iron to build another fleet; and taxed almost every article used by his people, even to their wigs. They obeyed silently, thinking him perhaps mad, but glorious. Baron Georg von Görtz, now his chief minister, labored to break up the coalition. Noting that George I was quarreling with Peter over the division of the spoils, he tried to make peace between Sweden and Russia, and aid the Stuart revolt in England; but his plans failed. By the fall of 1717 Charles had assembled an army of twenty thousand men. That year, and again in 1718, he invaded Norway, hoping to win territory that might compensate for his mainland losses. In December he laid siege to the fortress of Fredrikssten. On the twelfth he raised his head for a moment over the parapet of the foremost trench. A Norwegian bullet struck him in the right temple and killed him instantly. He was thirty-six years old.

He died as he had lived, stupefied with bravery. He was a great general, and won unbelievable victories against great odds; but he loved war to intoxication, never had victories enough, and, in search of them, planned campaigns to the verge of insanity. His generosity was spoiled by his pride; he gave much, but demanded more; and time and again he prevented peace by refusing concessions that might have saved his empire and his face. History pardons him because it was not he who had begun this "Great Northern War" that he refused to finish except with victory.

The Swedish government, seldom extreme, hastened negotiations for peace. By the Treaties of Stockholm (November 20, 1719, and February 1, 1720) it yielded Bremen and Verden to Hanover, and Stettin to Prussia. At first it refused Peter's demands for all the Swedish territory in the eastern

Baltic. Russian armies three times invaded a Sweden bled white with war, and devastated her coastal lands and cities. Finally, by the Treaty of Nystad (August 30, 1721), Russia obtained Livonia, Esthonia, Ingria, and part of Finland. The struggle for the Baltic had left Russia victorious, and had made her a "Great Power."

The weary, aging, but triumphant Czar, arriving at Petersburg with the news and cry of "*Mir! Mir!*" (Peace! Peace!), was hailed by his people as Father of his Country, Emperor of All the Russias, and Peter the Great.

CHAPTER XIII

Peter the Great

1698–1725

I. THE BARBARIAN

VOLTAIRE wanted "to know what were the steps by which men passed from barbarism to civilization."[1] No wonder he was interested in Peter, for Peter embodied, if not that process, at least that effort, in his flesh and soul and people. Or hear another "Great," Frederick II of Prussia, writing about Peter to Voltaire, a bit confusedly:

> He was the only truly educated prince. He was not only the legislator of his country, but he understood perfectly all naval science. He was an architect, an anatomist, a surgeon, . . . an expert soldier, a consummate economist. . . . To make him the model of all princes he only needed an education less barbarous and ferocious.[2]

We have noted that barbarous and ferocious education, the violence and bloodshed that surrounded Peter's childhood, shocking his nervous system and accustoming him to brutality. Even in youth he suffered from a nervous tic, which may have been aggravated later by heavy drinking and venereal disease.[3] "He is subject to convulsions all over his body," reported Burnet after visiting him in England in 1698.[4] "It is well known," said an eighteenth-century Russian, "that this monarch . . . was subject to short but frequent brain attacks, of a somewhat violent kind. A sort of convulsion seized him, which for a certain time, and sometimes even for hours, threw him into such a distressing condition that he could not bear the sight of anyone, not even his nearest friends. This paroxysm was always preceded by a strong contortion of the neck towards the left side, and by a violent contraction of the muscles of the face."[5] Yet he was robust and powerful. We are told that when he and Augustus II met they rivaled each other in crumpling silver plate in their hands. Kneller in 1698 pictured him as a youth in arms and regalia, quite incredibly gentle and innocent; later we find him more realistically portrayed as a stooping giant, six feet eight and a half inches tall, with full round face, large eyes and nose, and brown hair falling in curls rarely cut. His look of stern command hardly harmonized with his careless and untidy dress, his coarse, darned socks, his rudely cobbled shoes. While he put a nation in order he left his immediate surroundings in disorder wherever he went. He was so immersed in large endeavors that he grudged all time given to little things.

His manners, like his dress, were so informal that he might have been taken for a peasant rather than a king—except that he had none of the muzhik's stolid patience. Sometimes his manners were worse than a peasant's, because unrestrained by fear of a master or the law. Seeing a phallus in a collection of antiquities at Berlin, he ordered his wife to kiss it; when Catherine refused he threatened to have her beheaded; she still refused, and he was calmed only by receiving the object as a present to adorn his private room.[6] In his conversation and correspondence he allowed himself the crudest obscenities. Time and again he reproved his closest friends with blows of his massive fist; he gave Menshikov a bloody nose, and kicked Lefort. His fondness for practical jokes occasionally took cruel forms; so he forced one of his aides to eat tortoises, another to drink a whole flask of vinegar, and young girls to down a soldier's ration of brandy. He took undue pleasure in practicing dentistry, and those near him had to guard against the slightest complaint of a toothache; his forceps were always at hand. When his valet complained that his wife, on the score of pretended toothache, refused him the consolations of matrimony, he sent for her, forcibly extracted a sound tooth, and told her that more would be forthcoming if she continued celibate.[7]

His lawless cruelty exceeded the degree in which it might be excused as normal or necessary in his time and land. The Russians were accustomed to cruelty, and were probably less sensitive to pain than persons of a subtler nervous organization; they may have needed a harsh discipline; but Peter's almost personal massacre of the Streltsi suggests a sadistic pleasure in cruelty, an orgasm of blood; and no need of the state required to have two conspirators sliced to death inch by inch.[8] Peter was immune to pity or sentiment, and lacked the sense of justice that checked the whims of Louis XIV or Frederick the Great. His violations of his solemn word, however, were fully in the manner of the age.

Like the muzhik, Peter thought intoxication was a reasonable vacation from reality. He had taken upon himself all the burdens of the state, and the far greater task of transforming an Oriental people into Western civilization; festive drinking with his friends seemed a merited relief from these undertakings. He heartily accepted the peasant adage that drinking is the Russian's joy. The ability to hold liquor was one of his measures of a man. When he was in Paris he wagered that his priest-confessor could drink more and remain stable than the priest-secretary of the French ministry; the contest went on for an hour; when the abbé rolled under the table Peter hugged his priest for having "saved the honor of Russia."[9] About 1690 Peter and his intimates formed a band called the "Most

Drunken Assembly [*sobor*] of Fools and Jesters." Prince Feodor Romodanovsky was elected czar of the *sobor;* Peter accepted a subordinate position (as he did in the army and navy), and often in real life he pretended that Romodanovsky was Czar of Russia. The *sobor* of drunkards was formally dedicated to the worship of Bacchus and Venus; it had an elaborate ritual, mimicking with grossness and obscenity those of the Russian Orthodox and Roman Catholic churches; and much of this mock ritual was composed by Peter himself. The *sobor* took part in many official state celebrations. When its mock patriarch, Nikita Zatov, aged eighty-four, married a bride of sixty, Peter designed and commanded an ornate ribald ceremonial (1715), in which the dignitaries and ladies of the court were to take part along with bears and stags and goats, and ambassadors playing flutes or the hurdy-gurdy, and Peter beating a drum.[10]

His sense of humor was hilarious and unrestrained, often stooping to buffoonery. His court was crowded with jesters and dwarfs, who seemed indispensable to every ceremony. Once the Czar, nearly seven feet tall, playing Gulliver to his Lilliputians, rode in a procession at the head of twenty-four mounted dwarfs. At one time Peter had seventy-two dwarfs at his court, some of whom were served up at table in gigantic pies. There were giants too, but most of these were sent as gifts to Frederick William of Prussia to join his army of obelisks. Several Negroes were presented to Peter. He held them in high esteem, and sent some of them to Paris for an education. One of them became a Russian general, the great-grandfather of the poet Pushkin.

So far we picture Peter as still very much a barbarian, an Ivan the Terrible but humorous; anxious to be civilized, but envying the West not for its graces and arts but for its armies and navies, its commerce and industry and wealth. His virtues were directed to these ends as the prerequisites of civilization. Hence his insatiable curiosity. Of everything he wanted to know how it worked, and then how it could be made to work better. On his travels he exhausted his aides by running about to see this and that, even through the night. He was swamped with ideas, thereby amazing Leibniz, who had a swamp of his own; but Peter's ideas were frankly utilitarian. He had an open mind for anything that could make his country catch up to the West. In a nation gloomily religious and fanatically hostile to foreign creeds and ways, he was as unprejudiced as a child or a sage, sampling Catholicism, Protestantism, even free thought. He was rather imitative than original; he transplanted ideas rather than conceived them; but in attempting to raise his nation to a competitive level with the West it was wiser to absorb first the best that the West could teach, and then try to surpass it. Never had imitation been so original.

His indefatigable devotion to his purpose raised him out of barbarism to greatness. If he conscripted and consumed millions of Russians to his ends, he used himself up, too, in the effort to give Russia a modern army, a more efficient government, more varied and productive industries, wider commerce, and ports that could reach the world. He was economical of everything except human life, which was Russia's one abundant commodity. Almost his first measures on reaching power were to dismiss the horde of servants and palace officials that had cluttered the royal household; to sell three thousand horses from the royal stables; to sweep away three hundred cooks and kitchen boys; to reduce the royal table, even on feast days, to sixteen places at most; to dispense with formal receptions and balls; and to make over to the state the sums that had heretofore been allotted to these luxuries. His father, Alexis, had left him a personal property of 10,734 dessiatines (28,982 acres) of cultivated land and fifty thousand houses, bringing in a revenue of 200,000 rubles yearly; Peter turned nearly all this over to the state treasury, reserving as his own only the ancient patrimony of the Romanov family—eight hundred "souls" in the province of Novgorod. In effect, and in sharp contrast to Louis XIV, the greatest of the czars reduced his court to a few friends, with an occasional festival, informal and sometimes hilarious, to brighten Moscow's monotony. Often his economy became parsimony. He underpaid his palace staff, meted out mathematically its daily allowance of food, invited his friends not to dinner but to picnics where each would pay his share; and when the prostitutes who served him bemoaned their modest honorariums he replied that he paid them as much as he paid a grenadier, whose services were far more valuable.

Women, with one exception, were minor incidents in his life. He was not keenly sensitive to beauty. He had sexual needs, but he dispatched them without ritual. He did not like to sleep alone, but this had nothing to do with sex; usually he had a servant share his bed, probably he wanted someone near him in case he should have a convulsion during the night. At seventeen, to quiet his mother, he married Eudoxia Lopukhina, who was described as "beautiful but stupid"; finding one quality more lasting than the other, he neglected her, and went back to his friends and his ships. He took a succession of transient mistresses, nearly always of lowly origin and condition. When Frederick II of Denmark jested with him about having a mistress, Peter answered, "Brother, my harlots do not cost me much, but yours cost you thousands of crowns, which you could spend in a better way."[11] Both Lefort and Menshikov served the Czar as procurers, and Menshikov surrendered his own mistress to be Peter's second wife. There must have been remarkable ability in her to raise her, like Justinian's Theodora, from strumpet to empress.

The future Catherine I was born about 1685 in Livonia of humble stock.

Left an orphan, she was brought up as a servant by the Lutheran Pastor Glück in Marienburg. He taught her the catechism but not the alphabet; she never learned to read. In 1702 a Russian army under Sheremetiev besieged Marienburg. Despairing of defense, the commander of the garrison decided to blow up his fortress and himself. Pastor Glück, informed of his intention, took his family and his servant and fled to the Russian camp. He was sent on to Moscow, but Catherine was kept as a solace for the soldiers. She graduated through them to Sheremetiev to Menshikov to Peter. In those wars and regions a simple woman had to be complaisant in order to eat. For a time Catherine seems to have served both Menshikov and the Czar. They liked her because she was neat, cheerful, kind, and understanding; for example, she did not insist on being sole mistress. Peter found her a gay relief after the alarums of politics or war and the tantrums of jealous concubines. She accompanied him on campaigns, lived like a soldier, cut her hair, slept on the ground, and did not flinch when she saw men shot down at her side. When a convulsion seized Peter, and all others were afraid to touch him, she would speak to him soothingly, caress him, calm him, and let him sleep with his head on her breast. When they were apart he wrote to his "Katierinoushka" letters of playful and yet sincere tenderness. She became indispensable to him. By 1710 she was his wife in everything but law. She bore him several children. In 1711 she helped to save him at the Prut. In 1712 he publicly acknowledged her as his wife. In 1722 he crowned her empress.

Her influence over him was good in many ways. She, the peasant girl, improved the manners of the royal boor. She moderated his drinking; on several occasions she entered the room where he was carousing with friends, and quietly commanded him, *"Pora domoï, batioushka"* (Come home, little father), and he obeyed. She winked at his postmarital flirtations. She made no attempt to influence politics, but she saw to it that the Czar provided for her future, her relatives, and her friends. She overcame widespread resentment of her elevation by acting as an angel of mercy; in several instances she saved persons from the penalties to which Peter wished to condemn them; and when he insisted on severity he had to conceal it from her. She abused her power over him by selling her intercession; in this way she amassed a secret fortune, part of which she judiciously invested under assumed names at Hamburg or Amsterdam. Shall we blame her for seeking some security at a time when everything depended upon one man's whim, and all Russia was in flux?

II. THE PETRINE REVOLUTION

Peter had inherited absolute power, took it for granted, and never doubted its necessity. Rule by the *duma* of boyars would restore feudal separatism and national chaos or stagnation; rule by a democratic assembly was impossible in a country still mentally and morally primitive; Peter agreed with Cromwell and Louis XIV that only the concentration of authority and responsibility could organize the human motley into a state strong enough to control the passions of the people and repel the attacks of land-hungry enemies. He thought of himself not as a despot but as a servant of the nation and its future; and in large measure this was an honest belief, at least half true.

He worked as hard as the simplest peasant in his realm. Normally he rose at five in the morning and labored fourteen hours a day. He slept only six hours at night, but took a siesta after noon. Such a program was not impracticable in the St. Petersburg summers, when daylight began at 3 A.M. and lasted till 10 P.M.; but in winter much of it had to go on during the night, which began about three in the afternoon and continued till nine the next morning.

St. Petersburg was the symbol and Archimedean fulcrum of his revolution. It was not an ideal site for a capital, being too close to the coast; even so, it was twenty-five miles from the sea, at a point where the River Neva split into two branches; and Peter hoped to protect it by the fortress of Kronstadt that he raised (1710) on an island at the entrance to the bay. The city itself was founded in 1703, on the model of Amsterdam. Since much of the site was marshy (*neva* is Swedish for mud), St. Petersburg was built upon piles—or, as a sad Russian saying had it, upon the bones of the thousands of laborers who were conscripted to lay those foundations and rear the town. In 1708 some 40,000 men were sent to the task; in 1709 another 40,000; in 1711, 46,000; in 1713, 40,000 more. They were paid half a ruble per month, which they had to supplement with begging and thieving. Swedish prisoners of war employed in the construction died by the thousands. As there were no wheelbarrows, the men transported the materials in their uplifted caftans. Stone too was conscripted; a ukase of 1714 forbade the erection of stone houses anywhere in Russia except in St. Petersburg; but there every nobleman in the land was commanded to raise a dwelling of stone. The nobles did it under protest, hating the climate and not sharing Peter's love of the sea. For himself Peter had some Dutch artisans put together a cottage like those that he had seen at Zaandam, with log walls, shingle roof, and small rooms. He disliked palaces, but allowed three at Peterhof (now Petrodvorets), on the southern outskirts of the city, for ceremonial occasions; this "Summer Palace" was destroyed in the Second World War. In a nearby suburb, Tsarskoe Selo (now Pushkin), he built a summer cottage for his Katierinoushka.

He did not at first intend to make St. Petersburg a capital as well as a port; it was too close to hostile Sweden; but after his victory over Charles XII at Poltava he decided to make the change. He longed to get away from the somber ecclesiastical atmosphere of Moscow and its narrow nationalism, and he wanted the conservative nobles to feel progressive winds from the West. So in 1712 he made it his capital. The Muscovites mourned, and predicted that God would soon destroy the half-heathen city. "Before the new capital," wrote Pushkin, "Moscow bowed her head, as an imperial widow bows before a young tsaritsa."[12] Peter was so anxious to Westernize Russia that he dragged it, so to speak, to the Baltic and bade it look through his "window on the West."* To this purpose, and to have a base for his fleet and a port for foreign trade, he sacrificed all other considerations. The port would be icebound five months in the year, but it would face the West and touch the sea. As the Dnieper had made Russia Byzantine and the Volga had made it Asiatic, so now the Neva would invite it to be European.[14]

The next step was to build a navy that would guard the lanes of Russian commerce through the Baltic to the West. Peter achieved this for a time by building in the course of his reign a thousand galleys; but they were hastily and badly constructed, their timbers rotted, their masts broke in the wind; and after his death Russia reconciled herself to being what geography had made it, a landlocked country shut off from the Atlantic, and waiting for the conquest of the air to overleap its barriers into the world. In this sense Moscow was right: Russia's power and defense had to be on land, through its armies and its space. So, in 1917, Moscow had its revenge, and became the capital again.

Peter's most permanent reform was the reorganization of the army. Before him it had depended upon levies of peasants led by their feudal lords, loyal chiefly to them, poorly disciplined, and poorly armed. Peter undermined the boyars by establishing a standing army manned by conscription, equipped with the latest weapons of the West, officered by men who had passed through the ranks, and disciplined in the new ideal of proudly serving Russia rather than a narrow province or a hated lord. It was military necessity that dictated Peter's revolution. He could not develop Russia without opening a way to the Baltic or the Mediterranean; he could not do this without a modern army; he could not maintain such an army without transforming the Russian economy and government; and

---

* This phrase was apparently first used by Count Francesco Algarotti in 1739.[13]

he could not transform these without remaking the Russian people in manners, aims, and soul. It was too great a task for one man, or for one generation.

He began, in his whimsical impulsive way, with the beards and dress of the men around him. In 1698, soon after returning from the West, he had his own sparse beard shaved, and commanded all who wished to keep his favor to do the same, excepting only the Patriarch of the Orthodox Church. Soon an edict went throughout Russia that all laymen were to shave their chins; mustaches might remain. The beard had been almost a religious symbol in Russia; it had been worn by the Prophets and the Apostles; and the reigning Patriarch, Adrian, only eight years before, had condemned the shaving of the beard as irreligious and heretical. Peter accepted the challenge: beardlessness was to be a sign of modernity, of willingness to enter into Western civilization. Those laymen who felt a dire need of whiskers might keep them by paying an annual tax rising from one kopek for a peasant to a hundred rubles for a rich merchant. "There were many old Russians," says an old history, "who, after having their beards shaved off, saved them preciously, in order to have them placed in their coffins, fearing that they would not be allowed to enter heaven without them."[15]

Next to go was the Russian costume. Here too Peter felt that internal resistance to Westernization would be reduced by wearing Western garb. He himself cut off the long sleeves of the army officers who appeared before him. "See," he said to one of them, "these things are in your way. You are safe nowhere with them. At one moment you upset a glass, then you forgetfully dip them in the sauce. Get gaiters made of them."[16] So an order went forth (January, 1700) commanding all courtiers and officials in Russia to adopt Western dress. All persons entering or leaving Moscow had to choose between having their ankle-long caftans cut at the knees or paying a fine. The women were likewise urged to adopt Western costume; they resisted less than the men, for in dress women are annual revolutionists.

Not so much by decrees as by the example of his family, Peter ended the seclusion of Russia's women. His father, Alexis, and his mother, Natalia, had led the way; his half-sister Sophia had broadened it; now Peter invited women to social gatherings, encouraged them to remove their veils, to dance, to make music, and to seek education, even if only through tutors. He issued edicts forbidding parents to marry their children against their will, and requiring an interval of six weeks between betrothal and marriage; in that period the engaged couple should be allowed to see each other frequently, and to break off the engagement if they wished. The women were glad to emerge from the *terem;* they began a race to adopt new fashions; and some increase in illegitimate births gave the clergy a weapon against Peter's revolution.

The resistance of religion was his greatest obstacle. The clergy realized that his reforms would lessen their prestige and power. They bemoaned his toleration of Western faiths in Russia, and they suspected that he himself had no religious belief. They heard with horror of the parodies with which he and his intimates mocked the Orthodox ritual. For his part Peter resented the diversion of manpower into the vast and innumerable monasteries, and he coveted the enormous revenues that these institutions enjoyed. When the Patriarch Adrian died (October, 1700), Peter deliberately refrained from appointing a successor; he himself, like Henry VIII in England, became head of the church, and led a Reformation in Russia. For twenty-one years the office of patriarch remained vacant, depriving the Orthodox Church of a leader against the Petrine reforms. In 1721 Peter abolished the office altogether, and replaced it with a "Holy Synod" of ecclesiastics appointed by the Czar and subject to a lay procurator. In 1701 he transferred the administration of ecclesiastical properties to a department of the government. The jurisdiction of the ecclesiastical courts was curtailed. The appointment of bishops was made subject to governmental approval. Further edicts forbade the ordination of mystics or fanatics, and limited the number of miracle-working centers. Men were not to take monastic vows before the age of thirty; women were not to take final vows as nuns before the age of fifty.[17] Monks were to be compelled to do useful work. A census of monastic properties and revenues was taken by the government; a part of this income was left to the monasteries, the rest was devoted to the establishment of schools and hospitals.[18]

Most of the clergy resigned themselves to this Russian Reformation, which, again like that of Henry VIII, left doctrine unchanged. Some Raskolniki (dissenters) denounced Peter as Antichrist, and urged the people to refuse him obedience or taxes. He had the leaders of this rebellion arrested, and dealt with them after his usual fashion: some were knouted and banished to Siberia, some were imprisoned for life, one died of torture, two were slowly burned to death.[19]

For the rest, Peter was abreast of the West in religious toleration. He protected the Raskolniki from persecution as long as they abstained from politics. In St. Petersburg, to encourage foreign trade, he allowed Calvinist, Lutheran, and Catholic churches to be built on the Nevski Prospekt, which came to be called the "Prospect of Tolerance."[20] He protected the Capuchin monks who entered Russia, but banished the Jesuits (1710) as too sedulous in propaganda for the Roman Church. In general the religious reforms of Peter were the most lasting of all. They ended the Middle Ages in Russia.

A vast process of secularization changed the life and spirit of Russia from domination by priests and landlords to rule, almost regimentation, by the state. Peter subordinated the boyars to his will, made them serve the public, and reorganized social ranks according to the importance of the social service performed. A new aristocracy arose, composed of officials in the army, the navy, and the bureaucracy. The government was headed by a Senate of nine (later twenty) men appointed by the Czar; it was administered by nine "colleges" directing respectively taxation and revenue, expenditure, audit and control, commerce, industry, foreign relations, war, navy, and law. Responsible to the Senate were the governors of the twelve provinces, or guberniyas, and the councils that ruled the cities. The population of each city was divided into three classes: rich merchants and the professions, teachers and craftsmen, wage earners and laborers; only the first class could be elected to the municipal council (*magistrat*), only the first two classes could vote, but all male taxpayers could take part in the town meetings. The mir, or village community, took form not as a democratic institution, but as a body collectively responsible for the poll tax introduced in 1719. Local autonomy was checked by central control, and there was no thought of democracy. The rapid transformation that Peter planned could be achieved, if at all, only by dictatorial power.

That transformation had to be economic as well as political, for no purely agricultural society could long maintain its independence against states enriched and armed by industry. A German economist of the time pointed out what the next two hundred years would prove—that a nation exporting chiefly raw material and agricultural products would soon become vassal to states producing and exporting chiefly manufactured goods.[21] For agriculture, therefore, Peter did little. Instead of reducing serfdom he extended it to industry. By his own example he taught the peasants how to cut their corn, and he commanded the replacement of sickles with scythes. The Russians were accustomed to burn the woodlands to provide fertilizing ashes for the soil; Peter forbade this, needing lumber for his ships, trees for his masts. He introduced the cultivation of the tobacco plant, the mulberry, and the vine, and began the Russian breeding of horses and sheep.

But his chief aim was rapid industrialization. The first problem was to provide raw materials. He spurred the spread of mining; he gave stimulating rewards to men like Nikita Demidov and Aleksandr Stroganov who showed enterprise and skill in mining and metallurgy; he urged landowners to encourage or allow the extraction of minerals from their soils, and decreed that if they neglected to do this their soil might be mined by others by paying them merely a nominal fee. By 1710 Russia ceased to import iron; before Peter's death it was exporting it.[22]

He brought in foreign artisans and managers, and prodded the Russians of every rank to learn the industrial arts. An Englishman opened in Moscow a factory for treating hides and making shoes; Peter commanded every town in Russia to send a delegation of cobblers to Moscow to learn the latest methods of making boots and shoes, and held the galleys as a threat over shoemakers who clung to their old ways. To encourage the Russian textile industry he wore, after this was functioning, only native-made cloth, and forbade the Muscovites to buy imported stockings. Soon the Russians were making good textiles. An admiral shocked tradition and delighted the Czar by manufacturing silk brocades. A muzhik developed a lacquer superior to any similar product in "Europe" except the Venetian. Before the reign was over there were 233 factories in Russia. Some were quite large: the Moscow manufacture of sailcloth employed 1,162 workers; one textile mill used 742 men; another, 730; one metallurgical establishment had 683 employees.[23] There had been factories in Russia before Peter, but not on this scale. Many of the new plants were started by the government and were later sold to private management; but even then they received state subsidies, and were subject to detailed supervision by the government. High protective tariffs shielded the incipient industries from foreign competition.

To man the factories Peter resorted to conscription. Since there were few free laborers available, peasants were converted, willy-nilly, into industrial workers. Manufacturers were empowered to buy serfs from landlords, and put them to work in the factories. Large-scale undertakings were supplied with peasants transferred from state lands and farms.[24] As in most governmental attempts at rapid industrialization, the leaders could not wait for the acquisitive instinct to overcome habit and tradition and lead workers from old fields and ways to new tasks and disciplines. An industrial serfdom was developed, more or less reluctantly by Peter, deliberately by his successors. Peter apologized in an edict of 1723:

> Is not everything done [at first] by compulsion? That there are few people willing to go into business [industry] is true, for our people are like children, who never want to begin the alphabet unless they are compelled by their teachers. It seems very hard to them at first, but when they have learnt it they are thankful. Already much thanksgiving is heard for what has already borne fruit. . . . So in manufacturing affairs we must act and compel, and help by teaching.[25]

But industry could not develop without commerce to sell its products. To encourage commerce Peter raised the social status of the merchant class. He forced the growth of a great shipbuilding industry at Archangel and St. Petersburg. He tried (and failed) to establish a merchant marine to carry Russian goods in Russian ships; the muzhik, rooted and locked in his land, did not take willingly or ably to the sea. Within Russia itself trade was discouraged by great distances and forbidding roads. But rivers abounded, fed by the snows of the north and the rains of the south; and when the rivers froze they froze so firmly that they, like the frozen roads, could carry heavy loads. What was needed was to bind these rivers with canals—to lead the Neva and the Dvina to the Volga, and the Volga to the Don, and so unite the Baltic and the White Sea with the Black Sea and the Caspian. Peter laid the foundation of the great system, and opened in 1708 the link between the Neva and the Volga; but several reigns had to pass before the network was complete, and thousands of workers died in the attempt.

War and his multifarious enterprises compelled Peter to raise capital in quantities unprecedented in Russia. Part of this he secured by giving the government a monopoly in the production and sale of salt, tobacco, tar, fats, potash, resin, glue, rhubarb, caviar, even of oak coffins. These coffins were sold at a profit of four hundred per cent; salt made a modest one hundred per cent. But the Czar realized that monopolies discouraged both industry and trade, and after peace was signed with Sweden he abolished them at one stroke, leaving internal trade free. Foreign trade remained subject to import and export duties, but it multiplied almost tenfold between 1700 and Peter's death in 1725. Most of it was carried in foreign vessels, and what remained in Russian hands was hampered by widespread bribery that even Peter's draconic penalties could not suppress.

Taxation was exhaustive. A special group of governmental appointees was charged with devising and administering new taxes. There were taxes on hats, boots, beehives, rooms, cellars, chimneys, births, marriages, beards. A tax on households was frustrated by whole and chaotic migrations; Peter changed it to a tax on "souls" wherever found; this did not apply to the nobility or the clergy. The revenues of the state rose from 1,400,000 rubles in 1680 to 8,500,000 in 1724—of which seventy-five per cent went to the army and navy. Half of the increase was unreal, being due to a fifty per cent depreciation of the currency during Peter's reign, for he could not resist the temptation to make a temporary profit by debasing the coinage.

From monarch to muzhik dishonesty clogged the economy, the collection of taxes, the decisions of the courts, the administration of the laws. Peter decreed death for all officials who accepted "gifts," but one of his aides warned him that if he enforced this decree he would soon have none but dead officials. He killed some of them nevertheless. Prince Matvei Gagarin, governor of Siberia, became too conspicuously rich; he adorned his statue of the Virgin with jewels worth 130,000 rubles; Peter wanted to know how the Virgin got them; when he found out he had Gagarin hanged. In 1714 several high officials were arrested for stealing from the government and the people; they included the vice-governor of St. Petersburg, the head of the state commissary, the head of the admiralty, the commandants of Narva and Revel, and several senators. Some were hanged, some were given life imprisonment, some had their noses slit, some were beaten with rods. When Peter gave the order to halt the punishment, the soldiers who had administered it begged him, "Father, allow us to flog a little more, for the thieves [have] stolen even our bread."[26] Corruption continued. A Russian proverb said that Christ himself would steal if his hands were not tied to the Cross.

Amid this struggle of one will to change the economic and political life of half a continent, Peter found time to attempt a cultural revolution too. He hated superstition, and longed to replace it with education and science. The Russians had heretofore dated the years from the supposed creation of the world, and had begun them with September. Peter, in 1699, brought the Russian calendar in harmony with the Julian, as used by the Protestant states; hereafter the year was to begin with January, and be dated from the birth of Christ. The people complained; how could God have chosen midwinter as the time of Creation? Peter had his way, but he did not dare adopt the Gregorian calendar, which Catholic Europe had accepted in 1582. The elimination of ten days, as required by that "papistical trick," would have robbed several Orthodox saints of their holydays.

The restless Czar succeeded in the equally difficult enterprise of reforming the alphabet. The Orthodox Church used the old Slavonic alphabet, but the business classes had adopted an alphabet based on the Greek. Peter ordered all secular works to be printed in this new form. He imported printing presses and printers from the Netherlands; he started (1703) the first Russian newspaper, the *Gazette of St. Petersburg;* he ordered and financed the publication of books on technology and science; he founded the Library of St. Petersburg, and established the Russian Archives by gathering into the library the manuscripts, records, and chronicles of the monasteries. He opened several technical institutes, and ordered the sons of the aristocracy to enter them. He tried to set up in each province a "mathematical school," and in Moscow he provided a *gymnasium* after the German model, to teach languages, literature, and philosophy; but these schools did not long survive. In 1724 he organized the Academy of St. Petersburg; to this he brought such distinguished savants as Joseph Delisle to teach astronomy, and Daniel Bernoulli for mathematics. On Leibniz' prompting he commissioned (1724) Vitus Bering, the Danish navigator, to lead an expedition to Kamchatka to find out whether Asia and America were physically united. Bering sailed after Peter's death.

Under Alexis the Russian theater had given only private performances. Peter licensed a theater on the Red Square and opened it to the public;

he imported German players, who presented fifteen tragedies and comedies, including some of Molière. Foreign musicians were brought in to provide orchestras; the sonata and the concerto were introduced into Russia, and Russian secular music took European forms of harmony and counterpoint. Peter commissioned the purchase of paintings and statues, chiefly Italian, gathered these and other works into a museum of art in St. Petersburg, opened the museum to all visitors without charge, and had refreshments served to them.[27] Foreign painters came to paint portraits in Western style. Some churches were built during the reigns of Alexis, hardly any under Peter; architects now found it more profitable to build palaces.

No great literature flowered during this uprooting revolution; time would be needed before the stimulus of Peter would be felt in poetry. One brave book appeared in the year before Peter's death. Ivan Possoshkov's *Book of Poverty and Wealth* chided the Russians for barbarism and illiteracy, and strongly supported the Czar's reforms. "Unhappily," it said, "our great monarch is almost alone, with ten others, in pulling upwards, while millions of individuals pull downwards."[28] Ivan denounced the oppression of the peasantry, demanded an impartial administration of justice by courts free from class domination, and shocked the Czar by asking that representatives of all classes be brought together to write a new constitution and code of laws for Russia. A few months after Peter's death Possoshkov was arrested; he died in prison in 1726.

III. AFTERMATH

The resistance to Peter's reforms rose from year to year. The Russians were accustomed to poverty, suffering, and despotism, but not even under Ivan the Terrible had they borne such burdens, or paid such taxes, or died in such numbers not only in battle but in forced labor, from hunger, cold, exhaustion, and disease. "Misery increases from day to day," wrote Peter's beloved Lefort in 1723; "the streets are full of people who try to sell their children . . . The government pays neither the troops, nor the navy, nor the [administrative] colleges, nor anybody."[29] The Czar, bewildered by the growth of poverty amid his reforms, made it a crime to beg, or to give to beggars, and set up sixty organizations to distribute charity.

Begging continued, and crime spread. Serfs fleeing from servitude, soldiers and conscript laborers deserting their camps at the risk of their lives, almost ruled the roads. Sometimes they organized themselves into regiments, several hundred strong, which besieged and captured cities. "Moscow," reported a general in 1718, "is a hotbed of brigandage, everything is devastated, the number of lawbreakers is multiplying, and executions never stop." Some streets in Moscow were barricaded by the citizens, some houses were surrounded with high fences, to keep thieves out. Peter tried to suppress robbery by severity: captured brigands were to be hanged, housebreakers were to have their noses cut off to the bone, etc. The criminals were not deterred. Life was so hard for the poor that they looked upon capital punishment as hardly distinguishable from the life imprisonment of serfdom or forced toil, and they bore the most appalling tortures with the stoicism of deadened nerves.

Peter was so unpopular that many wondered that no one killed him. The nobles hated him for compelling them to serve the state, and for raising up the business classes to prominence and wealth; the peasants hated him for conscripting them into labor that uprooted them from their homes, often from their families; churchmen hated him as the Beast of the Apocalypse, who had made Christ himself the servant of the government; nearly all Russians distrusted him for consorting with foreigners and importing "heathen" ideas; all Russia feared him because of his violence and savage penalties. Russia did not want to be Westernized; it abominated the West; to preserve its own national spirit it had to be "Slavophil." Desperate revolts broke out in Moscow in 1698, in Astrakhan in 1705, along the Volga in 1707, and sporadically throughout the empire and the reign.

Peter symbolized and intensified the conflict by twice returning to the West. In the fall of 1711 he went to Germany to preside at Torgau over the marriage of his son. There he received Leibniz, who proposed to him the establishment of a Russian Academy, of which the polymorphous philosopher hoped to be president. The Czar was back in St. Petersburg in January, 1712, but in October, amid a campaign against Sweden, he took the waters at Carlsbad, and visited Wittenberg. Some Lutheran clergymen took him to the house in which Luther had flung an inkwell at the Devil, and they showed him the ink spot on the wall. They asked him to write some comment on the wall; he wrote: "The ink is quite fresh, so that the story is evidently not true."[30] Peter returned to his new capital in April, 1713. In February, 1716, he was off to the West again; he visited Germany and Holland, and in May, 1717, reached Paris, hoping to marry his daughter Elizabeth to Louis XV. Meeting the seven-year-old King, Peter lifted him up to embrace him; a few days later, received by Louis before the royal palace, Peter raised him like an infant and carried him up the steps, setting the court atremble. He spent six weeks in Paris as a sightseer, absorbing every aspect of the political, economic, and cultural life of the city. He had his portrait painted by Rigaud and by Nattier. He visited the aged Mme. de Maintenon at St.-Cyr. From Paris he went to Spa, and for five weeks he drank the waters there, for by this time he was suffering from a dozen ailments. At Berlin his wife, Catherine, joined him. She discovered that he had a mistress, but she forgave this as in the best traditions of European royalty. When they reached St. Petersburg (October 20, 1716) Peter faced one of the worst crises of his career.

His son Alexis, to whom he had hoped to bequeath the realm and the advancement of his reforms, had come to dislike many of those innovations, and the methods by which they were enforced. Physically and mentally Alexis was the son of Eudoxia rather than of Peter. He was small, timid, and weak, fond of books, and devoted to the Orthodox Church, for he had been reared in piety while Peter went off to war and the West. At the age of nine Alexis saw his mother dismissed to a convent (1699); when he was eleven he heard the priests mourning the melting of church bells for cannon; he asked his father why Russians should go out of Russia to fight for so distant a city as Narva; Peter was disgusted to find that his heir had no taste for bloodshed.

While Peter busied himself building St. Petersburg, Alexis remained in Moscow, loving its churches and ancient ways. He resented the disruption of the patriarchate and the confiscation of monastic property by the state. His confessor taught him always to defend the church, at whatever cost. Alexis became the idol and hope of the ecclesiastical and aristocratic groups that hated Peter's secularization and Westernization of Russia, and they waited impatiently for the time when this religious and manageable youth would succeed to the throne. Peter seldom saw him, and then usually scolded him, sometimes struck him, as when the Czar found that the boy had secretly visited his mother in her nunnery. The youth's disaffection came near to hatred. He admitted to his confessor Ignatiev that he wished his father were dead. Ignatiev thought this no sin. "God will forgive you," he told Alexis; "we all wish for his death, because the people have to bear such heavy burdens."[31]

In 1708 Peter sent his son to Dresden to study geometry and fortification. At Torgau in 1711 Alexis married Princess Charlotte Christina Sophia of Brunswick-Wolfenbüttel. He could not pardon her refusal to abandon her Lutheran faith for the Russian Orthodox religion. He took mistresses, even from brothels, and drank heavily. Shortly after Charlotte had borne him a child he visited her in the company of a courtesan.[32] A year later his wife died in childbirth (1715). Peter summoned him to St. Petersburg in an angry letter containing ominous words: "I do not spare my own life, nor that of any of my subjects; I will make no exception in your case. You will mend your ways, and you will make yourself useful to the state; otherwise you shall be disinherited."[33] Alexis sought to appease his father by resigning his rights to the throne; he would be satisfied, he said, to lead a quiet life in the country. Peter felt that this was no solution. On January 30, 1716, he wrote to Alexis:

I cannot believe your oath. . . . David said that all men are liars, so that [even] if you wished to keep it you could be dissuaded by the long-beards. . . . It is known to everyone that you hate my deeds, which I do for the people of this nation, not sparing my health, and after my death you will destroy them. For that reason, to stay as you would like to be, neither fish nor flesh, is impossible. Therefore either change your character, and without hypocrisy be my worthy successor, or become a monk. Give me immediately an answer. . . . If you do not do this, I will treat you as a criminal.[34]

Alexis' friends advised him to become a monk. "A monk's cowl is not nailed on a man," said one of them; "it can be laid aside again." Alexis wrote to his father that he was willing to become a monk. Peter relented, and told him to take half a year to make up his mind. The Czar went off to the West (February, 1716). On June 29 Peter's sister Natalia counseled Alexis to leave Russia and put himself under the protection of the Emperor. In September Peter wrote to his son from Copenhagen saying that the half year was up, and that Alexis must enter a monastery at once, or join his father in Denmark, prepared for military service. Alexis pretended that he was going to his father; he obtained funds from Menshikov and the Senate, and proceeded not to Copenhagen but to Vienna (November 10). He begged the Imperial Vice-Chancellor to secure for him the protection of the Emperor Charles VI. "My father," he said, "is incredibly wrathful and vengeful, and spares no man; and if the Emperor gives me back to my father it is all the same as taking my life."[35] The Vice-Chancellor sent him to the Castle of Ehrenberg in the Tirol. There Alexis remained in concealment and disguise, under surveillance but supplied with all comforts, and allowed to keep with him his mistress Afrosinia, dressed as a page. Peter's agents traced him there; Alexis, warned, fled to Naples, where he was guarded in the Castel Sant' Elmo. Peter's agents found him and urged him to return to Russia in confidence of his father's mercy. He consented, on condition that Peter allow him to live with Afrosinia in rural retirement. Peter so promised in a letter of November 28, 1717. Alexis arranged to have Afrosinia stay in Italy till she bore her child. On his long journey to Russia he sent her the tenderest letters.

He reached Moscow at the end of January. On February 3 Peter received him in a solemn assembly of the leading dignitaries of state and church. Alexis, kneeling and in tears, asked pardon. Peter granted it, but disinherited him, and declared Catherine's son Peter Petrovich, now in his third year, heir to the throne. Alexis pledged allegiance to the new Czarevich. Peter now made his pardon conditional on Alexis' confession of his accomplices in the opposition to his father's reforms. Alexis implicated many; they were arrested and were tortured to elicit further details; several were banished to Siberia, some were executed after the most barbarous torments. Alexis, in apparent freedom, was installed in a house near the Czar's palace in St. Petersburg, and was allotted an annual pension of forty thousand rubles. He wrote to Afrosinia that his father treated him well and had invited him to his table. He looked forward to her coming, and to happiness with her in rural peace.

She arrived in April. She was at once arrested; she was subjected not to torture but to a severe examination; she broke down, and confessed that Alexis had rejoiced at news of rebellions against his father, that he had expressed his intention, on coming to power, to abandon St. Petersburg and the navy, and to reduce the army to the needs of defense. This was nothing worse than what Peter already knew, and he left Alexis at liberty for two months more. Then, spurred on by new revelations not known to us, he announced that since his pardon of Alexis had presumed a full confession, and he now had evidence that the confession had been insincere and incomplete, he withdrew the pardon. On June 14 Alexis was arrested, and was confined in the SS. Peter and Paul Fortress.

On June 19, 1718, after examination by the High Court of Justice, he was put to the torture for the first time, receiving twenty-five blows of the knout. He confessed that he had desired his father's death, and that his confessor had told him, "We all wish for his death." He was confronted with Afrosinia, who repeated what she had told the Czar; nevertheless he vowed that he would love her till his death. He admitted, "By degrees not only everything about my father, but his very person, became odious to me." He acknowledged that he would have used the Emperor's help "to conquer the crown by main force."[36] On June 24 a further torture by fifteen blows of the knout drew from him nothing more. The High Court pronounced him guilty of treason, and condemned him to death. Alexis begged to be allowed to embrace his mistress before his execution; we do not know if this was granted him. Peter did not sign the sentence. Twice again (June 25 and 26) Alexis was interrogated under torture, the second time in the presence of the Czar and members of the court; and Lefort later reported, "Though I am not sure of this, I am assured that his father struck the first blows."[37] That afternoon Alexis died in prison, apparently from the effects of torture. One story says that Catherine bade the doctors open his veins; we cannot say whether this was an act of mercy or of ambition for her son. Afrosinia received a share of Alexis' property, married an officer of the guard, and lived comfortably in St. Petersburg for thirty years more.

Peter hoped to raise Catherine's son to succeed him, but the boy died in 1719. Catherine bore two more sons, Peter and Paul, but both died before the Czar. He consoled himself with the majestic titles awarded him after the peace with Sweden. In that year 1721 the Senate and the Holy

Synod conferred the title of empress upon Catherine. After allowing Russia its one year of peace since the beginning of his active rule, Peter turned his forces against Persia. He hoped to clear and control a caravan route to Central Asia, at last to India; his informants told him that gold could be found on the way; and he anticipated the industrial possibilities of Caucasian and Middle Eastern oil.[38] In 1722 he sent a fleet over the Caspian to attack Persia. It captured Baku and some of the Persian Caspian coast; but storms destroyed most of the ships, disease decimated the army, and Peter returned from the campaign of 1724 exhausted, pessimistic, and near death.

He had for years been suffering from syphilis,[39] and from the medicines taken to cure it. Heavy drinking had made matters worse, and the excitements of war, revolution, revolts, and terroristic violence had finally exhausted his giant physique. In November, 1724, he jumped into the icy Neva to help rescue sailors on a grounded vessel. He worked through a whole night in water up to his waist. On the next day he had a fever, but he survived it, and resumed a heavy schedule of activities. On January 25 he took to his bed with painful inflammation of the bladder. Not till February 2 would he admit that death was upon him. He confessed some of his sins, and received the sacraments. On the sixth he signed a proclamation freeing all prisoners except those condemned for murder or offenses against the state. He startled his attendants with his cries of pain. He called for a slate on which to write his will; but when he had written only the words "Give all," the pen fell from his hand. Soon he lapsed into a coma, which continued thirty-six hours, and from which he did not awake. He was pronounced dead on February 8, 1725. He was fifty-two years old.

Russia breathed with relief, as if a long and terrible nightmare had ended at last. The Kings of Sweden and Poland rejoiced; they expected Russia to fall into anarchy, and be no longer a danger to the West. The old medieval Russia raised its head and begged for a return to the past. The nation had been too violently propelled, and it had been hurt in its soul and pride by too indiscriminate an imitation of the West. Reaction was widespread and victorious. Many of the reforms were allowed to die from lack of support. The administrative bureaucracy was reduced, but its framework endured till 1917. The nobles regained much of their old power; they recovered their rights to the timber and minerals on their lands. The business class, so suddenly elevated by Peter, returned to its former subjection. Many of the new industries collapsed through inadequate machinery, or incompetence in labor or management. The incipient capitalism faded away, and economic Russia remained for another two hundred years essentially as she had been before the Petrine revolution. The commercial reforms had better success; trade with the West continued to increase. Some improvement of manners resulted from the contacts with Europe, but the old native costumes returned under Catherine II (1762–96), and beards came back into style with Alexander II (1855–81). Corruption continued. Morals showed no gain, and perhaps Peter's example of drunkenness, licentiousness, and brutality left his people morally worse than before. Only those changes survived that had sunk their roots in time.

Peter was among the less lovable figures of modern history. And yet his achievement was immense. His failures attest the limitations of genius as a factor in history, but the mark that he left upon Russia is a tribute to the power of personality. He gave Russia an army and navy; he opened the ports that allowed her to trade goods and ideas with the West; he established mining and metallurgy; he founded schools and an academy. With one savage pull he drew Russia out of Asia into Europe and made her a factor in European affairs. Henceforth Europe would have to reckon more and more with that vast heartland, those hardy, patient, stoic multitudes, and their imperious and inescapable destiny.

CHAPTER XIV

The Changing Empire

1648–1715

I. THE REORGANIZATION OF GERMANY

THE Thirty Years' War had cut the population of Germany from
20,000,000 to 13,500,000. The soil, fertilized by human blood, recovered in a year, but it waited for men. Of women there was an excess,
of men a dearth. The triumphant princes met this biological crisis by a return to Biblical polygamy. At the Congress of Franconia, held in February,
1650, at Nuremberg, they adopted a resolution that

> men under sixty years of age shall not be admitted to monasteries.
> . . . Priests and curates (if not ordained), and the canons of religious
> establishments, shall marry . . . Every male shall be allowed to marry
> two wives; and each and every male is earnestly reminded, and shall
> often be warned from the pulpit, to so comport himself in this matter.[1]

Taxes were imposed upon unmarried women.[2] Soon the new births restored the approximate equality of the sexes, and wives insisted on whole
husbands. Population rapidly recovered, and by 1700 Germany again had
20,000,000 souls. Magdeburg was rebuilt; Leipzig and Frankfurt-am-Main
were reinvigorated by their fairs; Hamburg and Bremen emerged stronger
than before. Industry and commerce, however, took over a hundred years
to regain their sixteenth-century level. The Swedes and the Dutch controlled the mouths of the Oder, the Elbe, and the Rhine, and oceanic transport was leaving inland traffic relatively becalmed. The middle classes
declined. The towns were now ruled not by businessmen but by the territorial princes or their appointees.

The war had ended in disaster for the Imperial Hapsburg power. France
had humbled it, and had humbled the Empire's ally, Spain. The German
princes were now collectively stronger than the emperor. They had their
own armies, courts, and coinage, determined their own foreign policies,
formed their own alliances with non-German states, even against the Imperial interest. There were now some two hundred "temporal" principalities enjoying such independence; sixty-three ecclesiastical states ruled by
Roman Catholic archbishops, bishops, or abbots; and fifty-one "free cities,"

subject only to the emperor, and only formally to him. France rejoiced to see so many Germanies rather than one.

The margraviate of Brandenburg was the symbol of the Empire dying, of a new Germany taking form. There, far from the emperor, facing Sweden and an ocean of Slavs, the Hohenzollern family learned that their little state could survive only through its own resources and force. Back in the tenth century Henry the Fowler had established the "Northern Mark [i.e., frontier] of the Saxons" along the Elbe as a bulwark against the Slavic inundation. He wrested from the Slavic Wends their fortress and capital of Brennibor (from which the name Brandenburg was derived), and drove them back to the Oder. For centuries the territory between the Elbe and the Oder changed hands between the Germans and the Slavs. The margraviate came more actively into history when Frederick of Hohenzollern, in 1411–17, purchased it and its electoral vote in the Imperial Diet. From that time onward the house of Hohenzollern governed Brandenburg till it became Prussia, and Prussia till the abdication of William II in 1918. Rarely has a family been so long and so intimately associated with a state, or devoted itself so zealously and effectively to a nation's prosperity and aggrandizement. Under the Elector John Sigismund (1608–19) Brandenburg acquired the duchy of Cleve in the west and the duchy of East Prussia in the east, so that the margraviate already presaged the kingdom of Prussia. One of the weakest members of the family was the Elector George William (1619–40), whose vacillations in the Thirty Years' War led to the devastation of Brandenburg by Swedish troops. Villages and towns were deserted, Berlin was laid waste, industry almost disappeared; the population of the margraviate fell from 600,000 to 210,000. Inheriting this desolation (1640), Frederick William accomplished in his reign of forty-eight years such a miracle of restoration and development that even his contemporaries yielded him the name "Great Elector." Without him Frederick the Great (as Frederick the Great admitted[3]) would have been impossible.

He was twenty when he came to power—a handsome, black-haired, dark-eyed youth breaking authority. He had been reared in piety and discipline, and had completed his schooling at the University of Leiden. Anticipating Peter of Russia, he admired the Dutch people, their sturdy courage and industrious ways; later he brought in thousands of them to repopulate his man-hungry land. At the Peace of Westphalia he obtained eastern (Farther) Pomerania, the bishoprics of Minden and Halberstadt, and the right of succession to the important archbishopric of Magdeburg; this fell to him in 1680, and Frederick William ended his reign with a scattered realm already straining to be a kingdom. As early as 1654 his chief minister, Count George Frederick of Waldeck, proposed to unite all Germany under the Hohenzollern house.[4] Frederick William seemed the man to undertake this protective union. When Augustus the Strong of Saxony became a Catholic to be King of Poland, the road to Protestant leadership of Germany lay open—except for Swedish power.

For the treaties of 1648 had left some of the most strategic points in Germany under Swedish control, and Sweden claimed the leadership of Protestant Germany by right of its sacrifices and victories in the Thirty Years' War. How could Brandenburg-Prussia, with its constituent parts hedged in by rival states from one end of Germany to the other, become strong enough to defend itself against domination by Sweden, or by a Saxony central and unified? Frederick William began with a plan and a will, which are the first principle of statesmanship; then, by taxes and French subsidies, he raised money, which is the second principle of statesmanship; then, with money, he organized an Army, which is the third principle of statesmanship. By 1656 he had the first standing army in Europe —eighteen thousand trained men permanently in arms. With this persuasive he induced his constituent states to pay an annual "contribution" to the central government at Berlin; with these revenues he became independent of the power of the purse in the provincial diets; and he achieved what appeared to him to be the only practical form of government in the existing stage of political and intellectual development—absolute and centralized rule. He exempted the nobles from direct taxation, but required their sons to serve him as *Junker* in the higher ranks of the army and the administration. These "juniors" at first resented such service; but he gave them splendid uniforms and social prominence, trained them in competence and pride, and developed in them an *esprit de corps* that replaced the feudal loyalties of the old regime and made the army serve not the landowners but the government. So began the military and social machine that enabled Frederick the Great to stand up against half of Europe, and that prepared Germany for the First World War.

One quality Frederick William did not have—the military genius of the Swedish kings. For twenty years he shifted his force from side to side in the conflicts of Sweden with Poland and of the Empire with France, barely preserving himself by diplomacy. But when Charles XI invaded Brandenburg, Frederick William's army justified itself by defeating the Swedes at Fehrbellin (1675); it was this victory that won him the title of Great Elector. In the end, despite his fluctuating policies and narrow resources, he added forty thousand square miles to his state.

More important were his economic and administrative reforms. Under his urging the nobles improved agricultural methods, and expanded the yield, on their estates. He developed a prosperous silk industry by the extensive planting of mulberry trees. He reversed the trend to deforestation by requiring peasants to plant twelve trees before they married. He planned and financed the building of the Frederick William Canal to connect the Oder with the Spree. When Louis XIV revoked the Edict of Nantes, the Great Elector issued an "Edict of Potsdam" (November, 1685), inviting the distressed Huguenots to come and settle in Brandenburg-Prussia; he sent agents to guide and finance their migration;[5] twenty thousand came, proved a spur to Prussian industry, and formed five regiments in the Prussian army. Frederick William himself, like his descendant Frederick the Great, labored assiduously in administration, and established the principle, later accepted by Peter of Russia and the "enlightened despots" of the eighteenth century, that the ruler should be the dedicated servant of the state. He recognized that religious intolerance was an obstacle to economic and political development; he distinguished himself in Germany by allowing his people to remain Lutheran while he himself remained Calvinist; and he gave religious freedom to Catholics, Unitarians, and Jews.

He died in 1688, aged sixty-eight. His will, dividing his several states among his sons, would have canceled the unifying effect of his rule, but his successor repudiated the document and maintained the central power. Frederick III earned the good will of the Emperor Leopold I by joining him against France; for this, and eight thousand soldiers, Leopold granted him the title of *König in Preussen*. He was crowned Frederick I at Königsberg on January 18, 1701, and Prussia began its career toward Bismarck and German unity.

It is a plume in Frederick's record that he founded the University of Halle; another that he supported the efforts of his second wife to promote the intellectual graces in Berlin. Sophia Charlotte, daughter of the Electress Sophia of Hanover, was reputed to be the prettiest and wittiest woman in Germany. From her long stay in Paris she brought to the court of Berlin an attractive union of culture and charm. Urged on by her and Leibniz, Frederick established the Berlin Academy of Sciences, destined to make history under Frederick II. For her the Elector built (1696) the famous *Schloss*—castle or palace—in the suburb that took her name, Charlottenburg. To her salon in the Schloss Charlottenburg came scientists, philosophers, freethinkers, Jesuits, and Lutheran ministers; Charlotte loved to prod them into theological battles that sometimes lasted through the night. There her sister-in-law, Queen Caroline of England, drank in the learning and art that were to startle England. When Charlotte died (if we may believe her grandson Frederick the Great) she rejected both Catholic and Protestant offers of religious ministrations; she told the divines that she was dying in peace, and rather in curiosity than in hope or fear; now, she said, she would satisfy her inquisitiveness about the origin of things, "which even Leibniz could never explain to me"; and she consoled her ceremony-loving husband with the thought that her death would "afford him the opportunity of giving me a magnificent funeral."[6] Sophia Charlotte was among the many women of character and education who adorned Germany as the seventeenth slipped into the eighteenth century.

The court of Berlin, among the more than three hundred that then consumed the revenues of the Empire, was rivaled only by the Saxon court at Dresden. Augustus the Strong, who ruled Saxony (1694–1733) as Elector Frederick Augustus I, bequeathed to Europe a bevy of bastards, among them the famous Maréchal de Saxe. He made his capital "the prettiest city in Germany,"[7] the center and pride of the minor arts; but the Saxons could not forgive him his change of faith, his use of their money and men in Poland's wars, and the costly luxuries of his court.

The Electorate of Hanover contributed to history in this period by sheltering Leibniz and annexing England. In 1658 Sophia, the dethroned Princess Palatine, daughter of Elizabeth Stuart (Queen of Bohemia), married Ernest Augustus, who became Elector of Hanover. Her erudition discomfited her husband, for she spoke five languages with few interruptions, and knew more English history than the English ambassadors at her court. For a time she maintained at Hanover a salon of scholars and philosophers. But her consuming passion was to secure the throne of England for her son George; her blood tingled with royalty, for she never forgot that she was the granddaughter of James I. In 1701 the English Parliament, as we have seen, settled the succession to the throne upon Sophia and "the heirs of her body, being Protestant." She contemplated with pleasure the future of her son as George I, but without pleasure the prospect of her daughter-in-law, Sophia Dorothea, as a queen; and she looked with equanimity upon the breakup of their marriage. George, suspecting his wife of adultery with Count Philipp von Königsmarck, had him killed, divorced Sophia Dorothea, and imprisoned her from 1694 till her death in 1726. Meanwhile the Electress Dowager died in June, 1714, aged eighty-four, just two months before the crown of England descended upon the head of her son. So the great god Chance, from his ubiquitous throne, shuffled the fates and states and men.

II. THE GERMAN SOUL

The struggle between Catholicism and Protestantism for the soul of Germany was moderating its violence, for the Thirty Years' War had brought theological hatreds to a *reductio ad absurdum*. Largely through Jesuit persuasion some Protestant princes went over to the Roman Church in this period. Calvinism gained on Lutheranism, which tended to a stiff Scholastic dogmatism. Chiefly in reaction to this formalism the Pietist movement spread, seeking to replace outward observances with an inner spirit of union with God. In the second half of the seventeenth century George Fox, William Penn, and Robert Barclay carried their Quaker gospel to Germany, and perhaps this missionary movement shared in developing Pietism there; we note that Philipp Jakob Spener's *Pia desideria* (1675) appeared four years after Penn's first visit. Spener, as pastor of a Lutheran church in Frankfurt-am-Main, supplemented its services with the mystic devotions of private assemblies (*collegia pietatis*) in his home. The name Pietist, like Puritan and Methodist, was given to these devotees by their critics as a term of ridicule; it was accepted by them, and became a badge of humble pride. They clung with fervor to the millenarian hopes that had consoled some of the German masses during the war. They thought of the Second Advent not as a vague doctrine of theology, but as a warm and active inspiration of their daily lives. At any moment now Christ would reappear on earth; he would still the strife of faiths and end the reign of force and war; he would establish a purely "spiritual church," without organization, without ritual, without priests, but practicing with joy a generous Christianity of the heart.

August Francke carried on the movement with the ardor of a prophet. Many women were touched by his practical Christianity and enlisted in the cause of personal piety and public charity. Influenced by English Puritanism and French Quietism, the movement in turn influenced English Methodism and German poetry, and made itself felt in America, where Cotton Mather hailed it hopefully: "The world begins to feel a warmth from the fire of God, which thus flames in the heart of Germany."[8] But Pietism, like Puritanism, injured itself by making its piety public and professional, sometimes falling into affectation and cant. In the eighteenth century it was swamped by the rationalist flood that poured in from France.

The successes of Richelieu, Mazarin, and Louis XIV, and the growing wealth and splendor of the French court, had an irresistible influence upon German society in the century following the Peace of Westphalia. For a time cosmopolitanism overcame nationalism. French ways dominated the princely courts in language, literature, liaisons, manners, dances, art, philosophy, wine, and wigs. The German aristocracy now spoke German chiefly to servants. German authors wrote in French for the upper classes or in Latin for the learned world. Leibniz, who wrote mostly in French, admitted that German "manners have been somewhat modified toward elegance and politeness" by French example, but mourned the replacement or infiltration of German speech by the language or phrases of France.[9]

Only one German book of this age has survived—the *Simplicius Simplicissimus* (1669) of Hans von Grimmelshausen. In form it is the picaresque episodic autobiography of Melchior von Fuchshaim, who is one-quarter fool, one-quarter philosopher, and one-half rogue. In spirit it is a good-humored but pessimistic satire on the Germany that was left barely alive after thirty years of war. Melchior begins as the foster child of a peasant, whose life is described in courtly terms:

> Instead of pages, lackeys, and hostlers my sire had sheep, goats, and pigs, and each waited upon me on the chase until I drove them home. His armory was well provided with plows, mattocks, axes, hoes, shovels, dung forks and hay forks, wherewith he practiced every day, for hoeing and digging were his *disciplina militaris;* . . . drawing out manure was his science of fortification, holding the plow his strategy, cleaning out the stable his knightly diversion, his tournament.[10]

A band of soldiers breaks into this peasant paradise, and tortures the family to make it reveal nonexistent hoards. Melchior escapes and finds refuge with an old hermit, who gives him his first lessons in theology. Asked for his name, he answers, "Rascal or scape-gallows," for he has never heard himself otherwise addressed; his foster-father's name, on the same basis, was "clown, ruffian, drunken dog." Captured by soldiers, he is taken to the court of the governor of Hanau; there he is trained to be a fool, and is christened Simplicius Simplicissimus. He is kidnaped, becomes a thief, finds a hidden treasure, becomes a gentleman, seduces a girl, is forced to marry her, deserts her, becomes a Catholic, visits the center of the earth, loses his fortune, recoups it by quackery, wearies of wandering, and retires to lead the life of a hermit disillusioned with the world. This is *Candide* a century before Voltaire, except that its satire is softened with German humor rather than graced with Gallic wit. The book was condemned by the critics, and became a classic, the most famous production of German literature between Luther and Lessing.

We must not take it as a fair picture of Germany in the generation after the war. The German might be too fond of drink, but he kept his bubbling good humor even in his cups; his wife might call him a drunken dog, but she loved him *faute de mieux*, and reared his children sturdily. Perhaps there was a more wholesome morality in the Germany of this age than in France. Poor Charlotte Elisabeth, Princess Palatine, married (1671) against her wishes to "Monsieur" Philippe d'Orléans, the invert widower of "Madame" Henrietta, never forgot the cool loveliness of Heidelberg; and after forty-three years of uncomfortable living with the comforts of the French court, she still longed for "a good dish of sauerkraut and smoked sausages" as far preferable to the coffee, tea, or chocolate of Paris or Versailles.[11] Her stoic fidelity to her worthless husband, and her patience with the royal brother-in-law who ordered or permitted the devastation of the Palatinate, show us that even amid the ruins of Germany there were women who could teach decency and humanity to beribboned, embroidered, periwigged, perfumed kings.

III. THE ARTS IN GERMANY

Moreover, and contrary to all reasonable expectations, this age was one of the most productive in German architecture. It saw the first flowering of German baroque, which gave a new front of charm and gaiety to Karlsruhe, Mannheim, Dresden, Bayreuth, Würzburg, and Vienna. It was the time of builders like Johann Fischer von Erlach, Jakob Prandtauer, Johann and Kilian and Cristoph Dientzenhofer, and Andreas Schlüter, whose names would be as well known to English-speaking peoples as those of Wren and Inigo Jones, were it not for the prison of frontiers and the babel of tongues. Some of their work, however, was destroyed in the invasions of Germany by French armies (1689), and some in the Second World War.[12] History is a race between art and war.

Some lovely churches rose amid the poverty and desolation. We should dishonor our record if we found no line for Johann Dientzenhofer's cathedral at Fulda or his abbey church at Banz, or for the work of Christoph and Kilian Dientzenhofer on the churches of St. Nicholas and St. John in Prague. In 1663 the Italian architect Agostino Barelli began the Nymphenburg Palace outside Munich, and Joseph Effner completed its interior in a successful merger of classic pilasters and baroque decoration. Ornament was the besetting temptation of baroque; it went to excess in the Festsaal, or Festival Salon, of the Schloss Berlin, and in the pavilion of the Zwinger Palace built at Dresden by Matthäus Daniel Pöppelmann for Augustus the Strong; here baroque passed into a pretty rococo rather befitting a boudoir interior than a palace front. This was mostly destroyed in the Second World War; so were the Schloss Charlottenburg and the Schloss Berlin, the royal palace begun by Andreas Schlüter in 1698.

Schlüter was the outstanding German sculptor of the age. All Germany was thrilled by his equestrian statue of the Great Elector, *Der Grosse Kurfürst*, which withstood all the bombs of war, and now rides the Charlottenburg plaza outside Berlin. At Königsberg Schlüter set up an equally imposing figure of Frederick I, just made King of Prussia. Julius Glessker carved a quietly mourning *Head of Mary* for a Crucifixion group in the cathedral at Bamberg. The wood carvers showed their skill in the magnificent choir stalls of the *Klosterkirche* in Silesia, but they went to excess in the extravagantly carved furniture demanded by patrons who had more pride than taste.

German painting begot no masterpieces in this period, unless we count as such a charming *Young Man with a Gray Hat* by Christoph Paradiso.[13] The tapestries designed for the Würzburg Palace by Rudolf Byss are among the finest; and Paul Decker's engravings in copper were near the top of their kind. The little town of Warmbrunn—the Warm Springs of Silesia—was famous for its cut glass; Dresden made "Dresden china" fashionable; Augustus the Strong was also *le roi de faïence;* and at Meissen, suitable clays having been found nearby, he established (1709) the kilns that produced the first hard porcelain in Europe.

But it is in music that the German spirit found its most characteristic expression; this, so to speak, was the eve of Johann Sebastian Bach. The forms and instruments came from Italy, but the Germans poured into them their own tender sentiment and massive piety, so that while Italy excelled in melody and France in graceful rhythm, Germany moved toward primacy in lieder, organ music, and chorales. In G. F. Krieger's *12 Suonate a due Violini* (1688) the sonata sequence is already established in three movements—allegro, largo, and presto. Instrumental music, rising out of dance forms (pavan, saraband, gavotte, *gigue*, etc.), was declaring its independence of both dance and voice.

Italian musicians were still in demand in Germany. Cavalli reigned in Munich, as Vivaldi later in Darmstadt. Italian opera was imported, and had its first performance in Germany at Torgau (1627); others followed at Regensburg, Vienna, and Munich. The first German opera, called a *Singspiel*, was Johann Theile's *Adam und Eva*, produced at Hamburg in 1678; from that time, for half a century, Hamburg held the leadership in German opera and drama. There Handel brought out his *Almira* and *Nero* in 1705, and his *Daphne* and *Florinda* in 1706, before going to conquer England. The great name in the German opera of this period is Reinhard Keiser, who produced 116 operas for the Hamburg company.

After 1644 German composers won pre-eminence from the Italians in compositions for the organ and the church. The hymns of Paul Gerhardt expressed his uncompromising Lutheranism. Jan Reinken dominated the organ in the Katherinenkirche at Hamburg from 1663 till his death at the age of ninety-nine in 1722. Dietrich Buxtehude, born in Denmark, became organist in the Marienkirche at Lübeck in 1668; his performances there, and especially his *Abendmusik* concerts for organ, orchestra, and chorus, were so renowned that in 1705 the great Bach walked fifty miles from Arnstadt to Lübeck to hear him play.[14] Nearly seventy of his compositions for the organ have survived; many are still performed; and his chorales shared in forming Johann Sebastian's style. Johann Kuhnau preceded Bach as organist at the Thomaskirche in Leipzig; he developed the sonata for the clavier, and composed *Partien* of the same type as Bach's suites.

The Bach family was now entering upon the musical scene in bewildering profusion. We know of some four hundred Bachs between 1550 and 1850: all musicians, sixty of them holding important posts in the musical world of their time. They formed a kind of family guild, meeting periodically at their headquarters in Eisenach, Arnstadt, or Erfurt. They constitute unquestionably the most extensive and remarkable dynasty in cultural history, impressive not merely by their number, but by devotion to their art, by a typically Germanic steadiness of purpose, and by their productivity and influence. They do not come prominently into musical annals until their fifth generation, with Johann Christoph and Johann Michael Bach, sons of Heinrich Bach, organist at Arnstadt. Johann Christoph was chief organist at Eisenach for thirty-eight years: a simple, serious, painstaking man who trained choirs and composed for organ and for orchestra. His brother Johann Michael became organist at Gehren in 1673, remained there till his death in 1694, and gave his fifth daughter to be the first wife of Johann Sebastian. Heinrich's brother Christoph Bach, organist at Weimar, had twin sons who were violinists; one of them, Ambrosius, was Johann Sebastian's father. Johann Bach, brother of Heinrich and Christoph, was organist at Erfurt from 1647 till 1673, when he was succeeded by his son Johann Christian Bach, who in 1682 was succeeded by his brother Johann Egidius Bach. All the forces of nature seem to have been directed to produce and prepare Johann Sebastian Bach.

IV. AUSTRIA AND THE TURKS

Vienna is so beautiful today that we find it hard to picture it after the Thirty Years' War. Austria had not suffered so severely as Germany, but its treasury was exhausted, its armies were in disgrace, and the Peace of Westphalia had lowered the prestige and power of the emperors. One circumstance was favorable: Leopold I succeeded his father Ferdinand III on the Imperial throne in 1658, and held it for forty-seven years; and though that long reign heard the Turks again knocking at Vienna's gates, the recovery of Austria was proceeding rapidly. Only formally sovereign over the German principalities, Leopold was actual king of Bohemia and western Hungary, and governed the duchies of Styria, Carinthia, and Carniola, and the county of Tirol. He was not a great ruler; he labored dutifully in administration and the formation of policy, but he lacked the far vision of his Hapsburg forebears, inheriting only their theology and their chin. He had originally been trained for the priesthood; he never lost his affection for the Jesuits, or strayed much from their guidance. Though himself of irreproachable morals, he accepted the principle that all his subjects must be made Catholic; and he enforced this policy with hard autocracy in Bohemia and Hungary. He was inclined to peace, but was forced or led into a succession of wars by the aggressions of Louis XIV and the Turks. Between these bloodlettings he found time for poetry, art, and music; he composed music himself, and encouraged opera in Vienna; four hundred new operas were presented there in the fifty years after his accession. An engraving of 1667 shows already a sumptuous opera house, with three tiers of boxes, every seat taken; so old is that pleasant scaffolding for song.

We must think of Austria in this age as defending the West against resurgent Turkey, and harassed by the enmity of the strongest ruler in the West; the struggle of Christendom against Islam was hampered and confused by the old conflict of the Hapsburgs with France. Hungary further complicated the problem, for only the western third of it was under the emperor, part of this was Protestant, and all of it longed to be free. The Hungarians had their own nationalist sentiment, fed by their literature and their proud traditions of Hunyadi János and Matthias Corvinus; only recently (1651) Miklós Zrinyi had published an epic throbbing with patriotism. Insulted and oppressed by Austrian rule and Catholic domination, the Hungarians were half inclined to welcome the Turks when these decided to attempt the conquest of all Hungary.

A succession of powerful viziers had interrupted the decline of Turkey, and resumed the harrowing of the West. It was one symptom of the recovery that a major Turkish poet, Nabi, sang the praises of the viziers who filled his palm; another that Turkish funds and taste and piety could raise the lovely Mosque of Yeni-Validé in Stamboul (1651–80). Sultan Mohammed IV appointed as his grand vizier (1656) Mohammed Kuprili, who at the age of seventy inaugurated half a century of rule by his Albanian family. His own vizierate lasted only five years, but in that quinquennium he had 36,000 persons executed for crimes ranging from theft to treason; his chief executioner averaged three stranglings per day. Corruption in the administration and political intrigue in the harem were frightened into moderation, discipline was restored in the army, and the provincal pashas reduced their independence and embezzlements. When George Rákóczy II, Prince of Transylvania, repudiated Turkish suzerainty, Kuprili overwhelmed the revolt with an army under his own leadership, deposed Rákóczy, exacted a heavy indemnity, and increased from fifteen thousand to fifty thousand florins Transylvania's annual tribute to the Sultan.

The terrible septuagenarian was succeeded as vizier by his son Ahmed Kuprili. When another revolt broke out in Transylvania, led by John Keményi, Emperor Leopold sent to its support ten thousand men under one of the outstanding generals of this age, the Italian Count Raimondo di

Montecucculi. Ahmed retaliated by leading 120,000 troops in an effort to complete the conquest of Hungary. Leopold appealed for help; the German states, Protestant as well as Catholic, responded with money and men; and Louis XIV, abandoning his alliance with Turkey, contributed four thousand soldiers. Even so, resistance seemed hopeless; Europe expected Vienna to fall; Leopold prepared to abandon his capital. Montecucculi's forces were far outnumbered, but better equipped with artillery. Not daring to meet the Turks in open terrain, where numbers would count, he maneuvered them into an attempted crossing of the River Rába at Szentgotthárd, some eighty miles south of Vienna, and attacked each Turkish detachment as it arrived on the left bank. His strategy, and the special heroism of the French contingent, won the day (August 1, 1664) in a battle that again saved Europe from Moslem inundation.

But just as, a century before (1571), the victory of Lepanto had left the Turks still strong and rapidly recovering, so now their power of recuperation, their still immense army, and the unreliability of Leopold's allies, anxious to return home, led the Emperor to sign with the Sultan a twenty-year truce (August 10, 1664) which left most of Hungary under Turkish rule, acknowledged Turkish sovereignty over Transylvania, and paid the Sultan a "gift" of 200,000 florins. Ahmed Kuprili, having lost the battle and won the war, returned to Constantinople in triumph.

The attack of Louis XIV upon the Netherlands (1667) ended for the time being the Christian union against the Turks. In 1669 Ahmed took command of the long siege of Crete, and forced the Venetians to surrender the island; the Turkish fleet was again dominant in the Mediterranean. Only John Sobieski, King of Poland, had a stomach strong enough, he felt, to swallow Turkey. He announced his aim bravely: "To give the barbarian conquest for conquest, to pursue him from victory to victory, over the very frontier that belched him forth from Europe, . . . to hurl him back into the deserts, to exterminate him, to raise upon his ruins the Empire of Byzantium: this enterprise alone is Christian; this alone is noble, wise."[15] However, Leopold encouraged the Turks to attack Poland, and Louis urged them to attack Leopold.[16]

Ahmed Kuprili died in 1676, worn out at the age of forty-one by so many brilliant defeats, having lost "decisive battles" and extended the Turkish dominion to its European maximum. Sultan Mohammed IV gave the vizierate to his son-in-law Kara Mustafa, who delighted Louis XIV by promising to renew the war against Austria.[17] Kara was encouraged by a revolt (1678) of Hungarian nationalists under Imre Thököly, who so resented the violent suppression of nationalism and Protestantism in Austrian Hungary that he offered to recognize Turkish suzerainty over all Hungary if the Turks would aid his rebellion. Leopold, too late, abandoned the policy of repression, and proclaimed religious toleration in Hungary. Louis XIV sent financial support to Thököly,[18] and promised Sobieski the possession of Silesia and Hungary if he would ally Poland with France against the Emperor. Leopold could only offer Sobieski an archduchess as bride for his son, and a pledge to support Sobieski's effort to make the Polish throne hereditary in his famliy line. We do not fully know the King's motives in coming to the aid of Austria against the Turks; we can only say that it was one of the most dramatic and pivotal events in modern history.

Kara Mustafa felt that the feuds between Hapsburg and Bourbon, between Catholicism and Protestantism, offered him an opportunity to take Vienna, perhaps all Europe. The Turks boasted that in the fifteenth century they had turned Constantinople, capital of the Eastern Roman Empire, into a Moslem citadel, and St. Sophia's into a mosque; so now, they declared, they would not stop till they had taken Rome and stabled their horses in St. Peter's nave.[19] In 1682 Kara assembled at Adrianople his levies of men and supplies from Arabia, Syria, the Caucasus, Asia Minor, and European Turkey, pretending that he planned to attack Poland. On March 31, 1683, the Sultan and the Vizier started on their long march to Vienna. As the army advanced it added reinforcements from each Turkish province on the way; Wallachian, Moldavian, and Transylvanian contingents joined it; when it reached Osijek (Eszék) on the Drava, it numbered 250,000 men, and included camels, elephants, muezzins, eunuchs, and a harem.[20] There Thököly issued a manifesto, calling upon the surrounding Christians to support the attack upon Austria, and promising them security of life and property, and freedom of religious worship, under the Sultan. Many towns opened their gates to the invaders.

Leopold again appealed to the German principalities; they responded sluggishly. He placed his 40,000 troops under the command of Charles V, Duke of Lorraine, whom Voltaire described as one of the noblest princes in Christendom.[21] Leaving a garrison of 13,000 in Vienna, Charles retreated with his main force to Tuln, where he waited for the Poles. Leopold fled to Passau, while his people condemned him for having failed to prepare his capital for the long-expected siege. Its fortifications were dilapidated, its garrison was not a tenth of the advancing foe. On July 14 the Turks appeared before the walls. Leopold sent messengers to Sobieski begging him to come at once, ahead of his slowly moving infantry; "your name alone, so terrible to the enemy, will ensure a victory."[22] Sobieski came with 3,000 cavalry. On September 5 his infantry arrived, 23,000 strong. Two days later 18,000 men came from the German states; the Christian army now numbered 60,000. But by this time Vienna was starving, its forts were crumbling under the Turkish artillery; another week of siege, and the city would fall.

Early on September 12 the Christians, now under the supreme command of Sobieski, attacked the besiegers. Kara Mustafa had not believed that the Poles would come, much less that the Christian forces would take the initiative; he had organized everything for siege rather than for battle; his officers had adorned their trenches with tapestries and tiles, and he himself had equipped his tent with baths, fountains, gardens, and concubines. His best troops, caught by surprise in their trenches, were cut to pieces. His motley army, gathered from provinces unstirred with loyalty to the distant Sultan, fell into disorder before Christians inspired by the feeling that they were saving Europe and Christianity. After eight hours darkness interrupted the conflict. When the next dawn came the Christians, still uncertain of victory, discovered to their joy that the Turks had fled, leaving 10,000 dead, and most of the army's materials behind in the camp. The Christians lost 3,000 men.

Sobieski wanted to pursue, but the Polish soldiers begged him to let them go home now that their main task was done. The victorious King entered Vienna and its cathedral to give thanks to God; on his route the grateful people hailed him as a divine deliverer, and struggled to touch his garment and kiss his feet;[23] they felt that nothing in the annals of chivalry could outshine his deed. When Leopold returned to his capital (September 15) he was coldly received by the populace. He inquired of his aides whether a merely elective monarch had ever been received by an emperor, and what formalities should be observed; he delayed meeting Sobieski, and finally greeted him with quite moderate gratitude; he suspected that the hero's desire to pursue the Turks was due to a plan to carve out an added kingdom for himself and his family.[24] So the pursuit was not begun till September 17, and not till ten days later was contact made with the retreating Turks. At Parkány, near the Danube, Sobieski and Charles again won a decisive victory. Then, his army weakened with marching, fighting, and dysentery, the King led it back to Poland, entering Cracow on Christmas Eve, 1683. On the following day the Sultan put Kara Mustafa to death.

At the urging of Pope Innocent XI Austria, Poland and Venice formed a Holy League to carry on the war against the Turks (1684). Francesco Morosini reconquered the Morea (the Peloponnesus) for Venice; in 1687 he laid siege to Athens, and captured it on September 28; in the process his artillery ruined the Propylaea and the Parthenon, which the Turks had used as a magazine for their powder. The Turks recaptured Athens and Attica in 1688, the Morea in 1715. Meanwhile Charles of Lorraine defeated the Turks at Gran (Esztergom) in 1685, and in the same year, after ten weeks' siege, took Buda—the ancient capital of Hungary—which the Turks had held since 1541. In 1687 Charles led the Austrian forces to triumph at Harkány, near Mohács, where the victory of Suleiman the Magnificent in 1526 had begun the Turkish ascendancy. This "second Mohács" ended the Turkish power in Hungary, which now became a possession of the Austrian monarchy. Transylvania acknowledged the suzerainty of the Hapsburg emperor, and was incorporated (1690) into the Austro-Hungarian Empire. In 1688 Max Emanuel of Bavaria took Belgrade. Leopold proclaimed that now the road was open to Constantinople, and that the time and opportunity had come to drive the Turks from Europe.

Louis XIV came to their rescue. The war of Bourbon against Hapsburg seemed to the "Most Christian King" more important than the conflict between Christianity and Islam. He looked with mounting jealousy upon the successes of the Holy League and the extension of the Hapsburg realm and prestige. In 1688, ignoring the fact that only four years previously he had signed a twenty years' truce with the Emperor, he resumed his war against the Empire, and sent an army into the Palatinate. Leopold dispatched Charles and Max Emanuel to meet the attack upon the Rhine; the advance against the Turks ceased; Turkish assault was renewed.

The new Sultan, Suleiman II, called to the vizierate another Kuprili, Mustafa, brother of Ahmed. Mustafa pacified the Christians in European Turkey with extended freedom of worship, organized a new army, and recaptured Belgrade (1690); but a year later he was killed, and the Turks were routed, at Slankamen. Sultan Mustafa II took the lead of the army in person, but was defeated at Senta (1697) by the Christians under Prince Eugene of Savoy. Mustafa sued for peace; and Leopold, glad to be freed for action against Louis, signed with Turkey, Poland, and Venice the Treaty of Karlowitz (1699). Turkey renounced all claims to Transylvania and Hungary (except for the banat of Temesvár), ceded the western Ukraine to Poland, and surrendered the Morea and northern Dalmatia to Venice. It still retained nearly all the Balkans—southern Dalmatia, Bosnia, Serbia, Bulgaria, Romania, and most of Greece; but this treaty marked the end of the Turkish danger to Christendom.

What had caused the decline of the Ottoman power from its zenith under Suleiman I? Nothing fails like success. The opportunities for enjoyment that had come from victory and wealth proved too tempting; the sultans dissipated in the harem the energy needed to discipline the army, the bureaucracy, and the viziers. Their empire had grown too large for effective administration, for the rapid communication of commands and transfer of soldiery; the provinces were ruled by pashas whose distance from Constantinople made them almost independent of the sultans. No longer stimulated by hunger or threatened by enemies, the Turks slacked down into laziness and venality; bribery corrupted the government while debasement of the currency disordered the economy and the army. The Janissaries, paid in depreciated coinage, repeatedly rebelled; they discovered their power, and abused it in the measure of its increase. They won the right to marry, and obtained for their sons and others admission into their once select corps; they repudiated the strict training and discipline that had made the Janissaries the best soldiers in Europe. Their leaders, become experts in venery, failed to keep abreast of military science and weaponry. While the Christian West made better guns, and developed superior strategy and tactics, in the life-and-death struggle of the Thirty Years' War, the Turks, who under Mohammed II had had the best artillery in the world, found themselves, as at Lepanto, inferior in fire power and strategy. War, which had strengthened the Ottoman state when the sultans led their armies in person, exhausted the state when they preferred the easy triumphs of the harem to the ordeal of battle. Domination of life and thought by a fatalistic and unprogressive religion stifled Islamic science, which in the Middle Ages had been pre-eminent; knowledge grew in the West and lagged in the East. The Christians improved their shipbuilding as well as their gunnery. Their commerce advanced to all the continents, plowing new roads through the sea, while most Ottoman commerce crawled in caravans over the land. Lazy administrators allowed aqueducts and canals to decay, while a peasantry disordered by war waited humbly for rain. Westward the course of empire took its way, until one day, still moving westward, it would find itself again in the East.

For the West the repulse of the Turks was an invitation to internecine war. Freed from the pressure of Islam, Austria and Germany turned to face the ambitions of Louis XIV, who was stretching his arms into the Netherlands, the Rhineland, the Palatinate, Italy, and Spain. These blows from the West completed the disintegration of the Holy Roman Empire; nothing remained of it but the form. The emperor came to think of himself not as Roman but as Austrian; the Austro-Hungarian Empire replaced the Holy Roman. The three thrones of Austria, Hungary, and Bohemia were made hereditary in the Hapsburg family (1713), annulling the traditional rights of the Bohemian and Hungarian Estates to elect their kings. Hungary revolted again (1703–11) under Francis Rákóczy II, but the revolt was suppressed, leaving the longing for freedom to echo in poetry and song.

Austria manipulated the economies of Hungary and Bohemia to her own advantage, and her upper classes enjoyed a new affluence. Splendid palaces rose for the aristocracy; beautiful churches and monumental monasteries housed the triumphant priests and monks. Prince Pál Esterházy rebuilt his great castle at Eisenstadt, where Haydn would someday conduct and compose. In Vienna Domenico Martinelli designed the Liechtenstein Palace and, for Eugene of Savoy, the Belvedere Palace; Johann Fischer von Erlach raised for the same prince a sumptuous Winter Palace, and laid the plans for the Royal Library, and the Imperial Palace of Schönbrunn. In 1715 this greatest of Austrian architects began work on the Karlskirche at Vienna, in the style of St. Peter's at Rome. On the banks of the Danube some forty miles west of Vienna, Jakob Prandtauer built the vast Kloster Melk, the largest and most impressive Benedictine abbey in German lands; this is the zenith of Austrian baroque. In the aftermath of victory the able and lordly Archbishop Johann Ernst Thun laid out the famous Mirabell Garden of Salzburg, with sculptures by Fischer von Erlach. Proud and splendid, Austria moved into its greatest century.

CHAPTER XV

The Fallow South

1648–1715

I. CATHOLIC ITALY

IT IS part of the wordless wisdom of the peasant that soil nearing exhaustion from abundant bearing may be restored by letting it lie fallow for a season, plowed, perhaps, but not sown. Italy, after the consuming fertility of the Renaissance, rested. Her incredible vitality subsided to a quieter pace, as if gathering strength for new achievements to come. So we must not expect from the Italy of this and the succeeding age—between Bernini and Bonaparte—such fruits as poured from her horn of plenty in her golden centuries. We visit her again, satisfied if now and then, in cities echoing with history, we can hear minor voices attesting unextinguished life.

She was, of course, still Catholic; this is part of her soul, and could hardly be taken from her without violating her spirit. The poor were abused by the rich, who naturally controlled the governments and made the laws. The rich explained that if the poor were better paid they would become disorderly and insolent. The women, except in the flowering of their beauty, were exploited by the men and the race. Under these conditions the lower classes and the then weaker sex found solace in the ministrations of the Church. Their faith in the divine justice upheld them against the inhumanity of man; the sins of their hot tongues and pagan flesh were readily pardoned by the lenient priests and amiable monks whom they fed so hopefully; their burdened days were gratefully interrupted by the lazy festivals of their protective saints. Those saints and the compassionate Virgin Mother, by intercession at the throne of God, would save them from the horrors of hell; the indulgences distributed by the Church would shorten their stay in purgatory; sooner or later they would be admitted to a Paradise—even more beautiful than Italy—where there would be no landlords, no taxes, no tithes, no toil, no war, no grief, and no pain.

So they bore with patience, humor, and song the exactions of their omnipresent clergy, who absorbed at least a third of the nation's revenues. They loved their churches as isles of peace in the war of life. They saw with pride, not resentment, the splendor of St. Peter's and the Vatican; these were the product of their pennies and their artisans; they belonged to the poor even more than to the rich; and they were not too grand for the tomb of the first Apostle, or for the home of the head of Christendom, the Servant of the Servants of God. If that Holy Father punished attacks upon the Church, it was only to prevent fools from destroying the moral edifice built upon religious belief, only to preserve the faith that made a heroic poem from the prose of toil.

The Italian Inquisition was relatively human in this age. Its most famous victim was a Spanish priest, Miguel de Molinos, born in Saragossa, domiciled in Rome. In 1675 he published a *Guida spirituale,* which argued that though devotion to Jesus and the Church was a help toward the highest religious state, yet the worshiper who had given himself to direct communion with God might safely ignore all priestly intermediation and all churchly ritual. In a further tract Molinos opined that a devotee confident in his freedom from mortal sin might rightly receive the Eucharist without previously confessing to a priest. Molinos' *Guide* proved especially attractive to women; hundreds of them—including Princess Borghese and Queen Christina—sought his counsel and sent him gifts. Many nuns took to the new quietism, discarded their rosaries, and wrapt themselves in a proud liaison with God. Several Italian bishops, complaining of a movement that minimized church services and contributions, appealed to Innocent XI to suppress it.[1] Jesuits and Franciscans attacked Molinos as putting an almost Protestant emphasis upon faith above "works." The Pope for a time protected him, but in 1685 the Roman Inquisition arrested him, and soon thereafter almost a hundred of his followers. He had amassed four thousand gold crowns ($50,000?) by levying a small charge for his epistolary advice; we may judge the number of correspondents from the cost, twenty-three ducats ($287.50?), of the postage on letters received by him on the single day of his arrest.[2]

After examining the prisoners the Inquisition drew up a series of accusations: chiefly that Molinos had justified the breaking of crucifixes and religious images as impeding the quiet of union with God; that he had discouraged persons from taking religious vows or entering religious orders; and that he had led his disciples to believe that nothing done by them after attaining divine union could be a sin. Perhaps under stress of imprisonment, torture, or fear, he confessed to excusing the destruction of images, and to dissuading from monastic vows persons whom he thought unfit; he admitted that for many years he had practiced "the most indecent acts with two women"; he "had not deemed this sinful, but a purification of the soul"; and thereby "he enjoyed a closer union with God."[3] The Inquisition condemned sixty-eight propositions found in Molinos' books, letters, or confessions, and on September 3, 1687, it indicted him in a public auto-da-fé. A great crowd attended, and demanded that he be burned; but the Inquisition contented itself with ordering his confinement for life. He died in prison in 1697.

Our sympathies may go more readily to those Alpine "heretics" whom Milton mourned in his sonnet "On the Late Massacher in Piedmont." In the valleys hiding between Savoyard Piedmont and French Dauphiné dwelt the Vaudois, descendants of the Waldenses who had preceded and survived the Reformation, and who had preserved their Protestant faith through a hundred fluctuations of law and government. In 1655 Duke Charles Emmanuel II of Savoy joined Louis XIV in organizing an army to force the conversion of these Vaudois. The resultant slaughter aroused the indignation of Cromwell, who secured from Mazarin an order ending the persecution. But after the deaths of the Protector and the Cardinal the oppression was renewed, and when the Edict of Nantes was revoked the French state resumed its effort to exterminate Protestantism from the province. The Vaudois laid down their arms on a promise of amnesty; then, unarmed, three thousand of them, including women, children, and old men, were massacred (1686). The still unconverted survivors were allowed to migrate to the environs of Geneva. A later Duke of Savoy, Victor Amadeus, finding himself, in the kaleidoscope of politics, allied not with France but against her, invited the Vaudois to return to their valleys (1696). They came, fought in his service, and thereafter were allowed to worship the Unknown in their own trusting way.

The poor were as poor in the Papal States as elsewhere in Italy. The Curia, or papal court, like any government, taxed its subjects to the point of diminishing returns, and never had funds enough for its purposes and personnel. Cardinal Sacchetti warned Pope Alexander VII (1663) that the tax collectors were impoverishing the population to the verge of despair. "The people, having no more silver or copper or linen or furniture to satisfy the rapacity of the commissioners, will be next obliged to sell themselves to meet the burdens laid upon them by the Camera" (the legislative chamber of the Curia).[4] The Cardinal complained of venality in the papal judiciary, of verdicts bought and sold, of suits prolonged for years, of violence and tyranny experienced by losers who dared to appeal from a lower to a higher official. These "oppressions," said Sacchetti, "exceed those inflicted upon the Israelites in Egypt. People not conquered by the sword, but subjected to the Holy See, . . . are more inhumanly treated than the slaves in Syria or Africa. Who can witness these things without tears of sorrow?"[5] Amid the poverty of the masses several noble families related to popes or cardinals received rich gifts from the revenues of the Church.

The popes of this period were neither ascetics like Pius V nor statesmen like Sixtus V; they were usually good men too weak to overcome the human vices around them, or to keep an eye upon the thousand loopholes and crannies that let corruption pass or hide in the administration of the

Church. Perhaps no institution so vast in its scope and tasks can be kept clear of the faults inherent in the nature of man. Innocent X (1644-55), "blameless of life and upright in principle,"[6] labored to moderate taxation, to check the exploitation of papal revenues by greedy nobles, and to maintain order and justice in his states. As pictured by Velázquez he has every semblance of a powerful character, but he allowed others to govern for him, and let Olimpia Maidalchini, his ambitious and acquisitive sister-in-law, influence his appointments and policies. Cardinals and envoys humbled themselves before her, and she became scandalously wealthy on their gifts; but when Innocent died she professed herself too poor to pay for his funeral.[7]

In the conclave that chose his successor a cardinal is said to have exclaimed, "This time we must seek an honest man."[8] They found him in Fabio Chigi, who became Alexander VII (1655-67). He did his best to cleanse the papal administration of venality and delay; he banished his esurient nephews to Siena; he reduced the public debt. But the corruption around him was too extensive and pervasive to be overcome. He yielded, let his nephews return to Rome, and gave them lucrative posts; one of them soon amassed a fortune.[9] Power passed from Alexander's tired hands to the cardinals, who claimed more and more authority in the government of the Church. An aristocracy of families boasting cardinals replaced the absolute monarchy that the Council of Trent had confirmed to the popes.

Clement IX (1667-69) renewed the struggle against nepotism. He allowed his relatives some modest privileges, but he turned his back upon petitioners for place. Hundreds had come from his native Pistoia, confident that he would raise them to affluence; he refused them; they lampooned him; we perceive again that the nature of man is the same in the oppressor and the oppressed, and that the people are the chief source of the evils that surround them. The new Pope was a man of peace and justice. Whereas his predecessor, at the urging of Louis XIV, had issued a troublemaking bull against the Jansenists, Clement effected a truce in that quarrel within the Church. It was a misfortune that he died after only two years of rule.

Clement X (1670-76) was eighty at his accession; he left matters to the cardinals (as they had planned), but he concluded his pontificate without reproach. Innocent XI (1676-89), says the Protestant Ranke, was a man "remarkable for humility, . . . most gentle and placid in disposition," conscientious in morals and resolute in reforms.[10] He discontinued the "college" of apostolic notaries, "of which," says a Catholic historian, "the appointments were regularly bought and sold."[11] He abolished many useless offices, privileges, and exemptions, balanced the papal budget for the first time in many years, and established such a reputation for fiscal integrity that the Curia was now able to borrow money at three per cent. He was "a virtuous man," wrote Voltaire, "a wise pontiff, a poor theologian, a courageous, resolute, and magnificent prince."[12] He tried in vain to moderate the precipitation of James II in Catholicizing England. He condemned the violence used by Louis XIV against the Huguenots; men "must be led to the temple," he said, "not dragged into it."[13] He had no reason to love the proud King who claimed over the Church in France almost as full authority as that which Henry VIII had asserted in England. To reduce crime in Rome Innocent XI annulled the right of asylum previously accorded to the residences of ambassadors; Louis insisted on retaining that right for his envoys, and even for the streets adjacent to the French embassy, and in 1687 his ambassador entered Rome with a regiment of cavalry to enforce the royal claim. The Pope censured the ambassador, and laid an interdict upon the Church of St. Louis, where the ambassador worshiped in Rome. Louis appealed to a general council, imprisoned the papal nuncio in France, and seized the territory of Avignon, which had belonged to the papacy since 1348. Hence Innocent XI looked with equanimity upon the expedition of Protestant William III of Orange to unseat Catholic James II and bring England into a coalition against France. He co-operated with the efforts of Leibniz to reunite Catholicism and Protestantism; he sanctioned concessions which were pronounced satisfactory in the uiversities of Protestant Germany; an Englishman called him "a Protestant pope."[14]

Innocent XI died before he could see the triumph of his aims; but during the pontificates of Alexander VIII (1689–91) and Innocent XII (1691–1700) the French ambassador relinquished the right of asylum, Avignon was returned to the papacy, the French clergy transferred its allegiance from king to pope, and the Grand Alliance restored the balance of power against aggressive France. In the War of the Spanish Succession Clement XI (1700–21) found himself caught between the violent divisions of Europe; he threw his influence hesitantly now upon one side, now upon the other; in the end the kings divided the spoils—even Sicily and Sardinia, technically papal fiefs—without consulting him. In like manner the Treaty of Westphalia had ignored the protests of Innocent X. The intensification of nationalism involved the weakening of the papacy, and shared with the growth of science in promoting secularism and lessening the role of religion in European life.

II. ITALIAN ART

Art as well as politics felt this mounting rivalry between the sacred and the profane. Ecclesiastics were still the richest patrons, commissioning structures, paintings, statuary, metalwork, and decoration; but the aristocracy now multiplied palaces faster than churches, courted posterity with portraits, and dowered it with collections of art. In seventeenth-century Italy the two streams of patronage ran side by side in a colorful descent from the Renaissance.

Turin was rising to affluence under the Savoy dukes. For the Cathedral of San Giovanni Battista, Guarino Guarini designed the Cappella del Santissimo Sudario, the Chapel of the Most Holy Shroud (in which, the faithful believed, Joseph of Arimathea had wrapped the corpse of Christ). The dome of the great Church of San Filippo, begun by Guarini, collapsed as it neared completion; it was restored by Filippo Iuvara, who was born (1676) seven years before Guarini's death. Perhaps we shall meet Iuvara again.

In Genoa the master building of this time was the Palazzo Durazzo, built by Falcone and Cantone in 1650, bought by the house of Savoy in 1817, and thenceforth serving as the Palazzo Reale; its famous Hall of Mirrors, foreshadowing the Galerie des Glaces (1678) of Versailles, was shattered in the Second World War; it is not true that Mars ever loved Venus. The outstanding Genoese painter was now Alessandro Magnasco, whom we may sample by the *Synagogue* in the Chicago Art Institute, or by the *Bohemian Repast* in the Louvre.

Venice persisted in breeding heroes and artists. What could be more heroic than the defense of Candia against the Turks? Through a quarter of a century the soldiers and sailors of the Porte assailed Crete, then a Venetian colony; 100,000 Turks died in those passionate campaigns;[15] and though a Turkish army of 50,000 men took some minor cities in the island, the capital stood siege for twenty years, repulsing thirty-two attacks. In 1667 Francesco Morosini was sent to command the starving garrison. It surrendered at last (1668), but no one spoke any longer of Venetian degeneration. In 1693, when Morosini, aged seventy-five, took charge of the Venetian fleet, the Turks withdrew at its approach, awed by his very name. He was still the sort of man portrayed by Tintoretto and Veronese—courage incarnate and merciless.

Baldassare Longhena was another of this septuagenarian mold. Many years back (1632) he had designed that stately mistress of the lagoons, Santa Maria della Salute; now, forty-seven years later, he built the Palazzo Pesaro on the Grand Canal—powerful and beautiful with its double columns and multiple cornices; and in 1680 (aged seventy-six) the Palazzo Rezzonico, where Browning was to die. Sebastiano Ricci, another hardy plant, bore the Venetian seed through half the Continent. Born (1659) at Belluno in the province of Venezia, he went to Florence to decorate the Palazzo Marucelli, then followed the line of least starvation to Milan, Bologna, Piacenza, Rome, Vienna, London. He spent ten years in England, painted in Chelsea Hospital, Burlington House, and Hampton Court Palace, and narrowly missed appointment to decorate the new St. Paul's. Then to Paris, where he was elected to the Académie des Beaux-Arts. His *Diana and Nymphs*[16] is as voluptuous as Boucher, as gracious as Correggio. Surviving till 1734, Ricci transmitted his skills to the eighteenth century, and prepared for the Indian summer of Venetian painting under Tiepolo.

The Bolognese school had not quite spent its force. Carlo Cignani won fame with his frescoes in the cathedral at Forlì. Giuseppe Maria Crespi ("Lo Spagnuolo") revealed in his *Self-Portrait*[17] a man absorbed, forgetting all troubles if allowed to paint. Giovanni Battista Salvi ("Il Sassoferrato") rendered the selflessness of devotion in *The Madonna Praying*,[18] and showed us, in his *Virgin and Child*,[19] just such a simple mother, happy in her *bambino*, as one may see any day among the poor of Italy.

Two reigns of Tuscan grand dukes carried Florence, Pisa, and Siena through this age: Ferdinand II and Cosimo III. In 1659 Siena began its renowned *palio*: the ten wards provided a procession, in picturesque costumes, along streets adorned with architecture, bunting, flowers, and vivacious women alluringly dressed; then the chosen horsemen of the wards competed madly in a race for the cloak (*palio*) of the Madonna to whom the devout city had long since dedicated its life and soul. Florence had now only minor painters. Carlo Dolci continued, with lessened art, the senti-mental, heaven-brooding Virgins and saints of Guido Reni; all the world knows his *St. Cecilia*.[20] Justus Sustermans, who migrated from Flanders to Florence, painted portraits that are among the arresting surprises in the Pitti Gallery—not least the majestic head of Galileo. So, and not as in the horned monster of Michelangelo, Moses might have looked, giving laws.

In Rome art was recovering from the restraints of the Counter Reforma-tion. The popes returned in subdued measure to the spirit of the Renais-sance, encouraging literature, drama, architecture, sculpture, and painting. Innocent X restored the Capitol and the Church of San Giovanni in Laterano. Alexander VII commissioned Bernini to raise a quadruple cordon of granite guardsmen around St. Peter's Square (1655–67)—284 columns and 88 pilasters, successfully transmuting gold into stone. In the same reign Pietro da Cortona rebuilt the Church of Santa Maria della Pace, where Raphael's Sibyls still pondered fate; and Girolamo Rainaldi joined with his son Carlo in erecting the handsome Church of Sant' Agnese in the Piazza Navona. Father and son collaborated again in designing the Church of Gesù e Maria; and Carlo reared the shrine of Santa Maria in Campitelli to shelter an image of the Virgin which was believed to have stopped the plague of 1656. Cardinals and nobles housed and buried themselves palatially. Now rose the Palazzo Doria and the exuberantly baroque gallery in the Palazzo Colonna; and for the Bolognetti family, in the Church of

Gesù e Maria, Francesco Cavallini carved a tomb that must have made the living envious of the dead.

Many painters testified to the survival of their art in Rome. Carlo Maratti was courted there, in the second half of the seventeenth century, as the pictorial protagonist of late baroque. His portrait of Clement IX[21] remembered Velázquez' *Innocent X*, but it came off well enough; his *Madonna with Saints in Paradise*[22] repeated a hundred such, but it is beautiful. When Clement XI wished to have Raphael's Vatican frescoes restored he assigned to Maratti this delicate operation, dangerous to the restorer as well as to the pictures; and it was competently done. Giovanni Battista Gaulli ("Il Baciccio") was chosen by the Jesuits to paint the vault of their mother church, Il Gesù, but they had in their own order one of the ablest artists of the time. Andrea Pozzo, who joined them at the age of twenty-three, designed in Il Gesù the altar of St. Ignatius—one of the *chefs-d'oeuvres* of baroque. In 1692 Pozzo published a treatise, *Perspectiva pictorum et architectorum*, which made a stir in several languages. As fascinated with his subject as Uccello had been two centuries before, Andrea developed his studies with subtleties of illusionism, as in his frescoes in Frascati. Invited to Vienna by Prince von Liechtenstein, he exhausted himself with a multiplicity of undertakings, and died there in 1709, aged sixty-seven.

The greatest Italian painters were now in Naples. Everything flourished there—music, art, literature, politics, drama, hunger, murder, and always the gay, furious, melodious pursuit of feminine curves by agitated men. Salvator Rosa was moved by all these elements of life. His father was an architect, an uncle taught him painting, his brother-in-law was a pupil of Ribera, and Salvator himself was in time admitted to that august studio. Another teacher transmitted to him the technique of drawing battle scenes. Salvator became especially famous for such pictures, which can be seen in the Naples Museo Nazionale or the Louvre. From battles he passed to landscapes, but there too his wild spirit favored Nature in her tantrums, as in the Louvre canvas of heavy clouds and darkened earth abruptly illuminated by lightning that in a moment shatters rocks and withers trees. Lanfranco persuaded him to go to Rome and cultivate cardinals; he went and prospered, but in 1646 he hurried back to Naples to participate in Masaniello's revolt. When that collapsed he returned to Rome, painted high ecclesiastics, and wrote a scornful satire of ecclesiastical luxury. He accepted the invitation of Cardinal Giancarlo de' Medici to come and live with him in Florence; there he remained nine years, painting, playing music, writing poetry, taking part in plays. Again in Rome, he took a house on the Pincian Hill, where Poussin and Lorrain had lived. The dignitaries of the Church, smiling at his tirades, and loving his brush more than his pen, flocked to him for portraits; for a decade he was the most popular painter in Italy. He made the customary pictures of saints and myths, but in his etchings he indulged his sympathy for poor soldiers and harassed peasants; and these etchings are among his finest works.

His fame was rivaled only by another Neapolitan. Luca Giordano was already an artist at eight; then he painted, in the Church of Santa Maria la Nuova, two angels so graceful that the Viceroy, seeing them, marveled, and sent the boy some gold pieces, with a recommendation to Ribera. For nine years Luca studied with that brooding master, astonishing everyone with his readiness in copying masterpieces and imitating styles. He longed to go to Rome and examine the famous frescoes of Raphael, but his father, who lived by selling Luca's paintings and drawings, protested. Luca absconded secretly; soon he was copying *con furia* in the Vatican, in St. Peter's, in the Palazzo Farnese. His father followed him, and again lived by selling his son's *obiter picta;* a story has it that Luca got his nickname, Fa-Presto, from his father's urging him to speed.

Having absorbed Rome, he went on to Venice and painted, in the manner of Titian and Correggio, pictures hardly distinguishable from their masterpieces. But he painted originals too, which won acclaim; we may judge them from the powerful *Crucifixion* and *Deposition from the Cross* in the Venetian Academy. Returning to Naples, he decorated a dozen churches and palaces with a competence and celerity that reduced his rivals to picking flaws. Invited to Florence by Cosimo III (1679), he won plaudits for his frescoes in the Cappella Corsini. His friend Carlo Dolci fell into such deep melancholy at seeing Luca's success that he soon died;[23] fond Italy tells as many legends about her artists as about her saints. In another story the Spanish Viceroy at Naples commissioned a large panel for the Church of St. Francis Xavier; raged when, after long deferments, he found no work done on the assignment; and was amazed, two days later, to find it complete and beautiful. "The painter of this picture," exclaimed the Viceroy, "is either an angel or a demon."[24]

The fame of the demonic angel reached Madrid; soon Luca was pressed with invitations from Charles II to join the Spanish court. Though the King was approaching bankruptcy, he sent the artist a gratuity of fifteen hundred ducats, and put a royal galley at Luca's disposal for the trip. When Giordano neared Madrid (1692), six royal coaches met him on the road. Soon thereafter, aged sixty-seven, Giordano began work in the Escorial. He adorned with frescoes the grand staircase of the monastery; and on the vault of the church he painted a "facsimile" of the heavens, showing Charles V and Philip II in Paradise—all their sins forgiven as a courtesy from the Trinity to the Hapsburgs. In the next two years he executed a large number of frescoes, which Spanish historians of art rank as the best ever made in the Escorial.[25] There and in the Alcazar, or royal palace, at Madrid, and at Buen Retiro and in the churches of Toledo and the capital, he painted so many pictures, with such industry, that his rivals taunted him with working eight hours a day and on holydays. Nor did it please them that he amassed an unseemly fortune, living abstemiously but buying costly jewels as a safe investment, since everything would change but human vanity. All the court honored him, and Charles II, in a lucid moment, called him greater than a king.

Charles died in 1700. Giordano remained in Spain despite the consequent War of the Spanish Succession, and when Philip V came to the throne he continued to receive lucrative and difficult commissions. In 1702 he returned to Italy, stopped in Rome to kiss the papal foot, and reached Naples in triumph. On ceilings in the Certosa, or Carthusian Monastery, of San Martino, overlooking the city, he painted in forty-eight hours a series of frescoes that displayed an energy and skill almost incredible in a man of seventy-two years (1704). A year later he died, sighing, "*O Napoli, sospiro mio!*" (O Naples, breath of my life!)[26]

At his death his fame was equaled by that of no other artist in his generation. Dutch burgomasters competed with emperors and kings to buy his paintings, and in far-off England Matthew Prior sang the praises of "divine Jordain." Laymen admired the richness of his colors, the force of his figures, the grandeur of his conceptions, the power of his presentation. But artists, recovering from this *stupor mundi*, pointed to the signs of haste in Luca Fa-Presto's work, the incongruous mingling of pagan and Christian ideas or subjects in the same scene, the strained or affected attitudes, the excessive glare of light, the absence of harmony and repose. Luca had long since replied to his critics by defining a good painter as one whom the public likes.[27] It is difficult to refute such a definition, since there is no objective standard of excellence or good taste; but we may find the least subjective test of greatness in the extent of a man's influence in space and time, and the least subjective measure of a reputation in its ability to survive. Giordano had the happiness of a successful life, and feels no hurt from his dying fame.

Francesco Solimena was forty-eight when Fa-Presto died, but his four-score years and ten carried the Neapolitan school almost to the middle of the eighteenth century. Luca had painted the nave of the monastery at Monte Cassino; Francesco painted the choir; both works succumbed in the Second World War. But the museums preserve Solimena's art: in Vienna *The Rape of Oreithyia*, a fleshly rapture of male muscles and female contours; in the Louvre an echo and challenge of Raphael in *Heliodorus Driven from the Temple;* and in Cremona a *Madonna Addolorata* accompanied by an angel so delectable that if heaven has many such we shall be reconciled to immortality.

III. THE CHRISTINE ODYSSEY

The arts were now but a small part of the cultural life of Rome. Here were also hundreds of musicians, poets, dramatists, scholars, and historians. Museums, libraries, and colleges offered the treasures of the past to the student, and academies gave encouragement to literature and science. The decorative conceits of Marini still infected Italian verse, but the sting of Tassoni's satires, the fire of Marini's sensualism, and the bubbling flow of Tasso's stanzas had given Italian poetry a stimulus and an afflatus still felt in lyric souls.

The greatest lyric poet of modern times, should we believe Macaulay,[28] was Vincenzo da Filicaia. He celebrated in grateful odes the deliverance of Vienna by Sobieski, he welcomed Christina to Rome with ecstatic flattery, and he voiced with angry shame the subjection of his country to foreign arms:

> Italia, O Italia, doomed to wear
> 　The fatal wreath of loveliness, and so
> 　The record of illimitable woe
> Branded forever on thy brow to bear!
> Would that less beauty and more vigor were
> 　Thy heritage! that they who madly glow
> 　For that which their own fury layeth low
> More terrible might find thee, or less fair![29]

Henry Hallam, after wandering as a learned linguist through all the literature of Europe, thought that not Filicaia but Carlo Alessandro Guidi had "raised himself to the highest point that any lyric poet of Italy has attained," and that "his ode on Fortune [was] at least equal to any in the Italian language."[30] No one still uncomfortable in Italian can settle this dispute between Macaulay and Hallam, between Guidi and Petrarch, between Filicaia and Byron or Shelley or Keats.

Guidi was one of several poets who warbled their rhymes in Christina's Roman salon. The Queen of Sweden had formerly won renown not only as head of a great power but as a patron and paragon of learning, the eager hostess of Salmasius and Descartes. Now her abandonment of a crown for a faith, her conversion from the Protestantism that her father had died to save, and her pilgrimage through the courts of Europe to kiss the feet of the Pope—these were events that rivaled wars and revolutions in fascinating the European mind.

She was twenty-eight years old when she left Sweden (1654). Her cousin Charles X, whom she had nominated to her throne, gave her fifty thousand crowns to gild her journey, and the Swedish Diet voted her a substantial income, and the rights of a queen over her retinue. Hurrying through Denmark, she reached Hamburg, where she scandalized the natives by putting up at the house of a Jewish financier, who as her financial agent had served her faithfully. She passed incognita through Protestant Holland, but in Catholic Antwerp she assumed her own dress. There she royally received the Archduke Leopold, and Elizabeth of Bohemia (another dethroned Queen), and Elizabeth's daughter the Princess Elizabeth (another pupil of Descartes). Then to Brussels, where she was hailed with bonfires, fireworks, cannon salvos, and applauding crowds. For a time she gave herself joyously to balls, tournaments, hunting parties, and plays; Mazarin sent a company of actors from Paris to entertain her. On Christmas Eve she made private abjuration of the Lutheran faith, and announced her resolve to "listen to no more sermons."[31] She dallied in Flanders while the Roman Curia prepared plans for her official reception into the Church and Italy. Leaving Brussels, she traveled leisurely into Austria. "At Innsbruck she made her formal profession of the Catholic creed. Her progress through Italy to Rome was as glorious as that of a victorious Caesar. Town after town adorned itself to greet her; fetes and spectacles were arranged in her honor at Mantua, Bologna, Faenza, Rimini, Pesaro, Ancona; at last (December 19, 1655) she entered Rome amid a blaze of illuminations that made a game of her disguise. On the morrow she proceeded to the Vatican and was welcomed by Alexander VII. After she had been three days in Rome she was escorted from it to make the formal entry that had been scheduled by the high ecclesiastics. Riding a white horse in prancing state, she passed through a triumphal arch and the Porta del Popolo into the city, between lines of soldiery and crowds of populace. It was as if the old Church felt that in the abjuration of one woman the whole Protestant Reformation had been annulled.

All that consummated, Christina was allowed to rule her own days, receiving prelates, potentates, and pundits, visiting museums, libraries, academies, and ruins, and astonishing her guides by her knowledge of Italian history, literature, and art. The great families overwhelmed her with banquets, gifts, and compliments; Cardinal Colonna, aged fifty, fell in love with her, serenaded her, and had to be banished to save the dignity of the Church. Soon she found herself entangled in the rivalries of French and Spanish factions at the papal court. Sweden, financing with difficulty a war with Poland, interrupted the payment of her allotted revenue. She pawned her jewels, and received a loan from the Pope.

In July, 1656, she set out on a visit to France. There too she was honored as a queen. She entered Paris on a white charger richly caparisoned;

a thousand cavaliers rode forth to meet her; crowds cheered her; officials smothered her with oratorical flowers. The current Duc de Guise, sent by Mazarin to escort her, described her as

> not tall, but she has a plump waist and large hips, handsome arms, a white and well-made hand, but more that of a man than a woman. . . . The face is large without being out of shape. . . . Nose aquiline, mouth rather big but not disagreeable; . . . eyes very fine and full of fire. . . . A very odd headgear . . . : a man s wig, thick and high. . . . She is shod like a man, and she has the tone of voice and nearly all the actions of a man. She affects to play the amazon . . . She is very civil and cajoling, speaks eight languages, principally French—as well as if she were born in Paris. She knows more than our Academy with the Sorbonne added; understands painting admirably, as she does all other things. A very extraordinary person.[32]

She was lodged in the King's apartment in the Louvre. Later the Duc de Guise led her to Compiègne, where she was received by Louis XIV, then a handsome lad of eighteen. Court ladies fluttered about her, but were disconcerted by her masculine dress and speech. Mme. de Motteville thought she "looked at first sight like a disreputable gypsy," but "after . . . I began to get accustomed to her clothes . . . I noticed that her eyes were fine and sparkling, that there was gentleness in her face, and kindness mingled with pride. Finally I perceived with amazement that she pleased me."[33] Generally, however, the women who embroidered French manners, fashions, gaiety, tact, and grace were offended by Christina's carelessness in dress, her "immoderate laughter, [and] her freethinking in speech, as much on religion as on topics about which the proprieties of her sex demanded more reserve. . . . She professed to despise all women on account of their ignorance, and took pleasure in conversing with men, on evil topics as much as good ones. She observed none of the rules."[34] Voltaire thought that the ladies of France judged this unruly queen too harshly for her failure to follow the norm. "There was not," he said, "one woman at the French court whose intellect was equal to hers."[35] Christina, for her part, set down the court ladies as too affected, the men as too feminine, and both as insincere. At Senlis, on the way back from Compiègne to Paris, she asked to see "a demoiselle named Ninon [de Lenclos], celebrated for her vice, her loose way of living, her beauty, and her wit. To her alone, of all the women she saw in France, did she show any signs of regard."[36] She found Ninon temporarily confined to a convent. Christina conversed gaily with her, and approved her avoidance of marriage.[37] After visiting the cultural institutions and notable art of France, Christina returned to Italy (November, 1656).

In September, 1657, she visited France again. She was not as formally received as before, but she was lodged semiregally at Fontainebleau. There she alarmed France by what she appears to have thought a legitimate use of her royal rights over her retinue. The Marchese Monaldeschi, her equerry, entered into a conspiracy against her, which she detected by intercepting his letters. He made matters worse by accusing another on her staff of the plot. She confronted him with his incriminating letters; she ordered a priest to hear his confession and give him absolution, and then she had the Marchese put to death by her guards. France was shocked, and even those who recognized the rights which the Swedish Diet had granted her over her attendants were scandalized that so sudden and arbitrary a use of her authority had been made in rooms belonging to the King of France. Though Christina was allowed to spend that winter in Paris, enjoying plays and balls, the court was much relieved when she left for Italy (May, 1658).

The interruption of her income from Sweden placed her in such straits that she is said to have asked the Emperor Leopold I for an army which she herself would lead against Charles X; she was dissuaded from this martial enterprise by an annuity of twelve thousand scudi from Pope Alexander VII. Twice she visited Sweden (1660, 1667) to regain her revenues, and perhaps her crown. The revenues were restored to her, but she was not welcomed in Stockholm; the Lutheran clergy accused her of plotting to convert the nation to Catholicism, and she was forbidden to hear Mass in her apartments. After each of these visits to Sweden she retired to Hamburg. Thence in 1668 she sent agents to Warsaw to enter her candidacy for the Polish throne, left vacant by the abdication of John Casimir; Pope Clement IX supported her claim, but the Polish Diet rejected her for many reasons, one of which was her refusal to marry; not all the empire of the world, she said, would reconcile her to matrimony.[38] She returned to Italy in November, 1668, and remained there till her death.

Those final twenty years were the most gracious of her life. Her apartments in the Palazzo Corsini became the leading salon in Rome, the rendezvous of prelates, scholars, composers, nobles, and foreign diplomats. There she welcomed Alessandro Scarlatti, and received from Arcangelo Corelli the dedication of his first published sonatas. Her rooms were embellished with paintings, statues, and other forms of art chosen with a taste admired by conoisseurs; and the manuscripts she collected were later reckoned among the choicest in the Vatican Library. She discouraged the artificial style that had developed in Italian verse, and influenced Guidi to lead a movement back to the purity of language, and directness of expression, prevalent under the Medici. Her own memoirs were a model of simple and forceful speech, and her *Aphorisms* were the sharp and pithy pronouncements of a woman of the world who did not let her piety hamper her enjoyment of life. She was no bigot. She condemned the violence of French Catholics in enforcing the Revocation of the Edict of Nantes. "I look upon France," she wrote, "as a sick person, whose arms and legs have been cut off in order to treat her for a disorder of which she would have been completely cured by the exercise of gentleness and patience."[39] Bayle thought these sentiments a remnant of her Protestant rearing; she reproved him for this interpretation; he wrote her an apology; she forgave him on condition that he send her new or curious books.[40]

She died in 1689, aged sixty-three, and was buried in St. Peter's. Three years after her death Giovanni Maria Crescimbeni founded in her memory the Arcadian Academy, whose first members were chiefly those who had formerly gathered under her wing. They continued the old association of poetry with pastoralism; they called themselves shepherds, took bucolic names, and held their meetings in the fields. They established branches in the principal cities of Italy, and, despite their constitutional artifice, they ended the reign of conceits in Italian poetry.

IV. FROM MONTEVERDI TO SCARLATTI

In that gay society of seventeenth-century Italy music was the note and air of life. A passionate people, kept in unwilling peace by Spain and the papacy, waged wars in operas, and fought love combats in madrigals.

Musical instruments took a hundred forms. The organ was now an embellished bellows with two keyboards for the hands and one for the feet, plus diverse stops; and of course there were "portative" organs for the street. As early as 1598 we hear of another keyboard instrument, called *piano e forte*, which was listed as owned and played by Duke Alfonso II at Modena; but how far this differed from the *clavicembalo* (harpsichord) and the *spinetta* is still a mystery. A century passes before we hear of the pianoforte again. In 1709 Bartolommeo Cristofori, instrument maker to the music-loving Prince Ferdinand de' Medici at Florence, displayed what he called a *"gravicembalo col piano e forte."* This differed slightly and yet vitally from the harpsichord: the note was sounded by a little hammer rising to strike a string, and the sound could be made low or loud by varying the touch of the fingers on the key—whereas in previous keyboard instruments the note had been produced by a plectrum (of quill or hard leather) rising to pluck the string, and no variation was possible in the force of the sound.* The pianoforte slowly replaced the harpsichord in the

---

* One of Cristofori's pianofortes, dated 1720, is in the Metropolitan Museum of Art in New York.

eighteenth century, not only because it could play "soft and loud," but because the hammers wore out less rapidly than the plectra.

The violin had evolved out of the lyre in the sixteenth century, chiefly at Brescia.* Andrea Amati had brought the art of violinmaking to Cremona, and there his grandson Nicolò surpassed all rivals in the craft until he himself was excelled by his pupils Andrea Guarneri and Antonio Stradivari. The Guarneri too were a dynasty: Andrea and his sons Pietro "de Mantua" and Giuseppe I, his grandson Pietro II "de Venezia," and his grandnephew Giuseppe II "del Gesù"—who made the violin preferred by Paganini to all others. The oldest violin signed by Stradivari is dated 1666, when he was twenty-two years old; it was labeled ANTONIUS STRADIVARIUS CREMONENSIS ALUMNUS NICOLI AMATI FACIEBAT ANNO 1666, followed by his personal symbol—a Maltese cross and his initials, A.S., enclosed in a double circle. Later he signed himself with proud simplicity "Stradivarius." He worked incessantly, ate frugally, lived ninety-three years, and amassed such a fortune by the superior beauty, construction, tone, and finish of his instruments that *ricco come Stradivari* became Cremonese for opulence. He is known to have made 1,116 violins, violas, and violoncellos; 540 of his violins exist today; some have sold for ten thousand dollars.[41] The secret of his varnish has been lost.

The improvement in instruments encouraged the development of the orchestra, and the composition and performance of instrumental music. Composers and virtuosos discovered in the violin a flexibility of movement and range of tone impossible for the human voice; they could run up and down the chromatic scale with literally ineffable ease; they could build and frolic with variations; they could escape from the grooves of melody and launch upon new rhythms, evolutions, and experiments. When many instruments were combined the composition could be freed from the dance as well as from song, and could mount on its own wings in new sequences, combinations, and forms. Tommaso Vitali led the way with violin sonatas of unprecedented richness of invention, and helped to establish the progression of quick, slow, and lively movements. Arcangelo Corelli, as composer and virtuoso, prepared for eighteenth-century chamber music with his sonatas for the violin; he and Vitali in Italy, Kuhnau and Heinrich von Biber in Germany, gave structure and form to the sonata as a piece to be *sounded* by instruments only, in contrast to cantatas as compositions to be sung by the voice. It was Corelli who set the form of the *concerto grosso* —two violins and one violoncello leading an orchestra of strings—with such simple and melodious productions as his *Christmas Concerto* (1712); so he opened a path for the concertos of Vivaldi and Handel and the suites of Bach. Corelli's compositions retained their popularity so far into the

* Wlodzimierz Kaminski in 1961 claimed to have found descriptions of the violin in fourteenth-century Polish manuscripts.—Los Angeles *Times*, August 11, 1961.

eighteenth century that Burney, writing about 1780, thought their fame would endure "as long as the present system of music shall continue to delight the ears of mankind."[42]

As Corelli was now the favorite composer for the violin, so Alessandro Stradella, with solos, duets, trios, and oratorios, dominated the vocal music of this age. His life itself was a music drama, and has been made into a play and an opera. As a teacher of singing at Venice he achieved a tragic success. One of his aristocratic pupils, Ortensia, though affianced to the Venetian senator Alvise Contarini, eloped with Alessandro to Rome. The senator sent assassins to slay them. These sensitive cutthroats, hearing him sing the leading part in his "Oratorio di San Giovanni Battista" in the Church of San Giovanni in Laterano, were so touched by the music that (so the story avers) they abandoned their assignment and warned Stradella and his mistress to seek some safe obscurity. The lovers fled to Turin, but soon Alessandro became dangerously famous there by his compositions and his voice. Contarini sent two unmusical ruffians to kill him; they attacked him, and left him for dead. He recovered, married Ortensia, and moved with her to Genoa. There the senatorial hirelings found them, and stabbed them both to death (1682).[43] The oratorio that allegedly saved his life remained popular for a century, and prepared the way for Handel.

Opera had by this time become a craze in Italy. Venice alone had sixteen opera houses in 1699, and heard nearly a hundred different operas between 1662 and 1680.[44] The melodious spectacle was only slightly less fashionable in Naples. In Rome it symbolized the advancing secularization of music; Clement IX himself, before his elevation to the papacy, composed some musical comedies.[45] There was a temporary decline in the quality of Italian opera after Monteverdi; the plots lost in dignity and significance, but gained in absurdity and violence. Francesco Cavalli, a pupil of Monteverdi, developed the solo aria as the most delectable feature of the performance; soon the audiences demanded a succession of dramatic airs, and bore the intervals impatiently. Castrated boys or men took many soprano or contralto parts, but prima donnas now began to rival queens. Milton addressed Latin lyrics to Leonora Baroni, and Naples turned out en masse to welcome Leonora's mother, Adriana Basile, the most thrilling soprano of her time. Stage machinery probably reached its *ne plus ultra* in this age: in seventeenth-century Venice, according to Molmenti, the Theater of San Cassiano could show on demand a royal palace, a forest, an ocean, Olympus, and heaven; and in one case a ballroom, fully illuminated, with all its furniture and dancers, was suspended over the permanent stage, and was lowered to it, or raised out of view, as the story required.[46] Marcantonio Cesti sought to rescue opera from the aria; he gave more scope and prominence to the overture, more logic and sobriety to the story, and varied the singing with recitative. Both Cesti and Corelli were musical missionaries, bringing Italian opera the one to Paris under Louis XIV, the other to Vienna under Leopold I. Operatically Europe north of the Alps was an Italian colony.[47]

The dominant figure in the composition of operas was now Alessandro Scarlatti. His son Domenico has crowded out the father in current repute, but until recently "Scarlatti" meant Alessandro, and Domenico was an arpeggio to a famous name. Born in Sicily (1659), Alessandro came to Rome when he was thirteen, studied for a while under Carissimi, composed cantatas, was stirred by the work and career of Stradella, and, at the age of twenty, produced his first known opera, *L'errore innocente*. Christina of Sweden liked it, took Alessandro under her wing, and produced his next operas in her private theater. In 1684 he accepted appointment as *maestro di cappella* to the Spanish Viceroy at Naples. He remained there for eighteen years, producing operas in such rapid succession that by the time of his death they numbered at least 114, of which only half survive. It was probably in this period that Solimena painted the remarkable portrait that hangs in the Naples Conservatorio di Musica—a slender face, all sensitivity, concentration, and resolution.

The War of the Spanish Succession disturbed Naples, and threw Scarlatti's salary so far in arrears that he removed to Florence with his wife and family, and composed and produced operas under the patronage of Prince Ferdinand. A year later he passed to Rome as *maestro di cappella* to Cardinal Pietro Ottoboni, a gay and accomplished ecclesiastic who had succeeded Christina as center and patron of the arts in Rome, and who divided his profane energies among art, literature, music, and mistresses.[48] In 1707 Alessandro went to Venice, where he produced his masterpiece, *Mitridate Eupatore*, an opera distinguished by complete absence of love interest. In that year Naples came under Austrian rule; the new Viceroy invited Scarlatti to return to his former post; he agreed, and spent there the next decade of his life, at the zenith of his fame.

His operas set a style that endured for half a century. Scarlatti made the overture a substantial composition unconnected with the opera, and divided it into three movements that remained standard till Mozart: allegro, adagio, and allegro. To the aria he gave its typical eighteenth-century dominance and its *da capo* form, in which the third section repeats the first; he infused it with passion, tenderness, and romantic coloratura, and made it a vehicle for *castrato* feats of virtuosity and improvisation, but its frequency artificially interrupted the feeling and the action. He resisted for a time the popular demand for sentimental airs; finally he yielded to it, and for fifty years the music drama enjoyed a thousand triumphs without producing works capable of buffeting the tides of taste. Opera declined till Gluck startled it to new life and form, in Vienna (1762) and Paris, with the haunting loveliness of *Orfeo ed Euridice*.

V. PORTUGAL: 1640–1700

When the Duke of Braganza was crowned as John IV (1640) Portugal began twenty-eight years of war to defend her restored independence from Spain. France helped her till 1659, when Mazarin, in the Peace of the Pyrenees, agreed to give no further aid to Portugal. Alfonso VI turned to England for help; Catherine of Braganza was sent to London as the bride of Charles II (1663), bringing as her dowry Bombay, Tangier, and £500,000; in return, England sent troops and arms. With this and other support, but above all by their own efforts, leadership, and discipline, the Portuguese drove back one Spanish army after another, until, by the Treaty of Lisbon (1668), Spain formally recognized the independence of Portugal.

Pedro II strengthened the ties with England by the Methuen Treaty (1703): each nation agreed to give preferential tariffs to the other; Portugal would import manufactured goods from England, England would import wine and fruit from Portugal; so the eighteenth-century English drank port wine from Oporto, instead of "clear" claret from Bordeaux. This economic alliance gave Portugal and her remaining colonies a lasting protection from Spain and France.

In 1693 the gold fields of Minas Gerais were discovered in Brazil; soon they brought to Pedro II such bullion that after 1697 he ruled without summoning the Cortes to vote him funds, and maintained at Lisbon one of the most sumptuous courts in Europe. American gold, however, produced the same results in Portugal as in Spain: it was used to pay for manufactured articles from abroad, instead of financing industrial enterprise at home; the native economy remained listlessly agricultural; and even the vineyards around Oporto fell into English hands, being bought with Portuguese gold secured in English trade.

Portuguese authors continued to enliven letters with deeds. Francisco Manuel de Melo of Lisbon, after studying at the Jesuit College of S. Antão, joined Spanish regiments bound for Flanders, survived several battles, fought for the Spanish King in the Catalan rebellion, and wrote its history (*Historia de la guerra de Cataluña*) in one of the many classics contributed by the Portuguese to Spanish literature. When Portugal declared itself free from Spain he offered his services to John IV; welcomed, he equipped and led a Portuguese fleet. Having fallen in love with the intoxicating Countess of Villa Nova, he was arrested on the instigation of her husband, and spent nine years in jail. Released on condition of exile to Brazil, he went to live at Bahia (Baía), where he wrote his *Apologos dialogaes*. He was allowed to return in 1659. In his remaining seven years he published works on morals and literature, some poetry, and a play that anticipated the theme and humor of Molière's *Le Bourgeois Gentilhomme*. Though he wrote in Spanish, Portugal properly claims him as among her most brilliant sons.

Antonio Vieira was another. Born in Lisbon (1608), he was taken in childhood to Brazil, was educated by the Jesuits at Bahia, entered their order, and astonished everyone by proposing, in eloquent sermons and pamphlets, that Christianity be practiced by governments. Sent on a mission to Portugal (1641), he so impressed John IV by the integrity of his character and the variety of his powers that he was made a member of the royal Council; there he had no small part in planning the victories that restored the independence of his country. He disturbed established ideas by advocating the reform of the Inquisition, the taxation of all persons regardless of class, the admission of Jewish merchants to Portugal, and the abolition of the distinction between "Old Christians" and "New Christians" (converted Jews). He was one example, in many, of the vitality, versatility, and frequent liberalism of the Jesuits.

Back in Brazil (1652), he was sent as a missionary to Maranhão, but he so uncompromisingly condemned the barbarity and morals of the slave-owners that they had him banished to Portugal (1654). He pleaded before the King the cause of the oppressed Indians, and secured some amelioration of their condition. Returning to South America (1655), he spent six years as "the Apostle of Brazil," traveling hundreds of miles on the Amazon and its tributaries, risking his life daily among savage tribes and natural perils, teaching the arts of civilization to the natives, and so courageously defending them against their overlords that these again secured his transfer to Portugal (1661). There the Inquisition arrested him on the charge that his writings contained dangerous heresies and reprehensible extravagances (1665). He was horrified by the conditions in the prisons of the Inquisition—five men crowded into a cell nine feet by eleven, where the sole natural light came from a slit in the ceiling, and the vessels were changed only once a week.[49] He was released after two years, but was forbidden to write or preach or teach. He went to Rome (1669), was welcomed and honored by Clement X, and fascinated cardinals and commoners with his eloquence. Christina of Sweden vainly begged him to be her spiritual director. He laid before the Pope a detailed indictment of the Inquisition as a blot on the honor of the Church and a blight on the prosperity of Portugal. Clement ordered that all cases before the Portuguese Inquisition be referred to Rome, and Innocent XI suspended that body for five years.

Victorious but lonesome for Indians, Vieira sailed once more to Brazil (1681), and labored there as Jesuit teacher and missionary till his death at eighty-nine. His works, in twenty-seven volumes, contain much mystical abracadabra, but his sermons, which have been compared with Bossuet's, have given him rank as "one of the great classics of the Portuguese language";[50] and his services as a patriot and reformer led the Protestant Southey to number him among the greatest statesmen of his country and time.[51]

VI. THE COLLAPSE OF SPAIN: 1665–1700

In 1665 Spain was still the greatest empire in Christendom. She ruled the southern Netherlands, Sardinia, Sicily, the kingdom of Naples, the duchy of Milan, and vast areas in North and South America. But she had lost the naval and military power needed to control the commerce and destiny of this scattered realm. Her costly armadas had been destroyed by the English (1588) and the Dutch (1639); her armies had suffered decisive defeats at Rocroi (1643) and Lens (1648); her diplomats, in the Peace of the Pyrenees (1659), had acknowledged the triumph of France. Her economy depended upon the influx of gold and silver from America, and that flow was repeatedly interrupted by Dutch or English fleets. Her reliance on foreign gold, and the scorn of her people for trade, had stunted her commerce and her industries. Much Spanish commerce was carried in foreign vessels. Spanish shipping plying between Spain and America was seventy-five per cent less in 1700 than in 1600. Manufactured articles were imported from England and Holland, and were paid for only in part by the export of wine, oil, iron, or wool; the balance was paid in bullion, so that American gold merely passed through Spain and Portugal on the way to England, France, and the United Provinces. Cordova and Valencia, once famous for their crafts, were in conscious and querulous decay. The expulsion of the Moriscos had injured agriculture, and the frequent debasement of the coinage had demoralized finance. Roads were so bad, transport so primitive, that towns near the sea or on navigable rivers found it cheaper to import goods, even grain, from abroad than to bring them in from sources in Spain. Exorbitant taxes, including a sales tax of fourteen per cent, strove to sustain the wars of Spain against incredibly unyielding enemies presumably cursed by God. The standard of living was so reduced that countless Spaniards abandoned their farms, their shops, at last their country. Infantile mortality was high, and there was apparently some furtive limitation of the family. Thousands of men and women became barren monks or nuns, and other thousands went off to adventure in distant lands. Seville, Toledo, Burgos, and Segovia lost part of their population; Madrid, in the seventeenth century, fell from 400,000 to 200,000.[54] Spain was dying of gold.

Amid the spreading and intensifying poverty the upper classes both hoarded and displayed their wealth. Long enriched by native exploitation or imported treasure, the nobles kept their wealth from investment in industry or commerce, and dazzled one another with gems and precious metal, with costly entertainments and magnificent equipage. The Duke of Alva had 7,200 plates and 9,600 other vessels of silver; the Prince of Stigliano made for his wife a sedan chair of gold and coral, so heavy that it was unfit for use. The Church too remained rich, grew richer,[53] amid surrounding penury. The Archbishop of Santiago proposed to build an entire chapel of silver; dissuaded, he built it all of marble.[54] The blood of the people was the soil of wealth and the glory of God.

The Inquisition was as strong as ever, stronger than the government. Autos-da-fé were less frequent than before, but only because heresy had been burned out. The disabilities of Catholics in England could hardly compare with the perils of Protestants in Spain. Cromwell was unable to protect English merchants there. The English ambassador's Protestant servant was arrested by the Inquisition in 1691, and in that year the corpse of the ambassador's Anglican chaplain was exhumed and mutilated by the people. The burning of converted Jews accused of secret Judaism continued. In Majorca the Inquisition built for itself a handsome palace from the wealth confiscated in a single investigation.[55] The populace warmly approved such bonfires, though many nobles sought to discourage them. When in 1680 Charles II expressed the wish to see an auto-da-fé, the artisans of Madrid volunteered to erect an amphitheater for the sacred spectacle; during their work they cheered one another to haste and industry by devout exhortations; it was truly a labor of love. Charles and his young bride attended in full regalia; 120 prisoners were judged, and twenty-one were burned to death in a caldron in the Plaza Major; it was the greatest and most splendid auto-da-fé in the history of Spain; and a book of 308 pages was published describing and commemorating the event.[56] In 1696 Charles appointed a Junta Magna to examine the abuses of the Inquisition; it submitted a report revealing and condemning many evils, but the Inquisitor General persuaded the King to consign the "terrible indictment" to oblivion; when, in 1701, Philip V called for it, no copy could be found.[57] The Inquisition, however, moved thereafter with more measured pace, and abated its conflagrations.

The Church tried to redeem its wealth, and buttress the faith, by financing art. In 1677 Francisco de Herrera el Mozo designed the second cathedral of Saragossa, called *del Pilar* from its boasting a pillar on which the Virgin was believed to have descended from heaven. Baroque architecture now came to Spain; almost overnight the Spanish mood passed from Gothic gloom to decorative extravagance. The great name here is José

Churriguera; *churrigueresca* became for a time a name for Spanish baroque. Born at Salamanca in 1665, he expressed his exuberant energy in architecture, sculpture, cabinetry, and painting. Coming to Madrid at the age of twenty-three, he entered a competition to design a catafalque for the obsequies of Queen María Luisa; he won, and the confused structure,[58] formed with fantastic pillars and broken cornices, and embellished with skeletons, crossbones, and skulls, established his reputation for fantastic skill. About 1690 he returned to Salamanca, and for ten years labored there, adorning the cathedral, building the high altar in the Church of San Esteban, and the magnificent hall of the city council. In Madrid, toward the close of his life, he designed the façade of the Church of San Tomás; dying (1725), he left the further construction to his sons, Gerónimo and Nicolás; during their operations the dome fell, crushing many workers and worshipers. A relatively moderate form of Churrigueresque migrated to Mexico, where it produced some of the loveliest buildings in North America.

Sculpture continued to be a powerful expression of the Spanish spirit. Sometimes the power came from a bizarre realism, as when it showed in gory detail the head of John the Baptist or some other severed saint. The Museum of Valladolid had two such heads of St. Paul.[58] Altar screens were still a favorite form; so Pedro Roldan carved the great screens in the parish church of the cathedral, and in the Hospital de la Caridad, at Seville; and his daughter Luisa Roldana, the outstanding woman sculptor of Spain, raised in the cathedral of Cádiz a group centering about Nuestra Señora de las Angustias—"Our Lady of the Sorrows." Pedro de Mena dominated the age with his nudes (so rare in Spanish art), his Virgins, and his choir stalls in the Málaga cathedral, while his *San Francisco*, in the Seville cathedral, is among the finest examples of Hispanic sculpture. Toward the end of the seventeenth century the art shared in the general deterioration. Panels were loaded with ornament, images were equipped with mechanisms for moving the head, the eyes, and the mouth; real hair and dresses, and always color, were added in efforts to reach the simplest public imagination and taste.

The age of the giants was past in Spanish painting, but many minor heroes remained. Juan Carreño de Miranda, who succeeded Velázquez as court painter, was almost as loved as he; a man modest and kindly, and so absorbed in his work that at times he could not recall whether he had eaten or not. His portraits of Charles II and the court so pleased the young King that he was offered knighthood and the Cross of Santiago; Carreño refused the distinction as beyond his merit. Madrid in those days delighted in the story of *el cantarillo de miel*, the jar of honey. Gregorio Utande, an obscure artist, had painted for the Carmelite nuns a picture for which he asked a hundred ducats; they thought this too much, but agreed to let Carreño decide. Before Carreño heard of this, Utande presented him a jar of honey, and begged him to retouch the picture. This was done, much to its improvement. Carreño was surprised when the nuns called upon him to appraise it. He refused, but a third artist valued it at two hundred ducats, and the secret was kept till the price was paid.

In his later years Carreño eased the way for one of his successors. Claudio Coello worked day and night at his easel, with indifferent results. Carreño befriended him, and secured permission for him to study and copy the works of Titian, Rubens, and Vandyck in the royal galleries. The experience helped Claudio to mature, and in 1684, a year before Carreño's death, Coello was appointed painter to the King. He achieved national renown by his *Sagrada Forma*, which showed the "Sacred Wafer" being presented to Charles II for an altar in the Escorial. The legend behind the picture expresses the temper of Spain. In the war with the Dutch (said the story) a consecrated Host had been trodden underfoot by some impious Calvinists; drops of blood had flowed from the injured wafer, at once converting one of the desecrators; the rescued Host had been reverently carried to Vienna, and had been sent as a gift to Philip II; since then it had been periodically exhibited, stained with Christ's blood, to awed worshipers. Coello showed the King and his principal courtiers kneeling in adoration before the miraculous bread; half a hundred figures appeared in the picture, nearly all individualized, and arranged in a perspective of remarkably illusory depth.[60] After this work, which he had taken two years to complete, Coello was the undisputed master of all artists in the capital. Six years later (1692) he was suddenly eclipsed by the arrival of Luca Fa-Presto Giordano from Italy; Luca was at once given the leading role in redecorating the Escorial. Luca made matters worse by praising Claudio's pictures. Coello finished the painting on which he was engaged, but then laid aside his brush. A year after Giordano's arrival Coello died, aged fifty-one, allegedly of disappointment and jealousy.[61]

Meanwhile Seville had seen the birth and death (1630–90) of the last great figure in Spanish painting before Goya. Juan de Valdés Leal, like Coello, was of Portuguese parentage and Spanish birth. After some years in Cordova, he moved to Seville to challenge the ascendancy of Murillo. He was too proud to offer to his patrons the sentimental loveliness of demure Madonnas. He painted the Virgin in her Assumption, but his heart and power went rather into uncompromising pictures belittling the pleasures of life and pointing to inevitable death. He showed St. Anthony turning in terror from the beauty of women.[62] *In Ictu Oculi* (*In the Twinkling of an Eye*) represented Death as a skeleton putting out life's candle, whose brief illumination reveals, in chaos on the floor, the apparatus of worldly pursuits and glory—books, armor, a bishop's miter, a king's crown, a chain of the order of the Golden Fleece. In a variation on this idea Leal showed a charnel pit littered with corpses, skeletons, and skulls, and, above these, a fair hand holding a balance in which one scale contains the symbols of a knight, the other the insignia of a bishop; the one scale labeled NIMAS (no more), the other labeled NIMENOS (no less)—layman and ecclesiastic alike found wanting in the scales of God. Murillo, viewing the first of these two paintings, said to Valdés, "Comrade, it is a picture which cannot be looked at without holding one's nose"[63]—which might have been praise of the painter's realism, or the reaction of a healthy mind to decadent art.

Decadence was the order of the day. No great literary figure dignified the age, no great drama took the stage. The universities were languishing amid the general destitution and obscurantism; at Salamanca, in this period, the enrollment of students fell from 7,800 to 2,076.[64] The Inquisition and the Index Librorum Prohibitorum labored successfully to exclude from Spain all literature displeasing to the Church; for a century Spain was hermetically sealed against the movements of the European mind. And decadence in person sat symbolically on the throne.

Charles II became king at the age of four (1665). During his minority the country was formally ruled by his mother, Queen Mariana, actually by her Jesuit confessor, Johannes Eberhard Nithard, then by her lover Fernando Valenzuela. Disorder mounted, and the competent ministry of another Don Juan of Austria was too brief to halt decay. In 1677 the sixteen-year-old King assumed the government and presided helplessly over the debacle. Persistent intermarriage within the Hapsburg family may have contributed to his debility of body and mind. The Hapsburg chin was in Charles so prognathous that he could not chew; his tongue was so large that his speech could hardly be understood. Till the age of ten he had been treated as an infant in arms. He could barely read; he had received little education; and the superstitions and legends of his faith were his dearest heritage. A leading Spanish historian describes him as "sickly, imbecile, and highly superstitious"; he "believed himself to be possessed by the Devil, and was the plaything of the ambitions of all who surrounded him."[65] He married twice, but "it was a matter of public knowledge that he could not expect to have a child."[66] Short, lame, epileptic, senile and completely bald before thirty-five, he was always on the verge of death, but repeatedly baffled Christendom by continuing to live.

The disintegration of Spain now became a European tragedy. Despite taxation, inflation, and the exploitation of American mines, the government was so near to bankruptcy that it could not pay the interest on its debt, and even the royal table had to stint the service of the King. The administrative bureaucracy, underpaid, was venal and indolent. Poverty was so desperate that people murdered for bread; bands of starving people broke into homes to rob and kill; and twenty thousand beggars roamed the streets of Madrid. The police, unable to obtain their pay, disbanded and joined the criminals.

Amid the chaos, insecurity, and desolation the poor, crippled, half-demented King, feeling death upon him, faced in bewilderment and vacillation the problem of fixing the succession to his throne. His power being theoretically absolute, one line of his writing would suffice to bequeath his empire in four continents to either Austria or France. His mother pleaded for Austria, but Charles resented her scheming, and the shrewish rapacity of his German wife. The French ambassador reminded him that since the dowry of Louis XIV's Spanish bride had not yet been paid, her renunciation of the succession was annulled; Louis was urging her rights, and had the power to enforce them. If Charles overrode those rights, Europe would flame into war, and Spain might be torn to pieces in the strife. Charles broke down under the burden of decision; he wept, and complained that some witch had laid unbearable misfortunes upon him. While he listened to confusing arguments rioters besieged his palace, crying out for bread.

In September, 1700, Charles took to his bed of death. The French party among the factions surrounding him won the Archbishop of Toledo, primate of Spain, to its side; he remained day and night with the dying King, and reminded him that only Louis XIV had the power to keep the Spanish empire intact, and to use it as a bastion of the Catholic Church. Pope Innocent XII, under the urging of Louis, advised Charles to favor France. At last Charles yielded, and signed the fatal will that left all his dominions to Philip, Duke of Anjou, grandson of the French King (October 3, 1700). On November 1 Charles died, aged thirty-nine but seeming to be eighty. The race of the Spanish Hapsburgs came to an end in a sunset red with the threat of war.

CHAPTER XVI

The Jewish Enclaves

1564–1715

I. THE SEPHARDIM*

THE survival of the Jews through nineteen centuries of hardship and revenge is a somber strain in the history of ignorance, hatred, courage, and resilience. Deprived of their national home, forced to find shelter in ethnic pockets among unrelenting foes, subject at every turn to contumely and oppression, to sudden confiscation, expulsion, or massacre, holding no weapon of defense but patience, subtlety, desperate resolution, and religious faith, they lived through such adversities as no other people in history has borne; their will was never broken; and out of their poverty and grief they raised up poets and philosophers recalling the Hebrew legislators and prophets who had prepared the spiritual foundations of the Western world.

In Spain the extinction of the Jews was now apparently complete; they remained only as a hidden current in the Spanish blood. By 1595 a Spanish bishop could express satisfaction that converted Jews had been successfully assimilated by intermarriage, and that their descendants were now good Christians.[2] The Inquisition did not agree with him. In 1654 ten men were burned in Cuenca and twelve in Granada, in 1660 eighty-one were arrested in Seville, and seven burned, on the charge of secretly adhering to Jewish rites.[3]

In Portugal, especially, many seeming converts (*conversos*, Marranos) continued to practice and transmit Judaism in the privacy of their homes; over a hundred of them, as *relapsos*, fell victims to the Inquisition between 1565 and 1595.[4] Despite all dangers of detection, crypto-Jews found precarious place in Portuguese life as writers, professors, merchants, financiers, even as monks and priests. The most prominent physicians were secret Jews; and at Lisbon the Mendes family developed one of the greatest banking firms in Europe.

After the absorption of Portugal into Spain (1580), the activity of the Portuguese Inquisition increased; in the next twenty years there were fifty

* *Sepharad* appears in the Bible[1] as the name of a district in western Asia, where Jewish deportees were settled after the Babylonian capture of Jerusalem. Later it became a Hebrew term for Spain, and the Jews of Spanish or Portuguese origin were called Sephardim.

autos-da-fé, with 162 condemnations to death, and 2,979 penitents. A Franciscan friar, Diogo da Assumçao, aged twenty-five, was burned at Lisbon (1603) after revealing his conversion to Judaism.[5] Many Marranos, finding the Portuguese Inquisition more ferocious than the Spanish, migrated to Spain. In 1604, by a bribe of 1,860,000 ducats paid to Philip III, and lesser bribes to his ministers, they persuaded the King to obtain from Pope Clement VIII a bull directing the Portuguese inquisitors to release all their Marrano prisoners with merely spiritual penances. In one day (January 16, 1605) 410 such victims were freed. But the efficacy of such bribes diminished with time, and soon after the death of Philip III (1621) the Portuguese Terror was renewed. In 1623 a hundred "New Christians" were arrested in the little town of Montemor o Novo. At Coimbra, the cultural center of the kingdom, there were 247 such arrests in 1626, 218 in 1629, 247 in 1631. In twenty years (1620–40) 230 Portuguese Jews were burned in person, 161 in effigy, having escaped; and 4,995 were "reconciled" with lesser penalties.[6] Risking life and abandoning property, thousands of Marranos fled from Portugal, as formerly from Spain, to all quarters of the world.

The great majority of the Sephardic exiles sought refuge in Islam, and formed or joined Jewish settlements in North Africa, Salonika, Cairo, Constantinople, Adrianople, Smyrna, Aleppo, and Iran. In these centers the Jews were subject to political and economic disabilities, but rarely to physical persecution. Jews rose to prominence not only as physicians but in affairs of state. Joseph Nassi, a Marrano, was a favorite of Selim II, and as Duke of Naxos (1566) he received the revenues of ten islands in the Aegean.[7] A German Jew, Solomon ben Nathan Ashkenazi, was Turkey's ambassador to Vienna in 1571, and negotiated there the peace that for a time ended war with the Porte.

In Italy the fortunes of the Jews fluctuated with the needs and moods of dukes and popes. In Milan and Naples, ruled by Spain, life was almost impossible for them; in 1669 an explicit decree expelled them from all Spanish possessions. In Pisa and Livorno (Leghorn) the Tuscan grand dukes gave them nearly complete liberty, being anxious to develop the commerce of these free ports. A charter granted in 1593 to merchants in these cities was in effect an invitation to Marranos: "We desire that . . . no Inquisition, Visitation, Denunciation, or Accusal shall be made against you or your families, even though, during the past, they may have lived outside our dominions in the guise of Christians, or with the name of being such."[8] The plan succeeded; Livorno flourished; and the Jewish community there, exceeded in number only by those in Rome and Venice, became famous for its culture as well as its wealth.

The Venetian Senate, fearing the relationships of the Jews with Turkey, repeatedly expelled them, and repeatedly allowed them to return as a valuable element not only in commerce and finance but in industry; Jewish enterprises in Venice employed four thousand Christian workingmen.[9] German and Oriental, as well as Sephardic, Jews settled there, and the Senate protected them from the Inquisition. They lived nearly all in the Giudecca, or Jewish quarter, but were not confined to it; this "ghetto" included many rich families, fine homes, and a luxuriously furnished synagogue built in 1584, and rebuilt in 1655 under the supervision of the famous architect Baldassare Longhena. The six thousand Jews of Venice had the highest cultural level of any Jewish community in this age.

At Ferrara a colony of Marranos from Portugal settled about 1560, but it was dispersed in 1581 by order of the Pope, who acted under pressure by the Portuguese Inquisition. In Mantua the Gonzaga dukes protected the Jews, but periodically mulcted them with contributions and "loans"; and in 1610 all Mantuan Jews were compelled to reside in a walled ghetto whose gates were locked at sunset and opened at dawn.[10] When plague came to Mantua the Jews were accused of having brought it in; and when, in the War of the Mantuan Succession, the troops of the Emperor took the city, they sacked the ghetto thoroughly, appropriated 800,000 scudi in jewels and money, and ordered the Jews to leave Mantua within three days with only such property as they could carry.[11]

In Rome, where previously the papacy had usually protected the Jews, the popes after 1565, with the exception of Sixtus V, issued a long succession of hostile decrees. Pius V (1566) commanded all Catholic powers to enforce to the full the canonical restrictions and disabilities of the Jews. They were hereafter to be confined to ghettos physically closed off from the Christian population; they were to wear a distinctive badge or garb; they were to be excluded from the ownership of land; and they were not to have more than one synagogue in any city. In 1569, in a bull accusing them of usury, procuring, witchcraft, and magic arts, Pius V directed that all Jews be expelled from the Papal States, except from the cities of Ancona and Rome.[12] Gregory XIII (1581) forbade the Christian employment of Jewish physicians, ordered the confiscation of Hebrew books, and (1584) renewed the compulsion laid upon the Jews to hear sermons aimed at their conversion. Sixtus V ended the persecution for a time. He opened the ghetto (1586), allowed the Jews to reside anywhere in the Papal States, dispensed them from wearing a distinctive mark or dress, permitted them to print the Talmud and other Hebrew literature, granted them full freedom of worship, and bade the Christians treat the Jews and their synagogues with humane respect.[13] But this Christian pontificate was brief. Clement VIII renewed the edict of expulsion (1593). By 1640 nearly all the Jews of Italy were living in ghettos; when stepping outside these they were to wear some badge of their tribe; they were excluded from agriculture and the guilds. Montaigne, touring Rome in 1581, described how the Jews, on their Sabbath, were required to send sixty of their youths to the Church of Sant' Angelo in Pescheria to hear exhortations to conversion.[14] John Evelyn saw such a ceremony in Rome (January 7, 1645), and observed that "a conversion is very rare." Many of the less pleasant characteristics of the Jews in body and character were the result of long confinement, humiliation, and poverty.

In France the Jews were theoretically subject to all the restrictions called for by Pius V; actually their importance in industry, commerce, and finance earned them a tacit toleration. In one of his ordinances Colbert emphasized the benefits accruing to Marseilles from the mercantile enterprises of the Jews.[15] Marrano refugees established themselves in Bordeaux and Bayonne, and contributed so much to the economic life of southwestern France that they were allowed to practice their Judaic rituals with less and less concealment. When an army of mercenaries invaded Bordeaux in 1675, the town council feared that the exodus of frightened Jews would cripple the prosperity of the city; without them, reported a *sous-intendant*, "the trade of Bordeaux and of the whole province would be inevitably ruined."[16] Louis XIV took the Jewish community at Metz under his protection; when local magistrates tortured to death (1670) a Jew accused of ritual child murder, the King condemned the execution as judicial slaughter, and ordered that henceforth criminal charges against Jews were to be brought before the royal Council.[17] Toward the end of Louis' reign, when the War of the Spanish Succession had brought the French government close to bankruptcy, Samuel Bernard, a Jewish financier, put his fortune at the King's disposal; and the proud monarch was grateful for the aid of "the greatest banker in Europe."[18]

II. THE DUTCH JERUSALEM

The migration of the Jews from Spain and Portugal played a part (sometimes exaggerated)[19] in the passage of commercial leadership from those countries to the Netherlands. There the exiled Jews went first to Antwerp; but in 1549 Charles V ordered the expulsion from the Low Countries of all Marranos who had entered from Portugal in the preceding five years. The burgomasters of Antwerp pleaded for exemption from this edict; it was enforced, and the new immigrants resumed their search for a home. Antwerp lost its commercial prominence not from this partial migration but through the disasters that befell the city in the war of liberation and the Treaty of Westphalia, which closed the Scheldt to navigation.

The imperfect but growing freedom of religion in the United Provinces attracted Jews to the Dutch towns—The Hague, Rotterdam, Haarlem, and, above all, Amsterdam. Marrano Jews appeared there in 1593; four years later they opened a synagogue. Hebrew was their language in worship, Spanish or Portuguese in their daily life. In 1615, after a report drawn up by Hugo Grotius, the city authorities formally authorized the Jewish community, granting freedom of worship but forbidding intermarriage with Christians and attacks upon the Christian religion;[20] hence the trepidation of the synagogue leaders when the heresies of Uriel Acosta and Baruch Spinoza touched the fundamentals of the Christian creed.

The Jews included some of the wealthiest merchants in the thriving port. They managed a substantial segment of Dutch trade with the Spanish Peninsula, and with the East and West Indies. On one occasion, at the wedding of a Jewish girl, forty of the guests had fortunes totaling forty million florins.[21] In 1688, when Stadholder William III was planning his expedition to capture the crown of England, Isaac Suasso, we are told, advanced him two million florins without interest, saying, "If you are fortunate, you will repay them to me; if not, I am willing to lose them."[22] Some of this wealth was made too conspicuous; David Pinto adorned his home so gaudily that the civic authorities reproved him;[23] we should add, however, that the Pinto family gave millions to Jewish and Christian charities.[24] Behind this economic front was a busy cultural life, with scholars, rabbis, physicians, poets, mathematicians, and philosophers. Schools provided education, and a Hebrew printing press founded by Manasseh ben Israel in 1627 issued a great number of books and pamphlets; for the next two centuries Amsterdam was to be the center of the Jewish book trade. In 1671–75 the Portuguese-Jewish community, numbering four thousand families, signalized its prosperity by building the beautiful synagogue that is still one of the sights of Amsterdam; Christians, we are told, took part in the dedication. It was a happy moment in the life of the modern Jews.

There were spots on this sun. About 1630 Ashkenazic, or Eastern, Jews* came into Amsterdam from Poland and Germany. They had their own dialect of German, and set up their own synagogue; they multiplied rapidly, and aroused much antipathy among the Sephardic Jews, who were proud

* The name *Ashkenaz* appears first in Genesis x, 3, as a great-grandson of Noah; in Jeremiah LI, 27, it is the name of a kingdom in western Asia; among the medieval rabbis, for reasons unknown, it was the name for Germany; and *Ashkenazim* became a synonym for the Jews of Germany, Poland, and Russia.

of their superior language, culture, dress, and wealth, and looked upon marriage with an Ashkenazic Jew as almost apostasy. Within the Sephardic group itself a class division formed: the small trades and proliferating poor denounced the "millionaires" who controlled the politics and personnel of the synagogue. "The dollar binds and looses," said a contemporary satire; "it raises the ignorant to the chief offices in the community."[25] The intellectual leaders—Saul Levi Morteira, Isaac Aboab da Fonseca, and Manasseh ben Israel—were men of ability and integrity; but they were cautiously conservative in politics, religion, and morals. They became as dogmatic as the Spanish persecutors of their forebears, and they exercised a watchful inquisition over potential heresies.[26]

Manasseh ben Israel left his mark upon history by reopening England to the Jews. Born in La Rochelle of Marrano parents recently arrived from Lisbon, he was brought to Amsterdam in childhood, became a devoted student in Hebrew, Spanish, Portuguese, Latin, and English, and at eighteen was chosen preacher of the congregation Neveh Shalom. He pleased Christians as well as Jews by writing *El Conciliador* to reconcile alleged discrepancies in the Bible. He had many Christian correspondents and friends —Huet, Grotius, Christina of Sweden, Dionysius Vossius, who translated his book into Latin, and Rembrandt, who etched his portrait in 1636. Above all he attracted the interest of Christian visionaries because he preached the early coming of a Messiah who would rule the earth.

For Manasseh was a Cabalist and mystic idealist, who dreamed that soon the lost ten tribes of Israel would be found and be united, that they were probably the American Indians, that the Jews would be readmitted to England and Scandinavia, and that the Holy Land would then be restored to Israel in full Messianic glory. Puritans of the Fifth Monarchy sect in England corresponded with Manasseh, and though their Messiah was not his they welcomed his views on the early coming of the Kingdom of God. So encouraged, he published (1650) a treatise, *Esperança de Israel*, pleading for the re-entry of Jews into England. For a Latin translation of this book he wrote a preface addressed to the English Parliament; he explained that according to Scriptural prophecies the return of the Jews to their homeland would be preceded by their dispersion into all countries; he begged the English government to help realize this preliminary condition by receiving the Jews into England and letting them freely exercise their religion and build their synagogues. He expressed the hope that he might be allowed to come to England to prepare the establishment of a Hebrew community.

Cromwell was favorably disposed. "Great is my sympathy with this poor people," he said, "whom God chose, and to whom He gave His Law."[27] Lord Middlesex, perhaps representing the Parliament, sent a letter of acknowledgment and thanks "to my dear brother, the Hebrew philosopher, Manasseh ben Israel." The English ambassador in Holland visited Manasseh, and was received with Hebrew music and prayer (August, 1651). But in October Parliament passed a Navigation Act obviously aimed at Dutch trade; commercial competition led to the First Dutch War (1652–54), and Manasseh had to bide his time. "Barebone's Parliament" (1653) received with favor his renewed plea; a safe-conduct was dispatched to him; when peace came Cromwell seconded the invitation; and in October, 1655, Manasseh and his son crossed to England.

III. ENGLAND AND THE JEWS

Between the expulsion of the Jews from England in 1290 and the accession of Cromwell in 1649, no Jews were legally permitted there. Some Jewish peddlers may have appeared in the villages, some merchants and physicians in the towns; but nearly all that the Elizabethan knew or thought of Jews was derived from Christian gossip or literature. From such sources Marlowe drew his Barabas and Shakespeare his Shylock.

Some critics[28] have thought that Shakespeare wrote *The Merchant of Venice* at his company's suggestion to profit from the storm of anti-Semitism just aroused in England by the case of Rodrigo Lopez, executed in 1594 for allegedly trying to poison Queen Elizabeth. Born in Portugal of Jewish parents, Lopez settled in London in 1559, and made his way to prominence in the medical profession. Engaged as physician to the Earl of Leicester, he was accused of helping him to remove enemies by poison. In 1586 he became chief physician to the Queen. He treated, among others, the second Earl of Essex, but earned his enmity by revealing his ailments to others. About 1590 he joined Francis Walsingham in intrigues with the court of Spain against Dom Antônio, pretender to the Portuguese crown, and he received, apparently from agents of Philip II, a diamond ring then valued at a hundred pounds. In 1593 Esteban da Gama was seized in Lopez' house on a charge of conspiring against Antônio; others were arrested, and some of the confessions implicated Lopez in a plot against Elizabeth. Essex, who had supported Antônio, led the prosecution of the physician. Put on the rack, Lopez confessed to having received and concealed an offer of fifty thousand ducats to poison the Queen; but he claimed that his intention had been merely to mulct the Spanish King. He and two others were hanged, drawn, and quartered. With his last breath he declared, to the derision of the spectators, that he loved the Queen as well as he loved Jesus Christ.[29] Shakespeare, friendly to Essex, produced *The Merchant of Venice* two months after the execution; and many auditors must have noted that Shylock's intended victim was called Antonio.

The spread of the Bible, accelerated by the King James Version, modified anti-Semitism by giving England a closer acquaintance with the Old Testament. The ideas and feelings of the ancient Hebrews entered intimately into the thought and phrases of the Puritans. The wars of the Jews seemed to them to prefigure their own wars against Charles I; somehow Jehovah the God of Hosts fitted their needs better than the Prince of Peace described in the New Testament. Many Puritan regiments inscribed their banners with the Lion of Judah, and Cromwell's Ironsides marched to battle singing Biblical songs. Accepting the magnificent literature of the Old Testament as literally the Word of God, the Puritans felt constrained to acknowledge the Jews as chosen by God to be the immediate recipients of His revelation; one preacher told his congregation that the Jews should still be honored as the select of God; and some Levellers called themselves Jews.[30] Many Puritans perceived that Christ's explicit confirmation of the Mosaic Law outweighed Paul's rejection of it and laid upon all Biblical Christians the obligation to practice that Law; one Puritan leader, Major General Thomas Harrison, close aide to Cromwell, proposed that the Mosaic Code be made part of English law.[31] In 1649 a bill was introduced into the House of Commons to change the Lord's day from the pagan Sunday to the Jewish Sabbath. Now, said the Puritans, the English too were the chosen people of God.

During the reign of James I (1603–25) a small group of Marranos had settled in London. At first they attended Christian services, but later they made little effort to conceal their fidelity to Judaism. Jewish financiers like Antonio Carvajal shared in meeting the monetary needs of the Long Parliament and the Commonwealth.[32] When Cromwell came to power he used Marrano merchants as sources of economic and political information regarding Holland and Spain. He noted with some envy the prosperity that had come to Dutch commerce partly through the influx and international connections of the Jews.

Soon after Manasseh ben Israel's arrival in England Cromwell received him, and put a London residence at his disposal. Manasseh presented a petition, and circulated through the press a "Declaration" stating the religious and economic case for the admission of Jews into England. He explained why the Jews, through their legal disabilities and physical and financial insecurity, had been forced to abstain from agriculture and take to trade. He pointed out that the Amsterdam Jews lived by commercial investment rather than by moneylending, that they practiced no usury, but placed their liquid funds in banks and were satisfied with five per cent interest on these deposits. He showed the baselessness of the legend that Jews murdered Christian children to use their blood in religious rituals. He assured Christians that Jews made no attempt to secure converts. He concluded by asking that Jews be admitted to England on condition of taking an oath of loyalty to the realm; that they receive religious freedom, and protection from violence; and that their internal disputes be settled by their rabbis and laws without prejudice to English law and interests.

On December 4, 1655, Cromwell assembled at Whitehall a conference of jurists, officials, and clergymen to consider the admission of the Jews. He himself defended the idea with force and eloquence, stressing not the economic but the religious aspect: the pure Gospel must be preached to the Jews, but "can we preach to them, if we will not tolerate them among us?"[33] His arguments met with little sympathy. The clergymen insisted that Jews had no place in a Christian commonwealth; representatives of commerce objected that Jewish merchants would deflect trade and wealth from English hands. The conference voted that Jews could not settle in England "except by private sufferance of His Highness."[34]

Public opinion was predominantly hostile to admission. Rumors were spread that the Jews, if allowed into England, would turn St. Paul's Cathedral into a synagogue. William Prynne, who had made a stir twenty-seven years earlier by his *Historiomastix* attack upon the English theater, issued (1655–56) a *Short Demurrer* renewing old charges that the Jews were counterfeiters of coinage and murderers of children. A passionate Puritan, Thomas Collyer, answered Prynne, but weakened his case by urging that the Jews be honored as the chosen people of God. Manasseh himself published (1656) a *Vindication* appealing to the English people's sense of justice. Could they really believe "that strange and horrid accusation . . . that the Jews are wont to celebrate the Feast of Unleavened Bread [by] fermenting it with the blood of some Christians whom they have for that purpose killed?" He showed how often in history such accusations had been made by false witnesses, or supported only by confessions under torture, and how often the innocence of Jews so accused had been brought to light after their execution. He concluded with touching faith and fervor:

> And to the highly honored nation of England I make my most humble request, that they would read over my arguments impartially, . . . effectually recommending me to their grace and favor, and earnestly beseeching God that He would be pleased to hasten the time promised by Zephaniah, wherein we shall all serve Him with one consent, after the same manner, and shall be all of the same judgment; that as His name is one, so His fear may be also one, and that we may all see the goodness of the Lord (blessed forever!) and the consolations of Zion.[35]

The English people were not won over by this plea, and Manasseh obtained no formal admission of the Jews. Cromwell, absorbed in protecting his government and his life, put the problem aside; however, he awarded Manasseh a yearly pension of a hundred pounds (which was never paid) out of the public treasury. In September, 1657, Manasseh's son died. With the aid of a grant from the Protector he took the body to Holland for burial. Exhausted with travel and grief, the Apostle to England died at Middelburg November 20, leaving not enough money to pay for his own funeral.

He had not really failed in his mission. Evelyn's *Diary* remarks, under December 14, 1655, "Now were the Jews admitted." No decree of the Protector, no enactment of Parliament, legalized their return; but more and more of them came in with the tacit approval of Cromwell. In 1657 he allowed the Jews of London to establish their own burial ground, not as Christians but as Jews; soon thereafter they opened a synagogue and quietly practiced their ritual. When the Restoration came, Charles II remembered the financial support given him in his Dutch exile by Mendes da Costa and other Hebrews; he perceived the advantages that had already accrued to England from the mercantile enterprises of the London Jews; and he winked an eye on further immigration. William III, also recalling Jewish help, continued this tolerant attitude, despite the repeated complaints of English merchants and clergymen. Solomon Medina earned the first Jewish knighthood by his services as army contractor for William III and Marlborough.[36] By 1715 Jewish brokers were on the London Exchange, and Jewish financiers were a minor power in the land. In 1904 the English Jews celebrated the tercentenary of Manasseh's birth.

IV. THE ASHKENAZIM

Despite medieval crusades and a thousand vicissitudes, there remained in 1564 substantial Jewish settlements in Germany, above all in Frankfurt-am-Main, Hamburg, and Worms. But the Reformation had intensified rather than moderated the Christian hatred of the strange people that could not accept Christ as the Son of God. At Frankfurt the Jews were forbidden to leave the ghetto except on urgent business, and could not receive out-of-town guests without the knowledge of the magistrates; their clothing had to have a special mark or color; their houses were to bear distinctive emblems, often grotesque. Bribery of town officials sometimes bought exemptions from these humiliations, but the hostility of simple folk was a perpetual menace to Jewish life and property. So in September, 1614, while most Frankfurt Jews were at prayer, a Christian crowd forced an entry into the ghetto; after enjoying a night of plunder and destruction, it compelled 1,380 Jews to leave the city with no other belongings than the clothes on their backs. Several Christian families sheltered and fed the fugitives; and the Archbishop of Mainz compelled the municipality of Frankfurt to restore them to their homes, to indemnify them for their losses, and to hang the leader of the mob.[37] A year later, at Worms, a similar uprising drove the Jews from the city and desecrated their synagogues and cemeteries; but the Archbishop of Worms and the Landgrave of Hesse-Darmstadt gave refuge to the exiles, and the Elector Palatine protected their return. In general the higher clergy and classes were inclined to toleration, but the lower clergy and the masses were easily stirred to the ecstasy of hate. Old disabilities, even when relaxed, always hung over Jewish heads, and insult and injury were the possibilities of any day. Some ardent Christians snatched Jewish infants from their mothers' breasts and forcibly baptized them.[38] If there were no ignorance there would be no history.

The Thirty Years' War left the Jews of Germany relatively unharmed. Protestants and Catholics were so engrossed in mutual murder that they almost forgot to kill Jews, even when these had lent them money. The Emperor Ferdinand I had imposed burdensome regulations upon the Jews of Austria, and had expelled them from Bohemia (1559); but Ferdinand II protected them, allowed them, in Catholic Vienna, to build a synagogue and discard the badge, and permitted the return of Jews to Bohemia. The Bohemian Jews pledged forty thousand gulden yearly to the Imperial cause in the great war. To soothe Christians who complained of his tolerant policy, Ferdinand II (1630) ruled that the Jews of Prague should listen every Sunday to Christian sermons, and fines were levied for truancy or sleeping.

After the Peace of Westphalia the Hebrew settlements in Germany expanded rapidly. The excesses of the war had in some measure discredited bigotry and persecution; hundreds of Jews came in from Poland after the pogroms that followed the Cossack revolt of 1648. Between 1675 and 1720 an annual average of 648 Jewish merchants attended the Leipzig fairs. German princes found uses for Jewish skill in the management of finances and the organization of supplies for armies and courts. So Samuel Oppenheimer superintended the Imperial fisc during the campaigns that closed the seventeenth century, and Samson Wertheimer supervised the Imperial commissariat in the War of the Spanish Succession. The influence of the Spanish-born and Jesuit-inspired Empress Margaret Theresa upon her husband Leopold I resulted in the banishment of the Jews from Austria, but the Great Elector Frederick William welcomed many of the exiles into Brandenburg, and the Jewish community in Berlin grew into one of the largest in Europe.

Ever since the twelfth century the Jews of Central Europe had been developing their own Yiddish (*Jüdisch*) dialect, composed mostly of German words with Hebrew and Slavic additions, and written in Hebrew characters. Literate Jews continued to study Hebrew, but the secular publications of the Ashkenazim became predominantly Yiddish. A Yiddish literature arose, rich in wry humor and domestic sentiment, in folk tales transmitted across centuries and frontiers, in *Purimspiele*, or playlets for the gay spring festival, and in proverbs of homely wisdom ("One father supports ten children, but ten children do not support one father").[39] Before 1715 this literature could boast of only one notable author, Elijah Bochur, a scholar in Hebrew and a poet in Yiddish, who wrote fantastic romances in ottava rima, and rendered the Psalms into popular speech. A Yiddish version of the Pentateuch appeared in 1544, only fifteen years after Luther's German Bible, and a Yiddish translation of the entire Old Testament was published at Amsterdam in 1676-79. The German Jews were on their way to the cultural leadership of their people.

Jews had entered Poland from Germany in the tenth century. Despite an occasional massacre they prospered and increased under the protection of the government. In 1501 there were some fifty thousand Jews in Poland; in 1648, half a million.[40] The gentry (szlachta) controlling the Sejm supported the Jews, because landlords found them especially competent in collecting rents and taxes, and managing estates. With some exceptions, the rulers of Poland in the sixteenth and seventeenth centuries were among the most liberal monarchs of their time. Stephen Báthory issued two edicts confirming the commercial rights of the Jews, and branding ritual-murder charges as cruel "calumnies" not to be admitted in Polish courts (1576).[41] But popular animosity remained. Only a year after these edicts a mob attacked the Jewish quarter in Poznań, pillaged homes, and killed many Jews. Báthory imposed a fine upon the city officials for having failed to stop the riot. Sigismund III continued royal toleration.

Two factors contributed to end this era of governmental good will. German merchants in Poland resented Jewish competition; they fomented popular outbreaks in Poznań and Wilno, where a synagogue was demolished and the houses of Jews were sacked (1592); and they submitted to the King a petition *de non tolerandis Judaeis* (1619). The Jesuits, brought in by Báthory, and soon taking intellectual lead of the Catholics in Poland, joined in the campaign to discontinue toleration. Accusations of ritual murder now won governmental recognition. In 1598, at Lublin, the corpse of a boy having been found in a swamp, three Jews were forced by torture to confess that they had slain him; they were hanged, drawn, and quartered; and the body, preserved in a Catholic church, became an object of religious veneration. Anti-Semitic literature grew in ferocity.

In 1618 Sebastian Michiński of Cracow published *A Mirror of the Polish*

Crown, in which he charged the Jews with child murder, witchcraft, robbery, swindling, and treason, and called upon the Sejm to expel all Jews from Poland. The pamphlet aroused such public feeling that Sigismund ordered its suppression. A Polish physician accused Jewish doctors of systematically poisoning Catholics (1623). King Ladislas IV directed municipal authorities to protect the Jews against popular uprisings, and tried to lessen Christian hostility by forbidding Jews to take homes in Christian neighborhoods, or to build new synagogues, or open new cemeteries, without royal license. The Sejm of 1643 required all merchants to limit themselves to a maximum profit of seven per cent if they were Christians, three per cent if they were Jews; the result was that Christians bought from the Jews, who prospered and incurred more hate.

Despite hatred, restrictions, tribulations, and poverty, the Polish Jews multiplied. They built temples and schools, transmitted their stabilizing traditions, morals, and laws, and cherished their comforting faith. Elementary schools were organized by private teachers paid by the parents per pupil and term; for pupils who could not pay, most Jewish communities maintained a school from public funds. Attendance at elementary school was compulsory for boys from their sixth to their thirteenth year. Higher education was provided in a college (*yeshibah*) under rabbinical control. A contemporary rabbi describes the system (1653):

> Every Jewish community supported *bahurs* (college students), giving them a certain amount of money per week. . . . Every one of these *bahurs* was made to instruct at least two boys. . . . A community of fifty Jewish families would support no less than thirty of these young men and boys, one family supplying board for one college student and his two pupils, the former sitting at the family table like one of the sons. . . . There was scarcely a house . . . where the Torah was not studied, and where either the head of the family or his son or his son-in-law, or the *yeshibah* student boarding with him, was not an expert in Jewish learning.[42]

From our later and secular standpoint the education and literature of Polish Jewry was narrowly rabbinical, being almost confined to the Talmud, the Bible, the Cabala, and Hebrew. But since the Talmud contained Jewish law as well as Jewish religion and history, it served as a severe and deepening discipline of the mind; and the harassed communities doubtless felt that only an intense religious faith, and a study rooted in the traditions and mores of the tribe, could generate the strength to bear persistent contumely, persecution, hardship, and insecurity. The Polish Jews remained medieval until modernity became modern enough to give them liberty—or death.

The year 1648 brought them a terrible reminder of their precarious status in Christendom. In the revolt that then flared up among the Cossacks against their Polish or Lithuanian landlords, the Jews who had served as stewards and taxgatherers for the estates bore the brunt of the rebellion. In Pereyaslav, Piryatin, Lubny, and other towns thousands of Jews were massacred, whether or not they had served the nobility. Some survived by accepting conversion to the Greek Orthodox faith, some by taking refuge among the Tatars, who sold them as slaves. The pent-up resentment of the Cossacks ran mad in incredible ferocity. Says a Russian historian:

> Killing was accompanied by barbarous tortures: the victims were flayed alive, split asunder, clubbed to death, roasted on coals, or scalded with boiling water. . . . The most terrible cruelty, however, was shown to the Jews. They were destined to utter annihilation, and the slightest pity shown to them was looked upon as treason. Scrolls of the Law were taken out of the synagogues by Cossacks, who danced on them while drinking whiskey. After this Jews were laid upon them and butchered without mercy. Thousands of Jewish infants were thrown into wells, or buried alive.[43]

In one city alone, Niemirov, 6,000 Jews were said to have perished in this revolt. At Tulchyn 1,500 Jews were rounded up in a park, and were offered a choice between conversion and death; if one may believe the Jewish chronicler 1,500 chose death. In the town of Polonnoye, we are told, 10,000(?) Jews were killed by Cossacks or taken prisoner by Tatars. Lesser pogroms raged in other Ukrainian towns. When the Cossacks, faced by the Polish army, allied themselves with Russia (1654), Muscovite troops joined Cossacks in killing or expelling the Jews of Moghilev, Vitebsk, Wilno, and other cities taken from the Lithuanians or the Poles.

In 1655 the invasion of Poland by Charles X of Sweden created another problem for the Jews. Like many Poles, they accepted the Swedish conqueror without resistance, as a savior from the dreaded Russians. When a new Polish army rose and drove out the Swedes, it massacred the Jews throughout the provinces of Poznań, Kalisz, Cracow, and Piotrków, excepting the city of Poznań itself. Altogether, these disasters of 1648–58 in Poland, Lithuania, and Russia were, till our own time, the bloodiest in the history of the European Jews, exceeding in terror and mortality the massacres of the Crusades and the Black Death. A conservative estimate has reckoned 34,719 Jewish lives lost, and 531 Jewish communities wiped out.[44] It was this tragic decade that began the mass migration of Jews from Slavic lands into Western Europe and North America, resulting in a complete redistribution of Jewish population on the globe.

In Poland the surviving Jews returned to their homes and patiently rebuilt their devastated communities. King John Casimir declared his resolve to compensate his Jewish subjects, so far as he could, for the calamaties they had borne; he gave them new charters of rights and protection, and temporary exemption from taxes in those centers that had suffered most. But popular and theological hostility remained, graced now and then with Christian commiseration. In 1660 two rabbis were executed on the old charge, so repeatedly repudiated by the popes, of ritual murder; and in 1663 a Jewish apothecary at Cracow, on the unproved accusation that he had written a diatribe against worship of the Virgin Mary, suffered death in the barbarous sequence ordered by the court: his lips were cut off, his hand was burned, his tongue was cut out, and his body was burned at the stake.[45] The general of the Dominican order sent from Rome (February 9, 1664) a letter urging the Dominican monks of Cracow "to defend the hapless Jews from every calumny invented against them."[46] At Lvov the pupils of a Jesuit academy invaded the Jewish quarter, killed a hundred Jews, demolished houses, and desecrated synagogues (1664); but at Wilno Jesuit students protected Jews from riotous mobs (1682).[47] The generous Sobieski (1674–96) labored to comfort the Jews of Poland: he reaffirmed their violated rights, freed them from the jurisdiction of municipal authorities subject to popular passions, and gave sympathetic audience to the syndics who presented the petitions of the Jews to his court. By the end of his reign the Polish Jews had recovered, in number, from the bitter decade, but the horror of it remained for generations in Hebrew memory.

Legally there were no Jews in Russia before 1772. Ivan the Terrible gave his view of them in answering a request from Sigismund II that Lithuanian Jews be admitted to Russia for business purposes (1550):

> It is not convenient to allow Jews to come with their goods to Russia, since many evils result from them. For they import poisonous herbs into our realm, and lead astray the Russians from Christianity. Therefore he, the King, should no more write about these Jews.[48]

When Russian troops occupied the Polish border city of Polotsk (1565), Ivan sent orders to have all local Jews converted or drowned. In the war of 1654 with Poland the Russians were astonished to find many cities in Lithuania and the Ukraine with entire sections populated by Jews. They murdered some of these "dangerous heretics," and took others prisoner to Moscow, where these became the nucleus of a small and illegal Jewish colony. In 1698 Peter the Great, in Holland, received through the burgomaster of Amsterdam a petition from some Jews to allow them to enter Russia. He replied:

> My dear Witsen, you know the Jews, and you know their character and habits; you also know the Russians. I know both; and believe me,

the time has not yet come to unite the two nationalities. Tell the Jews that I am obliged to them for their proposal, and that I realize how advantageous their services would be to me, but I should have pity on them were they to live in the midst of the Russians.[49]

This Russian policy of Jewish exclusion continued till the first partition of Poland (1772).

V. THE INSPIRATIONS OF FAITH

To understand the hostility of Christians to Jews, we must go back into the mind of the medieval Catholic and the Reformation Protestant. They remembered the Crucifixion, but they did not remember the large crowds of Jews that had heard Christ gladly and had welcomed him into Jerusalem. They thought of Jesus as the Anointed One, the Son of God; but the Jews could not see in Christ the Messiah promised by their prophets, the savior who would free them from bondage and make them again a nation erect and free. It was difficult for Christians to look with brotherly tolerance upon a minority whose monotheism was no distant rivalry like that of Mohammedanism, but a passionate cry, heard from synagogues multiplying in Christendom itself—"Hear, O Israel! Adonai, our God, is One!" That proud Semitic creed was felt as an ever present challenge to the fundamental Christian belief that the Son of Man who had died on the Cross was in full truth the Son of God, whose infinite sacrifice had atoned for man's sins, and had opened the gates of Paradise. Could anything in life be more precious and sustaining than that faith?

To protect that faith the Christians of Europe sought to isolate the Jews with geographical barriers, political disabilities, intellectual censorship, and economic restraints. Nowhere in Christian Europe before the French Revolution—not even in Amsterdam—were they allowed full citizenship and its rights. They were shut out from public office, the army, the schools and universities, and the practice of law in Christian courts. They were heavily taxed, they were subject to forced loans, they might at any time suffer confiscation of their property. They were excluded from agriculture by restrictions on the ownership of land, and by the haunting insecurity that forced them to put their savings in currency or movable goods. They were ineligible to the guilds, for these were partly religious in form and purpose, and required Christian oaths and rituals. Limited to petty industry, to commerce and finance, they found themselves harassed even in these occupations by special prohibitions varying in place and changeable at any time: in one district they could not be peddlers, in another they could not be shopkeepers, in another they must not deal in leather or wool.[50] So most Jews lived as small tradesmen, peddlers, dealers in secondhand goods or old clothes, tailors, servants of their richer fellow men, craftsmen making goods for Jews. From these occupations, and the humiliations of the ghetto, the poorer Jews developed those habits of dress and speech, those tricks of trade and qualities of mind, that were so distasteful to other peoples and higher ranks.

Above this lowly majority were the rabbis, physicians, merchants, and financiers. The activity of Jewish exporters and importers played a significant part in the prosperity of Hamburg and Amsterdam. One twelfth of England's foreign trade passed through Jewish hands in the first half of the seventeenth century.[51] Jews predominated in the import of gems and textiles from the East. The Jews profited, in international commerce, from their family relations in divers states, and their superior knowledge of languages; they had their own channels of information, which guided them, occasionally, to anticipations profitable on the bourse.[52] These foreign connections enabled them to develop letters of credit and bills of exchange.[53] The Jews, of course, were not the inventors of modern capitalism; we have seen that system grow quite independently of them, and rather in manufacturing than in finance; and even in finance they played a minor role as compared with the Medici of Florence, the Grimaldi of Genoa, or the Fuggers of Augsburg. Jewish moneylenders charged high rates of interest, but no higher than Christian bankers facing equal risks.

The Jewish mind, sharpened by hardship, oppression, and study, developed in trade and finance an acquisitive subtlety never forgiven by their competitors. The ethics of the Jews, like those of the Puritans, placed no stigma upon wealth; the rabbis recognized it as the support of charity, the sinews of the synagogue, and the last resort to buy off persecuting kings or populace. Nevertheless it is true that in the Jewish communities of Holland, Germany, Poland and Turkey there were men who made the making of money not only their tribe's protection but their soul's delight, who used more craft than conscience in amassing it, who gave to their fellow men the corrosive spectacle of great wealth tarnished with conspicuous luxury, and only partly redeemed by substantial charities. Around them, in the ghetto, a third of their fellows lived in a poverty that only charity kept this side of starvation.[54]

The religion of the Jews, like their character, suffered from the poverty, introversion, and contumely of ghetto life. The rabbis, who in the Middle Ages had been men of courage and wisdom, became in this age devotees of a mysticism that fled from the hell of persecution and penury into a heaven of compensatory dreams. The Talmud in the Middle Ages had replaced the Bible as the soul of Judaism; now the Cabala replaced the

Talmud. A Frankfurt author of the seventeenth century alleged that in his day there were many rabbis who had never seen a Bible.[55] Solomon Luria (1510–72) marked the transition; he began with the Talmud, and based upon it his *Yam shel Shelomo* (*Sea of Solomon*), but even his subtle mind finally succumbed to the Cabala. This was the "Secret Tradition" of medieval Jewish mystics who believed that they had found a divine revelation concealed in the symbolism of numbers, letters, and words, above all in the letters composing Yahveh's ineffable name. Scholar after scholar in the ghetto lost himself in such fancies, until one of them declared that he who neglects the esoteric wisdom of the Cabal deserves excommunication.[56] In the sixteenth and seventeenth centuries, says the chief of modern Jewish historians, "the parasitic Kabbala choked the whole religious life of the Jews. Almost all rabbis and leaders of Jewish communities . . . were ensnared" by it, from Amsterdam to Poland to Palestine.[57]

To the Jews so dispersed, and so often destitute and maligned, the prop of life was the faith that someday soon the real Messiah would come to raise them out of misery and ignominy to power and glory. It is pitiful to see how, in century after century, some impostor or fanatic was accepted by the Jews as this long-awaited savior. We have seen elsewhere how, in 1524, David Reubeni of Arabia was hailed by Mediterranean Hebrews as the Messiah, though he himself made no such pretense. Now, in 1648, a Jew of Smyrna, Sabbatai Zevi, announced that he was the promised Redeemer.

Physically he seemed to be an admirable choice: tall, shapely, handsome, with the fine black hair and beard of a Sephardic youth.[58] Drawn to the Cabala by the writings of Solomon Luria, he subjected himself to an ascetic regimen in the hope that this would make him worthy of the Secret Tradition in its fullest revelation. He mortified his body, bathed frequently in the sea at all seasons, and kept himself so clean that his followers celebrated the fragrance of his flesh. He felt no attraction to women; he married early in obedience to Jewish custom, but his wife soon divorced him for his failure to perform his marital duties. He married again, with the same result. Young men gathered about him, admiring the melodious voice in which he sang Cabalistic songs, and wondering was he not a heaven-sent saint. His father was one of a group who believed that the Messiah was coming soon—not later than 1666. Sabbatai heard them predicting that the great redemption would be effected by a man of pure soul and profound piety, initiated in the Cabala, and capable of drawing together all good men into the millennium. The thought came to Sabbatai that he, purified by asceticism, was this divine Redeemer. The *Zohar*, the thirteenth-century text of Cabala, had specified the Jewish year 5408 (A.D. 1648) as inaugurating the era of redemption. In that year Sabbatai, aged twenty-two, proclaimed himself the Messiah.

A little band of disciples took him at his word. The rabbinate of Smyrna condemned them as blasphemers; they persisted, and were banished. Moving to Salonika, Sabbatai performed a Cabalistic ceremony marrying himself to the Torah; the rabbis of Salonika expelled him. He passed to Athens; then to Cairo, where he gained a rich adherent, Raphael Chelebi; then to Jerusalem, where his ascetic practices impressed even the rabbis. Impoverished by the cessation of alms from the stricken Jews of the Ukraine, the Jerusalem community sent Sabbatai to seek aid in Cairo. He returned to Jerusalem not only with funds but with a third wife, Sarah, whose beauty shed luster on his claims. At Gaza, on the way, he received another rich recruit, Nathan Ghazati, who announced that he himself was Elijah, reborn to make straight the way for the Messiah, and that within a year the Messiah would overthrow the Sultan and establish the Kingdom of Heaven. Believing him, thousands of Jews mortified their bodies to atone for their sins and be worthy of the earthly paradise. Back in Smyrna, Sabbatai in 1665 entered the synagogue on the Jewish New Year, and again declared himself the Messiah. Now he was accepted by a multitude delirious with joy. When an old rabbi denounced him as an impostor Sabbatai had him banished from Smyrna.

Throughout western Asia the news that the Messiah had come electrified the Jewish communities. Merchants from Egypt, Italy, Holland, Germany, and Poland brought the glad tidings back to their lands, and told of the miracles that in rising number were ascribed to Sabbatai. A few Jews were skeptical, but thousands, prepared by Cabalistic prophecies and ardent hopes, believed. Even some Christians shared in the exultation, saying that the Smyrna Messiah was really the reborn Christ. Henry Oldenburg, writing to Spinoza from London (December, 1665) reported: "All the world here is talking of a rumor of the return of the Israelites, dispersed for more than two thousand years, to their own country. Few believe it, but many wish it . . . . Should the news be confirmed, it may bring about a revolution in all things."[59] In Amsterdam prominent rabbis declared for Sabbatai; the coming of the Kingdom was celebrated in the synagogue with music and dance; prayer books were printed to teach believers the penances and chants preparatory to entering the Promised Land. In the Hamburg synagogue Jewish worshipers of all ages hopped, jumped, and danced with the scroll of the Law in their hands. In Poland many Jews abandoned their homes and property and refused to work, saying that the Messiah would soon come in person and lead them in triumph to Jerusalem.[60] Thousands of Jews—sometimes whole communities, like that of Avignon—made ready to move to Palestine. At Smyrna some enthusiasts, excited by the world-wide homage to their leader, proposed that Jewish prayers henceforth be addressed not to Yahveh, but to "the first-begotten Son of God, Sabbatai Zevi, Messiah and Redeemer" (so Christians prayed more often to Christ or the Virgin than to God). Word was sent out from Smyrna that the Jewish holydays of mourning were hereafter to be celebrated as feasts of joy, and that soon all the laborious prescriptions of the Law were to be abrogated in the security and happiness of the Kingdom.

Apparently Sabbatai had himself come to believe in his miraculous powers. He announced that he was going to Constantinople, presumably to fulfill the prophecy of Ghazati that the Messiah would peacefully take the crown of the Ottoman Empire (including Palestine) from the Sultan. (Some said, however, that the cadi, or Turkish magistrate, in Smyrna had ordered him to present himself before high officials in the capital.) Before leaving Smyrna, Sabbatai divided the world and its government among his most faithful aides. With a band of disciples in his train, he set out on January 1, 1666. He had predicted the day of his arrival, but a tempest delayed his vessel; his companions turned the miscalculation into an added proof of his divinity by telling how, with a divine word, he had stilled the storm.

When he landed on the shore of the Dardanelles he was arrested, was brought in fetters to Constantinople, and was put in prison. Two months later he was transferred to a milder confinement at Abydos. His wife was allowed to join him; his friends came from all quarters to comfort him, to do him homage, and to bring him funds. His followers did not lose faith in him; they pointed out that according to the best predictions the Messiah would be at first rejected by the secular authorities, who would subject him to sufferings and indignities. Throughout Europe the Jews expected that at any moment he would be released, and would realize happier prophecies. His initials, S and Z, were posted in synagogues. In Amsterdam, Leghorn, and Hamburg Jewish business came almost to a standstill, so warm was the belief that soon all Jews would be returned to the Holy Land. Jews who expressed doubt that Sabbatai was the Messiah were in daily peril of their lives.

Puzzled by the excitement that was disturbing the economic life of many Ottoman communities, and yet afraid that the execution of Sabbatai as a rebel and impostor would sanctify him as a martyr and turn his movement into a costly rebellion, the Turkish authorities decided to try a peaceful solution. Sabbatai was taken to Adrianople. There he was told that a decree condemned him to be dragged through the streets and scourged with burning torches; this, however, he could avoid, and he would acquire high honors in Islam, by accepting conversion to the Mohammedan faith. He agreed. On September 14, 1666, he appeared before the Sultan, and confirmed his apostasy by removing his Jewish garments and donning

Turkish dress. The Sultan gave him the name Mehmed Effendi, and appointed him his doorkeeper, with a handsome salary. Sarah, also converted, received rich gifts from the Sultana.

The news of this apostasy was greeted with incredulity by the Jews of Asia, Europe, and Africa; but when at last it was established it almost broke the heart of Jewry. The leading rabbi of Smyrna, who after much doubt had accepted Sabbatai, nearly died of shame. Jews became everywhere the butt of Moslem and Christian ridicule. Sabbatai's aides sought to comfort his followers by explaining that the conversion was part of his subtle plan to win Mohammedans to Judaism, and that soon he would reappear as a Jew, with all Islam in his train. Sabbatai obtained permission to preach to the Jews of Adrianople, assuring the Turkish authorities that he would convert his auditors to Islam; at the same time he issued secret messages to the Jews that he was still the Messiah, and that they must not lose faith in him. But neither at Adrianople nor elsewhere did the Jews give any sign of accepting Mohammed. Disappointed, the Ottoman government deported Sabbatai to Ulcinj in Albania, where no Jews dwelt. There in 1676 the broken Messiah died. For half a century believers continued his movement, affirming his sanctity, and promising his resurrection from the dead.

VI. HERETICS

Knowing that in Jewish communities encompassed by unrelenting enemies religion was the prop of life and the life of the Law, the rabbis discouraged secular studies that might open a cranny to religious doubt. Joel Sirkis, chief rabbi at Cracow, condemned philosophy as the mother of heresy, the fatal "harlot" of whom Solomon had said, "None that go unto her return again";[61] and he proposed to excommunicate any Jew within his jurisdiction who became addicted to philosophy. Joseph Solomon Delmedigo, coming to Poland (1620) from an Italy still warm with the Renaissance, was dismayed by the exclusion of science from the curriculum and reading of the Jews. "Behold," he wrote, "darkness covers the land, and the ignorant are numerous, . . . saying, The Lord takes no delight in the sharpened arrows of the grammarians, poets, and logicians, nor in the measurements of the mathematicians, and the calculations of the astronomers."[62]

Delmedigo was the great-grandson of the Elijah del Medigo who had taught Hebrew in the circles of the Medici. He began his deviations by learning Greek as well as the Talmud from his father, a rabbi in Crete; and he obtained some scientific education at the progressive University of Padua, where Galileo was his tutor. He took up the practice of medicine, which gave him a living and his Italian name; but science—mathematics above all—continued to lure him, and in its pursuit he shed some of his religious faith. Such molting leaves a sensitive skin, and may for a time unsettle character. Uprooted and restless, Joseph moved from city to city. Transiently he attached himself at Cairo and Constantinople to the Karaite sect, Jews who (like the Protestants) rejected ecclesiastical traditions and emendations and clung to the Bible as the sole source of their theology. In Hamburg and Amsterdam he found his medical knowledge so far behind that of the Jewish physicians there that for bread's sake he turned orthodox, joined the rabbinate, and finally defended the Cabala. He died as an obscure physician in Prague (1655).

Leo ben Isaac Modena was a subtler and profounder spirit. He took his Italian name from the town to which his family had migrated in the expulsion of the Jews from France. He was a child prodigy, reading the Prophets in his third year, preaching in his tenth, and writing his first published work at thirteen. It was a dialogue against gambling, on which Leo was an authority, for he remained its devotee to the end of his life. Greatest of his gambles was his marriage in 1590, aged nineteen. Of his three sons one died at twenty-six, one was killed in a brawl, one took to dissipation and disappeared in Brazil. One of his two daughters died during his lifetime; the other, having lost her husband, became dependent upon her father, whose wife became insane. Amid these buffets Leo was excommunicated for persistent gambling at cards. He wrote a dissertation proving that the rabbis had gone beyond the Law in their decree, which was soon revoked.

Meanwhile he had mastered Biblical, Talmudic, and rabbinical literature, had studied physics and philosophy, and had written in Hebrew and Italian some passable poetry. Admitted to the rabbinate in Venice, he delivered Italian addresses of such learning and eloquence that many Christians were drawn to his audience. One of his Christian friends, an English nobleman, engaged him to write an Italian exposition of Jewish ritual. In preparing this *Historia dei riti ebraici* (1637), Leo came to the conclusion that many of the traditional ceremonies, now divorced from their original purpose, had lost much of their significance. In an anonymous work, *Kol Sakal*, he proposed that Hebrew prayers and rites be revised and simplified, the dietary laws abrogated, and the holydays reduced in number and austerity. In this same book he criticized rabbinical Judaism as a mass of unwarranted complications added to the authentic Jewish Law; he urged a return from the Talmud to the Bible, but he extended his heresies to the Bible itself, even to the entire Mosaic revelation. He left this revolutionary pronunciamento unpublished; and when it was found among his papers after his death (1648), it was accompanied by a companion treatise defending orthodox Judaism. Neither saw print till 1852. Had Leo dared to publish *Kol Sakal* in his lifetime, Reform Judaism might have begun in the seventeenth century. He was too clever to anticipate history.

The most tragic of the Jewish heretics was Uriel Acosta of Amsterdam. His father came of a Marrano family that had settled in Oporto and had fully adjusted itself to the Catholic faith. Gabriel, as the youth was called in Portugal, was educated by the Jesuits, who terrified him with sermons on hell but sharpened his mind with Scholastic philosophy. Studying the Bible, he was impressed by the fact that the Church recognized the Old Testament as the Word of God, and that Christ and the twelve Apostles had accepted the Mosaic Law. He concluded that Judaism was divine; he questioned the right of St. Paul to divorce Christianity from Judaism; and he resolved at the first opportunity to return to the faith of his ancestors. He persuaded his mother and his brothers (his father was now dead) to join in an attempt to elude the Inquisition and escape from Portugal. After many perils they reached Amsterdam (c. 1617). There Gabriel changed his name to Uriel, and the family became members of the Portuguese congregation.

But the same spirit of inquiry and independent thought that had led him to leave the Church made him uncomfortable within the equally rigorous dogmas of the synagogue. He was shocked by the addiction of even the learned rabbis of Amsterdam to the intellectual puerilities of the Cabala. He boldly reproved his new associates for rites and regulations that had no apparent basis in the Bible, and that sometimes, in his judgment, ran quite counter to Biblical ways. As he had little sense of history, he thought it a great mistake that Jewish ritual and belief had altered in the course of nineteen hundred years. As formerly he had returned from the New Testament to the Old, so now he urged a return from the Talmud to the Bible. In 1616 he had published at Hamburg a Portuguese tract, *Propostas contra a tradição* —arguments against the traditions upon which the Talmud was based. He sent a copy to the Jewish congregation in Venice; it proclaimed a ban against him (1618); and Leo Modena, himself a heretic, was required, by his position in the rabbinate, to refute Acosta's claim that the ordinances of the rabbis had in many cases no warrant in Scripture. The Amsterdam rabbis, whom he called Pharisees, warned Acosta that they too would ban him unless he retracted. He refused, and openly ignored the regulations of the synagogue. Excommunication was pronounced against him (1623), excluding him from all relations with his fellow Jews. Even his relatives now shunned him; and as he had not yet learned Dutch, he found himself without a single friend. Children stoned him in the streets.

In the bitterness of his isolation he proceeded (like Spinoza a generation later), to a heresy that attacked a fundamental belief of nearly every person in Europe. He let it be known that he rejected, as quite alien to the Old Testament, the immortality of the soul; the soul, he said, is merely the vital spirit flowing in the blood, and dies with the body.[63] Seeking to answer Acosta's contentions, a Jewish physician, Samuel da Silva, published a Portuguese *Treatise on the Immortality of the Soul* (1623), in which he called Acosta ignorant, incompetent, and blind. Uriel countered with *An Examination of the Pharisaic Traditions . . . and a Reply to Samuel da Silva, the False Calumniator* (1624). The leaders of the Jewish community, to protect its religious freedom, notified the Amsterdam magistracy that Acosta, in denying immortality, was undermining Christianity as well as Judaism. The magistrates arrested him, fined him three hundred gulden, and burned his book. He was soon released, and apparently suffered no physical harm.

His punishment was economic and social. His younger brothers became dependent upon him, and therefore upon his freedom—now forbidden—to engage in economic relations with his fellows. Perhaps for this reason, and because he wished to marry again, Uriel decided to submit to the synagogue, to recant his heresies, and, as he put it, "to become an ape among apes."[64] His recantation was accepted (1633), and for a time the passionate skeptic lived in relative peace. But secretly his heresies continued, and broadened. "I doubted," he later wrote, "whether Moses' Law was in reality God's law, and decided that it was of human origin."[65] Now he cast aside all religion except a vague belief in a God identical with nature (as in Spinoza). He neglected the burdensome religious usages required of an orthodox Jew. When two Christians came to him and professed a desire to adopt Judaism, he dissuaded them, warning them that they were laying a heavy yoke upon their necks. They reported this to the synagogue. The rabbis summoned and questioned him; they found him unrepentant, and now they pronounced against him a second and severer excommunication (1639). Again his relatives excluded him from their lives, and his brother Joseph joined in persecuting him.[66]

He bore this isolation for seven years, and then, finding himself grievously hampered in business and law, he offered to submit. Angered by his long and troublesome resistance, the Jewish leaders condemned him to a form of recantation and penance imitated from the Portuguese Inquisition.[67] As in an auto-da-fé, he was made to mount a platform in the synagogue, to read before a full congregation a confession of his errors and sins, and to solemnly promise that henceforth he would obey all regulations of the community, and live as a true Jew. Then he was stripped to the waist and was scourged with thirty-nine stripes. Finally he was made to lie across the threshold of the synagogue, and those present, including his hostile brother, stepped over him as they left.

He rose from this humiliation not reconciled but furious. Going home, he shut himself up in his study for several days and nights, and wrote his last and bitterest denunciation of the Judaism which he had sacrificed much to adopt, but whose introverted history, and protective rigorism under centuries of oppression, he had never sympathetically understood. In this sarcastic *Exemplar humanae Vitae* he told his intellectual autobiography as an example of what happens to the man who thinks. "All evils," he felt, "come from not following Right Reason and the Law of Nature."[68] He contrasted "natural" with revealed religion, and claimed that the latter taught men hatred as the former taught men love. Having finished his manuscript, he loaded two pistols, waited at his window till he saw his brother Joseph pass, fired at him, and missed.[69] Then he shot himself (1647?).

The Jewish community tried to bury this tragedy in silence, but some members must have found it hard to forget. Spinoza was a lad of fifteen when that excommunication rite was performed; he may have been in the congregation that saw it performed; he may have walked in awe and horror over the prostrate heretic. Through that youth the vision of Acosta, cleansed of its anger, entered into the heritage of philosophy.[70]

BOOK IV

THE INTELLECTUAL ADVENTURE

1648–1715

CHAPTER XVII

From Superstition to Scholarship

1648–1715

I. IMPEDIMENTS

NATURE, as conceived by all but a small minority of Europeans in the seventeenth century, was the product or battleground of supernatural beings benevolent or malevolent, inhabiting human bodies as souls, or dwelling in trees, woods, rivers, and winds as animating spirits, or entering organisms as angels or demons, or roaming the air as michievous elves. None of these spirits was subject to inviolable or calculable law; any of them could intervene miraculously in the operations of stones or stars, animals or men; and events not visibly due to the natural or regular behavior of bodies or minds were attributed to such supernatural powers taking a mysterious part, portentous or prophetic, in the affairs of the world. All natural objects, all planets and their denizens, all constellations and galaxies, were helpless islands in a supernatural sea.

We have seen some forms of superstition in earlier ages. Most of them survived the coming of modern science in Copernicus, Vesalius, and Galileo; some flourished in Newton himself. Astrology and alchemy continued their decline, but astrologers were numerous at the court of Louis XIV;[1] and at Vienna, reported Lady Mary Wortley Montagu in 1717, "there was a prodigious number of alchemists."[2] Sturdy Britons still believed in ghosts, watched for omens, paid for horoscopes, took their dreams as prophecies, calculated lucky and unlucky days; and less sturdy Britons begged their king to cure their scrofula with his touch. The seventh number of *The Spectator* described the upheaval caused in a British family by the spilling of a little salt, or by laying a knife and a fork across each other on a plate, or by allowing thirteen persons in a room or company. (Note the absence of a thirteenth floor in some twentieth-century hotels.) In France Jacques Aymer was the hero of his time (1692) because by the twitching of a hazel twig held in his hand he could (many believed) detect the nearness of a criminal.[3] In Germany a magic wand was used to end hemorrhages, heal wounds, and reset bones.[4] In Sweden Stiernhielm was accused of witchcraft when he burned a peasant's beard with a magnifying glass; the experimenter was saved from death only by the interposition of Queen Christina.[5]

Skeptics of witchcraft were multiplying, but were probably far outnumbered by believers. The courtiers of Charles II took little stock in any goblins that might spoil their sport, but the "immense majority," and the most prominent authors among the English clergy, still held that human beings might league themselves with the Devil and thereby acquire supernatural powers.[6] Joseph Glanvill, an Anglican clergyman of brilliant mind and forceful style, in *Philosophical Considerations touching Witches and Witchcraft* (1666), counted it a shocking wonder that "men otherwise witty [intelligent] and ingenious are fallen into the conceit that there is no such thing as a witch or apparition"; doubts of this kind, he warned, would lead to atheism. Another famous divine, Ralph Cudworth, in his *True Intellectual System of the Universe* (1678), denounced as atheists all who denied the reality of witches.[7] The Cambridge Platonist Henry More, in his *Antidote to Atheism* (1668?), warmly defended the story of a "witch" who had been married to Satan for thirty years; and he thought it sheer blasphemy to question the ability of witches to raise storms by incantation, or ride the air on a broom.[8]

The persecution of witches tapered off. The Scottish clergy, however, distinguished themselves by their burning zeal. At Leith, in 1652, a variety of tortures induced six women to confess witchcraft; they were hung up by the thumbs and were flogged; lighted candles were placed under their feet and in their forcibly opened mouths; four of the six died of their torments.[9] In 1661 there were fourteen courts trying witches in Scotland; in 1664 nine women were burned together in Leith. Such executions continued sporadically in Scotland till 1722. In England two witches were hanged at Bury St. Edmunds in 1664; three were put to death in 1682, and an uncertain number in 1712. The arguments of Weir and Spee, of Hobbes and Spinoza and others, gradually undermined the witchcraft delusion in the educated laity. Lawyers and magistrates increasingly withstood the theologians, and refused to prosecute or convict. In 1712 a jury of simple Englishmen adjudged Jane Wenham guilty of witchcraft; the judge refused to sentence her; the local clergy denounced him;[10] but there were no executions for witchcraft in England after that year. In France Colbert secured from Louis XIV an edict (1672) forbidding condemnations for witchcraft.[11] The Parlement of Rouen protested that this prohibition violated the Biblical injunction "Thou shalt not suffer a witch to live" (Exodus XXII, 18), and some local authorities managed to burn seven "sorcerers" in France between 1680 and 1700; but we hear of no executions after 1718. The belief in witchcraft continued until the temporary triumph of rationalism in the eighteenth-century Enlightenment: here and there it still exists.

Censorship and intolerance co-operated with superstition to check the growth and spread of knowledge. In France the conflicts between kings and popes, between the Gallican Church and the papacy, between Jansenists and Jesuits, between Catholics and Huguenots, prevented that unity, consistency, and thoroughness of censorship which in this age isolated Spain from the movements of the European mind. Heretical authors found ways of evading the censors, and perhaps French wit was stimulated by the necessity of expressing ideas too subtly for officials to comprehend. In Catholic Cologne the Archbishop Elector censored all speech or publications on religion. In Protestant Brandenburg the Great Elector, to quiet religious strife, ordered a thorough censorship. In England, despite the Act of Toleration (1689), the government continued to imprison obnoxious authors and burn heretical books.[12] Nevertheless, the diversity of sects in Protestant lands made censorship less effective there than in Catholic countries; partly for this reason England and Holland, in the seventeenth century, excelled in science and philosophy.

The competing faiths agreed on intolerance. The Catholic Church argued quite cogently that since nearly all Christians accepted the Bible as the word of God, and as, according to the Bible, the Son of God had founded the Church, it was clearly her right and duty to suppress heresy. Protestant denominations came to a similar but less sanguinary conclusion: since the Bible was God's word, anyone deviating from its teachings (as officially interpreted) should at least be suppressed, and be thankful that he was not killed. The Treaty of Westphalia (1648) recognized three religions as legal in Germany: Catholicism, Lutheranism, and Calvinism; each ruler was left free to choose any one of these, and to enforce it upon his subjects. The Scandinavian countries allowed no religious faith but the Lutheran. Switzerland permitted each canton to determine its own creed. France led the way to toleration by the Edict of Nantes (1598), and led the way back by the Revocation (1685). England, after 1689, eased the disabilities of Dissenters, continued those of Catholics, and exterminated a third of all Catholics in Ireland. The rationalist Hobbes agreed with the popes on the necessity of intolerance.

However, toleration grew. The critical study of the Bible began in this age to free men to admire it as literature while suspecting it as science, and the multiplication of sects made social order increasingly difficult without mutual toleration. In New England Roger Williams announced (1644) that it was "the will and command of God" that "permission of the most paganish, Jewish, Turkish, or Antichristian consciences and worships be granted to all men in all nations."[13] John Milton pleaded for "unlicensed printing" (1644), and Jeremy Taylor defended "liberty of prophesying" (1646). James Harrington (1656) allowed no limits to religious freedom: "Where civil liberty is entire, it includes liberty of conscience; where liberty of conscience is entire . . . , a man, according to the dictates of his own conscience, may have the full exercise of his religion, without impediment to his preferment or employment in the state."[14] In commercial countries like Holland, and even in Catholic Venice, the necessities of trade compelled tolerance of the diverse religions of merchants from alien lands. It was in liberal Holland that Spinoza published in his *Tractatus theologico-politicus* (1670) a plea for the full toleration of heretical ideas; in Holland Bayle defended toleration in his *Philosophical Commentary on the Text, Compel them to come in* (1686); and it was after years of residence in Holland that Locke issued his *Letters on Toleration* (1689). Decade after decade the demand for intellectual freedom rose, and by the end of the seventeenth century no church would have dared to do what had been done to Bruno in 1600, or to Galileo in 1633. *Eppur si muove.*

II. EDUCATION

Knowledge was slowly spreading, through newspapers, journals, pamphlets, books, libraries, schools, academies, universities. News, in the seventeenth century, became a commodity bought and sold, first to bankers, then to statesmen, then to anyone. In 1711 the total circulation of British newspapers, daily or weekly, was 44,000.[15]

The Journal des savants, founded in 1665, recognized that events in the world of literature and scholarship could also be news; soon it established itself as an international medium of scholars, scientists, and literary men. Within a few years it had competitors: the *Giornale de' letterati* of Rome (1668), the *Giornale Veneto* of Venice (1671), and the *Acta Eruditorum* of Leipzig (1682). Bayle founded a famous review at Rotterdam in 1684, *Nouvelles de la République des Lettres;* and two years later Jean Le Clerc began the monthly *Bibliothèque universelle;* some of the most important pronouncements of Locke and Leibniz were made in these periodicals.

The circulation of books was growing rapidly. In 1701 there were 178 master booksellers in Paris, thirty-six of them printers and publishers.[16] Libraries old and new were making their treasures more widely available. In 1610 Sir Thomas Bodley obtained from the Stationers' Company a grant whereby the Bodleian Library that he had established at Oxford (1598) was to receive a copy of every book published in England; so in 1930 it had 1,250,000 volumes. In 1617 a decree of Louis XIII ordered that two copies of every new publication in France be deposited in the Bibliothèque Royale (now Nationale) at Paris. In 1622 this collection had 6,000 volumes; in 1715, largely through the zeal of Colbert, 70,000; in 1926, 4,400,000. The Great Elector of Brandenburg founded a national library at Berlin in 1661. In that year Mazarin bequeathed his costly library of 40,000 volumes to

Louis XIV and France, and in 1700 the descendants of Sir Robert Bruce Cotton deeded the Cottonian Library to the British Museum. The first English library open to the general public was opened by Thomas Tenison in London in 1695.

Education was laboring to redeem the losses it had sustained from the Religious Wars in France, the Civil War in England, and the Thirty Years' War in Germany. Not till Lessing (1729–81) did German schools and literature regain the stature they had reached with Luther, Ulrich von Hutten, and Melanchthon two centuries before. In the interval a mediocre Latin remained the esoteric language of the literary few, while German, so lusty in Luther, became a merely plebeian instrument; and not a single writer of German rose to international repute during the long penance for a generation of fratricidal war. The German nobility, disdaining the Latin pedantry of the universities, sent their sons to *Ritterakademien*—knight schools—or engaged private tutors to prepare pedigreed youth for the tasks and graces of princely courts. At the other end of the social scale August Francke, the Pietist, organized at Halle his *Stiftungen*, charitable institutions ridiculed by cynics as "ragged schools," where, through thirty-two years (1695–1727), he fed, clothed, and taught the children of the poor. Soon he added a *Hauptschule* for the secondary education of his brightest boys, and a *höhere Töchterschule* for his brightest girls. All these schools gave half their time to religion.

The secular spirit in Germany found voice in Christian Thomasius. We shall commemorate him later as a philosopher; here we see him as the greatest German educator of his time. Driven from his native Leipzig because of his heresies, he moved to Halle, in the rising state of Brandenburg-Prussia (1690); his lectures there led to the founding of the university; he became its most famous professor, and the protagonist in making it the first "modern" university. He laughed Scholasticism out of face, replaced Latin with German as the language of instruction, published a German magazine, introduced science courses into the curriculum, and fought for the freedom of teachers and students to think. Frederick the Great called him the father of the *Aufklärung*, the German Enlightenment.

Elementary education was made universal and compulsory for both sexes in the duchy of Württemberg in 1565, in the Dutch Republic in 1618, in the duchy of Weimar in 1619, in Scotland in 1696, in France in 1698, in England in 1876. The delay in England was due to the wide extension of voluntary education through private religious agencies, and to the feeling in the ruling classes that in the prevailing economic system the education of the poor was unnecessary and probably undesirable. The Society for Promoting Christian Knowledge began in 1699 to establish "charity schools" for poor children, chiefly to transmit Christian theology and discipline; all teachers were to be members of the Church of England, and required a license from the bishop. Bernard Mandeville, who made a stir in 1714 with his *Fable of the Bees*, denounced these schools as a waste of money; if parents were too poor to pay for the education of their children, he said, "it is impudence in them to aspire any further."[17]

In France every parish had to maintain an elementary school. The teacher was usually a layman, but he was chosen and controlled by the bishop, and instruction was firmly Catholic. The *petites écoles* of Port-Royal reached only a few selected boys. In 1684 Jean Baptiste de La Salle founded the Frères des Écoles Chrétiennes, soon to be known as the Frères Chrétiens. La Salle, an ascetic priest, made religion the pervading essence of the education which these "Christian Brothers" offered gratis to the children of the poor. Four hours a day were devoted to religious exercises; reading, writing, and arithmetic were added; but the never forgotten aim was to train loyal Catholics, and to save souls from worldly riot and everlasting hell. Flogging was found useful for these purposes. Teachers were exhorted to teach by example rather than precept. In 1685 the Christian Brothers opened what was probably the first modern institution for the training of elementary-school teachers.

Secondary education in France remained in the hands of the Jesuits, and was still the best in Christendom. Their Collegium Societatis Jesu, directly behind the Sorbonne, changed its name to Collegium Ludovici Magni, or Collège Louis-le-Grand, after the King attended a play produced there by the pupils in 1674. At the urging of Mme. de Maintenon Louis XIV in 1686 opened at St.-Cyr (three miles from Versailles) the first French boarding school for girls. Nunneries provided higher education for elite paying girls, always with the emphasis on religion. Catholic and Protestant authorities agreed in the conviction that human nature was so ill adjusted to civilized restraints that it could be molded to morality and order only through the fear of God. The attempt to educate character without the aid of religion is still in the experimental stage.

Except in the Dutch Republic, universities were now in decline, purged by victorious sects, disordered by riotous students, and dominated by barren theological disputes. In France and Germany university degrees were sold for cash. None of the great philosophers of the period, and few of the leading scientists, were on university staffs, and Hobbes, Leibniz, and Bayle all spoke of the professors with a contempt that made no allowance for public pressures upon public employees. Some new universities were opened in this period: Duisberg (1655), Durham (1657), Kiel (1665), Lund (1666), Innsbruck (1673), Halle (1694), and Breslau (1702). These were mostly small establishments, seldom having more than twenty professors or four hundred pupils. In nearly all of them the curriculum had stiffened with age, and the requirements of orthodoxy cramped students and teachers alike. Milton complained that the English universities took "from young men the use of their reason by certain charms compounded of metaphysics, miracles, traditions, and absurd scriptures"; he felt that he had misspent his years at Cambridge trying to digest "an asinine feast of sour thistles and bramble," and other "sophistical trash."[18] This bondage of tradition continued in Oxford and Cambridge until the example of the Royal Society, and the professorate of Newton at Trinity College (1669–1702), stirred Cambridge to give a daring prominence to science.

Poets, priests, journalists, and philosophers struggled to reinvigorate education. We have summarized Milton's "Letter to Mr. Hartlib" (1644) on the ideal school; his prescriptions had no influence upon actual teaching. In France the most attractive contribution was Fénelon's little *Traité de l'éducation des filles* (1687). Mme. de Beauvilliers had asked him to outline some principles to guide the instruction of her daughters. The priest naturally stressed the religious reinforcement of the moral code, but he deprecated the austerities and seclusion of conventual schooling; nunneries, he felt, "provided no preparation for life in the world, into which the convent graduate entered as one emerging into full daylight from a cave."[19] He pleaded for gentle methods in teaching; education should suit itself to the nature, interests, and sensitivity of the child, rather than bend all pupils to one inflexible rule. Let us teach the way nature teaches—not by abstractions but by leading children into the middle of things; let their games and their natural interests be used as means of instruction. (Here were Rousseau's pedagogy, and the "progressive education" of the twentieth century, expounded by a priest of the seventeenth.) Fénelon wished girls to read the classics, if possible in the original languages; they ought to learn some history, and enough law to govern an estate; but they should not meddle with science—a young woman should show a certain "modesty about science" (*une pudeur sur la science*). The handsome priest was sensitive to feminine charms, and did not want them clothed in algebra; he would never have understood Voltaire's love for that professor of Newtonian mechanics, Mme. du Châtelet.

Ten years after Fénelon's *Traité*, Defoe published his appeal for the higher education of women. Except in rich homes, English girls of the seventeenth century found little opportunity for secondary education. Like Esther Johnson with Jonathan Swift, they had to rely on tutors, or, like Evelyn's favorite daughter, they had to purloin knowledge by private enterprise. Macaulay judged that "even in the highest ranks the English women of that generation [1685–1715] were decidedly worse educated than they have been at any other time since the Revival of Learning."[20] Swift estimated that hardly one gentlewoman in a thousand was taught to read or spell;[21] but that gloomy Dean throve on exaggerations. In any case Defoe thought the neglect of feminine education a barbarous inequity. "I cannot think that God Almighty ever made women so delicate, so glorious creatures, and furnished them with such charms . . . to be only stewards of our houses, cooks, and slaves." So he proposed for girls an academy similar to the "public" schools of England. There they should learn not merely music and dancing, but "languages, as particularly French and Italian; and I venture the injury of giving a woman more tongues than one." They should study history, and acquire all the graces and courtesies of speech. The gallant novelist concluded that "a woman well bred and well taught, furnished with the additional accomplishments of knowledge and behavior, is a creature without comparison, . . . the finest and most delicate part of God's creation"; and that "the man that has such a one to his portion has nothing to do but rejoice in her and be thankful."[22]

By far the best considered and most influential contribution to pedagogical theory in this age of Louis XIV was John Locke's *Some Thoughts concerning Education* (1693),[23] written after the author had served several years as tutor in the family of the first Earl of Shaftesbury. Taking cues from Montaigne, the philosopher proposed that the teacher should first aim at physical health and stamina; a sound body is prerequisite to a sound mind. So his pupils are to eat a simple diet, accustom themselves to scanty clothing, hard beds, cold weather, fresh air, plenty of exercise, regular sleep, no wine or liquor, and "very little or no physick" (medicine). Second in time but first in importance is the formation of character; all education, physical and mental as well as moral, should be a discipline in virtue. And as the body is to be trained to health by hardships, so character is to be molded by inculcating self-denial in all things that run counter to mature reason. "Children should be used to submit their desires, and go without their longings, even from their very cradles"; the discipline of desire is the backbone of character. This discipline is to be made as pleasant as possible, but it is to be insisted upon throughout. Nor will single good actions suffice; the pupil must be formed by the repetition of virtuous actions into good *habits*; for "habits work more constantly and with greater facility than reason, which, when we have most need of it, is seldom fairly consulted, and more rarely obeyed." Locke oscillates between Aristotle and Rousseau. He prefers a libertarian education to one that ignores the bent and individuality of the child; lessons should be made interesting, and discipline humane; but he accepts the occasional desirability of physical punishments for conscious misbehavior. Moreover, "inuring children gently to suffer some degrees of pain without shrinking is a way to gain firmness for their minds, and lay a foundation for courage and resolution in the future part of their lives."

The education of the intellect should be a discipline in methods of thought and rigor of reasoning, not a digest of classics or a bandying of languages. French and Latin should be taught to the children at an early age, and by conversation rather than by grammar. Greek, Hebrew, and Arabic should be left to professional scholars. It would be better to give time to geography, mathematics, astronomy, and anatomy; later to ethics and law; finally to philosophy. "The business of education is not to make the young perfect in any one of the sciences, but so to open and dispose their minds as may best make them capable of any, when they shall apply themselves to it." And as virtue is to be trained by habit, so thought is to be trained by repeated reasonings:

> Nothing does this better than mathematics, which therefore, I think, should be taught to all those who have the time and opportunity, not so much to make them mathematicians as to make them reasonable creatures. . . . We are born to be, if we please, reasonable creatures, but it is use and exercise that makes us so, and we are indeed so no further than industry and application has carried us. . . . I have mentioned mathematics as a way to settle in the mind a habit of reasoning closely and in train . . . ; that, having got the way of reasoning which that study naturally brings the mind to, they might be able to transfer it to other parts of knowledge as they shall have occasion.[24]

Locke's treatise was designed for a "liberal education"—i.e., one chiefly in arts, literature, and manners; it was intended to produce a gentleman— i.e., a man of "gentle" birth, who would never have to work for a living.* Its curriculum, while admitting some sciences, generally adhered to the "humanities"—the studies favored by the Renaissance humanists. It included also dancing, riding, wrestling, fencing, and even "a manual trade, nay two or three," but as helps to health and character, not as means of livelihood. The arts were to be taught as recreations, not as professions; the young gentleman was not to take such affairs very seriously; he should enjoy poetry, but not write it except as a pastime; he should be taught to enjoy music, but not to seek proficiency on any instrument; this would take too much time, and, besides, it would put the youth into "such odd company." So Locke's treatise was both conservative and liberal. In its repudiation of Scholastic absorption in ancient languages, its lessened stress on religion and theology, its emphasis on health and character, and its effort to prepare well-born youth for public life and service, it pointed to the future, and had immense influence in England and America. It shared in forming the physical and moral side of education in the English "public"

---

* *Gentlemen* goes back to the Latin *gens,* a clan or family line of freemen. A "liberal" education was originally one intended for freemen (*liberi*).

schools. Translated into French (1695), it went through five editions in fifty years, and gave many suggestions to Rousseau. Locke's own pupil, the third Earl of Shaftesbury, whom we shall meet again, did credit to his teacher's theories and character.

III. THE SCHOLARS

Despite their apparent preoccupation with dying languages and dead debates, great scholars continued to mold the future by illuminating the past; and some found themselves embattled in the struggle of Christianity against free thought.

Certain minor devotees merit a passing reverence. Charles du Fresne, Sieur du Cange, astonished his contemporaries—who knew him as a lawyer in the Paris Parlement—by issuing (1678) a dictionary of late and medieval Latin in three volumes so meticulous in scholarship that they are still the authority in their field. Pierre Huet discovered and edited a major manuscript of Origen, learned Syriac, Arabic, and chemistry, made eight hundred anatomical dissections, wrote poetry and fiction, and shared with the learned Mme. Dacier in editing for the instruction of the Dauphin the famous sixty-volume "Delphin" edition of Latin classics; he was made bishop of Avranches, and, dying, left the library that is now a treasured part of the Bibliothèque Nationale. The Jesuit "Bollandists" continued their centipedalian *Acta Sanctorum*. In Paris, under the lead of Jean Mabillon, the Benedictine Congregation of St.-Maur compiled (1668–1702) a twenty-volume history of Benedictine saints; in the process they shed precious light upon the annals and literature of medieval France. Mabillon himself gave a new form to Latin paleography by his *De Re diplomatica* (1681)— not a manual of diplomacy but a treatise on the date, character, and authenticity of old charters and manuscripts. Completing one of his fat folios, Mabillon wrote: "May it please God not to impute it to me as a crime that I have passed so many years studying the acts of the saints, and yet resemble them so little."[25]

The giant of classical erudition in this age was Richard Bentley, stern master of Trinity College, Cambridge, for forty-two years. His youth was consumed in consuming the Bodleian Library; at twenty-nine he was already among the most learned pundits of Europe in Greek, Latin, and Hebrew literature and antiquities. In that year (1691) he published a hundred-page *Epistola ad Millium*, a letter to an early John Mill, so accurate and recondite in its scholarship that it gave him a European fame. At thirty he was chosen to give the first series of the lectures for which funds and a name had been provided in the will of the pious chemist Robert Boyle.

He responded by arguing powerfully that the cosmic order revealed in Newton's recent *Principia* proved the existence of God. This was a great comfort to Newton, who had been accused of atheism. Bentley was appointed to the post of royal librarian, with an apartment in St. James's Palace. There he met frequently Newton, Locke, Evelyn, and Wren; and from that citadel he fought one of the famous battles in British scholarship.

The contest arose from the English share in the debate on the relative merits of ancient versus modern literature. Sir William Temple opened fire with the essay *Of Ancient and Modern Learning* (1690), defending antiquity. Bentley would probably have praised the essay had it not praised Phalaris as an example of Greek superiority in literature. Phalaris was a dictator who governed Akragas (Agrigento) in Greek Sicily in the sixth century before Christ. History or legend described him as roasting his enemies in the belly of a brazen bull; but it honored him as a patron of literature, and 148 letters had come down the centuries allegedly from his pen. Charles Boyle, an undergraduate at Christ Church College, Oxford, published the letters in 1695. William Wotton, preparing a second edition (1697) of his *Reflections upon Ancient and Modern Learning*, in which he opposed Temple, asked Bentley to judge the authenticity of the letters. Bentley replied that their attribution to Phalaris was a mistake, that they were written in the second century A.D.; incidentally he pointed out some errors in Charles Boyle's edition. Boyle and his teachers issued a hot defense of Phalaris' authorship. Jonathan Swift, secretary to Temple, entered the fracas on his master's side by ridiculing Bentley in *The Battle of the Books*. The general opinion of scholars supported Boyle, and Bentley's friends bemoaned the apparent collapse of his reputation. His answer to them deserves remembrance: "No man was ever written out of reputation but by himself."[26] In 1699 he issued an enlarged *Dissertation on the Epistles of Phalaris*. Not only did it prove his case, but it shed so much light on the evolution of the Greek language that the world of scholarship acclaimed him as worthy to join the line of the Scaligers, Casaubon and Salmasius. Even the style of the letters betrayed their century, said Bentley, and he added:

> Every living language, like the perspiring bodies of living creatures, is in perpetual motion and alteration; some words go off and become obsolete; others are taken in and by degrees grow into common use; or the same word is inverted to a new sense and notion, which in tract of time makes as observable a change in the air and features of a language as age makes in the lines and mien of a face. All are sensible of this in their own native tongues, where continual use makes every man a critic. For what Englishman does not think himself able, from the very turn and fashion of the style, to distinguish a fresh English composi-

tion from another a hundred years old? Now, there are as real and sensible differences in the several ages of Greek. . . , but very few are so versed and practised in that language as ever to arrive at that subtlety of taste.[27]

Here was a scholar who could write English as well as read Greek.

In 1699 the unanimous vote of the six bishops appointed by William III to nominate for the vacancy raised Bentley to the mastership of Trinity College, Cambridge. He reformed student discipline, improved the curriculum, and built an "elaboratory" for chemistry and an observatory for astronomy; but he so alienated the faculty by his pomp and overbearing ways, and his affection for money, that he was twice sentenced to removal from his office; he fought back, and kept his post to the end. Meanwhile he edited a large number of Greek and Latin classics, encouraged and financed the second edition of Newton's *Principia*, demolished Anthony Collins in *Remarks on a Late Discourse of Freethinking* (1713), and ventured rashly from his field by editing *Paradise Lost* with pedantic corrections of Milton's grammar and text. He made an enemy of Alexander Pope by saying of his translation of the *Iliad*, "A pretty poem, Mr. Pope, but you must not call it Homer." "The portentous cub," Bentley reported, never forgave him. In *The Dunciad* (April, 1742) Pope ridiculed him as

> The mighty scholiast, whose unwearied pains
> Made Horace dull, and humbled Milton's strains.[28]

In July Bentley died from a complication of Pope and pleurisy. He was the greatest and most insufferable scholar that England ever produced.

Meanwhile another Englishman, Thomas Stanley, broadened the British mind with the first English *History of Philosophy* (1655–62), and surprised his readers by devoting the last of its four volumes to "Chaldaic [Arabic] Philosophy." Scholarship was venturing beyond ancient Rome and Greece to the Near and Middle East, with disturbing results. Edward Pococke discovered and edited four Syrian versions of the New Testament Epistles (1630); for him Oxford established its first chair of Arabic, and his lectures there opened English eyes to Islamic civilization. In France Barthélemy d'Herbelot's lifework, an immense *Bibliothèque orientale* (1697)—subtitled *Universal Dictionary Containing Generally All That Concerns a Knowledge of . . . the Orient*—was a revelation of Arabic history and learning, and played a part in that broadening of intellectual horizons which burst all bonds in the eighteenth-century Enlightenment. Students wondered at the wealth of Arabic poetry, historiography, philosophy, and science; they noted how the Arabs had preserved Greek science and philosophy while these were being forgotten in the Dark Ages of

Western Europe; they learned that Mohammed was no mere imposter but a subtle statesman; and they were puzzled to find no more crime, and no less virtue, in Islam than in Christendom. The relativity of morals and theology became a dissolving ferment in the Christian mind.

Studies of Oriental—including Egyptian and Chinese—chronology undermined the Jewish calculation that the world had been created in 3761 B.C., and the computation (1650) of James Ussher, Anglican Archbishop of Armagh in Ireland, that the Creation had occurred "at the beginning of the night before Monday, the 23rd of October, 4004 B.C."[29] Spinoza, as we shall presently see, was inaugurating (1670) the "higher criticism" of the Bible—the study of it as a human production rich in grandeur and nobility, in errors and absurdities.

The most learned Biblical critic of the seventeenth century, in an attempt to answer Spinoza, brought down upon his head the thunder of Bossuet for finally conceding much of what the philosopher had claimed. Richard Simon, a blacksmith's son, had joined the Oratory at Paris, and had been ordained a priest (1670). In that year he wrote a pamphlet defending the Jews of Metz, who had been accused of murdering a Christian child. In 1678, after years of research including studies with several rabbis, he prepared to publish his *Histoire critique du Vieux Testament*. He proposed *en passant* to refute Spinoza's arguments against the divine inspiration of the Scriptures. He admitted that the books of the Old Testament were not entirely the work of the authors to whom they were ascribed; that Moses could not have written all the Pentateuch (which described Moses' death); and that the Biblical books had been considerably altered from their first form by the scribes and editors who had transmitted them. Simon struggled to keep his orthodoxy and imprimatur by holding that these revisers too had been divinely inspired; but he confessed that all existing copies of the Old Testament were so mangled with repetitions, contradictions, obscurities, and other difficulties that they could offer only a frail basis for a dogmatic theology. He thought to turn this point against the Protestants by contending that their belief in the verbal inspiration of the Scriptures left them helpless against textual criticism, while a loyal Catholic could survive such scholarship by accepting the interpretation put upon the text by the Roman Church. In any case, Simon concluded, the divine inspiration of the Bible applied only to matters of faith.

The general of the Oratory sanctioned the publication of Simon's book. But while it was in the press some of the proof sheets came under the eye of the "Great" Arnauld of Port-Royal. He was alarmed. He showed the sheets to Bossuet, who at once denounced the volume as "a tissue of impieties and a bulwark of free thought," which would "destroy the authority of canonical scripture."[30] Bossuet appealed to the secular authorities to prevent publication of the book. They confiscated the entire issue of thirteen hundred copies, and reduced them to pulp. Simon retired to an obscure curacy in Normandy, but he found ways of having his manuscript printed in Rotterdam (1685). Four years later he published his *Histoire critique du Nouveau Testament*. He proposed to complete his labors with a new translation of the Bible; he finished his version of the New Testament; but Bossuet, shocked by the freedom with which Simon handled the sacred text, persuaded the Chancellor to suppress the book (1703). Simon abandoned his enterprise, burned his papers, and died (1712).

His work on the Old Testament elicited forty refutations, indicating its irrefutability. With Spinoza's *Tractatus theologico-politicus* it remains one of the landmarks in the modern study of the Bible. Leibniz, reading these early critiques, warned that this line of inquiry, if continued, would destroy Christianity.[31] It is still too early to say whether Leibniz was right.

CHAPTER XVIII

The Scientific Quest

1648–1715

I. THE INTERNATIONAL OF SCIENCE

SLOWLY the mood of Europe, for better or for worse, was changing from supernaturalism to secularism, from theology to science, from hopes of heaven and fears of hell to plans for the enlargement of knowledge and the improvement of human life. The upper classes, pursuing their epicurean ways, made little protest against a religious faith which they conceived to be salutary for the unfortunate masses excluded from the paradise of pedigree; yet even among the gilded few there were some who played at science, balanced equations, burned their fingers or sniffed their noses in laboratories, or gazed in puzzlement at the multiplying stars. In Paris fashionable ladies crowded to Lémery's lectures on chemistry, to Du Verney's demonstrations in anatomy; Condé invited Lémery to his very exclusive salon, and Louis XIV appointed Du Verney to aid in educating the heir to the throne. In England Charles II had a "chimical laboratory" of his own; barons, bishops, and barristers contrived experiments; elegant mistresses came in their carriages to observe the marvels of magnetism; Evelyn dabbled in physics, and proposed to establish an institute for scientific research; Pepys, between ships and skirts, plied the microscope, the air pump, and the dissecting knife, and became president of the Royal Society.

The universities lagged behind the public in the new interest, but private academies took it up. First, apparently, the Academia Secretorum Naturae at Naples (1560); then the Accademia dei Lincei at Rome (1603), to which Galileo belonged; then the Accademia del Cimento which his disciples Viviani and Torricelli founded at Florence (1657). This last institute was dedicated by its name to experiment, and took Cartesian doubt as its starting point; nothing was to be received on faith; every problem was to be investigated without regard to any existing sect or philosophy.[1] Some of these academies were short-lived, but they left successors when they died. Academies were established at Schweinfurt (1652), Altdorf (1672), and Uppsala (1710); in 1700, after thirty years of pleading by Leibniz, the Berlin Academy took form; and to Leibniz' credit we must ascribe also the Academy of St. Petersburg (1724).

In France the Académie des Sciences developed from the meetings (1631–38) of Mersenne, Roberval, Desargues, and other scientists in the home of Pascal's father in Paris, or in Mersenne's monastic cell. It formulated a program "to work for the perfection of the sciences and the arts, and to seek generally for all that can be of use or convenience to the human race"; it resolved also "to disabuse the world of all those common errors that have long passed for truth," but it counseled its members to avoid discussion of religion or politics.[2] In 1666 the Academy received a royal charter, and a room in the Bibliothèque Royale; at Versailles we may still see a large canvas, by Testelin, in which Louis XIV presents this charter to a group headed by Christian Huygens and Claude Perrault. Each of the twenty-one members received an annual salary from the government, and funds for expenses; in effect the Academy became a department of the state. Louis was especially kind to astronomers. He invited Cassini from Italy, Roemer from Denmark, Huygens from Holland, and built for them a splendid observatory. When Hevelius of Danzig, who had distinguished himself by his studies of the moon, lost his precious library in a fire, the King sent him a substantial gift to repair the loss.[3] Laplace credited the Académie with most of the scientific advances made in France; but its dependence upon a King closely allied with the Church proved detrimental to the progress of French science,[4] and the English forged ahead.

It was characteristic of England that its scientific academies were private foundations only incidentally indebted to the government. About 1645, according to John Wallis, he became acquainted in London with "divers worthy persons, inquisitive into natural philosophy and other parts of human learning, and particularly . . . Experimental Philosophy."[5] They agreed to meet once a week to discuss mathematics, astronomy, magnetics, navigation, physics, mechanics, chemistry, the circulation of the blood, and other such subjects. This "Invisible College," as it was then called, took its inspiration from the House of Solomon in Bacon's *New Atlantis*. When Wallis removed to Oxford as professor of mathematics, the association divided into two sections, one of which met in the lodgings of Robert Boyle at the University, the other in Gresham's College, London; Wren and Evelyn were early members there. The political turmoil intervening between the death of Cromwell and the Restoration interrupted these London meetings, but they were resumed soon after the accession of Charles II; and on July 15, 1662, the King conferred an official charter upon the "Royal Society of London for Improving Natural Knowledge." The ninety-eight "original fellows" included not only scientists like Boyle and Hooke, but poets like Dryden and Waller, Wren the architect, Evelyn, fourteen peers, and several bishops. Between 1663 and 1686 some three hundred additional fellows were enrolled. No class distinctions divided them; dukes and commoners rubbed elbows in the enterprise; and poor members were exempt from dues.[6] In 1673 Leibniz, admitted to membership, declared the Royal Society the most respected intellectual authority in Europe. As early as 1667 Thomas Sprat published his excellent *History of the Royal Society*; he too, though he became bishop of Rochester, was stirred by the Baconian breezes that were blowing over England.

Some theologians complained that the new institute would undermine respect for the universities and the Established Church, but the moderation and caution of the Society soon calmed ecclesiastical opposition. Its strange experiments amused the court and the King, who laughed when he heard that it was weighing air and meditating mechanical flight. Swift satirized it in *Gulliver's Travels*[7] as the Grand Academy of Lagado, whose members made plans for extracting sunshine from cucumbers, and for building houses from the roof downward; and Samuel Butler, author of *Hudibras*, told how a club of scientists was excited by discovering an elephant in the moon, only to find that it was a mouse in their telescope.[8] But it was under the auspices of the Royal Society that Evelyn improved English husbandry, that Sir William Petty established the science of statistics, that English science and medicine advanced beyond anything known in contemporary France or Germany, that Boyle almost founded chemistry, that Ray revolutionized botany, Woodward geology, and Newton astronomy. The Society made thousands of experiments in chemistry and physics; it received, dissected, and studied the bodies of executed criminals; it became a repository of clinical reports from physicians in all parts of the country; it collected reports of technological developments; it kept in touch with scientific research abroad. Its emphasis on natural processes and law discredited superstition and the witchcraft persecution.

In 1665 Henry Oldenburg, its secretary, began to publish *The Philosophical Transactions of the Royal Society*, which has continued to our own day. It invited and received contributions from abroad; it was among the first to print the findings of Malpighi and Leeuwenhoek. Oldenburg had come to England in 1653 to negotiate a trade treaty for his native Bremen; he remained, and became a friend of Milton, Hobbes, Newton, and Boyle; he corresponded actively with scientists and philosophers in all parts of the world. The members of the Royal Society, he said, "have taken to task the whole universe";[9] and he wrote to Spinoza:

> We feel certain that the forms and qualities of things can best be explained by the principles of mechanics, and that all effects of Nature are produced by motion, figure, texture, and the varying combinations of these; and that there is no need to have recourse to inexplicable forms and occult qualities, as to a refuge from ignorance.[10]

Through these *Philosophical Transactions*, the *Journal des savants*, the *Giornale de' letterati*, and the *Acta Eruditorum* the scientists and scholars of Europe were able to overcome national boundaries, to keep in touch with one another's work and findings, and to form a united army of advance in a vast creative enterprise. Almost hidden away in their studies, laboratories, and expeditions, ignoring or surviving the clatter of politics, the march of regiments, the din of dogma, the mists of superstition, and the prying agents of civil or ecclesiastical censorship, they pored over texts, test tubes, and microscopes, mingled chemicals curiously, measured forces and magnitudes, plotted equations and diagrams, peered into the mysteries of the cell, burrowed into the strata of the earth, charted the movements of the stars, until all the motions of matter seemed to fall into an order of law, and the overwhelming immensity of the universe seemed to obey the predictions of the amazing human mind. In France Fermat, Pascal, Roberval, Mariotte, Perrault, and whole families of Cassinis; in Switzerland the Bernoullis; in Germany Guericke, Leibniz, Tschirnhaus, Fahrenheit; in Holland Huygens and Leeuwenhoek; in Italy Viviani and Torricelli; in Denmark Steno; in Scotland James and David Gregory; in England Wallis, Lister, Boyle, Hooke, Flamsteed, Halley, Newton: these and many others, in this brief period of Europe's history from 1648 to 1715, labored apart and together, solitary and conspiring, to build, day by day, night after night, the mathematics, astronomy, geology, geography, physics, chemistry, biology, anatomy, and physiology that were to effect a fateful revolution in the modern soul. Oldenburg, feeling this internationalism of science, and never dreaming that nationalism might make science itself a partisan and cataclysmic tool, saw in this inspiring co-operation an omen of a better life. "I hope," he wrote to Huygens, "that in time all nations, even the less civilized, will embrace each other as dear comrades, and will join forces, both intellectual and material, to banish ignorance and to make true and useful philosophy regnant."[11] It is still the hope of the world.

II. MATHEMATICS

First, the new international sharpened its instruments. Pascal, Hooke, and Guericke developed the barometer; Guericke's air pump explored the possibility of a vacuum; Gregory, Newton, and others made better telescopes than those of Kepler and Galileo; Newton invented the sextant; Hooke improved the compound microscope, which transformed the study of the cell; the thermometer became more reliable and accurate under Guericke and Amontons, and in 1714 Fahrenheit gave it its English-American form by using mercury instead of alcohol as the expanding medium, and dividing its scale at zero, 32 degrees, and 96 degrees (which he assumed to be the normal temperature of the human body).

The greatest instrument of all was mathematics, for this gave experience a quantitative and measured form, and in a thousand ways enabled it to predict, even to control, the future. "Nature plays the mathematician," said Boyle; and Leibniz added, "Natural science is naught but applied mathematics."[12] Historians of mathematics acclaim the seventeenth century as especially fruitful in their field, for it was the century of Descartes, Napier, Cavalieri, Fermat, Pascal, Newton, Leibniz, and Desargues. Ladies perfumed with pedigree attended lectures on mathematics; some of them, joked the *Journal des savants*, made the squaring of the circle the sole passport to their favors;[13] this may explain Hobbes's persistent efforts to solve that baffling problem.

Pierre de Fermat fathered the modern theory of numbers (the study of their classes, characteristics, and relationships), conceived analytical geometry independently of—perhaps before—Descartes, invented the calculus of probabilities independently of Pascal, and anticipated the differential calculus of Newton and Leibniz. Yet he lived in comparative obscurity as a counselor of the Parlement of Toulouse, and formulated his contributions to mathematics only in letters to his friends—which were not published till 1679, fourteen years after his death. We catch the mathematical ecstasy in one of these letters: "I have found a very great number of exceedingly beautiful theorems."[14] He was delighted by every new trick or surprising regularity in numbers. He challenged the mathematicians of the world "to separate a cube into two cubes, a fourth power into two fourth powers," etc.; "I have discovered," he wrote, "a truly marvelous demonstration" of this, now known as "Fermat's last theorem"; but neither his nor any conclusive proof of it has yet been found. A German professor in 1908 left 100,000 marks to the first person who should prove Fermat's proposition; no one has yet claimed the reward, perhaps discouraged by the depreciation of marks.

Christian Huygens, barring only one, was the outstanding scientist of this age—*facile secundus* to Newton. His father, Constantijn Huygens, was one of the most distinguished of Holland's poets and statesmen. Born at The Hague in 1629, Christiaan (as the Dutch spelled him) began at the age of twenty-two to publish mathematical treatises. His discoveries in astronomy and physics soon won him a European renown; he was elected a fellow of the Royal Society in London in 1663, and in 1665 he was invited by Colbert to join the Académie des Sciences in Paris. He moved to the French capital, received a liberal pension, and remained there till 1681; then, uncomfortable under a King turned persecutor of Protestants, he returned to Holland. His correspondence in six languages with Descartes,

Roberval, Mersenne, Fermat, Pascal, Newton, Boyle, and many others illustrated the growing unity of the scientific fraternity. "The world is my country," he said, and "to promote science is my religion."[15] His *mens sana in corpore aegro* was one of the marvels of his time—his body always ailing, his mind creative till his death at sixty-six. His work in mathematics was the least part of his achievement; yet geometry, logarithms, and calculus all profited from his labors. In 1673 he established that "law of inverse squares" (that the attraction of bodies for one another varies inversely as the square of the distance between them) which became so vital to Newton's astronomy.

Newton, of course, was now the central luminary in the galaxy of British science; he deserves a separate chapter; but there were satellites to his star. His friend John Wallis, an Anglican priest, became Savilian professor of geometry at Oxford in 1649 at the age of thirty-three, and held that chair for fifty-four years. Grammar, logic, and theology diverted his pen from science; nevertheless he wrote effectively on mathematics, mechanics, acoustics, astronomy, tides, botany, physiology, geology, and music; he lacked only some amours and wars to make him a full man. His *De Algebra Tractatus Historicus et Practicus* (1673) not only contributed original ideas to that science, but was the first serious attempt in England to write the history of mathematics. His contemporaries were delighted by his prolonged controversy with Hobbes over the quadrature of the circle; Wallis scored his point, but the old philosopher fought on to the end of his ninety-first year. History remembers Wallis chiefly for his *Arithmetica Infinitorum* (1655), which applied Cavalieri's method of indivisibles to the quadrature of curves, and so prepared for infinitesimal calculus.

Calculus meant originally a small stone used by the ancient Romans in calculating; but only the devotees of calculus can now define their science properly.* Archimedes had glimpsed it, Kepler had approached it, Fermat had discovered it but had not published his findings; Cavalieri and Torricelli in Italy, Pascal and Roberval in France, John Wallis and Isaac Barrow in England, James and David Gregory in Scotland, had all carried bricks to the building in this astonishing co-operation of a continent. Newton and Leibniz brought the work to fulfillment.

---

* For us who are not initiates, differential calculus may be described as the calculation of variable quantities, as of weight, distance, or time. So the level of water poured at a uniform rate into an inverted cone will rise less and less rapidly; differential calculus determines how much the level will rise in any given unit of time. A body falling in a *resistance-free* medium will increase its rate of fall with each increment of time; calculus determines how far it will fall in any stated interval. More complicated forms of calculus deal with the construction of tangents to curves, the areas enclosed by a curve, the approximation of indefinitely multiplied straight lines to a circle. . . . Infinitesimal calculus calculates a variable quantity by reducing it without limit to so infinitesimal a part that the rate of variation may be ignored. Integral calculus calculates a quantity from knowledge of its rate of change. All these methods of reckoning have proved invaluable in engineering.

The term *calculus* was suggested to Leibniz by Johann Bernoulli, member of a family as remarkable as the Bachs, the Brueghels, and the Couperins for the social heredity of genius. Nikolaus Bernoulli (1623–1708), like his ancestors, was a merchant. In his son Jakob Bernoulli I (1654–1705) mercantile accounting passed into higher forms of reckoning. Taking as his motto *Invito patre sidera verso*—"Against my father's will I study the stars"—Jakob dabbled in astronomy, contributed to analytical geometry, advanced the calculus of variations, and became professor of mathematics at the University of Basel. His studies of catenary curves (curves described by a uniform chain suspended between two points) came to later fruition in the designing of suspension bridges and high-voltage transmission lines. His brother Johann (1667–1748), also against paternal plans, took up medicine, then mathematics, and succeeded Jakob as professor at Basel; he contributed to physics, optics, chemistry, astronomy, the theory of tides, and the mathematics of sails; he invented exponential calculus, constructed the first system of integral calculus, and introduced the use of the word *integral* in this sense. Another brother, Nikolaus I (1662–1716), took his doctor's degree in philosophy at sixteen, in law at twenty, taught law at Bern and mathematics in St. Petersburg. We shall find six more Bernoulli mathematicians in the eighteenth century, and there were two in the nineteenth. By that time the Bernoulli battery had run down.

The establishment of statistics as almost a science was among the achievements of this age. John Graunt, a haberdasher, amused himself by collecting and studying the burial records of London parishes. Usually these records stated the reported cause of death, including "dead in the street and starved," "executed and prest to death," "King's evil," "starved at nurse," and "made away themselves."[16] In 1662 Graunt published his *Natural and Political Observations . . . upon the Bills of Mortality*; this is the beginning of modern statistics. He concluded from his tables that *thirty-six per cent of all children died before the age of six*, twenty-four per cent died in the next ten years, fifteen per cent in the next ten, etc.;[17] the infantile mortality seems much exaggerated here, but suggests the labor of love in keeping up with the angel of death. "Among the several casualties," said Graunt, "some bear a constant proportion unto the whole number of burials; such are chronical diseases, and the diseases whereunto the city is most subject, as, for example, consumptions, dropsies, jaundice, etc.";[18] i.e., certain diseases, and other social phenomena, though incalculable in individuals, may be precalculated with relative accuracy for a large community; this principle, here formulated by Graunt, became a foundation of statistical prediction. He noted that in many years the burials in London exceeded the christenings; he concluded that London was especially rich in opportunities for death, as from business anxieties, "smokes, stinks, close air," and "intemperance in feeding." As the population of London grew nevertheless, Graunt ascribed the increase to immigration from the countryside and the lesser towns. He reckoned the population of the capital in 1662 at some 384,000 souls.

Statistics were applied to politics by Graunt's friend Sir William Petty. Again exemplifying a versatility impossible today, Petty, after studying at Caen, Utrecht, Leiden, Amsterdam, and Paris, taught anatomy at Oxford and music at Gresham College, London, and won fortune and knighthood as physician to the royal army in Ireland.* In 1676 he wrote the second classic in English statistics, *Political Arithmetic*. Politics, Petty held, could approach to a science only by basing its conclusions on quantitative measurements. Therefore he pleaded for a periodical census that would record the birth, sex, marital condition, titles, occupation, religion, etc., of every inhabitant of England. On the basis of mortality bills, number of houses, and annual excess of births over deaths, he estimated the population of London at 696,000 in 1682; of Paris, 488,000; Amsterdam, 187,000; Rome, 125,000. Like Giovanni Botero in 1589 and Thomas Malthus in 1798, Petty thought that population tends to increase faster than the means of subsistence, that this leads to war, and that by the year 3682 the habitable earth would be dangerously overcrowded, with one person to every two acres of land.[20]

Insurance companies used statistics to turn their business into an art and science that took account of everything except inflation. From the mortality reports of Breslau Edmund Halley drew up (1693) a table of expectable deaths for all years between one and eighty-four; on its basis he calculated the odds against persons of a given age dying during the calendar year, and deduced the logical price of a policy. The first life insurance companies established in London in the eighteenth century made use of Halley's tables, and turned mathematics into gold.

III. ASTRONOMY

The stars were subjected to science in a hundred countries. In Italy the Jesuit astronomer Riccioli (1650) discovered the first double star—i.e., a star which to the eye seems one but is seen through the telescope as two stars apparently revolving around each other. In Danzig Johannes Hevelius built an observatory in his own home, made his own instruments, catalogued 1,564 stars, discovered four comets, observed the transit of Mercury,

---

* At Oxford, says Aubrey, "he kept a body . . . soused or pickled." One of the corpses turned over to him for dissection was that of Nan Green, who had murdered her bastard child; Petty found her still breathing, and brought her back to life.[19]

noted the moon's librations (periodic alternations in the visibility of its parts), charted its surface, and gave to several of its features names that remain on lunar maps today. When he announced to Europe's stargazers that he could distinguish stellar positions as accurately with a diopter (a sight using only one lens or prism) as with a compound telescope, Robert Hooke challenged the claim; Halley traveled from London to Danzig to test it, and reported that Hevelius had told the truth.[21]

Recognizing the importance of astronomy for navigation, Louis XIV provided funds to raise and equip an observatory at Paris (1667–72). From that center Jean Picard led or sent expeditions to study the skies from different points on the earth; he went to Uraniborg to note the exact location from which Tycho Brahe had made his classic map of the stars; and, by a variety of observations ranging from Paris to Amiens, he measured a degree of longitude with such accuracy (within a few yards of the current figure, 69.5 miles) that Newton is supposed to have used Picard's results to estimate the mass of the earth and verify the theory of gravitation. By similar observations Picard reckoned the equatorial diameter of the earth at 7,801 miles—not far from our present computation of 7,913 miles.[22] These findings made it possible for a ship at sea to determine its location with unprecedented precision. So the commercial expansion and industrial development of Europe urged on the scientific revolution, and profited from it.

At Picard's suggestion Louis XIV invited to France the Italian astronomer Giovanni Domenico Cassini, who had already acquired European fame by discovering the spheroidal form of Jupiter and the periodic rotation of Jupiter and Mars. Arrived in Paris (1669), he was received by the King as a prince of science.[23] In 1672 he and Picard sent Jean Richer to Cayenne, in South America, to observe Mars at its maximum "opposition" to the sun and nearness to the earth; Cassini noted the same opposition from Paris. The comparison of the simultaneous observations from these two separate points gave new and more precise values to the parallax of Mars and the sun and their distance from the earth, and revealed vaster dimensions in the solar system than had been estimated before. As a pendulum was found to beat more slowly at Cayenne than a similar pendulum at Paris, the astronomers concluded that gravity was less intense near the equator than in higher latitudes; and this suggested that the earth was not a perfect sphere. Cassini thought it was flattened at the equator; Newton thought it was flattened at the poles; further research supported Newton. Meanwhile Cassini discovered four new satellites of Saturn, and the division (now known by his name) of Saturn's ring into two. After Cassini's death in 1712 he was succeeded in the Paris observatory by his son Jacques, who measured the arc of the meridian from Dunkirk to Perpignan, and published the first tables of the satellites of Saturn.

Christian Huygens, before joining the cosmopolitan assemblage of scientists in Paris, made at The Hague some important contributions to astronomy. With his brother Constantijn he developed a new method of grinding and polishing lenses; with these he constructed telescopes of greater power and clarity than any known before; thereby he discovered (1655) the sixth satellite of Saturn, and that planet's mysterious ring. A year later he made the first delineation of the bright region (now bearing his name) in the Orion nebula, and detected the multiple character of its nuclear star.

The great rival to the Paris astronomers was the remarkable group that gathered mostly around Halley and Newton in England. James Gregory of Edinburgh lent distant aid by designing the first reflecting telescope (1663)—i.e., one in which the rays of light from the object are concentrated by a curved mirror instead of a lens; Newton improved this in 1668. In 1675 John Flamsteed and others addressed to Charles II a memorial asking him to finance the building of a national observatory, so that better methods of calculating longitude might guide the English shipping that was now plowing the seas. The King provided for the building, which was raised in the borough of Greenwich near southeast London; this came to be used as the point of zero longitude and standard time. Charles offered Flamsteed a small salary as director, but nothing to pay for assistants or instruments. Flamsteed, frail and sickly, gave his life to that observatory. He took pupils, bought instruments out of his personal funds, received others as gifts from friends, and set himself patiently to chart the sky as seen from Greenwich. Before he died (1719) he had made the most extensive and accurate star catalogue yet known, considerably improving on that which Tycho Brahe had left to Kepler in 1601. Harassed by lack of aid, doing himself the paperwork usually left to assistants, Flamsteed angered Halley and Newton by delays in the calculation and announcement of his results; at last Halley published them without Flamsteed's permission, and the ailing astronomer shook the stars with his wrath.

Nevertheless Edmund Halley was the finest gentleman of them all. An enthusiastic schoolboy student of the sky, he published at twenty a paper on the planetary orbits; and in that same year (1676) he set out to see how the heavens looked from the southern hemisphere of the earth. On the island of St. Helena he charted the behavior of 341 stars. On the eve of his twenty-first birthday he made the first full observation of a transit of Mercury. Back in England, he was elected a fellow of the Royal Society at twenty-two. He recognized Newton's genius, financed the first edition of the costly *Principia*, and prefixed to it some complimentary verse in splendid Latin, ending in the line, *Nec fas est proprius mortali attingere divos* (It is not allowed to any mortal to come closer to the gods).[24] Halley edited the Greek text of the *Conics* of Apollonius of Perga, and learned Arabic to translate Greek treatises preserved only in that language.

He wrote his name in the sky by one of the most successful predictions in history. Borelli had paved the way by discovering the parabolic form of cometary paths (1665). When a comet appeared in 1682 Halley found similarities in its course with comets recorded in 1456, 1531, and 1607; he noted that these manifestations had come at intervals of some seventy-five years, and he predicted a reappearance in 1758. He could not live to see the fulfillment of his prophecy, but when the comet returned it received his name, and added to the rising prestige of science. Until late in the seventeenth century comets were considered to be direct acts of God, portending great calamities to mankind; the essays of Bayle and Fontenelle, and the prediction of Halley, laid this superstition. Halley identified another comet, seen in 1680, with one observed in the year of Christ's death; he traced its recurrence every 575 years, and from this periodicity he computed its orbit and speed around the sun. Commenting on these calculations, Newton concluded that "the bodies of comets are solid, compact, fixed, and durable, like the bodies of the planets," and are not "vapors or exhalations of the earth, of the sun, and other planets."[25]*

In 1691 Halley was refused the Savilian chair of astronomy at Oxford on suspicion of being a materialist.[26] In 1698, on a commission from William III, he sailed far into the South Atlantic, studied the variations of the compass, and charted stars as seen from the Antarctic. (Compared with this expedition, said Voltaire, "the voyage of the Argonauts was but the crossing of a bark from one side of a river to the other."[27]) In 1718 Halley pointed out that several of the supposedly "fixed stars" had altered their positions since Greek times, and that one of them, Sirius, had changed since Brahe; allowing for errors of observation, he concluded that the stars vary their positions relative to one another over great periods of time; and these "proper motions" are now accepted as real. In 1721 he was appointed to succeed Flamsteed as astronomer royal; but Flamsteed had died so poor that his creditors seized his instruments, and Halley found his own work hampered by inadequate equipment as well as by his own declining energies; nevertheless he began, at sixty-four, to observe and record the phenomena of the moon through its complete cycle of eighteen years. He died in 1742, aged eighty-six, after wisely drinking a glass of wine against his doctor's orders. Life, like wine, should not be taken in excess.

---

* Dryden, in *Absalom and Achitophel* (1681), had recently described comets as "rising from earthy vapours ere they shine in the skies."

IV. THE EARTH

In love with science, Halley had ventured into the mists of meteorology with an essay (1697) on trade winds, and a chart that for the first time mapped the movements of the air. He attributed these movements to differences in the temperature and pressure of the atmosphere; so the sun, moving apparently westward, carried heat with it, especially along the equatorial regions of the earth; the air rarefied by this heat sucked in less rarefied air from the east, and created the prevailing equatorial winds that Columbus had relied on to sail from east to west. Francis Bacon had suggested a similar explanation. George Hadley was to develop it in 1735 by adding that the greater eastward speed of the earth's rotation at the equator creates a contrary westward flow of air.

The development of the barometer and the thermometer made meteorology a science. Guericke's barometer rightly forecast a severe storm in 1660. Various hygrometers were invented in the sixteenth century to measure humidity. The Accademia del Cimento used a graduated vessel that received the moisture dripping from the outside of an ice-filled metallic cone. Hooke attached a grain bristle, or "beard"—which swelled and bent with increasing moisture in the air—to an indicator needle that turned as the bristle swelled. Hooke invented also a wind gauge, a wheel barometer, and a weather clock. This last instrument, designed on a commission from the Royal Society (1678), measured and recorded the velocity and direction of the wind, the pressure and humidity of the atmosphere, the temperature of the air, and the amount of rainfall; for literal good measure it gave the time of day. Armed with improved instruments, weather stations in diverse cities began to record and compare their simultaneous observations, as between Paris and Stockholm in 1649. Grand Duke Ferdinand II of Tuscany, patron of the Cimento, sent barometers, thermometers, and hygrometers to chosen observers at Paris, Warsaw, Innsbruck, and elsewhere, with instructions for recording meteorological data daily, and transmitting a copy to Florence for comparison. Leibniz persuaded the weather stations at Hanover and Kiel to keep daily records from 1679 to 1714.

The ingenious and inconclusive Hooke opened a hundred promising avenues of investigation, but was too poor in funds or patience to follow them to famous ends. We find him everywhere in the history of British science in the second half of the seventeenth century. Son of a minister who "died by suspending himself,"[28] he prefigured his vacillating diversity by painting pictures, playing the organ, and inventing thirty different ways of flying. At Oxford he took to chemistry, serving as assistant to Robert

Boyle. In 1662 he was appointed "curator of experiments" for the Royal Society; in 1665 he was professor of geometry in Gresham College; in 1666, after the Great Fire of London, he took to architecture and designed several major buildings—Montagu House, the College of Physicians, and Bethlehem Hospital ("Bedlam"). After long poring through microscopes, he published his *chef-d'oeuvre, Micrographia* (1665), containing a number of suggestive ideas in biology. He proposed a wave theory of light, helped Newton in optics, and anticipated both the law of inverse squares and the theory of gravitation. He discovered the fifth star in Orion, and made the first attempts to determine by telescope the parallax of a fixed star. He propounded a kinetic theory of gases in 1678, and described a system of telegraphy in 1684. He was among the first to apply the spring to regulate watches; he laid down the principle of the sextant for measuring angular distances; he made a dozen scientific instruments. He was probably the most original mind in all that galaxy of geniuses that for a time made the Royal Society the pacemaker of European science; but his somber and nervous nature kept him from the acclaim that he deserved.

Even in geology he had his moment of truth. He argued that fossils proved for the earth and for life an antiquity quite incompatible with the Book of Genesis; and he foresaw that the chronology of terrestrial life would someday be calculated from the differing fossils of successive strata. Most seventeenth-century writers still accepted the Biblical account of Creation, and some of them struggled to reconcile Genesis with the sporadic discoveries of geology. In *An Essay towards a Natural History of the Earth* (1695) John Woodward, after long study of his large collection of fossils, restored Leonardo da Vinci's interpretation of them as the relics of plants or animals that had once lived on the earth, but even he thought that the distribution of fossils was a result of Noah's Flood. An Anglican clergyman, Thomas Burnet, proposed (1680) a reconciliation between Genesis and geology by stretching the "days" of the Biblican Creation myth into epochs; this subterfuge proved acceptable; but when Thomas, gathering courage, went on to explain the story of Adam's fall as an allegory, he found himself barred from ecclesiastical advancement.

Athanasius Kircher was both a good Jesuit and a great scientist; we shall find him brilliant in a dozen fields. His *Mundus subterraneus* (1665) charted ocean currents, suggested that underground streams were fed from the sea, and ascribed volcanic eruptions and hot springs to subterranean fires; this seemed to confirm the popular belief that hell was in the center of the earth. Pierre Perrault (1674) rejected the idea that springs and rivers have subterranean sources, and upheld the now accepted view that they are the product of rain and snow. Martin Lister explained volcanic eruptions as due to the heating and consequent explosion of the sulphur in iron pyrites;

and experiment showed that a mixture of iron filings, sulphur, and water, buried in the earth, became heated, cracked the earth above it, and burst into flames.

The most prominent figure in the geology of this age was known to Denmark as Niels Stensen, and to the international of science as Nicolaus Steno. Born in Copenhagen, he studied medicine there and in Leiden, where he numbered Spinoza among his friends.[29] Migrating to Italy, he accepted Catholicism and became court physician to Ferdinand II at Florence. In 1669 he published a small volume, *De solido intra solidum naturaliter contento*, which one student has ranked as "the most important geological document of that century."[30] Its purpose was to confirm the new view of fossils; but as a prelude Steno for the first time formulated principles to explain the evolution of the earth's crust. Studying the geology of Tuscany, he found six successive strata. He analyzed their structure and contents, the formation of mountains and valleys, the causes of volcanoes and earthquakes, and the fossil evidence for formerly higher levels of rivers and the sea. The reputation earned by this book, and by Steno's anatomical studies, led King Christian IV to offer him the chair of anatomy in the University of Copenhagen. He accepted, but his zealous Catholicism caused some friction; he returned to Florence, passed from science to religion, and ended as bishop of Titopolis and vicar apostolic for north Europe.

Meanwhile geography was growing, usually as a by-product of missionary, military, or commercial enterprise. The Jesuits were almost as devoted to science as to religion or politics; many of them belonged to learned societies, which welcomed their geographical and ethnographical reports. As missionaries they ventured into Canada, Mexico, Brazil, Tibet, Mongolia, China . . . They gathered and remitted much useful knowledge, and made the best maps of the areas they visited. In 1651 Martino Martini published his *Atlas sinensis*, the fullest geographical description of China yet printed; and in 1667 Athanasius Kircher issued a magnificent *China illustrata*. Louis XIV sent six Jesuit scientists, equipped with the latest instruments, to map China again; in 1718 they issued a vast map in 120 sheets, covering China, Manchuria, Mongolia, and Tibet; this remained for two centuries the basis of all later maps of those areas. The cartographical wonder of the age was the map, twenty-four feet in diameter, which Giovanni Cassini and his aides drew in ink on the floor of the Paris observatory (c. 1690), showing the precise location, in latitude and longitude, of all important places on the earth.[31]

Some famous travelers belong to this period. We have already helped ourselves to Tavernier's *Six Voyages through Europe into Asia* (1670), and Chardin's *Travels in Persia* (1686). "In my six voyages," wrote Tavernier, "and traveling by different roads, I had the leisure and opportunity to see all Turkey, all Persia, and all India. . . . The last three times I went beyond Ganges to the island of Java, so that for the space of forty years I have traveled above sixty thousand leagues by land."[32] Chardin in one sentence anticipated Montesquieu's *Spirit of Laws*: "The climate of each particular race is . . . always the primary cause of the inclinations and customs of its people."[33] In 1670–71 François Bernier published an account of his travels and studies in India, and was accused of having shed his Christianity en route.[34] William Dampier buccaneered in a hundred lands and seas, wrote *A New Voyage round the World* (1697), and gave a cue to Defoe by telling how, on one of his later sallies, he piloted the vessel that rescued Alexander Selkirk from an otherwise uninhabited island (1709).

Geography played its part in the erosion of Christian theology. As accounts of other continents accumulated, the educated classes of Europe could not but marvel at the variety of religious beliefs on the earth, the similarity of religious myths, the confidence of each cult in the truth of its creed, and the moral level of Mohammedan or Buddhist societies that in some respects shamed the gory wars and murderous intolerance of peoples dowered with the Christian faith. Baron de Lahontan, traveling in Canada in 1683, reported that he had much difficulty in meeting criticisms of Christianity by Indian natives.[35] Bayle again and again quoted the customs and ideas of the Chinese or the Japanese in criticizing European beliefs and ways. The relativity of morals became an axiom of eighteenth-century philosophy; one wit described the travels of Jacques Seden the hermaphrodite, who, to his delight, found a country where all the inhabitants were homosexuals, who looked upon Europe's heterosexuals as immoral and disgusting monstrosities.[36]

V. PHYSICS

Physics and chemistry conflicted less visibly than geography and biology with the ancient creed, for they dealt with solids, liquids, and gases that apparently had no connection with theology; but even in that material realm the progress of science was enlarging the rule of law, and weakening the faith in miracles. The study of physics rested on no philosophical interests, but on commercial and industrial needs.

Navigators, having induced astronomers to chart the skies more accurately, now offered rewards for a clock that would aid in finding longitude despite the perturbations of the sea. Longitude at sea could be determined by comparing the moment of sunrise or meridian with the time shown at that instant by a clock set to keep Greenwich or Paris time; but unless the clock was accurate the calculation would be dangerously wrong.

In 1657 Huygens contrived a reliable clock by attaching a pendulum to a toothed escapement wheel, but such a clock was useless on a rolling and pitching ship.* After many trials, Huygens constructed a successful marine clock by substituting for the pendulum a balance wheel worked by two springs. This was among the illuminating suggestions expounded by him in one of the classics of modern science, the *Horologium oscillatorium (The Pendulum Clock)* published in Paris in 1673. Three years later Hooke invented the anchor escapement of clocks, applied spiral springs to the balance wheel of watches, and expounded the action of the springs on the principle *Ut tensio sic vis*—"As the tension, so the force"; this is still called Hooke's law. Pocket watches could now be made more competently and cheaply than before.

In the *Horologium* and a special monograph Huygens studied the law of centrifugal force—that every particle of a rotating body not lying in the axis of rotation is subject to a centrifugal force which increases with its distance from the axis, and with the speed of rotation. He set a clay sphere rotating rapidly, and found that it assumed the form of a spheroid flattened at both ends of the axis. On this centrifugal principle he explained the polar flattening of the planet Jupiter, and by analogy he concluded that the earth too must be slightly flattened at the poles.

Huygens' *Tractatus de Motu Corporum ex Percussione* (1703), published eight years after his death, continued the studies of Galileo, Descartes, and Wallis on the problems of impact. These presented intriguing mysteries, from the play of billiards to the collision of stars. How is force transmitted from a moving object to an object that it strikes? Huygens did not solve the mystery, but he stated some basic principles:

> I. If upon a body at rest another body equal to it impinges, the latter will come to rest after the impact, while the body initially at rest will acquire the velocity of the impinging body.
>
> II. If two equal bodies collide with unequal velocities, they will move, after impact, with interchanged velocities. . . .
>
> XI. In the mutual impact of two bodies the sum of the products of the masses into the squares of the relative velocities is the same before and after impact.

These propositions, formulated by Huygens in 1669, gave partial expression to the most comprehensive principle of modern physics, the conservation of energy. They were, however, only ideally true, since they assumed

---

* Leonardo da Vinci, about 1500, made drawings of a pendulum and an escapement mechanism. Galileo formulated some laws of the pendulum, and conceived the idea of a pendulum clock in 1641, but he died before applying the idea in practice. Camerini in 1656 made a small pendulum clock just a few months before Huygens.

complete elasticity in bodies. As no body in nature is perfectly elastic, the relative velocity of impinging objects is diminished according to the substance of which they are composed. Newton determined this rate of diminution for wood, cork, steel, and glass in the introductory scholium to Book I of his *Principia* (1687).

Another line of investigation flowed from the experiments of Torricelli and Pascal on atmospheric pressure. Pascal had announced in 1647 that "any vessel, however large, can be made empty of all matter known in nature and perceptible to the senses."[37] For hundreds of years European philosophy had proclaimed that *natura abhorrat vacuum;* even now a Paris professor informed Pascal that the angels themselves could not produce a vacuum, and Descartes scornfully remarked that the only existing vacuum was in Pascal's head. But about 1650 Otto von Guericke constructed at Magdeburg an air pump which produced so nearly complete a vacuum that he astonished the dignitaries of his country, and the luminaries of the scientific world, with a famous experiment known as "the Magdeburg hemispheres" (1654). In the presence of the Emperor Ferdinand III and the Imperial Diet at Ratisbon, he brought two bronze hemispherical shells together in such a way that they were hermetically sealed but not mechanically connected at their edges; he pumped nearly all the air from their united interiors; then he showed that the combined strength of sixteen horses—eight pulling in one direction, eight in the opposite direction— could not separate the two halves of the sphere; but when a stopcock in one hemisphere was opened, admitting air, the shells could be separated by hand.

Guericke had a flair for making physics intelligible to emperors. By emptying a copper sphere of water and air he caused it to collapse with a loud and startling noise; so he demonstrated the pressure of the atmosphere. He balanced two equal globes, and made one fall by pumping air from the other; so he proved that air has weight. He confessed that all vacuums were incomplete, but he showed that in his imperfect vacuums a flame would be extinguished, animals would suffocate, and a striking clock would make no sound; so he prepared for the discovery of oxygen, and revealed air as the medium of sound. He used the suction of a vacuum to pump water and raise weights, and shared in preparing for the steam engine. Having become burgomaster of Magdeburg, he delayed publishing his discoveries till 1672; but he communicated them to Kaspar Schott, Jesuit professor of physics at Würzburg, who printed an account of them in 1657. It was this publication that stimulated Boyle to the researches leading to the law of atmospheric pressure.

Robert Boyle was a prime factor in the flowering of English science in the second half of the seventeenth century. His father, Richard Boyle, Earl of Cork, had acquired a large estate in Ireland, and Robert inherited most of this at the age of seventeen (1644). On frequent visits to London he became acquainted with Wallis, Hooke, Wren, and other members of the "Invisible College." Fascinated by their work and their aspirations, he moved to Oxford and built a laboratory there (1654). He was a man of warm enthusiasms and of a piety that no science could destroy. He refused to communicate further (through Oldenburg) with Spinoza when he learned that the philosopher worshiped "substance" as God; but he placed much of his fortune at the service of science, and helped many friends. Tall and lean, frail and often ill, he held death at a distance by resolute diet and regimen. He found in his laboratory "that water of Lethe which causes me to forget everything but the joy of making experiments."[38]

Having read of Guericke's air pump, Boyle devised, with Hooke's help (1657), a "pneumatic engine" to study the properties of the atmosphere. With this and later pumps he proved that the column of mercury in a barometer is supported by atmospheric pressure, and he measured roughly the density of the air. He advanced upon Galileo's alleged experiment at Pisa by showing that even in an incomplete vacuum a bunch of feathers fell as rapidly as a stone. He showed that light is not affected by a vacuum, and therefore does not, like sound, use air as its medium of transmission; and he confirmed Guericke's demonstration that air is indispensable to life. (When a mouse fainted in the vacuum chamber he stopped the experiment and revived it by letting in air.) We see the international of science in action when we learn that Guericke was stimulated by Boyle's work to contrive a better air pump and resume his scientific studies; and that Huygens, visiting Boyle in 1661, was led to make similar instruments and tests.

Boyle went on to creative inquiries into refraction, crystals, specific gravities, hydrostatics, and heat. He crowned his contributions to physics by formulating the law that bears his name: that the pressure of air or any gas varies inversely as its volume—or that at a constant temperature the pressure of a gas, multiplied by its volume, is constant. He first announced this principle in 1662, and generously credited it to his pupil Richard Towneley. Hooke had reached the same formula in 1660 by independent experiments, but did not make it known till 1665. A French priest, Edme Mariotte, about the same time as Boyle, arrived at a similar conclusion— "air is compressed according to the weight acting upon it"; he published this in 1676; and on the Continent his name, rather than Boyle's, is attached to the law of atmospheric pressure. Whatever its parentage, it was one of the progenitors of the steam engine and the Industrial Revolution.

Boyle and Hooke followed up Bacon's view that "heat is a motion of expansion not uniformly of the whole body, but in the smaller parts of it."[39] Describing heat as "a property arising in a body from the motion or agitation of its parts," Hooke distinguished it from fire and flame, which he attributed to the action of air on heated bodies. "All bodies," said Hooke, "have some degree of heat in them," for "the parts of all bodies, though never so solid, do yet vibrate";[40] cold is merely a negative conception. Mariotte amused his friends by showing that "cold" could burn: with a concave slab of ice he focused sunlight upon gunpowder, causing it to explode. Spinoza's friend Count Ehrenfried Walter von Tschirnhaus melted porcelain and silver dollars by focusing upon them the light of the sun.

In the physics of sound two Englishmen, William Noble and Thomas Pigot, separately showed (c. 1673) that not only the whole, but different parts of a string may vibrate with diverse overtones, in sympathy with a near and related string plucked, struck, or bowed. Descartes had suggested this to Mersenne, and Joseph Sauveur, working on this idea, arrived independently at results similar to those of the Englishmen (1700); we should note in passing that Sauveur, who first used the word *acoustics,* had been a deaf mute from infancy.[41] In 1711 John Shore invented the tuning fork. Attempts to find the velocity of sound were made in this period by Borelli, Viviani, Picard, Cassini, Huygens, Flamsteed, Boyle, Halley, and Newton; Boyle, reckoning it at 1,126 feet per second, came closest to our current estimate. William Derham pointed out (1708) that this knowledge could be used to calculate the distance of a storm by observing the time interval between the lightning flash and the thunderclap.

The second half of the seventeenth century was probably the most brilliant epoch in the history of the physics of light. First, what was light itself? Hooke, always ready to delve into difficulties, hazarded the view that light is "nothing else but a peculiar motion of the parts of the luminous body"[42]—i.e., light differs from heat only in the more rapid motion of the body's constituent particles.* Second, how fast does it move? Scientists had heretofore assumed that the speed of light was infinite, and even the venturesome Hooke had regarded it as in any case too great for measurement. In 1675 Olaus Roemer, a Danish astronomer brought to Paris by Picard, proved the finite velocity of light by noting that the period of eclipse of Jupiter's innermost satellite varied according as the earth was moving toward or away from that planet; by computations based on the time of the satellite's revolution and the diameter of the earth's orbit, he showed that the variation in the observed time of the eclipse was due to the time taken by light from the satellite to traverse the orbit of the earth; and

---

* Cf. our current conception of light as visible radiant energy. All bodies are assumed to be continually emitting radiant energy. Radiation from objects warmer than the human body are felt by the skin as heat; but if the temperature of the object is sufficiently increased it will become luminous—i.e., some of its emitted radiation will be felt by the eye as light.

on that slender basis he calculated the speed of light at some 120,000 miles per second. (The current estimate is 186,000 miles.)

But how was light transmitted? Did it move in straight lines? If so, how did it get around corners? Francesco Grimaldi, Jesuit professor at Bologna, discovered and named (1665) the phenomena of diffraction—that rays of light passing through a small opening into a dark room spread more widely on the opposite wall than straight lines from source to wall would warrant, and that rays of light are slightly deflected from a straight line when they pass by the edges of an opaque body; these and other findings led Grimaldi to accept Leonardo da Vinci's suggestion that light moves in expanding waves. Hooke agreed, but it was Huygens who established the wave theory still popular among physicists. In another classic of modern science, *Traité de la lumière* (1690), Huygens reported the conclusions he had reached from studies begun twelve years before: that light is transmitted by a hypothetical substance which he called *aether* (from the Greek word for the sky), and which he conceived as made up of small, hard, elastic bodies transmitting light in successive spherical waves spreading out from the luminous source. On this theory he formulated laws of reflection, refraction, and double refraction; he ascribed to the enveloping motion of the waves the ability of light to move around corners and opaque objects; and he explained translucence by supposing the ether particles to be so minute that they can travel around and between the particles composing transparent liquids and solids. But he confessed himself unable to explain polarization; this was one of the reasons why Newton rejected the wave hypothesis and preferred the corpuscular theory of light.

The seventeenth century made only modest advances in the study of electricity after the work of Gilbert and Kircher on magnetism, and of Cabeo on electrical repulsion. Halley studied the influence of terrestrial magnetism on compass needles, and was the first to recognize a connection between the magnetism of the earth and the aurora borealis (1692). Guericke reported in 1672 some experiments in frictional electricity. A ball of sulphur, after being rotated against his hand, attracted paper, feathers, and other light objects, and carried them around with it in its rotation; he likened this to the action of the earth carrying along with it the objects on or near its surface. He verified electrical repulsion by showing that a feather, placed between the electrified ball and the floor, jumped up and down from one to the other. He pioneered in studying conduction by proving that an electric charge could travel along a linen thread, and that bodies could become electrified by being brought near to the electrified ball. Francis Hauksbee, of the Royal Society, developed (1705–9) a better method of generating electricity by rapidly rotating an exhausted glass ball, and then applying it to his hand; the contacts gave off sparks an inch long, providing light enough for reading. Another Englishman, Wall, having produced similar sparks, likened their sound and light to thunder and lightning (1708). Newton made the same comparison in 1716; Franklin confirmed the relation in 1749. So, year by year, and mind by mind, the impenetrable immensity surrenders some teasing, luring fragment of its mystery.

VI. CHEMISTRY

This remarkable century saw the science of chemistry evolve from the experiments and vagaries of alchemy. Industry had long been accumulating chemical knowledge through such operations as smelting iron, tanning leather, mixing dyes, brewing beer; but the investigation of substances in their composition, combination, and transformation had been for the most part left to alchemists seeking gold, or to pharmacologists concocting drugs, or to philosophers, from Democritus to Descartes, puzzling over the constitution of matter. Some approach to chemistry had been made by Andreas Libavius in 1597 and by Jan van Helmont in 1640; but both of these men shared the alchemist's hope of transmuting "base" metal into gold. Boyle himself made experiments with this aim. In 1689 he secured repeal of an old English statute against "multiplying gold and silver,"[43] and at his death (1691) he left to his executors a quantity of red earth with instructions for trying to turn it into gold.[44] Now that the transmutation of metals is a cliché of chemistry we can applaud the science in alchemy while condemning and concealing the itch for gold.

The greatest blow to alchemy was the publication of Boyle's *Sceptical Chymist* (1661)—the prime classic in the history of chemistry. He apologized for "suffering" his treatise "to pass abroad so maimed and imperfect,"[45] but, with his many ailments, he was never confident of much longer life. He was consoled to "observe that of late chymistry begins, as indeed it deserves, to be cultivated by learned men who before despised it."[46] He called his chemistry skeptical because he proposed to reject all mystical explanations and occult qualities as the "sanctuary of ignorance," and was resolved to rely upon "experiments rather than syllogisms."[47] He abandoned the traditional division of matter into the four elements of air, fire, water, and earth; these, he argued, were compounds, not elements; the real elements were rather "certain primitive and simple, or perfectly unmingled bodies, which, not being made of any other bodies or of one another," are the ingredients of all compounds, and into which all compounds may be resolved. He did not mean that the elements were the ultimate constituents of matter; these *minima naturalia*, he thought, were tiny particles, invisible to the eye, and differing in shape and size, like the atoms of Leucippus. From the diversity and motion of these particles, and their union in "corpuscles," all bodies, and all their qualities and conditions, like color, magnetism, heat, and fire, arise by purely mechanical means and laws.

Fire was as fascinating to scientists as to dreamers at the hearth. What made a substance burn? How explain those ever-changing tongues of flame, beautiful, imperious, and terrible? In 1669 a German chemist, Johann Joachim Becher, reduced all "elements" to two—water and earth; one form of the latter he called "oily earth," which he believed present in all combustible bodies; this it was that burned. In the eighteenth century Georg Stahl, following this false lead, was to set chemistry askew for decades with his similar theory of "phlogiston." Boyle took another cue. Noting that various burning substances ceased to burn in a vacuum, he concluded that "there is in the air a little vital quintessence . . . which serves to the refreshment and restoration of our vital spirits."[48] His younger contemporary John Mayow, also of the Royal Society, advanced (1647) toward our current theory of fire by positing among the constituents of air a substance that unites with metals when they are calcined (oxidized); and he believed that a similar substance, entering our bodies, changes venous into arterial blood. A hundred years had to pass before Scheele and Priestley would definitely discover oxygen.

About 1670 a German alchemist, Hennig Brand, discovered that he could obtain from human urine a chemical that glowed in the dark without preliminary exposure to light. A Dresden chemist, Kraft, exhibited the new product before Charles II at London in 1677. Boyle drew from the secretive Kraft only the admission that the luminous substance "was somewhat that belonged to the body of man."[49] The hint proved enough: Boyle soon obtained his own supply of phosphorus, and by a series of experiments he established all that is yet known about the glowing of that element. The new product cost its purchasers six guineas ($315?) per ounce, despite the abundance of the source.

VII. TECHNOLOGY

Until the nineteenth century more stimulus was given by industry to science than by science to industry; and until the twentieth century inventions were made less often in the laboratory than in the shop or field. In the most important case of all, the development of the steam engine, the two processes may have proceeded hand in hand.

Hero of Alexandria, in or before the third century A.D., made several steam engines, but, so far as we know, these were used as toys or marvels to amuse the multitude rather than as mechanisms replacing human energy. Early in the sixteenth century Leonardo da Vinci described a gun which by steam pressure could propel an iron bolt twelve hundred yards; but his scientific manuscripts remained unpublished till 1880. Some of Hero's Greek writings were translated into Latin in 1575, and into Italian in 1589. Jerome Cardan (1550) and Giambattista della Porta (1601) pointed out that a vacuum could be produced by the condensation of steam, and Porta described a machine for using the pressure of steam to raise a column of water. Similar applications of expanding steam were proposed by Salomon de Caus at Paris in 1615 and by Branca at Rome in 1629; and in 1630 David Ramsay obtained from Charles I of England a patent for machines "to raise water from low pits by fire . . . to make any sort of mills to go on standing waters by continual motion, without help of wind, waite [weight?], or horse."[50] In 1663 Edward Somerset, Marquis of Worcester, received from Parliament a ninety-nine-year monopoly on "the most stupendous work in the whole world"—a "water-commanding engine" that raised water to a height of forty feet;[51] by this mechanism he proposed to operate waterworks for a large part of London, but he died before he could put his plans into effect. About 1675 Samuel Morland, master mechanic to Charles II, invented the plunger pump, and in 1685 he published the first accurate description of the expansive power of steam. In 1680 Huygens made the first gas engine with cylinder and piston driven by the expansive force of exploding gunpowder.

Huygens' French assistant, Denis Papin, went to England, worked with Boyle, and published in 1681 an account of a "digester"—a pressure cooker —to soften bones by water boiling in a closed vessel. To prevent explosion he attached to the top of the vessel a tube that could be opened when the pressure reached a certain point; this first "safety valve" played a saving role in the development of the steam engine. Papin went on to show that the power of expanding steam could be piped pneumatically from one place to another. Moving to Marburg in Germany, he demonstrated (1690) the first engine in which the condensation of steam, producing a vacuum, was used to drive a piston. He suggested the possibilities of this machine for throwing bombs, raising water from mines, and propelling ships by paddle wheels; and in 1707 (precisely a century before Fulton's *Clermont* moved up the Hudson River) he used his steam engine to drive a paddle-wheel boat on the River Fulda at Cassel.[52] This boat, however, was wrecked, and the German authorities, comfortable in the *status quo,* and perhaps fearing the spread of unemployment, discouraged the development of mechanical power.[53]

A similar apparatus had been offered to the Navy Board in England about 1700 by Thomas Savery, but had been turned down with the alleged comment, "What have interloping people, that have no concern with us, to do to pretend to contrive or invent things for us?"[54] Savery demonstrated his device on the Thames, but the Navy again rejected it. In 1698 Savery patented the first steam engine actually employed to pump water out of mines. In 1699 he was awarded a patent granting him for fourteen years "the sole exercise of a new invention . . . for raising water and occasioning motion by the impellant force of fire; which will be of great use for draining mines, serving towns with water, and for the working of all sorts of mills."[55] Savery's engines, however, proved costly and dangerous: they had gauge cocks but no safety valves; they were subject to boiler explosions; and though they were used in some mines to pump out water, the mine owners soon returned to the employment of horses.

At this point in the story we again meet Robert Hooke. About 1702, according to a reliable contemporary, he corresponded with a Dartmouth ironmonger and blacksmith, Thomas Newcomen, on the possibility of using the air-pump principle to produce mechanical power. "Could you make a speedy vacuum under your second cylinder," he wrote, "your work is done."[56] Apparently Newcomen had been experimenting with a steam engine; here science and industry visibly touched. Hooke was skeptical, let the matter drop, and again missed an opportunity. Newcomen joined with a plumber, John Cawley, to build (1712) a steam engine—with rocking beam, piston, and safety valve—that could be trusted to do heavy work without danger of explosion, and with fully automatic control. Newcomen continued till his death (1729) to improve his engine; but we may date from Savery's patent in 1699, and Newcomen's engine of 1712, the beginnings of the Industrial Revolution that in the next two centuries would change the face and air of the world.

VIII. BIOLOGY

The remarkable group of investigators that made the glory of the Royal Society extended its researches into the sciences of life. The omnipresent Hooke demonstrated experimentally what Sir Kenelm Digby—that "arrant mountebank," as Evelyn called him[51]—had already pointed out: that plants need air for their life. He sowed lettuce seed in soil under the open sky, and, at the same time, similar seed in similar soil in a vacuum chamber; the first grew an inch and a half in eight days, the other not at all. Hooke identified the part of the air used up in combustion with the part used up in plant and animal respiration, and described this used part as nitrous in character (1665). He showed that animals which had stopped breathing could be kept alive by blowing air into their lungs with bellows. He discovered the cellular structure of living tissue, and invented the term *cell* for its organic constituents. Through his microscope the members of the Society saw with delight the cells of cork, whereof, Hooke estimated, one cubic inch contained 1,200,000,000 cells. He studied the histology of insects and plants, and gave novel drawings of them in his *Micrographia*. Hooke was always on the verge of ranking with Galileo and Newton.

Another member of the society, John Ray, shared in giving its modern form to the science of botany. He was the son of a blacksmith, but he made his way to Cambridge, became a fellow of Trinity College, and was ordained an Anglican priest. Like Boyle, he gave his devotion to religion as well as to science. Because he would not sign the Act of Uniformity (1662) pledging nonresistance to Charles II, he resigned his fellowship, and set out with his pupil Francis Willughby on a tour of Europe to gather data for a systematic description of the animal and plant kingdoms. Willughby undertook the zoology, but died after completing the sections on birds and fishes. In 1670 Ray issued a *Catalogus Plantarum Angliae*, which became the frame of English botany. Helped by the improved terminology and classification established in 1678 by Joachim Jungius, Ray proposed a *Methodus Plantarum Nova* (1682), which divided all flowering plants into dicotyledons and monocotyledons according to their having two seed leaves or only one. He completed his great task in one of the *chefs-d'oeuvre* of modern science, the massive three-volume *Historia Generalis Plantarum* (1682–1704), which described 18,625 species of plants. Ray was the first to use the word *species* in its biological sense, as a group of organisms derived from similar parents and capable of reproducing their kind. This definition, and the later classification by Linnaeus (1751), set the stage for the controversy over the origin and mutability of species. Meanwhile Ray edited Willughby's manuscripts on ichthyology and ornithology, and added a *Synopsis Methodica Animalium Quadrupedum* (1693), providing for modern zoology the first really scientific classification of animals.[58] Order was Ray's first law.

Even in antiquity botanists had recognized that some plants might be termed female because they bore fruit, and others male because they did not, and Theophrastus, in the third century before Christ, had observed that the female date palm produces fruit only if the dust of the male date palm has been shaken over it; but these ideas had been almost forgotten. In 1682 Nehemiah Grew, of the Royal Society, gave a new charm to flowers by definitely affirming the sexuality of plants. Studying plant tissues under the microscope, he noted the pores in the upper surface of leaves, and suggested that leaves are organs of respiration. Flowers he described as organs of reproduction: the pistils as female, the stamens as male, the pollen as seed. He mistakenly assumed that all plants are hermaphrodites, uniting male and female structures in one organism. In 1691 Rudolf Camerarius, professor of botany at Tübingen, definitely proved the sexuality of plants by showing that they would bear no fruit after the removal of their anthers—the pollen-containing part of the stamens.

On the same day (December 7, 1671) that the Royal Society of London received Grew's first essay (*The Anatomy of Vegetables Begun*) it received also a manuscript from Marcello Malpighi of Bologna. The Society published it (1675) as *Anatomes Plantarum Idea;* the use of Latin was still facilitating the international of science. Malpighi divided with Grew the honor of establishing the histology of plants, but his major contribution was to zoology. In 1676 Mariotte, by chemically analyzing the residue of plants and the soil in which they had grown, showed that they absorb nutritive elements in the water that they suck from the earth. Neither Mariotte nor Grew nor Malpighi recognized the power of plants to take nourishment from the air; but the processes of nutrition and reproduction now discovered were a vast advance upon Aristotle's vague explanation of plant growth by the expansive ambitions of the "vegetable soul."

An old and popular notion received in 1668 the first of several shocks when Francesco Redi of Arezzo published his *Esperienze intorno alla generazione degli insetti*—experiments tending to disprove abiogenesis, or the spontaneous generation of living organisms from nonliving matter. Until the second half of the seventeenth century it was almost universally believed (William Harvey an outstanding exception) that minute animals and plants could be generated in dirt or slime, and especially in decaying flesh; so Shakespeare spoke of "the sun breeding maggots in dead dogs."[59] Redi showed that maggots did not form on meat that was protected from insects, but did form on meat exposed. He formulated his conclusion in the phrase *Omne vivum ex ovo*—"Every living thing comes from an egg or a seed." When protozoa were discovered, the argument for abiogenesis was revived; Spallanzani answered it in 1767, and Pasteur again in 1861.

The discovery of those single-celled organisms which were later termed protozoa was the major contribution of this age to zoology. Anton van Leeuwenhoek was a Dutchman of Delft, but he reported through the Royal Society at London his scientific results through forty of his ninety-one years. Coming of a family of rich brewers, he was able to accept employments that offered him more leisure than pay, and he gave himself with fascinated pertinacity to studying the new world of life revealed by the microscope. He had 247 of these instruments, most of them made by himself, and his laboratory sparkled with 419 lenses, some of which may have been ground by Spinoza, who had been born in the same year (1632) and the same land as he. Peter the Great, when in Delft in 1698, made it a point to peer through Leeuwenhoek's microscopes. When (1675) the scientist turned one of these to the study of some rain water that had fallen into a pot a few days before, he was astonished to see "little animals appearing to me ten thousand times less than those represented by Mons. Swammerdam and by him called water fleas or water lice, which may be perceived in the water with the naked eye";[60] and he proceeded to describe an organism that we now recognize as the bell animalcule (*Vorticella*). This was apparently the earliest description of a protozoon. In 1683 Leeuwenhoek discovered still tinier organisms—bacteria. He found them first on his own teeth, "though my teeth," he protested, "are kept usually very clean"; and he startled some neighbors by examining their spittle and showing them, under the microscope, "a great many living creatures" therein.[61] In 1677 he discovered spermatozoa in semen. He marveled at nature's profuse equipment for reproduction: in a small quantity of human semen he estimated a thousand spermatozoa; and he calculated that in the milt of a single codfish there were 150 billion sperm—more than ten times the number of inhabitants that the earth would contain if all the land were as thickly populated as the Netherlands.

Jan Swammerdam was five years younger than Leeuwenhoek, but preceded him by forty-three years to the grave; he was a man of nerves, passions, ailments, and fluctuating purposes, who stopped his scientific work at thirty-six and burned himself out at forty-three (1680). He was intended for the ministry, but abandoned theology for medicine. Having secured his medical degree, he devoted himself to anatomy. He became enamored of bees, and especially of their intestines; he spent his days in dissecting them, his nights in reporting and illustrating his findings. When he had finished his classic treatise on bees (1673) he broke down physically; soon thereafter he gave up science as too worldly a pursuit, and returned to religion. Fifty-seven years after his death his manuscripts were collected and published as *Biblia Naturae*, the Bible of nature. This contained, in remarkably exact detail, the life history of a dozen typical insects, including the May fly and the honey bee, and microscopic studies of the squid, the snail, the clam, and the frog. Here, too, were descriptions of the experiments by which Swammerdam proved that muscles in tissues cut off from an animal's body could be made to contract by stimulation of the connecting nerve. Like Redi he rejected abiogenesis; he went further, and showed that instead of decaying flesh producing minute organisms, it is these that produce decay in organic matter. In his brief career Swammerdam founded modern entomology, and established himself as one of the most accurate observers in the history of science. His return from science to religion personified the hesitation of modern man between a search for truth that smiles at hope and a retreat to hopes that shy from truth.

IX. ANATOMY AND PHYSIOLOGY

The human body, subjected to the microscope, gave up some of its intimate secrets to the advancing army of science. In 1651 Jean Pecquet of Paris traced the course of the lacteal vessels; in 1653 Olof Rudbeck of Uppsala discovered, and Thomas Bartholin of Copenhagen described, the lymphatic system; and in 1664 Swammerdam detected the lymphatic valves. In that year his friend Regnier de Graaf demonstrated the function and operation of the pancreas and the bile. In 1661 Nicolaus Steno, another friend, discovered the duct (still bearing his name) of the parotid gland, and a year later the lachrymal ducts of the eye. Graaf studied especially the anatomy of testicles and ovaries; in 1672 he gave the first account of those ovum-bearing sacs which Haller in his honor called the Graafian follicles. Bartholin left his card on two oval bodies adjoining the vagina, and William Cowper (physician, not poet) found (1702), and gave his name to, the glands that discharge into the urethra. Franciscus Sylvius (beloved teacher of Graaf, Swammerdam, Steno, and Willis at Leiden) left his signature on a fissure of the brain (1663). Thomas Willis, a founder of the Royal Society, published in 1664 a *Cerebri Anatome* which was the most complete account yet given of the nervous system; his name is still borne by the "circle of Willis," a hexagonal network of arteries at the base of the brain.

The outstanding anatomist of the age was Marcello Malpighi. Born near Bologna in 1628, he took his degree in medicine there; after some professorial years in Pisa and Messina he returned to Bologna, and taught medicine in the university for twenty-five years. After working on the microscopic anatomy of plants he turned his lenses upon the silkworm, and recorded his findings in a classic monograph. In this investigation he nearly lost his eyesight; nevertheless, "in performing these researches," he wrote, "so many marvels of nature were spread before my eyes that I experienced an internal pleasure that my pen could not describe."[62] He must have felt like Keats first looking into Chapman's Homer when (1661) he saw, in the lungs of the frog, how the blood passed from the arteries into the veins through vessels so fine that he called them "capillaries"; he found a network of such "little hairs" wherever arterial became venous blood; now, for the first time, the circulatory system was demonstrated in its course.

This was but a part, though the most important, of Malpighi's contributions to anatomy. He was the first to prove that the papillae of the tongue are organs of taste; the first to distinguish the red corpuscles in the blood (but he mistook them to be globules of fat); the first to give an accurate account of the nervous and circulatory systems in the embryo; the first to describe the histology of the cortex and the spinal cord; the first to make possible a practical theory of respiration by describing with precision the vesicular structure of the lungs. Justly his name is scattered over our flesh in the "Malpighian tufts," or loops of capillaries, in the kidneys, in the "Malpighian corpuscles" of the spleen, in the "Malpighian layer" of the skin. Many of his revelations and interpretations were challenged by his contemporaries; he defended himself vigorously, and won his battles at some cost to his nerves. As if laying these matters before the supreme court of science in his age, he sent to the Royal Society at London an account of his labors, discoveries, and controversies; the Society published this as his autobiography. In 1691 he was appointed personal physician to Pope Innocent XII, but he died in 1694 of an apoplectic stroke. His detection of the capillaries is one of the landmarks in the history of anatomy; his work as a whole established the science of histology.

As anatomical research progressed it revealed so many similarities between human and animal organs that some students were led close to a theory of evolution. Edward Tyson (whose name is given to the sebaceous glands of the foreskin) published in 1699 *Orang-Outang, sive Homo Sylvestris,* describing the orangutan as a "man of the woods"; he compared the anatomy of man with that of the monkey, and reckoned the chimpanzee to be intermediate between the two. Only the fear of a theological earthquake kept biology from anticipating Darwin in the seventeenth century.

From anatomy and structure the researchers passed to physiology and function. Till about 1660 respiration had been interpreted as a cooling process; now the experimenters likened it to combustion. Hooke proved that the essence of respiration is the exposure of venous blood to fresh air in the lungs. Richard Lower, also of the Royal Society, showed (1669) that venous blood could be changed to arterial by aeration, and that arterial blood became venous when persistently kept from contact with air. He suggested that the chief agent in aeration is a "nitrous spirit" in the atmosphere. Following these leads, Lower's friend John Mayow described this active factor as "nitro-aerial particles." In respiration, he believed, the nitrous particles are absorbed from the air into the blood; hence air exhaled is lighter in weight and less in volume than the same air inhaled. Animal heat is due to the union of nitrous particles with combustible elements in the blood; increased heat after exercise results from the extra intake of nitrous particles through increased respiration. These nitrous particles, said Mayow, play the leading role in the life of animals and plants.

The interpretation of vital processes led to one of the most indestructible controversies in the history of modern science. As physiology delved more and more curiously into the human anatomy, one after another function of the body seemed to yield to a mechanical interpretation in terms of physics and chemistry. Respiration appeared to be a combination of expansion, aeration, and contraction; the functions of the saliva, the bile, and the pancreatic juice were obviously chemical; and Gian Alfonso Borelli apparently brought to completion (1679) the mechanical analysis of muscular action. Steno, the fervent Catholic, adopted the mechanical view of physiological processes, and dismissed as "mere words meaning nothing" such vague phrases as Galen's "animal spirits." Descartes' conception of the body as a machine seemed now fully justified.

Nevertheless most scientists felt that these bodily mechanisms were merely the instruments of some vital principle beyond analysis in physicochemical terms. Francis Glisson, a founder of the Royal Society, ascribed to all living substance a characteristic "irritability"—susceptibility to stimulation—which he thought to be absent from nonliving matter. Just as Newton, after reducing the cosmos to mechanism, ascribed the initial impetus of the world machine to God, so Borelli, after giving a mechanical explanation of the muscular processes, posited within the human body a soul from which all animal motion took its origin.[63] Claude Perrault, architect and physician, suggested (1680) that physiological actions that now seem mechanical were formerly voluntary, guided by a soul, but became mechanical through frequent repetition, like the formation of habits; perhaps even the heart had once been controlled by the will.[64] Georg Stahl argued (1702) that the chemical changes in living tissue are different from those seen in laboratories, for in living animals, he believed, the chemical changes are governed by an *anima sensitiva* which pervades all parts of the body. The soul, said Stahl, directs every physiological function, even digestion and respiration; it builds each organ, indeed the whole body, as an instrument of desire.[65] Diseases, he surmised, are processes by which the soul strives to remove something that hinders its operations; and he foreshadowed a twentieth-century "psychosomatic" theory by holding that disturbances of the "sensitive soul" can produce bodily ailments.[66]

In one form or another vitalistic conceptions held the ascendancy in science till the second half of the nineteenth century. They yielded for a time to the rising prestige of mechanical physics; and they were revived, with the charm of literature, in Bergson's *Creative Evolution* (1906). The debate will go on until the part understands the whole.

X. MEDICINE

The strongest stimulus to the biological sciences came from the needs of medicine. Botany, before Ray, had been the handmaiden of pharmacy.

Health was the *summum bonum*, and men, women, and children sought it through prayers, stars, kings, toads, and science. One physician, before prescribing, "went to his closet to pray," says Aubrey,[67] so that at last "his knees were horny" with orisons. Astrology still took a hand in medicine; the surgeon in ordinary of Louis XIV advised that the King be bled only in the first and last quarters of the moon, "because at this time the humors have retired to the center of the body."[68] Defoe thought that the money spent upon quacks would have paid off the national debt.[69] Flamsteed, the astronomer royal, traveled miles to have his back stroked by the famous quack Valentine Greatrakes, who proposed so simply to cure scrofula. Perhaps Flamsteed was among the 100,000 whom Charles II touched for scrofula—the "King's evil." In the one year 1682 the complaisant ruler touched 8,500 sufferers; in 1684 the press to get to him was so great that six of the sick were trampled to death. William III refused to go on with the play. "It is a silly superstition," he exlaimed when a crowd besieged his palace. "Give the poor creatures some money, and send them away." On another occasion, when he was importuned to lay his hand on a patient, he yielded, but said, "God give you better health and more sense." The people denounced him as an infidel.[70]

Defects of personal hygiene and public sanitation co-operated with the resilient ingenuity of disease. Prostitution spread syphilis in cities and camps. It was especially rife among actors and actresses, as we gather from a subtle story in Mme. de Sévigné of "a player who, being resolved to marry though he labored under a certain dangerous disorder, one of his companions said to him, 'Zounds! can't you wait till you are cured? You will be the ruin of us all.' "[71] The French general Vendôme appeared at court without a nose, having sacrificed it to the spirochetes.[72] Cancer was on its way; Mme. de Motteville describes a cancer of the breast.[73] Yellow fever was first described in 1694. Smallpox was especially widespread in England; no cure was yet known for it; Queen Mary died of it, and Marlborough's son. Epidemics, particularly of malaria, ran through whole countries; in 1657, reported Thomas Willis, almost all England was a hospital treating malarial fever.[74] Plague devastated London in 1665, killed 100,000 in Vienna in 1679, and 83,000 in Prague in 1681.[75] Occupational diseases increased with industry: Bernardino Ramazzini, professor of medicine at Padua, issued in 1700 a classic treatise, *De morbis artificum*, on the damage done to painters by the chemicals in their paint, to workers in colored glass from antimony, to masons and miners from tuberculosis, to potters from vertigo, to printers from eye troubles, to physicians from the mercury they applied.

Amid ignorance and poverty the science of medicine slowly advanced. The thirst for money hampered the profession; some doctors who had made successful cures refused to reveal to other doctors the treatment they had used.[76] The medical members of the Royal Society rose above this greed, and zealously shared their discoveries with their fellows. There were now good medical schools, led by those at Leiden, Bologna, and Montpellier; and generally a degree from a recognized institution was required for the legal practice of medicine in Western Europe. The teachers of the art continued their division into two schools of treatment. Borelli defended "iatrophysical" therapy, proposing to deal with diseases as derangements of the body's mechanism. Sylvius, developing the arguments of Paracelsus and Helmont, advocated the "iatrochemical" method of using drugs to counteract disturbances in the "humours" of the body; most of these, he thought, were due to hyperacidity. More fruitful than these general theories were discoveries in the causes of specific diseases; so Sylvius first described tubercles in the lungs, and related these morbid growths to consumption.

One of the most basic discoveries of this age was the work of that remarkable Jesuit, Athanasius Kircher of Fulda, mathematician, physicist, Orientalist, musician, and physician, and apparently the first to use the microscope in investigating disease.[77] With this aid he found that the blood of plague victims contained numberless "worms" invisible to the naked eye. He saw similar animalcules in putrefying matter, and ascribed putrefaction and many diseases to their activity. He reported his findings in *Scrutinium pestis* (Rome, 1658), which first stated in explicit terms what Fracastoro had only suggested in 1546—the doctrine that the transfer of noxious organisms from one person or animal to another is the cause of infectious disease.[78]

Medical treatment lagged behind medical research, for those who excelled in research tended to form a class distinct from those who practiced, and their communication was imperfect. Some medieval cures were still prescribed. Aubrey records an untimely success: "A woman . . . endeavored to poison her husband (who was a dropsical man) by boiling a toad in his potage; which cured him; and this was the occasion of finding out the medicine."[79] Some new drugs entered the pharmacopoeia in the second half of the seventeenth century: ipecacuanha, cascara, peppermint . . . Dutch physicians, favoring Dutch commerce, prescribed tea as almost a panacea.[80]

Two Dutchmen were the greatest medical teachers of the age: Sylvius and Boerhaave, both at Leiden. Hermann Boerhaave taught chemistry, physics, and botany as well; students came to him from all northern Europe; and he raised the status of clinical medicine by taking his maturer pupils with him on his daily rounds of the hospital beds, instructing them by direct observation and specific treatment of each individual case. His works were translated into all major European languages, even Turkish; his reputation reached to China itself.

In England clinical medicine had its finest exponent in Thomas Sydenham. After two stays at Oxford, separated by terms of service in the army, he settled in London as a general practitioner. With little theory and much experience, he came to his philosophy of disease, which he defined as "an effort of nature striving with all her might to restore the health of the patient by eliminating morbid matter."[81] He distinguished "essential" symptoms as those caused by the foreign substance, and "accidental" as those caused by the body's resistance to it; so fever is not an illness but a device of the organism in its self-defense. The problem of the physician is to help this process of defense. Hence Sydenham praised Hippocrates because the "Father of Medicine"

> required no more of art than to assist nature when she languished, and to check her when her efforts were too violent. . . . For this sagacious observer found that nature alone terminates distemper, and works a cure with the assistance of a few simple medicines, and sometimes even without any medicines at all.[82]

Sydenham's distinction lay in recognizing that each major disease has many varieties; he studied each case with its clinical record, in order to diagnose the special form of the disease involved; and he adjusted the treatment to the specific differences of the ailment. So he separated scarlatina from measles, and gave it its current name. He was known to his profession as "the English Hippocrates," because he subordinated theory to observation, general ideas to particular cases, and drugs to natural cures. His *Processus Integri* remained for a century the English practitioner's manual of therapy.

Surgery continued to struggle for recognition as a reputable science. Its ablest representatives found themselves pressed on either side by the hostility of physicians and the envy of barbers—who still performed some minor operations, including dentistry. Guy Patin, dean of the faculty of medicine in the University of Paris, could not forgive surgeons for assuming the dress and manners of the medical profession, and he denounced all surgeons as "a race of evil, extravagant coxcombs who wear mustaches and flourish razors."[83] But in 1686 the surgeon Félix operated successfully upon Louis XIV's fistula; the King was so pleased that he gave Félix fifteen thousand louis d'or, a country estate, and a patent of nobility. This elevation raised the social status of surgeons in France. In 1699 surgery was decreed to be a liberal art, and its exponents began to assume a high rank in French society. Voltaire called surgery "the most useful of all the arts," and "the one in which the French excelled all other nations in the world."[84]

English surgery, however, had at least two credits in this age: in 1662 J. D. Major made the first successful intravenous injection in man, and in

1665–67 Richard Lower succeeded in transfusing blood from one animal into the veins of another; Pepys noted this latter event in his diary.[85] From that private gossip sheet we gather that operations were usually performed with only feeble anesthetics or none: when Pepys was operated on for stone in his bladder he received no chloroform and no antiseptics, but only "a soothing draught."[86]

Satires of the physician continued as in every generation. People resented his fees, his pompous dress in gown, wig, and conical hat, his grandiloquent speech, and his sometimes mortal mistakes. Boyle said that many people feared the doctor more than the disease.[87] Molière's caricatures of the great profession were for the most part the good-natured fun of a man who nevertheless took care to keep on amiable terms with his physician. After all darts had been thrown it remained that the seventeenth century had seen a creditable advance in medical science through a hundred discoveries in anatomy, physiology, and chemistry, that the international exchange of medical knowledge was increasing, that notable teachers were sending out able pupils to all parts of Western Europe, that surgery was improving its methods and status, that specialists were developing greater knowledge and skill, and that more measures were being taken to promote public health. Municipal governments legislated sanitation. In 1656, when plague appeared in Rome, Monsignor Gastaldi, papal commissioner of health, made mandatory the cleansing of streets and sewers, the regular inspection of aqueducts, the provision of public facilities for the disinfection of clothing, and the requirement of health certificates from all persons entering the city.[88] As wealth rose, men built sturdier houses that could keep rats at a respectful distance and so reduce the spread of plague. Better supplies of water—the first necessity of civilization—enabled the willing body to be clean. For more and more people it was becoming physically possible to be civilized.

XI. RESULTS

All in all, the seventeenth century was one of the peak periods in the history of science. See it in its arching gamut, from Bacon calling men to labor for the advancement of learning, and Descartes marrying algebra to geometry; through the improvement of telescopes, microscopes, barometers, thermometers, air pumps and mathematics; through Kepler's planetary laws, Galileo's swelling firmament, Harvey's charting of the blood, Guericke's obstinate hemispheres, Boyle's skeptical chemistry, Huygens' multifarious physics, Hooke's polymorphous tentatives, and Halley's cometary predictions, culminating in Leibniz' notational calculus and Newton's cosmic synthesis: what previous century had equaled that performance? The modern mind, said Alfred North Whitehead, has "been living upon the accumulated capital of ideas provided for it by the genius of the seventeenth century" in science, literature, and philosophy.[89]

The influence of science spread in widening arcs. It affected industry by supplying the physics and chemistry for new ventures in technology. In education it compelled a lessening of emphasis on the humanities—on literature, history, and philosophy; for the development of industry, commerce, and navigation demanded practical knowledge and minds. Literature itself felt the new influence: the scientist's pursuit of order, precision, and clarity suggested similar virtues in poetry and prose, and accorded well with the classic style exemplified by Molière, Boileau, and Racine, by Addison, Swift, and Pope. The Royal Society, according to its historian, required of its members "a close, naked, natural way of speaking, . . . bringing all things as near to mathematical plainness as they can."[90]

The triumphs of mathematics and physics, giving period to comets and laws to stars, affected philosophy and religion. Descartes and Spinoza accepted geometry as the ideal of philosophy and exposition. There seemed no need, henceforth, to posit in the universe anything but matter and motion. Descartes saw all the world, except the human and divine mind, as a machine; Hobbes challenged the exception, and formulated a materialism in which even religion would be a tool of the state for manipulating human machines. The new physics, chemistry, and astronomy seemed to show a universe operating according to invariable laws; this cosmos allowed no miracles, therefore answered no prayers, therefore needed no God. Perhaps He could be kept to give the world machine an inaugural push; but thereafter he might retire to be an Epicurean-Lucretian deity, mindless of the world and men. Halley was said to have assured a friend of Berkeley that "the doctrines of Christianity" were now "inconceivable."[91] Boyle, however, saw in the revelations of science additional evidence of the existence of God. "The world," he wrote, "behaves as if there were diffused throughout the universe an intelligent being"; and in a sentence recalling Pascal he added, "The soul of man [is] a nobler and more valuable being than the whole corporeal world."[92] Dying, Boyle left a fund to finance lectures that would demonstrate the truth of Christianity against "notorious infidels, viz., atheists, theists, pagans, Jews, and Mohammedans," to which he added a proviso that the lectures must not mention the controversies among Christians.[93]

Many scientists agreed with Boyle, and many believing Christians joined in praising science. "In these last hundred years," said Dryden at the close of the century, "almost a new Nature has been revealed to us—more errors . . . have been detected, more useful experiments have been made, more noble secrets in optics, medicine, anatomy, and astronomy have been discovered, than in all these doting and credulous ages from Aristotle to us."[94] This was a wild but significant exaggeration, revealing the conviction of the "moderns" that they had won the battle of the books with the "ancients." In any case men could not but see that the sciences were increasing human knowledge while religions quarreled and statesmen warred. Science now rose to a new status of honor among human enterprises; indeed, by the end of this epoch it was already being hailed as the harbinger of Utopia and the savior of mankind. "The application of science to nature," said Fontenelle in 1702, "will constantly grow in scope and intensity, and we shall go on from one marvel to another. The day will come when man will be able to fly by fitting on wings to keep him in the air; the art will increase, . . . till one day we shall be able to fly to the moon."[95] Everything was progressing except man.

CHAPTER XIX

Isaac Newton

1642–1727

I. THE MATHEMATICIAN

HE WAS born in a small farm at Woolsthorpe, in the county of Lincoln, on December 25, 1642 (Old Style)—the year in which Galileo died; cultural, like economic, leadership was passing from the south to the north. At birth he was so small that (his mother later told him) he might have been put into a quart mug, and so weak that no one thought he would live beyond a few days.[1] As his father had died some months earlier, the boy was brought up by his mother and an uncle.

At twelve he was sent to the public school at Grantham. He did not do well there; he was reported as "idle" and "inattentive," neglecting prescribed studies for subjects that appealed to him, and giving much time to mechanical contrivances like sundials, water wheels, and homemade clocks. After two years at Grantham he was taken from school to help his mother on the farm, but again he skimped his duties to read books and do mathematical problems. Another uncle, recognizing his ability, sent him back to school, and arranged for Newton's admission to Trinity College, Cambridge (1661), as a subsizar—a student who earned his expenses by various services. He took his degree four years later, and was soon thereafter elected a fellow of the college. He dealt chiefly with mathematics, optics, astronomy, and astrology; in this last study he maintained interest till late in his life.

In 1669 his mathematics teacher, Isaac Barrow, resigned; and on Barrow's recommendation of him as an "unparalleled genius," Newton was appointed to succeed him; he held this chair at Trinity for thirty-four years. He was not a successful teacher. "So few went to hear him," his secretary recalled, "and fewer that understood him, that ofttimes he did in a manner, for want of hearers, read to the walls."[2] On some occasions he had no auditors at all, and returned sadly to his room. There he built a laboratory—the only one then to be found in Cambridge. He made many experiments, mainly in alchemy, "the transmuting of metals being his chief design";[3] but also he was interested in the "elixir of life" and the "philosopher's stone."[4] He continued his alchemist studies from 1661 to 1692, and even while writing the *Principia*;[5] he left unpublished manuscripts on alchemy totaling 100,000 words or more, "wholly devoid of value."[6] Boyle and other members of the Royal Society were feverishly engaged in the same quest for manufacturing gold. Newton's aim was not clearly commercial; he never showed any eagerness for material gains; probably he was seeking some law or process by which the elements could be interpreted as transmutable variations of one basic substance. We cannot be sure that he was wrong.

Outside his rooms at Cambridge he had a small garden; there he took short walks, soon interrupted by some idea which he hurried to his desk to record. He sat little, but rather walked about his room so much that (said his secretary) "you might have thought him . . . among the Aristotelian sect" of Peripatetics.[7] He ate sparingly, often skipped a meal, forgot that he had missed it, and grudged the time he had to give to eating and sleeping. "He rarely went to dine in the hall; and then, if he had not been [re]minded, would go very carelessly, with shoes down at the heels, stockings untied . . . and his head scarcely combed."[8] Many stories were told, and many were invented, about his absent-mindedness. On awakening from sleep, we are assured, he might sit on his bed for hours undressed, engrossed in thought.[9] When he had visitors he would sometimes disappear into another room, jot down ideas, and quite forget his company.[10]

During those thirty-five years at Cambridge he was a monk of science. He drew up "rules of philosophizing"—i.e., of scientific method and research. He rejected the rules which Descartes in his *Discours* had set up as a priori principles from which all major truths were to be derived by deduction. When Newton said, *"Non fingo hypotheses"*—I do not invent hypotheses[11]—he meant that he offered no theories as to anything beyond observation of phenomena; so he would hazard no guess as to the nature of gravitation, but would only describe its behavior and formulate its laws. He did not pretend to avoid hypotheses as cues to experiments; on the contrary, his laboratory was devoted to testing a thousand ideas and possibilities, and his record was littered with hypotheses tried and rejected. Nor did he repudiate deduction; he merely insisted that it should start from facts and lead to principles. His method was to conceive possible solutions of a problem, work out their mathematical implications, and test these by computation and experiment. "The whole burden of [natural] philosophy," he wrote, "seems to consist in this—from the phenomena of motions to investigate the forces of nature, and then from these forces to demonstrate the other phenomena."[12] He was a compound of mathematics and imagination, and no one can understand him who does not possess both.

Nevertheless we proceed. His fame has two foci—calculus and gravitation. He began his work on the calculus in 1665 by finding the tangent and radius of curvature at any point on a curve. He called his method not calculus but "fluxions," and gave for this term an explanation upon which we cannot improve:

> Lines are described, and thereby generated, not by the apposition of parts, but by the continued motion of points; superficies [planes] by the motion of lines; solids by the motion of superficies; angles by the rotation of the sides; portions of time by continual flux; and so in other quantities . . . Therefore, considering that quantities, which increase in equal times, and by increasing are generated, became greater or less according to the greater or less velocity with which they increase or are generated, I sought a method of determining quantities from the velocities of the motions or increments with which they are generated; and calling these velocities of the motions or increments *Fluxions*, and the generated quantities *Fluents*, I fell by degrees upon the Method of Fluxions . . . in the years 1665 and 1666.[13]

Newton described his method in a letter to Barrow in 1669, and referred to it in a letter to John Collins in 1672. He probably used the method in reaching some of the results in his *Principia* (1687), but his exposition there (probably for the convenience of his readers) followed accepted geometrical formulas. He contributed a statement of his fluxions procedure —but not over his own name—to Wallis' *Algebra* in 1693. Not till 1704, in an appendix to his *Opticks*, did he publish the account just quoted. It was characteristic of Newton to delay publication of his theories; perhaps he wished first to resolve the difficulties suggested by them. So he waited till 1676 to announce his binomial theorem,* though he had probably formulated it in 1665.

These deferments embroiled the mathematicians of Europe in a disgraceful controversy that for a generation disrupted the international of science. For between Newton's communication of his "fluxions" to his friends in 1669 and the publishing of the new method in 1704, Leibniz developed a rival system at Mainz and Paris. In 1671 he sent to the Académie des Sciences a paper containing the germ of the differential calculus.[14] On a visit to London, January to March, 1673, Leibniz met Oldenburg; he had already corresponded with him and Boyle; Newton's friends later believed—historians now doubt[15]—that Leibniz on this trip received some suggestion of Newton's fluxions. In June, 1676, at the request of Oldenburg and Collins, Newton wrote a letter for transmission to Leibniz, explaining his method of analysis. In August Leibniz replied to Oldenburg, including some examples of his own work in calculus; and in June, 1677, in a further

---

* By which any power of a binomial (an algebraic expression composed of two terms connected by a plus or minus sign) can be found by an algebraic formula instead of being worked out by multiplication. Newton had been partly anticipated in this theorem by Viète and Pascal.

letter to Oldenburg, he described his form of differential calculus, and his system of notation, which differed from Newton's. In the *Acta Eruditorum* for October, 1684, he again expounded the differential calculus, and in 1686 he published his system of integral calculus. In the first edition of the *Principia* (1687) Newton apparently accepted Leibniz's independent discovery of calculus:

> In letters which went between me and that most excellent geometer, G. W. Leibniz, ten years ago, when I signified that I was in the knowledge of a method of determining maxima and minima, of drawing tangents, and the like, . . . that most distinguished man wrote back that he had also fallen upon a method of the same kind, and communicated his method, which hardly differed from mine except . . . in his forms of words and symbols.[16]

This gentlemanly acknowledgment should have contracepted controversy. But in 1699 a Swiss mathematician, in a communication to the Royal Society, suggested that Leibniz had borrowed his calculus from Newton. In 1705 Leibniz, in an anonymous review of Newton's *Opticks*, implied that Newton's fluxions were an adaptation of the Leibnizian calculus. In 1712 the Royal Society appointed a committee to examine the documents involved. Before the year was out the Society published a report, *Commercium Epistolicum*, asserting the priority of Newton, but leaving open the question of Leibniz' originality. In a letter of April 9, 1716, to an Italian priest in London, Leibniz protested that Newton's scholium had settled the question. Leibniz died November 14, 1716. Soon afterward Newton denied that the scholium "allowed him [Leibniz] the invention of the *calculus differentialis* independently of my own." In the third edition of the *Principia* (1726) the scholium was omitted.[17] The dispute was hardly worthy of philosophers, since either claimant might have bowed to Fermat's priority.

II. THE PHYSICIST

Mathematics, however wonderful, was only a tool for calculating quantities; it did not profess to understand or describe reality. When Newton turned from the tool to the ultimate quest, he addressed himself first to the mystery of light. His first lectures at Cambridge were on light, color, and vision; characteristically he did not publish his *Opticks* till thirty-five years later, 1704. He had no itch to print.

In 1666 he bought a prism at Stourbridge Fair, and began optical experiments. From 1668 onward he made a succession of telescopes. Hoping to avoid some defects persisting in the refracting telescope, he made with his own hands a reflecting telescope, on theorems set forth by Mersenne (1639) and James Gregory (1662), and presented it to the Royal Society at its request in 1671. On January 11, 1672, he was elected to membership in the Society.

Even before making telescopes he had reached (1666) one of his basic discoveries—that white light, or sunlight, is not simple or homogeneous, but is a compound of red, orange, yellow, green, blue, indigo, and violet. When he passed a small ray of sunlight through a transparent prism he found that the apparently monochrome light divided into all these colors of the rainbow; that each component color emerged from the prism at its own specific angle or degree or refraction; and that the colors arranged themselves in a row of bands, forming a continuous spectrum, with red at one end and violet at the other. Later investigators showed that various substances, when made luminous by burning, give different spectra; by comparing these spectra with the one made by a given star, it became possible to analyze in some degree the star's chemical constituents. Still more delicate observations of a star's spectrum indicated its approximate rate of motion toward or from the earth; and from these calculations the distance of the star was theoretically deduced. Newton's revelation of the composition of light, and its refraction in the spectrum, has therefore had almost cosmic consequences in astronomy.

Hardly foreseeing these results, but feeling (as he wrote to Oldenburg) that he had made "the oddest if not the most considerable detection which hath hitherto been made in the operations of nature,"[18] Newton sent to the Royal Society early in 1672 a paper entitled "New Theory about Light and Colors." It was read to the members on February 8, and aroused a controversy that crossed the Channel to the Continent. Hooke had described in his *Micrographia* (1664) an experiment similar to Newton's with the prism; he had not deduced from it a successful theory of color, but he felt slighted by Newton's ignoring his priority, and he joined with other members of the Society in criticizing Newton's conclusions. The dispute lingered on for three years. "I am so persecuted," wrote the thin-skinned Newton, "with discussions arising out of my theory of light that I blamed my own imprudence for parting with so substantial a blessing as my quiet to run after a shadow."[19] For a time he was inclined to "resolutely bid adieu to philosophy eternally except what I do for my own satisfaction."[20]

Another point of controversy with Hooke concerned the medium through which light is transmitted. Hooke had adopted Huygens' theory that light traveled on the waves of an "ether." Newton argued that such a theory could not explain why light traveled in straight lines. He proposed instead a "corpuscular theory": light is due to the emission, by a luminous body, of innumerable tiny particles traveling in straight lines through empty space with a speed of 190,000 miles per second. He rejected ether as a medium of light, but later accepted it as a medium of gravitational force.*

Newton gathered his discussions of light into the *Opticks* of 1704. Significantly, it was written in English (the *Principia* was in Latin), and was addressed "to Readers of quick Wit and Understanding not yet versed in Opticks." At the end of the book he listed thirty-one queries for further consideration. Query I suggested prophetically: "Do not bodies act upon light at a distance, and by their action bend its rays, and is not this action strongest at the least distance?"† And Query XXX: "Why may not Nature change bodies into light, and light into bodies?"

III. THE GENEALOGY OF GRAVITATION

The year 1666 was germinal for Newton. It saw the beginning of his work in optics; but also, he later recalled, in May "I had entrance into the inverse method of Fluxions; and in the same year I began to think of gravity extending to the orbit of the moon, . . . having thereby compared the force requisite to keep the moon in her orbit with the force of gravity at the surface of the earth, and found them to answer pretty nearly. . . . In those years I was in the prime of my age."[21]

In 1666 the plague reached Cambridge, and for safety's sake Newton returned to his native Woolsthorpe. At this point we come upon a pretty story. Wrote Voltaire, in his *Philosophie de Newton* (1738):

> One day, in the year 1666, Newton, then retired to the country, seeing some fruit fall from a tree, as I was told by his niece, Mme. Conduit, fell into a profound meditation upon the cause which draws all bodies in a line which, if prolonged, would pass very nearly through the center of the earth.[22]

This is the oldest known mention of the apple story. It does not appear in Newton's early biographers, nor in his own account of how he came to the idea of universal gravitation; it is now generally regarded as a legend. More likely is another story in Voltaire: that when a stranger asked Newton how he had discovered the laws of gravitation, he replied, "By thinking

---

* Later physicists preferred Huygens' undulating theory on the ground that Newton's corpuscular hypothesis did not account satisfactorily for phenomena of diffraction, interference, and polarization. Contemporary physics would like to combine the two views to explain phenomena apparently involving both corpuscles and waves. The photons or quanta of today recall Newton's corpuscles. The ether is at present in disrepute.

† Cf. Albert Einstein, *Relativity* (New York, 1900), 88.

of them without ceasing."[23] It is fairly clear that by 1666 Newton had calculated the force of attraction holding the planets in their orbits as varying inversely with the square of their distance from the sun.[24] But he could not as yet reconcile the theory with his mathematical reckonings. He laid it aside, and published nothing about it for the next eighteen years.

The idea of interstellar gravitation was by no means original with Newton. Some fifteenth-century astronomers thought that the heavens exert a force upon the earth like that of the magnet upon iron, and that, since the earth is equally attracted from every direction, it remains suspended in the sum total of all these forces.[25] Gilbert's *De Magnete* (1600) had set many minds thinking about the magnetic influences surrounding every body, and he himself had written, in a work that would be published (1651) forty-eight years after his death:

> The force which emanates from the moon reaches to the earth, and, in like manner, the magnetic virtue of the earth pervades the region of the moon; both correspond and conspire by the joint action of both, according to a proportion and conformity of motions; but the earth has more effect, in consequence of its superior mass.[26]

Ismaelis Bouillard, in his *Astronomia philolaica* (1645), had held that the mutual attraction of the planets varies inversely as the square of the distance between them.[27] Alfonso Borelli, in *Theories of the Medicean Planets* (1666), held "that every planet and satellite revolves round some principal globe of the universe as a fountain of virtue [force], which so draws and holds them that they cannot by any means be separated from it, but are compelled to follow it wherever it goes, in constant and continuous revolutions"; and he explained the orbits of these planets and satellites as the resultant of the centrifugal force of their revolution ("as we find in a wheel, or a stone whirled in a sling") countered by the centripetal attraction of their sun.[28] Kepler considered gravity inherent in all celestial bodies, and for a while he reckoned its force as varying inversely with the square of the intervening distance; this would have clearly anticipated Newton; but later he rejected this formula, and supposed the attraction to be diminished in direct proportion as the distance increased.[29] These approaches to a gravitational theory were deflected by Descartes' hypothesis of vortices forming in a primeval mass and then determining the action and orbit of each part.

Many of the alert inquirers in the Royal Society puzzled over the mathematics of gravitation. In 1674 Hooke, in *An Attempt to Prove the Annual Motion of the Earth*, anticipated by eleven years Newton's *announcement* of the gravitation theory:

I shall explain a system of the world, differing in many particulars from any yet known, answering in all things to the common rules of mechanical motions. This depends upon three suppositions: first, that all celestial bodies whatsoever have an attractive or gravitating power towards their centers, whereby they attract not only their own parts, and keep them from flying from them, . . . but that they do also attract all other celestial bodies that are within the sphere of their activity. . . . The second suggestion is this, that all bodies whatsoever, that are put into direct and simple motion, will so continue to move forward in a straight line, till they are by some other effectual powers deflected. . . . The third supposition is, that these attractive powers are so much the more powerful in operating, by how much nearer the body wrought upon is to their own centers.[30]

Hooke did not, in this treatise, reckon the attraction as varying inversely with the square of the distance; but, if we may believe Aubrey, he communicated this principle to Newton, who had already arrived at it independently.[31] In January, 1684, Hooke propounded the formula of inverse squares to Wren and Halley, who themselves had already accepted it. They pointed out to Hooke that what was needed was no mere supposition, but a mathematical demonstration that the principle of gravitation would explain the paths of the planets. Wren offered to Hooke and Halley a reward of forty shillings ($100) if either would bring him, within two months, a mathematical proof of gravitation. So far as we know, none came.[32]

Sometime in August, 1684, Halley went to Cambridge, and asked Newton what would be the orbit of a planet if its attraction by the sun varied inversely as the square of the distance between them. Newton replied, an ellipse. As Kepler had concluded, from his mathematical study of Tycho Brahe's observations, that the planetary orbits are elliptical, astronomy seemed now confirmed by mathematics, and vice versa. Newton added that he had worked out the calculations in detail in 1679, but had laid them aside, partly because they did not fully accord with the then current estimates of the earth's diameter and the distance of the earth from the moon; more probably because he was not sure that he could treat the sun, the planets, and the moon as single points in measuring their attractive force. But in 1671 Picard announced his new measurements of the earth's radius and a degree of longitude, which last he calculated at 69.1 English statute miles; and in 1672 Picard's mission to Cayenne enabled him to estimate the distance of the sun from the earth as 87,000,000 miles (the present figure is 92,000,000). These new estimates harmonized well with Newton's mathematics of gravitation; and further calculations in 1685 convinced him that a sphere attracts bodies as though all its mass were gathered at its center. Now he felt more confidence in his hypothesis.

He compared the rate of fall in a stone dropped to the earth with the rate at which the moon would fall toward the earth if the gravitational pull of the earth upon the moon diminished with the square of the distance between them. He found that his results agreed with the latest astronomical data. He concluded that the force making the stone fall, and the force drawing the moon toward the earth despite the moon's centrifugal impetus, were one and the same. His achievement lay in applying this conclusion to all bodies in space, in conceiving all the heavenly bodies as bound in a mesh of gravitational influences, and in showing how his mathematical and mechanical calculations tallied with the observations of the astronomers, and especially with Kepler's planetary laws.*

Newton worked out his calculations anew, and communicated them to Halley in November, 1684. Recognizing their importance, Halley urged him to submit them to the Royal Society. He complied by sending the Society a treatise, *Propositiones de Motu* (February, 1685), which summarized his views on motion and gravitation. In March, 1686, he began a fuller exposition, and on April 28, 1686, he presented to the Society, in manuscript, Book I (*De Motu Corporum*) of *Philosophiae Naturalis Principia Mathematica*. Hooke at once pointed out that he had anticipated Newton in 1674. Newton answered, in a letter to Halley, that Hooke had taken the idea of inverse squares from Borelli and Bouillard. The dispute waxed to mutual irritation; Halley acted as peacemaker, and Newton soothed Hooke by inserting into his manuscript, under Proposition IV, a scholium in which he credited "our friends Wren, Hooke, and Halley" as having "already inferred" the law of inverse squares. But the dispute so irked him that when he announced to Halley (June 20, 1687), that Book II was ready, he added, "The third I now design to suppress. Philosophy is such an impertinently litigious lady that a man had as good be engaged in lawsuits as have to do with her." Halley persuaded him to continue; and in September, 1687, the entire work was published under the imprint of the Royal Society and its current president, Samuel Pepys. The Society being short of funds, Halley paid for the publication entirely out of his own pocket, though he was not a man of means. So at last, after twenty years of preparation, appeared the most important book of seventeenth-century science, rivaled, in the magnitude of its effects upon the mind of literate Europe, only by the *De revolutionibus orbium coelestium* (1543)

---

* Kepler's laws (1609, 1619): 1. The planets describe elliptical orbits, in which the sun is one focus. 2. The line joining a planet to the sun sweeps over equal areas in equal times. 3. The square of the period of revolution of a planet is proportional to the cube of its average distance from the sun. This last formula led to the law of inverse squares.

of Copernicus and *The Origin of Species* (1859) of Darwin. These three books are the basic events in the history of modern Europe.

IV. THE *PRINCIPIA*

The preface explained the title:

> Since the ancients (as we are told by Pappus) made great account of the science of mechanics in the investigation of natural things; and the moderns, laying aside substantial forms [of the Scholastics] and occult qualities, have endeavored to subject the phenomena of nature to the laws of mathematics, I have in this treatise cultivated mathematics as far as it regards [natural] philosophy.... Therefore we offer this work as mathematical principles of philosophy; for all the difficulty of philosophy seems to consist in this—from the phenomena of motions to investigate the forces of nature, and then from these forces to demonstrate the other phenomena.

The viewpoint is to be strictly mechanical:

> I wish we could derive the rest of the phenomena of nature by the same kind of reasoning from mechanical principles, for I am induced by many reasons to suspect that they may all depend upon certain forces by which the particles of bodies, by some causes hitherto unknown, are either mutually impelled towards each other, and cohere in regular figures, or are repelled and recede from each other; which forces being unknown, philosophers have hitherto attempted the search of nature in vain; but I hope the principles here laid down will afford some light either to that or some truer method of philosophy.

After laying down some definitions and axioms, Newton formulated three laws of motion:

> 1. Every body continues in its state of rest, or of uniform motion in a straight line, unless it is compelled to change that state by forces impressed upon it.
> 2. The change of motion is proportional to the motive force impressed, and is made in the direction of the straight line in which that force is impressed.
> 3. To every action there is always opposed an equal reaction.

Armed with these laws, and the rule of inverse squares, Newton proceeded to formulate the principle of gravitation. Its current form, that every particle of matter attracts every other particle with a force varying directly as the product of their masses and inversely as the square of the distance between them, is nowhere found in these words in the *Principia;* but Newton expressed the idea in the general scholium that closes Book II: "Gravity . . . operates . . . according to the quantity of the solid matter which they [the sun and the planets] contain, and propagates its virtue on all sides, . . . decreasing always as the inverse square of the distances."[33] He applied this principle, and his laws of motion, to the planetary orbits, and found that his mathematical calculations harmonized with the elliptical orbits deduced by Kepler. He argued that the planets are deflected from rectilinear motions, and are kept in their orbits, by a force tending toward the sun and varying inversely as the square of their distances from the center of the sun. On similar principles he explained the attraction of Jupiter upon its satellites, and of the earth upon the moon. He showed that Descartes' theory of vortices as the first form of the cosmos could not be reconciled with Kepler's laws. He calculated the mass of each planet, and figured the density of the earth as between five and six times that of water. (The current figure is 5.5.) He accounted mathematically for the flattening of the earth at the poles, and ascribed the bulge of the earth at the equator to the gravitational attraction of the sun. He worked out the mathematics of tides as due to the combined pull of the sun and the moon upon the seas; and by similar "lunisolar" action he explained the precession of the equinoctial points. He reduced the trajectories of comets to regular orbits, and so confirmed Halley's prediction. By attributing gravitational attraction to all planets and stars, he pictured a universe mechanically far more complex than had been supposed; for now every planet or star was viewed as influenced by every other. But into this complex multitude of heavenly bodies Newton placed law: the most distant star was subject to the same mechanics and mathematics as the smallest particles on the earth. Never had man's vision of law ventured so far or so boldly into space.

The first edition of the *Principia* was soon sold out, but no second edition appeared till 1713. Copies became so scarce and hard to secure that one scientist transcribed the whole work with his own hand.[34] It was recognized as an intellectual enterprise of the highest order, but some notes of criticism soured the praise. France, clinging to Descartes' vortices, rejected the Newtonian system until Voltaire gave it a worshipful exposition in 1738. Cassini and Fontenelle objected that gravitation was just one more occult force or quality; Newton propounded certain relationships among the heavenly bodies, but he had not revealed the nature of gravitation, which remained as mysterious as God. Leibniz argued that unless Newton could show the mechanism by which gravitation could act through apparently empty space upon objects millions of miles away, gravitation could not be accepted as anything more than a word.[35]

Even in England the new theory was not readily received. Voltaire claimed that forty years after its first publication hardly twenty scientists could be found favorable to it. Whereas in France critics complained that the theory was insufficiently mechanical as compared with Descartes' primeval whirlpools, in England the objections were predominantly religious. George Berkeley, in *Principles of Human Knowledge* (1710), regretted that Newton had thought of space, time, and motion as absolute, apparently eternal, and existing independently of divine support. Mechanism so pervaded the Newtonian system that there seemed no place in it for God.

When Newton, after characteristic delays, agreed to prepare a second edition, he tried to appease his critics. He assured Leibniz and the French that he did not assume a force acting at a distance through empty space; he believed in an intervening medium of transmission, though he would not attempt to describe it; and he frankly confessed that he did not know the nature of gravitation. It was in this connection that he wrote in the second edition the oft misunderstood words "*Non fingo hypotheses.*"[36] "Gravity," he added, "must be caused by an agent acting constantly according to certain laws; but whether this agent be material or immaterial I have left to the consideration of my readers."[37]

To further meet religious objections he appended to the second edition a general scholium on the role of God in his system. He restricted his mechanistic explanations to the physical world; even in that world he saw evidences of divine design; the great machine required some initial source of its motion, which must be God; moreover there were, in the solar system, certain irregularities of behavior which God periodically corrected as they arose.[38] To make room for such miraculous interpositions Newton surrendered the principle of the conservation of energy. The world machine, he now supposed, lost energy in time, and would run down if God did not intervene to restore its force.[39] "This most beautiful system of the sun, planets, and comets," he concluded, "could only proceed from the counsel and dominion of an intelligent and powerful Being."[40] Finally he moved toward a philosophy that could be interpreted in either a vitalistic or a mechanistic sense:

> And now we might add something concerning a certain most subtle spirit which pervades and hides in all gross bodies; by the force and action of which spirit the particles of bodies attract one another at near distances, and cohere if contiguous; and electric bodies operate to greater distances, as well repelling as attracting the neighboring corpuscles; and light is emitted, reflected, refracted, inflected, and heats bodies; and all sensation is excited, and the members of animal

bodies move at the command of the will, namely by the vibrations of this spirit, mutually propagated along the solid filaments of the nerves, from the outward organs of sense to the brain, and from the brain into the muscles. But these are things that cannot be explained in a few words, nor are we furnished with that sufficiency of experiments which is required to an accurate determination and demonstration of the laws by which this electric and elastic spirit operates.[41]

What was his actual religious faith? His professorship at Cambridge required allegiance to the Established Church, and he attended Anglican services regularly; but, says his secretary, "as for his private prayers, I can say nothing of them; I am apt to believe his intense studies deprived him of the better part."[42] Yet he studied the Bible as zealously as he studied the universe. An archbishop complimented him—"You know more divinity than all of us put together";[43] and Locke said of his knowledge of the Scriptures, "I know few his equals."[44] He left theological writings greater in bulk than all his scientific works.

His studies led him to semi-Arian conclusions much like those of Milton: that Christ, though the Son of God, was not equal in time or power with God the Father.[45] For the rest, Newton was, or became, quite orthodox. He seems to have taken every word of the Bible as the word of God, and to have accepted the books of Daniel and Revelation as literal truth. The greatest scientist of his age was a mystic who lovingly copied out large passages from Jakob Böhme, and who asked Locke to discuss with him the meaning of the "White Horse" in the Apocalypse. He encouraged his friend John Craig to write *Theologiae Christianae Principia Mathematica* (1699), which sought to prove mathematically the date of Christ's second coming, and the ratio between the highest attainable earthly happiness and the believer's rewarding bliss in Paradise.[46] He wrote a commentary on the Apocalypse, and argued that the Antichrist therein predicted was the pope of Rome. Newton's mind was a mixture of Galileo's mechanics and Kepler's laws with Böhme's theology. We shall not soon see his like again.

V. EVENING

He was in another sense an anomalous mixture: a man apparently absorbed in mathematical and mystical theory, and yet possessed of practical ability and common sense. In 1687 he was chosen by the University of Cambridge to go with others and protest to James II the King's attempt to have the University admit a Benedictine monk to a degree without taking the usual oaths impossible to a Catholic. The mission failed to dissuade the King, but the University must have approved Newton's conduct of it, for he was chosen member for Cambridge in the Parliament of 1689. He served till the dissolution in 1690, and was re-elected in 1701, but he took no memorable part in politics.

His career was interrupted in 1692 by two years of physical and mental illness. He addressed to Pepys and Locke letters complaining of sleeplessness and melancholia, expressing fears of persecution, and mourning that he had lost "the former consistency of his mind."[47] On September 16, 1693, he wrote to Locke:

> SIR:
>   Being of opinion that you endeavored to embroil me with women and by other means, I was so much affected that when one told me you were sickly and would not live, I answered, 'twere better if you were dead. I desire you to forgive me for this uncharitableness. For I am now satisfied that what you have done is just, and I beg your pardon for having hard thoughts of you for it, and for representing that you struck at the root of morality in a principle you laid down in your book of ideas, and designed to pursue in another book, and that I took you for a Hobbist. I beg your pardon also for saying or thinking that there was a design to sell me an office, or to embroil me.
>   I am your most humble
>   and unfortunate servant,
>   Is. NEWTON[48]

Pepys, in a letter of September 26, 1693, mentioned "a discomposure in . . . head or mind" evidenced by a message he had received from Newton. Huygens left at his death (1695) a manuscript in which he noted, under date of May 29, 1694, that "M. Colin, a Scotchman, informed me that eighteen months ago the illustrious geometer, Isaac Newton, had become insane," but had "so far recovered his health that he began to understand the *Principia*." Huygens sent the report to Leibniz in a letter of June 8, 1694: "The good Mr. Newton has had an attack of phrenitis which lasted eighteen months, and of which they say his friends have cured him by means of remedies and keeping him shut up."[49] Some have supposed that this nervous breakdown led Newton from science to the Apocalypse, but we cannot say. It was said that "he never again concentrated after the old fashion, or did any fresh work";[50] yet he solved almost at once, in 1696, a mathematical problem proposed by Johann Bernoulli "to the acutest mathematicians in the world"; and he did likewise with a problem set by Leibniz in 1716.[51] His answer to Bernoulli was sent anonymously through the Royal Society, but Bernoulli at once guessed the author to be Newton, recognizing, he said, *"tanquam ex ungue leonem"*—the lion from his toenail. In 1700 he discovered the theory of the sextant; he let it remain unknown except by a letter to Halley, and it had to be reinvented in 1730. And he seems to have filled creditably the difficult positions to which he was presently appointed by the state.

Locke, Pepys, and other friends had for some time negotiated to secure for Newton a governmental position that would get him away from the confinement of his room and laboratory at Cambridge. In 1695 they persuaded Lord Halifax to offer him the post of warden of the Mint. The appointment was no sinecure, and no act of charity; the government wished to use Newton's knowledge of chemistry and metallurgy in minting a new coinage. In 1695 he moved to London, where he lived with his niece Catherine Barton, the mistress of Halifax.[52] Voltaire felt that the charm of this niece led Halifax, as chancellor of the exchequer, to make Newton master of the Mint in 1699;[53] but this bit of gossip hardly explains why Newton continued to hold that office through his remaining twenty-eight years, and to the general satisfaction.

His old age should have been happy. He was honored as the greatest of living scientists; not till our own time did any man of science enjoy such wide acclaim. He was elected president of the Royal Society in 1703, and annually thereafter till his death. In 1705 he was knighted by Queen Anne. When he rode in his carriage through the London streets people gazed with awe upon his pink face, majestic and benevolent under a mass of white hair; and they could not always see that he had expanded out of proportion to his modest height. He enjoyed a good salary, £1,200 a year, and invested his savings so wisely that he left £32,000 when he died,[54] though he had been generous in gifts and charity. He surmounted successfully the South Sea Company fiasco. However, he was moody, sometimes irritable, suspicious, secretive, always timid but proud.[55] He loved privacy, and did not make friends readily. In 1700 he proposed to a rich widow; nothing came of it, and he never married. Highstrung and morbidly sensitive, he bore criticism painfully, resented it sharply, and fought back stoutly in controversy. He was conscious of his own work and ability, but he lived modestly until his salary and his savings enabled him to have six servants and enjoy a high place in London society.

In his seventy-ninth year he began to repay his debt to nature. Diseases that respect no genius afflicted him—stone in the bladder and urinary incontinence; at the age of eighty-three he suffered from gout, and at eighty-four from hemorrhoids. On March 19, 1727, the pains from the stone were so severe that he lost consciousness. He never regained it, but died the next day, in his eighty-fifth year. He was buried in Westminster Abbey after a funeral led by statesmen, nobles, and philosophers, in a pall borne by dukes and earls. Poets swathed him in elegies, and Pope composed a famous epitaph:

> Nature and Nature's laws lay hid in night;
> God said, Let Newton be! and all was light.

Voltaire even in old age was moved when he told how, in his English exile, he had seen a mathematician buried with the honors of a king.[56]

Newton's fame grew to almost absurd heights. Leibniz judged his rival's contributions to mathematics to be equal in value to all previous work in that science.[57] Hume considered Newton "the greatest and rarest genius that ever rose for the adornment and instruction of the species,"[58] and Voltaire modestly agreed.[59] Lagrange called the *Principia* "the greatest production of the human mind," and Laplace assured it for all time "a pre-eminence above all other productions of the human intellect"; Newton, he added, was the most fortunate of men, for there is only one universe, and one ultimate principle in it, and Newton discovered that principle.[60] Such judgments are precarious, for "truth," even in science, wilts like a flower.

If we rank the greatness of a man by the least subjective test, the spread and duration of his influence, Newton can be compared only with the founders of world religions and pivotal philosophies. For a time his influence upon English mathematics was harmful, for his "fluxions" and their notation proved less convenient than the calculus and notation with which Leibniz prevailed on the Continent. For a century his corpuscular theory of light seems to have impeded the progress of optics, though some students now find much help in Newton's view.[61] In mechanics his work has proved endlessly creative. "All that has been accomplished in mechanics since his day," wrote Ernst Mach, "has been a deductive, formal, and mathematical development . . . on the basis of Newton's laws."[62]

Theologians at first feared the influence of the *Principia* on religion; but Bentley's Boyle lectures (1692), encouraged by Newton, turned the new world-view to the support of faith by stressing the apparent unity, order, and grandeur of the universe as evidences of the wisdom, power, and majesty of God. However, the same Newtonian system was accepted by the deists as strengthening their replacement of the Christian theology with a simple acceptance of one God, or even their identification of God with Nature and her laws. Probably the final influence of Newton on religion was injurious; despite his protests, and his million words of theological writings, freethinkers supposed that he had conceived a self-subsistent world, and had brought deity into it as a comforting afterthought. In France especially, Newton's cosmology, though presented deistically by

Voltaire, encouraged the mechanistic atheism of many *philosophes*.

Between the decline of the Cartesian cosmogony in France (c. 1740) and the rise of relativity theories and quantum mechanics in the twentieth century, Newton's "System of the World" met no serious challenge, and seemed to be verified by every advance or discovery in physics or astronomy. So far as an outsider can understand such arcana, the principal dissents of contemporary physicists from Newton's mechanics are:

1. Newton took space and distance, time and motion, as absolute—i.e., not varying in quantity according to anything outside themselves.[63] Einstein considered them relative—varying with the position and motion of the observer in space and time.

2. Newton's first law of motion apparently assumed that a body might "continue in a state of rest, or of uniform motion in a straight line." But "rest" is always relative, like the rest of a traveler in a speeding plane; all things move, and never in a straight line, for every line of motion or action is deflected by surrounding bodies (as Newton realized).

3. Newton thought of mass as a constant; some contemporary physicists think of it as varying with the relative velocity of observer and object.

4. "Force" is now looked upon as a convenient but not necessary concept in science, which aims to content itself with describing sequences, relations, and results. We do not and need not (we are told) know what "it" is that passes from a moving object to an object that it strikes; we need only record the sequences, and assume (never with absolute certainty) that these will be in the future what they have appeared to be in the past. Gravitation, in this view, is not a force but a system of relationships among events in space and time.

It is a consolation to learn that these and other emendations of Newton's mechanics are of importance only in fields (such as electromagnetic phenomena) where particles seem to move with a speed approaching the velocity of light; elsewhere the divergence between the old physics and the new may be safely ignored. Philosophers, cured of certainty by history, may still retain a humble skepticism about contemporary ideas, including their own; they will sense a fluent relativity in relativity formulas; and they will remind all delvers in atoms and stars of Newton's own final estimate of his epochal achievement:

> I do not know what I may appear to the world; but to myself I seem to have been only like a boy playing on the seashore, and diverting myself in now and then finding a smoother pebble or a prettier shell than ordinary, while the great ocean of truth lay all undiscovered before me.[64]

CHAPTER XX

English Philosophy

1648–1715

I. THOMAS HOBBES: 1588–1679

1. Formative Influences

H E WAS born aforetime on April 5, 1588; his mother attributed his
premature birth to her fright at the coming of the Spanish Armada
and the threat of a large-scale invasion by murderous idolaters. To this
unpremeditated expulsion into life the philosopher ascribed his timorous
disposition, but he was the boldest heretic of his age. His father, an
Anglican clergyman at Malmesbury in Wiltshire, may have transmitted
some pugnacity to the son, for he engaged in a brawl at the door of his
church and then disappeared, leaving his three children to be brought up
by a brother.

The brother prospered, and at fifteen Thomas entered Magdalen College, Oxford, doubtless as timid as any youth venturing into caves dedicated to the idols of the tribe. He found little to his liking in the philosophy
taught there; he consoled himself with extracurricular reading, and gained
a firsthand acquaintance with Greek and Latin classics. Graduating at
twenty, he had the good fortune to be employed as private tutor to William
Cavendish, who became second Earl of Devonshire; the protection given
him by that family proved precious to him in the days of his heresies.
With his pupil he traveled on the Continent (1610). On his return he
served for a while as secretary to Francis Bacon; that stimulating experience may have shared in forming his thoroughly empirical philosophy.
About this time, Aubrey tells us, "Mr. Benjamin Johnson, Poet Laureate,
was his loving and familiar friend,"[1] more learned than Hobbes, and not
yet tough. Soon he was back with the Cavendish family; he retained relations with it for three generations; and probably from these generous
and well-entrenched patrons he adopted the royalist and High Church
views that won pardon for his materialistic metaphysics, and kept him
from burning.

His discovery of Euclid was a turning point in his mental biography.
He was forty years old when, in a private library, he saw the *Elements*

open at Proposition XLVII of Book I. Reading it, he cried out, "By God, this is impossible!" The demonstration referred for its proof to an earlier proposition, and this to another, and so backward to the initial definitions and axioms. He was delighted with this logical architecture, and fell in love with geometry.[2] But, Aubrey adds, he "was much addicted to music, and practiced on the bass viol." In 1629 he published a translation of Thucydides, with the professed aim of scaring England away from democracy. In that year he resumed his travels, now as tutor to his first pupil's son, the third Earl of Devonshire. His visit to Galileo (1636) may have strengthened his inclination to interpret the universe in mechanical terms.

He returned to England in 1637. As the conflict between Parliament and Charles I progressed, Hobbes wrote an essay, *The Elements of Law, Natural and Politique*, defending the absolute authority of the King as indispensable to social order and national unity. This was circulated in manuscript, and might have led to the author's arrest had not Charles dissolved the Parliament. As the temper of the conflict rose, Hobbes thought it discreet to retire to the Continent (1640). He remained there, chiefly in Paris, for the next eleven years. In Paris he won the friendship of Mersenne and Gassendi, and the hostility of Descartes. Mersenne invited him to submit comments on Descartes' *Meditations;* he did, with some courtesy but too much point, and Descartes never forgave him. When civil war came to England (1642), Royalist emigrés formed a colony in France, and Hobbes may have taken from them some added rubbing of monarchist sentiment. For two years (1646–48) he was tutor in mathematics to the exiled Prince of Wales, the future Charles II. The outbreak of the Fronde in France—aiming, like the revolt in England, to limit royal power—confirmed his conviction that only an absolute monarchy could maintain stability and internal peace.

He arrived very slowly at the definitive expression of his philosophy. "He walked much and contemplated," says Aubrey, "and he had in the head of his staff [cane] a pen and inkhorn, carried always a notebook in his pocket, and as soon as a notion darted, he presently entered it into his book, or else he should perhaps have lost it."[3] He issued a series of minor works,* most of which are now negligible; but in 1651 he gathered his thoughts into a reckless masterpiece of thought and style: *The Leviathan, or The Matter, Form, and Power of a Commonwealth, Ecclesiastical and Civil.* This is one of the landmarks in the history of philosophy; we must tarry with it leisurely.

---

* Chiefly *De Cive* (1642, 1647); *The Elements of Law*, published in two parts (1650) as *Human Nature* and *De Corpore Politico; Philosophical Rudiments* (1651); *Elementorum Philosophiae, Sectio Prima: De Corpore* (1655); *De Homine* (1658); many fragments on mathematics; translations of the *Iliad* and the *Odyssey; Behemoth* (1670); and an autobiography in verse (1679).

2. Logic and Psychology

The style is almost as good as Bacon's: not as rich in illuminating images, but every bit as pithy, idiomatic, forceful, and direct, with now and then a tang of pointed irony. There is no ornament here, no show of eloquence, only the clear expression of clear thought with a stoic economy of verbal means. "Words," said Hobbes, "are wise men's counters, they do but reckon by them; but they are the money of fools that value them by the authority of an Aristotle, a Cicero, or a Thomas."[4] With that new razor he cut down many a weed of pretentious and meaningless speech. When he came upon St. Thomas Aquinas' definition of *eternity* as *nunc stans,* or "everlasting now," he shrugged it off as "easy enough to say, but though I fain would, yet I never could conceive it; they that can are happier than I." Therefore Hobbes is a blunt nominalist: class or abstract nouns like *man* or *virtue* are merely names for generalizing ideas; they do not represent objects; all objects are individual entities—individual virtuous actions, individual men . . .

He defines his terms carefully, and on the first page of his book he defines "Leviathan" as "a commonwealth or state." He found the word in Job (xli), where God used it for an unspecified sea monster as an image of the divine power. Hobbes proposed to make the state a great organism that should absorb and direct all human activity. But before coming to his main thesis he swept through logic and psychology with a merciless hand.

He understood by philosophy what we should now call science: "the knowledge of effects, or of appearances, acquired from the knowledge . . . of their causes, and, conversely, of possible causes from their known effects."[5] He followed Bacon in expecting from such a study great practical benefits to human life. But he ignored Bacon's call to inductive reasoning; he was all for "true ratiocination," i.e., deduction from experience; and in his admiration for mathematics he added that "ratiocination is the same with addition and subtraction"—i.e., the combination or separation of images or ideas. He thought that what we lack is not experience, but proper reasoning about experience. If we could clear away the miasma of meaningless words from metaphysics, and the prejudices transmitted by custom, education, and partisan spirit, what a load of error would fall away! Reason, however, is fallible, and, except in mathematics, can never give us certainty. "The knowledge of consequence, which I have said before is called science, is not absolute, but conditional. No man can know by discourse [reasoning] that this or that is, has been, or will be, which is to know absolutely; but only that if this be, that is; if this has been, that has been; if this shall be, that shall be; which is to know conditionally."[6]

As that passage foresaw Hume's argument that we know only sequences, not causes, so Hobbes anticipated Locke's sensationist psychology. All knowledge begins with sensation. "There is no conception in a man's mind which hath not at first, totally or by parts, been begotten upon the organs of sense."[7] It is a frankly materialistic psychology: nothing exists, outside us or within us, except matter and motion. "All qualities called sensible," or sensory (light, color, form, hardness, softness, sound, odor, taste, heat, cold), "are, in the object that causeth them, but so many several motions of the matter, by which it presseth our organs diversely. Neither, in us that are pressed, are they anything else but divers motions, for motion produceth nothing but motion."[8] Motion in the form of change is necessary to sensation; *"semper idem sentire idem est ac nihil sentire"* (Hobbes could be epigrammatic in Latin too)—always to feel the same thing is the same as to feel nothing.[9] (So neither the white man nor the colored man is conscious of his own odor, since it is always under his nose.)

From sensation Hobbes proceeds to derive imagination and memory through a peculiar application of what came to be Newton's first law of motion:

> That when a thing lies still, unless somewhat else stir it, it will lie still forever, is a truth that no man doubts of. But that when a thing is in motion it will eternally be in motion unless somewhat else stay it, though the reason be the same (namely, that nothing can change itself), is not so easily assented to. . . .
>
> When a body is once in motion it moveth (unless something else hinder it) eternally; and whatsoever hindreth it cannot in an instant, but [only] in time and by degrees, quite extinguish it. And as we see in the water, though the wind cease, the waves give not over rolling for a long time after; so also it happeneth in that motion which is made in the internal parts of a man, then when he sees, dreams, etc. For after the object is removed, or the eye shut, we still retain an image of the things seen, though more obscure than when we see it. And this is it the Latins call Imagination. . . . Imagination, therefore, is nothing but *decaying sense*. . . . When we would express the decay, and signifying that the sense is fading, old, and past, it is called Memory. . . . Much Memory, or memory of many things, is called Experience.[10]

Ideas are imaginations produced by sensation or memory. Thought is a sequence of such imaginations. That sequence is determined not by a free will but by mechanical laws governing the association of ideas.

Not every thought to every thought succeeds indifferently. But as
we have no imagination whereof we have not formerly had sense
in whole or in parts, so we have no transition from one imagination
to another whereof we never had the like before in our senses. The
reason whereof is this: All fancies [imaginations, ideas] are motions
within us, relics of those made in the sense; and those motions that
immediately succeeded one another in the sense, continue also together after sense. . . . But because in sense, to one and the same
thing perceived, sometimes one thing, sometimes another, succeeds, it
comes to pass in time that, in the imaging of anything, there is no certainty what we shall imagine next; only this is certain, it shall be
something that succeeded the same before, at one time or another.[11]

Such a train of thoughts may be unguided, as in dreams, or "regulated
by some desire and design." In dreams the images lying dormant in the
brain are aroused by some "agitation of the inward parts of man's body."
For all parts of the body are connected in some way with certain parts of
the brain. "I believe there is a reciprocation of motion from the brain to
the vital parts, and back from the vital parts to the brain, whereby not
only imagination [or idea] begetteth motion in those parts, but also motion
in those parts begetteth imagination like to that by which it was begotten."[12]
"Our dreams are the reverse of our waking imaginations: the motion, when
we are awake, beginning at one end, and, when we dream, at another."[13]
The illogical sequence of images in dreams is due to the absence of any
external sensation to check them, or of any purpose to guide them.

There is no place in Hobbes's psychology for free will. The will itself
is no separate faculty or entity, but merely the last desire or aversion in
the process of deliberation; and deliberation is an alternation of desires or
aversions, which ends when one impulse lasts long enough to flow into
action. "In deliberation the last appetite or aversion immediately adhering
to the action or the omission thereof is that we call the will."[14] "Appetite,
fear, hope, or the rest of the passions are not called voluntary, for they
proceed not from, but are, the will, and the will is not voluntary."[15] "Because every act of man's will, and every desire and inclination, proceedeth
from some cause, and that from another cause, in a continual chain (whose
first link is in the hand of God the first of all causes), they proceed from
necessity. So that to him that could see the connection of those causes, the
necessity of all men's voluntary actions would appear manifest."[16] Throughout the universe there is an unbroken chain of causes and effects. Nothing
is contingent or miraculous or due to chance.

The world is a machine of matter in motion according to law, and man
himself is a similar machine. Sensations enter him as motions, and beget
images or ideas; each idea is the beginning of a motion, and becomes an

action if not impeded by another idea.[17] Every idea, however abstract, moves the body in some degree, however unseen. The nervous system is a mechanism for transforming sensory motion into muscular motion. Spirits exist, but they are merely subtle forms of matter.[18] The soul and the mind are not immaterial; they are names for the vital processes of the body and operations of the brain. Hobbes makes no attempt to explain why consciousness should have developed in such a mechanical process of sensation-to-idea-to-response. And by reducing all perceived qualities of objects to images in the "mind," he comes close to the position that Berkeley would later take in refuting materialism—that all reality known to us is perception, mind.

3. Ethics and Politics

Like Descartes before him and Spinoza after him, Hobbes undertakes an analysis of the passions, for he finds in them the sources of all human actions. All three philosophers use the word *passion* broadly to mean any basic instinct, feeling, or emotion—chiefly appetite (or desire) and aversion, love and hate, delight and fear. Behind all these are pleasure and pain —physiological processes raising or lowering the vitality of the organism. Appetite is the beginning of a motion toward something that promises pleasure; love is such an appetite directed to one person. All impulses (as La Rochefoucauld would argue fourteen years later) are forms of self-love, and derive from the instinct of self-preservation. Pity is the imagination of future calamity to ourselves, aroused by perceiving another's calamity; charity is the satisfied feeling of power in helping others. Gratitude sometimes includes a certain hostility. "To have received from one, to whom we think ourselves equal, greater benefits than there is hope to requite, disposeth to counterfeit love but really secret hatred, and puts a man into the estate of a desperate debtor, that, in declining the sight of his creditor, tacitly wishes him there where he might never see him more. For benefits oblige, and obligation is thralldom."[19] The basic aversion is fear, the basic appetite is for power. "I put for a general inclination of all mankind a perpetual and restless desire of power after power, that ceaseth only in death."[20] We desire riches and knowledge as means to power, and honors as evidence of power; and we desire power because we fear insecurity. Laughter is an expression of superiority and power.

> The passion of laughter is nothing else but sudden glory [self-satisfaction] arising from a sudden conception of some eminency in ourselves by comparison with the infirmity of others, or with our

own formerly; for men laugh at the follies of themselves past, when these come suddenly to remembrance, except they bring with them any present dishonor. . . . Laughter is incident most to them that are conscious of the fewest abilities in themselves, who are forced to keep themselves in their own favor by observing the imperfections of other men. And therefore much laughter at the defects of others is a sign of pusillanimity. For of great minds one of the proper works is to help and free others from scorn, and compare themselves only with the most able.[21]

Good and *bad* are subjective terms, varying in content not only from place to place and from time to time, but from person to person. "The object of any appetite or desire . . . a man calleth the *good;* the object of his hate or aversion, *evil;* for these words . . . are ever used with relation to the person that useth them, there being nothing simply and absolutely so, nor any common rule of good and evil to be taken from the nature of the objects themselves."[22] Strength of passions may be good, and lead to greatness. "He who has no great passion for . . . power, riches, knowledge, or honor . . . cannot possibly have a great fancy or much judgment." To have weak passions is dullness; to have passions abnormally strong is madness; "to have no desires is to be dead."[23]

> The felicity of this life consisteth not in the repose of a mind satisfied. For there is no such *finis ultimus* (utmost aim) nor *summum bonum* (greatest good) as is spoken of in the books of the old moral philosophers. . . . Felicity is a continual progress of the desire, from one object to another, the obtaining of the former being still but the way to the latter.[24]

The government of men so constituted, so acquisitive and competitive, so hot with passions and prone to strife, is the most complex and arduous of all human tasks, and to those who undertake it we must allow every weapon of psychology and power. Though the human will is not free, society is justified in encouraging certain actions by calling them virtuous and rewarding them, and in discouraging some actions by calling them wicked and punishing them. There is no contradiction here with determinism: these social approvals and condemnations are added, for the good of the group, to the motives influencing conduct. "The world is governed by opinion";[25] government, religion, and the moral code are in large part the manipulation of opinion to reduce the necessity and area of force.

Government is necessary, not because man is naturally bad—for "the desires and other passions . . . are in themselves no sin"[26]—but because man is by nature more individualistic than social. Hobbes did not agree with Aristotle that man is "a political animal"—i.e., a being equipped by nature for society. On the contrary, he conceived an original "state of nature" (and therefore the original nature of man) as a condition of competition and mutual aggression checked only by fear, not yet by law. We can visualize that hypothetical condition (said Hobbes) by observing international relations in our own age: nations are still for the most part in "a state of nature," not yet subject to a superimposed law or power.

> In all times kings and persons of sovereign authority, because of their independency, are in continual jealousies, and in the state and posture of gladiators; having their weapons pointed, and their eyes fixed, on one another—that is, their forts, garrisons, and guns on the frontiers of their kingdoms—and continual spies upon their neighbors; which is a posture of war. . . . Where there is no common power there is no law, no injustice. Force and fraud are in war the cardinal virtues.[27]

So, Hobbes believed, individuals and families, before the coming of social organization, had lived in a condition of perpetual war, actual or potential, "every man against every man."[28] "War consisteth not in battle only, . . . but in a tract of time wherein the will to contend by battle is sufficiently shown."[29] He rejected the theory of Roman jurists and Christian philosophers that there is, or ever was, a "law of nature" in the sense of laws of right and wrong based upon the nature of man as a "reasonable animal"; he admitted that man was occasionally rational, but saw him rather as a creature of passions—above all, the will to power—using reason as a tool of desire, and controlled only by fear of force. Primitive life—i.e., life before social organization—was lawless, violent, fearful, "nasty, brutish, and short."[30]

From this hypothetical "state of nature," men, in Hobbes's vision, had emerged by an implicit agreement one with another to submit to a common power. This is the "social-contract" theory made popular by Rousseau's treatise under that title (1762), but already old and battered in Hobbes's day. Milton, in his tract *On the Tenure of Kings and Magistrates* (1649), had just interpreted the contract as an agreement between a king and his subjects—that they would obey him, and that he would properly fulfill the duties of his office; if he failed in this, said Milton (like Buchanan, Mariana, and many others), the people would be justified in deposing him. Hobbes objected to this form of the theory on the ground that it established no authority empowered to enforce the contract, or to determine when it had been broken. He preferred to think of the social compact as made not between ruler and ruled, but among the ruled, who agreed

> to confer all their power and strength [their right to the use of force upon one another] upon one man, or upon one assembly of men. . . .

> This done, the multitude so united in one person is called a COMMON-WEALTH. This is the generation of the great LEVIATHAN, or rather ... of that Mortal God to which we owe, under the *Immortal God*, our peace and defense. For by this authority, given him by every ... man in the Commonwealth, he hath the use of so much power and strength conferred on him, that by terror thereof he is enabled to form the wills of them all ... to the end he may use the strength and means of them all, as he shall think expedient, for their peace and common defense. And he that carryeth this Person is called Sovereign, and said to have Sovereign Power; and every one besides, his Subject.[31]

The theory rashly assumed, among the "nasty and brutish" savages aforementioned, a degree of order, rationality and humility sufficient for an agreement to surrender their powers. Hobbes wisely allowed for alternative origins of the state:

> The attaining to this Sovereign Power is by two ways. One, by natural force, as when a man ... maketh his children to submit themselves, and their children, to his government, as being able to destroy them if they refuse; or by war subdueth his enemies to his will. ... The other is when men agree among themselves to submit to some man, or assembly of men, voluntarily, on confidence to be protected by him against all others. This latter may be called a Political Commonwealth.[32]

However based, the sovereign, to be really sovereign, must have absolute power, for without it he cannot ensure individual security and public peace. To resist him is to violate the social contract which every person in the community has implicitly agreed to by accepting the protection of its head. The theoretical absolutism may admit of some actual limitations: a sovereign may be resisted if he orders a man to kill or maim himself, or to confess a crime, or if the ruler is no longer able to protect his subjects. "The obligation of subjects to the Sovereign is understood to last as long and no longer than the power lasteth by which he is able to protect them." Revolution is always a crime until it succeeds. It is always unlawful and unjust, for both law and justice are determined by the Sovereign; but if a revolution establishes a stable and effective government, the subject is bound to obey the new power.

The king does not rule by divine right, since his power is derived from the people; but his authority must not be limited by a popular assembly, or by law, or by the Church. It should extend also to property; the sovereign should determine property rights, and may reappropriate private property for what he deems the public good.[34] Absolutism is necessary, for when power is shared, as between king and parliament, there will soon be conflict, then civil war, then chaos, then insecurity of life and property; and since security and peace are the ultimate needs of a society, there should be no separation, but full unity and concentration, of governmental powers. Where powers are divided there is no sovereign, and where there is no sovereign there will soon be no state.[35]

Consequently the only logical form of government is monarchy. It should be hereditary, for the right to choose his successor is part of the sovereign's sovereignty; again the alternative is anarchy.[36] Government by an assembly might serve, but only on condition that its power be absolute, not subject to the shifting desires of an uninformed populace. "A democracy is no more than an aristocracy of orators."[37] The people are so readily moved by demagogues that control must be exercised by the government over speech and press; there should be strict censorship of the publication, importation, and reading of books.[38] There is to be no nonsense about individual liberty, private judgment, or conscience; anything that threatens the sovereign authority, and therefore the public peace, should be contracepted at the source.[39] How could a state be governed, or protected in its foreign relations, if every individual remained free to obey or not to obey the law according to his private opinion?

4. Religion and the State

The sovereign must also control the religion of his people, for this, when taken to heart, can be a disruptively explosive force. Hobbes offers a summary definition: "Fear of power invisible, feigned by the mind, or imagined from tales publicly allowed [is] Religion; not allowed, Superstition."[40] This reduces religion to fear, imagination, and pretense; but elsewhere Hobbes ascribes it to an anxious inquiry into the causes and beginnings of things and events.[41] Ultimately this pursuit of causes leads to the belief that "there must be (as even the heathen philosophers confessed) one First Mover, i.e., a First and an eternal cause of all things; which is that which men mean by the name of God."[42] Men naturally supposed that this First Cause was like themselves, a person, soul, and will, only much more powerful. They attributed to this Cause all events whose natural determinants they could not yet discern, and they saw, in strange events, portents and prophecies of the divine will.

In these four things, opinion of ghosts [spirits], ignorance of second causes, devotion towards what men fear, and taking of things casual for prognostications, consisteth the natural seed of religion, which, by reason of different fancies, judgments, and passions of several men, hath grown up into ceremonies so different, that those which are used by one man are for the most part ridiculous to another.[43]

Hobbes was a deist rather than an atheist. He acknowledged an intelligent Supreme Being,[44] but added, "Men . . . may naturally know that God is, though not what he is."[45] We must not conceive of God as having figure, for all figure is finite; or as having parts; or as being in this or that place, "for whatsoever is in place is bounded and finite"; nor that he moves or rests, for these ascribe to him place; nor (except by metaphor) that he partakes of grief, repentance, anger, mercy, want, appetite, hope, or any desire.[46] Hobbes concluded that "the nature of God is incomprehensible."[47] He would not describe God as incorporeal, for we cannot conceive anything to be without body; probably every "spirit" is subtly corporeal.[48]

Having put religion and God in their place, Hobbes proposed to make use of them as instruments and servants of government. For this he claimed prestigious precedents.

> The first founders and legislators of commonwealths amongst the Gentiles, whose ends were only to keep the people in obedience and peace, have in all places taken care: First, to imprint in their minds a belief that those precepts which they gave concerning religion might not be thought to proceed from their own device, but from the dictates of some God, or other Spirit; or else that they themselves were of a higher nature than mere mortals, that their laws might be more easily received: So Numa Pompilius pretended to receive the ceremonies he instituted among the Romans from the nymph Egeria; and the first king and founder of the Kingdom of Peru pretended himself and his wife to be the children of the sun; and Mahomet, to set up his new religion, pretended to have conferences with the Holy Ghost in the form of a dove. Secondly, they have had a care to make it believed that the same things were displeasing to the gods, which were forbidden by the laws.[49]

Lest anyone conclude that Moses used similar devices in ascribing his laws to God, Hobbes adds, with a certain allergy to fire, that "God himself, by supernatural revelation, planted religion" among the Jews.

But he feels himself justified, by historical examples, in recommending that religion be made an instrument of government, and that, in consequence, its doctrines and observances be dictated by the sovereign. If the Church were independent of the state there would be two sovereigns, therefore no sovereign; and subjects would be torn between two masters.

> Seeing the ghostly [spiritual] power challenges [assumes] the right
> to declare what is sin, it challenges by consequence to declare what
> is law (sin being nothing but the transgression of the law). . . .
> When these two powers [Church and state] oppose one another, the
> Commonwealth cannot but be in great danger of civil war, and dis-
> solution.[50]

In such a conflict the Church will have an advantage, "for every man, if he
be in his wits, will in all things yield that man an absolute obedience, by
virtue of whose sentence he believes himself to be either saved or damned."
When the spiritual power moves the subjects "by the terror of punishment
and hope of reward" of this supernatural sort, "and by strange and hard
words suffocates their understanding, it must needs thereby distract the
people, and either overwhelm the commonwealth by oppression, or cast it
into the fire of civil war."[51] The only escape from such turmoil, Hobbes
thinks, is to make the Church subject to the state. As the Catholic Church
had the opposite solution, Hobbes, in Part IV of *The Leviathan*, attacks it
as the ultimate and most powerful foe of his philosophy.

He enters upon some "Higher Criticism" of the Bible—questions Moses'
authorship of the Pentateuch, and dates the historical books much later
than in orthodox tradition. He suggests that Christianity should require of
its adherents only a faith in "Jesus the Christ," and that for the rest it should
allow public opinion to vary within the safe bounds of public order. To a
creed so chastened he offers not only the support of the government, but
the full force of the state to propagate it. He agrees with the pope that only
one religion should be tolerated in a state.[52] He advises the citizens to accept
the theology of their sovereign without critical hesitation, as a duty to
morality and the state. "For it is with the mysteries of our religion as with
wholesome pills for the sick, which, swallowed whole, have the virtue to
cure, but, chewed, are for the most part cast up again without effect."[53]
The most powerful assault that any Englishman had yet made upon Christianity ended with Christianity established as the inescapable law of an
absolute state.

5. Baiting the Bear

"And thus," said the final paragraph of *The Leviathan*, "I have brought
to an end my Discourse of Civil and Ecclesiastical Government, occasioned
by the disorders of the present time, without partiality . . . and without
other design than to set before men's eyes the mutual relation between protection and obedience."

The impartiality was not widely recognized. The emigrés who gathered about Charles II in France welcomed Hobbes's defense of royalty, but condemned his materialism as indiscreet if not blasphemous, and they regretted that their unmanageable philosopher had spent reams attacking the Catholic Church just when they were soliciting the aid of a Catholic king. The Anglican divines who were among the refugees from the triumphant Puritans raised such an outcry against the book that Hobbes "was ordered to come no more to court."[54] Finding himself now friendless and unprotected in France, Hobbes decided to make his peace with Cromwell and return to England. According to Bishop Burnet, he made some changes in the text of The Leviathan "to gratify the Republicans."[55] This is not certain; certain it is, however, that the doctrine of revolution as unlawful in origin, but sanctified by success, fitted imperfectly, like patchwork, with the basic doctrine of absolute obedience to an absolute monarch. The final "Review and Conclusion," which looks like an afterthought, explained the conditions under which a subject formerly loyal to a king might in time gracefully submit to the new regime that had deposed the king. The book was published in London (1651) while Hobbes was still in Paris. At the end of that year, amid a severe winter, he crossed to England, and found a familiar haven with the Earl of Devonshire, who had long since submitted to the revolutionary Parliament. Hobbes sent in his own submission; it was accepted; and the philosopher, supported by a small pension from the Earl, moved to a house in London, because in the countryside "the want of learned conversation was a very great inconvenience."[56] He was now sixty-three years old.

Slowly, as his book found readers, a swarm of critics gathered around his head. One clergyman after another came to the defense of Christianity, and asked who was this "Malmesbury animal" who set himself up against Aristotle, Oxford, Parliament, and God? Hobbes was timid, but he was a fighter; in 1655 he restated, in The Elements of Philosophy, his materialistic and deterministic views. John Bramhall, the learned bishop of Derry, cast his hook for Hobbes in The Catching of the Leviathan (1658), and aimed so well, according to another bishop, that "the hook is still in Hobbes's nose."[57] The attacks continued in almost every year till Hobbes's death. The Earl of Clarendon, after his fall from power as chancellor, amused his exile by publishing A Brief View and Survey of the Dangerous and Pernicious Errors, in Church and State, in Mr. Hobbes's Book entitled Leviathan (1676); through 322 pages it followed the volumes systematically, answering argument with argument in lucid and majestic prose. Clarendon spoke as a man with long experience in political office, and smiled Hobbes's philosophy away as that of one who had had no responsible posts to temper his theorems with practice; and he hoped that "Mr. Hobbes might have a place in Parliament, and sit in Council, and be present in Courts of Justice and other Tribunals, whereby it is probable he would find that his solitary cogitations, how deep soever, and his too peremptory adhering to some Philosophical Notions, and even Rules of Geometry, have misled him in the investigation of Policy."[58]

Not all the attacks were so even-tempered. In 1666 the House of Commons ordered one of its committees "to receive information touching such books as tend to atheism, blasphemy, and profaneness, or against the essence and attributes of God, and in particular the book published in the name of White [a former Catholic priest who questioned the immortality of the soul], and the book of Hobbes called *The Leviathan*."[59] "There was a report (and surely true)," says Aubrey, "that in Parliament . . . some of the bishops made a motion to have the good old Gentleman burnt for a heretic."[60] Hobbes destroyed such of his unpublished papers as might further embroil him, and wrote three dialogues arguing learnedly that no court in England could try him for heresy.

The restored King came to his rescue. Shortly after reaching London, Charles II noticed Hobbes in the street, recognized him as his former tutor, and welcomed him to the court. The Restoration court, already inclined to religious skepticism, and defending royal absolutism against Parliament, found some congenial elements in Hobbes's philosophy. But his bald head, white hair, and Puritanlike garb invited taunting. Charles himself called him "the Bear," and, as Hobbes neared, said, "Here comes the Bear to be baited."[61] Nonetheless the witty King relished Hobbes's ready repartees. He had the old man's portrait painted, placed it in his private chambers, and gave him a pension of a hundred pounds a year. Though this was irregularly paid, it sufficed, with fifty pounds a year from the Cavendish family, to meet the philosopher's simple needs.

Aubrey describes him as sickly in youth but healthy and vigorous in old age. He played tennis till he was seventy-five; when a tennis court was not available he took a daily walk long and brisk enough to give him a "great sweat, and then he gave the servant some money to rub him." He ate and drank moderately; after seventy no meat and no wine. He bragged that he "had been in excess in his life a hundred times," but Aubrey calculated that as this came to little more than once a year, it was not egregious. He never married. He appears to have had an illegitimate daughter, for whom he made generous provision.[62] He read little in these later years, and "was wont to say that if he had read as much as other men, he should have known no more than" they. "At night, when he was abed, and the doors made fast, and was sure nobody heard him, he sang aloud (not that he had a very good voice, but) for his health's sake; he did believe it did his lungs good, and conduced much to prolong his life."[63] However, as early as 1650, "he had a shaking palsy in his hands," which grew so bad that by 1666 his writing became almost illegible.

He continued to write nevertheless. Reverting from philosophy to mathematics, he slipped incautiously into controversy with an expert, John Wallis, who made short work of the old man's claim to square the circle. In 1670, aged eighty-two, he published *Behemoth*, a history of the Civil War; he wrote several replies to his critics, and lovingly translated *The Leviathan* into Latin. In 1675 he composed an autobiography in verse, and rendered all the *Iliad* and the *Odyssey* into English rhymes (1675), because "there is nothing else for me to do."

In that year, aged eighty-seven, he returned from London to the country, and he spent the remainder of his life at the Cavendish estate in Derbyshire. Meanwhile his palsy increased, and he suffered from strangury—painful difficulty in urination. When the current Earl moved from Chatsworth to Hardwick Hall, Hobbes insisted on going with him. The trip proved exhausting. A week later his paralysis spread, putting an end to his speech. On December 4, 1679, having received the Sacrament as an obedient Anglican, he died, four months short of completing his ninety-second year.

6. Results

Hobbes's psychology was a masterpiece of deduction from inadequate premises. Logical as it seems at first view, its joints creak with loose assumptions that further inquiry might have corrected. Determinism is logical, but it may be determined by the mold of our logic, formed by dealing with things rather than ideas. Hobbes found difficulty in conceiving anything to be incorporeal; it seems equally difficult to conceive thought or consciousness as corporeal; yet these are the only realities directly known to us— everything else is hypothesis. Hobbes passed from object to sensation to idea without shedding much light upon the mysterious process whereby the apparently corporeal object generates the apparently incorporeal thought. Mechanistic psychology falters in the face of consciousness.

Nevertheless it was in psychology that Hobbes contributed most to our legacy. He cleared the field of some metaphysical ghosts like the Scholastic "faculties"—though these could be readily interpreted not as separate mental entities but as aspects of mental activity. He established the more evident principles of association, but underestimated the role of purpose and attention in determining the selection, sequence and persistence of ideas. He gave a helpful description of deliberation and volition. His analysis and defense of the passions was a brilliant summary, and it paid to Spinoza the debt that it owed to Descartes. From these psychological pages Locke developed his more careful and detailed *Essay concerning Human Understanding*. It was in answering Hobbes (rather than Filmer) that Locke evolved his treatises on government.

Hobbes's political philosophy reformulated Machiavelli in terms of Charles I. It stemmed from the successful absolutism of Henry VIII and Elizabeth in England, and of Henry IV and Richelieu in France; and doubtless it took some warmth from ducal friends and royal refugees. In immediate effect it seemed justified by the happy restoration of a Stuart King still claiming unlimited authority, and ending an erosive anarchy. But some able Englishmen felt that if the consent of "nasty and brutish" savages sufficed to create a government, the consent of men in a presumably more advanced condition might rightly check or topple it. So in the Glorious Revolution of 1688 the philosophy of absolutism fell before the reassertion of Parliament, and was soon replaced by the liberalism of Locke preaching the limitation and separation of powers. After a nineteenth century of relative democracy growing in an England guarded by the Channel and in an America protected by the seas, a modified absolutism returned in totalitarian states exercising governmental control over life, property, industry, religion, education, publication, and thought. Invention transcended mountains and moats, frontiers vanished, national isolation and security disappeared. The absolutist polity is a child of war, and democracy is a luxury of peace.

We do not know if Hobbes's "state of nature" ever existed; perhaps social organization antedated man. The tribe preceded the state, and custom is older, wider, deeper than law. The family is the biological ground of an altruism that enlarges the ego and its loyalties; Hobbes's ethic might have been kindlier if he had brought up a family. To let the state define morality (though this too has passed into the totalitarian regimes) is to destroy one of the forces improving the state. The moral sense sometimes enlarges its area of co-operation or devotion, and then prods the law to widen its protection accordingly. In a distant future it may be possible for a state to be Christian, as was once that of Ashoka, who was a Buddhist.

Hobbes's strongest influence was his materialism. From intellectual groups "Hobbism" flowed into the professional and business classes; the irate Bentley reported in 1693 that "the taverns and coffeehouses, nay, Westminster Hall [Parliament], and the very churches, were full of it."[64] Many men in the government privately accepted it, but publicly covered it with a conspicuous respect for the Established Church as a beneficent form of social control that only reckless fools would destroy. In France the materialistic philosophy affected Bayle's skepticism, and came to bolder developments in La Mettrie, d'Holbach, and Diderot.

Bayle ranked Hobbes as "one of the greatest geniuses of the seventeenth century."[65] Honored or denounced, he was recognized as the most power-ful philosopher that England had produced since Bacon, and as the first Englishman to present a formal treatise in political theory. One clear debt we owe him: he formulated his philosophy in logical order and lucid prose. Reading him and Bacon and Locke, or Fontenelle and Bayle and Voltaire, we perceive again what the Germans had made us forget, that obscurity need not be the distinguishing mark of a philosopher, and that every art should accept the moral obligation to be intelligible or silent.

II. HARRINGTON'S UTOPIA

While Hobbes defended an ailing monarchy, James Harrington proposed a democratic utopia. Now that exploration and commerce were opening up remote areas of the globe, and legends came to Europe with any cargo from overseas, it was a simple matter for imaginative wordsmen to voyage in fancy to some happy corner of the map—or, like Cyrano de Bergerac and Tommaso Campanella, to the moon or the sun—whose political and social customs would shame the tyranny and misery of men under "civiliza-tion." The cult of antiquity by the Renaissance gave way to a futuristic romance of more or less perfect states in distant and uncorrupted lands. So in 1656 Harrington offered his *Oceana* to the coffeehouses of London.

Born among the gentry, he naturally moved toward a political philosophy favoring the minor landlords of England. After leaving Oxford he traveled widely on the Continent, admired the Dutch Republic, served in the Dutch army, visited Venice, was impressed by its "republican" institutions, saw the Pope, refused to kiss the papal toe, and, returning to England, had all his sins forgiven when he explained to Charles I that he could not think of kissing the foot of a foreign prince after having kissed the hand of Eng-land's King. When Charles was arrested, Harrington was appointed by Parliament to attend him. He loved the unhappy prisoner, but explained to him the desirability of a republic. He accompanied Charles to the end, was on the scaffold at the execution, and, we are told, nearly died of grief.[66] Comforted by the birth of the English republic, he set himself to expound his republican ideas in fictional form. But while Harrington wrote, Crom-well changed the new republic into a semimonarchical protectorate; and when *The Commonwealth of Oceana* was passing through the press the Protector ordered it suppressed. Cromwell's favorite daughter, Mrs. Clay-pole, interceded for the book, Harrington dedicated it to her father, and it saw the light in 1656.

"Oceana" is England as the author hoped that Cromwell would remake it. He lays down a principle which, two centuries later, was expanded into the economic interpretation of history: political supremacy, says Harrington, naturally and rightly follows economic supremacy; only in that accord can a state enjoy stability. "Such as is the proportion of property in land, such is the nature of the empire"—i.e., the government.[67] If one man (as in Turkey) owns all the land, the government will be an absolute monarchy; if a few own it, the government will be a "mixed monarchy" supported and limited by an aristocracy; "and if the whole people be landlords, or hold the lands so divided among them that no one man or number of men . . . overbalance them, the empire (without the imposition of force) is a commonwealth."[68] To Hobbes, who thought that all government rests on force, Harrington answered that armies had to be fed and armed, so power goes to those who can raise the money to feed and arm them.[69] A change in the form or direction of the government is merely an adjustment to a change in the distribution of property. On this basis Harrington explained the victory of the Long Parliament, as representing the gentry, over the King as representing the major landowners.

To prevent the government from being an oligarchy of large estates, Harrington proposed an "equal agrarian" law limiting any one person to land yielding no more than two thousand pounds a year. Actual democracy requires a wide distribution of property; and the best democracy will be one in which every landowner has a turn in government. In the true English republic the citizens will send landowners to serve in a popular assembly and a senate. The senate alone will propose laws, the assembly alone will pass or reject them. The senators will nominate candidates for public office; from that list the citizens will elect the magistrates by secret ballot.[70] Each year one third of the assemblymen, the senators, and the magistrates will be replaced by other men in a new election; by this rotation all landowners will ultimately have a term in the government. Popular election will protect the community against lawyers serving private interests, and against the clergy—"those declared and inveterate enemies of popular power."[71] There will be universal education in national schools and colleges, and complete freedom of religion.

"The Doctrine was very taking," reported Aubrey, and soon found enthusiastic supporters. Harrington gathered some of these (including Aubrey) in a "Rota" club (1659), which agitated for parliamentary enactment of his rotarian republic. He ascribed the current collapse of the Commonwealth to its failure to confiscate the large estates and redistribute the land in smaller parcels among the people; that failure left the nobles still powerful, and the people still poor and powerless; on the principle that property dictates government, the restoration of an oligarchic monarchy was inevitable unless Parliament voted the "agrarian law." "But," says Aubrey, "the greatest part of the Parliament-men perfectly hated this design of Rotation by Ballotting, for they were cursed tyrants and in love with their power";[72] they preferred to recall Charles II. As Harrington continued to propagate his plan even after the Restoration, the King had him committed to the Tower on a charge of conspiracy (1661). When efforts were made to free him by habeas corpus, he was transported to closer confinement on an island off Plymouth. There he fell into spells of insanity. He was released, but he never regained his health.

His utopia was more practical than most, and much of it has been realized. Perhaps one weakness lay in its assumption that land is the only form of wealth. Harrington mentioned the power of money in commerce and industry, but did not foresee its rise to political power; he may have felt that even commercial and industrial wealth is ultimately subject to owners of the land. The gradual extension of the franchise, and the secrecy of the ballot, were in line with his hopes; and though Britain rejected rotation in office as an annual dismemberment of experience, the United States accepted it in the periodical election of a part of Congress; and Locke, Montesquieu, and America approved his separation of governmental powers. Let not dreamers despair; time may surprise them with fulfillments, and turn their poetry into prose.

III. THE DEISTS

As the religious wars injured religious belief in France, so the Civil War in England shared in generating theological doubts. Memories of the Puritan regime made irreligion popular among the triumphant royalists, and made atheism ribald and boisterous at the Restoration court. The first Earl of Shaftesbury, the second Duke of Buckingham, and the second Earl of Rochester were suspected of atheism; so, later, were Halifax and Bolingbroke.

The extension of geographical, historical, and scientific knowledge widened the skeptical current. Every day some traveler or chronicler told of great nations whose religion and morals were shockingly different from the Christian, but usually as virtuous, and seldom as homicidal. The mechanical view of the world encouraged by the pious Descartes and the apocalyptic Newton seemed to be pushing Providence out of sight; the discovery of law in nature was making miracles indigestible; the slow triumph of Copernicus and the dramatic prosecution of Galileo contributed to the erosion of belief. The brave attempt of many Christian theologians to demonstrate the creed by reason weakened the creed; no one, said Anthony Collins, doubted the existence of God until the Boyle lecturers undertook to prove it.[73]

The refutations of atheism attested its spread. Sir William Temple wrote
(1672) "of those who would pass for wits . . . by saying things which,
David tells us, the fool hath said in his heart."[74] In the same year Sir Charles
Wolseley remarked that "irreligion in its practice hath been the companion
of every age, but its open and public defense seems to be peculiar to this."[75]
According to Archdeacon Samuel Parker (1681),

> . . . the ignorant and unlearned among ourselves are become the
> greatest pretenders to skepticism and infidelity. . . . Atheism and ir-
> religion are at length become as common as vice and debauchery. . . .
> Plebeians and mechanics have philosophized themselves into principles
> of impiety, and read their lectures of atheism in the streets and high-
> ways. And they are able to demonstrate out of *The Leviathan* that
> there is no God.[76]

Among the educated classes doubt sought a compromise in Unitarianism,
"natural religion," and deism. The Unitarians questioned the equality of
Christ with the Father, but they usually accepted the divine authority of
the Bible. The advocates of natural religion preferred a faith independent
of Scripture and limited to beliefs which they thought universal—in God
and immortality. The deists, who made their chief stir in England, required only a belief in God, whom they sometimes depersonalized into a
synonym for Nature, or the Prime Pusher of the Cartesian or Newtonian
world machine. The word *deist* first came into prominence in 1677,
through Archdeacon Edward Stillingfleet's *Letter to a Deist*, but the deistic
literature had begun with Lord Herbert of Cherbury's *De Veritate* in 1624.

Lord Herbert's disciple, Charles Blount, carried on with *Anima Mundi*
(1679). All organized religion, ran the argument, was the creation of impostors seeking political power or material gain; heaven and hell were
among their clever inventions to control and milk the populace. The soul
dies with the body. Men and beasts are so alike that "some authors are of
opinion that man is nothing but an ape cultivated." In *Great Is Diana of
the Ephesians, or The Origin of Idolatry* (1680), Blount made priests themselves the tools of privileged classes that fattened on the patient labor and
credulity of the people. With impish subtlety he translated Philostratus'
Life of Apollonius of Tyana, indicated the similarities between the miracles
ascribed to the pagan wonder-worker and those attributed to Christians,
and gently suggested their equal incredibility. In *A Summary Account of
the Deists' Religion* (1686) Blount proposed a religion free from all cult
and ritual, and consisting only of the worship of God by a moral life. In
The Oracles of Reason (1693) he pointed out that the Christian theology
was at first based upon the erroneous expectation of an early end to the
world. He ridiculed the Biblical stories of Creation. of Eve's birth from

Adam's rib, of original sin, of the stopping of the sun by Joshua, as childish absurdities, and suggested that "to believe our modern earth (a blind and sordid particle of the universe, inferior to each of the fixed stars as well in bulk as in dignity) to be the heart, the most noble and vital part, of so vast a body, is irrational and repugnant to the nature of things." An anonymous work uncertainly ascribed to Blount, *Miracles No Violations of the Laws of Nature* (1683), tried to explain many miracle stories as honest misconceptions, by simple minds, of natural causes and events. The Bible, it added, was written to "excite pious affections," not to teach physics, and it should be interpreted accordingly. "Whatever is against Nature is against Reason, and whatever is against Reason is absurd, and should be rejected."[77] Blount himself did not worship reason to the end, if we may believe the report that he killed himself (1693) because English law would not let him marry his deceased wife's sister.

John Toland continued the campaign. Born in Ireland, he was brought up as a Roman Catholic, but was converted to Protestantism in his youth. He studied at Glasgow, Leiden, and Oxford. At twenty-six he issued anonymously *Christianity Not Mysterious* (1696), which he described as "a treatise showing that there is nothing in the Gospel contrary to reason, nor above it." Accepting Locke's recent *Essay concerning Human Understanding* as having proved the sense origin of all knowledge, he drew from it a thoroughgoing rationalism:

> We hold that Reason is the only foundation of all our certitude, and that nothing revealed . . . is more exempted from its disquisitions than the ordinary phenomena of Nature. . . . To believe the divinity of Scripture, or the sense of any passage thereof, without rational proof and an evident consistency, is a blamable credulity . . . ordinarily grounded upon an ignorant and willful disposition, but more generally maintained out of a gainful prospect.[78]

This was a declaration of war, but as Toland proceeded he unveiled an olive branch by arguing that the basic doctrines of Christianity, excepting transubstantiation, are quite reasonable. Nevertheless his challenge was not ignored. The grand juries of Middlesex and Dublin joined hands across the Irish Sea to condemn the book; it was officially burned before the doors of the Irish Parliament, and Toland was sentenced to jail. He escaped to England, but, unable to secure employment there, he migrated to the Continent. For a time he found welcome with Electress Sophia of Hanover and her daughter Sophia Charlotte, Queen of Prussia.

To the latter he addressed *Letters to Serena* (1704). One of these tried to trace the origin and growth of the belief in immortality; this was among the first attempts at a natural history of supernatural beliefs. Another letter disputed the view that matter is by itself inert and motionless; motion, said Toland, is inherent in matter, and no body is in absolute rest. All objective phenomena are the motions of matter, including the actions of animals, and this might be true of man as well.[79] Here, however, Toland checked himself; such thoughts should not be publicly expressed, for the uneducated multitude must be left in undisturbed orthodoxy as a means of moral and social control. Freethinking should be the duty, and the exclusive privilege, of the educated minority. Among these there should be no censorship; "let all men freely speak what they think, without being ever branded or punished but for wicked practices."[80] The terms *freethinker* and *pantheist* were apparently coined by Toland.[81]

His essay *Nazarenus* (1718) suggested that Christ had not intended to separate his followers from Judaism, and that the Jewish Christians, who continued to observe the Mosaic Law, represented "the true original plan of Christianity." A pamphlet, *Pantheisticus*, expounded the creed and ritual of an imaginary secret society; perhaps Toland was a member of the "Mother Grand Lodge" of Freemasonry which was established in London in 1717. The society described by Toland rejected all supernatural revelations, proposed a new religion agreeing with philosophy, identified God with the universe, and replaced the saints of the Christian calendar with the heroes of liberty and thought. The society allowed its members to conform to the popular worship so long as, through their political influence, they could render fanaticism harmless.[82]

After a fitful and varied career Toland retired to a life of poverty in England, kept from starvation by Lord Molesworth and the philosopher Shaftesbury. He bore up stoutly under the storm of refutations (fifty-four in sixty years) that fell upon his books. He claimed that philosophy had granted him "perfect tranquillity," and had freed him from "the terrors of death."[83] Attacked by an incurable disease at the age of fifty-two (1722), he composed his own proud epitaph:

> Here lies John Toland, who was born . . . near Londonderry. . . . He cultivated the various literatures, and was acquainted with more than ten languages. The Champion of Truth, the Defender of Liberty, he bound himself to no man, on no man did he fawn. Neither threats nor misfortunes deterred him from his appointed course, which he pursued to the very end, subordinating his own interest to the pursuit of the Good. His soul is united with the Heavenly Father, from whom he first proceeded. Beyond all doubt he will live again unto all eternity, yet never will there be another Toland. . . . For the rest consult his writings.[84]

Anthony Collins took up the deist cause with more skill and modesty. He had the advantages of money, a house in the country, a house in the town; he could not be refuted by starvation. He was a man of fine manners and irreproachable character. Locke, who knew him well, wrote to him: "To love truth for truth's sake is the principal part of human perfection in this world, and the seed-plot of all other virtues; and, if I mistake not, you have as much of it as ever I met with in anybody."[85] Collins' *Discourse of Freethinking* (1713) was the ablest exposition that deism received in this age.

He defined freethinking as "the use of the understanding in endeavoring to find out the meaning of any proposition whatsoever, in considering the nature of the evidence for or against it, and in judging of it according to the seeming force or weakness of the evidence. . . . There is no other way to discover the truth."[86] The diversity of creeds, and the contradictory interpretations of Biblical passages, compel us to accept the judgment of reason; to what other court can we turn, unless it be to the arbitrament of force? How, except by evidence and reasoning, can we decide which books of the Bible are to be accepted as authentic, and which should be set aside as apocryphal? Collins quotes a divine as estimating at thirty thousand the number of different readings proposed by scholars for the text of the New Testament alone; and he refers to Richard Simon's textual criticism of the Scriptures.[87]

He tries to answer the objections that cautious men advanced against free thought: that most people have not the capacity to think both freely and harmlessly about fundamental problems; that such freedom would lead to endless divisions of opinion and sects, and therefore to disorders in society; that freethinking may conduce to atheism in religion and libertinism in morals. He gives ancient Greece and modern Turkey as examples of social order maintained despite freedom of opinion or diversity of faiths. He denies that freethinking makes for atheism; he quotes and supports Bacon's aphorism about a little thought inclining us to atheism, and more thought turning us away from it; ignorance, he adds, with apparent sincerity, "is the foundation of atheism, and freethinking the cure for it."[88] He lists freethinkers who were "the most virtuous people in all ages": Socrates, Plato, Aristotle, Epicurus, Plutarch, Varro, Cato Censor, Cato of Utica, Cicero, Seneca, Solomon, the Prophets, Origen, Erasmus, Montaigne, Bacon, Hobbes, Milton, Tillotson, Locke; here and in Toland we have a model for Comte's calendar of positivist saints. And (Collins suggests) another list could be made of those foes of free thought who disgraced humanity with barbarous cruelties under the pretext of glorifying God.

So many replies rained down upon him from pulpits and universities that Collins thought discretion required travel. His stay in Holland may have left upon him some influence from Spinoza and Bayle. Returning to England, he raised another storm with an *Inquiry concerning Human Liberty* (1715), which stated with clarity and force the case for determinism; Collins found himself a freethinker slave to an unfree will. Nine years later he set the theological air astir by a *Discourse on the Grounds and Reason of the Christian Religion*. He quoted the Apostles and Pascal as basing their demonstration of Christianity on Old Testament prophecies which the new dispensation had seemingly fulfilled, and he argued that these predictions had no reference to Christianity or Christ. Thirty-five theologians answered him in thirty-five tracts. The controversy was still alive when Voltaire reached England in 1726; he enjoyed it mischievously, and imported it into France, where it entered into the skeptical Enlightenment.

The deistic movement was continued in England by William Whiston, Matthew Tindal, Thomas Chubb, and Conyers Middleton, and passed down through Bolingbroke and the philosopher Shaftesbury to Gibbon and Hume. It became unpopular with the ruling classes when they suspected it of encouraging democratic ideas; but its immediate influence was felt in a temporary decline of religious belief. In 1711 an official report on the subject was drawn up for the Upper House of Convocation of the English clergy in the province of Canterbury. It described a wide spread of unbelief and profanity, denials of Biblical inspiration, rejection of miracles as fables, ridicule of the doctrine of the Trinity, doubts of immortality, and much decrying of priests as impostors.[89] By the beginning of the eighteenth century in England "religion had sunk to deism."[90] It was in this crisis that some of the ablest minds in Britain rose vigorously to the defense of Christianity.

IV. DEFENDERS OF THE FAITH

Most of them were willing to meet their assailants on the grounds of reason, scholarship, and history; this in itself betrayed the spirit of the age.

Charles Leslie led the defense with *A Short and Easy Method with the Deists* (1697), intended originally as a reply to Blount. The evidences for the Biblical narratives, he argued, were of the same nature, and as convincing, as for the careers of Alexander and Caesar; the miracles were attested by testimony as plentiful and reliable as that which is accepted as adequate in English courts; priests could never have persuaded peoples of such miracles as the parting of the Red Sea unless many eyewitnesses had corroborated them. Leslie rounded out his argument by portraying Judaism as a primitive covenant superseded by the coming of Christ, Mohammedanism as an ungrateful imitation of Christianity by an ambitious impostor, and paganism as a mass of fables too childish for rational belief. Only the Christian religion met all the tests of evidence and reason.

Samuel Clarke, who knew enough mathematics and physics to defend Newton against Leibniz, undertook to prove the Christian creed by demonstrations as rigorous as geometry. In his Boyle lectures of 1704 he forged a chain of twelve propositions which in his judgment established the existence, omnipresence, omnipotence, omniscience, and benevolence of God. The chain of contingent or dependent beings and causes, he supposed, compels us to assume a necessary and independent being who is the first cause of all causes. God must have intelligence, for there is intelligence in created beings, and the creator must be more perfect than the creature; God must be free, for otherwise His intelligence would be a senseless slavery. This, of course, added nothing to ancient or medieval philosophy; but in the second series of his Boyle lectures Clarke proposed to prove "the truth and certainty of the Christian revelation." Moral principles, he thought, are as absolute as the laws of nature; man's depraved nature, however, can be led to obey these moral rules only through the inculcation of religious beliefs; hence it was necessary that God give us the Bible, and the doctrines of heaven and hell. History, with its usual humor, adds that Clarke was dismissed by Queen Anne as her chaplain because he was suspected of doubting the Trinity. In the next reign, according to the impish Voltaire, he was prevented from becoming archbishop of Canterbury because a bishop informed Princess Caroline that Clarke was the most learned man in England, but had one defect—he was not a Christian.[91]

The still more learned Bentley had already demonstrated "the Folly and Unreasonableness of Atheism" in the Boyle lectures of 1692–93. Twenty years later he was aroused by Collins' book to issue some *Remarks on a Late Discourse of Freethinking*. This chiefly consisted of exposing errors in Collins' scholarship; the argument seemed overwhelming, and the senate of Cambridge University gave Bentley a unanimous vote of thanks. Jonathan Swift, who was then serving the deist Bolingbroke, thought that Collins, for having revealed a secret that all gentlemen kept to themselves, deserved additional chastisement; this he administered in a tract called *Mr. Collins' Discourse of Freethinking, Put into Plain English . . . for the Use of the Poor*. He burlesqued Collins' arguments by humorous exaggerations; he added that since most men are fools, it would be disastrous to leave them free to think; "the bulk of mankind is as well qualified for flying as for thinking"[92]—which is now a more hopeful statement than Swift intended it to be. He agreed with Hobbes that dictatorship, even *in spiritualibus*, is the sole alternative to anarchy. We have seen that the

Irish Anglicans thought the gloomy Dean would make an excellent prelate if he believed in God.

The Cambridge Platonists defended Christianity with less wit and more sincerity. They went back to Plato and Plotinus to find a bridge between reason and God, and they illustrated their faith not so much by arguments as by the integrity and devotion of their lives. They had so strong a sense of divinity surrounding them that this seemed to them the most immediate testimony of reason. Hence their first leader, Benjamin Whichcote, claimed that "reason is the voice of God."[93]

Henry More, the outstanding member of this once famous group, went beyond the philosophies of Europe to an almost Hindu sense of the vanity, the literal emptiness, of sense knowledge, its incapacity to satisfy the longing of the solitary soul for some companionship and significance in the universe. The cosmic mechanism of Descartes gave him no comfort; he found more to his needs in the Neoplatonists, the Jewish mystics, and Jakob Böhme. He wondered "whether the knowledge of things was really that supreme felicity of man, or something greater and more divine was; or, supposing it to be so, whether it was to be acquired by such an eagerness or intentness in the reading of authors, or contemplating of things; or by the purging of the mind from all sorts of vices whatsoever."[94] He resolved to cleanse himself of all self-seeking, all worldliness, all intellectual curiosity. "When this inordinate desire after the knowledge of things was thus allayed in me, and I aspired after nothing but this sole purity and simplicity of mind, there shone in upon me daily a greater assurance than ever I could have expected, even of those things which before I had the greatest desire to know."[95] Gradually, he tells us, he so purified himself in body and soul that his flesh, in the spring season, gave forth a sweet odor, and his urine had the fragrance of violets.[96]

So cleansed, he seemed to feel the reality of spirit in himself as the most convincing experience possible to man; and from this conviction he passed readily to the belief that the world was peopled by other spirits, of ascending grades, from the lowest to God Himself. All motion in matter, he thought, is the operation of some species of spirit. Instead of the material plenum of Hobbes, More proposed a spiritual universe in which matter was merely the tool and vehicle of spirit. This animating *anima* occasionally expanded beyond its habitation; how else explain magnetism, electricity, and gravity? More went on to accept the reality of devils, witches, and ghosts. He was an amiable and unselfish soul, refusing the worldly preferments offered him, and remaining on friendly terms with materialist Hobbes. Hobbes said that if he ever found his own opinions untenable, he "would embrace the philosophy of Dr. More."[97]

Ralph Cudworth, the most learned of the Cambridge Platonists, undertook to prove Hobbes's opinions untenable. *The True Intellectual System of the Universe* (1678) challenged Hobbes to explain why, in addition to the various sensory and muscular motions to which he had reduced the operations of the mind, there is also, in many cases, an *awareness* of these motions; how can a materialist philosophy find room and function for consciousness? If all is matter in motion, why should not the nervous system, through sensation and response, as in reflexes, attend to everything, and not be bothered with a superfluous consciousness? How can we deny reality—even primacy—to a consciousness without which no reality whatever could be known? Knowledge is no passive receptacle of sensations, it is the active transformation of sensations into ideas.[98] Here, in Cudworth, we have, long in advance, the answer of Berkeley and Kant to Hobbes and Hume.

Joseph Glanvill, chaplain to Charles II, was not geographically one of the Cambridge Platonists, but he strongly agreed with them. In *The Vanity of Dogmatizing* (1661) he turned the guilt of dogmatism upon science and philosophy, arguing that they had built up grandiose systems of doctrine upon insecure foundations. So the notion of cause (which Glanvill supposed indispensable to science) is an unwarrantable assumption; we know sequences, relations, and occasions, but we have no idea of what it is in one thing that produces an effect in itself or another (another premonition of Hume). Consider, says Glanvill, how ignorant we are of the most basic things—the nature and origin of the soul, and its relation to the body. "How should a thought be united to . . . a lump of clay? The freezing of the words in the air in northern climes is as inconceivable as this strange union. . . . And to hang weights on the wings·of the wind seems far more intelligible."[99] Anticipating Bergson, Glanvill charges the intellect with being a constitutional materialist—so used to dealing with matter that it loses capacity to think of other realities except by a "return to material phantasms," or images.[100] How fallible our senses are! They make it appear that the earth is at rest in space, whereas the latest pundits assure us that it is dizzy with a variety of simultaneous motions. And even supposing that our senses have not deceived us, how often do we reason wrongly from correct premises! Our feelings time and again mislead us; "we easily believe what we wish." And our mental environment often dominates our reasoning.

> Opinions have their climes and national diversities. . . . They that never peeped beyond the common belief in which their easy understandings were at first indoctrinated, are indubitably assured of the Truth and comparative excellency of their receptions. . . . The larger souls, that have traveled the divers climates of opinion [here is born

a famous phrase] are more cautious in their resolves, and more sparing to determine.[101]

Despite these warnings to science, Glanvill was a zealous member of the Royal Society, defended it against charges of irreligion, applauded its achievements, and looked forward to a world of marvels to come from scientific research:

> I doubt not but posterity will find many things, that are now but rumors, verified into practical realities. It may be, some ages hence, a voyage to the Southern unknown tracts, yea possibly to the moon, will not be more strange than one to America. To them that come after us it may be as ordinary to buy a pair of wings to fly into remotest regions, as now a pair of boots to ride a journey. And to confer at the distance of the Indies by sympathetic conveyances may be as usual to future times, as to us in a literary correspondence. The restoration of gray hairs to juvenility, and renewing the exhausted marrow, may at length be effected without a miracle; and the turning of the now comparatively desert world into a paradise may not improbably be expected from late agriculture.[102]

We must add that Glanvill, like Cudworth and Henry More, believed in witches. They argued that if there is a spiritual as well as a material world, there must be spirits as well as bodies in the universe; and judging from the parlous state of things some of these spirits must be devilish. If pious people communicate with God or saints or angels, why should not wicked people communicate with Satan and his demons? The Devil's last stratagem, said Glanvill, is to spread the belief that he does not exist. "Those that dare not bluntly say, There is no God, content themselves (for a fair step and introduction) to deny that there are spirits and witches."[103] Satan had to be rescued for God's sake.

V. JOHN LOCKE: 1632–1704

1. Biography

The most influential philosopher of this age was born at Wrington, near Bristol, in the same year as Spinoza. He grew up in an England that made a bloody revolution and killed its King; he became the voice of a peaceful revolution and an age of moderation and tolerance, and represented English compromise at its sanest and best. His father was a Puritan attorney, who at some sacrifice supported the Parliamentary cause, and expounded to his son the doctrines of popular sovereignty and representative government. Locke remained faithful to these lessons, and grateful for the paternal discipline that trained him to sobriety, simplicity, and industry. Lady Masham said of Locke's father that he

> used a conduct towards him when young that he [the son] often spoke of afterwards with great approbation. It was the being severe to him by keeping him in much awe and at a distance when he was a boy, but relaxing still by degrees of that severity as he grew up to be a man, till, he being become capable of it, he lived perfectly with him as a friend.[104]

Locke bore no similar gratitude toward his teachers. At Westminster School he was choked with Latin, Greek, Hebrew, and Arabic, and was probably not allowed to witness the execution of Charles I (1649) in nearby Whitehall Palace Yard; but that event left a mark on his philosophy. The turmoil of the Civil War delayed his entry into Christ College, Oxford, till he was twenty years old. There he studied Aristotle as dressed in Latin Scholastic form; more Greek; some geometry and rhetoric; much logic and ethics, most of which he later disgorged as antequated in substance and indigestible in form. After taking his master's degree (1658) he remained at Oxford as a don, tutoring and lecturing. He had a love affair which for a time "robbed me of the use of my reason";[105] he regained his reason and lost the lady. Like nearly all the philosophers in this period—Malebranche, Bayle, Fontenelle, Hobbes, Spinoza, Leibniz—he never married. He was advised to enter the ministry, but he demurred at "being lifted into a place which perhaps I cannot fill, and from whence there is no descending without tumbling."[106]

In 1661 his father died of tuberculosis, leaving him with a small fortune and weak lungs. He studied medicine, but did not take the medical degree till 1674. Meanwhile he read Descartes, and felt the fascination of philosophy when it spoke intelligibly. He helped Robert Boyle in laboratory experiments, and acquired an admiration for scientific method. In 1667 he received an invitation to come and live at Exeter House as personal physician to Anthony Ashley Cooper, soon to be first Earl of Shaftesbury, member of the Cabal ministry under Charles II. From that time onward, though keeping Oxford as his legal home till 1683, Locke found himself in the stream of English politics, whose events and figures molded his thought.

As physician he saved Shaftesbury's life by a skillful operation for tumor (1668). He helped to negotiate the marriage of the Earl's son, attended the daughter-in-law in her confinement, and directed the education of the

grandson, his successor in philosophy. "Mr. Locke," recalled this third
Earl of Shaftesbury,

> grew so much in esteem with my grandfather that, as great a man as
> he experienced him in physic, he looked upon this as but his least part.
> He encouraged him to turn his thoughts another way; nor would he
> suffer him to practice physic except in his own family, and as a kind-
> ness to some particular friend. He put him upon the study of the
> religious and civil affairs of the nation, with whatsoever related to
> the business of a minister of state; in which he was so successful that
> my grandfather began to use him as a friend, and consult with him
> on all occasions of that kind.[107]

For two years (1673-75) Locke served as secretary to the Council of
Trade and Plantations (Colonies), of which Shaftesbury was president.
He helped Shaftesbury to draft a constitution for Carolina, of which the
Earl was a founder and a chief proprietor; these "Fundamental Institutions"
were not generally carried out in the colony, but the freedom of conscience
provided in them was largely accepted by the new settlement.[108]

When Shaftesbury fell from office in 1675 Locke traveled and studied in
France. There he met François Bernier, who introduced him to the philosophy of Gassendi; therein he found a reasoned rejection of "innate ideas,"
the comparison of the unborn child's mind to a *tabula rasa*, or clean slate,
and the key sentence that was to be later bandied across the Channel:
Nihil est in intellectu nisi quod prius fuerit in sensu—"There is nothing in
the mind except what was first in the senses."

Locke returned to London and Shaftesbury in 1679, but as the Earl
ventured closer and closer to revolution, Locke retired to Oxford (1680),
and resumed the life of a scholar. Shaftesbury's arrest, escape, and flight
to Holland cast royal suspicion upon his friends. Spies were sent to Oxford
to catch Locke in remarks that might serve as a basis for prosecuting him.[109]
Feeling insecure, and foreseeing the accession of his enemy James II,
Locke too sought refuge in Holland (1683). The abortive revolution of
the Duke of Monmouth (1685) provoked James to demand from the
Dutch government the extradition of eighty-five Englishmen on the charge
that they had shared in the plot to overthrow the new King; Locke was
named among them. He hid, and took a false name. A year later James
sent him an offer of pardon, but Locke preferred to remain in Holland.
Living in Utrecht, Amsterdam, and Rotterdam, he enjoyed the friendship
not only of English refugees but of Dutch scholars like Jean Le Clerc
and Philip van Limborch, both of them leaders in the liberal Arminian
theology. In that environment Locke found much encouragement for his
ideas of popular sovereignty and religious freedom. There he wrote his

Essay concerning Human Understanding, and the first drafts of his treatises on education and toleration.

In 1687 he joined in the plot to replace James II with William III on the throne of England.[110] When the expedition of the Stadholder succeeded in this enterprise, Locke sailed to England (1689) on the same vessel that carried the future Queen Mary.[111] Before leaving Holland he wrote to Limborch, in Latin, a letter whose warmth of sentiment may correct the supposition that his habitual moderation stemmed from coldness of character:

> In going away, I almost feel as though I were leaving my own country and my own kinsfolk; for everything that belongs to kinship, good will, love, kindness—everything that binds men together with ties stronger than that of blood—I have found among you in abundance. I leave behind me friends whom I can never forget, and I shall never cease to wish for an opportunity of coming back to enjoy once more the genuine fellowship of men who have been such friends that, while far away from my own connections, while suffering in every other way, I have never felt sick at heart. As for you, best, dearest, and most worthy of men, when I think of your learning, your wisdom, your kindness and candor and gentleness, I seem to have found in your friendship alone enough to make me always rejoice that I was forced to pass so many years amongst you.[112]

In an England governed by his friends, Locke passed through a succession of official employments. In 1690 he was a commissioner of appeals; in 1696–1700 he was a commissioner of trade and plantations. He was intimate with John Somers, attorney general, with Charles Montagu, first Earl of Halifax, and with Isaac Newton, whom he aided in reforming the coinage. After 1691 he lived most of the time at Oates Manor in Essex with Sir Francis Masham and his wife, Lady Damaris Masham, a daughter of Ralph Cudworth. He remained in that quiet haven, writing and rewriting, till his death.

2. Government and Property

When he came back from exile he was already fifty-six years old. So far he had published only some minor articles, and a French epitome of his *Essay* in Le Clerc's *Bibliothèque universelle* (1688). He was not yet known as a philosopher except to a few friends. Then, all in one *annus mirabilis*, he sent to the press three works that made him a major figure in European thought. In March, 1689, his *Epistola de Tolerantia* appeared in Holland; it was translated into English in the fall; and it was followed in 1690 by a *Second Letter concerning Toleration*. In February, 1690, he issued his two *Treatises on Government*, the cornerstone of modern democratic theory in England and America; and a month later the *Essay concerning Human Understanding*, the most influential book in modern psychology. Though this had been completed before he left Holland, he preceded it in print by the *Treatises on Government* because he was anxious to provide a philosophical basis for the Glorious Revolution of 1688–89. This purpose was frankly stated in the preface to the first treatise: "to establish the throne of our great restorer, our present William III; to make good his title in the consent of the people . . . and to justify to the world the people of England, whose love of their just and natural rights, with their resolution to preserve them, saved the nation when it was on the brink of slavery and ruin."[113]

The first and lesser treatise undertook to answer the *Patriarcha, or The Natural Power of Kings Asserted*, which Sir Robert Filmer had written about 1642 to uphold the divine right of Charles I, but which had only recently (1680) reached print in the heyday of Charles II's triumphant absolutism. It was not the best of Sir Robert's writings. He published anonymously in 1648 *The Anarchy of a Limited Mixed Monarchy*, anticipating Hobbes's views. Though he suffered imprisonment for his defense of a losing cause, he defended it again in *Observations upon Aristotle's Politiques*, published anonymously in 1652, a year before the author's death.

Filmer presented government as an extension of the family. God conferred sovereignty over the first human family upon Adam, from whom it descended to the patriarchs. Those who (like Filmer's opponents) believe in the divine inspiration of the Bible must admit that the patriarchal family, and the power of the patriarch, were sanctioned by God. From the patriarchs this sovereignty passed to kings; the early kings were patriarchs, and their authority was a form and derivative of parental rule. Monarchy, therefore, goes back to Adam, and so to God; its sovereignty, except when it commands an explicit violation of God's law, is divine and absolute; and rebellion against it is a sin as well as a crime.[114]

Against the theory that man is born free, Filmer points out that man is born subject to the customs and laws of the group, and to the natural and legal rights of parents over their children; "natural freedom" is a romantic myth. It is also a myth that government was originally established by the consent and agreement of the people. "Representative government" is another myth; actually the representative is chosen by a small and active minority in each constituency.[115] All government is of a majority by a minority. It is in the nature of government to be above the laws, for by definition a legislature is empowered to make and unmake laws. "We do but flatter ourselves if we hope ever to be governed without an arbitrary power."[116] If government is to depend upon the will of the governed, there will soon be no government, for every individual or group will claim the right to rebel according to "conscience." That would be anarchy, or mob rule; and "there is no tyranny to be compared to the tyranny of the multitude."[117]

Locke felt that his first task, as defender of the Glorious Revolution, was to dispose of Filmer's arguments. He thought "there was never so much glib nonsense put together in well-sounding English" as in Sir Robert's discourses.[118] "I should not speak so plainly of a gentleman long since past answering, had not the pulpit, of late years, publicly owned his doctrine and made it the current divinity of the times"—i.e., had not the Anglican clergy upheld the divine right of kings even under Catholic James II. Locke proceeded with playful, sometimes ungracious, sarcasm to question Filmer's derivation of royal authority from the supposed sovereignty of Adam and the patriarchs; we need not follow him in his long Biblical refutation; today we rationalize our political prejudices by other than Scriptural means. Something of Filmer remains after Locke's rough handling of him—the attempt, however mistaken in detail, to illuminate the nature of government by seeking its origins in history, even in biology. Probably both Filmer and Locke underestimated the role of conquest and force in the establishment of states.

In the *Second Treatise of Civil Government* Locke turned to the task of finding for the rule of William III in England some more defensible basis than a divine right that would unfortunately return the power to James II. In deriving William's title from the consent of the governed he assumed more than he could historically prove: the people had not given their consent to William's conquest of England, and the aristocrats who had maneuvered it had thought not of securing popular consent, but only of avoiding public resistance. Nevertheless, in building a philosophical prop for William's power, Locke raised an impressive defense of popular sovereignty. While defending a monarch he developed the theory of representative government; and while offering a rationale to the Whigs and the defenders of property he formulated the gospel of political liberty. He ended, in English political philosophy, the ascendancy of Hobbes.

He followed Hobbes in assuming a primitive "state of nature" before the rise of states; like Hobbes and Filmer he fashioned history to his purpose; but, unlike Hobbes, he imagined that individuals in the "state of nature" were free and equal; he used this word as Jefferson was to use it in following him, to mean that no man had by nature more "rights" than any other; and he allows to man in the "natural condition" certain social instincts as a psychological preparation for society. Occasionally Locke makes some amiable assumptions—"Every man being . . . naturally free, and nothing being able to put him into subjection to any earthly power without his consent . . ."[119] The state of nature, in this theory, was not a Hobbesian war of each against all, for the "law of nature" supported the rights of men as reasoning animals. By reason (Locke supposed) men came to an agreement—made a "social contract" with one another—to surrender their individual rights of judging and punishing not to a king but to the community as a whole. Hence the community is the real sovereign. By its majority vote it selects a chief administrator to implement its will.[120] He may be called king, but, like any other citizen, he is bound to obey the laws enacted by the community. If (like James II) he seeks to violate or circumvent them, the community has the right to withdraw from him the authority which it has conferred.

Locke was really defending not William against James, but (the now victorious) Parliament against any king. The highest power in a state should be the legislature. It should be chosen by the unpurchased vote of the people, and the laws should punish severely any attempt to buy the vote of a citizen or a legislator; Locke did not foresee that his admired William III would be forced to buy the vote of M.P.s, and that powerful families would continue for yet 140 years to control and dispose of the vote of "rotten boroughs." The functions of the legislature should be strictly separate from those of the executive, and each of these branches of the government should serve as a check upon the other.

"Government," said Locke, "has no other end but the preservation of property."[121] There had once been a primitive communism, when food grew without planting and men could live without toil; but when labor began communism ended, for a man naturally claimed as his separate property anything whose value had been created by his work. Labor, then, is the source of "ninety-nine hundredths" of all physical values.[122] (Here, quite without intending it, Locke offered one of its basic tenets to modern socialism.) Civilization grows through labor, and therefore through the institution of property as the product of labor. Theoretically no man should have more property than he can use;[123] but the invention of money enabled him to sell such surplus product of his labor as he could not utilize; and in this way there developed the great inequality of possessions among men. We might have expected at this point some criticism of the concentration of wealth; instead, Locke looked upon property, however unequally distributed, as natural and sacred; the continuance of social order and civilization requires that the protection of property shall be the paramount purpose of the state. "The supreme power cannot take from any man part of his property without his consent."[124]

On this basis Locke could not admit any revolution involving the expropriation of property. But as the "prophet and voice of the Glorious Revolution"[125] he could not deny the right to overthrow a government. "The people are absolved from obedience when illegal attempts are made upon their liberties or properties," for "the end of government is the good of mankind. And which is best for mankind? That the people should be always exposed to the boundless will of tyranny, or that the rulers should be sometimes liable to be opposed when they grow exorbitant in the use of their power and employ it for the destruction and not the preservation of the properties of their people?"[126] Whereas some Huguenot and some Jesuit philosophers had sanctioned revolution to protect the one true religion, Locke sanctions it only to protect property. Secularization was changing the locus and definition of sanctity.

Locke's influence on political thought remained supreme till Karl Marx. His philosophy of the state was so well suited to the Whig ascendancy and the English character that for a century its faults were ignored as trivial blemishes in a magnificent Magna Carta of the bourgeoisie. It provided a halo not only to 1689 but, by remarkable anticipation, to 1776 and 1789—i.e., to the three stages in the revolt of business against birth, of money against land. Today critics smile at Locke's derivation of government from the consent of free men in a state of nature, just as he smiled at Filmer's derivation of it from the patriarchs, Adam, and God. "Natural rights" are suspect and theoretical; in a lawless society the only natural right is superior might, as now among states; and in civilization a right is a liberty desired by the individual and not injurious to the group. Rule by the majority may exist in small communities on less than vital concerns; usually rule is by an organized minority. Governments now recognize greater obligations than the protection of property.

Nevertheless, the achievement of that second treatise remains immense. It broadened the victory of Parliament and the Whigs over the monarchy and the Tories into a theory of representative and responsible government that inspired one people after another in its climb to liberty. England rejected Locke's separation of powers, and subordinated all government to the legislature; but his doctrine had aimed to check the executive, and that aim was completely achieved. Much of his trust in human reasonableness and decency, and his moderation in applying theory to practice, became standard procedure in English politics, making revolution imperceptible while real.

From England the ideas of Locke passed to France with Voltaire in 1729; they were taken up by Montesquieu on his visit to England in 1729-31; they found voice in Rousseau and others before and during the French Revolution, and appeared in full blast in the Constituent Assembly's

Declaration of the Rights of Man in 1789. When the American colonists rebelled against the resurgent monarchy of George III, they adopted the ideas, the formulas, almost the words, of Locke to express their Declaration of Independence. The rights that Locke had vindicated became the Bill of Rights in the first ten amendments to the American Constitution. His separation of governmental powers, as extended to the judiciary by Montesquieu, became a living factor in the American form of government; his solicitude for property passed into American legislation; his essays on toleration influenced the founding fathers in separating Church from state and decreeing religious liberty. Rarely in the history of political philosophy has one man had such lasting influence.

3. Mind and Matter

Locke's influence was as extensive and profound in psychology as in the theory of government. He had been writing the *Essay concerning Human Understanding* since 1670; characteristically he sent it to the printer only after twenty years of revision; and then, for this masterpiece of psychological analysis, he received thirty pounds. He himself ascribed the inception of the *Essay* to a conversation in London in 1670:

> Five or six friends meeting at my chamber, and discoursing on a subject very remote from this, found themselves quickly at a stand, by the difficulties that rose on every side. After we had a while puzzled ourselves, without coming any nearer a solution of those doubts . . . it came into my thoughts that we took a wrong course, and that before we set ourselves upon inquiries of that nature, it was necessary to examine our own abilities, and see what *objects* our understandings were, or were not, fitted to deal with. This I proposed to the company, who all readily assented; and thereupon it was agreed that this should be our first inquiry. Some hasty and undigested thoughts . . . which I set down against our next meeting gave the first entrance into this discourse.[127]

Apparently the stimulus to the *Essay* was the contention of the Cambridge Platonists—who here followed the Scholastic philosophers—that we derive our ideas of God and morality not from experience but from introspection, and that these ideas are innate with us, part of our mental equipment, however unconscious, at our birth. This view, rather than Descartes' incidental statements on "innate ideas," led Locke to consider whether there were any ideas whatever that were not the result of impressions from the external world.[128] Locke came to the conclusion that all knowledge—including our ideas of God and right and wrong—is derived from our experience, and is not part of the inborn structure of the mind. He knew that in arguing for this empirical position he would offend many of his contemporaries, who felt that morality required the support of religion, and that both morality and religion would be weakened if their basic ideas had any less noble origin than God Himself. He asked his readers to be patient with him; and for his own part he approached the dangerous discussion in a spirit of modest uncertainty. "I pretend not to teach, but to inquire."[129] He spoke quietly, moderately, leisurely. And he confessed that he was "too lazy, and too busy," to be brief.[130]

But at least he would define his terms. He protests against the "affected obscurity" of some philosophers.[131] "The knowing precisely what our words stand for would . . . in many cases . . . end the dispute."[132] It must be allowed that Locke's teaching in this particular is better than his practice. He defines *understanding* as "the power of perception," but he uses *perception* to include (1) the perception of ideas in our minds; (2) the perception of the signification of signs (words); and (3) the perception of the agreement or disagreement between ideas.[133] But what is idea? Locke uses the term to mean (1) the impress of external objects upon our senses (what we should call sensation); or (2) the internal awareness of this impress (what we should call perception); or (3) the image or memory connected with the idea (what we should call idea); or (4) the "notion" that combines many individual images into a general or abstract or "universal" concept of a class of similar objects. Locke does not always make clear in which sense he uses this troublesome term.*

He begins by rejecting "innate principles." "It is an established opinion, amongst some men, that there are in the understanding certain innate *principles*, some primary notions . . . stamped upon the mind of man, which the soul receives in its very first being, and brings into the world with it." He proposes to show "the falseness of this supposition."[135] He does not deny innate *tendencies*—what were later called tropisms, reflexes, or instincts; but these, in his view, are physiological habits, not ideas. Following Hobbes, he describes such processes as "trains of motion in the animal spirits, which, once set going, continue in the steps they have been used to, which, by often treading, are worn into a smooth path, and the motion in it becomes easy, and as it were natural" or inborn.[136] He is inclined to reduce the associations of ideas to such physiological paths.

---

* In discussing the subjectivity of general or class ideas, Locke points out that the term *species*, as applied to organisms, is a mental construct and convenience; that the objective world contains no separate species but only separate individuals, all descending "by easy steps and a continued series of things that in each remove differ very little one from all other . . . till we come to the lowest and most inorganical parts of matter. . . . The boundaries of the species, whereby men sort them, are made by men."[134]

Descartes had supposed that the idea of God is innate in us; Locke denies this. Some tribes have been found without it, and those that profess it have such different conceptions and images of the deity that it is wiser to reject the notion of innateness, and rest our belief in God upon "the visible marks of extraordinary wisdom and power . . . in all the works of crea- tion"[137]—i.e., upon experience. Likewise there are "no innate practical principles"—no inborn conceptions of right and wrong; history shows so great, sometimes so contradictory, a variety of moral judgments that they cannot be a part of man's natural inheritance; they are a social inheritance, differing from place to place and from time to time.[138]

Having disposed of innate ideas, Locke proceeds to inquire how ideas are generated. "Let us then suppose the mind [at birth] to be, as we say, white paper, void of all characters, without any ideas; how comes it to be furnished? . . . To this we answer in one word, from experience; in that all our knowledge is founded, and from that it ultimately derives itself."[139] All ideas are derived either from sensation or from reflection on the products of sensation. Sensations themselves are physical; their mental re- sult is perception, which is "the first faculty of the mind."[140]

Locke saw no reason to doubt that we can have true or valid knowledge of the external world, but he accepted the long-established distinction be- tween the primary and secondary qualities of objects perceived. Primary qualities are "such as are utterly inseparable from the body, in what state soever it be": solidity, extension, figure, number, and motion or rest. Secondary qualities "are nothing in the objects themselves but powers to produce various sensations in us by their primary qualities"; so colors, sounds, tastes, and odors are secondary qualities produced in us by the bulk, figure, texture, or motion of objects; the objects themselves have no color, weight, taste, smell, sound, or warmth. This distinction, as old as Albertus Magnus and Thomas Aquinas, had been accepted by Descartes, Galileo, Hobbes, Boyle, and Newton; Locke's exposition and emphasis gave it new and wider currency; theoretically the external world was now imagined by science as a colorless and silent neutrality, whose flowers and fruit had lost all fragrance and flavor. Poetry may have been depressed by this conception into the prosy verse of the "Augustan Age"—the early eighteenth century in England; but it ultimately discovered that qualities felt are as real as the objects themselves; and romanticism revenged itself on classicism by making feelings the supreme reality.

The analysis of an object into qualities led to the question, What is the substance in which the primary qualities seem to inhere? Locke confessed that we know nothing of that mysterious substratum except its qualities; take these away, and the *substance*—the underlying ground of the quali- ties—loses all meaning, apparently all existence.[141] Berkeley entered here.

If we know only the qualities of objects, and know these only as ideas, then all reality is perception; and Locke, the great champion of empiricism —of experience as the source of all knowledge—becomes an *idea*list, reducing matter to idea. Moreover, the "mind" is as suppostitious as substance, body, or matter. In a remarkable passage Locke overleaps Berkeley and anticipates Hume:

> The same thing happens concerning the operations of the mind, viz. thinking, reasoning, fearing, etc., which we, concluding not to subsist of themselves, nor apprehending how they can belong to body or be produced by it, are apt to think the actions of some other *substance,* which we call *spirit,* whereby yet it is evident that, having no other idea or notion of matter but something wherein those many sensible qualities which affect our senses do subsist, [so] by supposing a substance wherein thinking, knowing, doubting, and a power of moving, etc., do subsist, we have as clear a notion of spirit as we have of body: the one being supposed to be (without knowing what it is) the *substratum* to those simple ideas we have derived from without; and the other supposed (with a like ignorance of what it is) to be the *substratum* to those operations we experiment [experience] in ourselves within.[142]

Admitting, then, that "our idea of substance is equally obscure, or none at all, in both" worlds, and that "it is but a supposed I know not what to support those ideas we call accidents," Locke concludes that in both cases we are warranted in believing in a substance, though we cannot know it: in a matter behind and emitting the sensory qualities, and in a mind behind and possessing the ideas—a spiritual agent performing the various operations of perceiving, thinking, feeling, and willing.[143]

Whatever the mind is, its operations are all of one kind—the play of ideas. Locke rejects the Scholastic notion of "faculties" in the mind, such as thought, feeling, and will. Thought is the combination of ideas, feeling is the physiological reverberation of an idea; will is an idea flowing into action, as all ideas tend to do unless checked by another idea.* But how can an idea become an action—how can a "spiritual" process become a physiological process and a physical motion? Locke reluctantly accepts the dualism of corporeal body and incorporeal mind; but in an imprudent moment he suggests that "mind" might be a form of "matter." This is a *locus classicus* in Locke:

> Possibly we shall never be able to know whether any mere material being thinks or no; it being impossible for us, by the contemplation

---

* In the first edition of the *Essay* Locke admitted no "free will" except as freedom from external restraint. In later editions he modified this determinism to allow that the mind can suspend the execution and satisfaction of its desires.[144]

of our own ideas, without revelation, to discover whether Omnipo-
tency has not given to some systems of matter, fitly disposed, a power
to perceive and think, or else joined and fixed to matter, so disposed,
a thinking immaterial substance; it being, in respect of our notions, not
much more remote from our comprehension to conceive that God
can, if He pleases, superadd to matter a *faculty of thinking*, than that
He should add to it *another substance with a faculty of thinking*. . . .
He that considers how hardly sensation is, in our thoughts, reconcil-
able to extended matter, or existence to anything that has no extension
at all, will confess that he is very far from certainly knowing what
his soul is. . . . He who will give himself leave to consider freely . . .
will scarce find his reason able to determine him fixedly for or against
the soul's materiality.[145]

Though Hobbes had already leaped upon the materialistic horn of the
dilemma, the suggestion of its possible truth was, in the intellectual context of Locke's time, so offensive to orthodoxy that a hundred defenders
of religion attacked him as playing recklessly into the hands of the atheists.
They paid little attention to his passing obeisance to revelation, or to his
earlier statement that "the more probable opinion is that consciousness is
annexed to, and the affection of, one individual immaterial substance."[146]
Perhaps they foresaw how La Mettrie, d'Holbach, Diderot, and other materialists would see in Locke's suggestion a secret inclination to their view.
Bishop Stillingfleet accused him of precisely such a tendency, and warned
him that it endangered the whole Christian theology. Forgetting his usual
caution, Locke warmly reasserted the *possibility* of the material hypothesis,
in a controversy that lasted, with Stillingfleet and others, till 1697.

Despite its critics, its occasional contradictions, obscurities, and other
faults, the *Essay* gathered prestige and influence with every year. Four
editions of it were called for in the fourteen years between its publication
and Locke's death. A French edition appeared in 1700, and was greeted
with enthusiastic admiration. It became a topic in English drawing rooms;
Tristram Shandy assured his hearers that a reference to the *Essay* would
enable anyone to cut "no contemptible figure in a metaphysical circle."[147]
The influence of the *Essay* on Berkeley and Hume was so great that we
might date from it the turn of British philosophy from metaphysics to
epistemology. Perhaps Pope had Locke in mind when he wrote that "the
proper study of mankind is man."

A French edition appeared in 1700, and was greeted with enthusiastic
hyperboles. "After so many speculative gentlemen had formed the romance
of the soul," wrote Voltaire, "one truly wise man appeared who has, in
the most modest manner imaginable, given us its real history. Mr. Locke
has laid open to man the anatomy of the soul, just as some learned anatomist
would have done that of the body."[148] And again, "Locke alone has de-

veloped the human understanding in a book where there is nothing but truths, a book made perfect by the fact that these truths are stated clearly."[149] The *Essay* became the psychological bible of the French Enlightenment. Condillac adopted and extended Locke's sensationism, and thought nothing had been done in psychology between Aristotle and Locke[150]—a manifest injustice to the Scholastics and Hobbes. D'Alembert, in the *discours préliminaire* of the *Encyclopédie*, credited Locke with having created scientific philosophy as Newton (he supposed) had created scientific physics. Despite its professions of orthodoxy, the *Essay* made for a rationalistic empiricism that soon discarded the soul as a needless hypothesis, and passed on to apply the same reasoning to God.

4. Religion and Toleration

Locke himself had no sympathy with such extremes. Whatever his private doubts, he felt, like an English gentleman, that good manners and morals required public support of the Christian church. If philosophy should take from the people their faith in a divine justice standing behind the apparent injustices and sufferings of life, what could it offer to sustain the hopes and courage of men? A slow progress toward a democratic utopia? But in that utopia would not the natural greed and inequality of men forge new means for the use and abuse of the simple or the weak by the clever or the strong?

His first concern was to "lay down the measures and boundaries between faith and reason"; and this he aimed to do in Chapter 18 of Book IV of the *Essay*. "I find every sect, as far as reason will help them, make use of it gladly; and where it fails them, they cry out, It is a matter of faith, and above reason."[151] "Whatever God hath revealed is certainly true,"[152] but only reasoning on the available evidence can tell us whether a scripture is the word of God, and "no proposition can be received for divine revelation if it be contrary to our clear intuitive knowledge."[153] When a matter can be decided by such direct observation, our knowledge is above any supposed revelation, for it is clearer than any certainty we can have that the revelation in question is really divine. However, "there being many things wherein we have very imperfect notions, or none at all; and other things, of whose past, present, or future existence, by the natural use of our faculties, we can have no knowledge at all; these, as being . . . *above reason*, are, when revealed, *the proper matter of faith*."[154] Locke concludes: "Nothing that is contrary to, and inconsistent with, the clear and self-evident dictates of reason, has a right to be urged or asserted as a matter of faith wherein reason hath nothing to do."[155] "One unerring mark of" the love of truth is "not entertaining any proposition with greater assurance than the proofs it is built upon will warrant."[156] "Reason must be our last judge and guide in everything."[157]

So, in 1695, Locke published *The Reasonableness of Christianity as Delivered in the Scriptures*. He read the New Testament again, as one might read a new book, putting aside (as he thought) all dogmas and commentaries. He was overwhelmed by the lovable nobility of Christ, and the beauty of nearly all his teaching as the best and brightest hope of mankind. If anything could be a divine revelation, this narrative and doctrine seemed divine. Locke proposed to accept it as divine, but also to prove it, in all its essentials, to be in the profoundest agreement with reason.

But those essentials, it seemed to him, were far more modest and simple than the complex theology of the Thirty-nine Articles, the Westminster Confession, or the Athanasian Creed. He quoted passage after passage from the New Testament requiring of a Christian only the belief in God and in Christ as his divine messenger or Messiah. Here, said Locke, is a plain and intelligible religion, fit for any man, and independent of all learning and theology. As to the existence of God, he felt that "the works of nature in every part of them sufficiently evidence a Deity";[158] from his own existence he argued to a First Cause; and since he found perception and knowledge in himself, he concluded that such attributes must also belong to God; God is "eternal Mind."[159] When Locke's critics complained that he had left out such vital doctrines as the immortality of the soul and everlasting punishments and rewards, he replied that in accepting Christ he accepted Christ's teachings, in which those doctrines were included. So Locke came out by the same door wherein he went.

However, he insisted that all forms of Christianity except Catholicism should enjoy full liberty in England. He had written an essay on toleration as early as 1666. When he moved to Holland (1683) he found much more freedom of worship than in England; and while he was there he must have noted Bayle's powerful defense of toleration (1686). Moved by the persecution and migration of the Huguenots (1685), he wrote a letter to his friend Limborch, who urged its publication; it was printed in Latin in 1689 as *Epistola de Tolerantia*, and appeared in an English translation before the year was out. An Oxford don denounced it; Locke, now in England, defended it in a second and third *Letter concerning Toleration* (1690, 1692). The Toleration Act of 1689 fell far short of his proposals; it excluded Catholics, Unitarians, Jews, and pagans, and barred Dissenters from public affairs. Locke also made exceptions: he would not tolerate atheists, because he thought their word could not be trusted, since they feared no God; or any religion that did physical harm, as by human sacrifice; or any religion demanding allegiance to a foreign power; he gave Mohammedanism as an example, but was understood to mean Catholicism too.[160] He explicitly called for toleration of Presbyterians, Independents, Anabaptists, Arminians, and Quakers. He did not dare include Unitarians, though the first Shaftesbury, dying in Amsterdam (1683), said he had imbibed Arianism and Socinianism (Unitarianism) from his secretary Locke.[161]

The law, said Locke, should concern itself only with the preservation of social order; it has a right to suppress expressions destructive of the state, but it has no jurisdiction over men's souls. No church should have the power to compel adherence. How ridiculous to punish persons in Denmark for not being Lutherans, in Geneva for not being Calvinists, in Vienna for not being Catholics! After all, which individual or group can have the full truth about human life and destiny? Locke noted that most of the religions demanded toleration when they were weak, but refused it when they were strong. Persecution, he felt, comes from lust for power, and from jealousy masquerading as religious zeal. Persecution creates hypocrites, toleration promotes knowledge and truth. And how can a Christian persecute, being pledged to charity?

Locke continued his campaign for toleration till the close of his life. He was engaged in writing a fourth letter on the subject when his time ran out. Death came to him (1704) while he sat quietly listening to Lady Masham reading Psalms.

Even before his death he had reached in philosophy a reputation surpassed only by Newton's in science; men already spoke of him as *the philosopher.* While he ended in almost orthodox piety, his books, unable to change with age, passed through editions and translations into the thought of educated Europe. "The Western Enlightenment," said Spengler, "is of English origin. The rationalism of the Continent comes wholly from Locke."[162] Of course not wholly. But of whom else would one now risk such hyperbole?

VI. SHAFTESBURY: 1671–1713

His pupil, Anthony Ashley Cooper, third Earl of Shaftesbury, was a credit to Locke the educator. Not that Locke was responsible for Shaftesbury's style; the explorative psychologist wrote a pedestrian prose, simple and usually clear (this side the stake), but seldom beautiful; Shaftesbury, a man of wealth and leisure, wrote with confident urbanity, tolerant humor, and almost Gallic grace—the English seigneur condescending to be a philosopher. We must stay with him a while, for he almost founded aesthetics in modern philosophy, and, by rescuing feeling and sympathy from the cold hands of Hobbes and Locke, fed the stream of sentiment that culminated in Rousseau.

Under Locke's supervision, and on Locke's scheme of teaching a language by conversation, Elizabeth Birch, skilled in Greek and Latin, enabled Anthony to read both these languages with ease by the age of eleven. Then off to Winchester School; then three years of travel, during which he learned French and French ways, and acquired such a flair for art as must have seemed unseemly in an English lord. He served for a year in Parliament—long enough to note "the injustice and corruption of both parties";[163] but London smoke so aggravated his asthma that he retreated to Holland, where he found the intellectual air vibrant with Spinoza and Bayle. Having succeeded to the earldom (1699), he spent the remainder of his life at his country estate. Four years before his death he married, and was astonished to find himself as happy as before.[164] In 1711 he published his collected essays under the omnibus title *Characteristics of Men, Manners, Opinions, and Times.* In 1713, only forty-two years old, he died.

It was not to be expected that a man who had inherited such a fortune on the earth should bother much about heaven. He deprecated the "enthusiasm"—by which his time meant fanaticism—of those Englishmen who thought that they exhaled divine revelations. Any form of violent emotion or speech was in his judgment a mark of ill-breeding. But he thought it wiser to smile at such people than to persecute them; indeed, wit and humor, which he made the subject of an originative essay, appeared to him the best approach to everything, even to theology. He agreed with Bayle that atheists could be decent citizens, and that they had done less harm to religion and morality than the brutality of faiths wielding power.[165] He protested against "the adoration and love of a God whose character it is to be captious and of high resentment, subject to wrath and anger, furious and revengeful . . . , encouraging deceit and treachery amongst men, favorable to a few . . . and cruel to the rest."[166] He wondered what effect such a conception of the deity had had upon human character and conduct. He thought it abject and cowardly to be virtuous from hope of heaven or fear of hell; virtue is real only when practiced for its own sake. However, man being what he is, it is necessary to inculcate belief in such future punishments and rewards.[167] " 'Tis real humanity and kindness to hide strong truths from tender eyes. . . . It may be necessary . . . for wise men to speak in parables."[168] So Shaftesbury defended an established church, and tried to reconcile evil and theism with an optimistic philosophy that reduced evil to a human prejudice.[169] Nevertheless Alexander Pope thought that the *Characteristics* had done more harm to revealed religion in England than all the works of explicit infidels.[170]

Shaftesbury agreed with Aristotle and Locke that happiness is the rightful aim of human actions; he defined philosophy as "the study of happiness."[171] But he opposed the reduction of all human motives to egoism or self-interest. According to that analysis (recently expounded by Hobbes and La Rochefoucauld),

> civility, hospitality, humanity towards strangers or people in distress, is only a more deliberate selfishness. An honest heart is only a more cunning one; and honesty and good nature a . . . better regulated self-love. The love of kindred, children, and posterity is purely love of self and one's own immediate blood. . . . Magnanimity and courage, no doubt, are modifications of this universal self-love![172]

Against this view Shaftesbury alleged the double equipment of human nature with instincts for personal gain and instincts for living in a group. He believed that society and the state had originated not in a social contract but in the "herding principle and associating inclination . . . so natural and strong in most men."[173] There are "natural affections . . . founded in love, complacency, goodwill, and sympathy with the kind. . . . To have these natural and good affections in full strength is to have the chief means of self-enjoyment; to want them is certain misery and ill."[174] To be "good" is to have one's inclinations consistently directed toward the good of the group: the larger the group that inspires these feelings, the better the man. The consciousness of such social sympathy is the moral sense. This is innate, not in its specific commands (which vary from group to group), but in its instinctive ground, "the sense of right and wrong . . . being as natural to us as natural affection itself, and being a first principle in our constitution."[175]

Shaftesbury passed from ethics to aesthetics by identifying them. The good and the beautiful are one: morality is "the taste of beauty and the relish of what is decent"; so we speak of some unsocial acts as ugly, for we feel that they offend that harmony of the part with the whole which is both goodness and beauty. A man can make his life a work of art—of unity and harmony—by developing an aesthetic sense in which morality will be an element; a man "of thorough good breeding" (our aristocrat believed) does this, and is by training "incapable of doing a rude or brutal action";[176] his formed good taste will guide him in conduct as in art. Truth too is a kind of beauty, a harmony of the parts of knowledge with the whole. Hence Shaftesbury took readily the side of classicism in art: form, unity, and harmony seemed to him the essentials of excellence in poetry, architecture, and sculpture; and in painting color is less basic and noble than line. He was the first modern who made beauty a fundamental problem in philosophy; he began the discussion that at the end of the eighteenth century culminated in Lord Kames and Burke.

This was one line of Shaftesbury's influence; there were many others. His emphasis on feeling affected the romantic movement, especially in Germany through Lessing, Schiller, Goethe, and Herder—who called him "Europe's amiable Plato."[177] In France this influence appeared in Diderot as well as in Rousseau. His interpretation of religion as theoretically weak but morally indispensable touched Kant's practical nerve. His stress on sympathy as the basis of morals reappeared in Hume and Adam Smith. His ideas on art shared in forming Winckelmann's classical ecstasy. Beginning as a pupil of the intellectual and not too aesthetic Locke, he became (perhaps by the natural resistance of every generation to its generators) the philosopher of feeling, sentiment, and beauty. Lover of the classic style in art, he became a source of the romantic revival on the Continent, though in England poetry and architecture followed his classic bent. And he had the distinction of making philosophy shine with a grace of style reminiscent of Plato, and then rivaled only by Berkeley.

VII. GEORGE BERKELEY: 1685–1753

He was born at Dysert Castle in County Kilkenny. At fifteen he entered Trinity College, Dublin. At twenty he formed a club to study "the new philosophy," which meant Locke. At twenty-one he entered into his "commonplace book" the idea which, he hoped, would crush materialism forever: that nothing exists except by being perceived, that therefore mind is the only reality, and matter is a myth.

> As . . . the doctrine of matter, or corporeal substance [has been] the main pillar and support of skepticism, so likewise upon the same faith have been raised all the impious schemes of atheism and irreligion. . . . How great a friend material substance hath been to atheists in all ages, were needless to relate. All their monstrous systems have so visible and necessary a dependence on it, that when this cornerstone is once removed, the whole fabric cannot choose but fall to the ground; insomuch that it is no longer worth while to bestow a particular consideration on the absurdities of every wretched sect of atheists.[178]

So in the next seven years, and before completing his twenty-ninth birthday, Berkeley issued his most important works: *An Essay towards a New Theory of Vision* (1709), *A Treatise concerning the Principles of Human Knowledge* (1710), and *Three Dialogues between Hylas and Philonous, in Opposition to Sceptics and Atheists* (1713). The first was a brilliant contribution to psychology and optics; the others profoundly stirred the waters of modern philosophy.

The essay on vision stemmed from a passage in Locke,[179] which told how William Molyneux (a tutor in Trinity College, Dublin) had posed a problem to him: Would a man born blind be able, on recovering his sight, to distinguish by sight alone a sphere from a cube if both of these were of like material and size? Molyneux and Locke had concurred in the negative; Berkeley agreed with them and added his own analysis. Sight gives us no perception of the distance, size, relative positions, or movements of objects, except after correction by the sense of touch; through repeated experiences this correction becomes almost instantaneous; and sight then gives us such a judgment of the shape, distance, place, and motion of objects seen as we should have if we touched them.

> A man born blind, being made to see, would at first have no idea of distance by sight; the sun and stars, the remotest objects as well as the nearer, would all seem to be in his eye, or rather in his mind. The objects intromitted by sight would seem to him (as in truth they are) no other than a new set of thoughts or sensations, each whereof is as near to him as the perception of pain or pleasure or the most inward passions of the soul. For our judging objects perceived by sight to be at any distance, or without the mind, is entirely the effect of experience.[180]

Space, then, is a mental construct; it is a system of relationships built up in the course of experience to co-ordinate our perceptions of sight and touch. Operations reported by the Royal Society (1709, 1728) confirmed this view: when a congenitally blind person was surgically given sight, he was at first "so far from making any judgment about distances that he thought all objects whatever touched his eyes. . . . He knew not the shape of anything, nor any one thing from another, however different in shape or magnitude."[181]

The Principles of Human Knowledge was a remarkable product for a lad of twenty-five. Again Berkeley took a leap out of Locke's *Essay*. If all knowledge comes from the senses, nothing has reality for us unless we perceive or have perceived it; *esse est percipi*—to be is to be perceived. Locke had supposed that perceptions were caused by external objects pressing upon our sense organs. How do you know, asked Berkeley, that such objects exist? Have we not in our dreams ideas as vivid as in our waking hours? Locke tried to save the independent reality of objects by distinguishing between their primary and secondary qualities: the latter were subjective, "in the mind"; the others—extension, solidity, figure, number, motion, rest—were objective; they subsisted in some mysterious substratum of which Locke confessed himself ignorant, but which he and the world identified with "matter." Berkeley now announced that the primary qualities are as subjective as the secondary; that we know the extension, solidity, figure, number, motion, and rest of objects only through perception; that therefore these primary qualities too are subjective, are ideas. The world is for us just a bundle of perceptions. "It is the mind that frames all that variety of bodies which compose the visible world, any one whereof does not exist longer than it is perceived."[182] Take away from "matter" the primary as well as the secondary qualities, and "matter" becomes a meaningless nonentity. The materialist is left mouthing nothings.[183]

Berkeley was well aware that others besides materialists would protest against this sleight-of-hand evaporation of the external world. He was not at a loss when asked if the furniture in our rooms ceases to exist when no one is there to perceive it.[184] He did not deny the reality of an external world, an external source for our perceptions;[185] he merely denied the materiality of that world. External objects may continue to exist when we do not perceive them, but that is only because they exist as percepts in the mind of God.[186] And in truth (he went on) our sensations are caused not by external matter, but by the divine power acting upon our senses. Only spirit can act upon spirit; God is the sole source of our sensations and ideas.[187]*

Berkeley's contemporaries thought this was all an Irish lark. Lord Chesterfield wrote to his son that

> Doctor Berkeley, a very worthy, ingenious, and learned man, has written a book to prove that there is no such thing as matter, and that nothing exists but an idea. . . . His arguments are, strictly speaking, unanswerable; but yet I am so far from being convinced by them that I am determined to go on to eat and drink, and walk and ride, in order to keep that *matter*, which I so mistakenly imagine my body at present to consist of, in as good plight as possible.[188]

And all the world knows what pains Dr. Johnson took to answer Dr. Berkeley:

> After we came out of church [says Boswell] we stood talking for some time together of Bishop Berkeley's ingenious sophistry to prove the non-existence of matter, and that everything in the universe is merely ideal. I observed that though we are satisfied his doctrine is not true, it is impossible to refute it. I shall never forget the alacrity with which Johnson answered, striking his foot with mighty force against a large stone, till he rebounded from it, "I refute it thus!"[189]

Berkeley, of course, would have pointed out to the Great Cham that all that he knew of the stone, including the pain in his toe, was subjective: a bundle of perceptions called a stone, mingling with a bundle of auditory

---

* In the latest physics our sensations are caused not by any known "matter," but by subtle energies whose material substratum is unknown and hypothetical.

sensations called Boswell and a bundle of indoctrinated ideas called philosophy, had generated a response resulting in another bundle of sensations.
Hume agreed with Boswell and Chesterfield: Berkeley's arguments "admit
of no answer and produce no conviction."[190]

Hume found Berkeley's puzzle fascinating, but drew from it a devastating conclusion. He admitted that "matter" vanishes when we divest it of
all the qualities which our perceptions ascribe to it, but he suggested that
the same could be said of "mind." We have seen Locke's preview of this
point; but Berkeley foresaw it, too. In the third of the *Dialogues* he makes
Hylas challenge Philonous:

> You acknowledge you have, properly speaking, no idea of your own
> soul. . . . You admit, nevertheless, that there is a spiritual substance,
> although you have no idea of it; while you deny there can be such a
> thing as material substance, because you have no notion or idea of it.
> Is this fair dealing? . . . To me it seems that according to your own
> way of thinking, and in consequence of your own principles, it should
> follow that you are only a system of floating ideas, without any sub-
> stance to support them. Words are not to be used without a meaning.
> And as there is no more meaning in spiritual substance than in material
> substance, the one is to be exploded as well as the other.[191]

Philonous (lover of mind) answers Hylas (Mr. Matter):

> How often must I repeat, that I know or am conscious of my own
> being; and that I myself and not my ideas, but somewhat else, a think-
> ing, active principle that perceives, knows, wills, and operates about
> ideas? I know that I, one and the same self, perceive both colors and
> sounds; that a color cannot perceive a sound, nor a sound a color;
> that I am therefore one individual principle, distinct from color and
> sound.[192]

Hume was not convinced by this reply; he concluded that Berkeley, willy-
nilly, had destroyed both matter and soul, and that the writings of the
brilliant bishop, who had longed to defend religion, "form the best lessons
of skepticism which are to be found either among the ancient or modern
philosophers, Bayle not excepted."[193]

Forty years remained to Berkeley after publishing his three treatises. In
1724 he was appointed dean of Derry. In 1728, on a promise of funds from
the government, he sailed to found a college in Bermuda for "the reformation of manners among the English in our western plantations, and the
propagation of the Gospel among the American savages."[194] Having
reached Newport, Rhode Island, he waited for the promised twenty thousand pounds, none of which ever came. While there he composed *Alci-*

phron, or The Minute Philosopher (1732), to put an end to all religious doubt. He left his mark upon the mind of Jonathan Edwards, and wrote a famous line: "Westward the course of empire takes its way." After three years of vain expectations he returned to England. In 1734 he was appointed bishop of Cloyne. We have seen how Swift's Vanessa made him one of her executors, and left him half her property. In 1744 he issued a strange treatise, *Siris, . . . the Virtues of Tar-Water*—to which he had been introduced by the aforesaid savages, and which he now recommended as a cure for smallpox. He died at Oxford in 1753, aged sixty-eight.

No man ever surpassed him in proving the unreality of the real. In his effort to restore religious belief, and to exorcise the Hobbesian materialism that was infecting England, he turned philosophy outside in, and made "all the choir of heaven and furniture of the earth, . . . all those bodies which compose the mighty frame of the world,"[195] to exist for man as merely ideas in his mind. It was a risky enterprise, and Berkeley would have shuddered to see Hume and Kant draw from his pious principles a critique of reason that left no basic dogma undislodged in the ancient and beloved edifice of the Christian faith. We admire the subtlety of his web-weaving, and concede that no one since Plato had written nonsense so charmingly. We shall find his influence everywhere in Britain and Germany in the eighteenth century, less in France, but rising again in the epistemological abracadabra of nineteenth-century Kantians. Even today European philosophy has not yet quite made up its mind that the external world exists. Until it reconciles itself to the extreme probability thereof, and faces the problems of life and death, the world will pass it by.

All in all, this was the finest epoch in the history of English philosophy. The bell that Francis Bacon had rung to call the wits together had been heard after the subsiding fury of the Civil War. Hobbes was the bridge over that mindless void, Newton was the lever by which mechanics moved theology, Locke was the peak from which the problems of modern philosophy came clearly into view. From that English quartet, soon abetted by the canny, uncanny Hume, came a powerful influence into France and Germany. The French thinkers of this period were not so profound or original as the English, but more brilliant, partly because they were Gauls, partly because a more stringent censorship compelled them to spend their substance upon form and dispense their wisdom in wit. Then in 1726 Voltaire came to England. When he returned he carried Newton, Locke, Bacon, Hobbes, and other contraband in his bags; and France for half a century thereafter used English science and philosophy as weapons to *écraser l'infâme* of superstition, obscurantism, and ignorance. An English midwife served at the accouchement of the French Enlightenment.

CHAPTER XXI

Faith and Reason in France

1648–1715

I. THE VICISSITUDES OF CARTESIANISM

THE dictionary of the French Academy in 1694 defined *philosopher* as

> one who devotes himself to research work in connection with the various sciences, and who seeks from their effects to trace their causes and principles. A name [also] applied to one who lives a quiet and secluded life remote from the stir and troubles of the world. It is occasionally used to denote someone of undisciplined mind who regards himself as above the responsibilities and duties of civil life.[1]

From the first part of this definition it is clear that philosophy and science were not yet distinguished; science, as "natural philosophy," would remain a branch of philosophy till the nineteenth century. From the final portion of the definition we gather that the Forty Immortals, under Louis XIV, sniffed a revolutionary odor in the philosophic air, as if the harbingers of the Enlightenment had already spoken their prologue.

Between three horns of the definition the intellectual legacy of René Descartes meandered through renown to repudiation. The legacy itself had three horns: one sounded the trumpet of doubt as the prelude to all philosophy; another announced the universal mechanism of the external world; the third played the welcome tunes of the traditional creed, and drew God, free will, and immortality out of the vortices of the world. Descartes had begun with doubt and ended with piety; and his heirs could take him at either end. The ladies of the early salons—the *femmes savantes* satirized by Molière in 1672—found some exciting respite from the rosary in the whirlpools of the new cosmology. Mme. de Sévigné reported the Cartesian philosophy as an after-dinner topic in her circle; she and Mmes. de Grignan, de Sablé, and de La Fayette were all *cartésiennes*. Fragrant women attended the lectures given in Paris by followers of Descartes.[2] Great nobles took up the philosophic mode; Cartesian discourses were pronounced each week in the château of the Duc de Luynes, and in the Paris palace of the Prince de Condé, and in "the most magnificent *hôtels* of the capital."[3] Religious orders—Oratorians, Benedictines, Augustinians—

taught the new philosophy in their schools. It became the fashion to praise reason in science and human affairs, while carefully subordinating it, in religion, to divine revelation as interpreted by the Catholic Church. The Jansenists and Port-Royal accepted Cartesianism as an elegant reconciliation of religion and philosophy.

But their most brilliant convert, Blaise Pascal, denounced Cartesianism as the vestibule of atheism. "I cannot pardon Descartes," he said; "he would have been glad, in all his philosophy, to dispense with God; but he could not avoid allowing him a fillip [a snap of the finger released from the thumb] to put the world in motion; after that he had no use for God."[4] On this point the Jesuits agreed with Pascal; after 1650 they rejected Cartesianism as a subtle, even if unintended, corrosive of religious faith. The Sorbonne wished to proscribe Descartes; Boileau defended him; Ninon de Lenclos and others persuaded Molière to write a satire on the Sorbonne; the Sorbonne deferred its censure.[5] The learned Huet, after long accepting Cartesianism, turned against it as blowing hot and cold for and against Christianity. Theologians were increasingly alarmed by the difficulty of reconciling transubstantiation with Descartes' view of matter as pure extension. In 1665 Louis XIV forbade the teaching of the ambivalent philosophy in the Collège Royal, and in 1671 he extended the prohibition to the University of Paris. In 1687 Bossuet joined in the attack.

These condemnations revived interest in Cartesianism, and drew attention to its skeptical overture, the *Discours de la méthode;* the initial doubt of that essay spread subterraneanly; its orthodox appendages withered away; in the eighteenth century hardly anything remained of the once victorious system except its attempt to reduce the external world to a mechanism obeying the laws of physics and chemistry. Every new discovery of science seemed to support this Cartesian mechanism and to discredit the Cartesian theology. The God of Abraham, Isaac, and Jacob found no place in Descartes' picture of the cosmos; nor was Christ there; all that remained was a *dieu fainéant* who gave the world an initial push and then retired from the scene except as a guarantor of Descartes' intuitions. This was not the majestic and awful God of the Old Testament, nor the merciful Father of the New; he was the God of deism, impersonal, functionless, negligible, subject to invariable laws; who would think of praying to such an Epicurean futility? Already in 1669 and 1678 the books of Guillaume Lamy, professor on the medical faculty at the University of Paris, expounded a completely mechanistic psychology anticipating Condillac's *Traité des sensations* (1754), and a materialistic philosophy anticipating La Mettrie's *L'Homme machine* (1748). And amid the fracas Cyrano de Bergerac made his scandalous voyages to the moon and the sun.

II. CYRANO DE BERGERAC: 1619-55

For most of us he is the lover travestied by Rostand, and losing every race to Venus by a nose. The real Cyrano was not quite frustrated; he played vivaciously with life and love, and frittered away his time to the top of his bent. To the usual education of a wellborn lad he added (with Molière) eager attendance on the lectures of Pierre Gassendi, the amiable priest who liked Epicurus the materialist and Lucretius the atheist. Cyrano became an *esprit* especially *fort*, a *libertin* in both senses, as freethinker and loose liver. He joined in Paris a company of sacrilegious roisterers, earned repute as a duelist, served in the army, was for a while incapacitated by his wounds, and retired from active venery to philosophy. He wrote the first French philosophical play, and opened the road to Swift by making fun of mankind via travels to unfrequented parts of the cosmos. He laughed at the venerable St. Augustine, "that grand personage who assures us, though his mind was illuminated by the Holy Ghost, that in his time the earth was as flat as an oven, and that it floated on the water like half an orange."[6]

Cyrano tried his pen in almost every literary form, seldom seriously, but usually finding the nerve. His comedy, *Le Pédant joué*, seemed to Molière good enough for poaching a scene or two. His tragedy, *La Mort d'Agrippine*, was acted once in 1640, was immediately proscribed by the authorities, and had to wait till 1960 to reach the boards again. But it was published in 1654, and soon the wild young men of Paris were shouting the atheistic lines of its Séjan:

> *Que sont-ils donc ces dieux? Des enfants de l'effroi;*
> *Des beaux riens qu'on adore et sans savoir pourquoi . . .;*
> *Des dieux que l'homme fait, et qui n'ont pas fait l'homme*

—"What, then, are these gods? The offspring of our fears; pretty nothings that we adore without knowing why. . . ; Gods whom man has made, and who never made man." And on immortality:

> *Une heure après la mort notre âme évanouie*
> *Sera ce qu'elle était une heure avant la vie*

—"One hour after death our vanished soul will be that which it was an hour before life."

Soon after this play was printed, Cyrano was struck on the head by a falling beam, and died of the blow, aged thirty-six. He left a manuscript which was published in two parts: *Histoire comique des états et empires de la lune,* (1657), and *Histoire comique des états et empires du soleil* (1662). They were a comic kind of science fiction, based upon the Cartesian cosmology, and deriving the planets from vortices formed by the revolutionary agitation of primeval matter. Cyrano suggested that the planets had once blazed like the sun, but,

> in the compass of time, suffered so great a loss of light and heat by the continual emission of the corpuscles causing such phenomena, that they have become cold, dark, and almost powerless pulps. We find even that sun spots . . . increase in size from day to day. Now who knows if these are not a crust forming on the sun's surface from its mass that cools in proportion as light is lost, and if the sun will not become . . . an opaque globe like the earth?[7]

Propelled by rockets, Cyrano leaves the earth, and swiftly reaches the moon. He notes that through three quarters of the way he feels the earth drawing him backward, then, through the final quarter, he feels the attraction of the moon. "This, I told myself, was because the mass of the moon was less than that of the earth; hence the sphere of its action was correspondingly less in space."[8] Landing dazed, he finds himself in a Garden of Eden. He falls into an argument with Elijah about original sin, and is expelled from the garden into the primitive wastelands of the satellite. There he encounters a tribe of animals twelve cubits long, fashioned like men but walking on all fours. One of these, having served in Athens as the daemon of Socrates, speaks philosophic Greek. He informs Cyrano that walking on all fours is the natural and healthy way; that these lunar gentlemen have a hundred senses, not five or six, and perceive countless realities hidden from mankind. (Fontenelle, Voltaire, and Diderot will play with this speculation.) Cyrano's fancy runs wild: the lunars feed only on vapors pressed from foods, not on foods themselves; hence they are saved the nuisance and noises of digestion, the indignities and anachronisms of elimination. The lunar laws are made by the young, who are revered by the old; celibacy and chastity are condemned; suicide, cremation, and large noses are praised. The aforesaid daemon of Socrates explains that the world was not created, but is eternal; that creation out of nothing (taught by the Scholastics) is inconceivable; that the eternity of the universe is no more difficult to accept than the eternity of God; indeed, the hypothesis of a God is quite unnecessary, since the world is a self-propelled and self-perpetuating machine. Cyrano argues that there must be a God, for he has with his own eyes seen miraculous cures; the daemon laughs these away as due to suggestion or imagination. Orthodoxy is revenged by a powerful Ethiopian, who grasps Cyrano in one arm, the daemon in the other, carries the daemon to hell, and, en route, deposits Cyrano in Italy, where all the neighborhood dogs howl at him because he smells of the moon. Jonathan Swift was attracted, too.

III. MALEBRANCHE: 1638–1715

Against the infidel progeny of Gassendi and Descartes the faith found powerful defenders not only in Pascal, Bossuet, and Fénelon, but in one of the subtlest metaphysicians of modern times.

Nicolas de Malebranche was an almost exact contemporary of Louis XIV: born a month before him, dying a month after him. There was no further resemblance. Nicolas was gentle of spirit and pure of life. As his father was secretary to Louis XIII, and his uncle was viceroy of Canada, he had every advantage of birth and rearing except health; his body was feeble and deformed, and only a frugal regimen in the routine and peace of monastic life can explain his seventy-seven years. At twenty-two he joined the Congregation of the Oratory, a religious order dedicated to meditation and preaching. At twenty-six he was ordained priest.

In that same year he came upon Descartes' *Traité de l'homme*. He was transported by both its argument and its style. He became a Cartesian with a sublime faith in reason; and he at once resolved to prove by reason the Catholic creed in which he had rooted his life and his hopes. This was a brave move away from Pascal back to St. Thomas Aquinas; it showed the splendid confidence of youth, but it exposed the citadel of faith to the inroads of reason. After ten years of study and writing, Malebranche issued in four volumes (1674) one of the classics of French philosophy, *De la Recherche de la vérité* (*The Search for Truth*). Here, as by all the philosophers of France, the moral obligation to be intelligible was accepted, and philosophy became literature.

Descartes had not only begun his lucubrations with the self, but had set such a gulf between the body physical and mechanical and the mind spiritual and free, that no interaction between them could be conceived. And yet that interaction seemed indisputable: an idea could move an arm or an army, and a drug could muddle the mind. Half the puzzling of Descartes' successors was devoted to bridging the gap between flesh and thought.

A Flemish philosopher, Arnold Geulincx, prepared for Malebranche—and for Spinoza and Leibniz—by denying the interaction. The material body does not act upon the immaterial mind or vice versa; when either seems to act upon the other it is only because God has created reality in two distinct streams of events, the one physical, the other mental; their synchronism is like that of two clocks, set to the same second and speed and striking the same hours simultaneously, but operating quite independently of each other except that both have one source—the intelligence that set and started them. So God is the sole source of both the physical and mental series of causes and effects; the mental state is the occasion, not the cause, of the apparently resultant physical motion; and the physical motion—event or sensation—is merely the occasion of the mental state that it seems to cause; in each case God alone is the cause.* At this point Geulincx, fearful of determinism, broke into his system by allowing that in conscious actions the human will, co-operating with God, can be a real cause of physical results.

Malebranche made this hesitant "occasionalism" complete. God is always the cause of both the physical act and the mental state; their interaction is illusory; neither ever acts upon the other.† "God alone drives back the air which He Himself has made me breathe. . . . It is not I who breathe; I breathe despite myself. It is not I who speak to you; I merely wish to speak to you."[9] God [the total energy of the universe] is the only power. Whatever moves or thinks does so because the divine power acts through the physical and mental processes. Motion is God acting in material forms; thought is God thinking in us.

In this apparently deterministic philosophy there are countless difficulties, which in later treatises Malebranche tried to resolve. He struggled to harmonize some degree of free will in man with the universal agency of God, and to reconcile evil and suffering and multitudinous deviltry with the sole and omnipresent causality of an omnipotent and omniscient benevolence; we shall not follow him into these labyrinths. But in the course of his wandering he leaves a helpful thread of psychology. Sensations, he thinks, are in the body, not in the mind; the mind has ideas, and knows objects only as bundles of ideas—of structure, size, color, odor, solidity, sound, temperature, taste. These idea complexes are built up not merely from the object; most of the qualities here named are not in the object; and many of our judgments about the object—that it is large, small, bright, dim, heavy, light, hot, cold, quickly moving or slow—describe the position, condition, and attitude of the observer rather than the attributes of the thing observed. We do not know things; we know only our prejudiced and transformed perceptions and ideas. (All this a generation before Locke and Berkeley.)

---

* Spinoza's emendation of this "psychophysical parallelism" may help us to see some sense in Geulincx. God, or nature, acts in two concurrent aspects and streams: the physical sequences of the objective world, including our bodies; and the mental sequences of the subjective world, including our feelings, thoughts, and volitions. Neither of the two streams ever causes the other, for both are merely two sides—the outside and the inside—of one process, one duplex stream of events.

† Compare this theological statement with the determinist doctrine that every motion in matter, and every mental state, is caused by the total past, and that the immediate physical agents, and the self and "free will," are the instruments of this total force, or cosmic energy, acting through matter and mind.

Despite his spiritualistic background, Malebranche, after Descartes and Hobbes, gives physiological explanations of habit, memory, and association of ideas. Habit is a readiness with which the animal spirits, as the result of similar experiences or actions often repeated, flow in certain grooves or channels of the body. Memory is the reactivation of associations created in experience. Ideas tend to be associated according to their past sequence or contiguity. Strength of character, power of will, are the force of animal spirits flowing along the fibers of the brain, deepening the grooves of association and the vividness of imagination.

Pious though Malebranche was, there were many elements in his philosophy that disturbed that alert watchman of orthodoxy, Bénigne Bossuet. In a clever move to divert the passionate pen of Antoine Arnauld from the logic of Jansenism to the succor of the proper faith, he persuaded him to comb Malebranche for hidden heresies. The philosopher defended himself in a series of treatises as eloquent and incredible as the first; and the controversy continued from 1683 to 1697. Bossuet brought Fénelon's light artillery to the attack. Mme. de Sévigné, seeing that mice were devouring her crops and caterpillars her trees, complained that she found little consolation in Malebranche's view of evil as a necessary element in the best of all possible worlds.[10]

To offset these critics Malebranche had many fervent friends. Young men and old women found in his doctrine of God as the only agent in all actions a mystic pleasure of surrender and divine union. Frenchmen and foreigners wore a path to his cell; one Englishman said that he came to France to see only two celebrities, Louis XIV and Malebranche.[11] Berkeley came, all reverence, and engaged the old priest in a long discussion. Soon afterward Malebranche, seventy-seven, weakened; he grew thinner every day, until his mind had hardly any body left to serve as occasion for his thought. On October 13, 1715, he passed away in his sleep.

His fame faded rapidly after his death, for his religious philosophy was not in tune with the skepticism and revelry of the Regency, and still less with the ensuing tendency of the *philosophes* to replace divine Providence with a world machine. But his influence appeared in Leibniz' attempt to show that the actual was the best possible world; in Berkeley's view that things exist only in our perception or in God's; in Hume's destructive analysis of cause as an occult quality; in Kant's emphasis on the subjective elements in the formation of knowledge; even in the determinism of the Enlightenment. For to say that God is the only cause of all motions, volitions, and ideas is not far different from saying that every change in matter or mind is the inevitable result of the total forces operating in the universe at that moment. In Malebranche's ecstasy he had approached—though he denied it—a determinism that made man an automaton.

Above all, the system of occasionalism served as a halfway house between Descartes and Spinoza. Descartes saw mechanism in matter, but liberty in mind; Malebranche saw God as sole cause in every action of every mind; Spinoza, quite as "God-intoxicated" as the monk, agreed with him that the mental and physical series were parallel products of one creative force. Unwittingly the pious Oratorian, seeing God everywhere, had taught, even to the faithful, a pantheism that needed only the phrase *Deus sive natura*—God *or* nature—to become the philosophy of Spinoza, and of the Enlightenment.

IV. PIERRE BAYLE: 1647–1706

The "Father of the Enlightenment" was the son of a Huguenot minister serving the town of Carla in the countship of Foix, under the Pyrenees. Pierre lived there his first twenty-two years, imbibing Greek, Latin, and Calvinism. He was a sensitive, impressionable youth. Sent to the Jesuit college at Toulouse (1669) to get the best classical education within his family's reach and means, he fell in love with his teachers, and was soon converted to Catholicism—so fervently that he tried to convert his father and brother. They bore with him patiently, and seventeen months later he returned to the parental faith. But now, as a relapsed heretic, he was subject to prosecution by the Roman Church. To protect him the father sent him to the Calvinist University of Geneva (1670), hoping that Pierre would enter the Protestant ministry. There, however, Bayle discovered the works of Descartes, and began to doubt all forms of Christianity.

His schooling completed, he lived as a tutor in Geneva, Rouen, and Paris, and rose to a professorship in philosophy at a Huguenot seminary in Sedan (1675). In 1681 the seminary was closed by order of Louis XIV, as part of his war of attrition against the Edict of Nantes. Bayle found refuge in Rotterdam, and a berth as professor of history and philosophy in the École Illustre, the municipal academy. He was among the first of many intellectual emigrés who in this age made the Dutch Republic a citadel of independent thought.

His salary was small, but he was content to live simply so long as he had access to books. He never married, preferring a library to a wife. He was not unmindful of feminine graces and charms, and would have been grateful for the tender solicitude of a good woman, but he suffered all his life from headaches and an associated "megrim," or melancholia, and doubtless he hesitated to bind another spirit to his ills. He had his cynical moments, however, for when a French Jesuit, Father Maimbourg, in a *History of Calvinism*, argued that Catholic priests had accepted conversion to Protestantism in order to marry, Bayle asked how could this be, "for what greater cross is there than marriage?"[12]

He reviewed Maimbourg's book in a volume of letters that appeared in 1682. He wondered whether any man strongly attached to a special faith could write impartial or truthful history. How could one trust a historian who, like Maimbourg, called Louis XIV's treatment of the Huguenots [before 1682] "just, gentle, and charitable?" Turning to Louis himself, Bayle, writing from a Holland so recently and flagrantly assailed by France, asked, What right had any king to force his own religion upon his subjects? If he had such a right, then the Roman emperors were justified in persecuting Christianity. Conscience, Bayle thought, should be the only ruler over a man's beliefs. Maimbourg answered conclusively by procuring from Louis XIV an order that any copy of Bayle's book found in France should be publicly burned by the common hangman.

In that same year 1682 Bayle issued his first major work, *Pensées diverses sur la comète*—miscellaneous thoughts on the comet that had crossed the sky in December, 1680. All Europe had been frightened by that star, whose tail of fire seemed to herald the conflagration of the world. Only if we put ourselves back into the fears of that age—when Catholic and Protestant alike interpreted such phenomena as divine warnings, and believed that any moment would bring upon a sinful earth the thunderbolts of God—can we understand the terror with which that flaming apparition had been viewed, or appreciate the courage and wisdom of Bayle's comments. Even the learned Milton had recently told how "the comet from its horrid hair shakes pestilence and war."[13] Basing his discussion upon the recent studies of astronomers (but Halley's comet of 1682 had not yet appeared), Bayle assured his readers that comets move through the heavens according to fixed laws, and have nothing to do with the misery or happiness of mankind. He mourned the pertinacity of superstition. "He who would find all the causes of popular errors will never be finished."[14] He rejected all miracles except those of the New Testament (without this exception his book could not have been printed in Holland). "In sound philosophy Nature is nothing else than God Himself acting by certain laws which He has established of his own free will. So that the works of Nature are not less the effect of the power of God than miracles, and suppose as great a power as miracles, it being altogether as difficult to form a man by natural laws of generation as to raise him from the dead."[15]

Bayle passed boldly to one of the most difficult problems of history: Is a natural ethic possible—can a moral code be maintained without the aid of supernatural belief? Did atheism lead to corrupt morals? If that were so, said Bayle, one would have to conclude, from the crime, corruption, and immorality prevalent in Europe, that most Christians are secret atheists.

Jews, Mohammedans, Christians, and infidels differ in creeds, but not in deeds. Apparently religious belief—and ideas in general—have little influence upon conduct; this flows from desires and passions usually stronger than beliefs. What influence had the precepts of Christ upon the European conception of courage and honor?—which praised most the man who promptly and violently avenged insults and injuries, who excelled in war, inventing an infinity of machines to make sieges more murderous and frightful; "it is from us that infidels learn to use better arms."[16] Bayle concluded that a society of atheists would have no worse morals than a society of Christians. What keeps most of us in order is not the distant and uncertain terror of hell so much as the fear of the policeman and the law, of social condemnation and disgrace, of the hangman; take away these secular deterrents, and you would have chaos; keep them, and a society of atheists would be possible; indeed, it might contain many men of high honor, and women of chastity.[17] We hear of such exemplary atheists in antiquity, like Epicurus and both Plinys; and in modern times, like Michel de l'Hôpital and Spinoza. (Whether the morals of the average man would be worse than they are if religion did not supplement law is a question that Bayle leaves untouched.)

This tract on the comet was published anonymously. Bayle took the same precaution when he inaugurated one of the major periodicals of the time, *Nouvelles de la République des Lettres*. Its first number, running to 104 pages, appeared in Amsterdam in March, 1684. The magazine proposed to keep its readers informed on all significant developments in literature, science, philosophy, scholarship, exploration, and historiography. So far as we know, Bayle himself wrote all the contents, month after month for three years; we may imagine the industry this entailed. His reviews of books soon became a power in the literary world. In 1685 he took courage, and acknowledged his authorship. Two years later his health broke down, and he surrendered the editorship to other hands.

Meanwhile the persecution of Huguenots in France found four victims in Bayle's family. As a direct or indirect result of the dragonnades his mother died in 1681, his father in 1685; in that year his brother was imprisoned, and died of the cruelties inflicted upon him. Six days later (October 18) the Edict of Nantes was revoked. Bayle was shocked by these developments. Like Voltaire, he had no weapon but his pen. In 1686 he challenged the persecutors with one of the classics in the literature of toleration.

He called it *Commentaire philosophique sur ces paroles de Jésus-Christ: Contrains-les d'entrer (Philosophical Commentary on These Words of Jesus Christ: "Compel Them to Come In")*. The persecutors had claimed to find a divine warrant for their procedure in the parable told by Christ of the man who, when the guests whom he had invited to a feast failed to come, said to his servant, "Go out quickly into the streets and lanes of the city, and bring in hither the poor, and the maimed, and the halt, and the blind. . . . Compel them to come in, that my house may be filled."[18] Bayle had no trouble in showing that these words had nothing to do with compelling unity of religious faith. On the contrary, the attempts to enforce unity of belief had bloodied half of Europe, and the diversity of religions in a state prevented any one creed from being strong enough to persecute. Besides, which of us can be so sure that he has the truth as to warrant injuring another for differing from him? Bayle condemned persecution by Protestants as well as by Catholics, and of non-Christians by Christians in general. Unlike Locke, he proposed to extend freedom of worship or nonworship to Jews, Mohammedans, and freethinkers. Forgetting his claim that atheists were as likely as Christians to be good citizens, he advised against tolerating sects that had no belief in Providence and a punishing deity; these, undeterred from perjury by fear of God, would make difficult the enforcement of the law.[19] For the rest, only intolerance should be exempt from toleration. Should a Protestant state tolerate the rise of a Catholicism that defended intolerance on the ground that it alone had the true faith? Bayle thought that in such cases Catholics "should be deprived of the power of doing mischief. . . . Yet I should never be for leaving them exposed to personal insult, or for disturbing their enjoyment of property or the exercise of their religion, or allow any injustice in their appeals to law."[20]

The Protestants were no better pleased than the Catholics by this program of toleration. Pierre Jurieu, who had been Bayle's friend and professorial associate in Sedan, and was now pastor of a Calvinist congregation in Rotterdam, attacked Bayle in a tract on *The Rights of the Two Sovereigns in the Matter of Religion—the Conscience and the Prince* (1687). Jurieu proposed "to destroy the dogma of the indifference of religions, and of universal tolerance, against a book entitled *A Philosophical Commentary*." He agreed with the popes that rulers had full right to destroy a false religion; and he was especially shocked by the idea of tolerating Jews, Mohammedans, Socinians, and pagans. In 1691 Jurieu appealed to the burgomasters of Rotterdam to dismiss Bayle from his professorship. They refused; but in 1693 an election changed the official personnel; Jurieu renewed his campaign, charging Bayle with atheism, and Bayle was dismissed. "God preserve us from the Protestant Inquisition," said the philosopher; "another five or six years, and it will have become so terrible that people will be longing to have the Roman back again."[21]

Soon recovering his perspective and good humor, Bayle adjusted himself to the situation. It was sufficient consolation that now he could devote all his working hours to the epochal *Dictionnaire* that he had already begun.

He accustomed himself to live on his savings, and a few honorariums from his publishers. He received offers of patronage from the French ambassador in Holland, and from three English earls; he courteously declined, and even refused the Earl of Shrewsbury's proffered gift of two hundred guineas for the dedication of the *Dictionary*. He had friends, but few distractions. "Public amusements, games, country jaunts . . . and other recreations . . . were none of my business. I waste no time on them, nor in any domestic cares, never soliciting for any preferment. . . . I find sweetness and repose in the studies in which I have engaged myself, and which are my delight. . . . *Canem mihi et Musis*—I will sing to myself and the Muses."[22]

So he remained quietly in his room, working fourteen hours a day, adding page after page to the strange volumes that were to become a fountainhead of the Enlightenment. The two massive folios, totaling 2,600 pages, appeared at Rotterdam in 1697. He called them *Dictionnaire historique et critique;* not a vocabulary of words, but a critical considera- tion of persons, places, and ideas in history, geography, mythology, theology, morals, literature, and philosophy. "*Iacta est alea!*" he cried as he dispatched the final proof sheets to the printer—"The die is cast!" It was a heavy gamble with life and liberty, for it contained more heresies than any other book of its century, perhaps more than its grandchild, the *Encyclopédie* (1751) of Diderot and d'Alembert.

Bayle had begun with the limited aim of correcting the errors and supplying the omissions in the *Grand Dictionnaire historique* that Louis Moréri had published in 1674 from the viewpoint of Catholic orthodoxy; but his aim widened as he progressed. He never pretended to encyclopedic coverage; where he had nothing to say he said nothing; so there were no articles on Cicero, Bacon, Montaigne, Galileo, Horace, Nero, Thomas More. Science and art were largely ignored; on the other hand, there were articles on such recondite notables as Akiba, Uriel Acosta, and Isaac Abrabanel. Space was allotted not according to historical importance but according to Bayle's interest; so Erasmus, who had been allotted one page in Moreri, received fifteen in Bayle, and Abélard eighteen. The arrangement was alphabetical but semi-Talmudic: the main facts were stated in the text, but in many cases Bayle appended in smaller type a note in which he let himself go into "a miscellany of proofs and discussions . . . , even sometimes a train of philosophical reflections." It was in this fine print that he draped his heresies from the common view. In the margins he indicated his sources; altogether these display a range of reading and learning hardly possible in one lifetime. Some notes contained risqué anecdotes; Bayle hoped these would help his sales, but doubtless, in his baccalaureal solitude, he enjoyed them for their own sake. Readers took gratefully to his racy, rambling, saucy style, his sly exposure of weaknesses in current creeds, and his tongue-in-cheek professions of Calvinist orthodoxy. The original issue of one thousand copies was sold out in four months.

Bayle's method was to collate authorities, ferret out the facts, expound rival and contradictory opinions, follow reason to its conclusions, and then, if these wounded orthodoxy, reject them piously in favor of Scripture and faith. Jurieu angrily asked, "Can a word in passing in favor of faith over reason oblige men to renounce the objections that Bayle has called invincible?"[23] Otherwise there is little order in his *Dictionnaire*. Some of its major discussions emerge under trivial topics or misleading heads. "I cannot meditate with much regularity on one subject; I am too fond of change. I often wander from the subject, and jump into places of which it might be difficult to guess the way out."[24] Usually the argument was courteous, modest, undogmatic, and good-humored; now and then, however, Bayle sharpened his tongue, and the article on St. Augustine did not spare the great Calvinist for his long deferment of chastity, his gloomy theology, and his religious intolerance. Bayle professed to accept the Bible as the Word of God, but he slyly pointed out that we would never believe some of its miracle stories had they not had so distinguished an author. He put pagan legends—e.g., Hercules swallowed by a whale—beside similar tales in the Bible, and let the reader puzzle why one story should be rejected and the other received. In the most famous of his articles he recounted the massacres, treacheries, and adulteries of King David, and left the reader to wonder why such a crowned scoundrel should be honored by Christians as the ancestor of Christ.

He found it easier to swallow both Jonah and the whale than the fall of Eve and Adam. How could an omnipotent deity create them, foreseeing that they would taint the whole human race with "original sin" and curse it with a million miseries?

> If man is the creature of one principle perfectly good, most holy and omnipotent, can he be exposed to diseases, to heat and cold, hunger and thirst, pain and grief? Can he have so many bad inclinations? Can he commit so many crimes? Can perfect holiness produce a criminal creature? Can perfect goodness produce an unhappy creature? Would not omnipotence, joined with infinite goodness, furnish his own work plentifully with good things, and secure it from everything that might be offensive or vexatious?[25]

The God of Genesis was either a cruel deity or one of limited power. So Bayle expounded with much sympathy and force the Manichean conception of two gods, one good, the other evil, fighting to control the world and man. As "the Papists and the Protestants agree that very few people escape damnation," it would seem that the Devil is winning the battle against Christ; moreover, his victories are everlasting, for, the theologians assure us, there is no escape from hell. Since there is, or will be, more souls in hell than in heaven, and those in hell "eternally curse the name of God, there will be more creatures who will hate God than those who will love him." Bayle maliciously concluded that "we must not engage with the Manicheans until we have first laid down the doctrine of the exaltation of faith and the abasing of reason."[26]

The article on Pyrrho expressed doubts about the Trinity, for "things which do not differ from a third do not differ from each other."[27] And as to transubstantiation, "the modes of a substance"—and therefore the appearances of bread and wine—"cannot subsist without the substance which they modify."[28] As to all men inheriting the guilt of Adam and Eve: "A creature which does not exist cannot be an accomplice of an ill action."[29] But all these doubts were placed by him in other mouths than his own, and were repudiated by him in the name of faith. Bayle quoted as "most falsely said by impious men" that "religion is a mere human invention, set up by sovereigns to keep their subjects within the bounds of obedience."[30] In the article on Spinoza he went out of his way to condemn the Jewish pantheist as an atheist; yet he must have found something fascinating in him, for this is the longest article in the *Dictionary*. Bayle pretended to reassure the theologians by telling them that the doubts expressed in his book would never destroy religion—because these matters were beyond the understanding of the people.[31]

Faguet thought Bayle "unquestionably an atheist,"[32] but it would be fairer to call him a skeptic, and to remember that he was skeptical of skepticism too. Since secondary sense qualities are largely subjective, the objective world is quite different from what it appears to us. "The absolute nature of things is unknown to us; we know only some relations they have one to another."[33] Amid 2,600 pages of reasoning he confessed the weakness of reason; it too, like the senses upon which it depends, may deceive us, for it is often clouded by passion, and it is desire and passion, rather than reason, that determine our conduct. Reason can teach us to doubt, but it rarely moves us to act.

> The reasons for doubting are doubtful themselves; one must therefore doubt whether he ought to doubt. What chaos! What torment for the mind! . . . Our reason is the way to wander, since, when it displays itself with the greatest subtlety, it throws us into such an abyss. . . . Human reason is a principle of destruction and not of edification; it is only fit to start doubts, and to turn itself all manner of ways to perpetuate a dispute.[34]

Consequently Bayle counseled philosophers not to set a high value on philosophy, and he advised reformers not to expect much of reforms. Since human nature is apparently the same in all centuries, it will continue, through greed, pugnacity, and erotic appetite, to produce the problems that disorder societies and cause the infantile mortality of utopias. Men do not learn from history; every generation shows the same passions, delusions, and crimes. Therefore democracy is all the more a mistake in proportion as it is real: to allow the busy, ill-informed, and impulsive multitude to choose rulers and policies would be the suicide of a state. Some kind of monarchy is necessary, even under democratic forms.[35] Progress too is a delusion; we mistake movement for advance, but probably it is merely oscillation.[36] The best we can hope for is a government that, though manned by corrupt and imperfect men, will provide enough law and order to enable us to cultivate our gardens in security, and pursue our studies or hobbies in peace.

No such peace was left to Bayle in the nine years that remained to him. As his readers passed from his large to his fine print, a wave of resentment rose. The consistory of the Walloon church in Rotterdam summoned Bayle —a member of the congregation—to appear before it and answer charges that his *Dictionary* contained "indecent expressions and questions, a great many obscene quotations," offensive remarks on atheism and Epicurus, and especially objectionable articles on David, Pyrrho, and the Manichees. Bayle promised that he "would meditate further on the doctrine of the Manichees," and if he "found any replies, or if the ministers of the consistory would furnish him with some," he "would be glad to put them in the best form possible."[37] For the second edition of the *Dictionary* (1702) he rewrote and softened the article on David. Jurieu, unmollified, renewed the assault, and published in 1706 a blast entitled *The Philosopher of Rotterdam Accused, Attacked, and Convicted.*

After that second edition Bayle's health failed. Like Spinoza, he suffered from tuberculosis. In these later years he coughed almost constantly, fell into repeated fevers, and grew despondent with headaches. Convinced that his disease was incurable, he resigned himself to death, retired more and more to the confinement of his room, and worked day and night on the reply that he was making to his critics. On December 27, 1706, he sent his final sheets to the printer. The next morning his friends found him dead in his bed.

His influence pervaded the eighteenth century. His *Dictionary*, repeatedly reissued, became a secret delight to thousands of rebel minds. By 1750 nine editions had appeared in French, three in English, one in German. In Rotterdam his admirers wished to raise a statue to him alongside that of Erasmus,[38] and they induced the publishers to reprint the original article on David. Within a decade of his death students stood in line at the Mazarin

Library in Paris, waiting their turn to read the *Dictionnaire*.[39] A survey of private libraries in France found it in more of them than any other work.[40] Almost every thinker of consequence felt his influence. Most of Leibniz' *Theodicy* was explicitly an attempt to answer Bayle. Lessing's mental emancipation, and his defense of tolerance, stemmed from Bayle. Frederick the Great probably derived his skepticism originally from Bayle rather than from Voltaire; he called the *Dictionary* "the breviary of good sense,"[41] had four sets of it in his library, and supervised the publication of a cheaper and abbreviated two-volume edition to attract a wider range of readers.[42] Shaftesbury and Locke were touched by Bayle more lightly; both of them knew him in Holland, and Locke's *Epistola de Tolerantia* (1689) walked in the footsteps of Bayle's *Commentaire* (1686).

But of course the greatest influence of Bayle was on the *philosophes* of the Enlightenment; they were weaned on the *Dictionnaire*. It was probably from Bayle that Montesquieu and Voltaire took the device of invoking Asiatic comparisons and criticisms of European institutions. The *Encyclopédie* of 1751 was not, as Faguet judged, "merely a revised, corrected, and slightly augmented edition of Bayle's *Dictionary*,"[43] but much of its standpoint and many of its guiding ideas came from those two volumes; and its article on toleration perhaps too generously referred the reader to Bayle's *Commentaire* as "exhausting the subject." Diderot acknowledged his indebtedness with his usual candor, and hailed Bayle as "the most redoubtable exponent of skepticism in either ancient or modern times."[44] Voltaire was Bayle reborn with better lungs, more energy, years, wealth, and wit. The *Dictionnaire philosophique* has been rightly called an echo of Bayle's.[45] The delicious monkey of Ferney often differed from Bayle; for example, Voltaire thought that religion had helped to foster morality, and that if Bayle had had five or six hundred peasants to govern, he would not have hesitated to announce to them a god who punishes and rewards;[46] but he reckoned Bayle as "the greatest dialectician who has ever written."[47] Altogether, the philosophy of France in the eighteenth century was Bayle in an explosive proliferation. With Hobbes, Spinoza, Bayle, and Fontenelle the seventeenth century opened, between Christianity and philosophy, the long and bitter war that would culminate in the fall of the Bastille and the feast of the Goddess of Reason.

V. FONTENELLE: 1657–1757

In the first forty of his hundred years Bernard Le Bovier de Fontenelle waged the philosophic war, independently of Bayle, sometimes before him; and he continued the war, *un poco adagio*, for half a century after Bayle's death. He was one of the phenomena of longevity, bridging the gap between Bossuet and Diderot, and carrying into the intellectual turmoil of the eighteenth century the milder and more cautious skepticism of the seventeenth.

He was born at Rouen February 11, 1657, so frail that he was baptized at once in fear that he would die before the day was out. He remained frail through all his circuit; his lungs were bad, and he spat blood if he exerted himself even to play billiards; but by measuring out his forces sparingly, avoiding marriage, starving his passions and indulging his sleep, he outlived all his contemporaries, and remembered Molière while he spoke to Voltaire.

He had some impetus to letters as the nephew of Corneille. He too dreamed dramas, but the plays and operas that he composed, his eclogues, love poems, and *bergeries* lacked passion, and died of the cold. French literature was losing art and gaining ideas, and Fontenelle found himself only when he discovered that science could be a more astonishing revelation than the Apocalypse, and that philosophy was a ruthful battle transcending all wars. Not that he was a warrior; he was too genial for strife, too much a man of the world to lose his temper in debate, and too conscious of the relativity of truth to tie his thought to an absolute. And yet he "sowed dragon's teeth."[48] Where he walked in feigned discourse with his imaginary Marquise, the army of the Enlightenment would rise with the dashing light horse of Voltaire, the heavy infantry of d'Holbach, the sappers of the *Encyclopédie*, and the artillery of Diderot.

His first sally into philosophy was a fifteen-page essay, *L'Origine des fables*, in effect a sociological inquiry into the origin of gods. We can hardly believe his biographer that this was composed at the age of twenty-three, though prudently left in manuscript till the censorship was relaxed in 1724. It is almost completely "modern" in spirit, tracing myths not to priestly invention but to primitive imagination—above all, to the readiness of simple minds to personify processes. So a river flowed because a god poured out its water; all natural operations were the actions of deities.

> Men beheld many wonders beyond their own power: to hurl thunderbolts, raise the winds and the waves . . . Men imagined beings more powerful than themselves, capable of producing these effects. These superior beings had to have human form, for what other form could be imagined? . . . So the gods were human, but endowed with superior power. . . . Primitive men could conceive no quality more admirable than physical force; they had not yet conceived, had not yet words for, wisdom and justice.[49]

Half a century before Rousseau, Fontenelle rejected Rousseau's idealization of the savage; primitive men were stupid and barbarous. But, he added,

"All men are so much alike that there is no race whose follies should not make us tremble."[50] He took care to add that his naturalistic interpretation of the gods did not apply to the Christian or Jewish deity.

Putting that little essay aside for safer times, Fontenelle took a leaf and a title from Lucian, and published in January, 1683, a little book called *Dialogues des morts*. These imaginary conversations between dead celebrities proved so popular that a second edition was called for in March, and a third soon afterward. Bayle praised it enthusiastically in his *Nouvelles*. Before the year ran out it was translated into Italian and English, and Fontenelle, at twenty-six, reached European fame. The dialogue form was handy in a world infested with censors; almost any notion could be expressed by one of the speakers, "refuted" by another, and disclaimed by the author. Fontenelle, however, was in a mood for humor rather than heresy; the ideas he discussed were moderate, and left no miters crushed. So Milo, the vegetarian athlete of Crotona, plumes himself with having carried an ox on his shoulders at the Olympic games; Smindiride, from neighboring Sybaris, taunts him with developing his muscles at the expense of his mind; but the sybarite confesses that the epicurean life is also vain, since it dulls pleasure with frequency, and multiplies the sources and degrees of pain. Homer compliments Aesop on teaching truth with fables, but warns him that truth is the last thing desired by mankind. "The spirit of man is extremely sympathetic to falsehood. . . . Truth must borrow the figure of the false to be agreeably received by the human mind."[51] "If," said Fontenelle, "I had all truth in my hands, I would be careful not to open them";[52] but probably that would be out of sympathy for mankind, as well as from reckless love of the pursuit.

In the most delightful of the *Dialogues* Montaigne meets Socrates, doubtless in hell, and discusses the idea of progress:

MONTAIGNE. Is this you, divine Socrates? What a joy it is to see you! I've just entered this region, and ever since I've been looking for you. At last, after filling my book with your name and praise, I can talk with you.

SOCRATES. I am happy to see a dead man who appears to have been a philosopher. But since you have come so recently from up there . . . let me ask you the news. How goes the world? Hasn't it changed a great deal?

MONTAIGNE. Much indeed. You wouldn't recognize it.

SOCRATES. I am delighted to hear it. I have never doubted that it must become better or wiser than in my time.

MONTAIGNE. What are you saying? It is crazier and more corrupt than ever. That is the change I wanted to discuss with you; and I have been waiting to hear from you an account of the age in which you lived, and in which so much honesty and justice reigned.

SOCRATES. And I, on the contrary, have been waiting to learn about the marvels of the age in which you have just lived. What? Men have not yet corrected the follies of antiquity? . . . I hoped that things would take a turn toward reason, and that men would profit from the experience of so many years.

MONTAIGNE. Eh? Men profit from experience? They are like birds that repeatedly let themselves be caught in the same nets that have already taken a hundred thousand birds of the same species. Everyone enters new into life, and the mistakes of the parents are lost on the children. . . . Men of all centuries have the same inclinations, over which reason has no power. Hence, wherever there are men there are follies, even the same follies. . . .

SOCRATES. You idealized antiquity because you were angry at your own time. . . . When we were alive we esteemed our ancestors more than they deserved, and now our posterity exalts us beyond our merits: but our ancestors, ourselves, and our posterity are quite equal. . . .

MONTAIGNE. But aren't some ages more virtuous, and others more wicked?

SOCRATES. Not necessarily. Clothes change, but that is not to say that the figure of the body changes, too. Politeness or grossness, knowledge or ignorance, . . . are but the outside of man, and all that changes; but the heart changes not at all; and all of man is in the heart. . . . Among the vast multitude of foolish men born in a hundred years, nature may have scattered here and there . . . two or three dozen reasonable men.[53]

Some years after this pessimistic conclusion, Fontenelle took a slightly more optimistic view in a *Digression sur les Anciens et les Modernes* (January, 1688). There he drew a helpful distinction: in poetry and art there had been no visible progress, for these depend upon feeling and imagination, which hardly change from generation to generation; but in science and learning, which depend upon the slow accumulation of knowledge, we may expect to surpass antiquity. Each nation, Fontenelle suggested, goes through stages like an individual: in infancy it devotes itself to meeting its physical wants; in youth it adds imagination, poetry, and art; in maturity it may reach science and philosophy.[54] Fontenelle thought that he saw truths growing through the gradual elimination of erroneous views. "We are under an obligation to the ancients for having exhausted almost all the false theories that could be formed"—which is to forget that for every truth there is an indefinite number of possible errors. He supposed that Descartes had found a new and better mode of reasoning—the mathematical; now, he hoped, science would grow by leaps.

> When we behold the progress the sciences have made during the last hundred years, in spite of prejudices, obstacles, and the small number of scientific men, we might almost be tempted to let our hopes for the future rise too high. We shall see new sciences springing out of nothingness, while ours are still in the cradle.[55]

So Fontenelle formulated a theory of progress, *le progrès des choses;* and, like Condorcet a century later, he conceived it as having no assignable limit in the future; here already was the "indefinite perfectibility of mankind." The idea of progress was now fully launched, and sailed on through the eighteenth century to become one of the fairest vehicles of modern thought.

Meanwhile, Fontenelle, whose brilliant fancy was ever straining at the leash of caution, had come close to the Bastille. About 1685 he published a brief *Relation de l'île de Bornéo*, an imaginary voyage so realistically described (anticipating the verisimilitude of Defoe and Swift) that Bayle printed it as an actual history in his *Nouvelles*. But the conflict which it described between Eénegu and Mréo was an evident satire on the theological strife between Geneva and Rome. When the French authorities saw through the anagrams, the arrest of Fontenelle seemed inevitable, for the skit appeared on the very heels of the Revocation of the Edict of Nantes. He hurriedly issued a poem lauding "the Triumph of Religion under Louis the Great." His apology was accepted, and thereafter Fontenelle saw to it that his philosophy should be unintelligible to governments.

He returned to science, and made himself its missionary to French society. He was too fond of ease to engage directly in experiment or research, but he understood the sciences well, and presented them to his growing audiences in small doses coated with literary art. To popularize the Copernican astronomy he composed *Entretiens sur la pluralité des mondes* (1686)—*Conversations on the Plurality of Worlds*. Though 143 years had passed since the appearance of Copernicus' *De revolutionibus orbium coelestium*, very few people in France, even among college graduates, accepted the heliocentric theory. Galileo had been condemned by the Church (1633) for assuming that the hypothesis was a fact; and Descartes had not dared to publish his treatise *Le Monde*, in which the Copernican view had been taken for granted.

Fontenelle approached the subject with disarming gallantry. He imagined himself discussing it with a pretty marquise; her figure—unseen but not unfelt—moved through the discourse alluringly; for when beauty has a title it can dim the stars. The six "conversations" were *soirs*, "evenings"; the scene was the garden of the marquise's château near Rouen. The purpose was to get the people of France—or at least the ladies of the salons—to understand the rotation and revolution of the earth, and the Cartesian theory of vortices. As an added lure, Fontenelle raised the question whether the moon and the planets are inhabited. He was inclined to think so; but, remembering that some readers might be disturbed by the notion that there were in the world men and women not descended from Adam and Eve, he prudently explained that these lunar or planetary populations were not really human. However, he suggested that they might have other senses, perhaps finer senses, than ours; if so, they would see objects differently than we do; would truth, then, be relative? This would upset everything, even more than Copernicus had done. Fontenelle saved the situation by pointing out the beauty and order of the cosmos, comparing it to a watch, and deducing from the cosmic mechanisms a divine artificer of supreme intelligence.

As the desire to teach is among our strongest itches, Fontenelle again risked the Bastille by issuing anonymously, in December, 1688, the boldest of his little treatises, *L'Histoire des oracles*. He confessed to having taken his material from the *De Oraculis* of a Dutch scholar, van Dael; but he transformed it by the clarity and gaiety of his style. "*Il nous enjôle à la vérité*," said a reader—"He cajoles us to the truth." So he compared mathematicians with lovers: "Grant a mathematician the least principle, and he will draw from it a consequence which you must also grant him, and from this consequence another . . ."[56] Theologians had accepted some pagan oracles as authentic, but had ascribed their occasional accuracy to Satanic inspiration; and they had held it a proof of the Church's divine origin that these oracles had ceased to operate after the coming of Christ. But Fontenelle showed that they had continued as late as the fifth century A.D. He exonerated Satan as their *deus ex machina;* the oracles were tricks of pagan priests moving in the temples to work apparent miracles, or to appropriate the food offered by worshipers to the gods. He pretended that he spoke only of pagan oracles, and explicitly excepted Christian oracles and priests from his analysis. This essay, and the *Origine des fables*, were not only subtle blows struck for enlightenment; they were examples of a new historical approach to theological questions—to explain the human sources of transmundane beliefs, and thereby naturalize the supernatural.

L'Histoire des oracles was the last of Fontenelle's sapping operations. In 1691 he was elected to the French Academy, over the opposition of Racine and Boileau. In 1697 he became, and for forty-two years he remained, "perpetual secretary" of the Académie des Sciences. He wrote its history, and composed gracious and illuminating *éloges* of members who had died; these constitute a lucid record and exposition of French science through almost half a century. From such séances of the sciences Fontenelle could pass with equal pleasure to the salons—first that of Mme. de Lambert, then Mme. de Tencin's, then Mme. Geoffrin's. He was always welcomed, not merely because of his fame as a writer, but because his courtesy never lapsed. He dispensed truth with discretion, he refused to sour conversation with controversy, and his wit had no sting. "No man of his time was more open-minded and free from prejudice."[57] Mme. de Tencin, who had been a firefly of passion, foolishly accused him of having another brain where his heart should have been.[58] And the young God-killers who were grow-ing up around him could no more understand his moderation than he could relish their dogmatism and violence. *"Je suis effrayé de la conviction qui règne autour de moi"* (I am frightened by the certainties that reign around me).[59] He did not see an unmixed evil in the decay of his hearing as he grew old.

About the age of fifty he apparently decided to give thereafter none but platonic services to the ladies. But his gallantry never faltered. At ninety, being introduced to a young and pretty woman, he remarked, "Ah, if I were only eighty now!"[60] Nearly ninety-eight, he opened a New Year's ball by dancing with the one-and-a-half-year-old daughter of Helvétius.[61] When Mme. Grimaud, almost as old as he, said, wonderingly, "Well, here we are, both still alive," he put a finger to his lips, and whispered, "Hush, madame, death has forgotten us."[62]

It found him at last, January 9, 1757, and took him quietly, after he had been ill but a day. He explained to his friends that he was "suffering from being" (*"Je souffre d'être"*); he may have felt that he had carried longevity to excess. He fell short by thirty-three days of rounding out a century. He had been born before Louis XIV had begun to govern; he had grown up amid the triumphs of Bossuet, the Revocation, and the dragonnades; he had lived to see the *Encyclopédie*, and to hear Voltaire summon the philoso-phers to war upon *l'infame*.

CHAPTER XXII

Spinoza

1632–77

I. THE YOUNG HERETIC

THIS strange and lovable character, who made the boldest attempt in modern history to find a philosophy that could take the place of a lost religious faith, was born in Amsterdam on November 24, 1632. His ancestors can be traced to the town of Espinosa, near Burgos, in the Spanish province of León. They were Jews who, as *conversos* to Christianity, included scholars, priests, and Cardinal Diego d'Espinosa, onetime grand inquisitor.[1] Part of the family, presumably to escape the Spanish Inquisition, migrated to Portugal. After a period of residence there, at Vidigueira, near Beja, the grandfather and father of the philosopher moved to Nantes in France, and thence, in 1593, to Amsterdam. They were among the first Jews who settled in that city, eager to enjoy the religious freedom guaranteed in 1579 by the Union of Utrecht. By 1628 the grandfather was regarded as head of the Sephardic community in Amsterdam; at various times the father was warden of the Jewish school there and president of the organized charities of the Portuguese synagogue. The mother, Hana Debora d'Espinoza, came to Amsterdam from Lisbon. She died when Baruch was six years old, leaving him a consumptive heredity. He was brought up by the father and a third wife. As "Baruch" was Hebrew for blessed, the boy was later named Benedictus in official and Latin documents.

In the synagogue school Baruch was given a predominantly religious education, based upon the Old Testament and the Talmud; there was also some study of Hebrew philosophers, especially Abraham ibn Ezra, Moses ben Maimon, and Hasdai Crescas, with perhaps some dippings into the Cabala. Among his teachers were two men of prominence and ability in the community, Saul Morteira and Manasseh ben Israel. Outside of school Baruch received, in Spanish, considerable instruction in secular subjects, since his father wished to prepare him for a business career. In addition to Spanish and Hebrew he learned Portuguese, Dutch, and Latin, with later a touch of Italian and French. He developed a fondness for mathematics, and made geometry the ideal of his philosophical method and thought.

It was natural that a youth of exceptionally active mind should raise some questions about the doctrines transmitted to him in the synagogue school. Perhaps even there he had heard of Hebrew heresies. Ibn Ezra had long ago pointed out the difficulties involved in ascribing to Moses the later parts of the Pentateuch; Maimonides had proposed allegorical interpretations of some otherwise indigestible passages in the Bible,[2] and had suggested some doubts about personal immortality,[3] and about Creation as against the eternity of the world.[4] Crescas had ascribed extension to God, and had rejected all attempts to prove by reason the freedom of the will, the survival of the soul, and even the existence of God. In addition to these predominantly orthodox Jews, Spinoza must have read Levi ben Gerson, who had reduced Biblical miracles to natural causes, and had subordinated faith to reason, saying, "The Torah cannot prevent us from considering to be true that which our reason urges us to believe."[5] And only recently, in this Amsterdam community, Uriel Acosta had challenged the belief in immortality, and, humiliated by excommunication, had shot himself (1647). The vague recollection of that tragedy must have deepened the turmoil in Spinoza's mind when he felt slipping from him the upholding theology of his people and his family.

In 1654 his father died. A daughter claimed the whole estate; Spinoza contested her claim in court, won his case, and then turned over to her all of the legacy but a bed. Now dependent upon himself, he earned his bread by grinding and polishing lenses for spectacles, microscopes, and telescopes. In addition to tutoring some private pupils, he became an instructor in the Latin school of Frans van den Ende, ex-Jesuit, freethinker, dramatist, and revolutionary.* There Spinoza improved his Latin; perhaps he was stimulated by van den Ende to study Descartes, Bacon, and Hobbes; he may now have dipped into the *Summa theologiae* of Thomas Aquinas. He seems to have fallen in love with the headmaster's daughter; she preferred a more affluent suitor, and Spinoza, so far as we know, made no further move toward marriage.

Meanwhile he had begun to lose his faith. Probably before reaching the age of twenty he had ventured, with all the pain and trepidation that such moltings bring to sensitive spirits, upon some exciting ideas—that matter may be the body of God, that angels may be phantoms of the imagination, that the Bible said nothing of immortality, that the soul is identical with life.[7] He might have kept these proud heresies to himself had his father lived; and even after his father's death he might have remained silent had not some friends importuned him with questions. After much hesitation, he confessed to them the tremors of his faith. They reported him to the synagogue.

It has often been pointed out, but must always be borne in mind, that

---

* Later van den Ende served the Dutch as a secret agent in Paris; he was captured by the French government, and was hanged (1676).[6]

the leaders of the Jewish community in Amsterdam were in a difficult position in dealing with heresies that attacked the fundamentals of the Christian as well as the Jewish creed. The Jews enjoyed in the Dutch Republic a religious toleration denied them elsewhere in Christendom; but that could be withdrawn if they tolerated among themselves ideas that might unsettle the religious basis of morality and social order. According to the biography of Spinoza written in the year of his death by a French refugee in Holland, Jean Maximilien Lucas, the students who reported Baruch's doubts falsely added the charge that he had expressed scorn of the Jewish people for thinking itself especially chosen by God, and for believing that God was the author of the Mosaic Code.[8] We do not know how far we can trust this account. In any case the Jewish leaders must have resented any disruption of the faith that had been a tower of strength and a well of comfort to the Jews through centuries of bitter suffering.

The rabbis summoned Spinoza, and chided him for disappointing the bright hopes that his teachers had held for his future in the community. One of these teachers, Manasseh ben Israel, was absent in London. Another, Saul Morteira, pleaded with the youth to abandon his heresies. In fairness to the rabbis we must note that Lucas, though strongly sympathetic with Spinoza, records that when Morteira recalled the loving care he had given to the education of his favorite pupil, Baruch "answered that in return for the trouble Morteira had taken in teaching him the Hebrew language, he [Spinoza] would now be glad to teach his instructor how to excommunicate."[9] This seems quite out of character with all else that we hear of Spinoza, but we must not let our affections select the evidence; and (to vary a remark of Cicero's) there is hardly anything so foolish but we can find it in the lives of the philosophers.

We are told that the synagogue leaders offered Spinoza an annual pension of a thousand gulden if he would promise to take no hostile step against Judaism, and would show himself from time to time in the synagogue.[10] The rabbis appear to have invoked against him at first only the "lesser excommunication," which merely excluded him, for thirty days, from intercourse with the Jewish community.[11] We are told that he accepted this sentence with a light heart, saying, "Good; they are forcing me to do nothing that I would not have done of my own free will";[12] probably he was already living outside the Jewish quarter of the city. A fanatic tried to assassinate him, but the weapon only tore Spinoza's coat. On July 24, 1656, the religious and secular authorities of the Jewish community solemnly pronounced from the pulpit of the Portuguese synagogue the full excommunication of "Baruch d'Espinosa," with all the customary curses and prohibitions: no one was to speak or write to him, or do him any service, or read his writings, or come within the space of four cubits' distance from him.[13] Morteira went before the Amsterdam officials, notified them of the charges and the excommunication, and asked that Spinoza be expelled from the city. They sentenced Spinoza to "an exile of some months."[14] He went to the nearby village of Ouderkerk, but soon returned to Amsterdam.

His knowledge of Hebrew won him several friends in a little circle of students led by Lodewijk Meyer and Simon de Vries. Meyer had degrees in philosophy and medicine; in 1666 he published *Philosophiae Sacrae Scripturae interpres*, which subordinated the Bible to reason; it may have reflected—or influenced—the views of Spinoza. De Vries, a prosperous merchant, was so fond of Spinoza that he wished to give him two thousand florins; Spinoza refused to take them. When de Vries neared death (1667) he proposed, being unmarried, to make Spinoza his heir; Spinoza persuaded him to leave the entire estate to a brother; the gratified brother offered him an annuity of five hundred florins; Spinoza accepted three hundred.[15] Another Amsterdam friend, Johan Bouwmeester, wrote to Spinoza, "Love me, for I love you with all my heart."[16] Next to philosophy, friendship was the chief support of Spinoza's life. In one of his letters he wrote:

> Of all the things that are beyond my power, I value nothing more highly than to be allowed the honor of entering into bonds of friendship with people who sincerely love truth. For, of things beyond our power, I believe there is nothing in the world which we can love with tranquility except such men.[17]

He was not quite a recluse, nor an ascetic. He approved "good food and drink, the enjoyment of beauty and growing plants, the hearing of music, visits to the theater";[18] it was on such a visit that the attempt had been made to kill him. He had still to fear attack; on his signet ring was one word: *Caute*, carefully.[19] But far more than amusements, more even than friendship, he loved privacy and study and the peace of a simple life. According to Bayle it was "because the visits of his friends too much interrupted his speculations"[20] that Spinoza in 1660 left Amsterdam to live in the quiet village of Rijnsburg—"town on the Rhine"—six miles from Leiden. The Collegiants, a Mennonite sect resembling the Quakers, made their headquarters there, and Spinoza found welcome in one of their families.

In that modest dwelling, now preserved as the Spinozahuis, the philosopher wrote several minor works, and Book I of the *Ethics*. He composed in 1662 a *Short Treatise on God, Man, and His Well-Being*; but this was largely a reflection of Descartes. More interesting is the fragment *De Intellectus Emendatione* (*On the Improvement of the Intellect*), which was set aside, unfinished, in that same year. Within its forty pages we get a preview of Spinoza's philosophy. We feel the loneliness of the out-cast in its first sentences:

> After experience had taught me that all things that frequently take place in ordinary life are vain and futile; when I saw that all the things I feared, and which feared me, had nothing good or bad in them save in so far as the mind was affected by them, I determined at last to inquire whether there might be anything which might be truly good and able to communicate its goodness, and by which the mind might be affected to the exclusion of all other things.

He felt that riches could not do this, nor fame (*honor*), nor the pleasures of the flesh (*libido*); turmoil and grief are too often mingled with these delights. "Only the love towards a thing eternal and infinite feeds the mind with pleasure . . . free from all pain."[21] This could have been written by Thomas à Kempis or Jakob Böhme; and indeed there always remained in Spinoza a note and mood of mysticism that may have come to him from the Cabala, and now found nourishment in his solitude. The "eternal and infinite good" which he had in mind could be termed God, but only in Spinoza's later definition of God as one with nature in its creative powers and its laws. "The greatest good," says the *Emendatione*, ". . . is the knowledge of the union which the mind has with the whole of nature. . . . The more the mind understands the order of nature, the more easily it will be able to liberate itself from useless things";[23] here is Spinoza's first phrasing of the "intellectual love of God"—the reconciliation of the indi-vidual with the nature of things and the laws of the universe.

This eloquent little treatise states also the aim of Spinoza's thinking, and his understanding of science and philosophy. "I wish to direct all sciences in one direction or to one end, namely, to attain the greatest possible human perfection; and thus everything in the sciences that does not pro-mote this endeavor must be rejected as useless."[23] Here is quite a different strain from that which we heard in Francis Bacon; the progress of the sciences is a delusion if they merely increase man's power over things with-out improving his character and desires. That is why the *chef-d'oeuvre* of modern philosophy will be called *Ethics* despite its long metaphysical prelude, and why so much of it will analyze the bondage of man to desire, and his liberation through reason.

II. THEOLOGY AND POLITICS

The circle of gentlemen students whom Spinoza had left behind in Amsterdam heard that he had begun, for a pupil in Rijnsburg, a geometrical version of Descartes' *Principia philosophiae*. They importuned him to complete it and send it to them. He did, and they financed its publication (1663) as *Renati Des Cartes Principia Philosophiae more geometrico demonstrata*. We need note only three things about it: that it expressed Descartes' views (for example, on free will), not Spinoza's; that it was the only book of Spinoza's printed in his lifetime over his own name; and that in an appended fragment, *Cogitata metaphysica*, he suggested that time was not an objective reality, but a mode of thinking.[24] This is one of several Kantian elements in Spinoza's philosophy.

In Rijnsburg he made some new friends. The great anatomist Steno became acquainted with him there. Henry Oldenburg, of the Royal Society, coming to Leiden in 1661, went out of his way to visit Spinoza, and was deeply impressed; returning to London, he began a long correspondence with the unprinted but already famous philosopher. Another Rijnsburg friend, Adriaan Koerbagh, was summoned before an Amsterdam court (1668), charged with "intemperate" opposition to the prevailing theology; one magistrate sought to implicate Spinoza as the source of Koerbagh's heresies; Koerbagh denied this, and Spinoza was spared; but the young heretic was sentenced to ten years in prison, where he died after he had served fifteen months of his term.[25] We can understand why Spinoza did not rush into print.

In June, 1663, he moved to Voorburg, near The Hague. For six years he lived in the home of an artist, still polishing lenses and composing the *Ethics*. The desperate defensive war of the United Provinces against Louis XIV frightened the Dutch government into tighter restrictions on the expression of ideas. Nevertheless Spinoza published anonymously, in 1670, a *Treatise on Theology and Politics* that became a milestone in Biblical criticism. The title page of this *Tractatus theologico-politicus* stated the purpose: "to set forth that freedom of thought and speech not only may, without prejudice to piety and the public peace, be granted, but that also it may not, without danger to piety and the public peace. be withheld." Spinoza disclaimed atheism, supported the fundamentals of religious belief, but undertook to show the human fallibility of those Scriptures upon which the Calvinist clergy based their theology and intolerance. The clergy in Holland were using their influence, and their Biblical texts, to oppose the party led by the de Witts, which favored liberal thought and negotiations for peace; and Spinoza was warmly devoted to that party and to Jan de Witt.

> As I marked the fierce controversies of philosophers raging in Church and state, the source of bitter hatred and dissension . . . , I determined to examine the Bible afresh in a careful, impartial, and

unfettered spirit, making no assumptions concerning it, and attributing to it no doctrines which I do not find clearly therein set down. With these precautions I constructed a method of scriptural interpretation.[26]

He noted and illustrated the difficulty of understanding the Hebrew of the Old Testament; the Masoretic text—which filled in the vowels and accents omitted by the original writers—was partly guesswork, and could hardly give us an indisputable prototype. He profited much, in the earlier chapters of this treatise, from Maimonides' *Guide to the Perplexed*. He followed Abraham ibn Ezra and others in questioning the Mosaic authorship of the Pentateuch. He denied that Joshua had composed the Book of Joshua; and he ascribed the historical books of the Old Testament to the priest-scribe Ezra, of the fifth century B.C. The Book of Job, he thought, was a Gentile production translated into Hebrew. Not all these conclusions have been accepted by later research; but they were a brave advance toward understanding the composition of the Bible; and they preceded by eight years the more scholarly *Critique du Vieux Testament* (1678) of Richard Simon. Spinoza pointed out that in several instances the same story or passage was repeated in different places in the Bible, sometimes in the same words, sometimes in divergent versions; the one case suggesting common borrowing from an earlier manuscript, the other raising the question as to which account was the Word of God.[27] There were chronological impossibilities and contradictions. In his Epistle to the Romans (III, 20–28) Paul taught that man can be saved only by faith, not by works; the Epistle of the Apostle James (II, 24) taught precisely the opposite; which was God's view and Word? Such diverse texts, the philosopher pointed out, have generated bitterest—even murderous—quarrels among theologians, not the good conduct that a religion should inspire.

Were the Old Testament prophets the voice of God? Evidently they were not ahead of the knowledge shared by the educated classes of their time; "Joshua," for example, took it for granted that the sun, until he "stopped" it, revolved around the earth.[28] The prophets excelled not in learning but in intensity of imagination, enthusiasm, and feeling; they were great poets and orators. They may have been divinely inspired, but if so it was by a process that Spinoza confessed himself unable to understand.[29] Perhaps they dreamed that they saw God; and they may have believed in the reality of their dream. So we read of Abimelech that "God said unto him in a dream" (Gen. xx, 6). The divine element in the prophets was not their prophecies but their virtuous lives; and the theme of their preaching was that religion lies in good conduct, not in sedulous ritual.

Were the miracles recorded in the Bible real interruptions of the normal course of nature? Did the sins of men bring down fire and flood, and did the prayers of men give fertility to the earth? Such stories, Spinoza suggested, were used by the Scriptural authors to reach the understanding of simple men and move them to virtue or devotion; we must not take them literally.

> When, therefore, the Bible says that the earth is barren because of men's sins, or that the blind were healed by faith, we ought to take no more notice than when it says that God is angry at men's sins, that he is sad, that he repents of the good he has promised or done, or that, on seeing a sign, he remembers something he had promised; these and similar expressions are either thrown out poetically, or related according to the opinions and prejudices of the writer. We may be absolutely certain that every event which is truly described in Scripture necessarily happened—like everything else—according to natural law; and if anything is there set down which can be proved in set terms to contravene the order of nature, or not to be deducible therefrom, we must believe it to have been foisted into the sacred writings by irreligious hands; for whatsoever is contrary to nature is contrary to reason, and whatsoever is contrary to reason is absurd.[30]

This was probably the most forthright declaration of independence yet made for reason by a modern philosopher. So far as it was accepted, it involved a revolution of profounder significance and results than all the wars and politics of the time.

In what sense, then, is the Bible the Word of God? Only in this: that it contains a moral code that can form men to virtue. It contains also many things that have led—or been adapted—to human deviltry. For the generality of men (too obsessed with daily cares to have leisure or capacity for intellectual development) the Biblical stories can be a beneficent aid to morality. But the emphasis of religious teaching should always be upon conduct rather than creed. It is a sufficient creed to believe in "a God, that is, a supreme being who loves justice and charity," and whose proper worship "consists in the practice of justice and love towards one's neighbor." No other doctrine is necessary.[31]

Aside from that doctrine, thought should be free. The Bible was not intended to be a textbook of science or philosophy; these are revealed to us in nature, and this natural revelation is the truest and most universal voice of God.

> Between faith or theology and philosophy . . . there is no connection, or affinity. . . . Philosophy has no end in view save truth; faith . . . looks for nothing but obedience and piety. . . . Faith, therefore, allows the greatest latitude in philosophical speculation, allowing us without

blame to think what we like about anything, and only condemning, as heretics and schismatics, those who teach opinions that tend to produce hatred, anger, and strife.[32]

So Spinoza, in his own optimistic variation, renewed Pomponazzi's distinction between two truths, the theological and the philosophical, each of which, though contradictory, may be allowed to the same person in the one case as a citizen, in the other as a philosopher. Spinoza would allow to secular officials the right to compel obedience to the laws; the state, like the individual, has the right of self-preservation. But he adds:

> With religion the case is widely different. Since it consists not so much in outward action as in simplicity and truth of character, it stands outside the sphere of law and public authority. Simplicity and truth of character are not produced by the constraint of laws, nor by the authority of the state; no one the whole world over can be forced or legislated into a state of blessedness; the means required for such a consummation are faithful and brotherly admonition, sound education, and, above all, free use of the individual judgment. . . . It is in every man's power to wield the supreme right and authority of free judgment . . . and to explain and interpret religion for himself.[33]

The public practice of religion should be subject to state control, for though religion may be a vital force in molding morality, the state must remain supreme in all matters affecting public conduct. Spinoza was as firm an Erastian as Hobbes, and followed him in subordinating the Church to the state, but he cautioned his readers, "I speak here only of the outward observances, . . . not of . . . the inward worship."[34] And (probably having Louis XIV in mind) he rose to hot indignation in denouncing the use of religion by the state for purposes contrary to what he conceives as basic religion—justice and benevolence.

> If, in despotic statecraft, the supreme and essential mystery be to hoodwink the subjects, and to mask the fear, which keeps them down, with the specious garb of religion, so that men may fight as bravely for slavery as for safety, and count it not shame but highest honor to risk their blood and their lives for the vainglory of a tyrant; yet in a free state no more mischievous expedient could be planned or attempted. [It is] wholy repugnant to the general freedom . . . when law enters the domain of speculative thought, and opinions are put on trial and condemned on the same footing as crimes, while those who defend and follow them are sacrificed not to public safety, but to their opponents' hatred and cruelty. If deeds alone could be made the ground of criminal charges, and words were always allowed to pass free, . . . seditions would be divested of every semblance of justification,

and would be separated from mere controversy by a hard and fast line.[35]

In examining the Scriptures Spinoza faced the fundamental issue between Christians and Jews: Had Christianity been unfaithful to Christ in rejecting the Mosaic Law? In his opinion that Law was intended for the Jews in their own state, and not for other nations, not even for the Jews themselves when living in an alien society; only the moral laws in the Mosaic Code (like the Ten Commandments) have eternal and universal validity.[36] Some passages in Spinoza's discussion of Judaism reveal a strong resentment of his excommunication, and an anxiety to justify his rejection of the synagogue's teachings. But he joined the Jews in hoping for their early restoration to an autonomous Israel. "I would go so far as to believe that . . . they may even raise up their state anew, and God may elect them a second time."[37]

He made several approaches to Christianity. He apparently read the New Testament with increasing admiration for Christ. He rejected the notion of Christ's physical resurrection from the dead,[38] but he found himself in such sympathy with the preaching of Jesus that he conceded to him a special revelation from God:

A man who can by pure intuition comprehend ideas which are neither contained in, nor deducible from, the foundation of our natural knowledge, must necessarily possess a mind far superior to those of his fellow men; nor do I believe that any have been so endowed save Christ. To him the ordinances of God leading to salvation were revealed directly without words or visions, so that God manifested himself to the Apostles through the mind of Christ, as he formerly did to Moses through the supernatural voice. In this sense the voice of Christ, like the voice which Moses heard, may be called the voice of God; and it may be said that the wisdom of God (wisdom more than human*) took upon itself in Christ human nature, and that Christ was the way of salvation. I must at this juncture declare that those doctrines, which certain churches put forward concerning Christ, I neither affirm nor deny, for I freely confess that I do not understand them. . . . Christ communed with God mind to mind. Thus we may conclude that no one except Christ received the revelation of God without the aid of imagination, whether in words or vision.[39]

This olive branch offered to the Christian leaders could not conceal from them that the *Tractatus theologico-politicus* was one of the boldest pronouncements yet made in the conflict between religion and philosophy.

---

* Cf. the *Sophia* of the Book of Wisdom, and the *Logos* of the Fourth Gospel.

Hardly had it appeared when the church council of Amsterdam (June 30, 1670) protested to the Grand Pensionary of Holland that so heretical a volume should be allowed to circulate in a Christian state. A synod at The Hague, petitioned him to ban and confiscate "such soul-destroying books."[40] Lay critics joined in the attack upon Spinoza; one called him Satan incarnate;[41] Jean Le Clerc described him as "the most famous atheist of our time";[42] Lambert van Velthuysen accused him of "craftily introducing atheism . . . destroying all worship and religion from the very foundation."[43] Luckily for Spinoza, the Grand Pensionary, Jan de Witt, was one of his admirers, who had already conferred upon him a small pension. As long as de Witt lived and ruled, Spinoza could rely on his protection. That was to be for only two years.

III. THE PHILOSOPHER

In May, 1670, shortly after publication of the *Tractatus*, Spinoza moved to The Hague, perhaps to be nearer to de Witt and other influential friends. For a year he stayed in the house of the Widow van Velen; then he passed to the home of Hendrik van der Spyck on the Pavilioensgracht; this building was bought in 1927 by an international committee, and is preserved as the Domus Spinozana. There he remained to the end of his life. He occupied one room on the top floor, and slept in a bed that during the day could be folded into the wall.[44] He "was sometimes three whole months without stepping out of doors," Bayle tells; perhaps his consumptive lungs made him fearful of the winter damp. But he had many visitors, and (again according to Bayle) he occasionally "visited persons of importance . . . to discourse of state affairs," which "he understood well."[45] He continued to polish lenses; Christian Huygens commented on their excellence.[46] He kept an account of his expenditures; we learn therefrom that he lived on four and a half sous per day. His friends insisted on helping him, for they must have seen that his confinement to the house, and the dust from his lens polishing, were aggravating his constitutional ailment.

The protection that he received from Jan de Witt ended when a mob assassinated both the de Witt brothers in the streets of The Hague (August 20, 1672). Hearing of the murder, Spinoza wished to go out and denounce the crowd to its face as *ultimi barbarorum*, the lowest barbarians, but his host locked the door and prevented him from leaving the house.[47] Jan de Witt's will left Spinoza an annuity of two hundred francs.[48]* After the

---

* Some scholars question the acquaintance of Spinoza with Jan de Witt. Cf. Clark, *The Seventeenth Century*, 223n.

death of de Witt the civil power fell to Prince William Henry, who needed the support of the Calvinist clergy. When a second edition of the *Tractatus theologico-politicus* appeared in 1674, the Prince and the Council of Holland issued a decree prohibiting the sale of the book; and in 1675 the Calvinist consistory of The Hague published a proclamation bidding all citizens to report at once any attempt to print any writing by Spinoza.[49] Between 1650 and 1680 there were some fifty edicts, by church authorities, against the reading or circulation of the philosopher's works.[50]

Perhaps such prohibitions shared in spreading his fame into Germany, England, and France. On February 16, 1673, Johann Fabritius, professor in the University of Heidelberg, wrote "to the very acute and renowned Philosopher Benedictus de Spinoza" in the name of the liberal Elector of the Palatinate, Prince Charles Louis:

> His Serene Highness . . . has commanded me to write to you . . . and ask whether you are willing to accept an ordinary professorship of philosophy in his illustrious university. You will be paid the annual salary which the ordinary professors enjoy today. You will not find elsewhere a prince more favorable to distinguished geniuses, among whom he reckons you. You will have the utmost freedom of philosophizing, which he believes you will not misuse to disturb the publicly established religion . . .

Spinoza replied on March 30:

> MOST HONORABLE SIR:
>
> If I had ever experienced a wish to take on a professorship in any faculty, I could have desired no other than that which is offered me through you by his Serene Highness the Elector Palatine. . . . Since, however, it was never my intention to give public instruction, I cannot be induced to embrace this glorious opportunity . . . For first, I think that if I want to find time for instructing youth, then I must desist from developing my philosophy. Secondly, . . . I do not know within what limits that freedom of philosophizing ought to be confined in order to avoid the appearance of wishing to disturb the publicly established religion. For schisms arise not so much from an ardent love of religion as from men's various dispositions, or the love of contradiction. . . . I have already experienced these things while leading a private and solitary life; much more then are they to be feared after I shall have risen to this degree of dignity. Thus you see, Most Honored Sir, that I am not holding back in the hope of some better fortune, but from love of peace.[51]

Spinoza was fortunate in his refusal, for in the following year Turenne devastated the Palatinate, and the university was closed.

In May, 1673, amid the invasion of the United Provinces by a French army, an invitation came to Spinoza from a colonel in that army to visit the Great Condé at Utrecht. Spinoza consulted the Dutch authorities, who may have seen in the invitation an opportunity to open negotiations for a desperately needed truce. Both sides gave him safe-conducts, and the philosopher made his way to Utrecht. Meanwhile Condé had been sent elsewhere by Louis XIV; he sent word (according to Lucas[52]) asking Spinoza to wait for him; but after several weeks another message said that he was indefinitely delayed. It was apparently at this time that Maréchal de Luxembourg advised Spinoza to dedicate a book to Louis, assuring him of a liberal response from the King.[53] Nothing came of the proposal. Spinoza returned to The Hague, to find that many citizens suspected him of treason. A hostile crowd gathered about his house, shouting insults and throwing stones. "Do not be troubled," he told his landlord; "I am innocent, and there are many . . . in high places who well know why I went to Utrecht. As soon as you hear any disturbance at your door I will go out to the people, even if they should treat me as they treated the good de Witt. I am an honest republican, and the welfare of the Republic is my aim."[54] His host would not let him go, and the crowd dispersed.

He was now forty-one. A portrait in the Domus Spinozana at The Hague shows him as a fine type of Sephardic Jew, with flowing black hair, heavy eyebrows, black, bright, and slightly somber eyes, a long straight nose, altogether a rather handsome face, if only in comparison with Hals's *Descartes*. "He was extremely neat in his appearance," reported Lucas, "and never left his house without wearing clothes that distinguished the gentleman from the pedant."[55] His manners were grave but amiable. Oldenburg noted his "solid learning combined with humanity and refinement."[56] "Those who have been acquainted with Spinoza," wrote Bayle, ". . . all say that he was sociable, affable, honest, friendly, and a good moral man."[57] To his neighbors he spoke no heresy; on the contrary, he encouraged them to continue their church attendance, and occasionally he accompanied them to hear a sermon.[58] More than any other modern philosopher he achieved a tranquillity born of self-control. He rarely replied to criticism; he dealt with ideas rather than personalities. Despite his determinism, his uprooting from his people, and his illness, he was far from being a pessimist. "Act well," he said, "and rejoice."[59] To know the worst and believe the best might have been the motto of his thought.

Friends and admirers made a path to his door. Walter von Tschirnhaus persuaded him to let him see the manuscript of the *Ethics*. "I beg you," wrote the mathematician-physicist, "to help me with your usual courtesy wherever I do not rightly grasp your meaning."[60] Probably through this eager student Leibniz won access to Spinoza (1676), and presumably to the still unpublished masterpiece. The surviving members of Dr. Meyer's circle in Amsterdam came to see him, or were among his correspondents. His letters to and from European scholars shed unexpected light upon the intellectual climate of the time. Hugo Boxel repeatedly urged him to admit the reality of ghosts. In 1675 the anatomist Steno sent from Florence a touching appeal for Spinoza's conversion to Catholicism:

> If you wish, I shall willingly take upon myself the task of showing you . . . wherein your teachings are behind ours, although I should wish that you . . . would offer to God a refutation of your own errors . . . in order that if your first writings have turned aside a thousand souls from the true knowledge of God, the recantation of them, reinforced by your own example, may lead back to him a thousand thousand with you as with another Augustine. I pray with all my heart that this grace may be yours. Farewell.[61]

The fascination of Catholicism captured also Albert Burgh, son of Spinoza's friend Conrad Burgh, treasurer general of the United Provinces. Albert, like Steno, had become a convert while traveling in Italy. In September, 1675, he wrote to Spinoza not so much soliciting as challenging him to accept the Roman Catholic faith:

> How do you know that your philosophy is the best among all those which have ever been taught in the world, or are actually taught now, or ever will be taught in the future? . . . Have you examined all those philosophies, ancient as well as modern, which are taught here and in India and everywhere throughout the world? And even if you have duly examined them, how do you know that you have chosen the best? . . .
>
> If, however, you do not believe in Christ, you are more wretched than I can say. But the remedy is easy: return from your sins, and realize the fatal arrogance of your wretched and insane reasoning. . . . Will you, you wretched little man, vile worm of the earth, . . . dare, in your unspeakable blasphemy, to put yourself above the Incarnate, Infinite Wisdom? . . .
>
> From your principles you will not explain thoroughly even one of those things which are accomplished in witchcraft . . . , nor will you be able to explain any of the stupendous phenomena among those who are possessed by demons, of all of which I have myself seen various instances, and I have heard most certain evidence.[62]

Spinoza, in part, replied (December, 1675):

> What I could scarcely believe when it was related me by others, I at last understand from your letter; that is, that not only have you

become a member of the Roman Church . . . but that you are a very
keen champion of it, and have already learned to curse and rage
petulantly against your opponents. I had not intended to reply to your
letter, . . . but certain friends who with me had formed great hopes
for you from your natural talent, earnestly prayed me not to fail in
the duty of a friend, and to think rather of what you recently were
than of what you now are. . . . I have been induced by these arguments
to write to you these words, earnestly begging you to be kind enough
to read them with a calm mind.

I will not here recount the vices of priests and popes to turn you
away from them, as the opponents of the Roman Church are wont to
do. For they usually publish these things from ill-feeling, and . . . in
order to annoy rather than instruct. Indeed, I will admit that there are
found more men of great learning, and of an upright life, in the Roman
than in any other Christian Church; for since there are more . . . members of this Church, there will also be found in it more men of every
condition. . . . In every Church there are many very honest men who
worship God with justice and charity . . . For justice and charity are
the surest sign of the true Catholic faith . . . , and wherever these are
found, there Christ really is, and where they are lacking, there Christ
also is not. For by the spirit of Christ alone can we be led to the love
of justice and charity. If you had been willing duly to ponder these
facts within yourself, you would not have been lost, nor would you
have caused bitter sorrow to your parents. . . .

Your asked me, how I know that my philosophy is the best among
all those which have ever been taught in the world, or are taught now,
or will be taught in the future. This, indeed, I can ask you with far
better right. For I do not presume that I have found the best philosophy, but I know that I think [it] the true one. . . . But you who presume that you have at last found the best religion, or rather the best
men, to whom you have given over your credulity, how do you know
that they are the best among all those who have taught other religions,
or are teaching them now, or will teach them in the future? Have
you examined all those religions, both ancient and modern, which
are taught here and in India, and everywhere throughout the world?
And even if you have duly examined them, how do you know that
you have chosen the best? . . .

Do you regard it as arrogance and pride because I use my reason,
and acquiesce in that true Word of God which is in the mind and can
never be depraved or corrupted? Away with this deadly superstition;
acknowledge the reason which God has given you, and cultivate it, if
you would not be numbered among the brutes. . . . If you will . . .
examine the histories of the Church (of which I see you are most
ignorant), in order to see how false are many of the Pontifical traditions, and by what . . . arts the Roman Pontiff, six hundred years after
the birth of Christ, obtained sovereignty over the Church, I doubt not

that you will at last come to your senses. That this may be so, I wish you from my heart. Farewell.[63]

Burgh joined the Franciscan order, and died in a monastery in Rome.

Most of Spinoza's extant correspondence was with Oldenburg. We are surprised to find that much of it deals with science, that Spinoza carried on experiments in physics and chemistry, and that his letters are illustrated with many diagrams. This correspondence was interrupted in 1665. Oldenburg was arrested in 1667, and was held in the Tower of London on suspicion of dealing with a foreign power. On his release he turned to religion, and when he resumed correspondence with Spinoza (1675) he joined in the effort to win him back to some form of orthodox Christianity. He begged him to take the story of Christ's resurrection not allegorically but literally. "The whole Christian religion and its truth," he thought, "rests on this article of the Resurrection; and if it is taken away, the mission of Christ and his heavenly teaching collapse."[64] He finally gave up Spinoza as a lost soul, and discontinued the correspondence (1677).

All through the years from 1662 Spinoza had been working on the *Ethics*. As early as April, 1662, he wrote to Oldenburg that he was thinking of publishing it, but "I am naturally afraid lest the theologians . . . take offense, and with their usual hatred attack me, who utterly loathe quarrels."[65] Oldenburg urged him to publish, "however much the theological quacks may growl,"[66] but Spinoza still hesitated. He allowed some friends to read parts of the manuscript, and probably profited from their comments, for he repeatedly revised the treatise. The clamor aroused by the *Tractatus theologico-politicus* justified his caution. The murder of the de Witts, and the suspicions directed against him after his visit to the French army, further troubled him; and it was not till 1675 that he made another move to put the *Ethics* into print. He reported the results to Oldenburg:

> At the time when I received your letter of 22 July, I was setting out for Amsterdam with the intention of getting printed the work about which I have written to you. While I was engaged in this matter a rumor was spread everywhere that a book of mine about God was in the press, and that in it I endeavored to show that there is no God. This rumor was believed by many. Therefore certain theologians . . . seized the opportunity of bringing complaints against me before the Prince and the magistrates. . . . When I heard all this . . . I decided to postpone the publication I was preparing.[67]

He put the manuscript away, and turned to writing a treatise on the state, *Tractatus politicus*, but death came upon him before he could finish it.

On February 6, 1677, Georg Hermann Schuller, a young physician, wrote to Leibniz: "I fear that Mr. Benedictus Spinoza will soon leave us, as the consumption . . . seems to grow worse every day."[68] Two weeks later, while the rest of the household were absent, the philosopher entered upon his final suffering. Schuller alone (not Meyer, as formerly supposed) was with him at the time. Spinoza left instructions that his modest belongings be sold to pay his debts, and that such manuscripts as he had not burned be published anonymously. He died on February 20, 1677, without any religious ministrations.[69] He was buried in a cemetery of the New Church of The Hague, near the tomb of Jan de Witt. The manuscripts—chiefly the *Ethics*, the *Tractatus politicus*, and the treatise *On the Improvement of the Intellect*—were prepared for the press by Meyer, Schuller, and others, and were printed at Amsterdam toward the end of 1677.

And so we come at last to the book into which Spinoza had poured his life and solitary soul.

IV. GOD

He called it *Ethica ordine geometrico demonstrata*, first because he thought of all philosophy as a preparation for right conduct and wise living, and second because, like Descartes, he envied the intellectual asceticism and logical sequence of geometry. He hoped to build, on the model of Euclid, a structure of reasoning in which every step would follow logically from preceding proofs, and these would at last be irrefutably derived from axioms universally received. He knew that this was an ideal, and he could hardly have supposed it proof against error, for he had by a similar method expounded the Cartesian philosophy, with which he did not agree. At least the geometrical scheme would make for clarity; it would check the confusion of reason by passion, and the concealment of sophistry with eloquence. He proposed to discuss the behavior of men, and even the nature of God, as calmly and objectively as if he were dealing with circles, triangles, and squares. His procedure was not faultless, but it led him to rear an edifice of reason imposing in its architectural grandeur and unity. The method is deductive, and would have been frowned upon by Francis Bacon; but it claimed to be in harmony with all experience.

Spinoza began with definitions, mostly taken from medieval philosophy. The words he used have changed their meaning since his day, and now some of them obscure his thought. The third definition is fundamental: "I understand Substance to be that which is in itself and is conceived through itself; I mean that, the conception of which does not depend upon the conception of another thing from which it must be formed." He does not mean substance in the modern sense of material constituents; our use of the word to mean essence or basic significance comes closer to his intent. If we take literally his Latin term *substantia*, it indicates that which stands under, underlies, supports. In his correspondence[70] he speaks of "substance or being"; i.e., he identifies substance with existence or reality. Hence he can say that "existence appertains to the nature of substance," that in substance, essence and existence are one.[71] We may conclude that in Spinoza *substance* means the essential reality underlying all things.

This reality is perceived by us in two forms: as extension or matter, and as thought or mind. These two are "attributes" of substance; not as qualities residing in it, but as the same reality perceived externally by our senses as matter, and internally by our consciousness as thought. Spinoza is a complete monist: these two aspects of reality—matter and thought— are not distinct and separate entities, they are two sides, the outside and the inside, of one reality; so are body and mind, so is physiological action and the corresponding mental state. Strictly speaking, Spinoza, so far from being a materialist, is an *idea*list: he defines an attribute as "that which the intellect apprehends of substance as constituting its essence";[72] he admits (long before Berkeley was born) that we know reality, whether as matter or as thought, only through perception or idea. He believes that reality expresses itself in endless aspects through an "infinite number of attributes," of which we imperfect organisms perceive only two. So far, then, substance, or reality, is that which appears to us as matter or mind. Substance and its attributes are one: reality is a union of matter and mind; and these are distinct only in our manner of perceiving substance. To put it not quite Spinozistically, matter is reality externally perceived; mind is reality internally perceived. If we could perceive all things in the same double way—externally and internally—as we perceive ourselves, we should, Spinoza believes, find that "all things are in some manner animate" (*omnia quodammodo animata*)[73]; there is some form or degree of mind or life in everything. Substance is always active: matter is always in motion; mind is always perceiving or feeling or thinking or desiring or imagining or remembering, awake or in sleep. The world is in every part of it alive.

God, in Spinoza, is identical with substance; He is the reality underlying and uniting matter and mind. God is not identical with matter (therefore Spinoza is not a materialist), but matter is an inherent and essential attribute or aspect of God (here one of Spinoza's youthful heresies reappears). God is not identical with mind (therefore Spinoza is not a spiritualist), but mind is an inherent and essential attribute or aspect of God. God and substance are identical with nature (*Deus sive substantia sive natura*) and the totality of all being (therefore Spinoza is a pantheist).

Nature has two aspects. As the power of motion in bodies, and as the power of generation, growth, and feeling in organisms, it is *natura naturans*

—nature "creating" or giving birth. As the sum of all individual things, of all bodies, plants, animals, and men, it is *natura naturata*—generated or "created" nature. These individual entities in generated nature are called by Spinoza *modi*, modes—transient modifications and embodiments of substance, reality, matter-mind, God. They are part of substance, but in our perception we distinguish them as passing, fleeting forms of an eternal whole. This stone, this tree, this man, this planet, this star—all this marvelous kaleidoscope of appearing and dissolving individual forms—constitute that "temporal order" which, in *On the Improvement of the Intellect*, Spinoza contrasted with the "eternal order" that in a stricter sense is the underlying reality and God:

> By series of causes and real entities I do not understand . . . a series of individual mutable things, but the series of fixed and eternal things. For it would be impossible for human weakness to follow up the series of individual mutable things [every stone, every flower, every man] . . . Their existence has no connection with their essence [they *may* exist, but *need* not], or . . . is not an eternal truth . . . This [essence] is only to be sought from fixed and eternal things, and from the laws inscribed in those things as in their true codes, according to which all individual things are made and arranged; nay, these individual and mutable things depend so intimately and essentially (so to speak) on these fixed ones, that without them they can neither exist nor be conceived.[74]

So a single, specific triangle is a mode; it may but need not exist; but if it does it will have to obey the laws—and will have the powers—of the triangle in general. A specific man is a mode; he may or may not exist; but if he does he will share in the essence and power of matter-mind, and will have to obey the laws that govern the operations of bodies and thoughts. These powers and laws constitute the order of nature as *natura naturans*; they constitute, in theological terms, the will of God. The modes of matter in their totality are the body of God; the modes of mind in their totality, are the mind of God; substance or reality, in all its modes and attributes, is God; "whatever is, is in God."[75]

Spinoza agrees with the Scholastic philosophers that in God essence and existence are one—His existence is involved in our conception of His essence, for he conceives God as all existence itself. He agrees with the Scholastics that God is *causa sui*, self-caused, for there is nothing outside him. He agrees with the Scholastics that we can know the existence of God, but not his real nature in all his attributes. He agrees with St. Thomas Aquinas that to apply the masculine pronouns to God is absurd but convenient.* He agrees with Maimonides that most of the qualities we ascribe to God are conceived by weak analogy with human qualities.

> God is described as the lawgiver or prince, and styled just, merciful, etc., merely in concession to popular understanding and the imperfection of popular knowledge[77] . . . God is free from passions, nor is he affected with any emotion [*affectus*] of joy or sorrow[78] . . . Those who confuse divine with human nature easily attribute human passions to God, especially if they do not know how passions are produced in the mind.[79]

God is not a person, for that means a particular and finite mind; but God is the total of all the mind (all the animation, sensitivity, and thought)— as well as of all the matter—in existence.[80] "The human mind is part of a certain infinite intellect"[81] (as in the Aristotelian-Alexandrian tradition). But "if intellect and will appertain to the eternal essence of God, something far else must be understood by these two attributes than what is commonly understood by men."[82] "The actual intellect, . . . together with will, desire, love, etc., must be referred to the *natura naturata*, not to the *natura naturans*";[83] that is, individual minds, with their desires, emotions, and volitions, are modes or modifications, contained in God as the totality of things, but not pertaining to Him as the law and life of the world. There is will in God, but only in the sense of the laws operating everywhere. His will is law.

God is not a bearded patriarch sitting on a cloud and ruling the universe; He is "the indwelling, not the transient, cause of all things."[84] There is no Creation, except in the sense that the infinite reality—matter-mind— is ever taking new individual forms or modes. "God is not in any one place, but is everywhere according to his essence."[85] Indeed, the word *cause* is out of place here; God is the universal cause not in the sense of a cause preceding its effect, but only in the sense that the behavior of anything follows necessarily from its nature. God is the cause of all events in the same way that the nature of a triangle is the cause of its properties and behavior. God is "free" only in the sense that He is not subject to any external cause or force, and is determined only by His own essence or nature; but He "does not act from freedom of will";[86] all His actions are determined by His essence—which is the same as to say that all events are determined by the inherent nature and properties of things. There is no design in nature in the sense that God desires some end; He has no

---

* Language usually makes Nature feminine and God masculine; by identifying them Spinoza does more justice to the female or productive principle in reality. Perhaps the masculinization of God was part of the patriarchal subordination of woman, who is, after all, the main stream of human reality.

desires or designs, except as the totality contains all the desires and designs of all modes and therefore of all organisms. In nature there are only effects following inevitably from antecedent causes and inherent properties. There are no miracles, for the will of God and the "fixed and unchanged order of nature" are one;[87] any break in "the chain of natural events" would be a self-contradiction.

Man is only a small part of the universe. Nature is neutral as between man and other forms. We must not apply to nature or to God such words as *good* or *evil, beautiful* or *ugly;* these are subjective terms, as much so as *hot* or *cold;* they are determined by the contribution of the external world to our advantage or displeasure.

> The perfection of things is to be judged by their nature and power alone; nor are they more or less perfect because they delight or offend the human senses, or because they are beneficial or prejudicial to human nature[88] . . . If, therefore, anything in nature seems to us ridiculous, absurd, or evil, it is because we know only in part, and are almost entirely ignorant of, the order and interdependence of nature as a whole; and also because we want everything to be arranged according to the dictates of our human reason. In reality that which reason considers evil is not evil in respect to the order and laws of nature as a whole, but only in respect to the laws of our reason.[89]

Likewise there is no beauty or ugliness in nature.

> Beauty . . . is not so much a quality of the object beheld, as an effect in him who beholds it. If our sight were longer or shorter, if our constitutions were different, what we now think beautiful we should think ugly. . . . The most beautiful hand, seen through the microscope, will appear horrible[90] . . . I do not attribute to nature either beauty or deformity, order or confusion. Only in relation to our imagination can things be called beautiful or ugly, well-formed, or confused.[91]

Order is objective only in the sense that all things cohere in one system of law; but in that order a destructive storm is as natural as the splendor of a sunset or the sublimity of the sea.

Are we justified, on the basis of this "theology," in calling Spinoza an atheist? We have seen that he was not a materialist, for he did not identify God with matter; he says quite clearly that "those who think that the *Tractatus* [*theologico-politicus*] rests on the identification of God with nature—taking nature in the sense of a certain mass of corporeal matter— are entirely wrong."[92] He conceived God as mind as well as matter, and he did not reduce mind to matter; he acknowledged that mind is the only reality directly known. He thought that something akin to mind is mingled with all matter; in this respect he was a panpsychist. He was a pantheist, seeing God in all things, and all things in God. Bayle, Hume, and others[93] considered him an atheist; and this term might seem justified by Spinoza's denial of feeling, desire, or purpose in God.[94] He himself, however, objected to "the opinion which the common people have of me, who do not cease to accuse me falsely of atheism."[95] Apparently he felt that his ascription of mind and intelligence to God absolved him from the charge of atheism. And it must be admitted that he spoke repeatedly of his God in terms of religious reverence, often in terms quite consonant with the conception of God in Maimonides or Aquinas. Novalis would call Spinoza "*der Gottbetrunkene Mensch*," the God-intoxicated man.

Actually he was intoxicated with the whole order of nature, which in its eternal consistency and movement seemed to him admirable and sublime; and in Book I of the *Ethics* he wrote both a system of theology and the metaphysics of science. In the world of law he felt a divine revelation greater than any book, however noble and beautiful. The scientist who studies that law, even in its pettiest and most prosaic detail, is deciphering that revelation, for "the more we understand individual objects, the more we understand God."[96] (This sentence struck Goethe as one of the profoundest in all literature.) It seemed to Spinoza that he had honestly accepted and met the challenge implicit in Copernicus—to reconceive deity in terms worthy of the universe now progressively revealed. In Spinoza science and religion are no longer in conflict; they are one.

V. MIND

Next to the nature and operation of the cosmos the greatest puzzle in philosophy and science is the nature and operation of the mind. If it is difficult to reconcile an omnipotent benevolence with the neutrality of nature and the fatality of suffering, it seems just as hard to understand how an apparently external and material object in space can generate an apparently immaterial and spaceless idea, or how an idea in the mind can become a motion in the body, or how idea can contemplate idea in the mystery of consciousness.

Spinoza tries to avoid some of these problems by rejecting Descartes' assumption that body and mind are two different substances. Body and mind, he believes, are one and the same reality, perceived under two different aspects or attributes, just as extension and thought are one in God. There is then no problem of how body acts upon mind or vice versa; every action is the simultaneous and unified operation of both body and mind. Spinoza defines mind as "the idea of the body";[97] i.e., it is the psychological (not necessarily the conscious) correlate or accompaniment of a physiological process. The mind is the body felt from within; the body is the mind seen from without. A mental state is the inside, or internal aspect, of bodily action. An act of "will" is the mental accompaniment of a bodily desire that is moving into physical expression. There is no action of the "will" upon the body; there is a single action of the psychophysical (mental-material) organism; the "will" is not the cause, it is the consciousness of the action. "The decision of the mind, and the desire and determination of the body are . . . one and the same thing, which, when considered under the attribute of thought . . . , we call a decision (*decretum*), and which, when considered under the attribute of extension, and deduced from the laws of motion and rest, is called a determination" (a finished action).[98] Hence "the order of the actions and passions [movements] of our body are simultaneous in nature with the order and passions of the mind."[99] In all cases of the supposed interaction of mind and body the actual process is not the interplay of two distinct realities, substances, or agents, but the single action of one substance, which, seen from outside, we call body, and which, seen from within, we call mind. To every process in the body there is a corresponding process in the mind; "nothing can happen in the body which is not perceived by the mind."[100] But this mental correlate need not be a thought; it may be a feeling; and it need not be conscious; so a sleepwalker performs any number of actions while he is "unconscious."[101] This theory has been called "psychophysical parallelism"; however, it supposes parallel processes not in two different entities, but in one psychophysical unity doubly seen.

On this basis Spinoza proceeds to a mechanistic description of the knowledge process. Probably following Hobbes, he defines sensation, memory, and imagination in physical terms.[102] He takes it as evident that most knowledge originates in impressions made upon us by external objects; but he admits to the idealist that "the human mind perceives no external body as actually existing save through ideas of modifications in its body."[103] Perception and reason, two forms of knowledge, are derived from sensation; but a third and higher form, "intuitive knowledge," is derived (Spinoza thinks) not from sensation but from a clear, distinct, immediate, and comprehensive awareness of an idea or event as part of a universal system of law.

Anticipating Locke and Hume, Spinoza rejects the notion that the mind is an agent or entity possessing ideas; "mind" is a general or abstract term for the succession of perceptions, memories, imaginations, feelings, and other mental states. "The idea of the mind, and the mind itself" at any moment, "are one and the same thing."[104] Nor are there any distinct "faculties" such as intellect or will; these also are abstract terms for the sum of cognitions or volitions; "intellect or will have reference in the same manner to this or that idea, or to this or that volition, as 'stoniness' to this or that stone, or 'man' to Peter or Paul."[105] Neither do idea and volition differ; a volition or act of "will" is merely an idea that has "affirmed itself"[106] (i.e., has lasted long enough to complete itself in an action, as ideas, if unimpeded, automatically do). "The decision of the mind . . . is nothing but the affirmation which the idea necessarily involves insofar as it is an idea[107] . . . Will and intellect are one and the same thing."[108]

From another standpoint what we call will is simply the sum and play of desires. "By desire . . . I understand all the efforts, impulses, appetites, and volitions of a man, which . . . not infrequently are so opposed to one another that he is drawn hither and thither, and knows not where to turn."[109] Deliberation is the alternating domination of body-and-thought by conflicting desires; it ends when one desire proves powerful enough to maintain its corresponding mental state long enough to pass into action. Obviously (says Spinoza) there is no "free will"; the will at any moment is just the strongest desire. We are free insofar as we are allowed to express our nature or our desires without external hindrance; we are not free to choose our own nature or our desires; we *are* our desires. "There is in no mind absolute or free will, but the mind is determined for willing this or that by a cause which is determined in its turn by another cause, and this again by another, and so on to infinity."[110] "Men think themselves free because they are conscious of their volitions and desires, but are ignorant of the causes by which they are led to wish and desire";[111] it is as if a stone flung through space should think it is moving and falling of its own will.[112]

Possibly the Calvinist fatalism in the "climate of opinion" that Descartes and Spinoza lived in as residents of Holland may have shared with the Galilean mechanics (Newton's *Principia* had not yet appeared) in molding the mechanistic theory in Descartes and the determinist psychology in Spinoza. Determinism is predestinarianism without theology; it substitutes the primeval vortex or nebula for God. Spinoza followed the logic of mechanism to its bitter end; he did not, like Descartes, confine it to bodies and animals; he applied it to minds as well, as he had to, since to him mind and body were one. He concluded that the body is a machine,[113] but he denied that determinism makes morality useless or insincere. The exhortations of the moralist, the ideals of the philosophers, the stigma of public condemnation, and the penalties of the courts are still valuable and necessary; they enter into the heritage and experience of the growing individual, and therefore into the factors that form his desires and determine his will.

VI. MAN

Into this apparently static philosophy Spinoza inserts two dynamic elements: first and generally, that matter and mind are everywhere united, that all things are animated, that they have in them something akin to what in ourselves we call mind or will; second and specifically, that this vital element includes in everything a *conatus sese preservandi*—an "effort at self-preservation." "Everything insofar as it is in itself endeavors to preserve its own being," and "the power or endeavor of anything . . . to persist in its own being is nothing else than . . . the essence of that . . . thing."[114] Like the Scholastic philosophers who said that *esse est agere* (to be is to act) and that God is *actus purus* (pure activity); like Schopenhauer, who saw in will the essence of all things; like those modern physicists who reduce matter to energy—Spinoza defines the essence of each being through its powers of action; "the power of God is the same as his essence";[115] in this aspect God is energy (and energy might be named, in addition to matter and mind, as a third attribute which we perceive as constituting the essence of substance or reality). Spinoza follows Hobbes in ranking entities according to their capacity for action and effectiveness. "The perfection of things is estimated solely from their nature and power"[116]—but in Spinoza *perfect* means *per-factum*, complete.

Consequently he defines virtue as a power of acting or doing; "by virtue and power (*potentia*) I understand the same thing";[117] but we shall see that this "potency" means power over ourselves perhaps even more than power over others.[118] "The more each one seeks what is useful to him— i.e., the more he endeavors and is able to preserve his being—the more he is endowed with virtue. . . . The endeavor to preserve oneself is the only basis of virtue."[119] In Spinoza virtue is biological, almost Darwinian; it is any quality that makes for survival. In this sense, at least, virtue is its own reward; "it is to be desired for its own sake; nor is there anything more excellent or more useful to us . . . for the sake of which virtue ought to be desired."[120]

As the endeavor for self-preservation (the "struggle for existence") is the active essence of anything, all motives derive from it, and are ultimately self-seeking. "Since reason postulates nothing against nature, it postulates, therefore, that each man should love himself, and seek what is useful to him—I mean what is truly useful to him—and desire whatever leads man truly to a greater state of perfection [completion], and finally that each one should endeavor to preserve his being as far as in him lies."[121] These desires need not be conscious; they may be unconscious appetites lodged in our flesh. Taken altogether, they constitute the essence of man.[122] We judge all things in terms of our desires. "We do not strive for, wish, seek, or desire anything because we think it to be good; we judge a thing to be good because we . . . desire it."[123] "By good (*bonum*) I understand that which we certainly know to be useful to us."[124] (Here is Bentham's utilitarianism in one sentence.)

All our desires aim at pleasure or the avoidance of pain. "Pleasure is man's transition from a lesser state of perfection [completion, fulfillment]."[125] Pleasure accompanies any experience or feeling that enhances the bodily-mental processes of activity and self-advancement.[126] "Joy consists in this, that one's power is increased."[127]* Any feeling that depresses our vitality is a weakness rather than a virtue. The healthy man will soon slough off the feelings of sadness, repentance, humility, and pity;[129] however, he will be readier than the weak man to render aid, for generosity is the superabundance of confident strength. Any pleasure is legitimate if it does not hinder a greater or more lasting pleasure. Spinoza, like Epicurus, recommends intellectual pleasures as the best, but he has a good word for a great variety of pleasures.

> There cannot be too much merriment. . . . Nothing save gloomy . . . superstition prohibits laughter. . . . To make use of things, and take delight in them as much as possible (not indeed to satiety, for that is not . . . delight), is the part of a wise man; . . . to feed himself with moderate pleasant food and drink, and to take pleasure with perfumes, . . . plants, dress, music, sports, and theaters.[130]

The trouble with the conception of pleasure as the realization of desires is that desires may conflict; only in the wise man do they fall into a harmonious hierarchy. A desire is usually the conscious correlate of an appetite which is rooted in the body; and so much of the appetite may remain unconscious that we have only "confused and inadequate ideas" of its causes and results. Such confused desires Spinoza called *affectus*, which may be translated by emotions. He defines these as "modifications of the body by which the power of action in the body is increased or diminished . . . and at the same time the ideas of these modifications"[131]—a definition vaguely recognizing the role of internal (endocrine) secretions in emotion, and remarkably anticipating the theory of C. G. Lange and William James that the bodily expression of an emotion is the direct and instinctive result of the cause, and that the conscious feeling is an accompaniment or result, not a cause, of the bodily expression and response. Spinoza proposed to study the emotions—love, hate, anger, fear, etc.—and the power of reason over

---

* Nietzsche echoes these definitions. "What is good? All that enhances the feeling of power . . . What is happiness? The feeling that power is increasing."[128]

them, "in the same manner . . . as if I were dealing with lines, planes, and bodies";[132] not to praise or denounce them but to understand them; for "the more an emotion becomes known to us, the more it is within our power, and the less the mind is passive to it."[133] The resulting analysis of the emotions owed something to Descartes, perhaps more to Hobbes, but it so improved upon them that when Johannes Müller, in his epochal *Physiologie des Menschen* (1840), came to treat of the emotions, he wrote: "With regard to the relations of the passions to one another, apart from their physiological conditions, it is impossible to give any better account than that which Spinoza has laid down with unsurpassed mastery"[134]—and he proceeded to quote extensively from the *Ethics*.

An emotion becomes a passion when, through our confused and inadequate ideas of its origin and significance, its external cause dictates our feeling and response, as in hatred, anger, or fear. "The mind is more or less subject to passions according as it has more or less adequate ideas."[135] A man with poor powers of perception and thought is especially subject to passion; it is such a life that Spinoza describes in his classic Book IV, "Of Human Bondage." Such a man, however violent his action may be, is really passive—is swept along by an external stimulus instead of holding his hand and taking thought. "We are driven about by external causes in many ways, and, like waves driven by contrary winds, we waver and are unconscious of the issue and our fate."[136]

Can we free ourselves from this bondage, and become in some measure the masters of our lives?

VII. REASON

Never completely, for we remain part of nature, subject (as Napoleon was to say) to "the nature of things." And since the emotions are our motive force, and reason can be only a light and not a fire, "an emotion can neither be hindered nor removed save by a contrary and stronger emotion."[137] Hence society rightly seeks to moderate our passions by appealing to our love of praise and rewards, our fear of blame and punishment.[138] And society rightly labors to instill in us a sense of right and wrong as another check to passion. Conscience, of course, is a social product, not an innate endowment or divine gift.[139]

But to use the imaginary rewards and punishments of a life after death as stimulants to morality is an encouragement to superstition and quite unworthy of a mature society. Virtue should be—and is—its own reward, if we define it, like men, as ability, intelligence, and strength, and not, like cowards, as obedience, humility, and fear. Spinoza resented the Christian view of life as a vale of tears, and of death as a door to heaven or hell; this, he felt, casts a pall over human affairs, clouding with the notion of sin the legitimate aspirations and enjoyments of men. To be daily thinking of death is an insult to life. "A free man thinks of nothing less than of death, and his wisdom is a meditation not on death but on life."[140]

Nevertheless Spinoza seems at times to flutter around the idea of immortality. His theory of mind and body as two aspects of the same reality committed him in logic to view their death as simultaneous. He affirms this quite clearly: "The present existence of the mind, and its power of imagining, are taken away as soon as the mind ceases to affirm the present existence of the body";[141] and again: "The mind can imagine nothing, nor can it recollect anything that is past, except while the body exists."[142] In Book V some hazy distinctions appear. "If we look at the common opinion of men, we shall see that they are indeed conscious of the eternity of their minds, but they confound this with duration, and attribute it to imagination and memory, which they believe remain after death."[143] Insofar as the mind is a series of temporal ideas, memories, and imaginations connected with a particular body, it ceases to exist when that body dies; this is the mortal *duration* of the mind. But insofar as the human mind conceives things in their eternal relationships as part of the universal and unchanging system of natural law, it sees things as in God; it becomes to that extent part of the divine eternal mind, and is eternal.

> Things are conceived as actual in two ways by us, either insofar as we conceive them to exist with relation to certain time and space, or insofar as we conceive them to be contained in God [the eternal order and laws], and to follow from the necessity of the divine nature [those laws]. But those things which are conceived in this second manner as true or real we conceive under a certain species of eternity [*sub quadam specie eternitatis*—in their eternal aspect], and their ideas involve the eternal and infinite essence of God.[144]

When we see things in that timeless way we see them as God sees them; our minds to that extent become part of the divine mind, and share eternity.

> We attribute to the human mind no duration which can be defined by time. But as there is nevertheless something else which is conceived under a certain eternal necessity through the essence of God, this something will be necessarily the eternal part which appertains to the mind[145] . . . We are certain that the mind is eternal insofar as it conceives things under the species of eternity.[146]

Let us suppose that in contemplating the majestic sequence of apparent cause and effect according to apparently everlasting laws, Spinoza felt that through "divine philosophy" he had escaped, like some sinless Buddha, from the chain of time, and had shared in the viewpoint and tranquillity of an eternal mind.

Despite this seeming reach for the moon, Spinoza devoted most of his concluding Book V, "Of Human Liberty," to formulating a natural ethic, a fount and system of morals independent of survival after death, though fondly using religious terms. One sentence reveals his starting point: "An emotion which is a passion ceases to be a passion as soon as we form a clear and distinct idea of it"[147]—that is, an emotion aroused in us by external events can be reduced from passion to controlled feeling by letting our knowledge play upon it until its cause and nature become clear, and its result in action can, through remembered experience, be foreseen. One method of clearing up an emotional state is to see the events that begot it as part of a chain of natural causes and necessary effects. "Insofar as the mind understands all things as necessary, it has more power over the emotions, and is less passive to them"[148]—less given to passions. No one becomes passionate at what he considers natural and necessary. Anger at an insult can be cooled by viewing the offender as the product of circumstances outreaching his control; grief over the passing of aged parents can be moderated by realizing the naturalness of death. "The endeavor to understand is the first and only basis of virtue,"[149] in Spinoza's sense of this word, for it reduces our subjection to external factors, and increases our power to control and preserve ourselves. Knowledge is power; but the best and most useful form of that power is power over ourselves.

So Spinoza works his Euclidean way to the life of reason. Recalling his three kinds of knowledge, he describes merely sensory knowledge as leaving us too open to domination by external influences; rational knowledge (reached by reasoning) as gradually freeing us from bondage to the passions by letting us see the impersonal and determined causes of events; and intuitive knowledge—direct awareness of the cosmic order—as making us feel ourselves part of that order and "one with God." "We should expect and bear both faces of fortune with an equal mind; for all things follow by the eternal decree of God in the same way as it follows from the essence of a triangle that its three angles will make two right angles."[150] This escape from thoughtless passion is the only true freedom;[151] and he who achieves it, as the Stoics used to say, can be free in almost any condition in any state. The greatest gift that knowledge can give us is to see ourselves as reason sees us.

On this naturalistic basis Spinoza arrives at some ethical conclusions surprisingly like Christ's:

> He who rightly knows that all things follow from the necessity of divine nature, and come to pass according to eternal, natural, and

regular laws, will find nothing at all that is worthy of hatred, laughter, or contempt, nor will he deplore anyone; but as far as human virtue can go, he will endeavor to act well . . . and rejoice.[152] . . . Those who cavil at men, and prefer rather to reprobate vices than to inculcate virtues . . . , are a nuisance both to themselves and to others.[153] . . . A strong man hates no one, is enraged with no one, envies no one, is indignant with no one, and is in no wise proud.[154] . . . He who lives under the guidance of reason endeavors as much as possible to repay hatred, rage, contempt, etc., with love and nobleness. . . . He who wishes to avenge injuries by reciprocal hatred will live in misery. Hatred is increased by reciprocated hatred, and, on the contrary, can be demolished by love.[155] . . . Men under the guidance of reason . . . desire nothing for themselves which they do not also desire for the rest of mankind.[156]

Does this control of emotion by reason contradict, as some[157] have thought, Spinoza's admission that only an emotion can overcome an emotion? It would unless the following of reason could itself be raised to an emotional level and warmth. "A true knowledge of good and evil cannot restrain any emotion insofar as the knowledge is true, but only insofar as it is considered as an emotion."[158] This need, and perhaps a desire to kindle reason with phrases hallowed by piety and time, led Spinoza to the final and culminating thought of his work—that the life of reason must be inspired and ennobled by the "intellectual love of God." Since God, in Spinoza, is the basic reality and invariable law of the cosmos itself, this *amor intellectualis dei* is not the abject propitiation of some nebular sultan, but the wise and willing adjustment of our ideas and conduct to the nature of things and the order of the world. Reverence for the will of God and an understanding acceptance of the laws of nature are one and the same thing. Just as the mathematician finds a certain awe and ecstasy in viewing the world as subject to mathematical regularities, so the philosopher may take the deepest pleasure in contemplating the grandeur of a universe moving imperturbably in the rhythm of universal law. Since "love is pleasure accompanied by the idea of an external cause,"[159] the pleasure we derive from viewing—and adapting ourselves to—the cosmic order rises to the emotion of love toward the God who is the order and life of the whole. Then "love toward a being eternal and infinite fills the mind completely with joy."[160] This contemplation of the world as a necessary result of its own nature—of the nature of God—is the ultimate source of content in the mind of the sage; it brings him the peace of understanding, of limitations recognized, of truth accepted and loved. "The highest good (*summum bonum*) of the mind is the knowledge of God, and the highest virtue of the mind is to know God."[161]

Thus Spinoza mated the mathematician and the mystic in his soul. He still refused to see in his God a spirit capable of returning man's love, or of rewarding litanies with miracles; but he applied to his deity the tender terms that for thousands of years had inspired and comforted the simplest devotees and the profoundest mystics of Buddhism, Judaism, Christianity, and Islam. Cold in the solitude of his philosophic empyrean, longing to find something in the universe to receive his adoration and his confidence, the gentle heretic who had viewed the cosmos as a geometrical diagram ended by seeing and losing all things in God, by becoming, to the confusion of posterity, the God-intoxicated "atheist." The compulsion to find meaning in the universe made the exile from every faith conclude his seeking with the vision of an omnipresent divinity, and an exalting sense that, if only for a moment, he had touched eternity.

VIII. THE STATE

Perhaps, when Spinoza had finished the *Ethics,* he felt that, like most Christian saints, he had formulated a philosophy for the use and salvation of the individual rather than for the guidance of citizens in a state. So, toward 1675, he set himself to consider man as a "political animal," and to apply reason to the problems of society. He began his fragmentary *Tractatus politicus* with the same resolve that he had made in analyzing the passions—to be as objective as a geometer or a physicist:

> That I might investigate the subject matter of this science with the same freedom of spirit as we generally use in mathematics, I have labored carefully not to mock, lament, or execrate human actions, but to understand them; and to this end I have looked upon passions, such as love, hatred, anger, envy, ambition, pity, and the other perturbations of the mind, not in the light of vices of human nature, but as properties just as pertinent to it as are heat, cold, storm, thunder, and the like to the nature of the atmosphere.[162]

Since human nature is the material of politics, Spinoza felt that a study of the state should begin by considering the basic character of man. We might understand this better if we could imagine man before social organization modified his conduct by force, morality, and law; and if we would remember that underneath his general and reluctant submission to these socializing influences he is still agitated by the lawless impulses that in the "state of nature" were restrained only by fear of hostile power. Spinoza follows Hobbes and many others in supposing that man once existed in such a condition, and his picture of this hypothetical savage is almost as dark as in *The Leviathan*. In that Garden of Evil the might of the individual was the only right; nothing was a crime, because there was no law; and nothing was just or unjust, right or wrong, because there was no moral code. Consequently "the law and ordinance of *nature* . . . forbids nothing . . . and is not opposed to strife, hatred, anger, treachery, or in general anything that appetite suggests."[163] By "natural right," then—i.e., by the operations of "nature" as distinct from the rules and laws of society—every man is entitled to whatever he is strong enough to get and to hold; and this is still assumed between species and between states;[164] hence man has a "natural right" to use animals for his service or his food.[165]

Spinoza moderates this savage picture by suggesting that man, even in his first appearance on the earth, may have been already living in social groups. "Since fear of solitude exists in all men—because no one in solitude is strong enough to defend himself and procure the necessaries of life—it follows that men by nature tend towards social organization."[166] Men, then, have social as well as individualistic instincts, and society and the state have some roots in the nature of man. However and whenever it came about, men and families united in groups, and the "natural right" or might of the individual was now limited by the right or might of the community. Doubtless men accepted these restrictions reluctantly, but they accepted them when they learned that social organization was their most powerful tool for individual survival and development. So the definition of virtue as any quality that makes for survival—as "the endeavor to preserve oneself"[167]— has to be enlarged to include any quality that makes for the survival of the group. Social organization, the state despite its restraints, civilization despite its artifices—these are the greatest inventions that man has made for his preservation and development.

Therefore Spinoza anticipates Voltaire's answer to Rousseau:

> Let satirists laugh to their hearts' content at human affairs, let theologians revile them, let the melancholy praise as much as they can the rude and barbarous isolated life, let them despise men and admire the brutes; despite all this, men will find that they can prepare with mutual aid far more easily what they need. . . . A man who is guided by reason is freer in a state where he lives according to common law than in solitude where he is subject to no law.[168]

And Spinoza rejects also the other end of the law-less dream—the utopia of the philosophical anarchist:

> Reason, can, indeed, do much to restrain and moderate the passions, but we saw . . . that the road which reason herself points out is very steep; so that such as persuade themselves that the multitude . . . can

ever be induced to live according to the bare dictates of reason must
be dreaming of the poetic golden age, or of some stage play.[169]

The purpose and function of the state should be to enable its members to
live the life of reason.

> The last end of the state is not to dominate men, nor to restrain
> them by fear; rather it is to set free each man from fear, that he may
> live and act with full security and without injury to himself or his
> neighbor. The end of the state . . . is not to make rational beings into
> brute beasts and machines [as in war]; it is to enable their bodies and
> their minds to function safely. It is to lead men to live by, and to
> exercise, a true reason. . . . The end of the state is really liberty.[170]

Consequently Spinoza renews his plea for freedom of speech, or at least of
thought. But yielding, like Hobbes, to fear of theological fanaticism and
strife, he proposes not merely to subject the church to state control, but to
have the state determine what religious doctrines shall be taught to the
people. *Quandoque dormitat Homerus.*

He proceeds to discuss the traditional forms of government. As became
a Dutch patriot resenting the invasion of Holland by Louis XIV, he had
no admiration for monarchy, and he sharply counters Hobbes's absolutism:

> Experience is supposed to teach that it makes for peace and concord
> when all authority is conferred upon one man. For no political order
> has stood so long without notable change as that of the Turks, while
> none have been so short-lived, nay, so vexed by seditions, as popular
> or democratic states. But if slavery, barbarism, and desolation are to
> be called peace, then peace is the worst misfortune that can befall a
> state. . . . Slavery, not peace, comes from the giving of all power to
> one man. For peace consists not in the absence of war, but in a union
> and harmony of men's souls.[171]

Aristocracy, as "government by the best," would be fine if the best were
not subject to class spirit, violent faction, and individual or family greed.
"If patricians . . . were free from all passion, and guided by mere zeal for
the public welfare . . . , no dominion could be compared with aristocracy.
But experience itself teaches us only too well that things pass in quite a
contrary manner."[172]

And so Spinoza, in his dying days, began to outline his hopes for democracy. He who had loved the mob-murdered de Witt had no delusions about
the multitude. "Those who have had experience of how changeful the
temper of the people is, are almost in despair. For the populace is governed
not by reason but by emotion; it is headlong in everything, and easily cor-

rupted by avarice and luxury."[173] Yet "I believe democracy to be of all forms of government the most natural, and the most consonant with individual liberty. In it no one transfers his natural right so absolutely that he has no further voice in affairs; he only hands it over to the majority."[174] Spinoza proposed to admit to the suffrage all males except minors, criminals, and slaves. He excluded women because he judged them by their nature and their burdens to be less fit than men for deliberation and government.[175] He thought that ruling officials would be encouraged to good behavior and peaceful policies if "the militia should be composed of the citizens only, and none of them be exempted; for an armed man is more independent than a man unarmed."[176] The care of the poor, he felt, was an obligation incumbent on the society as a whole.[177] And there should be but a single tax:

> The fields, and the whole soil, and, if it can be managed, the houses, should be public property, that is, the property of him who holds the right of the commonwealth; and let him lease them at a yearly rent to the citizens. . . . With this exception, let them all be free and exempt from every kind of taxation in time of peace.[178]

Then, just as he was entering upon the most precious part of his treatise, death took the pen from his hand.

IX. THE CHAIN OF INFLUENCE

In the great chain of ideas that binds the history of philosophy into one noble groping of baffled human thought, we can see Spinoza's system forming in twenty centuries behind him, and sharing in shaping the modern world. First, of course, he was a Jew. Excommunicated though he was, he could not shed that intensive heritage, nor forget his years of poring over the Old Testament and the Talmud and the Jewish philosophers. Recall again the heresies that must have startled his attention in Ibn Ezra, Maimonides, Hasdai Crescas, Levi ben Gerson, and Uriel Acosta. His training in the Talmud must have helped to sharpen that logical sense which made the *Ethics* a classic temple of reason. "Some begin" their philosophy "from created things," he said, "and some from the human mind. I begin from God."[179] That was the Jewish way.

From the philosophers traditionally most admired he took little—though in his distinction between the world of passing things and the divine world of eternal laws we may find another form of Plato's division between individual entities and their archetypes in the mind of God. Spinoza's analysis of the virtues has been traced to Aristotle's *Nicomachean Ethics*.[180] But "the authority of Plato, Aristotle, and Socrates," he told a friend, "has not much weight with me."[181] Like Bacon and Hobbes, he preferred Democritus, Epicurus, and Lucretius. His ethical ideal may echo the Stoics; we hear in it some tones of Marcus Aurelius; but it was fully consistent with Epicurus.

He owed more to the Scholastic philosophers than he realized, for they came to him through the medium of Descartes. They too, like Thomas Aquinas in the great *Summa*, had attempted a geometrical exposition of philosophy. They gave him such terms as *substantia, natura naturans, attributum, essentia, summum bonum*, and many more. Their identification of existence and essence in God became his identification of existence and essence in substance. He extended to man their merger of intellect and will in God.

Perhaps (as Bayle thought) Spinoza read Bruno. He accepted Giordano's distinction between *natura naturans* and *natura naturata;* he may have taken term and idea from Bruno's *conato de conservarsi;*[182] he may have found in the Italian the unity of body and mind, of matter and spirit, of world and God, and the conception of the highest knowledge as that which sees all things in God—though the German mystics must have spread that view even into commercial Amsterdam.

More immediately, Descartes inspired him with philosophical ideals, and repelled him with theological platitudes. He was inspired by Descartes' ambition to make philosophy march with Euclid in form and clarity. He probably followed Descartes in drawing up rules to guide his life and work. He adopted too readily Descartes' notion that an idea must be true if it is "clear and distinct." He accepted and universalized the Cartesian view of the world as a mechanism of cause and effect reaching from some primeval vortex right up to the pineal gland. He acknowledged his indebtedness to Descartes' analysis of the passions.[183]

The *Leviathan* of Hobbes, in Latin translation, obviously evoked much welcome in Spinoza's thought. Here the conception of mechanism was worked out without mercy or fear. The mind, which in Descartes was distinct from the body and was endowed with freedom and immortality, became, in Hobbes and Spinoza, subject to universal law, and capable of only an impersonal immortality or none at all. Spinoza found in *The Leviathan* an acceptable analysis of sensation, perception, memory, and idea, and an unsentimental analysis of human nature. From the common starting point of a "state of nature" and a "social compact" the two thinkers came to contrary conclusions: Hobbes, from his royalist circles, to monarchy; Spinoza, from his Dutch patriotism, to democracy. Perhaps it was through Hobbes that the gentle Jew was led to Machiavelli; he refers to him as "that most acute Florentine," and again as "that most ingenious . . . , foreseeing man."[184] But he escaped the confusion of right with might, recognizing that this is forgivable only among individuals in the "state of nature," and among states before the establishment of effective international law.

All these influences were tempered and molded by Spinoza into a structure of thought awe-inspiring in its apparent logic, harmony, and unity. There were cracks in the temple, as friends and enemies pointed out: Oldenburg ably criticized the opening axioms and propositions of the *Ethics*,[185] and Überweg subjected them to a Germanically meticulous analysis.[186] The logic was brilliant, but perilously deductive; though based upon personal experience, it was an artistry of thought resting upon internal consistency rather than objective fact. Spinoza's trust in his reasoning (though what other guide could he have?) was his sole immodesty. He expressed his confidence that man can understand God, or essential reality and universal law; he repeatedly avowed his conviction that he had proved his doctrines beyond all question or obscurity; and sometimes he spoke with an assurance unbecoming in a spray of foam analyzing the sea. What if all logic is an intellectual convenience, a heuristic tool of the seeking mind, rather than the structure of the world? So the inescapable logic of determinism reduces consciousness (as Huxley confessed) to an epiphenomenon—an apparently superfluous appendage of psychophysical processes which, by the mechanics of cause and effect, would go on just as well without it; and yet nothing seems more real, nothing more impressive, than consciousness. After logic has had its say, the mystery, *tam grande secretum*, remains.

These difficulties may have shared in the unpopularity of Spinoza's philosophy in the first century after his death; but resentment was more violently directed against his critique of the Bible, prophecies, and miracles, and his conception of God as lovable but impersonal and deaf. The Jews thought of their son as a traitor to his people; the Christians cursed him as a very Satan among philosophers, an Antichrist who sought to rob the world of all meaning, mercy, and hope. Even the heretics condemned him. Bayle was repelled by Spinoza's view that all things and all men are modes of the one and only substance, cause, or God; then, said Bayle, God is the real agent of all actions, the real cause of all evil, all crimes and wars; and when a Turk slays a Hungarian it is God slaying Himself; this, Bayle protested (forgetting the subjectivity of evil) was a "most absurd and monstrous hypothesis."[187] Leibniz was for a decade (1676–86) strongly influenced by Spinoza. The doctrine of monads as centers of psychic force may owe something to *omnia quodammodo animata*. At one time Leibniz declared that only one feature of Spinoza's philosophy offended him—the rejection of final causes, or providential design, in the cosmic process.[188] When the outcry against Spinoza's "atheism" became universal, Leibniz joined in it as part of his own *conatus sese preservandi*.

Spinoza had a modest, almost a concealed, share in generating the French Enlightenment. The leaders of that combustion used Spinoza's Biblical criticism as a weapon in their war against the Church, and they admired his determinism, his naturalistic ethic, his rejection of design in nature. But they were baffled by the religious terminology and apparent mysticism of the *Ethics*. We can imagine the reaction of Voltaire or Diderot, of Helvétius or d'Holbach, to such statements as "The mental intellectual love towards God is the very love of God with which God loves himself."[189]

The German spirit was more responsive to this side of Spinoza's thought. According to a conversation (1780) reported by Friedrich Jacobi, Lessing not only confessed that he had been a Spinozist through all his mature life, but affirmed that "there is no other philosophy than Spinoza's."[190] It was precisely the pantheistic identification of nature and God that thrilled the Germany of the romantic movement after the *Aufklärung* under Frederick the Great had run its course. Jacobi, champion of the new *Gefühlsphilosophie*, was among the first defenders of Spinoza (1785); it was another German romantic, Novalis, who called Spinoza *"der Gottbetrunkene Mensch"*; Herder thought that he had found in the *Ethics* the reconciliation of religion and philosophy; and Schleiermacher, the liberal theologian, wrote of "the holy and excommunicated Spinoza."[191] The young Goethe was "converted" (he tells us) at his first reading of the *Ethics*; henceforth Spinozism pervaded his (nonsexual) poetry and prose; it was partly by breathing the calm air of the *Ethics* that he grew out of the wild romanticism of *Götz von Berlichingen* and *Die Leiden des jungen Werthers* to the Olympian poise of his later life. Kant interrupted this stream of influence for a while; but Hegel professed that "to be a philosopher one must first be a Spinozist"; and he rephrased Spinoza's God as "Absolute Reason." Probably something of Spinoza's *conatus sese preservandi* entered into Schopenhauer's "will to live" and Nietzsche's "will to power."

England for a century knew Spinoza chiefly through hearsay, and denounced him as a distant and terrible ogre. Stillingfleet (1677) referred to him vaguely as "a late author [who] I hear is mightily in vogue among many who cry up anything on the atheistical side." A Scottish professor, George Sinclair (1685), wrote of "a monstrous rabble of men who, following the Hobbesian and Spinosian principle, slight religion and undervalue the Scripture." Sir John Evelyn (1690?) spoke of the *Tractatus theologico-politicus* as "that infamous book," a "wretched obstacle to the searchers of holy truth." Berkeley (1732), while ranking Spinoza among "weak and wicked writers," thought him "the great leader of our modern infidels."[192] As late as 1739 the agnostic Hume shuddered cautiously at the "hideous hypothesis" of "that famous atheist," the "universally infamous Spinoza."[193] Not till the romantic movement at the turn of the eighteenth into the nineteenth century did Spinoza really reach the English mind. Then he, more than any other philosopher, inspired the youthful metaphysics of Wordsworth, Coleridge, Shelley and Byron. Shelley quoted the *Tractatus theologico-politicus* in the original notes to *Queen Mab*, and began a translation of it, for which Byron pledged a preface; a fragment of this version came into the hands of an English critic, who, taking it for a work by Shelley himself, called it a "schoolboy speculation . . . too crude for publication entire." George Eliot translated the *Ethics* with virile resolution, and James Froude[194] and Matthew Arnold[195] acknowledged the influence of Spinoza on their mental development. Of all the intellectual products of man, religion and philosophy seem to endure the longest. Pericles is famous because he lived in the days of Socrates.

We love Spinoza especially among the philosophers because he was also a saint, because he lived, as well as wrote, philosophy. The virtues praised by the great religions were honored and embodied in the outcast who could find a home in none of the religions, since none would let him conceive God in terms that science could accept. Looking back upon that dedicated life and concentrated thought, we feel in them an element of nobility that encourages us to think well of mankind. Let us admit half of the terrible picture that Swift drew of humanity; let us agree that in every generation of man's history, and almost everywhere, we find superstition, hypocrisy, corruption, cruelty, crime, and war: in the balance against them we place the long roster of poets, composers, artists, scientists, philosophers, and saints. That same species upon which poor Swift revenged the frustrations of his flesh wrote the plays of Shakespeare, the music of Bach and Handel, the odes of Keats, the *Republic* of Plato, the *Principia* of Newton, and the *Ethics* of Spinoza; it built the Parthenon and painted the ceiling of the Sistine Chapel; it conceived and cherished, even if it crucified, Christ. Man did all this; let him never despair.

CHAPTER XXIII

Leibniz

1646–1716

I. THE PHILOSOPHY OF LAW

A CHASM of character and thought separates Spinoza from Leibniz. The solitary Jew, cast out by Judaism, not accepting Christianity, living in poverty in an attic room, finishing only two books, slowly evolving a boldly original philosophy that would alienate all the religions, and dying of consumption at forty-four; the German man of the world, busy with statesmen and courts, traveling through nearly all of Western Europe, spreading his feelers into Russia and China, accepting both Protestantism and Catholicism, welcoming and using a dozen systems of thought, writing half a hundred treatises, embracing God and the world with desperate optimism, living out his threescore years and ten, and resembling his predecessor only in the loneliness of his funeral: here in one generation are the antipodes of modern philosophy.

But before we come to this protean mosaic of a man, let us acknowledge some minor credits to German thought. Samuel von Pufendorf began his trajectory in 1632, in the same year as Spinoza and Locke. After studying at Leipzig and Jena he went to Copenhagen as tutor in the family of a Swedish diplomat; was arrested with him when Sweden declared war upon Denmark; and tempered the tedium of imprisonment by constructing a system of international law. Released, he moved to Leiden, where he published the results as *Elementa Jurisprudentiae universalis* (1661), which so pleased Charles Louis of the Palatinate (the same who later invited Spinoza) that the Elector called him to Heidelberg, and created for him a professorship in natural and international law—the first such chair in history. There Pufendorf composed a study of the German realm, *De Statu Imperii Germanici, Liber Unus* (1667), which shocked Leopold I by attacking the Holy Roman Empire and its emperors. Pufendorf migrated to Sweden and the University of Lund (1670), where he published his *chef d'oeuvre, De Iure Naturae et Gentium* (1672). Attempting to mediate between Hobbes and Grotius, Pufendorf identified the "law of nature" not with the "war of each against all," but with the dictates of "right reason." He extended "natural rights" (rights belonging to all rational beings) to Jews and Turks, and argued that international law should hold not only among Christian states, but equally in their relations with "infidels." He preceded Jean Jacques Rousseau by almost a century in declaring that the will of the state is, and should be, the sum of the wills of its constituent individuals; but he thought slavery desirable as a way of reducing the number of beggars, tramps and thieves.[1]

Some Swedish pastors thought these theories made too little account of God and the Bible in political philosophy; they urged that Pufendorf be returned to Germany; but Charles XI called him to Stockholm and made him historiographer royal. The professor repaid him by writing a biography of the King and a history of Sweden. In 1687, perhaps with an eye to travel, Pufendorf dedicated to the Great Elector of Brandenburg a treatise on the relation of the Christian religion to civil life (De Habitu christianae Religionis ad Vitam civilem), defending toleration. He soon accepted a call to Berlin, became historiographer to Frederick William, was made a baron, and died (1694). His writings remained for half a century the dominant works in political and legal philosophy in Protestant Europe, and their realistic analysis of social relations helped events to deflate the theory of the divine right of kings.

The decline in the theological interpretation of human affairs was accentuated by the careers of Balthasar Bekker and Christian Thomasius. Bekker was a Dutch pastor ministering to a flock in Friesland. Having spoiled his faith with Descartes, he proposed to apply reason to Scripture. He interpreted Biblical devils as popular delusions or metaphors; he traced the pre-Christian history of the idea of Satan, held it an interpolation into Christianity, concluded that the Devil was a myth, and blasted him out of existence in a Dutch manifesto, De betooverte Wereld (The Bedeviled World, 1691). The Church severely censured Bekker, feeling that fear of the Devil is the beginning of wisdom. The Devil suffered some loss in prestige, but not in devotees.

Thomasius carried on the battle. While continuing to accept the Scriptures as a guide to religion and salvation, he aspired to follow the rule of reason, to believe only up to the evidence, and to encourage religious toleration. As professor of natural law at Leipzig (1684–90), he offended the faculty and the ministry by the originality of his views, methods, and language. He countered the superstitions of his time with lusty German laughter; he agreed with Bekker in exorcizing the Devil from religion; he denounced the belief in witchcraft as shameful ignorance, and the persecution of "witches" as criminal brutality; through his influence trials for sorcery were ended in Germany. To make matters worse, he lectured his students in German instead of Latin, taking half the dignity out of pedagogy. In 1688 he began to pubish a periodical review of books and ideas; we should have called it the first serious journal in German, but it took its erudition with a light heart, coated scholarship with humor, and called itself *Scherzhafte und ernsthafte, vernünftige und einfältige Gedanken über allerhand lustige und nützliche Bücher und Fragen* (*Jocose and Earnest, Rational and Silly Thoughts on All Kinds of Pleasant and Useful Books and Questions*). His defense of the Pietists against the orthodox clergy, and of intermarriage between Lutherans and Calvinists, so alarmed the authorities that they forbade him to write or lecture, and finally ordered his arrest (1690). He escaped to Berlin; the Elector Frederick III gave him a professorship at Halle; he took part in organizing the university there, and soon made it the liveliest intellectual center in Germany. In 1709 Leipzig invited him to return; he refused, and remained at Halle thirty-four years, to the end of his life. He inaugurated the *Aufklärung* which produced Lessing and Frederick the Great.

Some of the enthusiasts pushed their revolt to the extremes of atheism. Matthias Knutzen of Holstein discarded all supernatural belief; *"insuper Deum negamus"*—above all we deny God.[2] He proposed to replace Christianity, its churches, and its priests with a positivist "religion of humanity" in full anticipation of Auguste Comte, and to base morality solely on the naturalistic education of conscience (1674). He claimed seven hundred followers; this was probably an exaggeration; but we observe that between 1662 and 1713 at least twenty-two works were published in Germany aiming to spread or refute atheism.[3]

Leibniz deplored "the apparent triumph of freethinkers." "In our day," he wrote, toward 1700, "many people have scant respect for Revelation . . . or miracles."[4] And he added, in 1715: "Natural religion is growing very much weaker. Many hold that souls are corporeal; others that God Himself is corporeal. Mr. Locke and his followers are doubtful whether souls are not material and naturally perishable."[5] Leibniz was not too firm in his own faith; but as a man of the world and its courts, he wondered where the rising rationalism would end, and what it would do to churches, morals, and thrones. Could the rationalists be answered in their own terms, and the faith of the fathers be rescued for the health of the children?

II. WANDERJAHRE

Gottfried Wilhelm Leibniz was two years old when the Thirty Years' War ended; he grew up in one of the most barren and unhappy periods of German history. But he had every educational opportunity then available, for his father was professor of moral philosophy at the University of Leipzig. Gottfried was a *Wunderkind*, eager for knowledge and in love with books. The paternal library was opened to him with the invitation

"*Tolle, lege*" (Take and read). He began Latin at eight, Greek at twelve; he devoured history; he became a "polymath"—learned in many fields. At fifteen he entered the university, where the stimulating Thomasius was one of his teachers. At twenty he applied for the doctor's degree in law; Leipzig refused it because of his youth, but he received it soon afterward from Nuremberg's university at Altdorf. His doctoral dissertation there made such an impression that he was at once offered a professorship. He declined, saying that he had "different things in view." Very few of the major philosophers have held university chairs.

Economically secure, intellectually free, he now dipped into all the movements and philosophies that were agitating renascent Germany. He had studied the Scholastic systems at Leipzig; he kept their terminology and many of their ideas, like the ontological proof for the existence of God. He imbibed the full Cartesian tradition, but salted it with Gassendi's objections and atomism. He passed on to Hobbes, praised him as *subtilissimus*, and flirted with materialism.[6] Living for a time (1666–67) in Nuremberg, he sampled the mysticism of the Rosicrucians (Fraternitas Rosae Crucis), that Brotherhood of the Rosy Cross which alchemists, physicians, and clergymen had founded about 1654; he became its secretary and delved into alchemy, very much as his future rival Newton was doing at Cambridge. He left no idea untouched or unborrowed. Before he was twenty-two he had written several treatises, small in scope but swelling with confidence.

One of these, *Novus Methodus docendi discendique Iuris* (*A New Method of Teaching and Learning Law*) attracted the attention of a diplomat then staying in Nuremberg, Johann von Boineburg, who advised the young author to dedicate it to the Archbishop Elector of Mainz, and arranged to have it presented in person. The plan worked, and in 1667 Leibniz entered the service of the Elector, first as assistant in revising the laws, then as councilor. He remained at Mainz five years. He became familiar with Catholic clergymen, theology, and ritual, and began to dream of reuniting the sundered Christian creeds. The Elector, however, was more interested in Louis XIV than in Luther, for the insatiable King was spreading his armies into the Low Countries and Lorraine, too close to Germany, and was obviously anxious to swallow the Rhine. How could he be stopped?

Leibniz had a plan for that—indeed, two plans, brilliant enough for a lad of twenty-four. The first was to unite the western German states in a *Rheinbund* for mutual defense (1670). The second was to deflect Louis from Germany by persuading him to seize Egypt from the Turks. Relations between France and Turkey were at that time strained; if Louis (anticipating Napoleon by 128 years) were to send an expedition to conquer Egypt, he would capture control of the commerce—including Dutch commerce—that went from Europe through Egypt to the East, he would keep the soil of France free of war, he would end the Ottoman threat to Christendom, he would be the honored savior, instead of the dreaded scourge, of Europe. Boineburg so wrote to Louis, enclosing an outline of the plan from Leinbniz' pen.* Simon Arnaud de Pomponne, the French foreign minister, invited Leibniz (February, 1672) to come and offer the plan to the King. In March the twenty-six-year-old statesman set out for Paris.

The generals foiled him and themselves. By the time Leibniz reached Paris Louis had mended his quarrel with Turkey, and had decided to attack Holland; on April 6 he declared war. Pomponne informed Leibniz that crusades were out of fashion, and he refused to let him see the King. Still hoping, the philosopher drew up for the French government a memorial, of which he sent a summary—the *Consilium Aegyptiacum*—to Boineburg. If the proposal had been carried out to success, France, rather than England, might have captured India and the rule of the seas. Louis' decision, said Admiral Mahan, "which killed Colbert and ruined the prosperity of France, was felt in its consequences from generation to generation."[8]

Boineburg died before the *Consilium* reached him, and Leibniz mourned the loss of an unselfish friend. Partly for this reason he did not return to Mainz; moreover, he had been caught in the intellectual currents of Paris, and found them more stimulating than those that surrounded even the liberal and enlightened Elector. Now he met Antoine Arnauld of Port-Royal, and Malebranche, and Christian Huygens, and Bossuet. Huygens drew him into higher mathematics, and Leibniz began those infinitesimal calculations that were to lead him to the calculus.

In January, 1673, on a mission from the Elector of Mainz to Charles II, he crossed the Channel to England. In London he made the acquaintance of Oldenburg and Boyle, and felt the zest of awakening science. Returning to Paris in March, he gave more and more of his time to mathematics. He contrived a computing machine that improved upon Pascal's by performing multiplication and division as well as addition and subtraction. In April he was elected, in absence, a member of the Royal Society. By 1675 he had discovered the differential calculus, by 1676 the infinitesimal calculus, and he had formulated his successful notation. No one any longer charges Leibniz with having plagiarized his calculus from Newton's.[9] Newton had apparently made his discovery in 1666, but he did not publish it till 1692; Leibniz published his differential calculus in 1684, his integral calculus in 1686.[10] There remains no doubt that Newton was first in the discovery, that

---

* "Even this early," said Spengler, "Leibniz laid down the principle that Napoleon grasped . . . more clearly after Wagram, viz., that acquisitions on the Rhine and in Belgium would not permanently better the position of France, and that the neck of Suez would one day be the key of world-dominance."[7]

Leibniz reached his own discovery independently, that he antedated Newton in publishing the discovery, and that Leibniz' system of notation proved superior to Newton's.[11]

The Archbishop of Mainz died in March, 1673, leaving Leibniz without official employment. Soon he signed an agreement to serve Duke John Frederick of Brunswick-Lüneburg as curator of the ducal library at Hanover. Still fascinated by Paris, Leibniz remained there till 1676, then traveled leisurely to Hanover via London, Amsterdam, and The Hague. At Amsterdam he talked with Spinoza's disciples, and at The Hague with the philosopher himself. Spinoza hesitated to confide in him, for Leibniz was proposing to reconcile Catholicism and Protestantism, which might then join in suppressing freedom of thought.[12] Leibniz overcame these suspicions, and Spinoza allowed him to read—even to copy passages from —the manuscript *Ethica*.[13] The two men had several long conversations. Leibniz had much trouble, after Spinoza's death, in concealing how deeply he had been influenced by the saintly Jew.

He reached Hanover toward the end of 1676, and remained in the employ of successive Brunswick princes through the remaining forty years of his life. He had hoped to be accepted as a councilor of state, but the dukes assigned him to care for their libraries and write the history of their house. He performed these tasks intermittently well. His voluminous history (*Annales Brunsvicenses*) was weighted and illuminated with original documents assiduously obtained; his genealogical researches in Italy established the common origin of the Este and Brunswick dynasties; and though the subject of his book was uncomfortably confining for so ambitious a genius, he lived to see the Brunswick family inherit England. He tried hard to be a German patriot; he pleaded with the Germans to use their vernacular in law; but he wrote his treatises in Latin or French, and was a shining exemplar of the "good European" and the cosmopolitan mind. He warned the German princes that their divisive jealousies, and their deliberate weakening of the Imperial power, condemned Germany to be the victim of better centralized states, and the battleground of repeated wars between France, England, and Spain.[14]

His secret hope was to serve the Emperor and the Empire rather than the princes of the separate states. He had a hundred plans for political, economic, religious, and educational reform, and he agreed with Voltaire that it was easier to reform a state by converting its ruler than by slowly educating the masses, who are too harassed with board and bed to have much time for thought.[15] In 1680, when the Imperial librarian died, Leibniz offered himself for the post, but he added that he would not want it unless it carried with it membership in the Emperor's Privy Council. His application was rejected. Returning to Hanover, he found some solace in the friendship of the Electress Sophia, and, later, of her daughter Sophia Charlotte, who gave him entree to the Prussian court, helped him to found the Berlin Academy (1700), and inspired him to write his *Théodicée*. For the rest he ennobled his modest position by corresponding with the leading thinkers of Europe, by making major contributions to philosophy, and by advancing a brave plan for the religious reunification of Christendom.

III. LEIBNIZ AND CHRISTIANITY

Was he himself a Christian? Outwardly yes, of course; a man with his zeal to pass from philosophy to statesmanship had to robe himself in the theology of his time and place. "I have endeavoured in all things," said his preface to the *Theodicy* "to consider the need for edification."[16] The writings that he published during his life were exemplary in their faith; they defended the Trinity, miracles, divine grace, free will, immortality; and they attacked the freethinkers of the age as undermining the moral bases of social order. However, "he went to church little . . . and for many years did not communicate";[17] the simple people of Hanover nicknamed him Lövenix (i.e., *glaubt nichts*—believes nothing).[18] Some students have credited him with two opposed philosophies: one for public consumption and the comforting of princesses; the other "a clear-cut affirmation of all the principles of Spinozism."[19] "Leibniz fell into Spinozism whenever he allowed himself to be logical; in his published works, accordingly, he took care to be illogical."[20]

His efforts to reconcile Catholicism and Protestantism subjected him to the charge of indifferentism.[21] His passion for unity and compromise dominated his theology; while avoiding preachers, he labored to bring them together. Because he saw deeply he minimized surface diversities; if Christianity was a form of government, its creedal varieties seemed to him not instruments of piety and good will but obstacles to order and peace.

In 1677 the Emperor Leopold I sent Christopher Rojas de Spinola, titular bishop of Tina in Croatia, to the court of Hanover to suggest to the Duke, John Frederick, himself a convert to Catholicism, that he join in a campaign to reunite Protestants with Rome. Probably the plan had political fringes: the Elector at the time desired the support of the Emperor, and Leopold hoped for a stronger German unity and spirit against the Turks. For a while Spinola commuted between Vienna and Hanover, and the affair progressed. When Bossuet (1682) formulated the Gallican Declarations by which the French clergy defied the Pope, Leibniz may have been led to hope that France would join with Germany in a Catholicism sufficiently independent of the papacy to soften Protestant hostility to the ancient creed. In 1683, as the Turks were marching to the siege of Vienna, Spinola assembled at Hanover a conference of Protestant and Catholic theologians, and submitted to them "rules for the ecclesiastical union of all Christians."

It was probably for this meeting[22] that Leibniz anonymously composed the strangest of the many documents that were found among his papers after his death. It was called *Systema Theologicum*, and purported to be such a statement of Catholic doctrine as any Protestant of good will might accept. In 1819 a Catholic editor published it as evidence that Leibniz had been secretly converted; more likely it was a diplomatic effort to reduce the theological gap between the two communions, but the editor was justified in considering the paper overwhelmingly Catholic. It began with brief impartiality:

> After invoking the divine aid by long and earnest prayer, putting aside, so far as is humanly possible, all party spirit, looking at the religious controversies as though I had come from another planet, a humble learner, unacquainted with any of the various communions, bound by no obligations, I have, after due consideration, arrived at the conclusions hereinafter set forth. I have deemed it incumbent upon me to embrace them because Holy Writ, immemorial religious tradition, the dictates of reason, and the sure testimony of the facts, seem to me to concur in establishing them in the mind of any unprejudiced human being.[23]

Thereupon followed a profession of faith in God, Creation, original sin, purgatory, transubstantiation, monastic vows, invocation of saints, use of incense, religious images, ecclesiastical vestments, and the subordination of the state to the Church.[24] This generosity to Catholicism might cast doubt on the document, but its authenticity as a work of Leibniz is generally accepted today.[25] Perhaps he hoped, by so supporting the Catholic view, to prepare for himself a commodious berth at the court of the Catholic Emperor in Vienna. And, like any good skeptic, Leibniz admired the sight, sound, and smell of Catholic ritual.

> Thus the strains of music, the sweet concord of voices, the poetry of the hymns, the beauty of the liturgy, the blaze of lights, the fragrant perfumes, the rich vestments, the sacred vessels adorned with precious stones, the costly offerings, the statues and the pictures that awaken holy thoughts, the glorious creations of artistic genius, . . . the stately splendor of public processions, the rich draperies adorning the streets, the music of bells, in a word all the gifts and marks of honor which the pious instincts of the people prompt them to pour forth with lavish hand, do not, I trow, excite in God's mind the dis-

dain which the stark simplicity of some of our contemporaries would
have us believe they do. That, at all events, is what reason and experience alike confirm.[26]

All these arguments failed to move the Protestants. Louis XIV disrupted
the décor by revoking the Edict of Nantes and making brutal war upon
French Protestants. Leibniz set aside his agape for more gracious times.

In 1687, to consult scattered archives for his *Annals of the House of
Brunswick*, he set out on three years of travel through Germany, Austria,
and Italy. In Rome, on the assumption that he would accept conversion,
the authorities offered him the curatorship of the Vatican Library; he
declined. He made a brave attempt to obtain cancellation of the ecclesiastical decrees against Copernicus and Galileo.[27] After his return to Hanover he
began (1691) three years of correspondence with Bossuet in the hope of
reviving the movement for the reunion of Christendom. Could not the
Roman Church call a really ecumenical council, one including Protestant as
well as Catholic leaders, to reconsider and revoke the Council of Trent's
harsh branding of Protestants as heretics? The bishop, who had just
bombarded these "heretics" with his *Variations des églises protestantes*
(1688), replied uncompromisingly: if the Protestants wished to re-enter
the sacred fold, let them accept conversion and end the debate. Leibniz
begged him to reconsider. Bossuet held out hope: "I enter into the scheme.
... You shall shortly hear what I think."[28] In 1691 Leibniz wrote to Mme.
Brinon with his usual optimism:

> The Emperor is favorably disposed; Pope Innocent XI and a number
> of cardinals, generals of monastic orders, ... and many grave theo-
> logians, having carefully considered the matter, have expressed them-
> selves in the most encouraging terms. ... It is no exaggeration to say
> that if the King of France and the prelates ... who have his ear in
> this matter were to take concerted action the thing would not be
> merely feasible, it would be as good as done.[29]

When Bossuet's answer came it was crushing: the decisions of the Council
of Trent were irrevocable; they had rightly held the Protestants to be
heretics; the Church is infallible; no conference between Catholic and
Protestant leaders could reach any constructive result unless the Protestants
would agree in advance to adopt the decisions of the Church on the matters
at issue.[30] Leibniz replied that the Church had often changed her views
and teaching, had contradicted herself, and had condemned and excommunicated persons without just cause. He declared that he "washed his
hands of all responsibility for whatever further ills the existing schism may
have in store for the Christian Church."[31] He turned to the apparently
more hopeful task of reconciling the Lutheran and Calvinist branches of

Protestantism, but here he met with an intransigence as hard and proud as Bossuet's. At last he privately called down a plague upon all the rival theologies, and proclaimed that there were only two kinds of books with any value: those reporting scientific demonstrations or experiments, and those containing history, politics, or geography.[32] Outwardly, and laxly, he remained a Lutheran to the end of his life.

IV. LOCKE REVIEWED

Half of Leibniz' product was an *argumentum ad hominem*, undertaken more or less incidentally as a discussion of some other writer's ideas. His greatest book, which grew to 590 pages, began in 1696 as a seven-page review of Locke's *Essay concerning Human Understanding* (1690), known then to Leibniz only from an abstract in Le Clerc's *Bibliothèque universelle*. When the *Essay* appeared in a French translation (1700), Leibniz reviewed it again for a German magazine. He was quick to recognize the importance of Locke's analysis, and generously praised its style. In 1703 he set himself to comment on it chapter by chapter; it is these comments that constitute Leibniz' *Nouveaux Essais sur l'entendement humain* (*New Essays on Human Understanding*). When he learned of Locke's death (1704), he left the commentary unfinished. It was not published till 1765, too late to interfere with the pervasive influence of Locke upon Voltaire and other luminaries of the French Enlightenment, but in time to share in molding Kant's epochal *Critique of Pure Reason*. It is among the most important productions in the history of psychology.

In form it is a dialogue between Philalethes (Lover of Truth), repre-senting Locke, and Theophilus (Lover of God), representing Leibniz. The dialogue is vigorously sustained, and still makes good reading for any person of keen mind and endless leisure. The preface shows Leibniz in his most courteous mood, professing modestly to win readers by attaching his discourse to "the *Essay on the Understanding* by a distinguished English-man, one of the most beautiful and esteemed works of this period." The question to be discussed is stated with laudable clarity: "To know whether the soul in itself is entirely empty as the tablets upon which as yet nothing has been written (*tabula rasa*), according to Aristotle and the author of the *Essay*, and whether all that is traced thereon comes solely from the senses and experience; or whether the soul contains originally the *principles* of many ideas and doctrines which external objects merely call up on occasion, as I believe with Plato."[33]* The mind, in Leibniz' view, is not a passive

---

* Locke wrote of the mind at birth as "white paper,"[34] but did not use the phrase *tabula rasa* (clean slate), which was Aquinas' translation of a passage in Aristotle's *De anima*.[35]

receptacle of experience; it is a complex organ that by its structure and functions transforms the data of sensation, just as the digestive tract is no empty sack but a system of organs for the digestion of food and its transformation into the needs and organs of the body. In a famous epigram Leibniz summarized and amended Locke: *Nihil est in intellectu quod non fuerit in sensu, nisi ipse intellectus*—"Nothing is in the mind that has not been in the senses, *except the mind itself*."[36] Locke, as Leibniz noted, had recognized that ideas could come from introspective "reflection" as well as from external sensation, but had ascribed to a sensory origin all elements entering into reflection. Leibniz, on the contrary, argued that the mind of itself supplies certain principles or categories of thought, such as "being, substance, unity, identity, cause, perception, reason, and many other notions which the senses cannot give";[37] and that these tools of understanding, these organs of mental digestion, are "innate," not in the sense that we are conscious of them at birth, or always conscious of them when we use them, but in the sense that they are part of the native structure or "natural aptitudes" of the mind. Locke felt that these supposedly inborn principles were gradually developed by the interplay, in thought, of ideas originally sensory. But without such principles, Leibniz urged, there would be no ideas, only a disorderly succession of sensations; just as, without the action and digestive juices of the stomach, food would not feed us, and would not be food. In this measure, he boldly added, all *ideas* are innate—i.e., the result of the transforming action of the mind upon sensations. But he admitted that the innate principles are at birth confused and indistinct, and become clear only through experience and use.

The inherent principles, in Leibniz' judgment, include all "necessary truths, such as are found in pure mathematics,"[38] for it is the mind, not sensation, that supplies the principle of necessity; everything sensory is individual and contingent, and gives us, at best, repeated sequence but not necessary sequence or cause.[39] (Locke had conceded this.[40]) Leibniz considered innate all our instincts, our preference of pleasure to pain, and all the laws of reason[41]—though these become clear only with experience. Among the innate laws of thought two are especially basic: the principle of contradiction—that contradictory statements cannot be true at the same time ("if A is a circle it is not a square"); and the principle of sufficient reason—"that nothing happens without a reason why it should be so rather than otherwise."[42] Human intelligence, Leibniz thought, differs from animal knowledge by deducing general ideas from particular experiences through the use of innate principles of reason; brutes are pure empirics, guiding themselves solely by examples; "so far as we can judge of them, they never attain to the formation of necessary propositions."[43]

The principle of sufficient reason suffices to "demonstrate the being of a

God, and all the other parts of metaphysics or natural theology."[44] In this
sense our idea of God is innate, though in some minds or tribes the idea may
be unconscious or confused; and we may say the same of the idea of
immortality.[45] The moral sense is innate, not in its specific content or
judgments, which may vary in time and place, but as consciousness of a
difference between right and wrong; this consciousness is universal.[46]

In Leibniz' psychology the mind is active not only as entering by its
structure and functioning into the making of every idea, but also in the
incessant continuance of its activity. Using the word *think* in Descartes'
broad sense as including all mental operations, Leibniz agreed with the
Cartesians that the mind is always thinking, whether awake, unconscious,
or asleep. "A state without thought in the soul, and an absolute repose in
the body, appear to me equally contrary to nature, and without example in
the world."[47] Some mental operations are subconscious; "it is a great error
to believe that there is no perception in the soul besides those of which it
is conscious."[48] It is with such propositions in Leibniz that modern psychology began its efforts to delve into what some students called unconscious mind, and what *esprits forts* considered to be merely cerebral or
other bodily processes that did not evoke consciousness.

Leibniz has much to say about the relation between body and soul, but
there he leaves psychology, soars into metaphysics, and asks us to see all
the world as psychophysical monads, like ourselves.

V. MONADS

When he was in Vienna in 1714 he met Eugene of Savoy, who, with
Marlborough, had saved Europe from subjection to Louis XIV. The Prince
asked the philosopher for a brief statement of his philosophy in a form
intelligible to a general. Leibniz responded by composing a compact
treatise of ninety paragraphs, which he left among his papers at his death.
A German translation was published in 1720, but the original French text
was not printed till 1839, and then it was the editor who christened it
La Monadologie. Leibniz could have taken the term *monad* from Giordano
Bruno,[49] or from Frans (son of the chemist J. B.) van Helmont,[50] who
used the word to describe the minute "seeds" which alone were directly
created by God, and which developed into all the forms of matter and
life. An English physician, Francis Glisson, had attributed not only force
but instinct and ideas to all substances (1672). A similar theory had germi-
nated in Leibniz' roving and receptive mind since 1686. He may have been
influenced by the recent work of microscopists, who had shown such
throbbing life in the smallest cells. Leibniz concluded that "there is a

world of created beings—living things, animals . . . , souls . . . , in the least part of matter."[51] Every portion of matter may be conceived as a pond full of fishes, and every drop of blood in one of these microscopic fishes is another pond full of fishes, and so on *ad infinitum*. He was moved —as Pascal had been appalled—by the indefinite divisibility of every extended thing.

This endless divisibility, Leibniz suggested, is a puzzle arising from our conception of reality as matter, therefore as extended, therefore as divisible *ad nauseam*. If we consider the ultimate reality as energy, and conceive the world as composed of centers of force, the mystery of divisibility vanishes, because force, like thought, does not imply extension. So he rejected the atoms of Democritus as the ultimate components of the universe, and replaced them with monads, unextended units of force; he defined substance not as matter but as energy. (Up to this point Leibniz' conception was quite in accord with twentieth-century physics.) "Matter" is everywhere instinct with motion, activity, and life. Every monad feels or perceives; it has inchoate or incipient mind, in the sense that it is susceptible—and responds—to external changes.

We shall understand the monads better if we think of them "in imitation of the notion that we have of souls."[52] As each soul is "a simple, separate Person,"[53] a solitary ego, *solus contra mundum*, fighting its way by its own internal will against everything outside it, so each monad is essentially alone, a separate, independent center of force against all other centers of force; reality is a universe of individual powers, unified and harmonized only through the laws of the whole, or God. As every soul is different from all others, so is every monad unique; in the entire cosmos there are no two beings completely alike, for their differences constitute their individuality; two things having all the same qualities would be indistinguishable, identical, one ("the law of indiscernibles").[54] As each soul feels or perceives the reality surrounding it, and, ever less clearly, the reality progressively distant from it, but feels all reality in some degree, so each monad feels, however confusedly and unconsciously, the whole universe; in this way it is a mirror more or less obscurely reflecting and representing the world. And as no individual mind can really look into another mind, so no single monad can see into another; it has no window or other opening for such direct communication; and therefore it cannot directly produce any change in any other monad.

The monads do change, for change is essential to their life; but the changes come from their own inner striving.[55] For just as each self is desire and will, so each monad contains—is—an inner purpose and will, an effort to develop; this is the "entelechy" that Aristotle spoke of as the core of every life; in this sense [as Schopenhauer was to say] force and will are two forms or degrees of the same fundamental reality.[56] There is an immanent teleology in nature: there is in everything a seeking, an "appetition," a guiding, molding purpose, even though that purpose, that will, acts within the limits, and by means, of mechanical law. Just as, in ourselves, the bodily movement is the visible and mechanical expression of an internal will or desire, so in the monads the mechanical process that we see from without is only the outer form and shell of an inner force: "That which is exhibited mechanically, or by extension, in matter, is concentrated dynamically and monadically in the entelechy [or inner striving] itself."[57] In our confused perception we identify external things with "matter" because we see their outer mechanism only; we do not, as in introspection, see the inner and formative vitality. In this philosophy the passive and helpless atoms of the materialists give place to monads, or units, that are living centers of individuality and force; the world ceases to be a dead machine, and becomes the stage of diverse and palpitating life.

In that diversity the most important feature is the degree in which the "mind" of the monad is conscious. All monads have mind, in the sense of sensitivity and response; but not all mind is conscious. Even we marvelous human beings go through many mental processes without consciousness, as in dreams; or as when, in our intense attention to certain aspects of a situation, we are not aware that we are perceiving many other elements in the scene—elements which may nevertheless be deposited in memory, enter into our dreams, or emerge from hidden corners of the mind into later consciousness; or as when, conscious of the roar and hiss of the surf, we do not realize that each wave, and each particle of each wave, is beating upon our ears to produce a thousand individual impressions that become our hearing of the sea. So the simplest monads feel and perceive everything about them, but so confusedly that they have no consciousness. In plants the feelings become clearer and more specialized, and lead to more specific responses. In the monad that is the soul of an animal the echoing perceptions become memories, whose interplay begets consciousness. Man is a colony of monads [cells?], each with its own hunger, needs, and purposes; but these particles become a unified community of living organisms under the direction of a dominating monad which is man's entelechy and soul.[58] "When this soul is raised to the level of reason, it is . . . reckoned as mind,"[59] and rises in rank in the measure of its perceiving necessary relations and eternal truths; when it perceives the order and mind of the universe it becomes the mirror of God. God, the Prime Monad, is pure and fully conscious Mind, free from mechanism and body.[60]

The most difficult aspect of this philosophy is Leibniz' theory of "preestablished harmony." What is the relation between the inner life of a monad and its outward manifestation, or material shell? And how shall we explain the apparent interaction of physical body and spiritual mind in man? Descartes had delegated this problem helplessly to the pineal gland; Spinoza had answered it by denying any separation or interaction of matter and mind, since these were, in his view, merely the outside and inside aspects of one process and reality. Leibniz restored the problem by thinking of the two aspects as separate and distinct; he denied their interaction, but ascribed the simultaneity of the physical and the mental processes as due to a continuous collusion marvelously prearranged by God:

> The soul follows its own laws, and the body its own likewise, and they accord by virtue of the harmony *pre-established* among all substances, since they are all representations of one and the same universe.[61] . . . Bodies act as though, *per impossibile*, there were no souls, and souls act as if there were no bodies, and both act *as if* each influenced the other.[62] . . . I am . . . asked how it happens that God is not content to produce all the thoughts and modifications of the soul without these useless bodies which the soul (it is said) can neither move nor know. The answer is easy. It is that it was God's will that there should be a greater rather than a lesser number of substances, and He found it good that these modifications should correspond to something outside.[63]

Suspecting that this debonair exploitation of deity as a substitute for thought might not win universal applause, Leibniz embellished it with the occasionalism and timepieces of Geulincx: body and mind, each operating independently of the other and yet in puzzling harmony, are like two clocks so skillfully constructed, wound, and set that they tick off the seconds and strike the hours in perfect agreement, without any interaction or mutual influence; so the physical and psychical processes, though quite independent, and never acting upon each other, accord through a "harmony pre-established by a divine anticipatory artifice."[64]

Let us assume that what Leibniz had in view, but did not care to say, was that the apparently separate but synchronous processes of mechanism and life, of action and thought, are one and the same process, seen externally as matter, internally as mind. But to have said this would have been to repeat Spinoza, and share his fate.

VI. WAS GOD JUST?

This need to put theological clothing upon philosophical nudities led Leibniz to write the book that drew the ire and wit of Voltaire, and almost lost a really profound thinker in the caricature of Professor Pangloss defending the best of all possible worlds. The only complete philosophical work published by Leibniz in his lifetime was called *Essais de Théodicée sur la bonté de Dieu, la liberté de l'homme, et l'origine du mal* (1710)— almost as comforting a promissory note as Descartes' *Principles of First Philosophy, in Which are Demonstrated the Existence of God and the Immortality of the Soul* (1641). "Theodicy," of course, meant the justice, or justification, of God.

This book, like the others, had an occasional origin. In an article ("Hieronymus Rorarius") in the *Dictionnaire historique et critique* Bayle, while expressing great admiration for Leibniz, questioned the philosopher's view that faith can be reconciled with reason, or man's freedom with God's omnipotence, or earthly evil with divine goodness and power. We had better, said Bayle, give up the idea of proving religious creeds; it merely brings the difficulties into clearer light. Leibniz replied in an essay (1698) contributed to Jacques Basnage's journal, *Histoire des ouvrages des savants.* In the second edition of his *Dictionary* Bayle added to the article on Rorarius a substantial note again hailing Leibniz as "that great philosopher," but pointing out further obscurities, especially in the theory of pre-established harmony. Leibniz sent (1702) his rejoinder directly to Bayle, but did not print it. In that same year he wrote again to the Rotterdam scholar, complimenting him on his "striking reflections" and "boundless researches."[65] Few episodes in the history of philosophy are so pleasant as the mutual courtesy in this exchange of ideas. Sophia Charlotte, Queen of Prussia, expressed her desire to know Leibniz' answers to Bayle's doubts. He was preparing such a statement when news came to him that Bayle had died. He revised and extended his replies, and published them as the *Théodicée.* He was now sixty-four years old, felt the nearness of the "Great Perhaps," and may have longed to believe in the justice of God to man. How had it come about that a world created by an omnipotent and benevolent deity had been sullied with such martial massacres, political corruption, human cruelty and suffering, earthquakes, famines, poverty, and disease?

The "preliminary dissertation on the confronting of faith with reason" described reason and the Bible as being both of them divine revelations, and therefore unlikely to contradict each other. Bayle had wondered how a good God, presumably foreseeing all "the fruit thereof," could have allowed the temptation of Eve; Leibniz answered that to make man capable of morality God had to give him free will, and therefore freedom to sin. It is true that free will seems incompatible with both science and theology: science sees everywhere the rule of invariable law, and human freedom seems lost in God's foreknowledge and predestination of all events. But (said Leibniz) we are obstinately and directly conscious that we are free.

Though we cannot prove this freedom, we must accept it as a prerequisite to any sense of moral responsibility, and as the only alternative to viewing man as a ridiculously helpless physiological machine.

As to the existence of God, Leibniz is content with traditional Scholastic arguments. We conceive a perfect being, and since existence is a necessary element in perfection, a perfect being must exist. There must be a necessary and uncaused being behind all proximate causes and contingent events. It is inconceivable that the grandeur and order of nature should have any other source than a Supreme Intelligence. The Creator must contain in Himself, in an infinite degree, the power, knowledge, and will discoverable in His creatures. Divine design and cosmic mechanism are not contradictory: Providence uses mechanism its wonders to perform; and God can interrupt the world machine now and then to work a miracle or two.[66]

Of course the soul is immortal. Death, like birth, is only a change of form in an assemblage of monads; the inherent soul and energy remain. Soul, except in God, is always attached to body, and body to soul; but there will be a resurrection of the body as well as of the soul.[67] (Leibniz is here a good Catholic.) Below man the immortality of the soul is impersonal [merely a redistribution of energy?]; only the rational soul of man will enjoy a conscious immortality.

Good and evil are human terms, defined according to our pleasure and pain; these terms cannot be applied to the universe without presuming for man an omniscience possible only to God. "Imperfection in the part may be required for a greater perfection in the whole"[68]; so sin is an evil, but is a result of free will, which is a good; and even the sin of Adam and Eve was in some sense a *felix culpa*, a happy fault, since it resulted in the coming of Christ.[69] "There is in the universe . . . no chaos, no confusion, save in appearance."[70] The afflictions of men "contribute to the greater good of those who suffer them."[71] Even

> holding . . . to the established doctrine that the number of men damned eternally will be incomparably greater than that of the saved, we must say that the evil could not but seem to be almost as nothing in comparison with the good, when one contemplates the true vastness of the City of God. . . . Since the proportion of that part of the universe which we know is almost lost in nothing compared with that which is unknown, . . . it may be that all evils are almost nothingness in comparison with the good things which are in the universe.[72] . . . One need not even agree that there is more evil than good in the human kind. For it is possible, and even a very reasonable thing, that the glory and perfection of the blessed may be incomparably greater than the misery and imperfection of the damned.[73]

Imperfect as it may seem to our selfish sight, this world is the best that God could have created so long as He left men human and free. If a better world had been possible, we may be sure God would have created it.

> It follows from the supreme perfection of God that in producing the universe He chose the best possible plan, containing the greatest variety, together with the greatest order; the best-arranged situation, place, and time; the greatest effect produced by the simplest means; the most power, the most knowledge, the most happiness and goodness in created things, of which the universe admitted. For as all possible things have a claim to existence in the understanding of God in proportion to their perfections, the result of all these claims must be the most perfect actual world which is possible.[74]

We cannot recommend any further reading of Leibniz' *Theodicy* today, except to those who would appreciate to the full the bitter laughter of *Candide*.

VII. PARALIPOMENA

Nevertheless, the *Théodicée* became the most widely read of Leibniz' books, and succeeding generations knew him as "the best-of-all-possible-worlds man." If we must regret the edifying absurdity of that performance, our respect for the author revives when we contemplate the prodigious variety of his intellectual interests. Though science was but one corner of his thought, he was fascinated by it; if he had to live another life, he told Bayle, he would have been a biologist.[75] He was one of the profoundest mathematicians of an age rich in mathematicians. He bettered Descartes' formula for measuring force.* His conception of matter as energy seemed to his time a bravura of metaphysics, but it is now a commonplace of physics. He described matter as our confused perception of the operations of force. Like our contemporary theorists he rejected the "absolute motion" assumed by Newton; motion, said Leibniz, "is simply change in the relative position of bodies, and thus is nothing absolute, but consists in a relation."[76] Anticipating Kant, he interpreted space and time not as objective realities but as perceptual relations: space as perceived coexistence, time as perceived succession—views adopted in relativity theories today. In his final year (1715) Leibniz entered into a long correspondence with Samuel Clarke about gravitation; this seemed to him another occult quality,

---

* Descartes' formula was mv—force is mass times velocity. Leibniz, on the basis of Galileo's work, changed this to mv^2. The current formula is $\frac{1}{2}mv^2$.

acting at enormous distances through an apparent void; it would be, he objected, a perpetual miracle; no greater, replied Clarke, than "pre-established harmony."[77] Leibniz feared that Newton's theory of the cosmic mechanism would make many atheists; on the contrary, said Clarke, the majestic order revealed by Newton would strengthen the belief in God;[78] the aftermath justified Leibniz.

In biology Leibniz vaguely visioned evolution. Like many thinkers before and after him he saw a "law of continuity" running through the organic world; but he extended the concept to the supposedly inorganic world as well. Everything is a point or stage in an endless series, and is connected with everything else through an infinite number of intermediate forms;[79] there is, so to speak, an infinitesimal calculus running through reality.

> Nothing is accomplished all at once, and it is one of my great maxims . . . that nature makes no leaps. . . . This law of continuity declares that we pass from the small to the great—and the reverse— through the medium, in degree as well as in parts.[80] [This is now questioned by many physicists.] . . . Men are linked with animals, these with plants, and these again with fossils, which in their turn are connected with those bodies which sense and imagination represent to us as completely dead and inorganic.[81]

In this majestic continuity all antitheses dissolve through a great chain of being and hardly perceptible differences, from the simplest matter to the most complex, from the lowliest animalcule to the greatest ruler, genius, or saint.

Leibniz' mind seemed to span the whole continuity that he described. He was *au courant* with every science; he knew the history of nations and of philosophy; he touched the worldly affairs of a dozen states; he was at home with atoms and with God. In 1693 he published a paper on the beginnings of the earth, quietly ignoring Genesis, and he developed his geological ideas in a treatise, *Protogaea*, which was published (1749) after his death. Our planet, he thought, had once been an incandescent globe; it gradually cooled, contracted, and formed a crust; as it cooled, the vapor surrounding it condensed into water and oceans—which became salty by dissolving minerals in the crust. Subsequent geological changes were due either to the action of water flooding the surface, leaving sedimentary formations, or to the explosion of subterranean gases, leaving igneous rocks. The same treatise gave an excellent explanation of fossils,[82] and advanced toward a theory of evolution. It seemed to him "worthy of belief that in the course of vast changes" in the crust of the earth "even the species of animals have many times been transformed."[83] He thought it probable that the earliest animals were marine forms, and that the amphibia and land animals were descended from these.[84] Like some optimists of the nineteenth century, he saw in this evolutionary transformism one basis for faith in "a perpetual and unrestricted progress of the universe. . . . Progress will never come to an end."[85]

From biology Leibniz jumped to Roman law, and from this to Chinese philosophy. His *Novissima Sinaica* (1697)—"the latest news from China" —eagerly took up the reports that missionaries and merchants were sending from the "Middle Kingdom." He held it probable that in philosophy, mathematics, and medicine the Chinese had made discoveries which might be of great help to Western civilization, and he urged cultural links with Russia partly as a means of opening cultural communication with the East. He corresponded with scholars, scientists, and statesmen in twenty countries and three languages. He wrote some three hundred letters every year; fifteen thousand of them have been preserved;[86] Voltaire's correspondence rivals this in quantity, but yields to it in intellectual diversity. Leibniz suggested an international culture bourse, or exchange, through which men of learning could compare notes and ideas.[87] He planned an international language—"*characteristica universalis*"—in which each idea in philosophy and science would have its symbol or character, so that thinkers could manipulate notions by this *ars combinatoria*, just as mathematicians used signs for quantities; so he came close to founding mathematical or symbolic logic.[88] By a kind of noble futility he distributed himself into so many areas that he left hardly anything but fragments behind him.

Our eager polymath found no time for marriage. At last, aged fifty, he proposed; but, says Fontenelle, "the lady asked for time to take the matter into consideration, and as Leibniz thus obtained leisure to consider the matter again, he never married."[89] After his travels, and his flights into diplomacy, he treasured the privacy of his study, and he who had touched half the world with the tentacles of his mind now kept his friends at a distance as enemies to his work. He lost himself in reading and writing, often through the night, seldom taking note of Sundays or holidays. He had no servant; he sent out for his meal, and ate it alone in his room.[90] If he stirred out it was to make researches, or pursue his schemes for the advancement of learning, science, or amity.

He dreamed of establishing academies in the great capitals, and succeeded in one. The Berlin Academy was founded (1700) on his initiative, and elected him its first president. He met Peter the Great at Torgau (1712), and again at Carlsbad and Pyrmont; he proposed a similar academy for St. Petersburg; the Czar loaded him with gifts, and adopted his suggestion for governing Russia through administrative "colleges"; but Leibniz did not live to see the Academy of St. Petersburg take form in 1724. In

1712 we find him in Vienna, itching for an Imperial post and pregnant with another academy; he submitted to Charles VI a plan for an institution that would promote not only science but education, agriculture, and industry; and he offered his services to direct it. The Emperor raised him to the ranks of the nobility, and made him an Imperial councilor (1712).

His long absences from Hanover angered the new Elector George; Leibniz' salary was for a period discontinued, and he was warned that it was time, after a quarter century of interruptions, that he should finish his history of the house of Brunswick. When Queen Anne died, George left Hanover to take the throne of England. Three days after this departure Leibniz arrived from Vienna (1714). He had hoped to be taken to London and enjoy there some loftier office and emoluments; he sent conciliatory letters to the new King; but George I answered that until the *Annals* were complete Leibniz had better remain in Hanover.[91] Besides, England had not forgiven him for disputing with Newton the parentage of calculus.

Disappointed and lonely, he struggled for two years more to believe in the good intentions of the universe. The man who was remembered in the eighteenth century as the apostle of optimism died in pain of gout and stone at Hanover on November 14, 1716. His death was not noticed by the Berlin Academy, nor by the German courtiers in London, nor by any friends at home, for these had been alienated by his absences and his privacy. No clergyman came to administer religious rites to the philosopher who had defended religion against philosophy. One man alone, his former secretary, attended the funeral. A Scotsman then in Hanover wrote that Leibniz "was buried more like a robber than what he really was, the ornament of his country."[92]

We must not spend space marking the flaws in this polymorphous multitude of ideas; time has long since performed these unpleasant obsequies. Critics have charged Leibniz with ubiquitous borrowing: they have found his psychology in Plato, his theodicy in the Scholastics, his monads in Bruno, his metaphysics, ethics, and mind-and-body relation in Spinoza. But who can say anything on these problems but what has been said a hundred times before? It is easier to be original and foolish than to be original and wise; there are a thousand possible errors for every truth, and mankind, with all its efforts, has not yet exhausted the possibilities. There is much nonsense in Leibniz, but we cannot quite decide whether it was honest nonsense or protective discoloration. So he tells us that when God created the world He saw in a flash, in its most minute detail, everything that was to happen in history.[93] "I always begin as a philosopher," he said, "but I always end up as a theologian"[94]—i.e., he felt that philosophy missed its aim if it did not lead to virtue and piety.

His long and genial debate with Locke gave him one of his many claims to significant thought. He may have exaggerated the innateness of "innate ideas," but he admitted that they were capacities, instincts, or aptitudes rather than ideas; and he succeeded in showing that Locke's sensationism had oversimplified the process of knowledge, and that "mind" is by its nature—if only crudely at birth—an organ for the active reception, manipulation, and transformation of sensations; here, as in his views of space and time, Leibniz stands high as a precursor of Kant. The doctrine of monads is shot through with difficulties (if they are not extended, how can any number of them produce extension? if they "perceive" the universe, how can they be immune to external influence?), but it was an illuminating attempt to bridge the chasm between mind and matter by making matter mental rather than mind material. Of course Leibniz failed to reconcile mechanism and design in nature, or mechanism in the body with freedom in the will; and his reseparation of mind and body after Spinoza had united them in one two-sided process was a step backward in philosophy. His pretense that this is the best of all possible worlds was the gallant or hopeful effort of a courtier to comfort a queen. The most learned of philosophers ("a whole academy in himself," Frederick the Great called him) wrote theology as if nothing had happened in the history of thought since St. Augustine. But with all his shortcomings his achievements in science and philosophy were immense. Patriot and yet "good European," he restored Germany to a high place in the development of Western civilization. "Of all who made Germany illustrious," wrote Frederick II, "those rendering the greatest service to the human spirit were Thomasius and Leibniz."[95]

His influence diminished as his theology lost face before the moral consciousness of mankind. Within a generation after his death his philosoph was given a systematic reformulation by Christian von Wolff, and in th. modified form it became the dominant fashion of thought in the German universities. Outside Germany his influence was slight. Though most of his writings were in French, they were too fragmentary to exert any consistent or concentrated force; no collected edition appeared till 1768, and even then some important but heterodox items were excluded, and had to wait till 1901 to venture into print. His calculus notation was destined to victory, but for half a century his rivals, Newton and Locke, carried everything before them, and became the idols of the French Enlightenment. Yet even amid that ecstasy of reason Buffon ranked Leibniz as the greatest genius of his age.[96] The outstanding German thinker of the twentieth century, Oswald Spengler, considered Leibniz "without doubt the greatest intellect in Western philosophy."[97]

To round out these superlatives we may add that, all in all, the seventeenth century was the most productive in the history of modern thought. Bacon, Descartes, Hobbes, Spinoza, Locke, Bayle, Leibniz: here was a majestic sequence of men warm with the wine of reason, joyfully confident (most of them) that they could understand the universe, even to forming "clear and distinct ideas" about God, and leading—all but the last—to that heady Enlightenment which was to convulse both religion and government in the French Revolution. Leibniz foresaw that terminus; and while he continued to the end to defend freedom of speech,[98] he urged freethinkers to consider the effect of their spoken or written words upon the morals and spirit of the people. About 1700, in the *Nouveaux Essais,* he uttered a remarkable warning:

> If fairness wishes to spare persons (freethinkers), piety demands the representation, where it is fitting, of the bad effects of their dogmas when they are . . . contrary to [belief in] the providence of a perfectly wise, good, and just God, and contrary to that immortality of souls which renders them susceptible to the effects of His justice, not to speak of other opinions dangerous as regards morality and the police. I know that excellent and well-meaning men maintain that these theoretic opinions have less influence upon practice than is thought, and I also know that there are persons of an excellent disposition whom these opinions will never make do anything unworthy of themselves. . . . It may be said that Epicurus and Spinoza, for example, have led a life wholly exemplary. But these reasons cease most frequently in their disciples or imitators, who, believing themselves released from the troublesome fear of an overseeing Providence and of a menacing future, give loose reins to their brutish passions, and turn their minds to the seduction and corruption of others; and if they are ambitious, and of a disposition somewhat harsh, they will be capable, for their pleasure or advancement, of setting on fire the four corners of the earth. I have known this from the character of some whom death has swept away. I find also that similar opinions, insinuating themselves little by little into the minds of men of high life who rule others, and upon whom affairs depend, and slipping into the books of fashion, dispose all things to the general revolution with which Europe is threatened.[99]

There is a spirit of sincere concern in these lines, and we must respect the counsel of caution that they express. And yet, even after the Enlightenment had crumbled creeds, and the French Revolution had set on fire the four corners of the earth, and the September massacres had transiently sated the thirst of the gods, a major historian could look back to this first

age of modern science and philosophy and see its adventurers not as
destroyers of civilization but as liberators of mankind. Said Lecky:

> It was thus that the great teachers of the seventeenth century . . .
> disciplined the minds of men for impartial inquiry, and, having broken
> the spell that so long had bound them, produced a passionate love of
> truth which has revolutionized all departments of knowledge. It is to
> the impulse which was then communicated that may be traced a great
> critical movement which has renovated all history, all science, all
> theology—which has penetrated into the obscurest recesses, destroy-
> ing old prejudices, dispelling illusions, rearranging . . . our knowledge,
> and altering the whole scope and character of our sympathies. But all
> this would have been impossible but for the diffusion of a rationalistic
> spirit.[100]

So, for good or ill, the seventeenth century laid the foundations of
modern thought. The Renaissance was tied to classical antiquity and to
Catholic ritual and art; the Reformation was bound to primitive Christianity and a medieval creed. Now this rich and fateful era, from Galileo
to Newton, from Descartes to Bayle, from Bacon to Locke, turned its
face toward an uncharted future that promised all the dangers of liberty.
It deserved, perhaps even more than the eighteenth century, the name Age
of Reason; for though its thinkers were still the voices of a small minority,
they displayed a wiser moderation, a deeper sounding of the limits and
difficulties of reason and freedom, than the unmoored protagonists of the
French Enlightenment. In any case the greatest drama in modern history
had played its second act, and moved on to its fulfillment.

BOOK V

FRANCE AGAINST EUROPE

1683–1715

CHAPTER XXIV

The Sun Sets

I. MME. DE MAINTENON

AFTER the death of Marie Thérèse (July 30, 1683), the uncrowned Queen of France was the "Widow Scarron," the Marquise de Maintenon, governess of the King's bastards, soon (January, 1684?) his morganatic wife, and henceforth the strongest personal influence in the reign.

It is difficult today to know her real character, and historians still debate it. She had many enemies who resented her rise and power; some of them wrote history, and handed her down to us as a selfish, scheming villain. However, when she might have replaced Mme. de Montespan as royal mistress—with all the influence that this would bring—she refused, and, instead, persuaded the King to return to the bed of the Queen (August, 1680). The Queen was then forty-two, three years younger than La Maintenon, and there was no reason to expect her early death; at this point, apparently, the Marquise preferred virtue to power. When death took the Queen the governess still refused to become a mistress; she played for higher stakes, risking her present place. If her virtue was ambition, it was no more sullied by it than the modesty of a prudent maiden who has only her charms to bargain for her life, and thinks a night's lodging less security than a wedding ring. When Louis married Maintenon she was forty-eight years old; Mignard pictured her as an amiable matron long past the age of physical allure. At best she was sincerely pious; at worst she took a brave gamble, and won.

Placed now in an apartment near the King's, she lived in the Palace of Versailles with an almost bourgeois simplicity. "Court life was irksome to her, and she had no pleasure in ostentation."[1] She did not accumulate wealth; even at the crest of her curve she owned little more than the Château of Maintenon, which she left unfurnished and unused. In their later years Louis is reported to have said to her, "But, madame, you have nothing, and if I die you will be destitute. Tell me what I can do for you."[2] She asked some modest favors for her relatives, and considerable sums for her pet enterprise, the college that in 1686 she established at St.-Cyr for girls of good family but straitened means. It was not her vanity, but the King's that conscripted labor and money for the abortive aqueduct that took her name.

In many ways she was a good wife. Her constant occupation, through

685

a busy day, was to serve as a buffer between the King and the world, to maintain peace amid the ambitions and intrigues of courtiers, to humor a swarm of place-seekers, to serve as a kindly aunt to her husband's grandchildren, to meet his masculine needs, to comfort him in his failures and defeats, to amuse "the man most difficult to amuse in all his kingdom,"[3] and to bring an atmosphere of domestic calm into a life that in almost every hour had to make decisions affecting a million lives. Among her private papers found after her death was this prayer, apparently composed soon after her marriage:

> Lord God, Thou hast placed me where I am, and I submit myself to Thy providence without reserve. Grant me grace that as a Christian I may support its sorrows, sanctify its pleasures, seek in everything Thy glory, and . . . help the salvation of the King. Prevent me from giving way to the agitations of a restless mind. . . . Thy will, O God, not mine, be done; for the sole happiness in this world and the next is to submit to it without reserve. Fill me with this wisdom, and all other spiritual gifts necessary to the high place to which Thou hast called me; make fruitful the talents Thou hast been pleased to give me. Thou who holdest in Thy hands the hearts of kings, open that of the King that I may set therein the good that Thou desirest; enable me to please, console, encourage, and even, if it be necessary to Thy glory, to sadden him. Let me hide none of the things he might learn from me which others have not the courage to tell him. Let me save myself together with him; [let me] love him in Thee and for Thee; and let him love me in the same way. Grant that we may walk together in Thy paths without reproach until the day of Thy coming.[4]

This is beautiful, as beautiful as any letter of Héloïse to Abélard, and, we hope, more authentic; such a prayer can give strength regardless of any external response. Perhaps there is a secret will to power in the desire to reform and guide others; but Maintenon's remaining years proved the sincerity, as well as the narrowness, of her piety. "She found a King," said Saint-Simon, "who believed himself an apostle because he had all his life persecuted Jansenism. . . . This indicated to her with what grain she could sow the field most profitably."[5]

Did she encourage the persecution of the Huguenots? Saint-Simon thought so,[6] but later investigation tends to clear her of this inhumanity, in which Louvois, her consistent enemy, was the protagonist. Lord Acton, a Catholic historian seldom pro-Catholic, judged her

> the most cultivated, thoughtful, and observant of women. She had been a Protestant, and retained for a long time the zeal of a convert. She was strongly opposed to Jansenists, and was much in the con-

fidence of the best men among the clergy. It was universally believed
that she promoted persecution and urged the King to revoke the Edict
of Nantes. Her letters are produced in evidence. But her letters have
been tampered with by an editor who was a forger and a falsifier.[7] *

Like Fénelon, Mme. de Sévigné, and nearly all Catholics at the time, she
approved the Revocation, but she used her influence—often successfully,
says the Protestant Michelet—to check the cruelty of the persecution.[8]

Lest a romantic tendency to idealize woman should color the picture
with roses, let us look at the Marquise through other prejudices. Saint-
Simon's ducal pride could never forgive the rise of the lowly *bourgeoise*
to be mistress of France:

> The distress and poverty in which she had so long lived had nar-
> rowed her mind, and abased her heart and her sentiments. Her feelings
> and her thoughts were so circumscribed that she was in truth always
> less even than Mme. Scarron. . . . Nothing was more repelling than
> this meanness [low origin] joined to a situation so radiant.[9]

Even so the Duke found some virtues amid her faults:

> Mme. de Maintenon was a woman of much wit, which the good
> company in which she had at first been merely suffered, but in which
> she soon shone, had much polished and ornamented with knowledge
> of the world, and which gallantry had rendered of the most agreeable
> kind. The various positions she held had rendered her flattering, in-
> sinuating, complacent, always seeking to please. The need she had of
> intrigues, those she had seen of all kinds, and been mixed up in for
> herself and for others, had given her the taste, the ability, and the
> habit of them. Incomparable grace, an easy manner, and yet measured
> and respectful, which, in consequence of her long obscurity, had
> become natural to her, marvelously aided her talents; with language
> gentle, exact, well expressed, and naturally eloquent and brief. Her
> best time, for she was three or four years older than the King, had been
> the dainty-phrase period—the superfine gallantry days. . . . She put
> on afterwards an air of importance, but this gradually gave place to
> one of devoutness that she wore admirably. She was not absolutely
> false by disposition, but necessity had made her so, and her natural
> flightiness made her appear twice as false as she was.[10]

---

* Cf. Jacques Boulenger, *The Seventeenth Century* (New York, 1920), 243: "It is evident
that she had nothing to do with the Revocation of the Edict of Nantes." And the *Encyclopaedia Britannica*, XIV, 693a: "The Revocation and the dragonnades have been unjustly
laid to her charge." Voltaire had long ago concluded likewise (*Works*, [New York, 1927]
XXIa-290).

Macaulay, from the pathos of distance, took a more chivalrous view; perhaps he felt that much could be forgiven in a woman who was both "eloquent and brief":

> When she attracted the notice of her sovereign she could no longer boast of youth or beauty; but she possessed in an extraordinary degree those more lasting charms which men of sense . . . prize most highly in a female companion. . . . A just understanding, an inexhaustible yet never redundant flow of rational, gentle, and sprightly conversation; a temper of which the serenity was never for a moment ruffled; a tact which surpassed the tact of her sex as much as the tact of her sex surpasses the tact of ours: such were the qualities which made the widow of a buffoon first the confidential friend, and then the spouse, of the proudest and most powerful of European kings.[11]

Finally, see her through the eyes of Henri Martin, a French historian of inadequately recognized excellence:

> There was a harmony of mind and manners between them [the Marquise and the King] which was destined to increase with age; and her regular, gentle, and serious beauty, heightened by rare natural dignity, was essentially fitted to please Louis. She loved *consideration* as he loved *glory;* like him reserved, circumspect, and yet full of attraction and grace, she had the same charm of conversation, and sustained this charm longer by the resources of a richer imagination and a more varied education. Like him she had the individuality of vigorous and self-seeking organizations, yet she was capable of lasting and solid, if not ardent, affections. She was at once less passionate and more constant than the King, who was to be, in friendship as in love, truly constant to her alone; but she had never known what it was to sacrifice to her feelings either her interests or her repose; contrary to Louis XIV, she was devoted in small things and devoid of generosity in great ones. . . . Her calm reflective, reasoning character, incapable of impulse and of illusion, aided her to defend a virture often besieged.[12]

In any case there must have been many admirable qualities in a woman whom so masterful a king could choose as his wife, and whom he trusted with cognizance of the most intimate affairs of state. Usually he met his ministers in her private room, in her presence and hearing; and though she maintained a discreet distance and silence, busying herself with her needlework, Louis "sometimes turned to her and asked her judgment"[13]—which he valued so highly that he called her *"Votre Solidité."* Skeptics called her "Madame de Maintenant" (Madame Now), presuming that she would

soon be joined or displaced by rivals; on the contrary, the King remained
her loving husband till his death.

Her influence grew with every year, and was as beneficent as her piety
would permit. She tried to moderate the King's extravagance, and to divert
him from war; hence the hostility of Louvois. She secured royal support
for charities—hospitals, convents, help for bankrupt nobles, dowries for
demoiselles.[14] None but good Catholics could win her recommendation for
office. She had vines or drapes drawn over the more vital nudities in the
art that decorated Versailles.[15] She changed St.-Cyr from a college to a
convent (1693), whose doors were henceforth closed to the world. She
herself became almost a nun in a palace; "with her shut-in life, spending
hours in solitude, she seemed to have one foot in a nunnery."[16]

The King began by laughing at her piety, he ended by imitating it this
side of humility. The priests about him rejoiced to see the regularity with
which he performed the rituals of devotion, but she understood him well;
the King, she said, "never misses a station of the cross, or a penance, but
he cannot understand the necessity of humbling himself and acquiring the
true spirit of repentance."[17] Pope Alexander VIII, however, was satisfied,
and congratulated Madame upon reforming the once antipapal Gallican.
Perhaps the decline of his physical energy after 1684, and his sufferings
from an anal fistula, furthered the King's piety by reminding him of his
mortality. On November 18, 1686, he submitted to a painful operation,
which he bore with class-conscious courage. For a time the anti-French
coalition rejoiced in the rumor that he was dying.[18] He survived; and when
he went to Notre Dame (January 30, 1687) to thank God for his cure, all
Catholic France hailed his recovery with festive joy.

"From that time," said Voltaire, "the King no longer went to the
theater."[19] The gaiety-in-dignity that had characterized the earlier half of
his reign gave way to a seriousness that sometimes neared austerity, but
permitted occasional excesses of bed and board.[20] Prompted by fatigue,
seconded by Maintenon, he reduced the parade and ceremony of the court,
and retired to a more private life, content with the domesticity to which
his wife had accustomed him. He was still extravagant in his expenditures
on palaces and gardens, still as proud as his scepter and as sensual as his
jowls. In March, 1686, he allowed an obsequious courtier, François
d'Aubusson, later Duc de La Feuillade, to erect on the Place des Victoires
a statue dedicated to him as "the immortal man"; we must add, however,
that when d'Aubusson wished to provide a votive lamp to be kept lighted
before the statue night and day, the King forbade this premature assumption of divinity.

An inner circle of devout aristocrats, led by the Duke and Duchess of
Chevreuse, the Duchesses of Beauvilliers and Mortemart, and the three

daughters of Colbert, formed around the King and his wife a *cordon sanitaire* of *dévots*, many of them sincerely religious, and some of them adopting the mystic quietism of Mme. Guyon. The world-famous hymn "Adeste Fideles" was composed by an unknown French poet about this time. The remainder of the court joined, only outwardly, in the new mood of the King. It abandoned its frivolity, went more frequently to Mass and Communion, less and less to the opera and the theater, which now rapidly declined from their heyday under Lully and Molière. Hunts, costly banquets and balls, and card-playing for high stakes went on, but in an atmosphere of moderation touched with reminiscent gloom. The roisterers and freethinkers of Paris hid their heads, waiting for revenge under an impatiently expected Regency. But the people of France rejoiced in the saintliness of their ruler, and silently bore, in death and taxes, the swelling levies of war.

II. THE GRAND ALLIANCE: 1689–97

Taxes rose even as prosperity declined. Colbert's massive system of state-regulated commerce and industry had begun to collapse before his death (1683). Partly it died through the drain of men from farms and factories to camps and battlefields. Chiefly it died through self-strangulation: governmental regulations stifled the growth that might have come under less supervision and restraint, more liberty to breathe, to experiment, and to err. Enterprise found itself bound by a maze of orders and penalties; the complex mechanism of economic activity, moved by the toilsome hunger of the many and the inventive greed of the few, groaned and stumbled under a mountain of rules, and threatened to halt. So soon as 1685 we hear the cry of *laissez faire*, sixty-five years before Quesnay and Turgot, ninety-one before Adam Smith. "The supreme secret," said one of Louis XIV's intendants, "is to allow complete freedom of trade. Never had manufacturers and commerce so wasted away in this realm as since we have taken it into our heads to build them up by the decrees of the state."[21] Other factors contributed to decay. Huguenots fleeing from persecution took with them their economic skills, and sometimes their savings too. Commerce suffered from the King's desire to conquer rather than to trade. Exports were balked by foreign tariffs retaliating against French import dues. The English and the Dutch proved to be better seamen and colonizers than the proud and impatient Gauls; the Compagnie des Indes failed. Taxes discouraged agriculture, and a dishonest currency confused and palsied finance.

The ministers who served Louis after the death of Colbert could not compare in ability with those whom the King had inherited from Richelieu and Mazarin. Colbert's son Jean Baptiste, the Marquis de Seignelay, received the ministries of commerce and marine; Claude Le Peletier took charge of finance, but was soon succeeded by Louis Phélypeaux, Seigneur de Pontchartrain; Louvois remained minister of war. The new men were awed by Louis XIV's accumulated glory and authority; they feared to make decisions, and the machine of state waited upon the burdened mind of the King. Only Louvois had a will of his own, and it was all for war— against the Huguenots, against the Netherlands, against any prince or people that stood in the path of expanding France. For Louvois had built the finest army in Europe; he had trained it to discipline and bravery, had equipped it with the latest weapons, and had taught it the gentle art of the bayonet.* How could such a force be fed, or keep its morale, unless it fought and won?

France looked upon that army with pride, all the rest of Europe heard of it with anger and dread. When, in May, 1685, Louis claimed part of the Elector Palatine's estate as the inheritance of the dead Elector's sister Charlotte Elisabeth, now Duchesse d'Orléans, the princes of the Empire wondered what demands would come next from the aggressive King. The tension rose when Louis in effect bound Cologne, Hildesheim, and Münster to France by securing the election of his nominees as their episcopal princes (1686). On July 6 the Catholic Emperor Leopold I and the Catholic Elector Maximilian II Emanuel of Bavaria joined the Protestant Great Elector of Brandenburg, the Protestant King Charles XI of Sweden, and the Protestant Stadholder William III of the United Provinces in forming the League of Augsburg for defense against any attack upon their territories or their powers. The Emperor was still busy with the retreating Turks, but their defeat at the "second Mohács" (1687) and at Belgrade (1688) freed the Imperial troops for action on the Empire's western front.

The King of France now made the pivotal mistake of his military career. The Stadholder had expected him to renew the assault upon Holland; instead, Louis decided to invade Germany before the Imperial forces could be assembled on his frontier. On September 22, 1688, he dispatched his main divisions toward the Rhine, with a characteristic speech to the twenty-seven-year-old Dauphin: "My son, in sending you to command my armies, I give you opportunities of making your merit known; show it to all Europe, so that when I come to die, no one will perceive that the King is dead."[23] On September 25 the French army swept into Germany. Within a month it took Kaiserslautern, Neustadt, Worms, Bingen, Mainz, and

---

* The *baïonette* was manufactured at Bayonne as early as 1500, but seems to have had its first large-scale use at Ypres in 1647.[22]

Heidelberg; on October 29 the strategic fortress of Philippsburg fell; on November 4 the triumphant Dauphin advanced to attack Mannheim.

Perhaps it was these victories that began the downfall of the King. For they committed him to a long war with a swelling host of foes; they freed Holland from fear of an early invasion; they induced the States-General of the United Provinces to give its consent and support to the conquest of England by William III. As soon as he had certified his power, William turned England from a dependency into an enemy of France, and pleaded with his new subjects co take their part in defending the political and religious liberty of Europe. Parliament hesitated; it suspected that William's main interest was to save Holland; and Holland was England's greatest commercial competitor. But again the victories of France strengthened William's plea.

Louvois had urged Louis to let him devastate the Palatinate in order to deprive the oncoming enemy of any local means of subsistence. Louis reluctantly agreed. In March, 1689, the French army sacked and burned Heidelberg and Mannheim, then Speyer, Worms, Oppenheim, parts of the archbishopric of Trier and the margraviate of Baden; nearly all the German Rhineland was ruined. Voltaire described the atrocity with the conscience of a good European:

> It was in the heart of winter. The French generals could not but obey; and accordingly they announced to the citizens of those flourishing and well-ordered towns, to the inhabitants of the villages, and to the masters of more than fifty castles, that they would have to leave their homes, which were to be destroyed by fire and sword. Men, women, old people, and children departed in haste. Some went wandering about the countryside; others sought refuge in neighboring territory, while the soldiery . . . burnt and sacked the country. They began with Mannheim and Heidelberg, the seats of the Electors; their palaces, as well as the houses of the common citizens, were destroyed. . . . For the second time this beautiful country was ravaged by Louis XIV; but the flames of the two towns and twenty villages which Turenne had burned in [the 1674 devastation of] the Palatinate were but sparks compared with this conflagration.[24]

From all Germany, the Netherlands, and England a cry rose for vengeance against the King of France. German pamphleteers denounced the French soldiers as Huns dead to any human feelings; they described Louis as a monster, a blasphemer, a barbarian worse than any Turk. German historians taunted the French people with having received their civilization from the Franks (i.e., Germans) and their universities from the Holy Roman emperors (i.e., Germans).[25] Pierre Jurieu, Huguenot exile in Holland, had already published there a powerful diatribe, *Les Soupirs de la France esclave* (*The Sighs of a France Enslaved*), branding Louis as a bigoted tyrant, and calling upon the French people to depose him and establish a constitutional monarchy. The French press replied with appeals to the citizens to hurl back these insults into the face of the enemy, and come to the rescue of their brave, beleaguered, beloved King. On May 12, 1689, England joined the Empire, Spain, the United Provinces, Denmark, and Savoy in the first Grand Alliance, which pledged itself to defend each of its members against external aggression. The war was now of Europe against France.

Louis responded by raising his armies to 450,000 men, his navy to 100,000 personnel; Europe had never seen such armed hosts before. The King melted down his silverware to help taxation pay the cost of these multitudes; he ordered all private individuals, and many churches, to do the same; and he allowed Pontchartrain to remint and depreciate the currency by ten per cent. The minister created new offices, restored old ones that had lapsed, and sold them to place-seekers infatuated with titles. "Every time your Majesty creates an office," he said to Louis, "God creates a fool to purchase it."[26]

Seignelay advised the King to order his fleet to cut off Ireland from England. It might have been done, for on June 30, 1690, Admiral de Tourville, with seventy-five ships, defeated a combined Dutch and English fleet at Beachy Head, off the East Sussex coast. But Louis sent only two thousand men to support James II in Ireland; a larger force might have won the battle of the Boyne (July 1, 1690), and might have kept England and its Dutch King too busy in Ireland to fight on the Continent. William III, by the victory, was free to go to Holland (1691) and lead English and Dutch troops against the French. In 1692 Louis attempted an invasion of England; a fleet from Toulon was ordered to sail north and join a fleet under Tourville at Brest; together they were to beat down any English resistance, and carry thirty thousand troops across the Channel. The squadron from Toulon, checked by a storm at Gibraltar, failed to reach Tourville, who had to fight unaided the united Dutch and English fleets; he was defeated in a decisive engagement off La Hogue, near Cherbourg (May 19, 1692), and the invasion was turned back. After this victory England remained mistress of the seas, free to capture from France one after another of her colonies. The Channel protected England till our time.

On land the French continued their victories, though at enormous cost in materials and men. In April, 1691, proud to anesthesia under the eyes of their King, they besieged and took strategic Mons. Louvois died on July 7, but Louis was not quite displeased at being freed from his aggressive minister of war; he proposed henceforth to guide all military policy himself. He observed an old French custom when he gave Louvois' post to Louvois' son, the amiable and tractable twenty-four-year-old Marquis de Barbezieux. In June, 1692, Louis led his troops in person to the capture of Namur; then, leaving the command to the Duc de Luxembourg, he returned to sip his glory at Versailles. William III surprised the Duke at Steenkerke in July; the French, at first routed, recovered order and courage under the direction and example of their ill but invincible general; once more the victory was French but dearly bought. There Philippe II d'Orléans, future regent of France but not yet fifteen, fought in the van, was wounded, and returned to fight again. There young Louis, Duc de Bourbon-Condé (grandson of the Great Condé), veteran of three sieges, and François Louis de Bourbon, Prince de Conti, and Louis Joseph Duc de Vendôme (great-grandson of Henry IV), and many others of the French nobility displayed the gallant bravery that made them, despite their idle extravagance in peace, the idols of their people in war, and exemplars even to the enemy. "What a nation you are!" exclaimed Count Salm, one of their prisoners. "There are no foes more to be feared in battle, and no more generous friends in victory."[27]

A year later the same French army, under the same general, defeated William at Neerwinden, near Brussels; here too the slaughter was immense —twenty thousand of the Allies, eight thousand of the French. No matter how often William was beaten, he soon appeared with a new army and fresh funds. In August, 1694, he recaptured Namur, and France discovered that after five years of bloodshed it had failed to conquer even the Spanish Netherlands. Other French armies won victories in Italy and Spain, but found it hard to hold their gains against foes and supplies rising replenished on every side. In July, 1694, an English fleet sailed to attack Brest; some friends in England (including, it was said, Marlborough himself[28]) had betrayed the plan to James II; so forewarned, the French lined the coast at Brest with guns, and the English were repulsed with heavy losses.

In January, 1695, the Maréchal de Luxembourg died, and Louis was left with only second-rate generals. Though its soil had been hardly touched by the Allies, France was feeling the burden of a new kind of war, in which no hired mercenaries fought the battles, but whole nations were conscripted for competitive massacre. Even while they acclaimed their generals, their heroes, and their victories, the French people, taxed as never before, were nearing exhaustion in body and spirit. In 1694 famine was added to destitution; in one diocese alone there were 450 deaths from starvation.[29] The national economy verged on collapse. Transportation was in chaos, for the repair of bridges and roads had almost stopped during the war. Internal trade was choked by tolls exacted at a hundred places

on rivers or land. Foreign commerce, already hampered by import and
export dues, was made almost impossible by enemy fleets and privateers.
Those who had lived by coastal fishing or trade were ruined. Hundreds
of towns were depleted of their resources by their support of troops
quartered upon them. Poverty, famine, disease, and war reduced the population of France from some 23,000,000 in 1670 to some 19,000,000 in
1700.[30] The province of Touraine lost a fourth of its people; its capital,
Tours, had only 33,000 left of the 80,000 who had peopled it under Colbert. Hear the reports of intendants from various parts of France toward
the end of the seventeenth century:

> This town, formerly rich and flourishing, is today without any
> industry. . . . There were formerly manufactures in this province, but
> today they have been abandoned. . . . The inhabitants formerly ob-
> tained much more from the soil than they do at present; agriculture
> was infinitely more flourishing twenty years ago. . . . Population and
> production have diminished by one fifth these last thirty years . . .[31]

In 1694 Fénelon, soon to be archbishop of Cambrai, addressed to Louis
XIV an anonymous letter which is one of the high-water marks of the
French spirit:

> SIRE, he who takes the liberty to write you this letter has no worldly
> interest. He writes through neither disappointment nor amibition,
> nor through desire to mingle in great affairs. He loves you without
> being known to you; he sees God in your person. . . . There is no
> evil that he would not gladly suffer to make you recognize the truths
> necessary to your salvation. If he speaks strongly to you, do not be
> surprised; it is only because truth is free and strong. You are not used
> to hearing it. People accustomed to be flattered mistake for resent-
> ment, bitterness, or excess that which is only pure truth. It would be
> treason to the truth not to show it to you. . . . God is witness that he
> who now speaks to you does so with a heart full of zeal, of respect, of
> fidelity and devotion for everything that concerns your real inter-
> est. . . .
> For some thirty years past your chief ministers have overturned all
> the ancient maxims of state to raise your authority to the utmost, be-
> cause it was in their hands. No one spoke any more of the state and its
> laws; they spoke only of the King and his good pleasure. They have
> extended your revenues and your expenditure without limit. They
> have raised you to the skies in order, they say, to efface the grandeur
> of all your predecessors combined, but actually they have impoverished
> all France to establish at the court a monstrous and incurable luxury.
> They have wished to elevate you upon the ruin of every class in the

state—as if you could be great while ruining all the subjects upon whom your greatness depends. True, you have been jealous of authority, . . . but in reality each minister has been master within the scope of his administration. . . . They have been hard, haughty, unjust, violent, and of bad faith. In domestic and foreign affairs they have known no rule but to threaten, remove, or destroy everything that opposed them. . . . They have accustomed you constantly to receive extreme praises verging upon idolatry, which, for your own honor, you should have rejected with indignation. They have made your name hateful—and the whole French nation unbearable—to neighboring peoples. They have retained none of our old allies, because they wanted only slaves. They have been the cause, through twenty years, of bloody wars . . . whose only motives were glory and vengeance. . . . All the frontiers that have been extended by war have been unjustly acquired. You have always wished to dictate peace, to impose conditions, instead of arranging them with moderation; that is why no peace has endured. Your enemies, shamefully struck down, have only one thought: to stand up again and unite themselves against you. Is it surprising? You have not even stayed within the limits of the peace terms that you so proudly dictated. In time of peace you have made war and immense conquests. . . . Such conduct has aroused and united all Europe against you.

Meanwhile your people, whom you should have loved as your children, and who have till now been so devoted to you, are dying of hunger. The cultivation of the earth is almost abandoned; the towns and the countryside are depopulated; all industry languishes, and no longer supports the workers. All commerce is destroyed. You have consumed half the wealth and vitality of the nation to make and defend vain conquests abroad. . . . All France is now but a vast hospital, desolate and without provisions. The magistrates are worn out and despised. . . . Popular uprisings, so long unknown, increase in frequency. Paris itself, so near you, is not exempt; its officials must tolerate the insolence of rebels, and spread money to appease them. You are reduced to the sad and disgraceful extremity of letting sedition go unpunished and therefore grow, or to slaughter without pity people whom you have driven to despair by snatching from them, through taxes for war, the bread that they toil to earn by the sweat of their brows. . . .

For a long time now the arm of God has been raised above you, but He is slow to strike because He pities a prince who all his life has been surrounded by sycophants, and because, also, your enemies are His. . . . You do not love God, you only fear Him, and with a slavish fear. . . . Your only religion consists in superstitions, in petty superficial observances . . . You love only your glory and your gain. You bring back everything to yourself, as if you were the god of the earth, and everything else were made to be sacrificed to you. On the contrary, God has put you in this world only for your people. . . .

We have hoped, Sire, that your Council would draw you away from the wrong road; but it has neither the courage nor the strength. At least Mme. de M. [Maintenon] and M. le D. de B. [Beauvilliers] might use the confidence you place in them to undeceive you; but their weakness and timidity are a disgrace and scandal before the world. . . . You ask, perhaps, Sire, what it is they should do. This: they should show you that you must humble yourself under the powerful hand of God, if you do not wish Him to humble you; that you must ask for peace, and expiate by that humiliation all the glory which you have made your idol . . . ; that to save the state you must as soon as possible restore to your enemies all that you cannot with justice retain.

Sire, he who tells you these truths, far from opposing your interests, would give his life to see you such as God wishes you to be; and he will not cease to pray for you.*

Fénelon did not dare send this letter directly to the King; he had it delivered to Mme. de Maintenon, perhaps hoping that though she might not show it to Louis, she would be moved by it, as reflecting the mood of the people, to use her influence for peace. She turned it over to Archbishop de Noailles, with this comment: "It is well written, but such truths only irritate or discourage the King. . . . We must lead him gently in the way he should go."[33] She had written in 1692: "The King knows the sufferings of his people, and he seeks all means of relieving them."[34] Doubtless she knew what reply he would have made to Fénelon: that the maxims of Christianity could not be used in dealing with states; that a generation of Frenchmen might justly be sacrificed if thereby the future of France could be ensured by natural and more defensible boundaries; and that an attempt to secure peace from the united and vengeful allies would open France to invasion and dismemberment. Caught in the conflict between the religion of brotherhood and the philosophy of war, Maintenon went more and more frequently to St.-Cyr, and sought in the fellowship of the young nuns the happiness that she had not found in power.[35]

Toward the close of the war Pierre Le Pesant, Sieur de Boisguillebert, *lieutenant général* of the region around Rouen, brought to Pontchartrain a plan to mitigate the economic chaos and public destitution. "Listen to me patiently," he urged the finance minister; "you will at first take me for a fool; then you will see that I deserve attention; finally you will be

---

* From the French text in Fellows and Torrey, *The Age of Enlightenment*, 91-95. The letter was first published by d'Alembert in 1787. Its authenticity remained doubtful until 1825, when a copy of it was found in Fénelon's own hand.[32]

satisfied with my ideas." Pontchartrain laughed at him and sent him away. The angry magistrate published his rejected manuscript as *Le Détail de la France* (1697). It denounced the multiplicity of taxes, which fell heavily upon the poor, lightly upon the rich; it condemned the Church for absorbing so much land and wealth; it excoriated the financiers whose sticky fingers clung to the taxes they collected for the King.[36] The argument was weakened by exaggerations, careless statistics, and erroneous views of French economic history before Colbert; but it was sharpened by insights that a government accustomed to regulate everything was not equipped to understand. Boisguillebert was among the first to reject the mercantilist delusion that the precious metals are in themselves wealth, and that the purpose of trade is to accumulate gold. Wealth, he held, is an abundance of goods and of the power to produce them. The ultimate wealth is land; the farmer is the base of the economy, and his ruin involves the ruin of all; ultimately all classes are bound in a community of interests. Every producer is a consumer, and any advantage that he secures as a producer is sooner or later annulled by his disadvantage as a consumer. Colbert's regulatory system was a mistake; it was hampering production and hardening the arteries of trade. The wisest way is to let men produce, sell, and buy freely within the state. Let the natural ambition and acquisitiveness of men operate with a minimum of legal restraint; so freed, they will invent new methods, enterprises, uses, tools; they will multiply the fertility of land, the products of industry, and the range and activity of commerce; and the resultant increase of wealth will provide new revenue for the state. Inequities will arise, but the economic process itself will remedy them. Here again was *laissez-faire*, two centuries before the heyday of free-enterprise capitalism in the Western world.

The King and his ministers might be forgiven if they felt that a war against half of Europe was no time to attempt so far-reaching an economic revolution. Instead of reforming the economy they raised taxes. In 1695 a poll or head tax was decreed, supposedly for every male adult in France; it was excused as temporary, it continued till 1789. In theory nobles, priests, and magistrates were to be subject to it; actually the clergy bought exemption with a moderate subsidy, while nobles and financiers found loopholes in the law. Every device was used to elicit money from the people. Lotteries were organized, offices were sold, the currency was debased, rich men were courted and prodded for loans. The King himself entertained the banker Samuel Bernard, luring millions from him by the hypnotism of the royal aura and charm. Despite taxes and devices old and new, the total revenue of the state in 1697 was 81,000,000 livres; the expenses were 219,000,000.

At last Louis confessed that his victories were bleeding the life from

France. He bade his diplomats come to terms with his enemies. Their skill in a measure rescued him. In 1696 they persuaded the Duke of Savoy to sign a separate peace. Louis let it be whispered that he would end his support of the Stuarts and would recognize William III as King of England. William himself was finding that money was dearer than blood. "My poverty is incredible," he complained, but Parliament grew more and more reluctant to pour out pounds to supply his troops. He required, as a preliminary to peace, the expulsion of James II from France. Louis refused, but he offered to restore nearly all the cities and terrain that his armies had won during the war. On September 20, 1697, the Peace of Ryswick (near The Hague) ended the "War of the Palatinate" with England, Holland, and Spain. France kept Strasbourg and Franche-Comté, and regained Pondicherry in India and Nova Scotia in America, but French tariffs were lowered to Dutch trade. On October 30 a supplementary peace was signed with the Empire. Both the Emperor and the King of France expected the early death of Charles II of Spain; and the chancelleries of Europe understood quite well that what had been signed was only a truce in preparation for a greater war, in which the prize would be the richest empire in the world.

III. THE SPANISH PROBLEM: 1698–1700

Charles II, childless, was nearing death; who would inherit his possessions, ranging from the Philippines through Italy and Sicily to North and South America? Louis claimed them, not only as the son of the eldest daughter of Philip III of Spain, but through the rights of his dead wife, Marie Thérèse, eldest daughter of Philip IV. True enough, Marie Thérèse at her marriage had renounced all claim to the Spanish throne; but that renunciation had been made on condition that the Spanish government pay 500,000 gold crowns to France as her dowry. Those crowns had never been paid, for Spain was bankrupt.

The Emperor Leopold I had counterclaims. He was the son of Maria Anna, younger daughter of Philip III; in 1666 he had married Margaret Theresa, younger daughter of Philip IV; and neither of these ladies had renounced her rights of possible succession to the Spanish crown. Always harassed by the Turks, Leopold, for the sake of peace with France, compromised his claims by signing with Louis XIV (January 19, 1668) a secret treaty for the eventual partition of the Spanish Empire. By this pact, says a British historian, "he virtually admitted the force of Louis XIV's contention that the French Queen's renunciation of her claims was invalid."[37]

When, by a second marriage, Leopold had a second son, he renewed his claims, but offered to resign them in favor of this new Archduke Karl.

England, the United Provinces, and the German principalities saw with dread the possibility that the vast realm of Spain would fall to France or to Austria, in either case toppling the balance of power: if Louis won, he would dominate Europe and imperil Protestantism; if Leopold won, the Emperor, holding the Spanish Netherlands, would threaten the Dutch Republic, and would soon reduce the autonomy of the German states. Commercial as well as dynastic interests were involved: English and Dutch exporters supplied most of the market for industrial goods in Spain and her colonies, and received considerable gold and silver in exchange; they were loath to let that trade become a French monopoly. "The preservation of the commerce between the kingdom of Great Britain and Spain," the British government stated in 1716, "was one of the chief motives that induced our two royal predecessors to enter the late, long, expensive war."[38]

Anxious to satisfy the merchants of both his native and his adopted lands, and to preserve the balance of power on the Continent, William III proposed to Louis that France waive her claim and agree with England that Spain, the Indies, Sardinia, and the Spanish Netherlands should be resigned to Joseph Ferdinand, Electoral Prince of Bavaria, grandson of Leopold; that the Dauphin of France should receive the Tuscan ports and the "Two Sicilies" (Italy south of the Papal States); while the Archduke Karl should be appeased with the duchy of Milan. Louis accepted the proposal, and signed with William (October 11, 1698) the First Treaty for the Partition of Spain. Leopold angrily rejected the plan. Hoping to keep the Spanish empire from such fragmentation, Charles II drew up a will (November 14, 1698) making the Electoral Prince of Bavaria his universal heir. The Prince confused the situation by dying (February 5).

Louis offered William a new division: the Dauphin to receive the Tuscan ports, the "Two Sicilies," and the duchy of Lorraine; the Duke of Lorraine to be compensated with Milan; all the rest of the Spanish empire, including America and the Spanish Netherlands, to go to the Archduke Karl. William and Louis signed this Second Partition Treaty on June 11, 1699. The United Provinces agreed to it, but Charles II protested against any dismemberment of his possessions, and the Emperor, hoping to win all for his son, supported the Spanish position and refused to accept the partition. Charles, as a Hapsburg, was inclined to leave all to the Archduke; as a Spaniard, however, he hated the Austrians, and as a Latin he preferred the French. As a fervent Catholic he asked the advice of the Pope; Innocent XII replied (September 27, 1700) that the best plan would be to bequeath the Spanish empire to a Bourbon prince, who should renounce any right to the throne of France; so Spain would retain its integrity. Apparently the

French diplomats outwitted the Austrians in Madrid as well as in Rome. Public opinion in Spain, alienated by the arrogant manners of its German Queen, agreed with the Pope. "The general inclination," reported the English ambassador at Madrid, "is altogether French."[39] On October 1 Charles signed the fateful will that bequeathed all Spain and its territories to the seventeen-year-old Philip, Duke of Anjou, second son of the Dauphin, with the proviso that the crowns of France and Spain should never be united under one head. On November 1 Charles died.

When news of the will reached Paris Louis was pleased but hesitant. He knew that the passage of Spain from the Hapsburgs to the Bourbons would be violently opposed by the Emperor, and that England and Holland would join in resistance. A German historian gives Louis credit, at this juncture, for pacific aims:

> It would be unjust to say of Louis XIV that his intention had been from the beginning to throw over the Partition Treaty so soon as a will favorable to his House should be in his hands. Even when he was sure of such a will, while King Charles was still alive, he ordered his ambassador in Holland to assure the Pensionary that it was his intention to adhere to his engagements, rather than accept any offers that might be made to him. In addition to this, he still continued his efforts to obtain the accession of the Court of Vienna to the Treaty of Partition.[40]

On October 6 Louis sent an urgent appeal to the Emperor to accept that Second Treaty of Partition.[41] Leopold refused. Louis henceforth considered the treaty void.

Immediately after the death of Charles, the Spanish Junta, or Regency, dispatched a courier to Paris to notify Louis that his grandson would be accepted as King of Spain as soon as he came and took the oath to observe the laws of the realm. The Spanish ambassador at Paris was instructed, in case of a French refusal, to bid the courier hasten to Vienna and submit the same offer to the Archduke;[42] in any case the Spanish empire must not be partitioned. On November 9 Louis called the Dauphin, his Chancellor Pontchartrain, the Duc de Beauvilliers, and the Marquis de Torcy, foreign minister, to a council in the apartment of Mme. de Maintenon, and asked their advice. Beauvilliers pleaded for a rejection of the Spanish offer as sure to lead to war with the Empire, England, and the United Provinces, and he reminded the King that France was in no condition to face such a coalition. Torcy argued for acceptance; war, he held, was inevitable in any event; Leopold would fight both the Partition Treaty and the will; besides, if the offer should be rejected by the King it would certainly be welcomed by the Emperor, and France would again be surrounded by that same cordon—Spain, north Italy, Austria, and the Spanish Netherlands—which during the last two hundred years it had cost France so much blood to break. Better go to war for a just cause—the will—than in an attempt to enforce the partition of Spain against the desire of its government and its people.[43]

After three days of further deliberation, Louis announced to the Spanish envoys his acceptance of the will. On November 16, 1700, he presented the Duke of Anjou to the court assembled at Versailles. "Gentlemen," he said, "you see here the King of Spain. His descent called him to that crown; the deceased King so ordered it in his testament; the whole [Spanish] nation desired it, and earnestly entreated me to give my assent. Such was the will of Heaven; I have fulfilled it with joy." And to the young monarch he added, "Be a good Spaniard—that is now your first duty; but remember that you were born a Frenchman, and maintain unity between the two nations; this is the way to make them happy, and to preserve the peace of Europe."[44] The Spanish Regency proclaimed Philip at Madrid, and all sections of Spain and her dominions soon declared their consent. One government after another recognized the new King: Savoy, Denmark, Portugal, the United Provinces, England, several Italian and German states; even the Elector of Bavaria—who thought his son had been poisoned by the Emperor—was among the first princes to offer recognition. The crisis seemed surmounted, and the century-long enmity between Spain and France seemed peacefully healed. The Spanish ambassador at Versailles knelt in homage to his new sovereign, and uttered famous words that Voltaire mistakenly attributed to Louis XIV: "*Il n'y a plus de Pyrénées*" (There are no more Pyrenees).[45]

IV. THE GRAND ALLIANCE: 1701–2

Philip V, beginning the Spanish Bourbons, was "quietly and cheerfully received in Spain," wrote Lord Chesterfield, "and was acknowledged as king of it by most of those powers who afterwards joined in an alliance to dethrone him."[46] But the Emperor Leopold felt that this virtual union of France and Spain, if allowed to continue, would be a disaster for the house of Hapsburg, so long accustomed to rule both the "Holy Roman" and the Spanish empires. Reflecting his resentment, pamphleteers roused and expressed public sentiment in Austria by pointing out that Charles II had not been of sound mind when he bequeathed Spain to her ancient foe; indeed, they claimed, a post-mortem showed the King's brain and heart grievously infected with disease; therefore his testament was null and void, and the Spanish dominions belonged to Leopold by the unrenounced rights of his mother and his wife. Leopold urged his former allies—Holland and England—to join him in denying or withdrawing recognition of Philip V, even if this meant war.

The leader of the United Provinces at this time was Antonius Heinsius, who had been chosen grand pensionary after William's departure for England. In earlier days, as Dutch envoy to France, he had been threatened with arrest by Louvois in violation of diplomatic immunity, and he had never forgotten that indignity. Now aged fifty-nine, he lived in a modest house at The Hague, cherished books, walked daily to his office, worked ten hours a day, and served as a living challenge of bourgeois simplicity and republican government to luxurious aristocrats and absolute kings. In November, 1700, under instruction by the States-General, he sent to Louis XIV a memorial entreating him to reject the will of Charles II as vitally injurious to the Emperor, and to return to a policy of partition. Louis replied (December 4, 1700) that his acceptance of the will had been made necessary by the Emperor's repeated rejection of a partition plan, and by the certainty that if France refused the Spanish offer the Emperor would accept it.

The actions of Louis heightened Europe's fear of French power. On February 1, 1701, he caused the Paris Parlement to register a royal decree reserving the eventual rights of Philip and his line to the crown of France. This did not necessarily mean that Louis looked toward the union of France and Spain under one king; it was probably intended to ensure an orderly succession to the French throne in case all prior heirs to it should be deceased; in that emergency Philip could surrender the Spanish crown for that of his native land, and so continue the Bourbon line without interruption. But a further procedure of the King justified a hostile interpretation. A treaty with Spain had confirmed the right of the Dutch to guard against the invasion of Holland by maintaining armed garrisons in some "barrier towns" of the Spanish Netherlands. On February 5, by an understanding between Louis and the Elector of Bavaria, who was then governing the Spanish Netherlands, French troops entered these towns and ordered the Dutch garrisons to depart. The Spanish ambassador at The Hague informed the States-General that this had been done by the desire of the Spanish government. The States-General, protesting, submitted, but Heinsius agreed with William III that the Grand Alliance against France must be renewed.

William took the position that the Second Partition Treaty had been an agreement between himself and Louis; that it had remained valid whether Leopold signed it or not; and that French acceptance of the Spanish bequest had broken a solemn pact. Parliament, however, was loath to resume the expensive struggle with France. When the French government notified

England of Philip V's succession to the Spanish throne, William resigned himself to congratulating his "very dear brother the King of Spain" on his "happy accession"[47]—thus giving formal recognition to the new Bourbon regime (April 17, 1701).[48] But as the immense consequences of the Franco-Spanish union came more clearly into view—as the occupation of Flanders by French troops brought Louis XIV closer to Holland, and his possession of Antwerp gave him control over English commerce using that port—the English began to realize that the issue was not merely between Bourbon and Hapsburg, nor only between Catholicism resurgent and Protestantism at bay, but between English and French domination of the seas, of Europe's colonies, and of world trade. In June, 1701, without declaring war, Parliament engaged to sustain William in all alliances that he might contract for the purpose of limiting the exorbitant power of France. To implement this aim it sanctioned the recruiting of 30,000 seamen and voted £2,700,000. In response to an appeal from the States-General William ordered twenty ships and 10,000 men to Holland, and in July he himself crossed to The Hague.

The Emperor, claiming the entire Spanish dominion, was already at war. In May, 1701, he sent an army of 6,000 horse and 16,000 foot to seize the possessions of Spain in north Italy. He placed in command a young prince who was destined to rival Marlborough himself as a general—Eugene of Savoy. Eugene's grandfather was Charles Emmanuel, Duke of Savoy; his father, Prince Eugène Maurice, settled in France as Count of Soissons; his mother was Olympe Mancini, one of the alluring nieces of Mazarin. Eugene himself, aged twenty (1683), asked Louis XIV to give him command of a regiment; refused as too young, he renounced France and entered the Imperial service. He joined with Sobieski in the relief of Vienna and the pursuit of the Turks; he was wounded in the capture of Buda, and again in the siege of Belgrade; he led the Imperial army to its decisive victory over the Turks at Senta (1697). He had every charm except those of features and physique. An unsympathetic Gaul described him as "this ugly little man with a turned-up nose over an upper lip too short to conceal his teeth";[49] but Voltaire recognized in him "the qualities of a hero in war and a great man in peace, a mind imbued with a high sense of justice and pride, and a courage unshaken in the command of armies."[50] Now, aged thirty-eight, he guided his forces over the Alps, outmaneuvered the French detachments there, and, with successive victories over Catinat and Villeroi, won for the Emperor nearly the whole duchy of Mantua (September, 1701), long before the War of the Spanish Succession had been declared.

Meanwhile diplomacy had prepared a decade of massacre. In August Spain granted to France the lucrative *asiento*—the "contract" to supply slaves to the Spanish colonists in America; evidently France intended to use her overriding influence in Spain to capture the commerce of its possessions on three continents. On September 7 the representatives of England, the United Provinces, and the Empire signed the Treaty of The Hague, forming a second Grand Alliance. Article Two declared it essential to the peace of Europe that the Emperor obtain satisfaction for his rights to the Spanish succession, and that England and the United Provinces be made secure in their dominions, navigation, and trade. The treaty promised to the Emperor the Spanish possessions in Italy and the Low Countries, but it left open the possibility that Philip V might be recognized as King of Spain. The contracting states pledged themselves to undertake no separate negotiations, to sign no separate peace, to prevent the union of the French and Spanish crowns, to bar French trade from the Spanish colonies, and to defend and maintain any conquests that England or the United Provinces should make in the Spanish Indies.[51] Two months were granted France to accept these terms; failing this, the signatories would declare war.

Louis met the challenge with characteristic pride. He proclaimed himself in honor bound to defend the will of Charles II, and the resolve of the Spanish people that their Empire should not be dismembered. Too confident in the power and righteousness of his cause, he appeared at the bedside of the dying James II, and comforted him with the promise that he would recognize and uphold James III as King of England. When the father died Louis kept the promise; we do not know whether this was a "magnanimous action" (as a magnanimous English historian called it[52]), or a surrender to the tearful pleas of the widow,[53] or a military measure designed to divide England into supporters of William and Jacobite supporters of a second Stuart restoration. In any case the War of the Spanish Succession was also a war for the English succession, even for the English soul; for a restored Stuart might resume the attempt to make England Catholic. Though France felt that the action of the allies violated the recognition that nearly all of them had given to Philip V as King of Spain, most of England felt that Louis had violated the Treaty of Ryswick, in which he had recognized William III as King of England; and the recognition of James III was resented as a presumptuous interference in English affairs. A clause was added to the terms of the Grand Alliance binding its signatories to make no peace with France till William should have received satisfaction for the insult offered him by Louis' action. In January, 1702, Parliament attainted James III—i.e., declared him a traitor and an outlaw. At the same time, by a majority of one, it passed an Abjuration Act requiring all Englishmen to repudiate the "Pretender," and to swear fealty to William III and his heirs. On March 8, 1702, William died, aged fifty-two, too soon to know that he had welded an alliance that for half a century would determine the map of Europe. On May 15 the Emperor, the States-General of the United

Provinces, and the Parliament of England simultaneously declared war upon France.

V. THE WAR OF THE SPANISH SUCCESSION: 1702–13

Practically all of Europe west of Poland and the Ottoman Empire was involved. The Alliance was joined by Denmark, Prussia, Hanover, the episcopate of Münster, the elecorates of Mainz and the Palatinate, and some minor German states; to these in 1703 were added Savoy and Portugal. Together they mustered 250,000 men, and assembled a navy far superior to the French in numbers, equipment, and leadership. France had now 200,-000 men in her armies, but these were distributed along many fronts in the Rhine region, Italy, and Spain. Her only allies were Spain, Bavaria, Cologne, and, for a year, Savoy. Spain was a liability, requiring French armies to defend it; and the Spanish colonies were at the mercy of the Dutch and English fleets.

We must not lose ourselves in the royal game of human chess that ensued, sanguinary almost beyond precedent. Now came the masterly and gory campaigns of Marlborough and Eugene of Savoy. Perhaps never since Caesar had the genius of war been so combined with the art of diplomacy as in Marlborough: skilled in the strategy of planning operations and moving armies, in the tactics of manipulating infantry, cavalry, and artillery with rapidity of perception and decision, as the needs of battle changed; and yet also patient and tactful in dealing with the governments behind him, the personalities around him, even with the enemies that looked to him as a statesman conscious of realities and possessed of authority. He was sometimes merciless, and often unscrupulous; he poured out the blood of his soldiers in any quantity needed for success; and he communicated with James II and III to gild his own fate should the Stuarts return to power. But he was the organizer of victory.

Louis XIV, perceiving that the whole splendor of his reign now hung in the balance, and that the dispute over Spain had become a contest for continents, called upon France to send him her sons and her gold. By 1704 he had 450,000 men under arms—as many as all his foes combined.[54] Hoping to bring the costly conflict to an early issue, he ordered his main force to march through friendly Bavaria and attack the final citadel of the enemy, Vienna itself, which even the Turkish hordes had failed to take. An insurrection in Hungary occupied Imperial forces in the east, and left their capital almost denuded of defense. While a French army under Villeroi was supposed to chain Marlborough to the Low Countries, French troops under Marsin and Tallard joined those of the Bavarian Elector and pressed farther and farther into Austria. The Emperor again, as in 1683, fled from Vienna, knowing that his capture by the enemy would be a disaster to the allies' cause.

In this crisis Marlborough, against the pleas of the Dutch States-General, but with the secret consent of Heinsius, decided to risk the invasion of Holland by Villeroi, and march night and day from the North Sea to the Danube (May to June, 1704) to save Vienna. Pretending to seek a crossing of the Moselle, he moved southward along the river, luring Villeroi into a parallel movement on the other side. Then suddenly, at Coblenz, he turned east, crossed the Rhine on a floating bridge, marched down to Mainz, crossed the Main to Heidelberg, crossed the Neckar to Rastadt. Now he effected critical junctions with reinforcements from Holland, with an Imperial army under Eugene of Savoy, and with another under Margrave Louis William I of Baden-Baden. The French and the Bavarians were astonished to find Marlborough so far from the positions where Villeroi had been expected to contain him. Marsin, Tallard, and the Elector of Bavaria gathered 35,000 infantry and 18,000 cavalry between Lutzingen and Blindheim (Blenheim) on the left bank of the Danube. There, on August 13, 1704, Marlborough and Eugene, with 33,000 foot and 29,000 horse, engaged them in what France tries to forget as the battle of Höchstädt, and what England celebrates as the victory of Blenheim. Marlborough's superior cavalry overwhelmed the French center and drove Tallard's routed army into Blenheim, where its surviving 12,000 men surrendered, Tallard himself being captured; then Marlborough's horsemen rode to the support of hard-pressed Eugene on the right, and helped him force Marsin into an orderly retreat. The human loss was heavy: 12,000 casualties on the allied side, 14,000 on the Franco-Bavarian. The surrender of twenty-seven battalions of infantry and twelve squadrons of mounted men shattered the reputation of French arms. The Elector of Bavaria fled to Brussels; Bavaria was occupied by an Imperial army; nearly three hundred square miles of terrain were cleared of French troops. Leopold returned in safety to his capital.

On August 4 an Anglo-Dutch fleet marked another date in history by capturing the barren Rock of Gibraltar. The English turned it into a fortress that for two centuries made them masters of the Mediterranean. Not knowing that it had been decided by these two victories, the war continued for nine more years. An English fleet took Barcelona (October 9, 1705); an allied army protected a revolt of Catalonia against Philip V, and established the Archduke Karl at Madrid as Charles III (June 25, 1706). But the sight of Austrians and Englishmen ruling the country roused the Spanish from their unworldly torpor; even the ecclesiastics urged them on to resistance. The peasants armed themselves as best they could, and cut the allied line of communications between Barcelona and Madrid; the English Duke of Berwick, James Fitzjames, natural son of James II, led a Franco-Spanish force from the west, recovered Madrid for Philip V (September 22), and drove the Archduke and his English "heretics" back to Catalonia.

Meanwhile Marlborough, after overcoming political obstacles in London and The Hague, assembled an army of 60,000 English, Dutch, and Danes, and marched into the Spanish Netherlands. On May 23, 1706, he met the main French army of 58,000 men under Villeroi at Ramillies, near Namur. In the ecstasy of battle, and forgetting that generals must die in bed, he dashed to the front, and was knocked from his horse. His aide, while helping the Duke to another mount, had his head blown off by a cannon ball. Marlborough recovered, realigned his troops, and led them to another bloody victory; his army suffered 5,000 casualties, the French 15,000. He advanced through negligible resistance to the capture of Antwerp, Bruges, and Ostend; there he had a direct line of communications with England, and was only twenty miles from France. Marshal Villeroi, sixty-two, retired to his estate in grief, but with no reproof from the King, who told him sadly, "There is no more luck at our age."[55]

Everywhere now, except in Spain, the French were in peril or retreat. In Vienna Joseph I, twenty-seven, succeeded (1705) his father as emperor, and gave vigorous support to his generals. Eugene of Savoy drove the French from Turin (1706), then from all Italy (1707). By the Convention of Milan the duchies of Milan and Mantua became parts of the Austrian Empire, and the rule of the Mantuan Gonzagas, begun in 1328, came to an end. The kingdom of Naples, so long a viceroyalty of Spain, fell in its turn to Austrian arms, though it continued to be formally a papal fief. The Papal States remained papal by permission of the Emperor, whose German troops had marched through them against the will of the helpless Pope.[56] Venice and Tuscany preserved a precarious independence.

Louis XIV was a changed man. The pride of power had almost left him, but he maintained the calm dignity of his state. In 1706 he offered the allies terms of peace that five years earlier they might have been glad to accept: Spain to be surrendered to Archduke Karl; Philip to be content with Milan, Naples, and Sicily; barrier towns and fortresses to be restored to Dutch control in the Spanish Netherlands. The Dutch were disposed to negotiate; the English and the Emperor refused. Louis turned wearily to recruiting new armies and levying new taxes; even baptisms and marriages, to be legal, had now to pay a tax. The population of France, desperate in poverty, baptized its own children and married without priestly aid, though the offspring of such unions were officially branded as illegitimate.[57]

Revolts broke out at Cahors, in Quercy, in Périgord; peasant mobs seized town offices and seignorial châteaux. Living skeletons (squelettes) of starving people clamored at the gates of Versailles for bread; the Swiss Guard drove them away. Placards appeared on Paris walls warning Louis that there were still Ravaillacs in France—i.e., men willing to kill a king.[58] The new taxes were abandoned.

Early in 1707 the Marquis de Vauban, whose military engineering had been a vital element in French victories a generation earlier, published in his seventy-fourth year a proposal for a juster tax—*Projet d'une dîme royale*. He described the misery of France: "Nearly a tenth of the people are reduced to beggary, and of the other nine tenths the majority are more in a condition to receive charity than to give it. . . . It is certain that the evil has been pushed to excess, and that if no remedy is applied the people will fall into such destitution that they will never recover." He reminded the King that "it is the lower class of the people which, by their labor and industry, and their contributions to the royal treasury, enrich the sovereign and his realm"; yet "it is that class which now, through the demands of war and the taxation of its savings, is reduced to living in rags and crumbling cottages while its lands lie fallow" in the absence of its recruited sons.[59] To relieve these most productive classes Vauban, adopting some ideas from Boisguillebert, proposed to abolish all existing taxes and replace them with a graduated income tax, exempting no class; landowners to pay five to ten per cent, workers not more than three and a half per cent. The state should maintain its monopoly on salt, but custom dues were to be charged only at national frontiers.[60]

Saint-Simon describes the book and its reception:

> It was full of information and figures, all arranged with the utmost clearness, simplicity, and exactitude. But it had a grand fault. It described a course which, if followed, would have ruined an army of financiers, of clerks, of functionaries of all kinds: it would have forced them to live at their own expense, instead of at the expense of the people, and it would have sapped the foundation of those immense fortunes that are seen to grow up in such short time. This was enough to cause its failure. All the people interested in opposing the work set up a cry. . . . What wonder, then, that the King, who was surrounded by these people, listened to their reasons, and received with very ill grace Maréchal Vauban when he presented his book to him.[61]

Louis reproached him as a dreamer whose plan would have upset the finances of the kingdom in the crisis of war. A decree in council (February 14, 1707) ordered the book to be seized and exposed in a pillory. Six weeks later, disheartened by his disgrace, the old Marshal died. The King uttered some words of tardy regret: "I lose a man well affected to my person and to the state."[62]

The taxes and the war continued. In August, 1707, Victor Amadeus II,

Duke of Savoy, who had begun as an ally of France, joined Eugene of Savoy and an English fleet in besieging Toulon by land and sea. If this fell they planned to attack Marseilles; if that too fell, France would be shut out from the Mediterranean. A new French army was raised, and was sent to thrust back the invaders; it succeeded; but in that campaign much of Provence was laid waste. In 1708 the King mustered an army of 80,000 men, placed it under Marshal Vendôme and the Dauphin's son, the popular Duke of Burgundy, and dispatched them to stop the allied advance in Flanders. Marlborough and Eugene, likewise with 80,000 men, met them at Audenaarde on the Scheldt (July 11, 1708). The French were overwhelmed, losing 20,000 in dead or wounded, and 7,000 prisoners. Marlborough wished to push on to Paris, but Eugene prevailed upon him to besiege Lille first, lest its garrison cut the allies' line of communications and supplies. Lille was taken, but after a siege of two months, and at the cost of 15,000 men.

Louis felt that France could fight no more. The misery of his people was made crueler by the severest winter in their memory (1708–9). For two months all rivers froze; even the seas froze along the coasts, so that heavily laden carts moved safely on the ocean ice.[63] Almost all vegetation was killed, including the hardiest fruit trees, and all grain in the earth. Nearly all newborn infants died in that terrible season;[64] one exception was the King's great-grandson, the future Louis XV, born to the Duke of Burgundy on February 15, 1709. Famine followed in the spring and summer. Monopolists cornered the bread supply and kept the price high; Saint-Simon, usually hostile to the King, reported that Louis himself was accused of sharing in the profits of the monopolists;[65] but, says Henri Martin, "history is too deliberate to take the gloomy imagination of Saint-Simon without distrust."[66] The situation was saved by importing twelve million kilograms of grain from the Barbary States and elsewhere, and by planting barley as soon as the ground thawed.[67]

Humbled by the defeats of his armies and the calamities of his people, Louis sent the Marquis de Torcy to The Hague (May 22, 1709) to ask for peace. Torcy was instructed to offer the surrender of all the Spanish empire to the allies, to cede Newfoundland to England, to restore the barrier towns to the Dutch, and to end all French support of the Jacobite cause. He tried to bribe Marlborough, but failed.[68] On May 28 the allies presented to Torcy an ultimatum requiring not only that Spain and all its possessions be yielded to the Archduke, but that if Philip should not have quit Spain within two months, the French army was to join the allies in expelling him; else (they argued) France would be left free to reorganize its fighting power while the allies were engaged in the Peninsula. Louis replied that it was too much to ask of him that he should use force to expel his own grandson from a Spain that had just rallied to Philip's support. "If I must fight [on]," he said, "it shall be with my enemies rather than with my children."[69]

The demands of the allies aroused the resentment of France. Recruits came more willingly to the colors, if only to find food; nobles sent their silver to the mint; and French vessels, eluding the British and the Dutch, brought from America bullion worth thirty million francs. A fresh army was raised, 90,000 strong, and was placed under Marshal Villars, who had never yet been defeated by the allies. At the same time Marlborough assembled 110,000 men. The two swarms met at Malplaquet (just within the French frontier against Belgium) in the bloodiest battle of the eighteenth century. Marlborough lost 22,000 men in this his final victory; the French suffered 12,000 casualties, including the brave Villars, who, fifty-six years old, charged at the head of his troops, and was borne from the field with one knee shattered by a cannon ball. The French retreated in good order, but the allies went on to capture Mons. "God Almighty be praised," wrote Marlborough to his Sarah; "it is now in our power to have what peace we please."[70]

It seemed so, for France had apparently made her last effort. How could she find another army among her depleted families, or feed it from her abandoned fields? Agriculture, industry, transport, commerce, finance— all were in chaos, all were caught in a spreading disintegration that invited the occupation and dismemberment of the country by its advancing foes. The King, once the "God-given" idol of his people, was losing their affection, even their respect. He had always shunned Paris, remembering the hostile horde of the Fronde; the city had resented his long resentment; and the wit and insults of pamphlets and placards had stung his absolutist pride.[71] Men wondered why, amid the destitution of France, the halls of Versailles were still thronged by idle, costly, gambling courtiers; though the King and his wife were now pious and subdued, "the expenses and personnel of the court remained undiminished to the last."[72] Some breadless Parisians chanted a revised version of the Lord's Prayer, sparing neither Louis nor his mate nor his new minister of war and finance:

> Our Father which are at Versailles, thy name is no longer hallowed, thy kingdom is no longer so great, thy will is no longer done on earth or on the sea. Give us our bread, which on every side we lack. Forgive our enemies who have beaten us, and not thy generals who allowed them to do so. Do not succumb to all the temptations of La Maintenon, but deliver us from Chamillard.[73]

"The King," mourned Madame, "is reproached for all his expenditure; they would like to do away with his horses, his dogs, his servants . . . They would like to stone me because they imagine that I never tell him anything unpleasant, for fear of grieving him."[74]

The nobles were still loyal to the King who entertained and protected them, but their patriotism flagged when, as a last resort, he asked for a tenth of their income (1710). The universal *dîme* that Vauban, three years before, had proposed as a substitute for all other taxes, was now added to all other taxes; and the poor had the consolation of seeing the hated tax-gatherers enter the homes, and scrutinize the accounts, of the rich. The King was loath to invade gilded privacy, but his confessor, Father Le Tellier, assured him that, in the opinion of the doctors of the Sorbonne, "all the wealth of his subjects was his, and when he took it he only took what belonged to him."[75] The upper middle classes likewise suffered some cooling of martial ardor when interest ceased to be paid on government bonds. The recoinage and debasement of the currency "brought some profit to the King," reported Saint-Simon, "but ruin to private people, and a disorder to trade which completed its annihilation."[76] Great bankers like Samuel Bernard declared bankruptcy, disrupting nearly all business in Lyons. "All was perishing step by step; the realm was entirely exhausted; the troops were not paid, though no one could imagine what was done with the millions that came into the King's coffers."[77]

In March, 1710, Louis again asked the allies for peace. He offered to acknowledge the Archduke as King of Spain, to give no assistance to Philip, even to contribute funds to aid in dethroning him. He would surrender Strasbourg, Breisach, Alsace, Lille, Tournai, Ypres, Meenen, Furnes, and Maubeuge to the Allies. They offered him not peace, but a two months truce; in that period Louis, with French forces unaided by any other, was to expel Philip from Spain; if he failed to achieve this within the truce period, they would resume the war.[78] Louis published these terms to his people, who agreed with him that they were impossible.

Somehow France raised new armies. When the Archduke again invaded Spain with a force of Austrian and English troops, and fought his way to oust Philip once more from Madrid, Louis sent to his grandson 25,000 men under the Duc de Vendôme. Aided by Spanish volunteers, the Duke defeated the invaders at Brihuega and Villaviciosa (December, 1710), and so definitely restored Philip to his throne that Spain remained Bourbon till 1931.

Meanwhile the political wind was veering in England. In 1706 Queen Anne had written: "I have no ambition . . . but to see an honorable peace, that whenever it please God I shall die I may have the satisfaction of leaving my poor country and all my friends in peace and quiet."[79] Anne had been kept to the war policy by Marlborough's fiery Duchess; that influence now waned; in 1710 the Queen dismissed Sarah, and openly sided with the

Tories. The merchants, manufacturers, and financiers had profited from the war,[80] and had supported the warmaking Whigs; the landowners had lost as war raised taxes and inflated the currency; they seconded the Queen's longing for peace. On August 8 she dismissed Godolphin, Marlborough's right-hand man; Harley headed a Tory ministry; England turned toward peace.

In January, 1711, the English government secretly sent to Paris a French priest, the Abbé Gaulthier, who had long resided in London. Gaulthier went to Torcy at Versailles. "Do you want peace?" he asked. "I come to bring you the means of concluding it, independently of the Dutch."[81] Negotiations proceeded slowly. Suddenly, at the surprisingly early age of thirty-two, Joseph I died (April 17, 1711); the Archduke became the Emperor Charles VI; the English and the Dutch, who had promised him all Spain, found that their costly victories were confronting them with a new Hapsburg Empire as vast as that of Charles V, and as dangerous to Protestant nations and liberties. The English government now offered Louis recognition of Philip V as King of Spain and the Spanish possessions in America on relatively moderate conditions: securities against the union of France and Spain under one crown; barrier fortresses to protect the United Provinces and Germany from any future French invasion; the restitution of French conquests; the recognition of the Protestant succession in England, and the expulsion of James III from France; the dismantling of Dunkirk; the confirmation of Gibraltar, Newfoundland, and the Hudson Bay region as English property; and the transfer from France to England of the right to sell slaves to Spanish America. Louis assented with minor modifications; England notified The Hague that she favored making peace on these terms; the Dutch agreed to them as a basis for negotiation, and plans were made for a peace congress at Utrecht. Marlborough, who had found war profitable, was dismissed (December 31, 1711) and was replaced by James Butler, second Duke of Ormonde, with instructions not to hazard English troops in battle until further orders should be received.

While the congress assembled at Utrecht (January 1, 1712), Eugene of Savoy, considering the English terms of peace to be a betrayal of the Imperial cause, continued the war. Day after day he pushed forward against the line of defenses built by the industrious Villars. On July 16 Ormonde was notified by London that England and France had signed an armistice, and that consequently his English regiments must be withdrawn to Dunkirk. These obeyed, but most of the Continental contingents under Ormonde's command denounced the English as deserters, and placed themselves under Eugene's command. The Prince had now some 130,000 men, Villars 90,000; but on July 24 the alert Maréchal pounced upon a detachment of 12,000 Dutch at Denain (near Lille), and annihilated it before Eugene could come to its aid. The Prince retired across the Scheldt to reorganize his unwieldy army; Villars advanced to capture Douai, Le Quesnoy, and Bouchain. Louis and France took heart. These were the only French victories of the war on the northern front, but with the successes of Vendôme in Spain they gave new strength to the French negotiators at Utrecht.

After fifteen months of protocol, punctilio, and agrument, all parties to the war except the Emperor signed the Peace of Utrecht (April 11, 1713). France yielded to Britain all that she had promised in the preliminaries, including that precious *asiento*, or slave-trade monopoly, which lies like a badge of shame upon that age; and the ancient enemies made mutual concessions on import dues. The Dutch restored to France Lille, Aire, and Béthune, but kept control of all the Netherlands until peace should be made with the Empire; meanwhile the Elector of Bavaria was to hold Charleroi, Luxembourg, and Namur. Nice was returned to the Duke of Savoy. Philip V retained Spain and Spanish America; he refused, then (July 13) consented, to cede Gibraltar and Minorca to England. Eugene of Savoy fought on, bitter against the British for signing a separate peace; but the Imperial treasury was empty, his army was reduced to 40,000 troops, and Villars was advancing against him with 120,000 men. Finally he accepted the invitation of Louis XIV to meet Villars and work out terms of peace. By the Treaty of Rastatt (March 6, 1714) France retained Alsace and Strasbourg, but she restored to the Empire all French conquests on the right bank of the Rhine, and she recognized the replacement of Spanish by Austrian rule in Italy and Belgium.

So the treaties of Utrecht and Rastatt achieved little more than what diplomacy might have peacefully achieved in 1701. After thirteen years of slaughter, impoverishment, and devastation, these pacts settled for twenty-six years the map of Europe, as the Treaties of Westphalia had settled it for a generation after the Thirty Years' War. In both cases the task was to establish a balance of power between Hapsburg and Bourbon; it was done. Between France and England in America a balance was established which would hold till the Seven Years' War (1756–63).

The chief losers in the sanguinary contest for the Spanish succession were Holland and France. The Dutch Republic had gained terrain on land and lost power on the sea; it could no longer match England in shipping, seamanship, resources, or war; its victory exhausted it and began its decline. France too was weakened, almost fatally. She had kept her nominee on the throne of Spain, but she had failed to preserve his empire intact; and for this tarnished triumph she paid with a million lives, the loss of her sea power, and the temporary collapse of her economic life. Not till Napoleon would France recover from Louis XIV, only to repeat his tragedy.

The victors of the war were Austria on the Continent, and England everywhere else. Austria now held Milan, Naples, Sicily, and Belgium; she would be the strongest force in Europe until the accession of Frederick the Great (1740). England thought more of controlling the sea than of expanding on land; she acquired Newfoundland and Nova Scotia, but valued more her mastery in the avenues of trade. She compelled France to lower her tariffs, and to dismantle the fort and port of Dunkirk, which had been a threat to English shipping. With Gibraltar in Spain and Port Mahon in Minorca, England held the Mediterranean in fief. These gains made no spectacular show in 1713; their results would be written in the history of the eighteenth century. Meanwhile the Protestant faith and succession had been made secure in Britain against everything but the birth rate.

A chief product of the war was the intensification of nationalism and international hate. Each nation forgot its gains and remembered its wounds. Germany would never forgive the double devastation of the Palatinate; France would not soon forget the unprecedented slaughter in Marlborough's victories; Spain suffered every day the indignity of Gibraltar in alien hands. Each nation bided its time for revenge.

Some gentle souls, thinking that Europe was a continent of Christians, dreamed of a substitute for war. Charles Castel, Abbé de Saint-Pierre, accompanied the French delegation to Utrecht. Returning, he published his *Projet ... pour rendre la paix perpetuelle* (1713)—a plan for perpetuating the new-found peace. Let the nations of Europe confederate in a league of nations with a permanent congress of representatives, a senate for the arbitration of disputes, a code of international law, a combined military force for action against any rebellious state, the reduction of each national army to six thousand men, and the establishment of uniform measures and currency throughout Europe.[82] Saint-Pierre expounded his scheme to Leibniz, who, no longer so sure that this was the best of all possible worlds, sadly reminded the abbé that "some sinister fate was always interposing betwixt man and the attainment of his happiness."[83] Man is a competitive animal, and his character is his fate.

VI. TWILIGHT OF THE GOD: 1713-15

Judged in terms of his time, Louis XIV was not the ogre that hostile historians have made him; he merely applied on a larger scale, and for a while with invidious success, the same methods of absolute rule, territorial expansion, and martial conquest that characterized the conduct, or the aspirations, of his enemies. Even the cruelty of his armies in the Palatinate had a precedent in the sack of Magdeburg (1631), and an epilogue in the massacres of Marlborough. Louis had the distinction of living so long that the Furies could revenge upon him in person, rather than upon his children, the sins of his pride and power.

History has not withheld from him some admiration for the courage and dignity that he showed in defeat, and it has allowed him some pity in the disasters that almost destroyed his children simultaneously with his armies and fleets. In 1711 his only legitimate son, "Le Grand Dauphin" Louis, died, leaving the King with two grandsons—Louis, Duke of Burgundy, and Charles, Duke of Berry. The younger Louis developed good qualities under Fénelon's tutelage, and became the solace of the monarch's old age. In 1697 he married Marie Adélaïde of Savoy, whose beauty, wit, and charm reminded the King of Madame Henrietta and his happy youth. But on February 12, 1712, this gay spirit succumbed to spotted fever at the age of twenty-six. Her devoted husband had refused to leave her sickbed; he contracted the disease, and died of it on February 18, aged twenty-nine, only a year after his father's death. Their two sons caught the infection from them; one died on March 8, at the age of eight; the younger survived, but remained so weak that no one dreamed that he would live to rule France as Louis XV till 1774. If this frail lad should collapse, the heir to the throne would be Charles, Duke of Berry, but Charles died in 1714.

There was another possible successor—Philip V of Spain, younger son of Le Grand Dauphin; but half of Europe was pledged to keep him from uniting the two crowns. Next in line was Philippe, Duc d'Orléans, grandson of Louis XIII, and nephew and son-in-law of the King. But this Philippe had a laboratory, carried on experiments in chemistry, and was therefore accused, in public gossip, of having poisoned the Duke and Duchess of Burgundy and their eldest son. The physicians who performed the three autopsies were divided on the question whether poison had been used. Philippe, furious under these suspicions, asked the King to give him a public trial; Louis believed him innocent, and refused to lay upon him the burden and stigma of such an ordeal.

Should these lines of succession fail, a last resort remained. The King had legitimized his illegitimate sons, the Duke of Maine and the Count of Toulouse. Now (July, 1714) he issued an edict—which the Parlement of Paris registered without protest—that, in default of princes of the blood royal, these quondam bastards should inherit his throne; and a year later, to the horror of Saint-Simon and other nobles, he decreed that their rank should be equal in law to that of the legitimate princes.[84] Their mother, Mme. de Montespan, was dead, but their foster mother, the wife of the

King, loved them as her own, and used her influence to promote them in honors and power.

It was amid these problems and bereavements that Louis faced the final crisis of the war. When he bade farewell to Villars, who was leaving to meet the advance of Eugene on the Belgian front, the King, now seventy-four years old, for a moment broke down. "You see my condition, Maréchal," he said. "There have been few examples of what has happened to me—to lose in the same month my grandson, my granddaughter, and their son, all of great promise, and all most tenderly loved. God is punishing me. I have well deserved it; I shall suffer less in the next world." Then, recovering himself, he continued: "Let us leave my domestic misfortunes, and see how to avert those of the kingdom. I confide to you the forces and salvation of the state. Fortune may be adverse to you. If this misfortune should happen to the army you command, what would be your feeling as to the course which I should take in person?" Villars did not reply. "I am not surprised," said the King, "that you do not answer me at once. While waiting for you to tell your idea I will tell you mine. I know the reasonings of the courtiers; almost all wish me to retire to Blois if my army should be defeated. For my part, I know that armies of such size are never so much defeated that the greater part could not fall back upon the Somme, a river very difficult to cross. I should go to Péronne or St.-Quentin, gather there all the troops I might have, make a last effort with you, and we would perish together or save the state."[85]

Villars' victory at Denain cheated the King of such a heroic death. He survived that battle by three years, and the peace by two. Excepting the anal fistula, long since cured, his health had maintained itself reasonably well for seventy years. He ate immoderately, but never grew fat; he drank moderately; he let few days pass without some active exercise in the open air, even in the severe winter of 1708-9. It is difficult to know if he might have lived longer with fewer physicians, and whether the purges, bleedings, and sweats to which they treated him were a greater curse than the ills they were intended to relieve. One doctor in 1688 gave him so strong a laxative that it acted on him eleven times in eight hours; after which, we are told, he felt somewhat fatigued.[86] When Rigaud in 1701 made the painting that stands so prominently in the Louvre, he pictured Louis as still insolent with strength and victory and robes of state, black wig concealing white hairs, and swollen cheeks attesting appetite. Seven years later Coysevox, in the splendid statue in Notre Dame, showed him kneeling in prayer, but still more conscious of royalty than of death. Perhaps the artists clothed him in prouder pride than he felt, for in those failing years and mounting trials he had learned to accept reproof humbly, at least from Maintenon.[87] He became as a child in the hands of the fanatic Jesuit Le

Tellier, who had succeeded Père La Chaise as the King's confessor in 1709; "the inheritor of Charlemagne asked pardon for his sins from the son of a peasant."[88] The strong infusion of Catholic faith and piety that he had received from his mother rose to the surface now that passion ebbed and glory lost its glow. Rumor said that the King, in the surge of his devotion, had become a Jesuit affiliate in 1705; and in his final illness it added that he took the fourth vow as a full member of the Society of Jesus.[89]

In January 1715 he lost his famous appetite, and ailed so visibly that in Holland and England wagers were laid that he would not survive the year.[90] Reading news dispatches to this effect, he laughed them off, and continued his routine of conferences, reception of ambassadors, reviewing of troops, hunting, and ending the day with his seventy-nine-year-old wife, the faithful, weary Maintenon. On August 2 he drew up a will naming the Duke of Maine guardian to Louis XV, and appointing the Duke to a Council of Regency that should rule France till the boy should come of age. On August 12 sores broke out on his leg. They became gangrenous and malodorous; fever set in, and he took to his bed. On August 25 he wrote a codicil to his will, naming Philippe d'Orléans chief of the Council of Regency, with a deciding vote in a division. To two magistrates who received this document, he said, "I have made a testament; they"—presumably Mme. de Maintenon, the Duke and Duchess of Maine, and their supporters—"insisted that I should make it; I had to purchase my repose; but as soon as I am dead it will be of no account. I know too well what became of my father's testament."[91] That confused will was destined to write a chapter in French history.

He died like a king. After receiving the sacraments he addressed to the ecclesiastics at his bedside a supplementary and unwelcome confession:

> I am sorry to leave the affairs of the Church in their present state. I am perfectly ignorant in the matter, as you know; and I call you to witness that I have done nothing therein but what you wanted, and have done all that you wanted; it is you who will answer before God for all that has been done. I charge you with it before him, and I have a clear conscience. I am but a know-nothing who have left myself to your guidance.[92]

To his courtiers he said:

> Gentlemen, I ask your pardon for the bad example I have set you. I have to thank you sincerely for the manner in which you have served me, and the fidelity you have always shown to me. I ask you to give the same zeal and devotion to my grandson which you have given me. He is a child who may have to suffer much. I hope you will all work

for union, and that should anyone fail in this, you will seek to call him back to his duty. I perceive that I am allowing my feelings to overcome me, and am causing you to do the same. I ask your pardon for all this. Farewell, gentlemen; I trust that you will sometimes remember me.[93]

He asked the Duchess of Ventadour to bring in his grandson, now five years old. To him (according to the Duchess) he said:

My child, you are going to be a great king. Do not imitate me in the taste that I have had for building or for war; try, on the contrary, to be at peace with your neighbors. Render to God what you owe Him; recognize the obligations you are under to Him; make Him honored by your subjects. Try to comfort your people, which unhappily I have not done. . . . My dear child, I give you my benediction with all my heart.[94]

To two servants whom he saw in tears: "Why do you weep? Did you think me immortal?"[95] And reassuringly to Mme. de Maintenon: "I thought it would be harder to die than this. I assure you it is not a very terrible business; it does not seem to me difficult at all."[96] He asked her to leave him, as if he were aware that after his death she would be a lost soul in a class-conscious court. She retired to her apartment, divided its furniture among her attendants, and departed for St.-Cyr, which she would never leave till her death (1719).

The King had spoken too confidently; he suffered a long night of agony before he died, September 1, 1715. Of his seventy-seven years he had spent seventy-two on the throne—the longest reign in European history. Even before his last hour the courtiers, anxious for their berths, had deserted him to pay homage to Philippe d'Orléans and the Duke of Maine. Some Jesuits gathered around the corpse and performed the ceremonies customary for one who had died in their order.[97] News of the King's death was received by the people of Paris as a blessed deliverance from a reign that had lasted too long and had seen its glory tarnished with misery and defeat. Very little pomp was wasted on the funeral that bore to St.-Denis, on September 9, the corpse of the most famous king in the history of France. "Along the route," said Voltaire, "I saw small tents set up where people drank and sang and laughed."[98] Duclos, then eleven, later recalled that "many persons were unworthy enough to pour forth insults on seeing the hearse pass by."[99]

At that moment the Parisians remembered his faults with a blinding clarity. They felt that his love of power and glory had led France to the brink of ruin. They resented the pride that had destroyed local self-government and had centered all rule in one unchallengeable will. They mourned the millions of francs and the thousands of lives that had been spent in beautifying Versailles; and they cursed the neglect with which the King had treated his turbulent capital. A small minority rejoiced that the persecution of the Jansenists might now cease; a large majority still applauded the expulsion of the Huguenots. In retrospect it was clear that the invasion of Holland in 1672, the invasion of Germany in 1688, and the hasty seizure of the barrier towns in 1701 had been massive blunders, raising a swarm of foes around France. But how many Frenchmen had condemned those invasions, or spoken a word of conscience about the double devastation of the Palatinate? The nation had been as guilty as its King, and held against him not his crimes but his defeats. Barring a few priests, it had not condemned his adulteries, and had shown no enthusiasm over his moral reform, his piety, or his fidelity to his morganatic wife. It forgot now that for many years he had graced his power with courtesy and humanity;[100] that, until the demon of war enthralled him, he had supported Colbert in developing French industry and trade; that he had protected Molière against the bigots, and Racine against the cliques; that his extravagant expenditures had not merely indulged his own luxury but had dowered France with a new heritage of art.

What the people felt most keenly and most justly was the immense price they had paid in blood and treasure for the glory that had now collapsed in the death of the King and the desolation of France. There was hardly a family in the nation that had not lost a son to the wars. Population had been so reduced that the government now gave rewards to the parents of ten children. Taxes had stifled economic incentive, war had blocked the avenues of commerce and had closed foreign markets to French goods. The state was not only bankrupt; it owed three billion francs.[101] The nobility had lost its usefulness by being turned from local administration to prancing about the court; it had shone only in its expensive dress and its martial bravery. A new nobility had been created by wholesale auction of titles to rich commoners; in one year alone the King had ennobled five hundred persons at six thousand livres each; so some ancient families fell vassal to the sons of serfs. As war became no distant contest of mercenaries and gladiators but a pervasive and exhausting test of national resources and economies, the middle classes rose in number and power to challenge the baron and the priest, and financiers prospered amid the general decline. For in modern states the men who can manage men manage the men who can manage only things; and the men who can manage money manage all.

In judging Louis XIV we must remember Goethe's humane dictum that a man's vices are usually the influence of his time, while his virtues are his own; or, as the Romans had put it with characteristic brevity, *vitium est temporis potius quam hominis*—"vices are of the age rather than of the man."[102] The absolutism, the persecuting bigotry, the lust for glory, the taste for war, were in him as a child of his time and his Church; his generosity and magnanimity and courtliness, his appreciation and stimulation of literature and art, his ability to carry a burden of concentrated and far-reaching government, were his personal qualities, making him every inch a king. In Louis XIV, Goethe wrote, nature produced the consummate specimen of the monarchical type, and, in so doing, exhausted herself and broke the mold.[103] "Louis XIV," said Napoleon, "was a great king. It was he who raised France to the first rank among nations. What king of France since Charlemagne can be compared with him in all his aspects?"[104] "He was," in Lord Acton's judgment, "by far the ablest man who was born in modern times on the steps of a throne."[105] He waged devastating wars, indulged his pride extravagantly in building and luxury, stifled philosophy, and taxed his people to destitution; but he gave France an orderly government, a national unity, and a cultural splendor that won for her the unquestioned leadership of the Western world. He became the head and symbol of his country's supreme epoch; and France, which lives on glory, has learned to forgive him for almost destroying her to make her great.

Bibliographical Guide

to editions referred to in the notes

AARON, R. J., *John Locke*. Oxford University Press, 1937.
ABBOTT, G. F., *Israel in Egypt*. London, 1907.
ACTON, JOHN EMERICH, LORD, *Lectures on Modern History*. London, 1950.
ADDISON, JOSEPH, and others, *The Spectator*, 8v. New York, 1881.
ALDIS, JANET, *Mme. Geoffrin: Her Salon and Her Times*. New York, 1905.
ALLEN, J. W., *English Political Thought, 1603 to 1660*. London, 1938.
ALTAMIRA, R., *History of Spain*, tr. Muna Lee. New York, 1955.
———, *History of Spanish Civilization*. London, 1930.
ANDRADE, E. N., *Sir Isaac Newton*. London, 1954.
ARNOLD, MATTHEW, *Essays in Criticism*, 1st series, New York, n.d.
ASHTON, JOHN, *Social Life in the Reign of Queen Anne*. London, 1883.
AUBREY, JOHN, *Brief Lives*, ed. O. L. Dick. Ann Arbor, Mich., 1957.

BABBITT, IRVING, *The Spanish Character and Other Essays*. Boston, 1940.
BACON, FRANCIS, *Essays*. Everyman's Library.
———, *Philosophical Works*, ed. J. M. Robertson. London, 1905.
BAIN, F. W., *Christina, Queen of Sweden*. London, 1890.
BARINE, ARVÈDE, *La Grande Mademoiselle*, tr. Helen Meyer. New York, 1902.
BARON, S. W., *Social and Religious History of the Jews*, 3v. New York, 1937.
BAYLE, PIERRE, *Dictionnaire historique et critique*, 16v. Paris, 1820.
———, *Selections from the Dictionary*. Princeton, N. J., 1952.
BEARD, CHARLES, *Port Royal*, 2v. London, 1873.
BEARD, MIRIAM, *History of the Business Man*. New York, 1938.
BEBEL, AUGUSTE, *Woman under Socialism*. New York, 1923.
BELL, AUBREY, *Portuguese Literature*. Oxford, 1922.
BELL, E. T., *Men of Mathematics*. New York, 1937.
BENOIST, LUCIEN, *Coysevox*. Paris, 1930.
BERKELEY, GEORGE, *A New Theory of Vision, and Other Writings*. Everyman's Library.
BESANT, SIR WALTER, *London in the Time of the Stuarts*. London, 1903.
BEVAN, EDWYN, and SINGER, CHARLES, *The Legacy of Israel*. Oxford, 1927.
BIDNEY, DAVID, *The Psychology and Ethics of Spinoza*. Yale University Press, 1940.
BISHOP, A. THORNTON, *Renaissance Architecture of England*. New York, 1938.
BISHOP, MORRIS, *Life and Adventures of La Rochefoucauld*. New York, 1951.
BLOMFIELD, SIR REGINALD, *Three Hundred Years of French Architecture: 1494-1794*. London, 1936.
BOILEAU-DESPRÉAUX, NICOLAS, *Poèmes*. Vol. VII of *Poètes français*. Paris, 1913.
BOISSIER, GASTON, *Madame de Sévigné*, tr. M. B. Anderson. Chicago, 1888.
BOSSUET, JACQUES, *Oraisons funèbres et sermons*. Paris: Librairie Larousse, n.d.
BOSWELL, JAMES, *Life of Samuel Johnson*. Modern Library.

BOULENGER, JACQUES, *The Seventeenth Century*. New York, 1920.
BOURGEOIS, ÉMILE, *Le Grand Siècle: Louis XIV*. Paris, 1896.
BOWEN, MARJORIE, *William [III] Prince of Orange*. London, 1928.
BOWLE, JOHN, *Hobbes and His Critics*. London, 1951.
———, *Western Political Thought*. London, 1954.
BOYLE, ROBERT, *The Sceptical Chymist*. Everyman's Library.
BRANDES, GEORG, *Main Currents in Nineteenth-Century Literature*, 6v. New York, 1905.
———, *Wolfgang Goethe*. New York, 1924.
BRERETON, GEOFFREY, *Jean Racine*. London, 1951.
BRETT, G. S., *History of Psychology*. London, 1953.
BREWSTER, SIR DAVID, *Memoirs of the Life, Writings, and Discoveries of Sir Isaac Newton*, 2v. Edinburgh, 1855.
BRINTON, SELWYN, *The Gonzaga—Lords of Mantua*. London, 1927.
BROCKELMANN, CARL, *History of the Islamic Peoples*. New York, 1947.
BROCKWAY, WALLACE, and WEINSTOCK, HERBERT, *The Opera*. New York, 1941.
BROCKWAY, WALLACE, and WINER, BART, *A Second Treasury of the World's Great Letters*. New York, 1941.
BROWNE, LEWIS, *The Wisdom of Israel*. New York, 1945.
BROWNE, SIR THOMAS, *Religio Medici*. Everyman's Library.
BRUNSCHVIGG, LEON, *Spinoza et ses contemporains*. Paris, 1951.
BRYANT, SIR ARTHUR, *King Charles II*. London, 1955.
———, *Samuel Pepys*. New York, 1934.
BUCKLE, HENRY THOMAS, *Introduction to the History of Civilization in England*, 4v. New York, 1913.
BUNYAN, JOHN, *Entire Works*, 4v. London: Virtue & Co., n.d.
———, *Pilgrim's Progress*. Everyman's Library.
BURNET, GILBERT, BISHOP, *History of His Own Times*. Everyman's Library.
BURNEY, CHARLES, *General History of Music*, 2v. New York, 1957.
BURY, J. B., *The Idea of Progress*. New York, 1955.
BUTLER, SAMUEL, *Hudibras*. Cambridge University Press, 1905.
BUTTERFIELD, H., *The Origins of Modern Science*. New York, 1951.

CALVERT, A. F., *Sculpture in Spain*. London, 1912.
Cambridge History of English Literature, 14v. London, 1910.
Cambridge History of Poland, 2v. Cambridge University Press, 1950.
Cambridge Modern History, 12v. New York, 1907.
CAMPBELL, THOMAS J., *The Jesuits*. New York, 1921.
CARLYLE, THOMAS, *Oliver Cromwell's Letters and Speeches*, 4v. New York, 1901.
CARTWRIGHT, JULIA, *Madame: A Life of Henrietta, Daughter of Charles I, Duchess of Orléans*. New York, 1901.
CASSIRER, ERNST, *The Philosophy of the Enlightenment*. Princeton, N. J., 1951.
———, *The Platonic Renaissance in England*. Austin, Tex., 1953.
CASTIGLIONI, ARTURO, *A History of Medicine*. New York, 1941.
Catholic Encyclopedia. New York, 1912.
CHESTERFIELD, PHILIP STANHOPE, EARL OF, *Letters to His Son*. New York, 1901.
CHURCHILL, SIR WINSTON, *History of the English-speaking Peoples*, 3v. London, 1957.

————, *Marlborough: His Life and Times*, 2v. London, 1947.

CLARK, BARRETT, *Great Short Biographies of the World*. New York, 1928.

CLARK, G. N., *The Seventeenth Century*. Oxford University Press, 1929.

COLLINS, ANTHONY, *A Discourse of Free-thinking*. London, 1713.

COULTON, G. G., *Life in the Middle Ages*, 4v. Cambridge University Press, 1930.

COXE, WILLIAM, *History of the House of Austria*, 3v. London, 1847.

CRUTTWELL, MAUD, *Madame de Maintenon*. London, 1930.

CUNNINGHAM, W. C., *Western Civilization in Its Economic Aspects*, 2v. Cambridge University Press, 1900–1902.

D'ALTON, REV. E. A., *History of Ireland*, 6v. Dublin, n.d.

DAMPIER, SIR WILLIAM, *History of Science*. Cambridge University Press, 1948.

DAY, CLIVE, *History of Commerce*. London, 1926.

DAY, LILLIAN, *Ninon: A Courtesan of Quality*. New York, 1957.

DEFOE, DANIEL, *Journal of the Plague Year*. Everyman's Library.

————, *Moll Flanders*. Everyman's Library.

DESNOIRESTERRES, GUSTAV, *Voltaire et la société française au xviiie siècle*, 8v. Paris, 1871.

DEWEY, JOHN, and others, *Studies in the History of Ideas*, 2v. Columbia University Press, 1935.

DILLON, EDWARD, *Glass*. New York, 1907.

DISRAELI, ISAAC, *Curiosities of Literature*, 3v. London: Frederick Warne & Co., n.d.

DRYDEN, JOHN, *Essays*. Everyman's Library.

————, *Poems*. New York: Cassell's National Library, n.d.

DUBNOW, S. M., *History of the Jews in Russia and Poland*, 3v. Philadelphia, 1916.

DUCLOS, CHARLES P., *Secret Memoirs of the Regency*. New York, 1910.

DUNNING, W. A., *History of Political Theories from Luther to Montesquieu*. New York, 1905.

EDWARDS, H. S., *Idols of the French Stage*, 2v. London, 1889.

Encyclopaedia Britannica, 14th ed.

EVELYN, JOHN, *Diary*, 2v. Everyman's Library.

FAGUET, ÉMILE, *Dix-huitième Siècle: Études littéraires*. Paris: Boivin et Cie, n.d.

————, *Dix-septième Siècle: Études et portraits littéraires*. Paris: Boivin et Cie., n.d.

————, *Literary History of France*. New York, 1907.

FELLOWS, OTIS, and TORREY, NORMAN, *The Age of the Enlightenment*. New York, 1942.

FÉNELON, FRANÇOIS DE SALIGNAC DE LA MOTHE-, *Les Aventures de Télémaque*. Paris, 1869.

FERGUSSON, JAMES, *History of Modern Styles of Architecture*. London, 1873.

FERVAL, CLAUDE, *Life of Louise de La Vallière*. New York, 1914.

FINKELSTEIN, LOUIS, ed., *The Jews: Their History, Culture, and Religion*, 2v. New York, 1949.

FIRTH, SIR CHARLES, *Oliver Cromwell and the Rule of the Puritans in England.* Oxford University Press, 1953.
FISCHER, KUNO, *Descartes and His School.* London, 1887.
FLINT, ROBERT, *History of the Philosophy of History.* New York, 1894.
FLORINSKY, MICHAEL T., *Russia: A History and an Interpretation,* 2v. New York, 1955.
FOX, GEORGE, *Journal.* Everyman's Library.
FOXE-BOURNE, H. R., *Life of John Locke,* 2v. London, 1876.
FRANCE, ANATOLE, *Nicolas Fouquet.* New York, 1930.
FRANCKE, KUNO, *History of German Literature.* New York, 1901.
FROUDE, J. A., *Bunyan.* New York: Harper, n.d.
———, *Short Studies on Great Subjects,* 2v. Everyman's Library.
FÜLOP-MILLER, RENÉ, *The Power and Secret of the Jesuits.* New York, 1930.
FUNCK-BRENTANO, FRANTZ, *L'Ancien Régime.* Paris, 1926.
FUNK, F. X., *Manual of Church History,* 2v. London, 1910.

GARDINER, S. R., *History of the Commonwealth and Protectorate,* 3v. London, 1901.
GARLAND, H. B., *Lessing.* Cambridge University Press, 1949.
GARNETT, RICHARD, *History of Italian Literature.* New York, 1898.
GARRISON, F., *History of Medicine.* Philadelphia, 1929.
GOOCH, G. P., *English Democratic Ideas in the Seventeenth Century.* Cambridge University Press, 1927.
GOSSE, EDMUND, ed., *A Volume of Restoration Plays.* Everyman's Library.
GRAETZ, H., *History of the Jews,* 6v. Philadelphia, 1891.
GRAMONT, PHILIBERT DE, *Memoirs of the Comte de Grammont* (by Anthony Hamilton). London, 1876.
GREEN, J. R., *Short History of the English People,* 3v. London, 1898.
GROOM, ARTHUR, *History of Money.* New York, 1958.
Grove's Dictionary of Music and Musicians, 5v. New York, 1927.
GUÉRARD, ALBERT, *Life and Death of an Ideal: France in the Classical Age.* New York, 1928.
GUIZOT, F., *History of Civilization,* 3v. London, 1898.
———, *History of France,* 8v. London, 1872.

HALLAM, HENRY, *Constitutional History of England,* 3v. New York, 1862.
———, *Introduction to the Literature of Europe in the Fifteenth, Sixteenth, and Seventeenth Centuries,* 4v. in 2. New York, 1880.
HARDING, T. SWANN, *Fads, Frauds, and Physicians.* New York, 1930.
HARDY, EVELYN, *The Conjured Spirit: Swift.* London, 1949.
HARRINGTON, JAMES, *Oceana,* in *Ideal Commonwealths.* New York, 1901.
HAUSER, ARNOLD, *Social History of Art,* 2v. New York, 1952.
HAVENS, GEORGE, *The Age of Ideas.* New York, 1955.
HAZARD, PAUL, *The European Mind: The Critical Years (1680–1715).* Yale University Press, 1953.
HEARNSHAW, F. J., *Social and Political Ideas of Some English Thinkers of the Augustan Age.* New York, 1950.
History Today. London.

HOBBES, THOMAS, *Elements of Law, Natural and Political.* Cambridge University Press, 1928.
———, *Leviathan.* Everyman's Library.
———, *The Metaphysical System of Thomas Hobbes,* ed. Mary W. Calkins. Chicago, 1913.
HOLZKNECHT, KARL, *Backgrounds of Shakespeare's Plays.* New York, 1950.
HOOVER, HERBERT, and GIBBONS, H. A., *Conditions of a Lasting Peace.* New York, 1939.
HUME, DAVID, *Enquiries concerning the Human Understanding and concerning the Principles of Morals.* Oxford University Press, 1955.
———, *Essays, Literary, Moral, and Political.* London: Ward, Lock & Co., n.d.
———, *History of England,* 5v. Philadelphia: Porter & Coates, n.d.
HUME, MARTIN, *Spain: Its Greatness and Decay.* Cambridge University Press, 1899.
HÜRLIMANN, MARTIN, *Germany.* London, 1957.
HUTCHINSON, F. E., *Milton and the English Mind.* New York, 1948.

JAMES, B. B., *Women of England.* Philadelphia, 1908.
Jewish Encyclopedia. New York, 1901.
JOHNSON, SAMUEL, *Lives of the Poets,* 2v. Everyman's Library.
JORDAN, G. J., *The Reunion of the Churches: A Study of G. W. Leibnitz and His Great Attempt.* London, 1927.
JOSEPH, H. W., *Lectures on the Philosophy of Leibniz.* Oxford, 1949.
JUSTI, CARL, *Diego Velázquez and His Times.* London, 1889.

KAYSER, RUDOLF, *Spinoza.* New York, 1946.
KESTEN, HERMANN, *Copernicus and His World.* New York, 1945.
KING, JAMES E., *Science and Rationalism in the Government of Louis XIV.* Baltimore, 1949.
KIRBY, R. S., *Engineering in History.* New York, 1956.
KIRKPATRICK, RALPH, *Domenico Scarlatti.* Princeton, N. J., 1953.
KLUCHEVSKY, V. O., *History of Russia,* 3v. London, 1912.
KRONENBERGER, LOUIS, *Marlborough's Duchess.* New York, 1958.

LA BRUYÈRE, JEAN DE, *Characters.* New York, 1929.
LACROIX, PAUL, *The Eighteenth Century in France.* London: Bickens & Sons, n.d.
LA FARGE, HENRY, *Lost Treasures of Europe.* New York, 1946.
LA FAYETTE, MME. MARIE MADELEINE DE, *La Princesse de Clèves.* Paris: Classiques Larousse, n.d.
LA FONTAINE, JEAN DE, *Choix de contes et nouvelles.* Paris: Librairie Gründ, n.d.
———, *Fables,* Paris, 1813.
LANE-POOLE, STANLEY, *Story of Turkey.* New York, 1895.
LANFREY, P., *Histoire politique des papes,* 2v. in 1. Paris, 1873.
LANG, ANDREW, *History of Scotland,* 4v. Edinburgh, 1902.
LANGE, F. E., *History of Materialism,* 2v. in 1. New York, 1925.
LA ROCHEFOUCAULD, FRANÇOIS, DUC DE, *Moral Reflections and Maxims.* London, 1930.
LEA, H. C., *History of the Inquisition in Spain,* 4v. New York, 1906.

LECKY, W. E., *History of England in the Eighteenth Century*, 8v. London, 1888.

———, *History of the Rise and Influence of the Spirit of Rationalism in Europe*. London, 1910.

LEIBNIZ, GOTTFRIED WILHELM VON, *Monadology*. Oxford, 1951.

———, *New Essays concerning Human Understanding*. La Salle, Ill., 1949.

———, *Philosophical Writings*. Everyman's Library.

———, *Theodicy*. London, 1951.

Leibniz-Clarke Correspondence. University of Manchester, 1956.

LEVASSEUR, ÉMILE, *Histoire des classes ouvrières et de l'industrie en France avant 1789*, 2v. Paris, 1900.

LEWIS, W. H., *The Splendid Century*. New York, 1954.

LINGARD, JOHN, *History of England*, 9v. London, 1855.

LIPSON, E., *Growth of English Society*. London, 1949.

LOCKE, JOHN, *Essay concerning Human Understanding*. Everyman's Library.

———, *Two Treatises on Government*. New York, 1947.

LOCY, W. A., *Growth of Biology*. New York, 1925.

LOUIS XIV, *Mémoires . . . , Réflexions . . . , Instructions . . .* Paris, 1923.

LUCRETIUS, *De Rerum Natura*. London: Loeb Library, 1931.

MACAULAY, THOMAS BABINGTON, *Essays*, 2v. Everyman's Library.

———, *History of England*, 4v. Everyman's Library.

MACLAURIN, C., *Post Mortem*. New York: George Doran, n.d.

MAHAN, A. T., *Influence of Sea Power in History: 1660–1783*. New York, 1950.

MAIMONIDES, *Guide to the Perplexed*, 3v. London, 1885.

MANTOUX, PAUL, *The Industrial Revolution in the Eighteenth Century*. London, 1955.

MANTZIUS, KARL, *History of Theatrical Art*, 6v. New York, 1937.

MARKUN, LEO, *Mrs. Grundy: A History of Four Centuries of Morals*. New York, 1930.

MARTIN, HENRI, *The Age of Louis XIV*, 2v. Boston, 1865.

———, *Histoire de France*, 16v. Paris, 1860.

MARX, KARL, *Capital*, 2v. Chicago, 1919.

MASSON, DAVID, *Life of John Milton*, 6v. New York, 1946.

MATHER, F. J., JR., *Western European Painting of the Renaissance*. New York, 1948.

MAVERICK, L. A., *China a Model for Europe*. San Antonio, Tex., 1946.

MAVOR, JAMES, *Economic History of Russia*, 2v. London, 1925.

MAYER, JOSEPH, *Seven Seals of Science*. New York, 1927.

McCABE, JOSEPH, *Candid History of the Jesuits*. New York, 1913.

———, *Crises in the History of the Papacy*. New York, 1916.

MENCKEN, H. L., *New Dictionary of Quotations*. New York, 1942.

MESNARD, JEAN, *Pascal*. New York, 1952.

MEYER, R. W., *Leibniz and the Seventeenth-Century Revolution*. Cambridge University Press, 1952.

MICHELET, JULES, *Histoire de France*, 5v. Paris: J. Hetzel et Cie., n.d.

MILTON, JOHN, *Areopagitica and Other Prose Works*. Everyman's Library.

———, *Poetical Works*. Oxford University Press, 1935.

MODDER, MONTAGU, *The Jews in the Literature of England*. Philadelphia, 1939.

MOLIÈRE, *Le Misanthrope*. Paris: Classiques Larousse, n.d.
———, *Plays*. Everyman's Library.
———, *Théâtre*, 4v. Paris: Hachette, n.d.
MONROE, PAUL, *Text-Book in the History of Education*. New York, 1928.
MONTAGU, LADY MARY WORTLEY, *Letters and Works*, 2v. London, 1893, 1908.
MONTAIGNE, MICHEL EYQUEM DE, *Diary of a Journey to Italy*. New York, 1929.
MONTALEMBERT, CHARLES, COMTE DE, *The Monks of the West*, 2v. Boston: Marlier, Callanan & Co., n.d.
MORLEY, JOHN, *Oliver Cromwell*. New York, 1902.
MORNET, DANIEL, *Les Origines intellectuelles de la Révolution française*. Paris, 1933.
———, *Short History of French Literature*. New York, 1935.
MORTON, J. B., *Sobieski*. London, 1932.
MOTTEVILLE, MME. FRANÇOISE DE, *Memoirs*, 3v. Boston, 1901.
MOUSNIER, ROLAND, *Histoire générale des civilisations, Tome IV: Les xvie et xviie Siècles*. Paris, 1956.
MUMFORD, LEWIS, *Technics and Civilization*. New York, 1934.

NETTLETON, G. H., *English Drama of the Restoration*. New York, 1914.
New Cambridge Modern History, Vol. VII. Cambridge University Press, 1957.
NEWMAN, JAMES R., *The World of Mathematics*, 4v. New York, 1956.
NEWTON, ISAAC, *Mathematical Principles of Natural Philosophy*, tr. Andrew Motte, ed. Florian Cajori. University of California Press, 1946. Refered to as *Principia*.
NIETZSCHE, FRIEDRICH WILHELM, *Antichrist*. Edinburgh, 1915.
NOYES, ALFRED, *Voltaire*. New York, 1936.
NUSSBAUM, F. L., *History of the Economic Institutions of Modern Europe*. New York, 1937.

OGG, DAVID, *Europe in the Seventeenth Century*. London, 1956.
OLSCHKI, LEONARDO, *The Genius of Italy*. Oxford University Press, 1949.
OWEN, JOHN, *Skeptics of the French Renaissance*. London, 1893.

PALGRAVE, F. T., *Golden Treasury*. London, 1901.
PALMER, JOHN, *Molière*. New York, 1930.
PARTON, JAMES, *Life of Voltaire*, 2v. Boston, 1882.
PASCAL, BLAISE, *Pensées*, ed. Havet, 2v. Paris, 1887.
———, *Pensées*. Everyman's Library.
———, *Provincial Letters*. Boston, 1887.
PASTOR, LUDWIG, *History of the Popes*, 22v. St. Louis, 1898.
PATTISON, MARK, *Milton*. London, 1883.
PEPYS, SAMUEL, *Diary*, 4v. London: Nottingham Society, n.d.
PETERSON, HOUSTON, ed., *Treasury of the World's Great Speeches*. New York, 1954.
PLATO, *Dialogues*, tr. Jowett, 4v. Boston: Jefferson Press, n.d.
Poètes français, 10v. Paris, 1813.
POKROVSKY, M. N., *History of Russia*. New York, 1931.
POLLOCK, SIR FREDERICK, *Introduction to the History of the Science of Politics*. London, 1897.

POPE, ALEXANDER, *Collected Poems, Epistles, and Satires.* Everyman's Library.
PRADEL, PIERRE, *L'Art au siècle de Louis XIV.* Paris, 1949.
PRATT, WALDO SELDEN, *History of Music.* New York, 1927.
PUTNAM, G. H., *Censorship of the Church of Rome,* 2v. New York, 1906.

QUENNELL, PETER, *Caroline of England.* New York, 1940.

RABELAIS, *Gargantua* and *Pantagruel,* ed. Cluny. Paris, 1939.
RACINE, JEAN, *Oeuvres complètes,* 2v. Paris, 1956.
RAMBAUD, ALFRED, *History of Russia,* 3v. Boston, 1879.
RANKE, LEOPOLD, *History of the Popes,* 3v. London, 1878.
REA, LILIAN, *Life and Times of Marie Madeleine, Countess of La Fayette.*
    London, 1908.
RÉAU, LOUIS, *L'Art russe,* 2v. Paris, 1921.
RENARD, G., and WEULERSEE, G., *Life and Work in Modern Europe.* London,
    1926.
RETZ, PAUL DE GONDI, CARDINAL DE, *Memoirs.* London: Grolier Society, n.d.
RICHARD, ERNST, *History of German Civilization.* New York, 1911.
ROBERTSON, J. M., *Short History of Freethought,* 2v. London, 1914.
ROBINSON, D. S., *Anthology of Modern Philosophy.* New York, 1931.
ROBINSON, HOWARD, *Bayle the Sceptic.* New York, 1931.
ROBINSON, J. H., *Readings in European History.* Boston, 1906.
ROCKER, RUDOLF, *Nationalism and Culture.* Los Angeles, 1937.
ROGERS, JAMES EDWIN THOROLD, *Economic Interpretation of History,* London,
    1891.
———, *Six Centuries of Work and Wages.* New York, 1890.
ROTH, CECIL, *History of the Marranos.* Philadelphia, 1941.
———, *The Jewish Contribution to Civilization.* Oxford University Press, 1945.
ROTH, LEON, *Spinoza.* Boston, 1929.
ROWSE, A. L., *The Early Churchills.* New York, 1956.
RUSSELL, BERTRAND, *Critical Exposition of the Philosophy of Leibniz.* London,
    1949.
———, *History of Western Philosophy.* New York, 1945.

SAINT-AMAND, IMBERT DE, *Court of Louis XIV.* New York, 1900.
SAINTE-BEUVE, CHARLES AUGUSTIN, *Portraits of the Seventeenth Century,* 2v.
    in 1. New York, 1904.
———, *Port-Royal,* 5v. Paris, 1867.
SAINTSBURY, GEORGE, *Dryden.* New York: Harper, n.d.
———, *History of Criticism,* 3v. New York, 1900.
———, *History of Elizabethan Literature.* London, 1893.
SAINT-SIMON, LOUIS DE ROUVROY, DUC DE, *Memoirs of Louis XIV and the
    Regency,* 3v. Washington, 1901.
SANDERS, E. K., *Bossuet.* London, 1921.
SAW, RUTH, *Leibniz.* Pelican Books, 1954.
SCHOENFELD, HERMANN, *Women of the Teutonic Nations.* Philadelphia, 1908.
SCHUYLER, EUGENE, *Peter the Great,* 2v. London, 1884.
SCOTT, SIR WALTER, *The Pirate.* New York: Lovell, n.d.

SÉE, HENRI, *Economic and Social Conditions in France during the Eighteenth Century.* New York, 1935.

SEMPLE, ELLEN, *The Geography of the Mediterranean Region,* New York, 1931.

SÉVIGNÉ, MARIE DE RABUTIN-CHANTAL, MARQUISE DE, *Letters,* 10v. London, 1927.

SHAFTESBURY, ANTHONY ASHLEY COOPER, EARL OF, *Characteristics,* 2v. London, 1900.

SHREWSBURY, CHARLES TALBOT, DUKE OF, *Correspondence.* London, 1821.

SIDGWICK, HENRY, *Outlines of the History of Ethics.* London, 1949.

SISMONDI, J. C., *History of the Italian Republics.* London: Routledge, n.d.

SMITH, ADAM, *Theory of Moral Sentiments.* London, 1801.

SMITH, D. E., *History of Mathematics,* 2v. Boston, 1923.

SMITH, D. E., and others, *Sir Isaac Newton.* Baltimore, 1928.

SMITH, PRESERVED, *History of Modern Culture,* 2v. New York, 1930.

SOMBART, WERNER, *The Jews and Modern Capitalism.* Glencoe, Ill., 1951.

SPENGLER, OSWALD, *The Decline of the West,* 2v. New York, 1928.

SPINOZA, BARUCH, *Correspondence.* London, 1928.

———, *Ethics* and *On the Improvement of the Intellect.* Everyman's Library. References to the *Ethics* are to part and proposition.

———, *Tractatus Theologico-Politicus* and *Tractatus Politicus.* London, 1895.

SPITTA, PHILIP, *Johann Sebastian Bach,* 3v. in 2. New York, 1951.

STEPHEN, LESLIE, *Alexander Pope.* New York, 1880.

———, *History of English Thought in the Eighteenth Century,* 2v. New York, 1902.

———, *Hobbes.* London, 1904.

———, *Swift.* New York, 1902.

STERNE, LAURENCE, *Life and Opinions of Tristram Shandy.* Everyman's Library.

STIRLING-MAXWELL, SIR WILLIAM, *Annals of the Artists of Spain,* 4v. London, 1891.

STRACHEY, LYTTON, *Books and Characters.* New York, 1922.

STRANAHAN, C. H., *History of French Painting.* New York, 1907.

SUMMERSON, JOHN, *Sir Christopher Wren.* London, 1954.

SWIFT, JONATHAN, *Journal to Stella.* Everyman's Library.

———, *Tale of a Tub, Battle of the Books, and Other Satires.* Everyman's Library.

———, *Travels into Several Remote Nations of the World by Lemuel Gulliver.* Everyman's Library.

TAINE, HIPPOLYTE, *History of English Literature.* New York, 1873.

TAVERNIER, JEAN BAPTISTE, *Six Voyages.* London, 1678.

THACKERAY, WILLIAM MAKEPEACE, *English Humorists,* in *Works.* Boston: Dana Estes & Co., n.d.

THIEME, HUGO, *Women of Modern France.* Philadelphia, 1908.

THORNDIKE, LYNN, *History of Magic and Experimental Science,* 4v. New York, 1929f.

TICKNOR, GEORGE, *History of Spanish Literature,* 3v. New York, 1854.

TOCQUEVILLE, ALEXIS DE, *L'Ancien Régime.* Oxford, 1937.

TOLAND, JOHN, *Christianity Not Mysterious.* London, 1702.

TOYNBEE, ARNOLD, J., *A Study of History*, 10v. Oxford University Press, 1935f.
————, *A Study of History*, Vols. I–VI, abridged by D. C. Somervell. Oxford University Press, 1947.
TRAILL, H. D., *Social England*, 6v. New York, 1902.
TREVELYAN, G. M., *England under the Stuarts*. New York, 1933.
————, *English Social History*. London, 1947.
TREVOR-ROPER, H. R., *Historical Essays*. London, 1957.
TURNER, E. S., *Call the Doctor*. London, 1958.

ÜBERWEG, FRIEDRICH, *History of Philosophy*, 2v. New York, 1871.
URE, PETER, *Seventeenth-Century Prose*. Pelican Books, 1956.

VAN LAUN, HENRI, *History of French Literature*, 3v. London, 1876.
VARTANIAN, ARAM, *Diderot and Descartes*. Princeton, 1953.
VOLTAIRE, *Age of Louis XIV*. Everyman's Library.
————, *History of Charles XII*. Everyman's Library.
————, *Works*, 44v. in 22. New York, 1927.
VOLTAIRE and FREDERICK THE GREAT, *Letters*, ed. Richard Aldington. New York, 1927.

WALISZEWSKI, K., *Peter the Great*. London, 1898.
WALPOLE, HORACE, *Anecdotes of Painting in England*, 3v. London, 1849.
WALTON, IZAAK, *The Complete Angler*. Boston, 1867.
WAXMAN, MEYER, *History of Jewish Literature*, 3v. New York, 1930.
WEBER, MAX, *The Protestant Ethic and the Spirit of Capitalism*. London, 1948.
WESTERMARCK, E., *History of Human Marriage*, 3v. London, 1921.
WHEWELL, WILLIAM, *History of the Inductive Sciences*, 2v. New York, 1859.
WHITEHEAD, ALFRED NORTH, *Science and the Modern World*. New York, 1926.
WILLEY, BASIL, *The Seventeenth-Century Background*. London, 1950.
WINGFIELD-STRATFORD, ESME, *History of British Civilization*. London, 1948.
WOLF, A., *History of Science, Technology, and Philosophy in the Sixteenth and Seventeenth Centuries*. New York, 1935.
————, *History of Science, Technology, and Philosophy in the Eighteenth Century*. New York, 1939.
WOLFSON, H. A., *The Philosophy of Spinoza*. Harvard University Press, 1948.
WOODS, G., WATT, H., and ANDERSON, G., *The Literature of England*, 2v. Chicago, 1936.
WORMELEY, K. P., *Correspondence of Madame Princess Palatine . . . and of Madame Maintenon*. Boston, 1902.

ZANGWILL, ISRAEL, *Dreamers of the Ghetto*. New York, 1923.
ZEITLIN, S., *Maimonides*. New York, 1935.

Notes

CHAPTER I

1. Motteville, Mme. de, *Memoirs*, I, 79.
2. Retz, Cardinal de, *Memoirs*, 103.
3. Motteville, I, 81.
4. Retz, 103.
5. Motteville, III, 232.
6. *History Today*, July 1959, p. 461.
7. Bishop, M., *Life and Adventures of La Rochefoucauld*, 149.
8. Voltaire, *Age of Louis XIV*, 36.
9. Retz, 281.
10. Sainte-Beuve, *Portraits of the Seventeenth Century*, I, 335.
11. Retz, 55, 73.
12. Voltaire, *Louis XIV*, 67.
13. Michelet, *Histoire de France*, IV, 388; Acton, *Lectures on Modern History*, 235.
14. Motteville, III, 237.
15. Palmer, *Molière*, 15.
16. Saint-Simon, *Memoirs*, II, 361.
17. Sainte-Beuve, I, 422.
18. *Ibid.*, 417.
19. *History Today*, March 1954, p. 149.
20. Voltaire, 256.
21. *Ibid.*, 69.
22. Rea, Lilian, *Countess of La Fayette*, 170.
23. Ferval, *Louise de La Vallière*, 55.
24. Saint-Simon, II, 369.
25. Sainte-Beuve, I, 413.
26. Saint-Simon, II, 361.
27. Sainte-Beuve, I, 423.
28. Louiv XIV, *Mémoires*, 35.
29. In Sainte-Beuve, I, 417.
30. Boulenger, *Seventeenth Century*, 178.
31. Motteville, III, 248.
32. Lewis, W. H., *Splendid Century*, 30.
33. Voltaire, 257.
34. Barine, *La Grande Mademoiselle*, 117.
35. Louis XIV, 76.
36. Martin, H., *Age of Louis XIV*, I, 63-65; Michelet, IV, 424-27.
37. Guizot, *History of Civilization*, I, 260.
38. Smith, Preserved, *History of Modern Culture*, I, 533.
39. Louis XIV, 96.
40. King, J. E., *Science and Rationalism in the Government of Louis XIV*, 87.
41. Saint-Simon, II, 34.
42. Louis XIV, 68.
43. King, 95.
44. Saint-Simon, II, 106, 370.
45. Guérard, *Life and Death of an Ideal*, 153.
46. Louis XIV, 70.
47. France, Anatole, *Nicolas Fouquet*, 258.
48. Voltaire, 262.
49. Martin, H., I, 23, quoting de Choisi.
50. Louis XIV, 74.
51. Martin, I, 22.
52. Sée, Henri, *Economic and Social Conditions in France during the 18th Century*, 93.
53. Martin, I, 34.
54. *Ibid.*, 33f.; Michelet, IV, 410.
55. Boulenger, 356.
56. Mousnier, R., *Histoire générale des civilisations*, IV, 148.
57. Voltaire, 324; Martin, I, 79.
58. Michelet, IV, 428.
59. Mousnier, IV, 148.
60. Voltaire, 273; Martin, I, 86.
61. Boulenger, 357; Lewis, *Splendid Century*, 81.
62. *History Today*, March 1954, p. 155.
63. Mousnier, IV, 252.
64. Nussbaum, *Economic Institutions of Modern Europe*, 154.
65. Mousnier, IV, 250; *Cambridge Modern History*, V, 11.
66. Boulenger, 355.
67. Levasseur, *Histoire des classes ouvrières et de l'industrie en France avant 1789*, I, 394.
68. Beard, Miriam, *History of the Business Man*, 366.
69. In Acton, *Lectures*, 326.
70. Martin, I, 489-90, 496.
71. Voltaire, 323.
72. Martin, I, 558.
73. Barine, 13.
74. Saint-Simon, I, 383; Voltaire, 288.
75. *Encyclopaedia Britannica*, XIII, 778c; Brereton, *Jean Racine*, 245-52.
76. Molière, *Théâtre: École des femmes*, I, i.
77. Sainte-Beuve, I, 250; Day, Lillian, *Ninon*, 34.
78. Sévigné, Mme. de, *Letters*, I, 98, April 1, 1671.
79. Day, *Ninon*, 141.
80. Parton, *Life of Voltaire*, I, 133.
81. Saint-Simon, I, 344.
82. Sévigné, I, 105, April 8, 1671; Day, *Ninon*, 242.
83. *Ibid.*, 80.
84. Saint-Simon, I, 344.
85. Day, 246.
86. *Ibid.*, 185.
87. Saint-Simon, I, 345.
88. Day, 260.
89. Sainte-Beuve, II, 199.

90. Boissier, *Mme. de Sévigné*, 109.
91. Michelet, V, 118.
92. Bourgeois, *Le Grand Siècle*, 74.
93. Boulenger, 349.
94. Bourgeois, 77; Guizot, *History of France*, IV, 587.
95. La Bruyère, *Characters*, chap. "Of the Gifts of Fortune."
96. Voltaire, 278.
97. Saint-Simon, II, 11.
98. Fülop-Miller, *Power and Secret of the Jesuits*, 415.
99. Martin, I, 172.
100. *Ibid.*, 171.
101. Stirling-Maxwell, *Annals of the Artists of Spain*, III, 942.
102. Day, *Ninon*, 163.
103. Cartwright, *Madame; A Life of Henrietta, Duchess of Orléans*, 89.
104. Racine, *Oeuvres: Andromaque*, Dedication.
105. Michelet, IV, 405.
106. *Ibid.*, V, 158.
107. Cartwright, 371; Voltaire, 284; Martin, I, 312.
108. Ferval, *La Vallière*, 67.
109. *Ibid.*, 302.
110. Voltaire, 282.
111. Michelet, IV, 437.
112. Saint-Simon, I, 391.
113. Boulenger, 192.
114. Cruttwell, *Mme. de Maintenon*, 29.
115. *Ibid.*, 46.
116. *Ibid.*, 53.
117. Michelet, V, 69; Martin, I, 535.
118. Saint-Amand, *Court of Louis XIV*, 46.
119. Cruttwell, 89; Martin, I, 530.
120. Boulenger, 195; Michelet, IV, 490; Cruttwell, 118-19.
121. Saint-Simon, II, 381.
122. *Ibid.*, III, 15.
123. Acton, 236; Ogg, *Europe in the 17th Century*, 231.
124. Louis XIV, 122-25.
125. Martin, I, 417.
126. Voltaire, 260; Martin, I, 40n.; *Enc. Brit.*, XII, 682c; Acton, 243.
127. *Camb. Mod. History*, V, 77.
128. Lewis, *Splendid Century*, 239.

CHAPTER II

1. Voltaire, *Age of Louis XIV*, 393; Guérard, 186-90.
2. Mesnard, *Pascal*, 99.
3. Campbell, *The Jesuits*, 259; Fülop-Miller, 195.
4. Voltaire, 430.
5. Saint-Simon, II, 84.
6. *Ibid.*, III, 37.
7. Louis XIV, 119.

8. Ranke, *History of the Popes*, II, 420.
9. Fülop-Miller, 105.
10. Sainte-Beuve, *Port-Royal*, I, 74f.
11. *Ibid.*, 83; Beard, Charles, *Port Royal*, II, 30.
12. Sainte-Beuve, *Port-Royal*, I, 89.
13. Beard, Charles, I, 30.
14. Sainte-Beuve, *Port-Royal*, I, 90.
15. *Ibid.*, II, 407n.
16. Beard, C., I, 52.
17. Sainte-Beauve, *Port-Royal*, I, 94.
18. Pascal, *Provincial Letters*, Introd., 97, and 421n.
19. Voltaire, 419; Beard, C., I, 260.
20. Pascal, *Letters*, Introd., 109.
21. Mesnard, *Pascal*, 12.
22. Mornet, Daniel, *Short History of French Literature*, 75.
23. Sainte-Beuve, *Port-Royal*, II, 379; Mesnard, 40.
24. Owen, John, *Skeptics of the French Renaissance*, 748.
25. Pascal, *Pensées*, Havet ed. Introd., p. civ.
26. Mesnard, 57.
27. *Ibid.*, 209.
28. Pascal, *Pensées*, Introd., p. cxxiii.
29. Pascal, *Provincial Letters*, 197.
30. *Ibid.*, 417.
31. *Ibid.*, 465; *Pensées*, II, 118.
32. McCabe, *Candid History of the Jesuits*, 235.
33. Mesnard, 92.
34. Voltaire, 424.
35. In Pascal, *Provincial Letters*, 127n.
36. Fülop-Miller, 195.
37. Voltaire, 424, 358.
38. Sainte-Beuve, *Port-Royal*, I, 118.
39. Voltaire, 359.
40. Sainte-Beuve, III, 173f.; Beard, C., I, 84.
41. Pascal, *Pensées*, Introd., xxviii; Mesnard, 137-38.
42. Cf. Rabelais, Book III, Ch. xiii.
43. *Pensées*, Introd., p. xxv; text, 17bis.
44. *Ibid.*, text, i, 1.
45. Sainte-Beuve, *Seventeenth Century*, 174.
46. *Pensées*, Everyman's Library, No. 82.
47. *Pensées*, Havet ed., Book III, No. 18.
48. Everyman ed., No. 4.
49. Havet ed., XVI, p. 1bis.
50. *Ibid.*, XX, p. 19.
51. *Ibid.*, I, p. 1.
52. Everyman ed., No. 349.
53. *Ibid.*, No. 418.
54. Havet ed., VIII, p. 1.
55. *Ibid.*, II, p. 8.
56. *Ibid.*, VI, p. 51; Everyman ed., No. 451.
57. Havet, IV, p. 1.
58. *Ibid.*, II, pp. 6, 2bis, 3.
59. Everyman, No. 402.

60. *Ibid.*, No. 397; Havet, I, p. 3.
61. Havet, I, p. 6; Everyman, No. 347.
62. Everyman, No. 277.
63. Havet, XXIV, p. 52.
64. *Ibid.*, X, p. 1; Everyman, No. 233.
65. Everyman, No. 233.
66. Havet, II, p. 8.
67. Sainte-Beuve, *Port-Royal*, II, 508.
68. Havet, IV, 7.
69. *Ibid.*, XIV, 2.
70. Robertson, J. M., *Short History of Freethought*, II, 124.
71. Owen, 800.
72. *Ibid.*, 775.
73. Sainte-Beuve, *Port-Royal*, III, 320.
74. Beard, C., II, 75.
75. *Provincial Letters*, 59.
76. *Pensées*, Havet, Introd., *cxii*.
77. Beard, C., II, 352.
78. Disraeli, Isaac, *Curiosities of Literature*, I, 97.
79. Saint-Simon, II, 12.
80. Boulenger, 284.
81. Michelet, V, 298.
82. In Martin, H., I, 231.
83. Lewis, *Splendid Century*, 108.
84. Sanders, *Bossuet*, 53.
85. *Camb. Mod. History*, V, 22.
86. Martin, I, 529.
87. *Ibid.*
88. *Ibid.*, 532.
89. Michelet, IV, 520.
90. Guizot, *History of France*, V, 23.
91. *Camb. Mod. History*, V, 23.
92. *Ibid.*
93. Boulenger, 263.
94. Martin, I, 552.
95. Ogg, *Seventeenth Century*, 305.
96. Martin, II, 33.
97. *Ibid.*, 43.
98. Buckle, H. T., *History of Civilization*, Ib, 492n., quoting Benoist, Élie, *Histoire de l'Édit de Nantes* (1695), V, 887f.
99. Michelet, IV, 507.
100. Voltaire, 409.
101. Martin, II, 44.
102. Robertson, J. M., II, 142.
103. Saint-Simon, III, 14.
104. Beard, Miriam, 373.
105. Bacon, "Of Unity in Religion," in *Essays*.
106. Sanders, *Bossuet*, 46.
107. Bossuet, *Oraisons funèbres et sermons*, 69.
108. *Ibid.*, 108.
109. Eccles. XVII, 14.
110. Romans XIII, 1.
111. Isaiah XIV, 1.
112. Sanders, 213.
113. Bossuet, in Ogg, 202.
114. Sanders, 260.
115. Buckle, Ib, 569.
116. Faguet, *Literary History of France*, 446.
117. Michelet, IV, 517.
118. Martin, II, 268.
119. Sanders, 280; Michelet, IV, 412.
120. Fénelon, *Télémaque*, end of Book IX.
121. *Ibid.*, Book XIII.
122. Faguet, *Literary History*, 446.
123. Hazard, *The European Mind: The Critical Years*, 208.
124. Sainte-Beuve, *Port-Royal*, II, 191.
125. Bayle, *Philosophical Commentary on . . . "Let Them Come in,"* in Robinson, H., *Bayle the Sceptic*, 73.
126. Bayle, *Dictionnaire historique et critique*, s.v. "Xénophanes."
127. Sainte-Beuve, *Port-Royal*, III, 302.
128. Mornet, *Les Origines intellectuelles de la Révolution française*, 24.
129. Meyer, R. W., *Leibniz and the 17th-Century Revolution*, 35.

CHAPTER III

1. Pradel, *L'Art au siècle de Louis XIV*, 101.
2. Voltaire, *Age of Louis XIV*, 376.
3. *Ibid.*, 325.
4. Wingfield-Stratford, *History of British Civilization*, 583.
5. Pradel, 96.
6. *Ibid.*, 99.
7. Boulenger, 365.
8. Fergusson, *History of the Modern Styles of Architecture*, 236-8.
9. Saint-Simon, I, 186.
10. Martin, II, 212; Blomfield, *Three Hundred Years of French Architecture*, 86.
11. Victoria and Albert Museum, London.
12. Dillon, *Glass*, 210.
13. Guizot, *History of France*, IV, 566.
14. Stranahan, *History of French Painting*, 50.
15. Louvre.
16. Dimier, Louis, *Histoire de la peinture française* (Paris, 1927), II, 45.
17. Versailles.
18. Benoist, *Coysevox*, 115; the bust is in the Louvre.
19. Louvre.
20. Louvre.
21. Louvre.
22. Louvre.
23. Louvre.

CHAPTER IV

1. Voltaire, *Age of Louis XIV*, 258.
2. Palmer, *Molière*, 46.

3. Mantzius, Karl, *History of Theatrical Art*, IV, 42.
4. Molière, *Le Misanthrope*, II, v, 711f.
5. Lucretius, *De rerum natura*, IV, 1155f.
6. Martin, I, 160; Sainte-Beuve, *Seventeenth Century*, II, 95-97.
7. Palmer, 59.
8. Voltaire, *Life of Molière*, in Clark, B. H., *Great Short Biographies of the World*, 628.
9. Palmer, 147.
10. *Les Précieuses ridicules*, scene iv, in Molière, *Plays*, Everyman's Library ed.
11. Sainte-Beuve, *Port-Royal*, III, 271.
12. Palmer, 145.
13. *Les Précieuses ridicules* (Everyman ed.), scene ix.
14. *L'École des maris* (Everyman), I, i.
15. *L'Impromptu de Versailles* (Everyman), I, i.
16. *L'École des femmes*, I, i.
17. *L'École des femmes* (Everyman) I, i.
18. *Critique de l'École des Femmes*, vi.
19. *Ibid.*
20. Michelet, IV, 419.
21. Molière, *Théâtre*, II, 40.
22. Palmer, 335.
23. *Tartuffe* (Everyman), I, vi.
24. *Ibid.*, III, ii.
25. III, vii.
26. IV, v.
27. *Le Festin de pierre* (Everyman), I, i.
28. *Ibid.*, III, i.
29. IV, ii.
30. Palmer, 380f.
31. As in the Everyman's Library edition.
32. *Le Festin de pierre* (Everyman), III, i.
33. Garrison, *History of Medicine*, 296.
34. *L'Amour médecin* (Everyman), II, v.
35. Palmer, 410.
36. *Le Misanthrope* (Everyman), II, i.
37. *Le Misanthrope*, I, i.
38. *Ibid.*, Classiques Larousse ed., 97-98.
39. In Sainte-Beuve, *Seventeenth Century*, II, 126-27.
40. *L'Avare*, II, vi.
41. *Le Bourgeois Gentilhomme* (Everyman), II, iv.
42. Guizot, *History of France*, IV, 560.
43. Michelet, IV, 421.
44. *Le Malade imaginaire* (Everyman), III, iii.
45. Edwards, *Idols of the French Stage*, I, 40.
46. *Ibid.*, 45.
47. *Le Bourgeois Gentilhomme* (Everyman), I, i.
48. *Critique de l'École des femmes* (Everyman), vi.
49. Sainte-Beuve, *Seventeenth Century*, II, 140.
50. Guérard, *Life and Death of an Ideal*, 204.

CHAPTER V

1. Martin, I, 142; Boulenger, 360; *Camb. Mod. History*, V, 152; Bourgeois, *Le Grand Siècle*, 93.
2. Guizot, *History of Civilization*, II, 231; Hauser, *Social History of Art*, I, 470.
3. Desnoiresterres, *Voltaire et la société française au xviiiᵉ siècle*, III, 404.
4. Van Laun, *History of French Literature*, II, 184.
5. *Enc. Brit.*, VI, 441b.
6. Sainte-Beuve, *Seventeenth Century*, II, 293; Brereton, *Racine*, 29.
7. Racine, Louis, *Mémoires sur la vie . . . de Jean Racine*, in Racine, Jean, *Oeuvres*, I, 42.
8. Brereton, 29.
9. Guizot, *History of France*, IV, 539.
10. Racine, *Andromaque*, I, iii.
11. Brereton, 154; Martin, I, 170.
12. Suetonius, *De vita Caesarum: Divus Titus*, VII, 2.
13. Racine, *Bérénice*, I, v.
14. Desnoiresterres, VI, 96.
15. Guizot, *France*, IV, 541.
16. Smith, Adam, *Theory of Moral Sentiments*, I, 255.
17. Racine, *Oeuvres*, I, 765.
18. Brereton, *Racine*, 245-52.
19. *Ibid.*, 19.
20. 2 Kings XI; 2 Chronicles XII.
21. Racine, *Athalie*, IV, iii.
22. Parton, *Voltaire*, I, 591; Mme. du Deffand, in Strachey, *Books and Characters*, 99; Guizot, *France*, IV, 546; Sainte-Beuve, *Port-Royal*, VI, 147; Faguet, *Dix-septième Siècle*, 314.
23. Guizot, *France*, IV, 548.
24. Racine, Louis, *Mémoires*, in Racine, *Oeuvres*, I, p. iii.
25. Saint-Simon, I, 155; Guizot, *France*, IV, 548-49; Sainte-Beuve, *Port-Royal*, VI, 153; Faguet, *Dix-septième Siècle*, 303.
26. Guizot, IV, 548.
27. *Ibid.*
28. Racine, L., *Mémoires*, in Racine, *Oeuvres*, I, 113.
29. Babbitt, Irving, *The Spanish Character*, 98.
30. *Brereton*, 143.
31. Sévigné, Mme. de, *Letters*, II, 210 (Mar. 16, 1672).
32. Desnoiresterres, VI, 102, 281.
33. Hume, "Of Civil Liberty," in *Essays*, 52.

34. La Fontaine, *Choix de contes*, 15f.
35. *Fables*, Preface.
36. Rea, *Life of ... Countess of La Fayette*, 230.
37. Guizot, IV, 552.
38. Sainte-Beuve, *Seventeenth Century*, II, 148.
39. Guizot, IV, 553.
40. Sainte-Beuve, *Port-Royal*, V, 24.
41. *Ibid.*
42. Faguet, *Dix-septième Siècle*, 238.
43. Boileau, Satire I, in *Poètes français*, VII, 21.
44. Satire IX.
45. *Poètes français*, VII, 182-85; *Enc. Brit.*, III, 790d.
46. Day, *Ninon*, 211.
47. Boileau, *L'Art poétique*, I, ll. 75-76.
48. *Ibid.*, ll. 171-74.
49. IV, 59-60.
50. IV, 125-26.
51. III, 45-46.
52. III, 391-94.
53. In Fischer, *Descartes and His School*, 511.
54. Guizot, *France*, IV, 551.
55. Sainte-Beuve, *Seventeenth Century*, II, 261.
56. Lewis, *Splendid Century*, 268.
57. Guizot, IV, 519.
58. La Fayette, Mme. de, *La Princesse de Clèves*, 104.
59. Rea, *Countess of La Fayette*, 284.
60. Bishop, *La Rochefoucauld*, 266.
61. Boissier, *Mme. de Sévigné*, 27.
62. Sévigné, *Letters*, I, 170 (June 10, 1671).
63. Letter of Jan. 20, 1672.
64. In Boissier, 145.
65. *Ibid.*, 145-47.
66. *Letters*, Introd., *xxxviii*.
67. Letter of July 5, 1761.
68. Apr. 8, 1761.
69. Boissier, 201; Sainte-Beuve, *Port-Royal*, I, 232.
70. Apr. 10, 1671.
71. Guizot, IV, 516.
72. Bishop, *La Rochefoucauld*, 128.
73. *Moral Maxims and Reflections*, 84.
74. *Ibid.*, 150.
75. 84.
76. 122.
77. 178.
78. 11.
79. 471.
80. 9.
81. 219.
82. 82, 465.
83. In Bishop, 68.
84. *Moral Maxims*, 15.
85. *Ibid.*, 77.
86. 138.

87. 140.
88. 74.
89. 367.
90. 436.
91. Preface to the first edition.
92. In Bishop, 244.
93. *Moral Maxims*, 688.
94. *Ibid.*, 70.
95. *Ibid.*, 658-59.
96. In Sainte-Beuve, *Seventeenth Century*, I, 380.
97. *Moral Maxims*, 476.
98. Rea, *Countess of La Fayette*, 265.
99. Sainte-Beuve, *loc. cit.*
100. Faguet, *Dix-septième Siècle*, 395.
101. La Bruyère, *Characters*, p. 273, Ch. xii, 7.
102. *Ibid.*, p. 492, Ch. xii, 7.
103. E.g., Ch. xi, 35, and Ch. xvii, 28, in La Bruyère, pp. 267, 469.
104. Guizot, *France*, IV, 528.
105. Motteville, *Memoirs*, I, 150.
106. French text in Fellows and Torrey, *The Age of the Enlightenment*, 35-39.
107. Hazard, *The Critical Years*, 127.
108. Saint-Évremond, Letter to de Créqui, in King, J., *Science and Rationalism*, 26.
109. Frederick II to Voltaire, Sept. 19, 1774, in Voltaire and Frederick the Great, *Letters*.
110. Lewis, *Splendid Century*, 282.
111. Voltaire, *Age of Louis XIV*, 1.

CHAPTER VI

1. A good example in Metropolitan Museum of Art, New York.
2. Vienna.
3. Dresden.
4. Madrid.
5. Louvre.
6. Wolf, *History of Science ... in the XVIth and XVIIth Centuries*, 626.
7. Beard, Miriam, 305.
8. Day, Clive, *History of Commerce*, 194; Marx, *Capital*, I, 826.
9. *Camb. Mod. History*, V, 12.
10. Adam Smith, in Nussbaum, *History of Economic Institutions*, 72.
11. Clark, G. N., *Seventeenth Century*, 44.
12. Spinoza, *Tractatus Theologico-Politicus*, Ch. xx.
13. Pepys, *Diary*, May 14, 1660.
14. Hazard, *Critical Years*, 93.
15. Graetz, H., *History of the Jews*, V. 20.
16. Hazard, 88.
17. Vienna.
18. The Hague.
19. New York.
20. Baron Thyssen Collection.
21. The Hague.
22. Mather, F. J., *Western European Paint-*

ing of the Renaissance, 549.
23. Czernin Collection, Vienna.
24. The Hague.
25. Edinburgh.
26. Frick Gallery, New York.
27. London.
28. Dresden.
29. Louvre.
30. New York.
31. Washington.
32. Chicago.
33. Budapest.
34. Frick Gallery.
35. Brussels.
36. Berlin.
37. London.
38. Louvre.
39. The Hague.
40. Amsterdam.
41. Dresden.
42. New York.
43. Mather, 590.
44. In Beard, Miriam, 288.
45. In Browne, Sir Thomas, *Religio Medici*, 19.
46. Voltaire, *Age of Louis XIV*, 94; Martin, *Louis XIV*, I, 333.
47. Voltaire, 93.
48. Bowen, Marjorie, *William Prince of Orange*, 196.
49. Martin, I, 347.
50. Bowen, 92.
51. *Camb. Mod. History*, V, 158.
52. Burnet, Bishop, *History of His Own Times*, 117.
53. *Camb. Mod. History*, V, 160; Acton, Lectures, 228.
54. Kronenberger, *Marlborough's Duchess*, 30.

CHAPTER VII

1. Firth, *Oliver Cromwell*, 228.
2. *Ibid.*, 230.
3. Trevor-Roper, *Historical Essays*, 218-219.
4. Firth, 244.
5. Gooch, *English Democratic Ideas in the 17th Century*, 168.
6. Trevelyan, *England under the Stuarts*, 294.
7. Carlyle, *Oliver Cromwell*, I, 427.
8. *Ibid.*, 428; Gardiner, S.R., *History of the Commonwealth and Protectorate*, I, 48.
9. Gooch, 183-84; Bowle, *Western Political Thought*, 343.
10. Gooch, 189-90.
11. D'Alton, *History of Ireland*, IV, 308.
12. *Camb. Mod. History*, IV, 533.
13. Carlyle, *Cromwell*, I, 458.

14. *Ibid.*
15. Firth, 255.
16. *Camb. Mod. History*, IV, 538.
17. Firth, 259.
18. Lingard, *History of England*, VIII, 178.
19. Churchill, Winston, *History of the English-speaking Peoples*, II, 235.
20. Lingard, VIII, 146.
21. Lang, Andrew, *History of Scotland*, III, 233.
22. Morley, John, *Oliver Cromwell*, 319.
23. Gooch, 165.
24. Lingard, VIII, 194-95.
25. Firth, 312; Hallam, *Constitutional History of England*, II, 229-30.
26. Gardiner, *History of the Commonwealth*, II, 208-10; *History Today*, October 1953, p. 690.
27. Morley, *Cromwell*, 336.
28. Firth, 319.
29. Hume, David, *History of England*, IV, 551n.
30. Churchill, II, 245.
31. Guizot, *History of Civilization*, I, 240-1.
32. Lingard, VIII, 207.
33. *Ibid.*, 211; Trevor-Roper, 188.
34. Morley, *Cromwell*, 427.
35. Firth, 445.
36. Hume, D., *History*, IV, 578.
37. Walpole, Horace, *Anecdotes of Painting in England*, I, 425.
38. Lingard, VIII, 271.
39. Hallam, *Constitutional History*, II, 241-243; Morley, *Cromwell*, 390.
40. Morley, 400.
41. Plato, *Republic*, §§556-65.
42. Evelyn, *Diary*, I, 331.
43. Morley, *Cromwell*, 413.
44. Macaulay, *History of England*, I, 128.
45. Lingard, VIII, 203.
46. Firth, 355; Morley, 412.
47. Hume, D., *History*, V, 45.
48. Churchill, II, 248.
49. Firth, 344.
50. In Masson, David, *Life of John Milton*, V, 23.
51. Fox, George, *Journal*, 34.
52. *Ibid.*, 4-5.
53. 8-9.
54. 11.
55. 12.
56. 20.
57. 22.
58. 27.
59. 36.
60. 43.
61. 51.
62. 105-6.
63. Firth, 357.
64. Lingard, VIII, 243-44.
65. Beard, Miriam, 397; Firth, 392.

66. Beard, 396.
67. Churchill, II, 249.
68. Hume, D., *History*, IV, 592.
69. Firth, 433.
70. Harding, T. S., *Fads, Frauds, and Physicians*, 118.
71. Lingard, VIII, 267.
72. *Ibid.*, 268.
73. Macaulay, *History*, I, 152.
74. *Enc. Brit.*, VI, 745d.
75. *Camb. Mod. History*, IV, 542.
76. Masson, *Milton*, V, 619.
77. Bowle, *Western Political Thought*, 337.
78. *Camb. Mod. History*, IV, 554; Bryant, Sir Arthur, *Charles II*, 58.
79. Lingard, VIII, 236.
80. Hallam, II, 328.
81. *Ibid.*, 329.
82. Bryant, 60.
83. Voltaire, *Age of Louis XIV*, 66.
84. Bryant, 64.
85. Lingard, VIII, 304.

CHAPTER VIII

1. Allen, J. W., *English Political Thought*, 268.
2. Walton, Izaak, *Complete Angler*, 15.
3. Palgrave, *Golden Treasury*, 67.
4. Bunyan, *Grace Abounding*, No. 2, in *Entire Works*, I, 5-6.
5. *Ibid.*, No. 4.
6. No. 8.
7. In Froude, *Bunyan*, p. 8.
8. Bunyan, *Grace Abounding*, No. 14.
9. *Ibid.*, No. 97.
10. No. 96.
11. No. 104.
12. Coulton, *Life in the Middle Ages*, I, p. 20.
13. *Grace Abounding*, No. 116.
14. Froude, *Bunyan*, p. 59.
15. *Ibid.*, 65.
16. 72.
17. 74-82.
18. *Pilgrim's Progress*, 7.
19. Acts xvi, 31.
20. *Pilgrim's Progress*, 169-71.
21. *Ibid.*, 193.
22. 196.
23. 11.
24. *Camb. History of English Literature*, VII, 197-98.
25. Froude, *Bunyan*, 86.
26. Milton, *Defensio Secunda*, in *Areopagitica and Other Works*, 291.
27. Johnson, Samuel, *Lives of the Poets*, I, 57.
28. Saintsbury, *History of English Literature*, 159.

29. Milton, *Reason of Church Government*, in *Areopagitica, etc.*, 305.
30. Milton, *Poetical Works*, 46.
31. *Comus*, ll. 768f.
32. *Defensio Secunda, loc. cit.*, 293.
33. *Reason of Church Government, loc. cit.*, 301.
34. "Letter to Mr. Hartlib," in *Areopagitica, etc.*, 46.
35. Johnson, *Lives*, I, 63.
36. Milton, "Letter to Mr. Hartlib," *loc. cit.*, 48.
37. As indicated in *Apology for Smectymnuus*, in *Areopagitica, etc.*, 113.
38. Masson, *Milton*, II, 215.
39. Milton, "Of Reformation," in *Areopagitica, etc.*, 58.
40. *Ibid.*, 102.
41. 103.
42. Masson, II, 257.
43. *Ibid.*, 390, 396.
44. Milton, in *Areopagitica, etc.*, 123.
45. *Ibid.*, 121.
46. 124.
47. 304.
48. *Reason of Church Government*, in Masson, II, 371.
49. *Areopagitica, etc.*, 302.
50. *Ibid.*, 303.
51. 304.
52. 146.
53. Masson, II, 487.
54. Aubrey, *Brief Lives*, 201.
55. Milton, *Doctrine and Discipline of Divorce*, in Taine, *History of English Literature*, 281.
56. Pattison, Mark, *Milton*, 58.
57. *Areopagitica, etc.*, 198.
58. *Ibid.*, 225.
59. 195.
60. Masson, III, 320-21.
61. *Ibid.*, 269.
62. *Areopagitica*, 4-5.
63. *Ibid.*, 21.
64. 13.
65. 35.
66. 36.
67. 38.
68. 34.
69. Masson, IV, 64.
70. *Ibid.*, 92.
71. *Areopagitica, etc.*, 4.
72. Masson, IV, 45n.
73. In *Areopagitica, etc.*, 289.
74. Masson, IV, 168.
75. *Ibid.*, 255-58.
76. 261.
77. 263-67.
78. Johnson, *Lives*, I, 69.
79. Masson, IV, 520.
80. *Defensio Secunda*, in Johnson, I, 72.

81. Masson, IV, 455-56.
82. *Ibid.*, 457.
83. *Ibid.*, 458.
84. Disraeli, *Curiosities*, I, 154.
85. Masson, IV, 627.
86. *Ibid.*, 582.
87. 588.
88. 605.
89. 612-15.
90. 609.
91. 610.
92. *Ibid.*
93. Masson, V, 206.
94. *Ibid.*, 215.
95. 369-70.
96. 573.
97. *Ready and Easy Way*, in *Areopagitica, etc.*, 166-69.
98. *Ibid.*, 186.
99. 181.
100. Masson, V, 603.
101. Aubrey, 202.
102. Masson, VI, 447, 649; Johnson, *Lives*, I, 87.
103. Pattison, *Milton*, 148.
104. Masson, VI, 476.
105. Aubrey, 201.
106. *Paradise Lost*, VII, 26.
107. Hutchinson, F. E., *Milton and the English Mind*, 118.
108. Johnson, I, 85.
109. *Ibid.*, 102, 108.
110. *Paradise Lost*, I, ll. 106f., 105-40.
111. *Ibid.*, I, 253-55.
112. IV, 800.
113. IV, 515f.
114. IX, 703-8.
115. VIII, 66f.
116. IV, 738f.
117. IX, 1051f.
118. X, 884, 888f.
119. Cf. IV, 634-38.
120. *Samson Agonistes*, 1053-60.
121. Masson, VI, p. 830.
122. *Paradise Lost*, III, l. 183; Masson, VI, p. 831.
123. Masson, 818.
124. *De Doctrina Christiana*, Ch. xxx, in Willey, *Seventeenth-Century Background*, 71-72.
125. Masson, VI, 827.
126. John Toland in Hutchinson, 152.
127. Johnson, I, 192.
128. Masson, VI, 683; Hutchinson, 104.
129. Aubrey, 201.
130. Masson, II, 473.
131. *Ibid.*, I, 312.
132. Johnson, I, 60.
133. *De Doctrina Christiana*, in Masson, VI, 837.
134. *Paradise Lost*, I, l. 496; IV, 765f.

135. Masson, VI, p. 654.
136. *Paradise Regained*, II, ll. 352f.
137. *Ibid.*, IV, 338.
138. IV, 606.
139. Masson, VI, p. 655.
140. Johnson, I, 88.
141. *Samson Agonistes*, ll. 68-72, 80-82.
142. *Ibid.*, 1034-60.
143. *Ibid.*, 597-98.
144. Masson, VI, p. 727.
145. Johnson, I, 92.
146. Dryden, *Essays*, 108.
147. *The Spectator*, Jan. 5–May 3, 1712.

CHAPTER IX

1. Evelyn, *Diary*, I, 341..
2. Bryant, *Charles II*, 85.
3. Gooch, *English Democratic Ideas in the 17th Century*, 271.
4. Taine, *English Literature*, 314.
5. Hume, *History of England*, V, 61.
6. Bryant, 90.
7. *Ibid.*, 89; Churchill, II, 264.
8. Cf. his speech in Peterson, H., *Treasury of the World's Great Speeches*, 96.
9. Pepys, *Diary*, Oct. 13, 1660.
10. Evelyn, *Diary*, I, 350.
11. As by Macaulay, *History of England*, I, 135; cf. Bryant, 128.
12. Burnet, *History of His Own Times*, 71.
13. Bryant, 133.
14. *Ibid.*, 159.
15. Pepys, July 27, 1667.
16. Burnet, 101.
17. *Grammont Memoirs*, 115n.
18. *Ibid.*, 116.
19. Pepys, May 19, 1668.
20. Bryant, 238.
21. Evelyn, Oct. 4, 1683.
22. Taine, *English Literature*, 314.
23. Bishop, A. T., *Renaissance Architecture of England*, 43.
24. Burnet, 103.
25. Evelyn, Feb. 4, 1685.
26. *Grammont Memoirs*, 350.
27. *Ibid.*, 356.
28. Aubrey, 288.
29. Bryant, 168.
30. Burnet, 33.
31. Bryant, 82.
32. Robertson, J. M., *Freethought*, II, 84.
33. Buckle, Ia, 261n.
34. In Robinson, J. H., *Readings in European History*, 363.
35. Voltaire, *Age of Louis XIV*, 137.
36. Hallam, *Constitutional History*, II, 327.
37. *Ibid.*
38. Burnet, 41.
39. Dick, O. L., Introd. to Aubrey, *Lives*, lxxviii.

40. Besant, Walter, *London in the Time of the Stuarts*, 87; Lecky, W. E., *History of . . . the Spirit of Rationalism in Europe*, II, 66.
41. Burnet, 45-46; Ure, Peter, *Seventeenth-Century Prose*, 136-38.
42. Burnet, 45.
43. Quoted on title page of Toland's *Christianity Not Mysterious*.
44. In Allen, J. W., *English Political Thought*, 297.
45. Markun, Leo, *Mrs. Grundy: A History of Four Centuries of Morals*, 122.
46. Weber, Max, *The Protestant Ethic and the Spirit of Capitalism*, 158-9.
47. Macaulay, *History*, I, 377-79.
48. Besant, *London in the Time of the Stuarts*, 152; Green, J. R., *Short History of the English People*, III, 1338.
49. *Ibid.*
50. Aubrey, 234; *Enc. Brit.*, XVII, 473d.
51. Buckle, Ia, 301n.
52. Churchill, II, 271.
53. Bryant, *Charles II*, 162n.
54. Fülop-Miller, *The Jesuits*, 344; Macaulay (*History*, III, 261) estimated the Catholics as 2 per cent of the population of England in 1690.
55. *History Today*, March 1954, p. 150.
56. Trevelyan, *English Social History*, 276; Clark, G. N., *Seventeenth Century*, 5; Macaulay, *History*, I, 221.
57. Toynbee, A. J., *Study of History*, ed. Somervell, 237.
58. Trevelyan, *Social History*, 322; Marx, *Capital*, 300n.
59. Nussbaum, *Economic Institutions*, 216.
60. Wolf, *History of Science . . . in the 16th and 17th Centuries*, 616.
61. Macaulay, *History*, I, 320.
62. Besant, *London in the Time of the Stuarts*, 287.
63. Macaulay, I, 324.
64. Mousnier, *Histoire générale*, 146.
65. Rogers, J. E. T., *Six Centuries of Work and Wages*, 267.
66. Rogers, *Economic Interpretation of History*, 267.
67. Nussbaum, 108.
68. Wingfield-Stratford, 579.
69. *Ibid.*, 577.
70. Lipson, E., *Growth of English Society*, 176-7.
71. *Ibid.*, 182.
72. Hume, *History*, V, 429; Cunningham, W. C., *Western Civilization in Its Economic Aspects*, II, 216; Lecky, *England in the 18th Century*, I, 194.
73. Bryant, *Charles II*, 278.
74. Besant, 184.
75. *Camb. Mod. History*, V, 206.
76. Rogers, *Economic Interpretation of History*, 212.
77. Besant, 122.
78. Ure, *Seventeenth-Century Prose*, 47; Los Angeles *Times*, Dec. 21, 1958.
79. Howard Kennedy in Los Angeles *Times*, March 2, 1958.
80. Besant, 223.
81. Defoe, *Journal of the Plague Year*, 7-8.
82. Evelyn, Feb. 7, 1666; *cf.* Pepys, Sept. 2, 1666.
83. Pepys, Sept. 2, 1666; Evelyn, Sept. 7, 1666; Lingard, IX, 65; Churchill, II, 277.
84. Besant, 251.
85. *Ibid.*, 245.
86. Summerson, *Sir Christopher Wren*, 55.
87. *Ibid.*, 134.
88. Fergusson, *History of Modern Styles of Architecture*, 294.
89. In Wingfield-Stratford, 605, where Riley is handsomely restored.
90. Duke of Marlborough Collection.
91. Pepys, Mar. 25, 1667.
92. *Ibid.*, Oct. 20, 1662.
93. London, National Portrait Gallery.
94. In Hampton Court Palace.
95. Pepys, Sept. 2, 1666.
96. *Ibid.*, Jan. 16, Feb. 3, Mar. 5, Apr. 9, 1660, etc.
97. Jan. 16, 1660.
98. Brockway and Weinstock, *The Opera*, 32.
99. Burney, Charles, *General History of Music*, II, 383.
100. *Ibid.*, 399.
101. Rowse, A. L., *The Early Churchills*, 98.
102. Hallam, *Constitutional History*, II, 344n.
103. Pepys, Mar. 26, 1666.
104. In *Grammont Memoirs*, 90; Macaulay, *History*, I, 561.
105. Taine, *English Literature*, 315.
106. *Grammont Memoirs*, 281f.
107. Pepys, Aug. 31, 1661; Nov. 9, 1663.
108. Pope, *Essay on Criticism*, ll. 536-43, in *Collected Poems*, p. 71.
109. *Grammont Memoirs*, 112.
110. *Ibid.*, 284n.
111. Evelyn, I, 366.
112. Ure, 36.
113. Markun, *Mrs. Grundy*, 127.
114. *History Today*, October 1958, p. 672.
115. Trevelyan, *Social History*, 313.
116. *History Today*, *loc. cit.*, 668.
117. Smith, Preserved, *History of Modern Culture*, I, 529.
118. James, B. B., *Women of England*, 295.
119. *Camb. Mod. History*, V, 213.
120. Besant, 345.
121. Macaulay, I, 327.
122. Saintsbury, *Dryden*, 182.

123. Bryant, 119; *Camb. Mod. History*, IV, 265.
124. Macaulay, I, 240; II, 426.
125. Hallam, II, 377.
126. Trevelyan, *England under the Stuarts*, 376.
127. *Camb. Mod. History*, V, 218.
128. Pepys, Nov. 2, 1663.
129. *Ibid.*, Aug. 18, 1664.
130. Besant, 303.
131. Day, *Ninon*, 182.
132. Traill, H. D., *Social England*, IV, 489.
133. Ashton, J., *Social Life in the Reign of Queen Anne*, 163.
134. Pepys, Sept. 25, 1666.
135. *Camb. Mod. History*, V, 108.
136. Pepys, June 1, 1667.
137. *Camb. Mod. History*, V, 202.
138. *Ibid.*; Lingard, IX, 85.
139. Text in Lingard, IX, Appendix; *cf.* Bryant, 168; Acton, *Lectures,* 210; *Camb. Mod. History*, V, 204.
140. *Ibid.*, 226; Lecky, *History of England*, I, 18.
141. Bryant, 183.
142. Burnet, 34.
143. Trevelyan, *England under the Stuarts*, 347.
144. Macaulay, I, 183.
145. *Camb. Mod. History*, V, 220.
146. *Enc. Brit.*, XVI, 662c.
147. Hallam, II, 413.
148. Macaulay, I, 186.
149. Trevelyan, *Stuarts*, 400-2.
150. Macaulay, I, 186; Bryant, 225.
151. Hume, *History*, V, 320.
152. Trevelyan, *Stuarts*, 387-88.
153. Hallam, II, 421.
154. Acton, 215.
155. Churchill, II, 298.
156. Acton, 215; Hume, V, 320.
157. *Enc. Brit.*, XX, 616b; Guizot, *History of Civilization*, I, 258.
158. Macaulay, *Essays*, I, 63; Wingfield-Stratford, 622; Lecky, *History of England*, III, 53.
159. Bryant, 270.
160. Mencken, H. L., *New Dictionary of Quotations*, 481.
161. Bryant, 283.
162. *Ibid.*, 282.
163. Turner, E. S., *Call the Doctor*, in *Time*, Dec. 8, 1958, p. 63.
164. Macaulay, *History*, I, 335; Bryant, 294.
165. Macaulay, I, 337; Bryant, 296.
166. Macaulay, I, 338.

CHAPTER X

1. Turin Gallery.
2. London National Gallery.
3. Macaulay, *History*, I, 560-64.
4. Burnet, 65.
5. *Camb. Mod. History*, V, 265, 268.
6. Macaulay, II, 387.
7. Rowse, *Early Churchills*, 152; Lingard, X, 90.
8. Hume, *History*, V, 359; Macaulay, I, 496.
9. Acton, 221; *Camb. Mod. History*, V, 233.
10. Hume, V, 345.
11. Lecky, *History of England*, I, 21.
12. Macaulay, I, 359, 525.
13. *Camb. Mod. History*, V, 239.
14. Hearnshaw, F. J., *Social and Political Ideas of Some English Thinkers of the Augustan Age*, 61.
15. Lingard, X, 128.
16. Macaulay, III, 170.
17. Lord Dartmouth's notes to Burnet's *History*, in Lingard, X, 136n.
18. Burnet, 251.
19. Lingard, X, 136.
20. *Ibid.*, 131.
21. Trevelyan, *Stuarts*, 441.
22. *Camb. Mod. History*, V, 243.
23. Shrewsbury, Duke of, *Correspondence*, 4.
24. Churchill, *Marlborough*, I, 263.
25. Robinson, J. H., *Readings*, 367-69.
26. Mantoux, *Industrial Revolution*, 97.
27. Macaulay detailed these in his essay on Hallam (1828), and countered them in his *History of England* (1848), end of Ch. X.
28. Halifax, *Thoughts and Reflexions*, in Hearnshaw, *Social and Political Ideas of . . . the Augustan Age*, 10.
29. *Ibid.*
30. Ure, *Seventeenth-Century Prose*, 72.
31. Hearnshaw, 60.
32. Halifax, *Character of a Trimmer*, in Trevor-Roper, 255.
33. Hearnshaw, 53.
34. Livy, *History of Rome*, v, 47.
35. Buckle, Ia, 297.
36. *Ibid.*, 298.
37. Bowen, *William Prince of Orange*, 277-8.
38. Burnet, 306.
39. Lecky, *England*, I, 275.
40. Voltaire, *Age of Louis XIV*, 141.
41. *Camb. Mod. History*, V, 317.
42. *Ibid.*, 321; Lecky, I, 279-80; D'Alton, *Ireland*, 467; Wingfield-Stratford, 665.
43. *Camb. Mod. History*, V, 323.
44. Renard and Weulersee, *Life and Work in Modern Europe*, 95.
45. Day, *History of Commerce*, 162.
46. Groom, *History of Money*, 41-46.
47. *Ibid.*

48. *Camb. Mod. History*, V, 249.
49. Macaulay, III, 418-19; Churchill, *Marlborough*, I, 302.
50. *Ibid.*, 348.
51. Rowse, 134.
52. Goldsmith, *Life of Bolingbroke*, in Clark, B. H., *Great Short Biographies*, 1032.
53. *Ibid.; cf.* Chesterfield, *Letters*, I, 261 (Dec. 22, 1749).
54. Lecky, *England*, I, 128.
55. *Enc. Brit.*, XXIII, 725.
56. Kronenberger, *Marlborough's Duchess*, 247.
57. Churchill, *English-speaking Peoples*, III, 76.
58. Rowse, 270.

CHAPTER XI

1. Mousnier, 308.
2. Desnoiresterres, I, 212.
3. Swift, *Journal to Stella*, Aug. 7, 1712.
4. Theater History Exhibition, New York Public Library, Sept. 28, 1956.
5. Johnson, *Lives*, I, 201.
6. Besant, *Stuarts*, 323.
7. Holzknecht, *Background of Shakespeare's Plays*, 417.
8. Besant, 321.
9. Hume, *History*, V, 436; *Camb. History of English Literature*, VIII, 209.
10. Farquhar, *Beaux' Stratagem*, I, i, in Gosse, *A Volume of Restoration Plays*.
11. Congreve, *Way of the World*, II, iv, in Gosse, 185.
12. Macaulay, *Essays*, II, 426.
13. Gosse, 161.
14. Vanbrugh, *The Relapse*, III, in Gosse.
15. *Ibid.*, IV, i.
16. Vanbrugh, *Provoked Wife*, I, i.
17. *Ibid.*, I, ii.
18. *Enc. Brit.*, XVI, 574b.
19. Johnson, *Lives*, II, 2.
20. Macaulay, *Essays*, II, 446.
21. *Enc. Brit.*, VI, 255d.
22. Congreve, *Way of the World*, II, v.
23. *Ibid.*, IV, v.
24. Macaulay, *Essays*, II, 449.
25. Thackeray, *English Humorists*, 139.
26. Lecky, *England*, I, 539.
27. Dryden, Preface to *Fables, Ancient and Modern*, in *Essays*, 290.,
28. Pepys, Feb. 23, 1663.
29. Nettleton, G. H., *English Drama of the Restoration*, 5.
30. Dryden, *All for Love*, IV, i, in Gosse.
31. *Camb. Mod. History*, V, 134.
32. Dryden, *Poems*, 75.
33. *Ibid.*, 78.
34. *Ibid.*, 89.

35. Pepys, Feb. 3, 1664.
36. Scott, *The Pirate*, 147-49.
37. Macaulay, *History*, I, 285.
38. Johnson, *Lives*, I, 187.
39. *Ibid.*, 219; *Camb. History of English Literature*, VIII, 231-32.
40. Johnson, I, 216.
41. As Macaulay believed (*History*, I, 657).
42. Dryden, *The Hind and the Panther*, in *Poems*, 123.
43. Butler, Samuel, *Hudibras*, 3-9.
44. Pepys, Dec. 10, 1663.
45. *Camb. History of English Literature*, VIII, 68.
46. An excellent edition, *Brief Lives*, appeared in 1957, with a lively and learned introduction by O. L. Dick.
47. *Camb. History of English Literature*, IX, 151.
48. A good example in Brockway and Winer, *Second Treasury of the World's Great Letters*, 131.
49. Macaulay, *Essays*, I, 195.
50. Temple, Sir William in Taine, *English Literature*, 333.
51. Evelyn, I, 229f. The passage on his son is under Jan. 27, 1658.
52. Pepys, June 13, 1662; June 17, 1663.
53. *Ibid.*, July 16, 1660.
54. Jan. 23, (1670).
55. Apr. 5, 1664.
56. Dec. 19, 1664.
57. Aug. 18, 1667.
58. Sept. 6, 1664.
59. July 15, 1660.
60. Aug. 23, 1663.
61. May 21, 1662.
62. July 30, 1663.
63. Sept. 4, 1660.
64. Sept. 24, 1663.
65. Feb. 28, 1662.
66. *Enc. Brit.*, VII, 139.
67. Defoe, *Moll Flanders*, 295.
68. Steele, *Tatler*, No. 151.
69. Thackeray, *English Humorists*, 183.
70. Steele, *Tatler*, No. 95.
71. Johnson, *Lives*, I, 330; Macaulay, *Essays*, II, 465.
72. *Ibid.*, 486; Johnson, I, 328.
73. Addison, *Spectator*, No. 4.
74. *Ibid.*
75. No. 112.
76. Macaulay, *Essays*, II, 499; Enc. Br. I, 161d.
77. Thackeray, 157n.
78. Voltaire, *Works*, XIXb, 137.
79. Stephen, Leslie, *Swift*, 82.
80. *Id.*, *Alexander Pope*, 60.
81. *Id.*, *Swift*, 15.
82. Hardy, Evelyn, *The Conjured Spirit: Swift*, 40.

83. *Ibid.*, 62.
84. Stephen, *Swift*, 52.
85. *Ibid.*, 37.
86. Swift, *Tale of a Tub, etc.*, 56.
87. *Ibid.*, 72.
88. 77.
89. 78.
90. 81.
91. 121.
92. 103.
93. 105.
94. 106.
95. 109.
96. 110.
97. Stephen, *Swift*, 42.
98. Rowse, 269.
99. Hardy, *Conjured Spirit*, 148.
100. Swift, "A Critical Essay upon the Faculties of the Mind," in *Tale of a Tub, etc.*, 192.
101. In Stephen, *Swift*, 47.
102. *Ibid.*, 161.
103. *Ibid.*, 57.
104. Hardy, 125.
105. In Trevelyan, *Social History*, 444.
106. In Rowse, 265.
107. *Ibid.*, 266.
108. *Ibid.*, 269.
109. Stephen, *Swift*, 103.
110. *Ibid.*, 102.
111. Swift, *Journal to Stella*, Letters XXVII and XXXIII.
112. *Ibid.*, 172 (Letter XXIII).
113. *Ibid.*, 203 (Letter XXVII).
114. Stephen, *Swift*, 143.
115. Hardy, 57.
116. Swift, "Strephron and Chloe," in Hardy, 59.
117. In Hardy, 176.
118. Stephen, *Swift*, 120.
119. *Journal to Stella*, Letter XVI.
120. Swift to Pope, Sept. 29, 1725, in Thackeray, *English Humorists*, 218n.
121. Stephen, *Swift*, 108.
122. Hardy, 164.
123. *Ibid.*, 157.
124. Stephen, 131.
125. Johnson, II, 258; Hardy, 174f; Stephen, 133f.
126. Hardy, 219.
127. Swift, *Gulliver's Travels*, Book II, Ch. vi, p. 120.
128. *Ibid.*, III, viii, p. 183.
129. III, x, pp. 198f.
130. IV, vii, p. 240.
131. IV, v, p. 250.
132. IV, xi, pp. 272-73.
133. Stephen, 168.
134. Hardy, 230.
135. Stephen, 160.
136. In Taine, *English Literature*, 436.

137. *Ibid.*
138. Stephen, 184.
139. *Ibid.*, 195.
140. In Woods, George, etc., *The Literature of England*, I, 813.
141. Stephen, 195.

CHAPTER XII

1. Morton, J. B., *Sobieski*, 41.
2. *Ibid.*, 57.
3. *Cambridge History of Poland*, I, 520.
4. Morton, 47.
5. *Camb. History of Poland*, I, 521.
6. *Ibid.*, 537.
7. Morton, 5.
8. *Camb. History of Poland*, I, 545.
9. *Ibid.*, 547.
10. *Ibid.*, 556.
11. Ogg, *Europe in the 17th Century*, 499.
12. Schoenfeld, H., *Women of the Teutonic Nations*, 263; Michelet, V, 154.
13. Kluchevsky, V., *History of Russia*, III, 334.
14. *Ibid.*, 282.
15. *Ibid.*, 367.
16. Waliszewski, *Peter the Great*, 63.
17. *Ibid.*, 75.
18. Florinsky, M. T., *Russia: History and an Interpretation*, I, 321.
19. Schuyler, E., *Peter the Great*, I, 350.
20. Waliszewski, 87.
21. *Ibid.*, 91.
22. Schuyler, I, 358.
23. *Ibid.*, 374.
24. Macaulay, *History*, IV, 374.
25. Voltaire, *Charles XII*, 37.
26. *Camb. Mod. History*, V, 595.
27. *Ibid.*; Schuyler, II, 85.
28. *Camb. Mod. History*, V, 596.
29. Waliszewski, 322.
30. Voltaire, *Charles XII*, 163; Schuyler, II, 138; *Camb. Mod. History*, V, 600.
31. Schuyler, II, 160.
32. *Ibid.*, 162.

CHAPTER XIII

1. In Buckle, *History of Civilization*, Ib, 580.
2. Frederick to Voltaire, Mar. 6, 1737, in Voltaire and Frederick, *Letters*, 55.
3. Florinsky, I, 327, 334.
4. Schuyler, I, 374.
5. Waliszewski, *Peter the Great*, 105.
6. *Ibid.*, 143.
7. 133.
8. 137.
9. 218.
10. 152-53, 161-63; Florinsky, I, 319; Schuyler, I, 422.

11. Schuyler, II, 405.
12. Rambaud, *History of Russia*, I, 104.
13. Réau, L., *L'Art russe*, II, 18n.
14. Semple, Ellen, *Geography of the Mediterranean Region*, 348.
15. Robinson, J.H., *Readings*, 390.
16. Schuyler, I, 412.
17. Waliszewski, 448f.
18. Ogg, 511.
19. Schuyler, II, 192.
20. Rambaud, I, 94.
21. Pokrovsky, M., *History of Russia*, 279.
22. *New Camb. Mod. History*, VII, 319.
23. Pokrovsky, 287; Florinsky, I, 380.
24. Mavor, *Economic History of Russia*, I, p. *xxxi*; *New Camb. Mod. History*, VII, 319.
25. Pokrovsky, 285; Schuyler, II, 471.
26. Schuyler, II, 453; Florinsky, I, 382.
27. Waliszewski, 436.
28. Rambaud, I, 99.
29. Schuyler, II, 609-10.
30. *Ibid.*, 283.
31. *Ibid.*, 338.
32. Waliszewski, 517.
33. *Ibid.*, 518.
34. Schuyler, II, 345.
35. *Ibid.*, 410.
36. Waliszewski, 534.
37. *Ibid.*, 538.
38. Toynbee, A., *Study of History*, VIII, 269.
39. Pokrovsky, 330; Florinsky, II, 334.

CHAPTER XIV

1. Westermarck, *History of Human Marriage*, III, 51; Bebel, *Woman under Socialism*, 71.
2. Rocker, *Nationalism and Culture*, 125.
3. *New Camb. Mod. History*, VII, 293.
4. *Camb. Mod. History*, IV, 426.
5. Acton, *Lectures*, 286.
6. Quennell, *Caroline of England*, 5-7.
7. Montagu, Lady Mary W., *Letters*.
8. Francke, K., *History of German Literature*, 175.
9. Richard, E., *History of German Civilization*, 332.
10. Thieme, *Women of Modern France*, 199.
11. Wormeley, *Correspondence of Mme. Princess Palatine*, letter of Nov. 22, 1714.
12. Hürlimann, *Germany*, 232; La Farge, H., *Lost Treasures of Europe*, 33.
13. Dresden.
14. Spitta, K., *Bach*, I, 257. The walking is doubtful.
15. Morton, *Sobieski*, 130.
16. *Ibid.*, 132.

17. *Camb. Mod. History*, V, 355.
18. *Ibid.*, 355-56; Ogg, 490.
19. Ogg, 488.
20. Lane-Poole, S., *Story of Turkey*, 226.
21. Voltaire, *Age of Louis XIV*, 165.
22. Coxe, W., *History of the House of Austria*, II, 445.
23. Morton, 202; Coxe, II, 447.
24. Ogg, 496.

CHAPTER XV

1. Lea, H. C., *History of the Inquisition in Spain*, IV, 53-54.
2. *Ibid.*, 49.
3. *Ibid.*, 57. Lea adds, "I cannot but regard this as a truthful report."
4. Ranke, *History of the Popes*, II, 381n.
5. *Ibid.*, 380; III, Appendix, 145.
6. Ranke, II, 325.
7. Funk, *Manual of Church History*, II, 148.
8. Ranke, II, 330.
9. *Ibid.*, 333; Funk, II, 177.
10. Ranke, II, 418.
11. Funk, II, 178.
12. Voltaire, *Age of Louis XIV*, 135.
13. Churchill, *English-speaking Peoples*, II, 317.
14. Acton, 226.
15. Sismondi, *History of the Italian Republics*, 789.
16. Bonacossi Collection, Florence.
17. Wadsworth Athenaeum, Hartford, Conn.
18. Dresden and Rome.
19. Wallace Collection.
20. Dresden.
21. Vatican.
22. Rome, Santa Maria in Vallicella.
23. Stirling-Maxwell, *Annals of the Artists of Spain*, III, 1152.
24. *Ibid.*, 1154.
25. *Ibid.*, 1101.
26. *Enc. Brit.*, X, 361b.
27. *Ibid.*
28. Garnett, *History of Italian Literature*, 283.
29. *Ibid.*, 284.
30. Hallam, *Literature of Europe*, IV, 213.
31. Bain, F. W., *Christina, Queen of Sweden*, 253.
32. Motteville, *Memoirs*, III, 104.
33. *Ibid.*, 106-8.
34. *Ibid.*, 109-10.
35. Voltaire, *Age of Louis XIV*, 60.
36. Motteville, III, 110.
37. Day, *Ninon*, 149.
38. Bain, 321.
39. In Voltaire, 405.
40. Bain, 339.

41. *Grove's Dictionary of Music*, V, 154.
42. Burney, *General History of Music*, II, 437.
43. *Ibid.*, 575; *Grove's*, V, 149.
44. Brockway and Weinstock, *Opera*, 11; Burney, II, 552.
45. Olschki, *Genius of Italy*, 423.
46. Brockway and Weinstock, *Opera*, 12.
47. Hazard, *The Critical Years*, 382.
48. Kirkpatrick, R., *Domenico Scarlatti*, 38.
49. Lea, *Inquisition in Spain*, III, 584.
50. Bell, Aubrey, *Portuguese Literature*, 267.
51. *Catholic Encyclopedia*, XV, 416b.
52. Buckle, IIa, 54.
53. *Camb. Mod. History*, V, 375.
54. Stirling-Maxwell, III, 1143-44.
55. Baron, S. W., *Social and Religious History of the Jews*, II, 7; Lea, *Inquisition in Spain*, III, 306.
56. Ticknor, G., *History of Spanish Literature*, III, 206; Hume, Martin, *Spain: Its Greatness and Decay*, 304; Ogg, 380.
57. Lea, I, 511.
58. Madrid, Church of the Incarnation.
59. Calvert, A., *Sculpture in Spain*, 115.
60. Still in the Escorial.
61. Stirling-Maxwell, III, 1200; Justi, C., *Diego Velázquez*, 137.
62. Seville Museum.
63. Stirling-Maxwell, III, 1069.
64. Altamira, R., *History of Spanish Civilization*, 142.
65. *Id.*, *History of Spain*, tr. Muna Lee, 398.
66. Ticknor, III, 203; Buckle, Ia, 60; *Camb. Mod. History*, V, 376.

CHAPTER XVI

1. Obadiah III, 20.
2. Lea, *Inquisition in Spain*, III. 236; Baron, *Social and Religious History of the Jews*, II, 68.
3. Lea, III, 298; Graetz, *History of the Jews*, V, 91, 111.
4. Roth, Cecil, *History of the Marranos*, 75.
5. *Ibid.*, 150.
6. Lc·, III, 273.
7. Brockelmann, C., *History of the Islamic Peoples*, 317; Finkelstein, L., *The Jews*, I, 247.
8. Roth, *Marranos*, 214.
9. Sombart, *The Jews and Modern Capitalism*, 69.
10. Brinton, *The Gonzaga*, 227.
11. *Ibid.*
12. Pastor, L., *History of the Popes*, XVII, 334; Graetz, IV, 590.
13. McCabe, *Crises in the History of the Papacy*, 343.
14. Montaigne, *Diary*, 154.
15. Sombart, 17.
16. *Ibid.*, 18.
17. Graetz, V, 176.
18. Sombart, 56.
19. As by Sombart, 14.
20. Roth, *Marranos*, 242.
21. *Ibid.*, 244.
22. Graetz, V, 205.
23. Roth, 244.
24. Graetz, V, 205.
25. *Ibid.*
26. Roth, 247.
27. Graetz, V, 27.
28. Modder, M. F., *The Jews in the Literature of England*, 24f.
29. *Jewish Encyclopedia*, VIII, 182.
30. Sombart, 250.
31. Graetz, V, 34.
32. Sombart, 54.
33. Graetz, V, 45.
34. Modder, 35-6.
35. Graetz, V, 49.
36. Sombart, 51.
37. Abbott, G. F., *Israel in Europe*, 229-31.
38. Schoenfeld, H., *Women of the Teutonic Nations*, 251.
39. Browne, Lewis, *Wisdom of Israel*, 638.
40. Dubnow, S. M., *History of the Jews in Russia and Poland*, I, 66.
41. *Ibid.*, 89.
42. Rabbi Nathan Hannover, in Dubnow, I, 116.
43. *Ibid.*, 145.
44. Baron, II, 169.
45. Dubnow, I, 164.
46. *Ibid.*, 165.
47. 161, 166.
48. 243.
49. 246.
50. Sombart, 178.
51. Nussbaum, *History of Economic Institutions*, 140.
52. Sombart, 172.
53. *Ibid.*, 65; Roth, C., *Jewish Contributions to Civilization*, 238-9.
54. Finkelstein, I, 258; Roth, *Jewish Contributions*, 229.
55. Baron, II, 127.
56. Dubnow, I, 133.
57. Graetz, V, 52.
58. The following account merely summarizes Graetz, V, 119-66.
59. *Ibid.*, 139.
60. Dubnow, I, 205.
61. Proverbs II, 19.
62. Dubnow, 133-34.
63. Wolfson, H., *Philosophy of Spinoza*, II, 323.

64. *Jewish Encyclopedia*, I, 168a.
65. *Ibid.*
66. Graetz, V, 64.
67. *Ibid.*, 63.
68. Zangwill, I, *Dreamers of the Ghetto*, 112.
69. Graetz, V, 64.
70. The life of Acosta was made into a play by Karl Gutzkow (1846), and into a fictionalized story by Israel Zangwill in *Dreamers of the Ghetto* (1898).

CHAPTER XVII

1. Voltaire, *Age of Louis XIV*, 271.
2. Brewster, Sir David, *Memoirs of . . . Sir Isaac Newton*, II, 375.
3. Hazard, *Critical Years*, 177.
4. *Ibid.*
5. Bain, *Christina*, 144.
6. Lecky, *Rationalism*, I, 45.
7. *Ibid.*, 43.
8. Smith, P., *History of Modern Culture*, I, 457.
9. Lang, Andrew, *History of Scotland*, III, 205.
10. Lecky, *Rationalism*, I, 44.
11. Voltaire, *Age of Louis XIV*, 355.
12. Putnam, G. H., *Censorship of the Church of Rome*, II, 264-65.
13. Smith, P., *Culture*, I, 491.
14. In Lecky, *Rationalism*, II, 28.
15. *Enc. Brit.*, XVI, 335d.
16. Parton, *Voltaire*, I, 71.
17. *Camb. History of English Literature*, IX, 454.
18. Smith, P., *Culture*, I, 344.
19. Martin, H., *Histoire de France*, XIV, 304.
20. Macaulay, *History*, I, 304.
21. Swift, "Of the Education of Girls," in Hardy, *Conjured Spirit*, 47.
22. Woods, etc., *Literature of England*, I, 787.
23. The following summary is based also on Locke's *Conduct of the Understanding*, published posthumously in 1706.
24. The quotations are from Monroe, Paul, *Text-Book in the History of Education*, 514-19, and Aaron, R. J., *John Locke*, 290-95.
25. Montalembert, *Monks of the West*, I, 141.
26. *Camb. History of English Literature*, IX, 373.
27. *Ibid.*, 374.
28. Pope, *The Dunciad*, IV, ll. 211-12.
29. Ussher, James, *Annals of the Old and New Testament* (1650-54), in Smith, P., I, 290.

30. *Ibid.*, 286-87; Martin, *Histoire de France*, XIV, 294; Hazard, *Critical Years*, 182-204.
31. Leibniz, *Sämtliche Schriften*, I, 148, in Smith, P. I, 286.

CHAPTER XVIII

1. Hallam, *Literature of Europe*, IV, 319.
2. Smith, P., I, 170.
3. Voltaire, *Age of Louis XIV*, 379.
4. Buckle, Ib, 500-504.
5. Smith, P., I, 166.
6. Wingfield-Stratford, 592.
7. Swift, *Gulliver's Travels*, Book III, Ch. v.
8. Smith, P., I, 169.
9. Spinoza, *Correspondence*, 35.
10. *Ibid.*, 80.
11. In Smith, P., I, 149.
12. *Ibid.*, 156.
13. Hazard, 306.
14. Bell, E. T., *Men of Mathematics*, 56.
15. Clark, *Seventeenth Century*, 251.
16. Wolf, *History of Science . . . in the 16th and 17th Centuries*, 594.
17. *Ibid.*, 609.
18. *Ibid.*, 595.
19. Aubrey, 238.
20. Smith, P., I, 251.
21. Wolf, 82.
22. Newman, J. R., *The World of Mathematics*, II, 792.
23. Martin, H., *Histoire*, XIII, 173.
24. Brewster, *Memoirs . . . of Newton*, I, 312.
25. Newton, I., *Mathematical Principles of Natural Philosophy*, Book III, Prop. 41, (p. 521).
26. Smith, D. E., *History of Mathematics*, I, 405.
27. Voltaire, *Age of Louis XIV*, 378.
28. Aubrey, 164.
29. Wolf, 358.
30. Mayer, Joseph, *Seven Seals of Science*, 109.
31. Newman, J. R., *World of Mathematics*, II, 794.
32. Tavernier, J. B., *Six Voyages*, Preface.
33. In Hazard, *Critical Years*, 12.
34. La Bruyère, *Characters*, xvii, 4.
35. Hazard, 13.
36. *Ibid.*, 25.
37. Smith, P., I, 79.
38. *History Today*, May 1957, p. 324.
39. Bacon, Francis, *Novum Organum*, II, 21.
40. Hooke, *Micrographia*, in Wolf, 278.
41. Pratt, W. S., *History of Music*, 325.
42. Wolf, 258.
43. *Enc. Brit.*, III, 994c.

44. Fox-Bourne, *John Locke*, II, 223-25.
45. Boyle, Robert, *Sceptical Chymist*, 1.
46. *Ibid.*, 2.
47. *Ibid.*, 17.
48. Butterfield, *Origins of Modern Science*, 105.
49. Wolf, 349.
50. *Ibid.*, 545.
51. Kirby, R. S., *Engineering in History*, 154.
52. Wolf, 550.
53. Beard, Miriam, 465.
54. Wolf, 551.
55. *Ibid.*, 552.
56. Wolf, A., *History of Science . . . in the 18th Century*, 611.
57. Evelyn, *Diary*, Nov. 7, 1651.
58. Wolf, *18th Century*, 406.
59. *Hamlet*, II, ii.
60. Locy, W. A., *Growth of Biology*, 212.
61. *Ibid.*, 214-16.
62. *Ibid.*, 236.
63. Castiglioni, *History of Medicine*, 537-538.
64. Brett, G. S., *History of Psychology*, 337.
65. *Ibid.*, 339; Sigerist, *The Great Doctors*, 184.
66. Garrison, *History of Medicine*, 313.
67. Dick in Aubrey, *xix*.
68. Lewis, *Splendid Century*, 181.
69. Harding, T. S., *Fads, Frauds, and Physicians*, 151.
70. Macaulay, *History*, III, 78.
71. Sévigné, *Letters*, I, 106 (April 8, 1671).
72. Michelet, *Histoire*, V, 29.
73. Motteville, *Memoirs*, I, 186.
74. Castiglioni, 560.
75. *Ibid.*, 562; Garrison, 304.
76. Dick in Aubrey, *xix*.
77. Garrison, 252.
78. *Ibid.*, 253.
79. Dick in Aubrey, *xix*.
80. Hallam, *Literature of Europe*, IV, 341.
81. Wolf, *16th Century*, 438.
82. *Ibid.*
83. Garrison, 295.
84. Voltaire, *Age of Louis XIV*, 374.
85. Pepys, Nov. 14, 1666.
86. MacLaurin, C., *Post Mortem*, 170f.
87. Dick in Aubrey, *xx*.
88. Castiglioni, 566.
89. Whitehead, Alfred North, *Science in the Modern World*, 58.
90. Sprat, *History of the Royal Society* (1667), 113, in Clark, G. N., *Seventeenth Century*, 336.
91. Newman, *World of Mathematics*, I, 286.
92. Wolf, *16th Century*, 668-70.
93. *Enc. Brit.*, V, 994c.
94. In Smith, P., I, 150.
95. In Hazard, *Critical Years*, 316; Mousnier, *Histoire générale*, IV, 331.

CHAPTER XIX

1. Brewster, *Newton*, I, 4.
2. *Ibid.*, 92.
3. Newton's secretary, in Brewster, II, 96.
4. Keynes, J. M., in Newman, J. R., *World of Mathematics*, I, 282.
5. Smith, D. E., *Isaac Newton*, 207.
6. Keynes in Newman, *loc. cit.*
7. Brewster, II, 96-97.
8. *Ibid.*, 93.
9. *Ibid.*, 413.
10. Andrade, E. N., *Sir Isaac Newton*, 77.
11. Newton, *Principia*, 546.
12. *Ibid.*, xvii, preface to first edition.
13. Newton, *Opticks*, Appendix "De Quadratura Curvarum," in Wolf, *16th Century*, 211.
14. Brewster, II, 24n.
15. Wolf, 217.
16. *Principia*, scholium to Prop. 7 of Book II.
17. Cf. *ibid.*, 656.
18. Wolf, 266.
19. *Enc. Brit.*, XVI, 361b.
20. Brewster, I, 96.
21. *Enc. Brit.*, XVI, 361b.
22. In Parton, *Voltaire*, I, 213.
23. *Ibid.*
24. Brewster, I, 26.
25. Thorndike, L., *History of Magic and Experimental Science*, IV, 158.
26. Gilbert, W., *De Mundo Nostro Sublunari Philosophia*, in Whewell, *Inductive Sciences*, I, 394.
27. Brewster, I, 282.
28. Whewell, I, 393.
29. Brewster, I, 287.
30. Aubrey, 166.
31. Butterfield, 118.
32. Brewster, I, 293.
33. *Principia*, 546.
34. Brewster, I, 337.
35. Leibniz, Letter to Hartsoeker, Feb. 10, 1711.
36. *Principia*, 546, General Scholium.
37. *Ibid.*, 634.
38. Cajori in *Principia*, 677.
39. Vartanian, A., *Diderot and Descartes*, 96.
40. General Scholium.
41. *Principia*, 547.
42. Brewster, II, 97.
43. *Ibid.*, 84.
44. Andrade, in Newman, I, 274.
45. Robertson, *Freethought*, II, 112-13.
46. Clark, G. N., *Seventeenth Century*, 249.

47. Keynes, address at tercentennial cele-
bration of Newton's birth by the Royal
Society, July 1946, in Newman, I, 283.
48. In Bell, E. T., *Men of Mathematics*,
113.
49. Brewster, II, 132-35.
50. Keynes, *loc. cit.*
51. Andrade, in Newman, I, 274.
52. Keynes, *loc. cit.*
53. Parton, *Voltaire*, I, 213.
54. Andrade, *Newton*, 121.
55. Keynes in Newman, I, 278; Locke in
Brewster, II, 163.
56. Parton, I, 213.
57. Smith, D. E., *History of Mathematics*,
I, 404.
58. Hume, *History of England*, V, 433.
59. Voltaire, *Works*, XXIb, 66.
60. Smith, D. E., *Newton*, 15; Brewster, I,
343.
61. S. Brodetsky in Smith, D. E., *Newton*,
8.
62. Andrade in Newman, I, 275.
63. *Principia*, First Scholium.
64. Andrade, *Newton*, 131.

CHAPTER XX

1. Aubrey, 157.
2. *Ibid.*, 150.
3. *Ibid.*, 151.
4. Hobbes, *Leviathan*, Ch. iv, p. 16.
5. Hobbes, *De Corpore*, i, 2, in *The Metaphysical System of Thomas Hobbes*,
ed. Mary W. Calkins, p. 6.
6. *Leviathan*, vii, p. 31.
7. *Ibid.*, i, p. 3.
8. *Ibid.*
9. *Elementorum Philosophiae*, in *Metaphysical System*, p. 119.
10. *Leviathan*, ii, pp. 4-5.
11. *Ibid.*, iii, p. 8.
12. Hobbes, *Elements of Law*, i, 3.
13. *Leviathan*, ii, p. 6.
14. *Ibid.*, vi, p. 28.
15. *Elements of Law*, i, 12.
16. *Leviathan*, xxi, p. 111.
17. *Ibid.*, vi, p. 23.
18. *Elements of Law*, i, 11.
19. *Leviathan*, xi, p. 50.
20. *Ibid.*, 49.
21. vi, p. 27.
22. Pp. 23-26.
23. viii, p. 35.
24. xi, p. 49.
25. *Elements of Law*, i, 12.
26. *Leviathan*, xiii, p. 65.
27. *Ibid.*
28. P. 64.
29. *Ibid.*
30. P. 65.

31. xvii, p. 89.
32. P. 90.
33. xxi, pp. 114-16.
34. xxix, p. 173.
35. P. 176.
36. xix, pp. 99, 101.
37. *Elements of Law*, ii, 2.
38. *Leviathan*, xviii, p. 93; xxix, p. 174.
39. P. 172.
40. vi, p. 26; xi, p. 54.
41. xii, pp. 54-55.
42. *Ibid.*
43. xii, p. 56.
44. Hobbes, *De Homine*, Ch. i.
45. *Leviathan*, xi, p. 53.
46. xxxi, p. 194.
47. xxxiv, p. 211.
48. Stephen, *Hobbes*, 151-52.
49. *Leviathan*, xii, p. 59.
50. xxix, p. 175.
51. Hobbes, *De Cive*, in Stephen, *Hobbes*,
222.
52. *Leviathan*, xxxi, p. 196.
53. xxxii, p. 199.
54. Bayle, *Selections*, article "Hobbes."
55. Burnet, *History of His Own Time*, 45.
56. Aubrey, 152.
57. Bowle, *Hobbes and His Critics*, 152.
58. *Ibid.*, 34.
59. *Enc. Brit.*, XI, 613b.
60. Aubrey, 156.
61. *Ibid.*, 153.
62. *Enc. Brit.*, XI, 613d.
63. Aubrey, 153-55.
64. Brewster, *Newton*, II, 149n; Stephen,
Hobbes, 68.
65. Bayle, article "Hobbes," *loc. cit.*
66. Aubrey, 124.
67. Harrington, *Oceana*, 186.
68. *Ibid.*, 186.
69. 187.
70. 197.
71. *Camb. Mod. History*, VI, 796.
72. Aubrey, 125.
73. Stephen, L., *History of English
Thought in the 18th Century*, II, 80.
74. Robertson, J. M., *Freethought*, II, 87;
Psalms XIV, L, LIII, L.
75. Robertson, II, 90.
76. *Ibid.*, 91.
77. *Ibid.*, 95; Smith, P., *Modern Culture*,
II, 482.
78. Toland, John, *Christianity Not Mysterious*, 6, 37.
79. Lange, F. E., *History of Materialism*, I,
328-29.
80. *Ibid.*, 325; Wolf, *History of Science ...
in the 18th Century*, 792.
81. *Ibid.*; *Enc. Brit.*, XXII, 270b.
82. Lange, I, 325.
83. Hazard, *Critical Years*, 264.

84. *Ibid.*, 152.
85. In Robertson, *Freethought*, II, 55.
86. Collins, Anthony, *Discourse of Free-thinking*, 5.
87. *Ibid.*, 88-89.
88. *Ibid.*, 105.
89. Robertson, II, 153.
90. Willey, *Seventeenth-Century Background*, 87.
91. *Leibniz-Clarke Correspondence*, p. xi.
92. In Stephen, *Eighteenth-Century Thought*, II, 210.
93. *Camb. Mod. History*, V, 750.
94. More, Henry, *Philosophical Poems*, in Willey, *Seventeenth Century*, 140.
95. In Willey, 161.
96. Disraeli, I., *Curiosities of Literature*, I, 210.
97. *Camb. Mod. History*, V, 751.
98. Cassirer, *Platonic Renaissance in England*, 62-64.
99. In Willey, 175.
100. *Ibid.*, 179.
101. *Ibid.*, 182, 193.
102. Glanvill, *Vanity of Dogmatizing*, in Mumford, *Technics and Civilization*, 58.
103. Glanvill, *Sadducismus Triumphatus*, in Willey, 195.
104. Fox-Bourne, *Locke*, I, 13.
105. Aaron, *Locke*, 6.
106. *Ibid.*
107. Fox-Bourne, I, 198.
108. Locke, *Two Treatises on Government*, Introd. xxxiii.
109. Macaulay, *History*, I, 417.
110. Aaron, 23.
111. *Enc. Brit.*, XIV, 271d.
112. Aaron, 24.
113. Locke, *Two Treatises*, 3.
114. Filmer. *Patriarcha*, in Locke, *Two Treatises*, 255f.
115. Filmer, *Observations upon Aristotle's Politics*, in Hearnshaw, *Thinkers of the Augustan Age*, 37.
116. *Ibid.*, 39.
117. Filmer, *Patriarcha, loc. cit.*, 278.
118. Locke, *Two Treatises*, 3.
119. *Second Treatise*, No. 119.
120. No. 85.
121. No. 94.
122. No. 40.
123. No. 36.
124. No. 138
125. Pollock, *Introd. to the History of the Science of Politics*, 65.
126. Locke, *Second Treatise*, Nos. 228-29.
127. Locke, *Essay concerning Human Understanding*, Epistle to the Reader, p. xx.
128. Lamprecht, S.P., in Dewey, *Studies in the History of Ideas*, III, 217.
129. Locke, *Essay*, II, xii, 17.
130. *Ibid.*, Epistle to the Reader, p. xx.
131. *Essay*, III, x, 5-14.
132. *Ibid.*, II, xiii, 27.
133. II, xxi, 6.
134. III, vi, 12, 37.
135. I, ii, 7.
136. II, xxxiii, 6.
137. I, iv, 8-9.
138. I, iii, 27.
139. II, i, 2.
140. II, ix, 1.
141. II, xxiii, 1-4.
142. *Ibid.*, 5.
143. 14-15.
144. II, xxi, 47-48, 52-53.
145. IV, iii, 6.
146. II, xxvii, 26.
147. Sterne, L., *Tristram Shandy*, 62.
148. Voltaire, *Letters on the English*, in *Works*, XIXb, 36.
149. Voltaire, *Age of Louis XIV*, 379.
150. Cassirer, *Philosophy of the Enlightenment*, 99.
151. Locke, *Essay*, IV, xviii, 2.
152. *Ibid.*, 10.
153. 5.
154. 6.
155. 10.
156. IV, xix, 1.
157. *Ibid.*, 14.
158. Locke, *Reasonableness of Christianity*, in Willey, 285.
159. *Essay*, IV, x, 12.
160. Aaron, *Locke*, 298.
161. *Ibid.*, 21.
162. Spengler, O., *Decline of the West*, II, 308.
163. Shaftesbury, *Characteristics*, I, xxii.
164. *Ibid.*, I, p. xii.
165. P. 237.
166. 263.
167. 267-70.
168. 45.
169. 239-46.
170. I, p. xxvii.
171. II, 150.
172. I, 79.
173. 75.
174. Sidgwick, *History of Ethics*, 186-87.
175. Shaftesbury, I, 260.
176. *Ibid.*, I, 86.
177. Cassirer, *Platonic Renaissance in England*, 199.
178. Berkeley, George, *Principles of Human Knowledge*, No. 92, in *New Theory of Vision*, p. 159.
179. Locke, *Essay*, II, ix, 8.

180. Berkeley, *New Theory of Vision*, No. 41.
181. Wolf, *Science . . . in the 18th Century*, 672.
182. Berkeley, *Principles of Human Knowledge*, No. 47.
183. *Ibid.*, Nos. 15-19.
184. 45-46.
185. 34-35; *Dialogues*, in *New Theory of Vision*, 274.
186. *Principles of Human Knowledge*, No. 90.
187. *Ibid.*, No. 57.
188. Chesterfield, Letter of Sept. 27, 1748.
189. Boswell, *Johnson*, 285.
190. Hume, D., *Enquiry concerning Human Understanding*, note to No. 122.
191. Berkeley, *Dialogues*, pp. 268-69.
192. *Ibid.*, p. 270.
193. Hume, *Enquiries*, No. 122, p. 155n.
194. *Camb. History of English Literature*, IX, 314.
195. Berkeley, *Principles of Human Knowledge*, No. 6.

CHAPTER XXI

1. Hazard, *Critical Years*, 330.
2. Vartanian, *Diderot and Descartes*, 25.
3. Mousnier, *Histoire générale*, IV, 309.
4. *Récit de Marguerite Périer* (Pascal's niece), in Robertson, *Freethought*, II, 121n.
5. Day, *Ninon*, 211.
6. Smith, P., *Modern Culture*, I, 407.
7. In Vartanian, 57.
8. In Fellows and Torrey, *Age of the Enlightenment*, 23.
9. Malebranche, *Dialogues on Metaphysics*, in Robinson, D.S., *Anthology of Modern Philosophy*, 227-34.
10. Sévigné, Letter of August 4, 1680.
11. Faguet, *Dix-septième Siècle*, 77.
12. Robinson, H., *Bayle*, 46.
13. *Ibid.*, 19.
14. Bayle, *Pensées diverses sur la comète*, Ch. 100, in Fellows and Torrey, 69.
15. Ch. 25, in Robinson, *Bayle*, 91.
16. Ch. 141, in Fellows and Torrey, 73.
17. Ch. 172, *ibid.*, 75.
18. Luke xiv, 16-23.
19. Bayle, *Selections*, xiv.
20. In Robinson, *Bayle*, 83.
21. Hazard, 93.
22. Disraeli, *Curiosities*, II, 391-92.
23. In Robinson, *Bayle*, 236.
24. Disraeli, II, 393.
25. Bayle, *Selections*, 173 (article "Manichees.").
26. *Ibid.*, 8-25 (article "Adam") and 157-83,

("Manichees"); Robinson, *Bayle*, 208-212.
27. *Selections*, 208 (article "Pyrrho").
28. *Ibid.*, 209.
29. 210.
30. 204 (article "Abdas").
31. 205 ("Pyrrho").
32. Faguet, *Dix-huitième Siècle*, 15.
33. *Selections*, 211 ("Pyrrho").
34. *Ibid.*, 214 ("Pyrrho") and 177 ("Manichees").
35. In Faguet, 18.
36. *Ibid.*, 10.
37. Havens, *Age of Ideas*, 35.
38. Hazard, 444.
39. Havens, 37.
40. *Selections*, Introd., xx.
41. Robinson, H., *Bayle*, 274.
42. *Selections*, Introd., xxx.
43. Faguet, 6.
44. *Selections*, Introd., xxvii.
45. Faguet, 6.
46. Robinson, *Bayle*, 294.
47. Noyes, A., *Voltaire*, 470.
48. Faguet, 54.
49. In Fellows and Torrey, 62.
50. Fontenelle, *Origine des fables*.
51. Fellows and Torrey, 43.
52. *Ibid.*, 60.
53. *Ibid.*, 44-46.
54. Flint, *History of the Philosophy of History*, 215.
55. In Lanfrey, *Historie politique des papes*, II, 138.
56. In Bell, *Men of Mathematics*, p. *xix*.
57. Bury, J.B., *The Idea of Progress*, 108.
58. Desnoiresterres, III, 239.
59. In Faguet, 21.
60. Havens, 60.
61. Aldis, *Mme. Geoffrin*, 25.
62. *Ibid.*, 30; Havens, 62.

CHAPTER XXII

1. Kayser, *Spinoza*, 41.
2. Maimonides, *Guide to the Perplexed*, I, Introd.; II, Props. 37-46; III, Props. 22, 30, etc.
3. *Ibid.*, II, pp. 17f.
4. II, Prop. 2, Introd.; Zeitlin, *Maimonides*, 151.
5. *Jewish Encyclopedia*, VIII, 29.
6. Martin, H., *Louis XIV*, I, 403.
7. Lucas, *Life of Spinoza*, in Clark, *Great Short Biographies*, 718.
8. *Ibid.*, 719.
9. 720.
10. Graetz, *History of the Jews*, V, 93.
11. *Ibid.*
12. Lucas, 720.
13. Graetz, V, 94.

14. Lucas, 722.
15. Wolf, A., in Spinoza, *Correspondence*, 49.
16. Kayser, 137.
17. Spinoza, *Correspondence*, 146, Letter XIX.
18. Spinoza, *Ethics*, Part IV, Prop. 45, Scholium II.
19. Waxman, *History of Jewish Literature*, II, 263.
20. Bayle, *Selections*, 305.
21. Spinoza, *On the Improvement of the Intellect*, Nos. 1-10.
22. *Ibid.*, Nos. 13 and 41.
23. No. 16.
24. Roth, Leon, *Spinoza*, p. 25.
25. Brunschvigg, L., *Spinoza et ses contemporains*, p. 138.
26. Spinoza, *Tractatus Theologico-Politicus*, Pref.
27. *Ibid.*, Ch. ix.
28. Ch. ii, p. 33.
29. Ch. i, p. 24.
30. Ch. vi, p. 92.
31. Ch. xiv, p. 186.
32. *Ibid.*, p. 189.
33. Ch. vii, p. 118.
34. Ch. xix, p. 245.
35. Preface, p. 5.
36. *Ibid.*, p. 8.
37. In Kayser, 202.
38. *Correspondence*, 348 (Letter LXXV).
39. *Tractatus*, Ch. i, p. 18.
40. Kayser, 247.
41. Meyer, R. W., *Leibniz and the 17th-Century Revolution*, 47.
42. *Ibid.*, 46.
43. Kayser, 168-69.
44. *Ibid.*, 231.
45. Bayle, *Selections*, 305-6.
46. Brunschvigg, 140.
47. *Ibid.*, 146.
48. Lucas, in Clark, 724.
49. Kayser, 249-51.
50. Putnam, *Censorship of the Church of Rome*, II, 255.
51. *Correspondence*, Letter XLVIII.
52. Lucas, 725.
53. Brunschvigg, 141.
54. Kayser, 262-65; *Enc. Brit.*, XXI, 234b.
55. Lucas, 725.
56. *Correspondence*, Letter I.
57. Bayle, *Selections*, 306.
58. *Ibid.*, 307.
59. Spinoza, *Ethics*, iv, 50, scholium.
60. *Correspondence*, Letter LXV.
61. Letter LXVII.
62. *Ibid.*
63. Letter LXXVI.
64. Letter LXXIX.
65. Letter VI.
66. Letter VII.
67. Letter LXVIII.
68. Kayser, 298.
69. Bayle, *Selections*, 308.
70. Letter IX.
71. *Ethics*, i, 8; Scholium II.
72. *Ibid.*, i; Definition IV.
73. ii, 13, scholium.
74. *On the Improvement of the Intellect*, Nos. 99-101.
75. *Ethics*, i, 15.
76. Letter LIV.
77. *Tractatus*, p. 65.
78. *Ethics*, v, 17.
79. *Ibid.*, i, 8; Scholium II.
80. *Cf.* Wolfson, H., *Philosophy of Spinoza*, II, 158.
81. Letter XXXII; *Ethics*, ii, 11, corollary.
82. *Ethics*, i, 17, note.
83. *Ibid.*, i, 31.
84. *Ibid.*, 18.
85. Letter LXXV.
86. *Ethics*, i, 32, Corollary I.
87. *Tractatus*, pp. 44, 92.
88. *Ethics*, i, appendix.
89. *Tractatus*, p. 202.
90. Letter LIV.
91. *Ethics*, i, appendix.
92. Letter LXXIII.
93. Including Wolfson, H., II, 348.
94. Letter XIX.
95. Letter XXX.
96. *Ethics*, v, 24.
97. ii, 13.
98. iii, 2, scholium.
99. *Ibid.*
100. ii, 12.
101. *Ibid.*
102. ii, 17-18.
103. ii, 26.
104. ii, 21.
105. ii, 48, scholium; Letter II.
106. *Ethics*, ii, 49.
107. iii, 2, scholium.
108. ii, 49, corollary.
109. iii, Definition I.
110. ii, 48.
111. i, appendix.
112. Letter LVIII.
113. *Ethics*, i, appendix.
114. iii, 6-7.
115. i, 34.
116. i, appendix.
117. iv, Definition VIII.
118. v, 20, scholium.
119. iv, 20, 22, corollary.
120. iv, 18, scholium.
121. *Ibid.*
122. iii, 59.
123. iii, 9, scholium.
124. iv, Definition I.

125. iii, appendix.
126. iii, 11, scholium; iv, 59.
127. iii, appendix.
128. Nietzsche, *Antichrist*, No. 2.
129. *Ethics*, iv, 45, scholium; iv, 50, 53-54.
130. iv, 42, 45, Scholium II.
131. iii, Definition III.
132. iii, Introd.
133. v, 3, corollary.
134. Müller, Johannes, *Physiologie des Menschen* (1840), II, 543-48.
135. *Ethics*, iii, 1, corollary.
136. iii, 59, scholium.
137. iv, 7.
138. iv, 51, scholium; 58, scholium.
139. iii, 59; Definition XXVII.
140. iv, 67.
141. iii, 12, scholium.
142. v, 21.
143. v, 34, scholium.
144. v, 29, scholium.
145. v, 23.
146. v, 31, scholium.
147. v, 3.
148. v, 6.
149. iv, 26.
150. ii, end.
151. iv, 68.
152. iv, 50, scholium.
153. iv, appendix, xiii.
154. iv, 73.
155. iv, 46.
156. iv, 48, scholium.
157. E.g., Bidney, *Psychology and Ethics of Spinoza*, 246.
158. *Ethics*, iv, 14.
159. *Ibid.*, iii, appendix, Definition VI.
160. *Improvement of the Intellect*, Introd.
161. *Ethics*, iv, 28.
162. *Tractatus Politicus*, i, 4.
163. *Ibid.*, ii, 8.
164. *Tractatus Theologico-Politicus*, Ch. xvi, p. 201; *Tractatus Politicus*, ii, 4.
165. *Ethics*, iv, 37, Scholium I.
166. *Tractatus Politicus*, vi, 1.
167. *Ethics*, iv, 20, 22.
168. *Ibid.*, 35, scholium; 73.
169. *Tractatus Politicus*, i, 5.
170. *Tractatus Theologico-Politicus*, Ch. xx, p. 259.
171. *Tractatus Politicus*, vi, 4.
172. *Ibid.*, xi, 2.
173. *Tractatus Theologico-Politicus*, Ch. xxvii.
174. *Ibid.*
175. *Tract. Pol.*, xi, 4.
176. *Ibid.*, vii, 17.
177. *Ethics*, iv, appendix, 17.
178. *Tract. Pol.*, vi, 12.
179. In Bevan and Singer, *Legacy of Israel*, 451.
180. Wolfson, H., *Spinoza*, II, 233f.
181. Letter to Hugo Boxel, in *Correspondence*, 290.
182. *Jewish Encyclopedia*, XI, 517.
183. *Ethics*, iii, preface; v, preface.
184. *Tract. Pol.*, x, 1; v, 7.
185. Oldenburg to Spinoza, in *Correspondence*, Letter III.
186. Uberweg, *History of Philosophy*, II, 64-74.
187. Bayle, article "Spinoza."
188. *Jewish Enc.*, XI, 519.
189. *Ethics*, v, 36.
190. Garland, *Lessing*, 174.
191. Brandes, G., *Main Currents of 19th-Century Literature*, I, 170; III, 257; IV, 75.
192. Robertson, *Freethought*, II, 168.
193. Hume, *Treatise on Human Nature*, Book I, Part iv, No. 5; Vol. I, pp. 228-29.
194. Froude, *Short Studies in Great Subjects*, I, 219-67.
195. Arnold, Matthew, "Spinoza," in *Essays in Criticism*.

CHAPTER XXIII

1. Dunning, *Political Theories from Luther to Montesquieu*, 321.
2. Robertson, *Freethought*, II, 296.
3. *Ibid.*, 298.
4. Leibniz, *New Essays on Human Understanding*, Introd., pp. 52 and 93; *Philosophical Writings*, 154, 166.
5. *Leibniz-Clarke Correspondence*, 192.
6. Meyer, *Leibniz and the 17th-Century Revolution*, 50.
7. Spengler, I, 42.
8. Mahan, A. T., *Influence of Sea Power in History*, 107.
9. Russell, Bertrand, *Critical Exposition of the Philosophy of Leibniz*, 6n.; *Camb. Mod. History*, V, 717.
10. *Ibid.*, 718; Meyer, 86.
11. Dampier, *History of Science*, 175; *Camb. Mod. History*, V, 717.
12. Wolf, A., in Spinoza, *Correspondence*, 47.
13. *Enc. Brit.*, XIII, 885c.
14. Jordan, G. J., *Reunion of the Churches: A Study of G. W. Leibnitz and His Great Attempt*, 42.
15. Meyer, 162.
16. Leibniz, *Theodicy*, 71.
17. Jordan, 36.
18. Robertson, *Freethought*, II, 300.
19. Piat, in Kayser, *Spinoza*, 206.
20. Russell, *Critical Exposition*, vii.
21. Meyer, 133.
22. *Ibid.*, 77.

23. Hazard, *Critical Years*, 223.
24. *Jordan*, 81-91.
25. *Ibid.*, 97.
26. Hazard, 224.
27. Kesten, H., *Copernicus and His World*, 400.
28. Hazard, 228.
29. *Ibid.*, 234.
30. 230; Martin, H., *Histoire de France*, XIV, 292.
31. Hazard, 231.
32. Leibniz, *Sämtliche Schriften*, I, 417, in Smith, P., *Modern Culture*, I, 318.
33. *New Essays*, Preface, p. 42.
34. Locke, *Essay*, II, i, 2.
35. Aristotle, *De anima*, III, 4.
36. Leibniz, *New Essays*, Book II, Ch. i, p. 111.
37. *Ibid.*
38. Preface, p. 43.
39. I, i, pp. 71, 81.
40. Locke, *Essay*, II, 21.
41. Leibniz, *New Essays*, I, ii, pp. 88, 95.
42. *Leibniz-Clarke Correspondence*, 16.
43. Leibniz, *Monadology*, Nos. 28-30; *New Essays*, Preface, p. 44.
44. *Leibniz-Clarke*, 16.
45. *New Essays*, I, ii, p. 94.
46. I, iii, p. 104.
47. II, i, p. 111.
48. II, i, p. 117.
49. Überweg, II, 107; Meyer, 152.
50. A. G. Langley in Leibniz, *New Essays*, p. 101n.
51. *Monadology*, No. 66.
52. Leibniz, *Système nouveau*, in Überweg, II, 109.
53. Walt Whitman.
54. *Monadology*, No. 9.
55. *Ibid.*, No. 11.
56. Nos. 18, 70.
57. Letter to Christian Wolff, in Cassirer, *Philosophy of the Enlightenment*, p. 83.
58. *Monadology*, No. 63.
59. *Principles of Nature and Grace*, No. 4.
60. *Monadology*, No. 72.
61. *Ibid.*, No. 78.
62. No. 81.
63. Leibniz, *Explanation of the New System*, in Cassirer, 111.
64. Letter of Mar. 3, 1696, in *Philosophical Writings*, 115.
65. Introd. to the *Theodicy*, 47.
66. *Monadology*, No. 41; *Theodicy*, p. 74.
67. *New Essays*, Preface, p. 52; *Monadology*, No. 77.
68. *Theodicy*, p. 378.
69. *Ibid.*
70. *Monadology*, No. 69.
71. *Philosophical Writings*, 40.
72. *Theodicy*, 134.

73. *Ibid.*, 379.
74. *Principles of Nature and Grace*, No. 10.
75. Letter to Bayle, 1702, in Introd. to the *Theodicy*, 47.
76. Couturat, *Opuscules . . . de Leibniz*, p. 590, in Joseph, H. W., *Lectures on the Philosophy of Leibniz*, 44.
77. *Leibniz-Clarke Correspondence*, x, xiv.
78. Meyer, 97f.
79. *New Essays*, III, vi, p. 333.
80. Preface, 50.
81. Letter to Guhrauer in *Monadology*, 38.
82. Wolf, A., *History of Science . . . in the 16th and 17th Centuries*, 391; *History of Science . . . in the 18th Century*, 352.
83. Leibniz, *Protogaea*, in Locy, *Growth of Biology*, 256.
84. *Ibid.*
85. 257.
86. Meyer, 103.
87. Maverick, L. A., *China a Model for Europe*, 14.
88. Russell, B., *History of Western Philosophy*, 591; Newman, J. R., *World of Mathematics*, III, 1861.
89. Brewster, *Newton*, II, 215.
90. Hazard, 234.
91. Meyer, 164.
92. *Ibid.*, 126.
93. Saw, Ruth, *Leibniz*, 147.
94. Meyer, 152.
95. In Robinson, *Bayle*, 268.
96. Hazard, 303.
97. Spengler, I, 42.
98. *New Essays*, II, xvi, p. 534.
99. *Ibid.*, IV, xvi, p. 535.
100. Lecky, *Rationalism*, I, 148.

CHAPTER XXIV

1. Boulenger, *Seventeenth Century*, 242.
2. Cruttwell, *Mme. de Maintenon*, 189.
3. *Ibid.*, 186.
4. *Ibid.*, 195, quoting Lavallée, *Lettres édifiantes*, 149.
5. Saint-Simon, III, 12.
6. *Ibid.*, 13.
7. Acton, *Lectures*, 244.
8. Martin, H., *Louis XIV*, I, 552; Michelet, V, 127-28.
9. Saint-Simon, III, 12.
10. *Ibid.*, 11.
11. Macaulay, *History*, II, 475.
12. Martin, I, 535.
13. *Ibid.*, II, 64.
14. Michelet, V, 16.
15. Benoist, *Coysevox*, 37.
16. Michelet, V, 6.
17. Boulenger, 239.
18. Martin, II, 65.

19. Voltaire, *Louis XIV*, 302.
20. Michelet, V, 39.
21. Clark, *Seventeenth Century*, 72.
22. *Enc. Brit.*, III, 242a.
23. *Voltaire*, 148.
24. *Ibid.*, 149.
25. Ogg, *Europe in the 17th Century*, 314.
26. Martin, II, 106.
27. Voltaire, 157.
28. *Enc. Brit.*, XIV, 923a. Sir Winston Churchill's gallant attempt to exonerate his ancestor is not convincing; *cf.* his *Marlborough*, II, 328, 373-86.
29. Nussbaum, *Economic Institutions*, 108.
30. Martin, II, 288.
31. Tocqueville, *L'Ancien Régime*, 179, Book III, Ch. iv.
32. Guérard, *Life and Death of an Ideal*, 208; Havens, *The Age of Ideas*, 52.
33. Cruttwell, 201.
34. Lewis, *Splendid Century*, 31.
35. Michelet, V, 14-15.
36. *Ibid.*, 36-37.
37. *Camb. Mod. History*, V, 349.
38. *Ibid.*, 378.
39. Ogg, 266.
40. Professor Wolfgang Michael in *Camb. Mod. History*, V, 393.
41. Martin, II, 314.
42. *Camb. Mod. History*, V, 394.
43. *Ibid.*
44. 395; Martin, II, 317.
45. Voltaire, 310; *Camb. Mod. History*, V, 396; Martin, II, 318n.
46. Chesterfield, Letter of May 31, 1752.
47. Martin, II, 325.
48. Ogg, 267; *Camb. Mod. History*, V, 401.
49. Boulenger, 291.
50. Voltaire, 186.
51. Mahan, 204; Ogg, 268; *Camb. Mod. History*, V, 398-9.
52. *Camb. Mod. History*, VI, 9.
53. Martin, II, 335.
54. Voltaire, 330.
55. Guizot, *History of France*, IV, 373.
56. Voltaire, 219.
57. Saint-Simon, I, 370.
58. Michelet, V, 86.
59. Funck - Brentano, *L'Ancien Régime*, 410; Lacroix, Paul, *Eighteenth Century*, 80.
60. *Camb. Mod. History*, V, 30.
61. Saint-Simon, I, 372.
62. Martin, II, 431.
63. Saint-Simon, II, 61.
64. Boulenger, 306.
65. Saint-Simon, II, 262.
66. Martin, II, 447.
67. *Ibid.*, 448.
68. Voltaire, 229.
69. *Ibid.*, 230.
70. Churchill, *English-speaking Peoples*, III, 68.
71. Saint-Simon, II, 68.
72. Lacroix, *Eighteenth Century*, 22.
73. Boulenger, 307.
74. *Ibid.*
75. Saint-Simon, II, 166.
76. *Ibid.*, 67.
77. *Ibid.*, 66.
78. Voltaire, 233; Michelet, V, 95.
79. Rowse, *Early Churchills*, 254.
80. Trevelyan, *English Social History*, 294.
81. Martin, II, 474.
82. In Hoover, H., and Gibbons, H. A., *Conditions of a Lasting Peace*, 33.
83. In Hazard, 437.
84. Voltaire, 306.
85. Martin, II, 493.
86. Lewis, *Splendid Century*, 181.
87. E.g., *cf.* Cruttwell, 284.
88. Saint-Amand, *Court of Louis XIV*, 51.
89. Martin, II, 540n.
90. Cruttwell, 347.
91. Martin, II, 539.
92. Saint-Simon, II, 354; Guizot, *History of France*, IV, 483.
93. Boulenger, 317.
94. Saint-Simon, II, 355.
95. *Ibid.*, 356.
96. Boulenger, 318.
97. Michelet, V, 125.
98. Martin, H., *Histoire de France*, XV, 7.
99. Duclos, *Secret Memoirs of the Regency*, 21.
100. Voltaire, 308-9.
101. Michelet, IV, 392.
102. Quoted by Voltaire, in *Works*, XIXb, 99.
103. Parton, *Life of Voltaire*, II, 493.
104. Saint-Amand, 53.
105. Acton, 234.

Index

Dates in parentheses following a name are of birth and death except when preceded by *r.*, when they indicate duration of reign for popes and rulers of states. A single date preceded by *fl.* denotes a *floruit.* A footnote is indicated by an asterisk. Italicized page numbers indicate principal treatment. All dates are A.D. unless otherwise noted.

About the Authors

WILL DURANT was born in North Adams, Massachusetts, on November 5, 1885. He was educated in the Catholic parochial schools there and in Kearny, New Jersey, and thereafter in St. Peter's (Jesuit) College, Jersey City, New Jersey, and Columbia University. New York. For a summer he served as a cub reporter on the New York *Journal*, in 1907, but finding the work too strenuous for his temperament, he settled down at Seton Hall College, South Orange, New Jersey, to teach Latin, French, English, and geometry (1907–11). He entered the seminary at Seton Hall in 1909, but withdrew in 1911 for reasons he has described in his book *Transition*. He passed from this quiet seminary to the most radical circles in New York, and became (1911–13) the teacher of the Ferrer Modern School, an experiment in libertarian education. In 1912 he toured Europe at the invitation and expense of Alden Freeman, who had befriended him and now undertook to broaden his borders.

Returning to the Ferrer School, he fell in love with one of his pupils—who had been born Ida Kaufman in Russia on May 10, 1898—resigned his position, and married her (1913). For four years he took graduate work at Columbia University, specializing in biology under Morgan and Calkins and in philosophy under Woodbridge and Dewey. He received the doctorate in philosophy in 1917, and taught philosophy at Columbia University for one year. In 1914, in a Presbyterian church in New York, he began those lectures on history, literature, and philosophy that, continuing twice weekly for thirteen years, provided the initial material for his later works.

The unexpected success of *The Story of Philosophy* (1926) enabled him to retire from teaching in 1927. Thenceforth, except for some incidental essays Mr. and Mrs. Durant gave nearly all their working hours (eight to fourteen daily) to *The Story of Civilization*. To better prepare themselves they toured Europe in 1927, went around the world in 1930 to study Egypt, the Near East, India, China, and Japan, and toured the globe again in 1932 to visit Japan, Manchuria, Siberia, Russia, and Poland. These travels provided the background for *Our Oriental Heritage* (1935) as the first volume in *The Story of Civilization*. Several further visits to Europe prepared for Volume 2, *The Life of Greece* (1939), and Volume 3, *Caesar and Christ* (1944). In 1948, six months in Turkey, Iraq, Iran, Egypt, and Europe provided perspective for Volume 4, *The Age of Faith* (1950). In 1951 Mr. and Mrs. Durant returned to Italy to add to a lifetime of gleanings for Volume 5, *The Renaissance* (1953); and in 1954 further studies in Italy, Switzerland, Germany, France, and England opened new vistas for Volume 6, *The Reformation* (1957).

Mrs. Durant's share in the preparation of these volumes became more and more substantial with each year, until in the case of Volume 7, *The Age of Reason Begins* (1961), it was so great that justice required the union of both names on the title page. And so it was on *The Age of Louis XIV* (1963), *The Age of Voltaire* (1965), and *Rousseau and Revolution* (winner of the Pulitzer Prize in 1968).

The publication of Volume 11, *The Age of Napoleon*, in 1975 concluded five decades of achievement. Ariel Durant died on October 25, 1981, at the age of 83; Will Durant died 13 days later, on November 7, aged 96. Their last published work was *A Dual Autobiography* (1977).

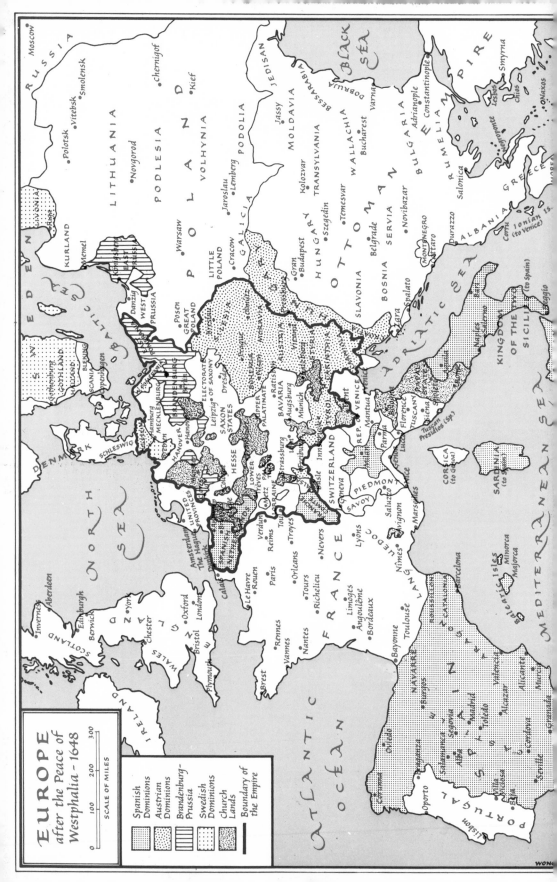

EUROPE
after the Peace of Westphalia - 1648

SCALE OF MILES

0   100   200   300

Spanish Dominions

Austrian Dominions

Brandenburg-Prussia

Swedish Dominions

Church Lands

Boundary of the Empire

RUSSIA

•Moscow

•Smolensk
•Vitebsk
•Polotsk
•Chernigof
•Kief

LITHUANIA

•Novgorod

KURLAND

LIVONIA
Riga

MEMEL

S W E D E N

BALTIC SEA

GOTHLAND
Gothenburg
HALLAND
SCANIA BLEKING
Copenhagen

DUCAL PRUSSIA
WEST PRUSSIA
Danzig

P O L A N D

PODLESIA

Warsaw•

POSEN
GREAT POLAND

LITTLE POLAND
Cracow•

VOLHYNIA

Jaroslau•
Lemberg•

GALICIA

PODOLIA

JEDISAN

BESSARABIA

MOLDAVIA
•Jassy

DOBRUJA

•Varna

BLACK SEA

Smyrna

Lesbos
Chios

•Naxos
Negroponte

•Constantinople

RUMELIA

Adrianople•

BULGARIA
•Salonica

SERVIA
•Novibazar

BOSNIA

SLAVONIA

TRANSYLVANIA
•Kolozvar

•Temesvar
•Szegedin

WALLACHIA
•Bucharest

Belgrade•
•Gran
•Budapest

HUNGARY

O T T O M A N

E M P I R E

GREECE

ALBANIA
Durazzo•

Corfu
IONIAN IS.
(to Venice)

MONTENEGRO
Cattaro•

Spalato•
Zara•

ADRIATIC SEA

DENMARK

SCHLESWIG

NORTH SEA

BRANDENBURG
Berlin

MECKLENBURG
Hamburg
Bremen
Lübeck

HANOVER

ELECTORATE OF SAXONY
Leipzig
Dresden

SAXON STATES

HESSE

UNITED PROVINCES
Amsterdam
The Hague
Dunkirk

SILESIA

BOHEMIA
Prague•

MORAVIA

AUSTRIA
Vienna•

STYRIA

BAVARIA
Munich•
Augsburg•

UPPER PALATINATE

Ratisbon•

TRENT

REP. OF VENICE
Venice•
Mantua•

Milan•
Parma•

Lucca•
Florence•
TUSCANY
Siena•

Tuscan Presidios (Sp.)

CORSICA
(to Genoa)

SARDINIA
(to Spain)

KINGDOM OF THE TWO SICILIES

Naples•

Bari•

Brindisi•

MEDITERRANEAN SEA

LOWER PALATINATE
Treves
Metz
Verdun
LORRAINE
Strassburg
Basle

SWITZERLAND
Geneva

SAVOY
PIEDMONT
Turin•
Saluzzo•
Marseilles•

F R A N C E

Calais
Reims•
Troyes•
Paris•
Orleans•
Tours•
Nevers•
Richelieu•
Lyons•

LANGUEDOC
Nîmes•
Toulouse•

NAVARRE
Bayonne•

Bordeaux•
Angoulême•
Limoges•

Le Havre
Rouen•

Brest•
Vannes•
Nantes•
Rennes•

ATLANTIC OCEAN

IRELAND

SCOTLAND
Inverness•
Aberdeen•
Edinburgh•
Berwick•

E N G L A N D
York•
Chester•
WALES
Oxford•
London•
Bristol•
Plymouth•

Moray Firth

P O R T U G A L
Lisbon
Oporto•

S P A I N

CATALONIA
Barcelona•

Burgos•
Segovia•
Toledo•
Valencia•
Cordova•
Seville•
Cadiz•

BALEARIC ISLES
Minorca
Majorca

WONG